HUMAN RESOURCE MANAGEMENT

A Contemporary Approach

Sixth edition

Edited by

Julie Beardwell and **Tim Claydon**

De Montfort University, Leicester

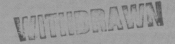

**Financial Times
Prentice Hall**
is an imprint of

Harlow, England • London • New York • Boston • San Francisco • Toronto • Sydney • Singapore • Hong Kong
Tokyo • Seoul • Taipei • New Delhi • Cape Town • Madrid • Mexico City • Amsterdam • Munich • Paris • Milan

Pearson Education Limited

Edinburgh Gate
Harlow
Essex CM20 2JE
England

and Associated Companies throughout the world

Visit us on the World Wide Web at:
www.pearsoned.co.uk

First published in Great Britain in 1994
Second edition 1997
Third edition 2001
Fourth edition 2004
Fifth edition 2007
Sixth edition published 2010

ISBN: 978-0-273-72285-4

British Library Cataloguing-in-Publication Data
A catalogue record for this book is available from the British Library

Library of Congress Cataloging-in-Publication Data
Human resource management : a contemporary approach / edited by Julie Beardwell, Tim
Claydon. -- 6th ed.
    p. cm.
  ISN 978-0-273-72285-4 (pbk.)
 1. Personnel management--Textbooks. I. Beardwell, Julie. II. Claydon, Tim, 1949–
   HF5549.H78413 2010
   658.3--dc22

                                                    2009050193

10 9 8 7 6 5 4 3 2 1
14 13 12 11 10

Typeset in 10/12pt Minion by 30.
Printed and bound by Rotolito Lombarda, Italy.

The publisher's policy is to use paper manufactured from sustainable forests.

HUMAN RESOURCE MANAGEMENT

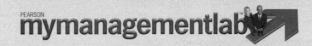

INSTANT ACCESS TO INTERACTIVE LEARNING
www.pearsoned.co.uk/mymanagementlab

With your purchase of this textbook, you received an access kit for **MyManagementLab** giving access to an unrivalled suite of online resources for both students and instructors:

Within a flexible course management platform, instructors can:

- Assess student progress through homework quizzes and tests that are easily set using the extensive pre-prepared question bank.
- Assign short answer, discussion and essay questions on key HRM topics for student homework or tutorial preparation.
- Track student activity and performance using detailed reporting capabilities.
- Communicate with students and teaching staff using email and announcement tools.

Students will benefit from a personalised learning experience, where they can:

- Complete a diagnostic 'pre-test' to generate a personal self-study plan that enables them to focus on the topics where their knowledge is weaker.
- Improve their understanding through a variety of practice activities including: revision flashcards, short answer questions, audio downloads and video cases.
- Measure their progress with a follow-up 'post-test' that not only ensures they have mastered key learning objectives but also gives them the confidence to move on to the next key topic.

A dedicated team is available to give you all the assistance you need to get online and make the most of **MyManagementLab**. Contact your sales representative for further details.

Brief contents

Contents

Contents

Part 4
THE EMPLOYMENT RELATIONSHIP

Contents

Preface

HRM is a continually evolving field of theory and practice. In its successive editions this book has tried to reflect critically on new developments as the issues and policies that have been associated with HRM have multiplied considerably. Previous editions have traced the debates over the role of the HRM specialist in organisations, the role and nature of HRM in relation to organisational change initiatives such as total quality management (TQM), and the strategic role of HRM and its effects on organisational performance. They also reflected on how in academic circles the search for a universal HRM paradigm has given way to an emphasis on understanding how HRM operates in diverse situations and what contribution it can make to organisational effectiveness and profitability, focusing on high performance work systems, the resource-based view of HRM and 'bundles' of HR policies.

More recent editions have also addressed issues raised by what has been variously termed as internationalisation and globalisation and the growing importance of multinational enterprises (MNEs). In the last edition we introduced new chapters that discussed whether distinctive national patterns of HRM can survive in the face of US-led globalisation, how HRM is developing in the rapidly growing economies of China and India, and the ways in which multinational companies are not only influencing HRM ideas and practice across the globe, but also the national and international policy environments in which HRM operates.

This edition continues to explore these themes, but we feel that it is time to move on from some aspects of the original HRM debate, such as the differences between HRM and Personnel Management, to extend our treatment of more contemporarily relevant issues such as the effects of HRM on organisational performance, the impact of HRM on HR professionals and work–life balance. Our concern to address contemporary developments has also led to new chapters on Talent Management, Performance Management and Employee Reward, and substantially recast chapters by Mairi Watson on Management Development and Sue Marlow, Bob Carter and Trevor Colling on the decline of collective bargaining and the emergence of a much more fragmented pattern of employment regulation in the UK. We know that a single volume cannot encompass the huge and expanding area in and around HRM and we apologise for any omissions. Nevertheless, we are confident that we have covered the broad sweep of the HRM field and some aspects of it in considerable detail.

As ever we thank our long-standing contributors and our new ones for their hard work and willing cooperation in getting this edition to press. We would also like to thank partners, family members and colleagues for their help and support in the arduous process of academic writing. Thanks too, to Pearson for their commitment to successive editions of this book and to our editors at Pearson for their enthusiastic help and encouragement. Finally, we would like to thank Mike Doyle, who contributed to every previous edition of the book but has now decided to call it a day. Thanks Mike.

Julie Beardwell
Tim Claydon

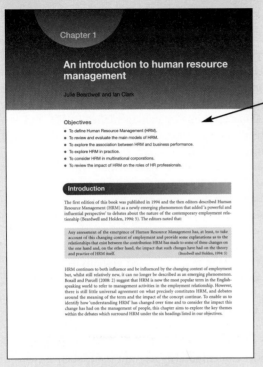

Objectives provide an overview of the topics to be covered in each chapter, giving a clear indication of what you should expect to learn.

Boxes contain a variety of business examples to put theory into practice.

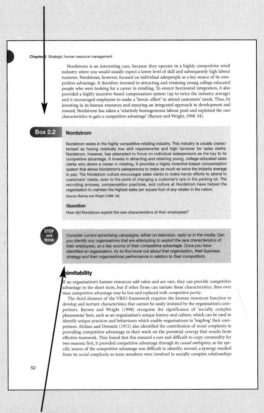

Figures are used to illustrate key points, models, theories and processes.

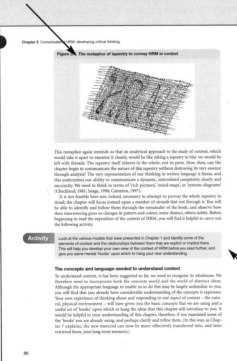

Stop and think: readers are frequently invited to reflect critically, challenge their assumptions and relate to their own experience.

Activities appear throughout the text to reinforce learning with problems and practical exercises.

Chapter **Summary** allows you to recap and review your understanding of the main points of the chapter.

Summary

change across countries. A more useful concept might be *hybridisation* (Kwon, 2004). In terms of Smith and Meiskins' framework, hybridisation can be seen as the interplay of dominance effects and societal effects. Dominance effects mean that national employment systems come to share more common influences such as lean production, shareholder value and labour flexibility but societal effects mean that the way governments, employers and other actors use these influences to achieve change continues to reflect features of the existing system.

In looking at recent patterns of change in Germany and Japan, we have seen that there is some evidence that dominance effects are at work in the diffusion of shareholder value ideas and pressures to increase labour flexibility. However, we have also noted the limited and partial nature of the changes that have taken place. Societal effects mean that there is still support for the social partnership principle in Germany and for welfare corporatism in Japan. While we cannot rule out the possibility that Germany and Japan will move closer to the American model in the future, the fact that employment systems are deeply embedded in wider societal institutions suggests that while the German and Japanese systems are likely to evolve in response to new global pressures, this is not to say that they will come to replicate the US model. Indeed, the difficulty of predicting the future shape of employment systems is compounded when we consider the possible effects of the emergence of China and India as leading players in the new global economy and the unfolding effects of the recent credit crunch and national and global responses to it.

Summary

- There are noticeable differences in the way the employment relationship is regulated in different countries such that we can identify different national employment systems.
- National employment systems can be compared on the basis of similarities and differences in the extent and patterns of institutionalised regulation of the employment relationship.
- Different countries' employment systems are embedded in and shaped by their wider business systems.
- Historically, Germany, Japan and the USA have adopted different employment paradigms based on respectively social partnership, welfare corporatism and a managerially led model.
- Each of the three paradigms has been embedded in distinctive business systems that have in turn produced and supported distinctive strategies for achieving competitiveness in domestic and international markets.
- Since the 1980s, each system has come under intense pressure to change in response to forces that many observers believe are encouraging the convergence of all employment systems towards the current US model.
- Globalisation if it means anything means that international competitive pressures and reactions to them override the priorities of national business and employment systems leading to the further marketisation of corporate governance and employment relations.
- In a global context financial performance becomes much more important than previously, particularly as the stock market and the market for corporate control increasingly discipline management to ensure managerial efficiency on the basis that investors and shareholders are the dominant stakeholders.
- The diffusion of investor and shareholder approaches to corporate performance, combined with external shocks such as the recession caused by the credit crunch, encourage employers to see labour as a cost rather than a productive resource, leading to changes in HRM. At the same time however, national systems of institutional regulation moderate this pressure.

601

Questions can be used for self-testing, class exercises or debates.

Case study

Activity Defining the effective human resource professional

What does an effective HR professional look like? What skills, competencies and knowledge do they require to become a business partner? Try to collect information from a range of sources, for example: organisational websites, HR practitioner journals, (*Personnel Today, People Management*), other journals (*Human Resource Management Journal, Management Learning*); the CIPD website and HRM textbooks to develop a profile of an effective HR professional in the twenty-first century. Which skills, competencies and knowledge would you identify as strategic HR competencies?

Questions

1 In what way does an understanding of strategic management contribute to your understanding of strategic human resource management?

2 How would you differentiate human resource management from strategic human resource management?

3 Compare and contrast the best fit and best practice approach to strategic human resource management.

4 Evaluate the relationship between strategic human resource management and organisational performance.

5 Why do human resources practitioners need to develop strategic capabilities?

Case study

Café Expresso

Café Expresso is one of the three main players in the 'coffee house' industry, which now has more than 6000 stores across the globe, 500 of which are in the UK and Ireland. They employ 7000 staff in the UK alone and serve 35 million customers in their stores across the globe each week.

The coffee industry is particularly robust, with coffee being the second most valuable commodity in the world after oil, with global retail sales estimated to be £39.2 billion. A total of 6.7 million tonnes of coffee were produced annually in 1998–2000, which is forecast to rise to 7 million tonnes by 2010.

The number of coffee bars in the high street has increased considerably in recent years, with the market being dominated by three main players. The 'coffee house' business therefore, is very competitive with coffee chains constantly looking for innovative ways of achieving sustainable competitive advantage, to remain ahead of their rivals.

Café Expresso had enjoyed first mover advantage in the marketplace and had rapidly grown to number one position, which they had retained for 15 years. In recent years, however, they have lost market share to rival competitors who have copied Café Expresso's business model and poached key staff to deliver it and subsequently customers had followed. This had resulted in Café Expresso slipping to the number three position. This loss of market share had forced them to rethink their strategy and a new charismatic chief executive, Ben Thomson, had been appointed in 2005 to turn the business around.

In reviewing Café Expresso's current strategy Ben Thomson embarked on an international fact finding tour of their coffee bars to meet staff and customers to get a feel for the nature of the business, together with rival coffee houses to gain an understanding of their source of competitive advantage. He wanted to return Café Expresso to the number one position in the marketplace. His review identified customers who were loyal to the brand of Café Expresso, but had been enticed away by the experience, the variety of coffee and level of customer service offered by their

75

Case studies, at the end of each chapter and part, help consolidate your learning of major themes by applying them to real-life examples.

References and further reading support the chapter by giving sources for additional study.

Chapter 6 Managing equality and diversity

Case study continued

'So don't they apply for sales advisor jobs?' asked Gordon.

'Yes, they apply, but they don't get them because they tend not to have the drive and hard-nosed attitude to sales. But we're not prejudiced here, it's just that skills are used where they are best suited. For instance, you'll see we've got some Asians in the office. They've got excellent contacts, particularly among their families, who have money and are willing to invest it in the financial products we sell. On the other hand, you won't see any black faces because they have a different attitude to investments and they aren't well-connected. Being well-connected to people with money to invest is one of the key factors for success in this job. In fact we've just recruited a couple of shirt-lifters because the company is hoping they'll bring in "pink cash" from their community.'

Dave checked his watch, and announced that it was time for them to finish off the interview in the bar across the road. He added, 'Besides, I'm desperate for a cigarette. That's one of the downsides of working here – it's a no-smoking office. Bloody discrimination if you ask me.'

Questions

1 Evaluate Dave's attitude using your knowledge of the social justice and business case arguments.

2 Evaluate the recruitment procedure used in this instance drawing upon your knowledge of equal opportunity best-practice guidelines.

3 Does Dave treat people according to principles of sameness or difference?

4 Assess whether or not there is evidence of institutional discrimination at Safe Future Finance.

5 Using Figure 6.2 as a process map, identify the critical junctures where problems have or could occur and where change interventions could/should be made.

References and further reading

Bradley, H. and Healy, G. (2008) *Ethnicity and Gender at Work*. London: Palgrave.

Cockburn, C. (1989) 'Equal opportunities: the short and long agenda', *Industrial Relations Journal*, 20, 3: 213–25.

Cockburn, C. (1991) *In the Way of Women*. Basingstoke: Macmillan.

Collinson, D.L., Knights, D. and Collinson, M. (1990) *Managing to Discriminate*. London: Routledge.

Cunningham, I. and James, P. (2001) 'Managing diversity and disability legislation', in M. Noon and E. Ogbonna (eds) *Equality, Diversity and Disadvantage in Employment*. Basingstoke: Palgrave, pp. 103–17.

Curran, M. (1988) 'Gender and recruitment: people and places in the labour market', *Work, Employment and Society*, 2, 3: 335–51.

Dickens, L. (1994) 'The business case for women's equality', *Employee Relations*, 16, 8: 5–18.

Dickens, L. (1999) 'Beyond the business case: a three-pronged approach to equality action', *Human Resource Management Journal*, 9, 1: 9–19.

Dickens, L. (2000) 'Still wasting resources? Equality in employment', in S. Bach and K. Sissons (eds) *Personnel Management*, 3rd edn. Oxford: Blackwell, pp. 137–69.

Healy, G. (1993) 'Business and discrimination' in Stacey, R. (ed.) *Strategic Thinking and the Management of Change*. London: Kogan Page, pp. 169–89.

Heery, E. and Noon, M. (2008) *A Dictionary of Human Resource Management*. Oxford: Oxford University Press.

Hoque, K. and Noon, M. (2004) 'Equal opportunities policy and practice in Britain: evaluating the "empty shell" hypothesis', *Work, Employment and Society* 18, 3: 481–506.

Kandola, R. and Fullerton, J. (1994) *Managing the Mosaic*. London: IPD.

Kandola, R., Fullerton, J. and Ahmed, Y. (1995) 'Managing diversity: succeeding where equal opportunities has failed', *Equal Opportunities Review*, 59: 31–36.

Kirton, G. and Greene, A-M. (2005) *The Dynamics of Managing Diversity*, 2nd edn. Oxford: Butterworth-Heinemann.

Liff, S. (2003) 'The industrial relations of a diverse workforce', in P. Edwards (ed.) *Industrial Relations*, 2nd edn. Oxford: Blackwell, pp. 420–46.

Liff, S. and Dale, K. (1994) 'Formal opportunity, informal barriers: Black women managers within a local authority', *Work, Employment and Society*, 8, 2: 177–98.

Liff, S. and Wajcman, J. (1996) '"Sameness" and "difference" revisited: which way forward for equal opportunity initiatives?', *Journal of Management Studies*, 33, 1: 79–94.

Modood, T., Berthoud, R., Lakey, J., Nazroo, J., Smith, P., Virdee, S. and Beishon, S. (1997) *Ethnic Minorities in Britain: Diversity and Disadvantage*. London: Policy Studies Institute.

Nazroo, J.Y. and Karlsen, S. (2003) 'Patterns of identity among ethnic minority people: Diversity and commonality', *Ethnic and Racial Studies*, 26, 5, 902–30.

Noon, M. (2007) 'The fatal flaws of diversity and the business case for ethnic minorities', *Work, Employment and Society*, 21, 4: 373–84.

Noon, M. and Blyton, P. (2007) *The Realities of Work*, 3rd edn. Basingstoke: Palgrave.

Noon, M. and Hoque, K. (2001) 'Ethnic minorities and equal treatment: the impact of gender, equal opportunities policies and trade union', *National Institute Economic Review*, 176: 105–16.

226

Plan of the book

Part 1		
HUMAN RESOURCE MANAGEMENT AND ITS ORGANISATIONAL CONTEXT		
Chapter 1 An introduction to human resource management	Chapter 2 Strategic human resource management	Chapter 3 Contextualising HRM: developing critical thinking

Part 2		
RESOURCING THE ORGANISATION		
Chapter 4 Human resource management and the labour market	Chapter 5 Talent management	Chapter 6 Managing equality and diversity

Part 3		
DEVELOPING THE HUMAN RESOURCE		
Chapter 7 Learning and development	Chapter 8 Human resource development: the organisational and national framework	Chapter 9 Management and leadership development

Part 4				
THE EMPLOYMENT RELATIONSHIP				
Chapter 10 The employment relationship and employee rights at work	Chapter 11 Establishing the terms and conditions of employment	Chapter 12 Performance management	Chapter 13 Employee reward	Chapter 14 Employee participation and involvement

Part 5		
INTERNATIONAL HUMAN RESOURCE MANAGEMENT		
Chapter 15 Trends and prospects in HRM systems: a comparitive pespective	Chapter 16 Human resource management in China and India	Chapter 17 International HRM

How to use this book

This text is designed to meet the needs of a range of students who are studying HRM either as a core or option subject on undergraduate degrees in Business and Social Science, MBAs, specialised Master's programmes, or for the CIPD's professional development scheme (PDS).

All the chapters are designed to take a critically evaluative approach to their subject material. This means that the book is not written in a prescriptive or descriptive style as are some other HRM textbooks, though there will be sections that must necessarily incorporate aspects of that approach. Some chapters will also be more easily absorbable by the novice student than others. For example. Chapters 1 (Introduction to HRM) and 2 (Strategic HRM) are good introductions to the subject, while Chapter 3 takes a more unusual perspective on contextualising HRM and developing critical thinking that will prove rewarding to the more able student. Likewise, Chapter 7 is a demanding and stimulating introduction to the processes of learning and development, whilst Chapter 8 contains more elements of what the student might expect in a chapter on HRD.

This edition features Activities and 'Stop and think' exercises throughout the text. These are to give readers pause for thought to help them absorb and understand the concepts and ideas in both a practical and theoretical context. As in earlier editions, there are case studies, exercises, activities and questions at the end of each part. These can be used by lecturers as course work exercises and the Lecturer's Guide that accompanies this edition gives detailed suggested answers. Additional material is also available on the companion website.

The outlines which follow are intended to indicate how the material in this book can be used to cover the requirements for a selection of post-graduate programmes. There is no corresponding outline for undergraduates because of the multiplicity of courses at this level which individual tutors will have devised. Nevertheless, it is hoped that these suggested 'routes' through the book will be helpful guidelines for tutors who have responsibility for some or all of these programmes.

MBA Route

Introduction: Chapters 1, 2, 3
Core: Chapters 4, 5, 8, 10, 11, 12, 13, 14, 15
Options: Chapters 6, 7, 9, 16, 17

MA/MSc Route

Introduction: Chapters 1, 2, 3, 4
Core: Chapters 5, 6, 9, 11, 12, 13, 14, 15
Options: Chapters 7, 8, 10, 16, 17

CIPD Professional Development Scheme

People Management and Development: Chapters 1, 2, 3, 4, 5, 6, 7, 9, 11, 12, 13
People Resourcing: Chapters 4, 5, 6, 13
Learning and Development: Chapters 7, 8, 9
Employee Relations: Chapters 6, 10, 11, 12, 14
Employee Reward: Chapter 13
Advanced Practitioner Standards: Chapters 1, 2, 15, 16, 17

CIPD specialist modules may be supported by the use of relevant chapters, for example:
Managing diversity and equality: Chapters 4, 6
Managing organisational learning and knowledge: Chapters 7, 8, 9.

Contributors

Phil Almond, BSc, MA, PhD, is Reader in International HRM at De Montfort University. His main research interests are international and comparative HRM and he also has an active research interest in industrial relations in France. His publications include *American Multinationals in Europe: Managing Employment Relations across National Borders*. Currently he is leading an ESRC-funded comparative study of relationships between multinational corporations and regional governance agencies in different countries.

Peter Butler, BA, MA, PhD is Senior Lecturer in Industrial Relations in the Department of Human Resource Management, De Montfort University. He teaches Industrial Relations at undergraduate and postgraduate level. Prior to his current appointment he was at the Centre for Labour Market Studies, University of Leicester, working on the ESRC-funded project *Learning to Work*. He has written on non-union employee representation and the management of managerial careers in US-owned multinational companies. He is currently working with Linda Glover and Olga Tregaskis on a longitudinal study of employee responses to organisational change in a major heavy engineering company.

Julie Beardwell, BA, MA, joined the Department of HRM at De Montfort University after ten years' experience in the retail sector. After a period of time as Associate Dean and Head of the School of Human Resource Management at Leeds Metropolitan University she has returned to De Montfort as Director of Corporate Programmes in the Department of Corporate Development, Her research interests include HRM in non-union firms and personnel careers.

Bob Carter BA (Soc Sci) PhD is Professor of Organisational Change Management in the Department of HRM at De Montfort University. His research interests centre on a range of issues connected to work and trade unions. He recently completed an ESRC-funded research project on workforce remodelling in schools and its possible affects on trade unions and industrial relations and a book based on the research, *Industrial Relations in Education: Transforming the School Workforce* is due to be published by Routledge in 2009. Currently he is working with a number of colleagues in other universities to investigate the effects of the introduction of lean production processes in the public sector.

Ian Clark, BA, MA, PGCE, PhD, is Senior Lecturer in Industrial Relations and HRM at Birmingham University, having left the Department of HRM at De Montfort University in 2005. Ian has written extensively on industrial relations and economic performance, and the influence of the US business system on HRM and industrial relations in the UK. His book on this subject, *Governance, The State, Regulation and Industrial Relations*, was published by Routledge in 2001, and Ian is recognised both nationally and internationally as an expert on Americanisation. Currently he is researching the impact of shareholder value approaches to corporate strategy on HRM and the role of private equity firms in the market for corporate control.

Tim Claydon, BSc, MSc (econ), PhD, is Head of the Department of Human Resource Management at De Montfort University. He has written on trade union history, union derecognition, union–management partnership and ethical issues in HRM. His current interests include perceptions of organisational justice and injustice, and the development of employment relations under New Labour.

Audrey Collin, BA, DipAn, PhD, is Emeritus Professor of Career Studies, De Montfort University. Her early career was in personnel management, and she is a member of the Chartered Institute of Personnel and Development. She was awarded a PhD for her study of mid-career change; she has researched and published on career and lifespan studies, mentoring, and the employment of older people. She has co-edited (with Richard A. Young) two books on career which reflect her questioning of traditional understandings of career and her commitment to interpretive research approaches. Now formally retired, she continues her writing on career for the international academic readership, while also addressing the relationship between theory and practice.

Trevor Colling, BA, MA, LLM is Senior Lecturer in Industrial Relations at the University of Warwick, having moved from De Montfort University in April 2005. He has written and published widely on public sector industrial relations, particularly the implications of privatisation and contracting out. More recently he has been researching and writing on employment practices of US multinationals and trade union roles in the enforcement of individual employment rights.

Linda Glover, BA, MBA, PhD, is Principal Lecturer in Human Resource Management, De Montfort University. She teaches on undergraduate and postgraduate programmes and is involved in a number of research projects. Linda is currently leading an industry-funded research project investigating employee responses to change initiatives and HRM in a major heavy engineering firm. She has also worked with Olga Tregaskis and Anthony Ferner on a project sponsored by the Chartered Institute of Personnel and Development examining the role of international HRM committees in transferring HR knowledge across borders within multinational companies. She has also collaborated with Noel Sui, of Hong Kong Baptist University, on a project examining the human resource issues associated with the management of quality in the People's Republic of China and she has written on the human resource problems associated with managing the subsidiaries of multinational companies.

Nicky Golding, BA, MSc, CIPD is a Senior Lecturer in Human Resource Management, De Montfort University. She lectures on a range of postgraduate and post experience courses in the area of Strategic Human Resource Management and Learning and Development. She has led and been involved in a range of consultancy projects in the public and private sector, advising senior management teams on SHRM and the management of change. Her current research interests are in exploring the relationship between SHRM and organisational performance.

Anita Hammer, BA (Hons.), MA, MSc, PhD, is a lecturer in International Human Resource Management in the Department of HRM, De Montfort University. Her research interests include globalisation and its impact on economic development and social change; multinational corporations and international HRM; comparative industrial relations and social movements; spatial globalisation, urban processes and politics; and the political economy of India. She has worked in industry and she teaches on a range of undergraduate and postgraduate management programmes.

Sue Marlow, BA, MA, PhD, is Professor of Small Business and Entrepreneurship at De Montfot University, Leicester. Sue has researched and published extensively in the area of small firms with a particular interest in women in self-employment, labour management, employment regulation, and training. She has recently co-edited a book for Routledge on employment relations in smaller firms and has been to the USA as a Visiting Professor to lecture on entrepreneurship and gender issues.

Mike Noon, BA, MSc, PhD, is Professor of Human Resource Management at Queen Mary, University of London. He has previously researched and taught at Imperial College London, Cardiff Business School, Lancaster University and De Montfort University. Mike's research explores the effects of contemporary management practices on the work of employees. One of his main areas of research covers equality, diversity and discrimination, exploring the effects of gender, ethnicity, disability and age on the work experiences of UK employees. As well as publishing numerous articles in academic journals, he has co-authored or co-edited three books: *The Realities of Work*, co-authored with Paul Blyton, the third edition of which was published by Palgrave in 2007, *Equality, Diversity and Disadvantage in Employment*, co-edited with Emmanuel Ogbonna and published by Palgrave in 2001, and *A Dictionary of Human Resource Management*, co-authored with Ed Heery, the second edition of which was published by Oxford University Press in 2008.

Julia Pointon, BA, MA, PGCE, D.Ed., CIPD, is Principal Lecturer in Organisational Behaviour and HRM in the Department of Human Resource Management at De Montfort University and a National Teacher Fellow. She teaches on a range of undergraduate and postgraduate courses and is Course Director of the MA in International Business and HRM and the MA in Personnel and Development. She is a committee member of the Chartered Institute of Personnel and Development (CIPD) National Upgrading Panel, serves on the CIPD membership and Education Committee and has also been Chair of the CIPD branch in Leicester.

Alan J. Ryan, BA, LLM, is Principal Lecturer in the Department of HRM at De Montfort University. His teaching is focused on the implications of legal change for the management of people at work and the development of managerial responses to legislative activity. He teaches courses at undergraduate and postgraduate level as well as delivering courses and programmes to corporate clients. His research interest lies in the development of soft systems analysis as a way of understanding changes in managerial behaviour following the introduction of legislation. He has undertaken some consultancy work in both the private and the voluntary sector. He has written on reward management, participation regimes in SMEs and the legal implications of flexibility.

Amanda Thompson, BA, MA, CertEd, FCIPD, is Principal Lecturer in Human Resource Management at Leicester Business School, De Montfort University. She teaches gender studies at undergraduate level and leads modules in employee resourcing on both taught and distance learning postgraduate programmes. She is also Programme Leader of the Postgraduate Diploma in Personnel Management. Amanda is currently involved in a research project with Professor Susan Marlow to explore labour management processes in medium-sized enterprises.

Olga Tregaskis, BSc, MSc, PhD is Reader in International Human Resource Management in the Department of HRM at De Montfort University, having previously worked at Cranfield School of Management, where she obtained her PhD. She has published numerous journal articles and book chapters on international and comparative HRM, with a particular focus on organisational learning in multinational companies. Her research has attracted funding from international and national bodies including the European Union and the Economic and Social Research Council and private companies, including the Chartered Institute of Personnel and Development.

Mairi Watson, LLB, LLM, MBA, PGCE, MCIM is Principal Lecturer in Organisational Behaviour and Human Resource Management at De Montfort University. Mairi brings her previous professional experience as a senior manager in the Prison Service and as Director of a management and leadership development consultancy to her role. She teaches on a range of undergraduate, postgraduate and professional programmes. Mairi's research interests are managerial perceptions of the process of change, organisational experiences of learning and development and the pedagogic impact of online learning.

Acknowledgements

Editors' acknowledgement

Many thanks to Steve Vaid, the Chief Executive of King's College London Student's Union and to Emily Ewins, Head of Human Resources for kindly permitting us to base the case study at the end of Chapter 13 on the review and re-design of their reward and recognition process.

Publisher's acknowledgements

Special thanks are due to the following reviewers, approached by the publishers, for their valued insightful and constructive comments that have helped shape the contents of this present edition:

David Banner, University of Westminster, Harrow Business School, UK

David Collins, University of Essex, UK

Susan Durbin, University of the West of England, Bristol, UK

Kim Hoque, Nottingham University Business School, UK

Jeanette Lemmergaard, University of Southern Denmark, Denmark

Iris Rittenhofer, Aarhus School of Business, Denmark

Chris Rowley, Cass Business School, UK

Bob Smale, University of Brighton, UK

We are grateful to the following for permission to reproduce copyright material:

Figures

Figure 1.1 adapted from *Managing Today and Tomorrow* Palgrave Macmillan (Stewart, R. 1993), reproduced with permission of Palgrave Macmillan; Figure 1.2 from M.A. Devanna, C.J. Fombrun and N.M. Tichy, A framework for strategic human resource management, in *Strategic Human Resource Management*, p. 35 (Fombrun, C.J., Tichy, N.M. and Devanna, M.A. (eds) 1984), Copyright © 1984 by John Wiley & Sons, Inc., reproduced with permission of John Wiley & Sons, Inc.; Figure 1.3 from *Managing Human Assets*, Free Press (Beer, M., Spector, B., Lawrence, P.R., Quinn Mills, D. and Walton, R.E. 1984) p. 16, Copyright © 1984 by The Free Press, reprinted with permission of The Free Press, a division of Simon & Schuster; Figure 1.4 from *Strategy and Human Resource Management*, 2nd ed., Palgrave Macmillan (Boxall, P. and Purcell, J. 2008) p. 84, reproduced with permission of Palgrave Macmillan; Figure 1.5 from *Strategy and Human Resource Management*, 2nd ed., Palgrave Macmillan (Boxall, P. and Purcell, J. 2008) p. 5, reproduced with permission of Palgrave Macmillan; Figure 1.6 from Commonalities and contradictions in HRM and performance research, *Human Resource Management Journal*, 15(3), pp. 67–94 (Boselie, P., Dietz, G. and Boon, C. 2005), Wiley-Blackwell, adapted from Strategic human resource management and performance: an introduction, *The International Journal of Human Resource Management*, 8(3), pp. 257–62 (Paauwe, J. and Richardson, R. 1997), http://www.tandfo.co.uk/journals; Figure 1.7 adapted from *The Changing HR Function: Survey Report*, CIPD (2007) p. 19, with the permission of the publisher, the Chartered Institute of Personnel and Development, London (www.cipd.co.uk); Figure 2.1 from *Contemporary Strategy Analysis: Concepts, Techniques, Applications*, 6th ed., Blackwell Publishing Ltd. (Grant, R.M. 2008) p. 7; Figure 2.2 from The Strategy Concept I: Five Ps For Strategy, *California Management Review*, 30 (1), pp. 11–24 (Mintzberg, H.), Copyright © 1987 by The Regents of the University of California, by permission of The Regents; Figure 2.3 from *What is Strategy and Does It Matter?*, 2nd ed., Thomson Learning (Whittington, R. 2001) p. 3; Figure 2.4 from *Human Resource Management*, 4th ed., Prentice Hall (Torrington, D. and Hall, L. 1998) p. 27; Figure 2.5 from Towards a unifying framework for exploring fit and flexibility in strategic human resource management, *Academy of Management Review*, 23(4), p. 758 (Wright, P. and Snell, S. 1998), Copyright 1998 by Academy of Management (NY), reproduced with permission of Academy of Management (NY) in the format Textbook via Copyright Clearance Center; Figure 2.6 from *Understanding the People and Performance Link: Unlocking the Black Box*, Chartered Institute of Personnel and Development (Purcell, J., Kinnie, N., Hutchinson, S., Rayton, B. and Swart, J. 2003), with the permission of the publisher, the Chartered Institute of Personnel and Development, London (www.cipd.co.uk); Figure 4.1 from *SCER Report 1 – Understanding the Labour Market*, Scottish Centre for Employment Research, University of Strathclyde (2001); Figure 4.2 from *The Realities of Work*, 3rd ed., Palgrave Macmillan (Noon, M. and Blyton, P. 2007) p. 368, reproduced with permission of Palgrave Macmillan; Figure 5.1 adapted from *Successful Selection Interviewing*, Blackwell (Anderson, N. and Shackleton, V. 1993) p.30, with permission from Professor Neil Anderson; Figure 5.2 from *Recruitment, Retention and Labour Turnover*, Survey Report, CIPD (2008) p. 25, with the permission of the publisher, the Chartered Institute of Personnel and Development, London (www.cipd.co.uk); Figure 5.3 from Quit stalling, *People Management*, p. 34 (Bevan, S. 1997), with permission from Stephen Bevan; Figure 6.2 from *The Realities of Work*, 3rd ed., Palgrave Macmillan (Noon, M. and Blyton, P. 2007), reproduced with permission of Palgrave Macmillan; Figure 7.1 from Design for learning in management training and development: a view, *Journal of European Industrial Training*, 4(8), p. 22 (Binsted, D.S. 1980), with permission from MCB University Press; Figure 8.4 from *Creating a Training and Development Strategy*, CIPD (Mayo, A. 2000), with the permission of the publisher, the Chartered Institute of Personnel and Development, London (www.cipd.co.uk); Figure 8.5 from *Learning and Development Survey*, CIPD (2009) p. 5, www.cipd.co.uk/subjects/lrnanddev/general/_learning_and_development_09, with the permission of the publisher, the Chartered Institute of Personnel and Development, London (www.cipd.co.uk); Figure 8.6 from *Effective Coaching: Lessons from the Coach's Coach*, 3rd ed. (Downey, M. 2003) p. 23, © 2003 South Western, a part of Cengage Learning, Inc., reproduced by permission of Cengage Learning, Inc., www.cengage.com/permissions, and the author; Figure 8.7a,b from *The Learning Company*, McGraw-Hill (Pedlar, M., Burgoyne, J. and Boydell, T. 1991) pp. 26–7 © 1991, reproduced with the kind permission of The McGraw-Hill Companies. All rights reserved; Figure 9.2 adapted from J. Burgoyne and B. Jackson, The arena thesis: management development as a pluralistic meeting point, in, *Management Learning: Integrating Perspectives in Theory and Practice*, p. 63 (Burgoyne, J. and Reynolds, M. (eds) 1997), Copyright © John Burgoyne and Brad Jackson 1997, Reproduced by permission of SAGE Publications, London, Los Angeles, New Delhi and Singapore; Figure 9.3 adapted from M. Clarke, D. Butcher and C. Bailey, Strategically aligned leadership development in, *Leadership in Organizations: Current Issues and Key Trends*, p.287 (Storey, J. (ed.) 2004), Routledge; Figure 10.1 from *Law Express: Employment Law*, Pearson Longman (Cabrelli, D. 2008) p.11; Figure 13.2 from *Paying for Contribution: Real Performance-Related Pay Strategies*, Kogan Page (Brown, D. and Armstrong, M. 1999) p. 81, reproduced with permission of D. Brown and M. Armstrong; Figure 13.3 from Figure 13.3 from J. Adams, Inequity in social exchange, in *Advances in experimental social psychology*, 2, pp. 267-96 (Berkowitz, L. (ed) 1965), Copyright © 1965 Academic Press Inc., with permission from Elsevier; Figure 13.7 adapted from *Paying for Contribution: Real Performance-Related Pay Strategies*, Kogan Page (Brown, D. and Armstrong, M. 1999) p. 137, reproduced with permission of D. Brown and M. Armstrong; Figure 14.1 adapted from *New Developments in Employee Involvement*, Department of Employment Research Series No. 2 (Marchington, M., Goodman, J., Wilkinson, A. and Ackers, P. 1992) p.7 HMSO, Crown Copyright material is reproduced with the permission of the Controller, Office of Public Sector Information (OPSI); Figure 16.1 from CEIC data, http://www.ceicdata.com/; Figure 17.2 from An integrative framework of strategic international human resource management, *Journal of Management*, 19(2), p. 422 (Schuler, R., Dowling, P. and De Cieri, H. 1993), copyright © 1993 Southern Management Association, reprinted by permission of SAGE Publications and the authors.

Tables

Table 1.1 from *Improving Health Through Human Resource Management: A Starting Point for Change*, Chartered Institute of Personnel and Development (Hyde, P., Boaden, R., Cortvriend, P., Harris, P., Marchington, M., Pass, S., Sparrow, P. and Sibald, B. 2006), with the permission of the publisher, the Chartered Institute of Personnel and Development, London (www.cipd.co.uk); Table 1.2 from Role call, *People Management*, 11(12), pp. 24–28 (Ulrich, D. and Brockbank, W. 2005), with permission from D. Ulrich and W. Brockbank; Table 2.1 adapted from *What is Strategy and Does It Matter?*, 2nd ed., Thomson Learning (Whittington, R. 2001) p. 39; Table 2.2 from Linking competitive strategies with human resource management, *Academy of Management Executive*, 1(3), pp. 207–219 (Schuler, R.S. and Jackson, S.E. 1987), Copyright 1987 by Academy of Management (NY), reproduced with permission of Academy of Management (NY) in the format Textbook via Copyright Clearance Center.; Table 2.3 from Modes of theorizing in strategic human resource management, *Academy of Management Journal*, 39(4), pp. 802–35 (Delery, J.E. and Doty, H. 1996), Copyright 1996 by Academy of Management (NY), reproduced with permission of Academy of Management (NY) in the format Textbook via Copyright Clearance Center; Table 2.4 from *Competing for the Future*, Harvard Business School Press, Boston, MA (Hamel, G. and Prahalad, C. 1994) pp. 217–18, Copyright © 1994 by the Harvard Business School Publishing Corporation, all rights reserved, reprinted by permission of Harvard Business School Press; Table 2.5 from *The Human Equation: Building Profits by Putting People First*, Harvard Business School Press, Boston, MA (Pfeffer, J. 1998) Copyright © 1998 by the Harvard Business School Publishing Corporation, all rights reserved, reprinted by permission of Harvard Business School Press; Table 2.7 from The romance of human resource management and business performance, and the case for big science, *Human Relations*, 58(4), pp. 429–63 (Wall, T.D. and Wood, S.J. 2005), copyright © 2005 The Tavistock Institute, reprinted by permission of SAGE Publications and the authors; Table on page 126 from *Census 2001*, Office for National Statistics (2001), Crown Copyright material is reproduced with the permission of the Controller, Office of Public Sector Information (OPSI); Table 4.1 from 2006-based national population projections, Office for National Statistics, Crown Copyright material is reproduced with the permission of the Controller, Office of Public Sector Information (OPSI); Table 4.2 from *Interim Life Tables 2005–07*, Office for National Statistics, Crown Copyright material is reproduced with the permission of the Controller, Office of Public Sector Information (OPSI); Table 4.3 from *Labour Force Survey*, Spring, Office for National Statistics (2008), Crown Copyright material is reproduced with the permission of the Controller, Office of Public Sector Information (OPSI); Table 4.4 from 2008, Equality and Human Rights Commission, reproduced by permission of the Equality and Human Rights Commission; Table 4.5 from *Ethnic Penalties in the Labour Market: Employers and Discrimination*, DWP Research Report 341 (Heath, A. and Cheung, S.Y. 2006) p. 15, Crown Copyright material is reproduced with the permission of the Controller, Office of Public Sector Information (OPSI).; Table 4.6 from *Working Futures: New*

Projections of Occupational Attainment by Sector and Region 2002–2012. Volume 1: National Report, Institute for Employment Research, University of Warwick (Wilson, R., Homenikou, K. and Dickerson, A. 2006) p. 26; Table 4.7 from *Working Futures: New Projections of Occupational Attainment by Sector and Region 2002–2012. Volume 1: National Report*, Institute for Employment Research, University of Warwick (Wilson, R., Homenikou, K. and Dickerson, A. 2006) p. 58; Table 4.8 from Family-friendly management: testing the various perspectives, *National Institute Economic Review*, 168(1), pp. 99–116 (Wood, S. 1999), Copyright © 1999 National Institute of Economic and Social Research, reprinted by permission of SAGE Publications and the author; Table 4.9 from *Inside the work place: findings from the 2004 Workplace Employment Relations Survey*, DTi (Kersley et al 2006) p. 206, Crown Copyright material is reproduced with the permission of the Controller, Office of Public Sector Information (OPSI); Table 4.10 from *The Third Work-Life Balance Employee Survey: Main Findings*, Institute for Employment Studies, Employment Relations Research Series No. 58 (Hooker, H., Neathley, F., Casebourne, J. and Munro, M. 2007) p. 69; Table 5.1 from Talent management for the twenty-first century, *Harvard Business Review*, March, p. 78 (Cappelli, P. 2008), Copyright © 2008 by the Harvard Business School Publishing Corporation, all rights reserved, reprinted by permission of Harvard Business Review; Table 5.2 from *Recruitment and Selection*, Advisory Booklet No. 6, Advisory, Conciliation and Arbitration Service (ACAS 1983), Crown Copyright material is reproduced with the permission of the Controller, Office of Public Sector Information (OPSI), © Acas, Euston Tower, 286 Euston Road, London NW1 3JJ; Table 5.3 from *Recruitment, Retention and Labour Turnover*, Survey Report, CIPD (2008) p. 10, with the permission of the publisher, the Chartered Institute of Personnel and Development, London (www.cipd.co.uk); Table 5.4 from *Recruitment, Retention and Labour Turnover*, Survey Report, CIPD (2008) p. 11, with the permission of the publisher, the Chartered Institute of Personnel and Development, London (www.cipd.co.uk); Table 5.5 from *Reflections on Talent Management*, Report, CIPD (2006) pp. 5-6, with the permission of the publisher, the Chartered Institute of Personnel and Development, London (www.cipd.co.uk); Table 9.1 from Management development for the individual and the organisation, *Personnel Management*, June, pp. 40–44 (Burgoyne, J. 1988), with permission from Dr J. G. Burgoyne; Table 9.2 from Comparing European approaches to management education, *Advances in Developing Human Resources*, 6(4), pp. 428–50 (Ramirez, M. 2004), copyright © 2004 reprinted by permission of SAGE Publications and the author; Table on page 417 from *Employment Tribunal Service Annual Report 2007/08*, Crown Copyright material is reproduced with the permission of the Controller, Office of Public Sector Information (OPSI); Tables 12.1, 14.2, 14.3 after *Workplace Employment Relations Survey 2004*, Crown Copyright material is reproduced with the permission of the Controller, Office of Public Sector Information (OPSI); Table 13.1 from *Reward Management: A CIPD Survey*, CIPD (2009) p.13, with the permission of the publisher, the Chartered Institute of Personnel and Development, London (www.cipd.co.uk); Table 13.2 from *Reward strategy: How to develop a reward strategy. A CIPD Practical Tool*, CIPD (2005) http://www.cipd.co.uk/subjects/pay/general/tools.htm?IsSrchRes=1, with the permission of the publisher, the Chartered Institute of Personnel and Development, London (www.cipd.co.uk); Table 13.3 from *Reward Strategy: 10 Common Mistakes*, Institute for Employment Studies (Bevan, S. 2000) p.3; Table 13.5 from *Employee Reward*, 3rd ed., CIPD (Armstrong, M. 2002) p. 306, with the permission of the publisher, the Chartered Institute of Personnel and Development, London (www.cipd.co.uk); Table 14.1 adapted from *Managing Employee Involvement and Participation*, Sage (Hyman, J. and Mason, B. 1995) p.25, Copyright © 1995, Reproduced by permission of SAGE Publications, London, Los Angeles, New Delhi and Singapore; Table 14.4 adapted from *All Change at Work? British Employment Relations 1980–1998, as Portrayed by the Workplace Industrial Relations Survey Series*, Routledge (Millward, N., Bryson, A. and Forth, J. 2000) p. 109; Table 14.5 adapted from *All Change at Work? British Employment Relations 1980–1998, as Portrayed by the Workplace Industrial Relations Survey Series*, Routledge (Millward, N., Bryson, A. and Forth, J. 2000) p. 96; Table 14.7 from Bouquets, brickbats and blinkers: TQM and employee involvement in practice, *Organisation Studies*, 18(5), pp. 799–819 (Wilkinson, A., Godfrey, G. and Marchington, M. 1997), with permission from G. Godfrey; Table 16.1 from Human resources in the People's Republic of China: the 'three systems reforms', *Human Resource Management Journal*, 6(2), p. 33 (Warner, M. 1996), John Wiley & Sons; Table 16.2 from Re-inventing China's industrial relations at enterprise level: an empirical field-study in four major cities, *Industrial Relations Journal*, 30(3), p. 247 (Ding, Z. and Warner, M. 1999), John Wiley & Sons; Table 17.2 from N. Adler and F. Ghadar, Strategic human resource management: a global perspective, in, *Human Resource Management: An International Comparison* (Pieper, R. (ed.) 1990), with permission of Walter de Gruyter & Co. and the authors.

Text

Box 2.1 from RBS was 'disaster waiting to happen', *Daily Telegraph*, 21 March 2009 (Winnett, R. and Corrigan, T.), copyright (c) Telegraph Media Group Limited 2009; Box 2.2 from On becoming a strategic partner: the role of human resources in gaining competitive advantage, *Human Resource Management*, 37(1), p. 34 (Barney, J.B. and Wright, P.M. 1998), Copyright 1998 by John Wiley & Sons, Inc., reprinted with permission of John Wiley & Sons, Inc.; Box 2.3 from On becoming a strategic partner: the role of human resources in gaining competitive advantage, *Human Resource Management*, 37(1), p. 35 (Barney, J.B. and Wright, P.M. 1998), Copyright © 1998 by John Wiley & Sons, Inc., reprinted with permission of John Wiley & Sons, Inc.; Box 2.4 from Toyota cuts production as car makers discuss

Government bail-out, *Daily Telegraph*, 11 March 2009 (Millward, D.), Copyright © Telegraph Media Group Limited 2009; Box 2.5 from *People Management*, 13 March 2006, reproduced with permission; Box 2.5 from CIPD report 2005, CIPD, with the permission of the publisher, the Chartered Institute of Personnel and Development, London (www.cipd.co.uk); Case Study on page 157 from Stuck on the 'mummy track' – why having a baby means lower pay and prospects, *The Guardian*, 20 January 2006 (Barkham, P.), Copyright Guardian News & Media Ltd 2006; Box 5.2 from *Recruitment, Retention and Labour Turnover*, Survey Report, CIPD (2008) p. 18, with the permission of the publisher, the Chartered Institute of Personnel and Development, London (www.cipd.co.uk); Box 5.6 from Caught by the fizz, *People Management*, 7 August 2008, p. 24 (Chynoweth, C.), with permission of the author; Case Study 8.1 from CIPD, Recruiting, training and developing referees at the Football Association, http://www.cipd.co.uk/helpingpeoplelearn/_lrncltreftbss.htm, with the permission of the publisher, the Chartered Institute of Personnel and Development, London (www.cipd.co.uk); Case Study on page 372 from Alignment and trust in the learning function at Tesco.com: the role of metrics and measures, http://www.cipd.co.uk/helpingpeoplelearn/_vlvtsc.htm, with the permission of the publisher, the Chartered Institute of Personnel and Development, London (www.cipd.co.uk); Box 9.4 from HM Prison Service Intensive Development Scheme, http://www.hmprisonservice.gov.uk/careersandjobs/typeswork/intensivedevelopmentscheme/, Crown Copyright material is reproduced with the permission of the Controller, Office of Public Sector Information (OPSI).; Case Study on page 458 from Teachers demand 10 per cent pay rise, *The Times*, 14 April 2009 (Woolcock, N.) © *The Times* 14 April 2009; Case Study on page 486 from CIPD case study site, with the permission of the publisher, the Chartered Institute of Personnel and Development, London (www.cipd.co.uk); Case Study on page 525 from KCLSU home page, http://www.kclsu.org/, thank you to Emily Ewins/Steve Vaid at KCLSU; General Displayed Text on page 573 from Alternatives to organisational downsizing: a German case study, *M@n@agement*, 2(3), pp. 263–86 (Kothen, G., McKinley, W. and Scherer, G. 1999), reproduced with kind permission from M@n@agement, Professor Andreas Georg Scherer and William McKinley; Box 15.1 from Mitsubishi's company man, *The Economist*, © The Economist Newspaper Limited, London (9 December 1985); Box 15.2 from Keidenran's Okuda lauds Japanese management for revival, *The Nikkei Weekly*, 16 January 2006.

The Financial Times

Case Study on page 26 from HR must raise its game, *Financial Times*, 17 February 2009, p. 38 (Stern, S.); Box 2.6 from Investors rebel over Shell executive pay, *Financial Times*, 20 May 2009 (Burgess, K. and Steen, M.); Case Study on page 112 from Fear and loathing after the credit crisis, *Financial Times*, 4 October 2008, p. 51 (Willman, J.); Case Study on page 117 from Human resources departments are unloved but not unnecessary, *Financial Times*, 18 April 2006 (Stern, S.); Case Study on page 192 from Engaging a worried workforce, *Financial Times*, 10 February 2009, p. 51 (Stern, S.); Case Study 7.1 from Investment banks battle for talent, *Financial Times*, 3 January 2007 (Sullivan, R.); Case Study 7.2 from A battle for talent, *Financial Times*, 20 March 2009 (Knight, R.); Case Study on page 371 from Ebay bids for a makeover, *Financial Times*, 25 January 2008 (Waters, R.)

In some instances we have been unable to trace the owners of copyright material, and we would appreciate any information that would enable us to do so.

Part 1

HUMAN RESOURCE MANAGEMENT AND ITS ORGANISATIONAL CONTEXT

1 An introduction to human resource management

2 Strategic human resource management

3 Contextualising HRM: developing critical thinking

Part 1 Case study

Introduction to Part 1

Human resource management has become a pervasive and influential approach to the management of employment in a wide range of market economies. The original US prescriptions of the early 1980s have become popularised and absorbed in a wide variety of economic settings: there are very few major economies where the nature of human resource management, to include its sources, operation and philosophy, is not actively discussed. As a result, the analysis and evaluation of HRM are major themes in academic, policy and practitioner literatures.

These first three chapters are strongly related in that they consider the nature of HRM from a number of perspectives. The first chapter outlines the different ways in which HRM has been interpreted and introduces two of the early influential models. It then explores the current preoccupation in the relationship between HRM and organisational performance. This raises question of why, given the growing body of evidence to suggest a positive link between HRM and enhanced organisational performance, is HRM only adopted in a minority of organisations? In exploring this question, the chapter considers the impact of context, including the context of multinational corporations. The chapter concludes by considering the impact of HRM on HR professionals.

The second chapter examines the strategic nature of HRM in more depth: how it is aligned to and configured with organisational strategy and how the debate incorporates multiple perspectives, including the 'best-fit', the 'configurational approach', the 'resource-based view' and 'best practice'. In considering claims for the importance of the strategic nature of HRM, it raises questions as to its efficacy in helping meet organisational objectives, creating competitive advantage and 'adding value' through 'high-performance' or 'high-commitment work practices'. Whether or not the claims for these approaches are supportable, it is becoming clear that no one system or approach can be applied to all organisations owing to the increasing complexity of organisational forms and organisational contexts.

The third chapter continues this contextual theme and examines the context in which human resource management has emerged and in which it operates. This is important in understanding some of the assumptions and philosophical stances that lie behind it. The purpose of the discussion is to create a critical awareness of the broader context in which HRM operates, not simply as a set of operational matters that describe the functional role of personnel management, but as part of a complex and sophisticated process that helps us to understand the nature of organisational life.

The type of questions raised by HRM indicates the extent to which it has disturbed many formerly accepted concepts in the employment relationship. For some it has become a model for action and application; for others it is no more than a map that indicates how the management of employees might be worked out in more specific ways than HRM as a set of general principles can adequately deal with.

Chapter 1

An introduction to human resource management

Julie Beardwell and Ian Clark

Objectives

- To define Human Resource Management (HRM).
- To review and evaluate the main models of HRM.
- To explore the association between HRM and business performance.
- To explore HRM in practice.
- To consider HRM in multinational corporations.
- To review the impact of HRM on the roles of HR professionals.

Introduction

The first edition of this book was published in 1994 and the then editors described Human Resource Management (HRM) as a newly emerging phenomenon that added 'a powerful and influential perspective' to debates about the nature of the contemporary employment relationship (Beardwell and Holden, 1994: 5). The editors noted that:

> Any assessment of the emergence of Human Resource Management has, at least, to take account of this changing context of employment and provide some explanations as to the relationships that exist between the contribution HRM has made to some of these changes on the one hand and, on the other hand, the impact that such changes have had on the theory and practice of HRM itself. (Beardwell and Holden, 1994: 5)

HRM continues to both influence and be influenced by the changing context of employment but, whilst still relatively new, it can no longer be described as an emerging phenomenon. Boxall and Purcell (2008: 2) suggest that HRM is now the most popular term in the English-speaking world to refer to management activities in the employment relationship. However, there is still little universal agreement on what precisely constitutes HRM, and debates around the meaning of the term and the impact of the concept continue. To enable us to identify how 'understanding HRM' has changed over time and to consider the impact this change has had on the management of people, this chapter aims to explore the key themes within the debates which surround HRM under the six headings listed in our objectives.

Definitions of HRM

Human resource management refers to a collection of policies used to organise work in the employment relationship and centres on the management of work and the management of people who undertake this work. Therefore, HRM is concerned with recruitment, selection, learning and development, reward, communication, teamwork and performance management. Whilst it is relatively easy to list activities that make up HRM, it is a subject that stimulates much debate and disagreement. Thus, despite the popularity of the term HRM, there is still no universally agreed definition of its meaning. Watson (2002: 369) suggests that a 'rather messy situation currently exists whereby the term HRM is used in a confusing variety of ways'. In its broadest sense HRM can be used as a generic term to describe any approach to managing people; for example, Boxall and Purcell (2008: 1) use the term to refer to 'all those activities associated with the management of employment relationships in the firm'.

In a similar vein, HRM can be used as a more contemporary phrase to describe the activities more commonly termed 'personnel management'. For others, though, HRM encompasses a new approach to managing people that is significantly different from more traditional practices. They claim that HRM offers two advantages over traditional approaches to managing people. First, it is more strategic in that HRM policies are designed to reinforce each other and support the organization's business strategy. Second, appropriately designed and integrated HRM policies create an organisational climate in which workers are more highly motivated and committed to cooperating with management to achieve organisational goals. This approach has been summed up by Storey as follows:

> a distinctive approach to employment management which seeks to achieve competitive advantage through the strategic deployment of a highly committed and capable workforce, using an array of cultural, structural and personnel techniques. (Storey, 2007: 7)

However, it begs the question of whether HRM policies designed to achieve strategic goals such as competitive costs or the ability to respond rapidly to changes in markets can also provide a climate of trust and cooperation between workers and managers. Some commentators have argued that HRM is essentially about creating a climate of employee commitment (e.g. Pfeffer, 1998) and cooperation, while others have maintained that the term HRM can relate to policies for managing people that are designed to further the strategic goals of the organisation (e.g. Legge, 2005; Huczynski and Buchanan, 2007). Consequently there is some ambiguity in the meaning of HRM, which has led to it becoming a contested concept.

This has led to various attempts to clarify the meaning or, indeed, the meanings of HRM. Some of the earliest contributions drew a distinction between 'soft' and 'hard' variants of HRM (Guest, 1987; Storey, 1992) with 'soft HRM' used to describe approaches aimed at enhancing the commitment, quality and flexibility of employees whilst 'hard HRM' describes the emphasis on strategy where human resources are deployed to achieve business goals in the same way as any other resource. 'Hard HRM' can also have a harsher interpretation associated with strategies of cost reduction (e.g. sub-contracting, out-sourcing, lower wages, minimal training and tighter monitoring and performance management) and lean production (downsizing, work intensification) associated with these strategies. However, this attempt at clarification is also problematic. For example, if hard HRM is used to describe a strategic approach to people management, then soft and hard HRM are 'not necessarily incompatible' (Legge, 2005). Hard variants can contain elements of soft practice, while soft variants can deliver hard outcomes in terms of tightness of fit with business strategy. However, if hard HRM is used to describe a cost minimisation approach, then soft and hard HRM may be 'diametrically opposed' (Truss *et al.*, 1997: 54).

As the debate on HRM continues, further terms have been introduced, for example 'high-commitment management (HCM)' and 'high-involvement management' have eclipsed soft HRM whereas 'strategic HRM' appears to have replaced hard HRM. Nonetheless, the underlying tensions within HRM that were captured in the 'hard' v. 'soft' dichotomy remain. More recently, preoccupation with the relationship between HR practices and improved business performance is reflected in the use of 'high-performance work practices (HPWP)' as a term to describe 'a set of complementary work practices covering three broad categories: high employee involvement practices, human resource practices, and reward and commitment practices' (Sung and Ashton, 2005). There are subtle variations in the meanings of these labels, but there is also considerable overlap and some authors (e.g. Pfeffer, 1998) use the terms interchangeably. Both the high-commitment and high-involvement models reflect 'a system of human resources practices thought to enhance employees' levels of skill, motivation, information and empowerment' (Guthrie, 2001: 180) and performance expectations are high in the commitment model (Walton, 1985). An element that all the models have in common is that they are seen as a contrast with a Taylorist, control type of management (Wood, 1999).

High commitment *vs* control

Walton (1985: 78) compared the high-commitment model with 'the traditional, control-oriented approach to workforce management'. This contrast can be misleading as high-commitment and control-based approaches to people management are both means of achieving organisational control, i.e. 'the regulation of organisational activities so that some targeted element of performance remains within acceptable limits' (Barney and Griffin, 1992: 329). What varies between them is the type of control exercised and the desired employee behaviours.

Stewart (1991) identifies three distinct control strategies: manager-directed control, bureaucratic control and employee-centred control. Rollinson and Dundon depict these strategies on a continuum, see Figure 1.1.

At the predictability end of the continuum, manager-directed control reflects Taylorist assumptions about worker competence and management authority. Control is exercised through supervisors giving direct instruction and closely monitoring work. The middle

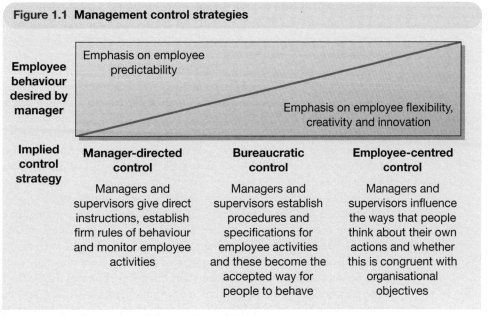

Figure 1.1 Management control strategies

Employee behaviour desired by manager	Emphasis on employee predictability Emphasis on employee flexibility, creativity and innovation		
Implied control strategy	**Manager-directed control**	**Bureaucratic control**	**Employee-centred control**
	Managers and supervisors give direct instructions, establish firm rules of behaviour and monitor employee activities	Managers and supervisors establish procedures and specifications for employee activities and these become the accepted way for people to behave	Managers and supervisors influence the ways that people think about their own actions and whether this is congruent with organisational objectives

Source: Adapted from Stewart 1991/3 in Rollinson and Dundon (2007: 344).

ground, bureaucratic control, relies less on close monitoring and seeks to limit employee discretion through fixed job definitions, reliance on rules and procedures, differentiated status, equitable pay and a restricted flow of information. Guest (1991) labels this the 'compliance' model. Employee-centred control, at the other end of the continuum, equates with the high-commitment model. This form of control emphasises employee discretion and aims to get employees to exercise self-control and behave in ways that are congruent with organisational objectives (Rollinson and Dundon, 2007).

The high-commitment/high-performance paradigm has come to be promoted as 'best practice' for both employers and employees. Employers are seen to benefit on the grounds that the practices associated with it yield performance levels above those associated with more traditional workplace practices (Godard, 2004: 349). Employees are seen to benefit from the ability to exercise discretion and experience high levels of trust. Guest and Conway (1999) found that employees in workplaces with a high number of HRM practices reported higher levels of job satisfaction and a more positive management–worker relationship than employees who did not. However, there is a danger that the terms used to define HRM imply positive outcomes that may not necessarily be warranted. For example, greater demands on employee commitment and tighter systems for performance management are likely to further the interests of the organisation, its owners and investors at the expense of employees. Enhancements in employee discretion, associated with 'high-commitment/involvement', practices may be achieved at the 'expense of stress, work intensification and job strain' (Ramsay *et al.*, 2000: 505). Similarly, Wall and Wood (2005: 432) challenge the assumption of an established link between HRM practices and organisational performance, implied in the 'high-performance' label.

The origins of HRM

There is rather more consensus that the origins of HRM lie within employment practices associated with welfare capitalist employers in the United States during the 1930s. Both Jacoby (1997, 2005) and Foulkes (1980) argue that this type of employer exhibited an ideological opposition to unionisation and collective employment relations. As an alternative, welfare capitalists believed the organisation, rather than third-party institutions such as the state or trade unions, should provide for the security and welfare of workers. To deter any propensity to unionise, especially once President Roosevelt's New Deal programme commenced after 1933, welfare capitalists often paid efficiency wages, introduced healthcare coverage, pension plans and provided lay-off pay. Equally, they conducted regular surveys of employee opinion and sought to secure employee commitment via the promotion of strong centralised corporate cultures and long-term permanent employment. Welfare capitalists pioneered individual performance-related pay, profit-sharing schemes and what is now termed team-working. This model of employment regulation had a pioneering role in the development in what is now termed HRM, but rested on structural features such as stable product markets and the absence of marked business cycles. While the presence of HRM was well established in the US business system before the 1980s, it was only after that period that HRM gained external recognition by academics and practitioners.

There are a number of reasons for its emergence since then, among the most important of which are the major pressures experienced in product markets during the recession of 1980–82, combined with a growing recognition in the USA that trade union influence was waning. By the 1980s the US economy was also being challenged by overseas competitors, most notably Japan. This led to discussions that focused on two issues: 'the productivity of the American worker', particularly compared with the Japanese worker, 'and the declining rate of innovation in American industries' (Devanna *et al.*, 1984: 33). From this sprang a desire to create a work situation free from conflict, in which both employers and employees worked in unity towards the same goal – the success of the organisation (Fombrun, 1984: 17). Beyond these prescriptive arguments and in a wide-ranging critique of institutional approaches to industrial relations analysis, Kaufman (1993) suggested that a preoccupation with pluralist industrial relations within and beyond the period of the New Deal excluded the non-union sector of the US economy for many years. He argued that this was a misreading of US employment relations because welfare capitalist employers (soft HRM) and anti-union employers (hard HRM or no HRM), are embedded features within the US business system, whereas the New Deal Model was a contingent response to economic crisis in the 1930s.

In the UK the business climate also began to favour changes in the employment relationship in the 1980s. As in the USA, this was partly driven by economic pressure in the form of increased product market competition, the recession in the early part of the decade and the introduction of new technology. However, a very significant factor in the UK, generally absent from the USA, was the desire of the government to reform and reshape the conventional model of industrial relations. This provided support for the development of more employer-oriented employment policies on the part of management (Beardwell, 1992, 1996). The restructuring of the economy saw a rapid decline in the old industries and a relative rise in the service sector and in new industries based on 'high-tech' products and services, many of which were comparatively free from the established patterns of what was sometimes termed the 'old' industrial relations. These changes were overseen by a muscular entrepreneurialism promoted by the Thatcher Conservative government in the form of privatisation and anti-union legislation 'which encouraged firms to introduce new labour practices and to re-order their collective bargaining arrangements' (Hendry and Pettigrew, 1990: 19).

At the same time the influence of the US 'excellence' literature (e.g. Peters and Waterman, 1982; Kanter, 1984) associated the success of 'leading edge' companies with the motivation of employees by involved management styles that also responded to market changes. Consequently, the concepts of employee commitment and 'empowerment' became another strand in the ongoing debate about management practice and HRM.

A review of these issues suggests that any discussion of HRM has to come to terms with at least three fundamental problems:

- that HRM is derived from a range of antecedents, the ultimate mix of which is wholly dependent upon the stance of the analyst, and which may be drawn from an eclectic range of sources;
- that HRM is itself a contributory factor in the analysis of the employment relationship, and sets part of the context in which that debate takes place;
- that it is difficult to distinguish where the significance of HRM lies – whether it is in its supposed transformation of styles of employee management in a specific sense, or whether in a broader sense it is in its capacity to sponsor a wholly redefined relationship between management and employees that overcomes the traditional issues of control and consent at work.

Models of HRM

Following from our earlier discussion of the different definitions and meanings of HRM, two broad models have become particularly influential, at least in academic circles, in the interpretation of HRM. On the one hand, contingency-based approaches have developed into strategic HRM to suggest that HRM must match with business strategy. On the other hand, what might be termed an absolute position – more is better – has developed around ideas of mutuality and stake-holding at organisation level.

create a work situation free from conflict, in which both employers and employees worked in unity towards the same goal – the success of the organisation (Fombrun, 1984: 17). Beyond these prescriptive arguments and in a wide-ranging critique of institutional approaches to industrial relations analysis, Kaufman (1993) suggested that a preoccupation with pluralist industrial relations within and beyond the period of the New Deal excluded the non-union sector of the US economy for many years. He argued that this was a misreading of US employment relations because welfare capitalist employers (soft HRM) and anti-union employers (hard HRM or no HRM), are embedded features within the US business system, whereas the New Deal Model was a contingent response to economic crisis in the 1930s.

In the UK the business climate also began to favour changes in the employment relationship in the 1980s. As in the USA, this was partly driven by economic pressure in the form of increased product market competition, the recession in the early part of the decade and the introduction of new technology. However, a very significant factor in the UK, generally absent from the USA, was the desire of the government to reform and reshape the conventional model of industrial relations. This provided support for the development of more employer-oriented employment policies on the part of management (Beardwell, 1992, 1996). The restructuring of the economy saw a rapid decline in the old industries and a relative rise in the service sector and in new industries based on 'high-tech' products and services, many of which were comparatively free from the established patterns of what was sometimes termed the 'old' industrial relations. These changes were overseen by a muscular entrepreneurialism promoted by the Thatcher Conservative government in the form of privatisation and anti-union legislation 'which encouraged firms to introduce new labour practices and to re-order their collective bargaining arrangements' (Hendry and Pettigrew, 1990: 19).

At the same time the influence of the US 'excellence' literature (e.g. Peters and Waterman, 1982; Kanter, 1984) associated the success of 'leading edge' companies with the motivation of employees by involved management styles that also responded to market changes. Consequently, the concepts of employee commitment and 'empowerment' became another strand in the ongoing debate about management practice and HRM.

A review of these issues suggests that any discussion of HRM has to come to terms with at least three fundamental problems:

- that HRM is derived from a range of antecedents, the ultimate mix of which is wholly dependent upon the stance of the analyst, and which may be drawn from an eclectic range of sources;
- that HRM is itself a contributory factor in the analysis of the employment relationship, and sets part of the context in which that debate takes place;
- that it is difficult to distinguish where the significance of HRM lies – whether it is in its supposed transformation of styles of employee management in a specific sense, or whether in a broader sense it is in its capacity to sponsor a wholly redefined relationship between management and employees that overcomes the traditional issues of control and consent at work.

Models of HRM

Following from our earlier discussion of the different definitions and meanings of HRM, two broad models have become particularly influential, at least in academic circles, in the interpretation of HRM. On the one hand, contingency-based approaches have developed into strategic HRM to suggest that HRM must match with business strategy. On the other hand, what might be termed an absolute position – more is better – has developed around ideas of mutuality and stake-holding at organisation level.

Contingency – The matching model

The 'matching' model, developed by academics at the Michigan Business School, introduced the concept of strategic human resource management in which HRM policies are inextricably linked to the 'formulation and implementation of strategic corporate and/or business objectives' (Devanna *et al.*, 1984: 34). The model is illustrated in Figure 1.2.

The authors emphasise the necessity of 'tight fit' between HR strategy and business strategy and the use of a set of HR policies and practices that are integrated with each other and with the goals of the organisation. Price (2004: 45–46) outlines the following key areas for the development of appropriate HR policies and systems:

- Selection of the most suitable people to meet business needs.
- Performance in the pursuit of business objectives.
- Appraisal, monitoring performance and providing feedback to the organisation and its employees.
- Rewards for appropriate performance.
- Development of the skills and knowledge required to meet business objectives.

The matching model is closely allied with the 'hard' interpretation of HRM; that is, the deployment of human resources to meet business objectives. Two assumptions underpin this model: the first is that the most effective means of managing people will vary from organisation to organisation and is dependent on organisational context. The second assumption is that of unitarism, that is the assumption that conflict or at least differing views cannot exist in the workplace because everyone (managers and employees) are working to achieve the

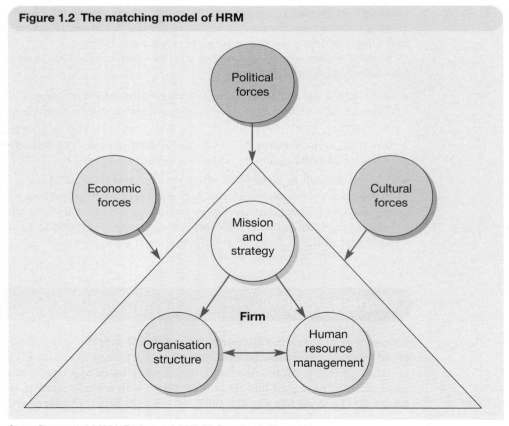

Figure 1.2 The matching model of HRM

Source: Devanna *et al.* (1984) in Fombrun *et al.* (1984: 35). Reproduced with permission.

same goal – the success of the organisation. This model has formed the basis of the 'best fit' school of HRM, discussed further in Chapter 2.

Universalism – more is better

A second influential model, illustrated in Figure 1.3, was developed by Beer *et al.* (1984) at Harvard University. 'The map of HRM territory', as the authors titled their model, recognises that there are a variety of 'stakeholders' in the organisation, which include shareholders, various groups of employees, the government and the community. The model recognises the legitimate interests of various groups, and assumes that the creation of HRM strategies will have to reflect these interests and fuse them as much as possible into the human resource strategy and ultimately the business strategy.

This recognition of stakeholders' interests raises a number of important questions for policy makers in the organisation:

> How much responsibility, authority and power should the organisation voluntarily delegate and to whom? If required by government legislation to bargain with the unions or consult with workers' councils, how should management enter into these institutional arrangements? Will they seek to minimize the power and influence of these legislated mechanisms? Or will they share influence and work to create greater congruence of interests between management and the employee groups represented through these mechanisms?
> (Beer *et al.*, 1984: 8)

Figure 1.3 The map of the HRM territory

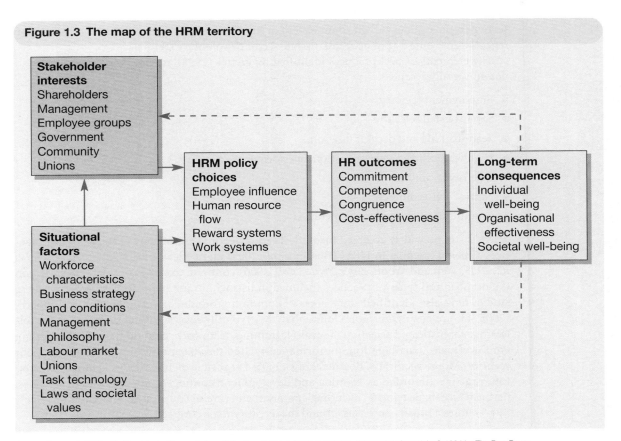

Source: Beer *et al.* (1984: 16). Reprinted with permission of The Free Press, a division of Simon & Schuster. Copyright © 1984 by The Free Press.

The recognition that employees and their representatives are important stakeholders who at least need to be included in the equation initially led to greater acceptance of this model by academics and commentators in the UK, although some still criticised it as being too unitarist (Hendry and Pettigrew, 1990). However, the main influence of this model is based less on considerations of stakeholder interests and situational factors and more on the benefits to employers of adopting a 'soft' approach to HRM that seeks to enhance the quality and commitment of the workforce. Building on this model, Guest (1989: 42) developed a set of propositions that combine to create more effective organisations:

- *Strategic integration* is defined as 'the ability of organisations to integrate HRM issues into their strategic plans to ensure that the various aspects of HRM cohere and for line managers to incorporate an HRM perspective into their decision making'.
- *High commitment* is defined as being 'concerned with both behavioural commitment to pursue agreed goals and attitudinal commitment reflected in a strong identification with the enterprise'.
- *High quality* 'refers to all aspects of managerial behaviour, including management of employees and investment in high-quality employees, which in turn will bear directly on the quality of the goods and services provided'.
- *Flexibility* is seen as being 'primarily concerned with what is sometimes called functional flexibility, but also with an adaptable organisational structure with the capacity to manage innovation'.

This reflects an assumption that it is possible to balance the strategic integration associated with the matching model and the high-commitment elements of the universal model.

The assumption of universalism that underlies the 'best practice' school of HRM is that a set of practices aimed at high commitment or high performance will benefit any organisation regardless of context (public sector, private sector or voluntary sector).

The elements of best practices identified by Pfeffer (1998) are now widely recognised, if not universally accepted:

- Employment security.
- Sophisticated selection.
- Teamworking and decentralisation.
- High wages linked to organisational performance.
- Extensive training.
- Narrow status differentials.
- Communication and involvement.

There is still no widely accepted theoretical rationale for favouring any particular set of practices as being essential to HRM (Boselie *et al.*, 2005) and reviews of the field (e.g. Boselie *et al.*, 2005; Wall and Wood, 2005; Hyde *et al.*, 2006) continue to show considerable variety in the number and types of practices included in lists within different studies. However, these studies have also identified some areas of common ground. For example, Wall and Wood's (2005: 435) review of 25 studies found that 'they typically cover a substantial range of the following: sophisticated selection, appraisal, training, teamwork, communication, job design, empowerment, participation, performance-related pay, harmonisation and employment security'. More specifically, Boselie *et al.*'s (2005: 73) review of 104 articles identified the top four practices, in order, as 'training and development, contingent pay and reward schemes, performance management (including appraisal) and careful recruitment and selection'. Guest (2001) notes a broad consensus around the territory to be covered:

> There is a plausible list of practices that includes selection, training, communication, job design and reward systems. There are also practices on the margin such as family-friendly and equal opportunity practices as well as some that cannot apply across all sectors, such as profit-related pay and employee-share ownership schemes. (Guest, 2001: 1096)

Best practice HRM is discussed more fully in Chapter 2 and will be revisited later in this chapter in relation to HRM and organisational performance. However, it is worth noting here that there are some challenges to the universal applicability of best practice HRM. For example, Marchington and Zagelmeyer (2005: 4) suggest that a high-commitment approach to HRM is dependent on the ability of employers to take a long-term perspective and on the prospect of future market growth. They also suggest that it is easier to engage in high-commitment HRM when labour costs form a low proportion of total costs. Boxall and Purcell (2008) agree that any list of best practices is unlikely to have universal application because of the influence of organisational context. However, they differentiate between the surface layer of policy and practice that is likely to be contingent on a range of internal and external factors and the underpinning layer that reflects 'certain *desirable* principles which, if applied, will bring about more effective management of people' (Boxall and Purcell, 2008: 84; see Figure 1.4).

Theoretical frameworks

At least part of the explanation of the lack of a universally agreed definition of HRM and the presence of competing models of HRM lies in the absence of 'a coherent theoretical basis for classifying HRM policy and practice' (Guest, 1997: 266). Nevertheless, it is possible to identify three theoretical frameworks that dominate the study of HRM: AMO theory (Appelbaum *et al.*, 2000), contingent theory and resource-based theory (Barney, 1991). AMO theory, which states that individual performance is a function of employee ability, motivation and opportunity, underpins many of the assumptions regarding which practices to include in a high-commitment/high-performance model, see Figure 1.5.

These aspects of performance are seen to contribute to organisational commitment, motivation and job satisfaction (e.g. Purcell *et al.*, 2003) and to enhance discretionary behaviour, a key factor in the link between individual and organisational performance (Appelbaum *et al.*, 2000). AMO theory underpins both 'best practice' and 'best fit' schools of thought, although they differ with respect to the precise nature of the HR practices required to enhance organisational performance. According to proponents of the 'best practice' or universal approach (e.g. Pfeffer, 1998), the adoption of a 'synergistic set of practices' (Wood, 1999) that fosters employee involvement and commitment will enhance performance regardless of organisational context.

Figure 1.4 The 'best fit' versus 'best practice' debate: two levels of analysis

Surface layer: HR policies and practices – heavily influenced by context (societal, sectoral, organisational)

Underpinning layer: generic HR processes and general principles of labour management

Source: Boxall and Purcell (2008: 84).

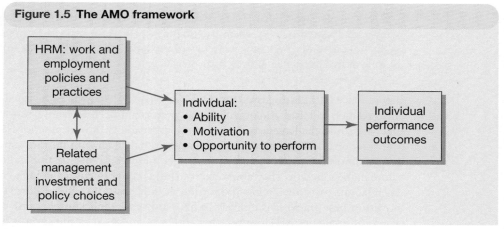

Figure 1.5 The AMO framework

Source: Boxall and Purcell (2008: 5).

In contrast, proponents of 'best fit' combine AMO with contingency theory and argue that there is no single best way; rather, people management practices need to be tailored to an organisation's specific circumstances. Thus different combinations of HRM practices may be effective and practices may change in response to specific external or internal influences. Well-known 'best fit' models are based on a variety of contextual factors, including life cycle (e.g. Kochan and Barocci, 1985); competitive advantage (e.g. Schuler, 1989; Sisson and Storey, 2000); and strategic configurations (e.g. Delery and Doty, 1996) and are discussed more fully in Chapter 2.

Resource-based theory, also discussed more fully in Chapter 2, states that a firm's human resources can be a source of sustained competitive advantage, particularly if they are 'inimitable' and 'non-substitutable' (Barney, 1991). The resource-based view also reflects elements of AMO and contingent theories, but here the set of HRM practices, which could be easily imitated (Wright *et al.*, 1994) is less important than the human and social capital held by the workforce. HR practices contribute to this through 'building the human capital pool and stimulating the kinds of human behaviour that actually constitute an advantage' (Boxall and Steeneveld, 1999: 445).

HRM and organisational performance

What distinguishes HRM from traditional approaches to people management is the idea that it must be central to organisational performance and have a strategic as well as an operational dimension. The strategic dimension incorporates vertical integration, i.e. the alignment of HR strategy with business strategies, whereas the operational dimension emphasises horizontal integration, i.e. HR policies and practices must be compatible with each other. In addition, HRM must contribute to organisational effectiveness beyond HR by enhancing other organisational practices such as supply chain management and total quality management. This raises the question of precisely how and indeed, whether, HRM has a positive effect on organisational performance (see, for example, Wall and Wood, 2005).

The view that HRM improves the performance of organisations is widespread, yet which aspects of performance are important and how they might be measured are not clearly defined. More critically, performance must relate to competitive advantage, particularly sustained competitive advantage, i.e. out-performing the market or improving market share. HRM may contribute to sustaining competitive advantage, but this does not necessarily have to rely on high-commitment HRM. A key issue relates to the type of sector and product market where a firm competes, broadly these fall into two categories. First, cost advantage, crucial to competitiveness in contexts where the imperative is cost control if not cost reduction, for example, mass service or mass production sectors. Second, labour differentiation, where quality and services are at a premium and the focus of HR strategies is to attract and retain good quality recruits and the design of superior organisational processes to promote both vertical and horizontal fit.

In the second half of the 1990s, the HRM debate turned away from attempts to define what its 'input' characteristics might be in favour of examining the results achieved by HRM when applied in different organisational contexts. Whereas earlier analysis of HRM had been primarily concerned with its architecture, the new emphasis on HRM 'outputs' focused on whether organisations with particular configurations of HRM practices enjoyed a competitive advantage over their rivals. Analysing the links between best practice (or high-commitment) HRM and organisational performance is now a major area of interest for research and policy (Marchington and Wilkinson, 2008). An overview of empirical work into the linkages between HRM and performance found 104 relevant articles published in 'pre-eminent, international refereed journals between 1994 and 2003' (Boselie *et al.*, 2005: 69).

The impetus for this approach is predominantly American, in particular the work of Arthur (1992, 1994), McDuffie (1995) and Huselid (1995). The unifying theme of these studies is that particular combinations of HRM practices, especially where they are refined and modified to fit with particular organisational contexts, can give quantifiable improvements in organisational performance. Arthur's work studied 54 mini-mills (new technology steel mills using smaller workforces and new working practices) and demonstrated that firms using a 'commitment' model of HRM saw higher productivity, lower labour turnover and lower rates of rejected production. McDuffie's work examined 70 plants in the world car industry, and the use of HR techniques that were regarded as innovative. His analysis argued that it is when practices are used together, rather than simply in isolation or only for the specific effect of some more than others, that superior performance can be achieved. An important part of this analysis is the extent to which employees gave 'extra' in the form of discretionary effort that would otherwise have not been forthcoming without the cumulative effect of the chosen practices. Three factors were noted in particular: *buffers* (the extent to which plants adopted flexibility), *work system* (the work arrangements that complemented flexibility), and *HRM policies* (the HRM practices that complemented flexibility). The marked effect on performance was in the combined impact of all three factors working together. Huselid's study examined the relationships between the HR system (the groups of practices rather than individual practices), outcome measures (such as financial performance as well as HR data on turnover and absence), and the fit between HR and competitive strategy in 986 US-owned firms employing more than 100 employees. Huselid's results indicated a lowering of labour turnover, higher sales performance, improved profitability and higher share valuations for those firms that performed well on his indices.

The benefits of adopting HRM are also evident in the study undertaken by Ichniowski *et al.* (1997). The authors identify four different types of HR system on the basis of innovative practices in relation to selection, reward, communication, work organisation, training and employment security. The HR systems are numbered from 1 to 4 with system 1 incorporating innovative practices in all areas and system 4, also labelled 'Traditional HRM', having no innovative practices. Systems 2 and 3 lie between the two extremes and have introduced innovative practices in some areas. The findings show a positive association between innovative HRM practices and both productivity and product quality. Furthermore, the authors claim that a move from system 4 to system 2, if maintained for ten years, would increase operating profits by over $10 million simply as a result of the HRM changes (Ichniowski *et al.*, 1997). A US study conducted by Chadwick and Cappelli (1998) identifies two approaches to managing people: an 'investment HR system' (including extensive training, employee involvement, teamworking) and a 'contractual HR system' (average pay, use of atypical workers, importance of industry credentials for selection). The findings suggest that not only are investment systems more likely to improve performance than contractual systems, but also that contractual systems can have a detrimental effect on performance.

Similar findings have emerged from the UK. Thompson's (1998) study of the aerospace industry found that innovative HRM practices were positively associated with higher added value per employee. A longitudinal study of single-site, single-product manufacturing firms (Patterson *et al.*, 1997) concluded that HRM practices account for 19 per cent of variation in profitability and 18 per cent of variation in productivity. More recently, a cross-sector study (Tamkin *et al.*, 2008) reports that increased investment in people, using measures associated with HRM, results in increased profits and sales growth. Positive results are not limited to manufacturing. In 2002, a study of HR practices in NHS acute hospital trusts found that certain HR practices (the sophistication and extensiveness of appraisal and training for hospital employees and the percentage of staff working in teams) were significantly associated with measures of patient mortality (West *et al.*, 2002).

The results of these studies would seem to provide convincing evidence that HRM has a positive impact on organisational performance. However, a literature review of empirical studies that examine the link between HRM and performance (Hyde *et al.*, 2006) finds little consistency in results. Training, pay, employee involvement and 'bundles' of HR practices are more likely to be positively associated with performance, but these same elements also have the highest number of non-significant associations with performance. Pay and employee involvement also have the highest number of negative associations with performance. Table 1.1 provides an overview of the results.

STOP and think — *What factors might account for the diversity of these results?*

Table 1.1 Numbers of empirical papers showing types of association between elements of HRM and performance

Element of HRM	Type of association			Main association between this element and performance	Total number of papers exploring this association
	Positive	Negative	Non-significant		
Training/development	24	1	19	Positive	44
Pay/incentives[1]	21	6	20	Positive	47
Involvement/voice[2]	16	5	17	Non-significant	38
Selection/recruitment	7	4	12	Non-significant	23
Teamworking	7	0	7	Positive or non-significant	14
Performance appraisal	6	0	12	Non-significant	18
HR index/bundle	37	3	20	Positive	60
Security	0	0	2	Non-significant	2
Job design (including work–life balance)	8	1	12	Non-significant	21
Equal opportunities	1	0	2	Non-significant	3
Career development (including mentoring)	2	0	6	Non-significant	8

[1] including 'pay for performance' [2] including 'information sharing/communication'

Source: from *Improving Health Through Human Resource Management: A Starting Point for Change*, Chartered Institute of Personnel and Development (Hyde, P., Boaden, R., Cortvriend, P., Harris, P., Marchington, M., Pass, S., Sparrow, P. and Sibald, B. 2006), with the permission of the publisher, the Chartered Institute of Personnel and Development, London (www.cipd.co.uk).

The extent to which it is possible to draw conclusions that can be generalised beyond specific studies on the association between HRM and business performance is limited for a number of reasons. First, there is a lack of consensus about which HR practices should be included. In their review of a range of studies into HRM and performance Marchington and Wilkinson (2008: 91) found that 'the number of HR practices in each of the lists varies substantially (from as few as six or seven to twenty or more) as does the inclusion or exclusion of specific techniques'. Second, there is considerable variety as to how these practices can be measured (Becker and Gerhart, 1996), (for a fuller discussion see Chapter 2) and little agreement about how organisational performance can be measured. The review of 97 academic papers undertaken by Hyde *et al.* (2006) found over 30 different performance measures used in the papers, with no single measure used in all the papers. There is also the danger that a concentration on the association between HRM and organisational performance can ignore other measures of managerial effectiveness and thus overstate the impact of HRM (Richardson and Thompson, 1999). A further concern relates to issues of causality: does the introduction of HRM practices lead to enhanced organisational performance or is it that better performing organisations can afford to invest in the more sophisticated practices associated with HRM? Figure 1.6 illustrates the association between HRM activities, HRM outcomes and business performance and 'indicates the possibility of two-way causation, i.e. that firm performance itself will give rise to a change (very often perceived as an improvement) in HRM practices' (Paauwe and Richardson, 1997).

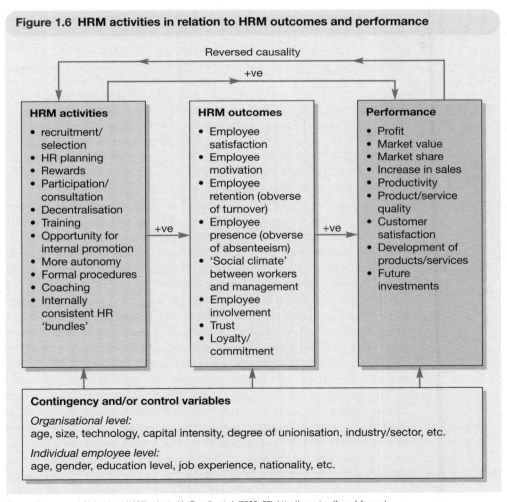

Figure 1.6 HRM activities in relation to HRM outcomes and performance

Source: Paauwe and Richardson (1997) adapted in Boselie *et al*. (2005: 68). http://www.tandf.co.uk/journals.

15

Issues about the direction of causality are revealed in a study exploring the relationship between HRM and performance in 366 UK companies in the manufacturing and service sectors (Guest *et al.*, 2003). The study covered nine main areas of HRM: recruitment and selection; training and development; appraisal; financial flexibility; job design; two-way communication; employment security and the internal labour market; single status and harmonisation; and quality. Measures of performance included employment relations items (e.g. labour turnover, absence and industrial conflict); labour productivity and financial performance compared to the average for the industry; and performance data such as value of sales and profit per employee. The findings show a positive association between HRM and profitability but appear to 'lend stronger support to the view that profitability creates scope for more HRM rather than vice versa' (p. 309). Overall, the results are described as 'very mixed and on balance predominantly negative':

> The tests of association show a positive relationship between the use of more HR practices and lower labour turnover and higher profitability, but show no association between HR and productivity. The test of whether the presence of more HR practices results in a change in performance shows no significant results.
>
> (Guest *et al.*, 2003: 307)

HRM, performance and the productivity gap

As Guest and his colleagues argue, the focus of research on HRM and performance over the past decade has been slightly schizophrenic; it appeared on the one hand to establish that HRM has a positive effect on organisational performance, but on the other hand as we establish in our summary of some of the recent research, such claims are premature. More critically, Wall and Wood (2005) demonstrate that the methodological limitations of most studies on HRM and performance undermine claims of any positive performance effect. In particular, Wall and Wood (2005: 450) claim that not all measures of improved performance, especially financial measures, are concurrent, that is they do not cover the same period of analysis. Thus, it is often the case that the data collected necessarily reflect prior performance and it follows from this that studies of HRM and performance may need to build a lag into their analysis. Alternatively, studies could be underestimating the strength of the relationship between HRM and performance because of inadequate measurement of HR practices.

The reason we make these points is because there are strong theoretical grounds for believing that the systematic deployment of HRM will not only improve employee involvement, but will also enhance organisational performance and productivity. More significantly than this, recently published contributions which evaluate the UK's productivity gap identify the significance of people management. For example, one contemporary focus in the evaluation of the UK productivity gap centres on the evaluation of micro-level productivity barriers/enhancers such as innovation, skill formation and management capability. In this respect the ESRC (2004) focuses not on the often quoted superior levels of capital investment in American or German firms, but on the fact that 50 per cent of the UK/US productivity gap relates to management, ways of working and the application of technology. In addition to this, the CIPD (2006) focuses on differences in productivity that relate to how available resources are used and managed and summarised as management capability.

The findings of the CIPD and the ESRC and other research such as the Conference Board (2005) make an important contribution to the wider debate about HRM and performance. First, the cited studies indicate that effective people management in conjunction with contemporary systems of work organisation can make a demonstrative difference to organisational performance and productivity. Second, if, as the cited studies demonstrate, effective people management does make a difference in terms of performance and productivity a key question for both academics and practitioners is why so few firms deploy these practices? Third, both the UK and the USA are frequently cited as liberal market economies where short-termism and shareholder capitalism predominate over longer-term stakeholder approaches to management. The established research on HRM in the US does suggest that high-performance, high-commitment approaches to HRM do not have a widespread presence; none-the-less their presence is greater than in the UK. So, while there is a strong case to be made that HRM may have a positive effect on performance, we are left with the question of why, in the UK, short-termism has generated such particularly strong barriers to its wider diffusion.

HRM in practice

Over ten years ago, the Sheffield study (Patterson *et al.*, 1997) concluded that the finding of a positive association between HRM and organisational performance was 'ironic, given that our research has also demonstrated that emphasis on HRM practices is one of the most neglected areas of managerial practice within organisations' (p. 21). Since then, empirical data (e.g. Guest *et al.*, 2000; Kersley *et al.*, 2006) continue to show that, although the use of individual practices is extensive, workplaces that adopt full-blown HRM, i.e. a high number of HRM practices, remain in the minority. The 1998 Workplace Employee Relations Survey (Cully *et al.*, 1999) investigated take-up of 16 practices commonly associated with HRM, including teamworking, employee involvement, guaranteed job security, etc. The survey found evidence of each of the 16 practices identified by the survey, suggesting that 'there is evidence that a number of practices consistent with a human resource management approach are well entrenched in many British workplaces' (Cully *et al.*, 1999: 82). However, only three of the practices (formal disciplinary and grievance procedures, team briefing and performance appraisal) were evident in the majority of workplaces and practices rated as significant for a high-commitment approach (e.g. job security, participation in problem-solving groups) were only evident in a small minority. Furthermore, only a fifth of workplaces had more than half of the 16 practices in place. At the other extreme, only 2 per cent of workplaces reported having none of these practices in place. Findings from the 2004 Workplace Employee Relations Survey (WERS) (Kersley *et al.*, 2006: 107) show a similar pattern, indicating that 'the diffusion of so-called high involvement management practices has been rather muted over recent years'. The low use of HRM practices is also highlighted in the Future of Work study:

> concentrating on a list of 18 typical practices, only 1 per cent of companies have more than three-quarters in place and applying to most workers, and only 26 per cent apply more than half of them. At the other extreme, 20 per cent of organisations make extensive use of less than a quarter of these practices.
>
> (Guest *et al.*, 2000: ix)

Sung and Ashton (2005) investigated the adoption of 35 'high performance work practices'. The findings show that the more of these practices an organisation uses, the more effective it is in delivering adequate training provision, motivating staff, managing change and providing career opportunities. However, the findings also show that about 60 per cent of the sample use less than 20 practices.

STOP and think

Why is the take-up of HRM practices generally low?

Sisson (2001: 80–81) proposes two explanations for the limited adoption of an integrated set of HRM practices. The first is that the time resources and costs associated with change may tempt managers to adopt an incremental approach, that is 'try one or two elements and assess their impact before going further, even though this means forgoing the benefits of the integration associated with "bundles" of complementary practices'. Findings from the 1998 and 2004 WERS show 'a degree of stability in the incidence of practices that are often cited as indicators of sophisticated human resource management' (Kersley *et al.*, 2006: 107), suggesting that any incremental path is progressing very slowly. The low take-up of HRM is also attributed to system inertia, particularly in established organisations. There are three possible causes of this inertia (CIPD/EEF, 2005): firms get locked into their initial choice of people management practices and face resistance to change; they experiment with change but abandon it when it does not appear to work; and change in people management practices may also require new production or distribution technologies and therefore will incur additional costs.

Another, and in Sisson's words, 'less comfortable' explanation is that 'competitive success based on the quality and upskilling that HRM implies is only one of a number of strategies available to organisations' and other strategies such as cost-cutting, new forms of Taylorism, mergers and joint ventures may be applied instead. Legge (1989: 30) suggests the potential incompatibility between business strategies and best practice HRM: 'if the business strategy should dictate the choice of HRM policies, will some strategies dictate policies that . . . fail to emphasise commitment, flexibility and quality?'

The attractiveness of HRM to employers can depend on human resource requirements. Marchington and Wilkinson (2008: 136) suggest the rationale for adopting 'best practice' HRM is hard to sustain in workplaces where the time taken to train new staff is relatively short, work performance can be assessed simply and speedily and there is a supply of substitutable labour readily available. McDuffie (1995: 199) suggests three conditions that enable HRM to contribute to improved economic performance:

- When employees possess knowledge and skills that managers lack.
- When employees are motivated to apply this skill and knowledge through discretionary effort.
- When the organisation's business strategy can only be achieved when employees contribute such discretionary effort.

In the absence of these conditions, the business case for investing in HRM may be weak.

Cost considerations are clearly important. Godard (2004) suggests that many of the claims about the positive association between HRM and business performance underestimate the costs involved in adopting HRM practices. 'These costs can reflect higher wages, more training, possible inefficiencies arising from participatory decision-making processes and various resource requirements needed to maintain high involvement levels' (p. 367). As a result, Godard suggests that, for most employers, the use of an integrated set of HRM practices often has little or no overall advantage over traditional personnel practices with a few high performance practices grafted on and may even have negative effects for some employers.

Contextual factors may also inhibit the adoption of HRM. Findings from WERS 2004 (Forth *et al.*, 2007) show that small and medium-sized enterprises (SMEs), which account for 94 per cent of all employers in the UK economy, are less likely than larger organisations to use a number of HRM practices such as sophisticated selection, extensive training, team-working, problem-solving and functional flexibility. WERS 2004 also shows differences in the approach to people management adopted in domestically owned and foreign-owned workplaces. The activities of foreign multinationals can be seen as an important source of innovation in a range of areas, including people management (Ferner, 2003) so it is on these workplaces that we now focus attention.

HRM in multinational corporations – international HRM?

International HRM is dealt with in more detail by our colleagues in Chapters 15 and 17. In summary, international HRM refers to a set of distinct activities, functions and processes that are directed towards attracting, developing and maintaining human resources in a multinational corporation. As a practitioner activity and as a field of research and scholarship, international HRM has developed from a focus on staffing decisions to the evaluation of international business and organisational strategy. Thus, the impact of globalisation in product and labour markets and the growth of multinational enterprises form another theme in the HRM debate. The employment relationship is materially affected and defined by national and related institutional contexts and these variations in labour markets and national business systems give rise to a wide variety of employment policies and strategies for the management of labour within broadly defined capitalist economies. As long as firms operate within the confines of their national business systems, the cultural and institutional characteristics of each system do not impinge on their neighbours. For example, the Americanness of American firms does not impinge on Canadian firms and their employment systems; similarly, the Britishness of British firms does not impinge on the Irish business system. In contrast to this, where employers operate across national borders these different cultural and institutional characteristics may become factors that an employer wishes to change or override. Thus multinational corporations (MNCs) may seek to deploy centralised – more homogenous – employment strategies, regardless of the institutional character of national business systems where they locate their subsidiary operations.

As global integration continues apace and more businesses from established and emerging industrial economies expand their operations across national borders, issues around HRM in multinational firms have become critical to organisational sustainability and success. The key issue is that HR practices originally developed in domestic contexts have now to operate across national and cultural boundaries. Since the early 1990s the focus of international HRM has moved towards the evaluation of strategic issues in multinational firms under four headings. First, the analysis and deployment of international business strategies (Bartlett and Ghosal, 1989); second, the transfer of management practices (see Hofstede, 1980, 1991); third, the evaluation of strategic issues relating to headquarters-subsidiary relations, for example, HQ central control and subsidiary autonomy (Dowling and Welch, 2004). Fourth, the evaluation of differences and similarities in national business systems and their effects on (international) HRM in multinationals firms (Whitley, 1999). Below these macro issues, more micro-empirical, firm-level issues in international HRM focus on the tensions between centralisation and global integration of business and HR strategies and the de-centralisation of these strategies to facilitate local responsiveness (see Ferner, *et al.*, 2004; Clark and Almond, 2004).

Multinational corporations are significant international actors in the world economy and play a key role in the trend towards 'globalisation', contributing to industrial development and restructuring within and across the borders of national business systems. But MNCs are not itinerant or transnational as is often suggested. Management style, strategies and policies are shaped by home business systems – the financial, institutional, legal and political frameworks in which they developed as domestic firms. Thus there is a persistent 'country of origin' effect in the behaviour of MNCs whereby the country where an MNC originates exerts a distinctive effect on management style, particularly the management of human resources. Hirst and Thompson (1999: 84) demonstrate that the majority of MNCs are disproportionately concentrated in their country of origin, sell the majority of their goods and services there and hold the majority of their assets there. In addition to this home country or country of origin effect, government regulation in countries where subsidiary operations of

MNCs are located may also have an effect on shaping company practices for the management of human resources. In some respects the impact of a 'host country' business system may constrain the preferred practices that reflect embedded patterns of regulation in an MNC's country of origin.

This interplay between home and host country influences raises important questions (for HR academics and practitioners employed in national and multinational firms) about the nature of international competitiveness and associated questions about how MNCs draw on and seek to diffuse competitive advantage from the business system in which they originate. International human resource management for global workforces is central to this question; policies to attract, retain, remunerate, develop and motivate staff are increasingly vital for the development of international competitive advantage. Thus the significance of these issues is not confined to theoretical debates on the nature and scope of globalisation; they are of considerable significance in respect of what becomes 'best practice' in and between different business systems. For example, there is evidence that US MNCs act as innovators in business systems where they operate. In the UK, US MNCs are widespread and account for approximately 50 per cent of foreign direct investment (Ferner, 2003). Productivity bargaining, performance-related pay, job evaluation, employee share option schemes, appraisal, single-status employment and direct employee involvement are now common in British firms, but were all pioneered in subsidiaries of US MNCs; see Edwards and Ferner (2002) for a review of empirical material on US MNCs.

In summary, MNCs may seek to deploy centralised employment policies to subsidiary operations, a tendency that is more pronounced in US and Japanese subsidiaries, but less so in the case of German MNCs. Some MNCs, notably US ones, have powerful corporate HR functions which 'roll out' programmatic approaches to HRM that monitor subsidiaries against an array of detailed performance targets. So within MNCs *international* HRM may create broad-based HR systems that minimise or override differences between national business systems and, instead, emphasise the importance of organisational cultures that are drawn from the strategic goals of the firm. Management style and practices for HRM in MNCs are shaped by the interplay between home and host country and, as Chapter 15 demonstrates, this interplay focuses on ongoing debates about the institutional embeddedness of national business systems and the cultural impact of MNCs in overseas economies.

Evidence of the shifts in HRM that can occur when businesses come under pressure are apparent from examples such as BMW's handling of the Rover group sale and Barclays' branch closure programme. In BMW's case it sought to fuse a European style of communication and involvement with the Japanese style already existing within Rover as a result of Rover's collaboration with Honda over the previous decade; in Barclays' case it saw the need to maintain its role as a 'big bank in a big world' by cutting 10 per cent of its branch network in one operation. Closures of plants owned by Corus, Ford and General Motors and relocation decisions made by the Prudential, British Telecom and Massey Ferguson demonstrate the UK's exposure to MNCs. Here an emergent pattern of strategic decision-making, sometimes made on a pan-European basis, illustrates some embedded characteristics of the British business system, such as comparatively loose redundancy laws, to demonstrate that host country characteristics need not constrain MNCs (see Almond *et al.*, 2003). In each case the competitive pressures associated with the value of sterling, comparative labour costs, skill levels and unit labour costs or delayed investment decisions overrode softer developmental aspects of HRM. This pattern illustrates how European consolidation in MNCs and the more general pursuit of 'shareholder value' further consolidate the cost-minimisation model of hard HRM.

The impact of HRM on the roles of HR professionals

'There have been notable attempts to capture the changing nature of personnel roles in response to major transformations in the workplace and the associated rise of HRM' (Caldwell, 2003: 983). In many organisations the personnel department was essentially an administrative support function, which focused on expert knowledge, procedural efficiency and compliance and was perceived as being remote from business performance issues (Storey, 2007). The emergence of HRM and the emphasis on its contribution to the achievement of business goals has been perceived by many practitioners as an opportunity to 'raise their game'. In order to overcome the traditional marginalisation and poor reputation of the personnel function, Ulrich (1998) proposed that HR professionals should become more proactive and strategic 'business partners' through the adoption of four key roles:

1 *Strategic partner* – working with senior and line managers in strategy execution. HR should identify the underlying model of the company's way of doing business, i.e. the organisational architecture, and undertake regular audits in order to identify aspects in need of change.

2 *Administrative expert* – improving administrative processes, often through the application of technology, in order to improve the efficiency of the HR function and the entire organisation.

3 *Employee champion* – ensuring that employees are 'engaged', i.e. feel committed to the organisation and contribute fully. This is achieved through acting as the voice for employees in management discussion as well as offering employees opportunities for personal and professional growth and providing the resources that help employees meet the demands put on them.

4 *Change agent* – building the organisation's capacity to embrace and capitalise on change by shaping processes by helping an organisation identify key success factors and assessing its strengths and weaknesses regarding each factor.

The 'Ulrich model of business partnering' has been widely espoused in the US and the UK, partly because of its rhetorical simplicity and its forceful message to change the HR function (Caldwell, 2008). In addition, steeply climbing salaries and an increased perception of status and prestige mean that the business partner term seems to have become the title of choice for ambitious HR practitioners (Francis and Keegan, 2006). However, not all aspects of the role have been embraced with equal enthusiasm. Although Ulrich (1998) suggests that the HR function needs to fulfil all four roles, empirical evidence suggests that HR practitioners are more likely to aspire to the strategic roles of strategic partner and change agent rather than the more operationally focused roles of administrative expert and employee champion. Survey findings in the UK (CIPD, 2003) show that a third of HR practitioners see their primary role as strategic partners and nearly three in five aspire to this role, whilst 28 per cent see themselves as change agents and a similar proportion (30 per cent) would like to play this role. In contrast, a quarter of respondents see their primary role as administrative expert and only 4 per cent would like to play this role and 12 per cent see themselves as employee champions and only 6 per cent would wish to do so.

Why do you think so few HR professionals want to be employee champions?

There is a danger that the emphasis in the HR literature on the achievement of business-oriented performance outcomes has minimised the contribution of the employee champion role and obscured the importance of employee well-being in its own right (Peccei, 2004 cited in Francis and Keegan, 2006). However, a number of studies (e.g. Guest and King, 2004;

Hope-Hailey *et al.*, 2005) show that the neglect of people-centred roles can have a negative effect on the sustainability of organisational performance.

Activity

Read the article by Hope-Hailey et al. (2005) 'The HR department's role in organisational performance', *Human Resource Management Journal*, 15, 3: 49–66.

What are the key problems caused by the HR department's adoption of a more strategic role and the relegation of the employee champion role to line managers?

How might these difficulties be overcome?

A more recent variant of this model (Ulrich and Brockbank, 2005a) redefines the employee champion and administrative expert roles, integrates the change agent role into the strategic partner role and introduces the new role of HR leader, see Table 1.2. These 'subtle but important changes' are described as reflecting the 'changing roles we are observing in the leading organisations with which we work' (p. 24), but also serve to correct the imbalances of business partnering roles (Caldwell, 2008). Ulrich and Brockbank (2005b: 201) argue that 'caring for, listening to, and responding to employees remains the centerpiece of HR work'. So, the employee champion role is enlarged and focuses on building the workforce of the future as well as addressing the employees' current needs. Functional experts are not only concerned with administrative efficiency, but also apply their expert knowledge to the design and implementation of HR practices that 'improve decisions and deliver results' (Ulrich and Brockbank, 2005a: 26). HR leaders are responsible for leading the HR function in order to enhance its credibility.

Table 1.2 Evolution of HR roles

Mid-1990s	Mid-2000s	Evolution of thinking
Employee champion	Employee advocate	Focuses on the needs of today's employee
	Human capital developer	Focuses on preparing employees to be successful in the future
Administrative expert	Functional expert	HR practices are central to HR value. Some HR practices are delivered though administrative efficiency and others through policies and interventions
Change agent	Strategic partner	Being a strategic partner has multiple dimensions: business expert, change agent, strategic HR planner, knowledge manager and consultant
Strategic partner	Strategic partner	As above
	Leader	Being an HR leader requires functioning in each of these four roles. However, being an HR leader also has implications for leading the HR function, collaborating with other functions, setting and enhancing the standards for strategic thinking and ensuring corporate governance

Source: from Role call, People Management. 11(12), pp. 24–28 (Ulrich, D. and Brockbank, W. 2005), with permission from D. Ulrich and W. Brockbank.

STOP and think

To what extent do these new titles increase the attractiveness of operational HR roles?

While many HR practitioners aspire to a more strategic role, survey data suggest that operational and administrative work is still dominant. The CIPD survey (2007) into the roles and responsibilities of HR practitioners asked respondents to identify the three most time-consuming activities and the three most important activities in terms of their contribution to the organisation. The results are shown in Figure 1.7. These findings help to illustrate the ongoing tensions between competing role demands on the HR function and the difficulties in creating an entirely new role and agenda for the function that 'focuses it not on traditional HR activities such as staffing and compensation, but on outcomes' (Ulrich, 1998: 124).

The findings may also reflect claims that although the role of the HR professional in contemporary organisations has become more multifaceted and complex, at least some of the negative counter-images of the past still remain (Caldwell, 2003: 983). Similar findings emerge from other studies. For example, Guest and King (2004) explore how far the advent of HRM offers a new basis for power and influence amongst HR professionals. From the findings they conclude that:

> While the rhetoric surrounding the importance of people management and people as key assets in the fight for competitive advantage has taken hold in industry, and while it is no longer quite right to claim that in the absence of a crisis HR is invariably a low priority for top management, neither is it a high priority.
> (Guest and King, 2004: 421)

Behavioural competence becomes more critical as people develop into senior roles and research suggests that HR professionals need to develop a broader skill-set if they are to meet the challenges facing business today (CIPD, 2009). Survey respondents (CIPD, 2007) identify the most important competencies for effective HR practitioners as strategic thinking, influencing/political skills and business knowledge. However, the respondents also consider that these are the most challenging to develop. The emphasis on critical behaviours, coupled with the rise of the 'HR business partner' has led to an enormous growth in HR competency

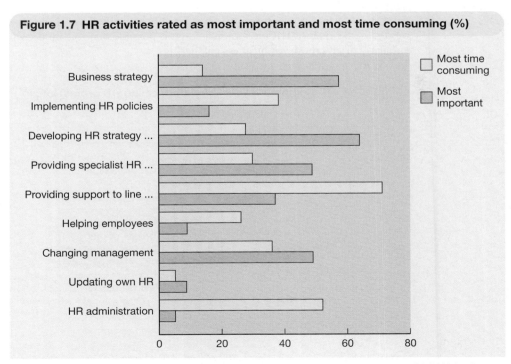

Figure 1.7 HR activities rated as most important and most time consuming (%)

Source: Adapted from *The Changing HR Function: Survey Report*, CIPD (CIPD 2007), p. 19, with the permission of the publisher, the Chartered Institute of Personnel and Development, London (www.cipd.co.uk).

models (see Caldwell, 2008). The Human Resource Competency Study (HRCS) led by Ulrich and Brockbank (reported in Grossman, 2007) looked at the competencies of HR professionals in over 400 companies in the US, Latin America, Europe, China, Australia and the Asian Pacific region. From their findings the researchers have identified six core competencies that high-performing HR professionals embody. These are depicted in Figure 1.8.

At the base of the pyramid are two competencies that Ulrich describes as 'table stakes – necessary but not sufficient' (Grossman, 2007: 61). In other words, these skills are required by all HR professionals but are insufficient on their own to deliver high performance:

- **Business ally** – knowledge and understanding of the business, its products and services, key customers, etc.
- **Operational executor** – competence in the effective and efficient delivery of transactional side of HR, concerned with the core activities of recruitment and selection, reward, development and employment relationship.

Three competencies are clustered together in the middle of the pyramid:

- **Strategy architect** – the ability to recognise key business trends, identify potential opportunities and likely obstacles.
- **Talent manager/organisational designer** – the ability to ensure the acquisition, development and retention of a high quality workforce and understanding of the organisational policies, practices and structures to support this.
- **Cultural steward** – the ability to shape company culture through facilitating change and fostering employee engagement. The HRCS identifies this role as the second highest predictor of performance of both HR professionals and HR departments (Grossman, 2007: 60).

The pinnacle of the pyramid, and therefore 'the top indicator in predicting overall outstanding performance' (Grossman, 2007: 59) is the:

- **Credible activist** – 'doing HR with attitude', delivering results with integrity, sharing information, building relationships of trust, taking appropriate risks, influencing others.

A number of larger organisations have already started to use these terms to describe the desired behaviours of HR professionals, so it is possible that this model will become as influential as Ulrich's model of business partnering.

Figure 1.8 HR Competencies of high performing HR professionals

Credible activist

Cultural steward
Talent manager
Strategy architect

Business ally
Operational
executor

Source: Adapted from Grossman (2007: 60)

Conclusion

HRM has now become the most popular term in the English-speaking world to refer to the activities of management in the employment relationship (Boxall and Purcell, 2008), but debates around the meaning of the term and the impact of the concept continue. In order to differentiate the generic use of the term, i.e. to cover all activities relating to people management and its more specific meaning as an approach focusing on enhancing the discretionary behaviour of individuals, a number of other terms have been introduced such as high-commitment management, high-involvement management and high-performance work systems. From its early origins a key theme in the HRM debate has concerned the relationship between HRM practice and organisational performance. The results are somewhat ambiguous in that, whilst there appear to be associations between HRM and organisational performance, a question remains over which comes first: does HRM lead to better organisational performance or are better-performing organisations more able to invest in HRM practices? Either way, it still seems that the majority of organisations have embraced HRM in a partial rather than a complete way. At the same time, it appears that the advent of HRM has had only partial impact on the role and status of the HR function and, while many HR practitioners aspire to more strategic roles, the operational focus continues to be dominant.

Overall, it seems that HRM as a term is widely used but subject to different interpretations so that 'it is easy to find slippage in its use' (Marchington and Wilkinson, 2008: 4). These different interpretations can be confusing, but they are also part of the attraction of HRM for academics and practitioners and help ensure that 'the domain remains lively, vibrant and contested' (Storey, 2007: 17). Whatever the perspective taken, it seems that the advent of HRM has raised questions about the nature of people management that have stimulated one of the most intense and active debates to have occurred in the subject in the last 40 years and there is every likelihood that the debate will continue for some considerable time yet.

Summary

- **Defining HRM**. There is no universally agreed definition of HRM and definitions can refer to people management activities in the broadest sense or in the specific meanings of high-commitment management or a strategic approach to people management.

- **Models of HRM**. By the early 1980s a number of US analysts were writing about HRM and devising models and explanations for its emergence which can be traced back to the 1930s. Among the most significant of these are Devanna (fit and the matching model) and Beer (the Harvard model).

- **HRM and business performance**. Over recent years attention has focused on the impact of HRM on business performance. Results from empirical studies suggest that there is some association between HRM practice and business performance but the direction of causality is less clear as is the assumption that a set of practices can have universal applicability.

- **HRM in practice**. Empirical evidence continues to show that although there is a high use of individual HRM practices, only a minority of workplaces appear to adopt a full-blown version of HRM. The general low level of take-up can be attributed to organisational inertia and cost considerations, but may also suggest that some organisations seek to achieve competitive advantage through a 'low-road' approach of cost-cutting or new forms of Taylorism rather than the 'high-road' approach of HRM.

- **IHRM in multinationals**. HRM in multinational corporations is shaped by the interplay between home and host country. Within MNCs *international* HRM may create broad-based HR systems that minimise differences between national business systems and emphasise the importance of organisational cultures that are drawn from the strategic goals of the firm.

- **HRM and the HR function?** The emergence of HRM and the emphasis on its contribution to the achievement of business goals has been perceived by many practitioners as an opportunity to improve the power and status of the HR function. One of the most influential models over years has been developed by Ulrich (1998). However, survey findings show that, whilst many practitioners aspire to adopt a more strategic role, the administrative role is still dominant. More recently, attention has moved towards the competencies required by HR professionals to meet the challenges of business today.

Case study

HR must raise its game

To adapt that key question concerning the Romans posed by Reg, the not very heroic leader of the People's Front of Judea in Monty Python's *Life of Brian*: 'What has HR ever done for us?'

We know the usual answer. It is delivered with a sneer and a derisive snort. HR managers are the 'abominable "No" men' (and women, too, of course). They get together to form 'business prevention units'. This relentless carping has undermined their self-confidence and surveys confirm that HR people worry that colleagues do not take them seriously. They struggle to influence the corporate agenda.

The financial crisis has only made things worse. HR is summoned to redundancy negotiations, but may then be ignored. And now questions are being asked about what HR did or did not do to help avert this crisis in the first place.

At a private meeting in London last week, hosted by the Corporate Research Forum (CRF), a management think-tank, senior HR professionals discussed whether they should have spoken up sooner about corporate excess. One said some HR directors at the banks had expressed regret at their failure to stay the hands of their chief executives – but added that another had admitted privately that, in his case, there would have been no point in trying.

Don't get the wrong idea. This gathering was pretty upbeat. There was a refreshing lack of traditional HR self-flagellation. Here was a group of people steeling themselves to make a much bigger impact on their organisations. But in addition to Reg's initial question we must also ask: to what problem is HR the solution? HR's true believers reply: without us there can be no sustained high performance.

CRF presented the meeting with a report on the future of HR. At its heart lay the question of gover-

nance. Some boards and senior management teams have failed to exercise proper control over their organisations in recent years. Those top-level discussions have been lacking something. Maybe a credible and influential HR director would be the best person to speak up.

Also attending the meeting was Patrick Wright, professor at Cornell university's school of industrial and labour relations, in the US. In his many discussions with business leaders he has found that there are concerns about the way ethical issues can get downplayed, or even completely ignored, because nobody else in a senior role will raise them. Guess who gets volunteered to do so? 'The HR director is told: "You need to get this on the table"', he says. Not easy – especially when you have little idea how much public support you will receive from your colleagues.

Perhaps, Professor Wright suggests, the HR director needs to become a kind of 'chief integrity officer', who could avoid being penalised if the chief executive's appetite for integrity turns out to be limited.

CRF's report makes other suggestions. The HR director should be involved in the selection and assessment of board members. He or she could monitor how well the board operates, design a performance management system and write development plans for each board member. And have a say in what they get paid.

The ultimate goal for HR, though, is 'organisational effectiveness' – helping to create a 'high-performance environment as well as a capable workforce', the CRF report suggests. Talent management, skills and leadership development, dealing with change – these and other 'people issues' are all on their agenda.

It seems plain that CEOs and other senior managers should focus more carefully on what they want the HR team to do for them. One HR director told last week's meeting that, on being appointed, the CEO had declared: 'I know what I don't want from you. But I'm not sure what I do want.'

Can the HR director act as a coach to the CEO and other senior managers? That will depend on the openness of the relationships at the top – and also on the courage of HR directors. One is quoted in the report as saying: 'My CEO expects to be challenged and receive insights about his leadership style. I tell him things he won't hear anywhere else. He has learned the hard way that this is in his own interests.' That may not sound like many HR directors you know. But speaking the truth to power ought to be part of any senior HR manager's job.

Still not convinced that HR has anything to offer you? Turn to last July's *Harvard Business Review*, where two recent Harvard MBAs, Matthew Breitfelder and Daisy Wademan, talk proudly about their commitment to their adopted discipline.

'In business school, we were trained to seek out underappreciated investment opportunities and to create value in surprising places,' they wrote. 'We see an undervalued and underpriced asset in the HR function itself, one that is poised to appreciate significantly.'

Ms Wademan is no fool. When she co-authored this article she was still a VP in HR for the investment bank Lehman Brothers. But by the end of the summer, before Lehman collapsed, she had secured a safe berth at Morgan Stanley. Human resourcefulness personified.

Source: from HR must raise its game, *Financial Times*, 17 February 2009, p. 38 (Stern, S.).

Questions

1 To what extent can HRM practices contribute to 'organisational effectiveness' as identified in this extract?

2 To what extent can the competencies identified by Ulrich help HR professionals make a bigger impact on their organisations?

3 Should HR be custodians of ethical issues in an organisation?

References and further reading

Those texts marked with an asterisk are recommended for further reading.

Almond, P., Edwards, T. and Clark, I. (2003) 'Multinationals and changing national business systems in Europe: towards the 'shareholder value' model'? *Industrial Relations Journal*, 34, 5.

Applebaum, E., Bailey, T., Berg, P. and Kalleberg, A. (2000) *Manufacturing Advantage: Why High-Performance Systems Pay Off*. Ithaca, NY: ILR Press.

Arthur, J.B. (1992) 'The link between business strategy and industrial relations systems in American steel mini-mills', *Industrial and Labour Relations Review*, 45, 3: 488–506.

Arthur, J.B. (1994) 'Effects of human resource systems on manufacturing performance and turnover', *Academy of Management Journal*, 37, 3: 670–87.

Barney, J. (1991) 'Firm resources and sustained competitive advantage', *Journal of Management*, 17, 1: 99–120.

Barney, J. and Griffin, R. (1992) *The Management of Organisations: Strategy, Structure, Behavior*, Boston, MA: Houghton Mifflin.

Bartlett, C. and Ghosal, S. (1989) *Managing Across Borders*. Harvard, MA: Transnational Solution.

Beardwell, I.J. (1992) 'The new industrial relations: a review of the debate', *Human Resource Management Journal*, 2, 2: 1–8.

Beardwell, I.J. (1996) 'How do we know how it really is?' in I.J. Beardwell (ed.) *Contemporary Industrial Relations*. Oxford: Oxford University Press, pp. 1–10.

Beardwell, I. and Holden, L. (1994) *Human Resource Management: A Contemporary Perspective*. London: Pitman.

Becker, B. and Gerhart, B. (1996) 'The impact of human resource management on organisational performance: progress and prospects' *Academy of Management Journal*, 39, 4: 779–801.

*Beer, M., Spector, B., Lawrence P.R., Quinn Mills, D. and Walton, R.E. (1984) *Managing Human Assets*. New York: Free Press.

Boselie, P., Dietz, G. and Boon, C. (2005) 'Commonalities and contradictions in HRM and performance research', *Human Resource Management Journal*, 15, 3: 67–94.

Boxall, P. and Purcell, J. (2008) *Strategy and Human Resource Management, 2nd edn*. Houndmills: Palgrave Macmillan.

Boxall, P. and Steeneveld, M. (1999) 'Human resource strategy and competitive advantage: a longitudinal study of engineering and competitive advantage: a longitudinal study of engineering consultancies', *Journal of Management Studies*, 36, 4: 443–63.

Caldwell, R. (2003) 'The changing role of personnel managers: old ambiguities, new uncertainties', *Journal of Management Studies*, 40, 4: 983–1004.

Caldwell, R. (2008) 'HR business partner competency models: re-contextualising effectiveness', *Human Resource Management Journal*, 18, 3: 275–94.

Chadwick, C. and Cappelli, P. (1998) 'Alternatives to generic strategy typologies in strategic human resource management' in P. Wright, L. Dyer, J. Boudreau and G. Milkovich (eds) *Research in Personnel and Human Resource Management*. Greenwich, CT: JAI Press.

Clark, I. and Almond, P. (2004) 'Dynamism and embeddedness: towards a lower road? British subsidiaries of American multinationals', *Industrial Relations Journal*, 35, 6: 536–57.

CIPD (2003) 'Where are we: where are we heading?'. *HR Survey*, London: CIPD.

CIPD (2006) *People, Productivity and Performance – Work Smart*. London: CIPD.

CIPD (2007) *The Changing HR Function*, Survey Report, September.

CIPD (2009) *Taking the Temperature on 'HR Skills for Survival'*, Survey Report, April.

CIPD/EEF (2005) *Maximising Employee Potential and Business Performance: The Role of High Performance Working*, CIPD Report, December.

Conference Board (2005) McGuckin, R. and van Ark, B. *Performance 2005: Productivity, Employment and Income in the World's Economies*. New York: Conference Board, August.

Cully, M., Woodland, S., O'Reilly, A. and Dix, G. (1999) *Britain at Work: As Depicted by the 1998 Workplace Employee Relations Survey*. London: Routledge.

Delery, J.E. and & Doty, H. (1996) 'Modes of theorizing in strategic human resource management: tests of universalistic, contingency and configurational performance predictions', *Academy of Management Journal*, 39, 4: 802–35.

*Devanna, M.A., Fombrun, C.J. and Tichy, N.M. (1984) 'A framework for strategic human resource management' in C.J. Fombrun, M.M. Tichy and M.A. Devanna (eds) *Strategic Human Resource Management*. New York: John Wiley.

Dowling, P. and Welch, D. (2004) *International Human Resource Management*, 4th edn. London: Thomson Learning.

Edwards, T. and Ferner, A. (2002) 'The renewed American challenge', *Industrial Relations Journal*, 33, 2: 94–111.

Employment Department (1992) 'People, jobs and opportunity', UK Government White Paper.

ESRC (2004) *The UK's Productivity Gap: What Research Tells Us and What We Need to Know*. Swindon: ESRC.

Ferner, A. (2003) 'Foreign multinationals and industrial relations innovation in Britain', in P. Edwards (ed.) *Industrial Relations in Britain*, 2nd edn. Oxford: Blackwell.

Ferner, A., Almond, P., Clark, I., Colling, T., Edwards, T., Holden, L. and Muller, M. (2004) 'The dynamics of central control and subsidiary autonomy in the management of human resources: case study evidence from US multinationals in the UK', *Organisational Studies*, 25, 3: 363–93.

Fombrun, C.J. (1984) 'The external context of human resource management' in C.J. Fombrun, N.M. Tichy and M.A. Devanna (eds) *Strategic Human Resource Management*. New York: John Wiley, pp. 1–18.

Forth, J., Bewley, H. and Bryson, A. (2007) *Small and Medium-sized Enterprises: Findings from the 2004 Workplace Employment Relations Survey*. London: Department for Business, Enterprise and Regulatory Reforms

Foulkes, F. (1980) *Personnel Policies in Large Non-Union Companies*. Englewood Cliffs, NJ: Prentice Hall.

Francis, H. and Keegan, A. (2006) 'The changing face of HRM: in search of balance', *Human Resource Management Journal*, 16, 3: 231–49.

Friedman, A. (1977) *Industry and Labour*. London: Macmillan.

Godard, J. (2004) 'A critical assessment of the high-performance paradigm', *British Journal of Industrial Relations*, 42, 2: 349–78.

Grossman, R. (2007) 'New competencies for HR', *HR Magazine*, June, 58-62.

Guest, D. (1987) 'Human resource management and industrial relations', *Journal of Management Studies*, 24, 5: 503–21.

Guest, D. (1989) 'Human resource management: its implications for industrial relations and trade unions' in J. Storey (ed.) *New Perspectives on Human Resource Management*. London: Routledge, pp. 41–55.

Guest, D. (1991) 'Personnel management: the end of orthodoxy?' *British Journal of Industrial Relations*, 29, 2: 149–75.

Guest, D. (1997) 'Human resource management and performance: a review and research agenda', *International Journal of Human Resource Management*, 8, 3: 263–76.

Guest, D. (2001) 'Industrial relations and human resource management', in J. Storey (ed.) *HRM: A Critical Text*. London: Thomson Learning.

Guest, D. and Conway, N. (1997) *Employee Motivation and the Psychological Contract, Issues in Personnel Management*, 21. London: IPD.

Guest, D. and Conway, N. (1999) 'Peering into the black hole: the downside of the new employment relations in the UK', *British Journal of Industrial Relations*, 37, 3: 367–89.

Guest, D. and King, Z. (2004) 'Power, innovation and problem solving: the personnel managers' three steps to heaven?' *Journal of Management Studies*, 41, 3: 401–23.

Guest, D., Michie, J., Conway, N. and Sheehan, M. (2003) 'Human resource management and corporate performance in the UK', *British Journal of Industrial Relations*, 41, 2: 291–314.

Guest, D., Michie, J., Sheehan, M., Conway, N. and Metochi, M. (2000) 'Effective people management: initial findings of the future of work study', *CIPD Research Report*. London: CIPD.

Guthrie, J. (2001) 'High-involvement work practices, turnover and productivity: evidence from New Zealand', *Academy of Management Journal*, 44, 1: 180-90.

Hendry, C. and Pettigrew, A. (1990) 'Human resource management: an agenda for the 1990s', *International Journal of Human Resource Management*, 1, 1: 17–43.

Hirst, P. and Thompson, G. (1999) *Globalization in Question*, 2nd edn. London: Polity.

Hofstede, G. (1980) *Culture's Consequences: International Differences in Work Related Values*. London: Sage.

Hofstede, G. (1991) *Cultures and Organizations: Software of the Mind*. London: McGraw-Hill.

Hope-Hailey, V., Farndale, E. and Truss, C. (2005) 'The HR department's role in organizational performance', *Human Resource Management Journal*, 15, 3: 49–66.

Huczynski, A. and Buchanan, D. (2007) *Organizational Behaviour*, 6th edn. Harlow: FT/Prentice Hall.

*Huselid, M. (1995) 'The impact of HRM practices on turnover, productivity and corporate financial performance', *Academy of Management Journal*, 38, 3: 635–72.

Hyde, P., Boaden, R., Cortvriend, P., Harris, C., Marchington, M., Pass, S., Sparrow, P. and Sibbald, B. (2006) 'Improving health through human resource management: a starting point for change', *Change Agenda*. London: CIPD.

Ichniowski, C., Shaw, K. and Prennushi, G. (1997) 'The effects of human resource management practices on productivity: a study of steel finishing lines', *American Economic Review*, 87, 291–313.

Jacoby, S. (1997) *Modern Manors: Welfare Capitalism Since the New Deal*. Princeton, NJ: Princeton University Press.

Jacoby, S. (2005) *The Embedded Corporation: Corporate Governance and Employment Relations in Japan and the United States*. Princeton, NJ: Princeton University Press.

Kanter, R. (1984) *The Change Masters*. London: Allen & Unwin.

Kaufman, B. (1993) *The Origins and Evolution of the Field of Industrial Relations*. New York: ILR Press.

Kersley, B., Alpin, C., Forth, J., Bryson, A., Bewley, H., Dix, G. and Oxenbridge, S. (2006) *Inside the Workplace: Findings from the 2004 Workplace Employment Relations Survey*. London: Routledge.

Kochan, T. and Barocci, T. (1985) *Human Resource Management and Industrial Relations*. Boston, MA: LittleBrown.

*Legge, K. (1989) 'Human resource management: a critical analysis' in J. Storey (ed.) *New Perspectives on Human Resource Management*. London: Routledge, pp. 19–40.

*Legge, K. (2005) *HRM: Rhetorics and Realities*. Basingstoke: Macmillan Business.

McDuffie, J.P. (1995) 'Human resource bundles and manufacturing performance', *Industrial and Labour Relations Review*, 48, 2: 197–221.

Marchington, M. and Wilkinson, A. (2008) *Human Resource Management at Work*, 4th edn. London: CIPD.

Marchington, M. and Zagelmeyer, S. (2005) 'Foreword: linking HRM and performance – a never-ending search?' *Human Resource Management Journal*, 15, 4: 3–8.

Paauwe, J. and Richardson, R. (1997) 'Introduction', *International Journal of Human Resource Management*, 8, 3: 257–62.

Patterson, M., West, M., Lawthorm, R. and Nickell, S. (1997) *The Impact of People Management Practices on Business Performance*, Issues in People Management, 22. London: IPD.

Peters, T.J. and Waterman, R.H. (1982) *In Search of Excellence: Lessons from America's Best Run Companies*. New York: Harper & Row.

Pfeffer, J. (1998) *The Human Equation*. Boston, MA: Harvard Business School Press.

Price, A. (2004) *Human Resource Management in a Business Context*, 2nd edn. London: Thomson Learning.

Purcell, J., Kinnie, N., Hutchinson, S., Rayton, B. and Swart, J. (2003) *Understanding the People and Performance Link: Unlocking the Black Box*. London, CIPD.

Ramsay, H., Scholarios, D. and Harley, B. (2000) 'Employees and high-performance work systems: testing inside the black box', *British Journal of Industrial Relations*, 38, 4: 501–31.

Richardson, R. and Thompson, P. (1999) *The impact of people management practices on business performance: a literature review*, Issues in People Management. London: IPD.

Rollinson, D. and Dundon, T. (2007) *Understanding Employment Relations*. London: McGraw-Hill.

Schuler, R. (1989) 'Strategic human resource management and industrial relations', *Human Relations*, 42, 2: 157–84.

*Sisson, K. (2001) 'Human resource management and the personnel function: a case of partial impact?' in J. Storey (ed.) *Human Resource Management: A Critical Text*, 2nd edn. London: Thomson Learning.

Sisson, K. and Storey, J. (2000) *The Realities of Human Resource Management*. Buckingham: Open University Press.

Stewart, R. (1991) *Managing Today and Tomorrow*. London: Macmillan.

Storey, J. (1992) *Developments in the Management of Human Resources: An Analytical Review*. London: Blackwell.

*Storey, J. (2007) 'Human resource management today: an assessment' in J. Storey (ed.) *Human Resource Management: A Critical Text*, 3rd edn. London: Thomson Learning.

Sung, J. and Ashton, D. (2005) '*High Performance Work Practices: Linking Strategy, Skills and Performance Outcomes*'. London: DTI/CIPD.

Tamkin, P., Cowling, H. and Hunt, W. (2008) *People and the Bottom Line, Report 448*. Brighton: IES.

Thompson, M. (1998) 'Jet setters', *People Management*, 4, 8: 38–41.

Truss, C., Gratton, L., Hope-Hailey, V., McGovern, P. and Stiles, P. (1997) 'Soft and hard models of human resource management: a reappraisal', *Journal of Management Studies*, 34, 1: 53–73.

Ulrich, D. (1998) *Human Resource Champions*. Boston, MA: Harvard Business School Press.

Ulrich, D. and Brockbank, W. (2005a) 'Role call', *People Management*, 11, 12: 24–28.

Ulrich, D and Brockbank, W. (2005b) *The HR Value Proposition*. Boston, MA: Harvard University Press.

Wall, T. and Wood, S. (2005) 'The romance of human resource management and business performance and the case for big science', *Human Relations*, 58, 4: 429–62.

Walton, R.E. (1985) 'From control to commitment in the workplace', *Harvard Business Review*, 63, 2: March–April, 76–84.

Watson, T. (2002) *Organising and Managing Work*. Harlow: FT/Prentice Hall.

West, M., Borrill, C., Dawson, J., Scully, J., Carter, M., Anelay, S., Patterson, M. and Waring, J. (2002) 'The link between the management of employees and patient mortality in acute hospitals', *International Journal of Human Resource Management*, 13, 8: 1299–310.

Whitley, R. (1999) *Divergent Capitalisms: The Social Structuring and Change of Business Systems*. Oxford: Oxford University Press.

Wood, S. (1999) 'Human resource management and performance', *International Journal of Management Reviews*, 1, 4: 367–413.

Wright, P., McMahan, G. and McWilliams, A. (1994) 'Human resources and sustained competitive advantage: a resource-based perspective', *International Journal of Human Resource Management*, 5, 2: 301–26.

For multiple-choice questions, exercises and annotated weblinks related to this topic, visit **www.pearsoned.co.uk/mymanagementlab**.

Chapter 2

Strategic human resource management

Nicky Golding

Objectives

- To indicate the significance of the business context in developing an understanding of the meaning and application of SHRM.
- To evaluate the relationship between strategic management and SHRM.
- To examine the different approaches to SHRM including:
  - the best fit approach to SHRM;
  - the configurational approach to SHRM;
  - the resource-based view of SHRM;
  - the best practice approach to SHRM.
- To evaluate the relationship between SHRM and organisational performance.
- To present a number of activities and case studies that will facilitate the reader's understanding of the nature and complexity of the SHRM debate, and enable the reader to apply their knowledge and understanding.

Introduction to strategic human resource management

This chapter charts the development of strategic human resource management. It assumes a certain familiarity with the evolution of HRM, early HRM models and frameworks and their theoretical underpinning as discussed in other chapters and particularly Chapter 1. The aim of this chapter is to provide a challenging and critical analysis of the strategic human resource management literature, so that you will be able to understand the synthesis both within and between strategic human resource management and strategic management in its various forms.

Since the early 1980s, when human resource management arrived on the managerial agenda, there has been considerable debate concerning its nature and its value to organisations. From the seminal works emerging from the Chicago School and the matching model of HRM (Fombrun *et al.*, 1984) the emphasis has very much concerned its *strategic* role in the organisation. Indeed, the now large literature rarely differentiates between human resource management (HRM) and strategic human resource management (SHRM). Some writers have associated HRM with the strategic aspects and concerns of 'best fit', in vertically aligning an organisation's human resources to the needs of the organisation as expressed in the organisational strategy (Fombrun, *et al.* 1984) or by creating 'congruence' or 'horizontal alignment' between various managerial and HRM policies (Beer, *et al.*, 1984; Walton, 1985). Others have focused on HRM as a means of gaining commitment and linked this to outcomes of enhanced organisational performance and business effectiveness (Beer *et al.*, 1984; Guest, 1987; Guest *et al.*, 2000a; Wood and De Menezes, 1998); through best practice models (Pfeffer, 1994; 1998; MacDuffie, 1995; Arthur, 1994) or high-performance work practices (Huselid, 1995; Guest, 1987). Others have recognised the 'harder' nature of strategic HRM (Storey, 1992) emphasising its contribution to business efficiency. Interlaced with this debate has been the wider controversy concerning the nature of business strategy itself, from which strategic HRM takes its theoretical constructs.

Add to this transformations in organisational forms, which have impacted simultaneously on both structures and relationships in organisations. The need for increased flexibility (Atkinson, 1984), or 'agility' (Rahrami, 1992: 35) in organisational structures and relationships, has led to 'delayering, team-based networks, alliances and partnerships and a new employer–employee covenant' or psychological contract. These changes in organisational structuring and employer–employee relationships, have led to difficulties finding new organisational forms that both foster creativity and avoid chaos. Thus tensions can arise between 'innovation and maintaining focus, between rapid response and avoiding duplication, between a focus on future products and meeting time to market criteria, between long-term vision and ensuring performance today'. These tensions have become more apparent with the global downturn in 2009, as organisations grapple with remaining lean and focused through 'rightsizing', yet needing to maintain a motivated core base of skill and knowledge capable of creativity and rapid response in the future. These dilemmas are not new to the strategic HRM literature, Kanter in 1989 noted contradictions between remaining 'lean, mean and fit' on the one hand, yet being seen as a great company to work for on the other.

Developments in SHRM thinking, explored in this chapter through the development of the best fit approach, the configurational approach, the resource-based approach and the best practice approach have a profound impact on our understanding of the contribution SHRM can make to organisational performance, through increased competitive advantage and added value. Indeed, it becomes clear that whether the focus of SHR practices is on alignment with the external context or on the internal context of the firm, the meaning of SHRM can only really be understood in the context of something else, namely organisational performance, whether that be in terms of economic value added and increased shareholder value; customer value added and increased market share or people added value through increased employee commitment and *reservoirs* of employee skills, knowledge and talent.

The debate therefore, becomes extremely complex in its ramifications for analysing processes, evaluating performance and assessing outcomes. The observer, therefore, must come to the view, in the best postmodern tradition, that the profusion and confusion of policy makes straightforward analysis of SHRM in empirical and analytical terms extremely difficult and contingent on positional stances of the actors and observers involved in the research process. However, some kind of analytical context is useful in beginning our evaluations.

In order to understand the development of strategic human resource management, and recognise that SHRM is more than traditional human resource management prefixed with the word 'strategic', it is necessary to consider the nature of strategic management. This will provide an understanding of the 'strategic' context within which strategic human resource management has developed, and enable us to understand the increasingly complex relationship between strategic management and strategic human resource management.

Understanding the business context

The nature of business strategy

Boxall (1996: 60) has commented that 'any credible attempt at model-building in strategic HRM involves taking a position on the difficult questions: what is strategy? (content) and how is strategy formed? (process)'. It is the intention of this section to explore these questions, and identify the difficulties and complexities involved in the 'strategy-making' process. This section provides an overview of some of the issues and debates, and sets the context for the SHRM debate discussed later in the chapter. It is not within the remit of this chapter, however, to provide a comprehensive review of strategic management theory. Readers are encouraged to seek further reading on strategic management, particularly if the material is completely new to you.

The roots of business strategy stretch far back into history (Alexander the Great 356–323 BC, Julius Caesar 100–44 BC), and early writers linked the term 'strategy' to the ancient Greek word 'strategos', which means 'general' and has connotations of 'to lead' and 'army'. Thus it is not surprising that many dictionary definitions convey a military perspective:

> Strategy. The art of war, especially the planning of movements of troops and ships etc. into favourable positions; plan of action or policy in business or politics etc.
>
> Oxford Pocket Dictionary

Early writings on business strategy adopted a military model combined with economics, particularly the notion of rational–economic man (Chandler, 1962; Sloan, 1963; Ansoff, 1965). This is known as the classical or rational-planning approach, and has influenced business thinking for many decades. The meaning of strategy has changed, however, and become more complex over the last 20 years or so, as the literature has moved from emphasising a long-term planning perspective (Chandler, 1962) to a more organic evolutionary process occupying a shorter time frame. (Ansoff and McDonnell, 1990; Aktouf 1996). Thus strategic management in the twenty-first century is seen to be as much about vision and direction as about planning, mechanisms and structure.

> Throughout the first half of our century and even into the early eighties, planning with its inevitable companion, strategy – has always been a key word, the core, the near ultimate weapon of 'good' and 'true' management. Yet many firms including Sony, Xerox, Texas Instruments ... have been remarkably successful ... with minimal official, rational and systematic planning.
>
> (Aktouf, 1996: 91)

Activity

How would you define the word 'strategy'? Note down five words you associate with strategy.

Strategy is a difficult concept to define, sometimes it is easier to think in terms of metaphors. We have already been introduced to the military metaphor of 'strategy as the art of war'. What other metaphors might you use to define strategy?

What metaphor would best describe the 'strategy-making' process in your organisation? If you are unable to use your organisation, you can use the case study at the end of this chapter.

Approaches to the strategy-making process

This chapter uses the four distinctive approaches to strategy-making identified by Whittington (1993, 2001) as a model of analysis. These are the *classical* or *rational-planning approach*, the *evolutionary approach*, the *processual approach* and the *systemic approach*. As you will see, an organisation's approach to its 'strategy-making' process has implications for our understanding and application of strategic human resource management.

The classical or rational-planning approach

This view suggests strategy is formed through a formal and rational decision-making process. The key stages of the strategy-making process emphasise a comprehensive analysis of the external and internal environment that then enables an organisation to evaluate and choose from a range of strategic choices that in turn allows for plans to be made to implement the strategy. With this approach, profitability is assumed to be the only goal of business and the rational-planning approach the means to achieve it. Alfred Chandler (1962), a business historian, Igor Ansoff (1965), a theorist and Alfred Sloan (1963), President of General Motors, identified these key characteristics of the classical approach in their work and writings. Chandler defined strategy as:

> the determination of the basic, long-term goals and objectives of an enterprise, and the adoption of courses of action and the allocation of resources necessary for those goals.
>
> (1962: 13)

Grant (2008) highlighted the classical approach in his model of common elements in successful strategies (Figure 2.1): where clear goals, understanding the competitive environment, resource appraisal and effective implementation form the basis of his analysis.

Within the classical perspective, strategy can and often is viewed at three levels. First, at the *corporate level*, which relates to the overall scope of the organisation, its structures, financing and distribution of key resources; second, at a *business level*, which relates to its competitive positioning in markets/products/services; third, at an *operational level*, which

Figure 2.1 Common elements in successful strategies

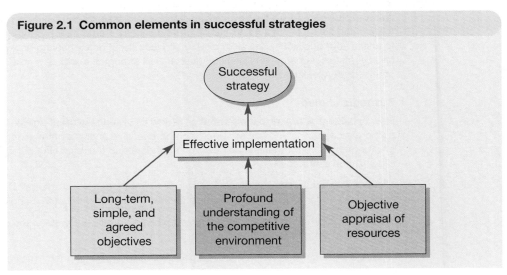

Source: Grant (2008: 7)

relates to the methods used by the various functions: marketing, finance, production and, of course, human resources to meet the objectives of the higher-level strategies. This approach tends to separate out operational practices from higher-level strategic planning. This is not always helpful in reality, as it is often operational practices and effective systems that are 'strategic' to success in organisations (Boxall and Purcell 2008), thus prompting Whittington (2001: 107) to comment that 'the rigid separation of strategy from operations is no longer valid in a knowledge-based age'. This is not to suggest that external analysis and planning should be ignored, but proposes a recognition that operational practices or 'tactical excellence' may provide sustainable competitive advantage by ensuring an organisation is adaptable and can flex with the environment. This becomes significant in contributing to our understanding of SHRM later in the chapter.

The classical approach, however, forms the basis of much of our early understanding of how organisations 'make strategy' and define competitive advantage. It is worth spending time on the activity below, which will enable you to understand and apply the strategic management process, from a classical rational-planning perspective. Drawing on Johnson and Scholes, (2002), it focuses on *strategic analysis*, which requires you to analyse the external and internal environment of an organisation and identify its key source of competitive advantage. This will then enable you to identify and evaluate the range of *strategic choices* open to the organisation, which in turn will enable you to consider the *implementation* stage of the strategy-making process in the organisation.

Activity | Analysing an organisation

Analyse the external environment

Analyse the external environment your business operates in. Consider the political, legal, technological, economic influences on your business. Now categorise these into opportunities and threats.

Analyse the internal environment

Now identify the internal strengths and weaknesses of the business. Consider the internal resources, structure, leadership, skills, knowledge, culture, etc.

Conduct a SWOT analysis

Put your analysis of the external and internal environment into a SWOT analysis. You might find it useful to prioritise the key strengths and weaknesses of the business, and the main threats and key opportunities available to the business. Remember it is important to be able to justify your decisions. You also need to be clear about differentiating between business and HR issues, although it is likely that certain HR strengths could be a core business competence/weakness.

Strategic choice

Now consider the organisation's strategy, review its vision statement, mission statement, corporate objectives and values. Does a comprehensive analysis of the external and internal environment of your organisation help you to understand the reasoning behind the organisation's strategy?

Can you identify the organisation's key sources of competitive advantage? Does this analysis help you to understand why the organisation has made certain strategic choices?

What other information do you think you would need to fully understand the strategy-making process in the organisation?

Do you think the organisation adopts a classical approach to 'strategy-making'?

Implementation

What changes has the organisation made in terms of culture, structures, leadership, functional strategies, specifically HR policies and practices to deliver their strategy. Have these changes been effective? Why? Why not?

You can either use the Case study at the end of this chapter to complete this exercise, or you can use the organisation you work for or one you are familiar with and for which you have access to company information.

In the previous activity, you have probably raised more questions than answers, and you have probably identified some of the short-comings of the classical approach. Mintzberg (1990), clearly identified the 'basic premises' of the classical approach as being the disciplined 'readiness and capacity of managers to adopt profit-maximising strategies through rational long-term planning' Whittington (2001: 15). He questioned the feasibility of adopting this approach as either a model for prescription of best practice or as a model of analysis, as he considered it to be an inflexible and oversimplified view of the 'strategy-making' process, relying too heavily on military models and their assumed culture of discipline. This can often lead to a disproportionate emphaisis on analysis and decision making about strategic choices at the expense of the key stage of implementation which, after all, delivers the results. Mintzberg (1987), therefore, argued that making strategy in practice tends to be complex and messy, and he preferred to think about strategy as 'crafting' rather than 'planning'.

The classical approach is, however, the basis for much strategy discussion and analysis, and, as we will see later, underpins much strategic HRM thinking, particularly the 'best fit' school of thought and the notion of vertical integration. If, however, we accept that devising and implementing strategies in organisations is a complex and organic process, then it highlights the complexity of both defining and applying strategic human resource management.

The evolutionary approach

An alternative view of the strategy-making process is the evolutionary approach. This suggests that strategy is made through an informal evolutionary process in which managers rely less upon top managers to plan and act rationally and more upon the markets to secure profit maximisation. Whittington (2001) highlights the links between the evolutionary approach and the 'natural law of the jungle'. Henderson (1989: 143), argued that 'Darwin is probably a better guide to business competition than economists are' as he recognised that markets are rarely static and indeed likened competition to a process of natural selection, where only the fittest survive. Darwin noted that more individuals of each species are born than can survive, thus there is a frequently recurring struggle for existence. Evolutionists, therefore, argue that markets not managers, choose the prevailing strategies. Thus in this approach the rational-planning models that analyse the external and internal environment in order to select the most appropriate strategic choices and then to identify and plan structural, product and service changes to meet market need, become irrelevant. The evolutionary approach suggests markets are too competitive for 'expensive strategizing and too unpredictable to outguess' (Whittington, 2001: 19). From this perspective sophisticated strategies can only deliver a temporary advantage, and some suggest focusing instead on efficiency and managing the 'transaction costs'.

The processual approach

Quinn (1978) recognised that in practice strategy formation tends to be fragmented, evolutionary and largely intuitive. His 'logical incrementalist' view, therefore, while acknowledging the value of the rational–analytical approach, identified the need to take account of the psychological, political and behavioural relationships which influence and contribute to strategy. Quinn's view fits well within Whittington's processual approach, which recognises 'organisations and markets' as 'sticky, messy phenomena, from which strategies emerge with much confusion and in small steps' (2001: 21).

The foundations of the processual school can be traced back to the work of the American Carnegie School according to Whittington (2001) and the work of Cyert and March (1956) and Simon (1947). They uncovered two key themes, first the cognitive limits of human action, and second, that human beings are influenced by 'bounded rationality' (Simon, 1947). Thus no single human being, whether he be the chief executive or a production worker, is likely to have all the answers to complex and difficult problems, and we all often have to act without knowing everything we would like to. Thus complexity, uncertainty and the need to take on board a range of interests become facts of life in strategic management and consequently in SHRM (Boxall and Purcell, 2008). It is important for organisations to recognise this to avoid falling into a fog of complacency or the 'success trap' (Barr *et al.*, 1992), and it also highlights the limitations of some of the prescriptions for success advocated both in the strategic management and SHRM literature. In practice, an organisation's approach to SHRM has considerable influence here on the strategic management process, as to effectively manage the environment better than their competitors, some writers would suggest that the organisation needs to adopt a learning and open systems perspective. Mintzberg (1987) recognised this in his ideas on 'crafting strategy', and the fluid and organic nature of the strategy-making process. He compared the skills required of those involved in the process to those of a traditional craftsperson – traditional skill, dedication, perfection, mastery of detail, sense of involvement and intimacy through experience and commitment. Thus he recognised that planned strategies are not always realised strategies, and that strategies can often emerge and evolve (Figure 2.2). Thus the classic sequence of plan first, implementation second can become blurred, as 'strategy is discovered in action' (March, 1976). Second, the processualists noted the significance of the micro-politics within organisations, a theme since developed by Pettigrew (1973, 1985) and Wilson (1992). This

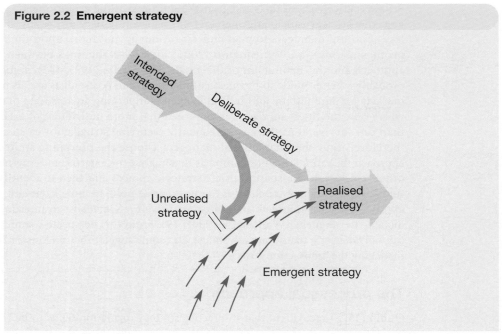

Figure 2.2 Emergent strategy

Source: from The Strategy Concept 1: Five Ps for Strategy, *California Management Review*, 30(1), pp. 11–24 (Mintzberg, H.), Copyright © 1987 by The Regents of the University of California, by permission of The Regents.

approach recognises the inherent rivalries and conflicting goals present within organisations and the impact this can have on strategy implementation. As we will see later in the chapter, it is these pluralist tensions that are sometimes ignored in certain branches of the SHRM literature, most notably the 'best practice' approach.

Can you think of reasons why an intended strategy might not be realised? Why do strategies sometimes emerge?

Illustrate your answers with examples from your own experience. If you do not have organisational examples, reflect upon your personal development so far.

What factors have influenced your choice of university? degree subject? career?, etc. Have you followed your original plans? What changes have you made? Have new strategies emerged? Using Mintzberg's model, you could plot your development so far on a time-line, identifying where and why planned strategies have failed to be realised while new ones have emerged

The systemic approach

This leads us on to the final perspective identified by Whittington (1993, 2001), the systemic approach. The systemic approach suggests that strategy is shaped by the social system it operates within. Strategic choices, therefore, are shaped by the cultural and institutional interests of a broader society. So for example, state intervention in France and Germany has shaped HRM in a way which is different from the USA and the UK. A key theme of the systemic approach is that 'decision makers are not detached, calculating individuals interacting in purely economic transactions' (Whittington, 2001: 26) but are members of a community 'rooted in a densely interwoven social system'. Therefore in reality, organisations and their members' choices are embedded in a network of social relations (Whittington, 1993). Thus according to this approach, organisations differ according to the social and economic systems in which they are embedded.

What are the implications for multinational organisations if we assume a systemic view of strategy?

What are the implications for the HR professional involved in mergers and acquisitions?

Box 2.1 RBS was 'disaster waiting to happen'

When the outgoing board of directors at RBS met for the final time in January 2009, the scale of the business disaster they had overseen was abundantly clear. The bank was preparing to announce the biggest British corporate loss in history; the Treasury was about to underwrite £325 billion of RBS's questionable assets; and even the Prime Minister had 'gone white' when given details of the bank's trading activities.

Gathered around the table at RBS's luxurious corporate headquarters, each member of the board was asked where they believed the mistakes had been made. 'You never stood a chance', said one non-executive director to the executives in charge of the day-to-day running of the bank. Another complained how the board was not given the information required to have questioned what are now seen as disastrous business decisions.

Box 2.1 continued

This weekend, attention is focused on the role of Sir Fred Goodwin, the ousted chief executive, and Larry Fish, the former head of Citizens Bank, an RBS subsidiary in America. The Financial Services Authority (FSA), the City regulator, is under pressure to investigate the meltdown of the bank. Senior insiders at the bank have told the *Daily Telegraph* that crucial information was not disclosed to board members. Concerns have also been raised about the 'culture' that developed within RBS and the way in which decisions were made.

However, although the board may have been unaware of what was happening, senior figures within the investment banking wing of RBS disclose today that the bank was 'a disaster waiting to happen'. In 1998, when Sir Fred joined Royal Bank of Scotland as the deputy chief executive, it was a modest high street bank with a celebrated history at the heart of Edinburgh and Scottish life. However, the youthful executive had ambitious plans to transform RBS into a global banking powerhouse.

Within three years of Sir Fred joining, RBS stunned the City of London by buying NatWest – in a deal that he masterminded. Sir Fred was charged with integrating the two institutions and soon earned his 'Fred the shred' nickname thanks to the ruthless zeal he showed for the task. By 2001, he was chief executive, flying around the world in the bank's private jet.

RBS prided itself as a cautious lender on the British high street, an image far removed from the scenes in the trading rooms of the investment banking division. Traders were under instructions to buy-up assets – office buildings, aircraft, ships and whatever else they could find. Huge private equity deals were financed and the mantra was 'accumulate assets'. At RBS Greenwich Capital in Stamford, Connecticut, the bank established what is reputed to be the 'largest trading floor in the world'. Those in charge were earning up to $25 million a year in cash bonuses. Another unit of RBS was also embarking on an equally risky strategy to move into sub-prime mortgages.

Citizens Bank was a well-established New England institution which had not engaged in the more risky mortgage businesses. It had been owned by RBS since the 1980s but during the past decade it took over several US regional banks. In 2007, it is understood to have begun buying up sub-prime mortgages from other banks. Although Citizens, headed by Larry Fish, was not offering sub-prime loans itself, it quickly amassed billions of pounds in sub-prime exposure. It is not known why it adopted this strategy, which was not authorised by the RBS board. It went disastrously wrong and Citizens is understood to have about £14 billion in 'toxic' loans.

Several senior executives at the bank were 'severely reprimanded' over the move into sub-prime. Mr Fish retired last year with a pension worth $27 million (£18.6 million) which pays him more than $2.2 million (£1.5 million) annually.

It is alleged that the way in which bonuses were paid – based on the interest earned on assets – encouraged traders to take on riskier prospects which offered higher rates of return. One former senior executive at the bank said: 'The place was totally dysfunctional. Everywhere you looked they were taking on assets – billions of dollars worth of planes, billions of dollars of ships, commercial real estate across America and Britain. They were buying everything to meet Goodwin's targets and his targets were assets.'

It was against this background that – despite Sir Fred's public statements – traders started buying into the American sub-prime mortgage market. In 2007, mortgage portfolios were bought from other banks and huge lines of credit offered to lenders with questionable records. Crucially, RBS was piling into the market as others were fleeing. The plan was to package up the sub-prime debts and sell them on, but RBS was unable to offload the 'toxic' mortgages. By the end of 2007, RBS was forced to begin announcing that the value of many of its assets was less than previously thought.

By last month, the bank admitted the scale of its disastrous mistakes, unveiling a £28 billion loss. The taxpayer now effectively owns the toxic debts. One former executive estimates that losses could total more than £100 billion before the end of the recession. Despite the huge public liabilities, political attention has focused on the £17 million pension awarded to Sir Fred after he was forced to step down from RBS last October. However, directors say that the pension row underlines the dysfunctional nature in which the bank was run. The board only learnt of the settlement at the January meeting.

Box 2.1 continued

Sir Fred's subordinates were terrified of bringing problems to his attention. 'The bank was all about what Sir Fred wanted,' said one insider. 'It was still being run like a small Scottish bank rather than a major multinational company.' Gordon Pell, the bank's deputy chief executive, said last week that the bank would scrap many of the business divisions blamed for its downfall. Meanwhile politicians from all parties are now pushing for an investigation into the downfall of RBS and other British banks.

Source: Winnett and Corrigan (2009).

Questions

1 What were the key influences on the development of RBS's corporate strategy?

2 Using Whittington's typology can you explain how and why RBS's strategy developed and failed?

The four approaches to strategy identified differ considerably in their implications for advice to management. Understanding that strategy formulation does not always occur in a rational, planned manner, due to complexities in both the external and internal environment is significant for our understanding of strategic human resource management. Whittington (1993) summarised his four generic approaches of *classical, evolutionary, systemic* and *processual* approaches discussed above, in the model below (Figure 2.3).

By plotting his model on two continua of outcomes (profit maximisation – pluralistic) and processes (deliberate – emergent), Whittington (1993, 2001) recognises that the strategy process changes depending upon the context and outcomes. In terms of strategic human resource management, therefore, the term 'strategic' has broader and more complex connotations than those advocated in the prescriptive 'classical' strategy literature. As turbulence in the environment increases, organisations are recognising the importance of human resources to the competitive performance of the organisation, and therefore its role at a strategic level rather than an operational one.

Figure 2.3 Whittington's model

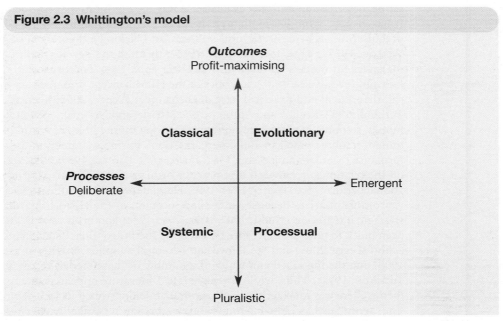

Source: Whittington (2001: 3).

Activity

Read the case study at the end of this chapter. Which of the approaches identified by Whittington (2001) best describes their approach to strategy formulation?

Why do you think it is important to consider the nature of strategy to aid our understanding of strategic human resource management?

By now you should be familiar with different approaches to understanding the nature of strategy and have gained an appreciation of the complexities involved in the strategic management process. You may have realised that our understanding and interpretation of SHRM will, to a certain extent, be influenced by our interpretation of the context of strategic management. It is to the definition and the various interpretations of strategic human resource management that we turn next.

The rise of strategic human resource management

In the past 20 years or so, the management of people within organisations has moved from the sidelines to centre stage. The contribution that human resources may make to an organisation's performance and effectiveness has become the subject of much scrutiny. Much of this change has been linked to changes in the business environment, with the impact of globalisation leading to the need for increased competitiveness, flexibility, responsiveness, quality and the need for all functions of the business to demonstrate their contribution to the bottom line. As we have already recognised, it is against this backdrop that the traditional separation between strategy and operational activities, such as HRM, has become blurred, particularly within a knowledge-based age.

There is confusion over the differentiation between human resource management and strategic human resource management. Part of the reason for this confusion will be familiar to you, as it arises from the varying stances of the literature, those of prescription, description or critical evaluation. Some writers see the two terms as synonymous (Mabey *et al.*, 1998), while others consider there are differences. A wealth of literature has appeared to prescribe, describe and critically evaluate the way organisations manage their human resources. It has evolved from being highly critical of the personnel function's contribution to the organisation, as being weak, non-strategic and lacking a theoretical base (Drucker, 1968; Watson, 1977; Legge, 1978; Purcell, 1985), through the development of human resource management models and frameworks (Beer *et al.* 1984; Fombrun *et al.* 1984; Schuler and Jackson, 1987; Guest, 1987), to critics of the HRM concept who question the empirical, ethical, theoretical and practical base of the subject (Legge, 2005; Keenoy, 1990; Blyton and Turnbull, 1992; Keenoy and Anthony, 1992; Clarke and Newman, 1997) to a wave of strategic human resource management literature focusing on the link or *vertical integration* between human resource practices and an organisation's business strategy, in order to enhance performance (Schuler and Jackson, 1987; Kochan and Barocci, 1985; Miles and Snow, 1984); and on the relationship between best practice or high-commitment HR practices and organisational performance (Pfeffer, 1994, 1998; Huselid, 1995; MacDuffie, 1995; Guest 2001).

Confusion arises because embedded in much of the HRM literature is the notion of strategic integration (Guest, 1987; Beer *et al.*, 1984; Fombrun *et al.*, 1984), but critics have been quick to note the difference between the rhetoric of policy statements and the reality of action (Legge, 2005) and the somewhat piecemeal adoption of HRM practices (Storey, 1992, 1995) and the ingrained ambiguity of a number of these models (Keenoy, 1990; Blyton and Turnbull, 1992). Thus, while the early HRM literature appeared to emphasise a strategic theme, there was much critical evaluation that demonstrated its lack of strategic integration. Thus terms such as 'old wine in new bottles' became a familiar explanation for the development of personnel to HRM to SHRM.

Activity

Consider the reading you have done in Chapter 1 and draw your own model of HRM, demonstrating its theoretical and applied origins.

● In what ways do you believe strategic HRM to be different to your model of HRM?

● Would you make any alterations to your model to ensure its strategic nature?

Exploring the relationship between strategic management and SHRM: the best fit school of SHRM

The best fit (or contingency) school of SHRM explores the close link between strategic management and HRM by assessing the extent to which there is *vertical integration* between an organisation's business strategy and its HRM policies and practices. This is where an understanding of the strategic management process and context can enhance our understanding of the development of SHRM, both as an academic field of study and in its application in organisations.

The notion of a link between business strategy and the performance of every individual in the organisation is central to 'fit' or vertical integration. Vertical integration can be explicitly demonstrated through the linking of a business goal to individual objective setting, to the measurement and rewarding of attainment of that business goal. Vertical integration between business strategy or the objectives of the business and individual behaviour and ultimately individual, team and organisational performance is at the core of many models of SHRM. Inherent in most treatments of fit is the premise that organisations are more efficient and/or effective when they achieve fit relative to when a lack of fit exists (Wright and Snell, 1998: 757). This vertical integration or 'fit' where 'leverage' is gained through procedures, policies and processes is widely acknowledged to be a crucial part of any strategic approach to the management of people (Dyer, 1984; Mahoney and Deckop, 1986; Schuler and Jackson, 1987; Fombrun *et al.* 1984, Gratton *et al.*, 1999). Vertical integration therefore ensures an explicit link or relationship between internal people processes and policies and the external market or business strategy, and thereby ensures that competences are created which have a potential to be a key source of competitive advantage (Wright *et al.*, 1994).

Tyson (1997) identifies the move towards greater vertical integration (between human resource management and business strategy) and horizontal integration (between HR policies themselves and with line managers) as a sign of 'HRM's coming of age'. In recognising certain shifts in the HRM paradigm, Tyson identified 'vertical integration' as the essential ingredient that enables the HR paradigm to become strategic. This requires in practice, not only a statement of strategic intent, but planning to ensure an integrated HR system can support the policies and processes in line with the business strategy. It is worthwhile considering the earlier discussions on the nature of strategic management here, as a number of critics, notably Legge (2005) have questioned the applicability of the classical–rational models on the grounds that there is a dearth of empirical evidence to support their credibility. Legge (2005: 135) tends to prefer the processual framework (Whittington, 1993), which is grounded in empirical work and recognises that 'integrating HRM and business strategy is a highly complex and iterative process, much dependent on the interplay and resources of different stakeholders'.

STOP and think

In what way does Whittington's typology (1993, 2001) of strategy impact on your understanding of 'vertical integration'? You may find it useful to use Table 2.1 to guide your thinking.

Table 2.1

	Classic	Processual	Evolutionary	Systemic
Strategy	Formal and planned	Crafted and emergent	Efficient	Embedded
Rationale	Profit maximisation	Vague	Survival of the fittest	Local
Focus	Fitting internal plans to external contexts	Internal (politics)	External (markets)	External (societies)
Processes	Analytical	Bargaining/learning	Darwinian	Social/cultural
Key influences	Economics/military	Psychology	Economics/biology	Sociology
Emergence	1960's	1970's	1980's	1990's

Source: Adapted from Whittington (2001: 39).

There have been a number of SHRM models that have attempted to explore the link between business strategy and HR policies and practices, and develop categories of integration or 'fit'. These include the lifecycle models (Kochan and Barocci, 1985; Lengnick Hall and Lengnick Hall, 1988; Sisson and Storey, 2000) and the competitive advantage models of Miles and Snow (1978) and Schuler and Jackson, (1987) based on the influential work of Porter (1985).

Lifecycle models

A number of researchers have attempted to apply business and product lifecycle thinking or 'models' to the selection and management of appropriate HR policies and practices that fit the relevant stage of an organisation's development or lifecycle (Baird and Meshoulam, 1988; Kochan and Barocci, 1985). So, for example, according to this approach, during the start-up phase of the business there is an emphasis on 'flexibility' in HR to enable the business to grow and foster entrepreneurialism. Whereas in the growth stage, once a business grows beyond a certain size, the emphasis would move to the development of more formal HR policies and procedures. In the maturity stage, as markets mature and margins decrease, and the performance of certain products or the organisation plateaus, the focus of the HR strategy may move to cost control. Finally, in the decline stage of a product or business, the emphasis shifts to rationalisation, with downsizing and redundancy implications for the HR function (Kochan and Barocci, 1985). The question for HR strategists here is first, how can HR strategy secure and retain the type of human resources that are necessary for the organisation's continued viability, as industries and sectors develop? Second, which HR policies and practices are more likely to contribute to sustainable competitive advantage as organisations go through their lifecycle (Boxall and Purcell, 2008)? Retaining viability and sustaining competitive advantage in the 'mature' stage of an organisation's development is at the heart of much SHRM literature. Baden-Fuller (1995) noted that there are two kinds of mature organisation that manage to survive industry development, 'one is the firm that succeeds in dominating the direction of industry change and the other is the firm that manages to adapt to the direction of change' (Boxall and Purcell, 2008: 198). Abell (1993), Boxall (1996) and Dyer and Shafer (1999) argue that the route to achieving human resource advantage as organisations develop and renew lies in the preparation for retaining viability and competitive advantage in the mature phase. The need for organisations to pursue 'dual' HR strategies, which enable them to master the present while preparing for and pre-empting the future, and avoiding becoming trapped in a single strategy is identified by Abell (1993), while Dyer and Shafer (1999) developed an approach that demonstrates how an organisation's HR strategy could contribute to what they termed 'organisational agility'. This implies an inbuilt capacity to flex and adapt to changes in the external context, which enables the business to change as a matter of course. Interestingly, this work appears to draw on the resource-based view and best practice view of SHRM discussed later in the chapter, as well as the best fit approach, reflecting the difficulty of viewing the various approaches to SHRM as distinct entities.

How does the lifecycle approach contribute to your understanding of SHRM? How could Café Expresso (case study at the end of this chapter) have prepared better for organisational renewal and industry changes?

Competitive advantage models

Competitive advantage models tend to apply Porter's (1985) ideas on strategic choice. Porter identified three key bases of competitive advantage: cost leadership, differentiation through quality and service and focus on 'niche' markets. Schuler and Jackson (1987) used these as a basis for their model of strategic human resource management, where they defined the appropriate HR policies and practices to 'fit' the generic strategies of cost reduction, quality enhancement and innovation. They argued that business performance will improve when HR practices mutually reinforce the organisation's choice of competitive strategy. Thus in Schuler and Jackson's model (see Table 2.2) the organisation's mission and values are expressed through their desired competitive strategy. This in turn leads to a set of required employee behaviours, which would be reinforced by an appropriate set of HR practices. The outcome of this would be desired employee behaviours that are aligned with the corporate goals, thus demonstrating the achievement of vertical integration.

As you can see, the 'cost-reduction'-led HR strategy is likely to focus on the delivery of *efficiency* through mainly 'hard' HR techniques, whereas the 'quality-enhancement'- and 'innovation'-led HR strategies to focus on the delivery of *added value* through 'softer' HR techniques and policies. Thus all three of these strategies can be deemed 'strategic' in linking HR policies and practices to the goals of the business and the external context of the firm, and in therefore contributing in different ways to 'bottom-line' performance. Another commonly cited competitive advantage framework is that of Miles and Snow (1978), who defined generic types of business strategy as *defenders, prospectors* and *analysers* and matched the generic strategies to appropriate HR strategies, policies and practices. The rationale being that if appropriate alignment is achieved between the organisation's business strategy and its HR policies and practices, a higher level of organisational performance will result.

What are the advantages and disadvantages inherent in the competitive advantage models?

Can you see any difficulties in applying them to organisations?

Configurational models

One criticism often levelled at the contingency or best fit school is that they tend to oversimplify organisational reality. In attempting to relate one dominant variable external to the organisation (for example, compete on innovation, quality or cost) to another internal variable (for example, human resource management), they tend to assume a linear, non-problematic relationship. It is unlikely, however, that an organisation will only pursues a single focus strategy, as organisations have to compete in an ever-changing external environment where new strategies are constantly evolving and emerging. Thus organisations tend to develop hybrid strategies where a quality-focused strategy, for example, will often be combined with elements of cost reduction and even innovation. How often in organisational change programmes have organisations issued new mission and value statements, proclaiming new organisational values of employee commitment, etc. on the one hand, with announcements of compulsory redundancies on the other? Thus cost-reduction reality and high-commitment rhetoric often go hand-in-hand, particularly in a short-termist economy. Delery and Doty (1996) noted the limitation of the contingency school, and proposed the notion of the configurational perspective. This approach focuses on how unique patterns or configurations of multiple independent variables are related to the dependent variable, by aiming to identify 'ideal type' categories of not only the organisation strategy but also the HR strategy. The significant difference here between the contingency approach and the configurational approach is that these configurations represent 'non-linear synergistic effects and higher-order interactions' that can result in maximum performance, Delery and Doty (1996: 808). As Marchington and Wilkinson (2008: 152) note, the key point about the configurational perspective is that it 'seeks to derive an internally consistent set of HR practices that maximise horizontal integration and then link these to alternative strategic configurations in order to maximise vertical integration'. Thus put simply, strategic human resource management according to configurational theorists, requires an organisation to develop a HR system that achieves both horizontal and vertical integration, or a form of 'idealised fit'. Delery and Doty use Miles and Snow's (1978) categories of 'defender' and 'prospector' to theoretically derive 'internal systems' or configurations of HR practices that maximise horizontal fit, and then link these to strategic configurations of, for example, 'defender' or 'prospector' to maximise vertical fit (Table 2.3).

Table 2.2 Business strategies and associated HR policies

Strategy	Employee role behaviour	HRM policies
Innovation	A high degree of creative behaviour	Jobs that require close interaction and coordination among groups of individuals
	Longer-term focus	Performance appraisals that are more likely to reflect long-term and group-based achievement
	A relatively high level of cooperative interdependent behaviour	Jobs that allow employees to develop skills that can be used in other positions in the firm
	A moderate degree of concern for quality	Pay rates that tend to be low, but allow employees to be stockholders and have more freedom to choose the mix of components that make up their pay package
	A moderate concern for quantity; an equal degree of concern for process and results	Broad career paths to reinforce the development of a broad range of skills
	A greater degree of risk-taking; a higher tolerance of ambiguity and unpredictability	
Quality enhancement	Relatively repetitive/predictable behaviours	Relatively fixed and explicit job descriptions
	A more long-term or immediate focus	High levels of employee participation in decisions
		Relevant to immediate work conditions and job itself
	A moderate amount of cooperative interdependent behaviour	A mix of individual and group criteria for performance appraisal that is mostly short-term and results-oriented
	A high concern for quality	Relatively egalitarian treatment of employees and some guarantees of job security
	A modest concern for quantity of output	Extensive and continuous training and development of employees
	High concern for process; low risk-taking activity; commitment to the goals of the organisation	

Table 2.2 *Continued*

Strategy	Employee role behaviour	HRM policies
Cost reduction	Relatively repetitive and predictable behaviour	Relatively fixed and explicit job descriptions that allow little room for ambiguity
	A rather short-term focus	Narrowly designed jobs and narrowly defined career paths that encourage specialisation expertise and efficiency
	Primarily autonomous or individual activity	Short-term results-oriented performance appraisals
	Moderate concern for quality	Close monitoring of market pay levels for use in making compensation decisions
	High concern for quantity of output	Minimal levels of employee training and development
	Primary concern for results; low risk-taking activity; relatively high degree of comfort with stability	

Source: Schuler and Jackson (1987: NY). Copyright 1987 by ACADEMY OF MANAGEMENT (NY). Reproduced with permission of ACADEMY OF MANAGEMENT (NY) in the format Textbook via Copyright Clearance Center.

The configurational approach provides an interesting variation on the contingency approach, and contributes to the strategic human resource management debate in recognising the need for organisations to achieve both vertical and horizontal fit through their HR practices, so as to contribute to an organisation's competitive advantage and therefore be deemed strategic. While Table 2.3 below only provides for the two polar opposites of 'de-fender' and 'prospector' type strategies, the approach does allow for deviation from these ideal-type strategies and recognises the need for proportionate deviation from the ideal-type HR systems.

Activity

Chart the differences between the two theoretical perspectives identified in the discussion so far (contingency and configurational approaches). In what ways have these approaches contributed to your understanding of *strategic* HRM?

Table 2.3 Gaining maximum vertical and horizontal fit through strategic configurations

HR practices	Internal career opportunities	Training and development	Performance management	Employment security	Participation	Role of HR
Defenders Low-risk strategies. Secure markets. Concentration on narrow segments. Focus on efficiency of systems	Sophisticated recruitment and selection systems. Build talent and skills. Career development opportunities. Retention of of key skills valued	Focus longer-term development for the future and emphasis on learning	Appraisals development oriented. Clear grading structure and transparency valued. Employee share schemes	Job security highly valued	Employee voice valued, through established systems of employee involvement, grievance, trade unions where recognised. Commitment to the organisation emphasised	Potential for strategic role. Well established department, with established HR systems

Table 2.3 *Continued*

HR practices	Internal career opportunities	Training and development	Performance management	Employment security	Participation	Role of HR
Prospectors Innovative high-risk strategies. Change and uncertainty. Focus on entering new markets	Buy-in talent and skills. Limited internal career paths	Focus short-term skill needs. Onus on individual to take responsibility for personal learning and development	Appraisals results-oriented Reward short-term incentive-based. Performance related pay based on bottom-line measures	Employability valued	Participation and employee voice limited	Administrative role. Support role

Source: Delery and Doty (1996: 802–35). Copyright 1996 by ACADEMY OF MANAGEMENT (NY). Reproduced with permission of ACADEMY OF MANAGEMENT (NY) in the format Textbook via Copyright Clearance Center.

In analysing the level of vertical integration evident in organisational practice, it soon becomes clear that organisations pursue and interpret vertical integration in different ways. Some organisations tend to adopt a top–down approach to HR 'strategy making', with senior management cascading defined strategic objectives to functional departments, who in turn cascade and roll out policies to employees, while other organisations might recognise HRM as a key business partner and involve HR in the strategic process. Torrington and Hall (2005) have explored the varying interpretations of 'fit' or 'integration' by attempting to qualify the degree or levels of integration between an organisation's business strategy and its human resources strategy. They identified five different relationships or levels of 'vertical integration' (see Figure 2.4).

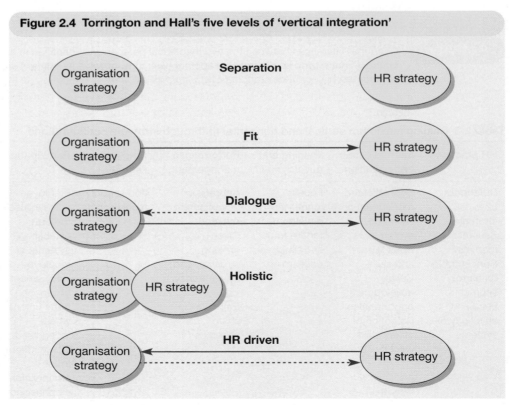

Figure 2.4 Torrington and Hall's five levels of 'vertical integration'

Source: Torrington and Hall (1998: 27).

In the separation model, there is clearly no vertical integration or relationship between those responsible for business strategy and those responsible for HR, thus there is unlikely to be any formal responsibility for human resources in the organisation. The 'fit' model according to Torrington and Hall, recognises that employees are key to achieving the business strategy, therefore the human resources strategy is designed to fit the requirements of the organisation's business strategy. This 'top–down' version of 'fit' can be seen in the matching model (Fombrun *et al.*, 1984) and in the best fit models of Schuler and Jackson (1987) and Kochan and Barocci (1985). As you have probably already identified, these models assume a classical approach to strategy. Thus they assume that business objectives are cascaded down from senior management through departments to individuals.

The 'dialogue' model recognises the need for a two-way relationship between those responsible for making business strategy decisions and those responsible for making HR decisions. In reality, however, in this model the HR role may be limited to passing on essential information to the board to enable them to make strategic decisions. The 'holistic' model, on the other hand, recognises employees as a key source of competitive advantage rather than just a mechanism for implementing an organisation's strategy. Human resource strategy in this model becomes critical, as people competences become key business competences. This is the underpinning assumption behind the resource-based view of the firm (Barney, 1991; Barney and Wright, 1998), discussed later in this chapter. The final degree of integration identified by Torrington and Hall is the HR driven model, which places HR as a key strategic partner.

STOP and think

Having considered Torrington and Hall's (1998, 2005) levels of vertical integration, which of these approaches to HR strategy represents your organisation's approach to developing HR strategy? Alternatively, you can use the case study 'Café Expresso' at the end of this chapter.

Limitations of the best-fit models of SHRM

Criticisms of the best fit approach have identified a number of problems, both in its underlying theoretical assumptions and its application to organisations. One of these key themes is the reliance on the classical rational-planning approach to strategy making, its reliance on determinism and the resulting lack of sophistication in its description of generic competitive strategies (Miller, 1992; Ritson, 1999; Boxall and Purcell, 2008), together with its rejection of societal and national cultural influences on HR strategy. As Boxall and Purcell (2008: 61) noted, the firm can never be the complete author of its own HRM. This criticism is partly answered by the configurational school, which recognises the prevalence of hybrid strategies and the need for HR to respond accordingly (Delery and Doty, 1996). A further criticism is that best fit models tend to ignore employee interests in the pursuit of enhanced economic performance. Thus, in reality, alignment tends to focus on 'fit' as defined by Torrington and Hall (1998), and relies on assumptions of unitarism rather than the alignment of mutual interests. It has been argued that 'multiple fits' are needed to take account of pluralist interests and conventions within an organisation, by ensuring that an organisation's HR strategy meets both the mutual interests of shareholders and employees. A third criticism could be levelled at the lack of emphasis on the internal context of individual businesses within the same sector and the unique characteristics and practices that might provide its main source of sustainable competitive advantage. Marchington and Wilkinson (2008: 158) ask, for example, why did Tesco choose to work closely with trade unions while Sainsbury's preferred to minimise union involvement? A number of these criticisms imply a lack of flexibility in the best fit school of SHRM as, while a 'tight' fit between an organisation's HR strategy and its business strategy may provide a key source of competitive advantage in a stable business

47

environment, in a dynamic changing environment it may prove to be a source of competitive disadvantage as the organisation cannot flex as quickly as its rivals. Some writers have argued that fit is sometimes not desirable and can be counter-productive in an environment of change (Lengnick Hall and Lengnick Hall, 1988). Wright and Snell (1998) drawing on the work of Milliman, Von Glinow and Nathan, 1991 suggest that this reflects an 'orthogonal perspective' suggesting fit and flexibility are at opposite ends of a continuum, and therefore cannot co-exist. They support the 'complementary perspective' (Milliman *et al.*, 1991) and propose that fit and flexibility can co-exist, and are both essential for organisational effectiveness. They argue that the strategic management challenge is to cope with change by continually adapting to achieve fit between the firm and its external environment (Wright and Snell, 1998: 757). Thus SHRM must promote organisational flexibility in order for the firm to achieve dynamic fit. Wright and Snell (1998: 759), drawing on the work of Schuler and Jackson (1987), Capelli and Singh (1992), Wright and McMahan (1992) and Truss and Gratton (1994) therefore propose a model of SHRM (Figure 2.5) which accounts for both fit and flexibility.

The model assumes a classical stance towards the strategic management process, as it demonstrates how the implementation of an organisation's human resource strategy needs to 'fit' the strategic choice made by the business in providing a process where the firm's strategy identifies the required or anticipated skills and behaviours, which then drive the intended HR practices, which in turn are operationalised in 'actual' HR practices, which influence the 'actual' skills and behaviours developed. When aligned, these then contribute to organisational performance. This alignment may endure and be effective in a stable and predictable environment because it supports the competitive needs of the organisation. Thus fit may exist without any need for flexibility being built into the system. However, when the environment becomes unpredictable it may become more difficult for managers to obtain the information they need and align the HR systems with the strategic process. Wright and Snell (2005) suggest that in such environments, achieving 'fit' over time may be dependent upon the extent to which flexibility exists in the system, thus requiring a flexible HR system. Flexibility is demonstrated in their model by developing HR systems that can be adapted quickly, by developing a human capital pool with a broad range of skills and by promoting behavioural flexibility among employees. Thus employees develop a repertoire of skills and behaviour which reflects their capability to react to and flex with strategic changes.

Activity

Reflect on Wright and Snell's fit/flexibility model (see Figure 2.5). How might an HR professional facilitate flexibility?

We have explored the best fit school of SHRM and its relationship to strategic management through the contingency and configurational approaches. The contingency approach recommends a strong relationship to strategic management, whether it be to an organisation's lifecycle or competitive forces. This obviously assumes a classical, rational-planning model of strategic management. We have considered this relationship or *vertical integration* between an organisation's business strategy and its human resource strategy in some detail, defining the varying degrees of 'fit' or vertical alignment, and have considered the possibility of providing both fit and flexibility alongside each other. The configurational approach attempts to answer some of the limitations of the contingency approach by identifying 'ideal type' categories of both the organisation strategy and the HR strategy. It 'seeks to derive an internally consistent set of HR practices that maximise horizontal integration and then link these to alternative strategic configurations in order to maximise vertical integration' and therefore organisational performance (Marchington and Wilkinson, 2008: 152). The configurational approach is further explored in the 'bundles' approach to SHRM, which is considered later in this chapter.

The best fit approach to strategic HRM utilises an 'outside-in' (Wright *et al.*, 2004: 37) perspective to explain how the strategic management of human resources can deliver com-

Figure 2.5 A fit/flexible model

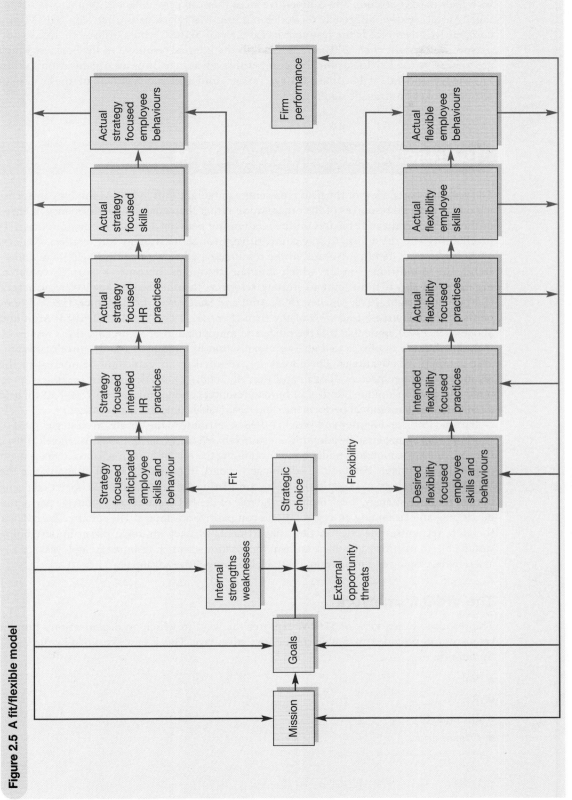

Source: Wright and Snell (1998: 758). Copyright 1998 by ACADEMY OF MANAGEMENT (NY). Reproduced with permssion of ACADEMY OF MANAGEMENT (NY) in the format Textbook via Copyright Clearance Center.

petitive advantage, thus by aligning an organisation's human resource policies and practices with their market position and competitive focus they can gain enhanced competitive advantage. An alternative approach to understanding the relationship between SHRM and competitive advantage is the resource-based view of SHRM, which utilises an 'inside-out' perspective (Wright *et al.*, 2004: 37), where it is the internal resources of the business which are viewed as the key to sustainable competitive advantage, thus an organisation's skills, knowledge and talent become 'strategic assets' and the management of these human resources takes on strategic significance.

The resource-based view of SHRM

The resource-based view of the firm represents a paradigm shift in SHRM thinking by focusing on the internal resources of the organisation rather than analysing performance in terms of the external context. It focuses on the relationship between a firm's internal resources, its profitability and the ability to stay competitive through its strategy formulation. (Delery, 1998; Ferris *et al.*, 1999). Advocates of the resource-based view on SHRM help us to understand the conditions under which human resources become a scarce, valuable, organisation-specific, difficult-to-imitate resource, in other words key 'strategic assets' (Barney and Wright, 1998; Mueller, 1998; Amit and Shoemaker, 1993; Winter, 1987). Proponents of the resource-based view of the firm (Penrose, 1959; Wernerfelt, 1984; Amit and Shoemaker, 1993) argue that it is the range and manipulation of an organisation's resources, including human resources that give an organisation its 'uniqueness' and source of sustainable competitive advantage. Their work has resulted in an 'explosion of interest in the resource-based perspective' (Boxall and Purcell, 2008: 72), particularly in seeking ways to build and develop 'unique bundles' of human resources and technical resources that will lead to enhanced organisational performance and sustainable competitive advantage.

Barney (1991) and Barney and Wright (1998) contribute to the debate on strategic HRM in two important ways. First, by adopting a resource-based view (Barney, 1991; Wernefelt, 1984), they provide an economic foundation for examining the role of human resource management in gaining sustainable competitive advantage. Second, in providing a tool of analysis in the VRIO framework (see next section), and by considering the implications for operationalising human resource strategy, they emphasise the role of the HR executive as a strategic partner in developing and sustaining an organisation's competitive advantage. The resource-based view therefore recognises the HR function (department) as a key 'strategic' player in developing sustainable competitive advantage and an organisation's human resources (employees) as key assets in developing and maintaining sustainable competitive advantage.

The VRIO framework

The resource-based view of SHRM explores the ways in which an organisation's human resources can provide sustainable competitive advantage. This is best explained by the VRIO framework:

- **Value**
- **Rarity**
- **Inimitability**
- **Organisation**

Value

Organisations need to consider how the human resources function can create value. It is quite common in organisations to reduce costs through HR such as the reduction in head-count and the introduction of flexible working practices etc., but it is also important to consider how they might increase revenue. Reicheld (1996) has identified human resources' contribution to the business as *efficiency*, but also as customer selection, customer retention and customer referral, thus highlighting the impact of HR's contribution through enhanced customer service and *customer added value*. This view is reflected by Thompson (2001) in recognising the paradigm shift from traditional added value through economy and efficiency to ensuring the potential value of outputs is maximised by ensuring they fully meet the needs of the customers that the product or service is intended for. The suggestion of the resource-based view is that if the human resources function wishes to be a 'strategic partner', they need to know which human resources contribute the most to *sustainable competitive advantage* in the business, as some human resources may provide greater leverage for competitive advantage than others. Hamel and Prahalad (1993), therefore, identify that productivity and performance can be improved by gaining the same output from fewer resources (*rightsizing*) and by achieving more output from given resources (*leveraging*). In order to achieve this, the human resources function must ask themselves the following questions:

- On what basis is the firm seeking to distinguish itself from its competitors? Production efficiency? Innovation? Customer Service?
- Where in the value chain is the greatest leverage for achieving differentiation?
- Which employees provide the greatest potential to differentiate a firm from its competitors?

Activity Try to answer these questions with regard to your organisation or one you are familiar with. Alternatively, you could use the case study 'Café Expresso' at the end of this chapter.

This approach has further implications for the role of human resource managers in a firm, as they need to understand the economic consequences of human resource practices and understand where they fit in the value chain. Barney and Wright (1998: 42) suggest that the human resources function needs to be able to explore the following questions:

- Who are your internal customers and how well do you know their part of the business?
- Are there organisational policies and practices that make it difficult for your internal clients to be successful?
- What services do you provide? What services should you provide? What services should you not provide?
- How do these services reduce internal customers' costs/increase their revenues?
- Can these services be provided more efficiently by outside vendors?
- Can you provide these services more efficiently?
- Do managers in the HR function understand the economic consequence of their jobs?

The value of an organisation's resources is not sufficient alone, however, for sustainable competitive advantage, because if other organisations possess the same value, then it will only provide *competitive parity*. Therefore an organisation needs to consider the next stage of the framework: rarity.

Rarity

The HR manager needs to consider how to develop and exploit rare characteristics of a firm's human resources to gain competitive advantage.

Nordstrom is an interesting case, because they operate in a highly competitive retail industry where you would usually expect a lower level of skill and subsequently high labour turnover. Nordstrom, however, focused on individual salespeople as a key source of its competitive advantage. It therefore invested in attracting and retaining young college-educated people who were looking for a career in retailing. To ensure horizontal integration, it also provided a highly incentive-based compensation system (up to twice the industry average) and it encouraged employees to make a 'heroic effort' to attend customers' needs. Thus, by investing in its human resources and ensuring an integrated approach to development and reward, Nordstrom has taken a 'relatively homogeneous labour pool and exploited the rare characteristics to gain a competitive advantage' (Barney and Wright, 1998: 34).

Box 2.2   **Nordstrom**

Nordstrom exists in the highly competitive retailing industry. This industry is usually characterised as having relatively low skill requirements and high turnover for sales clerks. Nordstrom, however, has attempted to focus on individual salespersons as the key to its competitive advantage. It invests in attracting and retaining young, college-educated sales clerks who desire a career in retailing. It provides a highly incentive-based compensation system that allows Nordstrom's salespersons to make as much as twice the industry average in pay. The Nordstrom culture encourages sales clerks to make heroic efforts to attend to customers' needs, even to the point of changing a customer's tyre in the parking lot. The recruiting process, compensation practices, and culture at Nordstrom have helped the organisation to maintain the highest sales per square foot of any retailer in the nation.

Source: Barney and Wright (1998: 34).

Question

How did Nordstrom exploit the rare characteristics of their employees?

Consider current advertising campaigns, either on television, radio or in the media. Can you identify any organisations that are attempting to exploit the rare characteristics of their employees, as a key source of their competitive advantage. Once you have identified an organisation, try to find more out about that organisation, their business strategy and their organisational performance in relation to their competitors.

Inimitability

If an organisation's human resources add value and are rare, they can provide competitive advantage in the short term, but if other firms can imitate these characteristics, then over time competitive advantage may be lost and replaced with *competitive parity*.

The third element of the VRIO framework requires the human resources function to develop and nurture characteristics that cannot be easily imitated by the organisation's competitors. Barney and Wright (1998) recognise the significance of 'socially complex phenomena' here, such as an organisation's unique history and culture, which can be used to identify unique practices and behaviours which enable organisations to 'leapfrog' their competitors. Alchian and Demsetz (1972) also identified the contribution of *social complexity* in providing competitive advantage in their work on the potential *synergy* that results from effective teamwork. They found that this ensured a rare and difficult-to-copy commodity for two reasons; first, it provided competitive advantage through its *causal ambiguity*, as the specific source of the competitive advantage was difficult to identify; second, a synergy resulted from its *social complexity* as team members were involved in socially complex relationships that are not transferable across organisations. So characteristics such as trust and good relationships become firm-specific assets that provide value, are rare and are difficult for competitors to copy.

Box 2.3 demonstrates the strength of *Inimitability*: SW Airlines exemplify the role that socially complex phenomena such as culture can play in gaining competitive advantage. Top management attribute the company's success to its 'personality', a culture of 'fun' and 'trust', that empowers employees to do what it takes to meet the customers' needs. This is reinforced through an extensive selection process, and a culture of trust and empowerment reinforced by the CEO. SW Airlines attribute its strong financial success to its 'personality', which CEO Kelleher believes cannot be imitated by its competitors. So the human resources of SW Airlines serve as a source of sustained competitive advantage because they create value, are rare and are virtually impossible to imitate.

Organisation

Finally, to ensure that the HR function can provide *sustainable* competitive advantage, the VRIO framework suggests organisations need to ensure that they are *organised* so that they can capitalise on adding value, rarity and imitability. This implies a focus on horizontal integration, or *integrated, coherent systems of HR practices* rather than individual practices, that enable employees to reach their potential (Guest, 1987; Gratton *et al.*, 1999; Wright and Snell, 1991; Wright *et al.* 1996). This requires organisations to ensure that their policies and practices in the HR functional areas are coordinated and coherent, and not contradictory. Adopting such a macro view, however, is relatively new to the field of SHRM, as 'each of the various HRM functions have evolved in isolation, with little coordination across the disci-

---

Box 2.3   Southwest Airlines

Southwest Airlines exemplifies the role that socially complex phenomena such as culture play in competitive advantage. According to the company's top management, the firm's success can be attributed to the 'personality' of the company; a culture of fun and trust that provides employees with both the desire and the discretion to do whatever it takes to meet the customers' needs. The 'fun' airline uses an extensive selection process for hiring flight attendants who will project the fun image of the airline. Applicants must go through a casting call type exercise where they are interviewed by a panel that includes current flight attendants, managers and customers . . . Those who make it through the panel interview are then examined against a psychological profile that distinguished outstanding past flight attendants from those who were mediocre or worse.

In addition to the extensive selection process, employees are empowered to create an entertaining travelling environment by a strong organisational culture that values customer satisfaction. Herb Kelleher, CEO, says:

> We tell our people that we value inconsistency. By that I mean that we're going to carry 20 million passengers this year and that I can't foresee all of the situations that will arise at the stations across our system. So what we tell our people is, 'Hey, we can't anticipate all of these things, you handle them the best way possible. You make a judgement and use your discretion; we trust you'll do the right thing. If we think you've done something erroneous, we'll let you know – without criticism, without backbiting.' (Quick, 1992)

The extensive selection process and the strong organisational culture contribute to the differentiated service that has made Southwest Airlines the most financially successful airline over the past 20 years ... with the fewest customer complaints.

Source: Barney and Wright (1998: 35).

Question

How did SW Airlines create a culture that was difficult to copy?

plines' (Wright and McMahan, 1992). Thus there is much best practice literature focusing on the micro perspective, for example, on identifying appropriate training systems, or conducting performance appraisals, or designing selection systems. Although this literature has now evolved and recognised the 'strategic' nature of the functional areas, it has tended to focus on vertical integration at the expense of horizontal integration, thus there is still limited development in the interplay between employee resourcing, employee development, performance, reward and employee relations strategies. This discussion is explored in more detail in the section: Best-practice SHRM, page 57.

To conclude our remarks on the VRIO framework, if there are aspects of human resources that do not provide value they can only be a source of competitive disadvantage and should be discarded. Aspects of the organisation's human resources that provide value and are rare provide competitive parity only, aspects that provide value, are rare but are easily copied provide temporary competitive advantage, but in time are likely to be imitated and then only provide parity. So to achieve competitive advantage that is sustainable over time, the HR function needs to ensure the organisation's human resources provide value, are rare, are difficult to copy and that there are appropriate HR systems and practices in place to capitalise on this.

> **STOP and think**
>
> *Which approach to strategic management identified by Whittington (1993) could be used to explain the resource-based view of SHRM?*
>
> *How does the resource-based view contribute to your understanding of strategic HRM?*
>
> *What implications does the resource-based view have for operationalising human resource strategy?*

Mueller (1998) in advocating the resource-based view of SHRM argues that 'the existing theorising in strategic HRM needs to be complemented by an evolutionary perspective on the creation of human resource competencies'. He echoes Mintzberg's concerns (1987), that an overly rationalistic approach to strategy-making tends to focus too much attention on past successes and failures, when what is really needed is a level of strategic thinking that is radically different from the past. He identifies a lack of theoretical and empirical evidence to justify the emphasis on rational, codified policies of HRM, and reflects Bamberger and Phillips (1991) in describing human resource strategy as an 'emergent pattern in a stream of human-resource related decisions occurring over time'. Thus the strategic planning approach may be viewed by some as a 'metaphor employed by senior management to legitimise emergent decisions and actions' (Giojia and Chittipeddi, 1991: 440). Unlike contingency and universalist theorists (Schuler and Jackson, 1987; Miles and Snow, 1978; Kochan and Barocci, 1985; Pfeffer, 1994, 1998; Huselid, 1995), Mueller (1998) is more wary of the claimed relationship between strategic HRM and the overall financial performance of an organisation. He recognises that enlightened best practice HR activities do not automatically translate into competitive superiority, but rather require more complex and subtle conditions for human resources to become 'strategic assets'. He defines these as 'the social architecture' or 'social patterns' within an organisation which build up incrementally over time and are therefore difficult to copy. The focus on 'social architecture' rather than culture is deliberate, as it provides an emphasis on developing and changing behaviours rather than values, which are notoriously difficult to change (Ogbonna, 1992). Mueller identifies an organisation's 'social architecture' as a key element in the resource-based view of SHRM. Together with an embedded 'persistent strategic intent' on the part of senior management and embedded learning in daily work routines, which enable the development of 'hidden reservoirs' of skills and knowledge, which in turn can be exploited by the organisation as 'strategic assets'. The role of human resources is then to channel these behaviours and skills so that the organisation can tap into these hidden reservoirs. This thinking is reflected in the work of Hamel and Prahalad (1993, 1994), discussed below.

STOP and think

How does Mueller's view on the rational-planning approach to strategic management aid your understanding of HR strategy in practice?

Compare Mueller's approach to Barney and Wright's VRIO framework.

Applying the resource based-view of SHRM

In adopting a focus on the internal context of the business, HR issues and practices are core to providing sustainable competitive advantage, as they focus on how organisations can define and build core competencies or capabilities which are superior to those of their competitors. One key framework here is the work of Hamel and Prahalad (1993, 1994) and their notion of 'core competencies' (Table 2.4) in their 'new strategy paradigm'. They argue that 'for most companies, the emphasis on competing in the present means that too much management energy is devoted to preserving the past and not enough to creating the future'. Thus it is organisations that focus on identifying and developing their core competencies that are more likely to be able to stay ahead of their competitors. The key point here is not to anticipate the future but to create it, by not only focusing on organisational transformation and competing for market share, but also regenerating strategies and competing for opportunity share. Thus in creating the future, strategy is not only seen as learning, positioning and planning but also forgetting, foresight and strategic architecture, where strategy goes beyond achieving 'fit' and resource allocation to achieving 'stretch' and resource 'leverage'. The level of both tacit and explicit knowledge within the firm, coupled with the ability of employees to learn becomes crucial. Indeed, Boxall and Purcell (2008) argue that there is little point in making a distinction between the resource-based view and the knowledge-based view of the firm, as both approaches advocate that it is a firm's ability to learn faster than its competitors that leads to sustainable competitive advantage.

Alternatively, Boxall and Purcell present Leonard's (1998) similar analysis based on 'capabilities'. These are 'knowledge sets' consisting of four dimensions: employee skills and knowledge, technical systems, managerial systems and values and norms. In this model, employee development and incentive systems become a key driving force of achieving sustainable competitive advantage through core capability. Interestingly, Leonard emphasises the interlocking, systemic nature of these dimensions and warns organisations of the need to build in opportunities for renewal to avoid stagnation.

When organisations grow through mergers or acquisitions, as they appear to increasingly (Hubbard, 1999), it has been argued that the resource-based view takes on further significance. When mergers and acquisitions fail, it is often not at the planning stage but at the implementation stage (Hunt *et al.* 1987) and people and employee issues have been noted as

Table 2.4 Hamel and Prahalad's notion of 'core competency'

A core competency:

- is a bundle of skills and technologies that enable a company to provide particular benefits to customers
- is not product specific
- represents . . . the sum of learning across individual skill sets and individual organisational units
- must be competitively unique
- is not an 'asset' in the accounting sense of the word
- represents a 'broad opportunity arena' or 'gateway' to the future

Source: from *Competing for the Future*, Harvard Business School Press, Boston, MA (Hamel, G. and Prahalad, C. 1994) pp. 217–18, Copyright © 1994 by the Harvard Business School Publishing Corporation, all rights reserved, reprinted by permission of Harvard Business School Press

the cause of one-third of such failures in one survey (Marks and Mirvis, 1982). Thus 'human factors' have been identified as crucial to successful mergers and acquisitions. The work of Hamel and Prahalad (1994) indicated that CEOs and directors of multi-divisional firms should be encouraged to identify clusters of 'know-how' in their organisations which 'transcend the artificial divisions of Strategic Business Units' or at least have the potential to do so. Thus the role of human resources shifts to a 'strategic' focus on 'managing capability' and 'know-how', and ensuring that organisations retain both tacit and explicit knowledge (Nonaka and Takeuchi, 1995) in order to become more innovative, as organisations move to knowledge-based strategies as opposed to product-based ones.

How does the work of Hamel and Prahalad (1993, 1994) contribute to the resource-based view debate?

Do you think the resource-based view model is appropriate for all organisational contexts?

The resource-based view of SHRM has recognised that both human capital and organisational processes can add value to an organisation, however, they are likely to be more powerful when they mutually reinforce and support one another. The role of the human resources function in ensuring that exceptional value is achieved and in assisting organisations to build competitive advantage lies in their ability to implement an integrated and mutually reinforcing HR system that ensures that appropriate talent is identified, developed, rewarded and managed in order to reach its full potential. This theme of *horizontal integration* or achieving congruence between HR policies and practices is developed further in the next section in the best practice approach to SHRM.

Limitations of the resource-based view

The resource-based view is not without its critics however, particularly in relation to the strong focus on the internal context of the business. Some writers have suggested that the effectiveness of the resource-based view approach is inextricably linked to the external context of the firm (Miller and Shamsie, 1996; Porter, 1991). They have recognised that the resource-based view approach provides more added value when the external environment is less predictable. Other writers have noted the tendency for advocates of the resource-based view to focus on differences between firms in the same sector as sources of sustainable competitive advantage. This sometimes ignores the value and significance of common 'base-line' or 'table stake' (Hamel and Prahalad, 1994) characteristics across industries, which account for their legitimacy in that particular industry. Thus in the retail sector, there are strong similarities in how the industry employs a mix of core and peripheral labour, with the periphery tending to be made up of relatively low-skilled employees who traditionally demonstrate higher rates of employee turnover. Thus in reality, economic performance and efficiency tends to be delivered through rightsizing, by gaining the same output from fewer and cheaper resources, rather than through leverage by achieving more output from given resources. The example of B&Q in the UK, employing more mature people as both their core and particularly their peripheral workforce, is a good example of how an organisation can partially differentiate themselves from their competitors by focusing on adding value through the knowledge and skills of their human resources. Thus leverage is gained as the knowledge of B&Q's human resources add value to the level of customer service provided, which theoretically in turn will enhance customer retention and therefore shareholder value. An exploration of the empirical evidence to support this relationship between SHRM and organisational performance is discussed in more detail in the next section: the best practice approach to strategic human resource management.

Best practice SHRM: high commitment models

The notion of best practice or 'high-commitment' HRM was identified initially in the early US models of HRM, many of which mooted the idea that the adoption of certain 'best' human resource practices would result in enhanced organisational performance, manifested in improved employee attitudes and behaviours, lower levels of absenteeism and turnover, higher levels of skills and therefore higher productivity, enhanced quality and efficiency. This can be identified as a key theme in the development of the SHRM debate, that of best practice SHRM or universalism. Here, it is argued that all organisations will benefit and see improvements in organisational performance if they identify, gain commitment to and implement a set of best HRM practices. Since the early work of Beer *et al.* (1984) and Guest (1987), there has been much work done on defining sets of HR practices that enhance organisational performance. These models of best practice can take many forms; while some have advocated a *universal* set of HR practices that would enhance the performance of all organisations they were applied to (Pfeffer, 1994, 1998); others have focused on high-commitment models (Walton, 1985; Wood and de Menezes, 1998; Guest, 2001) or 'human capital-enhancing' practices (Youndt, *et al.* 1996) and high involvement practices (Wood, 1999; Guthrie 2001) which reflect an underlying assumption that a strong commitment to the organisational goals and values will provide competitive advantage. Others have focused on 'high-performance work systems/practices' (Berg, 1999; Applebaum *et al.*, 2000) This work has been accompanied by a growing body of research exploring the relationship between these 'sets of HR practices' and organisational performance (Pfeffer, 1994; Huselid, 1995; Huselid and Becker, 1996; Huselid *et al.*, 1997; Patterson *et al.*, 1997; Guest, 2001; Guthrie, 2001; Batt, 2002; Guest *et al.*, 2003). Although there is a wealth of literature advocating the best practice approach, with supporting empirical evidence, it is still difficult to reach generalised conclusions from these studies. This is mainly as a result of conflicting views about what constitutes an ideal set of HR best practices, whether they should be horizontally integrated into 'bundles' that fit the organisational context or not and the contribution these sets of HR practices can make to organisational performance.

Universalism and high-commitment bundles

One of the best practice models most commonly cited is Pfeffer's (1994) universal 16 HR practices for 'competitive advantage through people' which he revised to seven practices for 'building profits by putting people first' in 1998. These have been adapted for the UK audience by Marchington and Wilkinson (2005), as shown in Table 2.5.

Pfeffer (1994) explains how changes in the external environment have reduced the impact of traditional sources of competitive advantage, and increased the significance of new sources of competitive advantage, namely human resources that enable an organisation to adapt and innovate. Pfeffer's relevance in a European context has been questioned due to his lack of commitment to independent worker representation and joint regulation (Boxall and Purcell, 2008), hence Marchington and Wilkinson's adaptation, highlighted in Table 2.5. With the universalist approach or 'ideal set of practices' (Guest, 1997), the concern is with how close organisations can get to the ideal set of practices, the hypothesis being that the closer an organisation gets, the better the organisation will perform in terms of higher productivity, service levels and profitability. The role of human resources therefore becomes one of identifying and gaining senior management commitment to a set of HR best practices and ensuring they are implemented and that reward is distributed accordingly. The key to Pfeffer's universal approach is the provision of employment security as this underpins the effectiveness of the other six practices. Pfeffer recognises that employees are unlikely to commit to the organisation and share their knowledge and ideas without some mutual recognition of employment security on the part of the organisation. Critics of Pfeffer have questioned the feasibility of providing employment security, particularly in a weak economic climate, as 'downsizing' or 'rightsizing' is often viewed as the favoured HR option when faced with an economic downturn. More recently, however, there have been examples of employers and employees negotiating reduced wages and hours to maintain employment security and employee commitment, thus reflecting Pfeffer's principle that job reductions should be avoided where possible (Box 2.4).

The first difficulty with the best practice approach is the variation in what constitutes best practice. Agreement on the underlying principles of the best practice approach is reflected in Youndt *et al*.'s (1996: 839) summary as follows:

> At the root, most [models] . . . focus on enhancing the skill base of employees through HR activities such as selective staffing, comprehensive training and broad developmental efforts like job rotation and cross-utilisation. Further [they] tend to promote empowerment, participative problem-solving and teamwork with job redesign, group based incentives and a transition from hourly to salaried compensation for production workers.

Lists of best practices, however, vary intensely in their constitution and in their relationship to organisational performance. A sample of these variations is provided in Table 2.6. This results in confusion about which particular HR practices constitute high-commitment, and a lack of empirical evidence and 'theoretical rigour' (Guest, 1987: 508) to support their universal application. Capelli and Crocker-Hefter (1996: 7) note:

> We believe that a single set of 'best' practices may, indeed, be overstated . . . We argue that (it is) distinctive human resource practices that help to create unique competencies that differentiate products and, in turn drive competitiveness.

Box 2.4 **Toyota cuts production as car makers discuss government bail-out**

Toyota has announced pay and production cuts as stricken car makers embarked on talks with the government over an industry bail-out. Workers at the Japanese company's plants at Burnaston, Derbyshire and Deeside, North Wales will take a 10 per cent pay cut for the next 12 months.

'Following extensive consultation with our employee representatives, and with input from all employees, it has been agreed that the best way to secure long-term employment is to temporarily reduce working hours and base pay by 10 per cent,' Toyota said in a statement.

'This work share arrangement will take effect from 1st April and will be in place for one year, during this time we will continue to monitor the market and company situation closely. We believe the measures we have announced give us a greater opportunity to maintain employment through this difficult period.'

Peter Tsouvallaris, a Unite representative at Toyota, said: 'Our members are reminded daily of the tremendous insecurity this recession has brought to our industry. The proposals put to the workforce today present a real opportunity to restore some measure of stability to Toyota in the coming months, and we will be recommending them to our members.'

The Toyota cuts were the latest demonstration of the crisis which has hit the motor industry over the last six months, which has seen a wave of lay-offs and production cuts by car makers across the country.

Source: Adapted from Millward (2009).

Question

To what extent do you think Pfeffer's notion of employment security and high-commitment HRM are illustrated in Toyota's HR response to the decline in car sales in the UK market? What are the advantages and challenges of this approach for Toyota?

Table 2.5

Building profits by putting people first	'High-commitment' HRM
Employment security	and internal labour markets
Selective hiring	and sophisticated selection
Extensive training	and learning and development
Sharing Information	Extensive involvement and voice
Self-managed teams/team working	Self-managed teams/team working and harmonisation
Reduction of status differentials	
High pay contingent on company performance	High compensation contingent on organisational performance

Source: from *The Human Equation: Building Profits by Putting People First*, Harvard Business School Press, Boston, MA (Pfeffer, J. 1998) Copyright © 1998 by the Harvard Business School Publishing Corporation, all rights reserved, reprinted by permission of Harvard Business School Press

Table 2.6

Pfeffer (1998)	MacDuffie (1995)	Huselid (1995)	Arthur (1994)	Delery and Doty (1996)	Luthans and Sommer (2005)	Stavrou and Brewster (2005)
Employment security	Self-directed work teams	Contingent pay	Self-directed work teams	Internal career opportunities	Information-sharing	Training
Selective hiring	Job rotation	Hours per year training	Problem-solving groups	Training	Job design programmes	Share-options
Extensive training	Problem-solving groups	Information sharing	Contingent pay	Results-oriented appraisals	Job analysis methods	Evaluation of HR
Sharing information	TQM	Job analysis	Hours per year training	Profit-sharing	Participation programmes	Profit-sharing
Self-managed teams	Suggestions forum	Selective hiring	Conflict resolution	Employment security	Incentive-based compensation bundle	Group bonus
High pay contingent on company performance	Contingent pay	Attitude surveys	Job design	Participation	Benefits	Merit pay
Reduction of status differentials	Hiring criteria, current job versus learning	Employment tests	Percentage of skilled workers	Job descriptions	Training	Joint HR-management bundle
	Induction and initial training provision	Grievance procedure	Supervisor span of control		Grievance	Communication on strategy
	Hours per year training	Formal performance appraisal	Social events		Selection and staffing	Communication on finance
		Promotion criteria	Average total labour costs		Performance appraisal	Communication on change
		Selection ratio				Communication on organisation of work
		Benefits/total labour costs				Career
						Wider-jobs
						Communication to management

Source: Adapted from Becker and Gerhart (1996: 785); Stavrou, E.T. and Brewster, C. (2005).

A key theme that emerges in relation to best practice HRM is that individual practices cannot be implemented effectively in isolation (Storey, 1992), but rather combining them into integrated and complementary bundles is crucial (MacDuffie, 1995). MacDuffie believes that a 'bundle' creates the multiple, reinforcing conditions that support employee motivation, given that employees have the necessary knowledge and skills to perform their jobs effectively (Stavrou and Brewster, 2005). Thus the notion of achieving horizontal integration within and between HR practices gains significance in the best-practice debate. Horizontal alignment with other functional areas has also been highlighted by some writers as a key element in enhancing the effectiveness of other organisational practices and therefore organisational performance. Lawler *et al.* (1995) identified the link between HRM and total quality management (TQM) and similarly MacDuffie (1995) identified human resource practices as integral to the effectiveness of lean production.

The need for *horizontal integration* in the application of SHRM principles is one element that is found in both the configurational school of thought, the resource-based view approach and in certain best practice models. It emphasises the coordination and congruence between HR practices through 'a pattern of planned action' (Wright and McMahan, 1999). In the configurational school, cohesion is thought likely to create synergistic benefits, which in turn enable the organisation's strategic goals to be met. Roche (1999: 669) in his study on Irish organisations noted that 'organisations with a relatively high degree of integration of human resource strategy into business strategy are much more likely to adopt commitment-oriented bundles of HRM practices'. Where some of the best practice models differ is in those that advocate the 'universal' application of SHRM, notably Pfeffer (1994, 1998). Pfeffer's argument is that best practice may be used in any organisation, irrespective of product lifecycle, market situation, workforce characteristics and improved performance will ensue. This approach ignores potentially significant differences between organisations, industries, sectors and countries however. The work of Delery and Doty (1996) has highlighted the complex relationship between the management of human resources and organisational performance, and their research supports the contingency approach (Schuler and Jackson, 1987) in indicating that there are some key HR practices, specifically internal career opportunities, results-oriented appraisals and participation/voice, that must be aligned with the business strategy or that, in other words, are context-specific. The best practice 'bundles' approach, however, is additive, and accepts that as long as there is a core of integrated high commitment practices, other practices can be added or ignored, and still produce enhanced performance. Guest *et al.*'s analysis of the WERS data (2000a: 15), for example, found that the 'only combination of practices that made any sense was a straightforward count of all the practices'. As with many high-commitment-based models, there is an underlying assumption of unitarism, which ignores the inherent pluralist values and tensions present in many organisations. Coupled with further criticisms of context avoidance and assumed rationality between implementation and performance, the best-practice advocates, particularly the universalists, are not without their critics.

Box 2.5 HR 'is still not strategic enough'

The annual Key Trends in Human Capital 2006 survey by Saratoga, the human capital metrics business of PricewaterhouseCoopers, found little evidence that the HR function was developing a higher level of strategic influence within the business.

The report stated: 'The centrality of human capital to organisational strategy would suggest that the HR function would move to a more influential position. There appears to be little evidence of this.'

In fact, although the number of HR professionals and managers has increased in Europe – from 62.1 per cent in 2003 to 64.5 per cent in 2004 – the findings do not suggest that their influence within the organisation has increased the same way.

Box 2.5 continued

The survey also found that the number of HR directors on the main boards of FTSE-100 companies had fallen to only six.

In the US, 63 per cent of HR directors report directly to the CEO, compared with 81 per cent in 2003.

Richard Phelps, partner in HR Services at PwC, said one of the reasons behind the trend was the lack of skilled, strategically minded HR professionals. 'Moving to a shared services model and outsourcing administrative duties is supposed to free up HR and allow it to be more strategic in the business, but we are finding that organisations are experiencing skill gaps there', he said (*People Management*, March 2006: 13).

Ulrich (1998) and Ulrich and Brockbank (2005) identified the need for HR professionals to move away from traditional HR specialisms and create a range of new roles which focused on business outcomes and organisational performance. Specifically he identified the need for HR professionals to become 'business' or 'strategic' partners who were crucially involved with senior managers and line managers in strategy execution and value delivery, a further key role was identified as that of enabling and driving change, together with being an employee champion and administrative/functional expert. Ulrich's work struck a chord with the HR community in the UK and the CIPD's HR Survey 2003: where are we, where are we heading? indicated that HR professionals in the UK were aware of these roles as one in three senior HR practitioners saw their role predominantly as that of business partner, while 56 per cent indicated they aspired to become strategic partners and more than one in four saw themselves as change agents.

Source: from CIPD report 2005, CIPD, with the permission of the publisher, the Chartered Institute of Personnel and Development, London (www.cipd.co.uk).

Questions

1 Why do you think, therefore, there is still a skills gap in Senior HR professionals?
2 What do you think a 'strategically minded HR professional would look like?
3 How would you define the role and what key skills and knowledge would you identify?

HRM and performance

In recognising HRM systems as 'strategic assets' and in identifying the strategic value of a skilled, motivated and adaptable workforce, the relationship between strategic human resource management and organisational performance moves to centre stage. The traditional HR function when viewed as a cost centre, focuses on transactions, practices and compliance. When this is replaced by a strategic HRM system it is viewed as an investment and focuses on developing and maintaining a firm's strategic infrastructure (Becker *et al.*, 1997). The strategic role of HRM then might be characterised as 'organisational systems designed to achieve *competitive advantage* through people' (Snell *et al.*, 1996: 62). In turn, competitive advantage may be defined as a set of capabilities or resources giving an organisation an advantage that leads to superior performance relative to that of its competitors (Wiggins and Ruefli, 2002: 84) thus the relationship between HRM and organisational performance becomes significant, both in terms of defining appropriate HR systems and in terms of identifying methods to evaluate and measure the contribution of HR systems.

It is not surprising, therefore that there is a growing body of work that focuses on the contribution of such HR systems to organisational performance (Stroh and Caligiuri, 1998; MacDuffie, 1995; Perry-Smith and Blum, 2000; Stavrou and Brewster, 2005). This systems approach and concentration on 'bundles' of integrated HR practices is at the centre of thinking on high-performance work practices. The seminal work of Huselid (1995) and Huselid and Becker (1996) identified integrated systems of high-performance work practices – those activities that improve employees' knowledge, skills and abilities and enhance employee motivation – as significant economic assets for organisations concluding that 'the magnitude of the return on investment in high performance work practices is substantial' (Huselid, 1995: 667) and that plausible changes in the quality of a firm's high performance work practices are associated with changes in market value of between $15,000 and $60,000 per employee. Zigarelli (1996: 63) identified that Huselid's study went beyond merely justifying the existence of the HR manager. In an increasingly competitive business environment where sources of competitive advantage are scarce, Huselid's work identified that strategic human resource management can provide such an edge, as a high quality, highly motivated workforce is a difficult advantage for competitors to replicate.

This differs from the universal approach, and is indicative of a configurational approach (Delery and Doty, 1996) in that high-performance work practices are recognised as being highly idiosyncratic and in need of being tailored to meet an individual organisation's specific context in order to provide maximum performance. These high-performance work practices will only have a strategic impact therefore, if they are aligned and integrated with each other and if the total HRM system supports key business priorities. Instead, therefore, of focusing on the effects of individual HR policies and practices on individual outcomes, it becomes necessary to explore the impact-specific configurations, or systems of HRM on organisational-level outcomes (Luthans and Sommer, 2005: 328). This requires a 'systems' thinking approach on the part of HR managers, which enables them to avoid 'deadly combinations' (Delery, 1998) of HR practices which work against each other, for example, team-based culture and individual performance-related pay, and seek out 'powerful connections' or synergies between practices, for example, building up new employees' expectations through sophisticated selection and meeting them through appropriate induction, personal development plans and reward strategies

The impact of human resource management practices on organisational performance has been recognised as a key element of differentiation between HRM and strategic human resource management. Much research interest has been generated in exploring the influence of 'high performance work practices' on shareholder value (Huselid, 1995) and in human capital management (Ulrich, 1997; Ulrich et al., 1995). For example, Youndt et al. (1996) demonstrated that productivity rates were higher in manufacturing plants where the HR strategy focused on enhancing human capital and Huselid et al. (1997) found that increased HRM effectiveness corresponded to a 5.2 per cent estimated increase in sales per employee, 16.3 per cent increase in cash flow and an estimated 6 per cent in market value. Recent studies in the UK have demonstrated similar findings. A survey by Patterson et al., (1997) published for the CIPD, cited evidence for human resource management as a key contributor to improved performance. Patterson argued that 17 per cent of the variation in company profitability could be explained by HRM practices and job design, as opposed to just 8 per cent from research and development, 2 per cent from strategy and 1 per cent from both quality and technology. Other studies have reviewed the links between high-commitment HRM and performance, and two recent studies by Guest et al. (2000a, 2000b) have argued the economic and business case for recognising people as a key source of competitive advantage in organisations and therefore a key contributor to enhanced organisational performance. Further, Gelade and Ivery (2003) noted significant correlations between work climate, human resource practices and business performance in the UK banking industry. Stavrou and Brewster (2005) however, have noted that while the connection between HRM and performance has been extensively researched in the US, there is a need for further studies to explore HRM approaches that are indigenous to the European Union.

In terms of HR managers, research has highlighted the need for the development of business-related capabilities (an understanding of the business context and the implementation of competitive strategies), alongside professional HRM capabilities. Huselid et al. (1997) concluded that while professional HRM capabilities are necessary but not sufficient for better firm performance, business-related capabilities are not only underdeveloped within most firms, but they represent the area of greatest economic opportunity. The important message for HR managers is not only to understand and implement a systems perspective, but to understand how HR can add value to their particular business, so that they can become key 'strategic assets'. HR professionals, therefore, need to develop internal consultancy skills in order to measure their impact on business outcomes, with increased emphasis on customer and market growth rather than cost reductions and efficiency measures (Gubman, 2004).

STOP and think

How can HR demonstrate their business capability? What systems and measurement processes do they need to put in place to demonstrate the contribution of HR practices to bottom-line performance?

Becker and Gerhart (1996: 793) argued that future work on the 'strategic' perspective of HRM 'must elaborate on the black box between a firm's HR systems and the firm's bottom line'. They recognized that there was a need to understand how and why HR policies influence performance which goes beyond a basic input–output model. It could be argued that the 'AMO' theory of Appelbaum *et al.* (2000) sets out to do this, where organisational performance is viewed as the sum of employees' abilities, motivations and opportunities to participate, which when managed appropriately will encourage employees to demonstrate discretionary behaviour. An employee's willingness to demonstrate discretionary behaviour was found to have clear links to organizational performance. As Boxall and Purcell(2008: 63) argue people will perform well when:

● they are able to do so (possess ability, necessary knowledge and skills);
● they have the motivation to do so (provided with appropriate engagement, reward);
● they have the opportunity to utilise their skills and knowledge and express their 'voice'.

Purcell *et al.* (2003) developed the AMO concept in their Bath People and Performance model, which identified 11 HR practices that contributed to organisational performance, through supporting the development of employee ability, motivation and providing opportunities to demonstrate discretionary behaviour (Figure 2.6). They reflected that the critical link in the HRM black box is how HR practices influence employee attitudes and improve worker performance in ways which are beneficial to the employing organization (Purcell and Hutchinson, 2007). This led to recognition of the key role of the front line manager in the SHRM/organisational performance equation. Front line managers were seen as key to enacting HR policy and practice and engaging in leadership behaviour that translate strategic HR choices to effective implementation thereby influencing employee attitude and behaviour. Thus, whilst much HR literature has focused on exploring the relationship with organisational performance in terms of HR strategic choices in relation to identifying appropriate HR roles (Ulrich and Brockbank, 2005); or in selecting appropriate HR practices that either 'fit' the business strategy (Schuler and Jackson, 1987) or generate high-commitment (Pfeffer, 1998; Macduffie, 1995; Huselid, 1995), there has not been much attention paid to the key influencers on the effective implementation of HR strategy, the role of the front line manager (Purcell and Hutchinson, 2007).

SHRM and performance: the critique

While research studies devoted to demonstrating the link between SHRM and performance have increased (Wright and Haggerty, 2005), there is still much critique aimed at these studies. Criticisms aimed at advocates of the high commitment/performance link are mainly

Figure 2.6 The Bath People and Performance Model

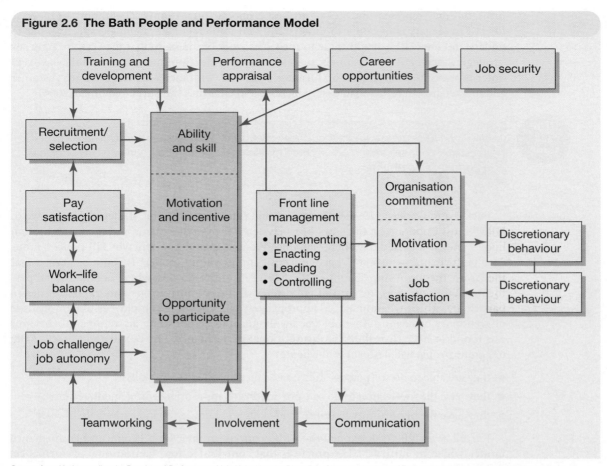

Source: from *Understanding the People and Performance Link: Unlocking the Black Box*, Chartered Institute of Personnel and Development (Purcell, J., Kinnie, N., Hutchinson, S., Rayton, B. and Swart, J. 2003), with the permission of the publisher, the Chartered Institute of Personnel and Development, London (www.cipd.co.uk).

centred on the validity of the research methods employed (Wall and Wood, 2005); the lack of theoretical underpinning (Becker and Gerhart, 1996; Dyer and Reeves, 1995; Wright *et al.*, 2003); problems associated with inconsistencies in the best practice models used (Becker and Gerhart, 1996; Marchington and Wilkinson, 2008; Wright and Gardner, 2003) and the lack of emphasis on the examination of the level of either vertical or horizontal alignment (Wall and Wood, 2005). This has led some researchers to be more circumspect in their analysis of the relationship between SHRM and performance (Marchington and Grugalis, 2000). In their 2003 study, Wright and Gardner suggest that HR practices are only 'weakly' related to firm performance (p. 312) and Godard (2004: 355) suggests that in liberal market economies the generalisability is likely to be low.

In terms of research methodology, Wall and Wood (2005), identified the least satisfactory survey method is to use single source respondents. In their review of 25 research studies, including many of the key studies on SHRM and performance, they identified that 21 of the studies had used single respondents as the sole source of data. A selection of the studies reviewed is included in Table 2.7. Wall and Wood (2005) therefore argue that future progress in justifying the relationship between SHRM and organisational performance depends on using large scale, long-term research or 'big science' in partnership between research, practitioner and government communities (Wall and Wood, 2005: 429).

In terms of evidence, it is difficult to pinpoint whether it is the HR practices that in turn lead to enhanced organisational performance or whether financial success has enabled the implementation of appropriate HR practices. It is difficult to see how organisations operating

Table 2.7 A review of research studies evaluating the SHRM/performance link

Research study and response rates	HRM dimensions	HRM measure and source	Dependent variable measures
Arthur (1994) 30 US mini steel mills: 56%	Control and commitment focus	Questionnaire: single source HR managers	Self-report: scrap rates and productivity
Guest and Hoque (1994) 119 UK manufacturing sites mainly: 39%	Four *a priori* types 2 × 2: whether or not claim HRM strategy and use more or less than half of 22 HRM practices	Questionnaire: single source principal HR manager or line manager	Self-report: productivity and quality
Huselid (1995) 968 companies with 100+ staff: 28%	Two scales: skills and structures (communication, QWL, training, grievance procedures) and motivation (performance appraisals, promotion on merit)	Questionnaire: single source mailed to senior HRM professional	Objective: productivity, Tobin's Q and GRATE
MacDuffie (1995) 62 car assembly plants worldwide: 69%	Two scales: work systems (participation, teams, quality role) and HRM policies (selection, performance-related pay, training)	Questionnaire: a contact person, often the plant manager, sections completed by different people	Objective: productivity (labour hours per vehicle)
Delaney and Huselid (1996) 50 for-profit and non-profit US firms: 51%	Five scales: staffing, selectivity, training, incentive pay, decentralisation, internal promotion	Telephone survey: single source, multiple respondents in a few cases	Self-report, organisational and market performance
Delery and Doty (1996) 216 US banks, 101 in some analyses: 18%	Seven scales: internal promotion, training, appraisal, profit-sharing, security, participation, job specification and two strategy measures	Questionnaire: single source, senior HR manager (+ strategy from president)	Objective: return on assets (ROA), return on equity (ROE)
Youndt *et al.* (1996) 897 manufacturing plants in US: 19%	Two scales: administrative HR (appraisal, incentives) and human capital enhancing HR (selection and training for problem-solving, salaried pay)	Questionnaire: multiple source (at least two respondents per per plant, mean score) general and functional managers	Self-report: customer alignment (quality), productivity and machine efficiency
Huselid *et al.* (1997) 9293 US firms (manufacturing, finance, miscellaneous) response rate unclear	Two scales: strategic HRM (teamwork, empowerment) and technical HRM (recruitment, training). Ratings of perceived effectiveness	Questionnaire: single source, executives in HR (92%) and line (8%) positions (effectiveness of HR practices)	Objectivity: productivity, GRATE and Tobins Q
Wood and de Menezes (1998) Representative sample of 1693 UK workplaces	Four types of workplace, ranging from high- to low high-commitment management	Interviews: single source, HR manager or senior manager responsible for HR	Self report: productivity, productivity change over last 3 years and financial performance

Table 2.7 Continued

Research study and response rates	HRM dimensions	HRM measure and source	Dependent variable measures
Hoque (1999) 209 UK hotels: 35%	Overall HRM (21 practices used, including harmonisation, job design, training, merit pay)	Questionnaire: single source, respondents unclear	Self-report: productivity, service quality and financial performance
Capelli and Neumark (2001) 433–666 US manufacturing plants: response rates unclear	Extent of job rotation, self-managed teams, teamwork training, cross-training pay for skill/knowledge, profit/gain	Telephone survey: single source: plant/site manager	Self-report: sales per employee, total labour cost per employee and sales/value/labour costs sharing, meetings and TQM
Guthrie (2001) 164 New Zealand firms, heterogeneous sample: 23%	Single high-involvement work practices (HIWP) scale based on 12 practices (e.g. performance-based promotion, skill-based pay, training participation)	Questionnaire: single source, various staff from CEO to junior manager	Self-report: productivity (annual sales per employee)
Batt (2002) 260 call centres: 54%	Skill level (education and training); job design (discretion and teamwork); HR incentives (supportive HR-training, feedback, high pay, security)	Telephone survey: single source, general managers	Self-report: percent change in sales in prior 2-year period
Wright *et al.* (2003) 50 business units, US food service companies: response rate unclear	Single overall HR practices scale: nine items covering selection, pay for performance, training, participation	Employee attitude survey: multiple source: rank and file employees	Objective (from company records), productivity and profit-subsequent for period 3–9 months after measurement of HR practices

Source: Wall and Wood (2005: 429–63).

in highly competitive markets, with tight financial control and margins would be able to invest in some of the HR practices advocated in the best-practice models. This is not to say that HR could not make a contribution in this type of business environment, but rather the contribution would not be that espoused by the best practice models. Here, the enhanced performance could be delivered through the efficiency and tight cost control more associated with 'hard' HR practices (Storey, 1995) and the contingency school. A further difficulty is the underlying theme of 'unitarism' pervading many of the best practice approaches. As Boxall and Purcell (2008) note, many advocates of best practice, high-commitment models, tend to 'fudge' the question of pluralist goals and interests. If the introduction of best practice HR could meet the goals of all stakeholders within the business equally, the implementation of such practices would not be problematic. However, it is unlikely that this would be the case, particularly within a short-termist-driven economy, where the majority of organisations are looking to primarily increase return on shareholder value. Thus if this return can best be met through cost reduction strategies or increasing leverage in a way that does not fit employees' goals or interests, how can these practices engender high-commitment and therefore be labelled 'best practice'? It is not surprising, therefore, that ethical differences between the *rhetoric* of human resource best practice and the *reality* of human resource real practices are highlighted (Legge, 1998). High-commitment models, therefore, which at first appear to satisfy ethical principles of deontology, in treating employees with respect and as ends in their own right, rather than as means to other ends (Legge, 1998), in reality can assume a utilitarian perspective, where it is deemed ethical to use employees as a means to an end, if it is for the greater good of the organisation. This might justify downsizing and rightsizing strategies, but it is difficult to see how this might justify recent tensions between shareholder interests and senior management goals. A common theme of the best-practice models is contingent pay, thus when an organisation is performing well, employees will be rewarded accordingly. There have been many recent cases, however, where senior managers of poorly performing organisations have been rewarded with large pay-offs (Box 2.5).

Box 2.6   **Investors rebel over Shell executive pay**

A global investor backlash over executive pay escalated on Tuesday when shareholders turned on Royal Dutch Shell and voted against its executive pay plan. In one of the biggest investor rebellions over directors' pay, about 59 per cent of the oil multinational's shareholders voted down the company's remuneration report.

They objected to the discretionary award to executive directors of bonuses for 2006–08 performance, which were made even though the company failed to meet targets. The scale of the No vote was strong evidence of the growing anger over remuneration and bonuses among shareholders, who have been criticised by regulators and politicians in the wake of the financial crisis for failing to hold boards to account.

Guy Jubb, head of corporate governance at Standard Life Investments, said he was 'dismayed' at the pay of Jeroen van der Veer, Shell's chief executive. He warned that shareholders would 'respond robustly' to 'persistent offenders'. Mr van der Veer, who steps down in June, received a bonus from the 2006–08 incentive scheme worth €1.35m (£1.19m). He was also paid €10.3m in 2008, up 58 per cent on his remuneration in 2007, according to Shell's annual report.

Institutional investors from the US, Europe and Canada, including Franklin Mutual as well as Standard Life Investments, lined up at Shell's annual meeting in The Hague and London to speak out against the report. Their biggest objection was the decision of the remuneration committee, led by Sir Peter Job, to award the performance bonuses. The Shell No vote was the second biggest against a UK company's remuneration report this year, topped only by the 80 per cent of votes cast against Royal Bank of Scotland acording to Manifest, the voting agency.

RiskMetrics, the proxy voting agency that advised investors to vote against Shell's report, said investors were uniting on pay issues in the UK and much of the rest of Europe. 'When dialogue has clearly failed, shareholders are now prepared to vote against,' said Jean-Nicolas Caprasse, its head of European and Middle Eastern business.

Source: from Investors rebel over Shell executive pay, *Financial Times*, 20 May 2009 (Burgess, K. and Steen, M.).

Time to thin down fat cat pay

Plato believed the income of the highest in society should never be more than five times that of the lowest. Ancient history, of course. In the past 10 years, median pay among FTSE 100 chief executives has grown by 92 per cent to £579,000, before bonuses and incentives, while male median pay sits at £21,000 having dribbled along with inflation.

According to pay consultants Hewitt, Bacon & Woodrow, in 84 per cent of European companies, decisions about executive pay are led by the remuneration committee, made up of non-executive directors. Yet in two or three meetings a year, these committees hardly have time to scratch the surface of what is a very complex subject, let alone go into the rival merits of an alphabet soup of performance indicators. In practice, they are heavily dependent on the advice they get. In 57 per cent of companies, that advice comes from the HR department. In 31 per cent HR commissions assistance from external consultants, but in 41 per cent HR actually designs the package.

Box 2.6 continued

HR is therefore complicit in the great fat cat pay heist. It is time it gave some thought to improving the link between performance and reward.

Source: Article by Stephen Overell, *Personnel Today*, February 2004.

Question

How do you think this tension between shareholder interests, employee interests and senior management interests should be managed in determining executive reward strategies and what role should HR play in the process?

Becker and Gerhart (1996) discuss and debate the impact of HRM on organisational performance further. They compare the views of those writers that advocate synergistic systems, holistic approaches, internal–external fit, and contingency factors on the one hand (Amit and Shoemaker, 1993; Delery and Doty, 1996; Dyer and Reeves, 1995; Huselid, 1995; Milgrom and Roberts, 1995) with those that suggest there is an identifiable set of best practices for managing employees that have universal, additive, positive effects on organisation performance on the other hand (Applebaum and Batt, 1994; Kochan and Osterman, 1994; Pfeffer, 1994). They provide a useful critique of the best practice school as they identify difficulties of generalisability in best-practice research and the inconsistencies in the best practice models (Ferris *et al.*, 1999; Boxall and Steeneveld, 1999), such as Arthur's (1994) low emphasis on variable pay, whereas Huselid (1995) and MacDuffie (1995) have a high emphasis on variable pay.

Box 2.7 | ### HR in practice – Rogas International

Rogas International (RI) owns a host of catalogue stores throughout Europe. They sell a broad range of goods from well-known electrical brands to children's toys to mobile phones at competitive prices. Rogas International operates stores in most medium-sized towns throughout the UK, as well as large stores in all major cities across Europe. Rogas has recently been taken over by a large multi-national retailer. The group trades in 1200 stores and online stores in 18 countries, and employs 30,000 people.

The challenge

As a result of the takeover, a two-year change programme has been announced. This has restructuring implications and it is anticipated that staff headcount in the major distribution centres will be reduced by 25 per cent. Some sites will be closed down, with approximately a further 1000 job losses. It is anticipated that new centres will be also be required and this will involve redeployment and recruitment of new staff.

The Managing Director of RI is keen to maintain morale and performance during the change period. He recognises the need to involve all staff in the change programme and communicate Rogas' new business strategy and values transparently. He recognises that employees need to understand the reasons for change and the possible implications for their future job roles. As the planned change is over a two-year programme, he wants to avoid a mass exodus of staff in the early stages due to fears over job security.

Sally Smart, the HR Director, shared the Managing Director's concerns and wanted to avoid losing people in a way that Rogas couldn't control – if employees reacted badly to the news and simply walked out, many of the high street stores would come to a standstill. Rogas needed to maintain and enhance performance whilst restructuring, and they also needed to ensure that they retained key skills and knowledge, which could then be transferred to the new sites.

Box 2.7 continued

The solution

Rogas invited 70 of their top managers to a two-day communication event. Sally Smart commented 'We delivered the news about the intended changes in the first hour and spent the rest of the two days trying to understand what their concerns were and how we could deal with them.'

To encourage buy-in to the new business strategy and the change programme, Rogas offered the managers a choice of personal and professional development courses so that if they did lose their job, they would feel better qualified to apply for another. For more junior staff, Rogas promised that if they could not find a role for them, they were entitled to £500-worth of training, their redundancy pay, a performance-related bonus and outplacement support.

'Most people don't like change, especially at work, the main reason they resist is because they feel they have no control. We wanted to make people feel more in control of their lives,' added Sally Smart.

One of the ways RI did this was by inviting a training and development consultancy Gomad (Go Make a Difference) into its centres to run a series of workshops and personal development focusing on dealing with and surviving change, and challenging self development boundaries.

Many blue collar staff were cynical initially. Workshops were organised to coincide with the different shift patterns and were voluntary. The HR team worked in partnership with the trade union, and trade union stewards led by example and attended the workshops. Change champions were appointed who promoted the workshops, and posters designed in the initial workshops were used to encourage all employees to attend. The workshops were subsequently well-attended and productive feedback sessions were organised with the senior management team.

Cross-functional project teams were established to consider change solutions. They were empowered to deal with 'real' change problems as they arose and resourced to implement solutions. Their successes were publicised throughout the centres and solutions were rolled out throughout the group.

Line managers were encouraged to identify key potential in personal development planning sessions, and recommend individuals for succession. The Managing Director supported a talent management programme to support and retain key knowledge and potential.

The outcome

The year to May 2006 was successful in terms of the distribution team's performance in terms of delivery efficiency and reduced costs, with 70 per cent of staff on track to earn their performance bonus. Shop sales were buoyant, employee turnover and sickness rates had improved and morale appeared strong.

The Gomad programme and talent management programme in particular proved popular with employees. In feedback surveys, 90 per cent of the attendees said they would apply what they had learned, while all participants said they would recommend them to someone else.

Finally HR and the trade union had forged a constructive partnership, and the HR Director had demonstrated to the Board how HR can add value to the business.

Questions

1 Which approach to SHRM discussed in this chapter best explains Rogas International's approach to strategic human resource management and change?

2 How has Rogas International enhanced organisational performance through the implementation of human resource systems and practices?

3 What human resources advice would you give to Rogas International, to ensure that they can manage the consolidation stage of their strategy effectively? Which approach to SHRM has influenced your thinking and why?

Measuring the impact of SHRM on performance

We have so far considered the complexity of the strategic human resource management debate and recognised that our understanding and application of strategic HRM principles is contingent upon the particular body of literature we cite our analysis in. What then are the implications for the HR professional? We started to consider the role of the HR professional at the end of our consideration of the best fit school. It is now appropriate to consider in more detail how strategic management processes in firms can be improved to deal more effectively with key HR issues and take advantage of HR opportunities. A study by Ernst & Young in 1997 cited in Armstrong and Baron (2002) found that more than a third of the data used to justify business analysts' decisions were non-financial, and that when non-financial factors, notably 'human resources', were taken into account better investment decisions were made. Their non-financial metrics most valued by investors are identified in Table 2.8 below.

This presents an opportunity for HR managers to develop business capability and demonstrate the contribution of SHRM to organisational performance. One method that is worthy of further consideration is the balanced score-card (Kaplan and Norton, 1996, 2001). This is also concerned with relating critical non-financial factors to financial outcomes by assisting firms to map the key cause–effect linkages in their desired strategies. Interestingly, Kaplan and Norton challenge the short-termism found in many Western traditional budgeting processes and as with the Ernst & Young study, they imply a central role for HRM in the strategic management of the firm and importantly suggest practical ways for bringing it about (Boxall and Purcell, 2008).

Kaplan and Norton identify the significance of executed strategy and the implementation stage of the strategic management process as key drivers in enhancing organisational performance. They recognise, along with Mintzberg (1987), that 'business failure is seen to stem mostly from failing to implement and not from failing to have wonderful visions' (Kaplan and Norton, 2001: 1). Therefore, as with the resource-based view, implementation is identified as a key process which is often poorly executed.

Kaplan and Norton adopt a stakeholder perspective, based on the premise that for an organisation to be considered successful it must satisfy the requirements of key stakeholders, namely investors, customers and employees. They suggest identifying objectives, measures, targets and initiatives on four key perspectives of business performance. These are:

Table 2.8 Non-financial metrics most valued by investors

Metric	Question to which measurable answers are required
1 Strategy	How well does management leverage its skills and experience? Gain employee commitment? Stay aligned with shareholder interests?
2 Management credibility	What is management's behaviour? And forthrightness in dealing with issues?
3 Quality of strategy	Does management have a vision for the future? Can it make tough decisions and quickly seize opportunities? How well does it allocate resources?
4 Innovativeness	Is the company a trendsetter or a follower? What's in the R&D pipeline? How readily does the company adapt to changing technology and markets?
5 Ability to attract talented people?	Is the company able to hire and retain the very best people? Does it reward them? Is it training the talent it will need for tomorrow?
6 Management experience	What is the management's history and background? How well have they performed?
7 Quality of Executive Compensation	Is executive pay tied to strategic goals? How well is it linked to the creation of shareholder value?
8 Research Leadership	How well does management understand the link between creating knowledge and using it?

Source: Adapted by Armstrong and Baron (2002) from Ernst & Young: Measures that Matter, Ernst & Young LLP. Boston: Mass.1997.

1 *Financial*: 'to succeed financially how should we appear to our shareholders'?

2 *Customer*: 'to achieve our vision how should we appear to our customers'?

3 *Internal business processes*: 'to satisfy our shareholders and customers what business processes must we excel at'?

4 *Learning and growth*: 'to achieve our vision, how will we sustain our ability to change and improve'?

They recognise that investors require financial performance, measured through profitability, market value and cash flow or EVA (economic value added). Customers require quality products and services, which can be measured by market share, customer service, customer retention and loyalty or CVA (customer value added). Employees require a healthy place to work, which recognises opportunities for personal development and growth. These can be measured by attitude surveys, skill audits, performance appraisal criteria, which recognise not only what they do, but what they know and how they feel or PVA (people value added). They can be delivered through appropriate and integrated systems, including HR systems. The balanced scorecard approach therefore provides an integrated framework for balancing shareholder and strategic goals, and extending those balanced performance measures down through the organisation, from corporate to divisional to functional departments and then on to individuals (Grant, 2008). By balancing a set of strategic and financial goals, the scorecard can be used to reward current practice and also offer incentives to invest in long-term effectiveness, by integrating financial measures of current performance with measures of 'future performance'. Thus it provides a template that can be adapted to provide the information that organisations require now and in the future for the creation of shareholder value. The balanced scorecard at Sears, for example (Yeung and Berman, 1997: 324; Rucci *et al.* 1998), focused on the creation of a vision that the company was 'a compelling place to invest', 'a compelling place to shop', and 'a compelling place to work', whereas the balanced scorecard at Mobil North American Marketing and Refining (Kaplan and Norton, 2001) focused on cascading down financial performance goals into specific operating goals, through which performance-related pay bonuses were determined. An abridged version of this, including some of the strategic objectives and measures in Mobil's Balanced Scorecard, is included in Table 2.9.

Kaplan and Norton (2001) recognise the impact key human resource activities can have on business performance in the learning and growth element of the balanced scorecard. Employee skills, knowledge and satisfaction are identified as improving internal processes, and therefore contributing to customer added value and economic added value. Thus the scorecard provides a mechanism for integrating key HR performance drivers into the strategic management process. Boxall and Purcell (2008) highlight the similarities between Kaplan and Norton's (2001: 93) learning and growth categories of *strategic competencies*, skills and knowledge required by employees to support the strategy, *strategic technologies*, information support systems required to support the strategy and *climate for action*, the cultural shifts needed to motivate, empower and align the workforce behind the strategy; with the *AMO theory of performance*, where performance is seen as a function of employee **ability**, **motivation** and **opportunity**. Thus the balanced scorecard contributes to the development of SHRM, not only in establishing goals and measures to demonstrate cause–effect linkages, but also in encouraging a process that stimulates debate and shared understanding between the different areas of the business. However, the balanced scorecard approach does not escape criticism, particularly in relation to the measurement of some HR activities which are not directly linked to productivity, thus requiring an acknowledgement of the multidimensional nature of organisational performance and a recognition of multiple 'bottom-lines' in SHRM. Boxall and Purcell (2008) suggest the use of two others besides *labour productivity*, these being *organisational flexibility* and *social legitimacy*. So although the balanced scorecard has taken account of the impact and influence of an organisation's human resources in achieving competitive advantage, there is still room for the process to become more HR driven.

Table 2.9 Abridged balanced scorecard for Mobil North American Marketing and Refining

Values	Strategic objectives	Strategic measures
Finance *To be financially strong*	ROCE Cash flow Profitability Lowest cost Profitable growth	ROCE Cash flow Net margins Cost per gallon delivered to customer Comparative volume growth rate
Customer *To delight the customer*	Continually delight targeted customer	Market share Mystery shopper rating
Organisation *To be a competitive supplier* *To be safe and reliable*	Reduce delivered costs Inventory management Improve health and safety and environment	Delivered cost per gallon vs customer's inventory level Number of incidents Days away from work
Learning and growth *To be motivated and prepared*	Organisation involvement Core competencies and skills Access to strategic information	Employee survey Strategic competitive availability Availability of strategic information

Source: Adapted from Grant (2008: 53) based on Kaplan and Norton (2001).

Activity

Either
Draw up a strategy map for your organisation or Café Expresso and identify appropriate balanced scorecard measures. Share your ideas with your colleagues and consider how you would audit HR.

Or
Evaluate your organisation's strategy map and balanced scorecard measures. How effective has this approach been in your organisation? Has it focused all stakeholders' attention on strategy implementation? Consult your colleagues, and prepare an audit of your HR provision.

Conclusion

Given the increasing profile of strategic human resource management in creating organis-ational competitive advantage and the subsequent complexity in interpreting and applying strategic human resource management principles, there appears to be agreement on the need for more theoretical development in the field, particularly on the relationship between strategic management and human resource management and the relationship between strategic human resource management and performance (Guest, 1997; Wright and Mc-Mahan, 1992; Wright and McMahan, 1999; Boxall and Purcell, 2008). This chapter has reviewed key developments and alternative frameworks in the field of strategic human resource management in an attempt to clarify its meaning so that the reader is able to make an informed judgement as to the meaning and intended outcomes of strategic human resource management. Thus strategic human resource management is differentiated from human resource management in a number of ways, particularly in its movement away from a micro perspective on individual HR functional areas to the adoption of a macro perspective (Butler *et al.* 1991; Wright and McMahan, 1992), with its emphasis on vertical integration

(Guest, 1989; Tyson, 1997; Schuler and Jackson, 1987) and horizontal integration (Baird and Meshoulam, 1988; MacDuffie, 1995). It therefore becomes apparent that the meaning of strategic human resource management tends to lie in the context of organisational perform-ance, although organisational performance can be interpreted and measured in a variety of ways. These may range from delivering efficiency and flexibility through cost reduction driven strategies through the implementation of what may be termed 'hard HR techniques' (Schuler and Jackson, 1987), to delivering employee commitment to organisational goals through 'universal sets' of HR practices (Pfeffer, 1994, 1998) or 'bundles' of integrated HR practices (Huselid, 1995; Delery and Doty, 1996), to viewing human resources as a source of human capital and sustainable competitive advantage (Barney, 1991; Barney and Wright, 1998) and a core business competence and a key strategic asset (Hamel and Prahalad, 1993, 1994). There are, therefore, conflicting views as to the meaning of SHRM and the contribu-tion strategic human resource management can make to an organisation. The implications of this are twofold: first, for academics and researchers there is a need for further theory devel-opment to define the relationship between strategic management and strategic human resource management and to ensure more rigorous research methodology in evaluating the SHRM– organisational performance link (Wall and Wood, 2005, Boselie *et al.*, 2005); and second for HR professionals, there is a need to develop strategic knowledge and capabilities and stakeholder awareness (Boxall and Purcell, 2008; Ulrich and Brockbank, 2005) so that they are credible strategic partners in the business.

Summary

- This chapter has charted the development of strategic human resource management, exploring the links between the strategic management literature and strategic human resource management. It has examined the different approaches to strategic human resource management identified in the literature, including the best fit approach, the best practice approach, the configurational approach and the resource-based view, in order to understand what makes human resource management strategic.

- A key claim of much strategic human resource management literature is a significant contribution to a firm's *competitive advantage*, whether it is through cost reduction methods or more often *added value* through best practice HR policies and practices. An understanding of the business context and particularly of the 'strategy-making' process is therefore considered central to developing an understanding of strategic human resource management.

- Whittington's typology (1993, 2001) was used to analyse the different approaches to 'strat-egy-making' experienced by organisations and to consider the impact this would have on our understanding of the development of strategic human resource management. The influence of the classical, rational-planning approach on the strategic management litera-ture and therefore strategic HRM literature was noted, with its inherent assumption that strategy-making was a rational, planned activity. This ignores some of the complexities and 'messiness' of the strategy-making process identified by Mintzberg and others. Other approaches that recognised the constituents of this 'messiness', namely the processual approach the evolutionary approach and the systemic approach, were identified. These took account of changes and competing interests both in the external and internal busi-ness environment. Significantly for human resource management, there is a recognition that it is not always appropriate to separate operational policies from higher-level strategic planning, as it is often operational policies and systems that may provide the source of 'tactical excellence', thus the traditional distinction between strategy and operations can become blurred.

- The best fit approach to strategic HRM explored the close relationship between strategic management and human resource management by considering the influence and nature of vertical integration. Vertical integration, where leverage is gained through the close link of HR policies and practices to the business objectives and therefore the external context of the firm, is considered to be a key theme of *strategic* HRM. Best fit was therefore explored in relation to lifecycle models and competitive advantage models and the associated difficulties of matching generic business type strategies to generic human resource management strategies were considered, particularly in their inherent assumptions of a classical approach to the strategy-making process. The inflexibility of 'tight' fit models in a dynamic, changing environment was evaluated, and consideration was given to achieving both fit and flexibity through complementary SHR systems.

- The configurational approach identifies the value of having a set of HR practices that are both vertically integrated to the business strategy and horizontally integrated with each other, in order to gain maximum performance or synergistic benefits. This approach recognises the complexities of hybrid business strategies and the need for HRM to respond accordingly. In advocating unique patterns or configurations of multiple independent variables, they provide an answer to the linear, deterministic relationship advocated by the best fit approach.

- The resource-based view represents a paradigm shift in strategic HRM thinking by focusing on the internal resources of the firm as a key source of sustainable competitive advantage, rather than focusing on the relationship between the firm and the external business context. Human resources, as scarce, valuable, organisation-specific and difficult-to-imitate resources, therefore become key strategic assets. The work of Hamel and Prahalad (1994) and the development of core competencies is considered significant here.

- The best practice approach highlights the relationship between 'sets' of good HR practices and organisational performance, mostly defined in terms of employee commitment and satisfaction. These sets of best practice can take many forms; some have advocated a universal set of practices that would enhance the performance of all organisations they were applied to (Pfeffer, 1994, 1998), others have focused on integrating the practices to the specific business context (high performance work practices). A key element of best practice is horizontal integration and congruence between policies. Difficulties arise here, as best practice models vary significantly in their constitution and in their relationship to organisational performance, which makes generalisations from research and empirical data difficult.

- In endeavouring to gain an understanding of the meaning of strategic human resource management, it soon becomes apparent that a common theme of all approaches is enhanced organisational performance and viability, whether this be in a 'hard' sense, through cost reduction and efficiency driven practices or through high-commitment and involvement driven value-added. This relationship is considered significant to understanding the context and meaning of strategic human resource management. The need to conduct further empirical research, particularly in Europe, is identified (Stavrou and Brewster, 2005) and the lack of methodological rigour and the extensive use of single source respondents in current research studies evaluating the SHRM/performance link is noted (Wall and Wood, 2005).

- Finally the need for further theory development in the field of strategic human resource management was noted, and the need for human resource practitioners to develop strategic capability.

Activity

Defining the effective human resource professional

What does an effective HR professional look like? What skills, competencies and knowledge do they require to become a business partner? Try to collect information from a range of sources, for example: organisational websites, HR practitioner journals, (*Personnel Today, People Management*), other journals (*Human Resource Management Journal, Management Learning*); the CIPD website and HRM textbooks to develop a profile of an effective HR professional in the twenty-first century. Which skills, competencies and knowledge would you identify as strategic HR competencies?

Questions

1 In what way does an understanding of strategic management contribute to your understanding of strategic human resource management?

2 How would you differentiate human resource management from strategic human resource management?

3 Compare and contrast the best fit and best practice approach to strategic human resource management.

4 Evaluate the relationship between strategic human resource management and organisational performance.

5 Why do human resources practitioners need to develop strategic capabilities?

Case study

Café Expresso

Café Expresso is one of the three main players in the 'coffee house' industry, which now has more than 6000 stores across the globe, 500 of which are in the UK and Ireland. They employ 7000 staff in the UK alone and serve 35 million customers in their stores across the globe each week.

The coffee industry is particularly robust, with coffee being the second most valuable commodity in the world after oil, with global retail sales estimated to be £39.2 billion. A total of 6.7 million tonnes of coffee were produced annually in 1998–2000, which is forecast to rise to 7 million tonnes by 2010.

The number of coffee bars in the high street has increased considerably in recent years, with the market being dominated by three main players. The 'coffee house' business therefore, is very competitive with coffee chains constantly looking for innovative ways of achieving sustainable competitive advantage, to remain ahead of their rivals.

Café Expresso had enjoyed first mover advantage in the marketplace and had rapidly grown to number one position, which they had retained for 15 years. In recent years, however, they have lost market share to rival competitors who have copied Café Expresso's business model and poached key staff to deliver it and subsequently customers had followed. This had resulted in Café Expresso slipping to the number three position. This loss of market share had forced them to rethink their strategy and a new charismatic chief executive, Ben Thomson, had been appointed in 2005 to turn the business around.

In reviewing Café Expresso's current strategy Ben Thomson embarked on an international fact finding tour of their coffee bars to meet staff and customers to get a feel for the nature of the business, together with rival coffee houses to gain an understanding of their source of competitive advantage. He wanted to return Café Expresso to the number one position in the marketplace. His review identified customers who were loyal to the brand of Café Expresso, but had been enticed away by the experience, the variety of coffee and level of customer service offered by their

Case study continued

competitors. His review of human resources found a high level of staff turnover, due to the minimum wage offered and the high percentage of international employees who tended to be employed on short-term contracts. The recent loss of market share and high employee turnover had led to low morale amongst remaining staff, as they felt Café Expresso's bars were dated and the range of coffees limited. Ben Thomson's review of the competitors supported this, as he identified the significance of the 'coffee drinking experience' which was delivered through appropriate décor, ambience, variety in the range of products and most importantly of all, the barista or 'coffee seller'. He identified these as key sources of added value and competitive advantage.

Ben Thomson decided to relaunch Café Expresso's business strategy with a new vision: 'To be the number one coffee house of choice across the globe' and identified the following mission: Experience Café Expresso, we don't just sell coffee we provide customers with an unforgettable experience. This was encapsulated in his value statement: 'Nowhere else makes you feel this good.' which he believed should apply to staff as well as customers. He was convinced that the success of coffee bars lay not just in selling coffee as a product, but in selling the 'coffee house' experience. To achieve this he felt that Café Expresso's human resources would be crucial to the success of his strategy. He recognised that human resources would face a difficult task, as the coffee house industry is traditionally renowned for low pay (minimum wage being the norm) and high employee turnover (50–100 per cent being the norm), yet the baristas (coffee sellers) are crucial to the success of the business and the selling of the coffee house experience.

He identified the following priorities:

Business

- To be the number one coffee house across the globe.
- To attract new customers through reputation for providing the coffee house experience.
- To retain existing customers through loyalty service.

Customer service

- Commitment to excellence.
- Internal and external customers valued.
- Sell the barista experience.

People

- Diversity and individuality valued.
- Knowledge and talent encouraged and retained.

- Pride and enthusiasm valued.
- Reward to retain.

Systems

- Customer feedback.
- Learning and development.
- Career and talent management.
- Performance management.
- Compensation and benefits.

Ben initiated a staged refurbishment programme starting with key stores and he appointed a new global HR director, Kam Patel, who came from a major airline, with a remit to introduce a new HR strategy to deliver Ben's vision of becoming the 'number one coffee house across the globe'. Kam Patel recognised the need to develop a human resource strategy which focused on the development and retention of key human resources, who could deliver the Café Expresso experience.

She reintroduced the HR strategy by relabelling the HR function as 'Partner Resources' and all staff became known as 'partners'. She decided to focus on key areas of human resources to deliver the business strategy, these were resourcing and retention, learning and development, talent management, employee involvement and communication and compensation and benefits, which she believed to be one of Partner Resources' most important roles in the company. Significantly, baristas were to be paid above minimum wage and store managers were offered a broad pay spectrum.

In terms of resourcing, Kam Patel focused on recruiting new 'partners' through window advertising and word of mouth. This was quite successful, and she acknowledged that a 'large number of their "partners" have grown to understand Café Expresso's market and approach through being a customer'. Store managers were responsible for interviewing and selection decisions and successful candidates were offered a half-day trial period.

The focus of the retention strategy is on the quality of compensation and range of benefits offered, particularly a share option scheme offered to all partners to encourage shared ownership in the business and reinforce the 'partner' ethos. A partner discount programme was also offered, which entitled staff to 30 per cent discount in stores.

All new recruits were encouraged to spend time 'on the floor' in the coffee bars, regardless of rank. They also spent a day at a central Café Expresso development centre learning about the company and the coffee industry. They also take part in the 'coffee

Case study continued

master' programme, enabling them to become a Café Expresso ambassador. This development is then further supported through a mentor system where each new recruit, both baristas and managers are appointed a 'buddy', who will support them in their role and provide further advice.

A performance management system was introduced where all partners agreed objectives and development needs, both in terms of technical skills and knowledge and behavioural skills. Performance was to be reviewed on a six-monthly basis, and manager, peer and customer reviews were included in the process.

Team briefings were introduced where regular information on the performance of the business and each store was conveyed to all partners, and upward feedback and ideas were encouraged. A suggestion scheme was introduced where ideas subsequently implemented were rewarded and recognised in the company magazine, Partner Voice. Kam Patel also introduced an engagement survey annually, and the results and feedback were published and provided to all partners in the *Partner Voice*.

Gradually customer service feedback improved, and market share increased. Employee turnover reduced to 25 per cent, and Café Expresso moved to number two in the industry. Ben Thomson and Kam Patel had recognised that the HR strategic changes had supported this improved level of service and customer attraction/retention. They recognised, however, that it would not be long before their competitors copied their initiatives, particularly in terms of reward and benefits, so they were concerned about how they might maintain and develop the extent of their competitive advantage.

Activity

1. Reflecting on the approaches to strategic human resource management discussed in this chapter (the best-fit approach; the configurational approach; the resource-based view; the best-practice approach), analyse the approach to SHRM adopted by Ben Thomson and Kam Patel at Café Expresso

2. Drawing on your answer to question 1, and the concerns raised by Ben Thomson and Kam Patel in the final paragraph, how would you develop the HR strategy to ensure Café Expresso continues to attract and retain customers.

Useful websites

www.cbi.org.uk	Confederation of British Industry
www.cipd.co.uk	Chartered Institute of Personnel and Development
www.berr.gov.uk	UK Department for Business, Enterprise & Regulatory Reform
www.managers.org.uk	Chartered Management Institute
www.personneltoday.com	*Personnel Today Journal*
www.strategicmanagement.net	Strategic Management Society

References and further reading

Those texts marked with an asterisk are recommended for further reading.

Abell, D.F. (1993) *Managing with Dual Strategies: Mastering the Present, Pre-empting the Future.* New York: Free Press.

Ahmad, S. and Schroeder, R.G. (2003) 'The impact of human resource management practices on operational performance: recognising country and industry differences', *Journal of Operations Management*, 21: 19–34.

Aktouf, O. (1996) *Traditional Management and Beyond: A Matter of Renewal.* Montreal: Gaetan Morin.

Alchian, A. and Demsetz, H. (1972) 'Production information costs and economic organisation', *American Economic Review*, 62: 777–95.

Amit, R. and Shoemaker, P. (1993) 'Strategic assets and organisational rent', *Strategic Management Journal*, 14: 33–46.

Ansoff, H.I. (1965) *Corporate Strategy.* Harmondsworth: Penguin.

Ansoff, H.I. and McDonnell, E. (1990) *Implanting Strategic Management*, 2nd edn. Hemel Hempstead: Prentice Hall.

Applebaum, E., Bailey, T., Berg, P. and Kalleberg, A. (2000) *Manufacturing Competitive Advantage: Why high-performance Systems Pay Off.* Ithaca, NY: ILR Press.

Applebaum, E. and Batt, R (1994) *The New American Workplace.* Ithaca, NY: ILR Press.

Armstrong, M. and Baron (2002) *Strategic Human Resource Management: A Guide to Action*, 2nd edn. London: CIPD.

Arthur, J. (1994) 'Effects of human resource systems on manufacturing performance and turnover', *Academy of Management Journal*, 37, 3: 670–87.

Atkinson, J. (1984) 'Manpower strategies for the flexible organisation', *Personnel Management*, August, 28–31.

Baden-Fuller, C. (1995) 'Strategic innovation, corporate entrepreneurship and matching outside-in to inside-out approaches to strategy research', *British Journal of Management*, 6 (special issue): 3–16.

Bae, J. and Lawler, J.J. (2000) 'Organisational and HRM strategies in Korea: impact on firm performance in an emerging economy', *Academy of Management Journal*, 43: 587–97.

Baird, L. and Meshoulam, I. (1988) 'Managing two fits of strategic human resource management', *Academy of Management Review*, 13, 1: 116–28.

Bamberger, P. and Phillips, B. (1991) 'Organisational environment and business strategy: parallel versus conflicting influences on human resource strategy in the pharmaceutical industry', *Human Resource Management*, 30, 2: 153–82.

Barney, J.B. (1991) 'Firm resources and sustained competitive advantage', *Journal of Management*, 17, 1: 99–120.

Barney, J. (1995) 'Looking inside for competitive advantage', *Academy of Management Executive*, 9, 4: 49–61.

Barney, J.B. and Wright, P.M. (1998) 'On becoming a strategic partner: the role of human resources in gaining competitive advantage', *Human Resource Management*, 37, 1: 31–46.

Barr, P., Stimpert, J. and Huff, A. (1992) 'Cognitive change, strategic action, and organisational renewal', *Strategic Management Journal*, 13: 15–36.

Batt, R. (2002). 'Managing customer services: human resource practices, quit rates and sales growth', *Academy of Management Journal*, 45: 587–97.

Becker, B. and Gerhart, B. (1996) 'The impact of human resource management on organisational performance: progress and prospects', *Academy of Management Journal*, 39, 4: 779–801.

Becker, B.E., Huselid, M.A., Pickus, P.S. and Spratt, M.F. (1997) 'HR as a source of shareholder value: research and recommendations', *Human Resource Management*, 36, 1: 39–47.

Beer, M., Spector, B., Lawrence, P.R., Quinn Mills, D. and Walton, R.E. (1984) *Managing Human Assets*. New York: Free Press.

Beer, M., Spector, B., Lawrence, P., Quinn Mills, D. and Walton, R., (1985) *Human Resource Management: A General Manager's Perspective*. New York: Free Press.

Berg, P. (1999) 'The effects of high performance work practices on job satisfaction in the US steel industry', *Industrial Relations*, 54: 111–35.

Blyton, P. and Turnbull, P. (1992) (eds) *Reassessing HRM*. London: Sage.

Boselie, P., Dietz, G. and Boon, C. (2005) 'Commonalities and contradictions in HRM and performance research', *Human Resource Journal*, 15, 3: 67–94.

Boxall, P. (1992) 'Strategic human resource management: beginnings of a new theoretical sophistication', *Human Resource Management Journal*, 2, 3: 60–79.

Boxall, P. (1996) 'The strategic HRM debate and the resource-based view of the firm', *Human Resource Management Journal*, 6, 3: 59–75.

Boxall, P. and Purcell, J. (2008) *Strategy and Human Resource Management*, Basingstoke, Palgrave MacMillan.

Boxall, P. and Steeneveld, M. (1999) 'Human resource strategy and competitive advantage: a longitudinal study of engineering consultancies', *Journal of Management Studies*, 36, 443–63.

Burgess, K. and Steen, M. (2009) 'Investors rebel over Shell executive pay', *Financial Times*, 20 May.

Butler, J.E., Ferris, G.R. and Napier, N.K. (1991) *Strategy and Human Resource Management*. Cincinnati, OH: Southwestern Publishing.

Capelli, P. and Crocker-Hefter, A. (1996) 'Distinctive human resources are firms' core competencies', *Organisational Dynamics*, 24, 3: 7–22.

Capelli, P. and Neumark, D. (2001). 'Do "High performance work practices" improve establishment-level outcomes?' *Industrial and Labor Relations Review*, 54, 737–75.

Capelli, P. and Singh, H. (1992) 'Integrating strategic human resources and strategic management' in D. Lewin, O.S. Mitchell and P. Sherer (eds) *Research Frontiers in Industrial Relations and Human Resources*. Madison, WI: Madison Industrial Relations Research Association, 165–92.

Chandler, A.D. (1962) *Strategy and Structure: Chapters in the History of the American Industrial Enterprise*. Cambridge, MA: MIT Press.

CIPD (2001) *Professional Standards for the Professional Development Scheme*, Chartered Institute of Personnel and Development. London: CIPD.

CIPD (2005) Fit for business: building a strategic HR function in the public sector. London: CIPD.

Clarke, J. and Newman, J. (1997) *The Managerial State*. London: Sage.

Cooper, C. (2000) 'In for the count', *People Management*, 28–34.

Cyert, R.M. and March, J.G. (1956) Organisational factors in the theory of monopoly, *Quarterly Journal of Economics*, 70, 1: 44–64.

Delaney, J.T. and Godard, J. (2001) 'An IR perspective on the high-performance paradigm', *Human Resource Management Review*, 40, 472–89.

Delaney, J.T. and Huselid, M.A. (1996) 'The impact of human resource management practices on perceptions of organisational performance', *Academy of Management Journal*, 39, 919–69.

Delery, J.E. (1998) 'Issues of fit in strategic human resource management: Implications of research', *HRM Review*, 8, 3: 289–309.

Delery, J. and Doty, H. (1996) 'Modes of theorizing in strategic human resource management', *Academy of Management Journal*, 39, 4: 802–35.

Drucker, P. (1968) *The Practice of Management*. London: Pan.

Dyer, L. (1984) 'Studying human resource strategy', *Industrial Relations*, 23, 2: 156–69.

Dyer, L. and Reeves, T. (1995) 'Human resource strategies and firm performance: what do we know and where do we need to go?' *International Journal of HRM*, 6, 3: 656–70.

Dyer, L. and Shafer, R. (1999) 'Creating organisational agility: implications for strategic human resource management' in P. Wright, L. Dyer, J. Boudreau and G. Milkovich (eds) *Research in Personnel and HRM*. Stamford, CT and London: JAI Press. *Supplement 4: Strategic Human Resource Management in the Twenty-first Century*.

Ferris, G.R., Hochwater, W.A., Buckley, M.N., Harrell-Cook, G. and Frink, D. (1999) 'Human resource management, some new direction', *Journal of Management*, 25, 385–418.

Fombrun C., Tichy, N. and Devanna, M. (eds) (1984) *Strategic Human Resource Management*. New York: Wiley.

Gelade, G. and Ivery, M. (2003) 'The impact of human resource management and work climate on organisational performance', *Personnel Psychology*, 56, 383–401.

Giojia, D.A. and Chittipeddi, K. (1991) 'Sensemaking and sensegiving in strategic change initiation', *Strategic Management Journal*, 12, 6: 433–48.

Godard, J.A. (2004) 'A critical assessment of the high performance paradigm', *British Journal of Industrial Relations*, 42, 349–78.

*Grant, R.M. (2008) *Contemporary Strategy Analysis: Concepts, Techniques, Applications*, 6th edn. Oxford: Blackwell.

Gratton, L., Hope-Hailey, V., Stiles, P. and Truss, C. (1999) 'Linking individual performance to business strategy: the people process model' in R.S. Schuler and S.E. Jackson (eds) *Strategic Human Resource Management*, pp. 142–58.

Gubman, E. (2004) 'HR strategy and planning: From birth to business results', *Human Resource Planning*, 27, 1: 13–23.

Guest, D. (1987) 'Human resource management and industrial relations', *Journal of Management Studies*, 24, 5: 503–21.

Guest, D. (1989) 'Personnel and HRM: Can you tell the difference?' *Personnel Management*, 21, 48–51.

Guest, D. (1997) 'Human resource management and performance: a review and research agenda', *International Journal of Human Resource Management*, 8, 3: 263–76.

Guest, D. (2001) 'Human resource management: When research confronts theory', *International Journal of Human Resource Management*, 12, 7: 1092–106.

Guest, D. and Hoque, K. (1994) 'The good, the bad and the ugly: Employee relations in new non-union workplaces', *Human Resource Management Journal*, 5: 1–14.

Guest, D.E., Michie, J., Conway, N. and Shehan, M. (2003) 'Human resource management and corporate performance in the UK', *British Journal of Industrial Relations*, 41, 291–314.

Guest, D., Michie, J., Sheehan, M. and Conway, N. (2000a) *Employment Relations, HRM and Business Performance: An Analysis of the 1998 Workplace Employee Relations Survey*. London: CIPD.

Guest, D., Michie, J., Sheehan, M., Conway, N. and Metochi, M. (2000b) *Effective People Management: Initial Findings of the future of Work Study*. London: CIPD.

Guthrie, J.P. (2001) 'High involvement work practices, turnover and productivity: Evidence from New Zealand', *Academy of Management Journal*, 44: 180–90.

Hamel, G. and Prahalad, C. (1993) 'Strategy as stretch and leverage', *Harvard Business Review*, 71, 2: 75–84.

Hamel, G. and Prahalad, C. (1994) *Competing for the Future*. Boston, MA: Harvard Business School Press.

Henderson, B.D. (1989) 'The origin of strategy', *Harvard Business Review*, November–December: 139–43.

Hoque, K. (1999). 'Human resource management and performance in the UK hotel industry', *British Journal of Industrial Relations*, 37, 419–443.

Hubbard, N. (1999) *Acquisition Strategy and Implementation*. Basingstoke: Macmillan.

Hunt, J., Lees, S., Grumber, J. and Vivian, P. (1987) *Acquisitions: The Human Factor*. London Business School and Egon Zehender International.

Huselid, M.A. (1995) 'The impact of human resource management on turnover, productivity, and corporate financial performance', *Academy of Management Journal*, 38: 635–72.

Huselid, M. and Becker, B. (1996) 'Methodological issues in cross-sectional and panel estimates of the HR-firm performance link', *Industrial Relations*, 35: 400–22.

Huselid, M.A., Jackson, S.E. and Schuler, R.S. (1997) 'Technical and strategic human resource management effectiveness as a determinant of firm performance', *Academy of Management Journal*, 40: 171–88.

Jackson, S.E. and Schuler R.S. (2000) *Managing Human Resources, A Partner Perspective*, 7th edn. Cincinatti, OH Southwestern Publishing.

Johnson G. and Scholes K. (2002) *Exploring Corporate Strategy*. London: Prentice Hall.

Kamoche, K.N. (2001) *Understanding Human Resource Management*. Buckingham: Open University Press.

Kanter, R. (1989) 'The new managerial work', *Harvard Business Review*, November–December: 85–92.

Kaplan, R. and Norton, D. (1996) *The Balanced Scorecard: Translating Strategy into Action*. Boston, MA: Harvard Business School Press.

Kaplan, R. and Norton, D. (2001) *The Strategy-Focussed Organisation*. Boston, MA: Harvard Business School Press.

Keenoy, T. (1990) 'HRM: A case of the wolf in sheep's clothing', *Personnel Review*, 19, 2: 3–9.

Keenoy, T. and Anthony, P. (1992) 'HRM: Metaphor, meaning and morality' in P. Blyton and P. Turnbull (eds) *Reassessing Human Resource Management*. London: Sage, pp. 233–55.

Kochan T. and Barocci, T. (1985) *Human Resource Management and Industrial Relations*. Boston, MA: LittleBrown.

Kochan, T.A. and Osterman, P. (1994) *The Mutual Gains Enterprise*. Boston, MA: Harvard Business School Press.

Lawler, E.E., Mohrman, S.A. and Ledford, G.E. (1995) *Creating High Performance Organisations*. San Francisco, CA: Jossey-Bass.

Legge, K. (1978) *Power, Innovation and Problem-Solving in Personnel Management*. London: McGraw-Hill.

Legge, K. (1998) 'The morality of HRM' in C. Mabey, G. Salaman and J. Storey (eds) *Strategic Human Resource Management, A Reader*. London: Open University/Sage, pp. 18–29.

Legge, K. (2005) *Human Resource Management: Rhetoric and Realities*. London: Macmillan.

Lengnick Hall, C.A. and Lengnick Hall, M.L. (1988) 'Strategic human resource management: A review of the literature and a proposed typology', *Academy of Management Review*, 13: 454–70.

Leonard, D. (1998) *Wellsprings of Knowledge: Building and Sustaining the Sources of Innovation*, Boston, MA: Harvard Business School Press.

Luthans, K.W. and Sommer, S.M. (2005) 'The impact of high peformance work on industry-level outcomes', *Journal of Managerial Issues*, 17, 3: 327–46.

Mabey, C., Salaman, G. and Storey, J. (eds) (1998) *Strategic Human Resource Management, A Reader*, London: Open University/Sage.

MacDuffie, J.P. (1995) 'Human resource bundles and manufacturing performance', *Industrial Relations Review*, 48, 2: 199–221.

Mahoney, T. and Deckop, J. (1986) 'Evolution of concept and practice in personnel administration/human resource management', *Journal of Management*, 12: 223–41.

March, J.G. (1976) 'The technology of foolishness' in J. Marsh and J. Olsen (eds) *Ambiguity and Choice in Organisations* Bergen: Universitetsforlaget.

Marchington, M. and Grugalis, I. (2000) 'Best practice human resource management: perfect opportunity or dangerous illusion?', *International Journal of Human Resource Management*, 11: 905–25.

Marchington, M. and Wilkinson, A. (2005) *Human Resource Management at Work: People Management and Development*, 3rd edn. London: CIPD.

Marchington, M. and Wilkinson, A. (2008) *Human Resource Management at Work: People Management and Development*, 4th edn, London: CIPD.

Marks, M. and Mirvis, P. (1982) 'Merging human resources: A review of current research', *Merger and Acquisitions*, 17, 2: 38–44.

Martin-Alcazar, F., Romero-Fernandez, P.M. and Sanchez-Gardey, G. (2005) 'Strategic human resource management: integrating the universalistic, contingent, configurational and contextual perspectives', *International Journal of HRM*, 16, 5: 633–59.

Miles, R. and Snow, C. (1978) *Organisational Strategy, Structure and Process.* New York: McGraw Hill.

Miles, R.E and Snow, C.C. (1984) 'Designing strategic human resource systems', *Organisational Dynamics*, Summer: 36–52.

Milgrom, P. and Roberts, J. (1995) 'Complementarities and fit: strategy, structure and organisational change in manufacturing', *Journal of Accounting and Economics*, 19, 2: 170–208.

Miller, D. (1992) 'Generic strategies; classification, combination and context', *Advances in Strategic Management*, 8, 391–408.

Miller, D. and Shamsie, J. (1996) 'The resource based view of the firm in two environments: The Hollywood Film Studios from 1936–1965', *Academy of Management Journal*, 39, 3: 519–43.

Miller, P. (1996) 'Strategy and the ethical management of human resources', *Human Resource Management Journal*, 6, 1: 5–18.

Milliman, J., Von Glinow, M.A. and Nathan, M. (1991) 'Organisational life cycles and international strategic human resource management in multinational companies: Implications for congruence theory', *Academy of Management Review*, 16, 318–39.

Millward, D. (2009) *Daily Telegraph*, 11 March.

Millward, N., Bryson A. and Forth, J. (2000) *All Change at Work, British Employment Relations, 1980–1998, as portrayed by the Workplace Employment Relations Series.* London: Routledge.

Mintzberg, H. (1987) 'Crafting strategy', *Harvard Business Review*, July–August: 65–75.

Mintzberg, H. (1990) 'The design school: reconsidering the basic premises of strategic management', *Strategic Management Journal*, 11: 171–95.

Mintzberg, H., Alhastrand, B. and Lampel, J. (1998) *Strategy Safari: a Guided Tour through the Wilds of Strategic Management.* London: Prentice Hall.

Mueller, F. (1998) 'Human resources as strategic assets: An evolutionary resource-based theory' in C. Mabey, G. Salaman and J. Storey (eds) *Strategic Human Resource Management: A Reader.* London: Open University/Sage, pp. 152–69.

Nonaka, I. and Takeuchi, H. (1995) *The Knowledge-Creating Company.* New York: Oxford University Press.

Ogbonna, E. (1992) 'Organisational culture and human resource management, dilemmas and contradictions' in P.

Blyton and P. Turnbull (eds) *Reassessing Human Resource Management.* London: Sage, pp. 74–96.

Patterson, M.G., West, M.A., Lawthom, R. and Nickell, S. (1997) *The Impact of People Management Practices on Business Performance.* London: IPD.

Penrose, E. (1959) *The Theory of the Growth of the Firm.* Oxford: Blackwell.

Perry-Smith, J. and Blum, T. (2000) 'Work-family human resource bundles and perceived organisational performance', *Academy of Management Journal*, 43: 1107–17.

Pettigrew, A.M. (1973) *The Politics of Organisational Decision-Making.* London: Tavistock.

Pettigrew, A.M. (1985) *The Awakening Giant: Continuity and Change in ICI.* Oxford: Blackwell.

Pfeffer, J. (1994) *Competitive Advantage through People.* Boston, MA: Harvard Business School Press.

Pfeffer, J. (1998) *The Human Equation: Building Profits by putting People First.* Boston, MA: Harvard Business School Press.

Porter, M. (1985) *Competitive Advantage: Creating and Sustaining Superior Performance.* New York: Free Press.

Porter, M. (1991) 'Towards a dynamic theory of strategy', *Strategic Management Journal*, 12 (Winter): 95–117.

Purcell, J. (1985) 'Is anybody listening to the corporate personnel department?' *Personnel Management*, September: 28–31.

Purcell , J. and Hutchinson, S. (2007) 'Front-line managers as agents in the HRM-performance causal chain: theory, analysis and evidence', *Human Resource Management Journal*, 17, 1: 3–20.

Purcell, J., Kinnie, N., Hutchinson, S., Rayton, B. and Swart, J. (2003) *Understanding the People and Performance Link: Unlocking the Black Box.* London: CIPD.

Quick, J. (1992) 'Crafting an organisational culture: Herb's hand at Southwest', *Organisational Dynamics*, 21: 45–56.

Quinn J.B. (1978) 'Strategic change: Logical incrementalism', *Sloan Management Review*, 1, 20: 7–21.

Rahrami, H. (1992) 'The emerging flexible organisation: perspectives from Silicon Valley', *California Management Review*, 34, 4: 33–48.

Reicheld, F. (1996) *The Loyalty Effect: The Hidden Force Behind Growth, Profits and Lasting Value.* Boston, MA: Harvard Business School Press.

Ritson, N. (1999) 'Corporate strategy and the role of HRM: critical cases in oil and chemicals', *Employee Relations*, 21, 2: 159–75.

Roche, W. (1999) 'In search of commitment-oriented HRM practices and the conditions that sustain them', *Journal of Management Studies*, 36, 5: 653–78.

Rucci, A. Kirn, S. and Quinn, R. (1998) 'The employee–customer–profit chain at Sears', *Harvard Business Review*, 76, 1: 82–97.

Schuler, R. and Jackson, S. (1987) 'Linking competitive strategies with human resource management', *Academy of Management Executive*, 1, 3: 207–19.

Schuler, R.S. and Jackson, S.E. (eds) (1999) *Strategic Human Resource Management.* Oxford: Blackwell Business.

Simon, H.A. (1947) *Administrative Behaviour.* New York: Free Press.

Sisson, K. and Storey, J. (2000) *The Realities of Human Resource Management.* Buckingham: Open University Press.

Sivasubramaniam, N. and Kroeck, K.G. (1995) 'The concept of fit in strategic human resource management', *Academy of Management Conference*, Vancouver.

Sloan, A.P. (1963) *My Years with General Motors*. London: Sidgwick & Jackson.

Snell, S.A., Youndt, M. and Wright, P.M. (1996) 'Establishing a framework for research in strategic human resource management: merging resource theory and organisation learning', *Research in Personnel and Human Resources Management*, 14: 61–90.

Stavrou, E.T. and Brewster, C. (2005) 'The configurational approach to linking strategic human resource management bundles with business performance: Myth or reality?', *Management Revue*, 16, 2: 186–202.

Storey, J. (1992) *Developments in the Management of Human Resources*. Blackwell: Oxford.

Storey, J. (1995) *Human Resource Management: A Critical Text*. London: Routledge.

Storey, J. (ed.) (2001) *Human Resource Management: A Critical Text*. London: Thomson Learning.

Stroh, L. and Caligiuri, P.M. (1998) 'Strategic human resources: A new source for competitive advantage in the global arena', *International Journal of Human Resource Management*, 9: 1–17.

Thompson, J. (2001) *Understanding Corporate Strategy*. London: Thomson Learning.

Torrington, D. and Hall, L. (1998) *Human Resource Management*, 4th edn. Europe: Prentice-Hall.

Torrington, D. and Hall, L. (2005) *Human Resource Management*, 5th edn. Europe: Prentice-Hall.

Truss, C. and Gratton, L. (1994) 'Strategic human resource management: A conceptual approach', *International Journal of Human Resource Management*, 5: 663–86.

Tyson, S. (1997) 'Human resource strategy: A process for managing the contribution of HRM to organisational performance', *International Journal of Human Resource Management*, 8, 3: 277–90.

Ulrich, D. (1997) 'Measuring human resources: An overview of practice and a prescription for results', *Human Resource Management*, 36, 3 (Fall): 303–20.

Ulrich, D. (1998) 'A new mandate for human resources', *Harvard Business Review*, January–February: 124–35.

Ulrich, D. and Brockbank, W. (2005) *The HR Value Proposition*. Boston, MA: Harvard Business Review School Press.

Ulrich, D., Brockbank, W., Yeung, A. and Lake, D. (1995) 'Human resource competencies: An empirical assessment', *Human Resource Management*, 34: 473–95.

Vandenberg, R.J., Richardson, H.A. and Eastman, L.J. (1999) 'The impact of high involvement work processes on organisational effectiveness', *Groups and Organisation Management*, 24: 300–99.

Ventrakaman, N. (1989) 'The concept of fit in strategy research: towards verbal and statistical correspondence', *Academy of Management Review*, 14: 423–44.

Wall, T.D. and Wood, S.J. (2005) 'The romance of human resource management and business performance, and the case for big science', *Human Relations*, 58, 4: 429–62.

Walton, J. (1999) *Strategic Human Resource Development*. London: FT Prentice Hall.

Walton R. (1985) 'From control to commitment in the workplace', *Harvard Business Review*, 63, March–April: 76–84.

Watson, J. (1977) *The Personnel Managers: A Study in the Sociology of Work and Employment*. London: Routledge & Kegan Paul.

Wernefelt, B. (1984) 'A resource based view of the firm', *Strategic Management Journal*, 5, 2: 171–80.

Whittington, R. (1992) 'Putting Giddens into action: social systems and managerial agency', *Journal of Management Studies*, 29, 6: 693–712.

Whittington, R. (1993) *What is Strategy and Does it Matter?* London: Routledge.

*Whittington, R. (2001) *What is Strategy and Does it Matter?* 2nd edn. London: Thomson Learning.

Winnett, R. and Corrigan, T. (2009) *Daily Telegraph*, 21 March.

Wiggins, R.R. and Ruefli, T.W. (2002) 'Sustained competitive advantage: temporal dynamics and the incidence and persistence of superior economic performance', *Organisation Science*, 13: 82–108.

Wilson, D. (1992) *A Strategy of Change*. London: Routledge.

Winter, S. (1987) 'Knowledge and competence as strategic assets' in D.J. Teece (ed.) *The Competitive Challenge: Strategies for Industrial Innovation and Renewal*. Cambridge, MA: Ballinger, pp. 159–84.

Wood, S. (1999) 'Human resource management and performance', *International Journal of Management Reviews*, 1, 4: 367–413.

Wood, S.J. and de Menezes, L. (1998) 'High commitment management in the UK: evidence from the workplace industrial relations survey and employers' manpower and skills practices survey', *Human Relations*, 51: 485–515.

Wright, M.W. and Haggerty, J.J. (2005) 'Missing variables in theories of strategic human resource management: time, cause and individuals', *Management Revue*, 16, 2: 164–74.

Wright, P.M. and Gardner, T.M. (2003) 'The human resource-firm performance relationship: methodological and theoretical challenges' in D. Holman, T.D. Wall, C.W. Clegg, P. Sparrow and A. Howard (eds) *The New Workplace: A Guide to the Human Impact of Modern Working Practices*. Chichester: Wiley.

Wright, P.M. and McMahan, G.C. (1992) 'Alternative theoretical perspectives for strategic human resource management', *Journal of Management*, 18: 295–320.

Wright, P.M. and McMahan, G.C. (1999) 'Theoretical perspectives for strategic human resource management' in R.S. Schuler and S.E. Jackson (eds) *Strategic Human Resource Management*. Oxford, Blackwell Business, pp. 49–72.

Wright, P. and Snell, S. (1991) 'Towards an integrative view of strategic human resource management', *Human Resource Management Review*, 1: 203–25.

Wright, P.M. and Snell, S.A. (1998) 'Towards a unifying framework for exploring fit and flexibility in strategic human resource management', *Academy of Management Review*, 23, 4: 756–72.

Wright, P.M. and Snell, S.A. (2005) 'Partner or guardian? HR's challenge in balancing value and values', *Human Resource Management Journal*, 44, 2: 177–82.

Wright, P.M., Gardner, T.M. and Moynihan, L.M. (2003) 'The impact of HR practices on the performance of business units', *Human Resource Management Journal*, 13: 21–36.

Wright, P., McCormick, B., Sherman, S. and McMahan, G. (1996) 'The role of human resource practices in petro-chemical refinery performance'. Paper presented at the 1996 Academy of Management, Cincinnati, OH.

Wright, P. McMahan, G. and McWilliams, A. (1994) 'Human resources and sustained competitive advantage: A resource-based perspective', *International Journal of Human Resource Management*, 5, 2: 301–26.

Wright, P., Snell, S. and Jacobsen, P. (2004) 'Current approaches to HR strategies: inside-out vs. outside-in', *Human Resource Planning*, 27: 36–46.

81

Yeung, A. and Berman, B. (1997) 'Adding value through human resources: Reorienting human resource management to drive business performance', *Human Resource Management*, 36, 3: 321–35.

Youndt, M., Snell, S., Dean, J. and Lepak, D. (1996) 'Human resource management, manufacturing strategy and firm performance', *Academy of Management Journal*, 39: 836–66.

Zigarelli, M. (1996) 'Human resources and the bottom line', *Academy of Management Executive*, 10: 63–64.

For multiple-choice questions, exercises and annotated weblinks related to this topic, visit **www.pearsoned.co.uk/mymanagementlab**.

Chapter 3

Contextualising HRM: developing critical thinking

Audrey Collin

Objectives

- To indicate the significance of context for the understanding of HRM.
- To discuss ways of conceptualising and representing the nature of context generally and this context in particular.
- To look at the nature of the immediate context of HRM: the problematical nature of organisations and the need for management.
- To indicate the nature of the wider context of HRM and illustrate this through selected examples.
- To examine how our ways of interpreting and defining reality for ourselves and for others construct and influence the way we understand and practise HRM.
- To suggest the implications for the readers of this book.
- To present a number of activities and a case study that will facilitate readers' understanding of the context of HRM.

Introduction

The significance and nature of context

> An event seen from one point-of-view gives one impression. Seen from another point-of-view it gives quite a different impression. But it's only when you get the whole picture you fully understand what's going on.
>
> (Reproduced with kind permission of DDB London, in memory of John Webster (1934–2006))

The need to be aware of the context of human affairs was demonstrated dramatically in this prize-winning advertisement for *The Guardian* newspaper that is still remembered today. We can easily misinterpret facts, events and people when we examine them out of context, for it is their context that provides us with the clues necessary to enable us to understand them. Context locates them in space and time and gives them a past and a future, as well as the present that we see. It gives us the language to understand them, the codes to decode them, the keys to their meaning.

This chapter will carry forward your thinking about the issues raised in Chapter 1 by exploring the various strands within the context of HRM that are woven together to form the pattern of meanings that constitute it. As that chapter explained, and the rest of the book will amplify, HRM is far more than a portfolio of policies, practices, procedures and prescriptions concerned with the management of the employment relationship. It is this, but more. And because it is more, it is loosely defined and difficult to pin down precisely, a basket of multiple, overlapping and shifting meanings, which users of the term do not always specify. Its 'brilliant ambiguity' (Keenoy, 1990) derives from the context in which it is embedded, a context within which there are multiple and often competing perspectives upon the employment relationship, some ideological, others theoretical, some conceptual. HRM is inevitably a contested terrain, and the various definitions of it reflect this.

From the various models of HRM in Chapter 1, you will recognise that the context of HRM is a highly complex one, not just because of its increasing diversity and dynamism, but also because it is multi-layered. The organisation constitutes the immediate context of the employment relationship, and it is here that the debate over how that relationship should be managed begins. The nature of organisation and the tensions between the stakeholders in it give rise to issues that have to be addressed by managers: for example, choices about how to orchestrate the activities of organisational members and whose interests to serve.

Beyond the organisation itself lie the economic, social, political and cultural layers, and beyond them again the historical, national and global layers of context. Considerable change is taking place within those layers, making the whole field dynamic. It is not the purpose of this chapter to register these many changes; you will become aware of some of them as you read the remainder of this book. However, we need to note here that the events and changes in the wider context have repercussions for organisations, and present further issues to be managed and choices to be made. Indeed, Mayo and Nohria (2005) argue that successful managers have what they have coined 'contextual intelligence' that enables them to be deeply sensitive to their organisation's context.

The various layers of context and the elements within them, however, exist in more than one conceptual plane. One has a concrete nature, like a local pool of labour, and the other is abstract, like the values and stereotypes that influence an employer's views of a particular class of person in the labour market. The abstract world of ideas and values overlays the various layers of the context of HRM: the ways of organising society, of acquiring and using power, and of distributing resources; the ways of relating to, understanding and valuing human beings and their activities; the ways of studying and understanding reality and of acquiring knowledge; the stocks of accumulated knowledge in theories and concepts.

It is the argument of this chapter that to understand HRM we need to be aware not just of the multiple layers of its context – rather like the skins of an onion – but also of these conceptual planes and the way they intersect. Hence, 'context' is being used here to mean more than the environment or the surrounding circumstances that exert 'external influences' on a given topic: context gives them a third dimension. The chapter is arguing, further, that events and experiences, ideas and ideologies are not discrete and isolatable, but are interwoven and interconnected, and that HRM itself is embedded in that context: it is part of that web and cannot, therefore, be meaningfully examined separately from it. Context is highly significant yet, as we shall see, very difficult to study. Hence this chapter will present you with some challenging and abstract material that will encourage you to be a more analytical thinker. This is necessary not only for those studying HRM; today it is becoming essential for practitioners, too. It is predicted that HR will see a major transformation in the next few years, with its core becoming more analytical and critical (Czerny, 2005) and turned 'from a department and a transaction into a philosophy leading the organisation' (Pickard, 2005: p. 15). And from 2005 the concept of the 'thinking performer', 'who applies a critically thoughtful approach to their job' (Whittaker and Johns, 2004: p. 32), underpins the professional standards of the Chartered Institute of Personnel and Development.

Conceptualising and representing context

How can we begin to understand anything that is embedded in a complex context? We seem to have awareness at an intuitive level, perceiving and acting upon the clues that context gives to arrive at the 'tacit knowledge' discussed later in Chapter 7. However, context challenges our formal thinking. First, we cannot stand back to take in the complete picture, which has traditionally been one way to gain objective knowledge of a situation. Because we are ourselves part of our context, as defined in this chapter, it is not possible for us to obtain a detached perspective upon it. In that respect we are like the fish in water that 'can have no understanding of the concept of "wetness" since it has no idea of what it means to be dry' (Southgate and Randall, 1981: 54). However, humans are very different from the 'fish in water'. We can be *reflexive*, recognising what our perspective is and what its implications are; *open*, seeking out and recognising other people's perspectives; and *critical*, entering into a dialogue with others' views and interrogating our own in the light of others', and vice versa. The 'Stop and think' boxes, Activities and Exercises throughout the chapter are there to encourage you in this direction.

Second, we need the conceptual tools to grasp the wholeness (and dynamic nature) of the picture. To understand a social phenomenon such as HRM, we cannot just wrench it from its context and examine it microscopically in isolation. To do this is to be like the child who digs up the newly planted and now germinating seed to see 'whether it is growing'. In the same way, if we analyse context into its various elements and layers, then we are already distorting our understanding of it, because it is an indivisible whole. Rather, we have to find ways to examine HRM's interconnectedness and interdependence with other phenomena in its context.

The study of context, therefore, is no easy task, and poses a major challenge to our established formal, detached and analytical ways of thinking. Nevertheless, as we shall discuss later in this chapter, there are ways forward that enable us to conceptualise the many loops and circularities of these complex interrelationships in an often dynamic context.

Before you continue, spend a few minutes reflecting upon this way of understanding context. How different is it from the way in which you would have defined context? Does this have any implications for you as you read this chapter?

Meanwhile, we shall try to conceptualise context through metaphor: that is, envisage it in terms of something concrete that we already understand. We have already used the metaphor of the many-skinned onion to depict the multiple layers of context, but context is more complex than that and we need another metaphor to suggest its interconnectedness and texture. We could, therefore, think of it as a tapestry. This is a 'thick hand-woven textile fabric in which design is formed by weft stitches across parts of warp' (*Concise OED*, 1982). The warp threads run the length of the tapestry, the weft are the lateral threads that weave through the warp to give colour, pattern and texture. This metaphor helps us to visualise how interwoven and interrelated are the various elements of the context of HRM, both the concrete and the abstract; and how the pattern of HRM itself is woven into them. In terms of this metaphor, our ways of seeing and thinking about our world – the assumptions we make about our reality – could be said to be the warp, the threads which run the length of the tapestry contributing to its basic form and texture. Ideologies and the rhetoric through which they are expressed – ways of defining reality for other people – are the weft threads that weave through the warp threads, and give the tapestry its basic pattern and texture. Events, people, ephemeral issues are the stitches sewn on to the surface of the tapestry to elaborate its pattern. We see this in Figure 3.1. In the case of the context of HRM, this tapestry is being woven continuously from threads of different colours and textures. At times one colour predominates, but then peters out. In parts of the tapestry patterns may be intentionally fashioned, while observers (such as the authors of this book) believe they can discern a recognisable pattern in other parts.

Figure 3.1 The metaphor of tapestry to convey HRM in context

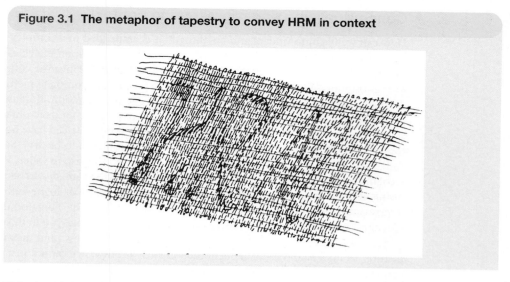

This metaphor again reminds us that an analytical approach to the study of context, which would take it apart to examine it closely, would be like taking a tapestry to bits: we would be left with threads. The tapestry itself inheres in the whole, not its parts. How, then, can the chapter begin to communicate the nature of this tapestry without destroying its very essence through analysis? The very representation of our thinking in written language is linear, and this undermines our ability to communicate a dynamic, interrelated complexity clearly and succinctly. We need to think in terms of 'rich pictures', 'mind-maps', or 'systems diagrams' (Checkland, 1981; Senge, 1990; Cameron, 1997).

It is not feasible here nor, indeed, necessary to attempt to portray the whole tapestry in detail; the chapter will focus instead upon a number of strands that run through it. You will be able to identify and follow them through the remainder of the book, and observe how their interweaving gives us changes in pattern and colour, some distinct, others subtle. Before beginning to read the exposition of the context of HRM, you will find it helpful to carry out the following activity.

Activity

Look at the various models that were presented in Chapter 1 and identify some of the elements of context and the relationships between them that are explicit or implied there. This will help you develop your own view of the context of HRM before you read further, and give you some mental 'hooks' upon which to hang your new understanding.

The concepts and language needed to understand context

To understand context, it has been suggested so far, we need to recognise its wholeness. We therefore need to incorporate both the concrete world and the world of abstract ideas. Although the appropriate language to enable us to do this may be largely unfamiliar to you, you will find that you already have considerable understanding of the concepts it expresses. Your own experience of thinking about and responding to one aspect of context – the natural, physical environment – will have given you the basic concepts that we are using and a useful set of 'hooks' upon which to hang the ideas that this chapter will introduce to you. It would be helpful to your understanding of this chapter, therefore, if you examined some of the 'hooks' you are already using, and perhaps clarify and refine them. (In this way, as Chapter 7 explains, the new material can now be more effectively transferred into, and later retrieved from, your long-term memory.)

Carry out the activity at the end of the chapter. This will focus your thinking and enable you to recognise that you already have the 'hooks' you will need to classify the material of this chapter in a meaningful way. It will show you that, although you may not customarily use the terminology below, from your present knowledge of the environment you already recognise that:

- Context is *multi-layered, multidimensional and interwoven.* In it, concrete events and abstract ideas intertwine to create issues; thinking, feeling, interpreting and behaving are all involved. It is like the tapestry described above.
- Our understanding depends upon our *perspective.*
- It also depends upon our *ideology.*
- Different groups in society have their own interpretations of events, stemming from their ideology. There are therefore *competing* or *contested interpretations* of events.
- These groups use *rhetoric* to express their own, and account for competing, interpretations, thus distorting, or even suppressing, the authentic expression of competing views.
- Powerful others often try to impose their interpretations of events, their version of reality, upon the less powerful majority: this is *hegemony.*

This subsection has perhaps given you a new language to describe what you already understand well. You will find some of these terms in the Glossary at the end of this book, and their definitions will be amplified in later sections of this chapter as it continues its exploration of the context of HRM.

The immediate context of HRM

Human resource management, however defined, concerns the management of the employment relationship: it is practised in organisations by managers. The nature of the organisation and the way it is managed therefore form the immediate context within which HRM is embedded, and generate the tensions that HRM policies and practices attempt to resolve.

The nature of organisations and the role of management

At its simplest, an organisation comes into existence when the efforts of two or more people are pooled to achieve an objective that one would be unable to complete alone. The achievement of this objective calls for the completion of a number of tasks. Depending upon their complexity and degree of interdependence, the availability of appropriate technology and the skills of the people involved, these tasks may be subdivided into a number of subtasks and more people employed to help carry them out. This division of labour constitutes the lateral dimension of the structure of the organisation. Its vertical dimension is constructed from the generally hierarchical relationships of power and authority between the owner or owners, the staff employed to complete these tasks, and the managers employed to coordinate and control the staff and their work. Working on behalf of the organisation's owners or shareholders and with the authority derived from them, managers draw upon a number of resources to enable them to complete their task: raw materials; finance; technology; appropriately skilled people; legitimacy, support and goodwill from the organisation's environment. They manage the organisation by ensuring that there are sufficient people with appropriate skills; that they work to the same ends and timetable; that they have the authority, information and other resources needed to complete their tasks; and that their tasks dovetail and are performed to the required standard and at the required pace.

The very nature of work organizations in a capitalist society therefore generates a number of significant tensions: between people with different stakes in the organisation, and therefore different perspectives upon and interests in it; between what owners and other members of the organisation might desire and what they can feasibly achieve; between the needs, capabilities and potentials of organisational members and what the organisation demands of and permits them. Management (see Watson, 2000) is the process that keeps the organisation from flying apart because of these tensions, that makes it work, secures its survival and, according to the type of organisation, its profitability or effectiveness. Inevitably, however, as Chapter 10 discusses, managerial control is a significant and often contentious issue. Until recently that had been seen in terms of managers controlling employees. The 2008/2009 banking crisis, however, now raises the issue of how senior managers are themselves controlled.

The management of people and relationships is intrinsic to the managing of an organisation, but the very nature of people and the way they constitute an organisation make management complex. Although the organisation of tasks packages people into organisational roles, individuals are larger and more organic than those roles have traditionally tended to be. The organisation, writes Barnard (1938, in Schein, 1978: 17) 'pays people only for certain of their activities. . . but it is whole persons who come to work'. Unlike other resources, people interact with those who manage them and among themselves; they have needs for autonomy and agency; they think and are creative; they have feelings; they need consideration for their emotional and their physical needs, security and protection. The management of people is therefore not only a more diffuse and complex activity than the management of other resources, but also an essentially moral one (again, see Watson, 2000). This greatly complicates the tasks of managers, who can only work with and through people to ensure that the organisation survives and thrives in the face of increasing pressures from its environment.

Owners and managers are confronted with choices about how to manage people and resolve organisational tensions. The next subsection examines some of these choices and the strategies adopted to handle them. Before then, however, it must be noted that as organisations become larger and more complex, the division of managerial labour often leads to a specialist 'people' function to advise and support line managers in the complex and demanding tasks of managing their staff. This is now commonly called 'HRM', which has developed a professional expertise in certain aspects of managing people, such as selection, training and industrial relations, which it offers in an advisory capacity to line managers, who nevertheless remain the prime managers of people. However, this division of managerial labour has fragmented the management of people: the development of human resource management beyond the original personnel approach can be seen as a strategy to reintegrate the management of people into the management of the organisation as a whole.

The approaches adopted by managers to resolve the tensions in organisations

The previous subsection suggested that there are inherent tensions in organisations. In brief, these are generated by:

- the existence of several stakeholders in the employment relationship;
- their differing perspectives upon events, experiences and relationships;
- their differing aims, interests and needs;
- the interplay between formal organisation and individual potential and needs.

In your own experience of being employed, however limited that might be so far, have you been aware of some of these tensions? What were their effects upon you and your colleagues at work? How did the management of the organisation appear to respond to these tensions? Has this coloured how you look at management and HRM?

Those tensions have to be resolved through the process of management or, rather, continuously resolved, for they are inherent in organisations. Thus Weick (1979: 44) writes that organising is a continuous process of meaning-making: 'organizations keep falling apart... require chronic rebuilding'. A continuing issue, therefore, is that of managerial control: how to orchestrate organisational activities in a way that meets the needs of the various stakeholders. The owners of organisations, or those who manage them on their behalf, have explored many ways to resolve these tensions: the emergence of HRM to develop alongside, subsume or replace personnel management is witness to this. The strategies they adopt are embodied in their employment policies and practices and the organisational systems they put in place (see also Chapter 10). They are also manifested in the psychological contract they have with their employees, the often unstated set of expectations between organisation and individual that embroiders the legal employment contract. (The notion of the psychological contract now in current use goes back to a much earlier literature – for example, Schein (1970) – and it is some of the earlier terminology that is used here.) This subsection will briefly outline some of the strategies that managers have adopted, while the next will discuss the interpretations by theorists and other commentators of those strategies. However, it must be kept in mind that managers are to some extent influenced by the concepts and language, if not the arguments, of these theorists.

In very crude terms, we can identify four strategies that managers have adopted to deal with these tensions. The first is represented by what is called scientific management, or the classical school of management theory. The second is the human relations approach, and the third is the human resource management approach. The fourth approach is perhaps more an ideal than a common reality. It must be emphasised that we cannot do justice here to the rich variety of approaches that can be found in organisations. You can elaborate upon the material here by reading about these differing views in an organisational behaviour textbook, such as Huczynski and Buchanan (2006) or Clark *et al.* (1994).

The first approach addressed the tensions in the organisation by striving to control people and keep down their costs: the *scientific management* approach. It emphasised the need for rationality, clear objectives, the managerial prerogative – the right of managers to manage – and adopted work study and similar methods. These led to the reduction of tasks to their basic elements and the grouping of similar elements together to produce low-skilled, low-paid jobs, epitomised by assembly-line working, with a large measure of interchangeability between workers. Workers tended to be treated relatively impersonally and collectively ('management and labour'), and the nature of the psychological contract with them was calculative (Schein, 1970), with a focus on extrinsic rewards and incentives. Such a strategy encouraged a collective response from workers, and hence the development of trade unions.

These views of management evolved in North America, and provided a firm foundation for modern bureaucracies (Clegg, 1990). In Britain they overlaid the norms of a complex, though changing, social class system that framed the relationships between managers and other employees (Child, 1969; Mant, 1979). This facilitated the acceptance of what Argyris (1960) saw were the negative outcomes of McGregor's (1960) X-theory of management which were hierarchy; paternalism; the attribution to workers of childlike qualities, laziness, limited aspirations and time horizons. While this strategy epitomised particularly the management approach of the first half of the twentieth century, it has left its legacy in many management practices, such as organisation and method study, job analysis and description, selection methods, an overriding concern for efficiency and the 'bottom line', appraisal and performance management. Moreover, it has not been completely abandoned (see Clegg, 1990; Ritzer, 1996 on 'McDonaldization'; and debates about employment in call centres, for example Callaghan and Thompson, 2002; Hatchett, 2000; Taylor *et al.*, 2002).

The *human relations* approach to the tensions in organisations emerged during the middle years of the twentieth century, and developed in parallel with an increasingly prosperous society in which there were strong trade unions and (later) a growing acceptance of the right of individuals to self-fulfilment. Child (1969) identifies its emergence in British management thinking as a response to growing labour tensions. It tempered scientific management by its recognition that people differed from other resources, that if they were treated as clock numbers rather than as human beings they would not be fully effective at work and could even fight back to the point of subverting management intentions. It also recognised the significance of social relationships at work – the informal organisation (Argyris, 1960). Managers therefore had to pay attention to the nature of supervision and the working of groups and teams, and to find ways of involving employees through job design (see Chapter 14), motivation, and a democratic, consultative or participative style of management. The nature of the psychological contract was cooperative (Schein, 1970).

The third and most recent major approach adopted by managers to address the tensions within the organisation has developed as major changes and threats have been experienced in the context of organisations (recession, international competition, and globalisation). It is a response to the need to achieve flexibility in the organisation and workforce (see Chapter 4) and improved performance through devolving decision-making and empowerment (see Chapter 14). As Chapter 7 notes, employees have had to become multi-skilled and to work across traditional boundaries. Unlike the other two strategies, the third approaches the organisation holistically and often with greater attention to its culture, leadership and 'vision', the 'soft' Ss of McKinsey's 'Seven S' framework (Pascale and Athos, 1982: 202–06). It attempts to integrate the needs of employees with those of the organisation in an explicit manner: the psychological contract embodies mutuality (Schein, 1970). It recognises that people should be invested in as assets so that they achieve their potential for the benefit of the organisation. It also pays greater attention to the individual rather than the collective, so that these notions of developing the individual's potential have been accompanied by individual contracts of employment (see Chapter 10), performance appraisal (see Chapter 13), and performance-related pay (see also Chapter 12).

The very title of *human resource management* suggests that this third approach to the management of organisational tensions is also an instrumental one. Although it differs greatly from the approaches that see labour as a 'cost', to be reduced or kept in check, it nevertheless construes the human being as a resource for the organisation to use. The fourth, idealistic, *humanistic* approach aims to construct the organisation as an appropriate environment for autonomous individuals to work together collaboratively for their common good. This is the approach of many cooperatives. It informed the early philosophy of organisation development (see Huse, 1980), although the practice of that is now largely instrumental. It also underpins the notion of the learning organisation (see Senge, 1990, and Chapters 7 and 8).

Although we have identified here four different strategies for managing the inherent tensions in organisations, they might be less easy to distinguish in practice. Some managers adopt a hybrid version more appropriate to their particular organisation. They will always be seeking new approaches to deal more effectively with those tensions, or to deal with variations in them as circumstances change (for example, with globalisation).

Activity **Comparing these managerial strategies**

Many of you have worked in a call centre, or know someone who does. Working on your own or in a group, examine your experiences of working there. Could you identify one or more of these managerial strategies in your workplace? What might have been your experiences had the management adopted a different strategy?

When we look more deeply into these four managerial strategies, we can recognise that they implicate some much deeper questions. Underlying the management of people in organisations are some fundamental assumptions about the nature of people and reality itself, and hence about organising and managing. For example, managers make assumptions about the nature of the organisation, many interpreting it as having an objective reality that exists separately from themselves and other organisational members – they reify it (see Glossary). They make assumptions about the nature of their own and the organisation's goals, which many interpret as rational and objective. They make assumptions about the appropriate distribution of limited power throughout the organisation, and how people in the organisation should be regarded and treated.

However, those assumptions are rarely made explicit, and are therefore rarely challenged. Moreover, many other members of the organisation appear to accept those premises on which they are managed, even though such assumptions might conflict with their own experiences, or virtually disempower or disenfranchise them. For example, many might assert the need for equal opportunities to jobs, training and promotion, but do not necessarily challenge the process of managing itself despite its often gender-blind nature (Hearn *et al.*, 1989; Hopfl and Hornby Atkinson, 2000). Nevertheless, those assumptions inform the practices and policies of management, and hence define the organisational and conceptual space that HRM fills, and generate the multiple meanings of which HRM is constructed. In terms of the metaphor used by this chapter, they constitute some of the warp and weft threads in the tapestry/context of HRM. They will be examined in greater detail in a later section.

Competing interpretations of organisations and management

When we turn from the concrete world of managing to the theories about organisations and management, we find that not only have very different interpretations been made over time, but that several strongly competing interpretations coexist. Again, this chapter can only skim over this material, but you can pursue the issues by reading, for example, Child (1969), who traces the development of management thought in Britain, or Morgan (1997), who sets out eight different metaphors for organisations through which he examines in a very accessible way the various ways in which theorists and others have construed organisations. Reed and Hughes (1992: 10–11) identify the changing focus of organisation theory over the past 30 or so years, from a concern with organisational stability, order and disorder, and then with organisational power and politics, to a concern with the construction of organisational reality.

The reification (see Glossary) of the organisation by managers and others, and the general acceptance of the need for it to have rational goals to drive it forward in an effective manner, have long been challenged. Simon (see Pugh *et al.*, 1983) recognised that rationality is 'bounded' – that managers make decisions on the basis of limited and imperfect knowledge. Cyert and March adopt a similar viewpoint: the many stakeholders in an organisation make it a 'shifting multigoal coalition' (see Pugh *et al.*, 1983: 108) that has to be managed in a pragmatic manner. Others (see Pfeffer, 1981; Morgan, 1997) recognise the essentially conflictual and political nature of organisations: goals, structures and processes are defined, manipulated and managed in the interests of those holding the power in the organisation. A range of different understandings of organisations has developed over time: the systems approach (Checkland, 1981), the learning organisation (Senge, 1990), transformational leadership and 'excellence' (Peters and Waterman, 1982; Kanter, 1983), knowledge management (see Chapter 7), the significance of rhetoric (see later, and Eccles and Nohria, 1992). This range is widening to include even more holistic approaches, with recent interest in the roles in the workplace of emotional intelligence (Cherniss and Goleman, 2001; Higgs and Dulewicz, 2002; Pickard, 1999), spirituality and love (Welch, 1998; Zohar and Marshall, 2001). The influence of many of these new ideas can be seen in the present concern for work–life balance (for example, CIPD, 2008).

The established views of managers are subject to further interpretations. Weick (1979) argues the need to focus upon the process of organising rather than its reified outcome, an organisation. As we noted earlier, he regards organising as a continuous process of meaning-making: '[p]rocesses continually need to be re-accomplished' (p. 44). Cooper and Fox (1990) and Hosking and Fineman (1990) adopt a similar interpretation in their discussion of the 'texture of organizing'.

Brunsson (1989) throws a different light on the nature and goals of organising, based on his research in Scandinavian municipal administrations. He suggests that the outputs of these kinds of organisations are 'talk, decisions and physical products'. He proposes two 'ideal types' of organisation: the *action* organisation, which depends on action for its legitimacy (and hence essential resources) in the eyes of its environment, and the *political* organisation, which depends on its reflection of environmental inconsistencies for its legitimacy. Talk and decisions in the action organisation (or an organisation in its action phase) lead to actions, whereas the outputs of the political organisation (or the organisation in its political phase) are talk and decisions that may or may not lead to action.

> … hypocrisy is a fundamental type of behaviour in the political organization: to talk in a way that satisfies one demand, to decide in a way that satisfies another, and to supply products in a way that satisfies a third.
>
> (p. 27)

There are similarly competing views upon organisational culture, as we see in Aldrich (1992) and Frost *et al.* (1991). The established view interprets it as a subsystem of the organisation that managers need to create and maintain through the promulgation and manipulation of values, norms, rites and symbols. The alternative view argues that culture is not something that an organisation has, but that it is.

Just as many managers leave their taken-for-granted assumptions unstated and unaddressed, so that their actions appear to themselves and others based upon reason and organisational necessity, so also do many theorists. Many traditional theorists leave unstated that the organisations of which they write exist within a capitalist economic system and have to meet the needs of capital. They ignore the material and status needs of owners and managers, and their emotional (Fineman, 1993) and moral selves (Watson, 2000). Many have also been gender-blind and take for granted a male world-view of organisations. These issues tend to be identified and discussed only by those writers who wish to persuade their readers to a different interpretation of organisations (for example, Braverman, 1974; Hearn *et al.*, 1989; Calas and Smircich, 1992).

At the close of the Introduction some of the concepts and terminology relevant to the understanding of context were noted. Have you been aware of any of these concepts in this discussion of the immediate context of HRM?

The wider context of HRM

Defining the wider context

The definition of the wider context of HRM could embrace innumerable topics (from, for example, demography to globalisation) and a long-time perspective (from the organisation of labour in prehistory, as at Stonehenge, to today). Such a vast range, however, could only be covered in such a perfunctory manner here that it render the exercise valueless. It is more appropriate to give examples of some of the influential elements and how they affect HRM, and to encourage you to identify others for yourself. You can read about some of them in Chapters 4 and 7).

Activity

Go back to the models of HRM presented in Chapter 1 and, working either individually or in a group, start to elaborate upon the various contextual elements that they include. Look, for example, at the external forces of the 'matching model' illustrated in Chapter 1, Figure 1.2.

Questions

1 What in detail constituted the elements of the economic, political and cultural forces at the time Devanna *et al.* were writing? What would they be now?

2 What other elements would you add to those, both then and now?

3 What are the relationships between them, both then and now?

4 And what, in your view, has been their influence upon HRM, both then and now?

Echoes from the wider context

Here the focus will be on distant events from the socio-political sphere that have nevertheless influenced the management of the employment relationship and still do so indirectly. Although what follows is not a complete analysis of these influences, it illustrates how the field of HRM resonates with events and ideas from its wider context.

The First and Second World Wars

The two world wars, though distant in time and removed from the area of activity of HRM, have nevertheless influenced it in clearly identifiable and very important ways, some direct and some indirect. These effects can be classified in terms of changed attitudes of managers to labour, changed labour management practices, the development of personnel techniques, and the development of the personnel profession. We shall now examine these, and then note how some outcomes of the Second World War continue, indirectly, to influence HRM.

Changed attitudes of managers to labour

According to Child (1969: 44), the impact of the First World War upon industry hastened changes in attitudes to the control of the workplace that had begun before 1914. The development of the shop stewards' movement during the war increased demand for workers' control; there was growing 'censure of older and harsher methods of managing labour'. The recognition of the need for improved working conditions in munitions factories was continued in the postwar reconstruction debates: Child (1969: 49) quotes a Ministry of Reconstruction pamphlet that advised that 'the good employer profits by his "goodness"'. The outcome of these various changes was a greater democratisation of the workplace (seen, for example, in works councils) and, for 'a number of prominent employers', a willingness 'to renounce autocratic methods of managing employees' and 'to treat labour on the basis of human rather than commodity market criteria' (pp. 45–46). These new values became incorporated in what was emerging as a distinctive body of management thought, practice and ideology (see Glossary and later section on 'Ways of seeing and thinking'), upon which later theory and practice are founded.

Changed labour management practices

The need to employ and deploy labour effectively led to increased attention to working conditions and practices during both wars; the changes that were introduced then continued and interacted with other social changes that ensued after the wars (Child, 1969). For example, the Health of Munitions Workers Committee, which encouraged the systematic study of human factors in stress and fatigue in the munitions factories during the First World War, was succeeded in 1918 by the Industrial Fatigue Research Board (DSIR, 1961; Child, 1969; Rose, 1978). During the postwar reconstruction period progressive employers advocated minimum wage levels, shorter working hours and improved security of tenure (Child, 1969).

'The proper use of manpower whether in mobilizing the nation or sustaining the war economy once reserves of strength were fully deployed' was national policy during the Second World War (Moxon, 1951). As examples of this policy, Moxon cites the part-time employment of married women, the growth of factory medical services, canteens, day nurseries and special leave of absence.

The development of personnel techniques

Both wars encouraged the application of psychological techniques to selection and training, and stimulated the development of new approaches. Rose (1978: 92) suggests that, in 1917, the American army tested 2 million men to identify 'subnormals and officer material'. Seymour (1959: 7–8) writes of the Second World War:

> the need to train millions of men and women for the fighting services led to a more detailed study of the skills required for handling modern weapons, and our understanding of human skill benefited greatly. . . Likewise, the shortage of labour in industry led . . . to experiments aimed at training munition workers to higher levels of output more quickly.

The wars further influenced the development of the ergonomic design of equipment, and encouraged the collaboration of engineers, psychologists and other social scientists (DSIR, 1961).

The exigencies of war ensured that attention and resources were focused upon activities that are of enormous significance to the field of employment, while the scale of operations guaranteed the availability for testing of numbers of candidates far in excess of those usually available to psychologists undertaking research.

The development of the personnel profession

Very significantly, the Second World War had a major influence on the development of the personnel profession. According to Moxon (1951: 7), the aims of national wartime policy were:

> (i) to see that the maximum use was made of each citizen, (ii) to see that working and living conditions were as satisfactory as possible, (iii) to see that individual rights were reasonably safeguarded and the democratic spirit preserved. The growth of personnel management was the direct result of the translation of this national policy by each industry and by each factory within an industry.

Child (1969: 11) reports how government concern in 1940 about appropriate working practices and conditions

> led to direct governmental action enforcing the appointment of personnel officers in all but small factories and the compulsory provision of minimum welfare amenities.

Moxon (1951) comments on the 'four-fold increase in the number of practising personnel managers' at this time (p. 7). Child (1969) records the membership of what was to become the Institute of Personnel Management as 760 in 1939, and 2993 in 1960 (p. 113). He also notes a similar increase in other management bodies. (The Institute has now become the Chartered Institute of Personnel and Development, with an individual membership of 133,000 in 2009.)

The postwar reconstruction of Japan

This subsection has so far noted some of the direct influences that the two world wars had upon the field of HRM. It now points to an indirect and still continuing influence. The foundation of the philosophy and practice of total quality management, which has been of considerable recent significance in HRM, was laid during the Second World War. Edward Deming and Joseph Juran were consultants to the US Defense Department and during the Second World War ran courses on their new approaches to quality control for firms supplying army ordnance (Pickard, 1992). Hodgson (1987: 40) reports that:

> Vast quantities of innovative and effective armaments were produced by a labour force starved of skill or manufacturing experience in the depression.

After the war, America 'could sell everything it could produce' and, because it was believed that 'improving quality adds to costs', the work of Deming and Juran was ignored in the West. However, Deming became an adviser to the Allied Powers Supreme Command and a member of the team advising the Japanese upon postwar reconstruction (Hodgson, 1987: 40–41). He told them that 'their war-ravaged country would become a major force in international trade' if they followed his approach to quality. They did.

Western organisations have since come to emulate the philosophy and practices of quality that proved so successful in Japan and that now feature among the preoccupations of human resource managers (see, for example, Chapter 14).

What other distant socio-political events have influenced HRM?

Contemporary influences on HRM

The topics to be examined now also come from fields distant from that of HRM but nevertheless influence it. However, they differ from those examined above. First, two of them belong primarily to the world of ideas, rather than action. Second, whereas the influences discussed above contributed to the incremental development of HRM thinking and practice, those discussed below have the potential to unsettle and possibly disrupt established thinking, and hence practice. Third, the two world wars are, for us, history: interpretations of them have by now become established and, to a large degree, generally accepted (though always open to question: see the later subsection 'Defining reality for others'). However, the first two to be discussed below are ideas of our own time, not yet fully formed or understood. They both originated in fields outside social science, but have been introduced into it because of their potential significance for the understanding of social phenomena. The third topic comes from significant events that are currently taking place.

'Postmodernism'

It was in the fields of art and architecture, in which there had been early twentieth-century schools of thought and expression regarded as 'modernism', that certain new approaches came to be labelled 'postmodern'. In due course, the concepts of 'modernism' and 'postmodernism' spread throughout the fields of culture (Harvey, 1990) and the social sciences. However, 'postmodernism' is proving to be a challenging and unsettling concept for those socialised into what would now be called a 'modern' understanding of the world. One way to appreciate it is through the 2006 film *A Cock and Bull Story*, with Steve Coogan and Rob Brydon, which is about the famously idiosyncratic eighteenth-century novel *Tristram Shandy* (Sterne, 1759–67). This stands out in the history of the novel for its reflexivity, the way the novelist shares with the reader his attempts to capture the wholeness of life in his pages. He wants to present his characters in context for, just as this chapter argues, without that understanding of them would be incomplete. So rather than following a traditional linear story-line, Sterne struggles to follow the interwoven threads of the tapestry of their life, causing him to digress and regress, and also to adopt unusual typography. Hence in the film

Coogan, playing himself as an actor as well as two of the novel's characters, declares *Tristram Shandy* to be 'postmodern' before 'modernism' even existed. The film does not attempt a full adaptation of the novel, but captures its 'postmodern' spirit by using a reflexive, fractured and many-layered narrative.

'Modernism' and 'postmodernism' are now used to express a critical perspective in organisation studies (for example, Gergen, 1992; Hassard and Parker, 1993; Hatch, 1997; Morgan, 1997) and in the HRM field (Legge, 1995; Townley, 1993). Connock (1992) includes 'postmodern' thinking among the contemporary 'big ideas' of significance to human resource managers, while Fox (1990) interprets strategic HRM as a self-reflective cultural intervention responding to 'postmodern' conditions. Although questions about 'postmodernism' merge with others on post-industrialism, post-Fordism, and the present stage of capitalism (see Legge, 1995; Reed and Hughes, 1992), here we focus only on 'postmodernism'.

There is considerable debate about it. Does it refer to an epoch (Hassard, 1993), a period of historical time, namely the 'post-modern' present which has succeeded 'modern times'? If so, does it represent a continuation of or a disjunction with the past? Or does it refer to a particular, and critical, perspective, which Hassard (1993) calls an 'epistemological position' (see Glossary)? Many, such as Legge (1995), distinguish this from the epochal 'post-modern' by omitting the hyphen ('postmodern').

An example of the epochal interpretation is Clegg's (1990: 180–81) discussion of 'post-modern' organisations, the characteristics of which he identifies by contrasting them with 'modern' organisations. For example, he suggests that the latter (that is, the organisations that we had been familiar with until the last decade or so of the twentieth century) were rigid, addressed mass markets and were premised on technological determinism; their jobs were 'highly differentiated, demarcated and de-skilled'. 'Post-modern' organisations, however, are flexible, address niche markets, and are premised on technological choices; their jobs are 'highly de-differentiated, de-demarcated and multiskilled'. Since Clegg's analysis, the hierarchy of 'modern' organisations has often been contrasted with 'post-modern' networking.

It is less easy to pin down 'postmodernism' as an epistemological position but, in brief, it is somewhat like the little boy's response to the 'emperor's new clothes'. Whereas 'modernism' was based on the belief that there existed a universal objective truth which we could come to know by means of rational, scientific approaches (though often only with the help of experts), 'postmodernism' denies that. It assumes that truth is local and socially constructed (see Glossary and later section) from a particular perspective. It asks: 'What truth?', 'Whose truth?', 'Who says so?' Hence it challenges the authority of the established view, for example, of the 'meta-narratives' of 'progress', 'the value of science' or 'Marxism vs capitalism' which had become the accepted framework of twentieth-century understanding. Instead it recognises the claims of diverse and competing interpretations, and accepts that everything is open to question, that there are always alternative interpretations.

Hence 'postmodernism' has considerable significance for HRM. It recognises that multiple and competing views of organisations and HRM are legitimate; that the significance of theory lies not in its 'truth' but in its usefulness for practice. (This, perhaps, is a significant issue for the learning organisation, which is discussed in Chapter 7.) Moreover, it throws into question (Hassard and Parker, 1993; Kvale, 1992) the traditional (Western) understanding of the individual as a '"natural entity", independent of society, with "attributes" which can be studied empirically' (Collin, 1996: 9). That 'modern' interpretation has underpinned the understanding and practices of HRM, such as psychometric testing: the 'postmodern' view challenges the accepted way of dealing with, for example, competencies and assessment (Brittain and Ryder, 1999).

Moreover, 'postmodernism' recognises that, far from being objective and universal as 'modernism' assumed, knowledge is constructed through the interplay of power relationships and often the dominance of the most powerful. This makes a critical interpretation of established bodies of thought such as psychology (Kvale, 1992), which could be seen as a Western cultural product (Stead and Watson, 1999). Thus, whereas 'modernism' often ignored or, indeed, disguised ideologies (see Glossary and the section later on 'Ways of seeing and thinking'), 'postmodernism' seeks to uncover them. It also encourages self-reflexivity and, therefore, a critical suspicion towards one's own interpretations, and an ironic and playful treatment of one's subject.

Another important difference between 'modernism' and 'postmodernism' lies in the way they regard *language*. 'Modernism' assumes that language is neutral, 'the vehicle for communicating independent "facts"' (Legge, 1995: 306). The 'postmodern' argument, however, is that this is not the case (see Reed and Hughes, 1992; Hassard and Parker, 1993). Language 'itself constitutes or produces the "real"' (Legge, 1995: 306). Moreover, it is 'ideological' (Gowler and Legge, 1989: 438): both the means through which ideologies are expressed and the embodiment of ideology (see Glossary and later subsection). This can be seen in sexist and racist language, and in 'management-speak'.

'Postmodernism' highlights the significance of *discourse*. 'Why do we find it so congenial to speak of organizations as structures but not as clouds, systems but not songs, weak or strong but not tender or passionate?' (Gergen, 1992: 207). The reason, Gergen goes on to say, is that we achieve understanding within a 'discursive context', and the organisational context understands structure. A discourse is a 'set of meanings, metaphors, representations, images, stories, statements and so on that in some way together produce a particular version of events' (Burr, 1995: 48), a version belonging to a particular group of people. It provides the language and meanings whereby members of that group can interpret and construct reality, and gives them an identifiable position to adopt upon a given subject, thereby constituting their own identity, behaviour and reality (Gavey, 1989). By interpreting competing positions in its own terms, the group's discourse shuts down all other possible interpretations but its own.

For example, in order to engage in academic discourse, academics have to learn

> a vocabulary and a set of analytic procedures for 'seeing' what is going on . . . in the appropriate professional terms. For we must see only the partially ordered affairs of everyday life, which are open to many interpretations . . . as if they are events of a certain well-defined kind.
>
> (Parker and Shotter, 1990: 9)

Parker and Shotter (1990: 2–3), using the contrast between 'everyday talk' and academic writing, explain how academic text standardises its interpretations:

> The strange and special thing about an academic text . . . is that by the use of certain strategies and devices, as well as already predetermined meanings, one is able to construct a text which can be understood (by those who are a party to such 'moves') in a way divorced from any reference to any local or immediate contexts. Textual communication can be (relatively) decontextualised. Everyday talk, on the other hand, is marked by its vagueness and openness, by the fact that only those taking part in it can understand its drift; the meanings concerned are not wholly predetermined, they are negotiated by those involved, on the spot, in relation to the circumstances in which they are involved . . . Everyday talk is situated or contextualised, and relies upon its situation (its circumstances) for its sense.

There are many discourses identifiable in the field of organisation and management studies – managerial, humanist, critical, industrial relations – that offer their own explanations and rhetoric. You can explore them further in, for example, the chapters that follow, and Clark *et al.* (1994), but you should remain aware that academic discourse itself enables writers to exercise power over the production of knowledge and to influence their readers. Awareness of discourse is also important for the understanding of organisations:

> organisational life is made up of many 'discourses' – that is, flows of beliefs, experiences, meanings and actions. Each of these discourses shapes the behaviour of the organisation and of teams and individuals within it. These discourses are in turn created and reworked by individuals' actions and their expressed beliefs. This may not sound much, but it shifts the management of change, for example, from a simplistic view of changing culture, processes and structures to one of altering these aspects of organisational life by building on and reshaping the various discourses flowing around a company. (Baxter, 1999: 49)

The notion of discourse is relevant to our understanding of HRM. From today's vantage point we can now perhaps recognise that the way in which we once conceptualised and managed the employment relationship was influenced by 'modernism'. However, Legge (1995: 324–25) considers HRM to be both 'post-modern' and 'postmodern'. 'From a managerialist view' it is 'post-modern' in terms of epoch and its basic assumptions (p. 324), whereas 'from a critical perspective' it is a 'postmodernist discourse' (p. 312). HRM, with its ambiguous, or contested, nature, discussed in Chapter 1, emerged alongside the spread of 'post-modern' organisations and 'postmodern epistemology'. The recognition of multiple, coexisting yet competing realities and interpretations, the constant reinterpretation, the eclecticism, the concern for presentation and re-presentation – all of which you will recognise in this book – can be interpreted as a 'postmodern' rendering of the debate about the nature of the employment relationship. We must therefore expect that there will be even more, perhaps very different, interpretations of HRM to be made.

The way David Brent, in Ricky Gervais's The Office, *communicates with his staff is a caricature of managerial discourse. Can you identify from that what kind of managerial strategy (see earlier) he appears to have adopted?*

The 'new science'

We shall now turn briefly to another possible source of influence upon the HRM field. The so-called 'new science' derives from new developments in the natural sciences that challenge some of the key assumptions of Newton's mechanistic notion of the universe (see Wheatley, 1992, for a simplified explanation). Traditionally, science has been 'reductionist' in its analysis into parts and search for 'the basic building blocks of matter' (Wheatley, 1992: 32). It has assumed that 'certainty, linearity, and predictability' (Elliott and Kiel, 1997: 1) are essential elements of the universe. However, new discoveries have questioned those assumptions, generating the theories of complexity and chaos. Complexity refers to a system's 'interrelatedness and interdependence of components as well as their freedom to interact, align, and organize into related configurations' (Lee, 1997: 20). 'Because of this internal complexity, random disturbances can produce unpredictable events and relationships that reverberate throughout a system, creating novel patterns of change... however,... despite all the unpredictability, coherent order *always* [emphasis in original] emerges out of the randomness and surface chaos' (Morgan, 1997: 262). To understand complexity, new approaches that recognise the whole rather than just its parts – a holistic approach – and attention to relationships between the parts are needed, and these are being developed.

Although theories of complexity and chaos are sometimes referred to as a 'postmodern science', this is a 'common misconception', for 'while recognizing the need for a modification of the reductionist classical model of science, [these theories] remain grounded within the "scientific" tradition' (Price, 1997: 3). They are, nevertheless, recognised as relevant to the understanding of complex social systems. For example, 'chaos theory appears to provide a means for understanding and examining many of the uncertainties, nonlinearities, and unpredictable aspects of social systems behavior' (Elliott and Kiel, 1997: 1). The literature on the application of these theories to social phenomena tends to be very demanding (for example,

Eve *et al.*, 1997; Kiel and Elliott, 1997). However, Morgan's (1997) and Wheatley's (1992) applications to organisations are more accessible. There has been some application in the HRM field. For example, Cooksey and Gates (1995) use non-linear dynamics and chaos theory as a way of conceptualising how common HRM practices translate into observable outcomes. Brittain and Ryder (1999: 51) draw on complexity theory in their attempt to improve the assessment of competencies, and conclude that 'HR professionals and psychologists need to challenge widely held beliefs about assessment processes, move away from simplistic assumptions about cause and effect and take a more complex view of the world.'

The failure of the US sub-prime mortgage market

As this chapter is being written, the whole world is experiencing the effects of the collapse of financial markets following disastrous investments in the American sub-prime mortgage market. Major firms are shrinking in size or disappearing altogether, small businesses are being lost, unemployment is rising alarmingly, and some taken-for-granted capitalist values are being challenged. The impact upon HRM, its practices, policies and strategies, is potentially enormous. It cannot be gauged at present because the story is still unfolding. However, you – who will probably come to have experience of the fall-out from these distant beginnings – will be able to follow how it influences HRM.

Ways of seeing and thinking

The chapter will now turn its attention to our ways of seeing and thinking about our world: ways that generate the language, the code, the keys we use in conceptualising and practising HRM. It is at this point that we become fully aware of the value of representing context as a tapestry rather than as a many-skinned onion, for we find here various strands of meaning that managers and academics are drawing upon to construct – that is, both to create and to make sense of – HRM. These ways of seeing are the warp, the threads running the length of the tapestry that give it its basic form and texture, but are generally not visible on its surface. They are more apparent, however, when we turn the tapestry over, as we shall do now, and examine how we perceive reality, make assumptions about it, and define it for ourselves. We shall then look at the weft threads of the tapestry as we examine how we define reality for others through ideology and rhetoric.

Perceiving reality

Perception

Human beings cannot approach reality directly, or in a completely detached and clinical manner. The barriers between ourselves and the world outside us operate at very basic levels:

> Despite the impression that we are in direct and immediate contact with the world, our perception is, in fact, separated from reality by a long chain of processing.
>
> (Medcof and Roth, 1979: 4)

Psychologists indicate that perception is a complex process involving the selection of stimuli to which to respond and the organisation and interpretation of them according to patterns we already recognise. (You can read more about this in Huczynski and Buchanan, 2006.) In other words, we develop a set of filters through which we make sense of our world. Kelly (1955) calls them our 'personal constructs', and they channel the ways we conceptualise and anticipate events (see Bannister and Fransella, 1971).

Defence mechanisms

Our approach to reality, however, is not just through cognitive processes. There is too much at stake for us, for our definition of reality has implications for our definitions of ourselves and for how we would wish others to see us. We therefore defend our sense of self – from what we interpret as threats from our environment or from our own inner urges – by means of what Freud called our 'ego defence mechanisms'. In his study of how such behaviour changes over time, Vaillant (1977: 7) wrote:

> Often such mechanisms are analogous to the means by which an oyster, confronted with a grain of sand, creates a pearl. Humans, too, when confronted with conflict, engage in unconscious but often creative behaviour.

Freudians and non-Freudians (see Peck and Whitlow, 1975: 39–40) have identified many forms of such unconscious adaptive behaviour, some regarded as healthy, others as unhealthy and distorting. We may not go to the lengths of the 'neurotic' defences which Vaillant (1977: 384–85) describes, but a very common approach to the threats of the complexity of intimacy or the responsibility for others is to separate our feelings from our thinking, to treat people and indeed parts of ourselves as objects rather than subjects. The scene is set for a detached, objective and scientific approach to reality in general, to organisations in particular, and to the possibility of treating human beings as 'resources' to be managed.

Making assumptions about reality

We noted earlier that the very term 'human resource management' confronts us with an assumption. This should cause us to recognise that the theory and practice of the employment relationship rest upon assumptions. The assumptions to be examined here are even more fundamental ones for they shape the very way we think. Some are so deeply engrained that they are difficult to identify and express, but they are nevertheless embodied in the way we approach life. They include the way we conceptualise, theorise about and manage the employment relationship, so our assumptions have important implications for our interpretation of HRM.

Writing about Kelly's (1955) personal construct theory, Bannister and Fransella (1971: 18) argue:

> we cannot contact an interpretation-free reality directly. We can only make assumptions about what reality is and then proceed to find out how useful or useless those assumptions are.

However, we have developed our assumptions from birth, and they have been refined and reinforced by socialisation and experience so that, generally, we are not even aware of them. We do not, therefore, generally concern ourselves with epistemology, the theory of knowledge, and often we find the discussion of philosophical issues difficult to follow. Nevertheless, we are undoubtedly making significant assumptions about 'what it is possible to know, how may we be certain that we know something' (Heather, 1976: 12–13). These assumptions underpin thinking and contribute to the filters of perception: they therefore frame any understanding of the world, including the ways in which researchers, theorists and practitioners construe HRM. To understand something of HRM we need at least to recognise some of the implications of these epistemological and philosophical issues.

Pepper's (1942) 'world hypotheses' help us distinguish some fundamentally different assumptions that can be made about the world. He classifies them as two pairs of polarised assumptions. The first pair is about the universe. At one pole is the assumption that there is an ordered and systematic universe, 'where facts occur in a determinate order, and where, if enough were known, they could be predicted, or at least described' (Pepper, 1942: 143). At the other pole, the universe is understood as a 'flowing and unbroken wholeness' (Morgan, 1997: 251), with 'real indeterminateness in the world' (Harré, 1981: 3), in which there are 'multitudes of facts rather loosely scattered and not necessarily determining one another to any considerable degree' (Pepper, 1942: 142–43). Pepper's second polarity is about how we approach the universe: through analysis, fragmenting a whole into its parts in order to examine it more closely, or through synthesis, examining it as a whole within its context.

Western thinking stands at the first pole in both pairs of assumptions: it takes an analytical approach to what is assumed to be an ordered universe. Hence 'we are taught to break apart problems, to fragment the world' (Senge, 1990: 3); we examine the parts separately from their context and from one another, 'wrenching units of behaviour, action or experience from one another' (Parker, 1990: 100). These approaches, which underpin the positivism discussed in the next subsection, lead us in our research to examine a world that we interpret as

> abstract, fragmented, precategorized, standardized, divorced from personal and local contexts or relevance, and with its meanings defined and controlled by researchers. (Mishler, 1986: 120)

By contrast, and of particular relevance to this chapter, is 'contextualism', Pepper's world hypothesis that espouses the assumptions at the second pole of both pairs above. This regards events and actions as processes that are woven into their wider context, and so have to be understood in terms of the multiplicity of interconnections and interrelationships within that context. This is what our tapestry metaphor has attempted to convey. We can use further metaphors to glimpse just how different this view is from our orthodox understanding of the world: from the user's perspective, the latter is like using a library, while the former is more like using the internet (Collin, 1997). The information in a library is structured and classified by experts in a hierarchical system according to agreed conventions; users have to follow that system, translating their needs for information into a form recognised by that system. The Internet, however, is an open-ended network of providers of information, non-linear, constantly changing and expanding. It presents users with a multitude of potential connections to be followed at will and, moreover, the opportunity to participate through dialogue with existing websites or through establishing their own web page or blog.

Differences as basic as those between Pepper's world hypotheses inevitably lead to very different ways of seeing and thinking about reality and, indeed, of understanding our own role in the universe. However, we are rarely aware of or have reason to question our deepest assumptions. Not only does our orthodox approach itself impede our recognition of these epistemological issues, but the processes of socialisation and education in any given society nudge its members in a particular direction (although some may wander off the highway into the byways or, like the author of *Zen and the Art of Motorcycle Maintenance* (Pirsig, 1976), into what are assumed to be badlands). It can be easier to discern these issues in the contrast offered by the epistemological positions adopted in other societies. We can, for example, recognise more of our own deeply embedded assumptions when we encounter a very different world view in an anthropologist's account (Castaneda, 1970) of his apprenticeship to a Yaqui sorceror. Of this, Goldschmidt (1970: 9–10) writes:

> Anthropology has taught us that the world is differently defined in different places. It is not only that people have different customs; it is not only that people believe in different gods and expect different post-mortem fates. It is, rather, that the worlds of different peoples have different shapes. The very metaphysical presuppositions differ: space does not conform to Euclidean geometry, time does not form a continuous unidirectional flow, causation does not conform to Aristotelian logic, man [*sic*] is not differentiated from non-man or life from death, as in our world . . . The central importance of entering worlds other than our own – and hence of anthropology itself – lies in the fact that the experience leads us to understand that our own world is also a cultural construct. By experiencing other worlds, then, we see our own for what it is…

Most of the epistemological threads in the tapestry examined in this chapter reflect Western orthodoxy. (Note how Western orthodoxy has exerted hegemony (see Glossary and below) over non-Western thinking (Stead and Watson, 1999).) And this orthodoxy itself might be gradually changing; some commentators have argued that it has reached a 'turning point' (Capra, 1983), that they can detect signs of a 'paradigm shift' (see Glossary). Indeed, over the last decade or so there have emerged new developments in the natural sciences (see the 'new science' above), and elsewhere (see feminist thinking: below) that challenge orthodoxy.

How could you use Pepper's ideas to explain the challenges of 'postmodernism' and the 'new science' to conventional thinking?

This chapter will now turn to a more accessible level of our thinking, easier to identify and understand, although again we do not customarily pay it much attention.

Defining reality for ourselves

The distinctions between the epistemological positions above and the philosophical stances examined here appear very blurred (Heather, 1976; Checkland, 1981). There is certainly considerable affinity between some of Pepper's (1942) 'world hypotheses' and the approaches noted below. The discussion here will be restricted to aspects of those approaches relevant to our understanding of concepts and practices like HRM.

Orthodox thinking

By orthodoxy we mean 'correct' or currently accepted opinions inculcated in the majority of members in any given society through the processes of socialisation and education and sustained through sanctions against deviation. In our society, for example, most people have traditionally trusted in rationality and 'orthodox medicine' and have had doubts about the paranormal and 'alternative medicine'. We do not generally question our orthodox beliefs: they 'stand to reason', they work, everyone else thinks in the same way. By definition, therefore, we do not pay much attention to them, nor consider how they frame the interpretations we make of our world, nor what other alternatives there could be. We shall therefore now first examine this orthodoxy and then some alternatives to it.

Activity

Either on your own or in a group, make a list of the characteristics of Western orthodoxy that have already been mentioned in this chapter.

The orthodox approach in Western thinking is based on positivism. Positivism forms the basis of scientific method, and applies the rational and ordered principles of the natural sciences to human affairs generally. It manifests itself (see Heather, 1976; Rose, 1978: 26) in a concern for objectivity, in the construction of testable hypotheses, in the collection of empirical data, in the search for causal relationships and in quantification. It is, therefore, uneasy with subjective experience, and attempts to maintain distance between the researcher and those studied (called 'subjects', though regarded more as objects). For example, the Western view is that the individual has (rather than is) a self, which is a natural object, bounded, re-ified, highly individualised, and autonomous (see Collin, 1996).

We can perceive the role of positivism in orthodoxy in the contrast Kelly draws between the assumptions underpinning his personal construct theory (see previous subsection) and those of orthodox science:

> A scientist... depends upon his [*sic*] facts to furnish the ultimate proof of his propositions... these shining nuggets of truth . . . To suggest [as Kelly does] . . . that further human reconstruction can completely alter the appearance of the precious fragments he has accumulated, as well as the direction of their arguments, is to threaten his scientific conclusions, his philosophical position, and even his moral security . . . our assumption that all facts are subject . . . to alternative constructions looms up as culpably subjective and dangerously subversive to the scientific establishment.   (Quoted in Bannister and Fransella, 1971: 17–18)

Positivism has informed most social science research, which in turn has reproduced, through the kind of new knowledge generated, Western orthodoxy. Hence, it 'reigns' in much HRM research (Legge, 1995: 308). It will be clear from the discussion of the immediate context of HRM that many managers and theorists of management espouse it. It underpins many organisational activities such as psychometric testing for selection and human resource planning models.

Challenging alternatives

There are several alternative ways of thinking that challenge orthodoxy, and you could read more about them in Denzin and Lincoln (1994). The approaches outlined here differ from one another, having different origins and, to some extent, values and constituencies, though they are largely similar in their express opposition to positivism. However, it is important to note that it is only the non-positivist forms of feminist and systems thinking that are covered here: in other words, there are also positivist versions.

Activity   Either on your own or in a group, make a list of the characteristics of alternatives to Western orthodoxy that have already been mentioned in this chapter.

Phenomenology, constructivism and social constructionism

These three approaches stand in marked contrast to positivism, being concerned not with objective reality, but with our lived, subjective, experience of it.

Phenomenology is concerned with understanding the individual's conscious experience. Rather than analysing this into fragments, it takes a holistic approach. It acknowledges the significance of subjectivity, which positivism subordinates to objectivity. Phenomenological researchers try to make explicit the conscious phenomena of experience of those they study, seeking access to them empathically, through shared meanings and intersubjectivity. This is not a commonplace approach in the field of HRM and management (Sanders, 1982), although it is sometimes discussed in qualitative research studies.

Constructivism is also concerned with individual experience, but emphasises the individual's cognitive processes. It does not deny the existence of an external reality, but holds that we cannot know it, only the models of it that we construct ourselves : 'each individual mentally constructs the world of experience . . . the mind is not a mirror of the world as it is, but functions to create the world as we know it' (Gergen, 1999: 236). (Note that some constructivists appear to retain something of the positivist approach.)

Social constructionism does not assume that a reality independent of the observer exists. Reality is only what we construct ourselves, and that not through our own cognitive processes, but through the social processes of language, discourse (see earlier), and social interaction. (See Raskin and Bridges, 2002.)

> Human beings in the social process are constantly creating the social world in interaction with others. They are negotiating their interpretations of reality, those multiple interpretations at the same time constituting the reality itself.   (Checkland, 1981: 277)

To make sense of our experiences, we have to interpret and negotiate meaning with others. There can be no single objective meaning but, Hoffman (1990: 3) suggests,

> an evolving set of meanings that emerge unendingly from the interactions between people. These meanings are not skull-bound and may not exist inside what we think of as an individual 'mind'. They are part of a general flow of constantly changing narratives.

Knowledge is thus a social phenomenon (Hoffman, 1990), and language, rather than depicting objective reality, itself constructs meaning. Weick (1979: 1) quotes a baseball story that illustrates this nicely:

> Three umpires disagreed about the task of calling balls and strikes. The first one said, 'I calls them as they is.' The second one said, 'I calls them as I sees them.' The third and cleverest umpire said, 'They ain't nothin' till I calls them.'

As also suggested by Pepper's (1942) contextualism, discussed earlier, this view of the social construction of meaning implies that we cannot separate ourselves from our created reality: 'man [*sic*] is an animal suspended in webs of significance he himself has spun' (Geertz, 1973: 5). Again as with contextualism, this approach emphasises the significance of perspective, the position from which an interpretation is made (remember *The Guardian* advertisement at the start of this chapter?). Further, it also draws attention to the way in which some people contrive to impose their interpretations upon, and so define the reality of, others, with the result that less powerful people are disempowered, overlooked, remain silent, are left without a 'voice' (Mishler, 1986; Bhavnani, 1990). This is a point to which the chapter returns later.

While the social construction of meaning appears a very abstract notion, it is apparent in everyday life in the stories we tell: narrative is how we make meaning (Polkinghorne, 1988). 'We dream in narrative, daydream in narrative, remember, anticipate, hope, despair, believe, doubt, plan, revise, criticize, construct, gossip, learn, hate, and love by narrative' (Hardy, 1968: 5). Listening to narratives is an approach increasingly favoured by those trying to understand organisations (Gabriel, 2000).

Can you identify social constructionist perspectives among the competing interpretations of organisations and management discussed earlier in the chapter?

Feminist thinking

Feminist thinking, which recognises differences between the world-views of women and men, challenges what is increasingly regarded as the male world-view of the positivist approach (Gilligan, 1982; Spender, 1985). Gilligan's (1982) landmark study concluded that women value relationship and connection, whereas men value independence, autonomy and control. Bakan (1966) made a distinction between 'agency' and 'communion', associating the former with maleness and the latter with femaleness. Agency is 'an expression of independence through self-protection, self-assertion and control of the environment' (Marshall, 1989: 279), whereas the basis of communion is integration with others.

> The agentic strategy reduces tension by changing the world about it; communion seeks union and cooperation as its way of coming to terms with uncertainty. While agency manifests itself in focus, closedness and separation, communion is characterized by contact, openness and fusion.
> (Marshall, 1989: 289)

Therefore, Marshall (1989) argues, feminist thinking 'represents a fundamental critique of knowledge as it is traditionally constructed . . . largely . . . by and about men' and either ignores or devalues the experience of women:

> its preoccupation with seeking universal, immutable truth, failing to accept diversity and change; its categorization of the world into opposites, valuing one pole and devaluing the other; its claims of detachment and objectivity; and the predominance of linear cause-and-effect thinking. These forms reflect male, agentic experiences and strategies for coping with uncertainty. By shaping academic theorizing and research activities, they build male power and domination into the structures of knowledge...
>
> (p. 281)

Calas and Smircich (1992: 227) discuss how gender has been 'mis- or under-represented' in organisation theory, and explore the effects of rewriting it in. Those would include the correction or completion of the organisational record from which women have been absent or excluded, the assessment of gender bias in current knowledge, and the making of a new, more diverse organisation theory that covers topics of concern to women. Hopfl and Hornby Atkinson (2000) point to the gendered assumptions made in organisations, while Hearn *et al.* (1989) identify similar shortcomings in organisation theory in their discussion of the sexuality of organisations.

Systems and ecological thinking

Systems thinking offers particularly useful insights into the understanding of context. As with feminist thinking, there are both positivist and alternative views of systems, but here we are concerned with the latter. For example, in his 'soft systems methodology', Checkland (1981) employs systems not as 'descriptions of actual real-world activity' (p. 314), but as 'tools of an epistemological kind which can be used in a process of exploration within social reality' (p. 249). (Note that his later book – Checkland and Scholes, 1990 – updates the methodology but does not repeat the discussion of its philosophical underpinnings.) As with feminist thinking, systems thinking gives us a different perspective from that of orthodox thinking. It allows us to see the whole rather than just its parts and to recognise that we are a part of that whole. It registers patterns of change, relationships rather than just individual elements, a web of interrelationships and reciprocal flows of influence rather than linear chains of cause and effect.

The concept of system denotes a whole, complex and coherent entity, comprising a hierarchy of subsystems, where the whole is greater than the sum of its parts. Much of what has been written about systems draws upon General Systems Theory, a meta-theory that offered a way to conceptualise phenomena in any disciplinary area. Very importantly, the systems approach does not argue that social phenomena are systems, but rather that they can be modelled (conceptualised, thought about) as though they had systemic properties. The concept of system used in the social sciences is therefore a very abstract kind of metaphor. However, we can give only a brief outline of systems concepts here: you will find further detail in Checkland (1981), Checkland and Scholes (1990), Senge (1990) and Morgan (1997).

Systems may be 'open' (like biological or social systems) or 'closed' to their environment (like many physical and mechanical systems). As shown in Figure 3.2, the open system imports from, exchanges with, its environment what it needs to meet its goals and to survive. It converts or transforms these inputs into a form that sustains its existence and generates outputs that are returned to the environment either in exchange for further inputs or as waste products. The environment itself comprises other systems that are also drawing in inputs and discharging outputs. Changes in remote parts of any given system's environment can therefore ripple through that environment to affect it eventually. There are feedback loops that enable the system to make appropriate modifications to its subsystems in the light of the changing environment. Thus the system constantly adjusts to achieve equilibrium internally and with its environment.

Figure 3.2 Model of an open system

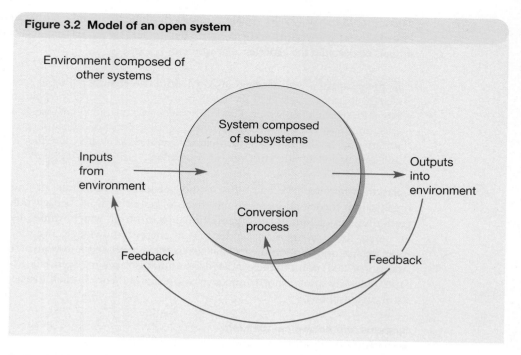

Reflecting upon the management approaches identified earlier, we can now recognise that the scientific management, human relations and perhaps also the humanistic approaches treated the organisation as a closed system, whereas the human resource approach recognises it as open to its environment. Brunsson's (1989) identification of the 'action' and 'political' organisations could also be seen as an open system approach.

The significance of systems thinking, then, lies in its ability to conceptualise complex, dynamic realities – the system and its internal and external relationships – and model them in a simple, coherent way that is yet pregnant with meaning and capable of further elaboration when necessary. This means that we can use it to hold in our minds such complex ideas as those discussed in this book, without diminishing our awareness of their complexity and interrelationships.

According to Senge (1990: 12–13), systems thinking – his 'fifth discipline' – is essential for the development of the effective organisation – the learning organisation (Chapter 7):

> At the heart of a learning organization is a shift of mind – from seeing ourselves as separate from the world to connected to the world, from seeing problems as caused by someone or something 'out there' to seeing how our own actions create the problems we experience. A learning organization is a place where people are continually discovering how they create their reality. And how they can change it.

What similarities do you see between systems thinking and the 'new science'?

Systems thinking therefore enables us to contextualise organisations and HRM. It conceptualises an organisation in an increasingly complex and dynamic relationship with its complex and dynamic global environment. Changes in one part of the environment – global warming, collapse of the banks, failed harvests, wars – can change the nature of the inputs – raw materials, money and other resources – into an organisation. This can lead to the need for adjustments in and between the subsystems – new marketing strategies, technologies, working practices – either to ensure the same output or to modify the output. The environment consists of other organisations, the outputs of which – whether intentionally or as by-products – constitute the inputs of others. A change in output, such as a new or improved product or service, however, will constitute a change in another organisation's input, leading to a further ripple of adjustments. Consider, for example, how flexible working practices and call centres have been developed. Sherwood (2002) illustrates how to apply systems thinking to practical HRM issues.

Activity

The organisation as an open system

How would you represent an organisation in a changing world in terms of the open systems model? Working individually or in groups, identify its inputs (where they come from, and how they could be changing), how it converts these, and what its (changing?) outputs might be. What are its feedback mechanisms?

Defining reality for others

This chapter has defined the warp of the tapestry of context as our ways of seeing and thinking. It will now examine some of the weft threads – the ways in which others define our reality (or we define reality for others): ideology, hegemony and rhetoric. These interweave through the warp to produce the basic pattern of the tapestry, but with differing colours and textures, and also differing lengths (durations), so that they do not necessarily appear throughout the tapestry. They constitute important contextual influences upon HRM, and in part account for the competing definitions of it.

Ideology

Gowler and Legge (1989) define ideology as 'sets of ideas involved in the framing of our experience, of making sense of the world, expressed through language' (p. 438). It has a narrower focus than the 'ways of thinking' we have been discussing above, and could be seen as a localised orthodoxy, a reasonably coherent set of ideas and beliefs that often goes unchallenged:

> Ideology operates as a reifying, congealing mechanism that imposes pseudoresolutions and compromises in the space where fluid, contradictory, and multivalent subjectivity could gain ground.
>
> (Sloan, 1992: 174)

Ideology purports to explain reality objectively, but within a pluralist society it actually represents and legitimates the interests of members of a subgroup. It is a 'subtle combination of facts and values' (Child, 1969: 224), and achieves its ends through language and rhetoric (see below). What we hear and what we read is conveying someone else's interpretations. The way those are expressed may obscure the ideology and vested interest in those interpretations. For example, in contrast to the orthodox view of culture, Jermier argues that culture is:

> the objectified product of the labor of human subjects . . . there is a profound forgetting of the fact that the world is socially constructed and can be remade . . . Exploitative practices are mystified and concealed.
>
> (Frost et al., 1991: 231)

As you will recognise from earlier in the chapter, the organisation is an arena in which ideologies of many kinds are in contest: capitalism and Marxism, humanism and scientific approaches to the individual, feminism and a gender-biased view.

Child (1969) discusses the ideology embodied in the development of management thinking, identifying how the human relations approach chose to ignore the difference of interests between managers and employees and how this dismissal of potential conflict influenced theory and practice. Commentators such as Braverman (1974), Frost et al. (1991) and Rose (1978), and many of the readings in Clark et al. (1994), will help you to recognise some of the ideologies at work in this field.

Hegemony

Hegemony is the imposition of the reality favoured by a powerful subgroup in society upon less powerful others. Such a group exerts its authority over subordinate groups by imposing its definition of reality over other possible definitions. This does not have to be achieved through direct coercion, but by 'winning the consent of the dominated majority so that the power of the dominant classes appears both legitimate and natural'. In this way, subordinate groups are 'contained within an ideological space which does not seem at all "ideological": which appears instead to be permanent and "natural" to lie outside history, to be beyond particular interests' (Hebdige, 1979: 15–16).

It is argued that gender issues are generally completely submerged in organisations and theories of them (Hearn *et al.*, 1989; Calas and Smirich, 1992; Hopfl and Hornby Atkinson, 2000) so that male-defined realities of organisations appear natural, and feminist views unnatural and shrill. You could use the readings in Clark *et al.* (1994) to identify instances of hegemony and the outcomes of power relations, such as the 'management prerogative'; Watson (2000) throws light on the manager's experience of these.

Rhetoric

Rhetoric is 'the art of using language to persuade, influence or manipulate' (Gowler and Legge, 1989: 438). Its 'high symbolic content' *allows it to reveal and conceal but above all develop and transform meaning*' (Gowler and Legge, 1989: 439, their italics). It '*heightens and transforms meaning by processes of association, involving both evocation and juxtaposition*'. In other words, its artfulness lies in playing with meanings, and can be used for various effects. It is something with which we are familiar, whether as political 'spin' or as the terminology used in effecting organisational change (Atkinson and Butcher, 1999). In the 'eco-climate' of an organisation, where meanings are shared and negotiated, power and knowledge relations are expressed rhetorically. For example, changes to structure and jobs might be described as 'flexibility' rather than as the casualisation of work (see, for example, Chapter 4), and increased pressures upon employees as 'empowerment' (see Chapter 14). Legge (1995) proposes that one way of interpreting HRM is to recognise it as 'a rhetoric about how employees should be managed to achieve competitive advantage' that both 'celebrates' the values of its stakeholders while 'at the same time mediating the contradictions of capitalism' (p. xiv). In other words, it allows those stakeholders to 'have their cake and eat it'. Nevertheless, Eccles and Nohria (1992: 10) regard rhetoric as

> something that can be used and abused, but it *cannot* be avoided [original italics]. Rather, it constantly serves to frame the way we see the world. In our view, rhetoric is used well when it mobilizes actions of people in a way that contributes both to the individuals as people and to the performance of organizations as a whole.

It is effective when it is flexible enough 'to incorporate the different meanings, emphases, and interpretations that different people will inevitably give it' (p. 35).

Conclusion... and a new beginning?

This chapter has examined something of the warp and weft that give the tapestry its basic form, pattern, colour and texture. To complete our understanding of the context of HRM we need to recognise that issues and people constitute the surface stitching that is drawn through the warp and weft to add further pattern and colour. You will be aware of examples from your own experience and the reading of this and other books, but we can instance the influences of recession, equal opportunities legislation, European directives, management gurus, Margaret Thatcher, 'New Labour', the euro debate, 11 September, that resonate with the warp and weft to produce the pattern that has come to be known as 'HRM'.

The tapestry of which HRM forms a part is continuously being woven, but we can now become aware of the sources of the differing approaches to organisation and management and of the contesting voices about the management of people. We can now recognise that their contest weaves multiple meanings into the organisational and conceptual pattern which is HRM. However, this awareness also allows us to recognise that yet other meanings, and hence potentials for the management of the employment relationship, remain to be constructed.

By pointing to the need to recognise the significance of the context of HRM, this chapter is also acknowledging that you will find therein more interpretations than this book of 'academic text' (Parker and Shotter, 1990: see 'Discourse' earlier), shaped by its writers' own agendas and values and the practicalities of commercial publication, can offer you. The process both of writing and of publication is that of decontextualisation, fragmentation, standardisation, and presentation of knowledge as 'entertaining education', in bite-sized chunks of knowledge or sound bites. But by urging you to become aware of the context of HRM, this chapter is at the same time inviting you to look beyond what this book has to say, to recognise the nature of its discourse or, rather, discourses, to challenge its assumptions (and, indeed, your own) and to use your own critical judgements informed by your wider reading and personal experience.

This, then, is why this book has begun its exploration of HRM by examining context. This chapter had a further aim (and this betrays this writer's 'agenda and values'). This is to orient your thinking generally towards an awareness of context, to think contextually, for ultimately awareness of context is empowering. One of the outcomes could well be greater knowledge but less certainty, the recognition that there could be competing interpretations of the topic you are considering, that the several perspectives upon the area could all yield different conclusions. Attention to context, therefore, encourages us not to be taken in by our initial interpretations, nor to accept unquestioningly the definitions of reality that others would have us adopt (the 'hegemony' of the previous section). There are, however, no easy answers, and we have to make the choice between alternatives. Reality is much messier and more tentative than theory and, like 'everyday talk', it is 'marked by its vagueness and openness', its meaning open to interpretation through negotiation with others. The acceptance of this, however, as we shall later see in Chapter 7, is one of the marks of the mature learner: the ability to recognise alternative viewpoints but, nevertheless, to take responsibility for committing oneself to one of them.

By definition, one chapter cannot begin to portray the details of the context of HRM. Those, after all, are constantly changing with time. It will have achieved its purpose if it causes you to recognise the significance of context and the need to adopt ways of thinking that enable you to conceptualise it. It can point you in some directions, and you will find many others in the chapters that follow, but there are no logical starting points, because context is indivisible; and you will never reach the end of the story for, from the perspective of context, the story is never-ending.

Summary

- The chapter argues that the keys to the understanding of human affairs, such as HRM, lie within their context. Although context is difficult to conceptualise and represent, readers can draw on their existing understanding of environmental issues to help them comprehend it. Awareness and comprehension of context are ultimately empowering because they sharpen critical thinking by challenging our own and others' assumptions.

- Multiple interests, conflict, and stressful and moral issues are inherent in the immediate context of HRM, which comprises the organisation (the nature of which generates a number of tensions) and management (defined as the continuous process of resolving those tensions). Over time, managers have adopted a range of approaches to their task, including scientific management; the human relations school; humanistic organisation development; and now HRM. To understand this layer of HRM's context calls for the recognition of the existence of some significant assumptions that inform managers' differing practices and the competing interpretations that theorists make of them.

- The wider social, economic, political and cultural context of HRM is diverse, complex and dynamic, but some very different and unconnected strands of it are pulled out for examination. The two world wars left legacies for the management of the employment relationship. 'Postmodern' experiences and critiques and the 'new science' locate HRM within a contemporary framework of ideas that could eventually challenge some assumptions about the management of the employment relationship, while the ongoing global financial crisis could influence the practices, policies and strategies of HRM.

- The chapter, however, finds it insufficient to conceptualise context as layered, like an onion. Rather, HRM is embedded in its context. The metaphor of a tapestry is therefore used to express the way in which its meaning is constructed from the interweaving and mutual influences of the assumptions deriving from basic perceptual, epistemological, philosophical and ideological positions. The notions of 'warp' and 'weft' are used to discuss such key contextual elements as positivism, phenomenology, constructivism, social constructionism, feminist thinking, systems thinking, ideology, hegemony, and rhetoric. People, events and issues are the surface stitching.

- The nature of this tapestry, with its multiple and often competing perspectives, ensures that HRM, as a concept, theory and practice, is a contested terrain. However, the chapter leaves readers to identify the implications of this through their critical reading of the book.

Activity

Drawing on your understanding of the environment

The nature of our environment concerns us all. As 'environment' and 'green issues' have crossed the threshold of public awareness to become big business, we have become concerned about our natural environment as no previous generations have been. We are now aware of the increasing complexity in the web of human affairs. We recognise the interrelationships within our 'global village', between the world's 'rich' North and the 'poor' South, and between politics, economics and the environment, and at home between, for example, health, unemployment, deprivation and crime. Another feature of our environment that we cannot ignore is its increasingly dynamic nature. Our world is changing before our very eyes. Comparing it with the world we knew even ten years ago, and certainly with that known by our parents when they were the age we are now, it has changed dramatically and in ways that could never have been anticipated.

1 You will have considerable knowledge, and perhaps personal experience, of many environmental issues. These might be the problems of climate change, waste disposal and pollution, genetically modified food, the impact on the countryside of the construction of new roads, or the threats to the survival of many species of animals and plants.

   As a step towards helping you understand better the nature of context as defined in this chapter, and working individually or in groups, choose two or three such issues for discussion, and consider the following points.

   (a) Identify those who are playing a part in them (the actors) and those who have an interest in them or are directly or indirectly affected by them (the stakeholders). How did the event or situation that has become an issue come about? Who started it? How do they explain it? Who benefits in this situation? How do they justify this? Who loses in it? What can they do about it? Why? Who is paying the cost? How and why?

(b) Look for concrete examples of the following statements.

- 'We have an impact upon the environment and cause it to change, both positively and negatively.'

- 'The environment and changes within it have an impact upon us and affect the quality of human life, both positively and negatively.'

- 'The interrelationships between events and elements in the environment are so complex that they are often difficult to untangle.'

- 'It may not be possible or even meaningful to identify the cause of events and their effects; the cause or causes may have to be inferred, the effects projected.'

- 'Sometimes their effects are manifested far into the future, and so are not easily identifiable now, though they may affect future generations.'

- 'Our relationship with our environment therefore has a moral dimension to it.'

- 'To deal with some of the negative causes may be gravely damaging to some other groups of people.'

- 'The understanding of these events will differ according to the particular perspective – whether of observer, actor, or stakeholder – and will arise from interpretation rather than ultimately verifiable "facts".'

- 'These issues often involve powerful power bases in society, each of which has its own interpretation of events, which it may wish others to accept.'

- 'The nature of our relationship with our environment challenges our traditional scientific ways of thinking, in which we value objectivity, analyse by breaking down a whole into its parts, and seek to identify cause and effect in a linear model.'

- 'It also therefore challenges our traditional methods of research and investigation, deduction and inference.'

2 The opening section of the chapter suggested that your examination of environmental issues would allow you to recognise that:

- Context is multilayered, multidimensional and interwoven, like a tapestry. Concrete events and abstract ideas intertwine to create issues, and thinking, feeling, interpreting and behaving are all involved.

- Our understanding of people and events depends upon our perspective.

- It also depends upon our ideology.

- There are therefore competing or contested interpretations of events.

- Different groups in society have their own interpretations of events, stemming from their *ideology*. Their *discourse* incorporates an explanation for competing interpretations. They use *rhetoric* to express their own interpretations and to explain those of other people, thus distorting, or even suppressing, the authentic expression of competing views.

- Powerful others often try to impose their interpretation of events, their version of reality, upon the less powerful majority: this is *hegemony*.

- From your knowledge of the environmental issues you have just discussed, can you give concrete examples of these points?

Questions

1 In what ways does the conceptualisation of context adopted by this chapter differ from more commonly used approaches (for example, in the models of HRM in Chapter 1)? Does it add to the understanding they give of HRM and, if so, in what way?

2 What assumptions and 'world hypotheses' underpin those models in Chapter 1, and what are the implications for your use of them?

3 What assumptions and 'world hypotheses' appear to underpin this chapter, and what are the implications for your use of the chapter?

4 Identify some recent events that are likely to play a significant part in the context of HRM.

5 This chapter has been written from a British perspective. If you were working from a different perspective – South African, perhaps, or Scandinavian – what elements of the context of HRM would you include?

6 The chapter has been written for students of HRM. Is it also relevant to practitioners of HRM and, if so, in what way?

Exercises

Having started to think in terms of context and to recognise the significance of our ways of thinking, you should be reading the rest of this book in this same critical manner. As you go through it, try to identify the following:

● the assumptions (at various levels) underlying the research and theory reported in the chapters that follow;

● the implications of these assumptions for the interpretations that the researchers and theorists are placing upon their material;

● the possibility of other interpretations deriving from other assumptions;

● the assumptions (at various levels) that the writers of the following chapters appear to hold;

● the implications of these assumptions for the interpretations that these writers are placing upon their material;

● the possibility of other interpretations deriving from other assumptions;

● the implications of the various alternatives for the practice of HRM.

Case study

Fear and loathing after the credit crisis

Historical events change behaviour and attitudes. The two world wars, the Great Depression of the 1930s and the 9/11 terrorist attacks on the US each shaped the way a generation thought and acted. The financial crisis will be no different.

Exactly how attitudes will change is not easy to forecast, however. As Niels Bohr, the Danish physicist, once observed, prediction is never easy – particularly about the future. But already some elements of the changed social landscape are emerging.

One is a deep scepticism – loathing, even – of the financial wizards who got the world's markets into this mess. When the House of Representatives voted down Hank Paulson's $700bn bank rescue package on

Case study continued

Monday, they did so because they feared the wrath of the voters.

Main Street faced economic ruin with the credit markets closed for business, but those who inhabit it were determined to block any measure that appeared to shore up Wall Street. New York had the feeling of a war zone, said one executive, as angry demonstrators jeered at shell-shocked bankers in the financial district.

The two archbishops at the head of the Church of England also caught the British public mood with their attacks on the City of London last week. Rowan Williams, archbishop of Canterbury and head of the Anglican church, said it was right to ban short selling, while John Sentamu, archbishop of York, called traders who cashed in on falling prices 'bank robbers and asset strippers'.

'We have all gone to this temple called money,' Dr Sentamu said in an interview. 'We have all worshipped at it. No one is guiltless.'

Full marks for honesty: the Church Commissioners who administer the church's assets had lent stock to short sellers, sold a mortgage portfolio last year and bought shares in the biggest listed hedge fund. But there is little doubt that the archbishops' sentiments were closer to the views of the parishioners who no longer attend their services than those who spoke up for short selling.

Bankers, in any case, have never been popular. In London and New York, they bid up the price of homes, forcing ordinary mortals to commute from ever more distant suburbs. And the arrogance and hubris of a group who felt themselves to be masters of the universe means they are winning no more sympathy in these straitened times that Sherman McCoy did when he fell from grace in Tom Wolfe's *Bonfire of the Vanities*.

A second consequence of the financial crisis, therefore, is likely to be a surge of recruits from the best universities into professions such as teaching, social work and public administration. Investment banking and its support industries have sucked up the talent for two decades, offering an appalling work–life balance in return for sufficient money to permit retirement at 30. Henceforth it will be the teachers and the engineers who will command the envy of the upwardly mobile, with their more secure careers and a positive contribution to society.

A third change is that no one will be able to borrow for many years to come the prodigious amounts of credit offered recently to people with no incomes, no jobs or assets – the so-called Ninjas. But few are likely to want to take out such massively leveraged loans either, given the misery already unfolding for the over-borrowed, and the happy fact that homes will be much more affordable as prices continue to plummet.

Lending institutions will return to prehistoric practices, such as requiring homebuyers to save some money before they take on such an expensive commitment. Potential borrowers are unlikely to demur, having become more risk-averse as a result of the credit crunch.

Savers are also becoming more risk-averse – understandably, given the runs on banks around the world. Soaring gold purchases are one symptom, but so are transfers of funds between savings institutions in search of a safe home for savings.

Northern Rock, the UK mortgage bank whose collapse was one of the first of the credit crunch, this week closed several savings accounts to new savers who saw a government-owned institution as a safe haven. Thousands queued to open post office savings accounts run by Bank of Ireland whose deposits are guaranteed by the Irish government.

Before Northern Rock, most savers had no idea about the interest rate on their nest-eggs and 42 per cent always used the same bank. A survey published yesterday by Mintel, the market research group, found most saying they now think carefully about where to save and invest.

Attitudes will also change to society's casualties, who have enjoyed less public sympathy when markets boomed and jobs were plentiful. If the slowdown turns into a recession, expect voters to be more amenable to increased welfare payments.

At the same time, they will become less supportive of public services, as household budgets come under strain and tax cuts look more compelling. Ipsos Mori's regular poll of British attitudes to social issues has already shown concern about the National Health Service, education and defence falling as concern about the economy rises to levels not seen in decades.

None of this will mean there will be no new global crisis in the future. The first world war was not 'the war to end all wars', and the dotcom bust only temporarily blighted the attractions of technology investments. But it will take many years for finance and its high priests to return to their position of unchallenged power – which will be no bad thing.

The writer is UK business editor.

Source: from Fear and loathing after the credit crisis, *Financial Times*, 4 October 2008, p. 51 (Willman, J.)

Case study continued

Questions

You can tackle these questions on your own or perhaps in a small group.

This article identifies some of the knock-on effects of the 2008/2009 global financial crisis that were being experienced in its early stages.

1 The crisis situation may have changed considerably by the time you are reading this. To up-date it, what other events would you need to note?

2 What are likely to be the most significant effects of this crisis on society?

3 What are likely to be the most significant effects of this crisis on individuals?

4 What are likely to be the most significant effects of this crisis on organisations?

5 In the light of those, make a systems map and use it to identify what are likely to be the most significant effects on HRM strategies, policies, and practice.

(If you are working in a group, split in two, one half looking at this from the perspective of an HR director of a large private sector organisation, and the other from that of an HR director of a public sector organisation. Compare the two models. Are there differences between them? Why?)

6 The colourful words used here to refer to bankers and their practices probably reflect some of the rhetoric and ideology of the banking industry. Can you identify this? Is a new rhetoric now developing?

References and further reading

Those texts marked with an asterisk are recommended for further reading.

Aldrich, H.E. (1992) 'Incommensurable paradigms? Vital signs from three perspectives' in M. Reed and M. Hughes (eds) *Rethinking Organization: New Directions in Organization Theory and Analysis.* London: Sage, pp. 17–45.

Argyris, C. (1960) *Understanding Organisational Behaviour.* London: Tavistock Dorsey.

Atkinson, S. and Butcher, D. (1999) 'The power of Babel: lingua franker', *People Management*, 5, 20, 14 October: 50–52.

Bakan, D. (1966) *The Duality of Human Existence.* Boston, MA: Beacon.

Bannister, D. and Fransella, F. (1971) *Inquiring Man: The Theory of Personal Constructs.* Harmondsworth: Penguin.

Baxter, B. (1999) 'What do postmodernism and complexity science mean?', *People Management*, 5, 23, 25 November: 49.

Bhavnani, K.-K. (1990) 'What's power got to do with it? Empowerment and social research' in I. Parker and J. Shotter (eds) *Deconstructing Social Psychology.* London: Routledge, pp. 141–52.

Braverman, H. (1974) *Labor and Monopoly Capital: The Degradation of Work in the Twentieth Century.* New York: Monthly Review Press.

Brittain, S. and Ryder, P. (1999) 'Get complex', *People Management*, 5, 23, 25 November: 48–51.

Brunsson, N. (1989) *The Organization of Hypocrisy: Talk, Decisions and Actions in Organizations.* Chichester: Wiley.

Burr, V. (1995) *An Introduction to Social Constructionism.* London: Routledge.

Calas, M.B. and Smircich, L. (1992) 'Re-writing gender into organizational theorizing: directions from feminist perspectives' in M. Reed and M. Hughes (eds) *Rethinking Organization: New Directions in Organization Theory and Analysis.* London: Sage, pp. 227–53.

Callaghan, G. and Thompson, P. (2002) 'We recruit attitude: the selection and shaping of routine call centre labour', *Journal of Management Studies*, 39, 2: 233–54.

Cameron, S. (1997) *The MBA Handbook: Study Skills for Managers*, 3rd edn. London: Pitman.

Capra, F. (1983) *The Turning Point: Science, Society and the Rising Cultures.* London: Fontana.

Castaneda, C. (1970) *The Teachings of Don Juan: A Yaqui Way of Knowledge.* Harmondsworth: Penguin.

Chartered Institute of Personnel and Development (2008) Factsheet *Work–Life Balance.* London: Chartered Institute of Personnel and Development (www.cipd.co.uk/subjects).

Checkland, P. (1981) *Systems Thinking, Systems Practice.* Chichester: Wiley.

Checkland, P. and Scholes, J. (1990) *Soft Systems Methodology in Action.* Chichester: Wiley.

Cherniss, C. and Goleman, D. (eds) (2001) *The Emotionally Intelligent Workplace: How to Select for, Measure, and Improve Emotional Intelligence in Individuals, Groups, and Organizations.* San Francisco, CA: Jossey-Bass.

Child, J. (1969) *British Management Thought: A Critical Analysis.* London: George Allen & Unwin.

*Clark, H., Chandler, J. and Barry, J. (1994) *Organisation and Identities: Text and Readings in Organisational Behaviour.* London: Chapman & Hall.

Clegg, S.R. (1990) *Modern Organizations: Organization Studies in the Postmodern World.* London: Sage.

Collin, A. (1996) 'Organizations and the end of the individual?', *Journal of Managerial Psychology*, 11, 7: 9–17.

Collin, A. (1997) 'Career in context', *British Journal of Guidance and Counselling*, 25, 4: 435–46.

Concise Oxford English Dictionary (1982) 7th edn. Oxford: Clarendon Press.

Connock, S. (1992) 'The importance of "big ideas" to HR managers', *Personnel Management*, June, pp. 24–27.

Cooksey, R.W. and Gates, G.R. (1995) 'HRM: A management science in need of discipline', *Asia Pacific Journal of Human Resources*, 33, 3: 15–38.

Cooper, R. and Fox, S. (1990) 'The "texture" of organizing', *Journal of Management Studies*, 27, 6: 575–82.

Czerny, A. (2005) 'Lean future looms for HR functions', *People Management*, 11, 11, 2 June: 9.

Denzin, N.K. and Lincoln, Y.S. (eds) (1994) *Handbook of Qualitative Research*. Thousand Oaks, CA: Sage.

Department of Scientific and Industrial Research (1961) *Human Sciences: Aid to Industry*. London: HMSO.

*Eccles, R.G. and Nohria, N. (1992) *Beyond the Hype: Rediscovering the Essence of Management*. Boston, MA: Harvard Business School Press.

Elliott, E. and Kiel, L.D. (1997) 'Introduction' in L.D. Kiel and E. Elliott (eds) *Chaos Theory in the Social Sciences: Foundations and Applications*. Ann Arbor, MI: University of Michigan Press, pp. 1–15.

Eve, R.A., Horsfall, S. and Lee, M.E. (eds) (1997) *Chaos, Complexity, and Sociology: Myths, Models, and Theories*. Thousand Oaks, CA: Sage.

Fineman, S. (ed.) (1993) *Emotion in Organizations*. London: Sage.

Fox, S. (1990) 'Strategic HRM: postmodern conditioning for the corporate culture', in S. Fox and G. Moult (eds) *Postmodern Culture and Management Development*, special edition: Management Education and Development, 21, 3: 192–206.

*Frost, P.J., Moore, L.F., Louis, M.R., Lundberg, C.C. and Martin, J. (1991) *Reframing Organizational Culture*. Newbury Park, CA: Sage.

Gabriel, Y. (2000) *Storytelling in Organizations: Facts, Fictions, and Fantasies*. Oxford: Oxford University Press.

Gavey, N. (1989) 'Feminist poststructuralism and discourse analysis: contributions to feminist psychology', *Psychology of Women Quarterly*, 13: 459–75.

Geertz, C. (1973) *The Interpretation of Cultures*. New York: Basic Books.

Gergen, K.J. (1992) 'Organization theory in the postmodern era', in M. Reed and M. Hughes (eds) *Rethinking Organization: New Directions in Organization Theory and Analysis*. London: Sage, pp. 207–26.

Gergen, K.J. (1999) *An Invitation to Social Construction*. London: Sage.

Gilligan, C. (1982) *In a Different Voice: Psychological Theory and Women's Development*. Cambridge, MA: Harvard University Press.

Goldschmidt, W. (1970) 'Foreword' in C. Castaneda, *The Teachings of Don Juan: A Yaqui Way of Knowledge*. Harmondsworth: Penguin, pp. 9–10.

Gowler, D. and Legge, K. (1989) 'Rhetoric in bureaucratic careers: managing the meaning of management success' in M.B. Arthur, D.T. Hall and B.S. Lawrence (eds) *Handbook of Career Theory*. Cambridge: Cambridge University Press, pp. 437–53.

Hardy, B. (1968) 'Towards a poetics of fiction: An approach through narrative'. *Novel*, 2: 5–14.

Harré, R. (1981) 'The positivist-empiricist approach and its alternative' in P. Reason and J. Rowan (eds) *Human Inquiry: A Sourcebook of New Paradigm Research*. Chichester: Wiley, pp. 3–17.

Harvey, D. (1990) *The Condition of Postmodernity*. Oxford: Blackwell.

Hassard, J. (1993) 'Postmodernism and organizational analysis: an overview' in J. Hassard and M. Parker (eds) (1993) *Postmodernism and Organizations*. London: Sage, pp. 1–23.

Hassard, J. and Parker, M. (eds) (1993) *Postmodernism and Organizations*. London: Sage.

Hatch, M.J. (1997) *Organization Theory: Modern, Symbolic and Postmodern Perspectives*. Oxford: Oxford University Press.

Hatchett, A. (2000) 'Call collective: ringing true', *People Management*, 6, 2, January: 40–42.

*Hearn, J., Sheppard, D.L., Tancred-Sheriff, P. and Burrell, G. (1989) *The Sexuality of Organization*. London: Sage.

Heather, N. (1976) *Radical Perspectives in Psychology*. London: Methuen.

Hebdige, D. (1979) *Subculture: The Meaning of Style*. London: Methuen.

Hendry, C. and Pettigrew, A. (1990) 'Human resource management: an agenda for the 1990s', *International Journal of Human Resource Management*, 1, 1: 17–43.

Higgs, M. and Dulewicz, V. (2002) *Making Sense of Emotional Intelligence*, 2nd edn. London: nferNelson.

Hodgson, A. (1987) 'Deming's never-ending road to quality', *Personnel Management*, July, pp. 40–44.

Hoffman, L. (1990) 'Constructing realities: an art of lenses', *Family Process*, 29, 1: 1–12.

Hopfl, H. and Hornby Atkinson, P. (2000) 'The future of women's career' in A. Collin and R.A. Young (eds) *The Future of Career*, Cambridge: Cambridge University Press, pp. 130–43.

Hosking, D. and Fineman, S. (1990) 'Organizing processes', *Journal of Management Studies*, 27, 6: 583–604.

Huczynski, A. and Buchanan, D. (2006) *Organizational Behaviour: An Introductory Text*, 6th edn. Harlow: FT/Prentice Hall.

Huse, E.F. (1980) *Organization Development and Change*, 2nd edn. St Paul, MN: West Publishing.

Kanter, R.M. (1983) *The Change Masters*. New York: Simon & Schuster.

Keenoy, T. (1990) 'Human resource management: rhetoric, reality and contradiction', *International Journal of Human Resource Management*, 1, 3: 363–84.

Kelly, G.A. (1955) *The Psychology of Personal Constructs*, Vols 1 and 2. New York: W.W. Norton.

Kiel, L.D. and Elliott, E. (eds) (1997) *Chaos Theory in the Social Sciences: Foundations and Applications*. Ann Arbor, MI: University of Michigan Press.

Kvale, S. (ed.) (1992) *Psychology and Postmodernism*. London: Sage.

Lee, M.E. (1997) 'From enlightenment to chaos: toward non-modern social theory', in R.A. Eve, S. Horsfall and M.E. Lee (eds) *Chaos, Complexity, and Sociology: Myths, Models, and Theories*. Thousand Oaks, CA: Sage, pp. 15–29.

Legge, K. (1995) *Human Resource Management: Rhetorics and Realities*. Basingstoke: Macmillan Business.

Mant, A. (1979) *The Rise and Fall of the British Manager*. London: Pan.

Marshall, J. (1989) 'Re-visioning career concepts: a feminist invitation', in M.B. Arthur, D.T. Hall and B.S. Lawrence (eds) *Handbook of Career Theory*. Cambridge: Cambridge University Press, pp. 275–91.

Mayo, A.J. and Nohria, N. (2005) *In Their Time: The Greatest Business Leaders of the 20th Century*. Boston, MA: Harvard Business School Press.

McGregor, D. (1960) *The Human Side of Enterprise*. New York: McGraw-Hill.

Medcof, J. and Roth, J. (eds) (1979) *Approaches to Psychology*. Milton Keynes: Open University Press.

Mishler, E.G. (1986) *Research Interviewing: Context and Narrative*. Cambridge, MA: Harvard University Press.

*Morgan, G. (1997) *Images of Organization*. Thousand Oaks, CA: Sage.

Moxon, G.R. (1951) *Functions of a Personnel Department*. London: Institute of Personnel Management.

Parker, I. (1990) 'The abstraction and representation of social psychology', in I. Parker and J. Shotter (eds) *Deconstructing Social Psychology*. London: Routledge, pp. 91–102.

Parker, I. and Shotter, J. (eds) (1990) 'Introduction' in *Deconstructing Social Psychology*. London: Routledge, pp. 1–14.

*Pascale, R.T. and Athos, A.G. (1982) *The Art of Japanese Management*. Harmondsworth: Penguin.

Peck, D. and Whitlow, D. (1975) *Approaches to Personality Theory*. London: Methuen.

People Management (2002) *The Guide to Work–Life Balance*. London: People Management (www.peoplemanagement. co.uk/work-life).

Pepper, S.C. (1942) *World Hypotheses*. Berkeley, CA: University of California Press.

Peters, T.J. and Waterman, R.H., Jr (1982) *In Search of Excellence: Lessons from America's Best Run Companies*. New York: Harper & Row.

Pfeffer, J. (1981) *Power in Organizations*. London: Pitman.

Pickard, J. (1992) 'Profile: W. Edward Deming', *Personnel Management*, June, p. 23.

Pickard, J. (1999) 'Emote possibilities: sense and sensitivity', *People Management*, 5, 21, 28 October: 48–56.

Pickard, J. (2005) 'HR will be a philosophy rather than a department', *People Management*, 11, 22, 10 November: 15.

Pirsig, R.M. (1976) *Zen and the Art of Motorcycle Maintenance*. London: Corgi.

Polkinghorne, D.E. (1988) *Narrative Knowing and the Human Sciences*. Albany, NY: State University of New York Press.

Price, B. (1997) 'The myth of postmodern science', in R.A. Eve, S. Horsfall and M.E. Lee (eds) *Chaos, Complexity, and Sociology: Myths, Models, and Theories*. Thousand Oaks, CA: Sage, pp. 3–14.

Pugh, D.S., Hickson, D.J. and Hinings, C.R. (1983) *Writers on Organizations*, 3rd edn. Harmondsworth: Penguin.

Raskin, J.D. and Bridges, S. K. (eds.) (2002) *Studies in Meaning: Exploring Constructivist Psychology*. New York: Pace University Press.

*Reed, M. and Hughes, M. (eds) (1992) *Rethinking Organization: New Directions in Organization Theory and Analysis*. London: Sage.

Ritzer, G. (1996) *The McDonaldization of Society: An Investigation into the Changing Character of Contemporary Social Life*. Thousand Oaks, CA: Pine Forge Press.

Rose, M. (1978) *Industrial Behaviour: Theoretical Development since Taylor*. Harmondsworth: Penguin.

Sanders, P. (1982) 'Phenomenology: a new way of viewing organizational research', *Academy of Management Review*, 7, 3: 353–60.

Schein, E.H. (1970) *Organizational Psychology*, 2nd edn. Englewood Cliffs, NJ: Prentice-Hall.

Schein, E.H. (1978) *Career Dynamics: Matching Individual and Organizational Needs*. Reading, MA: Addison-Wesley.

*Senge, P. (1990) *The Fifth Discipline: The Art and Practice of the Learning Organization*. London: Century.

Seymour, W.D. (1959) *Operator Training in Industry*. London: Institute of Personnel Management.

Sherwood, D. (2002) *Seeing the Forest for the Trees: A Manager's Guide to Applying Systems Thinking*. London: Nicholas Brealey.

Sloan, T. (1992) 'Career decisions: a critical psychology', in R.A. Young and A. Collin (eds) *Interpreting Career: Hermeneutical Studies of Lives in Context*. Westport, CT: Praeger, pp. 168–76.

Southgate, J. and Randall, R. (1981) 'The troubled fish: barriers to dialogue' in P. Reason and J. Rowan (eds) *Human Inquiry: A Sourcebook of New Paradigm Research*. Chichester: Wiley, pp. 53–61.

Spender, D. (1985) *For the Record: The Making and Meaning of Feminist Knowledge*. London: Women's Press.

Stead, G.B., and Watson, M.B. (1999) 'Indigenisation of psychology in South Africa' in G.B. Stead and M.B. Watson (eds) *Career Psychology in the South African Context*. Pretoria, South Africa: Van Schaik, pp. 214–25.

Sterne, L. (1759–67) *The Life and Opinions of Tristram Shandy, Gentleman*. Published by Penguin Classics, 1997, edited by M. New and J. New. Harmondsworth: Penguin.

Taylor, P., Mulvey, G., Hyman, J. and Bain, P. (2002) 'Work organisation, control and the experience of work in call centres', *Work, Employment and Society*, 16, 1: 133–50.

Townley, B. (1993) 'Foucault power/knowledge, and its relevance for human resource management', *Academy of Management Review*, 18, 3: 518–45.

Vaillant, G.E. (1977) *Adaptation to Life: How the Brightest and Best Came of Age*. Boston, MA: Little Brown.

*Watson, T.J. (2000) *In Search of Management: Culture, Chaos and Control in Managerial Work*. London: Thomson Learning.

*Weick, K.E. (1979) *The Social Psychology of Organizing*. New York: Random House.

Welch, J. (1998) 'The new seekers: creed is good', *People Management*, 4, 25, 24 December: 28–33.

Wheatley, M.J. (1992) *Leadership and the New Science: Learning about Organization from an orderly universe*. San Francisco, CA: Berrett-Koehler.

Whittaker, J. and Johns, T. (2004) 'Standards deliver', *People Management*, 10, 13, 30 June: 32–34.

Zohar, D. and Marshall, I. (2001) *Spiritual Intelligence: The Ultimate Intelligence*. London: Bloomsbury.

For multiple-choice questions, exercises and annotated weblinks related to this topic, visit **www.pearsoned.co.uk/mymanagementlab.**

How well are we doing at work?

FT

Some of the world's cleverest people have struggled to develop ways of measuring how well we are doing at work. You can choose from grand-sounding methodologies such as Economic Value Added or the Balanced Scorecard, among many others. But I always think the George Bailey test is pretty revealing.

Younger readers may need reminding that George Bailey is the hero of Frank Capra's classic 1946 film *It's A Wonderful Life*. In the film Bailey, played by James Stewart, is in despair on Christmas Eve and on the point of suicide when a guardian angel descends and takes him on a magical trip, showing him how dreadful life would have been in his home town had he not lived. Bailey is forced to reconsider his suicide plans and… well, it will be on again at Christmas, so why not watch it then?

In business, several disciplines pass the George Bailey test with ease. Without finance there are no accounts to file and no commercial record of performance. Without sales there is no business at all. But take away the human resources department and… what? Recruitment might seize up a bit. People will still get paid, presuming you have automated or outsourced these things. The employment lawyers will be busy clearing up some of the mess caused by untutored line managers. But how much would your company actually suffer? And would managers feel exposed or liberated by the sudden absence of their HR colleagues?

This is not going to be another of those 'Isn't HR rubbish?' articles. I raise these questions more in sorrow than in anger. The tragedy of HR is that it is, potentially, the most significant and rewarding work any manager could want to get involved in. Helping people to build a career and find work more fulfilling is a serious and worthwhile task. But HR is rarely discussed in these terms. Instead, people refer dismissively to the 'human remains' department. Less than 10 per cent of FTSE100 companies have an HR director on the board. The truth is the profession is at a crisis point, with its credibility – and future – at stake.

Yet HR's plight is not inevitable. A pathway to salvation has been plotted by Dave Ulrich, professor of business administration at the University of Michigan and HR's leading guru. In his 1997 book *Human Resources Champions*, he offers an ambitious, four-pillared approach to the task.

HR professionals, he says, need to be 'administrative experts', that is, make sure that the 'pay and rations' element of HR (what we used to call personnel) is in immaculate order. Second, HR needs to be a 'strategic partner': it must understand the commercial realities of the business and work with managers to help them execute the company's strategy.

Third, HR needs to be a 'change agent', helping the organisation understand the need for change and cope with it. And finally, HR should be the 'employee champion', listening and responding to employees, and making sure their voices are heard at the top table.

A fine model, we can all agree. But now look at the reality. Business leaders are simply not persuaded that most HR professionals have a serious contribution to make to the commercial success of their organisation. According to a recent UK survey carried out by PwC, while 73 per cent of HR directors say they see their role as strategic, 51 per cent of CEOs look on HR primarily as 'an administrative centre'.

Another survey, conducted by the Hay Group in the US last year, found that only about 50 per cent of workers below manager level believed their companies took a genuine interest in their well-being. Clearly, HR's performance is in doubt.

Why have HR managers failed to rise to the Ulrich challenge? Lack of nerve (and ability) maybe, but perhaps the hostility of some corporate environments has made it difficult for them to speak up. Clearly, if CEOs and finance chiefs do not really believe the phrases they sign off on the annual report – 'our people are our biggest asset', 'we are a people business' – then HR staff face a fairly hopeless task.

The difficulty of their position, in the UK at least, is symbolised by the unhappy fate of the operating and financial review (OFR), which was to come into force this year but has now been watered down.

Among other things, the OFR was an attempt to find better ways to account for the people side of business. HR professionals saw in it an opportunity finally to exert some influence at a strategic level. But like a hapless HR manager being excluded from a crucial meeting, OFRs were suddenly swept aside by government after a moment's reflection.

Nor does the fashionable debate over 'human capital management' seem to offer HR much encouragement.

According to a recent report by Saratoga, the human capital consultancy that is now part of PwC: 'The strategic importance of human capital may mean that CEOs and other senior executives are taking more personal responsibility and control over human capital issues.'

When line managers are competent it is hard to see what HR can add. But that is why we need HR. There is always management mess to clear up and hand-holding to be done. Sadly, this condemns HR to its traditional 'tea and sympathy' role.

As core administrative tasks are outsourced, and headcount in HR departments falls, those who remain will have to stand and deliver – preferably something that is valuable to the business.

But even if HR can, like George Bailey, pull itself back from the brink, there will always be that other unnerving question to answer – the one posed by the child who pointed at Lord Randolph Churchill when he was out campaigning, and said: 'Dearest Mama, pray tell me what is that man for?'

Source: from Human resources departments are unloved but not unnecessary, *Financial Times*, 18 April 2006 (Stern, S.).

Questions

1 Why do you think that the HR function failed to rise to the 'Ulrich challenge'?

2 Why does the HR function struggle to justify its contribution when finance and marketing functions do not?

3 Do contextual factors increase or decrease the need for a specialist HR function?

4 What effect are the different models of HRM discussed in this part of the book likely to have on the HR delivery?

Part 2

RESOURCING THE ORGANISATION

Introduction to Part 2

This part deals with how organisations define and meet their needs for labour and how they are influenced by factors internal and external to the organisation.

For students and practitioners of management, the main theme of the past decade has been change, uncertainty and risk. Technological change has transformed the nature of products and production systems, services and their delivery. Markets have become more unpredictable and competition more intense. The response has been to reduce the size of workforces and look for ways to achieve greater labour flexibility. These changes have called established approaches to the management of labour into question. At the same time, a tight labour market and growing competition for skilled workers increased the importance attached to effective recruitment and selection. However, as unemployment has begun to rise once again as the result of economic downturn, attention is focused upon staff utilisation, the management of talent and cost-effective approaches to staffing to help ease the tensions associated with recession.

Chapter 4 explains the labour market context within which employee resourcing decisions are taken. It starts by explaining the concept of the labour market and why different organisations adopt different approaches to recruitment, retention and reward. Next it examines the nature of labour supply and demand in the UK, looking at the determinants of labour supply and how the demand for labour is structured and how it has changed over the last two decades. Finally, it goes on to examine how developments in the nature of work and employment have influenced organizational requirements for labour and affected the quality of employment opportunities available to different labour market groups. It concludes with a critical assessment of workers' experiences of employment in contemporary Britain.

Chapter 5 takes up the theme of changing organisational requirements for labour by focusing on the growing interest in talent management. The need to attract, retain, motivate and develop individuals is of increasing importance as organisations seek to do more with less and this chapter explores the initiatives used to create and sustain a suitable talent pool to meet future requirements. The chapter also considers the relative merits of 'growing' or 'buying' talent and discusses whether talent management opportunities should apply to the total workforce or only a chosen few.

Chapter 6 picks up the themes of advantage and disadvantage in employment by examining the nature and effects of unfair discrimination in employment, why managers should act to promote fairness at work and the different, sometime conflicting ideas about how they should do so. It highlights the complex nature of the issues raised by attempts to tackle disadvantage due to unfair discrimination. For example, should managers treat all employees the same regardless of ethnicity or gender, or should they take these differences into account when framing their employment policies? Should policies for combating disadvantage aim at equality of opportunity or equality of outcome? It also discusses the significance of the recent tendency to shift the focus of discussion away from the traditional idea of 'equal opportunities' to the concept of 'managing diversity'.

Chapter 4

Human resource management and the labour market

Tim Claydon and Amanda Thompson

Objectives

- To explain the nature and composition of the UK labour market.
- To identify the major social forces responsible for shaping the nature and extent of people's engagement with paid employment.
- To highlight developments in the nature of work and employment in the late twentieth and early twenty-first centuries and to show how these trends have influenced organisational requirements for labour.
- To present a critical assessment of workers' experiences of employment in contemporary Britain.

Introduction

This chapter is concerned principally with the size, composition and condition of the UK labour market and more specifically with how the labour market shapes employers' choices concerning people management and utilisation. An appreciation of labour markets and how they operate is especially relevant for students of HRM, as it claims to offer a strategic approach to managing people. A strategic stance is considered attractive because it offers organisations scope to select an appropriate employment system and a set of complementary HR practices to 'fit' the external operating environment, placing the firm in a better position to exploit competitive advantage. From a practical perspective therefore, knowing and understanding labour market issues is likely to be of prime value to the organisation in its bid to formulate a strategic approach to HRM and support the wider aim of achieving superior business outcomes.

We divide the chapter into four main sections to draw upon a range of contemporary labour market issues and consider the significance of each for the practice of HRM. In the first we discuss the nature of labour markets and the considerations that influence the employment strategies of firms. In the second we explore recent political and social developments and the implications of these for the supply of labour. The third section explores the changing nature of work and employment and is designed to focus on emergent themes in employers' demand for labour. The final section of the chapter considers key dimensions of job quality and discusses these in relation to workers' experiences of employment in contemporary Britain.

The nature of labour markets

The most general definition of the labour market is that it consists of workers who are looking for paid employment and employers who are seeking to fill vacancies. The amount of labour that is available to firms – *labour supply* – is determined by the number of people of working age who are in employment or seeking employment and the number of hours that they are willing to work. This number will be determined by the size and age structure of the population and by the decisions made by individuals and households about the relative costs and benefits of taking paid employment. These decisions are influenced by various factors, one of which is the level of wages on offer. Generally speaking, a higher wage will attract more people into the labour market while a lower wage will attract fewer, as long as other factors, such as the level of welfare benefits and people's attitudes towards work, remain constant.

The number of jobs on offer to workers – *labour demand* – is the sum of people in employment plus the number of vacancies waiting to be filled. The demand for labour is determined by the level of demand for the goods and services produced by firms in the market. When sales and production are rising, firms' demand for labour rises. When sales fall and production is cut back, firms' demand for labour falls. This is illustrated by widespread job losses in the car industry during 2008–09, following a collapse of sales due to the recession. For example, BMW announced 850 job losses at its Mini production plant in Oxfordshire in February 2009 following a 35 per cent drop in sales.

The simplest view of the labour market is that it is an arena of competition. Workers enter the arena in search of jobs and employers enter it in search of workers. Competition between employers for workers and between workers for jobs results in a 'market wage' that adjusts to relative changes in labour demand and supply. Thus, when labour demand rises relative to labour supply, the market wage rises as firms try to outbid each other for scarce labour. When labour demand falls relative to labour supply, the market wage falls as workers compete with each other for the smaller number of available jobs.

Competition means that no individual firm can set a wage that is out of line with the competitive market wage. Neither can workers demand such a wage. Should a firm try to offer a wage that is below the market rate, it will be unable to hire workers. Should a firm set a wage above the market rate, it will go out of business because its costs of production will be above those of its competitors. For the same reason, workers who demand a wage higher than the market rate will price themselves out of jobs. No firm will hire them because to do so would increase their costs of production relative to those of their competitors.

While it is undeniable that competitive forces operate in the labour market to a degree, few would seriously pretend that this is a wholly accurate description of the real world. There are limits to competition between firms and among workers. Wages do not respond instantly to changes in labour demand. Nor is there a uniform wage in the labour market. Empirical research has shown that rates of pay vary between firms, even in the same industry and operating in the same local labour market (Nolan and Brown, 1983). Other employment policies also vary among firms. For example, some firms employ labour on a hire and fire basis and make heavy use of casualised forms of employment such as temporary work while others offer long-term employment security and career development. The policies that employers adopt are influenced to a great extent by the characteristics they seek in their workforce:

● **The need for a stable workforce**. A stable workforce is advantageous to employers because it reduces the costs of labour turnover, i.e. disruption of production due to the unplanned reductions in the workforce that result from workers leaving, costs of recruitment and selection, such as the financial costs of advertising for recruits and the cost in terms of management time spent in recruiting and selecting replacements, and the cost of training new recruits. These costs may be particularly high where skilled labour is scarce and replacements hard to find, or where employers have invested considerable amounts in training workers. In these situations employers have a strong interest in limiting the extent of labour turnover.

- **The need for worker cooperation in production.** A central issue in managing people at work is how to manage their performance. One way of trying to ensure that workers supply the required level of effort is by subjecting them to direct controls (Friedman, 1977). Traditionally, this took the form of direct personal supervision by a superior and externally imposed discipline. Today, direct supervision is supplemented with electronic surveillance, 'mystery customers' and customer questionnaire surveys in a managerial effort to make workers' effort levels increasingly visible. However, there are limits to the extent that employers can rely on direct controls. This is because the nature of the product or the production process often makes it difficult to define what the appropriate effort levels are for each worker and to measure how hard they are actually working. Therefore employers have to rely on sufficiently motivated workers using their initiative to ensure efficiency and quality in the production of goods and the delivery of services. This makes it difficult for managers to impose effort levels without the workers' agreement. Heavy reliance on supervision and surveillance may also be counterproductive because of the resistance that it can generate among workers. The alternative is to encourage workers to exercise *responsible autonomy* at work (Friedman, 1977). In other words, it may be more cost-effective for managers to offer positive incentives to ensure that workers cooperate voluntarily with management and use their job knowledge and their initiative to maintain and improve efficiency and quality.

What types of workforce will have low turnover costs and why? What types of workforce will have high turnover costs?

The greater the employer's need for a stable, highly cooperative workforce, the more likely they are to introduce policies to retain workers and create a basis for mutual trust and cooperation. These policies, which are associated with the 'best practice HRM' principle of treating employees as valued assets rather than disposable commodities (see Chapter 1), *internalise* employment by fostering long-term employment relationships and giving workers a degree of protection from external labour market pressures. They include guarantees of long-term employment security, opportunities for training and internal promotion, fringe benefits and pay that is higher than the market rate. However, these policies are themselves costly. Therefore the extent to which employers seek to internalise employment depends on the cost of labour turnover and the extent of the limits to direct control. Where these are low, employers are more likely to treat labour as a disposable commodity, in other words *externalising* the employment relationship.

Activity

Recently two academics undertook a study of how construction companies use contingent labour, i.e. subcontractors and workers supplied by agencies. They found widespread use of contingent labour, but many firms would have made less use of contingent labour had it not been for the difficulties they had in recruiting directly employed workers. The researchers also found that the vast majority of employers valued long-term relationships with workers even when using contingent contracts and tried to develop long-term relationships with suppliers, especially in the case of subcontract labour and to a lesser extent with temporary agencies.

Source: Forde and Mackenzie (2007).

Question

What advantages are there for construction industry employers in using contingent labour?

Why, in view of these advantages do the great majority of construction employers value long-term employment relationships and seek to foster long-term links with suppliers of contingent labour?

It is clear that employers make strategic choices concerning the extent to which they internalise or externalise employment but these choices are influenced by the specific labour market contexts in which individual firms operate. Two key elements of this context are the overall state of the labour market and the way in which the labour market is segmented, giving rise to advantaged and disadvantaged labour market groups. To be able to understand how these influences operate, we first need to examine the two sides of the labour market; labour supply and demand.

The supply of labour

'In being bought and sold in the labour market, labour becomes a commodity' (SCER (Scottish Centre for Employment Research), 2001: 5). It follows that firms in competition with one another for labour will be interested in the current and future availability of this commodity. Conventionally, the process of human resource planning involves forecasting the supply and demand for labour so that suitable plans can be put in place to address situations of labour shortage or surplus. Despite the apparent logic of this approach Taylor (2008) reports that the use of formalised human resource planning is in decline as employers find it impossible to predict labour supply and demand with any degree of accuracy in a climate of uncertainty. Even so, some understanding of where the future supply of labour can be sourced from and how plentiful that source is expected to be is important in informing employers' actions in the labour market.

The number of people seeking work in the labour market is influenced by factors relating to the size and composition of the population. Within this section of the chapter we consider the main demographic factors affecting total labour supply, namely population and population change, the age structure of the population, gender and ethnicity.

Population

National population trends

The supply side of the labour market derives from the country's population, specifically men aged between 16 and 64 years and women between the ages of 16 and 59 (working age), so information on the total size of the current population and predictions of future patterns of population growth and decline are important for estimating the current and future supply of labour.

Population is affected by birth and death rates. When live births exceed the number of deaths a net natural population increase arises and when mortality rates exceed birth rates a net natural decline in population occurs. Population change is also influenced by net migration; that is the effect caused by people moving into and out of the country. In the 1950s and 1960s population growth was largely attributable to net natural change. Within this period, a relatively stable death rate coupled with the baby boom that followed the Second World War triggered net natural growth. In the 1980s the net inflow of migrants began to increase, in other words the number of people coming to live in the United Kingdom began to surpass the number leaving, thus switching the key trigger for population growth from net natural change to the effects of migration. In 2004, for example, nearly 222,600 more people migrated to the United Kingdom than left it. This net inflow represents the highest since the present methods of estimation began in 1991. The net effects of migration are forecast to continue to play a significant role in population growth alongside net natural change (ONS, 2006). The ONS (Office for National Statistics) (2008a) projects that migration patterns coupled with an increased birth rate and lower deaths will result in a situation where natural change and net migration become roughly equally responsible for population growth during the period 2006 to 2011. However, in the following decade (2011 to 2021) natural change will once again be the main contributory factor to population change.

Latest data from the ONS (2008a) shows that the population of the United Kingdom has been climbing steadily since 1971 and had reached 60.6 million people by 2006. UK Snapshot (ONS, 2007) predicts that the population of the United Kingdom will grow by around 10.5 million in the period 2006–31, edging above the 71 million mark by 2031 (see Table 4.1 below).

As Table 4.1 shows, growth is expected to be greater in England compared with the rest of the United Kingdom and slowest in Scotland. In a slight move away from trends that began in the 1980s, where net migration has consistently been the key source of population growth in recent decades, from 2006 to 2031 net natural change in the population rather than net migration will be the main driver of population expansion (53 per cent of growth attributable to net natural change and 47 per cent to net migration). A main source of natural population growth in the United Kingdom over the period is predicted to be an increase in births to migrants. The overarching prediction is thus that as much as 69 per cent of the population growth experienced in the period 2006–2031 will be either directly or indirectly linked to migration.

The way in which the country's population expands, whether as a result of natural change or migration patterns, affects the gender composition, age profile and ethnic diversity of the labour market. Changes to the composition of the labour supply may call into question the appropriateness of established human resource management practices aimed at attracting and retaining suitable labour. At a local level, patterns of regional population density resulting from a combination of natural causes, international migration *and* internal migration (the movement of people between regions within the United Kingdom) lead to variations in the *amount* of labour available in different parts of the country. While labour tends to move to parts of the country where work is more plentiful (ONS, 2001), those organisations relying on local labour in areas of the country with low population density and/or net population loss are confronted with a different set of labour market circumstances from those operating in areas of higher population density. The age profile, ethnicity and skills mix of workers in local labour markets can also vary considerably, affecting the *type* of labour available. These factors combine to pose different employment challenges and opportunities for firms operating in different regions of the country.

Regional population trends

Regional populations form an interesting focal point for study with important implications for the supply of labour. ONS (2008a) shows that at Local Authority level in England the greatest net accumulation in population occurred in Milton Keynes, Buckinghamshire, where the population increased by over 78 per cent in the period 1981–2006. Next were Tower

Table 4.1 Projected populations of the constituent countries of the United Kingdom

						thousands
	2006	**2011**	**2016**	**2021**	**2026**	**2031**
United Kingdom	60587	62761	64975	67191	69260	71100
England	50763	52706	54727	56757	58682	60432
Wales	2966	3038	3113	3186	3248	3296
Scotland	5117	5206	5270	5326	5363	5374
Northern Ireland	1742	1812	1868	1922	1966	1999

Source: 2006-based national population projections, Office for National Statistics.

Hamlets (in London) and East Cambridgeshire; in both of these areas population rose by 47 per cent in 1981–2006. Regional populations reflect births and deaths and the effects of international and internal (within the UK) migration. Some interesting patterns are evident in terms of internal migration; the capital has seen the greatest net loss through internal migration for at least the last three decades, losing an average of 60,000 people annually to other parts of the UK, while the Devonshire Local Authority of Torridge was home to the highest net population gain from internal migration in 2006 (ONS, 2008a: 9). The effects of international migration can, of course, counter the net losses of within-UK (internal) migration, so whilst the number of people moving out of London to other parts of the UK exceed those moving to London from within the UK, London's population continues to rise as a consequence of the inflow of international migrants. In fact, London remains the most popular destination for international migrants with 170,000 of the 191,000 people coming in to the United Kingdom in 2006 settling in London (ONS, 2008a).

Age structure of the population

The age structure of the population is a key determinant of labour supply as firms draw employees from the portion of the total population that is of working age. The age structure is closely associated with past trends in migration; such trends, referred to in the section above, can also be used to explain regional differences in the population's age profile as migrants establish communities in certain areas of the country. ONS (2008a) shows that white ethnic groups, particularly the white Irish population, have an older age structure than other ethnic groups as a consequence of past fertility and immigration patterns. Among non-white ethnic groups, younger age profiles are exhibited within groups migrating to the United Kingdom relatively recently whilst, as might be expected, those groups with an earlier history of large-scale migration to the United Kingdom have now begun to contain larger proportions of people within older age brackets. For example in 2005, 32 per cent of the Pakistani community and 34 per cent of the Bangladeshi population in the United Kingdom was under the age of 16 and just 5 per cent and 4 per cent respectively of these groups were aged over 65. In the same year just 3 per cent of the country's Black African population were aged 65 and over. In contrast, 13 per cent of Black Caribbeans were aged 65 plus (ONS, 2008a), large-scale migration from countries such as Jamaica and Trinidad having taken place several decades prior to the large-scale arrival of migrants from Pakistan, Bangladesh and African countries.

Activity

Examine the information provided in the table below summarising the age structure of the populations of Eastbourne and Leicester at the time of the last census in April 2001. These Local Authorities are in very different parts of the country, Eastbourne is a seaside resort on the South coast of England and Leicester, a major city in the East Midlands. The ethnic profile of the two towns is also considerably different; according to Census data 2001 the population of Eastbourne is 92.47 per cent white British compared with 60.54 per cent in Leicester. Leicester has a large Indian population (25.7 per cent) and is home to other white and non-white ethnic groups.

Age structure of the population	Eastbourne	Leicester
% of the resident population aged 0–4	5.31	6.83
% of the resident population aged 5–15	12.69	15.46
% of the resident population aged 16–19	4.32	5.92
% of the resident population aged 20–44	30.49	38.75
% of the resident population aged 45–64	22.47	19.52
% of the resident population aged 65 or over	24.72	13.52
Average age of the population (years)	43.2	35.5

Source: Census 2001 (ONS, 2001).

As well as past trends in migration, the age structure of the total population and of regional populations is affected by trends in births and deaths. Records show a fairly erratic pattern in the number of live births occurring in the United Kingdom at different phases throughout the twentieth century (ONS, 2006). Notable decreases in the number of births occurred during the two world wars (1914–18 and 1939–45) and after a sharp increase immediately after the First World War, births fell again and remained relatively low for most of the inter-war period. A further baby boom occurred after the Second World War causing another, more modest, upsurge in the late 1980s and early 1990s as the baby boomer generation produced their own children. The smaller cohorts of women born in the 1970s (reaching their reproductive peak in the 1990s), coupled with lower fertility rates (fewer children born per woman), led to a decline in births by 2000 (ONS, 2008a). ONS data (2008a) shows that births reached their lowest point since 1977 in 2001 (at around 670,000) but have risen again every year since. Birth projections are set to follow an upward trajectory until 2020 before relapsing; the increased trend is attributed to an increase in births to mothers born outside of the UK whose child-bearing patterns perhaps bear more relation to norms in their country of origin than to the prevailing trend for lower fertility rates displayed among non-migrant women in the United Kingdom.

Together with birth rates, the age structure of the population is influenced by the death rate (number of deaths as a percentage of the population). The ONS (2008a) reports that every year since 1901, with the exception of 1976, there have been fewer deaths than births in the United Kingdom. In 2006 (ONS, 2008a) there were 572,000 deaths in the United Kingdom and deaths are expected to remain below 600,000 per annum until the late 2020s. After this time deaths are predicted to increase because those born in the postwar population boom in the 1950s and the 1960s baby boom years will be approaching old age. Effectively, death rates in the United Kingdom have fallen due to the combined factors of stable absolute death figures and a growing population. General improvements in living standards, changing occupational structure from hard physical labour to office/white collar work and advancements in health and medicine have contributed to increased life expectancy for both men and women. Recently figures also show that male life expectancy is increasing at a faster rate than women's, thus closing the gap between the sexes. Taking into account the continued improvements in mortality rates assumed in the 2006-based principal population projections, it is calculated that women born in the United Kingdom in 2006 can expect to live to the age of 91.5 and men to the age of 88.1 (ONS, 2008b); this contrasts sharply with the life expectancy of men and women born at the start of the last century, a time when boys could expect to live to just 45, and girls to 49. Projections of life expectancy based on 2006 data predict a continuation of past trends, adding some substance to the claim 'by this time tomorrow you can expect to live for five hours longer!' (Jah, 2006: 6).

We have seen in this section that the age structure of the population is affected by migration, births and deaths. While some non-white ethnic groups display relatively young age profiles, the overall picture in the United Kingdom is of an ageing population. In short, 'over the last 35 years the population aged under 16 has decreased from around 14.3 million to 11.5 million while the population aged 65 and over has increased by 2.3 million' (ONS, 2008a: 3). As we have seen, these recent trends in the age structure of the population can be attributed to lower fertility rates combined with declining mortality rates amongst the eld-

Table 4.2 UK life expectancy 2005–07

	Years			
	At birth		At age 65	
	Males	Females	Males	Females
United Kingdom	77.2	81.5	17.2	19.9
England	77.5	81.7	17.3	20.0
Wales	76.7	81.1	16.9	19.6
Scotland	74.8	79.7	16.0	18.7
Northern Ireland	76.2	81.2	16.8	19.7

Source: Office for National Statistics: Interim Life Tables 2005–07.

erly. Such trends show little sign of abating; on the contrary it is projected that the number of people over the age of 65 will exceed the number aged under 16 by 2021 (ONS, 2008a).

In terms of human resource management, the implications of changes in the age structure of the population are numerous, particularly where labour market conditions are tight. The following points indicate some of the challenges presented by an ageing population:

- The prospect of a shrinking pool of people of working age as the 'baby boomers' born in the 1950s and 1960s move into retirement.
- Intensified competition for school leavers/young workers.
- Identifying employment strategies to attract and retain older workers.
- Meeting the needs and aspirations of older workers in work.
- Career management and development.
- Managing sickness absence.
- Growing elder care responsibilities for those in employment.
- Concerns over the adequacy of pension arrangements.

In addition, employers are obliged to comply with the Employment Equality (Age) Regulations implemented on 1 October 2006. The regulations make it unlawful for employers to discriminate on the grounds of age by denying someone employment, dismissing someone, refusing to provide training, denying someone a promotion, retiring an employee before the employer's usual retirement age (if there is one) or retiring an employee before the default retirement age of 65 without an objective justification.

How might employees' care responsibilities for elderly relations impact upon their presence and attention to paid work?

Do you think elder care will soon begin to pose a greater challenge to employers and employees than childcare? Why?

What measures, if any, do you think employers should introduce to assist employees with elder care responsibilities?

The gender composition of the population

ONS (2008a) reports that more boys than girls have been born every year in the United Kingdom since 1922, however there are more females than males in the population. In 2006, there were 30.9 million females compared with 29.7 million males (ONS, 2008a: 2). Analysis of the country's population by gender and age in 2006 shows that although there are more male than female children, the number of women in the population overtakes the numbers of men by the 25–34 age group; this pattern is attributable to a higher mortality rate among young adult males in the 16–24 age group. In the older age groups (post-retirement age) the gap between the number of men and women in the population broadens; in 2006 there were three times as many women as men in the United Kingdom aged over 90 (ONS, 2008a). However, as we noted earlier, male life expectancy is improving at a faster rate than women's and so contributing to an expansion of the male population at older ages.

As 'the inflow of females has always been higher than the outflow' (ONS, 2006: 17) net in-migration further explains expansion in the country's female population. In every year since 1994 the outflow of males *and* females from the United Kingdom has been lower than the inflow of both sexes into the country, causing a net in-migration effect to both the male and female population with most of the increase being among the female population. In 2003 for example, the net gain for the United Kingdom's female population was more than 15,000 higher than the net gain to the male population (ONS, 2006: 17). It is highly probable that, at least in numerical terms, the labour market will benefit from net in-migration as migrants (both in and out) are least likely to be over the age of retirement, or children under the age of 15 (ONS, 2006: 18).

Later in the chapter we consider the ways in which gender shapes people's experiences of work. In particular, we explore the interplay of gender and age and look at gendered roles within the family to understand differences in the patterns of male and female participation in the labour market.

Ethnicity and the population

In previous sections we have referred to migration and demonstrated that in the postwar period the United Kingdom has granted residency to people from a variety of different countries including Pakistan, India, Bangladesh, China, parts of Africa and the Caribbean and more recently from countries within Eastern Europe. As a consequence, a number of distinct minority ethnic groups have joined the nation's historically white British heritage to form a more multicultural, ethnically and religiously diverse Britain. The census collects ethnicity data by asking people which group they see themselves belonging to. When the census was last conducted in April 2001 it showed England's population to be 87 per cent white British, 3.9 per cent white other, 1.3 per cent mixed, 4.6 per cent Asian, 2.3 per cent Black and 0.9 per cent Chinese and other (ONS, 2001). In terms of religious denomination, almost 70 per cent of respondents considered themselves to be of Christian religion and white British ethnicity. Other main faiths include Pakistani Muslims, Indian Hindus, black Caribbean Christians, Indian Sikhs and black African Christians. The next census, due to take place on 27 March 2011, will reveal changes to the ethnic composition of the United Kingdom over the decade.

While in general terms the total population is becoming more ethnically diverse, certain local authority districts contain high concentrations of (non-white) ethnic minority groups, in excess of the national average of 9 per cent non-white (ONS, 2001). The census conducted in 2001 shows that 16 of the 20 authorities with the highest concentrations of non-white ethnic minority groups are London boroughs (ONS, 2001); of these Newham and Brent both have a majority non-white population (61 per cent and 55 per cent respectively). Outside London, Leicester, Slough, Birmingham and Luton record the highest concentrations of non-white ethnic minority groups. In some other regions of the country (for example, the south-west and the north-east), non-white ethnic minority groups form a very small percentage of the population, significantly below the national average.

The limited geographical spread of non-white ethnic minority groups means that some local labour markets remain practically monocultural whilst others are considerably diverse. In 2003, a report by the Strategy Unit for the Cabinet Office on the position of ethnic minorities in the labour market showed that men and women from non-white ethnic minority groups tend to be disadvantaged in the labour market compared with whites. They were less likely to be active in the labour market than whites, more likely to suffer high levels of unemployment and when they were in work, people from ethnic minority groups as a whole had lower levels of occupational attainment and progression than white people. These results held even when factors such as age, gender and qualifications were controlled for and the report concluded that this was partially explained by racism and discrimination in the labour market (Strategy Unit, 2003).

Similarly, Heath and Cheung (2006), in a report commissioned by the Department for Work and Pensions, found ongoing evidence of 'ethnic penalties' in the labour market. In particular they found that a number of ethnic minority groups, notably Pakistani, Bangladeshi, Black Caribbean and Black African men, continue to experience higher unemployment rates, greater concentration in routine and semi-routine work and lower hourly earnings than members of the comparison group of British and other whites. Women from these ethnic minority groups also experience higher rates of unemployment than the comparison group but for those in work, average hourly earnings tend to match or exceed those of white women. Heath and Cheung drew particular attention to the levels of disadvantage experienced by Pakistani and Bangladeshi groups, where male unemployment and levels of male economic inactivity are high. In addition, where individuals from these groups are in employment they are disproportionately represented in semi-routine and routine work. The differentials Heath and Cheung found are not confined to those born and educated outside the United Kingdom; indeed the ethnic penalties they refer to also appear to be experienced by second generation ethnic minority groups who were born and schooled in the United Kingdom.

We return to the issues of disadvantage and discrimination in employment in Chapter 6, where the key subject of debate and discussion is the role of HRM in addressing workplace discrimination and embracing diversity.

The workforce

The workforce is conventionally drawn from the segment of the population between the ages of 16 and state retirement age, although some men and women will continue to work beyond the state pension age. However, not everyone of working age will be in employment at any one time. Figure 4.1 is a useful framework for analysing the activities of people of working age.

A proportion of those over the age of 16 will not be in work or seeking work; this portion of the workforce is classified as *economically inactive*. There are a number of reasons why people might be economically inactive. This group typically includes those with caring

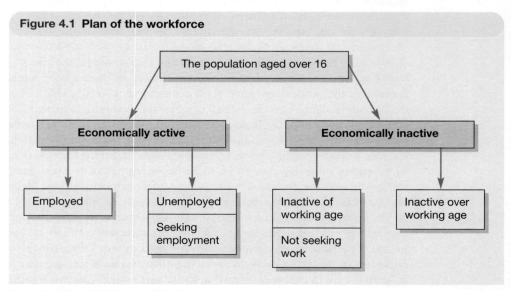

Figure 4.1 Plan of the workforce

Source: Adapted from *SCER Report* 1 (2001: 10).

responsibilities for children or other dependents, those who have retired from work, students, people who are incapacitated through ill-health or disability and those choosing not to work or seek work. People within this group may voluntarily decide to enter (or re-enter) the labour market once their circumstances alter. Others may need to be enticed back to work through incentives and/or government-orchestrated benefit reforms. The government is, at the time of writing, in the midst of reforming the welfare framework designed to help people into work, whilst supporting those who are genuinely incapacitated. An independent review commissioned by the Department for Work and Pensions (Gregg, 2008) sets out a vision for a more differentiated regime geared around the needs of three broad groups; a 'work-ready' group, a 'progression to work' group and a 'no conditionality' group. Those who fall into the last group include lone parents and partners with a youngest child under the age of one, and certain carers who would be eligible for Employment and Support Allowance (ESA) with no conditions attached. The proposals set out in the independent review are reflected in a White Paper currently making its way through Parliament. The revised benefits regime, expected to become law sometime in 2010, is part of the government's drive to get 1 million of the 2.6 incapacity benefit claimants back into work (Phillips, 2008).

The amount of labour available to firms at any one time is determined by the number of people of working age who are in employment or seeking employment, in other words those classified as *economically active*. ONS (2008a), using data drawn from the Labour Force Survey (LFS), shows that over the period 1971–2007 the number of both economically active and economically inactive people has increased. Much of the increase in the number of those in work or actively seeking work is attributable to the increased participation of women in the workforce since the 1970s. However, despite an increase in the number of those economically active, the economic activity rate (that is the percentage of the population in a given age group who are economically active) has not moved accordingly. This can be explained by an overall expansion in the working-age population in the corresponding period. By the second quarter of 2007 (ONS, 2008a) 29.5 million people of working age (16–64 for men and 16–59 for women) in the United Kingdom were economically active and 7.9 million people of working age were economically inactive.

The employed segment of the workforce contains those in paid work; this incorporates those working full time or part time, temporarily or permanently as employees (under a contract *of service*), workers (under a contract *for services*) or on a self-employed basis. A number of factors affect individuals' propensity to take work, including the availability and proximity of suitable employment opportunities, travel links, the levels of pay and benefits offered, the type of contract offered and so forth. These factors also influence people's decisions to move between jobs within the labour market.

The employment rate (the proportion of the working-age population of the United Kingdom in employment) is subject to fluctuations associated with the economic cycle and shows variations both within and between different regions of the country. There are also different trends for men and women, some differences according to educational attainment and differences at different age brackets. In the second quarter of 2007, the employment rate in the United Kingdom stood at 74 per cent, a full percentage point down on the previous quarter (ONS, 2008a) and the latest first release labour market statistics (ONS, 2009) show that the employment rate for the period November 2008 to January 2009 was 74.1 per cent. The employment rates of men and women of working age have converged considerably since 1971, the result of the male employment rate falling and women's employment rate rising. In the second quarter of 2007, the employment rate for working age women was 70 per cent whilst for men of working age it was just 9 percentage points higher at 79 per cent, this compares to a gulf between the sexes of 33 percentage points in 1971 (ONS, 2008a). In geographical terms there are also notable differences in employment rates, for example three London Boroughs, Hackney, Newham and Tower Hamlets had employment rates below 60 per cent in quarter two of 2007 whereas South Northamptonshire enjoyed an employment rate of 90 per cent; differences between Local Authorities are often more marked than differences between the regions of England (South West, East Anglia, North East etc.) or between England, Scotland and Wales (ONS, 2008a).

Those seeking work are typically registered as unemployed, but also include those who have recently left work but are not eligible to claim unemployment benefit, for example, those who have been made redundant. Job seekers might also include recent school leavers and those completing programmes of study in further and higher education. The term *unemployed* is used to describe those people who are currently not in work but would like to be. Unemployed workers must be able to show that they are actively seeking work as a condition for receiving unemployment benefits. The unemployed group consists of people affected by different types of unemployment:

- *Long-term unemployment or structural unemployment* – those unemployed as a result of the demise of whole industries or distinct occupations, for example mineworkers, shipbuilders, textile workers.
- *Frictional unemployment* – those temporarily out of work because they are between jobs.
- *Seasonal unemployment* – those made jobless as a result of seasonal fluctuations in the availability of work. Seasonal unemployment is characteristic of land workers and those whose work is connected with holiday seasons.

It is also likely that some of those registered unemployed will never work again as they lack the skills and competencies sought by employers. This group of unemployed workers is sometimes referred to as the *residual* unemployed.

Unemployment rates are also subject to variation across regions of the United Kingdom. Headline estimates for November 2008 to January 2009 (ONS, 2009) place the North East as the region suffering from the highest unemployment rate (8.8 per cent), whilst the rate is lowest in the South East at 4.4 per cent. Nationally the unemployment rate in the United Kingdom stood at 6.5 per cent (2.03 million people) in the period November 2008 to January 2009, an increase of 0.5 of a percentage point on the previous quarter (equivalent to 165,000 people). Although unemployment is rising and the economy officially slumped into recession in January 2009, following two successive quarters of negative economic growth, unemployment has yet to reach levels commensurate with those experienced in 1984 when 3.3 million were unemployed.

Patterns of labour market participation

This section of the chapter explores patterns of participation in paid employment by gender, parental/family status, age and ethnicity.

The operation of the labour market is influenced by broader societal developments, government ideology and policy, and the behaviour of employees and employers. In social terms, attitudes to marriage and partnership and men and women's respective responsibilities for childcare and domestic duties shape the labour market decisions made by individuals, couples and families. In so far as government policies are concerned, those concerning issues such as the school curriculum and funding for post-compulsory education affect the skills set and level of educational attainment with which young people join the labour market and also influence the age at which young people enter employment. As we saw earlier, the government also acts to stimulate labour supply by implementing policies designed to get the unemployed into work and schemes to encourage the economically inactive to enter into employment.

Some people's ability to find employment is constrained by their inability to understand the labour market and acquire and exploit 'social capital' (SCER, 2001: 17). In other words, some people will lack the necessary information and contacts to search for and take advantage of employment opportunities. The SCER notes that this is particularly likely to be the case for the unemployed and for new entrants to the labour market. However, the SCER also states that 'even with the right information, skills and qualifications, there still exist barriers to full or appropriate labour market participation for some people . . . one such barrier is discrimination, typically race and sex discrimination' (2001: 18). Whilst anti-discrimination legislation exists to help eradicate unfair discrimination in employment, employers' policies and practices may still harbour prejudice and unfairness, resulting in patterns of disadvantage in the labour market for certain groups and individuals.

Patterns of male and female participation in employment

Over the last 30 years or so the employment rates of men and women have converged considerably. A major doorway to the world of work has clearly opened up for women but, as we shall see, the career paths and fortunes of men and women in the labour market are often distinctly gendered.

One of the deeper influences attributable to gender that serves to structure women's participation in paid employment is domestic work. Women continue to perform the bulk of housework and to shoulder the primary responsibility for childcare in the majority of households and this shapes the amount of paid work they do. A glimmer of change is offered by Hardill *et al.* (1997) who present evidence of a small move towards more egalitarian relationships in professional/managerial, dual-career households, but this is dashed by Laurie and Gershuny (2000) who find that women continue to do more than 60 per cent of the domestic work even in couples where both partners work full time.

A major element of domestic work is childcare. Table 4.3 below (Labour Force Survey, 2008) clearly shows the differences in employment and unemployment rates, economic activity and economic inactivity rates of men and women of working age with and without responsibilities for the care of dependent children. It also shows differences between mothers and fathers in couples and lone mothers and lone fathers. This indicates that parenthood affects the employment rates of mothers and fathers in different ways; while mothers of working-age were marginally *less* likely to be in employment than working age women without any dependent children, fathers were much *more* likely to be in employment than men of working age without dependent children. Lone mothers experienced the lowest activity rate and employment rate of all groups and the highest economic inactivity rate.

STOP and think

Why might 'couple' mothers (but not lone mothers) display economic activity rates not dissimilar to women of working age without any dependent children?

While parenthood continues to affect women's employment rates disproportionately to men's, the proportion of working-age mothers with dependent children who are in employment has risen from 47 per cent in 1973 to 67 per cent in 2004 (EOC, 2006). In 2004, in all but the youngest age category (mothers aged 16–24 with dependent children) the majority of married *and* lone mothers of working age were engaged in paid employment. The employment rate of married and cohabiting mothers in the United Kingdom is particularly strong; in the second quarter of 2007 it was 72 per cent, 2 percentage points ahead of the employment rate for all women of working age (ONS, 2008a). The speed with which women return to work following maternity leave has also hastened significantly in the period since 1979; according to EOC figures (2006) 70 per cent of mothers are back at work eight months after giving birth, compared with just 15 per cent in 1979. The average amount of time women spend away from waged work for general family care is falling rapidly too (Bradley, 1999). Women have undoubtedly come a long way in terms of labour market participation but, as we shall see, there are still gender-based inequalities that segment the experiences of and opportunities for different sorts of women.

Table 4.3 Labour market summary for working-age people with and without dependent children, by sex[1,2] (United Kingdom, January–December 2008, not seasonally adjusted)

Thousands and per cent

	Couple parents with dependent children[3]			Lone parents with dependent children			People without dependent children[4]			All working-age people		
	Couple mothers	Couple fathers	Total	Lone mothers	Lone fathers	Total	Women	Men	Total	Women	Men	Total
Levels ('000s)												
Economically active	4,084	5,160	9,244	1,034	108	1,142	8,228	10,917	19,145	13,345	16,186	29,531
In employment	3,951	5,030	8,981	933	98	1,031	7,816	10,187	18,003	12,700	15,315	28,015
Unemployed	133	130	263	101	10	111	411	730	1,141	645	871	1,516
Economically inactive	1,447	345	1,792	651	41	692	2,582	2,976	5,558	4,680	3,362	8,042
Total	5,531	5,506	11,036	1,685	149	1,834	10,810	13,893	24,703	18,025	19,548	37,573
Rates (%)												
Economic activity rate	74	94	84	61	73	62	76	79	77	74	83	79
Employment rate	71	91	81	55	66	56	72	73	73	70	78	75
Unemployment rate	3	3	3	10	10	10	5	7	6	5	5	5
Economic inactivity rate	26	6	16	39	27	38	24	21	23	26	17	21

1 Men aged 16–64 and women aged 16–59.
2 Dependent children are children under 16 and those aged 16–18 who are never-married and in full-time education.
3 Includes people in married and cohabiting mixed-sex couples, same-sex couples and civil partnerships.
4 Figures for people without dependent children may include parents whose children live in a separate household from them. The Labour Force Survey does not ask people whether they have any children who live in a different household.
As with any sample survey, estimates from the Annual Population Survey are subject to a margin of uncertainty.

Source: Annual Population Survey Household Dataset, Labour Force Survey (2008)

Ethnicity and patterns of labour market participation

Employment participation rates for ethnic minorities are significantly lower than those for the population as a whole. In the first quarter of 2008, 68.1 per cent of ethnic minority people of working age were either in work or seeking work compared with 78.8 per cent among the population as a whole. The employment rate among ethnic minorities was 60.5 per cent as against 74.6 per cent for the population as a whole, while unemployment was higher among ethnic minorities at 11 per cent compared with 5.2 per cent of the entire workforce (ONS, 2008c). It has been argued that low participation rates among ethnic minorities are related to low levels of educational attainment and low skills, aspects of family structure, poor access to childcare, poor housing and a lack of public transport facilities (Strategy Unit, 2003). However, research by Wadsworth (2003) found that age, region and educational attainment explained hardly any of the difference in employment rates as between ethnic minorities and British-born whites.

There are noticeable variations in activity and employment rates as between different ethnic minority groups. For example, the employment rate among people of Indian origin is 69.4 per cent compared with just 42.9 per cent among Bangladeshis (ONS, 2008c). Activity and employment rates also vary within each ethnic group, generally being higher among British-born members of ethnic minorities than among immigrants (Wadsworth, 2003). Also, ethnic minority women are less likely to participate in employment than men, with the differential tending to be greater among immigrants relative to British-born ethnic minorities. Nonetheless, British-born Indian women had the same employment rate – 73 per cent – as British-born white women in 2002 (Wadsworth, 2003).

Labour demand

Aggregate demand for labour

The aggregate demand for labour consists of total employment plus unfilled vacancies. As the demand for labour is derived from the demand for goods and services it follows the economic cycle, rising in upswings and falling in recessions. Changes in labour demand are reflected in changes in the unemployment rate.

Low levels of unemployment are usually taken as a sign that the economy is growing and is in good shape. For employers however, the combination of record employment, low unemployment and high numbers of economically inactive people creates a labour market that is referred to as a 'tight labour market'. Tight labour markets mean that employers have to compete more actively for workers and workers have a wider choice of employment opportunities. This will lead to higher rates of labour turnover as workers leave organisations for better jobs elsewhere. In response, firms may be forced to increase pay. They may also adopt other policies aimed at retaining employees, since vacancies arising from labour turnover will be hard to fill. Therefore there will be more internal promotion and redeployment and this may necessitate increased investment in training. While these responses might be seen as moves towards internalising employment, they are not driven by the technical and skill requirements of production or a long-term employment strategy, but by immediate pressures from the labour market. These pressures may be reinforced by stronger trade union bargaining power as a result of low unemployment and unfilled vacancies. Once established, these employment practices may become embedded, although employers may seek to reverse them should labour demand slacken and unemployment rise.

Tight labour markets characterised the period from 2001 until 2008. There was low unemployment, a record number of people in employment and a large number of economically inactive people. All this meant that many employers experienced recruitment difficulties and skill shortages, although these problems were eased by an inflow of immigrant workers, including those from countries such as Latvia, Poland and Slovenia, which joined the EU on 1 May 2004 (CIPD, 2005). However, during 2008 the economy moved into recession as a result of the 'credit crunch', the ensuing financial crisis and global recession. As economic activity has slumped, unemployment has risen sharply, to 7.1 per cent in January–March 2009 compared with 5.4 per cent the year before. 286,000 workers were made redundant in January–March 2009 and the number of job vacancies was 232,000 fewer than in the same period in 2008 (ONS 2009a). The fall in labour demand has meant that tight labour market conditions have given way to a 'slack' labour market in which there are more people seeking work than there are jobs available. Employers do not replace workers who leave because they need a smaller workforce as demand for their product falls. Where they do need to fill vacancies, many prefer to hire on a temporary basis in view of uncertainties about future demand.

Whereas tight labour markets improve the bargaining position of workers relative to employers, the reverse is true when labour demand falls. Workers' and unions' anxiety about job losses may lead them to accept lower wage increases or even lower absolute wages in order to save jobs. They are also more likely to support changes to production methods in order to improve the chances of company survival, even if this leads to some job losses.

As well as examining changes in aggregate demand for labour we need to look at how the employment experience of different labour market groups varies as the result of structured patterns of inequality of employment opportunity. As we shall see, slack labour markets are likely to have disproportionate effects on those who are already disadvantaged in the labour market, such as those with little education and low skill levels and those who are subject to various forms of discrimination. We also need to examine the changing pattern of demand for labour in the long run and how it affects different labour market groups.

Labour market inequality

The quality of jobs on offer in the labour market varies. Some workers are in 'good jobs' with high earnings, good working conditions, employment security and opportunities for training and career development. Others are in 'bad jobs' with low status and pay, poor working conditions, little access to training and few if any opportunities for promotion. How good and bad jobs get created has been a matter of ongoing debate surrounding the theory of labour market segmentation. One line of explanation, advanced by two economists, Doeringer and Piore (1971), is based on the analysis of employers' labour requirements outlined earlier. Some firms face strong pressures to internalise the employment relationship in order to train, develop and retain suitably skilled workers and gain their voluntary cooperation in production. Others do not and are able to meet their labour requirements by following the commodity labour approach and externalising the employment relationship.

Another explanation (Gordon *et al.*, 1982) is that some firms enjoy monopoly power in their product markets and are able to use this power to increase the selling price of the product, thereby increasing profits. Some of these companies are faced by workers who have developed strong trade unions that can use their bargaining power to gain a share of these profits in the form of high wages and other benefits, including job security provisions. At the same time, management seeks to limit union solidarity and bargaining power by dividing the workforce into horizontal segments and offering the prospect of promotion to those who are cooperative and trustworthy. Firms that are unable to use monopoly power to raise their prices do not have surplus profits to share with trade unions, so terms and conditions of employment are less favourable. Since it is more likely that large, rather than small firms are able to exercise monopoly power, primary sector employment is concentrated in large, rather than small firms.

One of the central predictions of the labour segmentation thesis is that there will be little movement of workers between the primary and secondary sectors of the labour market. Workers in the primary sector are unwilling to move to the secondary sector and the high level of employment security that they enjoy means that they are unlikely to be forced to through job loss. Workers who make up the disadvantaged segments of the labour market are unable to move up into the primary sector because employers see them as undesirable candidates for jobs. Primary sector employers want disciplined, cooperative workers with good work habits, so when selecting from among applicants for jobs, primary sector employers will tend to reject those with unstable employment histories that involve frequent unemployment and job changes, because they will assume that this indicates a poor quality worker. This will automatically rule out secondary sector workers, regardless of their personal qualities, since by definition secondary workers are in unstable, insecure jobs. It is also the case however, that because of their experience of poor work, some secondary sector workers will tend to develop negative attitudes and poor patterns of work behaviour that reinforce employers' prejudices against secondary sector workers as a whole.

These explanations for labour market segmentation emphasise the way in which firms' employment decisions influence the wider labour market by dividing it into advantaged and disadvantaged groups. However, the question of whether the labour market *is* divided into primary and secondary sectors as a result of employers' labour policies has generated considerable debate. Numerous empirical studies to test the theory have been carried out in Britain and the United States, with mixed results (see Joll *et al.*, 1983; King, 1990 for a discussion of these).

What is not in doubt is that the quality of the jobs that people do is not determined simply by their abilities, educational attainment and skills acquired through training. The chances of someone being in a good or a bad job are also influenced by their membership of particular socio-economic groups. There is clear evidence that the labour market is segmented along lines that reflect 'broader social forces leading to discrimination within the labour market' (Rubery, 1994: 53).

Discrimination in the labour market means that workers' chances of gaining access to 'good' or 'bad' jobs are unfairly influenced by non-work characteristics such as gender, race, class, work-unrelated disability and age. Thus two equally skilled workers will find themselves in different sectors of the labour market because one is a white male from a middle-class social background and the other is a working-class black woman. This reflects deep-seated patterns of discrimination within society in general as well as in the labour market. Here we focus on how gender and ethnicity influence people's experiences in the labour market.

Women and ethnic minority groups occupy a disadvantaged place in the labour market. Women's employment disadvantage reflects deep-seated societal norms concerning the family and the respective roles of women and men in domestic roles and paid work. The domestic roles played by many women mean that their employment opportunities are restricted geographically and contractually. This is particularly true of women with children. In the absence of highly developed systems of state support for childcare, childcare responsibilities mean that many women cannot travel long distances to work and also that they cannot work 'standard' hours. Therefore they are invariably restricted to part-time work in the immediate locality. This means that they have limited choice of employment and therefore little bargaining power and may have to accept secondary sector terms and conditions of employment. Ethnic minority workers, as well as facing racial prejudice and discrimination, may be faced with additional limits to their choice of employment because they live in areas where business activity is low and public transport facilities are poor (Strategy Unit, 2003). For these reasons it is also likely that women and ethnic minority workers will be disproportionately affected by unemployment generated by recession. This is because they are less able to compete for such jobs as are available should they lose their current employment and it is easier for employers to discriminate against women and ethnic minorities when there are many people competing for a limited number of jobs. It is true that unemployment has risen faster for men than for women in the current recession with unemployment among men standing at 7.8 per cent and that for women at 6.1 per cent, but this reflects the different distribution of male and female employment across sectors, with men more commonly employed in manufacturing, construction and transport – the sectors hardest hit by recession – than women, who are disproportionately employed in the relatively more secure public sector areas of education, health and public administration (ONS, 2009b: 4.1).

Gender-based inequalities in employment opportunity

The social forces identified above mean that there are major differences in the types of work that men and women tend to do and the way in which male and female employment is segregated by time. Patterns of occupational segregation are strongly in evidence in the labour market, creating a division between male and female work. Bradley (1999) suggests that 66 per cent of men and 54 per cent of women work only or mainly with their own sex, with women typically crowded into administrative and secretarial work, catering, cleaning and caring occupations and men in skilled trades, construction and information technology (EOC, 2005). As shown in Table 4.4, patterns of vertical segregation also loom large with men continuing to dominate highly rewarded, senior roles in politics, business, media and culture and the public and voluntary sectors (Equality and Human Rights Commission, 2008: 5–7).

Men's and women's jobs are also segregated by hours of work. In 2007 there were 5.1 million female and 1.3 million male part-time workers clearly demonstrating that women are disproportionately represented in part-time work (ONS, 2008a). Generally women are more likely than men to work part-time, but particularly so if they have dependent children. Thirty eight per cent of women with dependent children worked part-time compared with only 4 per cent of men with dependent children (ONS, 2008d). Whilst part-time working is most closely associated with mothers, students and semi-retired older people are also attracted to working in this way (Hakim, 1998). Part-time working is invariably low-paid and this is reflected in the stubbornly persistent gender pay gap that exists between women working part-time and men working full-time (Longhi and Platt, 2009).

Table 4.4 Women's share of a selection of senior ranked roles in five consecutive years 2003–2008

Role	2003 % women	2004 % women	2005 % women	2006 % women	2007–08 % women
Members of parliament	18.1	18.1	19.7	19.5	19.3
Local Authority Council leaders	n/a	16.6	16.2	13.8	14.3
Directors in FTSE 100 companies (executive and non-executive directors)	8.6	9.7	10.5	10.4	11.0
Small businesses with women the majority of directors	12.3	14.4	12.0	14.0	n/a
Editors of national newspapers	9.1	9.1	13.0	17.4	13.6
Directors of major museums and art galleries	21.1	21.1	21.7	17.4	17.4
Chief executives of national sports bodies	14.3	6.3	6.7	6.7	13.3
Local authority chief executives	13.1	12.4	17.5	20.6	19.5
Senior ranks in the armed forces	0.6	0.8	0.8	0.4	0.4
Senior police officers	7.5	8.3	9.8	12.2	11.9
University vice chancellors	12.4	15.0	11.1	13.2	14.4
Health service chief executives	28.6	27.7	28.1	37.9	36.9

Source: Commission for Equality and Human Rights (2008: 9–7)

Female heterogeneity

The population, and hence the labour market, comprises different sorts of women, fractured by age, class, ethnicity, qualification level, background and experience. So, while generalisations about the relative positions of men and women in employment serve some purpose, an understanding of the different employment experiences of groups *within* these two broad categories is more useful.

While we have seen that women are typically casualties of segregation in employment, some women will be in a more advantageous labour market position than other women (and some men). For example, in quarter two of 2007, 86 per cent of women who had a degree were in employment compared with 39 per cent of women who did not have any qualifications (ONS, 2008a). Some of these female graduates will be mothers who have been able to return to well paid jobs following maternity leave, something women without qualifications are less likely to be able to do. Some women are making significant strides in training and occupations traditionally dominated by men, for example, women now comprise the majority of medical students, there was a 24 per cent rise in the number of female law students between 1971 and 1990, and a 61 per cent rise in women entering managerial work (Crompton, 1997).

Management is one of the areas in which women have made most progress. In 2004, 34 per cent of all managers or senior officials were female (ONS, 2005). However, a closer look at the gender composition at different levels of management and at management in different sectors reveals patterns of horizontal and vertical segregation *within* management careers. The dominance of men in the most senior management positions is aptly illustrated by the following findings from the Cranfield Female FTSE Index 2008 (Sealy, 2008):

- Alliance Trust tops the female FTSE index with three women on its board of seven members (43 per cent) including a female chairman and a female chief executive officer (CEO). AMEC and Marks and Spencer are joint second in the ranking with 33 per cent female boards. In joint fourth place each with three female directors (representing 30 per cent of the board) are RSA Insurance and Sainsbury's.

- Although there was an increase in the number of female CEOs in FTSE 100 companies between the 2007 index and the 2008 report, there are still only five female CEOs and three regional or divisional CEO posts held by women.

- 16 companies in the FTSE 100 have female executive directors – this is, however, only four more than in 1999 – the list includes Marks and Spencer, Pearson, Tesco, Lloyds TSB, HBOS, Royal and Sun Alliance, Legal and General.

- The total number of female executive directors across all FTSE 100 companies is 17 (4.8 per cent of the total).

- There are 114 female non-executive directors (NEDs) (14.9 per cent of the total).

- The total number of female directorships is 131 (11.7 per cent of the total).

- 22 FTSE 100 companies have exclusively all male boards.

- Of the 149 new appointees to the boards of FTSE 100 companies, only 16 (10.7 per cent) were female (the 2007 index showed 20 per cent of new FTSE 100 directorships going to women).

- Pearson (10th position with a 23 per cent female board) is the only FTSE 100 company with two female executive directors.

- There are only two female chairmen in the FTSE 100 (Baroness Hogg at 3i and Lesley Knox at Alliance Trust).

A similar picture emerges in the professions. Women make up some 40 per cent of those working in the autonomous liberal (traditional) professions, for example law, medicine, veterinary science, accountancy and teaching (EOC, 2001), but there are still some very entrenched areas such as engineering and sciences that are heavily male-dominated. Again, even where women formed a sizeable proportion of the profession as a whole, their share of higher-level jobs is low and they tend to be channelled into different branches of the profession to men as the following example illustrates:

- Women made up 34 per cent of hospital medical staff in 1999 (compared with 26 per cent in 1989).

- The number of female general practitioners increased by a similar amount in the same period.

But…

- Men made up 79 per cent of consultants (the highest grade) and 95 per cent of consultant surgeons.

- Women made up 38 per cent of paediatric consultants, 32 per cent of the psychiatry group and over 20 per cent of gynaecologists.

Source: EOC (2001)

A report by a working party of the Federation of Royal Colleges of Physicians (Federation of the Royal Colleges of Physicians of the United Kingdom, 2001) drew similar conclusions. It found that despite over 50 per cent of graduates being women, there were fewer women than might be expected in the acute medical specialties, academia and positions of seniority. Gender segregation is also evident in the teaching sector, where women remain over-represented in primary and nursery teaching and less well represented in secondary schools, further and higher education and in positions of leadership across the sector. Their pay and promotion prospects also lag behind men's (Shepherd, 2008).

Higher-level qualifications therefore, afford women greater opportunities within the labour market, but do not entirely safeguard against disadvantage. Even relatively advantaged women, such as those in the esteemed professions, find that their roles and opportunities for advancement are limited because of their gender; 'Women can stretch the ties that bind but cannot sever them' (Marlow and Carter, 2004: 16). Moreover, if highly educated women remain at a disadvantage in employment terms, this is even truer of less educated women from lower income and lower social class backgrounds (Taylor, 2002b).

Ethnically based labour market inequality

People from ethnic minorities experience disadvantage compared to whites in terms of their access to employment, their level of occupational attainment, and pay. Average unemployment among ethnic minority workers in autumn 2007 was 11.8 per cent compared with 5.9 per cent across the workforce as a whole (National Audit Office 2008: 14). Heath and Cheung have found that men and women in most ethnic minority groups face what they call 'ethnic penalties' in the labour market, i.e. disadvantages that cannot be explained by factors such as educational achievement and appear to be related to ethnicity alone. Ethnic minority men are paid less than white men. Ethnic minority women earn as much or more than white women, but this is mainly because they are more likely than white women to take full-time jobs, which are better paid than part-time jobs. Ethnic minorities in general are less likely than whites to be employed in professional and managerial occupations and more likely to be in semi-routine and routine occupations (Heath and Cheung, 2006).

These disadvantages could theoretically reflect differences in education and skills. We know that unemployment is higher and wages are lower among lower educated, unskilled workers. However, these disadvantages remain even when educational qualifications are taken into account. Most ethnic minority workers are paid less than white workers having the same educational qualifications. This means that the return to investments in education, that is the amount that each extra year of education beyond minimum school leaving age adds to lifetime earnings, is lower for most ethnic minority groups than for comparable white workers. Thus the National Audit Office report to Parliament in 2008 observed that:

> Employer discrimination puts ethnic minorities at a disadvantage. Research by the Department for Work and Pensions shows that ethnic penalties exist not only in accessing the labour market but also in occupational achievement and pay. There is considerable evidence that unequal treatment by employers on grounds of race or colour is likely to be a major factor underlying the pattern of ethnic penalties.
> (National Audit Office 2008: 18)

Ethnic heterogeneity

Although people from ethnic minorities as a whole are disadvantaged in the labour market, there is noticeable variation in the experience of different ethnic groups and between men and women within ethnic groups. Differences have also been found between members of ethnic minorities born in Britain and more recent immigrants (Wadsworth, 2003).

Unemployment varies considerably between groups; for example in Spring 2007 the unemployment rate among Bangladeshis at 18 per cent was more than twice as high as that for Indians at 8 per cent (National Audit Office 2008: 14). Levels of occupational attainment also vary between different ethnic minority groups, as shown in Table 4.5 below. Chinese and Indians of both sexes are more likely to be in professional and managerial occupations than whites, as are black African and black Caribbean women. With the exception of Indians and Chinese, ethnic minority workers are more likely to be in semi-routine or routine occupations than whites.

There are also variations in average earnings across ethnic minorities. Thus Indian and Chinese men's average hourly earnings in the period 2001–04 were 5 per cent higher and 11 per cent higher respectively than British and other white men's earnings. All other ethnic minority men earned less than British and other whites. Black Caribbean workers' average hourly earnings were 90 per cent of whites'; Pakistanis' earnings were 80 per cent and Bangladeshis received just 59 per cent. Ethnic minority women's earnings were as high or higher than those of British and other white women. Chinese earned 16 per cent more than whites while the lowest paid, the black Africans, earned 98 per cent (Heath and Cheung, 2006). At first glance this is surprising, but it is explained by the fact that ethnic minority women are less likely to take part-time jobs than white women. Full-time jobs are noticeably better paid than part-time jobs, and it is this that accounts largely for the apparent lack of pay disadvantage among ethnic minority women.

Table 4.5 Occupational attainment among ethnic groups in the UK 2001–2004

| | Proportion (per cent) of ethnic group in | | | |
| | High and low professional and managerial occupations | | Semi-routine and routine occupations | |
	Men	Women	Men	Women
British/other white	41.8	37	24.5	31.1
Black African	38.8	43	35.6	33.2
Black Caribbean	30.8	39.4	36.5	31.9
Indian	45.3	37	23.7	31.2
Pakistani	27.9	30	29.7	39
Bangladeshi	17.8	20.7	50.2	52.9
Chinese	46	41.6	18.2	26.7

Source: Heath and Cheung (2006: 15) .

All ethnic minorities apart from the Chinese experience ethnic penalties relating to access to employment. Once in employment, most groups – apart from Indians and Chinese – face ethnic penalties in terms of access to professional and managerial jobs and in terms of pay. Black Africans pay the highest penalty in this respect. From Table 4.5 this group appears quite successful, particularly women, who are more likely to be in professional and managerial roles than whites. However, they remain significantly under-represented when qualifications are taken into account. Black Africans are more highly qualified than whites in the UK. Some 27 per cent have degrees compared with 18 per cent of whites and only 11 per cent have low or no qualifications compared with 13 per cent of whites. On the basis of their qualifications a higher proportion of black Africans should be in professional and managerial occupations and black Africans should also have higher average earnings than whites, rather than lower.

The presence of disadvantaged groups in the labour market increases the range of options open to some employers by allowing them to fulfil their requirements for a stable, cooperative workforce without having to offer the positive incentives associated with internalised employment relationships (Rubery, 1994). This is because, as indicated above, disadvantaged groups have few employment alternatives so they have to take what they can get. The absence of better alternatives makes these jobs more attractive than they would otherwise be and therefore more highly valued by workers. This is reflected in the willingness of many disadvantaged workers to remain with their employer and cooperate with management in order to keep their jobs. This is illustrated in Box 4.1.

STOP
and
think

Is it rational for an employer to refuse to hire workers on the basis of their ethnicity or nationality? Do employers who hire ethnic minority workers nevertheless benefit from the presence of racism in society as a whole?

Changing patterns of demand

The period since the 1980s has seen significant changes in the pattern of demand for labour and therefore in the types of jobs available to workers. These shifts reflect inter-linked changes in the structure of the economy, government policy for the labour market, and employers' labour requirements.

A shift of employment from manufacturing to services

The proportion of workers employed in manufacturing has declined in the UK, USA and all the major European Union economies since the 1960s. This reflects the effects of economic

Box 4.1 Advantages to employers of using immigrant labour from Eastern Europe

Recent research carried out for the Joseph Rowntree Foundation into the position of Central and Eastern European immigrant workers in the UK found that immigrant workers from Central and Eastern Europe often had skills and qualifications that were significantly higher than those needed in their jobs. Many of these workers were willing to take low-paid work in the UK because there were even fewer employment opportunities in their home countries. The research also found that employers regarded them as 'high quality workers for low-skilled work' and that employers 'were often trying to balance the requirement for workers who were easy to hire and fire on the one hand but were also reliable and easy to retain'.

Source: Anderson *et al*. (2006: 115).

growth and rising incomes on people's consumption patterns. As people get richer, the proportion of their income that they spend on manufactured goods declines (although people may still spend more money on them in absolute terms) and the proportion spent on services increases. This means that output and hence employment grow faster in the service sector than the manufacturing sector. This trend is reinforced by the fact that the long-run rate of growth of labour productivity is higher in manufacturing than in services. Higher productivity growth plus slower growing demand mean slower growth or even decline of employment in manufacturing.

The decline of manufacturing has been particularly rapid in the UK since 1980. This has reflected additional forces such as the effects of government monetary and exchange rate policy during the 1980s, which raised the price of British exports in foreign markets and cheapened foreign imports; the long-term inability of UK manufacturing to respond adequately to foreign competition; and organisational restructuring whereby manufacturing firms have tried to cut costs by hiving off certain 'non-core' and specialist activities, such as security, cleaning and catering to outside suppliers of these services. This has meant that the workers who used to deliver these services are now counted as being in the service sector rather than manufacturing. The trend of employment away from manufacturing towards services is predicted to continue, as shown in Table 4.6.

The growth of service sector employment has been a major factor in the increase in part-time employment in the UK and has therefore expanded employment opportunities for women with dependent children and also, more recently, young people in full-time education.

STOP and think

How specifically has the growth of the service sector boosted part-time and female employment?

Changes in the occupational structure of employment

The occupational structure refers to how employment is apportioned among different jobs in the economy. Changes in the occupational structure of employment reflect changes in the types of skill demanded by employers. The declining relative importance of manufacturing means that, over time, the share of occupations associated with manufacturing has also declined while the share of occupations associated with the delivery of business services, retail services, etc. has increased. Changes in the occupational structure also reflect changes in the demand for skills *within* industries. These changes are generated by new technologies and by organisational changes that alter the way in which goods are produced and services delivered; for example, the introduction of new robotic equipment has reduced the requirement for semi-skilled workers in vehicle manufacture. Over the last 25 years the effect of technical

Table 4.6 Changes in the distribution of employment by broad sector 1982–2012 (percentage share of total employment)

	1982	1992	2002	2007*	2012*
Primary goods and utilities	5.2	3.5	2.2	2.0	1.8
Manufacturing	22.7	16.6	13.2	11.7	10.5
Construction	6.7	7.0	6.3	6.1	5.9
Distribution, transport, etc.	28.3	29.5	29.6	29.5	29.6
Business and other services	16.5	21.1	25.6	26.9	28.6
Non-marketed services	20.6	22.7	23.1	23.8	23.6

*Projected figures

Source: Wilson *et al.* (2006: 26)

change has been to increase demand for skilled workers relative to unskilled workers. A national survey of skills trends for the period 1986–2001 found evidence of an overall increase in the skill requirements of jobs, with the proportion of jobs requiring degree qualifications increasing from 9.7 per cent to 17.3 per cent over the period and the proportion requiring no qualifications falling from 38.4 per cent to 26.5 per cent. (Felstead *et al.*, 2002).

We can see further evidence of this in the way in which the occupational structure has changed since the early 1980s. From Table 4.7 we can see that the most highly skilled groups – managers and senior officials, professionals, and associate professional and technical occupations – increased their overall share of employment from 28.3 per cent in 1982 to 40.2 per cent in 2002. Meanwhile the share accounted for by the remaining categories fell from 71.8 per cent to 59.8 per cent. The projections suggest that by 2012 the three most highly skilled categories will have increased their share to 45.1 per cent while that of the rest will fall to 55 per cent.

We need to be careful in interpreting what these trends mean for actual employment opportunities. They do not mean that there will be no job vacancies in declining occupations. The figures in Table 4.7 refer to the total number of jobs in each occupation that results from its net expansion or decline – the 'expansion demand' (Wilson *et al.*, 2006). However, we also need to take account of the fact that in addition to net growth or decline, there will be a demand for workers to replace those leaving occupations, mainly for reasons of retirement. Replacement demand means that, although total employment in an occupation may be declining, there will still be a large number of jobs on offer within it at any one time. For example, employment in elementary clerical and service occupations (e.g. filing clerks, check-out operators) is predicted to fall by 408,000 over the period 2002–12 but replacement demand is estimated at 1,108,000. This means that there will be a net labour requirement of an extra 647,000 workers over that period, higher than for most of the professional and associated professional groups, which are predicted to grow (Wilson *et al.*, 2006: 73). It may be for this reason that employers report skill shortages in skilled trades and personal services. These reported shortages do not relate to a dearth of applicants to vacancies, but to what employers see as a lack of necessary skills among applicants. For example, the 2007 National Employers' Skills Survey reported that 48 per cent of applicants to skill shortage vacancies in skilled trades lacked technical and practical skills (Learning and Skills Council, 2008: 37).

Higgs (2004) observes that in response to a shortage of skills in certain areas, some employers have elected to focus on potential ability rather than current ability when hiring staff,

Table 4.7 Changes in the occupational structure (percentage share of total employment)

	1982	1992	2002	2007*	2012*
Managers and senior officials	10.7	12.6	14.9	15.4	16.2
Professional occupations	8.0	9.4	11.3	12.2	12.9
Associate professional and technical occupations	9.6	11.3	14.0	15.1	16.0
Administrative, clerical and secretarial occupations	15.5	15.8	13.2	12.2	11.4
Skilled trades	17.0	14.6	11.4	10.2	9.1
Personal service	3.7	4.9	7.3	8.2	9.4
Sales and customer service	6.1	6.7	7.9	8.5	9.0
Transport and machine operatives	11.8	9.7	8.4	7.7	7.2
Elementary occupations	17.7	15.0	11.6	10.4	8.9

*Projected figures

Source: Wilson *et al.* (2006: 58).

this approach, he suggests 'opens up a larger talent pool and at the same time offers potential employees skill development as part of the "deal" to attract and retain them' (Higgs, 2004: 20). However, in the light of the evidence of continuing discrimination against women and ethnic minorities in the labour market, employers could also put more effort into making fuller use of the skills and abilities of workers from disadvantaged labour market groups.

While employers claim to experience skill shortages in specific areas, there is evidence of a growing mismatch between the qualifications held by workers and those required in their jobs. The supply of workers with intermediate qualifications, i.e. Levels 2 and 3, is outstripping the demand for them and a growing proportion of workers as a whole are in jobs where they are over-qualified. This proportion increased from 30.6 per cent in 1986 to 37 per cent in 2001 (Felstead *et al.*, 2002). Bevan and Cowling (2007) cite studies that find that between 33 per cent and 55 per cent of workers in the UK are in jobs that under-utilise their skills. This suggests that, in general, the demand for skilled labour has not kept pace with the increased supply of qualified workers, so more people are experiencing job dissatisfaction as a result of the mismatch between their qualifications and the demands of their jobs. This is confirmed in the latest report of the UK Commission for Employment and Skills, which finds that there are 'too few high performance workplaces, too few employers producing high quality goods and services, too few businesses in high value-added sectors' (UKCES, 2009: 10).

This growing mismatch may be in part a reflection of a growing polarisation of employment in the UK (Bevan and Cowling, 2007). While there has been an overall shift in favour of more highly skilled jobs, some of the most rapid growth has been in low-skilled jobs such as sales assistants and check-out operators, telephone sales workers and security guards. One study found that employment growth was concentrated among the best paying and the worst paying jobs. Those in the top 20 per cent of the pay distribution and those in the bottom 10 per cent increased their share of total employment while the share of the rest declined (Goos and Manning, 2003). This suggests that the labour market is polarising into good jobs and bad jobs as intermediate jobs decline.

Activity

Review the sections of this chapter that discuss differences in employment opportunity between socio-economic groups and then consider the likely consequences of polarisation of employment for these different groups.

Changing forms of employment

During the 1980s and 1990s, senior managers initiated programmes of organisational change aimed at reducing costs and increasing the speed with which their organisations could respond to changes in market conditions. A central feature of organisational change programmes was workforce 'restructuring' that involved large-scale reductions in headcount, achieved partly through redundancies, early retirement and non-replacement of departing workers and partly by contracting out non-core and specialist services. This was accompanied by the reorganisation of work and in many cases, wider use of part-time, fixed-term contract and temporary labour and in a minority of cases, highly casualised forms of employment such as zero hours contracts (Cully *et al.*, 1999; Millward *et al.*, 2000). These changes were aimed at increasing managers' ability to achieve greater *numerical labour flexibility*, in other words to be able to adjust the size of the workforce more easily in response to changes in demand.

The result was that, although the total number of jobs grew, there was a net reduction in the number of *full-time* jobs in Britain during the 1990s. All of the growth in employment was accounted for by a growth of part-time jobs, which increased from 22.9 per cent of total employment in 1992 to 24.6 per cent in 1999. The early and mid-1990s also saw an increase in the share of fixed-term and temporary employment from 5.9 per cent in 1992 to 7.6 per cent in 1997. These developments led some to argue that the full-time, permanent job was likely to become the exception rather than the rule (Bayliss, 1998). However, while part-time employment continued to increase its share of total employment after 1997, reaching 25.8 per cent in 2004 before levelling off and dropping slightly to 25.5 per cent at the end of 2008, the trend of temporary and fixed-term employment has been downward, the share falling to 5.5 per cent in 2008 (ONS 2005, 2009c). Full-time, permanent jobs continue to be the most common form of employment.

What factors might explain why the share of employment accounted for by temporary and fixed-term jobs has fallen back in recent years while that of part-time jobs has continued to rise?

Labour market outcomes: the quality of employment

In this section of the chapter we examine how changes in the labour market have affected the quality of employment experience. How should we assess the quality of jobs? What indices should we use? Traditionally, economists have used pay as the measure of job quality. Other social scientists have stressed the level of skill as a key measure on the grounds that skilled work not only provides workers with better pay but also more variety, personal autonomy and involvement and ultimately more control over their effort. We have seen that there has been an overall trend towards increased skill requirements in jobs, so on the face of things at least it seems plausible that the quality of jobs available in the labour market has, on balance, improved. However, recent research has uncovered unexpected disjunctures between skill and other measures of job quality such as employment security, the ability to control one's level of effort and exercise control over how the job is done. In this section we review evidence relating to these dimensions of job quality to assess whether recent changes in the demand for labour have improved the quality of employment experience in the UK.

Job security

Job security is generally regarded as an important factor determining job quality. Employment security has also been linked positively to skill level, with skilled workers enjoying greater job security than unskilled workers. Management-led organisational change during the 1980s and 1990s led to a growth of concern at what appeared to be an increase in employment insecurity. It was argued widely in the press and by some academics that organisational restructuring and associated changes in patterns of labour demand were creating a new era of insecurity for workers, who were faced with higher risks of job loss and increased costs of job loss, leading to a subjective sense of employment insecurity (see Heery and Salmon (2000) for a review of these arguments).

The risk of job loss is affected by movements in the labour market, particularly changes in the rate of unemployment. The risk of job loss is greater when unemployment is rising than when it is constant or falling. However, during the 1990s some observers argued that the risk of job loss was increasing independently of the level of unemployment; in other words for any given level of unemployment the risk of job loss was higher than it used to be. Proponents of this argument pointed to redundancy dismissals and the replacement of permanent, full-time jobs with part-time and temporary jobs among previously secure groups such as managerial and professional workers and public sector workers, and some argued these developments marked the end of internalised employment relationships that offered 'jobs for life' and clear career paths linked to length of service. Supporters of the insecurity thesis also argued that the costs of job loss had risen because the level of social security payments had fallen relative to average wages and workers who had lost permanent full-time jobs were less able than previously to find equivalent replacements because of the trend away from full-time, permanent jobs to part-time and temporary jobs. They also argued that these developments generated heightened feelings of insecurity among workers. However, the idea that workers were entering a new age of employment insecurity was challenged by other observers, who argued that it was largely a media creation that had been fuelled by some well-publicised but unrepresentative instances where permanent, full-time employees had been replaced by freelance workers on fixed-term contracts, mostly in the media themselves (Doogan, 2001).

The empirical evidence showed that there had not been a step increase in employment insecurity during the 1990s. While there was a slight increase in the proportion of workers in jobs lasting less than one year between 1991 and 1998, there was also an increase in the proportion of people employed in long-term jobs, i.e. those lasting ten years or more (Sparrow and Cooper, 2003: 77). Neither was there a long-term increase in people's feelings of employment insecurity. In fact, fewer workers felt they were likely to lose their job in 2001 compared with 1987 or 1996 and more felt there was virtually no chance of losing their job (Green, 2004). The 'employment insecurity debate' subsided as quickly as it had arisen, figuring less and less in public discussion as we moved into the new millennium. However, while it is true that the structural basis for long-term employment has not been undermined, if the rise in unemployment that began in 2007–08 continues for another year or so, as seems likely at the time of writing, workers will feel more insecure as the chance of losing their job increases and the likelihood of finding another lessens. There is also evidence that the recession is forcing more male workers who really want permanent or full-time jobs to take part-time or temporary jobs (ONS, 2009c). For these workers, the quality of employment has declined.

Activity   Discuss with fellow students your perceptions of your own job security or insecurity. What factors influence your assessment?

Worker discretion and autonomy

Worker discretion and autonomy are usually associated with skill. In fact, the skill content of a job is partly defined in terms of the extent to which workers are required to exercise their own judgement in deciding how the job should be done, the other elements being task complexity and variety. The fewer the prescribed instructions to workers and the greater the number of decisions that workers have to make in the course of the job, the more skilled it is (Noon and Blyton, 1997). We have already seen that changes in the demand for labour have led to an increase in the average skill requirements of jobs. But does this mean that workers are enjoying increasing influence and control over how they work? The trend towards work intensification noted above suggests that workers have been losing control over effort levels and the pace of work. What has happened to their ability to influence other aspects of their work?

Various studies have cast doubt on how far recent upskilling of jobs has been accompanied by increased discretion and control for workers. Ramsay et al. (1991) found that white-collar workers in local government reported increased supervision following the introduction of information technology. Dent (1991) found that doctors and academics were being subject to increased bureaucratic control and a large survey carried out by Gallie et al. (1998) found that skilled workers were subject to increased supervision, particularly when they worked with new technology.

National survey data also show that the overall increase in skill levels has not been accompanied by increased worker discretion; if anything the reverse has occurred. The proportion of all workers reporting that they had a great deal of choice over the way they did their job fell from 51.8 per cent in 1986 to 38.6 per cent in 2001, a decline of 13.2 percentage points.

While all broad occupational categories reported a decline in discretion, it was most marked among professional workers, where the proportion reporting that they had a lot of choice over how they did their work fell from 71.5 per cent to 38.3 per cent, a drop of 33.4 percentage points (Green, 2006: 105).

Rather than the shift in favour of more skilled jobs providing workers with greater control over their work, there has been a marked overall decline in discretion, particularly among professionals, who are among the most highly skilled workers. The reasons for this probably include the effects of new technology, financial pressures in the public sector, the spread of subcontracting and the increased public accountability to which professions have been subjected in the interests of improving public services such as health and education. New technologies allow the implementation of routine processes and the closer monitoring of individual workers. Professional workers are also concentrated in the public sector, where government-imposed financial constraints have encouraged closer managerial control of professional workers. At the same time, political pressure to reform and improve public services has involved criticisms of established standards and practices among professional groups that have led to managerial interventions to limit professional autonomy.

Identify as many examples as you can of politically inspired managerial interventions that have affected public service sector professional workers. Here is one to start you off – the National Curriculum in schools.

Effort and work pressure

Since the 1980s, many have argued that work pressure has been increasing on two fronts in the UK. First, managers have been putting workers (and each other) under increasing pressure to work long hours. The prevalence of the 'long hours culture' in the UK is indicated by the fact that average working hours are higher than elsewhere in the European Union (EU). The British government has been accused of supporting a long hours culture by seeking to limit the effect of the EU Working Hours Directive in the UK. Second, since the mid-1980s analysts have argued that work is being intensified; in other words, workers are being made to work harder during their working hours.

Green (2006) notes that there is a widespread perception that work is encroaching on other aspects of life, restricting the time available for non-work activities and subjecting people to increased time pressures. This has fuelled recent discussion of 'work–life balance' (see below). Statistical evidence, however, shows that there has not been a long-term increase in average hours worked in the UK. Average hours worked per employed person fell from the 1950s to the 1980s. The decline was halted during the 1980s but has resumed since. In 2003, average annual hours worked per employed person were 1673 compared with 1767 in 1990, 1713 in 1983 and 1833 in 1979 (Green, 2006: 46). At the end of 2008, average weekly working hours for full-time workers stood at 37. What have increased are working hours per household as the proportion of households where all the adults are working has grown. The growing proportion of women with dependent children who are in work has been a major influence here. According to Green, it is the increase in the total hours worked per household rather than an increase in hours worked per worker that has made it more difficult to balance work and non-work activities and put people under pressure of time. Even so, there was widespread dissatisfaction over working hours among the UK workforce as a whole at the beginning of the millennium. Boheim and Taylor (2004) found that over 40 per cent of male and female full-time workers were dissatisfied with their hours of work, with the majority wanting to work fewer hours.

If the average amount of time that workers spend in work has not increased since the 1980s, people are nevertheless working harder during working time. Workers' self-reports during the 1990s showed that the amount of effort required of them increased, that they had to work faster to cope with their workload and that were increasingly working under a great deal of tension. Thus the proportion of workers reporting that they worked at very high speed all the time or almost all the time rose from 17.3 per cent in 1992 to 25.6 per cent in 2001 and the proportion agreeing or strongly agreeing that they worked under a great deal of tension rose from 48.4 per cent to 58.4 per cent over the same period (Green, 2006: 54). A growing proportion of workers also reported that they found it difficult to unwind after work, that they kept worrying about work problems after work and that they felt 'used up at the end of a workday' (Green, 2006: 156). Moreover, work pressure remains an important issue. The 2008 CIPD Absence Survey found that a third of responding organizations reported an increase in work-related stress over the previous year while only 11 per cent reported a decrease. The most common cause of work-related stress, cited by 56 per cent of respondents, was workload (CIPD, 2008: 26).

Work intensification has been driven mainly by the 'effort-biased' nature of technical change (Green, 2006), which enables management to exercise closer control over workers' effort. A clear example of this is the automated call distribution technology that is used in call centres. This ensures that call centre operators receive a continuous stream of incoming and outgoing calls, setting the pace of work in a similar way to the assembly line of an automated manufacturing plant. Another factor contributing to work intensification may be change in the labour market environment, particularly the decline of collective bargaining. This has given employers greater freedom to introduce new pay systems that are designed to extract higher effort from workers (Green, 2006).

STOP and think

Think about your own workplace. What systems and technologies are in place to regulate your effort? Have you noticed an increase or decrease in the intensity of your work over time?

Responses to work pressure – the quest for 'work–life balance'

Declining job satisfaction over hours and workload during the 1990s led to a growing demand for an improved balance between work and non-work aspects of life among workers generally. Therefore work–life balance is not just about finding ways of combining work with the need to care for children or older relatives. We need to take a wider view of work–life balance and not just see it in terms of the 'family friendly' agenda. Work–life balance is in fact a broader issue of how to deal with the conflicting demands of corporate profitability on the one hand and the concerns of workers who are under work pressure and strain on the other (Taylor, 2002a).

What do we mean by work–life balance?

Work–life balance is not an easily defined term. The word 'balance' suggests the search for equilibrium between work and life; a settled point perhaps at which work and the rest of life's activities can comfortably reside side by side. Noon and Blyton (2007) suggest work–life balance is about individuals being able to run their working lives and non-work lives without pressure from one detracting from the other. Part of the problem associated with the notion of striking a balance or equilibrium, however, is that work and non-work aspects of life are entwined rather than being separate, compartmentalised spheres. For example, we might read a report for work on the train on the way home, we may look up the cinema screening times on the internet at work or chat to colleagues about non-work related issues during working hours; in essence what we are doing is seeking to find ways to *integrate* work and other aspects of our lives in ways that are workable and beneficial. However, Noon and Blyton also point out that while individual and household adjustments to help bring about a better work–life balance are important, we also need to consider how they are shaped by action at community, organisational and societal levels. Consequently, they argue that it is necessary to consider four different levels of inter-related response to the problem of work–life imbalance to identify the conditions for achieving satisfactory work–life balance. These are shown in Figure 4.2 below.

The following sections briefly examine statutory intervention in the work–life balance arena and ways in which employers have responded to the work–life balance needs of employees.

Work–life balance and government policy

Legal imperatives for employers to address issues of work–life balance began to emerge at the end of the 1990s. In 1998 we saw the introduction of the Working Time Regulations, aimed at limiting the working week to a maximum of 48 hours and requiring employers to formally secure an 'opt-out' agreement with those employees willing to contract in excess of the 48-hour cap. On the heels of the Working Time Directive, the Employment Rights Act 1999 contained provisions to bolster the position of working parents and carers within the workplace whilst the Employment Act 2002 introduced a right to request flexible working for parents of children under the age of six, later to be extended to those with care responsibilities for adults (see Chapter 11 for further details of the legislation).

The UK government's concern for work–life balance was formally highlighted in Spring 2000 at the launch of the Work–Life Balance Campaign (Hogarth *et al.*, 2000). The campaign sought to alert employers to the business case in favour of introducing practices to help employees strike a better balance between work and other aspects of their lives. Importantly, the campaign sought to promote the merits of work–life balance *for all*, rather than just those with caring responsibilities. The Department for Education and Employment conducted a baseline study (Hogarth *et al.*, 2000) to assess how far employers operated work–life balance practices and to provide a comparator for future survey results. There have subsequently been two further surveys, one in 2003 conducted by MORI (Stevens *et al.*, 2004) and the

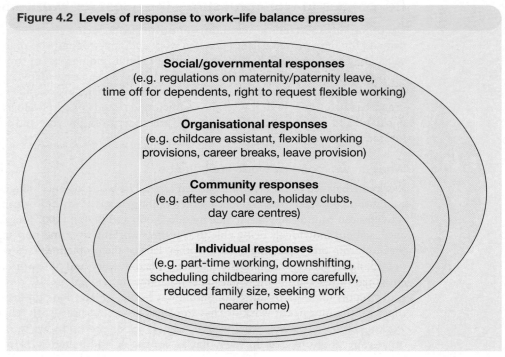

Figure 4.2 Levels of response to work–life balance pressures

Social/governmental responses
(e.g. regulations on maternity/paternity leave,
time off for dependents, right to request flexible working)

Organisational responses
(e.g. childcare assistant, flexible working
provisions, career breaks, leave provision)

Community responses
(e.g. after school care, holiday clubs,
day care centres)

Individual responses
(e.g. part-time working, downshifting,
scheduling childbearing more carefully,
reduced family size, seeking work
nearer home)

Source: Noon and Blyton (2007: 368).

latest in 2006 by researchers at the Institute for Employment Studies (Hooker *et al.*, 2007). The most recent survey is encouraging and appears to provide evidence that employers are engaging with the work–life balance agenda to the satisfaction of their employees. The availability of data from both the baseline survey and the second work–life balance survey has proved a useful source of comparison and has given analysts involved in the third survey the opportunity to begin to examine possible trends in the availability of, and demand for, flexible working arrangements, employees' perceived views of the feasibility of flexible working arrangements, take up patterns and so forth. Some of the key findings from the third survey are included within the following sub-section alongside other empirical evidence.

Organisational responses to work–life balance

There are potentially strong business reasons why employers should offer arrangements to employees to help achieve a better integration of work and non-work aspects of their lives. Clutterbuck (2004) suggests that creating an enabling culture in which employees can amend and re-apportion the time and attention they pay to work to meet their particular needs and circumstances can be a source of sustainable competitive advantage. More specifically, Edwards and Wajcman (2005) refer to international survey evidence to show that graduates care more about work–life balance than pay when they are selecting an employer, the implication being that employers who attend to the work–life balance needs of their employees are more likely to be employers of choice in the competitive graduate market. However, finding the right blend of organisational interventions to help individuals is complex; work–life balance is a movable target in the sense that different people have different ideas of what constitutes a satisfactory work–life balance. Sparrow and Cooper (2003) suggest that organisations can help employees to address work–life balance through practices that offer employees the opportunity to negotiate a wider range of options in relation to their patterns of work. They suggest two categories of practices. First, the provision of specific organisational arrangements to enable employees to split work and non-work aspects of their lives; for example, options to work part-time or full-time, to work in school term-time only or to job share. Second, practices that enable individuals to draw their own lines between and around work and non-work; for example, unpaid leave, career breaks, parental leave, sabbaticals, paid holidays. Work–life balance strategies are thus often associated with the provision of greater flexibility in terms of working arrangements.

In practice, employers' responses to work–life balance have been mixed. According to the WERS 2004 survey (Kersley *et al.* 2006), most managers (65 per cent) felt that it was up to individual employees to balance their work and family responsibilities. Managers in private sector organisations were more likely than those in the public sector to take this view and in line with this, fewer private sector than public sector employees reported finding their managers sympathetic to their work–life balance dilemmas. Managers in smaller workplaces, single independent establishments and non-union workplaces were more likely to say that it was up to individuals to manage their own work–life balance than were managers in larger workplaces, establishments that were part of a larger organisation, and workplaces where unions were recognised. Managers in organisations where more than half the workforce was female were less likely to believe individuals should take responsibility for their own work–life balance than workplaces that were male-dominated, so that more females than males found their managers to be understanding of their responsibilities outside of work. Nevertheless, comparison of WERS 2004 and WERS 1998 data show that some flexible working arrangements had become more widely available in 2004 (Kersley *et al.* 2006).

In work undertaken for the National Centre for Economic Research, Wood (1999) provides a framework for identifying and explaining why some firms seem to be willingly and proactively adopting work–life balance initiatives while others are more reluctant and reactive. Table 4.8 below presents Wood's four-fold theoretical classification of employers' motives for introducing work–life balance initiatives.

Table 4.8 Wood's theoretical classification of employers' responses to work–life balance

Institutional theory	Organisations whose behaviour shows them to be eager to reflect broader societal values in their practices conform to *institutional theory*. Typically these firms operate in the public sector and need to be seen to be proactive, or they are large private sector firms in the public gaze for whom there is visible kudos to be earned from setting the lead in developing and implementing work–life balance solutions. Additionally firms with trade union presence are more likely to conform.
Organisational adaption theory	Organisations in which societal norms are interpreted in ways that are seen to be consistent with the views and interests of senior management. Firms conforming to *organisational adaption theory* are likely to be drawn towards work–life balance initiatives because of specific organisational circumstances. Such firms may be especially reliant on a predominantly female workforce or require skill sets that are difficult to secure and retain so employee retention issues are critical. *Organisational adaption theory* also captures the propensity of firms to implement work–life balance initiatives when existing working patterns and systems are conducive to or compatible with them.
High-commitment theory	Organisations with developed HRM systems and practices, where it is understood that mechanisms to help employees achieve a better work–life balance may in turn engender greater levels of employee commitment.
Practical response theory	Organisations who display a rather more *ad hoc* approach to the development and introduction of work–life balance initiatives; resorting to implementing work–life balance practices if they are perceived to be beneficial in helping to address particular organisational difficulties.

Source: Wood (1999).

The WERS 2004 findings give some support to Wood's analysis. In line with the prediction of *institutional theory*, flexible working arrangements in support of work–life balance were generally found to be more prevalent in larger workplaces that were part of a wider organisation, large organisations, unionised organisations and the public sector. In addition, consistent with *organisational adaption theory*, most of the practices (with the exception of flexi-time and home-working) were more common where more than half of the workforce were female (Kersley *et al.*, 2006: 251).

Think of an organisation you have worked for where some work–life balance practices were available. Why do you think this organisation elected to develop and introduce WLB initiatives?

Trends in the provision and take-up of work–life balance initiatives

We have seen that the WERS 2004 survey showed that the majority of employers did not think they should take any responsibility for employees' work–life balance. However, the *Third Work–life Balance Survey* (Hooker *et al.*, 2007) reported a significant increase in the availability of most flexible working arrangements since 2003 (the time of the *Second Work–Life Balance Survey*, Stevens *et al.*, 2004). The most commonly available working arrangements cited by employees in the 2006 survey were part-time working (69 per cent said this would be available), the ability to reduce hours for limited periods (54 per cent) and flexi-time (53 per cent). Just over a third of employees thought their employers would be amenable to term-time working and a similar proportion said compressed hours would be an option (working normal weekly hours in a shorter time frame e.g. 37.5 hours over four days rather than five). If we compare these responses with the WERS 2004 data on the availability of different forms of flexible working, presented in Table 4.9 below, it appears that there are some significant mismatches between employees' perceptions of the likelihood of being able to taking advantage of certain forms of flexible working and what managers are willing to offer, particularly in relation to flexi-time, term-time working and compressed hours.

Take-up of these flexible working options, in other words the proportion of people making use of flexible working arrangements, has actually changed little since the *Second Work–Life Balance Survey* in 2003. Almost half (49 per cent) of those who had the option to use flexi-time had done so in the preceding 12 months, 44 per cent of those who could work from home made regular use of the arrangement, and 38 per cent took advantage of part-time working where it was available. Other flexible working practices were less commonly used; 24 per cent took advantage of compressed working hours where they were offered while under a fifth of employees who could reduce their hours for a limited period had done so in the preceding 12 months and just 12 per cent took their employers up on the option to job share. When employees were asked why they had not worked flexibly when they had the chance to do so, 41 per cent said that they were happy with their current working arrangements. Few mentioned organisational barriers to take-up and the survey also found that there were lower levels of unmet demand than reported in the 2003 survey, suggesting that more employees now have access to the working patterns they prefer.

These findings suggest that most employees do not think that their ability to take advantage of flexible working is being obstructed by their employer. In contrast however, another study into attitudes to flexible working and family life by Houston and Waumsley (2003) found that many employees feared that using flexible working practices would be career

Table 4.9 Availability of flexible working arrangements

Flexible working arrangements	Per cent of workplaces offering the arrangement to some employees
Reduced hours	70
Increased hours	57
Change working pattern	45
Flexi-time	35
Job sharing	31
Homeworking	26
Term-time only	20
Compressed hours	16

Source: Kersley *et al.* (2006: 206).

Table 4.10 Reasons given for not working flexibly by employees who had not worked any of the flexible arrangements

Concerned about career progression	1%	Other	3%
Concerned about job security	1%	Don't know	4%
No children/no childcare needs	1%	Employer would not allow it	6%
Hadn't thought of it	1%	Financial reasons	10%
On contract/fixed hours	1%	Doesn't suit domestic arrangements	11%
Just don't want to	1%	Job doesn't allow it	17%
Concerned about colleagues' workload	1%	Happy with current arrangements	41%
Want to work full-time	2%	No need/not necessary/not applicable	8%
Too much work to do	3%		

Source: Hooker *et al.* (2007: 69).

153

damaging. This was particularly true of managers, who were significantly more likely to feel that they had to put work before their family and personal life in order to progress than were skilled or semi-skilled workers, and more men were of this opinion than women. The reason for the discrepancy between the two studies is unclear but may be attributable to sampling and methodological differences.

Despite the optimistic findings of the *Third Work–Life Balance Survey*, progress in addressing work–life balance issues will continue to be uneven, given the trend to smaller workplaces combined with limited trade union presence. Moreover, even in those organis-ations where opportunities for flexible working are offered, barriers to their take-up by employees remain; 'organisations need not only to have policies for work–life balance in place, but also an underlying culture that supports employees who use flexible working options' (Noon and Blyton, 2007: 373). Obstacles to take-up include the irreducible nature of work tasks in many cases, possible damage to career prospects resulting from taking flexible work options and for low earners, loss of earnings resulting from some options. Workers may also be unwilling to take advantage of work–life balance initiatives because they are worried that it will generate hostile responses from colleagues who are unable or do not wish to do so (Sparrow and Cooper, 2003).

Job quality – an assessment

What can we conclude about the quality of working life at the end of the first decade of the new millennium? The evidence that we have reviewed in this section suggests that in impor-tant respects workers' experience of employment deteriorated during the 1980s and 1990s. Although there was no general, long-term increase in job insecurity, work became more intense and pressured and workers had less control over how they did their jobs. At the same time, the increase in the number of households where all adults are working led to difficulties of balancing work and non-work areas of life. These changes were responsible for a signifi-cant decline in job satisfaction among British workers, with just over 40 per cent of workers reporting high levels of job satisfaction in 2001 compared with just over 50 per cent in 1992 (Green, 2006: 154). More optimistically, since the end of the 1990s the incidence of long hours working has declined and the process of work intensification has halted. The propor-tion of workers working long hours peaked at 36 per cent in 1995 and fell to 30 per cent by the end of 2002 (Green, 2003: 140). While work was more intense in 2001 than in 1992, the trend to intensification halted in 1997 (Green, 2003: 144). Therefore we are working harder in 2009, though not on average longer, than in 1980 or 1990 and opportunities for flexible working are more readily available; we are subject to more extensive, if sometimes less obvi-ous, controls at work and more of us are likely to be in jobs for which we are over-qualified. This is not a particularly encouraging picture, especially when looked at alongside the increasing inequalities in income and wealth that have characterised the last 25 years.

Conclusion: labour market developments, job quality and the implications for the employment relationship

The evidence discussed in this chapter suggests that, despite the widespread rhetoric of high-commitment and high-involvement and the tendency among advocates and practitioners of HRM to present the employment relationship in terms of mutual consent, it continues to be characterised by conflicts of interest. Currently these centre on hours of work, work intensity, lack of discretion and control over how work is performed, and structured inequalities in the labour market.

The main labour market developments from 1997 to 2007 were sustained growth of employment accompanied by increasing inequality in the distribution of pay as a result of the polarised nature of employment growth. While employment and pay have risen for all groups of workers since 1993, the *relative* position of less-skilled workers in terms of unemployment, access to jobs, and pay is worse than it was at the start of the 1980s. This is despite recent government interventions such as the national minimum wage and measures aimed at improving the employability of young school leavers (Goos and Manning, 2003). Moreover, the 'credit crunch' and recession in 2008 have led to a rapid rise in unemployment that will have disproportionate effects on the most disadvantaged sections of the population.

In addition, long-standing patterns of inequality and disadvantage remain. The difference in employment rates between women and men has not really changed over the last ten years, the employment rate among women remaining 11 percentage points below that of men. Neither has there been much change in the quality of jobs occupied by women. They are still concentrated in occupations and industries where rates of pay are low and working conditions are poor. While the overall pay gap between women and men has narrowed, it is the minority of women who are working full-time in higher-paid occupations who have benefited. This group have also benefited from statutory maternity leave provisions, which have given them the right to return to their jobs after childbirth. The pay gap for the majority of working women, who are in part-time jobs, has not narrowed and may even have increased slightly (Robinson, 2003). Moreover the position of these women, employed mainly in low-skill occupations, has deteriorated to an even greater extent than that of low-skilled men in relation to unemployment, access to employment, and pay (Gregg and Wadsworth, 2003).

Established patterns of labour market inequality between ethnic minorities and whites have also persisted. There has been an increase in the employment rate and a consequent reduction in the employment gap relative to whites among some, but not all, British-born ethnic minority groups and a slight reduction in the degree of occupational segregation. However, there is less evidence for a reduction in the pay gap. The position of ethnic minority immigrants has shown no sign of improving relative to whites (Wadsworth, 2003).

These features of the contemporary labour market suggest that there are serious long-term issues to face. First, it is clear that there has been a mismatch between the way managers are organising work and designing jobs on the one hand and how workers' job aspirations are developing on the other. Widespread job dissatisfaction has weakened employees' commitment to their employers and eroded the goodwill that is necessary for cooperative behaviour in the workplace. Recent attention to work–life balance issues may go some way to addressing these issues but as long as, in the words of the UK Commission for Employment and Skills (2009: 10), there are 'too few high performance workplaces, too few employers producing high quality goods and services, too few businesses in high value-added sectors' there will continue to be too many people in jobs for which they are over-qualified and in which they find insufficient fulfilment.

Second, discrimination against ethnic minorities, women and older workers represents a waste of human resources since it leads to under-utilisation of skills possessed by these groups. However, employers individually may benefit from the presence of disadvantaged groups who can be exploited because they lack alternative job opportunities. Therefore there is a case for stronger state intervention to combat unfair discrimination in the labour market. There is also a case for strengthening workers' rights to trade union membership and representation.

Finally, the evidence reviewed in this chapter should lead you to think about the nature of HRM and the extent of its adoption in the UK. What do we consider to be HRM? Is it a set of practices aimed at generating high levels of employee commitment or high performance through employee involvement? If so, there would appear to be little evidence that it has spread widely in the UK since the 1980s.

Summary

- Labour markets are often seen as arenas of competition in which forces of supply and demand determine wage and employment levels. In reality however, there are limits to competition in labour markets.

- Employers have some freedom to make a strategic choice between internalising or externalising the employment relationship. Their choices are influenced although not completely determined by the nature of their labour requirements and by features of the labour market context in which they operate.

- The aggregate supply of labour – the size of the workforce – is determined by demographic factors such as the size and age structure of the population and by social and political factors that influence the participation rate of different socio-economic groups within the population. In the UK differential participation rates can be observed between men and women of different age groups and different ethnic groups.

- Aggregate labour demand consists of total employment plus unfilled vacancies. The demand for labour is derived from the demand for goods and services. In conditions of low unemployment – tight labour markets – employers have to compete more actively to attract and retain workers.

- The demand for labour is segmented into jobs offers of varying quality. Unfair discrimination along lines of gender and ethnicity mean that women and ethnic minorities are disadvantaged in terms of access to good jobs.

- There has been a long-term change in labour demand away from manufacturing to services. This has been an important force driving the long-term growth of part-time employment and women's employment.

- Since the 1980s there has been a shift in the occupational structure of labour demand mainly towards highly skilled occupations but also leading to the growth of some low-skilled occupations. There has been a relative decline in intermediate occupations.

- Since the 1980s managers have restructured their organisations and their workforces. This has involved a retreat from internalised employment relationships.

- Contrary to what might have been predicted from the overall trend towards more highly skilled work, the quality of jobs has deteriorated in terms of work pressure and worker autonomy, although not in terms of job stability leading to falling levels of job satisfaction compared with the early 1990s. The demand for better work–life balance is a recent response to growing work pressure.

- Declining job satisfaction and the presence of disadvantaged groups in the labour market indicate the continued presence of conflict in the employment relationship.

Questions

1 Explain the factors that influence the differential labour market participation rates of women and men and ethnic minorities and whites.

2 How has the structure of demand for labour changed since the 1980s?

3 Why have levels of job satisfaction declined since the early 1990s?

4 Who have been the main beneficiaries of changes in the labour market since the 1980s and who have been the main losers?

Case study

Stuck on the 'mummy track' – why having a baby means lower pay and prospects

From the moment they give birth, women get stuck on a 'mummy track' of low pay and low prospects as their wages fall and never fully recover – even when their children have left home, a new study has found.

Far from being a liberating release, the point when their children start school marks another sudden slump in the average growth of women's pay compared with male wages, according to the report by the Institute for Fiscal Studies.

Before they have children, the average hourly wage for female workers is 91 per cent of the male average but declines to 67 per cent for working mothers juggling jobs and childcare.

Their wages relative to men then stagnate for 10 years before showing a modest recovery, reports the study, *Newborns and New Schools*. But even when children have left home, the average hourly wage for their mothers remained at 72 per cent of the male average.

Rather than facilitate a large-scale return to the workforce for women, the moment their children enter full-time school accelerates relative wage decline. The average wage growth over two years for women before having children was 11 per cent, but fell to 8 per cent for women with newborn children. While it recovered to 9 per cent for those with pre-school children, it fell again to less than 5 per cent when their children entered school. The aggregate proportion of mothers in work before their children began school compared with afterwards only rose slightly from 53 per cent in June to 57 per cent when term began in September.

'There is a huge assumption that suddenly because the child is at school the mother can return to work,' said Gillian Paull, a co-author of the study for the Department for Work and Pensions. 'But school hours are far too short to cover most jobs and school brings with it a new set of responsibilities in terms of children needing input from parents and parents being involved in school life. Finding childcare that fits around school hours and the holidays is difficult unless you pay for expensive full-time care.'

Only a small part of this gender wage gap is because mothers choose to work part time. For full-time workers, the gender wage ratio suffered a similar slump between childless women and working mothers, with a decline from women commanding 94 per cent of male wages before children to just 74 per cent for those with children and 79 per cent for the group after children.

When researchers took account of other factors which might determine the gender wage gap such as gender differences in demographic background, educational attainment and work characteristics and conditions they still found 'a substantial "unexplained" gender wage gap' of 11 per cent for those before children, 30 per cent for those living with children and 23 per cent for those whose children have grown up or left home.

'The million-dollar question is: "Are the wage levels different because working mothers are treated differently or is it that they choose a different way to behave in the labour market?"' Dr Paull said.

Working mothers could be suffering a wide pay gap because of pure discrimination. Or, controversially, some employers claim they do not pay as much because working mothers are not as productive as men. Third, Dr Paull said, it could be that women were choosing jobs that fit in with the demands of motherhood, finding work that was less physically demanding, for instance, so they could devote more energy to their families.

'Too many women get stuck on a "mummy track" of low pay and low prospects. The pay gap for women working part-time, at nearly 40 per cent, has barely improved since the Sex Discrimination Act was introduced 30 years ago,' said Caroline Slocock, the chief executive of the Equal Opportunities Commission.

'Many women choose to work part-time, but they don't choose low pay. Four in five part-time workers – 5.6 million people, most of whom are women – are working in jobs which do not use their potential, because flexible and part-time work is too often low-status and underpaid. This is a colossal waste of talent for employers and the economy as well as individuals.'

The IFS study is published days before the Women and Work Commission reports to Tony Blair after spending 18 months looking at the problem of the gender pay gap. The Prime Minister is expected to help launch the report next month, which is expected to outline radical proposals to help women return to well-paid work.

Children represent a 'major part' of the gender pay gap, according to Margaret Prosser, who chairs the Women and Work Commission. 'Once women have

Case study continued

children, their job choices are hugely constrained, either because they have to choose local work which provides fewer options or choose part-time employment, where there are few jobs at a professional or senior level.'

Lady Prosser said she was not surprised that figures showed women's pay stagnating even years after they have raised young children.

'The majority of women who have children want to spend some time with those children. What they would like is work that is sufficiently flexible but what they do not want is work that is always at the bottom of the ladder.

'There is no silver bullet answer to this. There has to be a whole range of policy proposals around educational choices, encouragement for girls and more widely available childcare facilities.'

Source: from Stuck on the 'mummy track' – why having a baby means lower pay and prospects, *The Guardian*, 20 January 2006 (Barkham, P.), Copyright Guardian News & Media Ltd 2006.

Questions

1 To what extent do you believe that women get stuck on the 'mummy track' because they *choose* to prioritise responsibilities to their children over and above paid work?

2 Are New Labour's promises to improve access to affordable childcare and plans to introduce school

'wrap around time' (the provision of breakfast clubs and after school activities to extend the school day) the 'green light' needed for working mothers to be able to compete on equal terms with men in the workplace?

3 Whilst organisations might not deliberately set out to discriminate against working mothers, consider ways in which norms and expectations in the contemporary workplace may make it difficult for working mothers to gain promotion and hence access to better paid positions. What steps could organisations take to help more women off the 'mummy track'?

Activity

You have been invited to a campus debate to discuss the proposition outlined below:

Given employers' demand for low skill workers to fill low-paid jobs in the service sector, the existence of receptive pockets of labour (for example, working mothers, students, migrant workers) prepared to accept these jobs is beneficial for organisations and the economy at large.

Using the article 'Stuck on the Mummy track' as a starting point, consider positions both *in support of and against* the above statement. You should be able to draw upon several segments of this chapter to inform your arguments.

References and further reading

Adkins, L. (1995) *Gendered Work, Sexuality, Family and the Labour Market*. Buckingham: Oxford University Press.

Anderson, B., Ruhs, M., Rogaly, B. and Spencer, C. (2006) *Fair Enough? Central and Eastern European Migrants in Low-Wage Employment*. York: Joseph Rowntree Foundation.

Bayliss, V. (1998) *Redefining Work: An RSA Initiative*. London: Royal Society for the Encouragement of Arts, Manufactures and Commerce.

Bevan, S. and Cowling, M. (2007) *Job Matching in the UK and the European Union*. Research Report RR25 Sector Skills Development Agency. www.employment-studies.co.uk.

Boheim, R. and Taylor, M.P. (2004) 'Actual and preferred working hours', *British Journal of Industrial Relations*, 42, 1: 149–66.

Bradley, H. (1999), *Gender and Power in the Workplace: Analysing the Impact of Economic Change*. Basingstoke: Macmillan.

Browning, G. (2005) 'The search for meaning', *People Management*, 13 December: 38–39.

CIPD (2005) *A Barometer of HR Trends and Prospects, Overview of CIPD Surveys*. Wimbledon: CIPD.

CIPD (2006) 'Jobs blow to women as economic slowdown hits consumer services', Press Release, Wimbledon, CIPD, 15 March.

CIPD (2008) *Absence Management: Annual Survey Report 2008*. Wimbledon: CIPD.

CIPD and KPMG (2006) Labour Market Outlook, *Quarterly Survey Report*, Wimbledon, CIPD Spring.

Clutterbuck, D. (2004) *Managing Work–Life Balance in the 21st Century*. London: CIPD.

Connor, H., Tyers, C., Davis, S. and Tackey, N. (2003) *Minority Ethnic Students in Higher Education*. London: DfES.

Cooper, C. (2005) 'Another year down?' *People Management*, 13 December: 36–37.

Crompton, R. (1997) *Women and Work in Modern Britain*, Oxford: Oxford University Press.

Cully, M., Woodland, S., O'Reilly, A. and Dix, G. (1999) *Britain at Work. As Depicted by the 1998 Workplace Employee Relations Survey*. London: Routledge.

Dent, M. (1991) 'Autonomy and the medical profession: medical audit and management control' in C. Smith, D. Knights and H. Willmott (eds) *White-Collar Work: The Non-Manual Labour Process*. Basingstoke: Macmillan, pp. 65–88.

Doeringer, P.B. and Piore, M.J. (1971) *Internal Labor Markets and Manpower Analysis*. Lexington, MA: Heath.

Doogan, K. (2001) 'Insecurity and long term employment', *Work, Employment and Society*, 15, 3: 419–41.

Drucker, P. (2001) 'Beyond the information revolution' in A. Giddens (ed.) *Sociology: Introductory Readings*. Cambridge: Polity Press.

DWP (2005) Speech given by the Rt Hon Alan Johnson MP, Secretary of State for Work and Pensions, 7 February, www.dwp.gov.uk.

Edwards, P. and Wajcman, J. (2005) *The Politics of Working Life*. Oxford: Oxford University Press.

EOC (2001) *Women and Men in Britain: Professional Occupations*.

EOC (2005) *Facts about Men and Women in Britain 2005, an EOC Fact Sheet*.

EOC (2006) *Then and Now; 30 years of the Sex Discrimination Act, an EOC Fact Sheet*.

Equality and Human Rights Commission (2008) *Sex and Power 2008*. London: EHRC.

Federation of the Royal Colleges of Physicians of the United Kingdom (2001) *Women in Hospital Medicine: Career Choices and Opportunities*, Report of a Working Party of the Federation of Royal Colleges of Physicians. June.

Felstead, A., Gallie, D. and Green, F. (2002) *Work Skills in Britain 1986–2001*. Nottingham: DfES publications.

Forde, C. and Mackenzie, R. (2007) 'Getting the mix right? The use of labour contract alternatives in UK construction' *Personnel Review*, 36, 4: 549–63.

Friedman, A. (1977) *Industry and Labour*. London: Macmillan.

Gallie, D., White, M. and Cheng, Y. (1998) *Restructuring the Employment Relationship*. Oxford: Clarendon Press.

Goos, M. and Manning, A. (2003) 'McJobs and MacJobs: The growing polarisation of jobs in the UK' in R. Dickens, P. Gregg and J. Wadsworth (eds) *The Labour Market under New Labour: The State of Working Britain*. Basingstoke: Palgrave, pp. 70–85.

Gordon, D.M., Edwards, R. and Reich, M. (1982) *Segmented Work, Divided Workers: The Historical Transformation of Labor in the United States*. Cambridge: Cambridge University Press.

Green, F. (2003) 'The demands of work', in R. Dickens, P. Gregg and J. Wadsworth (eds) *The Labour Market under New Labour: The State of Working Britain*. Basingstoke: Palgrave, pp. 137–49.

Green, F. (2004) 'The rise and decline of job insecurity', *Department of Economics Discussion Paper*. Canterbury: Kent University.

Green, F. (2006) *Demanding Work: The Paradox of Job Quality in the Affluent Economy*. Oxford: Princeton University Press.

Gregg, P. (2008) *Realising Potential: A Vision for Personalized Conditionality and Support*. An Independent Report to the Department for Work and Pensions.

Gregg, P. and Wadsworth, J. (2003) 'Labour market prospects of less skilled workers over the recovery' in R. Dickens, P. Gregg and J. Wadsworth (eds) *The Labour Market Under New Labour: The State of Working Britain*. Basingstoke: Palgrave, pp. 87–97.

Hakim, C. (1998) *Social Change and Innovation in the Labour Market*. Oxford: Oxford University Press.

Hardill, I., Duddlestone, A. and Owen, D.W. (1997) 'Who decides what? Decision making in dual career households', *Work, Employment & Society*, 11, 2: 313–26.

Heath, A. and Cheung, S.Y. (2006) *Ethnic Penalties in the Labour Market: Employers and Discrimination*. DWP Research Report 341.

Heery, E. and Salmon, J. (2000) 'The insecurity thesis' in E. Heery and J. Salmon, (eds) *The Insecure Workforce*. London: Routledge, pp. 1–24.

Higgs, M. (2004) 'Future trends in HR' in D. Rees and R. McBain (eds) *People Management Challenges and Opportunities*. Basingstoke: Palgrave, pp. 15–31.

Hogarth, T., Hasluck, C., Pierre, G., Winterbotham, M. and Vivian, D. (2000) *Work–life Balance, 2000: Baseline Study of Work–Life Balance Practices in Great Britain*. Warwick: Institute for Employment Research, Warwick University.

Hooker, H., Neathley, F., Casebourne, J. and Munro, M. (2007) *The Third Work–Life Balance Employee Survey: Main Findings*, Institute for Employment Studies, Department of Trade and Industry, Employment Relations Research Series No. 58.

Houston, D., and Waumsley, J.A. (2003) *Attitudes to Flexible Working and Family Life*. Bristol: Policy Press.

Hudson, M. (1999) 'Disappearing pathways and the struggle for a fair day's pay', in B. Burchell, D. Day, M. Hudson, D. Ladipo, R. Mankelow, J. Nolan, H. Reed, I. Wichert and F. Wilkinson, *Job Insecurity and Work Intensification: Flexibility and the Changing Boundaries of Work*. York: Joseph Rowntree Foundation, pp. 77–93.

Jah, A. (2006) 'The future of old age', *The Guardian*, 8 March 2006, p. 6.

Joll, C., Mckenna, C., McNab, R. and Shorey, J. (1983) *Developments in Labour Market Analysis*. London: George Allen & Unwin.

Kersley, B., Alpin, C., Forth, J., Bryson, A., Bewley, H., Dix, G. and Oxenbridge, S. (2006) *Inside the Workplace: First Findings from the 2004 Workplace Employment Relations Survey*. London: DTI.

King, J.E. (1990) *Labour Economics*, 2nd edn. London: Macmillan.

Laurie, H. and Gershuny, J. (2000) 'Couples, work and money' in R. Berthoud and J. Gershuny (eds) *Seven Years in the Lives of British Families*. Bristol: Polity Press, pp. 45–72.

Learning and Skills Council (2008) *National Employer Skills Survey 2007: Main Report*. Coventry: Learning and Skills Council.

Leonard, D. and Speakman, M.A. (1986) 'Women in the family: companions or caretaker?' in V. Beechey and E. Whitelegg (eds) *Women in Britain Today*. Milton Keynes: Open University Press, pp. 8–76.

LFS (2008) Annual Population Survey, Office for National Statistics, www.statistics.gov.uk.

LFS (2006) 'Ethnic minorities in the labour market: Autumn 2005', *LFS Update*, www.emetaskforce.gov.uk.

Longhi, S. and Platt, L. (2009) *Pay Gaps and Pay Penalties by Gender and Ethnicity, Religion, Disability, Sexual Orientation and Age*. London: Equality and Human Rights Commission.

Marlow, S. and Carter, S. (2004) 'Accounting for change: professional status, gender disadvantage and self-employment', *Women in Management Review*, 19, 1: 5–17.

Miller, H. (1991) 'Academics and the labour process' in C. Smith, D. Knights and H. Willmott (eds) *White-Collar Work: The Non-Manual Labour Process*. Basingstoke: Macmillan, pp. 109–38.

Millward, N., Bryson, A. and Forth, J. (2000) *All Change at Work? British Employment Relations as Portrayed by the Workplace Industrial Relations Survey Series.* London: Routledge.

National Audit Office (2008) *Department for Work and Pensions. Increasing Employment Rates for Ethnic Minorities. Report by the Comptroller and Auditor General.* London: The Stationery Office.

Nolan, P. and Brown, W. (1983) 'Competition and workplace wage determination', *Oxford Bulletin of Economics and Statistics*, 45, 269–87.

Noon, M. and Blyton, P. (2007) *The Realities of Work: Experiencing Work and Employment in Contemporary Society*, 3rd edn. Basingstoke: Macmillan.

ONS (2001) Census 2001.

ONS (2005) *Labour Market Trends*, 113, 12.

ONS (2006) *Social Trends*, No. 36, 2006 edn, Office for National Statistics. Basingstoke: Palgrave MacMillan.

ONS (2007) *National Projections*, UK Snapshot, Population, www.statistics.gov.uk.

ONS (2008a) *Social Trends*, No. 38, 2008 edn. Office for National Statistics. Basingstoke: Palgrave MacMillan.

ONS (2008b) *Life Expectancy Continues to Rise*, UK Snapshot, Health, www.statistics.gov.uk.

ONS (2008c) *Labour Force Survey*, Spring 2008.

ONS (2008d) *More Women in Work But Half in Part-time Jobs.* Office for National Statistics News Release, 26 September 2008.

ONS (2009) *First Release Labour Market Statistics March 2009.* www.statistics.gov.uk 18 March 2009.

ONS (2009a) *National Statistics Online* 22 May www.statistics.gov.uk/cci.nugget.asp?ID=12.

ONS (2009b) *The Impact of the Recession on the Labour Market.* www.statistics.gov.uk/downloads/theme_labour/Impact-of-recession-on-LM.pdf.

ONS (2009c) *Economic and Labour Market Review*, April, Table 2.03. www.statistics.gov.uk/elmr/04_09/2.asp.

Phillips, L. (2008) 'Benefits claimants forced to look for work', *Personnel Management,* 29 December: 13.

Ramsay, H., Baldry, C., Connolly, A. and Lockyer, C. (1991) 'Multiple microchips: the computerised labour process in the public service sector', in C. Smith, D. Knights and H. Willmott (eds) *White-Collar Work: The Non-Manual Labour Process.* Basingstoke: Macmillan, pp. 35–64.

Robinson, H. (2003) 'Gender and labour market performance in the recovery', in R. Dickens, P. Gregg and J. Wadsworth (eds) *The Labour Market Under New Labour.* Basingstoke: Palgrave, pp. 232–47.

Rubery, J. (1994) 'Internal and external labour markets: towards an integrated analysis', in J. Rubery and F. Wilkinson (eds) *Employer Strategy and the Labour Market.* Oxford: Oxford University Press, pp. 37–68.

Scottish Centre for Employment Research (2001) *SCER Report 1 – Understanding the Labour Market*, Department of Human Resource Management, University of Strathclyde.

Sealy, R. (2008) *The Female FTSE Report 2008: A Decade of Delay.* Cranfield: Cranfield University.

Shepherd, J. (2008) 'Women teachers still losing out to men, says report', *Education Guardian*, 27 March.

Sparrow, P.R. and Cooper, C.L. (2003) *The Employment Relationship: Key Challenges for HR.* London: Butterworth Heinemann.

Stanworth, C. (2000) 'Flexible working patterns' in D. Winstanley and J. Woodall (eds) *Ethical Issues in Contemporary Human Resource Management.* Basingstoke: Palgrave, pp. 137–55.

Stevens, J. Brown, J. and Lee, C (2004) *The Second Work–Life Balance Study: Results from the Employees' Survey.* Department of Trade and Industry, Employment Relations Research Series No. 27.

Strategy Unit (2003) *Ethnic Minorities and the Labour Market: Final Report.* London: Cabinet Office.

Taylor, R. (2002a) *The Future of Work–Life Balance.* Swindon: Economic and Social Research Council.

Taylor, R. (2002b) *Britain's Diverse Labour Market.* Swindon: Economic and Social Research Council.

Taylor, S. (2008), *People Resourcing*, 4th edn. London: CIPD.

TUC (2005) *Challenging Times*, London: TUC.

UK Commission for Employment and Skills (2009) *Ambition 2020: World Class Skills and Jobs for the UK.* London: UKCES and www.ukces.org.uk.

Wadsworth, J. (2003) 'The labour market performance of ethnic minorities in the recovery' in R. Dickens, P. Gregg and J. Wadsworth *The Labour Market under New Labour: The State of Working Britain.* Basingstoke: Palgrave, pp. 116–33.

Wilson, R., Homenikou, K. and Dickerson, A. (2006) *Working Futures: New Projections of Occupational Attainment by Sector and Region 2002–2012.* Volume 1: *National Report.* Coventry: Institute for Employment Research, University of Warwick.

Wood, S. (1999) 'Family-friendly management; testing the various perspectives', *National Institute Economic Review*, 168 (1): 99–116.

For multiple-choice questions, exercises and annotated weblinks related to this topic, visit www.pearsoned.co.uk/mymanagementlab.

Chapter 5

Talent management

Julie Beardwell

Objectives

- To define talent and talent management.
- To consider ways of identifying talent to meet organisational requirements.
- To identify the contribution of recruitment and selection to talent management.
- To investigate initiatives designed to enhance employee retention and engagement.
- To identify the contribution of employee development activities and succession planning to talent management.

Introduction

A preoccupation with talent has grown considerably in recent years. At the time of writing this chapter, the TV programme 'Britain's got Talent' is just starting its third series in the UK, having already spawned spin-off talent programmes in over 20 countries. This interest in searching for and identifying talented individuals is not restricted to the media. Talent has become an important issue in the workplace and talent management is fast gaining top priority for organisations across many countries (Bhatnagar, 2008). A recent global study of HR leaders shows that talent management is *the* most critical issue facing HR departments worldwide. The study, conducted by the Boston Consulting Group and the World Federation of Personnel Management Associations (WFPMA), involved an on-line survey of nearly 5000 executives and over 200 in-depth interviews and the results reveal that talent management was at the top, or near the top, of executive agendas in almost all of the 83 countries surveyed (Phillips, 2008). Similar results were returned from a UK survey undertaken by the Chartered Institute of Personnel and Development (CIPD, 2006a) which shows that the vast majority of respondents (87 per cent) consider that talent management is a business priority for their organisations and almost all (94 per cent) agree that talent management can have a positive impact on an organisation's bottom line.

But what do we mean by talent management? The term was first coined by the McKinsey Group in the late 1990s when they warned that a 'War for Talent' was imminent due to a predicted shortage of people with leadership potential. Since then, the use of the term has become increasingly common but its meaning still remains somewhat elusive and open to a number of different interpretations. This chapter will therefore begin by defining the terms 'talent' and 'talent management' and will then explore the activities associated with talent management and their effectiveness.

Defining talent management

The Compact Oxford English Dictionary defines talent as 'natural aptitude or skill' and 'people possessing such aptitude and skill', so that talent can equally apply to specific skills and the people who possess these skills. In the workplace context, talent can be defined as 'those individuals who can make a difference to organisational performance, either through their immediate contribution or in the longer term by demonstrating the highest level of potential' (CIPD, 2006b: 3). Thus, talent can be used to refer to everyone, on the assumption that people all possess individual skills and abilities, or talent can be used in a more exclusive sense to only refer to those who can demonstrate high performance or potential. The initial McKinsey report focused on the recruitment and retention of 'A-players', the top performing 20 per cent of managers (Guthridge and Lawson, 2008) arguing that 'managerial talent is not the only type of talent that companies need to be successful, but it is a critical one' (Michaels et al., 2001). More recently, consideration of talent has broadened to reflect recognition of the valuable contribution of 'B-players', i.e. the capable, steady performers that make up the majority of the workforce (Guthridge and Lawson, 2008). A third interpretation suggests that the focus of any talent management activity should be on the key positions that are important to fill in any organization (CIPD, 2006a). Thus talent can be used in an exclusive sense, to refer to a select group of high-flyers; in an inclusive sense, to refer to all employees; or in a hybrid sense to refer to key workers or roles that are critical to organisational success but which may be at different levels of the organisation. A recent survey (Scott, 2007) found that fewer than half of respondents said that the word talent refers to all their staff; a fifth defined talent as those individuals with leadership potential at the mid-level of the organisation and 10 per cent reported that it only applied to senior leadership.

Talent management' can also be subject to broad or narrow interpretations. For example, compare these two definitions:

> Talent management is the use of an integrated set of activities to ensure that the organisation attracts, retains, motivates and develops the talented people it needs now and in the future. The aim is to secure the flow of talent, bearing in mind that talent is a major corporate resource.
> (Armstrong, 2006: 390)
>
> Talent management is the systematic attraction, retention, identification, development, engagement, retention and deployment of those individuals with high potential who are of particular value to the organisation.
> (CIPD, 2006b: 3)

Whilst there are subtle differences in the activities included under the talent management umbrella, both definitions include the need to attract, retain, motivate and develop individuals as core talent management activities. However, Armstrong's definition seems to imply a broad interpretation of talent whilst the CIPD's definition adopts a more exclusive focus, equating talent with high potential.

STOP and think

What impact might different interpretations of talent management have on organisational practice?

There is nothing particularly new about the individual activities that comprise talent management but what is different is that these activities are 'bundled together to produce a more coherent whole that can be a vehicle for the development and implementation of coordinated and mutually supporting approaches that help the organisation to get and keep the talented people that it needs' (Armstrong, 2006: 389). This implies that talent management is a strategic process closely aligned with business strategy so the chapter will now explore how far this is true in practice.

Talent management strategy

At its heart, talent management is simply a matter of anticipating the need for human capital and then setting out a plan to meet it (Cappelli, 2008). The now, rather clichéd, assertion that people are the prime source of competitive advantage can be seen to emphasise the need to adopt a strategic approach to talent management to ensure that the organisation has the 'right people in the right place at the right time' to fulfil its strategic goals. As Armstrong (2006) suggests:

> the aim of this strategy is… to ensure that a firm achieves competitive advantage by employing more capable people than its rivals. These people will have a wider and deeper range of skills and behave in ways that maximise their contribution. The organisation attracts such people by being 'the employer of choice'. It retains them by providing better opportunities and rewards than others, and by developing a positive psychological contract which increases commitment and creates mutual trust. Furthermore the organisation deploys its people in ways that maximise the added value they supply.
> (Armstrong, 2006: 371)

The existence of a strategy can support the development of plans which are concerned with attracting sufficient high-quality external applicants and making effective use of the internal labour market through the retention, deployment and engagement of the existing workforce. These plans are based on predictions of demand, i.e. the numbers of people and skills that the organisation will need in the future, and supply, i.e. the availability of those people and skills already in the organisation and in the external labour market. Reconciliation of these plans can help organisations to determine the optimum balance between external and internal recruitment. Some organisations prefer to fill as many vacancies as possible with existing employees in order to motivate and develop people and retain critical skills. This approach requires considerable investment in training and development and the support of a performance management system with an emphasis on identifying potential and on securing commitment from employees. However, the internal recruitment pool is likely to be relatively small so the potential downside of internal recruitment is that the organisation does not necessarily get the best person for the job.

An emphasis on external recruitment might help to bring new ideas and new styles of working into the organisation, but this approach may also reflect a short-term focus and an unwillingness or inability to invest in the existing workforce. Within the UK the unwillingness may arise from a fear of engaging in costly development activities with staff, which could make them attractive to competitors. Alternatively, management may believe that future changes can pose problems in offering long-term employability or promotion and do not wish to raise unrealistic expectations amongst the workforce. At the same time, rapidly changing organisational requirements may mean there is no time to develop the required competencies in-house. The CIPD *Recruitment, Retention and Labour Turnover Survey* (2008a) found that employers were more than twice as likely to respond to recruitment difficulties by 'appointing people who have the potential to grow but don't currently have all that is required' than to 'provide additional training to allow internal staff to fill posts' (CIPD, 2008a: 7). In practice, many organisations adopt a combination of both external and internal recruitment depending on the positions to be filled and the skills available in-house. Cappelli (2008) argues that adopting a supply chain perspective and applying operations principles to talent management can help to address the risks associated with estimating demand and the uncertainty of supply, see Table 5.1.

In many cases the decision to recruit externally or appoint internally may be a pragmatic response to specific circumstances as empirical evidence suggests that few organisations are adopting a strategic approach to talent management. Although, as discussed above, the majority of organisations agree that talent management is essential to business, survey data (CIPD, 2006a) show that 60 per cent of organisations have no formal talent management strategy and 80 per cent have no formal definition of talent management. The picture remains similar even if we narrow the focus to the exclusive definition of talent: a US study (Cohn *et al.*, 2005) found that although Chief Executives believe that having the right talent is crucial to the organisation's success, less than half had succession plans for vice presidents and above. Whether talent management is a strategic or reactive process, its key components are concerned with attracting, identifying, developing retaining and engaging talented individuals. The chapter will explore each of these activities in turn, considering the different methods that organisations may use and the effectiveness of different approaches.

Attracting talent

Attracting talent is primarily aimed at the external labour market and involves the use of recruitment and selection techniques to identify the skills required and then attract and choose the most suitable people to meet an organisation's human resource requirements. Recruitment

Table 5.1 Operations principles applied to talent management

Principle 1: Make and buy to manage talent	A deep bench of talent is expensive, so companies should undershoot their estimates of what will be needed and plan to hire from outside to make up for any shortfall. Some positions may be easier to fill from outside than others, so firms should be thoughtful about where they put their resources in development. Talent management is an investment, not an entitlement.
Principle 2: Adapt to the uncertainty in talent demand	Uncertainty in demand is a given, and smart companies find ways to adapt to it. One approach is to break up development programmes into shorter units. Rather than put management trainees through 3-year functional programmes, for instance, bring employees from all the functions together for an 18-month course that teaches general management skills, and then send them back to their functions to specialise. Another option is to create an organisation-wide talent pool that can be allocated among business units as the need arises.
Principle 3: Improve the return on investment in developing employees	One way to improve the payoff is to get employees to share in the costs of development. That might mean asking them to take on additional stretch assignments on a volunteer basis. Another approach is to maintain relationships with former employees in the hope that they may return someday, bringing back your investment in their skills.
Principle 4: Preserve the investment by balancing employee–employer interests	Arguably, the main reason good employees leave an organisation is that they find better opportunities elsewhere. This makes talent management a perishable commodity. The key to preserving your investment in development efforts as long as possible is to balance the interests of employees and employer by having them share in advancement decisions.

and selection are integrated activities, and where recruitment stops and selection begins is a moot point (Anderson, 1994). Nevertheless, it is useful to try to differentiate between the two areas: Whitehill (1991) describes the recruitment process as a positive one, 'building a roster of potentially qualified applicants', as opposed to the 'negative' process of selection. So a useful definition of recruitment is 'searching for and obtaining potential job candidates in sufficient numbers and quality so that the organisation can select the most appropriate people to fill its job needs' (Dowling and Schuler, 1990: 51). Selection is concerned more with 'predicting which candidates will make the most appropriate contribution to the organisation – now and in the future' (Hackett, 1991: 49), but also affects the ability to attract suitable candidates as applicants may be put off if the selection practices appears unfair or unprofessional.

External recruitment

The recruitment process involves identifying the skills and abilities required and then choosing the most effective recruitment methods to attract a pool of suitable candidates. When organisations choose to recruit externally rather than internally, the search takes place in local, regional, national and/or international labour markets, depending on numbers, skills, competences and experiences required, the potential financial costs involved and the perceived benefits involved to the organisation concerned. External recruitment often poses problems for organisations: 86 per cent of respondents to the CIPD *Recruitment, Retention and Labour Turnover Survey* (CIPD, 2008a) report recruitment difficulties. The main causes cited are:

- a lack of necessary specialist skills (70 per cent)
- applicants want more pay than can be offered (44 per cent)
- insufficient experience (42 per cent)
- no applicants (27 per cent).

The survey shows that the most commonly used initiatives in response to recruitment difficulties are:

- appointing people who have potential to grow but do not currently have all that is required (75 per cent)
- taking account of a broader range of qualities, such as personal skills instead of qualifications (48 per cent)
- redefining the job (43 per cent)
- increasing starting salaries or the benefits package (41 per cent)
- bounty payments to staff for introducing candidates (37 per cent).

However, when asked about initiatives that have the most positive impact, the results suggest that internal recruitment is more effective. The initiative rated positive by three-quarters of respondents is 'providing additional training to allow internal staff to fill posts' (CIPD, 2008a: 7) although only 33 per cent of respondents use this method. Other initiatives that rated highly in terms of a positive impact include:

- providing a realistic job preview – rated highly by 72 per cent and used by 22 per cent of respondents
- using employer brand as a recruitment tool – rated highly by 71 per cent and used by 33 per cent of respondents
- offering flexible working – rated highly by 70 per cent and used by 36 per cent of respondents.

Why might the initiatives rated as having the most positive impact not be the most popular responses to recruitment difficulties?

Realistic job previews

The purpose of a realistic job preview is to help prospective candidates to better understand the demands of the job and the culture and values of the organization. This can improve the 'fit' between employee and organisational expectations and reduce the numbers of employees who leave the organisation after a short time. Realistic job previews can be presented in a variety of ways, including on-line questionnaires, videos and workplace visits. The information included in a realistic job preview should be important to most recruits, not widely known outside the organisation and the reason why newcomers leave (Wanous, 2009). A study of the effectiveness of a realistic job preview for expatriate assignments in a multinational company (Caliguiri and Phillips, 2003) found that candidates who received a realistic job preview reported higher perceived ability to make an informed decision about whether to accept a global assignment than those who did not. The CIPD *Recruitment, Retention and Labour Turnover Survey* (2008a) shows that fewer than a quarter of employers currently use realistic job previews, suggesting that more organisations could benefit from doing so.

Employer branding

Over recent years, skills shortages and a tough economic environment have meant that employers are obliged to compete more fiercely with one another to attract and keep effective

---

Box 5.1 **Realistic job previews in the NHS**

NHS Jobs has launched a realistic job preview tool to help prospective applicants understand more about what it is like to work as a healthcare assistant in the NHS and decide whether they are likely to be suited to the role before they complete a job application.

The tool lists a range of scenarios commonly encountered by healthcare assistants and asks the candidate to select how they may react to the situation. After each scenario, the candidate receives some feedback on their response. Based on the feedback received, candidates can then make more informed decisions about whether to apply for the post or continue searching for roles that may be more suited to their skills and working preferences.

The realistic job preview tool was developed by NHS employers in partnership with SHL. The design of the tool involved:

- Job analysis with job holders, line managers and key stakeholders
- Expert design of questions and feedback
- Review by internal stakeholders.

Sample scenario: You have recently started working as a Healthcare Assistant. You are working with a patient who has just vomited. The patient, their bed and the floor are all covered in it. The smell is horrible. You are expected to clean up the mess. How do you feel about this?

A I don't mind cleaning up, it's all part of the job.

B I don't mind as I am new, and new people usually have to do the most unpleasant jobs.

C I feel that this is an unpleasant job, but know that it needs to be done.

Questions

1 What are the advantages and disadvantages of online realistic job previews for organisations and prospective employees?

2 What other methods could be used to give candidates an accurate picture of job requirements?

Source: www.nhsemployers.org/RecruitmentAndRetention/nhs-jobs accessed 24 April 2009.

staff, whilst often being constrained in the extent to which they can do this by paying higher salaries (CIPD, 2007a). One response to these difficulties has been to promote a strong employer brand that markets what the organisation has to offer potential and existing employees. Employer branding adopts similar techniques to those developed by marketeers to attract customers and maintain their loyalty but in this case applies them to employees. Employer branding can therefore be defined as:

> A set of attributes and qualities – often intangible – that makes an organisation distinctive, promises a particular kind of employment experience, and appeals to those people who will thrive and perform best in its culture.
>
> (CIPD, 2007b: 3)

All organisations have an employer brand, regardless of whether they have consciously sought to develop one. This brand will be based on the way they are perceived as a 'place to work' by potential recruits, existing employees and leavers (CIPD, 2009a). Developing an employer brand involves creating a compelling employer image and convincing employees and prospective employees of its worth (Suff, 2006a). A strong employer brand should therefore connect an organisation's values, its people management strategy and be intrinsically linked to a company brand (CIPD, 2007b). Employer branding also reflects recruitment and selection as a social process, i.e. recognising that it is not only the organisation that selects the applicant but also the applicant that selects the organisation (Nickson *et al.*, 2008).

Think about an organisation where you have worked or would like to work. How would you describe its brand? How is this brand communicated to potential and existing employees?

In addition to being able to attract high-quality applicants, organisations also have to be able to keep them. A strong employer brand is frequently associated with being an 'employer of choice' and is seen as a key element of winning the 'war for talent':

> In essence, creating a winning environment consists of developing a high-achieving company with values and brand images of which employees can be proud. At the same time, their jobs should permit a high degree of freedom, give them a chance to leave a personal mark and inject a constant flow of adrenalin. Leadership, of course, should be used to enhance, enable and empower, rather than to inhibit, constrain or diminish.
>
> (Williams, 2000: 31)

In the UK, the *Sunday Times* undertakes an annual survey to identify the best companies to work for. The results are based on employee responses to a range of questions covering the following key areas (www.bestcompanies.co.uk):

Leadership – measures how people feel about the head of their organisation, the senior management team and organisational values.

Well-being – measures stress, pressure, the balance between work and home life and the impact of these factors on personal health and performance.

My manager – measures whether people feel supported, trusted and cared for by their immediate manager.

My team – includes encouraging team spirit, feeling part of the organisation, having fun and belonging.

My company – focuses on how much people value their organisation, how proud they are to work there and whether they make a difference.

Personal growth – examines whether people feel challenged by their job, whether their skills are being utilised and their perceived opportunities for advancement.

Fair deal – includes how well employees feel they are treated and how their pay and benefits compare to similar organisations.

Giving something back – explores how much people think their organisation puts back into society and whether they believe this effort is driven by profit motives.

The 2009 winner is Beaverbrooks, a family-run, jewellery retailer with approximately 800 staff over sixty six sites. Almost half of the staff earn less than £15,000 a year and only 52 employees earn more than £35,000. Eighty-six per cent per cent of employees reported that they love to work for the company, suggesting that job satisfaction and company loyalty are based on more than financial rewards. Mark Addlestone, managing director and grandson of one of the three brothers who founded the business in 1919, explains:

> We look after people as if we were a family. We really do listen to our people. Our people become part of a family that has been in love with this business for ninety years. Our passion for jewellery is only matched by our passion for people.   (*Sunday Times*, 8 March 2009: 4)

Whether or not an organization is considered an employer of choice, the process of recruitment involves identifying the types of applicants that the organisation wants in terms of skills, experience and attributes. Traditionally, this approach has been very job-focused, i.e. identifying the specific vacancy to be filled and then identifying the person who can best meet the job requirements. More recently there has been a move towards being more people-focused, i.e. identifying the key attitudes and behaviours that will make a valuable employee and then training to match specific job needs. This chapter now considers the advantages and disadvantages associated with both approaches.

Defining the talent required

The traditional approach to defining the type of people an organisation wants to attract involves writing a comprehensive job description of the job to be filled. This enables the recruiter to know exactly what the purpose, duties and responsibilities of the vacant position will be and its location within the organisation structure. The next step involves drawing up a person specification that is based on the job description, and which identifies the personal characteristics required to perform the job adequately. Characteristics are usually described within a framework consisting of a number of broad headings. Two frequently cited frameworks are the seven-point plan (Rodger, 1952) and the five-fold grading system (Munro Fraser, 1954), illustrated in Table 5.2. Both frameworks are dated now, and some headings can appear to be potentially discriminatory (e.g. physical make-up and circumstances), but nevertheless they continue to form the basis of many person specifications in current use. It is common to differentiate between requirements that are essential to the job and those that are merely desirable.

Whatever exact format is used, the person specification can form the basis of the recruitment advertisement, it can help determine the most effective selection methods and, if applied correctly, can ensure that selection decisions are based on sound, justifiable criteria. However, the compilation of a person specification needs to be handled with care. Predetermined criteria can contribute to effective recruitment and selection only if full consideration has been given to the necessity and fairness of all the requirements. Preconceived or entrenched attitudes, prejudices and assumptions can lead, consciously or unconsciously, to requirements that are less job-related than aimed at meeting the assumed needs of customers, colleagues or the established culture of the organisation. Examples of this might include insistence on qualifications or experience that are not specifically required to undertake the role or sex role stereotyping.

Table 5.2 Person specification frameworks

Rodger (1952)	Munro Fraser (1954)
Physical make-up: health, appearance, bearing and speech	*Impact on others*: physical make-up, appearance, speech and manner
Attainments: education, qualifications, experience	*Acquired qualifications*: education, vocational training, work experience
General intelligence: intellectual capacity	
Special aptitudes: mechanical, manual dexterity, facility in use of words and figures	*Innate abilities*: quickness of comprehension and aptitude for learning
Interests: intellectual, practical, constructional, physically active, social, artistic	*Motivation*: individual goals, consistency and determination in following them up, success rate
Disposition: acceptability, influence over others, steadiness, dependability, self-reliance	*Adjustment*: emotional stability, ability to stand up to stress and ability to get on with people
Circumstances: any special demands of the job, such as ability to work unsocial hours, travel abroad	

Source: ACAS (1983)

The job-based approach to recruitment and selection can be inflexible in a number of ways. For example, the job description may fail to reflect potential changes in the key tasks or the list of duties and responsibilities may be too constraining, especially where teamworking is introduced. This concentration on a specific job and its place in a bureaucratic structure may be detrimental to the development of the skills and aptitudes needed for the long-term benefit of the organisation. In order to accommodate the need for greater flexibility and the desire to encourage working 'beyond contract', some organisations have replaced traditional job descriptions with more generic and concise job profiles, consisting of a list of 'bullet points' or accountability statements.

The recognition that jobs can be subject to frequent change can also reduce the importance of the job description and increase the relative importance of getting the 'right' person. This approach has the potential for greater flexibility as it enables organisations to focus 'more on the qualities of the jobholder and the person's potential suitability for other duties as jobs change' than on the job itself (IRS, 1999). For example, research into call centre recruitment and selection found that a positive attitude was more important in candidates than their ability to use a keyboard (Callaghan and Thompson, 2002).

In a talent management approach, a combination of the job-oriented and person-oriented approaches may be adopted in order to recruit people who can not only fill a specific vacancy but also contribute to the wider business goals of the organisation. One way to achieve this is via the use of competencies. The term has many definitions but most refer to 'the work-related personal attributes, knowledge, experience, skills and values that a person draws on to perform their work well' (Roberts, 1997: 6). Competencies can represent the language of performance in an organisation, articulating the expected outcomes of individuals' efforts and the manner in which these activities are carried out (CIPD, 2008b). Competency-based recruitment and selection involves the identification of a set of competencies that are seen as important across the organisation, such as planning and organising, managing relationships, gathering and analysing information and decision making. Each competency can then be divided into a number of different levels, and these can be matched to the requirements of a particular job.

Feltham (in Boam and Sparrow 1992) argues that a competency-based approach can contribute to the effectiveness of recruitment and selection in three main ways:

- the process of competency analysis helps an organisation to identify what it needs from its human resources and to specify the part that selection and recruitment can play;
- the implementation of competency-based recruitment and selection systems results in a number of direct practical benefits; and
- where systems are linked to competencies, aspects of fairness, effectiveness and validity become amenable to evaluation. These competence frameworks can be used for more than just recruitment and selection.

However, competency frameworks can be difficult to apply in practice and therefore may not achieve the goals of the organisation. The main reasons for this are that managers do not see the benefit of the competency framework and are not trained adequately in its use; there are not clear links to what the business is aiming to achieve; and many frameworks are a mix of different concepts which makes them unwieldy (Whiddett and Hollyforde, 2007).

What a competency-based approach may discover is that recruitment is not always the answer. There is usually a variety of strategies for achieving a particular competency mix and no 'right' solutions. For example, if specialist skills are scarce, an organisation may choose to replace the skills with new technology, train existing staff, or hire specialist consultants when needed in preference to employment of permanent staff (Feltham, 1992). Where recruitment and selection is deemed appropriate, a competency-based approach achieves a visible set of agreed standards which can form the basis of systematic, fair and consistent decision making.

Recruitment methods

The choice of methods and media used to attract candidates can have a significant influence on whether the right kinds of applicants are encouraged to apply and to persist with their application (Iles and Salaman, 1995). Organisations have a wide variety of methods to choose from, including the use of:

- informal personal contacts, such as word of mouth and speculative applications;
- formal personal contacts, such as employee referral schemes, careers fairs and open days;
- notice boards, accessible by current staff and/or the general public;
- advertising, including local and national press, specialist publications, radio and TV;
- the Internet; and
- external assistance, including job centres, careers service, employment agencies and 'head-hunters'.

The relative popularity of these different methods is shown in Table 5.3.

Decisions about the most appropriate method (or methods, as many organisations will use more than one) are likely to be influenced by the level of the vacancy and its importance within the organisation. Other factors to be taken into account when choosing the most

Table 5.3 Percentage of organisations using particular recruitment methods

Recruitment agencies	78	Links with schools/colleges/universities	36
Own corporate website	75	Search consultants	33
Local newspaper advertisements	74	Secondments	31
Specialist journals/trade press	62	Commercial job boards	25
Employee referral scheme	47	Apprentices	21
Speculative applications/word of mouth	47	Physical posters/billboards/vehicles	10
Jobcentre Plus	45	Radio or TV advertisements	6
National newspaper advertisements	42	Others	7

Number of employers in survey = 778

Source: from *Recruitment, Retention and Labour Turnover*, Survey Report, CIPD (2008) p. 10, with the permission of the publisher, the Chartered Institute of Personnel and Development, London (www.cipd.co.uk).

appropriate method include the resources available within the organisation (in terms of people and finance), the perceived target groups, and the organisation's stance on internal versus external recruitment. Human resource management literature emphasises the need to have well-developed internal labour market arrangements for promotion, training and career development, which would suggest that many openings can and should be filled internally (Beaumont, 1993). However, a number of organisations, particularly those in the public sector, have policies that require the majority of posts to be advertised externally. Findings from the 2004 *Workplace Employment Relations Survey* show that, although the majority of workplaces treat external and internal applicants equally, one-fifth give preference to internal candidates and one in ten prefer to recruit externally (Kersley *et al.*, 2006).

E-recruitment

Over recent years there has been a significant increase in use of technology to recruit candidates. On-line recruitment enables organisations to reduce the time and cost of recruitment and reach more potential applicants. Organisations can use on-line recruitment in a number of ways (CIPD, 2009b):

- to advertise vacancies on a corporate website, job sites or social networking sites;
- to deal with applications, e.g. email enquiries, emailed applications forms or CVs, online application forms;
- to enhance employer brand; and
- to create a personal relationship with the talent pool, e.g. through the use of recruitment blogs.

The impact of technology on the recruitment process can vary depending on whether online methods are used to supplement or replace more traditional approaches. For example, corporate and external websites can be used to advertise vacancies in addition to press adverts, while the handling of enquiries and applications via e-mail can lead to a duplication of activity (electronic as well as paper-based systems) rather than a replacement of one system with another.

STOP and think

What are the key advantages and disadvantages of using the Internet for recruitment?

The key advantages of online recruitment (CIPD, 2009b) are that it can:

- speed up the recruitment cycle and streamline administration;
- reduce recruitment costs;
- reach a wide pool of applicants;
- provide the image of an up-to-date organisation and reinforce employer branding;
- provide global coverage 24/7;
- be a cost-effective way to build a talent bank for future vacancies;
- help handle high-volume job applications in a consistent way;
- make internal vacancies known across multiple sites and separate divisions;
- provide more tailored information on the post and the organisation;
- build up a picture of the target audience to support an attraction strategy.

The key disadvantages (CIPD, 2009b) are that online recruitment can:

- limit the applicant audience as the internet is not the first choice for all job seekers;
- cause applications overload or inappropriate applications;
- exclude those who cannot or do not want to search for a new job online;

- give rise to allegations of discrimination, particularly in the use of limited key words to screen CVs;
- make the process impersonal which may be off-putting for some candidates;
- turn off candidates if the website is badly designed or technical difficulties are encountered;
- lose out on candidates particularly if the organisation's website is below the search engine ranking of competitors.

An IRS survey (IRS, 2005a: 48) compares online recruitment with more traditional methods and found that online recruitment is just as able to produce the most suitable candidate, even though the larger number of applicants sometimes means that recruiters are searching 'for a needle in a haystack'. Many respondents also find it easier to administer than traditional recruitment and the majority report that total costs are lower. The use of online recruitment is likely to continue to grow as the take up of broadband increases. A small number of organisations have started to use social networking sites to target potential employees. Social networking can help new recruits learn more about the organisation and its culture but there are employment law risks associated with using social networking sites to vet job candidates, including incorrect processing of data under the Data Protection Act 1998, breaching trust and confidence and claims for unlawful discrimination (Cronly-Dillon, 2007).

Recruitment documentation

The response to applicants should indicate the overall image that the organisation wishes to project. Some organisations prepare a package of documents, which may include the job description, the person specification, information about the organisation, the equal

---

Box 5.2 **Recruitment through social networking at T-Mobile**

T-Mobile International is one of the world's leading companies in mobile communications and the third biggest supplier in the UK. The company employs 5900 people at its head office in Hatfield. Hertfordshire and sites in Scotland, Wales and the North East of England.

T-Mobile seeks graduate recruits each year to join its UK workforce. The company seeks to attract a diverse pool of applicants but candidates need to be technically aware and attracted by the innovative approach and new economy values that T-Mobile represents. It is therefore important that recruitment practices reflect the T-Mobile brand and the company's values.

A facebook site has been created as part of the company's annual graduate recruitment round. Access is by invitation-only and the site is used to provide potential graduate recruits with information on selection procedures and processes, including recruitment criteria and assessment centre timetables. The site also allows potential recruits to communicate with each other. Tailored communications are posted for graduates at every point in the recruitment journey; e.g. press releases are reworded to ensure that graduates know what impact T-Mobile news will have on them. In this way the company ensures that the look, feel and tone of the brand and the messages remain consistent.

This tailored communication helps imbed the values of T-Mobile and creates a dialogue between the company and the graduates. As a result, graduates already feel valued and part of the organisation before even starting their first day. The use of social networking in the recruitment process appeals to the type of graduates that T-Mobile wishes to attract.

Source: from *Recruitment, Retention and Labour Turnover*, Survey Report, CIPD (2008) p. 18, with the permission of the publisher, the Chartered Institute of Personnel and Development, London (www.cipd.co.uk).

Question

1 What are the advantages and disadvantages of using social networking sites in the recruitment of graduates?

2 What factors should other organisations take into account when considering the use of social networking for recruitment?

opportunities policy, the rewards package available and possible future prospects. Some give candidates the opportunity to discuss the position with an organisational representative on an informal basis. This allows the candidate to withdraw from the process with the minimum activity and cost to the organisation. Much relevant information can now be supplied via the Internet: for example, the NHS provides online access to job details that were previously supplied in an information pack sent to all applicants (Suff, 2006b).

The design of application forms can vary considerably, but the traditional approach tends to concentrate on finding out about qualifications and work history, and usually includes a section in which candidates are encouraged to 'sell' their potential contribution to the organisation. A more recent development is the adoption of a competency-based focus, requiring candidates to answer a series of questions in which they describe how they have dealt with specific incidents such as solving a difficult problem, or demonstrating leadership skills. Some organisations, particularly in the retail sector, include a short questionnaire in which applicants are asked to indicate their preferred way of working.

A variant on the traditional application form, 'biodata' (short for biographical data), may also be used. Forms usually consist of a series of multiple-choice questions that are partly factual (e.g. number of brothers and sisters, position in the family) and partly about attitudes, values and preferences (Sadler and Milmer, 1993). The results are then compared against an 'ideal' profile, which has been compiled by identifying the competencies that differentiate between effective and non-effective job performance in existing employees. Biodata questionnaires are costly to develop and need to be designed separately for each job (Taylor, 2008). There are also problems with potential discrimination and intrusion into privacy, depending on the information that is sought. For these reasons, biodata is used by only a small number of employers.

STOP and think

How much time and effort does it take an individual to obtain details about a post and complete an application form that attempts to show how their skills and experiences match the requirements of the job?

Why is it important for an organisation to be aware of the answers to the above question?

Selecting talent

The stages described above constitute recruitment, and are primarily concerned with generating a sufficient pool of quality applicants. The focus now shifts to selection and the next stages concentrate on assessing the suitability of candidates.

Shortlisting

It is extremely unlikely that all job applicants will meet the necessary criteria, and so the initial step in selection is categorising candidates as probable, possible or unsuitable. This should be done by comparing the information provided on the application form or CV with the predetermined selection criteria. The criteria may either be explicit (detailed on the person specification) or implicit (only in the mind of the person doing the shortlisting). However, this latter approach is potentially discriminatory, and would provide no defence if an organisation was challenged on the grounds of unlawful discrimination. Potentially suitable candidates will continue to the next stage of the selection process. CIPD guidelines state that unsuccessful candidates should be informed as soon as possible. In practice, written notification of rejection is increasingly less common, and many application forms warn candidates that if they have not had a response by a set date they can assume they have been unsuccessful.

Other developments chiefly reflect a desire to reduce the time and effort involved in short-listing from large numbers of applicants. One option is to encourage unsuitable candidates to self-select themselves out of the process. The chapter has already discussed the use of realistic job previews that allow candidates to answer online questionnaires and receive feedback on their answers and potential suitability for the post prior to completing a job application. A variant on this is to use 'killer' questions; these are asked at certain stages of an online application process and an incorrect answer will terminate the application at that point (IRS, 2003). Another option is to use a software package that compares CVs with the selection criteria and separates the applications that match the criteria from those that do not. This has the advantage of removing some of the subjectivity inherent in human shortlisting, but does rely on the selection criteria being correctly identified in the first instance. It can also reject good candidates who have not used the right keywords so needs to be handled with caution. A third option is to reduce large numbers of applicants via random selection. Although there is concern that this may operate against equal opportunities, it is also claimed that 'randomised selection may produce a better shortlist than one based on human intervention where the wrong selection criteria are used consistently or where the correct selection criteria are applied inconsistently' (IRS, 1994: 6).

Selection techniques

Various selection techniques are available, and a selection procedure will frequently involve the use of more than one. The most popular techniques are outlined here, and their validity and effectiveness are discussed later in the chapter.

Interviews

Interviewing continues to be the most popular selection method. Torrington *et al.* (2002: 242) describe an interview as 'a controlled conversation with a purpose', but this broad definition encompasses a wide diversity of practice. Differences can include both the number of interviewers and the number of interview stages. The format can be biographical, i.e. following the contents of the application form or it can be based on the key competencies required for the job. Over the years interviews have received a relatively bad press as being overly subjective, prone to interviewer bias, and therefore unreliable predictors of future performance. Such criticisms are levelled particularly at unstructured interviews, and in response to this,

Table 5.4 Popularity of selection methods

	%
Interviews following contents of CV/application form (i.e. biographical)	72
Competency-based interviews	65
Structured interview (panel)	56
Tests for specific skills	48
General ability tests	41
Literacy and/or numeracy tests	40
Telephone interviews	36
Personality/aptitude questionnaires	35
Assessment centres	34
Group exercises (e.g. role-playing)	22
Pre-interview references	16
Online tests	15

N – 777

Source: from *Recruitment, Retention and Labour Turnover*, Survey Report, CIPD (2008) p. 11, with the permission of the publisher, the Chartered Institute of Personnel and Development, London (www.cipd.co.uk).

developments have focused on more formally structuring the interview or supplementing the interview with less subjective selection tools such as psychometric tests and work sampling.

There are different types of structured interview, but they have a number of common features (Anderson and Shackleton, 1993: 72):

- The interaction is standardised as much as possible.
- All candidates are asked the same series of questions.
- Replies are rated by the interviewer on preformatted rating scales.
- Dimensions for rating are derived from critical aspects of on-the-job behaviour.

The two most popular structured interview techniques are behavioural and situational interviews. Both use critical incident job analysis to determine aspects of job behaviour that distinguish between effective and ineffective performance (Anderson and Shackleton, 1993). The difference between them is that in behavioural interviews the questions focus on past behaviour (for example, 'Can you give an example of when you have had to deal with a difficult person? What did you do?'), whereas situational interviews use hypothetical questions ('What would you do if you had to deal with a team member who was uncooperative?').

Activity

Imagine you are responsible for selecting operators to work in a call centre. Prepare a set of behavioural questions suitable for the interview. You are looking for evidence of strong social skills, e.g. good verbal communication, positive attitude, good sense of humour, energy and enthusiasm; and good technical skills, e.g. numeracy and keyboard skills.

Test out these questions on friends and colleagues to assess their effectiveness. What do you see as the key strengths and weaknesses of this approach?

Tests

Tests have been used for selection purposes for over 50 years, but there has been a significant rise in test use over the last decade as the selection process has become more sophisticated and rigorous (CIPD, 2008c). The types of test used for selection are ability and aptitude tests, intelligence tests and personality questionnaires. Ability tests (such as typing tests) are concerned with skills and abilities already acquired by an individual, whereas aptitude tests (such as verbal reasoning tests or numerical aptitude) focus on an individual's potential to undertake specific tasks. Intelligence tests can give an indication of overall mental capacity, and have been used for selection purposes for some considerable time. Personality questionnaires allow quantification of characteristics that are important to job performance and difficult to measure by other methods (Lewis, 1985). The debate about the value of personality tests is ongoing, and centres around lack of agreement on four key issues (Taylor, 2008):

- the extent to which personality is measurable;
- the extent to which personality remains stable over time and across different situations;
- the extent to which certain personality characteristics can be identified as being necessary or desirable for a particular job;
- the extent to which completion of a questionnaire can provide sufficient information about an individual's personality to make meaningful inferences about their suitability for a job.

Tests have the benefit of providing objective measurement of individual characteristics, but they must be chosen with care. Armstrong (2006) lists four characteristics of a good test:

- It is a *sensitive* measuring instrument which discriminates well between subjects.
- It has been *standardised* on a representative and sizeable sample of the population for which it is intended so that any individual's score can be interpreted in relation to others.

- It is *reliable* in the sense that it always measures the same thing. A test aimed at measuring a particular characteristic should measure the same characteristic when applied to different people at the same time, or to the same person at different times.

- It is *valid* in the sense that it measures the characteristic which the test is intended to measure. Thus, an intelligence test should measure intelligence and not simply verbal facility (Armstrong, 2006: 462).

One relatively recent development has been the increased popularity of online testing, particularly in the recruitment of graduates and where employers are faced with high volumes of applicants (CIPD, 2008c). Online testing has the potential to reduce delivery costs, thus making testing more affordable for lower-paid jobs. However, there are also some potential disadvantages, including lack of control of the environment in which the test takes place, problems verifying candidates' identity and the need for candidates (under data protection legislation) to have access to any personal information stored about them (IRS, 2002a).

Assessment centres

An assessment centre is not a place but rather a process that 'consists of a small group of participants who undertake a series of tests and exercises under observation, with a view to the assessment of their skills and competencies, their suitability for particular roles and their potential for development' (Fowler, 1992). There are a number of defining characteristics of an assessment centre:

- A variety of individual and group exercises are used, at least one of which is a work simulation.

- Multiple assessors are used (frequently the ratio is one assessor per two candidates). These assessors should have received training prior to participating in the centre.

- Selection decisions are based on pooled information from assessors and techniques.

- Job analysis is used to identify the behaviours and characteristics to be measured by the assessment centre.

Assessment centres are used by a third of organisations (CIPD, 2008a), usually in the appointment of graduates or management positions. The assessment centre process allows organisations to observe candidate behaviour in a work-related setting. Typical exercises can include presentations, role-plays, group discussions as well as interviews and psychometric testing. Combining group and individual exercises can improve the consistency and objectivity of the selection process. In addition, the use of such a sophisticated technique, if handled

---

Box 5.3 **Online testing at Cadbury Schweppes**

Cadbury Schweppes receives around 4,000 applications each year for just 20 places on its graduate programme. Four years ago, the company moved its recruitment process online and has now gone even further and introduced online verbal and numerical reasoning tests in place of paper-based versions.

The company has always used psychometric assessment as part of its selection process. However, it was taking candidates in the region of 90 minutes to complete the paper-based tests during assessment centres. The company trialled an online test from assessment specialist PSL last year and has now cut this down to a 45-minute test that is conducted prior to the interview stage.

Source: IRS (2005b: 44).

Question

What are the advantages and disadvantages of this approach for the organisation and individual applicants?

Box 5.4 — International graduate recruitment at GKN

GKN is a global manufacturing and technological company. It recruits 20 engineering graduates each year to its 'International leadership development programme' (ILDP) and receives more than 1,000 applications for places on the programme. GKN recruits graduates from the UK, US, Germany, Italy, France and Spain. Assessment centres form a very important part of the selection process. Candidates invited to take part will already have successfully completed an initial interview with a member of the ILDP team and the results will have been considered by a pre-assessment centre board. Assessment centres are held over one and a half days and could take place at one of GKN's corporate sites or at a hotel or conference centre, depending on location. Typically, around 12 candidates attend each assessment centre.

The centre starts in the afternoon of the first day with a presentation about the GKN group and the ILDP programme. This is followed by a written in-tray exercise that lasts for 90 minutes and is based on similar tasks and scenarios to those the candidate would be likely to encounter in the role. The evening provides an opportunity for candidates to interact socially and they are often joined by current GKN employees who themselves joined the company through the ILDP route. The second day consists of two group exercises and a technical interview.

Internal staff act as assessors and observers at the centres and are typically quite senior people drawn from a range of business areas. Many have worked around the world and so are aware of cultural differences and may speak several languages. This can contribute to the fairness and the diversity of a process involving candidates from more than one country.

A competency-based approach is used to assess candidates. Candidates are rated against a competency framework that includes technical, personal and managerial competencies. A matrix profile is produced for each candidate to give the assessment team an overall picture of each individual's performance across all exercises. Feedback is given to both successful and unsuccessful candidates.

Source: IRS (2005c: 47).

Questions

1 What further action might GKN take to ensure that the selection process fully reflects the global nature of the business?

2 What criteria should GKN use to measure the effectiveness of the assessment centres?

well, can help the organisation to display a positive image to potential candidates. The drawbacks primarily relate to the costs and resources required. For this reason, assessment centres are most likely to be used in public sector organisations and by larger private sector employers.

References

These are used to obtain additional information about candidates from third parties such as previous employers, academic tutors, colleagues or acquaintances. The accuracy of the information is variable; Armstrong (2006) suggests that factual information (e.g. nature of previous job, time in employment, reason for leaving, salary, academic achievement) is essential, but opinions about character and suitability are less reliable. He goes on to say that 'personal referees are, of course, entirely useless. All they prove is that the applicant has at least one or two friends' (p. 435).

Almost 90 per cent of organisations take up candidate references mostly or always (CIPD, 2008a). References can be used at different stages in the selection process: many organisations use them only to confirm details of the chosen candidate after the position has been offered, whereas others will request references for shortlisted candidates prior to interview. The format may also vary, with some organisations requesting verbal references by telephone and others requiring written references. In either case, organisations may require referees to answer specific structured questions or provide some general comments on the candidate's performance and suitability. The most popular types of information requested by employers include most recent employment history and absence records.

Other methods

One of the more unconventional and controversial selection tools is graphology, based on the idea that handwriting analysis can reveal personal traits and characteristics. Although it is not widely used in the UK, its effectiveness as a selection tool has been the subject of considerable debate. Having reviewed the available data on graphology, the CIPD concludes that 'the evidence in favour is inconclusive, anecdotal and therefore prone to bias and misinterpretation' (CIPD, 2001b).

Factors influencing choice of selection techniques

What determines the choice of different techniques? One could reasonably assume that a key factor in determining the type of method would be its ability to predict who is suitable and unsuitable for the position. In other words, whatever technique is used, people who do well should be capable of doing the job and people who do badly should not.

Accuracy

'No single technique, regardless of how well it is designed and administered, is capable of producing perfect selection decisions that predict with certainty which individuals will perform well in a particular role' (Marchington and Wilkinson, 2008: 248). Figure 5.1 shows the accuracy of selection methods measured on the correlation coefficient between predicted and actual job performance, with zero for chance prediction and 1.0 for perfect prediction.

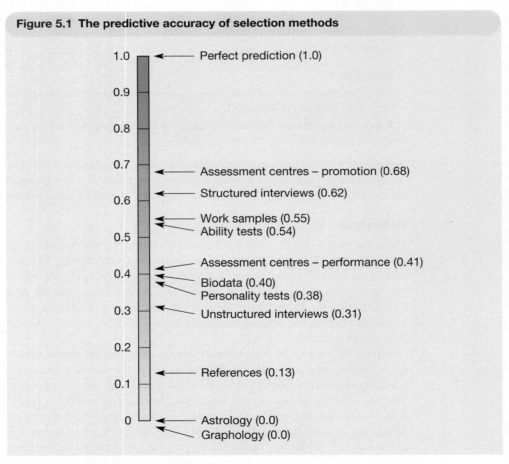

Figure 5.1 The predictive accuracy of selection methods

Source: Adapted from Anderson and Shackleton (1993: 30).

The increased use of more accurate methods such as assessment centres and selection testing can help to improve the effectiveness of the selection process, although findings from a CIPD survey (2005a) show that interviews are still rated as the most effective selection method for all occupational groups. Concerns about accuracy appear to have encouraged employers to adopt more structured interview formats or supplement the interview with other selection methods such as tests or work simulation. However, the extent to which the drive for accuracy is the key influence is open to question. A study into the use of selection tests (Wolf and Jenkins, 2006) suggests that their increased use is driven more by the desire of organisations to protect themselves from legal challenges to selection decisions and by the growing professionalism of HR departments than by considerations of tests' technical qualities and predictive validity. As a result the article concludes that 'further increases in test use are very likely, but . . . there is no reason . . . to expect that these will necessarily increase the effectiveness of the selection process' (p. 208).

Level of vacancy

The level of vacancy can have a significant influence on the choice of selection methods used. Assessment centres, in particular, are more likely to be used for managerial and graduate posts. This may indicate an organisation's willingness to invest more heavily in future managers than in other parts of the workforce, but may also be due to candidate expectations and the organisation's need to attract the highest-quality applicants for key positions.

Cost of selection techniques

There is no doubt that recruitment and selection can be costly activities, and the costs incurred by some selection techniques can make them prohibitive for all but a few 'key' vacancies in an organisation. For example, assessment centres require considerable investment of resources and are particularly demanding in terms of the time commitment required from assessors (IDS, 2002). However, in deciding on the most cost-effective methods, the 'up-front' costs need to be balanced against the costs of wrong decisions, which are estimated to lie anywhere between £5,000 and £50,000 depending on seniority and potential for business errors (CIPD, 2009b). Jaffee and Cohen (cited in Appelbaum et al., 1989: 60) suggest that consideration of costs should include some or all of the following:

- the start-up time required by a replacement for the jobholder;
- the downtime associated with the jobholder changing jobs internally or externally;
- training and/or retraining for the replacement and the jobholder;
- relocation expenses;
- the shortfall in productivity between an effective and ineffective jobholder; and
- the psychological impact on the 'failed' jobholder and the morale of others in the department.

The CIPD Recruitment and Retention Survey (CIPD, 2008a) estimates the average cost of recruitment as £4,667 per employee, rising to £5,800 if the associated costs of labour turnover are included.

Making the selection decision

The aim of the overall recruitment and selection process is to provide enough information to enable recruiters to differentiate between those who can do the job and those who cannot. The prescriptive approach stresses that the final decision should involve measuring each candidate against the selection criteria defined in the person specification and not against each other (Torrington et al., 2002). Searle (2003: 114–16) suggests a number of sources of error and bias in interviewers' decision-making process, including:

- 'similar to me effect', where interviewers enhance the ratings of those who look like themselves, respond in a similar way, or appear to have equivalent experiences;
- 'halo effect', where one aspect of the candidate's qualities (most commonly physical attractiveness) influences all other aspects and so boosts their overall rating;
- 'horns effect', where over-attention to some negative aspect reduces a candidate's overall rating.

The combination of a number of different selection methods and the increased use of more objective methods can enhance the quantity and quality of information about each candidate, although Anderson and Shackleton (1993) warn of the dangers of information overload in selection. Armstrong (2006) points out that the ultimate decision may be judgemental:

> There may be one outstanding candidate, but quite often there are two or three. In these circumstances you have to come to a balanced view of which one is more likely to fit the job and the organisation and have potential for a long-term career, if this is possible.
>
> (Armstrong, 2006: 459).

Retaining talent

Up until now, this chapter has focused on attracting new talent to the organisation. However, that is only part of the equation and talent management is also concerned with the ability to keep high-quality employees and continue to maximise their contribution to the organisation. Labour turnover is inevitable but, where it is high, organisations face a loss of corporate knowledge and a potential threat to their ability to meet business objectives (CIPD, 2008a: 20). Manfred Kets de Vries (cited in Williams, 2000: 28) stated that 'today's high performers are like frogs in a wheelbarrow: they can jump out at any time'. It seems that increasing numbers of organisations recognise this and the retention of key staff is a major component of talent management. Any retention strategy needs to have information on why employees leave the organisation. Investigating labour turnover can include the use of quantitative and qualitative techniques.

Investigating labour turnover – quantitative methods

The most common method of measuring labour turnover is to express leavers as a percentage of the average number of employees. The labour turnover index is usually calculated using the following formula:

$$\frac{\text{Number of leavers in a specified period}}{\text{Average number employed in the same period}} \times 100\%$$

This measure is used most effectively on a comparative basis and frequently provides the basis for external and internal benchmarking. Labour turnover can vary significantly between different sectors and industries; for example, a recent survey into labour turnover (CIPD, 2008a) reports that the average labour turnover rate in the UK is 17.3 per cent but this varies between different industries (e.g. 41 per cent in hotels, catering and leisure and 7.9 per cent in electricity, gas and water) and sectors (e.g. 20.4 per cent in private sector services and 13.5 per cent in public services). There is no single best level of labour turnover, but external comparisons can be useful to benchmark labour turnover against other organisations in the same industry, sector or location. However, even organisations with lower than average turnover rates can experience problems if people have left from critical jobs or from posts that are difficult to fill. Conversely, high turnover is not necessarily problematic and might even prove useful if an organisation is seeking to reduce the size of the workforce. The labour turnover index is a relatively crude measure that provides no data on the characteristics of leavers, their reasons for leaving, their length of service or the jobs they have left. So, while it may indicate that an organisation has a problem, it gives no indication about what the specific problem might be, nor what might be done to address it.

Knowledge about the location of leavers within an organisation can be gained by analysing labour turnover at department or business unit level or by job category. For example, managers generally have lower levels of resignation than other groups of employees (CIPD, 2005). Any areas with turnover levels significantly above or below organisational or job category averages can then be subject to further investigation. Most attention is levelled at the cost and potential disruption associated with high labour turnover, but low levels of labour turnover should not be ignored as they may be equally problematic.

What are the key problems associated with low labour turnover?

Low labour turnover can cause difficulties as a lack of people with new ideas, fresh ways of looking at things and different skills and experiences can cause organisations to become stale and rather complacent. It can also be difficult to create promotion and development opportunities for existing employees. Nevertheless, many organisations are keen for some levels of stability. While the labour turnover index focuses on leavers, the stability index focuses on the percentage of employees who have stayed throughout a particular period, often one year. This therefore allows organisations to assess the extent to which they are able to retain workers. The formula used to calculate stability is:

$$\frac{\text{Number of employees with 1 year's service at a given date}}{\text{Number employed 1 year ago}} \times 100\%$$

Quantitative methods of turnover analysis can be useful for benchmarking the organisation against competitors and for analysing the relative performance of different parts of the organisation. Year on year comparisons can also be used to monitor the effectiveness of any retention initiatives. The major drawback of quantitative methods is that they provide no information on the reasons why people are leaving. So, quantitative analyses can help to highlight problems but they give those responsible for talent management no indication about how these problems might be addressed.

Investigating labour turnover – qualitative methods

Investigations into reasons for turnover are usually undertaken via qualitative means. A variety of approaches are used in UK organisations. The most popular methods are shown in Figure 5.2.

Exit interviews are by far the most commonly used methods of finding out why people leave. The benefits of exit interviews are that they are flexible enough to investigate reasons for leaving, identify factors that could improve the situation in the future and gather information on the terms and conditions offered by other organisations. Generally, exit interviews collect information on the following (IRS, 2002b):

● reasons for leaving;
● conditions under which the exiting employee would have stayed;
● improvements the organisation can make for the future;
● the pay and benefits package in the new organisation.

There can also be a number of problems. The interview may not discover the real reason for leaving, either because the interviewer fails to ask the right questions or probe sufficiently or because some employees may be reluctant to state the real reason in case this affects any

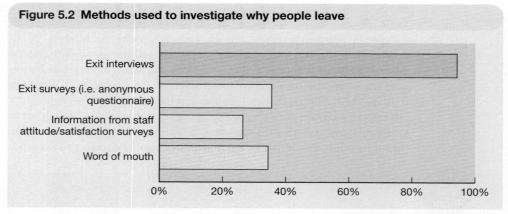

Figure 5.2 Methods used to investigate why people leave

Source: from *Recruitment, Retention and Labour Turnover*, Survey Report, CIPD (2008) p. 25, with the permission of the publisher, the Chartered Institute of Personnel and Development, London (www.cipd.co.uk).

future references or causes problems for colleagues who remain with the organisation, for example in instances of bullying or harassment. Conversely, some employees may choose this meeting to air any general grievances and exaggerate their complaints. Some organisations collect exit information via questionnaires. These can be completed during the exit interview or sent to people once they have left the organisation. They are often a series of tick boxes with some room for qualitative answers. The questionnaire format has the advantage of gathering data in a more systematic way which can make subsequent analysis easier. However, the standardisation of questions may reduce the amount of probing and self-completed questionnaires can suffer from a low response rate.

Reasons for leaving can generally be divided into four main categories:

● voluntary, controllable – people leaving the organisation due to factors within the organisation's control, e.g. dissatisfaction with pay, prospects, colleagues;

● voluntary, uncontrollable – people leaving the organisation due to factors beyond the organisation's control, e.g. relocation, ill-health;

● involuntary – determined by the organisation, e.g. dismissal, redundancy, retirement;

● other/unknown.

Attention is usually concentrated on leavers in the voluntary, controllable category as organisations can potentially take action to address the factors causing concern. However, distinctions between controllable and uncontrollable factors can become blurred. For example, in some instances, advances in technology and greater flexibility can facilitate the adoption of working methods and patterns to accommodate employees' domestic or personal circumstances. The involuntary category is also worthy of attention as high numbers of controlled leavers can be indicative of organisational problems, e.g. a high dismissal rate might be due to poor recruitment or lack of effective performance management.

The CIPD survey (CIPD, 2008a) asked organisations to identify the main reasons for employee turnover and the most commonly cited reasons were as follows:

● change of career (55 per cent);

● promotion outside the organisation (45 per cent);

● level of pay (41 per cent);

● lack of development or career opportunities (33 per cent);

● leaving to have/look after children (27 per cent).

However, whilst exit interviews or exit surveys can provide some information about why people are leaving, they do not necessarily identify the triggers that made someone decide to leave. For example, someone might say that they are leaving to go to a job with better pay, but this does not show what led the person to start looking for another job in the first place. In order to address labour turnover problems and improve retention, organisations need to differentiate between 'push' and 'pull' factors. Once an individual has decided to look for another job they are likely to base their decision on 'pull' factors, i.e. the attractions of the new job or organisation in relation to their existing circumstances. However, the decision to look for another job can be triggered by 'push' factors, that is factors within the organisation (e.g. poor line management, inadequate career opportunities, job insecurity, dissatisfaction with pay or hours of work) that weaken the psychological link between an individual and their employer (IRS, 2001a). A report from the HR benchmark group (cited in IRS, 2002b) listed the top five factors affecting an employee's decision to stay or leave an organisation as:

- the quality of the relationship with their supervisor or manager;
- an ability to balance work and home life;
- the amount of meaningful work and the feeling of making a difference;
- the level of cooperation with co-workers;
- the level of trust in the workplace.

One way to identify potential 'push' factors is to conduct attitude surveys within the organisation. Attitude surveys have an advantage over exit interviews and leaver questionnaires in that they can identify potential problems experienced by existing employees rather than those that have already decided to leave. This means that any response can be proactive rather than reactive. However, it also means that organisations can make problems worse if they do not act on the findings. 'Telling employees that an organisation cares enough to get their opinion and then doing nothing can exacerbate the negative feelings that already existed, or generate feelings that were not present beforehand' (IRS, 2002b: 40).

The final method to investigate labour turnover to be discussed here is risk analysis. This involves identifying two factors: the likelihood that an individual will leave and the consequences of the resignation (Bevan *et al.*, 1997). Statistically, people who are younger, better qualified and who have shorter service, few domestic responsibilities, marketable skills and relatively low morale are most likely to leave (IRS, 2001b). The consequences of any resignations are likely to be determined by their position in the organisation, performance levels and the ease with which they can be replaced. The risk analysis grid (Bevan, 1997) shows how the two factors can be combined (Figure 5.3). This then enables the organisation to target

Figure 5.3 Risk analysis grid

	Likelihood of leaving	
	High	*Low*
Impact on organisation — *High*	Danger zone	Watching brief
Impact on organisation — *Low*	'Thanks for all you've done'	No immediate danger

Source: from Quit stalling, *People Management*, p. 34 (Bevan, S. 1997), with permission from Stephen Bevan.

resources or action at the people it would be most costly to lose. However, the results should be treated with caution as the process does assume an element of predictability whereas research suggests that decisions to leave are often complex and dynamic, and may be unpredictable or precipitated by sudden events (Morrell and Arnold, 2007).

Information from current employees and leavers can help organisations determine the most effective steps to avoid high levels of turnover and improve employee retention. As well as keeping costs under control, retention initiatives can strengthen the internal employer brand and contribute to the organisation's ability to attract new talent (CIPD, 2008a: 26). Findings from the CIPD survey (2008a: 27) show the most common steps taken by organisations to improve retention:

- increased pay (53 per cent);
- increased learning and development opportunities (46 per cent);
- improved selection techniques (46 per cent);
- improved induction process (45 per cent);
- improved line management HR skills (37 per cent);
- improved benefits (36 per cent);
- changes to improve work–life balance (30 per cent);
- improved employee involvement (29 per cent);
- removed age-related policies and practices (26 per cent);
- offered coaching/mentoring/buddy systems (22 per cent).

How might these different practices improve retention? Which might be most effective for the retention of graduates?

Attention to the skills and abilities of managers is perceived by some as a key element of retention: 'put simply, employees leave managers not companies' (Buckingham, 2000: 45). Buckingham (2000) argues that employees are more likely to remain with an organisation if they believe that their manager shows interest and concern for them; if they know what is expected of them; if they are given a role that fits their capabilities; and if they receive regular positive feedback and recognition. However, he also suggests that 'most organisations currently devote far fewer resources to this level of management than they do to high-fliers' (p. 46).

Box 5.5   Improving retention at the Student Loans Company

The Student Loans Company employs approximately 600 staff at its call centre in Glasgow. The city is home to a large proportion of the UK's call centre operations and so the organisation faces stiff competition for staff and the risk of losing them to other companies is always present. As a non-departmental government body, the organisation is constrained in how it can compete with other companies, some of whom may be able to offer higher salaries and perks.

Staff retention is particularly important for the Student Loans Company because operator roles are complex and require in-depth knowledge. There is also a long training period and the annual cycle of student loans means that it takes a year for a new employee to experience the different demands and issues associated with the job. As a result of the lengthy training and the time it takes for employees to be fully productive, the organisation estimates the cost of labour turnover as almost £5,000 per person.

The Student Loans Company has introduced a competency-based approach to recruitment and selection, which enables the organisation to assess whether or not applicants can demonstrate competency in the necessary core qualities and thus helps to recruit the right people for the job. The complexity and knowledge requirements of the role mean that call centre operators enjoy more variation than in many call centres. However, the front-line nature of the work requires a certain amount of resilience.

The organisation is very supportive of new starters: induction begins with a formal two-week classroom-based programme before new employees join their teams in the call centre. This is followed by feedback meetings at the end of the first and second months of employment and a formal review at the end of the three-month probationary period. In addition, ongoing on-the-job training is provided by coaches and team leaders.

These improvements in recruitment and training have helped to reduce staff turnover from 40 per cent to 20 per cent.

Source: Based on IRS (2006).

Questions

1 What steps would you recommend to improve retention even further?

2 How might your recommendations be best implemented?

3 How would you monitor the effectiveness of action taken?

Engaging talent

Retention initiatives can help organisations to keep the skills, knowledge and experience required to fulfil long-term goals as well as reduce the costs and disruption associated with high labour turnover and frequent recruitment. However, in order to maximise employee contribution it is important that employees not only stay, but are actively engaged at work. Over the last few years increasing attention has been paid to the concept of employee engagement. The meaning of the term is still somewhat ambiguous, but definitions derived from academic and practitioner literature have a number of elements in common (Macey and Schneider, 2008: 4) in that employee engagement is seen as desirable; has an organisational purpose; and has both attitudinal and behavioural components. So for, example, the CIPD defines engagement as:

> a combination of commitment to the organisation and its values plus a willingness to help out colleagues (organisational citizenship). It goes beyond job satisfaction and is not simply motivation. Engagement is something the employee has to offer: it cannot be 'required' as part of the employment contract. (CIPD, 2009c)

The term 'employee engagement' has now become fairly widespread, but there is still relatively little academic research and much of the work on the subject has been undertaken by survey houses and consultancies (Robinson *et al.*, 2004). As a result, there is more description and prescription than critical analysis on the benefits of engagement to individuals and organisations. Engagement is closely linked to job satisfaction, so individuals are seen to benefit from having a job that they see as interesting and worthwhile, whilst organisations are seen to gain performance benefits from having employees who will give of their best and 'go the extra mile' (CIPD, 2009c).

Attitudinally, engagement is frequently associated with organisational commitment. However, a key distinction between the two concepts is that the attitudinal experience of commitment occurs apart from, or as a consequence of day-to-day work activity whereas engagement is developed and sustained through work and particularly the interaction with managers and co-workers (Jones and Harter, 2005). So, engaged employees are likely to display high levels of commitment, but not all committed employees are actively engaged. The extent to which engagement and commitment are aligned is dependent on the nature of commitment. Meyer and Allen (1991) identify three different types of commitment: normative commitment, continuance commitment and affective commitment. Normative or moral commitment occurs where an individual feels that they *ought* to be committed to the organisation, regardless of whether or not they actually believe in the organisation's values (Nickson *et al.*, 2008). Continuance commitment is where an individual chooses to remain with an organisation as long as they consider that the benefits of doing so outweigh the costs of leaving. With affective commitment, individuals feel an emotional attachment to the organisation. This type of commitment is most directly associated with engagement and is the form of commitment most likely to be measured by employers (Silverman, 2004). Individuals displaying affective commitment are more likely to go the extra mile for the organisation and so affective commitment is also closely associated with the behavioural component of employee engagement, frequently expressed as organisational citizenship behaviour.

The term organisational citizenship behaviour (OCB) covers a range of different behaviours but what they have in common is that they are discretionary and beyond the immediate demands of the job. As these types of behaviour are not usually part of the reward system, absence of such behaviours is not punishable by the organisation but performance of them should contribute to enhanced organisational performance (Barkworth, 2004). A review of the theoretical and empirical literature (Podsakoff *et al.*, 2000: 516–25) groups OCBs into seven key themes:

- **Helping behaviour** – voluntarily helping others with, or preventing the occurrence of, work related problems.
- **Sportsmanship** – maintaining a positive attitude even when things do not go your way, not being offended when others do not follow your suggestions, being willing to sacrifice personal interest for the good of the group.
- **Organisational loyalty** – promoting the organisation to outsiders, defending it against external threats, remaining committed to it even under adverse circumstances.
- **Organisational compliance** – scrupulous adherence to organisational regulations and procedures even when not being monitored or observed.
- **Individual initiative** – engaging in task-related behaviours at a level beyond generally expected levels, volunteering to take on extra responsibilities and encouraging others to do the same.
- **Civic virtue** – showing willingness to participate in organisational governance, monitoring the environment for threats and opportunities, to look out for the organisation's best interests.
- **Self-development** – engaging in voluntary activities to improve knowledge, skills and abilities.

How might OCBs help to improve organisational performance?

Enhancing employee engagement

Much of the appeal of employee engagement is driven by claims that it drives bottom-line results (Macey and Schneider, 2008). A study into almost 8000 business units in 36 companies (Harter *et al.*, 2002) found positive correlations between employee engagement and customer satisfaction and loyalty, profitability, productivity, employee turnover and safety outcomes. In addition, the study found that, within a given company, business units that scored above the company median for employee engagement realised 0.43 of a standard deviation higher performance in comparison to business units below the median.

However, despite the growing interest in employee engagement, levels remain relatively low. Results from a survey of working life in the UK (Truss *et al.*, 2006) found that only 35 per cent of employees are actively engaged and Gallup have estimated the cost of disengagement to the UK economy at over £37 billion (Fairhurst, 2008). So what can organisations do to improve levels of engagement? Research undertaken by the Institute of Employment Studies (Robinson *et al.*, 2004: 24) indicates that the following areas are of fundamental importance to engagement:

- **Good quality line management** – managers who care about their employees, treat them fairly, encourage them to perform well, take an interest in their career aspirations and provide opportunities for development.
- **Two-way, open communication** – allows employees to voice ideas and suggestions and keep employees informed about the things that are relevant to them.
- **Effective co-operation** – between different departments and between management and trade unions.
- **Focus on employee development** – providing training that employees need for their current role and fair access to development opportunities.
- **Commitment to employee well-being** – taking health and safety seriously, working to minimise accidents, injuries, violence and harassment, and taking effective action should a problem occur.
- **Clear, accessible HR policies and practices** – senior management and line management commitment to appraisals, equal opportunities and family friendliness.
- **Fair pay and benefits** – in terms of comparison inside and outside the organisation.
- **Harmonious working environment** – encouraging employees to respect and help each other.

The importance of effective management, clear and relevant communication, fairness and employee well-being are also identified in work undertaken for the CIPD. Case study research in two public sector organizations and two private sector firms (Gatenby *et al.*, 2009) identifies a number of barriers to employee engagement, including:

- leadership style during organisational change and periods of low performance;
- reactive decision-making that does not pick up problems until it is too late;
- inconsistent management style leading to perceptions of unfairness;
- low perceptions of senior management visibility and quality of downward communication;
- incoherent communication channels – increasing the amount of communication does not necessarily contribute to employee perceptions of communication; clarity and timeliness are more important;
- poor work–life balance due to long hours culture;
- few opportunities for leadership development resulting in limited internal progression.

Employee engagement is a key element of talent management: engaged employees feel positive about their job and identify with the organisation (Robinson *et al.*, 2004) and are less likely to leave (Harter *et al.*, 2002). A focus on employee development is a key element of engagement in order to help individuals improve in their current role and also to progress within the organisation. Employee development is also critical for the creation and maintenance of 'talent pipelines' designed to ensure that the organisation has sufficient people to fill critical roles. The chapter now provides a brief overview of popular methods used to develop talent and the use of succession planning to identify and develop high-potential employees.

Developing talent

Learning and performance improvement have always been an integral part of talent management (Frank and Taylor, 2004). Learning and development is discussed in detail in Chapter 7, so this section is just intended to highlight the key developmental practices associated with talent management. Research undertaken by CIPD (CIPD, 2006a) shows the most popular methods used to develop talent and respondents' assessment of their effectiveness, see Table 5.5.

The results show relatively high levels of satisfaction with the development methods used, although the methods rated most effective are not necessarily the most widely used.

STOP and think

Why might the methods achieving the highest ratings of effectiveness not necessarily be the most popular?

Different methods are suitable for different sets of circumstances so choosing when to employ the right methods, and why, is a critical consideration (Marchington and Wilkinson, 2008). The most appropriate methods are likely to be influenced by the size and nature of the talent pool, the organisation's focus on talent management, i.e. whether it is exclusive, inclusive or hybrid and by organisational context. For example, the survey findings show that small organisations (less than 250 employees) report that coaching is the most popular method, whereas larger organisations report that in-house development programmes are far more popular than other methods (CIPD, 2006a: 5). The survey also shows that, in the majority of UK organisations, talent management activities are aimed at developing high-potential individuals (67 per cent) and growing future managers (62 per cent) and so is frequently associated with succession planning.

Table 5.5 Talent development methods and their effectiveness

Activity	% of respondents	
	Frequently used	Rated as 'effective' 'very effective'
In-house development programmes	63	95
Coaching	43	87
Succession planning	34	62
Mentoring and buddying	32	80
Cross-functional project assignments	26	81
High-potential development schemes	26	78
Graduate development programmes	25	80
Courses at external institutions	25	87
Internal secondments	23	91
Assessment centres	20	81
360-degree feedback	20	81
Job rotation and shadowing	18	82
Development centres	15	76
MBAs	12	83
Action learning sets	11	75
External secondments	6	69

Source: from *Reflections on Talent Management*, Report, CIPD (2006) pp. 5–6, with the permission of the publisher, the Chartered Institute of Personnel and Development, London (www.cipd.co.uk).

Succession planning

Succession planning can be seen as a means of ensuring that an organisation is creating a 'talent pipeline', i.e. developing pool of individuals who are capable of filling key positions in the future. There is nothing new about organisations identifying and grooming people to fill key posts. The traditional approach to succession planning relied on identifying a few key individuals who would be ready to take on senior roles at certain points in time. However, to be effective, this requires a stable environment and long-term career plans. In response to a rapidly changing environment where the future is uncertain, the focus has moved away from identifying an individual to fill a specific job towards developing talent for groups of jobs as well as planning for jobs that do not yet exist. Succession planning can help retain talent by providing career development opportunities for individuals and make sure that the organis-ation has the skills it needs to respond to the rapidly shifting sands that make up today's business environment (Hills, 2009).

Succession planning is often linked to competency frameworks and the key challenge is to identify the competencies that will contribute to future organisational performance rather than those that have been valued in the past. For example, Astra Zeneca identifies seven core leadership competencies: provides clarity about strategic direction, builds relationships, ensures commitment, develops people, focuses on delivery, builds self-awareness and demon-strates personal conviction (IRS, 2002b: 42).

Box 5.6 **Creating a talent pipeline at Coca-Cola**

When soft drinks giant Coca-Cola was forced to look outside the organisation to recruit senior marketing professionals, it decided it was time to establish a programme to identify the talent it had internally. In 2005, the Group HR Director, Steven J. Sainte-Rose, attended the global marketing people development forum, a quarterly meeting of marketing leaders from each of Coca-Cola's eight geographical divisions. At this meeting they identified a par-ticular senior role – division marketing manager – as central to the company's succession planning in each region.

The next step was to create a joint job description so that each region had the same understanding of what the role required. Underlying these discussions was the information that had sparked concern in the first place: a worldwide engagement survey, which showed that marketing staff felt that the company was spending more time buying talent to fill roles as opposed to developing existing talent.

A global senior marketing leadership development centre was created which reflected Coca-Cola's marketing and core leadership competencies. Sainte-Rose and marketing leaders from around the business decided that testing for this critical combination of compe-tencies needed to be based on reality rather than a series of hypothetical situations, so the development centre includes actual events with the names and some information changed to protect confidentiality. The two-day development centre, which is shaped around a 'day in the life of' exercise, also includes dealing with an unexpected issue, coaching, developmen-tal sessions, presenting and feedback based on personality preferences and a 360-degree review. When participants leave the centre they are given feedback that links in to their exist-ing development programmes.

The development centre is now held twice a year and each geographical region nominates participants from their list of potential divisional marketing managers. This means that each event brings eight top people from across the globe into one place and so marketing leaders get to see the high calibre of talent internationally. As a result, there has been an increase in poaching talent from one region to another, but this is seen as a good thing as this movement creates a flow of fresh ideas for the company, benefits individual development and helps recruitment by showing the international opportunities available within the company.

Box 5.6 continued

Of the 31 participants who have taken part in the marketing development centre to date, 22 have been promoted or taken on significantly expanded job responsibilities.

Source: People Management (7 August 2008), p. 24.

Questions

1 What are the main benefits of this type of succession planning for the organisation and individuals?

2 What potential drawbacks also need to be considered?

A key issue in contemporary succession planning is the balance between internal and external labour markets, i.e. whether to grow or buy-in talent. Succession planning can be used as a means to retain and motivate key members of the existing workforce but there is a danger that the organisation can become stale in the absence of 'new blood'. Some senior external appointments are therefore necessary to improve diversity and to bring on board people with different skills and experience, but too many can result in frustration and the loss of some key talent.

A recent study of over 1000 employers in the UK (Parry, 2008) found that the majority of employers believe that internal development brings greater benefits to the organisation than external recruitment. The main benefits are perceived as cost effectiveness, better staff retention and increased employee motivation. However, the same study found that more than half fill their vacancies by external recruitment. A high proportion of organisations also appear to rely on external recruitment rather than succession planning to fill the most senior positions. For example, a study of chief executives in twenty large organisations in the US (Cohn *et al.*, 2005: 65) found that only a quarter have talent pipelines that extend three levels below them.

Concluding comments

Organisations appear to be sending out some mixed messages regarding talent management. On the one hand, survey respondents suggest that talent management is a top priority for the majority of organisations and most HR professionals consider that it can have a positive impact on an organisation's financial performance. On the other hand, most organisations do not have a talent management strategy and there appears to be a tendency to buy-in talent through external recruitment rather than 'grow your own' through employee development activities. For example, three-quarters of the respondents to the CIPD's *Recruitment, Retention and Labour Turnover Survey* (2008a) address recruitment difficulties by appointing people who do not currently have all that is required but are considered to have the potential to grow, whereas only a third provide additional training to enable internal staff to fill posts. The same survey shows that 45 per cent of leavers left their organisation for promotion and 33 per cent left due to lack of development and career opportunities. These results suggest that many organisations could benefit from paying the same attention to the talent within the existing workforce as they do to attracting talent externally. The majority of employers claim that internal recruitment brings greater benefits to the organisation than external recruitment (Parry, 2008) so why does there seem to be this gap between the rhetoric and the reality?

One explanation is that, whilst there have been a number of significant developments in the activities encompassed within the talent management umbrella, e.g. the growing interest in employer branding, employee engagement and the benefits of being an employer of choice, in many cases talent management activities lack the integration necessary to secure the flow of talent that organisations will require in the future (Armstrong, 2006). However, it may be that the difficult current economic circumstances might actually help some organisations to focus more attention on the talent that exists within the current workforce. In a recent survey conducted by CIPD on the effects of the economic downturn on talent management (CIPD, 2009e), over half (55 per cent) of respondents report that they are looking to develop more talent in-house; 45 per cent are focusing on essential development and 35 per cent are placing an increasing focus on employee retention (these figures add up to more than 100 per cent because some organisations are adopting multiple strategies). This does not mean the end of the external labour market: 43 per cent of respondents are still continuing to recruit key talent and some perceive greater opportunities to recruit talent discarded by their competitors. However, it does suggest that a number of organisations appear to be following the principles outlined by Cappelli at the beginning of the chapter. Time will tell whether the practice lives up to expectations.

Summary

- Talent can be used in an exclusive sense to refer to a select group of high-flyers; in an inclusive sense to refer to all employees; or in a hybrid sense to refer to key workers or roles that are critical to success, wherever they are in the organisation. The focus of talent management activities can therefore vary but definitions include the need to attract, retain, motivate and develop individuals.

- Methods used to identify the skills required can be job-based or person-based. The emphasis on identifying people with the 'right' attitudes has led to a growth in competency frameworks but these can be difficult to apply in practice.

- Recruitment activities can contribute to talent management by attracting a pool of suitable candidates. In recent years there has been significant growth in the use of e-recruitment, which can help organisations to reach more candidates and to develop a 'personal' relationship with the talent pool. The purpose of selection methods is to differentiate between suitable and unsuitable candidates and, if handled effectively and professionally, can also convey a strong image of the organisation.

- Employee retention and engagement are also key components of talent management as selecting and developing high quality employees is of limited value if the organisation then loses their skills and expertise. A number of initiatives have been introduced to aid retention but the most popular is to increase pay. Fair pay and benefits are important to employee engagement, but other significant factors are the quality of line management, the effectiveness of communication and a focus on employee development.

- Learning and performance improvement have always been an integral part of talent management. A combination of development activities and succession planning can be used to retain and motivate the workforce and ensure that the organisation has a talent pipeline to meet future requirements.

Case study

FT

Engaging a worried workforce

'Worried about the recession?' asked the nice young woman at the top of the stairs as I came out of the Tube station the other morning. She was offering little orange leaflets to my fellow commuters and she had a lot of takers. What were the leaflets advertising? Unemployment insurance.

But back on my desk in the office lay a pile of material on almost precisely the opposite subject: 'employee engagement'. This stuff had been building up over the past few weeks. It is clearly something that people are thinking about – when they are not worrying about losing their jobs.

Employee engagement is a venerable management theme. It has long been seen as a magic ingredient for corporate success. Build an engaged workforce, the gurus tell us, and all will be well.

But today you have to ask: engage with what (or with whom)? Employers are trying to disengage themselves from significant parts of their workforces. Contracts – both physical and psychological – are being torn up. The engagement is off. Is there anything managers can do to reinstate it?

Gallows humour prevails in many workplaces right now. People worry that they might be, as one newspaper executive used to put it, 'in the fingertip club'. When asked what he meant by that, the executive explained: 'You're hanging on to your job by your fingertips.'

Employers are in a lose–lose situation. Redundancies are necessary but disruptive. Survivors find little reassurance in what they see, perhaps rightly, as a temporary stay of execution. Yet, at the same time, they feel guilty about being spared, and wonder whose turn it will be next. The anxiety of not knowing your fate can be so intense that some, like the business psychologist Binna Kandola, argue that the certainty of getting fired is preferable to the uncertainty of not knowing your fate. 'We risk overengineering and mystifying what is at heart a pretty basic human response: the desire (or lack of it) to do a job well.'

Yes, times are bad. It was clearly the right moment to deal with the backlog of 'engagement' documents on my desk and see if there was anything important to understand about engaging the workforce. I dived in. I found quite a few interesting nuggets of information. And rather more that left me feeling underwhelmed.

The Engage Group, a London-based consultancy, says that a 'new inclusiveness' will help boost levels of employee engagement. This will involve – you may not like this – 'sharing power'.

Leaders will 'drive value by inviting employees who deliver the end result to contribute to day-to-day decisions, strategy and change in a well governed way', the Engage Group says. We need leaders who engage people in the decision-making process. 'The old model of the charismatic, controlling chief executive who leads from the front and barely looks back is not only dated but has a hugely negative impact on employee engagement,' they argue. So far, so plausible.

Colette Hill, chairman of the communications consultancy CHA, says (unsurprisingly) that, in worrying times such as these, clear, honest and timely communication is vital if you want people to remain engaged. You are steering the ship through very choppy waters. 'Will your employees act as your crew or will they become disgruntled passengers?' Ms Hill asks. Good question. We must hope, of course, that mutiny can be avoided.

But most spectacularly of all, Best Companies, the workplace consultancy, is launching an employee engagement 'experiential learning attraction' in April – a high-tech, interactive training programme that takes participants through a series of 'zones' that together are meant to show how employers can build greater engagement in their workforce. It will be a 3D, virtual reality extravaganza.

I think we risk overengineering and mystifying what is at heart a pretty basic human response: the desire (or lack of it) to do a job well. We have created an entire dictionary of terms to describe the same thing. Will colleagues 'go the extra mile'? Will they offer 'discretionary effort'? I heard a new one recently, based on the words of the old wartime song the Hokey-Cokey. Do your employees, asked Bruce Rayner of the consultancy You at Work, put their 'whole self in'?

There are two routes you can go down to win your employees' goodwill. You can splurge cash on them, as Wells Fargo, the rescued US bank, proposed to do, by taking colleagues on 'employee recognition outings' to fancy hotels in Las Vegas. This idea has now been dropped.

Or you could try telling the unvarnished truth. Last week, I met Archie Norman, the British businessman who famously led the hugely successful turnround of the Asda supermarket chain. How did he manage to get the buy-in of an anxious workforce?

'We stated it as it was,' he told me. 'You have to get people to face up to the reality. People will follow you...what they can't stand is unrealistic, deluded leadership. When we said that the situation was very bad, that we were in survival mode, we got three cheers from the front line,' Mr Norman explained. 'They said: "At last, somebody's arrived who realises what it's really like out there."'

Almost bankrupt and out of business in 1991, Asda was bought by Wal-Mart for £6.7bn eight years later.

Source: from Engaging a worried workforce, *Financial Times*, 10 February 2009, p. 51 (Stern, S.).

Questions

1 How do business conditions impact on employee engagement?

2 The example here emphasises the importance of communication. What other initiatives could be considered to retain levels of engagement?

3 What might be the consequences of a loss of employee engagement?

Questions

1 Compare and contrast an exclusive and inclusive approach to talent management. What factors might influence the approach adopted by an organisation?

2 What steps can organisations take to ensure that they have sufficient talent to meet future needs even when the future is uncertain?

3 How might the growth of social networking sites impact on talent management activities?

References and further reading

Those texts marked with an asterisk are recommended for further reading.

ACAS (1983) *Recruitment and Selection*, Advisory Booklet No. 6. London: Advisory, Conciliation & Arbitration Service.

Anderson, A.H. (1994) *Effective Personnel Management: A Skills and Activity-Based Approach*. Oxford: Blackwell Business.

*Anderson, N. and Shackleton, V. (1993) *Successful Selection Interviewing*. Oxford: Blackwell.

Anon (2008) 'Caught by the fizz', *People Management*, 7 August, 24.

Appelbaum, S., Kay, F. and Shapiro, B. (1989) 'The assessment centre is not dead! How to keep it alive and well', *Journal of Management Development*, 8, 5: 51–65.

Armstrong, M. (2006) *A Handbook of Human Resource Management Practice*, 10th edn. London: Kogan Page.

Barkworth, R. (2004) 'Appendix 2: organizational citizenship behaviour: a review of current research', *IES Report 408*. Brighton: IES: 41–51.

Bhatnagar, J. (2008) 'Managing capabilities for talent engagement and pipeline development', *Industrial and Commercial Training*, 40, 1: 19–28.

Beaumont, P. (1993) *Human Resource Management: Key Concepts and Skills*. London: Sage.

Bevan, S. (1997) 'Quit stalling', *People Management*, 20 November.

Bevan, S., Barber, I. and Robinson, D. (1997) *Keeping the Best: A Practical Guide to Retaining Key Employees*. London: Institute for Employment Studies.

Boam, R. and Sparrow, P. (eds) (1992) *Designing and Achieving Competency: A Competency-based Approach to Developing People and Organisations*. Maidenhead: McGraw-Hill.

Buckingham, G. (2000) 'Same indifference', *People Management*, 17 February: 44–46.

Callaghan, G. and Thompson, P. (2002) 'We recruit attitude: the selection and shaping of routine call centre labour', *Journal of Management Studies*, 39, 2: 233–54.

Caliguiri, P. and Phillips, J. (2003) 'An application of self-assessment realistic job previews to expatriate assignments', *International Journal of Human Resource Management*, 14, 7: 1102–16.

Cappelli, P. (2008) 'Talent management for the twenty-first century', *Harvard Business Review*, March: 74–81.

CIPD (2001b) Graphology, *Quick Facts*. London: CIPD.

CIPD (2005) *Recruitment, Retention and Labour Turnover*, Survey Report. London: CIPD.

CIPD (2006a) *Reflections on Talent Management*, Report, April.

CIPD (2006b) *Talent Management: Understanding the Dimensions*, Report, October.

CIPD (2007a) *Employer Branding: The Latest Fad or the Future for HR?* Research Insight Report, July.

CIPD (2007b) *Employer Branding: A No-nonsense Approach*, Report, October.

CIPD (2008a) *Recruitment, Retention and Labour Turnover*, Survey Report,

CIPD (2008b) *Competency and Competency Frameworks*, Factsheet, May.

CIPD (2008c) *Psychological Testing*, Factsheet, August.

CIPD (2009a) *Employer Brand*, Factsheet, January.

CIPD (2009b) *E-recruitment*, Factsheet, February.

CIPD (2009c) *Assessment Centres for Recruitment and Selection*, Factsheet, February.

CIPD (2009d) *Employee engagement*, Factsheet, January.

CIPD (2009e) *The War on Talent: Management Under Threat in Uncertain Times*, survey report, February.

Cohn, J., Rakesh, K. and Reeves, L. (2005) 'Growing talent as if your business depended on it', *Harvard Business Review*, October: 63–70.

Cronly-Dillon, M. (2007) 'Face up to rules on researching recruits on line', *People Management*, 13, 21: 20.

Dowling, P.J. and Schuler, R.S. (1990) *International Dimensions of HRM*. Boston, Mass: PWS-Kent.

Fairhurst, D. (2008) 'Am I "bovvered": Driving a performance culture through to the front line', *Human Resource Management Journal*, 18, 4: 321–26.

Feltham, R. (1992) 'Using competencies in selection and recruitment' in R. Boam and P. Sparrow *Designing and Achieving Competency: A Competency-based Approach to Developing People and Organisations*. Maidenhead: McGraw-Hill.

Fowler, A. (1992) 'How to plan an assessment centre', *PM Plus*, December: 21–23.

Frank, F. and Taylor, C. (2004) 'Talent management: trends that will shape the future HR', *Human Resource Planning*, 27, 1: 33–41.

Gatenby, M. Rees, C., Soane, E. and Truss, C. (2009) *Employee Engagement in Context*, CIPD Research Insight Report, January.

Guthridge, M. and Lawson, E. (2008) 'Divide and survive', *People Management*, 18 September: 40–44.

Hackett, P. (1991) *Personnel: The Department at Work*. London: IPM.

Harter, J., Schmidt, F. and Hayes, T. (2002) 'Business-unit-level relationship between employee satisfaction, employee engagement and business outcomes: a meta analysis', *Journal of Applied Psychology*, 87, 2: 268–79.

Hills, A. (2009) 'Succession planning – or smart talent management', *Industrial and Commercial Training*, 41, 1: 3–8.

IDS (2002) Assessment Centres, *Study 569*, January.

Iles, P. and Salaman, G. (1995) 'Recruitment, selection and assessment' in J. Storey (ed.) *Human Resource Management: A Critical Text*. London: Routledge, pp. 203–33.

IRS (1994) 'Ensuring effective recruitment' and 'Random selection', *Employee Development Bulletin 51*, March, pp. 2–8.

IRS (1999) 'The business of selection: an IRS survey', *Employee Development Bulletin 117*, September, pp. 5–16.

IRS (2001a) 'Benchmarking labour turnover 2001/02 part 1', *IRS Employment Review 741*, 3 December, pp. 31–38.

IRS (2001b) 'Risk analysis and job retention', *IRS Employee Development Bulletin 141*, September, pp. 3–4.

IRS (2002a) 'Psychometrics: the next generation', *IRS Employment Review 744*, 28 January: 36–40.

IRS (2002b) 'The changing face of succession planning', *IRS Employment Review 756*, 22 July: 37–42.

IRS (2003) 'Spinning the recruitment web', *IRS Employment Review 767*, 10 January: pp. 34–40.

IRS (2005a) 'E-recruitment', *IRS Employment Review 822*, 29 April, pp. 42–48.

IRS (2005b) 'Selecting graduates: doing it online, on time' *IRS Employment Review 836*, 2 December: 42–45.

IRS (2005c) 'Centres of attention', *IRS Employment Review 816*, 28 January: 43–47.

IRS (2006) 'Recruitment and retention', *IRS Employment Review 839*, 20 January, pp. 44–48.

Jones, J. and Harter, J. (2005) 'Race effects on the employee engagement-turnover intention relationship', *Journal of Leadership and Organizational Studies*, 11: 78–88.

Kersley, B., Alpin, C., Forth, J., Bryson, A., Bewley, H., Dix, G. and Oxenbridge, S. (2006) *Inside the Workplace: Findings from the 2004 Workplace Employment Relations Survey*. Abingdon: Routledge.

Lewis, C. (1985) *Employee Selection*. London: Hutchinson.

Macey, W. and Schneider, B. (2008) 'The meaning of employee engagement', *Industrial and Organizational Psychology*, 1: 3–30.

Marchington, M. and Wilkinson, A. (2008) *Human Resource Management at Work*, 4th edn. London: CIPD.

Meyer, J. and Allen, N. (1991) 'A three component conceptualization of organizational commitment', *Human Resource Management Review*, 1, 1: 61-89.

Michaels, E., Handfield-Jones, H. and Axelrod, E. (2001) *The War for Talent*. Boston, MA: Harvard Business School Press.

Morrell, K. and Arnold, J. (2007) 'Research article: look after they leap: illustrating the value of retrospective reports in employee turnover', *International Journal of Human Resource Management*, 18, 9: 1683–99.

Munro Fraser, J. (1954) *A Handbook of Employment Interviewing*. London: Macdonald & Evans.

Nickson, D., Warhurst, C., Dutton, E. and Hurrell, S. (2008) 'A job to believe in: recruitment in the Scottish voluntary sector', *Human Resource Management Journal*, 18, 1: 20–35.

Parry, E. (2008) *Nurturing Talent*, Cranfield Research Report, October.

Phillips, L. (2008) 'Talent management is a global preoccupation', *PM Online*, 14 April.

Podsakoff, P., MacKenzie, S., Paine, J. and Bacharach, D. (2000) 'Organizational citizenship behaviors: a critical review of the theoretical and empirical literature and suggestions for future research', *Journal of Management*, 26, 3: 513–65.

Roberts, G. (1997) *Recruitment and Selection: A Competency Approach*. London: IPD.

Robinson, D., Perryman, S. and Hayday, S. (2004) *The Drivers of Employee Engagement*, Report 408. Brighton: IES.

Rodger, A. (1952) *The Seven Point Plan*. London: National Institute of Industrial Psychology.

Sadler, P. and Milmer, K. (1993) *The Talent-intensive Organisation: Optimising your Company's Human Resource Strategies*, special report P659. London: The Economist Intelligence Unit.

Scott, A. (2007) 'Talent should be defined', *PM Online*, 22 June.

*Searle, R. (2003) *Selection and Recruitment: A Critical Text*. Milton Keynes: Open University Press.

Silverman, M. (2004) 'Appendix 1: Defining and creating employee commitment: a review of current research', *IES Report 408*. Brighton: IES.

Suff, R (2006a) 'More than just a pretty face: building an employer brand' *IRS Employment Review 857*, October: 42–45.

Suff, R. (2006b) 'Using employer websites to attract new recruits', *IRS Employment Review*, 845, April: 42–45.

*Taylor, S. (2008) *People Resourcing*, 4th edn. London: CIPD.

Torrington, D., Hall, L. and Taylor, S. (2002) *Human Resource Management*, 5th edn. Harlow: Prentice Hall.

Truss, C., Soane, E. and Edwards, C. (2006) *Working Life: Employee Attitudes and Engagement*, Research report. London: CIPD.

Wanous, J. (2009) 'Realistic job previews' in C. Cooper (ed.) *Blackwell Encyclopedia of Management*. Blackwell Reference Online, accessed at http://www.blackwellreference.com.

Whiddett, S. and Hollyforde, S. (2007) *Competencies*, Toolkit. London: CIPD.

Whitehill, A.M. (1991) *Japanese Management: Tradition and Transition*. London: Routledge.

Williams, M. (2000) 'Transfixed assets', *People Management*, 3 August: 28–33.

Wolf, A. and Jenkins, A. (2006) 'Explaining greater test use for selection: the role of HR professionals in a world of expanding regulation', *Human Resource Management Journal*, 16, 2: 193–213.

 For multiple-choice questions, exercises and annotated weblinks related to this topic, visit **www.pearsoned.co.uk/mymanagementlab**.

Chapter 6

Managing equality and diversity

Mike Noon

Objectives

- Define discrimination and describe its potential impact on different groups.
- Describe and compare the social justice and business case arguments for pursuing policies of equality and diversity.
- Explain the purpose of equality and diversity policies and assess their limitations.
- Explain the concepts of 'sameness' and 'difference', and evaluate their importance in guiding policy within organisations.
- Describe and critically evaluate the concept of institutional discrimination.
- Assess the process of discrimination in an organisation and outline its possible consequences.

Introduction

There is a short story by H.G. Wells called 'The Country of the Blind' in which a mountaineer falls into a hidden valley in South America where all the inhabitants have been blind for 15 generations. His initial reaction is that among such a disadvantaged group of people he can easily establish himself as superior because of his sight; indeed, as the saying expresses it, 'in the country of the blind the one-eyed man is king'. However, he soon learns that the whole of this society is constructed around the norm of blindness, so his sightedness provides no advantages and in many ways disadvantages him from becoming integrated and accepted into the community. For instance, all work is undertaken in the dark at night (when it is cool); there are no lights and the buildings have no windows; his descriptions and explanations based on sight, colour and so forth have no meaning to the inhabitants; and his under-developed alternative senses mean he cannot participate fully in the culture of the community. In the end, in order to fit in, he has to choose either to conform to the dominate norms and have his eyes removed or else leave the community.

The relevance of this story is that it illustrates how being different from the dominant social group can produce disadvantages for an individual irrespective of their qualities and abilities. In this example, the disadvantage suffered by the main character is due to his sight in a society in which sight is undervalued. In the real world, of course, key characteristics such as gender, race/ethnicity, disability, age, religion and sexual orientation are typically the bases for disadvantage. People can suffer rejection, non-acceptance and unfair treatment within a particular setting (especially the workplace) because they differ from the dominant social group across one of more of these characteristics. They can feel excluded and marginalised, or in extreme cases become the victims of abuse and harassment. This disadvantage can manifest itself in many of the key processes within organisations that are explained in other chapters: recruitment and selection, training and development; appraisals; promotion; career development; remuneration; and work organisation.

The purpose of this chapter is to explore how managers can take action to minimise the disadvantages and provide a working environment that supports equality and diversity. To investigate these issues the chapter is divided into six main sections. First, there is an examination of the meaning of discrimination; section two addresses the question of why managers should be concerned about equality and diversity; section three explains the role of equality and diversity policies; section four analyses the different approaches to devising such policies; section five evaluates the concept of institutional discrimination and section six explains the process of discrimination within organisations.

The nature of discrimination

'Discrimination' is the process of judging people according to particular criteria. For example, in the selection process for a teaching post, the appointment panel might discriminate in favour of a candidate who answers their questions clearly and concisely, and discriminate against a candidate who mutters and digresses from the point. However, when most people use the term discrimination they tend to mean *unfair* discrimination. The word is mainly used to denote that the criteria on which the discrimination has occurred are unjust. It is likely that most people would not describe the example above as 'discrimination' because they would not consider the criteria the panel used (clarity and conciseness) as unfair. However, if the criterion the appointment panel used to choose between candidates was gender or race, then most people would call it 'discrimination'.

Where can unfair discrimination occur?

In all of the chapters in this book you will have encountered issues where people (usually managers) are making choices that affect the lives of others in the workplace. It is at these decision points where judgements might be made that are unfairly discriminatory. In other words, there are numerous sites of potential unfair discrimination that you have already encountered. To illustrate, the list below shows some human resource management issues where equal opportunities must be considered unless the organisation wants to run the risk of legal action being taken against it by disgruntled employees (or prospective employees) who have been unfairly treated:

- advertising of posts
- recruitment procedures
- selection techniques
- contractual terms and conditions of employment
- pay
- dress codes
- working hours
- workplace disciplinary procedures
- appraisal interviews
- allowances and bonus payments
- dismissal procedures
- occupational pensions
- employee involvement arrangements
- training opportunities
- workplace culture and norms
- custom and practice arrangements
- promotion procedures

Consider the list of HRM issue above. Select five of these and in each case give an example of how equal opportunity considerations need to be taken into account. For instance, in considering the advertising of posts, managers might want to bear in mind the demographics of the readership of the newspaper or magazine where the advert is placed.

Who are the victims of unfair discrimination?

It is now popular to refer to the various strands of equality or diversity: sex/gender, race/ethnicity, disability, age, sexual orientation and religion/belief. Within the European Union all these strands are covered by legislation designed to protect people against unfair discrimination on these criteria. In other words, if someone considers they have been unfairly treated because of their sex, age, religion and so forth, they have a legal right to challenge their employer and seek compensation. There are other 'strands' that could be added to this list of six, such as size (both height and weight), appearance (tattoos, piercings, norms of attractiveness), health, class (socio-economic group), accent, schooling or university. None of these additional strands is covered directly by legislation, so it is often lawful for an employer to discriminate against someone on any of these grounds, although in some instances there might be some protection for the individual through indirect discrimination law (see below), or human rights legislation.

Activity

'Sizeism' or fair dismissal?

Nine Air India flight attendants were grounded for being too fat, and then dismissed when they were unable to lose weight. (BBC news online – 6 January 2009). An overweight firefighter in Scotland was dismissed. He had been given 3 months to improve his fitness level but failed to do so. (BBC news online – 15 January 2009)

Evaluate the fairness of these two scenarios.

One of the assumptions sometimes made is that discrimination based on sex, race/ethnicity, disability, age, religion/belief or sexual orientation is the same. While it is certainly the case that the effects of discrimination (the disadvantage suffered) are the same or very similar for the victims, the nature of the discrimination often differs and the response and attitudes of the social groups can also differ. It is important to elaborate these statements to show how there might be differences between these social groups and within these social groups. The term 'social group' refers to people who share similar characteristics; for example, it is possible to refer to women as a social group, or people with a disability as a social group. Of course, it would be possible to break these social groups down even further – for instance, white women; or muslim men with a disability; or even white, partially-sighted, lesbian, atheists, under 25. For our purposes at this stage, the social group is defined by one of the key characteristics (sex, age, ethnicity etc), although shortly we shall explore why this is an over simplification. These characteristics differ in terms of whether they can be considered *stable* and *visible*

● *Stable* characteristics are features such as race/ethnicity and sex – with the exception of the tiny minority of people that undergo gender reassignment. In contrast, a person's age differs throughout their life, thus everyone is susceptible to being a victim of ageism, and the type of ageism will change at different life stages.

● *Visible* characteristics are features that a person cannot hide – such as sex, race/ethnicity, some forms of disability, and religions that require certain codes of dress. Others, such as sexual orientation and some religion/beliefs can often be hidden and so although discrimination occurs, some potential victims can dodge it through behaviour that disguises their true identities.

A further consideration concerns the differences between the perpetrators and the victims. Whereas discrimination is perpetrated typically by one group against a different group (men over women, able-bodied over less able, ethnic majority over minority) this is not true of age discrimination. For instance, research by Oswick and Rosenthal (2001) reveals that older workers are frequently discriminated against by managers of similar ages; it is not simply the case that the 'old' are discriminated against by the 'young' (or vice versa). As the authors vividly express it, 'the purveyors of ageism are also in other circumstances its recipients' (Oswick and Rosenthal, 2001: 165). Thus there is 'same-group' discrimination, rather than 'different-group' discrimination.

STOP and think

Staff in a warehouse continuously taunt one of their co-workers for being gay. In fact he is not gay, and all his colleagues know that he is not gay. They consider his behaviour to be effeminate and hence he is a victim of verbal abuse – much of it vitriolic and intentionally hurtful.

Consider the basis for this discrimination and assess whether it is unfair.

Turning to the victims of discrimination it is important to recognise differences within social groups, rather than consider each group to be homogeneous. For instance, Reynolds *et al.* (2001) point out how disability can be a diverse and wide-ranging categorisation. People may move into a state of disability from ill-health, work accidents or ageing, and so while some people are 'born disabled', there is an increasing proportion of employees who 'become disabled'. Moreover, the needs of those with different 'disabilities' are so wide-ranging that it might be suggested there is very little meaning in such a broad category as 'disability'. The same conclusion might be reached for race/ethnicity. Commentators (for example, Modood *et al.* 1997; Pilkington 2001; Nazroo and Karlsen, 2003) argue that research evidence suggests there is so much ethnic diversity that to describe discrimination as being the same across different ethnic groups fails to take into account its differential impact. This means it is essential to recognise the differences between ethnic groups not only in terms of their experiences of discrimination, but also in their varied requirements for redressing the discrimination. Furthermore, it is possible to challenge the assumptions that a person's ethnic group can be clearly defined and remains stable (note the discussion above). First, there are increasingly people with multiple cultural identities who simply do not 'fit' the ethnic categories, and second, exposure to varied cultural influences means that ethnic identity is likely to change across one's lifetime.

It is important to acknowledge differences *between* social groups. If people within the *same* social group sometimes experience discrimination in different ways and in different circumstances, then people from *different* social groups will definitely have different experiences of discrimination. They may all be victims of discrimination but there is little reason to suppose that the experience of being discriminated against because you are a woman is the same as that of being discriminated against on the grounds of sexual orientation; or that the discrimination experienced by disabled employees is the same as that endured by ethnic minority employees.

A final issue to consider is that some people experience multi-discrimination. Academics often use the term 'intersectionality' to describe how the overlap between two or more characteristics (such as ethnicity and gender) creates further, more complex sets of disadvantage which, in turn, require different solutions to redress the inequality that occurs (see for example, Bradley and Healy, 2008). For example, an employee might be discriminated against because she is both a women and Asian, and might therefore not identify with or share the same concerns about, or experiences of, discrimination as her white women colleagues or black male colleagues. Similarly consider the following comment:

> I'm a 54 year old fitter who'd been made redundant, and I've been trying for months to get back into work. I've even done all these special courses at the Job Centre to make myself more employable and to practice interviews and things. The problem is that when an employer sees 54 on the application form the majority of them don't want to know – but of course I can't prove that.
>
> Then, after weeks of trying I got an interview, and I was really excited because it was a chance to get back to doing something useful and earning again. I can remember I was full of enthusiasm and hope when I walked into the interview room, but then I saw the look on the faces of the panel as I walked through the door and they realised I'm black.
>
> Noon, unpublished research notes.

What are the implications for managers?

The picture is of diversity in the nature of discrimination and difference in the needs of the various groups and individuals that experience discrimination. These are important issues because it means:

- Managers should not assume that discrimination means the same thing irrespective of the social group concerned.

- Managers should not assume that a policy solution for one social group (for example women) will be appropriate or welcomed by a different social group (for example disabled people).

- Managers should expect that attitudes will differ within social groups (for example, Asian employees and black employees).

The recognition of this diversity has led some commentators to argue that rather than defining people by their similarities to others, managers should see all employees as individuals with unique skills and needs. This is an issue that will be returned to later in the chapter.

On the basis of the preceding discussion reflect on your own experiences of disadvantage by identifying the ways you might have been disadvantaged personally in your past or current employment (or in any other aspect of your life). You do not necessarily need to restrict the criteria to the six strands noted above: there might be other features which you feel have resulted in negative treatment or disadvantage – for example, your accent, physical appearance (size, height, haircut, piercings, tattoos), class or social background, schooling or lack of belonging to the right social network.

Why be concerned with equality and diversity?

A key question that needs to be addressed is why managers should care whether some people are disadvantaged and suffer unfair treatment. In answering this question, it is useful to distinguish between two different sets of arguments, which can be labelled 'the social justice case' and 'the business case'.

The social justice case

The social justice case is that managers have a moral obligation to treat employees with fairness and dignity. Part of this involves ensuring that decisions are made without resorting to prejudice and stereotypes. You may already be familiar with these concepts, but in case not, the following definitions come from a dictionary of HRM.

Prejudice. Prejudice means holding negative attitudes towards a particular group, and viewing all members of that group in a negative light, irrespective of their individual qualities and attributes. Typically we think of prejudice as being against a particular group based on gender, race/ethnicity, religion, disability, age and sexual orientation. However, prejudice extends much further and is frequently directed at other groups based on features such as accent, height, weight, hair colour, beards, body piercings, tattoos and clothes. It is extremely rare to find a person who is not prejudiced against any group – although most of us are reluctant to admit to our prejudices. (Heery and Noon 2008: 359)

Stereotyping. Stereotyping is the act of judging people according to our assumptions about the group to which they belong. It is based on the belief that people from a specific group share similar traits and behave in a similar manner. Rather than looking at a person's individual qualities, stereotyping leads us to jump to conclusions about what someone is like. This might act against the person concerned (negative stereotype) or in their favour (positive stereotype). For example, the negative stereotype of an accountant is someone who is dull, uninteresting and shy – which, of course, is a slur on all the exciting, adventurous accountants in the world. A positive stereotype is that accountants are intelligent, conscientious and trustworthy – which is an equally inaccurate description of some of the accountants you are likely to encounter. The problem with stereotypes is that they are generalizations (so there are always exceptions) and can be based on ignorance and prejudice (so are often inaccurate). It is vital for managers to resist resorting to stereotyping when managing people; otherwise, they run the risk of treating employees unfairly and making poor-quality decisions that are detrimental to the organization. (Heery and Noon 2008: 443–44)

If decisions are made free from prejudice and stereotyping then there is a lower risk of any particular group being disadvantaged and therefore less chance of an individual feeling that he or she has been discriminated against.

A key concern for the social justice case is whether the focus should be on justice in terms of procedures ('a level playing field') or outcomes ('a fair share of the cake'). For example, in a recruitment process, this would mean either a person is selected according to merit (procedural justice) or they are selected in order to fill a quota (to ensure representativeness of different social groups). Selection on merit alone will not produce representativeness unless such merit is evenly distributed throughout all groups. Of course, such even distribution is highly unlikely due to structural disadvantages and inequalities (schooling, economics support, connections, social stereotypes, and so forth) which limit a person's potential to acquire meritorious characteristics (Noon and Ogbonna, 2001: 4).

As shall be seen later in the chapter, this dilemma leads to different policy suggestions as to how organisations should address the problem of ensuring fairness. Those who favour procedural intervention tend to advocate a 'light touch' in terms of legal regulation and best practice guidelines, while those who focus on outcomes advocate stronger legislation and/or more radical changes to organisational processes and practices.

Limitations of the social justice argument

Critics of the social justice case tend to argue that while the pursuit of fairness is laudable, it is not the prime concern of organisations. The goals of managers in organisations are profit and efficiency, rather than morality. If social justice were to guide their decision making it might have a detrimental effect on the operation of the business and ultimately the bottom line. This line of argument has led to an additional rationale for equality and diversity: the business case.

The business case

The second set of arguments that can be used to justify why managers should be concerned with eliminating disadvantage is based on making a business case. The point is that, aside from any concerns with social justice, fair treatment simply makes good business sense for four main reasons.

1 *It is a better use of human resources.* If managers discriminate on the basis of sex, race/ethnicity, disability, and so on, they run the risk of neglecting or overlooking talented employees. The consequence is that the organisation fails to maximise its full human resource potential and valuable resources are wasted through either under-utilising the competences of existing employees, or losing disgruntled, talented staff to other organisations.

2 *It leads to a wider customer base.* If managers broaden the diversity of the workforce, they might help the organisation to appeal to a greater range of customers. This might be particularly important where face-to-face service delivery is a central part of the business and requires an understanding of the diverse needs of customers.

3 *It creates a wider pool of labour for recruitment.* If managers are more open-minded about the people they could employ for various jobs, they will have a wider pool of talent from which to recruit. This is particularly important when an organisation is attempting to secure scarce resources, such as employees with specific skills or experience.

4 *It leads to a positive company image.* If there is a clear statement of the organisation's commitment to fair treatment, backed by meaningful practices that result in a diverse workforce, managers will be able to project a positive image of the organisation to customers, suppliers and potential employees. In terms of employees, the organisation will be perceived as good to work for because it values ability and talent, and so is more likely to attract and retain high-calibre people.

Limitations of the business case arguments

Although these arguments are quite persuasive, there might be some circumstances when 'good business sense' provides the justification for not acting in the interest of particular groups. For example, Cunningham and James (2001) find that line managers often justify the decision not to employ disabled people on the grounds that the necessary workplace adjustments would eat into their operating budgets. Indeed, equality and diversity initiatives often have a cost associated with them, the recovery of which cannot always be easily measured and might only be realised in the long term. The danger (highlighted by commentators such as Dickens, 1994, 2000; and Webb, 1997) is that such initiatives can only be justified as long as they contribute to profit. For example in Webb's (1997) case study of an international computing systems manufacturer, the corporate philosophy was to encourage employee diversity to bring in new ideas, meet customer needs and achieve success in the global market place. However, at divisional level in the UK, the requests from women for childcare provision and flexible hours were rejected on the basis that these would adversely affect profitability. Furthermore, although managerial opportunities were open to women this was clearly on men's terms, as Webb (1997: 165) explains.

Women graduate engineers are aware that they have to fit in as 'one of the boys' and however supportive the line manager, these are all men: 'I think the difficulty is still being able to sit down, map out your career and possibly say that at a certain time you many well wish to have a family . . . (graduate sales rep.). . . . Even for those willing to adopt male work norms, the corporate orientation to innovation and change mean that the uncertainties experienced by managers are likely to result in the continuing exclusion of women, who continue to be regarded as a riskier bet than men.

This type of problem is common and is expressed vividly by Liff and Wajcman (1996: 89) in the following quote.

Managers' perceptions of job requirements and procedures for assessing merit have been shown to be saturated with gendered assumptions… Feminists can argue (as they have for years) that not all women get pregnant, but it seems unlikely that this will stop managers thinking 'yes, but no men will'.

For an alternative example of how the business case argument can work against a particular group of employees, attempt the following activity.

Activity

The department store

The following quote is from a research interview with a personnel manager of a large departmental store in a city in the UK. She had been asked why there were no ethnic minority employees on the sales floor, even though the city had an ethnic minority population of over 5 per cent. She said:

> Our customers are mainly white, middle-class women. They would be uncomfortable being served by ethnic minorities and they would probably shop elsewhere. That is why we don't have black sales assistants and only have men in certain areas such as the electrical department. We have some Asian employees in the stockroom and doing other vital jobs behind the scenes.

Question

What are the potential problems for the organisation in taking this approach?

A further problem is the issue of measuring the effects of extending opportunities. The underlying assumption is that all initiatives will have a positive effect on business (hence they make good business sense). But this logic requires that they are subsequently measured and evaluated to assess their effects. This poses two difficulties:

1 *Finding a meaningful measure.* In some instances this is feasible. For example, it would be possible to recruit more Asian salespeople in order to increase sales to Asian customers, and in this case appropriate measures would be the number and value of sales and the number of Asian customers (identified by their family name). However, in other instances measurement is very difficult. For example, how would you measure the impact of ethnic-awareness training? Or the effects of flexible working arrangements? In both these cases it might be possible to measure the effects in terms of attitudes or changes in performance, but it would be more difficult to attribute these solely to the specific initiatives.

2 *Measuring in the short term.* In many instances the full effects of an equality or diversity initiative would only be realised in the long term. For many managers within organisations this would be a disincentive to invest in such initiatives, particularly if the performance of their department was measured in the short term. Moreover, it would be an even greater disincentive to invest if the manager's salary or bonus was affected by the short-term performance of their department.

Overall, the business case argument can make an impact – for example in circumstances of skills shortages, needs for particular types of employees, or local labour market conditions – but this is likely to be variable and patchy. As Dickens (1999: 10) states:

> The contingent and variable nature of the business case can be seen in the fact that business case arguments have greater salience for some organisations than others. . . . The appeal of a particular business case argument can also vary over time as labour or product markets change, giving rise to 'fair weather' equality action.

In summary, there are three sets of problems associated with the business case. The first is that there will not always be a business case for equality and diversity initiatives because it depends on the particular circumstances of the organisation. The second is that the business case might be difficult to prove (in quantitative terms), even if it seems persuasive. Third, even if there is a business case that can be proven at a given time, circumstances change (not least economic ones) so the particular business case might cease to have relevance. In contrast the social justice case is far more resilient since it is not affected by the vagaries of the market (see Noon, 2007).

Activity

Older workers at B&Q

The home improvement store, B&Q, have built a reputation for being willing to employ older workers. The engagement and diversity manager commented:

> At B&Q we've long realised the benefits of an age-diverse workforce. Faced with a reduced labour pool in the late 1980s we needed a fresh approach to recruitment. In 1989 we decided to test the true value of an older workforce by fully staffing a store with staff over the age of 50 – the results were compelling. Productivity increased, sales rose and absenteeism fell. Since then we have continued to promote age diversity across the business and today a quarter of our employees are over 50. The people we employ should reflect the people who shop with us. As society changes and grows older we should encourage other firms to reconsider their approach to recruiting older workers.
> *People Management*, 26 March 2009: 13)

Questions

1 What are the business case arguments being put forward?
2 To what extent are these arguments context-specific?

Justice and business sense

As you might have realised, the two sets of arguments are not necessarily mutually exclusive. Indeed, it is feasible and practical for managers to use both sets to justify equality or diversity initiatives in their organisations. By stressing both arguments there is more chance of gaining commitment to equality and diversity from a wider group of people. It does not really matter whether a manager is committed to equality for reasons of justice or because of a compelling business case – it is the fact they are committed that counts. Of course this is not quite as simple in practice, because once commitment has been gained, there is then the question of what policies to put in place.

Before proceeding with a discussion of policy choices, there is an important point to note that underpins much of the following discussion. Efforts to tackle unfair discrimination have not been able to develop through a simple reliance on voluntary commitment to social justice by managers or their rational acceptance of the business case. In most countries legislation has been introduced which sets limits to lawful managerial action and places obligations on managers to act in accordance with principles of fairness. In other words, some equality and diversity practices are the result of a legal obligation, rather than management choice. Bearing this general point in mind, you should also note the following:

- The type and extent of this legislation varies from country to country, so it is important to read about the specific legislation in your own national context.

- Opinion varies as to whether state regulation is necessary or the extent to which it is legitimate or practical to legislate to prevent discrimination and promote equality of opportunity.

- Even when legislation is in place there is no guarantee that this will ensure equality of opportunity. This might be because the legislation is ignored (unlawfully) or because it is ineffective (too weak, too many loopholes, difficult to enforce and so on).

In Europe there has been a move towards a common platform of human rights in relation to equality and fairness. One of the key developments has been the attempt to harmonise the protection against discrimination at work. Within each country there have been changes in national legislation – either amendments to existing laws or the introduction of new laws – in compliance with European Union directives. The basic principle behind the directives is a right to equal treatment irrespective of sex/gender, racial or ethnic origin, religion or belief, disability, age or sexual orientation. This principle is breached by direct and indirect discrimination, harassment or an instruction to discriminate. As well as providing a shared platform of protection, the directives have established common legal definitions of these four terms, such that they now have the same meaning in the different countries (although of course interpretation of the meaning might still vary in different judicial contexts).

1 *Direct discrimination* occurs when a person is treated less favourably than another is, has been or would be treated in a comparable situation on one of the grounds of sex/gender, racial or ethnic origin, religion or belief, disability, age or sexual orientation.

2 *Indirect discrimination* occurs where a provision, criterion or practice that appears to be neutral and non-discriminatory would, in fact, disadvantage someone of a particular sex/gender, racial or ethnic origin, religion or belief, disability, age or sexual orientation, compared to others, unless it is objectively justified by a legitimate aim and it is an appropriate and necessary means of achieving that aim. You should be aware that in the UK, there is no legal protection against indirect discrimination on the ground of disability; instead there is a separate category of protection against 'disability-related discrimination'.

3 *Harassment* is where unwanted conduct related to any of the listed grounds of discrimination takes place with the *purpose or effect* of violating someone's dignity and of creating an intimidating, hostile, degrading, humiliating or offensive environment.

4 *An instruction to discriminate* is where one person obliges another to act in a discriminatory manner against a third party on the grounds noted above.

Box 6.1   Direct and indirect discrimination

A Muslim woman applied for a job as a stylist in a hair salon, but she was rejected because she wore a headscarf and the salon owner argued that all the stylists should display their own hair. The Muslim woman claimed *direct discrimination* on the basis of her religion, but the employment tribunal ruled that there was no evidence of direct discrimination because the owner of the salon would have rejected a non-Muslim who wore a headscarf. She also claimed *indirect discrimination* because the salon owner's rule of no headscarves would affect Muslim women more than non-Muslims since it is a dress code observed by Muslim women only. In this claim she was successful because the salon owner failed to justify the requirement that stylists display their hair at work.

Equality and diversity policies

If the issue of disadvantage is to be addressed in a systemic and consistent way within an organisation, then it is essential to have an overall policy that guides decision-making and action. Increasingly, such policies are being created, although the terminology differs from organisation to organisation: some call them equal opportunity policies, others diversity policies and still others use both terms. The rationale for such policies can be based on a mix of justice and business sense arguments, as was noted above. The Equality and Human Rights Commission in the UK argues that organisations not only need an equality policy, but also an action plan to ensure that the policy is actually implemented (see Box 6.2).

Box 6.2 **Equality policy**

An equality policy states your organisation's attitude to rights and equality in the workplace. By drawing up an official policy you are making a commitment to rights and equality that you can be held accountable for.

An effective policy:

- states your values and how you intend to put them into practice
- shows people you are serious about fairness in the workplace
- helps people understand how they are expected to behave and what they can expect of your organisation
- helps to win new customers, especially from the public sector (who have a statutory duty to promote equality) and other large organisations
- supports your action plan.

Action plan
Your action plan takes the goals of your equality policy and specifies:

- what will be done to achieve these goals
- which senior person is responsible for each action
- deadlines and targets for achieving the goals
- how breaches of the policy will be tackled and rectified
- how success or failure will be measured
- how, and how often, progress will be reviewed.

A good action plan makes sure that your equality policy's goals are translated into real changes and improvements in your working practice.

You should make sure that all your employees are familiar with the policy and action plan, and how these will affect their work. This is particularly important for:

- senior staff who are responsible for carrying out your action plan
- staff involved in recruitment, appraisal and training.

Source: EHRC website (www.equalityhumanrights.com).

The form of equality policies varies between organisations, and Table 6.1 shows how organisations might be categorised according to the extent to which they are actively engaging with equality issues. At one extreme are those organisations that do the absolute minimum – barely meeting the legal requirements; and at the other extreme are those fully committed to an equality/diversity agenda.

Table 6.1 Types of equal opportunity organisation

The *negative* organisation	Has no equal opportunity policy
	Makes no claims of being an equal opportunity employer
	Might not be complying with the law
The *minimalist* organisation	Claims to be an equal opportunity employer
	Has no written equal opportunity policy
	Has no procedure or initiatives, but will react to claims of discrimination as they arise
The *compliant* organisation	Has a written equal opportunity policy
	Has procedures and initiatives in place to comply with some aspects of good practice recommendations
The *proactive* organisation	Has a written policy backed up with procedures and initiatives
	Monitors the outcomes of initiatives to assess their impact
	Promotes equality using full set of good practice guidelines, and might even go beyond these

Source: Based on Healy (1993) and Kirton and Greene (2005).

One particular technique recommended by advocates of equality and diversity as a way of embedding policy is 'discrimination proofing' the organisation. This entails auditing the human resource processes to assess the potential areas where unfair practice might occur. The identification of unfairness might signal the absence of clear policy or procedures, or the failure of existing procedures, often through a managerial lack of knowledge or training. The purpose of such an exercise is to identify the areas of vulnerability and to take action to make improvements where they carry an unacceptable level of risk.

STOP and think

In which category in Table 6.1 would you place your own organisation (or an organisation you are familiar with)?

Two key components: positive action and equality monitoring

To ensure the effectiveness of equal and diversity policies, there needs to be positive action initiatives and effective equality monitoring in place. These two components are a feature of those organisations with a 'proactive' approach to equality and diversity.

Positive action

Positive action (sometimes called affirmative action) means one or more specific initiatives designed to compensate for present or past disadvantages that have been caused by unfair discrimination. Typically, positive action initiatives encourage underrepresented groups to apply for jobs or promotion within the organisation. Positive action might also be concerned with making changes to working arrangements to encourage the retention of employees by making the environment more suited to the needs they have that differ from the majority of employees. Below are a few examples of the type of initiatives that could be described as 'positive action'.

- Launching a recruitment campaign in specific locations known to have a high density of ethnic minorities.
- Advertising in specialist media – such as the gay and lesbian press.

● Introducing a vocational training scheme open only to employees aged 55 or over.

● Adapting the uniform or dress code requirements to take into account religious requirements.

● Introducing flexible working hours to accommodate family needs.

● Providing a sign language interpreter for a training course.

Box 6.3 outlines a progressive positive action initiative that affects all public authorities in the UK. You will encounter other examples of positive action throughout the chapter, and there will be some subtle distinctions made between different types of positive action. For now, however, there is one important distinction that must be made: positive action is *not* the same as 'positive discrimination'. The latter means the preferential treatment of a person because of their sex, ethnicity, age and so forth, and this is unlawful under most discrimination law within Europe. For example, imagine that a school had no black or Asian teachers, so the governing body decided to shortlist only ethnic minority candidates for the next teaching post that became available. This would be positive discrimination and is unlawful because the candidates have been shortlisted due to their ethnicity, not due to their skills, experience, qualifications etc. On the other hand, an entirely lawful, positive action initiative would be for the school to state on the advert that 'applications from ethnic minorities would be particularly welcome'; and this could result in a preponderance of applications from black and Asian candidates with stronger CVs than white applicants and consequently an exclusively ethnic minority shortlist.

There is sometimes a fine line that distinguishes positive action from positive discrimination, but it should be drawn where the initiative goes beyond encouragement and persuasion. In other words, if an initiative means that a person is selected primarily because of their ethnicity, sex, age, religion or sexual orientation then this is likely to be unlawful positive discrimination. In the UK, the disability discrimination legislation allows employers to discriminate in favour of individuals because of their disability (and indeed there is no legal protection for someone to claim that they have been treated unfairly because they are *not* disabled). In France the positive action on disability is more like positive discrimination because there is a requirement for 6 per cent of the workforce to be disabled. There are also legal

---

Box 6.3   **The duty to promote equality**

Through legislation, the UK government has placed a range of duties on public authorities. Rather than simply encouraging public sector organisations to purse equal opportunities, the government now requires specific positive action in relation to the services public bodies provide and their own employment practices.

The key positive action initiative that affects the whole of the public sector in the UK is a 'general duty' in respect of sex/gender, race/ethnicity and disability. This obliges public bodies to:

● promote equality of opportunity and good relations

● eliminate harassment and unlawful discrimination.

In addition there are three main 'specific duties' that apply to a large number of public sector organisations.

1 public authorities must publish equality schemes or policies that describe the processes the organisation has established in order to ensure that it meets the requirement of the general duty.

2 public authorities must collect data to monitor the delivery of their services, and, in many cases, the composition of their workforce, in relation to the general duty.

3 public authorities must conduct *impact assessments* of all new and existing policies in order to identify their effects on equality.

exceptions in relation to the other social group characteristics where an organisation can claim there is a 'genuine occupational requirement' to take into account one of the characteristics: for example, a theatre company auditioning only male actors for the lead in Hamlet; a Chinese restaurant employing only Chinese waiters; or a refuge for battered women employing only female counsellors. The organisation must show that the requirement is really genuine for commercial or operating purposes, so, for example, it might be difficult for a computer games company to require all its game designers to be under the age of 25 or even a Catholic School to require all staff to be practising Catholics.

Positive action initiatives almost always meet with disapproval from those who will not benefit from them. So a recruitment campaign targeted at attracting women into a male-dominated workplace will be questioned by the men who see no need for change. However, if those who are openly hostile or resistant to the action are told what the social and organisational benefits are, they might moderate their position. Important in this respect is the production of the argument and evidence of the need for a change. As was noted above, business case arguments can sometimes be used to convince sceptics that there is a need to address equality of opportunity. In addition, the collection of data (particularly statistical information) is not only important for demonstrating current inequalities, but also vital as a tool for evaluating the effects of any positive action initiatives – and hence assessing their worth. The process of systematic data collection is called equality monitoring.

Activity

Positive discrimination in India

'Around half of all student places at Indian public universities will henceforth be allocated to members of specific lower castes. The groups that will benefit include those traditionally limited to work such as herding cattle, and the Dalit, the group once known as "untouchables".'

(*Times Higher Education*, 24 April 2008)

Question

What are the arguments for and against this positive discrimination initiative?

Equality monitoring

One of the key ways of helping to ensure the effectiveness of policies is through the use of equality monitoring. This is a process of systematically collecting and analysing data on the composition of the workforce, particularly with regard to recruitment and promotion. The rationale behind monitoring is that it is impossible for managers to make an assessment of what action to take (if any) unless they are aware of the current situation. Of course, the supposition behind this is that managers might want to take action – but if this is not the case, then logically managers might not see the value in collecting the data in the first place. Therefore, equality monitoring has both advocates and detractors who marshall different arguments to justify their position; these are summarised in Table 6.2. Once again there is also variation in practice, depending on the national context. For example, in France it is unlawful for data to be collected on the ethnic composition of the workforce because this contravenes French policy on ethnic integration. In contrast, in the UK, public authorities now have a legal requirement to collect ethnic monitoring data on staff in post, applications for employment, promotion and training, and then to analyse these data and act upon any evidence of unfairness or disadvantage.

Table 6.2 The arguments for and against monitoring

The case in favour of equal opportunities monitoring	The case against equal opportunities monitoring
It allows managers to demonstrate what is being done and identify particular problem areas so that they can take action	It stirs up trouble and discontent, and can create problems that would otherwise not arise
It encourages managers to think creatively about positive action initiatives	It puts undue pressure on managers, and might encourage them to lower standards or appoint for the wrong reasons
It removes the need for stronger legislation such as quotas (positive discrimination)	It is positive discrimination 'by the back door'
The data can be kept confidential, just like any other other information	It is an invasion of privacy and open to abuse
It provides useful information to help management decision making	It creates the requirement to collect information that is unnecessary
Organisations conducting their activities in line with the legal requirements have nothing to fear	Organisations with no problems regarding equal opportunities do not need this burdensome bureaucratic mechanism
The costs are modest	It is an unnecessary expenditure
It is good business practice	The business needs to focus on its commercial activities

Activity

Equality initiatives

Read these four examples of equality initiatives.

1 The big four accountancy firms – KPMG, Deloitte, Ernst & Young and PricewaterhouseCoopers – are actively seeking to recruit women and ethnic minorities because they are underrepresented in the organisations, especially at senior levels. Their tactics have been to hold career events specifically targeted at female and ethnic minority undergraduates.

2 The UK Environment Agency has set regional targets for recruiting ethnic minority employees and linked these to the bonuses of all executive managers. Within 18 months the percentage of black and ethnic minority applicants for advertised vacancies had doubled (from 3 to 7 per cent) and the number of ethnic minority candidates offered jobs increased from 2 to 5 per cent.

3 The disability charity Scope introduced a reserved-post policy which means that a certain percentage of jobs are to be filled by people who are registered disabled. The charity have set a target of 20 per cent of posts to be reserved for disabled employees.

4 Time Warner Books recognised how white-dominated their organisation was (along with most other book publishers) and decided to offer a paid internship to someone from an ethnic minority. The plan involved recruiting the person by word-of-mouth rather than formal advertising.

Questions

1 Which of the initiatives can be described as positive action and which are forms of positive discrimination?

2 Assess the pros and cons of each approach.

Criticism of equal and diversity policies

Naturally, there are some criticisms of equal and diversity policies. The first of these is that the policies are sometimes not worth the paper they are written on. Just because an organisation has a policy, it does not mean that the policy is effective. Indeed, research has found that in the majority of cases equality and diversity policies are not backed up with equality practices, so therefore lack substance and have little impact in ensuring that equality of opportunity prevails (Hoque and Noon, 2004). It might further be argued that in some organisations managers want to present the positive image of being aware of equality concerns, but do not wish to introduce procedures or initiatives that might (in their opinion) constrain or limit their decisions about who to appoint, train, promote and so on. However, when policies are backed up with strong equality practices, they can be very effective in ensuring equal treatment (Noon and Hoque, 2001).

A second criticism is that formal policies do not prevent managers from finding ways of evading or distorting the procedures. For example, in their case study of a local government authority in the UK, Liff and Dale (1994) interviewed a black woman on a clerical grade who had been told that she needed to get a professional qualification if she wanted promotion. 'After obtaining the qualification she was turned down again, this time in favour of a white woman without qualification: a decision justified [by the managers] on the grounds of "positive action" (*ibid.*: 187). In another study (Collinson *et al.*, 1990) even the personnel/HR managers, who are supposedly the guardians and promoters of good practice, were colluding with line managers to avoid equal opportunity guidelines.

A third criticism is that even where managers are working within the procedures, there is a huge amount of informal practice and discretion that means unfair treatment can persist. In the quote below, Liff (2003: 434) gives examples from two studies that show how this might occur during selection interviewing.

> Collinson *et al.* (1990) during detailed observation of interviews, found that managers used different (gender-based) criteria to assess whether applicants were able to meet the job requirements. For example, a form of behaviour described as 'showing initiative' and assessed as desirable when demonstrated by a male applicant, in a woman applicant was seen as 'pushy' and undesirable. Similarly Curran (1988: 344) showed that managers often found it hard to separate the assessment of a characteristic such as leadership from the concept of masculinity, or a 'requirement for a pleasant personality and one for a pretty girl with a smile'. What is important about these findings is that they show that for some managers at least, gender becomes part of their assessment of suitability criteria . . . Such findings also reduce the force of the prescriptive advice to excluded groups that they can succeed simply by gaining the necessary skills and demonstrating their ability at job-related tasks.

It will be noted that these three types of criticism are concerned with the ineffectiveness of equality and diversity policies, however, there are other critics who simply reject the whole idea of the needs for such policies. They tend to suggest that policies and positive action initiatives are providing special privileges for particular groups. It is a viewpoint that is common among those of an extreme, right-wing political persuasion and sometimes stems from a belief in the inferiority of some groups over others. Within organisations it can manifest itself in the form of verbal abuse and harassment – in these extreme circumstances the issue is not simply an organisational concern, but might also be a criminal matter. A dramatic example of the way that such extreme views can cause misery for employees is the case of a Ford UK employee.

Mr Parma suffered years of routine abuse by his foreman and his team leader. Once, he opened his sealed pay packet to find the word "Paki" scrawled inside. In another incident, he saw graffiti threatening to throw him to his death.[...]

On one occasion he was ordered into the "punishment cell", a small booth in which oil is sprayed over engines, but he was not allowed to wear protective clothing. He became ill and needed medical attention.

On another occasion Mr Parma had his lunch kicked out of his hands and was told: "We're not having any of that Indian shit in here." He was also warned that he would have his legs broken if he ever named any of his tormentors. The police were called in at one stage, but the Crown Prosecution Service decided to drop charges.

(Source: *The Independent*, 24 September 1999)

Incidents such as this may be extreme but their existence makes the case for all organisations both to have an equality/diversity policy and to ensure that it is enforced through positive action initiatives and audited through monitoring procedures.

Devising equality and diversity policies

It has been noted above that equality and diversity policies are seen as desirable and that recommendations are often made to organisations about how to frame such policies. Ultimately, however, it is up to the decision-makers within organisations to choose the form and content of their policies – although there will be certain legal requirements within which they are expected to operate.

When formulating policy, managers are faced with addressing the key question of how to treat people at work in order to ensure fairness. Or, to express this more specifically: to ensure fairness, should managers ignore the differences between people and treat them the same, or should managers acknowledge differences and treat people differently?

In many respects this is a key question that lies at the heart of any discussion about equality and diversity. The reason people often vehemently disagree about equality initiatives is because they are approaching the issue from very different perspectives. For example, if you believe that, men and women, or different ethnic groups are fundamentally (as human beings) the same, then you are approaching the issues from an alternative perspective to someone who sees people as fundamentally different because of characteristics such as sex and ethnicity.

These contrasting perspectives also lead to different ways of dealing with the issues of ensuring fairness at work. It is therefore important to understand the two perspectives and look at the organisational initiatives that each might lead towards. To help explain this, Figure 6.1 categorises the perspectives and the following sections analyse each category in detail.

The sameness perspective

A word of warning is needed here. This concept of 'sameness' acknowledges genuine differences between people, but suggests that attributes such as intelligence, potential to develop skills, values, emotions and so forth are distributed evenly across different social groups. Consequently, it is argued that any differences between people on these attributes are not determined by their gender, ethnicity, age, sexual orientation and so forth, but arise from their upbringing, experiences, socialisation and other contextual factors. Therefore, the important guiding principle for managers is that people should be treated equally regardless of their sex, ethnic group, age and so forth.

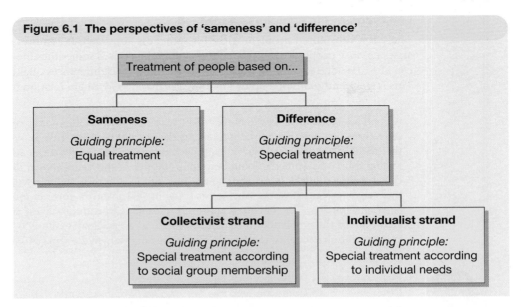

Figure 6.1 The perspectives of 'sameness' and 'difference'

Below are a few examples of the kinds of practices that this perspective might lead organisations to adopt.

- ensure that age is not used as a criterion to decide whether an employee is suitable for training
- ensure the same questions are asked of men and women during selection interviews
- ensure that gender-specific language does not appear in job adverts, job descriptions and other organisation documents
- ensure part-time working opportunities are available to men and women
- ensure any company benefits (for example, pensions, insurance rights, health scheme subsidies) are available to partners of non-married couples and same-sex partners
- ensure the same pay for the same job
- ensure the rules regarding the display of religious symbols apply to all employees regardless of their religion or beliefs.

The guiding policy behind these types of initiative is *equal treatment*. Obviously, any such organisational initiatives are influenced by the legal context in which the organisation is based. There is likely to be legislation that requires organisations to undertake some actions. For instance in the UK the legislation sets some of the parameters in the recruitment process (see Chapter 5) in terms and conditions of employment (Chapter 10) and in reward systems (Chapter 13).

Activity

Equality and diversity initiatives

1. Draw up a list of the initiatives designed to address equality and diversity in your organisation (if you work full-time or part-time) or an organisation with which you are familiar (if you are a full-time student). Your list does not need to be exhaustive, but try to include initiatives additional to the examples already given.

2. Which of the initiatives have arisen because of legal requirements and which have been introduced out of choice (i.e. voluntarily)?

3. Select one or two of those initiatives that have been introduced voluntarily and assess the influences that led to the initiatives being adopted. These could be internal or external pressures.

Limitation of the sameness approach

There is a substantial problem with this sameness approach. It assumes that disadvantage arises because people are not treated the same. While this is sometimes the case, disadvantage can also arise due to treating people the same when their differences ought to be considered. This is eloquently summed up by Liff and Wajcman (1996: 81) in relation to gender:

> All policies based on same/equal treatment require women to deny, or attempt to minimize, differences between themselves and men as the price of equality. This, it is suggested, is neither feasible nor desirable. Such an approach can never adequately take account of problems arising from, say, women's domestic responsibilities or their educational disadvantage. Nor does it take account of those who want to spend time with their children without this costing them advancement at work. Sameness is being judged against a norm of male characteristics and behaviour . . . [The sameness approach to equal opportunities takes] an over-simplistic view both of the problem of inequality (seeing it as a managerial failure to treat like as like) and its solution ('equality' can be achieved by treating women the same as men).

If you were to ask someone who has not studied human resource management how they would ensure equality of opportunity at work, they would very likely reply 'treat everyone the same'. This tends to be the 'common sense' view. If you were then to say to the person you have asked, 'So does this mean that if someone in a wheelchair applied for an office job you would expect them to walk up a flight of stairs to the interview room if there was no lift', you are most likely to get the answer 'no'. This means they are willing to make exceptions – hence they are accepting the principle that to ensure fair treatment sometimes people have to be treated differently.

Now try it out on a real person!

The difference perspective

The 'difference' perspective assumes that key differences exist between people and that these should be taken into account when managers are making decisions. Ignoring such differences can lead to people being disadvantaged.

Again there is a word of warning. There are two branches of this perspective: (1) the collectivist branch; (2) the individualist branch. This conceptual distinction must be made because each branch leads to different conclusions about the appropriate policy to put into place.

The collectivist branch

This approach argues that the differences between people are associated with the social groups to which a person belongs (based on gender, ethnicity disability etc.). For example, as the quote above from Liff and Wajcman (1996) underlines, women's domestic responsibilities are different in general from those of men – most notably in the time spent on childcare – so, to ignore this difference will disadvantage women. In practical terms it means that two candidates (one male, the other female) might be of the same age and both have children, but the female candidate is likely to have less direct work experience because she has had to take time out to have children and might have chosen to take extended maternity leave. By ignoring the differences associated with childbirth and childcare, the woman might appear a weaker candidate; by recognising the differences, the woman's achievements within her more restricted periods of employment can be assessed.

The collectivist branch therefore argues that differences between social groups exist and should be considered in relation to ensuring fairness at work. This means that it might be relevant to introduce practices that are based on recognising differences between social groups, rather than ignoring differences. Below are some examples of the types of initiatives that might arise from taking this collectivist difference perspective.

- single-sex training schemes (developing skills to allow access to a wide range of jobs)
- payment for jobs based on principles of equal value (see also, Chapter 13)
- job advertisements aimed at encouraging applications from under-represented groups
- reassessment of job requirements to open opportunities up to wider range of people
- choice of food in the workplace cafeteria that reflects different cultural needs

The guiding policy behind these types of positive action initiative is *special treatment according to social group membership*. There is a wide range of such initiatives, and the legal context must be taken into account because some principles, such as 'equal value', might be a legal requirement for all organisations, while others are left entirely to the discretion of managers within organisations. The most extreme type of initiative falling into the 'collectivist difference' category is the use of 'quotas' that set a requirement for organisations to recruit and promote a specific percentage of people from disadvantaged groups. For example, in Norway it is a legal requirement for large private companies to have at least 40 per cent of the board made up of women members. The penalty for non-compliance is the disbandment of the organisation. The Norwegian government argued that voluntary measures had failed, so legislation was necessary. Setting quotas in this way constitutes 'positive discrimination' which, as noted above, is unlawful in most European countries. Some of the most vehement critics of quota systems are the supposed beneficiaries of the systems, particular ethnic minorities. These critics argue that it demeans their achievements because it leads others to suspect that they only got the job or promotion to meet the required 'quota', rather than because they were the best candidate. Furthermore, some commentators argue that it is simply wrong in principle to redress the disadvantage suffered by one group of people because of favouritism and privilege with measures that are specifically designed to favour and privilege an alternative group of people. Indeed, this is the perspective of the UK's Chartered Institute of Personnel and Development who use the term 'reverse discrimination' to describe extreme measures such as quota systems.

In spite of the specific problem of quotas, the general policy of special treatment offers a persuasive approach because it recognises that disadvantage is often an intrinsic part of existing organisational structures, practices and culture. Simply adopting a policy of same treatment would not remove this existing disadvantage, instead something more radical has to be done to get to the root of the problem and redress the existing imbalance. A good example of this is the UK disability discrimination legislation which requires organisations to undertake reasonable adjustments to accommodate the needs of employees (and prospective employees) with disabilities. This 'special treatment' is not designed to give an advantage to such employees, but rather to recognise that the existing conditions mean that they are disadvantaged, so changes must me made in order to redress this unfairness.

Activity

A reasonable request?

A disabled worker has been awarded £6,000 damages after the world's most famous stairlift maker refused to install one of its own devices at its headquarters.

The Stannah employee was told a stairlift could not be fitted because 'everyone would want to ride on it and no work would get done', an employment tribunal was told.

The IT designer, who suffers back problems and uses crutches, told the hearing he had problems walking to and from his second floor office.

His boss laughed when he asked if the company could put in a stairlift, he alleged.

The company, based in Andover Hampshire, promptly terminated the employee's contract saying it had concerns about his conduct and training.

(*Metro*, 10 January 2007: 5).

Question

Evaluate this incident from the point of view of (a) the employer and (b) the employee.

The individualist branch

The second branch of the difference perspective focuses on the individual rather than the social group. This approach emphasises the individuality of all employees, pointing out that people have unique strengths and weaknesses, abilities and needs. It suggests that it is not important to focus on characteristics that associate people with a particular group – for instance their sex or whether they have a disability – but rather to concentrate on their individuality.

A label that is often associated with this approach is 'managing diversity'. It is increasingly being used by organisations as a term to describe their approach to ensure fairness and opportunities for all. However, a particular problem is that the term 'managing diversity' can have various meanings. It has become one of those widely used management phrases, so can mean different things in different organisations. At one extreme it is simply a synonym for 'equal opportunities' – used because the latter is seen as old-fashioned or backward looking – and therefore has no distinct or special meaning of its own. At the other extreme managing diversity represents a new approach to dealing with disadvantage at work.

A notable example of the new approach based on recognising individual differences is Kandola and Fullerton (1994). They argue that managing diversity is superior to previous approaches to equality at work for five reasons.

1 It ensures all employees maximise their potential and their contribution to the organisation.
2 It covers a broad range of people; no one is excluded.
3 It focuses on issues of movement within an organisation, the culture of the organisation, and the meeting of business objectives.
4 It becomes the concern of all employees and especially all managers.
5 It does not rely on positive action/affirmative action.

Below are some examples of the types of initiatives that might arise from taking this individualist difference perspective:

- Offer employees a choice of benefits from a 'menu' so they can tailor a package to suit their individual needs
- Devise training and development plans for each employee
- Provide training to ensure managers are aware of and can combat their prejudices based on stereotypes
- Explore and publicise ways that diversity within the organisation improves the organisation – for example, public perceptions, sensitivity to customer needs, wider range of views and ideas
- Re-evaluate the criteria for promotion and development and widen them by recognising a greater range of competences, experiences and career paths.

The guiding policy behind these types of initiative is *special treatment according to individual needs*. Of course, this approach has its critics, and in particular three objections can by raised.

1 *The approach tends to understate the extent to which people share common experiences.* It has a tendency to reject the idea of social groups which is somewhat counter to people's everyday experiences. For example, while several disabled people might differ considerably across a whole range of attributes and attitudes, their common experience of disability (even different forms of disability) might be sufficient to create a feeling of cohesion and solidarity. In particular some people might actively look for social group identity if they feel isolated or vulnerable.

2 *The approach ignores material similarities between social groups.* For example, Kirton and Greene (2005: 131) note that 'women of all ethnic groups typically take on the responsibility for childcare and elder care, and are less able to compete for jobs with men, not withstanding qualitative ethnic differences in how women . . . may "juggle" their multiple roles'.

3 *The approach has a tendency to emphasise the value of diversity in terms of the business sense arguments outlined earlier in the chapter.* As was noted such arguments have their limitations because they focus only on those initiatives that can be shown to contribute to the profitability or other performance indicators of the organisation. In practice this extends opportunities only to a selective number of individuals whose competencies are in short supply or have been identified as being of particular value.

Sameness and difference

As has been shown in the discussion above, disadvantage can arise by treating people the same or by treating people differently, so any policy that emphasises one perspective more than the other runs the risk of leaving some disadvantages unchecked. What is called for is a mixed policy because this recognises that to eliminate disadvantage it is necessary in some circumstances to treat people the same, and in other circumstances to treat people differently. Of course, this is a challenge in itself because in what circumstances do you apply one criterion and not the other? For example, imagine the following situation.

A woman applies for a job as an adviser selling financial products in a company that is dominated by men.

> *Scenario 1:* she has the same qualifications and experience as male applicants, but the all-male selection panel might reject her because they consider that she would not 'fit in' with the competitive, aggressive culture of the organisation.

> *Scenario 2:* she has the same qualifications as male applicants but has taken a career break for childcare purposes. The selection panel reject her because compared with men of the same age she has less work experience.

In the first scenario the panel are rejecting her by using the criterion of difference (recognising gender); in the second by using the criterion of sameness (ignoring gender). But if the panel were to reverse their logic of difference and sameness, it might lead them to different conclusions. In the first scenario, if the panel ignored gender, they would arrive at the conclusion that she was appointable. In the second scenario, if they recognised that, because of her gender, she has had extra domestic commitments so cannot be compared with men of the same age then again they might conclude she is appointable.

This illustrates that managers have a key role in dealing with disadvantage because they determine the criteria and define the circumstances in which sameness and difference are either recognised or ignored.

Institutional discrimination

One of key issues that managers must face is whether their organisation operates in ways that are fundamentally discriminatory. This is sometimes referred to as institutional racism, institutional sexism, institutional homophobia and so on. The term means that rather than discrimination being seen simply as the actions of individuals, it is deep-rooted in the processes and culture of the organisation.

Examples of processes that are sometimes described as evidence of institutional discrimination are:

- Word-of-mouth methods for recruitment
- Dress codes that prevent people practising their religious beliefs
- Promotions based on informal recommendations, rather than open competition
- Informal assessments rather than formal appraisals
- Assumptions about training capabilities
- Assumptions about language difficulties and attitudes.

Often these types of processes are not recognised as being discriminatory and have been in operation for many years. It is only when a company is faced with a legal challenge that such practices are seen to be having a discriminatory impact. Managers should regularly scrutinise organisational procedures, and the use of data collected through equality monitoring can be particularly effective in highlighting areas whether the processes might be disadvantaging particular groups.

Activity

Recruitment at SewCo

SewCo is a family-run business that makes garments. Most of its employees are sewing machine operators (all women) who assemble the garments. It has a stable, core workforce but there is fluctuation in demand for its products, so extra employees are brought in when the order books are full and 'let go' at slack periods. When managers need to recruit extra employees, or when they need to replace someone, they rely on word-of-mouth methods. This means that the women on the shopfloor ask around their friends and family. When likely candidates are identified their names are given to the factory manager. He calls them in for a chat and assesses their suitability. If he approves them he asks the supervisor to check if the candidate has the required sewing skills.

Question

1 Identify the problems with this approach to recruitment process in terms of equality and diversity.

2 Suggest an alternative approach that might address the problems you have identified.

Just as pernicious are workplace cultures that have the effect of excluding people from particular social groups by making them feel unwelcome or uncomfortable. This is a key issue for managers because organisations might have cultures that are long established and deeply embedded. An interesting review of the way organisational cultures can marginalise social groups is provided by Kirton and Greene (2005: 83–109). Most notable among their conclusions are the following points:

- Organisational cultures are infused with gendered meanings, which are often unarticulated and thus rendered invisible. The gendered hierarchy is an example, as are various unwritten codes, rules, customs and habits which guide gendered behaviour and underpin expectations of organisational members.

- Sexual harassment and the use of sexual humour are pervasive and the outcome of work-place gendered social relations, which are powerful mechanisms for the control and subordination of women.

- Stereotypes (based on gender, race, disability, sexual orientation and age) are reinforced through jokes and humour, leading to negative organisational experiences for some people.

- Non-disabled people's lack of contact with disability reinforces their fear and ignorance surrounding the issue.

- Employer ageism is often mediated by other factors, particular gender.

Consider whether your own employing organisation, university or college operates practices that might support institutionalised discrimination.

Problems with institutional discrimination

The first problem is inertia. Even when institutional discrimination has been identified there is no incentive to make changes because those people in positions of influence have benefited (and continue to benefit) from the system. Furthermore, those people most likely to change policies within the organisation (the 'victims' of discrimination) are denied access to decision-making processes.

The second problem is with the concept of institutional discrimination itself. Some critics argue that it can lead to a tendency to blame 'the system', rather than focusing on the people who shape and sustain the system. In some circumstances this can be helpful, because by removing blame from individuals it might be easier to encourage action to address the problem. In other circumstances it can result in nothing being done, because no one is deemed responsible or held accountable.

In defence of the concept of institutional discrimination, it can be argued that it alerts people to the way that the fundamental structures and processes can be detrimental to equality and diversity, and that unless action is taken to address these fundamentals, nothing will improve. This is an important point, because it suggests that in many instances the drive to equality and diversity requires some radical changes, rather than just equality/diversity statements and positive action initiatives.

The need for radical changes: the long agenda

The existence of institutional discrimination leads some commentators to argue that fundamental change is needed if the elimination of disadvantage is to be achieved. Foremost among these commentators is Cockburn (1989, 1991) who has pointed out that many of the positive action initiatives adopted by managers in organisations are concerned only with the short term. Typically these initiatives are fixing current problems, responding to outside pressures, or perhaps seeking to make a pre-emptive move to impress customers and clients. This ignores the possibilities of more radical, long-term initiatives that might fundamentally change the structures and processes that produce disadvantage.

The proposition forwarded by Cockburn is that as well as this short agenda (with its laudable aim of eliminating bias) there is the need to consider the long agenda. This would be a challenging project of organisational transformation, requiring fundamental changes to the processes, roles, norms, attitudes and relationships within organisations. Cockburn (1989: 218) explains:

> As such it brings into view the nature and purpose of institutions and the processes by which the power of some groups over others in institutions is built and renewed. It acknowledges the needs of disadvantaged groups for access to power. [. . .] But it also looks for change in the nature of power, in the control ordinary people of diverse kinds have over institutions, a melting away of the white male monoculture.

The obvious problem for enacting the long agenda is that those in positions of influence within organisations have little incentive to make changes that might challenge their own power and dominance. The long agenda therefore has to be led by activists and advocates. This might be through committed individuals within organisations, but it would also require collective voice and action. It might need a political context that encourages a more active approach by organisations to ensuring equality of opportunity – through, for example, compulsory monitoring or employment quotas for disadvantaged groups.

The process of discrimination in an organisation

The discussion so far has explored many of the complex and sometimes contradictory issues surrounding equality and diversity. It makes sense to bring this together by considering the range of pressures and influences that are brought to bear when managing equality and diversity. Figure 6.2 is a flowchart that maps the relationship between the key components and thereby show how the process of discrimination occurs in organisations (Noon and Blyton, 2007). Each of the components of this flowchart is discussed in this section, and is linked with many of the issues raised in the earlier part of the chapter.

At the centre of the process lie two vital questions: what should be the basis of any specific policy and is the policy fair. Try to envisage this in terms of specific policies, such as promotion, awarding of merit pay, entitlement to career development opportunities, and so on. The first question is of vital concern to managers since their decisions are going to shape a particular policy. However, as the diagram shows, such decisions are not made in isolation but are subject to a range of influences: personal influences (belief, values and political agenda), external pressures and organisational pressures.

1 *Personal influences.* A manager will have their individual beliefs and values that fundamentally guide behaviour and influence decisions. So, for instance, a strong belief in social justice is going to affect the choices that a manager makes, as is a particular prejudice or stereotype about a social group. Combined with this is the individual political agenda of the manager, which might moderate the values and beliefs in some way. For example, a male manager might believe that women do not make good leaders but knows that in order to get promotion he must suppress this view in order not to alienate his boss – who is a woman. This, of course, is the *realpolitik* of normal organisational life and will operate at all levels. This intermixing of beliefs, values and political manoeuvring is going to have an influence on the manager's decisions.

2 *External pressures.* In addition to these personal pressures, the manager is faced with external pressure. This could be legislation requiring (or prohibiting) certain action, public opinion, customer or client pressure, supplier influence, labour supply issues, and so forth. For instance, it was noted in the discussion about the business case how managers might adopt equal and diversity initiatives in order to improve the public image of their organisations, or access a wider customer base.

3 *Internal organisational pressures.* The final set of pressures arise from within the organisation. These pressures might come from other managers, employees (especially through satisfaction surveys and grievances), trade unions, works councils, and so forth. There might also be pressure as a result of data collected within the organisation. For example,

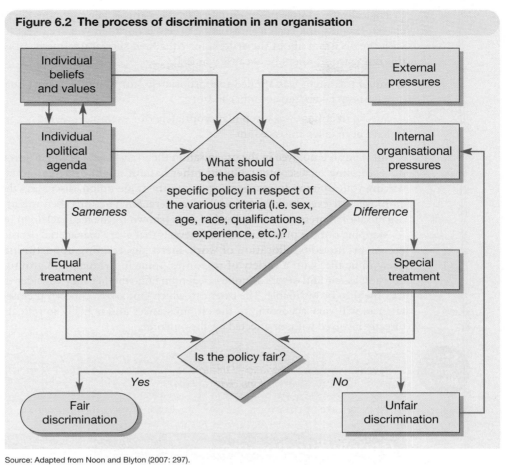

Figure 6.2 The process of discrimination in an organisation

Source: Adapted from Noon and Blyton (2007: 297).

high levels of employee turnover might encourage positive action initiatives that help to retain employees, develop and make better use of skills, and provide a more supportive and encouraging environment. In addition, there are likely to be pressures because of the workplace culture and traditions of the organisation – the sorts of issues that were discussed in the section on institutional discrimination.

These combined pressures establish the context in which decisions are made about specific policies within the organisation. As was noted earlier in the chapter, managers must make choices between people and therefore criteria have to be used to differentiate people. For example, imagine you are running a recruitment process and have received a pile of application forms. In deciding your shortlisting policy (that is, who to call for an interview) you might use the criterion of 'previous experience' as a way of choosing between applicants. Those who meet the minimum requirements are interviewed, those who do not are rejected. At the same time, you might think that formal qualifications are irrelevant for the particular job and so you do not take these into account when shortlisting the applicants. Hence your shortlisting policy is based on 'difference' with regard to experience, and 'sameness' with regard to formal qualifications. There is nothing wrong with this mixture – it reflects the possibility of combining principles of sameness and difference. The consequence of this combination is that someone with a university degree will be treated the same as someone without a degree (equal treatment), but if they have a previous work experience they will get treated more favourably (in this instance, shortlisted) compared with someone without appropriate previous experience.

Logically, this raises the question of whether this is fair (note the next stage in the flow-chart). If you think such a shortlisting policy is fair then you are likely to be in agreement with the decisions about the criteria for equal and special treatment. However, if you think this is unfair this might be because you feel:

- Equal treatment was applied inappropriately (for example, formal qualifications should have been taken into account) and/or

- Special treatment was given inappropriately (for example, previous experience should not have been taken into account).

If you were an employee in the organisation then this feeling of unfairness might simply produce a feeling of discontent. On the other hand it might drive you to take action such as voicing your opinion to managers, going to the trade union, discussing the issue with other employees or even looking for a job elsewhere. Such actions then might produce internal organisational pressures on future decisions (shown by the feedback loop in Figure 6.2).

Mapping out the process in this way reveals that every managerial decision about appointments, promotions, allocation of work, merit pay, training opportunities and so forth, is likely to be met with a variety of responses: some individuals and groups will interpret the decision as fair and others as unfair, depending on whether they consider the equal or special treatment to be justifiable. The extent to which employees concern themselves with issues of fairness will vary according to the circumstances and is likely to reflect whether they are directly involved with, or affected by, the outcome.

Have you directly experienced treatment you considered unfair? If so, what did you do about it? What other options did you have?

Concluding comment

It can be seen from the preceding sections that managing equality and diversity is about making choices between various courses of action. It was also shown that there are competing viewpoints as to why particular approaches should be taken. In many instances there is no clear-cut right or wrong method – rather it is a matter of judgement and conscience. What is important, however, is that any action or policy is backed up by a clear rationale.

Obviously, this chapter cannot conclude by recommending a particular approach because it depends on whether you are persuaded by the rationale behind that approach. The chapter's purpose has been to show you the approaches and provide you with an understanding of the key concepts and dilemmas. These should allow you to make your own choices and equip you to predict and challenge opposing viewpoints. The summary provides you with a review of the key points to reflect upon in forming your opinions.

Summary

- The differences that define disadvantaged groups are far more imprecise than might at first appear. It is important to recognise the diversity between social groups and within the same social group. Such diversity means policies need to be sensitive to different experiences of discrimination and different needs of disadvantaged groups and individuals.

- The reason for managers to intervene in order to prevent discrimination can be based on arguments of social justice or business needs – or both. The social justice case stresses the moral case for fairness, but critics argue that managers should be concerned with profit and efficiency, not morality. The business case stresses ways that equality and diversity are good for business, but critics point to instances where it can make good business sense *not* to act in the interests of equality and diversity.

- Equality and diversity policies vary between organisations; they range from those that are simply empty statements to others which are backed up by effective action programmes. For policies to be effective they need to have positive action initiatives to ensure policy is implemented, and monitoring to assess the effectiveness of the initiatives over time.

- When devising policies to ensure fairness, managers can base them on assumptions of sameness or assumptions of difference. These two perspectives help to explain why there is often a lack of agreement about how to ensure fairness. The sameness perspective emphasises similarities between people and advocates equal treatment. The difference perspective emphasises diversity either between social groups or between individuals. These two branches of the difference perspective are similar in that they both advocate special treatment that takes the differences between people into account, but they differ in their suggestions about the types of initiatives that organisations should adopt.

- The term managing diversity is often used to describe the approach to fairness that emphasises the individual differences between people. In some instances it an alternative approach advocated by commentators who think traditional equal opportunities policies have failed and are fundamentally flawed.

- It is important for managers to recognise that unfair treatment sometimes results from treating people differently when they ought to be treated the same, and sometimes from treating people the same when key differences ought to be recognised. Policies, procedures and attitudes within an organisation should therefore be based on recognising both the similarities and differences between people.

- Institutional discrimination is a term used to describe organisations that have processes and practices that are fundamentally discriminatory – sometimes without managers realising – and are reinforced through existing organisational structures and workplace cultures. Tackling such fundamental problems might require a more radical agenda than that being proposed by many advocates of equality and diversity.

- The process of discrimination can be seen as the combination of personal, external and internal pressures on managers to make choices according to principles of sameness or difference, in their decisions about appointments, promotions, allocation of work, training opportunities, and so forth. Perceptions of unfairness are the result of a mismatch between the expectations of employees and the manager's decisions. Viewed in this way, all decisions are susceptible to claims of unfairness, depending on the perspective of the individuals concerned, the perceived appropriateness of the criterion for the decision and the individual and social acceptability of the type of treatment (special or equal).

Questions

1 'We don't employ people over 50 years old because they find it difficult to learn new skills.' This statement was made by a training manager in a call centre.
   Comment on the statement using the concepts of stereotyping, prejudice, social justice and the business case.

2 What is the purpose of equality and diversity policies? Why do they sometimes fail to live up to expectations?

3 Without looking back through the chapter, give at least one example of a workplace initiative from each of the following approaches:

   (a) The sameness perspective.
   (b) The collectivist strand of the difference perspective.
   (c) The individualist strand of the difference perspective.

4 'I treat everyone the same – so that's how I ensure fairness.' This quote is from a section manager in a supermarket. Explain why such an approach can sometimes lead to unfairness.

5 'Everyone is unique. Everyone is an individual. As a manager you should treat them as such.' If you were being critical of this opinion, what points would you make?

6 The Fire Service in the UK has been described as institutionally racist, sexist and homophobic. What does this mean? How would you evaluate whether such a description was legitimate?

Case study 1

A clash of rights

In the UK in 2005 it became lawful for same-sex couples to join together in 'civil partnerships', which, in legal terms, are equivalent to a man and woman getting married. When a marriage ceremony is non-religious, it is conducted by a registrar, and so the civil partnership ceremonies are all undertaken by registrars. Ms Ladele was a registrar who did not wish to officiate at the ceremonies. She told her manager she would not be able to conduct civil partnerships because, she said, 'It states in the Bible that marriage occurs between a man and a women, not people of the same sex, and, as a Christian, I try to follow what the Bible teaches.'

Ms Ladele swapped with other registrars when she was scheduled to conduct civil partnerships, but over the next two years she was frequently challenged by her manager over her refusal and threatened with dismissal. She recalls, 'At one-to-one appraisals my manager would say things like "Don't expect to get promoted at any point" because she said that by refusing to perform the civil partnerships I was failing to do my job. She would say, "Nobody likes you, nobody wants to work with you."

'Sometimes she would say "Here comes po-face", when I walked in the room, and people would laugh, which was incredibly humiliating. Even going to ask for annual leave was difficult as she would tell me I couldn't have the weeks I was asking for, for no reason.'

Two of Ms Ladele's gay colleagues made an official complaint against her, stating that she was homophobic, and following a formal investigation, the Council (her employer) told her that she would be subject to disciplinary action.

She decided to take her employer to an employment tribunal. She said, 'I had tried again and again to rise above it all, but I couldn't allow myself to be sacked for something I knew wasn't right. How could it be right to ask me to choose between my religion or my job? I understand that gay people should have rights, just as we all should. But why should those rights be taken more seriously than my religious rights?'

Source: Summarised from the Mail Online, 13 July 2008.

Questions

1 What type of unfair treatment was Ms Ladele likely to have claimed at the tribunal?

2 Ms Ladele asks two questions in the final paragraph. What would be your answers to those questions?

3 To what extent should other sorts of non-religious beliefs be respected at work, for example, political or environmental beliefs?

4 To what extent should the religious beliefs of employees be accommodated in the tasks they do? For example, should a Muslim supermarket check-out operator be allowed not to handle alcohol?

Case study 2

Safe future finance

The following is a true story, although for legal reasons names have been changed.

Gordon Burrows graduated from university last year with a business degree, took some time out to go travelling around the world and then returned back to his University town. He was unsure about his career but he saw an advert pinned to the notice board in the University careers office that read as follows.

Are you qualified to degree level, highly self-motivated, diligent and keen to make a fortune? Then you could be the person for us!

We are looking for confident, young graduates to join our financial advisory team. Excellent prospects and high earning potentials. Call us to find out more.

With nothing to lose, Gordon made the phone call and within the week found himself outside the offices of Safe Future Finance, about to go for an interview with Mr Fletcher. The woman at reception escorted Gordon into a large open plan office, full of desks occupied by men in dark suits and brightly coloured ties. Mr Fletcher was among them and, it turned out, was not much older than Gordon.

'I have your interviewee, Mr Fletcher.'

'Thanks Brenda. Could you fetch us a couple of coffees? Is coffee okay for you Gordon? Sorry I can't offer you anything stronger! Call me Dave, by the way.'

Gordon soon learned that the job involved being part of Dave's team selling financial products – particularly investment plans with life cover. There was no fixed salary but he would be paid on a commission-only basis and would have 'self-employed' status. However, the bonuses were good; potentially they were very high if he reached Dave's level who, as a team leader, also received a percentage cut of all his sales team.

During the next half-an-hour Dave read through Gordon's application form and asked a series of questions. He enquired about Gordon's background and seemed particularly interested that Gordon had been to a private school. He also noted that Gordon was a keen golfer. The interview was not as Gordon had expected – it was more like a chat than the formal process he had learned about at business school.

'Right' said Dave, 'Let's give you a tour of the office then we'll finish this off in the bar across the road. That's where I can find out if you're the right man for the job – you know, find out if we'd be able to work together.'

As they wandered around the large air-conditioned office, Dave explained that the teams were in competition with each other so a good team spirit with everyone 'singing from the same hymn sheet' was essential. He added, 'There's no room for mavericks in my team. We work together and we play together – it's all part of building up good team spirit and getting sales. There's a lot of banter – you know nicknames, piss-taking, that sort of thing – but it's all part of the culture of the place. They must have taught you all about organisational culture at business school.'

Gordon nodded although this was not quite what he remembered about organisational culture.

As they walked between the desks Dave exchanged a few pleasantries and a few light-hearted insults with the various sales advisors. He explained to Gordon, 'One of the most important things you need to know about this place is that you are very much seen as an individual. Okay, you'd be part of my team but you work on your own and you sink or swim according to your own abilities. You could come to me for advice but I'd be expecting you to work your balls off. I've got no room for passengers on my team.'

Gordon was unsure whether to respond but commented. 'I work well on my own and I'm not scared of hard work.'

Dave nodded approvingly. 'Good. This is a tough job. It is all about closing a deal. I can teach you the basics but the drive comes from within. Sometimes you've got to be ruthless for the sake of your own bonus and the team. You see the chart on the wall over there? You see the long line?'

Gordon stared at a multicoloured chart that had everyone's name listed down the side and a performance line alongside. One of the lines stretched noticeably further than the rest.

'The longest line is me', said Dave loud enough for the men at the nearby desks to hear. 'I clean up on the amount of business I sign up. None of these tossers can get anywhere near me!' There were a few smirks and some obscene gestures before Dave said in a mocking tone, 'Come on, let's leave these ladies to it.'

'Funny you should say that', ventured Gordon. 'Aren't there any women working here?'

'Sure' said Dave, 'All the girls are on the next floor. They handle the paperwork.'

Case study continued

'So don't they apply for sales advisor jobs?' asked Gordon.

'Yes, they apply, but they don't get them because they tend not to have the drive and hard-nosed attitude to sales. But we're not prejudiced here, it's just that skills are used where they are best suited. For instance, you'll see we've got some Asians in the office. They've got excellent contacts, particularly among their families, who have money and are willing to invest it in the financial products we sell. On the other hand, you won't see any black faces because they have a different attitude to investments and they aren't well-connected. Being well-connected to people with money to invest is one of the key factors for success in this job. In fact we've just recruited a couple of shirt-lifters because the company is hoping they'll bring in "pink cash" from their community.'

Dave checked his watch, and announced that it was time for them to finish off the interview in the bar across the road. He added, 'Besides, I'm desperate for a cigarette. That's one of the downsides of working here – it's a no-smoking office. Bloody discrimination if you ask me.'

Questions

1 Evaluate Dave's attitude using your knowledge of the social justice and business case arguments.

2 Evaluate the recruitment procedure used in this instance drawing upon your knowledge of equal opportunity best-practice guidelines.

3 Does Dave treat people according to principles of sameness or difference?

4 Assess whether or not there is evidence of institutional discrimination at Safe Future Finance.

5 Using Figure 6.2 as a process map, identify the critical junctures where problems have or could occur and where change interventions could/should be made.

References and further reading

Bradley, H. and Healy, G. (2008) *Ethnicity and Gender at Work*. London: Palgrave.

Cockburn, C. (1989) 'Equal opportunities: the short and long agenda', *Industrial Relations Journal*, 20, 3: 213–25.

Cockburn, C. (1991) *In the Way of Women*. Basingstoke: Macmillan.

Collinson, D.L., Knights, D. and Collinson, M. (1990) *Managing to Discriminate*. London: Routledge.

Cunningham, I. and James, P. (2001) 'Managing diversity and disability legislation', in M. Noon and E. Ogbonna (eds) *Equality, Diversity and Disadvantage in Employment*. Basingstoke: Palgrave, pp. 103–17.

Curran, M. (1988) 'Gender and recruitment: people and places in the labour market', *Work, Employment and Society*, 2, 3: 335–51.

Dickens, L. (1994) 'The business case for women's equality', *Employee Relations*, 16, 8: 5–18.

Dickens, L. (1999) 'Beyond the business case: a three-pronged approach to equality action', *Human Resource Management Journal*, 9, 1: 9–19.

Dickens, L. (2000) 'Still wasting resources? Equality in employment', in S. Bach and K. Sissons (eds) *Personnel Management*, 3rd edn. Oxford: Blackwell, pp. 137–69.

Healy, G. (1993) 'Business and discrimination' in Stacey, R. (ed.) *Strategic Thinking and the Management of Change*. London: Kogan Page, pp. 169–89.

Heery, E. and Noon, M. (2008) *A Dictionary of Human Resource Management*. Oxford: Oxford University Press.

Hoque, K. and Noon, M. (2004) 'Equal opportunities policy and practice in Britain: evaluating the "empty shell" hypothesis', *Work, Employment and Society* 18, 3: 481–506.

Kandola, R. and Fullerton, J. (1994) *Managing the Mosaic*. London: IPD.

Kandola, R., Fullerton, J. and Ahmed, Y. (1995) 'Managing diversity: succeeding where equal opportunities has failed', *Equal Opportunities Review*, 59: 31–36.

Kirton, G. and Greene, A-M. (2005) *The Dynamics of Managing Diversity*, 2nd edn. Oxford: Butterworth-Heinemann.

Liff, S. (2003) 'The industrial relations of a diverse workforce', in P. Edwards (ed.) *Industrial Relations*, 2nd edn. Oxford: Blackwell, pp. 420–46.

Liff, S. and Dale, K. (1994) 'Formal opportunity, informal barriers: Black women managers within a local authority', *Work, Employment and Society*, 8, 2: 177–98.

Liff, S. and Wajcman, J. (1996) '"Sameness" and "difference" revisited: which way forward for equal opportunity initiatives?', *Journal of Management Studies*, 33, 1: 79–94.

Modood, T., Berthoud, R., Lakey, J., Nazroo, J., Smith, P., Virdee, S. and Beishon, S. (1997) *Ethnic Minorities in Britain: Diversity and Disadvantage*. London: Policy Studies Institute.

Nazroo, J.Y. and Karlsen, S. (2003) 'Patterns of identity among ethnic minority people: Diversity and commonality', *Ethnic and Racial Studies*, 26, 5, 902–30.

Noon, M. (2007) 'The fatal flaws of diversity and the business case for ethnic minorities', *Work, Employment and Society*, 21, 4: 373–84.

Noon, M. and Blyton, P. (2007) *The Realities of Work*, 3rd edn. Basingstoke: Palgrave.

Noon, M. and Hoque, K. (2001) 'Ethnic minorities and equal treatment: the impact of gender, equal opportunities policies and trade union', *National Institute Economic Review*, 176: 105–16.

Noon, M. and Ogbonna, E. (2001) 'Introduction: The key analytical themes', in M. Noon and E. Ogbonna (eds) *Equality, Diversity and Disadvantage in Employment*. Basingstoke: Palgrave, pp. 1–14.

Oswick, C. and Rosenthal, P. (2001) 'Towards a relevant theory of age discrimination in employment', in Noon, M. and Ogbonna, E. (eds) *Equality, Diversity and Disadvantage in Employment*. Basingstoke: Palgrave, pp. 156–71.

Pilkington, A. (2001) 'Beyond racial dualism: Racial disadvantage and ethnic diversity in the labour market', in M. Noon and E. Ogbonna (eds) *Equality, Diversity and Disadvantage in Employment*. Basingstoke: Palgrave, pp. 172–89.

Reynolds, G., Nicholls, P. and Alferoff, C. (2001) 'Disabled people, (re)training and employment: A qualitative exploration of exclusion', in Noon, M. and Ogbonna, E. (eds) *Equality, Diversity and Disadvantage in Employment*. Basingstoke: Palgrave, pp. 190–207.

Webb, J. (1997) 'The politics of equal opportunity', *Gender, Work and Organisation*, 4, 3: 159–69.

For multiple-choice questions, exercises and annotated weblinks related to this topic, visit **www.pearsoned.co.uk/mymanagementlab**.

Teacher shortages

Over the past 50 years, the UK has lurched from one crisis to another in the recruitment and retention of teachers, particularly for secondary schools. Now the shortage of teachers looks set to become even more of a problem as large numbers of people currently in the profession near retirement. Shortages are especially acute in subjects like maths, science and modern languages and in specific geographical areas like inner London, where there are many alternative careers. A growing body of economic research on the labour market for teachers is seeking to understand these shortages and provide insights into potential policy measures.

To some extent, the labour market for teachers functions like any other labour market, with schools acting as employers. But there are two notable characteristics shared with some other public service occupations like healthcare professionals. These are that the state has both monopoly power in the provision of credentials – the state determines who is qualified to teach – and near 'monopsony' (monopoly buyer) power in the recruitment of teachers – since most teachers are employed in state schools. What's more, teaching is highly unionised and the government generally determines pay.

England has an ageing teaching profession, especially in primary schools. 40 per cent of all teachers are aged 45–55, and those aged over 55 account for another 6 per cent of the workforce. Within the next ten years, nearly 50 per cent of the current workforce is likely to have retired. Currently, the official retirement age is 65 but teachers can retire as early as 55 and many do so. Since the number of pupils is not forecast to decrease significantly, at the current level of recruitment, there is likely to be a large shortage of teachers.

There has been an excess demand for teachers almost continuously throughout the post-war period. The main problem has been a shortage of secondary teachers, although the difference in excess demand between primary and secondary teachers disappeared towards the end of the 1990s.

Since 1992 teachers' pay has fallen by 6 per cent relative to average non-manual earnings (although the decline 'bottomed out' in the late 1990s. Over the longer run, teachers' pay follows a repetitive cyclical pattern; a period of sustained decline followed by a dramatic increase, usually as a result of a major government report on the crisis in teacher supply.

A key aspect of teacher supply is the relative popularity of the profession with women graduates. Feminisation of the teaching profession adds some difficulties to planning teacher supply as many women will at some point interrupt their career for family reasons. Women are also more likely to leave teaching than men so policies to facilitate work and child-rearing, such as subsidised childcare or reduced workload, may increase teacher supply.

As with other public sector service professions, there have also been shortages of teachers in certain areas of the country, most markedly in inner London and the South East. Official vacancy rates are two to three times higher than the national average in London despite it being the area that relies most on temporarily filled positions. Recruiting difficulties in London are thought to stem from the better alternative careers for potential teachers and the upward pressure on living costs associated with a more competitive labour market. But it is possible that recruiting difficulties in London have more to do with job conditions in inner city schools than outside job opportunities and living costs.

Most government policies to retain teachers concentrate on financial incentives but surveys of teachers reveal that pay is not the only determinant of their dissatisfaction. Compared with other graduates, teachers are more likely to claim to be dissatisfied with their hours of work. Compared with other employees, teachers' hours are concentrated during term time with an average working week of 52 hours.

It has long been asserted that many people become teachers because of the non-pecuniary benefits, such as long holidays. However, the national curriculum and rigours of the inspection procedure may have given teachers an excessive administrative burden. Interviews with teachers leaving the profession confirm that heavy workloads and other characteristics of schools rank higher than pay as a reason for quitting.

National recruitment and retention initiatives

Training bursaries

Training bursaries from the Teacher Development Agency (TDA) encourage recruitment into Initial Teacher Training (ITT) courses via postgraduate routes. It is not a loan and is tax-free for full-time postgraduate students. Bursaries from September 2006 are £9000 for maths, science and other secondary shortage subjects and £6000 for secondary non-shortage subjects and primary.

Golden hellos

This initiative was introduced to increase the number of trainees achieving Qualified Teacher Status (QTS) and finding employment in shortage subjects. Payment is made through salaries after a successful induction period – normally a year – and is taxable. From September 2006 'golden hello' payments are £5000 for maths and science and £2500 for secondary shortage subjects.

Payment of fees

From 2006–7 all trainees on postgraduate certificate in education (PGCE) courses will be required to pay variable fees. However, all PGCE students will be eligible for a £1200 grant from DfES to help pay for fees.

Graduate Teacher Programme (GTP)

The GTP is a one-year programme offering graduates the opportunity to train as a teacher and gain QTS while employed in a school. The school pays a salary at the rate for an unqualified teacher but receives a grant towards employment costs and training costs.

Registered Teacher Programme (RTP)

The RTP is normally a two-year programme, offering candidates who have completed two years of higher education (or equivalent) to train as a teacher and gain QTS while employed in a school. The school pays a salary at a rate for either a qualified or unqualified teacher and receives a grant to cover training costs.

Fast track teaching

The Fast Track Teacher programme is a leadership development programme providing professional development opportunities and coaching to help teachers reach leadership positions more quickly.

Overseas Trained Teachers Programme (OTTP)

The OTTP runs for a maximum of a year and offers teachers trained overseas the opportunity to gain QTS while working as a teacher. The school pays the salary at a rate for either a qualified or unqualified teacher.

Source: Employers Organisation (2005) Local government workforce profile and the top ten skills shortage areas – 2005: national recruitment and retention initiatives.

Questions

1 To what extent are these national initiatives likely to ease the shortages identified in the extract above?

2 What other options might be considered to improve recruitment and retention of teachers?

3 What are the cost implications of your recommendations?

Part 3

DEVELOPING THE HUMAN RESOURCE

Introduction to Part 3

Human resource development (HRD), like HRM, is a term that is often used loosely, and indeed poses problems of definition. Stewart and McGoldrick (1996: 1), who write authoritatively in the HRD area, suggest that the question of what it is 'is not yet amenable to a definitive answer', but offer the following 'tentative' definition:

> Human resource development encompasses activities and processes which are intended to have impact on organisational and individual learning. The term assumes that organisations can be constructively conceived of as learning entities, and that the learning processes of both organisations and individuals are capable of influence and direction through deliberate and planned interventions. Thus, HRD is constituted by planned interventions in organisational and individual processes.

This definition emphasises HRD of the individual and her or his relation to the organisation. It can, however, be viewed much more broadly than this. In Asian and African countries, for example, HRD encompasses government initiatives and policies to improve knowledge and skills to enhance economic growth. As Rao (1995: 15) states:

> at the national level HRD aims at ensuring that people in the country live longer; live happily; free of disease and hunger; have sufficient skill base to earn their livelihood and well being; have a sense of belongingness and pride through participation in determining their own destinies. The promotion of the well-being of individuals, families and societies provides a human resource agenda for all countries the world over.

And, indeed, over the last decade it has become recognised that the HRD that takes place in organisations can play an important role in the overall economy and hence in the well-being of society (see **www.ukces.org.uk**). This concept is represented by the three concentric circles in Figure P3.1. The more overlap (the shaded area) there is between these three elements, the more likely HRD is to be mutually beneficial for the individual, the organisation and the economy as a whole. It is therefore not surprising that training and development are important issues to which governments give careful consideration. For example, support from government initiatives, such as legislation on vocational training, enhances the skills and knowledge of those seeking work in the labour market, which enhances the efficiency of organisations, which in turn enhances the growth and development of the economy. For these reasons Part 3 looks beyond and beneath organisational HRD and examines both its national context and the basic processes that constitute it; where appropriate, it invites readers to reflect on their own individual learning and development.

Although Stewart and Harris (2003: 58) encountered an 'uneasy' relationship between HRM and HRD, with training 'the Cinderella of the HR function', HRD is now increasingly being recognised as having a significant part to play in achieving and maintaining the survival and success of an organisation. Managers have not only to acquire appropriate people to resource it, as discussed in Part 2, they also need to train and develop them, for the following reasons:

- New employees are, in some respects, like the organisation's raw materials. They have to be 'processed' to enable them to perform the tasks of their job adequately, to fit into their workgroup and into the organisation as a whole, but in a manner that respects their human qualities.

- Jobs and tasks may change over time, both quantitatively and qualitatively, and employees have to be updated to maintain adequate performance.

Figure P3.1 HRD: the individual, the organisation and the economy

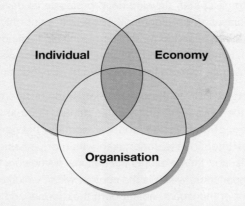

- New jobs and tasks may be introduced into the organisation, and be filled by existing employees, who need redirection.

- People need training to perform better in their existing jobs.

- People themselves change their interests, their skills, their confidence and aspirations, their circumstances.

- Some employees may move jobs within the organisation, on promotion or to widen their experience, and so need further training.

- The organisation itself, or its context, may change or be changed over time, so that employees have to be updated in their ways of working together.

- The organisation may wish to be ready for some future change, and require (some) employees to develop transferable skills.

- The organisation may wish to respond flexibly to its environment and so require (some) employees to develop flexibility and transferable skills.

- Management requires training and development. This will involve training for new managers, further development and training for managers, management succession, and the development of potential managers.

However, as the chapters that follow show, changes in the context of the organisation increase the need to train and develop its members to ensure effectiveness, quality and responsiveness. Because these changes are not being made once and for all, employees are having to adjust to continuous change, and their managers to pay greater attention to HRD than ever before. Nevertheless, HRD does not take place in an organisational vacuum. To be effective, it presupposes effective selection, effective supervision and an appropriate management style, the opportunity to transfer learning to the workplace, career paths and promotion possibilities, appropriate incentives and rewards. It also presupposes some degree of planning and linkage to the strategy of the organisation, and is therefore implicit within organisation development. Indeed, for the organisation that espouses 'human resource management' and addresses the human resource implications of its strategic positioning, training and development become investment decisions and operations that are as important as investments in new technology, relocation or entry into new markets.

Part 3 examines the several forms that HRD takes: the development of the employee both as an individual and as an employee; development of the employee by the employer or by self; training; education; career development; group development; staff development; professional development, management development and, even more widely, organisation development. These differ not only in terms of the hierarchical levels of the organisation but also in purpose and form. While recognising these different kinds of training and development in organisations, we have to understand that they are not necessarily easily distinguishable in practice, and that some activities contribute to more than one form of development.

Chapter 7 identifies the need for HRD in the organisation, and considers the basic processes of learning and development involved and the ways in which they can be facilitated in the organisation. This chapter underpins the subsequent chapters of Part 3 and introduces some of the concepts they use. Chapter 8 examines the processes and activities intentionally undertaken within organisations to enable employees to acquire, improve or update their skills, and then explores the national framework for vocational education and training, with some international comparisons, which is the context within which organisational HRD operates. Chapter 9 examines the development of managers, noting both their formal and informal modes of development, and relates management to organisation development. There is necessarily some overlap between the chapters of Part 3. Thus specific training to enable an employee to perform more effectively can now also contribute to that person's overall career development. What is intended as instrumental by the employer may be construed as empowering by the individual. This raises the question about who owns the individual's development, one of the controversial issues addressed in Chapter 7.

References and further reading

Rao, T.V. (1995) *Human Resource Development*. New Delhi: Sage.

Stewart, J. and Harris, L. (2003) 'HRD and HRM: an uneasy relationship', *People Management*, 9, 19, September: 58.

Stewart, J. and McGoldrick, J. (eds) (1996) *Human Resource Development: Perspectives, Strategies and Practice*. London: Pitman.

Chapter 7

Learning and development

Audrey Collin

Objectives

- To highlight the learning and development demanded by the significant changes taking place in organisations.
- To note the characteristics of different types of learners.
- To indicate the outcomes of learning.
- To outline the process of learning.
- To discuss the concept of development.
- To note various kinds of development.
- To discuss the implications of learning and development for human resource managers.
- To consider the context of learning and development within and beyond the organisation.
- To examine how learning and development can be facilitated and designed within organisations.
- To pose some controversial issues for reflection and discussion.
- To offer some activities that encourage readers to review their own learning and development.

Introduction

Learning is 'the central issue for the twenty-first century', asserts Honey (1998: 28–29):

> Changes are bigger and are happening faster, and learning is the way to keep ahead... to maintain employability in an era when jobs for life have gone. It enables organisations to sustain their edge as global competition increases. Learning to learn ... [is] the ultimate life skill.

This makes human resource development a key activity in today's organisations, and lifelong learning crucial for individuals.

Learning and development embodied in skills are also essential to the 'economic and social health of the UK': skills are 'the most important lever within our control to create wealth and to reduce social deprivation' (Leitch, 2006; see also **www.ukces.org/uk**). Moreover, the UK Commission for Employment and Skills (**www.ukces.org**) urges that employers do not cut training during the present recession (2009), but invest in it to 'build workforce talent and gain competitive advantage when recovery comes'.

The purpose of this chapter, which forms a foundation for Chapters 8 and 9, is to explain what learning and development are. It starts by identifying some of the ways in which work and organisations are changing, and why those changes demand continuous learning in individuals and organisations. It then explains what learning and development are, identifies how their context influences them, and examines how they can be facilitated in work organisations.

The changing world of work and organisations

By the end of the twentieth century, the firmly established nature of work and organisations was changing so dramatically that some observers had foreseen the 'end of work' (Rifkin, 1995) and workplaces without jobs (Bridges, 1995). Changes were being brought about through the new information and communications technologies, and through the way in which organisations were responding to the need to achieve and maintain their competitive edge in increasingly global markets. Globalisation affects employment, too: it is predicted that by 2030 50 per cent of the global workforce will be located in China and India (Smethurst, 2005). Castells (1996) argued that a new 'network society' was emerging. The new technologies have made economies interdependent, organised around global networks of capital, management and information, and thereby are profoundly transforming capital and labour. While capital and information flow around the globe, unconfined in space and time, labour is local: individuals live and work in time and place. 'Labor is disaggregated in its performance, fragmented in its organization, diversified in its existence, divided in its collective action' (Castells, 1996: 475).

Although great effort is made to understand what changes may take place (for example, the ESRC Future of Work Programme, **www.leeds.ac.uk/esrcfutureofwork/**), predictions about the future are difficult to make. Bayliss (1998) suggests that many of the traditional boundaries and distinctions – between organisations, between jobs, between employment and self-employment – will shift or become eroded. The relationship that individuals will have with employing organisations will change: individuals will move more frequently, have projects rather than long-term jobs, work in different locations and at different times, make their own work, no longer have fixed working lives. Many careers will be 'boundaryless', transcending traditional boundaries between organisations (Arthur and Rousseau, 1996). To express those changes in metaphors: whereas during much of the twentieth century jobs were like pigeon-holes, or boxes piled up to form organisations, at the start of the twenty-first century organisations are more like nets and networks.

In this changing context, organisations have had to become more flexible, innovative, quality-conscious, customer-oriented, constantly improving their performance to remain competitive. During the past 25 years or so they have undertaken what amount to massive experiments with ways of achieving those ends. During the 1980s the imperatives were excellence, world-class and 'lean' manufacturing (a collection of techniques contributing significantly to organisational performance), total quality management (TQM), downsizing, delayering, and the breaking of bureaucracies down into business units. During the early 1990s the new soft approaches were multi-skilling and the learning organisation, while the hard approach was business process re-engineering (BPR). In the later 1990s, attention turned to knowledge management and innovation, with a further emphasis on teamworking. As the twenty-first century opened, the key issues have become the management and measurement of human capital, 'the contribution of human skills and knowledge to the production of goods and services' (Scarborough, 2003: 32) and, more recently, the re-configuration of the HR function (Ulrich and Brockbank, 2005) and outsourcing (Pickard, 2006). Thus wave after wave of new approaches have brought about new tasks, new ways of working, new roles, relationships and skills, so that lifelong learning and human resource development are now central to the effectiveness of organisations.

For example, TQM (see also Chapter 14) holds that quality is achieved through continuous improvement in the processes, products and services of the organisation: Deming's 'journey of never-ending improvement' (Hodgson, 1987: 41). It requires new relationships between organisations and their suppliers and customers and the transformation of the management of people 'so that employees become involved in quality as the central part of their job' (Sheard, 1992: 33). BPR, which radically restructured bureaucratic organisations by focusing on their lateral processes rather than their vertical functions, not only 'downsized' organisations, but also redesigned the nature of jobs within them:

> For multi-dimensional and changing jobs, companies don't need people to fill a slot, because the slot will be only roughly defined. Companies need people who can figure out what the job takes and people to do it, people who can create the slot that fits them. Moreover, the slot will keep changing.
>
> (Hammer and Champy, 1994: 72)

Whereas work had previously been packaged into jobs, Martin (1995: 20) argues, it is now being reconstructed into the competences needed to achieve customer satisfaction. 'The future will see a world based more on skills than on organisations' (Tyson and Fell, 1995: 45).

If TQM and BPR can be seen as natural heirs – in spirit if not in practice – of scientific management and Taylorism (see Chapters 3 and 10), then knowledge management (Nonaka, 1991) could be recognised as an echo of Trist and the Tavistock school (Pugh *et al.*, 1983). They saw the working group as a socio-technical system: to be effective, the introduction of new technology had to take that into account. Fifty years later, it is once more being recognised (Malhotra, 1998) that it is people who make the difference. The wealth of information generated by information technology becomes meaningful and of competitive advantage to the organisation only when people share, interpret and elaborate it. This enables them to anticipate challenges to the organisation's goals and practices, and thus to adapt the organisation in appropriate and timely fashion.

> Creating, disseminating and embodying knowledge – tacit and explicit – becomes a key strategic resource to be leveraged. It holds the key to unlocking the organisation's ability to learn faster than its environment is changing. In summary, learning and development lie at the heart of innovation in organisations.
>
> (Guest *et al.*, 1997: 3)

Knowledge management embraces knowledge creation, validation, presentation, distribution, and application. In the first generation of knowledge management, its focus was on the role of information technology. The second generation recognised that different kinds of knowledge had to be managed in different ways. Some knowledge was explicit, and could easily be documented, whereas other knowledge was tacit. 'The knowledge needed to develop a new product is largely in people's heads . . . [it] cannot be written down, because an individual may not even know it is there until the situation demands a creative response' (Dixon, 2000: 37). The third generation (Snowden, 2002) is even more challenging to scientific management orthodoxy. Knowledge is now no longer regarded as 'abstract, objective' truth but a cultural construction within 'communities of practice', and hence 'essentially pragmatic, partial, tentative and always open to revision' (Blackler, 2000: 61). This view highlights the significance of organisational culture, meaning-making, narrative, context and systems thinking (see Chapter 3). The challenge to HRD is to promote the kind of learning that, through critical thinking and reflection, can recognise, appraise, transmit and apply contextually embedded meanings (Hwang, 2003). That calls for understanding of the process of learning, development of higher-order thinking skills and of the learning organisation.

Research suggests that financial results account for only 50 to 70 per cent of a firm's market value, the remainder being attributed to 'intangibles' (Ulrich and Smallwood, 2002), such as intellectual property and human capital. Scarborough (2003: 32–34) suggests that the human capital approach is 'more than a recycling of clichés about the importance of our employees. It also reflects a shift in thinking about ways to make the best use of the whole range of abilities that people bring to the workplace.' He cites the television programme *Jamie's Kitchen*, in which cook Jamie Oliver turned a team of inexperienced and unemployed young people into top-class chefs. 'This blending of new skills and attitudes into high-level performance sums up exactly what human capital can be and why it is so important to business' (Scarborough, 2003: 32). (See also CIPD Factsheet *Human Capital* (updated November 2008).)

Ulrich and Smallwood (2002: 43) include learning or knowledge management among the seven 'critical organisation capabilities that [create] intangible shareholder value': 'Learning capacity is an intangible value when organisations have the ability to move ideas across vertical, horizontal, external and global boundaries.' However, accountants have traditionally not found satisfactory ways of measuring human capital, and so have treated employees as costs to an organisation rather than assets. Considerable effort is being made to change that as the significance for competitiveness of investment in human capital is increasingly recognised (Manocha, 2005). Once again, this highlights the significance of HRD and the understanding and promotion of learning in organisations. It is also becoming clear that employees are beginning to recognise the need to invest in their own learning and development – their human capital – and so employers have to take steps to retain talent, nurture it, and manage it effectively, which in turn calls for effective means of measuring human capital (Mayo, 2002).

Activity

Identifying contextual changes leading to HRD

Before proceeding further, on your own or in a small group identify some of the changes taking place in organisations you know in response to changes in their context. What are the implications for human resource development and for the learning and development of individuals?

The strategic importance of learning and development

'Change matters more than ever before', said the president of the Chartered Institute of Personnel and Development (CIPD, formerly IPD) in his message in the Annual Report for 2000 (Beattie, 2002: 2–3). 'People are our only source of differentiation and sustainable competitive advantage. Essential to that is learning.' Hence the director general of the IPD claimed that 'staff management and development will become the primary weapon available to managers to generate success' (Rana, 2000). The continuous learning and development of individuals are, therefore, of crucial and strategic importance to organisations, and thereby also to the overall economy.

The new ways of working are demanding not just extensive training in new task skills, but completely new ways of thinking about work, doing work, and relating with one another. Individuals at all levels need to be able to challenge traditional ways of thinking and working; to think and work 'outside the box' of traditional job descriptions; work without prior experience, clear guidelines or close supervision; and to be flexible, prepared to change, undertake new tasks or move to a different organisation. In the struggle to 'think global and act local', organisations need people who have 'a "matrix of the mind"'; sharing learning and creating new knowledge are among the key capabilities that organisations must have (Ulrich and Stewart Black, 1999). Overall, this amounts to the need for using high levels of cognitive skills.

Human resource developers and trainers now have to address the new responsibilities of their increasingly strategic role (Chartered Institute of Personnel and Development, 2002a). That calls for more than training new employees: organisations have to invest in their human capital. It means that they have to train and develop their existing workforce, facilitate their learning within a learning culture, with appropriate resources, and develop a learning organisation (see Chapters 8 and 9). Hence human resource managers need to understand the processes and nature of the learning of the higher-order and other task skills in order to be able to facilitate that learning and development. It is the purpose of this chapter to explain these.

Importantly, organisations have to invest not just in their knowledge workers but in their lower-skilled employees as well (Chartered Institute of Personnel and Development, 2002a). For much of the industrial age, higher-order abilities were expected mainly in the upper echelons of organisations. However, in the twenty-first century, competitive organisations need to find those abilities much more widely in their workforce, in what Castells (1998: 341) calls the 'self-programmable' labour in the global economy. This has 'the capability constantly to redefine the necessary skills for a given task, and to access the sources for learning these skills'. Nevertheless, there will still be work that does not require those particular abilities – for example, serving in fast food outlets – jobs that will be undertaken by what Castells (1998: 341) calls 'generic' labour, which, lacking self-programmable skills, would be:

> 'human terminals' [which could] be replaced by machines, or by any other body around the city, the country, or the world, depending on business decisions. While they are collectively indispensable to the production process, they are individually expendable . . .

(It should not be assumed, however, that all jobs giving personal service demand low-level skills: they may require high levels of social, emotional and other non-cognitive intelligences (CIPD Factsheet *Emotional Intelligence*; Gardner, 1985, 1999; Pickard, 1999b).

However, although many employers had been recognising the value of their employees' learning, some are responding to the recession of 2008/2009 with lay-offs rather than investment in their human capital (see second case study at end of chapter). In this changed situation, the view that individuals must also take some responsibility and invest in their own learning and development to ensure their own employability (Arnold, 1997) becomes incontrovertible. This personal investment changes the balance of the 'psychological contract' (see Chapters 3 and 13), and raises the question of who owns the individual's learning (see Controversial issues on page 271 at the end of this chapter).

The need for higher order skills

According to Wisher (1994: 37), among the 'competencies that occur frequently in the most successful clusters of different organisations' are conceptual, 'helicopter' and analytical thinking. The Chartered Institute of Personnel and Development, for example, now underpins its professional standards with the concept of the 'thinking performer', 'who applies a critically thoughtful approach to their job' (Whittaker and Johns, 2004: 32). Organisations are thus now requiring higher-order thinking skills, and not just from their managers.

However, there is a long way to go for many organisations. According to Myers and Davids (1992: 47):

> workers are a resource which has not been well understood by management in the past. Blue-collar workers in particular have been regarded as a static commodity incapable of innovation and self-development. Consequently reservoirs of skill and ability remain untapped.

Cooley (1987) reports how the Lucas Aerospace Shop Stewards' Combine Committee, as long ago as 1975, recognised the value of human capital. It challenged the organisation not to lay off its highly skilled workforce when its market was failing, but to retain it by moving into new markets for 'socially useful' products:

239

> What the Lucas workers did was to embark on an exemplary project which would inflame the imagination of others. To do so, they realised that it was necessary to demonstrate in a very practical and direct way the creative power of 'ordinary people'. Further, their manner of doing it had to confirm for 'ordinary people' that they too had the capacity to change their situation, that they are not the objects of history but rather the subjects, capable of building their own futures.
>
> (Cooley, 1987: 139)

As this chapter reminds us, 'ordinary people' have the capacity to learn and develop.

The need for a learning society

The need for learning and development is not just an issue for individuals and their employers. It is now widely recognised that we need to become a learning society, in which there is a culture of, and opportunities for, lifelong learning in order to provide the skills required for competitiveness in a global economy. This national significance is now fully recognised by the government which has recently established the UK Commission for Employment and Skills (**www.ukces.org.uk**; see also **www.delni.gov.uk**). (See Chapter 8.)

What are the implications of the issues raised so far in this chapter for your own learning and development needs? How would you attempt to meet these needs? In the light of this, what would you seek from any prospective employer?

Learning and development

> Deep down, we are all learners. No one has to teach an infant to learn. In fact, no one has to teach infants anything. They are intrinsically inquisitive, masterful learners who learn to walk, speak . . . Learning organizations are possible because not only is it our nature to learn but we love to learn.
>
> (Senge, 1990: 4)

From birth, humans, like all animals, learn and develop: learning is a natural process in which we all engage. It is not just a cognitive activity, and it affects the person as a whole. Learning and development lead to skilful and effective adaptation to and manipulation of the environment, which is one element in a much-quoted definition of intelligence (Wechsler, 1958, in Ribeaux and Poppleton, 1978: 189). People continue learning throughout life, whether encouraged or not, whether formally taught or not, whether the outcomes are valued or not. Moreover, the process of their learning knows no boundaries: learning in one domain, such as employment, hobbies or maintenance of home and car, cross-fertilises that in another and thereby achieves a wider understanding and more finely honed skills.

> Most of us have learned a good deal more out of school than in it. We have learned from our families, our work, our friends. We have learned from problems resolved and tasks achieved but also from mistakes confronted and illusions unmasked. Intentionally or not, we have learned from the dilemmas our lives hand us daily.
>
> (Daloz, 1986: 1)

Society fosters and facilitates these activities of its members, but also channels and controls them through socialisation and education so that they yield outcomes that contribute to and are acceptable to it. However, although individuals have a lifetime's experience of being learners, some of their experiences (especially those in formal educational settings) might not have been happy ones (Honey, 1999). They might be experienced learners, but not necessarily competent or confident learners.

Defining learning and development

To understand the processes of learning and development and use this understanding to good effect in developing people and their organisations, you have to be able to think clearly about the concepts you are using. The concepts 'learning' and 'development' are frequently used loosely and even interchangeably, so it is important to define how they are being used here. The following definitions will enable you to distinguish them and understand the relationship between them.

Learning is

> a process within the organism which results in the capacity for changed performance which can be related to experience rather than maturation.   (Ribeaux and Poppleton, 1978: 38)

It is now widely recognised that intelligence is not just a unitary concept (see Gardner (1985, 1999) on multiple intelligences; Mayo and Nohria (2005) on 'contextual intelligence') nor just a cognitive capacity (see Pickard (1999b) on emotional intelligence). Hence learning is not just a cognitive process that involves the assimilation of information in symbolic form (as in book learning), but also an affective and physical process (Binsted, 1980). Our emotions, nerves and muscles are involved in the process, too. Learning leads to change, whether positive or negative for the learner. It is an experience after which an individual 'qualitatively [changes] the way he or she conceived something' (Burgoyne and Hodgson, 1983: 393) or experiences 'personal transformation' (Mezirow, 1977). Learning can be more or less effectively undertaken, and it could be more effective when it is paid conscious attention.

Development, however, is the process of becoming increasingly complex, more elaborate and differentiated, by virtue of learning and maturation. (As will be noted later, it is sometimes assumed that development connotes progression and advancement.) In an organism, greater complexity and differentiation among its parts leads to changes in the structure of the whole and to the way in which the whole functions (Reese and Overton, 1970: 126). In the individual, this greater complexity opens up the potential for new ways of acting and responding to the environment. This leads to the need and opportunity for even further learning, and so on.

Development, whether of an organism, individual or organisation, is a process of both continuity and discontinuity. Quantitative changes lead to qualitative changes or transformations; development is irreversible, although regression to earlier phases can occur.

> The disintegration of the old phase of functioning . . . creates the conditions for the discontinuous 'step-jump' to a new phase. This succeeding phase incorporates yet transforms the repertoire of principles, values, etc., of earlier phases and adds to them. The new phase is therefore not entirely new – it is a transformation. Each succeeding phase is more complex, integrating what has gone before.   (Pedler, 1988: 7–8)

Overall, then, learning contributes to development. It is not synonymous with it, but development cannot take place without learning of some kind. Lifelong learning means continuous adaptation. Increased knowledge and improved skills enlarge the individual's capacities to adapt to the environment and to change that environment. As the systems model in Chapter 3 implies, such external changes will lead on to further internal changes, allowing new possibilities for the individual to emerge. Moreover, these changes feed the

241

individual's self-esteem and confidence, and enhance social status. Hence learning generates potentially far-reaching changes in the individual: learning promotes development. In his very warm-hearted and insightful book on 'the transformational power of adult learning experiences', Daloz (1986: 24–26) draws on elements of traditional tales to convey the nature of this development:

> The journey tale begins with an old world, generally simple and uncomplicated, more often than not, home … The middle portion, beginning with departure from home, is character-ized by confusion, adventure, great highs and lows, struggle, uncertainty. The ways of the old world no longer hold, and the hero's task is to find a way through this strange middle land, generally in search of something lying at its heart. At the deepest point, the nadir of the descent, a transformation occurs, and the traveler moves out of the darkness toward a new world that often bears an ironic resemblance to the old.
>
> Nothing is different, yet all is transformed. It is seen differently . . . Our old life is still there, but its meaning has profoundly changed because we have left home, seen it from afar, and been transformed by that vision. You can't go home again.
>
> (Daloz, 1986: 24–26. Reprinted with permission of John Wiley & Sons, Inc.)

STOP and think

Has your learning caused you to develop? What has the experience of that been for you? Will you be able to 'go home again'?

The outcomes of a person's learning and development are the way they think, feel and inter-pret their world (their cognition, affect, attitudes, overall philosophy of life); the way they see themselves, their self-concept and self-esteem; and their ability to respond to and make their way in their particular environment (their perceptual-motor, intellectual, social and interper-sonal skills). Some of the transformational impact of learning can be seen in Daloz's description above of the journey of development. Learning and development are therefore significant experiences for individuals and hence for organisations. Following from this, it should also be noted, the facilitation of another's learning is a moral project: it has the poten-tial to promote changes that may have a profound effect in the other's life. This, too, has implications for the debate about the ownership of learning, one of the controversial issues at the end of the chapter.

Learning and development are processes that we all experience, active processes in which we all engage: we do not have learning and development done to us. However, we rarely pay con-scious attention to them and so might not fully understand them. This chapter therefore addresses you, the reader, directly, and here and throughout this chapter invites you to draw upon your own experience in order to understand and make use of the issues that are discussed.

Your very reading of this book might itself entail some of these issues. Before proceeding further, therefore, it makes sense to identify and reflect on them so that you will then have ready in your mind the 'hooks' on to which to hang the information this chapter will give you. In the language of a learning theory to be noted later, you will be ready to 'decode' these new 'signals'.

Activity | **Your aims and motivation for learning**

List your reasons for reading this book, noting:

- both short-term and long-term aims;

- those aims that are ends in themselves and those that are means to an end;

- the most important and the least important;

- the aims that you can achieve by yourself;
- those that require others to facilitate them;
- what else you need to achieve these aims;
- what initiated your pursuit of these aims;
- who or what has influenced you during this pursuit.

This chapter will examine how people learn, and what helps or hinders them. By paying attention now to how you are reading this book, you can begin to understand your own processes of learning and development. Later you will have the opportunity to identify those who benefit from and pay for your learning. This will help you to understand something of the problematical issues inherent in employee development.

Many types of learner

Much of what we know about learning and teaching derives from the study of children and young people (pedagogy). However, learners in organisations are not children, and have different needs and experiences.

From your own experience and observing others' behaviour, how do adult learners differ from young learners? What are likely to be the implications for human resource developers?

Adult learners

Instead of a pedagogical model of learning, an androgogical model is needed to understand adult learning. According to Knowles and Associates (1984), this needs to take into account that adult learners are self-directing, and motivated by their need to be recognised, to prove something to themselves and others, to better themselves, and achieve their potential. Their learning does not take place in a vacuum. Not only are they ready to learn when they recognise their need to know or do something, but they have experience on which to draw and to hang their new learning, and to assess its utility. Earlier (especially formal) learning experiences might have been far from effective or comfortable, so that many adults have developed poor learning habits or become apprehensive about further learning.

Human resource development has to address these various needs appropriately, as will be suggested in the later section on the organisation as a context for learning.

Learners in the organisation

Older workers

Traditionally, older people have been widely discriminated against when seeking employment and when employed (Naylor, 1987; Dennis, 1988; Laslett, 1989; Waskel, 1991). They have been commonly stereotyped as having failing cognitive and physical abilities, as being inflexible, unwilling and unable to learn new ways. However, the Carnegie Inquiry into the Third Age (Trinder *et al.*, 1992: 20) reports:

> There does seem to be a decline in performance with age . . . but such deterioration as there is, is less than the popular stereotype . . . Except where such abilities as muscular strength are of predominant importance, age is not a good discriminator of ability to work; nor of the ability to learn.

Trinder *et al.* (1992) also note that performance is influenced as much by experience and skill as by age: skill development in earlier years will encourage adaptability in later life.

Although older people are 'at a disadvantage with speedy and novel (unexpected) forms of presentation', Coleman (1990: 70–71) reports little or no decline with age in memory and learning, particularly 'if the material is fully learned initially'. (The role of rehearsal and revision in memory will be examined later in this chapter.) Pickard (1999a: 30), discussing changing attitudes to the employment of older people, and the possibility of retirement age rising to the upper 70s, quotes a 72-year-old Nobel prize-winning scientist as saying: 'You may forget where you were last week, but not the things that matter.' Coleman (1990) cites a study in which the majority of the 80 volunteers aged 63 to 91 years learned German from scratch, and in six months reached the level of skill in reading German normally achieved by schoolchildren in five years.

Until the 1990s, there were few examples to cite of organisations that employed older people. The do-it-yourself retail chain B&Q was a notable exception, staffing one store solely by people over the age of 50. It was 'an overwhelming success . . . In commercial terms the store has surpassed its trading targets' (Hogarth and Barth, 1991: 15). In this trial these older workers were found to be willing to train, although initially reluctant to use new technology, and did not require longer or different training from other workers. Since then, as Pickard (1999a) reports, B&Q has been joined by other employers in giving employment opportunities to older people. For example, BMW has an apprenticeship programme for older workers which is completed in 60 per cent of the time taken by the youth apprenticeship scheme. 'They already had life skills and were used to factory work, making it easier to acquire new skills. But they were also motivated and knew what they wanted to do' (*People Management*, 2005a: 17). These older workers demonstrate the ability to continue to learn through life. Their learning will be facilitated if employers adopt appropriate approaches, which will be examined in the section on the organisation as a context for learning.

However, traditional attitudes towards older workers are starting to change because of today's concern for knowledge management and investment in human capital (*People Management*, 2005b) and demographic changes. By 2020 young people are expected to comprise 11 per cent of the workforce compared with 16 per cent in 2005 (Griffiths, 2005a). At the same time, the proportion of older people in the population is growing, putting considerable pressure on pensions provision, and causing the government to raise the compulsory retirement age. Moreover, its legislation to deal with age discrimination will enable more older people to continue in employment. These changes have implications for HR managers, who have to consider introducing part-time working for older people, gradual retirement arrangements, the provision of career planning, continuing training opportunities (which have hitherto been scarce), and lifelong learning (Hope, 2005; Reday-Mulvey, 2005). Such ideas, and new appraisals of older workers, can be found in Smethurst (2006), via the Centre for Research into the Older Workforce at Surrey University, and via a CIPD Factsheet *Age and Employment*.

Other classes of employees

Three classes of people – disabled people, women, and individuals from cultural and ethnic minorities – are often socialised and educated in ways that do not advantage them in labour markets or organisations; they may develop correspondingly low expectations and aspirations. Negative stereotyping of them in employment is frequently discussed (Gallos, 1989; Thomas and Alderfer, 1989). This section will briefly note some aspects of their experience that will influence them as learners in the organisation: these need to be viewed in terms of the barriers to learning referred to later.

Until recently, little seems to have been written about the training of disabled people in organisations. Arkin (1995) summarised the implications for employers of the 1995 Disability Discrimination Act (DDA). The 2003 Amendment to the DDA is now raising further challenges to employers to treat disabled people as individuals, and it embraces training and career development (CIPD Factsheet *Disability and Employment* (updated July 2009),

Edwards, 2004; Griffiths, 2005b). A continuing impediment to providing opportunities for them is the attitudes of colleagues and customers, so organisations are providing for them awareness training on the difficulties faced by those with disabilities (Edwards, 2004). Nevertheless, e-learning (discussed later; see also Chapter 9) has the potential to enable those with disabilities to learn and update skills, though appropriate accessibility is not always available (Jarvis and Hooley, 2004).

There is now a considerable body of theory, including feminist critiques, that addresses the nature of women and their experiences in their own right, rather than as a subset of a supposed 'universal' (but often Eurocentric, middle-class male) nature. For example, as was noted in Chapter 3, Marshall (1989) states that knowledge is traditionally constructed from a male perspective, and Gilligan (1977: see Daloz, 1986: 134–35) argues that unlike men, who see their world as 'a hierarchy of power', women see theirs as 'a web of relationships'. The connected self interprets the environment differently, and so responds to it differently, from the separate self. These and other ways in which women may differ from men (Bartol, 1978) will influence their approach to, experience of, and outcomes from, learning; they may, indeed, give advantage in the development of some of the higher-order skills needed in organisations. However, it has also been suggested (Griffiths, 2005c) that competency frameworks may be biased against women.

Different cultures imbue their members with different basic assumptions about the nature of reality and the values and the roles in social life. Cultural experiences differ, hence the accumulated experience of the members will also differ. The concept of intelligence is not culture-free. Gardner (1985), who expounds a theory of multiple intelligences that include interpersonal and intrapersonal intelligence, recognises that

> because each culture has its own symbol systems, its own means for interpreting experiences, the 'raw materials' of the personal intelligences quickly get marshaled by systems of meaning that may be quite distinct from one another . . . the varieties of personal intelligence prove much more distinctive, less comparable, perhaps even unknowable to someone from an alien society. (p. 240)

Hence some members of cultural and ethnic minorities may have ways of learning that are dissimilar to those of the dominant culture, and also different outcomes from their learning. It is therefore important to assess such constructs as intelligence in as culture-fair a manner as possible (Sternberg, 1985: 77, 309), and to seek appropriate means to facilitate learning of the skills required in organisations. Clements and Jones (2002) point to the importance of self-learning when addressing diversity. Learning through action might also be particularly appropriate.

Understanding of and fluency with English are not the only language issues in organisations. As discussed in Chapter 3, language is ideological and can embody racism and sexism. Similarly, the construction of knowledge is a social and ideological process. Through the very nature of language and knowledge, these learners may be internalising constructions of themselves that ultimately undermine their self-esteem, alienate them from self-fulfilment, and erect barriers to their effective learning. Mentoring to support such learners could be particularly valuable.

The outcomes and process of learning

Managers responsible for human resource development need to understand the nature of learning and development. This section will, therefore, first examine the outcomes of learning, such as skill, competence and tacit knowledge, and employability, an indirect outcome. It will then look at the process of learning, the various levels of cognitive and other skills, at models of learning, and finally at barriers to learning.

The outcomes of learning

Skill

> ... the performance of any task which, for its successful and rapid completion, requires an improved organisation of responses making use of only those aspects of the stimulus which are essential to satisfactory performance. (Ribeaux and Poppleton, 1978: 53–54)

> ... an appearance of ease, of smoothness of movement, of confidence and the comparative absence of hesitation; it frequently gives the impression of being unhurried, while the actual pace of activity may of course be quite high ... increasing skill involves a widening of the range of possible disturbances that can be coped with without disrupting the performance.
>
> (Borger and Seaborne, 1966: 128–129)

These definitions are particularly appropriate to perceptual-motor skills, which involve physical, motor responses to perceived stimuli in the external world. Such skills are needed at every level of an organisation, from the senior manager's ability to operate a desktop computer to the cleaner's operation of a floor-scrubbing machine. High levels of such skills are particularly needed to operate complex and expensive technology. There are many other kinds of skills needed in organisations, such as cognitive, linguistic, social and interpersonal skills, that could also be defined in these terms. However, their complexity suggests that various levels of skill have to be recognised, which is what a later subsection will do in presenting some hierarchies of skills.

Competence

Competence – also referred to as competency in the literature – has been defined as:

> an underlying characteristic of a person which results in effective and/or superior performance in a job. (Boyatzis, 1982)

> the ability to perform the activities within an occupational area to the levels of performance expected in employment. (Training Commission, 1988)

The core of the definition is an ability to apply knowledge and skills with understanding to a work activity.

Competences are now a major element in the design of training and development in Britain (Cannell *et al.*, 1999), and seem to fit well with what is happening in organisations. Martin (1995: 20) proposes that they are a means of 'aligning what people can offer – their competencies – against the demands of customers rather than against the ill-fitting and ill-designed demands of jobs'. Nevertheless, the notions of competence and competency are still matters of debate: from the confusion suggested by differences between the definitions above (Woodruffe, 1991) to, arguably, some inherent weaknesses (see Ford, 2002), and the challenge of 'postmodern' (see Chapter 3) thinking (Brittain and Ryder, 1999). Despite considerable variation in the number of competences being used in competence frameworks (one study suggested between 21 and 30 and 300–400), and often a lack of validation of such frameworks, there is claimed to be a 'dramatic increase' in the number of companies using them. 'Personnel professionals must stop dismissing competencies as fads' (Walsh, 1998: 15). (See CIPD Factsheet *Competency and Competency Frameworks*.)

What needs to be noted at this point is that the concept of competence integrates knowledge and skill that are assessed via performance. This leads on to the distinction between formal knowledge and 'know-how', in which tacit knowledge has a significant part to play.

'Know-how' and tacit knowledge

'Knowing how to do something' is a very different matter from *knowing about* 'knowing how to do something'. This truism is captured in the everyday suspicion and disparagement of 'the ivory tower': 'those who can, do; those who can't, teach'.

Gardner (1985) makes the distinction between 'know-how' and 'know-that'. For him, 'know-how' is the tacit knowledge of how to execute something, whereas 'know-that' is the statement of formal thinking (propositional knowledge) about the actual set of procedures involved in the execution:

> Thus, many of us know how to ride a bicycle but lack the propositional knowledge of how that behaviour is carried out. In contrast, many of us have propositional knowledge about how to make a soufflé without knowing how to carry this task through to successful completion. (p. 68)

This distinction highlights the significance for learning of action. Book ('propositional') knowledge is not enough.

Tacit knowledge is an essential ingredient of 'know-how' and action. Sternberg (1985: 169) recognises this in his definition of practical intelligence:

> Underlying successful performance in many real-world tasks is tacit knowledge of a kind that is never explicitly taught and in many instances never even verbalized.

The example that he gives is of the tacit knowledge relevant to the management of one's career. The individual also draws upon tacit knowledge in the fluent performance of perceptual-motor skills, as seen in the definition of skill above; indeed, Myers and Davids (1992) write of 'tacit skills'. It would appear to be acquired through experience rather than through instruction, and is embedded in the context in which this experience is taking place. This can be seen in Stage 2 of the model of Dreyfus *et al.* (1986; see below), in which the learner becomes independent of instruction through the recognition of the contextual elements of the task, and thereafter develops the ability to register and 'read' contextual cues. However, unlike the formal knowledge that it accompanies, this tacit knowledge never becomes explicit, although it remains very significant. It has to be apprehended in context, and one way of doing this is to pay attention to the stories that are told in organisations (for example, Gabriel, 2000). Myers and Davids (1992: 47) question whether 'tacit skills' can be taught, and identify that they are often transmitted in 'an environment of intensive practical experience' and in task performance: 'We may yet be able to learn much from "sitting next to Nellie"!' They also note the need to take account of both formal and tacit knowledge in selection.

Traditionally, practical knowledge tends to feature at a lower level in any representation of the social hierarchy of skills, and is thereby institutionalised in lower-level occupations. In discussing the public's understanding of science, Collins (1993: 17) writes about:

> the all too invisible laboratory technician . . . Look into a laboratory and you will see it filled with fallible machines and the manifest recalcitrance of nature . . . Technicians make things work in the face of this . . . Notoriously, techniques that can be made to work by one technician in one place will not work elsewhere. The technician has a practical understanding of aspects of the craft of science beyond that of many scientists. But does the technician 'understand science'?

Cooley (1987: 10–13) draws attention to the way in which practical knowledge, craft skill, is devalued in the face of technological progress. This is the starting point for his reflections upon the way 'ordinary people' could achieve something extraordinary. He believes that technological systems

> tend to absorb the knowledge from ['ordinary people'], deny them the right to use their skill and judgement, and render them abject appendages to the machines and systems being developed.

Myers and Davids (1992: 47) come to a similar conclusion after their discussion of the significance of 'tacit skills'.

It is clear that organisations need both 'know-how' and 'know-that'. Hence the concept of competences, as defined above, is important, although it can be argued that the institutionalised, transorganisational process of identifying and defining them has wrenched them from their context and hence from the tacit knowledge that contributes so significantly to them. However, knowledge management, action learning, and mentoring all explicitly contextualise knowledge and learning and hence draw out tacit knowledge.

Employability

An indirect outcome of learning and development is employability, a notion that became current because of the proliferation of flexible contracts of employment and insecurity in employment during the 1990s. According to Kanter (1989a), employability was the 'new security': if individuals have acquired and maintained their employability then, should their job come to an end, they would be able to find employment elsewhere.

Employability results from investment in the human capital of skills and reputation. This means that individuals must engage in continuous learning and development, update their skills and acquire others that might be needed in the future by their current or future employer (Fonda and Guile, 1999). It is also argued that, as part of the 'new deal' in employment, good employers will ensure that their employees remain employable (Herriot and Pemberton, 1995) by keeping them up to date through training and development.

The process of learning

The chapter will now first consider theories of the process of learning and of elements within it, and then examine that process in terms of various levels, stages, and cyclical models of learning. This is a very rich and complex field, to which justice cannot be done here, and you are recommended to read a text such as Atkinson *et al.* (1999) or Ribeaux and Poppleton (1978).

Theories of the process of learning

Behaviourist approach to learning

The behaviourist approach has been one of the most influential in the field of psychology. It proposes that learning is the process by which a particular stimulus (S), repeatedly associated with, or conditioned by, desirable or undesirable experiences, comes to evoke a particular response (R). This conditioning can be of two kinds. Classical conditioning occurs when a stimulus leads automatically to a response. Dogs, for example, salivate at the presentation of food; Pavlov demonstrated that they could also be conditioned to salivate at the sound of a bell rung before food is presented. Operant conditioning (Skinner) takes place after a desired response, which is then reinforced, or rewarded, to increase the probability of the repetition of the same response when the stimulus recurs.

There has been much experimental research (including many animal studies) into such issues as the nature of the reinforcement (negative reinforcement, or punishment, is not as effective for learning as positive reward); the schedule of reinforcement (whether at fixed or variable intervals: intermittent reinforcement is more effective than continuous reinforcement). This form of conditioning is also used to shape behaviour: that is, to continue to reinforce responses that approximate to the desired behaviour until that behaviour is finally achieved. We are familiar with this kind of approach to the encouragement of simple behaviours: we use it with small children, with animals, and in basic forms of training.

Cognitive learning theory

The S–R approach pays no attention to the cognitive processes whereby the stimulus comes to be associated with a particular response: it does not investigate what is in the 'black box'. Cognitive learning theory, however, offers a more complex understanding of learning, proposing, again originally on the basis of animal studies, that what is learned is not an association of stimulus with response (S–R), but of stimulus with stimulus (S–S). The learner develops expectations that stimuli are linked; the result is a cognitive 'map' or latent learning. Hence insightful behaviour appropriate to a situation takes place without the strengthening association of S–R bonds. Social learning theory also addresses what is in the 'black box'. It recognises the role in learning of the observation and imitation of the behaviour of others, but as seen in, say, the debates over the influence of the media upon young people's behaviour, there are clearly many moderating variables.

Information-processing approach to learning

This approach regards learning as an information processing system in which a signal, containing information, is transmitted along a communication channel of limited capacity and subject to interference and 'noise' (Stammers and Patrick, 1975). The signal has to be decoded before it can be received, and then encoded to pass it on. In learning, data received through the senses are filtered, recognised and decoded through the interpretative process of perception; this information is then translated into action through the selection of appropriate responses. The effectiveness of learning depends on attention being paid only to the relevant parts of the stimuli, the rapid selection of appropriate responses, the efficient performance of them, and the feeding back of information about their effects into the system. Overload or breakdown of the system can occur at any of these stages.

Gagné (1974, in Fontana, 1981: 73) expresses this as a chain of events, some internal and others external to the learner. It begins with the learner's readiness to receive information (motivation or expectancy), and continues as the learner perceives it, distinguishes it from other stimuli, makes sense of it and relates it to what is already known. The information is then stored in short- or long-term memory. Thereafter it can be retrieved from memory, generalised to, and put into practice in, new situations. Its final phase is feedback from knowledge of the results obtained from this practice. Those concerned to facilitate learning in others can use their understanding of this chain to prevent failure to learn, which can take place at any one of these levels.

Elements in the process of learning

This subsection will deal briefly with other important elements in the process of learning that need to be taken into account when designing or facilitating learning.

Feedback (or knowledge of results)

The feedback to learners of the results of their performance is recognised as essential to their effective learning. This is discussed in Ribeaux and Poppleton (1978) and Stammers and Patrick (1975). Feedback will be either intrinsic or extrinsic (or augmented). Learners receive visual or kinaesthetic feedback (intrinsic) from their responses to stimuli in the learning situation; they need to be encouraged to 'listen' to such bodily cues in order to improve performance. They may also receive feedback (extrinsic, augmented) from an external source while they are performing (concurrent feedback) or after it (terminal). Learners may also benefit from receiving guidance before their performance about what to look out for during it. The sources cited above set out the characteristics, advantages and disadvantages of these different kinds of feedback.

The notion of feedback is frequently discussed in terms of learning perceptual-motor or similar skills. It is also of considerable importance in the learning of the higher-order skills discussed in this chapter, but here it is very complex in nature, and difficult for the learner to be aware and make sense of it. However, by reflecting and engaging in the whole-loop learning (see later), the learner will have opportunity to pay attention to both intrinsic and extrinsic feedback.

The choice of whole or part learning

Psychologists continue to debate the appropriateness of whole or part learning in learning to perform various tasks: that is, whether the task is learned as a whole, or in parts. Ribeaux and Poppleton (1978: 61) report on one approach that classifies tasks according to their 'complexity' (the difficulty of the component subtasks) and 'organisation' (the degree to which they are interrelated). Where complexity and organisation are both high, whole methods appear superior; where either is low, part methods are superior in most cases; when both are low, part and whole methods are equally successful. Stammers and Patrick (1975: 85–88), however, report on research that appears to draw opposite conclusions: where the elements of a task are highly independent the task is best learned as a whole, but where they are interdependent, they should be learned in parts.

It tends to be the whole method in operation when learning takes place during the performance of a job, through action learning, or through observing others.

The role of memory in learning

Memory plays a significant role in learning, and some understanding of it can therefore be used to make learning more effective. Once again, it is not possible to do more than present an outline here, but texts such as Stammers and Patrick (1975), Ribeaux and Poppleton (1978), Fontana (1981) and Atkinson *et al.* (1999) give further information.

Memory involves three kinds of information storage: the storage of sensory memories, short-term or primary memory, and long-term or secondary memory. Unless transferred to short-term memory, the sensory memory retains sense data for probably less than two seconds. Unless incoming information is paid particular attention or rehearsed, short-term memory holds it for up to 30 seconds and appears to have limited capacity, whereas long-term memory appears to have unlimited capacity and to hold information for years. What is therefore of concern for effective learning is the ability to transfer information to the long-term memory. There are two aspects to such transfer. The first is 'rehearsal' – that is, paying attention to and repeating the information until it is coded and enters the long-term store; it is otherwise displaced by new incoming information. The second aspect of the transfer of information to long-term memory is coding: the translation of information into the codes that enable it to be 'filed' into the memory's 'filing system'. Information is largely coded according to meaning (a semantic code) or through visual images, but sometimes (where the meaning itself is unclear) according to sound.

The ability to retrieve information from long-term memory depends in part upon how effectively it has been organised ('filed') in storage (for example, words may be stored according to sound and meaning), but also upon having the most appropriate retrieval cue. We experience this when we are searching for something that we have lost: we think systematically through what we were doing when we believe we last used the lost object. Recognition is easier than recall from memory because it follows the presentation of clear retrieval cues.

Difficulty in retrieving information, or forgetting, occurs for several reasons apart from those concerning the degree of organisation in storage. Interference from other information can disrupt long-term as well as short-term memory (where new items displace existing items in the limited capacity). Interference may be retroactive, when new information interferes with the recall of older material, or proactive, when earlier learning seems to inhibit the recall of later information. Forgetting also takes place through anxiety or unhappy associations with the material to be learned, which might become repressed. Unhappy childhood experiences, for example, might be repressed for many years.

Finally, memory does not just operate as a camera recording what is experienced: it is an active and a constructive process. This is particularly so when learning the kind of complex material that constitutes the world of organisations and human resource management. As well as recording its data inputs, the process of memory draws inferences from the data and so elaborates upon them, filtering them through the individual's stereotypes, mindset and world-view. What is then stored is this enhanced and repackaged material.

An understanding of the nature of memory suggests various ways in which it might be improved to make learning more effective. The transfer of new information to long-term memory is clearly crucial: attention, recitation, repetition and constant revision (known as *overlearning*) are needed. The coding and organisation of material to be stored are also important: this is helped by associating the new information with what is already familiar, especially using visual imagery, by attending to the context giving rise to the information to be learned, and by making the effort to understand the information so that it can be stored in the appropriate 'files'. Importantly, facilitators of learning need to ensure that the learning context or event does not provoke anxiety.

Levels of learning

This chapter has highlighted the need for organisational members to practise higher-order thinking skills. This implies that there are several types and levels of skill. This subsection presents several classifications, some of different types of skill, others of different levels or stages. Some are couched in terms of stages rather than levels: the individual can progress from the lower to the higher stages, but does not necessarily do so. The lower levels are prerequisites for, and subsumed by, the higher. (See The process of development on page 256 for a discussion of the concept of stages.)

Organisations require several types and levels of skills, not only the higher-level thinking skills. The human resource manager can therefore use these classifications, first to identify the prior learning needed before skills of various levels can be attained, and then to plan ways of facilitating their learning.

Fitts's stages of skills acquisition

Fitts (1962, in Stammers and Patrick, 1975) distinguished three stages of learning, in particular of perceptual-motor skills acquisition. It is recognised that they may overlap.

- *Cognitive stage.* The learner has to understand what is required, its rules and concepts, and how to achieve it.

- *Associative stage.* The learner has to establish through practice the stimulus–response links, the correct patterns of behaviour, gradually eliminating errors.

- *Autonomous stage.* The learner refines the motor patterns of behaviour until external sources of information become redundant and the capacity simultaneously to perform secondary tasks increases.

Dreyfus *et al.*'s stage model of skills acquisition

Dreyfus *et al.* (1986, in Cooley, 1987: 13–15 and Quinn *et al.*, 1990: 314–15) set out a more elaborate model of the acquisition of skills that is relevant to understanding the development of cognitive skills. Their five-stage model moves from the effective performance of lower- to higher-order skills.

- *Stage 1: the novice.* Novices follow context-free rules, with relevant components of the situation defined for them: hence they lack any coherent sense of the overall task.

- *Stage 2: the advanced beginner.* Through their practical experience in concrete situations learners begin to recognise the contextual elements of their task. They begin to perceive similarities between new and previous experiences.

- *Stage 3: competent.* They begin to recognise a wider range of cues, and become able to select and focus upon the most important of them. Their reliance upon rules lessens; they experiment and go beyond the rules, using trial and error.

- *Stage 4: proficient.* Those who arrive at this stage achieve the unconscious, fluid, effortless performance referred to in the definitions of skill given earlier. They still think analytically, but can now 'read' the evolving situation, picking up new cues and becoming aware of emerging patterns; they have an involved, intuitive and holistic grasp of the situation.

- *Stage 5: expert.* At this stage, according to Cooley (1987: 15), 'Highly experienced people seem to be able to recognise whole scenarios without decomposing them into elements or separate features'. They have 'multidimensional maps of the territory'; they 'frame and reframe strategies as they read changing cues' (Quinn *et al.*, 1990: 315). With this intuitive understanding of the implications of a situation, they can cope with uncertainty and unforeseen situations.

Managers' levels of learning (Burgoyne and Hodgson)

A similar hierarchy has been proposed specifically for the learning of managers. Burgoyne and Hodgson (1983) suggest that managers have a gradual build-up of experience created out of specific learning incidents, internalise this experience, and use it, both consciously and unconsciously, to guide their future action and decision-making. They identify three levels of this learning process:

- *Level 1 learning*, which occurs when managers simply take in some factual information or data that is immediately relevant but does not change their views of the world.

- *Level 2 learning*, which occurs at an unconscious or tacit level. Managers gradually build up a body of personal 'case law' that enables them to deal with future events.

- *Level 3 learning*, when managers consciously reflect on their conception of the world, how it is formed, and how they might change it.

Perry's continuum of intellectual and ethical development

Perry's (1968) schema (see Daloz, 1986) emerged from his research into his students' experiences. He interpreted their intellectual and ethical development as a continuum, and mapped out the way in which individuals develop multiple perspectives while at the same time becoming able to commit themselves to their own personal interpretation. At one extreme is basic dualism, where everything is seen as good or bad. This moves on to recognition of the diversity of opinion; recognition of extensive legitimate uncertainty; through recognition that all knowledge and values are contextual and relativistic; to the recognition of the need to make a commitment to a viewpoint; the making of that commitment; experiencing its implications; and, finally, to the affirmation of identity as this commitment is expressed through lifestyle.

Bloom et al.'s taxonomy of cognitive skills

Bloom *et al.* (1956) offer a classification of skills in which a hierarchy is implied:

- knowledge (simple knowledge of facts, of terms, of theories etc.);
- comprehension (an understanding of the meaning of this knowledge);
- application (the ability to apply this knowledge and comprehension in new concrete situations);
- analysis (the ability to break the material down into its constituent parts and to see the relationship between them);

- synthesis (the ability to reassemble these parts into a new and meaningful relationship, thus forming a new whole);
- evaluation (the ability to judge the value of material using explicit and coherent criteria, either of one's own devising or derived from the work of others) (Fontana, 1981: 71).

Single- and double-loop learning

Another useful classification of learning is found in the concept of two different types of learning: single- and double-loop learning. Individuals do not necessarily progress from single- to double-loop learning, nor is the former an essential prerequisite for the latter.

Single-loop learning refers to the detection and correction of deviances in performance from established (organisational or other) norms, whereas double-loop learning (Argyris and Schön, 1978) refers to the questioning of those very norms that define effective performance. Learning how to learn calls for double-loop learning.

Gagné's classification of learning

Gagné (1970, in Stammers and Patrick, 1975) studied both the process of learning and the most effective modes of instruction, and has made several classifications of types of learning, again implying a hierarchy. For example, he identified the ability to make a general response to a signal; to develop a chain of two or more stimulus–response links, including verbal chains and associations; to make different responses to similar though different stimuli; to achieve concept learning and identify a class of objects or events; to learn rules through the acquisition of a chain of two or more concepts; and, finally, to combine rules and so achieve problem-solving.

Gagné's classification allows us to identify the processes whereby skills of all levels are acquired, and hence suggests how to facilitate learning and prevent failure to learn at the various levels.

Activity | **Higher-order thinking skills**

On your own or in a small group, return to the section 'The changing world of work and organisations' and identify the higher-order thinking skills it suggests are now needed in organisations. Where would they be classified in the various classifications above? What does this tell you about those skills and how they could be developed?

Cyclical models of learning and learning styles

Another, and more dynamic, way of conceptualising the learning process is to see it as cyclical. The process has different identifiable phases, and individual learners have preferred learning styles. If methods appropriate to the various phases and individual styles are used, more effective learning will result. (The assumptions about phases echo those underlying the concept of development, which is to be discussed in the next section.) The various models below offer a number of important insights to the human resource manager concerned to facilitate higher-order skills in the organisation. They draw attention to the significance of learning through action and reflection, as well as through the traditional channels of teaching/learning. They recognise that individuals might prefer different phases of the cycle and have different styles: they offer means to identify those preferences; to engage in dialogue with individuals about their preferences; and to identify means of helping individuals to complete the whole cycle. (See CIPD Factsheet *Learning Styles* (updated August 2008).)

Kolb's learning cycle

The best-known learning cycle in the field in which we are interested is that of Kolb. There are two dimensions to learning (Kolb *et al.*, 1984): concrete/abstract (involvement/detachment) and active/reflective (actor/observer). Learning is an integrated cognitive and affective process moving in a cyclical manner from concrete experience (CE) through reflective observation (RO) and abstract conceptualisation (AC) to active experimentation (AE) and so on (Kolb, 1983).

Effective learning calls for learners:

- to become fully involved in concrete, new experiences (CE);
- to observe and reflect on these experiences from many perspectives (RO);
- to use concepts and theories to integrate their observations (AC);
- to use those theories for decision-making and problem-solving (AE).

However, many people have a preference for a particular phase and so do not complete the cycle: thus they do not learn as effectively or as comprehensively as they could. Kolb's Learning Styles Inventory identifies these preferences (Mumford, 1988: 27). The 'converger' (AC and AE) prefers the practical and specific; the 'diverger' (CE and RO) looks from different points of view and observes rather than acts; the 'assimilator' (AC and RO) is comfortable with concepts and abstract ideas; and the 'accommodator' (CE and AE) prefers to learn primarily from doing.

Honey and Mumford's learning styles

Honey and Mumford (1992) also identify four learning styles, based on the individual's preference for one element in the learning cycle, and have developed norms based on the results of those who have completed their Learning Styles Questionnaire. Their activists learn best when they are actively involved in concrete tasks; reflectors learn best through reviewing and reflecting upon what has happened and what they have done; theorists learn best when they can relate new information to concepts or theory; pragmatists learn best when they see relevance between new information and real-life issues or problems (Mumford, 1988). This information can be used to design effective learning events, including, Mumford (2002) reminds us, e-learning. Individuals, too, can use it to build on their strengths and reduce their weaknesses in learning.

The Lancaster cycle of learning

A cyclical model said to represent 'all forms of learning including cognitive, skill development and affective, by any process' (Binsted, 1980: 22) is the Lancaster model based on managers' learning. This identifies three different forms of learning: receipt of input/generation of output, discovery and reflection. As Figure 7.1 shows, they take place in both the inner and outer world of the individual. The receipt of input results from being taught or told information, or reading it in books. Learners follow the discovery loop (action and feedback) through action and experimentation, opening themselves to the new experiences generated, and becoming aware of the consequences of their actions. They follow the reflection loop (conceptualising and hypothesising) when making sense of the information they receive and the actions they undertake, and when, on the basis of this, theorising about past or future situations.

Each form of learning is cyclical, and the cycles can be linked in various ways (for example, learning in formal classroom settings links the receipt of input with reflection), but in effective learning the learner will complete the overall cycle.

The learning curve

Though not a cyclical model, the learning curve is included here for convenience. The notion of a curve is based on the recognition that there is a relationship between the rate of learning and the passage of time. Managers working on the introduction of a new system, for example, might say 'we are on a learning curve'. This curve is often represented as being S-shaped, that is, proficiency in a new skill begins slowly at first, increases steadily over time, and then remains on a plateau. However, since the shape of the curve must clearly depend on the nature and circumstances of the learning, this notion of a learning curve perhaps adds little of value to the understanding of learning.

Figure 7.1 The Lancaster model of the learning cycle

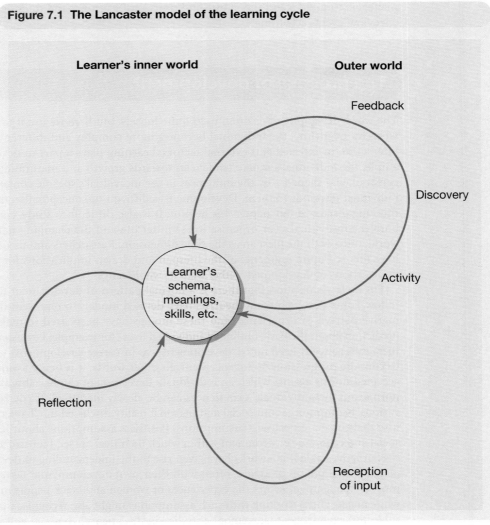

Source: Based on Binsted (1980: 21). Reproduced with permission of Emerald Group Publishing Limited.

Activity

Achieving effective learning

Reflect on your own learning about HRM. Identify where you are in terms of the classifications and cycles above. What do you have to do to make your learning more effective? Note this in your learning diary, and discuss with your mentor (see Exercises on page 275 at the end of this chapter).

Barriers to learning

Although learning is a natural process, people can experience significant barriers, particularly to their learning in formal settings such as school and work. Some of these barriers can be internal: the learner might have poor learning skills or habitual learning styles that constrain them; poor communications skills; unwillingness to take risks; fear or insecurity. Anxiety and lack of confidence are frequently emphasised as significant impediments to learning. Other barriers can be thrown up by the situation: lack of learning opportunities or of support, inappropriate time or place (see Mumford, 1988). This emphasises the need for HR managers to understand the nature and process of learning, and to design learning experiences and events accordingly.

The process of development

The word 'development' is often used quite loosely, but here we use it to mean the process whereby, over time, the individual becomes more complex and differentiated through the interaction of internal and external factors. Learning plays a part in development. For example, the individual's innate tendencies towards growth and maturation are facilitated or constrained – shaped – by the influences in the individual's specific context, and by how the individual responds to them. Development is difficult to conceptualise, though the systems thinking discussed in Chapter 3 is helpful. It is also difficult to study, embracing as it does both the individual's (or organisation's) inner life and the changing nature of a complex world, often with the lifespan as the time dimension. Researchers and theorists may therefore have focused upon segments of the lifespan and drawn implications for the remainder, or upon aspects of development rather than its whole range.

On their assumption that there is a normal pattern of development that all individuals follow, some developmental theorists have devised models to represent this universal, normative pattern of experience, and these models have been used to make some degree of prediction about the basic outline of individual lives (for example, Levinson *et al.*, 1978). Further, as has already been noted, development – as in 'career development' – is sometimes used to connote progression or advancement. In other words, it is being assumed that there are accepted norms against which an individual's development can be calibrated, and that those norms and the individuals' experiences can be clearly identified. If you recall the nature of various assumptions about social and personal reality discussed in Chapter 3, you will recognise that these are positivist assumptions. Positivist assumptions about individuals and the social and economic environment within which their lives are led (construed here as an objective, orderly, stable framework) have given rise to the understanding of development in terms of sequential phases or stages, often with their own developmental tasks. Moreover, those models frequently interpret the experiences of women and black people in terms of those of white males. Those working with such assumptions might also recognise that individuals have subjective experiences that cannot be studied in this scientific manner and so might disregard them, although individuals base decisions about their life on their subjective experiences.

However, as Chapter 3 outlined, there are alternative approaches. The phenomenological approach acknowledges the significance of a person's subjective experiences, and the social constructionist approach recognises that, because individual experiences are socially constructed, the context of the individual has to be taken into account. Such alternative assumptions lead to a focus upon individual cases and the search for insights rather than generalisable conclusions. They also emphasise the significance of context, and the dynamic, intersubjective processes through which individuals interpret and make decisions about their lives and careers.

When trying to understand development, then, it is important to be aware of the kind of assumptions that are being made about it. This may be particularly important if the present global recession (2009) badly disrupts what had become an accepted pattern of experience.

Lifespan development

Lifespan development embraces the total development of the individual over time, and results from the interweaving of the biological, social, economic and psychological strands of the individual's life. People develop through their lifespan, achieving greater degrees of complexity, even transformation. They are therefore continuously engaging in learning processes as they seek balance between changing self and changing environment. The theories and models of lifespan development have several implications for human resource development, for the organisation is one of the major arenas in which adult development takes place.

The influence of the socio-cultural context

One perspective upon the influence of the socio-cultural context on the individual's lifespan experiences interprets that there are tendencies towards common patterns in individual experiences resulting from socialisation. In any given social setting, whether culture, class or organisation, the members of a social group experience pressures to conform to certain patterns of behaviour or norms. Sometimes these pressures are expressed as legal constraints: the age of consent, marriage, attaining one's majority (becoming an adult); or as quasi-legal constraints such as the age at which the state pension is paid and hence at which most people retire from the labour force; or as social and peer group expectations. For example, Neugarten (1968) recognises how family, work and social statuses provide the 'major punctuation marks in the adult life', and the

> way of structuring the passage of time in the life span of the individual, providing a time clock that can be superimposed over the biological clock . . .   (p. 146)

Stable organisations in the past also had their own 'clocks'. Sofer (1970) writes of his respondents' 'sensitive awareness' of the relation between age and organisational grade, for they were:

> constantly mulling over this and asking themselves whether they were on schedule, in front of schedule or behind schedule, showing quite clearly that they had a set of norms in mind as to where one should be by a given age.   (p. 239)

There is another perspective, however, that emphasises that the environment offers different opportunities and threats for individual lives. The process of development or elaboration takes place as the individual's innate capacity to grow and mature unfolds within a particular context, which in turn facilitates or stunts growth, or prompts variations upon it. For example, it is argued that there are significant differences in physical, intellectual and socio-economic attainments between children from different social classes (Keil, 1981). The interaction and accommodation between individuals and their environment therefore cannot be meaningfully expressed in a model that is cross-cultural or universal. Hence Gallos (1989) questions the relevance of many of the accepted views of development to women's lives and careers, while Thomas and Alderfer (1989) note that 'the influence of race on the developmental process' is commonly ignored in the literature.

Models of lifespan development

There are many different models of the lifespan: here you can see two that have been influential in lifespan psychology. It is important to be aware of the assumptions underlying those models, as discussed above. Their implications for human resource development will be noted below.

Erikson's psychosocial model

Erikson (1950) conceives of development in terms of stages of ego development and the effects of maturation, experience and socialisation (see Levinson *et al.*, 1978; Wrightsman,

1988). Each stage builds on the ones before, and presents the expanding ego with a choice or 'crisis'. The successful resolution of that 'crisis' achieves a higher level of elaboration in individuality and adaptation to the demands of both inner and outer world, and hence the capacity to deal with the next stage. An unsuccessful or inadequate resolution hinders or distorts this process of effective adaptation in the subsequent stages.

For example, the adolescent strives for a coherent sense of self, or identity, perhaps experimenting with several different identities and as yet uncommitted to one; entry to work and choice of work role play a part here. A choice, however, has to be made and responsibility assumed for its consequences: unless this occurs, there is identity confusion. Young adults have to resolve another choice. This is between achieving closeness and intimate relationships *or* being ready to isolate themselves from others.

Erikson paid less attention to the remainder of the lifespan, but indicated that the choice for those aged 25 to 65 is between the stagnation that would result from concern only for self, indulging themselves as though they were 'their own only child' (Wrightsman, 1988: 66), *or* 'generativity'. This is the reaching out beyond the need to satisfy self in order to take responsibility in the adult world, and show care for others, the next generation, or the planet itself. The choice of the final stage is between construing life as having been well *or* ill spent.

The model of Levinson et al.

Levinson *et al.* (1978) studied the experiences of men in mid-life, and from those constructed a model of the male lifespan in terms of alternating, age-related, periods of stability and instability. In the stable period, lasting six to eight years, a man builds and enriches the structure of his life: work, personal relationships and community involvement. That structure, however, cannot last, and so there follows a transitional period, of four to five years, when the individual reappraises that structure and explores new possibilities. These can be uncomfortable or painful experiences, but they are the essential prelude to adapting or changing the life structure, and so achieving a further stable period.

You can read more about this model in Daloz (1986) and Wrightsman (1988), but should be aware of the assumptions underpinning it. Its definition of the periods within the lifespan in terms of chronological age – for example, between ages 22 and 28 a man embarks on a stable period and entry into the adult world, and between ages 33 and 40 enters another stable period in which he settles down – reflects its assumption about the universal, normative patterning of experiences.

What are the implications of your personal development so far for your effectiveness, or potential effectiveness, as an employee?

Career development

Individual development interacts with the organisation and its development through the individual's career. Career development therefore is of significance for both individual and organisation, and hence for human resource development.

Defining career

Although the term 'career' is well understood in everyday language, the concept is a complex one with several levels of meaning, making it open to several definitions (see Glossary, p. 682; Greenhaus and Callanan, 2006). The core of the concept suggests the experience of continuity and coherence while the individual moves through time and social space. As with development generally, an individual's career results from the interaction of internal and external factors. As individuals become more skilled and flexible through learning and development, they gain more opportunities for intra- or inter-organisational moves, including promotion. Their learning and development also influence the rewards they gain from their work, their relationship with their employer, the role of work in their lives, and the way they view themselves and are viewed by others. However, 'career' refers not only to their observable movement through and experiences in organisations and the social structure generally. That is their objective career, while the personal interpretation they make of those experiences, the private meaning and significance it has for them, is their subjective career.

Because career is such a broad, often ambiguous, yet widely used concept, there are many perspectives that can be taken upon it. For example, it can be considered as a concept in both social science and everyday speech. Collin and Young (2000) point out that there are various stakeholders in it, including the individual, the employer, the career counsellor, the government, and society itself, and draw attention to how power relationships are glossed over by its rhetorical use. (For a discussion of rhetoric see Chapter 3.) They also suggest that career may be changing from being a linear, future-oriented trajectory to becoming more of a collage of experiences. Another viewpoint upon career, found within vocational psychology, and underpinning career guidance theories and practice, focuses upon career choice and the most effective ways of matching people to jobs (for example, Holland, 1997). Or the concern may be with career development through life (for example, Cytrynbaum and Crites, 1989; Dalton, 1989). A further perspective looks at the nature and management of careers in organisations (for example, Arnold, 1997; Arthur *et al.*, 1989; Arthur and Rousseau, 1996; Chartered Institute of Personnel and Development, 2004; Hall and Associates, 1996; Jackson, 1999), while yet another adopts a self-help approach to careers (for example, Bolles, 1988).

Traditional theories of career development

There are many theories that have attempted to explain career. Although it is not possible to examine all these theories here (for further details see Arthur *et al.*, 1989; Greenhaus and Callanan, 2006; Watts *et al.*, 1996), by classifying them into families we can see something of their range and major concerns:

- Theories concerned with external influences upon the individual's career:
  - the economic system and labour markets;
  - social class, social structure and social mobility;
  - organisational and occupational structure and mobility.
- Theories concerned with factors internal to the individual:
  - factors such as age, gender;
  - psychoanalytical explanations;
  - personality traits;
  - lifespan development;
  - implementation of self-concept.
- Theories concerned with the interaction of internal and external factors:
  - decision-making;
  - social learning.
- Theories concerned with the interpretation of the individual's subjective experiences:
  - narrative approaches;
  - social constructionist approaches (see Chapter 3).

The theories of career development have similar characteristics to those of lifespan development. Because of the assumptions commonly made about objectivity and subjectivity (see Chapter 3, and the discussion about the concept of development above), frequently they:

- are formulated from a positivist rather than from a phenomenological or constructionist stance (see Chapter 3);
- focus upon objective rather than subjective experience;
- emphasise intra-individual rather than contextual factors;

- make assumptions about the universality of career, disregarding the significance of diversity: gender, race and social class (see Hopfl and Hornby Atkinson, 2000; Leong and Hartung, 2000; Marshall, 1989; Thomas, 1989).

When reading about career (for example, Greenhaus and Callanan, 2006), then, one must be aware of their underlying assumptions.

Careers in the twenty-first century

The theories above reflect long-established understandings of career. However, the flatter and more flexible forms of today's organisations, and the changing relationship between employees and employers ('the new deal', according to Herriot and Pemberton, 1995) could well change the nature of career dramatically. There are also some slow, deep-seated changes taking place in the context of career. Demographic changes and shifts in public and private values, for example, may over time have significant impacts upon individuals' opportunities, attitudes and aspirations. It is for this reason that questions have been asked not only about future careers (Chartered Institute of Personnel and Development, 2002b), but also about the future of the concept of career itself (Collin and Young, 2000). The present global disturbances taking place as this chapter is being written in 2009 make it unlikely that those questions can be answered for a long time.

The potentials and implications of some of these changes – for individuals, employers, educationalists, careers guidance practitioners and policy makers of various kinds – are being discussed widely (see Jackson *et al.*, 1996). It has been suggested that it is the traditional 'onward and upward' form of career that is under threat. However, Guest and McKenzie Davey (1996: 22), who have found little evidence of major organisational transformations in their own research, caution 'don't write off the traditional career'. Moreover, Moynagh and Worsley (2005), drawing on the ESRC's Future of Work research programme (**www.leeds.ac.uk/ esrcfutureofwork/**), also consider that long-term jobs and careers will continue to be found.

Theorists are attempting to understand what career is likely to become in the twenty-first century: three examples of their views are given here.

Bureaucratic, professional and entrepreneurial forms of career

Kanter (1989b: 508) draws our attention to the way in which, although only one of three forms of career, the '*bureaucratic*' form, defined by a 'logic of advancement', has come to dominate our view of organisational careers generally. The '*professional*' form of career (Kanter, 1989b: 516) is wider than that pursued by members of professional bodies. It is defined by craft or skill; occupational status is achieved through the 'monopolization of socially valued knowledge' and 'reputation' is a key resource for the individual. Career opportunities are not dependent in the same way as in the 'bureaucratic' career upon the development of the organisation, nor is satisfaction as dependent upon the availability of extrinsic rewards. Some professional careers may be only weakly connected to employing organisations. The '*entrepreneurial*' career develops 'through the creation of new value or new organisational capacity' (Kanter, 1989b: 516). Its key resource is the capacity to create valued outputs, and it offers freedom, independence and control over tasks and surroundings. However, while those with a 'bureaucratic' career have (relative) security, and 'professionals' can command a price in the marketplace, 'entrepreneurs' 'have only what they grow'.

It is the 'bureaucratic' form of career that is now under threat, but attributes of the 'professional' and 'entrepreneurial' forms are likely to be found far more extensively in the twenty-first century (Collin and Watts, 1996; Chartered Institute of Personnel and Development, 2002b).

The subjective career

Weick and Berlinger (1989) argue that in 'self-designing organisations' (the learning organisation of a later section), the focus will be on the subjective career. In the absence of the typical attributes of career such as advancement and stable pathways, 'the objective career dissolves' and the subjective career 'becomes externalized and treated as a framework for career growth' (Weick and Berlinger, 1989: 321), and a resource for the further organisational self-design. They liken career development in such organisations to what Hall (1976) describes as the 'Protean career', in which people engage in 'interminable series of experiments and explorations'. Such a career calls for frequent substantial career moves in order to incorporate a changing, complex and multi-layered sense of self; the 'decoupling' of identity from jobs; the preservation of the ability to make choices within the organisation; the identification of distinctive competence; and the synthesis of complex information (Weick and Berlinger, 1989: 323–26).

The boundaryless career

Arthur and Rousseau (1996: 3) indicate that whereas careers traditionally took place 'through orderly employment arrangements' within organisations, many are now 'boundaryless', crossing traditional boundaries – between organisations, and home and work.

How do you envisage your future career? How will it be likely to differ from the career of your parents' and grandparents' generations?

What are the implications for your learning and development needs?

Implications of the changing nature of career

Many have regarded the traditional career as elitist, available to only a few from a relatively privileged social background and education. The future career may also be elitist, available to a few, but perhaps a different few. At this point it is possible to identify some of the winners and losers from the changes that are taking place. So far the losers have included workers in manufacturing, unskilled workers of many kinds, clerical workers of many kinds, middle managers of many kinds, and full-time workers of many kinds; many of those have been men. The winners have been the knowledge workers, those with the skills required by the new technologies, those with the attitudes and skills needed in service jobs, those who are able (or want) to work only part time. Women may be benefiting from some of the changes. To be employed and to have a career in the future – to be self-programmable (Castells, 1998, see earlier) – individuals will have to remain employable, as this chapter has noted, with the ability to learn new knowledge and skills, and above all to learn how to learn. These are issues with which the present Labour government, which aims to achieve a high-skills and high-value-added economy, is greatly concerned. It recognises that, for individuals to get on in an imperfect labour market, both they and employers need encouragement and support. These will be delivered by the Adult Advancement and Careers Service for England, which is presently (2009) undergoing trials (Department of Innovation, Universities and Skills, 2008).

The changing nature of career is of considerable significance for society as a whole, as well as for individuals and for the economy. For example, the future orientation that a career gives an individual is essential when making decisions about such key issues as starting a family, taking out a mortgage, changing one's occupation, re-entering education, or retiring from employment. Uncertainty about career could therefore over time have effects on society.

Activity — Implications for human resource development

On your own or in a small group, identify and discuss the implications of an individual's

● lifespan development,

● career development

for the ways in which an organisation sets out to develop its employees

Development of the individual within organisations

We shall now note some ways in which individuals develop within organisations – or are developed by their organisations.

Employee development

Harrison (2005: 5) no longer uses the term 'employee development' because it 'smacks of the old "master-servant" relationship' and she now refers to it as 'learning and development'. Here, however, we want to mention it as one element of the latter, and so will use her 1992 definition of it. One definition of employee development is:

> . . . the skilful provision and organization of learning experiences in the workplace . . . [so that] performance can be improved . . . work goals can be achieved and that, through enhancing the skills, knowledge, learning ability and enthusiasm at every level, there can be continuous organizational as well as individual growth. Employee development must, therefore, be part of a wider strategy for the business, aligned with the organization's corporate mission and goals.
>
> (Harrison, 1992: 4)

Although, as the chapter has already argued, it is important for the organisation to develop its employees generally, many British employers have traditionally neglected employee development. This is reflected in the quotations from Cooley (1987) used in this chapter. However, recent interest in knowledge management, human capital and the learning organisation, and the establishment of the Investors in People award (see Chapter 8), are witness to employers' awareness of the need for employee development and the benefits that flow from it. Furthermore, those employers who have already recognised their own self-interest in their employees' continuous learning and employability often encourage their employees to engage in learning activities for self-development. Many organisations have now established learning centres that often support opportunities for learning beyond what those organisations specifically need. Others have set up corporate universities, such as Motorola and Unipart (Miller and Stewart, 1999; see also Coulson-Thomas, 2000). (See also CIPD Factsheet *Helping People Learn: Overview and Update* (updated 2009) and the subsection on e-learning.) Nevertheless, even though their employers may not formally 'develop' them or encourage them to develop themselves, people still continue to learn, as we shall note later in the chapter.

Staff development

This is similar to employee and professional development, but generally refers to the development of administrative, technical and professional staff in organisations, such as local authorities, in which such staff form a large proportion of those employed. Its aim is to enable such employees to perform their current and future roles effectively, but does not generally include their systematic development as managers.

Self-development

With the increasing flexibility of organisations and their contracts of employment, individuals need to engage in lifelong learning. However, many employees (including managers) do not receive from their employers the training and continuous development they need, and with the present (2009) uncertainty of employment, their need for self-development, associated with their need for employability, is likely in the future to be greater than ever.

'Self-development' is used to denote both 'of self' and 'by self' types of learning (Pedler, 1988). People developing themselves take responsibility for their own learning, identify their own learning needs and how to meet them, often through the performance of everyday work, monitor their own progress, assess the outcomes, and reassess their goals. The role of others in self-development is not to teach or to train, but perhaps to mentor, counsel or act as a resource.

Although self-development is regarded positively as proactive and entrepreneurial, it can be difficult for the individual to provide evidence of it without some form of accreditation. Once the study programmes available were largely dictated by the traditions and values of the educational providers, but now the Credit Accumulation and Transfer Scheme, and the Accreditation of Prior Learning and of Experiential Learning allow individuals to claim accreditation for a range of learning experiences, while S/NVQs (see Chapter 8) allow them to gain recognition for aspects of their work performance. Employee development schemes should also help individuals in their self-development, whether systematic or sporadic.

Management and organisation development

It should be noted that organisations, like people, need to develop to become more flexible, differentiated and adaptable to their environment. Indeed, the very development of organisational members will contribute to the development of the organisation itself, and the developing organisation can stimulate and foster individual learning. For example, as Chapter 9 recognises, management development is both needed by the developing organisation and sets in train further organisation development. However, it is not within the remit of this chapter to examine management development – this forms the subject of Chapter 9 – or organisation development, but they are included here for completeness.

Continuing professional development

Many professional institutions (see Arkin, 1992) require their members to engage in continuing professional development (CPD) because the changing environment is rendering obsolete some of their original professional skills and knowledge, and demanding the development of others. However, CPD is more than updating: it calls for a continuous process of learning and of learning-to-learn, and so is likely to have considerable benefits for organisations employing professionals, especially when part of the overall corporate strategy.

Likely to be of particular relevance to readers of this book is the requirement for CPD that the Chartered Institute of Personnel and Development (CIPD) places on its members. For the Institute, Whittaker (1992) states that CPD is needed to ensure that members remain up to date in a changing world and that the reputation of the profession is enhanced; and to encourage members to aspire to improved performance and become committed to learning as an integral part of their work. She identifies the following principles underlying CPD:

- development should always be continuous, the professional always actively seeking improved performance;
- development should be owned and managed by the learner;
- development should begin from the learner's current learning state – learning needs are individual;
- learning objectives should be clear, and where possible serve organisational as well as individual goals;
- investment in the time required for CPD should be regarded as being as important as investment in other activities.

Reflective learning is now also emphasised. CIPD members ensure their continuing development by engaging in professional activities, formal learning, and self-directed and informal learning (**www.cipd.co.uk/cpd**; Megginson and Whitaker, 2003). However, recent research (Rothwell and Arnold, 2005) indicated that, in practice, the high value that members attached to CPD has not translated into active engagement in it.

The subsection on career development referred briefly to the 'professional' form of career, and suggested that it might be more widely adopted in future. Continuing development, even where not required or monitored by a professional body, would be an important element of that.

The organisation as context for learning and development

This chapter has already noted how the process of learning knows no boundaries. People bring the fruits of this naturally occurring and continuous process into their place of work and so, as Cooley (1987: 169) shows, 'ordinary people' have the potential to contribute the knowledge, skills, attitudes and creative thinking that organisations need for survival, flexibility and development. Moreover, individuals' learning and development continue within the organisation, so here we shall examine how human resource managers can provide an environment in which the capacity to learn and adapt can be harnessed to benefit the organisation.

Employers benefit from – indeed, depend on – their employees' naturally occurring learning. Some recognise this and encourage, facilitate and extend those aspects of their employees' learning that are essential for the organisation, and support them informally or undertake formal employee development activities. However, organisations themselves can sometimes make inhospitable environments for the learning and development individuals bring to them (e.g. Honey, 2002). The section on learning and development noted that learning involves the whole person, but organisations are systems of roles (see Chapter 3), and those roles can distort or straitjacket individuals, as Argyris (1960) and McGregor (1960) argue. Moreover, some employers ignore the significance for the organisation of their employees' learning, and do little either to overcome the way in which the organisation may thwart the development of their employees, or to foster that learning and development. In those cases, employee development is not a planned or systematic process. It takes place nevertheless: employees learn for themselves how to carry out their jobs, or improve their performance; how to make job changes or achieve promotions; how to become managers and develop others. It must therefore be recognised that much employee learning might not be intended, planned or systematic. Nevertheless, individuals may:

- learn how to carry out their initial and subsequent jobs through doing and observing, through trial and error, through the influence of and feedback from their peers and supervisors, through modelling themselves on others, and through informal mentors;

- develop themselves through their own more or less systematic analysis of their learning needs;

- take the initiative to acquire additional skills, knowledge or understanding by attending educational and other courses, *via*, for example, learndirect (now Careers Advice Service, and to become the Adult Advancement and Careers Service) (see Career Development above, and Chapter 8).

Because of this, employee learning is problematical. Employers may receive many of its benefits without effort on their part, while at the same time, unlike recruitment and selection, they cannot fully control or contain it. Some employers might feel threatened by the potential of their employees' learning and development, seeing it as 'potentially subversive' (Garratt, in Pickard, 2005: 16), and not welcome significant changes in the people they had been at pains to select as employees. Through their work, employees might acquire knowledge and skills that make them marketable to other employers, and perhaps less than fully committed to their present employer. Equally, not exposed to best practice, they might learn poor lessons; they might also learn ineffectively and in an unnecessarily uncomfortable, effortful or wasteful manner. Thus they might not necessarily benefit from the learning and development they contribute to their organisation, although they would not be able to withhold some of its benefits from their employers.

To manage people effectively and fairly, and in a way that benefits the organisation, therefore, it is important to be aware of these thorny and, at times, moral issues. (You will have the opportunity to consider them in greater depth in the section on controversial issues.)

At the end of the twentieth century learning was advocated with missionary zeal, as is apparent in the words of Honey (1998: 28–29), quoted in the Introduction to this chapter, when setting out the Declaration of Learning drawn up by some of the 'leading thinkers on learning in organisations'. Many organisations heeded that message and, as many reports in *People Management* testify, are now committed to HRD. (See also CIPD's annual learning and development survey.) However, within a few years that Declaration had 'sunk without trace' (Pickard, 2005: 16). In a recent post-mortem, those same 'leading thinkers' discussed whether its demise might be due to HRD's tendency to control individuals through, for example, competency frameworks, rather than to develop them by developing the organisation. It was also suggested that, with the overall economy changing, HR was 'trying to make the industrial model work in the knowledge management world' (Burgoyne, in Pickard, 2005: 17). Nevertheless, the need for learning and development remains, and the organisation remains a significant context for it. It is, therefore, necessary to understand how the processes of learning and development can be facilitated in the organisation and, indeed, how the organisation itself can learn.

Influences upon learning and development from outside the organisation

Many significant influences upon learning and development emanate from outside the organisation. Government-driven education and training initiatives and changes, stemming from increasing concern over the country's need for learning and skills development, have contributed to the institutionalisation of competence-based education and training. The history, purpose and nature of these developments are discussed by Harrison (1992: 17–77; see also Harrison, 2005). Within a comprehensive and continually updating national framework agreed across all sectors and occupations (see Chapter 8), elements in an individual's learning and development, whether achieved through formal education, training or experiential learning across the lifespan, are identified and assessed against nationally agreed standards. The language, philosophy and procedures of this framework are likely to shape individuals' perceptions of their learning and learning needs, and to influence how employers articulate the learning needs of their employees. Moreover, the Investors in People initiative (see Chapter 8, Arkin, 1999 and CIPD Factsheet *Investors in People* (updated April 2008)) also both prompts, shapes and supports human resource development practices.

Facilitating learning and development within the organisation

Employees learn and develop through carrying out their jobs: this chapter has already noted the significance of action for learning. For example, the design of those jobs and the organisation structure, the degree to which it is centralised and bureaucratised, all influence employees' learning opportunities. People need to be able to grow in their jobs, and might outgrow their jobs as they learn, or to move into new jobs that would allow them to continue the process of their development. An organisation that is growing or changing is more likely to offer those opportunities than one that is static or declining.

Here, then, are some of the features of organisation and management that would facilitate learning and development within organisations.

The style of management

Reporting on the results of research by the New Learning for New Work Consortium, Fonda and Guile (1999) set out the guiding principles for managing 'capable' organisations that seek to develop the learning of their employees. These are 'respect for the views of the workforce and clarity about the capabilities that the whole workforce will need; the creation of both challenge and support for developing and sustaining these capabilities; and an individualised approach to potential' (p. 41). Thus, as well as specific training, individuals need feedback on their performance, encouragement, support, and resources to give them self-confidence, to stimulate and sustain their learning and development. To develop the higher-order skills needed in organisations, employees need the opportunity to take risks and hence to make mistakes. This presupposes not only a risk-taking and confident approach on the part of employees, but also a risk-taking and supportive management. Effective learning and development in the organisation therefore call for a managerial style that is compatible with this need. The existence and nature of an appraisal scheme (see Chapter 12) could have positive or negative effects upon employees' learning (Thatcher, 1996). Essentially, organisations that want to develop those characteristics need also themselves to learn to learn, to become learning organisations, to have a learning culture and a learning centre (Coulson-Thomas, 2000).

The learning organisation

The structure and operation of an organisation can influence the process of learning within it. It is evident that the human resource development argued for throughout this chapter would be achieved in a learning organisation. (See also Chapter 8.)

The concept of the learning organisation is open to criticism, not least because it is often expressed in theoretical terms. This is recognised by Senge (Pickard, 2000: 39), one of its early and influential proponents (Senge, 1990), who has since elaborated his thinking in more concrete terms (Senge *et al.*, 1998). Nevertheless, the learning organisation continues to be 'an aspirational concept' (Burgoyne, 1995: 24), a 'transitional myth' that makes sense both in the world that is passing and in the one that replaces it. Hence it enables people to bridge the gap – in this case as 'more emotionally involving, inclusive forms of organisation' emerge from the information-based organisation. However, Burgoyne (1999: 44), another early and key proponent, acknowledges that it has not 'delivered its full potential or lived up to all our expectations', and sets out what the characteristics of the second generation will have to be.

Today's interest in knowledge management gives new relevance to Morgan's (1997) 'holographic organisation'. Using the metaphor of the organisation as a brain, he offers a new way of appreciating how the organisation itself can facilitate, constrain or repress the learning of its members. Both brain and organisation can be understood as holograms, 'where qualities of the whole are enfolded in all the parts so that the system has an ability to self-organize and regenerate itself on a continuous basis' (p. 100). The holographic nature of the learning organisation provides the stimulus, prompts and cues for individuals to learn and develop the higher-order skills they need to sustain and develop the organisation in a changing world, and 'to develop a discursive, networking culture in which everyone constantly questioned their own assumptions' (Pickard, 2000: 39).

Reminding us that the brains of employees and the brain-like capacities of computers and the internet already have holographic features, Morgan considers how to design those features into organisations as well. He identifies five principles: the 'whole' built into the 'parts', redundant functions, requisite variety, minimum critical specification, and learning to learn.

Building the 'whole' into the 'parts'

One way of building the 'whole' into the parts of the organisation is through its culture. When that embodies the organisation's 'vision, values, and sense of purpose', then it will act like a 'corporate "DNA"' (Morgan, 1997: 102), which carries the holographic code of the human body in each of its parts. Another way is to network information throughout the organisation, so that it can be widely accessed, enabling organisational members 'to become full participants in an evolving system of organizational memory and intelligence' (Morgan, 1997: 104). Further ways are to have the kind of structure that allows the organisation to 'grow large while remaining small' (Morgan, 1997: 104), and to organise work tasks not into specialised jobs but into holistic teams of individuals having multiple skills.

Redundancy

In the traditional mechanistic design of organisations, each part has a specific function, with additional parts for backup or replacement. This allows a degree of passivity and neglect in the system ('"that's not my responsibility"', Morgan, 1997: 111). With the capacity for redesigning the system delegated to specialised parts, the capacity to self-organise is not generalised throughout the system. Instead, Morgan suggests that the organisation needs an 'excess capacity that can create room for innovation and development to occur' (1997: 108–10). It needs redundancy of functions rather than redundancy of parts (1997: 111–12). Where each part has additional functions currently redundant but potentially available – through multi-skilling and teamworking, for example – the capacities for the functioning of the whole are built into the parts. Thus the system as a whole has flexibility, with the capacity to reflect on and question how it is operating and to change its mode of operating.

Requisite variety

The internal diversity of a self-regulating system must match the variety and complexity of its environment in order to deal with the challenges from that environment. All elements of the organisation should therefore 'embody critical dimensions' of the environment with which they have to deal; this variety can be achieved, where appropriate, through 'multifunctioned teams' (Morgan, 1997: 112).

Minimum critical specification

Overdefinition and control, as in a bureaucracy, erode flexibility and stifle innovation. Hence the manager should define no more than is essential, but should instead focus on 'facilitation, orchestration and boundary management, creating "enabling conditions" that allow a system to find its own form' (Morgan, 1997: 114). The challenge is to avoid the extremes of anarchy and overcentralisation.

Learning to learn

Finally, the organisation needs to engage in double-loop learning (see earlier), allowing its operating norms and rules to change as the wider environment changes.

Morgan concludes by noting that these five interconnected principles should not be regarded as 'a blueprint or recipe' (Morgan, 1997: 115), but as a way of looking at how organisations could ensure that they remain adaptive.

Mentoring

Mentor was the friend to whom Ulysses entrusted the care of his young son before embarking on his epic voyages. Although the notion of mentoring is, therefore, a very old one, its value in organisations started to be recognised 25 or so years ago, and knowledge management now gives it particular relevance. You can read about mentoring in CIPD Factsheet *Mentoring*, Clutterbuck (2004), Collin (1988) Kram (1985).

The nature and purpose of mentoring

In organisations, mentors are more experienced employees (and often managers) who guide, encourage and support younger or less experienced employees, or 'protégés'. Their relationship is a developmental one that serves career-enhancing and psychosocial functions for the protégé while also benefiting the mentor. Overall, the mentor stimulates, encourages, guides, supports and cautions, acts as a role model, nurtures learning through action, learning-to-learn, and the adoption of a future orientation. While meeting the developmental needs of employees, mentoring is also contributing to the process of meaning-making in the organisation (see Chapter 3) and hence to its responsiveness to its environment. (Note that coaching, which is now gaining in popularity (CIPD Factsheet on *Mentoring* (updated February 2009), Clutterbuck and Megginson, 2005; Jarvis *et al.*, 2005), has traditionally differed from mentoring in its focus on role or task needs rather than the developmental needs of the protégé.)

Although being or having a mentor can occur naturally both outside and within organisations, this does not necessarily occur universally or systematically. To reap the benefits of mentoring, organisations set up formal programmes. Their purpose might be to support a graduate intake or other trainees and develop 'high fliers' or senior managers; encourage career advancement of women or those from minority groups (see Crofts, 1995); nurture employees with skills in short supply; stimulate and foster innovation in the organisation; and support managers in training, or other learners in the organisation. Examples are to be found in a wide range of private and public sector organisations in Britain, Europe and North America.

Protégés are not the only beneficiaries of mentoring: mentors also gain greatly from being challenged to understand their own jobs and the organisation, and to find ways of helping their protégés share this understanding and work effectively. Mentors might also find that they, too, need mentoring.

Have you had, or been, a mentor? What does your experience suggest would be the benefits of a mentoring programme in an organisation? How could it be made to work effectively?

The requirements for effective mentoring

This literature generally agrees on the following requirements for effective mentoring.

- *The status and characteristics of the mentor.* Mentors will generally be senior to protégés in status, experience and probably age; it is highly desirable that senior managers act as mentors, and that top management be involved with the programme. Mentors should have the skills and qualities that protégés respect, good empathic and people-developing skills, good organisational knowledge and personal networks, and patience and humility to be able to learn from the protégé. Not all managers, therefore, would make appropriate mentors. Mentors should not have a line relationship with their protégé because the element of control inherent in that would conflict with the developmental nature of the mentoring relationship.

- *The protégé.* Protégés should have potential, and be hungry to learn and develop in order to realise it. There will be many more potential protégés in the organisation than can be effectively mentored; it is therefore commonly noted that mentoring is elitist.

- *The relationship.* The relationship should be one of mutual trust, and will develop over time. Unless limits are set by a mentoring programme, it might continue until the protégé no longer needs its support. Sometimes it develops into a full friendship.

- *The activities.* Mentors encourage their protégés to analyse their task performance and to identify weaknesses and strengths. They give feedback and guidance on how weaknesses can be eliminated or neutralised. They help them recognise the tacit dimensions of the task skills, an important element in the development of competence and 'know-how'. Mentors act as a sounding board for their protégés' ideas, and support them as they try out new behaviours and take risks. They give honest, realistic but supportive feedback, an important element in learning generally and learning-to-learn in particular. They encourage their protégés to observe and analyse the organisation at work through their own and others' actions. Through this process the protégé begins to identify and then practise tacit knowledge and political skills. Mentors help protégés to identify and develop potentials, question and reflect on experiences and prospects within the organisation, apply formal learning to practice, and learn more widely about the organisation. Mentors draw upon their own networks to give experience and support to their protégés, and encourage them to develop networks of their own. In this way, the practice and benefits cascade through the organisation.

Activity **Developing higher-order skills through mentoring**

On your own or in a small group, identify the higher-order skills that mentoring could develop, and discuss how it might do so.

Designing learning in the organisation

Formal programmes

The messages about how to design effective learning are very consistent. For example, the advice that Sternberg (1985: 338–41), a theorist of intelligence, gives on how intelligent performance can be trained includes the following: make links with 'real-world' behaviour; deal explicitly with strategies and tactics for coping with novel tasks and situations; be sensitive to individual differences, and help individuals capitalise on their strengths and compensate for their weaknesses; be concerned with motivation. The implications of the androgogical model of learning for adults introduced in an earlier section (Knowles and Associates, 1984: 14–18) are that the facilitator of adult learning needs to:

- set a climate conducive to learning, both physical and psychological (one of mutual respect, collaborativeness, mutual trust, supportiveness, openness and authenticity, pleasure, 'humanness');
- involve learners in mutual planning of their learning;
- involve them in diagnosing their own learning needs;
- involve them in formulating their learning objectives;
- involve them in designing learning plans;
- help them carry out their learning plans – use learning contracts;
- involve them in evaluating their learning.

Belbin and Belbin (1972) draw upon their experience of studying training in industry for this advice on training 40- to 55-year-old adults:

1 Reduce anxiety and tension in the adult learner:
   – provide social support and allow social groups to form;
   – use acceptable instructors;
   – offer a secure future.
2 Create an adult atmosphere.
3 Arrange the schedule:
   – use sessions of appropriate length;
   – give preference to whole rather than part method;
   – start slowly.
4 Correct errors:
   – at the appropriate time.
5 Address individual differences:
   – different instructional approaches;
   – effects of previous education and work;
   – spare-time interests.
6 Follow up after training.

The value of these approaches is illustrated in the lessons drawn from the adoption in Britain of the Deming-inspired quality and continuous improvement programmes (Hodgson, 1987: 43):

> Train with extreme sensitivity – pick trainers who have operators' confidence, are alert to remedial training needs and people's fears about going back to class; minimise the gap between awareness, training and use; gear course contents to people's learning needs – don't impose blanket programmes.

However, if those principles of design are ignored, barriers to effective learning, such as anxiety and lack of confidence, would be set up (see earlier). Barry (1988: 47), for example, notes that the considerable apprehension felt by the fitters and electricians who were returning to college after 20 years was an obstacle in the introduction of a multi-skilling programme. Their anxieties were dissipated once they learned that some of the tutors belonged to the same union and had the same craft background as themselves.

e-learning

Information technology has provided the opportunity for e-learning, through which learning can be customised, and individuals can learn at their desks, rather than taking time out to study in a classroom (Sloman, 2001). For e-learning to be effective, it is not only the technology that has to be considered. The purpose of this form of learning has to be clear: it is more appropriate where knowledge is to be acquired than where interpersonal interactions are required.

Despite initial apparent enthusiasm for it, e-learning has not taken off as had been expected (Sloman, 2002). However, major lessons have been learned. An overall systematic approach, that includes e-learning, classroom and on-the-job learning, has to be developed, and it has to be recognised that e-learning is learner-centred, requiring new relationships between learners, trainers and line managers. Very importantly, it demands that effective support be provided for the learner (Sloman, 2002). (See also CIPD Factsheet *E-learning: Progress and Prospects*.)

Informal and tacit learning

Other people are major actors in the context of the individual's learning, and significant for an individual's learning and development, providing instruction and feedback (see earlier), support and encouragement, confidence-building, perhaps even inspiration. They might be, perhaps unknown to themselves, mentors, models or points of comparison for learners who learn not just from their formal instructors or supervisors, but also from peers and subordinates. This informal method of learning, including 'sitting next to Nellie', might have its weaknesses, but it also has strengths. It can offer whole rather than part learning, and the opportunity to apprehend tacit knowledge (see earlier).

Some organisations attempt to capture and use formally some of these otherwise informal ways of learning through people. Knowledge management and mentoring are examples of this. Shadowing is a method that gives the opportunity for a learner to observe the actions of a senior manager systematically and over a period of time. From this observation the learner can infer certain general principles, grounded in everyday organisational realities. However, as the novel *Nice Work* (Lodge, 1988) suggests, without feedback from the manager, the 'shadow' can misinterpret some of the situations witnessed.

Action learning

> There can be no action without learning, and no learning without action.   (Revans, 1983: 16)

Revans was the 'father of action learning' and 'one of the great unsung heroes of modern management' (Pedler *et al.*, 2003). His original concept (Pedler, 1983) has been adapted somewhat to changing circumstances, but as now applied is 'a method for individual and organisational development. Working in small groups [or 'learning sets'], people tackle important organisational issues or problems and learn from their attempts to change things' (Pedler *et al.*, 2003: 41).

Action learning (see also Chapter 9 and CIPD Factsheet *Action Learning* (updated July 2009)) embodies key aspects of learning that have been noted earlier. Whereas traditional instruction presents the kind of programmed knowledge needed to deal with puzzles that can be solved, action learning addresses problems for which there is no right answer, and which call for critical reflection and questioning insight (Pedler and Wilde, 2003). It stimulates learning through action, engages in double-loop learning as its participants start to examine their underlying assumptions, demands reflection, and draws on tacit knowledge. It offers human resource managers a way of developing the higher-order skills needed in an organisation.

Reflective practice

Reflection, as well as action, we have already noted, plays a key part in learning; the CIPD emphasises its significance in continuing professional development (see earlier). Schön (1983) suggested that effective professionals engage in reflective practice: they build reflection into their actions. When faced with a unique and uncertain situation, they enter into a 'reflective conversation' with it, hypothesise on the basis of their existing knowledge and theories about how it could be changed, reframe it, experiment to identify the consequences and implications of this frame, listen to the situation's 'talk back' and, if necessary, 'reframe' again.

Schön (1983) was writing particularly of professionsals, but other kinds of employee could also be encouraged to engage in reflective practice, thereby strengthening their learning to learn. See also Brockbank *et al.* (2002).

Controversial issues

Although the argument for the need for learning and development within organisations is incontrovertible, it nevertheless raises some controversial issues, which you should consider. For example,

- Who owns the employee's learning and development?
- As generally presented, the value and purpose of human resource development is not questioned. Are there other ways of interpreting it?

Activity

Who owns the employee's learning and development?

Reflect on your own experience. Then, on your own or in a small group, identify the stakeholders in the individual's learning and development.

Reflect on your own experience

- What is it costing you to learn? For example, take your reading of this book: what does this cost you?
- How do you benefit from your learning and development?

Who are the stakeholders in the individual's learning and development?

- What other costs are incurred in your learning and development? Who pays them?
- Who else benefits from your learning and development?
- What benefits do they receive?
- Who could impede your learning and development?

Activity

As generally presented, the value and purpose of human resource development is not questioned. Are there other ways of interpreting it?

The philosophy underpinning this chapter's presentation of its material is humanistic – learning and development have largely been interpreted as empowering of the individual. The chapter has not questioned whether the harnessing of individual learning and development by the organisation could be interpreted differently.

● Should the question that Legge (1995) asked of human resource management also be asked of human resource development – rhetoric or reality?

The awareness that the ownership of individual learning is a matter of debate, however, presents the opportunity to look for other interpretations. Consider this on your own or in a small group.

● What interpretations might the other chapters of this book make of human resource development?

● How idealistic or cynical are calls for activities such as mentoring and the learning organisation in today's flexible organisations?

● Is mentoring elitist or empowering?

● Is the learning organisation rhetoric or reality?

● Are there other possible interpretations?

(See the second case study below. You may find it helpful to return to the section on ideology and rhetoric in Chapter 3.)

Conclusions

This chapter has identified the significance of learning and development for individuals and organisations. Many organisations have recognised this, and have invested in their human resource development, as *People Management* reports in its regular company profiles and annual features on the National Training Awards. These reports suggest that both organisations and their employees have benefited.

However, by reflecting upon your own motivation and experiences, you will already have an insight into some of the thorny issues inherent in human resource development (others are discussed by Rainbird and Maguire, 1993). These issues can be summarised as follows:

● Learning and development take place throughout life, and in every aspect of life, as well as through performance of the job.

● Employer-initiated and sponsored and delivered learning can constitute only a small part of an individual's total learning.

● Some of such activities are undertaken as part of planned development; some are random or opportunistic.

● The employer cannot ring-fence such employer-provided learning.

● Employer-provided learning will be infiltrated by learning from other arenas – from home or social life, but also from undertaking the daily job, or observing boss or colleagues. Such learning may influence, strengthen, challenge or undermine employer-provided learning.

● The processes of learning and development might work counter to the processes of matching and control in which some employers invest heavily through the selection process.

- Learning and development are difficult to evaluate, because they often need an interval of time for their outcomes to be manifested.
- It is not easy to apportion their benefits to either employer or employee.
- It is not easy to calculate their costs, nor apportion them between employer and employee.
- Some of the costs are not borne by either of these; partners, families and the state through the educational and vocational training systems also pay some of the price of employee development.
- Individuals expect reward for their training or development – when they have put effort in, and become more skilled, they expect greater reward. This reward might be either extrinsic (promotion, increase in pay) or intrinsic (greater fulfilment through a more demanding or higher-status job).
- As employees learn and develop, they might become less compliant to their employer and more demanding of changes at work and further development.
- This might result in the employee's dissatisfaction with his or her present job or employer.
- Because of all the above, some employers might be reluctant to pay to develop their employees.
- Some of the processes, activities and benefits depend upon the individual's context (including the presence of significant others), age and stage of development in life.
- It is difficult formally to ensure effective learning – it often seems false in comparison with the ongoing spontaneous learning from life in general, and there are often difficulties in transferring from formal learning situations to everyday work.

The issue of the ownership of the learning and development of individuals, as employees, reminds us that managing people has a moral dimension – human resource management juggles with empowering and controlling. This is the unanswered (and unanswerable?) question at the heart of human resource development, and poses dilemmas to both employer and employee.

Summary

- This chapter addressed the issue of why individuals generally and human resource managers in particular need to understand learning and development.
- It began with a series of definitions of learning that rested on the view that the acquisition of knowledge and understanding facilitates change in perceptions and practice. Such acquisition is increasingly essential in today's world of work, in which employees are expected to cope with change and new technology, take more responsibility, become more skilled and knowledgeable, and develop the ability for problem solving and creative thinking.
- The attributes that today's organisations need for their survival were examined – in particular, the need for quality and continuous improvement, flexibility, adaptability, and the exploitation of knowledge. Individual employees therefore must engage in a continuous process of learning how to learn, and managers must learn how to facilitate this.
- The nature of the learner was examined; but it was also emphasised that learning is a life-long process that means making continuous adaptations. In many senses it is a journey. In the process of learning, many barriers are thrown up, including anxiety and lack of confidence on behalf of the learner. Discrimination also exists and often creates barriers for certain groups such as older workers, women, disabled people and cultural and ethnic minorities. This might impair their ability to learn by undermining their confidence and/or preventing them from taking courses and training programmes that will lead to greater opportunities. Many in those groups belong to the most disadvantaged in our society.

- The outcomes of learning – the acquisition of new skills, competence, 'know-how', tacit knowledge and employability – were highlighted. It is equally important for managers to have an awareness of the hierarchies of learning, the various levels of learning through which learners proceed. Each level adds a further layer of sophistication to that process, from the simple acquisition of knowledge of facts through to the ability to understand complicated analyses involving complex abstract processes. Such understanding will take the learner through the various stages of learning: novice, advanced beginner, competent, proficient and, finally, expert. Various theories and models of learning and learning styles were also examined.

- The concept of development was explored. It is a process in which the learner 'becomes increasingly complex, more elaborate and differentiated, and thereby able to adapt to the changing environment'. A number of theories and models of lifespan, career and other forms of development were then examined and their implications for human resource development noted.

- Much learning and development takes place within the organisational context, itself influenced from outside by national training initiatives. Although learning knows no frontiers, organisations can often make inhospitable environments for the learning and development of individuals, and with this in mind it must be recognised that learning has to be supported by managers, mentors, and the overall learning climate of a learning organisation.

- The final part of the chapter examined two controversies for the reader to reflect on. These questioned who owned the individual's learning and development, and whether human resource development should be accepted at face value. Rather than giving answers the author posed a number of probing questions for the reader to reflect upon – a form of self-development in itself.

Questions

1 What do human resource managers need to know about learning and development and how they take place? Draw up a list of questions that they could ask a learning specialist.

2 How can practical knowledge be developed in an organisation?

3 How might learning transform an individual? What are the implications of such transformation for an organisation?

4 What are the implications for an individual's career of new flexible forms of organisation?

5 The chapter has highlighted two controversial issues for discussion. What other thorny issues do learning and development in organisations raise?

Exercises

1 Keep a learning diary

Reflection is essential for effective learning. Systematically reflect upon what and how you learn by keeping a learning diary. It will also help you remember issues to discuss with your tutor (and, if you have one, mentor), and might also contribute to your continuing professional development portfolio. Spend half an hour every week recording the following:

- the most meaningful or stressful events of the week;
- how they came about and who was involved;

- your interpretation of them;
- the emotions evoked by them;
- how you dealt with them;
- the outcomes of your actions;
- your evaluation of your actions;
- what you would do or avoid doing in future;
- what further skills, knowledge and understanding you need to perform more effectively;
- how you could acquire these;
- your action plan.

2 Find yourself a mentor

- If you are not fortunate enough to have a mentor already, then find yourself one. Phillips-Jones (1982) suggests the following steps:
- Identify what (not who) you need.
- Evaluate yourself as a prospective protégé.
- Identify some mentor candidates.
- Prepare for the obstacles that they might raise.
- Approach your possible mentors.

3 How can you make and keep yourself employable?

- Assess your present employability.
- What do you need to do to achieve, maintain or improve this?
- What would be the implications for the nature and quality of your life overall if your career proved to be flexible and/or fragmented?

4 Review and make plans for your career development

To make effective plans for your future development, you need to be aware of how you have arrived at where you are and become who you are.

- Write a brief story of your life and career to date. Why and how have you become who you are today? What are your strengths and weaknesses?
- Now write your story again through the eyes of people who know you well: your parents or partner; your best friend or boss. Would they have a different interpretation of your life and career from you? Does that tell you anything about yourself that you might not have noticed before?
- Are you content with yourself and your present life? What would you like to be different? Why? What are the opportunities and threats to your life and career? What would you have to do (and forgo) to bring that change about? Would it be worth it? And what would the effect(s) be?
- Who else would such changes affect? Who could help or hinder you in those changes? What resources would you need to effect them? In what sequence would those changes have to come about, and how do they fit into the other timetables of your life?
- Now draw up an action plan, identifying the actions you will have to carry out over the short, medium and long term.
- Take the first step in implementing it today. Commit yourself to it by telling someone else about it and enlist their support to keep you motivated.
- At the end of the first month and every three months thereafter, review the progress of your plan and make any necessary adjustments.

Case study 1

FT

Investment banks battle for talent

The battle for talent among investment banks is set to intensify, say headhunters, who are gearing up for a hiring market fuelled by healthy banking revenues and a surge in mergers and acquisitions.

'It will be increasingly difficult to hire good people at the top, which will place enormous strain on the market,' said Simon Hall, global managing partner of financial services at headhunter Heidrick & Struggles.

Traditionally, from mid-January recruitment swings into action. Once the bonus season is over and bankers have weighed up the size of their rewards and cashed them, some begin to look for opportunities. Recruitment is difficult as investment banks plan to hire at the same time and are increasingly drawing from an overfished pool.

Bankers will be on the move to rival banks or seeking a different challenge in hedge funds or private equity. A growing number will move to real estate banking, an area that headhunters say has 'gone through the roof' in the past year but has a limited talent pool to draw from.

In the coming year there will also be a shortage of skills in emerging markets, especially Russia and the CIS states, India and the Middle East.

Fully trained bankers specialised in these areas are at a premium as business continues to grow.

Among those on the move will be managing directors, M&A bankers, directors and vice-presidents. 'Some junior bankers, vice-presidents and senior associate levels have never been paid so much,' says Lucia Ferreira, who has been in financial services recruitment for 15 years and is managing director of global banking and market practice at Russell Reynolds, the executive search firm. 'There is also a demand for seasoned M&A bankers who can perform client-facing roles,' says Ms Ferreira. She said banks were becoming more selective in their hiring, especially at managing director level.

Banks and financial groups have extended their search to the global marketplace and are looking as far afield as Asia-Pacific, India and China, which have shown unprecedented growth in head count in the financial services sector in recent years.

Specialist hedge fund recruiters are expecting increased competition for talent. Michael Goodman, a partner at hedge fund recruiter Long Ridge Partners, says hires in part will be made from the M&A and corporate financial sectors of investment banks and from proprietary trading desks.

However, he is expecting fewer senior bankers to make the move to hedge funds this year compared with last year because 'in some instances it is more lucrative to stay in banking'.

Good remuneration and high bonuses are not always enough to retain competent top employees, and headhunters say the best bankers do not leave just for money but for other incentives such as new challenges, credibility and internal equity.

'Everyone knows who the best players are but the problem is luring them away from their employers and retaining them,' says one leading international headhunter.

The challenge for this year will be sourcing talent to facilitate growth in financial services.

Robert Thesiger, chief executive of Morgan McKinley, the financial recruitment specialist, estimates that 2007 will be the third year in a row in which the City job market has expanded. 'The war for talent has been a constant theme in the City throughout 2006 and this will be the case in 2007.'

Source: from Investment banks battle for talent, *Financial Times*, 3 January 2007 (Sullivan, R.)

Questions

Working on your own or a small group, answer the following questions:

1 What changes have taken place since this article was published? Outline them briefly.

2 What skills are in demand here?

3 Based on this chapter, what advice on learning and development would you have given employees of investment banks in January 2007?

4 Based on this chapter, what advice on would you have given the banks in January 2007?

A battle for talent

It may be the worst job market since the Great Depression, but here is the good news: some companies are still hiring. But the reason they are hiring is because they are clearing out mediocre employees in the knowledge that they can hire better replacements.

In consultant-speak, it is called 'up-skilling'. Companies eager to take advantage of the surplus of talented workers looking for jobs are cutting more of their own employees to make room on the payroll for new hires with specialised skills.

'Organisations are taking this opportunity to upgrade their talent,' says Seymour Adler, a senior vice-president in Aon Consulting's human capital practice. 'They recognise that there are better people out there so they "over-correct" on the downside to take advantage.'

Of course, companies that shed jobs do so to save money. But according to human resources experts like Mr Adler, they often reduce their headcount more than they necessarily need to in order to re-stock their pipeline of fresh talent.

Last year, US companies shed 2.6m jobs, the largest number in a calendar year since 1945. The unemployment rate in the US now stands at 8.1 per cent, according to the US Department of Labor, and many economists predict it could reach 10 per cent this year.

'Companies are talking about exploiting the environment,' says Mr Adler. 'There are some highly qualified people out there, and companies are taking the opportunity to assemble an A-team. They are taking the Draconian, Jack Welch approach of cutting the bottom 5 or 10 per cent, and replacing them with people who are going to be top performers.'

Perhaps the biggest reason companies over-correct during tough economic times is that they can bring in new talent more easily – and often more cheaply – than they could in a good economy. Mr Adler says this is particularly true of newly minted MBAs, or entry-level positions for recent college graduates. 'They can be had for a starting salary of 10 to 20 per cent less than what the market would have demanded two or three years ago,' he says.

The trend is evident in industries from finance to marketing to IT but is most pronounced at technology companies and consulting firms. 'These companies are very attuned to the need for fresh blood, fresh ideas and innovation,' Mr Adler says. 'They realise they can bring in two bright people fresh out of school with the latest and greatest models for the price of one of their [current] employees.'

Mr Adler says most companies use a rule of thumb of 5 per cent, meaning that if the organisation aims to decrease its payroll by 10 per cent, it downsizes by 15 per cent. 'You do it in a way that it won't make a material difference to meeting the needs of the business,' he says. 'Organisations recognise that there are better people out there so they "over-correct" on the downside to take advantage.'

Simultaneous hiring and firing is standard business practice, but it has been exacerbated by the depth and severity of this recession, according to Emory Mulling, a consultant who runs an outplacement firm in Atlanta, Georgia.

Companies are not simply taking a hard look at their headcount but trying to think more strategically about their human capital: where they most need employees with specialised skills, and which departments are expendable. 'There's a saying that there's nothing quite like a recession to get a company in order,' says Mr Mulling.

Tough economic circumstances force companies to scrutinise employees – especially in the ranks of senior leadership – to determine whether they are the right candidate or whether there may be someone better, according to Elaine Eisenman, a former corporate human resources manager who runs the executive education programme at Babson's business school just outside Boston. In a robust economy, poor performers tend to be shuffled into different jobs or moved to different locations; in a bad economy, they are let go.

'These are typically opportune times. Suddenly, you can get poor performers out with a lucrative [severance package],' she says.

Companies are also more likely to announce mass job losses today than they were 20 or 30 years ago, which also enables them to over-correct, says Detlev Suderow, a professor at Brandeis International Business School who specialises in international human resource management.

Shedding thousands of workers at a time is not a stain on a company's record, and it does not damage its ability to recruit and retain workers. 'Most companies realise there is no shame in laying people off. It's normal, it's accepted. Companies used to hire employees for life, but that's not the case any more,' he says.

Some companies, however, can go too far by mistake. Rather than a strategic, thoughtful restructuring

Case study continued

of their workforce, they embark on a short-term cost-cutting exercise where they let workers go, but soon need to go on a hiring spree because there aren't enough employees left to do all the work.

'There are some companies that have cut the number of people, but don't reduce the work,' says Eric Abrahamson, a professor at Columbia Business School who studies techniques for managing organisations and their employees. 'That works for a while, but then the quality drops. There's a reflex of cutting costs by getting rid of people, but you have to rationalise the work, too.'

Source: from A battle for talent, *Financial Times*, 20 March 2009 (Knight, R.)

Questions

Working on your own or in a small group, answer the following questions:

1 The situations in the two case studies are totally different, but what do they have in common?

2 In the 2009 situation, which employees are at an advantage? Which at a disadvantage?

3 Based on this chapter, what advice would you give to organisations now?

4 Based on this chapter, what advice would you give to individuals now?

5 Do these two cases have any message for you?

Useful websites

CIPD factsheets:

www.cipd.co.uk/subjects

Future of work, skills required, and workplace learning:

www.cipd.co.uk
www.ukces.org.uk
www.delni.gov.uk
www.dius.gov.uk
www.tlrp.org
www.leeds.ac.uk/esrcfutureofwork/
www.toscagroup.com
www.TUC.org.uk
www.workforce-dev.com

Learning theories:

www.emtech.net/learning_theories.htm

Older workers:

www.agepositive.gov.uk
www.pjb.co.uk/npl/bp21.htm

Career management surveys:

www.cipd.co.uk/surveys

References and further reading

Those texts marked with an asterisk are recommended for further reading.

Argyris, C. (1960) *Understanding Organizational Behaviour*. London: Tavistock Dorsey.

Argyris, C. and Schön, D.A. (1978) *Organisational Learning: A Theory of Action Perspective*. Reading, MA: Addison-Wesley.

Arkin, A. (1992) 'What other institutes are doing', *Personnel Management*, March: 29.

Arkin, A. (1995) 'How the act will affect you', *People Management*, 16 November: 20, 23.

Arkin, A. (1999) 'Investors in future: above and beyond', *People Management*, 5, 3: 40–41.

Arnold, J. (1997) *Managing Careers into the 21st Century*. London: Paul Chapman.

Arthur, M.B., Hall, D.T. and Lawrence, B.S. (eds) (1989) *Handbook of Career Theory*. Cambridge: Cambridge University Press.

Arthur, M.B. and Rousseau, D.M. (1996) (eds) *The Boundaryless Career: A New Employment Principle for a New Organizational Era*. Oxford: Oxford University Press.

*Atkinson, R.L., Atkinson, R.C., Smith, E.E., Bem, D.J. and Nolen-Hoeksema, S. (1999) *Hilgard's Introduction to Psychology*, 13th edn. New York: Harcourt Brace College Publishing.

Barry, A. (1988) 'Twilight study sheds new light on craft development', *Personnel Management*, November: 46–49.

Bartol, K.N. (1978) 'The sex structuring of organizations: a search for possible causes', *Academy of Management Review*, October: 805–15.

Bayliss, V. (1998) *Redefining Work: An RSA Initiative*. London: The Royal Society for the Encouragement of the Arts, Manufactures and Commerce.

Beattie, D. (2002) *President's Message*, Annual Report 2002, London: Chartered Institute of Personnel and Development.

Belbin, E. and Belbin, R.M. (1972) *Problems in Adult Retraining*. London: Heinemann.

Binsted, D.S. (1980) 'Design for learning in management training and development: a view', *Journal of European Industrial Training*, 4, 8: whole issue.

Blackler, F. (2000) 'Collective wisdom', *People Management*, 22 June: 61.

Bloom, B.S. *et al.* (1956) *Taxonomy of Educational Objectives*, Handbook 1: *The Cognitive Domain*. London: Longmans Green.

Bolles, R.N. (1988) *What Color is Your Parachute?* Berkeley, CA: Ten Speed.

Borger, R. and Seaborne, A.E.M. (1966) *The Psychology of Learning*. Harmondsworth: Penguin.

Boyatzis, R.E. (1982) *The Competent Manager: A Model for Effective Performance*. New York: Wiley.

Bridges, W. (1995) *Job Shift: How to Prosper in a Workplace Without Jobs*. London: Nicholas Brealey.

Brittain, S. and Ryder, P. (1999) 'A certain *je ne sais quoi*: get complex', *People Management*, 25 November: 48–51.

Brockbank, A., McGill, I. and Beech, N. (2002) (eds) *Reflective Learning in Practice*. Aldershot: Gower.

Burgoyne, J. (1995) 'Feeding minds to grow the business', *People Management*, 21 September: 22–25.

Burgoyne, J. (1999) 'Better by design: design of the times', *People Management*, 3 June: 39–44.

Burgoyne, J.G. and Hodgson, V.E. (1983) 'Natural learning and managerial action: a phenomenological study in the field setting', *Journal of Management Studies*, 20, 3: 387–99.

Cannell, M., Ashton, D., Powell, M. and Sung, J. (1999) 'Training: auditory perceptions: ahead of the field', *People Management*, 22 April: 48–49.

Castells, M. (1996) *The Information Age: Economy, Society and Culture. I: The Rise of the Network Society*. Oxford: Blackwell.

Castells, M. (1998) *The Information Age: Economy, Society and Culture. III: End of Millennium*. Oxford: Blackwell.

Chartered Institute of Personnel and Development (2002a) *Training in the Knowledge Economy*. London: Chartered Institute of Personnel and Development.

*Chartered Institute of Personnel and Development (2002b) *The Future of Careers*. London: Chartered Institute of Personnel and Development.

Chartered Institute of Personnel and Development (2004) *Career Management: A Guide*. London: Chartered Institute of Personnel and Development.

Chartered Institute of Personnel and Development (ongoing) *Factsheets*. See 'Useful websites' above.

Clements, P. and Jones, J.J. (2002) *Diversity Training: A Practical Guide to Understanding and Changing Attitudes*. London: Kogan Page.

Clutterbuck, D. (2004) *Everyone Needs a Mentor*, 4th edn, London: Chartered Institute of Personnel and Development.

Clutterbuck, D. and Megginson, D. (2005) *Making Coaching Work*. London: Chartered Institute of Personnel and Development.

Coleman, P. (1990) 'Psychological ageing' in J. Bond and P. Coleman (eds) *Ageing and Society: An Introduction to Social Gerontology*. London: Sage, pp. 62–88.

Collin, A. (1988) 'Mentoring', *Industrial and Commercial Training*, 20, 2: 23–27.

Collin, A. and Watts, A.G. (1996) 'The death and transfiguration of career – and of career guidance?', *British Journal of Guidance and Counselling*, 24, 3: 385–98.

Collin, A. and Young, R.A. (eds) (2000) *The Future of Career*. Cambridge: Cambridge University Press.

Collins, H. (1993) 'Untidy minds in action', *Times Higher Education Supplement*, 1066, 9 April: 15, 17.

*Cooley, M. (1987) *Architect or Bee? The Human Price of Technology*. London: Hogarth Press.

Corney, M. (1995) 'Employee development schemes', *Employment Gazette*, 103, 10: 385–90.

Coulson-Thomas, C. (2000) 'Carry on campus', *People Management*, 17 February: 33.

Crofts, P. (1995) 'A helping hand up the career ladder', *People Management*, 7 September: 38–40.

Cytrynbaum, S. and Crites, J.O. (1989) 'The utility of adult development theory in understanding career adjustment process' in M.B. Arthur, D.T. Hall and B.S. Lawrence (eds) *Handbook of Career Theory*. Cambridge: Cambridge University Press, pp. 66–88.

*Daloz, L.A. (1986) *Effective Mentoring and Teaching*. San Francisco, CA: Jossey-Bass.

Dalton, G.W. (1989) 'Developmental views of careers in organizations' in M.B. Arthur, D.T. Hall and B.S. Lawrence (eds) *Handbook of Career Theory*. Cambridge: Cambridge University Press, pp. 89–109.

Dennis, H. (1988) *Fourteen Steps in Managing an Aging Work Force*. Lexington, MA: D.C. Heath.

Department of Innovation, Universities and Skills (2008) *Shaping the Future – A New Adult Advancement and Careers Service for England*. London: HMSO.

Dixon, N. (2000) 'Common knowledge: the insight track', *People Management*, 17 February: 34–39.

Dreyfus, H.L., Dreyfus, S.E. and Athanasion, T. (1986) *Mind Over Machine: The Power of Human Intuition and Expertise in the Era of the Computer*. New York: Free Press.

Edwards, C. (2004) 'Assister act', *People Management*, 10, 17, 2 September: 26–30.

Erikson, E. (1950) *Childhood and Society*. New York: W.W. Norton.

Fitts, P.M. (1962) 'Factors in complex skills training' in R. Glaser (ed.) *Training Research and Education*. New York: Wiley.

Fonda, N. and Guile, D. (1999) 'A real step change: joint learning adventures', *People Management*, 25 March: 38–44.

Fontana, D. (1981) 'Learning and teaching' in C.L. Cooper (ed.) *Psychology for Managers: A Text for Managers and Trade Unionists*. London: British Psychological Society and Macmillan, pp. 64–78.

Ford, J. (2002) 'The use of competency models is widespread, but new research highlights their shortcomings', *People Management*, 10 October: 56.

Gabriel, Y. (2000) *Storytelling in Organizations: Facts, Fictions, and Fantasies*, Oxford: Oxford University Press.

Gagné, R.M. (1970) *The Conditions of Learning*, 2nd edn. New York: Holt, Rinehart & Winston.

Gagné, R.M. (1974) *Essentials of Learning for Instruction*. Hinsdale, IL: Dryden Press.

Gallos, J.V. (1989) 'Exploring women's development: implications for career theory, practice, and research', in M.B. Arthur, D.T. Hall and B.S. Lawrence (eds) *Handbook of Career Theory*. Cambridge: Cambridge University Press, pp. 110–32.

Gardner, H. (1985) *Frames of Mind: The Theory of Multiple Intelligences.* London: Paladin.

Gardner, H. (1999) *Intelligence Reframed: Multiple Intelligences for the 21st Century.* New York: Basic Books.

Gilligan, C. (1977) 'In a different voice: women's conception of the self and of morality', *Harvard Educational Review,* 47: 481–517.

Greenhaus, J.H. and Callanan, G.A. (2006) (eds) *Encyclopedia of Career Development.* Thousand Oaks, CA: Sage.

Griffiths, J. (2005a) 'Firms must plan for dearth of young', *People Management,* 2 June: 10.

Griffiths, J. (2005b) 'Open and shut case', *People Management,* 1 September: 20–21.

Griffiths, J. (2005c) 'Masculine wiles', *People Management,* 27 October: 20–21.

Guest, D. and McKenzie Davey, K.M. (1996) 'Don't write off the traditional career', *People Management,* 22 February: 22–25.

Guest, D., Storey, Y. and Tate, W. (1997) *Opportunity Through People.* IPD Consultative Document, June. London: IPD.

Hall, D.T. (1976) *Careers in Organizations.* Pacific Palisades, CA: Goodyear.

Hall, D.T. and Associates (1996) *The Career is Dead – Long Live Career: A Relational Approach to Careers,* San Francisco, CA: Jossey-Bass.

Hammer, M. and Champy, J. (1994) *Reengineering the Corporation: A Manifesto for Business Revolution.* New York: Harper Business.

Harrison, R. (1992) *Employee Development.* London: Institute of Personnel Management.

Harrison, R. (2005) *Learning and Development,* 4th edn. London: Chartered Institute of Personnel and Development.

Herriot, P. and Pemberton, C. (1995) *New Deals: The Revolution in Managerial Careers.* Chichester: John Wiley.

Hodgson, A. (1987) 'Deming's never-ending road to quality', *Personnel Management,* July: 40–44.

Hogarth, T. and Barth, M.C. (1991) 'Costs and benefits of hiring older workers: a case study of B&Q', *International Journal of Manpower,* 12, 8: 5–17.

Holland, J.L. (1997) *Making Vocational Choices: A Theory of Vocational Personalities and Work Environments,* 3rd edn. Odessa, FL: Psychological Assessment Resources.

Honey, P. (1998) 'The debate starts here', *People Management,* 1 October: 28–29.

Honey, P. (1999) 'Not for the faint-hearted', *People Management,* 28 October: 39.

Honey, P. (2002) 'Tough love on learning', *People Management,* 2 May: 42.

Honey, P. and Mumford, A. (1992) *Manual of Learning Styles,* 3rd edn. London: Peter Honey.

Hope, K. (2005) 'New for old', *People Management,* 28 July: 14–15.

Hopfl, H. and Hornby Atkinson, P. (2000) 'The future of women's careers', in A. Collin and R.A. Young (eds) *The Future of Career,* Cambridge: Cambridge University Press, pp. 130–43.

Hwang, A.-S. (2003) 'Training strategies in the management of knowledge', *Journal of Knowledge Management,* 7, 3, July: 92–104.

Jackson, C., Arnold, J., Nicholson, N. and Watts, A.G. (1996) *Managing Careers in 2000 and Beyond.* Brighton: Institute for Employment Studies.

Jackson, T. (1999) *Career Development.* London: IPD.

Jarvis, J. and Hooley, A. (2004) 'Access all areas', *People Management,* 9 December: 40–42.

Jarvis, J., Lane, D. and Fillery-Travis, A. (2005) *The Case for Coaching.* London: Chartered Institute of Personnel and Development.

Kanter, R.M. (1989a) *When Giants Learn to Dance.* New York: Simon & Schuster.

Kanter, R.M. (1989b) 'Careers and the wealth of nations: a macro-perspective on the structure and implications of career forms' in M.B. Arthur, D.T. Hall and B.S. Lawrence (eds) *Handbook of Career Theory.* Cambridge: Cambridge University Press, pp. 506–21.

Keil, T. (1981) 'Social structure and status in career development' in A.G. Watts, D.E. Super and J.M. Kidd (eds) *Career Development in Britain: Some Contributions to Theory and Practice.* Cambridge: CRAC, Hobson's Press, pp. 155–92.

Knowles, M.S. and Associates (1984) *Androgogy in Action.* San Francisco, CA: Jossey-Bass.

Kolb, D.A. (1983) *Experiential Learning.* New York: Prentice-Hall.

Kolb, D.A., Rubin, I.M. and MacIntyre, J.M. (1984) *Organizational Psychology: An Experiential Approach,* 4th edn. New York: Prentice Hall.

Kram, K.E. (1985) *Mentoring At Work: Developmental Relationships in Organizational Life.* Glenview, IL: Scott, Foresman.

Laslett, P. (1989) *A Fresh Map of Life: The Emergence of the Third Age.* London: Weidenfeld & Nicolson.

Legge, K. (1995) *Human Resource Management: Rhetorics and Realities.* Basingstoke: Macmillan.

Leitch, S. (2006) *Leitch Review of Skills: Prosperity for All in the Global Economy – World Class Skills.* Final report. London: HMSO.

Leong, F.T.L. and P.J. Hartung (2000) 'Adapting to the changing multicultural context of career' in A. Collin and R.A. Young (eds) *The Future of Career,* Cambridge: Cambridge University Press, pp. 212–27.

Levinson, D.J., Darrow, C.M., Klein, E.B., Levinson, M.H. and McKee, B. (1978) *The Seasons of a Man's Life.* New York: Alfred A. Knopf.

Lodge, D. (1988) *Nice Work: A Novel.* London: Secker & Warburg.

Malhotra, Y. (1998) *Knowledge Management for the New World of Business,* WWW Virtual Library on Knowledge Management, **http://www.brint.com/km/.**

Manocha, R. (2005) 'Grand totals', *People Management,* 7 April: 26–31.

Marshall, J. (1989) 'Re-visioning career concepts: a feminist invitation' in M.B. Arthur, D.T. Hall and B.S. Lawrence (eds) *Handbook of Career Theory.* Cambridge: Cambridge University Press, pp. 275–91.

Martin, S. (1995) 'A futures market for competencies', *People Management,* 23 March: 20–24.

Mayo, A. (2002) 'A thorough evaluation', *People Management,* 4 April: 36–39.

Mayo, A.J. and Nohria, N. (2005) *In Their Time: The Greatest Business Leaders of the 20th Century.* Boston, MA: Harvard Business School Press.

McGregor, D. (1960) *The Human Side of Enterprise.* New York: McGraw-Hill.

Megginson, D. and Whitaker, V. (2003) *Continuing Professional Development.* Maidenhead: CIPD.

Mezirow, J. (1977) 'Personal transformation', *Studies in Adult Education* (Leicester: National Institute of Adult Education), 9, 2: 153–64.

Miller, R. and Stewart, J. (1999) 'U and improved: opened university', *People Management*, 5, 12, 17 June: 42–46.

*Morgan, G. (1997) *Images of Organization*, 2nd edn. Thousand Oaks, CA: Sage.

Moynagh, M. and Worsley, R. (2005) *Working in the Twenty-First Century*, Leeds/Norfolk: ESRC/The Tomorrow Project.

Mumford, A. (1988) 'Learning to learn and management self-development' in M. Pedler, J. Burgoyne and T. Boydell (eds) *Applying Self-Development in Organizations*. New York: Prentice Hall, pp. 22–27.

Mumford, A. (2002) 'Horses for courses', *People Management*, 27 June: 51.

Myers, C. and Davids, K. (1992) 'Knowing and doing: tacit skills at work', *Personnel Management*, February: 45–47.

Naylor, P. (1987) 'In praise of older workers', *Personnel Management*, November: 44–48.

Neugarten, B.L. (1968) 'Adult personality: toward a psychology of the life cycle' in B.L. Neugarten (ed.) *Middle Age and Aging: A Reader in Social Psychology*. Chicago, IL: University of Chicago Press, pp. 137–47.

Nonaka, I. (1991) 'The knowledge creating company' in *Harvard Business Review on Knowledge Management*. Cambridge, MA: Harvard Business School Press, pp. 21–45.

Pedler, M. (1988) 'Self-development and work organizations' in M. Pedler, J. Burgoyne and T. Boydell (eds) *Applying Self-Development in Organizations*. New York: Prentice-Hall, pp. 1–19.

Pedler, M. (ed.) (1983) *Action Learning in Practice*. Aldershot: Gower.

Pedler, M., Brook, C. and Burgoyne, J. (2003) 'Motion pictures', *People Management*, 17 April: 40–44.

Pedler, M., Burgoyne, J. and Boydell, T. (eds) (1988) *Applying Self-Development in Organizations*. New York: Prentice-Hall.

Pedler, M. and Wilde, A. (2003) *Action Learning Toolkit*, Ely, Cambs: Fenman.

People Management (2005a) 'Older staff train faster at BMW', 27 October: 17.

People Management (2005b) 'Troubleshooter', 27 October: 64–65.

Perry, W.G. (1968) *Forms of Intellectual and Ethical Development in the College Years: A Scheme*. New York: Holt, Rinehart & Winston.

Phillips-Jones, L. (1982) *Mentors and Protégés: How to Establish, Strengthen and Get the Most from a Mentor/Protégé Relationship*. New York: Arbor House.

Pickard, J. (1999a) 'Lifelong earning: grey areas', *People Management*, 29 July: 30–37.

Pickard, J. (1999b) 'Emote possibilities: sense and sensitivity', *People Management*, 28 October: 48–56.

Pickard, J. (2000) 'Profile: high-mileage meditations', *People Management*, 6, 7: 38–43.

Pickard, J. (2005) 'Out of control', *People Management*, 24 November: 16–17.

Pickard, J. (2006) 'Multiple choice', in *The Guide to HR Outsourcing, People Management*, London: Chartered Institute of Personnel and Development, pp. 7–11.

Pugh, D.S., Hickson, D.J. and Hinings, C.R. (eds) (1983) *Writers on Organizations*. Harmondsworth: Penguin.

Quinn, R.E., Faerman, S.R., Thompson, M.P. and McGrath, M.R. (1990) *Becoming a Master Manager*. New York: Wiley.

Rainbird, H. and Maguire, M. (1993) 'When corporate need supersedes employee development', *Personnel Management*, February, pp. 34–37.

Rana, E. (2000) '2000 predictions: Enter the people dimension', *People Management*, 6 January: 16–17.

Reday-Mulvey, G. (2005) 'The tide turns', *People Management*, 30 June: 36–38.

Reese, H.W. and Overton, W.F. (1970) 'Models of development and theories of development' in L.R. Goulet and P.B. Baltes (eds) *Life-Span Developmental Psychology: Theory and Research*. New York: Academic Press, pp. 115–45.

*Revans, R. (1983) *ABC of Action Learning*. Bromley: Chartwell-Bratt (Publishing and Training).

Ribeaux, P. and Poppleton, S.E. (1978) *Psychology and Work: An Introduction*. London: Macmillan.

Rifkin, J. (1995) *The End of Work: The Decline of the Global Labor Force and the Dawn of the Post-Market Era*. New York: Putnam.

Rothwell, A. and Arnold, J. (2005) 'How professionals rate "continuing professional development"', *Human Resource Management Journal*, 15, 3: 18–32.

Scarborough, H. (2003) 'Recipe for success', *People Management*, 23 January: 32–35.

Schön, D.A. (1983) *The Reflective Practitioner: How Professionals Think in Action*. New York: Basic Books.

*Senge, P. (1990) *The Fifth Discipline: The Art and Practice of the Learning Organization*. London: Century.

Senge, P., Kleiner, A., Roberts, C., Ross, R., Roth, G. and Smith, B. (1998) *The Dance of Change*. London: Nicholas Brealey.

Sheard, M. (1992) 'Two routes to quality: why Dow went for BS 5750', *Personnel Management*, November, pp. 33–34.

Sloman, M. (2001) *The E-Learning Revolution*. London: Chartered Institute of Personnel and Development.

Sloman, M. (2002) 'Don't believe the hype', *People Management*, 21 March: 40–42.

Smethurst, S. (2005) 'The great beyond', *People Management*, 27 January: 28–31.

Smethurst, S. (2006) 'State of mind', *People Management*, 12 January: 24–29.

Snowden, D. (2002) 'Complex acts of knowing: paradox and descriptive self-awareness', *Journal of Knowledge Management*, 6, 2, May: 100–11.

Sofer, C. (1970) *Men in Mid-Career*. Cambridge: Cambridge University Press.

Stammers, R. and Patrick, J. (1975) *The Psychology of Training*. London: Methuen.

Sternberg, R.J. (1985) *Beyond IQ: A Triarchic Theory of Human Intelligence*. Cambridge: Cambridge University Press.

Thatcher, M. (1996) 'Allowing everyone to have their say', *People Management*, 21 March: 28–30.

Thomas, D.A. and Alderfer, C.P. (1989) 'The influence of race on career dynamics: theory and research on minority career experiences' in M.B. Arthur, D.T. Hall and B.S. Lawrence (eds) *Handbook of Career Theory*. Cambridge: Cambridge University Press, pp. 133–58.

Thomas, R.J. (1989) 'Blue-collar careers: meaning and choice in a world of constraints' in M.B. Arthur, D.T. Hall and B.S. Lawrence (eds) *Handbook of Career Theory*. Cambridge: Cambridge University Press, pp. 354–79.

Training Commission (1988) *Classifying the Components of Management Competences*. Sheffield: Training Commission.

Trinder, C., Hulme, G. and McCarthy, U. (1992) *Employment: the Role of Work in the Third Age*, The Carnegie Inquiry into the Third Age, Research Paper Number 1. Dunfermline: The Carnegie United Kingdom Trust.

Tyson, S. and Fell, A. (1995) 'A focus on skills, not organis-ations', *People Management*, 19 October: 42–45.

Ulrich, D. and Brockbank, W. (2005) 'Role call', *People Management*, 16 June: 22–28.

Ulrich, D. and Smallwood, N. (2002) 'Seven up', *People Management*, 16 May: 42–44.

Ulrich, D. and Stewart Black, J. (1999) 'All around the world: worldly wise', *People Management*, 25 October: 42–46.

Walsh, J. (1998) 'Competency frameworks give companies the edge', *People Management*, 17 September: 15.

Waskel, S. A. (1991) *Mid-life Issues and the Workplace of the 90s: A Guide for Human Resource Specialists.* New York: Quorum.

Watts, A.G., Law, B., Killeen, J., Kidd, J.M. and Hawthorn, R. (1996) *Rethinking Careers Education and Guidance: Theory, Policy and Practice.* London: Routledge.

Wechsler, D. (1958) *The Measurement and Appraisal of Adult Intelligence*, 4th edn. London: Baillière, Tindall & Cox.

Weick, K.E. and Berlinger, L.R. (1989) 'Career improvisation in self-designing organizations' in M.B. Arthur, D.T. Hall and B.S. Lawrence (eds) *Handbook of Career Theory.* Cambridge: Cambridge University Press, pp. 313–28.

Whittaker, J. (1992) 'Making a policy of keeping up to date', *Personnel Management*, March, pp. 28–31.

Whittaker, J. and Johns, T. (2004) 'Standards deliver', *People Management*, 30 June: 32–34.

Wisher, V. (1994) 'Competencies: the precious seeds of growth', *Personnel Management*, July: 36–39.

Woodruffe, C. (1991) 'Competent by any other name', *Personnel Management*, September: 30–33.

Wrightsman, L.S. (1988) *Personality Development in Adulthood.* Newbury Park, CA: Sage.

Chapter 8

Human resource development: the organisational and national framework

Mairi Watson

Objectives

- To examine the strategic nature of HRD and its relationship to the organisational and UK national context.
- To outline and explain the development of HRD plans and the link to the organisational and national context.
- To examine the national framework for workforce development in the UK.
- To examine systems of national vocational education in Europe.
- To examine the implications of European comparisons for the UK.
- To identify future issues for HRD.

Introduction

As economic conditions become more challenging, and organisational ground shifts at extraordinary speeds, the context of HRD has become one where change and turbulence are the normal context. Despite these challenges, the vast majority of organisations have maintained budgets for training and development (CIPD, 2009). However, as organisations struggle for survival, the emphasis on demonstrating the value of the contribution of HRD to business strategy has become prominent in research and practice (Anderson, 2007).

As a consequence, the ways in which organisations develop their people have altered substantially. Three decades ago in the UK, the Employment and Training Act (1973) set the foundations for the transformation of the national and organisational learning and development landscape. Since then an 'evolution' has occurred as organisations have changed in size, purpose, structure, philosophy, work methods, technology and relationships (Garavan et al., 1995, Garavan, 2007). Approaches to learning have shifted as the practice and purpose of training and developing people have grown in importance, broadened in scope and become more sophisticated in method (Reid et al., 2004, CIPD, 2009). The change in strategic pressures for organisations has led to developments in training and learning technology, the role of external consultants, new perspectives on learning and knowledge, the increased emphasis on individual responsibility for learning, and an emphasis on developing skills for work.

While the environmental changes have had a significant impact on organisations at a general level, for human resource development (HRD) there appear to be three fundamental shifts in the way that the learning and development of people is managed and delivered:

- *From training to learning.* Training is defined as a set of activities which react to present needs and is focused on the instructor and contrasts with learning as a process that focuses on developing individual and organisational potential and building capabilities for the future (Reynolds, 2004: 1; Sloman, 2005: 2).

- *From human resource development to strategic human resource development.* This emphasises the link between how people in the organisation are developed and the achievement of organisational goals, and that competitive advantage comes from the strategic development of people.

- *From return on investment to return on expectation.* In this trend organisations are moving away from traditional evaluation using hard, financial measures to a set of measures that allow an assessment of the strategic value added to the business using both qualitative and quantitative measures (Anderson, 2007).

The underlying issues and broader implications of these three shifts are developed in this chapter. While the previous chapter considered the meanings, outcomes and processes of learning in the context of the organisation, this chapter explores this contemporary context at the organisational, strategic, national and international levels and considers the link between the development of people and organisations' business performance and competitiveness.

Training, learning, HRD and HRM

Training and learning

The role of formal training in organisations today appears to have declined significantly and has been replaced with an emphasis on developing skills (CIPD, 2009). The speed with which skills requirements change in some sectors means that formal, time-consuming, classroom based learning fails to deliver efficiently as required. Furthermore, the growing recognition of HRD as a tool to achieve competitive advantage has raised awareness of the need to embrace learning as a central strategic concern and to be part of the culture of the organisation (Senge, 1990; Pedlar *et al.*, 1997, Garavan, 2007) of which formal training is just one, often small, component. In addition, a government-policy-driven emphasis on individual responsibility for life-long learning and skills development (Leitch, 2006; DIUS, 2007b) gives individuals more responsibility for their own learning with spin-off benefits for the organisation, which reduces the relevance of off-the-shelf, one-size-fits-all group learning. On the other side of this coin is the need to provide employees with workplace-specific skills to reduce the 'poaching' of skilled employees which reduces the value of traditional training methods. Finally, the availability of more efficient and more effective alternatives (e.g. e-learning, distance learning, individualised learning, coaching and workplace learning) means that in achieving competitive advantage organisations can calculate a greater return on their investment with alternative methods of delivery and application. The extract in Box 8.1 emphasises that training as a standalone strategy for learning is likely to be worthless.

One allied issue which underpins the shift from training to learning is the growing and developing role of stakeholders in the process (Garavan *et al.*, 1998; Garavan, 2007). These stakeholders have varying degrees of power and influence, hold varying roles, have different values, use different tactics to achieve their aims, engage in different learning experiences, have different aims, objectives and structure, in different contexts and cultures, with different expectations. Employees, employers, managers, leaders, government, European and international bodies, customers, HRD specialists, consultants and trade unions all have a stake in developing the area to their advantage. Furthermore, investors value highly an organisation's ability to attract and retain the very best of people, and their investment in training them for the future (Ernst and Young, 1997; CIPD, 2006; CIPD, 2009).

| Box 8.1 | **The death of training?** |

The instructional side of training needs to be left behind, the Director of Learning and Strategy Evangelism at Microsoft has said. Bob Mosher told delegates that just as Microsoft's own learners had grown out of the classroom model, the same would happen in every organisation.

Quoting research from KPMG Consulting, which found that up to 80 per cent of learning occurred informally, Mosher questioned how many firms were actually supporting such learning. 'A lot should be, but most don't', he said.

And while Mosher admitted that there was still a place for instructor-led training at the beginning of someone's career, he argued that from then on, formal training failed to meet the needs of the learner.

He cited e-communities, peer support, internet references and electronic performance systems as tools to aid informal learning. These should also be used alongside formal training where it does occur, because employees need to be supported between courses.

'The average person gets 26 hours of instruction a year – but what are you doing to support them in between?' he asked.

Mosher also stressed the need to monitor informal learning. 'You can then help employees to choose learning that is appropriate for them,' he argued.

Source: Edwards (2005).

Questions

1 Given the emphasis on informal learning, what are the difficulties that organisations face in monitoring and controlling it?

2 As this chapter considers HRD to be a strategic resource, how can informal learning be linked to the strategy of the organisation?

One set of influential stakeholders are the professional organisations, and their impact is pervasive in this area. The Chartered Institute of Personnel Development's (CIPD) professional standards for 'Learning and Development' (2001a – due to be updated during 2010 to become Learning and Talent Development) established this phrase as one which intends to capture the breadth and depth of the role of learning and development in organisations underpinned by the assumption that if organisations make the shift from training to learning, and to the strategic development of learning, then they will achieve competitive advantage (Sloman, 2005: 1).

The performance indicators (shown below) allied to the CIPD's professional standards help to illustrate just how far the understanding of workplace training and learning has moved in the last three decades (CIPD, 2001a).

1 Integrating learning and development activity and organisational needs.

2 Providing a value-adding learning and development function.

3 Contributing to the recruitment and performance management processes.

4 Contributing to the retention of employees.

5 Contributing to building organisational capacity and facilitating change.

6 Stimulating strategic awareness and the development of knowledge.

7 Designing and delivering learning processes and activity.

8 Evaluating and assessing learning and development outcomes and investment.

9 Achieving ethical practice.

10 Ensuring continual professional self-development.

These indicate that 'learning and development' as a phenomenon exists, and exists on several levels:

- At the practical level of delivering or facilitating training, learning and development interventions, e.g. training, on-the-job learning, e-learning, coaching, mentoring, secondments, etc.

- At a professional level in hosting a set of plans, policies and strategies to achieve a predetermined set of strategic goals, to coordinate the production of information and evaluation, providing expertise and advice on learning and development as experts in the practice of ethical learning and development, who understand the nature of effective design and delivery.

- At a partnership level in building relationships intra-organisationally between HRD and HRM, HRD and the wider organisation.

- At a strategic level in ensuring that learning and development activity contributes to plugging performance gaps identified in strategic planning.

- At a cultural level in developing a culture that values learning and principles associated with it.

- At an extra-organisational level in building strategically beneficial relationships outside the organisation to ensure that learning and development in the organisation are up-to-date, relevant and appropriately develop the organisation's skills base.

Until 2006, the CIPD annually produced a 'Training and Development' Survey. During 2006 (and for the first time), the CIPD named the survey 'Learning and Development', perhaps representing the final nail in the coffin of an enduring emphasis on training as the primary mode of learning in the workplace. This is some way from the definition of an emphasis on training in the Employment and Training Act (1973) and demonstrates the growing importance of training and development for human resource management in companies (Sloman, 2002, Garavan, 2007; CIPD, 2009).

HRD and HRM

With the shift from training to learning comes the need to understand where HRD 'fits' in the organisation. The growing understanding of the contribution that HRD can make to organisational performance has much to do with the growth in interest in HRM and in the contribution that people can make to a business. Most of the models of HRM considered in Chapters 1 and 2 have as part of their aims, policies or outcomes that are directly related to HRD (Beer *et al.*, 1984; Storey, 1989; Storey, 1992). Approaches vary greatly, but organisations that demonstrate a high commitment to HRM policies include as part of this commitment extensive training learning and development (Sung and Ashton, 2004; Purcell, 2003; Pfeffer, 1998) enabling them to achieve superior performance through their people. In some organisations this is no small undertaking, and they have created their own 'Corporate Universities', for example UnipartU (**www.unipart.co.uk**) where training and learning, and ultimately, being a learning organisation are considered part of the company's competitive strategy. The commitment and involvement of line managers, as well as top management support are evident in companies that have a strong learning culture and a strategic approach to learning and development (McCracken and Wallace, 2000). Thus, some commentators argue that it is self-evident that HRD is not a subset of HRM, but that each has its own separate, equally important (and problematic) space (Stewart and McGoldrick, 1996; Hall, 1984; Nadler, 1984, Luoma, 2000; McCracken and Wallace, 2000; Garavan, 2007). They view HRM and HRD as separate but complementary processes in the analysis of contemporary organisations. However, it is more common to consider HRD as a section or part of an organisation's approach to HRM, one of the many tools at its disposal, and the existence of human resource management policies, generally, as being the distinguishing factor in successful organisations (Sloman, 2002).

The relationship between a business's strategy and HRD is, in practice, becoming increasingly important as financial conditions become more challenging. Two-thirds (65 per cent) of respondents in the CIPD's 2009 Learning and Development Survey anticipate that learning and development activity will become more closely integrated with business strategy and 60 per cent feel that there will be a greater emphasis on the evaluation of training effectiveness. Furthermore, while many organisations have a staff development budget, this is not uniform across sector or organisation size: voluntary sector organisations spend more per year on training than any other sector (CIPD, 2009). Overall, while seventy per cent of organisations had a specific training budget for the next 12 months, this represented a decrease of 7 per cent from last year's survey (CIPD, 2009).

HRD: The organisational context

Planning human resource development

Planning businesses are more likely to be training businesses.   (LSC, 2005: 52)

Businesses that engage in training planning are far more likely to have training expenditure in place (Shury *et al.*, 2008). Popular practitioner textbooks on HRD and learning and development (Harrison, 2009; Reid *et al.*, 2004; Mankin, 2009; Walton, 1999) recommend that in order to design, implement and evaluate effective learning events or HRD interventions (including training, but sometimes covering learning and development more broadly), a cyclical process or system of formal planning ought to be followed. However, the popularity of planning cycles are more evident in the rhetoric of the literature than in organisational reality with only 48 per cent of employers having a training plan specifying in advance the level and types of training employees will need in the coming year and only 36 per cent with a budget for training expenditure. Organisations with more than 25 people are much more likely to see these activities as 'standard' and to have them in place. Where businesses have a formal plan of business objectives, they are more likely to have a training plan, and where there is a training plan, it is more likely that there will be a training budget (Shury *et al.*, 2008).

Typically, the learning and development planning cycle (see Figure 8.1) comprises a number of logical stages in a step-by-step process to: ensure the consideration of the needs of the individual and the organisation at the early stages; establish appropriate aims and objectives; ensure optimum methods of design and delivery; and carry out effective evaluation of the learning intervention.

This approach stems from strategic planning approaches and has been popular for several decades (Rothwell and Kanazas, 1989; Walton, 1999). Its origins can be traced to the work of the Industrial Training Boards set up in 1964 and developed by Tom Boydell in 1971 (Harrison, 2009). It matches most organisations' tendency to treat strategic issues formally, using

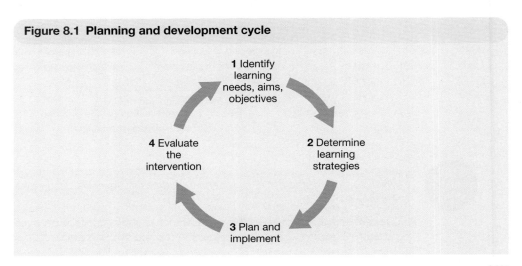

Figure 8.1 Planning and development cycle

1 Identify learning needs, aims, objectives

2 Determine learning strategies

3 Plan and implement

4 Evaluate the intervention

written documents with aims, objectives, targets, priorities and performance indicators. It relies heavily on analysis, planning and foresight, logical thinking and clarity of organisational objectives. As such the approach pays scant attention to the likelihood of iterations of or interruptions in or to the process, changes in aspects material to the process, and influences internal and external to the process. It does not take account of the need for evaluation to happen at all stages of the process, or the way that needs change and develop as the process moves on. It matches well the classical or rational planning approach to strategy which suggests that organisational strategy is formed through a formal, rational decision making process (see Chapter 2 on SHRM), but not with alternative approaches (e.g. evolutionary, processual or systemic (Whittington, 1993, outlined in Chapter 2) which conceptualise strategy as something more informal, fragmented and embedded in the social systems (cultural and institutional aspects) of the business.

Most commentators are not blind to the need to link the learning or training cycle to the strategic processes of the organisation. This consideration usually appears in the first stage of analysis of learning needs in the form of an organisational or strategic review, but it fails to appreciate the role of strategic considerations throughout the whole process, and doesn't account for other internal or external contextual issues such as power and politics, stakeholders, values, structure, culture, management perspectives and much, much more.

While the basic model is useful in order to structure consideration of the key aspects of planning HRD in organisations, the sequential presentation of the issues does not imply their sequential occurrence in practice. In particular, there is a need at all stages of the process to consider how the strategic intentions of the whole business are being served, and how this contribution will be measured. The adapted cycle shown in Figure 8.2 captures the overlapping and interactive nature of the development of HRD at a strategic level, and the concomitant consideration of needs. It underlines that this occurs in the internal and external context of the organisation. It goes on to emphasise the ongoing nature of evaluation, explored more fully below.

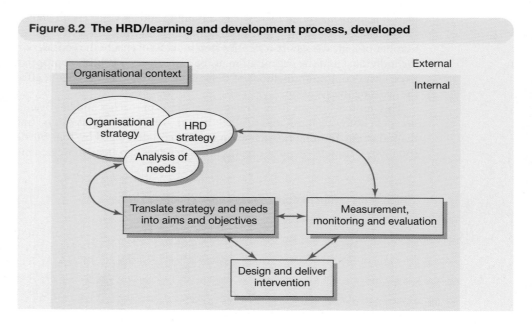

Figure 8.2 The HRD/learning and development process, developed

Which aspects of the cycle, or which interactions in the cycle, are likely to be neglected and why?

One of the areas that receives the least attention is closing the loop between evaluation and strategy. We explore this in detail below. Why do you think this area is paid so little attention?

Stages in the process

The next sections cover in sequence:

- Identifying learning needs, aims and objectives.
- Determining learning strategies.
- Planning and implementation.
- Evaluating L&D interventions.

Identifying learning needs

The purpose of identifying learning needs is to establish how learning and development strategies, policies, practices and activities can bridge the gap between where the organisation is now and where it needs to be in order to achieve its strategic objectives. A learning need exists when there is a gap between the future requirements of the job and the current capabilities of the incumbent, whether this is measured in terms of skills, attitudes or knowledge, and it is anticipated that a planned learning intervention will overcome the deficiency or barrier.

Given the multi-level nature of the learning and development process discussed above, one would expect multi-level analysis of learning and development needs. So, while this section considers the analysis of learning needs at just three levels: organisational, job and individual Harrison (2009), others consider more. McGoldrick *et al.* (2002), for example, offer a comprehensive structure which suggests seven levels of analysis:

- *Extra-organisational*: beyond organisational boundaries, attempting to understand, anticipate and create change in the environment and translate it into the advantage of the organisation. This involves practical and analytical research and learning and changing in response to this.
- *Inter-organisational*: between organisations, transferring learning and information, sharing best practices through collaboration and exchange.
- *Intra-organisational*: between departments, cross-fertilisation of ideas, encouraging diversity.
- *Organisational*: recognising the uniqueness of the organisation and responding to its needs for learning and change.
- *Departmental*: encouraging self-development and creativity through learning by experimentation.
- *Group*: through good communication identifying and solving problems to lead to learning and improvement.

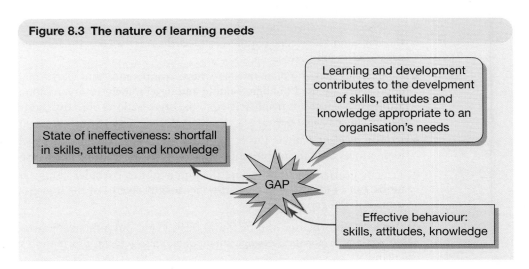

Figure 8.3 The nature of learning needs

State of ineffectiveness: shortfall in skills, attitudes and knowledge

Learning and development contributes to the develpment of skills, attitudes and knowledge appropriate to an organisation's needs

GAP

Effective behaviour: skills, attitudes, knowledge

- *Individual*: personal responsibility for identifying learning and improvement needs in knowledge, skills, aptitude and performance.

However, despite the aspirations of authors, articles and textbooks, very few organisations have developed or used appropriate measures (Anderson, 2007). Only half of employers (52 per cent) formally assess the extent to which employees currently have gaps in their skills against formal written job descriptions and 30 per cent do not have formal written job descriptions (Shury *et al.*, 2008).

For the organisation

The first level of analysis of the learning needs of the business is 'the identification of needed skills and active management of employees learning for their long-range future in relation to explicit corporate and business strategies' (Hall, 1984). This step provides the link between the broader strategy of the organisation and the HRD strategy and ensures that the learning processes, systems and interventions support the direction in which the business is heading and aims to identify the quantity and type of learning required to ensure all employees have the skills they need to do their jobs. This level of analysis may cover the shorter (a year) or longer term and will aid decisions about whether to develop existing staff or employ new talent (Taylor, 2008). However, it is not one that has always received attention:

> Many organisations invest considerable resources in training and development but never really examine how training and development can most effectively promote organisational objectives, or how developmental activities should be altered in the light of business plans.
>
> (Hall, 1984)

If learning and development are to be effective, then it is necessary to identify not only the needs of the individual and the job, but how these fit the overall organisational strategy and objectives. Therefore, this level of review has as its aim the identification of the learning needs of the whole organisation as evidenced in its strategy. This is also central to the 'Investors In People Standard' (considered below).

Considering what has been said here about the need to understand the broader context of the organisation, Hirsh and Reilly (1998: 40) warn that 'organisational structures and employee attitudes have an impact. Simply having appropriate skilled individuals does not automatically yield high performance'. Further, it is important that in the analysis of learning needs considers not only the 'fit' with the values and priorities of the organisation but also considers the feedback provided by evaluation of previous learning and development interventions.

In practice, this level of analysis can consist of (Reid *et al.*, 2004: 243):

- *A global review*: where the organisation examines its short- and longer-term objectives and the skills and knowledge required to meet them. This takes the form of a detailed whole-organisation job analysis.
- *Competence-based global review*: where competence and performance management approaches are used to align training and development to organisational objectives. It is attractive because it is firmly related to the organisation's objectives and can be the basis of performance related pay.
- *Critical incident analysis*: this is a positive, key event focused strategy which considers the main processes in the organisation and considers the learning needs associated with them.
- *Priority problem analysis*: where the aim is not to consider comprehensively learning needs, but to identify and prioritise the main problems of the organisation and respond using HRD interventions.

At this level, information can be found in strategic and human resource plans, succession planning data, performance management data, management information systems and financial plans.

Box 8.2

Practice in focus: how do we take a business goal and convert it to learning goals?

Andrew Mayo takes a refreshingly clear view of the link between organisational goals and learning goals. He suggests that managers easily fall into the trap of jumping to tried and trusted solutions, especially to training courses. He argues that we need to be very sure whether it is a learning solution that is needed or whether there is change required in resources or systems instead, or as well as. Only then, should managers proceed to set clear learning objectives and choose the most effective learning solution.

The eight steps shown in Figure 8.4 represent a methodology for doing this systematically.

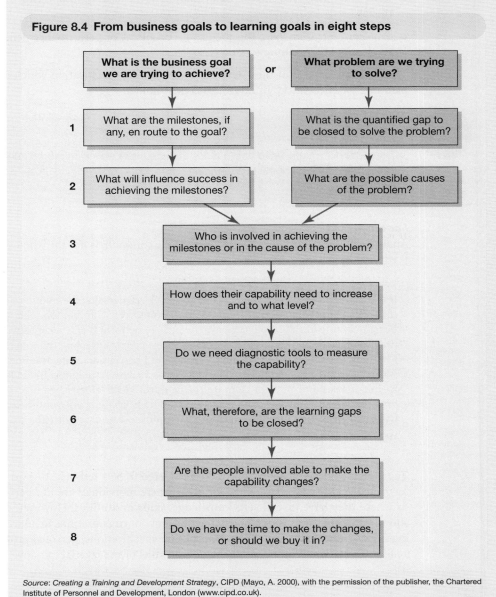

Figure 8.4 From business goals to learning goals in eight steps

Source: Creating a Training and Development Strategy, CIPD (Mayo, A. 2000), with the permission of the publisher, the Chartered Institute of Personnel and Development, London (www.cipd.co.uk).

For the job

Job level analysis has as its purpose the identification of the skills knowledge and attributes of the job. The outcomes of this level of analysis are usually a job description, job specification and job training specification. Job level analysis can be categorised on three levels (Stewart, 1999; Harrison, 2005):

- *Comprehensive analysis*: which consists of a full and exhaustive analysis of the job, producing a detailed job specification of all the tasks, roles and performance levels associated with the job and the level of knowledge, skills and attitudes required to perform the job effectively.

- *Key task analysis*: this consists of an analysis of the tasks central to effective performance of the job.

- *Problem-centred analysis*: this focuses on problems or performance deficiencies and seeks to identify HRD solutions.

The outcome of each of these levels is a job training specification which forms the basis of planning for HRD interventions for each post-holder.

How can you gather information to inform job analysis?

The most commonly used approaches include interviews with job holders, managers and supervisors, job logs, questionnaires and group discussions. What else can you think of?

For the individual

Analysis of training needs at the job level, while common, is not the whole picture, and nor is it without its critics:

It is tempting to address training needs at [job] level: deciding the training needed for particular roles then rolling out this training to all employees with that job. This approach has the benefit of ensuring all employees have the skills to perform their role effectively. Yet it also has drawbacks, with its 'sheep dip' tactics resulting in people attending training they do not need. The consequences are wasted training spend, poor perception of the training department and wasted working time. Addressing training needs analysis at the most individual level possible is time-consuming and can be more costly. But it yields greater benefits . . . financially . . . organisationally . . . and individually. What can make us more a part of the strategic direction of the organisation than delivering the employee resource with the exact skills profile required to realise it?

(Ashworth, 2006)

The individual level of analysis is often considered to be a response to gaps or failures in performance, identifying where there are areas where individuals are not performing effectively or where they have insufficient knowledge, skills or abilities. However, Ashworth (2006), above, argues that this is potentially the best way for organisations to address strategic learning needs. Information can come from person specifications, personal profiles, the appraisal system, assessment centres, and through individual or managerial initiative.

Determining learning strategies

Organisations have a choice about which learning strategy or intervention they identify to meet the needs established in the previous stage and the decision is highly circumstantial or contextual. Criteria can be employed to help to make the appropriate decision, which can include (Reid *et al.*, 2004):

● *The extent to which the learning intervention fits with objectives*: for example, if the objective is practical knowledge, then practical/hands-on experience should be sought, rather than classroom based education.

● *The extent to which the learning is likely to be transferred to the work place*: for example, whether the learning intervention is sufficiently related to the objectives that have to be met, and whether there are systems in place (such as coaching) to support transfer of learning on return to the workplace

● *Available resources*: for example, practical concerns such as time, money and the availability of internal or external expertise.

● *Learner-related factors*: for example, the learner's preferences in terms of time, location and learning, taking into account the nature of their contract and reasonable expectations on how they use their time.

What do organisations do?

Having briefly introduced the possibility that organisations have a choice of learning interventions, this chapter now turns to examining the different possibilities available. Given the extent of expenditure on training and learning activity in organisations (CIPD, 2009, LSC, 2008; Shury *et al.*, 2008), the cost effective use of training methods ought to be an investment which companies and organisations consider carefully. In the 12 months prior to the National Employers' Skills Survey in 2007 (LSC, 2008), a total of 218 million days of training were arranged or funded by employers, representing 9.8 days per annum for every worker in England, or 15.6 days for trainees. However, many commentators report that organisations choose inappropriate methods which are costly, time consuming, have a deleterious effect on employees' perceptions of the value of training and development and ultimately do little to increase skills levels in organisations (LSC, 2008).

The CIPD and the Learning Skills Council produce annual reports which include information on training and development activity in organisations. These are available online:

● *National Employers Skills Survey 200 (published May 2008)* **www.lsc.gov.uk**.

● *Annual Survey Report 2009: Learning and Development (published April 2009)* **www.cipd.co.uk**.

Compare and contrast the findings in each of the most recent surveys. Notice the different perspectives from which they are written and the different information presented.

Questions

1 *How can you account for the differences in findings?*

2 *How closely does your organisation match with organisations mentioned in the reports?*

3 *What can you learn from reading through the reports about the way your organisation needs to develop its people?*

The National Employer Skills Survey notes the division of training into (LSC, 2008):

● *Off-the-job training*: which takes place away from the individual's immediate work position.

● *On-the-job training*: defined as activities that would be recognised as training by staff, **but not** the sort of learning by experience which takes place on an ongoing basis. This type of training significantly increased between 2005 and 2007 (LSC, 2008).

The type of provision of training by employer varies, with 46 per cent providing off the job training and 54 per cent providing on the job training. (LSC, 2008). The CIPD (2009) reports that by far the most popular method of training is in-house development with a focus on coaching by line managers and on-the-job training (see Figure 8.5).

A summary of some of the main learning interventions is given below. In order to broaden the definitions and provide recognition of the many ways that staff are developed, here the reference is to on- and off-the-job *learning* rather than *training*.

On-the-job learning

One of the most popular ways of training and learning at work, on-the-job learning, includes staff meetings, discussion, reflection, observation, teamworking, undertaking a project, assignment or consultancy, taking on a new area of responsibility, changing work practices or systems and much more. It is popular because it is job-specific and relevant, immediate and flexible. In 2009, the CIPD survey identified that it was also one of the most *effective* methods of training, topped only by in house development programmes and coaching by line managers which have grown considerably in popularity in the last two years. However, both positive and negative behaviours and skills can be passed on, underlining the need for suitable role models and opportunities to be identified and developed as part of the

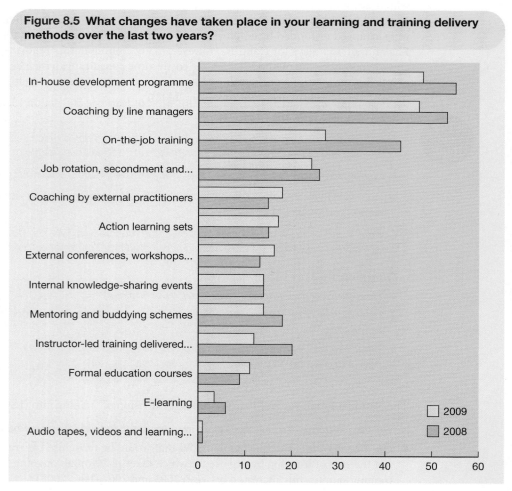

Figure 8.5 What changes have taken place in your learning and training delivery methods over the last two years?

Source: Learning and Development Survey, CIPD (2009) p. 5, www.cipd.co.uk/subjects/lrnanddev/general/_learning_and_development_09, with the permission of the publisher, the Chartered Institute of Personnel and Development, London (www.cipd.co.uk).

organisation's HRD strategy. On-the-job training ought not to be haphazard and accidental. The most commonly used planned methods are discussed under the following five headings.

Sitting by Nellie

Both the strengths and the limitations of this approach are based on its central premise – that people learn well by watching others. It is a truism that the majority of employees gain most of their job knowledge from colleagues and not from books or courses. It is popular because it is immediate and accessible to most employees. While much of this type of learning happens in an ad hoc, unplanned way, it can be a valid, planned way of transferring learning and knowledge in the workplace. In order to be effective, it relies on good structuring, planning and monitoring.

However, the limitations of this approach are well documented. The underlying assumption is that the role model is an experienced, well practiced and skilled performer who has a good understanding of what needs to be passed on. However, they may not be good at their job, may exhibit inefficient job practices or inappropriate behaviour. There might be someone else who is better, or the role model may not have been trained in the practices they are modelling. Often this is a result of poor structure, design and planning but it can result in the passing on of bad or even dangerous working practices (Cannell, 1997). That said it is how the vast majority of employees learn their job.

Reflective practice

Based on experiential learning theories (Kolb, 1984) reflective practice (Schön, 1983) includes both reflection-in-action (unplanned, spontaneous, ongoing, informal) which occurs in the midst of experience and conducted by the learner and planned reflection which occurs after the event to review the experience. The latter can be as 'coached reflection' with the support of another to assist the identification of learning and action (Seibert, 1999) or as any other planned reflective activity which is formal and structured. With the aim of identifying the learning from the event, this is commonly encouraged by professional organisations such as the CIPD and is central to their Professional Standards (CIPD, 2005a) and their assessment of continuing professional development (CPD). This is also discussed in Chapter 9.

Mentoring

The terms mentoring and coaching are sometimes used interchangeably, but there is a difference in the relationship between the participants in the process. The previous chapter gives a detailed consideration of mentoring, but a short summary is given here.

> The mentoring relationship is most often oriented towards an 'exchange of wisdom, support, learning or guidance for the purpose of . . . career growth; sometimes [it is] used to achieve strategic business goals . . . content can be wide ranging'.   (Parsloe and Wray, 2000: 12)

Thus, mentoring usually takes the form of a senior or experienced employee taking a supporting role in the development of a new or younger employee. It can be formal or informal and relies on the development of a positive advisory relationship. As such it includes the skills of coaching, facilitating, counselling and networking. Mentoring is part of a range of 'talent management' activities which organisations engage in to identify, develop, engage, retain and deploy the most talented individuals (Warren, 2006; CIPD, 2005d).

Coaching

> The coach does not need to impart knowledge, advice or even wisdom. What he or she must do is speak, and act, in such a way that others learn and perform at their best.
>
> (Downey, 2003: 17)

> Coaching . . . requires people to see things from others' perspectives, suspend their judgment and listen at a higher level.
>
> (Hall, 2005)

The coaching market has grown exponentially in the last decade. Coaching, along with e-learning, represents the largest growth area identified by subsequent CIPD Learning and Development Surveys (CIPD, 2005b, 2006, 2007, 2008a, 2009) with staying power that has outlived that expected by the critics. It is considered, along with in house development programmes to be the most effective method of learning and development (CIPD, 2009). Coaching is delivered either by in-house staff or external practitioners (Knights and Poppleton, 2008) and often forms part of managers' job descriptions.

At the centre of coaching are models of *structure* and *skills*. The **structure** of coaching, or the coaching process is firmly focused on the outcome or longer-term objective that the participants want to achieve. The most popular model is the 'GROW' model (Gallwey, 1986; Whitmore, 2002; Downey, 2003) (see Box 8.3). The model takes the participants through four overlapping stages in an iterative process of interaction between the coach and the coachee. Usually this takes the form of the coach asking questions in order to raise the awareness and responsibility of the coachee, and allows them to develop practicable solutions or actions in order to achieve the goal. It enables the coach to structure the conversation and deliver a result which emphasises the accountability and responsibility of the coachee and the will to achieve the outcome.

Within this conversational process the coach is using a range of **skills**: Downey (2003) suggests that the coach can use all of the skills on the spectrum shown in Figure 8.6. He indicates that the most effective skills of the coach lie at the non-directive end of the spectrum. For Downey, the skills of the coach are more valuable than his experience of the problem the coachee is attempting to resolve. He indicates that while there will be times when the coachee is stuck and the coach knows the solution, there are limitations to the directive approach – namely, the coach has to know the answer already or be able to work it out, the answer is unlikely to be the one that fits the problem best, and the experience of the coachee is excluded.

Coaching is beset by a number of debates, not least the one which concerns the appropriate way to regulate the profession and develop the skills of those who practice it (Hall, 2005). Many universities and professional bodies have introduced development programmes for would-be coaches, and most organisations have a system to measure the abilities or performance of the coaches they use.

Box 8.3   Typical Grow model

Goal: What is the longer term objective? What is the objective for *this* discussion?

Reality: What is the situation now? Who is involved? What is it costing? What is happening?

Options: What are the possible (not necessarily practicable) solutions? What could be done?

Will: What will be done? When? With whose support?

Figure 8.6 Spectrum of coaching skills

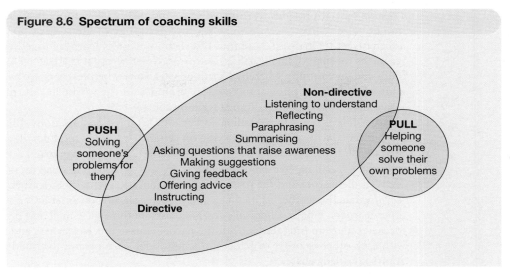

Source: from *Effective Coaching: Lessons from the Coach's Coach*, 3rd ed. (Downey, M.) p. 23, © 2003 South Western, a part of Cengage Learning, Inc., reproduced by permission of Cengage Learning, Inc., www.cengage.com/permissions and the author.

The emphasis has shifted in the last few years from developing effective coaches and processes to developing a coaching culture (CIPD, 2006; Clutterbuck and Megginson, 2005) with the aim of improving individual and organisational performance.

Job rotation, secondment and shadowing

Job rotation aims to reduce boredom, vary activities, and develop or increase skill levels by encouraging employees to change jobs periodically. Its popularity was established in the 1970s, and if properly structured can be a positive learning experience for employees and have spin-off benefits for business performance. It is usually part of a larger agenda of *job enrichment* which aims to motivate staff and increase productivity. However, it has been criticised for being insufficiently planned and structured, with less focus on employee development and more on achieving organisational outcomes of flexibility and efficiency.

Secondment encourages the cross-fertilisation of ideas, and usually involves an employee leaving, temporarily, their workplace to work for another organisation. Usually it will be a similar job in a different sector, or a similar area of work with a different focus, e.g. practical *vs* theoretical. It is usually for a fixed period of time with a structured procedure for feedback and learning.

Shadowing is another popular technique where employees gain an understanding of a job or role in a different department. Usually, the participant is not expected to carry out the job role they are shadowing, but learn about a job by walking through the work day as a shadow to a competent worker. Normally it is temporary, and allows the participant to view at first hand the work environment and skills in practice, with the intention of gaining skills and experience in that area in order to inform job choices, or to develop cross-departmental understanding.

e-learning

There is little doubt that e-learning is big business in the UK with almost 60 per cent of organisations using it (CIPD, 2008a). e-learning is, at its simplest, learning that uses information and communication technologies to achieve specified learning objectives. It can use the whole range of electronic resources, e.g. e-mail, intranet, internet, software packages, PDAs, CDs/DVDs and beyond as technologies develop and advance. It requires the learner to take a high level of responsibility for their own learning and motivation to learn. The paradox with e-learning is that while only 7 per cent of individuals or organisations? identify it as the most effective method of learning, 42 per cent identify that they have used it more in the last two years (CIPD, 2009).

At its best, it provides learning which is more accessible, more flexible and adaptable to individual circumstances, provides a broader range of alternatives and is cheaper than alternatives. Its greatest potential lies in how it links learners together and learners to resources through online learning platforms. Nonetheless, it is attractive because of its flexibility and accessibility whereby learning is available when learners are available to learn. It allows for learning to be completed in 'granules' in the workplace during working hours, rather than through the traditional training course.

According to a CIPD e-learning survey (2004a) most organisations still rely on CD-Roms (73 per cent), with around half relying on generic or specific modules. Reynolds *et al.* (2002) distinguish three types of e-learning: web-based learning, supported online learning, and informal e-learning. *Web-based learning* is content-focused and relies on minimal interaction between the learner and the tutor and no collaboration with other learners. *Supported online learning* has the learner as its focus and involves significant interaction with the tutor and other learners. Finally, *informal e-learning*, usually through e-mail and discussion boards, is focused on group interaction, with the participants acting as learners and tutors, interacting with each other in order to achieve organisational learning and the building of the organisation's knowledge base.

STOP and think

Can you find examples in your workplace or on the web of each of Reynolds et al.*'s three types of e-learning?*

1 *Web-based learning.*

2 *Supported online learning.*

3 *Informal e-learning.*

www.learndirect.co.uk *has hundreds of e-learning courses available on their website. You can find many examples of web-based learning and supported online learning there.*

However, its limitations lie in its use simply as a high-tech alternative to textbook learning and the most successful and effective reports of e-learning come from businesses which use a 'blended learning' approach (CIPD, 2008a) – e-learning combined with multiple additional routes that support and facilitate learning (Sloman and Rolph, 2003). This can be through e-learning supported by periodic face-to-face learning, or with the knowledge component

Box 8.4 | **e-learning – some secrets of success?**

E-learning reputedly works best when it doesn't stand alone. Thus, Smethurst (2006) reports the special measures that The Priory Group have taken to develop their e-learning solution into a 'blended learning system' and thus make essential efficiency savings. In combination with, and in support of, their online learning materials, they use face-to-face 30–40 minute modules to replace half or full day modules. Each employee has an individualised programme created for them based on a combination of line managers requests and some modules that everyone completes. Remarkably, no additional time is allocated for the completion of this learning. The aim is that 'downtime' in the working day, where employees have 10–20 minutes to log onto the system, is used to complete the learning process in small chunks (granules). Online learning administrators provide support through the e-learning sites. The mandatory evaluations, completed at the end of each module, show positive results so far.

A significant return on the investment is expected by the Group. 'Training costs were huge in the past and are expected to fall . . . we're not just seeing time savings. If you take a nurse off a ward, you have to replace her. Now they can usually fit training into the working day.'

Source: Smethurst (2006).

delivered through e-learning and skills component delivered face-to-face, perhaps supported by online discussions and resource links. The possibilities and combinations are endless and changing and it has been used by organisations as diverse as the National Health Service (Scott, 2008) and Councils (Phillips, 2008) and has demonstrable advantages for a diverse range of employees (Jarvis and Hooley, 2004).

Off-the-job learning

Off-the-job learning is simply learning which takes place away from the place of work of the employee. However, it is frequently pigeon-holed as the 'old' way of doing things – and typified as teacher-centred, classroom-based, process-focused and providing learning that is difficult to transfer to the workplace. It is often criticised as wasteful of time and money, taking the employee away from the practical context in which he or she will have to apply the theoretical knowledge. That said, learning which takes place away from the place of work gives the employee time and space to consider the new learning, and if the event includes learners from other departments, workplaces or sectors, allows the cross-fertilisation of ideas and innovations, the chance to consider notions free from distractions, and the opportunity to network with likeminded individuals. Off-the-job learning is epitomised by formal education courses or instructor-led training delivered off the job. Formal education courses normally take place in further or higher education colleges or universities. Instructor-led training is usually delivered by training professionals either directly employed by the organisations or contracted to deliver the event as a training consultant.

In order to make off-the-job learning credible and valuable, it has to be, like other learning interventions, identified as organisationally useful at the analysis stage of the process; providing training or learning opportunities which make little or no contribution to the business seriously affects the credibility of those in the organisation responsible for learning and development.

Consider an off-the-job learning experience you have had recently. Did you enjoy it? Did you learn something that you were able to apply to your job on return to the workplace? If it was successful, what contributed to this? If it was unsuccessful, why do you think this was the case?

Reading the previous chapter, you will see that the selection of training and learning methods is a complex business, and in order for learning to be effective, there has to be a match between the purpose of the event, your learning preferences and the learning methods employed.

What would be the advantages and disadvantages of each method of training delivery for the people in your organisation?

Which methods would be best for which skills?

Planning and implementation

Issues in the planning and implementation of learning and development are considered in depth in the previous chapter and will not be revisited here. However, the appropriate design of learning interventions is central to the learning and development process.

What impact can the learning theories discussed in the previous chapter have on the planning and implementation of learning interventions in your organisation?

Evaluating L&D interventions

> On the one hand, CEOs understand the essential strategic value of a skilled, motivated and flexible labour force. On the other hand, the traditional HRM function has not typically been thought of as a strategic asset, and consequently is under pressure to reduce expenses and demonstrate efficiency in the delivery of it services.
>
> (Becker and Huselid, 1998: 56)

> Organisations seriously committed to achieving competitive advantage through their people make measurement of their efforts a critical component of the overall process.
>
> (Pfeffer, 1994: 56)

The assumption that HRD can add something to 'the bottom line' of a business and that it can be measured springs from the literature on high performance work practices and the best-practice literature (see Chapter 2 on SHRM). The best-practice work (e.g. Beer *et al.* 1984, Guest, 1987) highlights the link between sets of good HR practices and organisational performance (e.g. productivity and quality) and argues these are applicable across all organisations. High performance work practices, typified by the work of Huselid (1995), sees integrated sets of HR practices as *economic* assets which are context specific, with a high potential magnitude of return on investment.

However, despite the strategic importance of HRD, the evaluation of it is rarely carried out in any organisationally useful way (Anderson, 2007). There are a number of reasons for this. Often it is simply because organisations are not sure how to do it, beyond tried and tested approaches and techniques, or, if sure how to do it, not sure what to do with the results. There is also a fear that it will be expensive and time-consuming, and offer little in the way of results. Finally, because evaluation is often tagged on at the end of training, learning or development, the event or intervention will not have been designed with the end (evaluation and feedback into the next intervention) in mind.

Green (1999) argues that businesses rarely give sufficient emphasis to researching the impact that specific interventions or tools can make to improved performance. He says that business success will be achieved by asking challenging questions such as: why is the organisation doing this activity? What difference does it make? Does the difference (return) justify the investment? Could we get the same results in a more cost-effective way? Does the difference anticipated align with our business strategy and objectives? These can be simplified to: why should we do this? What difference do we want? How are we going to measure it? Is it cost-effective?

Green's approach elevates the evaluation of learning and development to a strategic position and goes beyond considering the outcome of training courses and the transfer of learning to the workplace to considering how HRD can add value to the organisation. HRD can add value to an organisation by improving its position as an employer of choice, through a positive effect on motivation and morale, enhancing employee contribution, supporting the delivery of company objectives by developing the skills in line with organisational needs. It is a key part of the psychological contract in organisations and potentially skills the workforce to be better than the competition. At the very least, HRD sometimes means a business can operate within legal requirements. Measurements go beyond post-course evaluation to measuring wastage, error rates, cost benefit, customer satisfaction, staff opinions and motivation, and can attempt to link specific outcomes to the training delivered, analyse cost effectiveness, demonstrate contribution to strategic objectives, and linking HRD to performance via performance management system.

That said, evaluation is less of a calculation than it is a *judgement* (Kearns, 2005). A rigorous scientific approach to evaluation although in theory desirable, is not practicable (Kenney *et al.*, 1979). Therefore, it involves a number of subjective considerations – the measurement itself is subjective, the interpretation of the results is subjective, and the values and goals of the stakeholders in the process are different and potentially conflicting. Attaching a financial value to HRD, which means estimating the financial impact of employee behaviour, is at least challenging. However, one might argue, no less challenging than assessing the impact on the organisation of marketing efforts such as advertising or networking. Isolating the impact of HRD is therefore not insurmountable: for example, alongside the many tools suggested in this section, one might establish a control group, consider the impact of other influences (e.g. market or financial changes in the environment) or use professional judgement.

One remaining conundrum is that which concerns what evaluation purports to measure: most models we consider here are concerned with *intermediate* outcomes which may or may not lead to business success e.g. cost of training, reduction of turnover or absence, improved morale or motivation, all of which it is hoped will have some broader business impact. These *performance* indicators may not give the best information as they measure only the specific outcome they purport to measure and nothing more. Writers still struggle to elevate the measures associated with HRD to a higher, strategic level.

Such questions are at the heart of evaluation, and this section outlines some of the key models and approaches to judging the contribution HRD behaviour can make to organisational performance. Evaluation at its best flows throughout learning in the organisational context, and happens as events unfold using multiple methods of feedback and communication, rather than on a piece of paper at the end of a training course.

- *What are the benefits of investing in measuring the impact of training and learning on organisational outcomes?*
- *Why are most organisations reluctant to carry out any meaningful analysis?*
- *What evaluation techniques have you used or been subject to?*

Categorising evaluation

Three themes are apparent in the development of measurement and evaluation in HRD (Wang and Spitzer, 2005):

- *Practice-oriented stage*: typified by the seminal work of Kirkpatrick (1960) (see below) and considering the impact of (usually) training interventions.
- *Process-driven stage*: typified by the return on investment (ROI) work seeking to justify training and HRD expenditure based on the measurements of benefits *vs* costs of training.
- *Research-oriented, practice-driven stage*: based on an awareness of business reality and by extension, of the strategic contribution that HRD can make, which is still an emerging field of analysis.

Practice-oriented stage

This stage in the development of evaluation literature relies heavily on Kirkpatrick's (1960) enduring work, which, while criticised (Swanson and Holton, 2001), has had enviable staying power in the world of learning evaluation. Kirkpatrick proposed four levels of evaluation of learning and training. A close examination reveals that Kirkpatrick was more concerned with the transfer of learning to the workplace and organisational results than is often represented:

1 *Reactions* for Kirkpatrick are defined as 'how well the trainees liked a particular training program'. Reactions are typically measured formally, and immediately, at the end of training, but can be measured informally by the trainer/facilitator during the event.

    Measures include: reaction questionnaires, observation of reactions, relationships, body language, participant interactions, questioning by trainer and questions asked by participants.

2 *Learning* is defined by Kirkpatrick as the 'principles, facts, and techniques [that] were understood and absorbed by the conferees'. This has the purpose of measuring the change in the knowledge of the learner post-event, compared to the knowledge pre-event.

Measures include: written, verbal and practical tests, interviews with participants and managers at pre-determined times after the event, self-assessment, performance review procedures, questionnaires, interviews, peer group discussion.

3 *Behaviour* is about changes in on-the-job behaviour, which must be evaluated in the workplace itself.

Measures include: self, peer and manager appraisals, observation, measurement of outputs/results, interviews, product/service sampling.

4 *Results.* Kirkpatrick relied on a range of examples to make clear his meaning here: 'Reduction of costs; reduction of turnover and absenteeism; reduction of grievances; increase in quality and quantity or production; or improved morale which, it is hoped, will lead to some of the previously stated results.'

Measures include: measurement of performance indicators, e.g. absenteeism, grievances, production, customer satisfaction, turnover, targets, stakeholder feedback, return on investment measures (see below).

It is difficult to over-estimate the popularity of Kirkpatrick's model. Some 91 per cent of those surveyed in the CIPD's Learning and Development Survey 2006 evaluated training, learning and development activities and 98 per cent of those used exercises to measure Kirkpatrick's level 1 outcomes. Some 75 per cent used level 2 evaluation exercises, 62 per cent level 3 and 36 per cent go as far as level 4.

Missing from Kirkpatrick's model is any consideration of the pre-event state of affairs or an assessment of how level four results affect the business. Hamblin (1974) added this 'ultimate level' to consider the extent to which the event has affected the ultimate profitability and survival of the organisation.

Another popular model is from Warr *et al.*'s work in 1970. They suggested a similar four level model, considering:

- *Context*: conditions in the operational context, e.g. the aims and objectives, problems to be overcome, strengths and weaknesses of the approach chosen. This allows the evaluator to consider how the preparation underpinning the training did or did not support the achievement of the objectives of the event.

- *Input*: the processes and resources involved in the event itself, how these were chosen and deployed.

- *Reactions*: the reaction of the learners during and after the event, measuring what the participants feel, rather than what they have learned.

- *Outcome*: what happened as a result of the event, the learning and changes which can be related to the training. This comprises four stages – definition of training objectives, building evaluation tools, using them and reviewing the results.

These models have operational and practitioner appeal, and have a role in demonstrating the value that learning and development activities can add to organisations. Even at this level, organisations identify that their efforts to measure the impact of learning and development activities do not go far enough, and while there is an increasing emphasis on evaluation, cost, time, lack of effective measures, organisational priorities and lack of knowledge and understanding act against the best attempts of those who seek to establish the contribution that learning and development makes to business performance (CIPD, 2006).

Process-driven stage

This second stage in the development of evaluation was driven by an increasing awareness of the business reality of global competition, pressure from adverse economic conditions and increased demands for managerial accountability (Wang and Spitzer, 2005). Return on investment (ROI) measures represent the main theme of the work in this area, and these measures have stimulated much critical debate in the world of HRD (Phillips, 2005). At its simplest, ROI calculates of the costs and benefits of training events, and it is usually represented as an (apparently) straightforward formula:

$$\frac{\text{Benefits from training} - \text{Costs of training}}{\text{Costs of training} \times 100\%} = \% \text{ ROI}$$

There the simplicity ends, as measuring the costs and benefits of the training is often far from straightforward. Thompson (2005) argues that to measure ROI effectively, training has to be divided into two categories: knowledge and technical skills (content or 'hard' training), and attitude and interpersonal skills (process or 'soft' training). The former is fairly easy to assess for ROI purposes, but the latter (often the larger proportion of companies' training effort in terms of time, money or profile) is a 'problem area of evaluation'. Its complexity may be the cause of the limited use of ROI measures in practice; less than a fifth of those surveyed in the CIPD's Learning and Development survey (2006) used ROI as a measure of learning, training and development activities in their organisation.

The usefulness or otherwise of the measure is dependent on the quality of the information which feeds it. Sophisticated models (Phillips, 2002; Swanson, 2001; Kearns, 2005) emphasise the importance of:

- the collection of information post-event or programme, including evaluation instruments which are purposeful, timely, and multilevel;
- isolating the effects of the training or programme;
- converting the data to monetary value;
- calculating ROI;
- identifying other, intangible benefits.

Potentially, the sophisticated emphasis on financial and strategic measurement of outputs is at odds with the values-based practice of training and development and Dee and Hatton, 2006 argue for an incremental approach. 'Learning and Development should demonstrate a business benefit, but it is often impossible to go from training straight to ROI. A possible alternative is a staged process which focuses on improving the quality of programmes, increasing the transfer of learning to the workplace and measuring against specific metrics established from the outset' (Dee and Hatton, 2006).

Ford (1993) suggested measures (or metrics) covering three broad areas which he argues that most HRD practitioners find essential within the ROI calculation:

- *Measures of training activity*: how much training and development occurs? Percentage of payroll, training amount spent per employee per annum, average number of training days per employee/manager per annum, HRD staff per 100 employees.
- *Measures of training results*:
  - at reaction level: average percentage of positive course ratings;
  - at learning level: average percentage gain in learning per-course based on difference between pre- and post-course results;
  - at behaviour level: average percentage of improvement in on-the-job performance after training;
  - bottom line: profits per employee per year;
  - cost savings as a ratio of training expenses.
- *Measures of training efficiency*: training cost per delegate hour.

Despite the limitations, discussion of ROI has increased the awareness among HRD practitioners that in order to justify the existence of HRD interventions, there has to be some attempt to measure the financial contribution it makes to the organisations, however challenging this is in practice (Thompson, 2005; Phillips, 2005).

How would you gather the information required to inform an ROI judgement?

Thompson (2005) suggests five methods of gathering information to inform an ROI judgement:

- Refining end-of-course 'happy sheets' to ask 'What will you do/do differently as a result of this training?' and 'How exactly will each element of this course help you to do a better job?'
- Following up with line managers and participants at a later date asking for feedback on the things they have used from the training.
- E-mailing a sample of people, asking them about past 'critical incidents' (for example, in management of communication), what skills they used to deal with them, and where they acquired those skills without hinting that training could be the primary source.
- Interviewing participants, their managers and other significant stakeholders before and after training.
- Asking participants to complete pre- and post-event evaluations.

Benchmarking can also provide information on the evaluation of process in HRD, see Box 8.5. Benchmarking is a set of related activities which support and enhance strategies of imitation or collaboration leading to a competitive advantage (Ellis and Williams, 1995). Walton (1999: 303) notes that 'some organisations have relied excessively on comparative performance data as a key plank in their competitive strategy . . . this may help a company meet competitors' performance, but it is unlikely to reveal practices to beat them'. Harrison (2005: 250) also argues that benchmarking measures best-value or best-practice and not the value added to the organisation by the training or learning intervention. To measure added value, Harrison argues, means asking and answering a different question: 'what critical difference has the service made to the organisation's capability to differentiate itself from other similar organisations, thereby giving it a leading edge?'.

Box 8.5   Benchmarking

For HRD, Walton (1999: 313) suggests three levels at which benchmarking can operate:

1 *The level of organisational learning*:
   - How have other organisations generated a learning climate?
2 *The level of organisation-wide HRD processes*:
   - How have other organisations identified and developed competences for staff?
   - How have other organisations balanced on and off the job learning?
3 *The level of training and development activity and resource allocation*:
   - What percentage of payroll is devoted to training and development in other organisations?

Questions

1 How can you use this model of benchmarking in your organisation to assess the effectiveness of HRD activity?
2 Where can you find the information you need to answer the questions successfully?

There are three types of benchmarking: competitive benchmarking which assesses key parts of the organisation's processes, systems and procedures with those of chosen competitors in the field; best-practice/functional benchmarking which compares particular aspects of an organisation's product or service against organisations considered to be 'the best' in this area, and may involve collaboration; and internal benchmarking which considers and compares similar processes within an organisation to achieve internal best practice, e.g. induction, appraisal.

Green (1999) is not a supporter of an approach which values 'best practice' (above) as a guide for HR behaviour:

> The response that is often given by HR professionals when challenged on their activities is to refer to them as best practice, as if this in itself is enough to justify the often substantial investment. If probed further, it often turns out to mean 'everybody else is doing something on this, so we'd better too' . . . the eventual result of the best-practice syndrome is a cynical and negative view of the HR function as the purveyor of fads and gimmicks. But the best-practice approach also creates a defensive way of looking at HR needs and constrains the innovation and creativity that is needed now, more than ever, to make full use of people as the value drivers in organisations.
> (1999: 27)

This *added value* literature is often considered to be synonymous with the ROI literature, however, that is not the case. Commentators on added value focus on more than just financial metrics such as ROI, and usually go beyond to consider broader aspects of pre- and post-intervention measurement, with ROI as, if desired, a part of the broader measurement portfolio.

Green (1999) challenges the limited view that comes with approaches like those in the previous section and instead, he suggests that organisations ought to focus on taking a more 'offensive approach' to HR, and by extension to HRD. For him, measurement is a vital part of the picture but more is required. He argues that to establish added value, organisations must achieve:

- *alignment*, which means pointing people in the right direction;
- *engagement*, which means developing belief and a commitment to the organisation's purpose and direction; and
- *measurement*, which means providing data that demonstrates the improved results of this new approach.

Research-oriented, practice-driven stage

As a categorisation for evaluation of learning and development, this group is not closed, settled or firmly established (Wang and Spitzer, 2005). It has arisen as a result of the awareness of a need to demonstrate overall contribution to business performance in a way that goes beyond the previous section. Therefore, this section contains a number of approaches or ideas which attempt to go beyond measures of process and of intermediate outcomes, to measures of strategic contribution, added value or ultimate business performance outcomes.

STOP and think

In Chapter 2, you were introduced to the idea that the principal purpose of measuring HR performance is to drive performance improvement (Yeung and Berman, 1997) and to establish performance improvements from HR evaluation, organisations need to establish the timely and ongoing collection of data, analyse these data, and have managers accountable for those measures.

Question

How could the balanced scorecard approaches which are raised in this context be applied to HRD?

Holton (1996) raises similar issues in his critique of Kirkpatrick's model and refers to three primary learning outcome measures: learning: achievement of the learning outcomes desired in the intervention; individual performance: change in individual performance as a result of the learning being applied on the job; and organisational results: consequences of the change in individual performance. Holton, like many other writers in this area use outcome based models as the basis of their analysis.

Brinkerhoff (2005) supports this view that traditional evaluation models and methods do little to improve organisational performance. His 'success case method' argues that the main challenge for organisations is how to leverage learning – consistently, quickly and effectively – into improved performance. Responsibility for this does not lie solely with HRD professionals, and while the diffusion of responsibility poses challenges, especially for evaluation, it opens the way for a consideration of a 'whole organisation approach' to evaluation, which will ultimately be more effective in turning learning into organisational advantage. He uses the metaphor of marriage to explain that most evaluation considers the wedding (the training) whereas what we really need to know about is the whole marriage (the training, plus what comes afterwards), the entire training to organisational performance process.

The learning organisation

> The notion of the learning organisation is all about creating organisational results from individual learning.
>
> (Senge, 1990: 11)

The notion of the learning organisation has been, and continues to be an influential one. While its roots can be traced in literature on organisational excellence (Peters and Waterman, 1982), total quality management (Deming, 1986), action learning (Revans, 1982, 1983), and organisational learning (Argyris, 1992; Argyris and Schön, 1978), Peter Senge (1990) is usually credited with bringing the concept to organisational life in the early 1990s in the US. In the UK, the work of Pedlar, Burgoyne and Boydell (1991) on 'The Learning Company Project' in the late 1980s and early 1990s provided organisationally useful tools for establishing a *learning climate*.

It has at its heart a 'whole company' perspective (not just an HR one) on learning and development. It links the development of the potential of *everyone* (not just managers, or 'talent' in the business) to the development of the company as a whole. It emphasises the importance of organisational flexibility, responsiveness, adaptability and conscious approach to change (Senge, 1990) and underlines the importance of breaking down outmoded ideas, attitudes and practices before building new skills, structures and values (Pettigrew and Whipp, 1991). It is a 'systemic' rather than 'systematic' approach seeing everything as interconnected, rather than simple cause and effect, and because of this complexity, is probably much less commonly adopted than the rhetoric would suggest (Gibb and Megginson, 2001: 153).

Pedlar *et al.* (1991, 1997) explained that at its heart, the learning *company* was about releasing the 'massive underdeveloped potential in our organisations' (1997: 3) and seeking to differentiate the type of learning as one that happens 'at the whole organisation level' (1997: 3). For them, it is about being 'an organisation that facilitates the learning of all its members and consciously transforms itself and its context' (1997: 3) and is about 'understanding and mastering the art of corporate learning . . . as learning is the key to survival and development for the companies of today' (1997: 6).

Diagnostic tools are popular in the literature of the learning organisation. Pedlar *et al.* (1991, 1997) developed an 11-point diagnostic jigsaw (Figure 8.7). Honey and Mumford (1989) generated an 11-point checklist and Bartram *et al.* (1993) a 70-item questionnaire centred around seven broad categories (supportive management style, time pressures, degree of autonomy, encouraging team style, opportunities to develop, availability of written guidelines, atmosphere of satisfaction). These tools are intended as a structure for a gap analysis to establish the journey the business must make between where it is now and where it wants to be.

Figure 8.7a The learning company profile

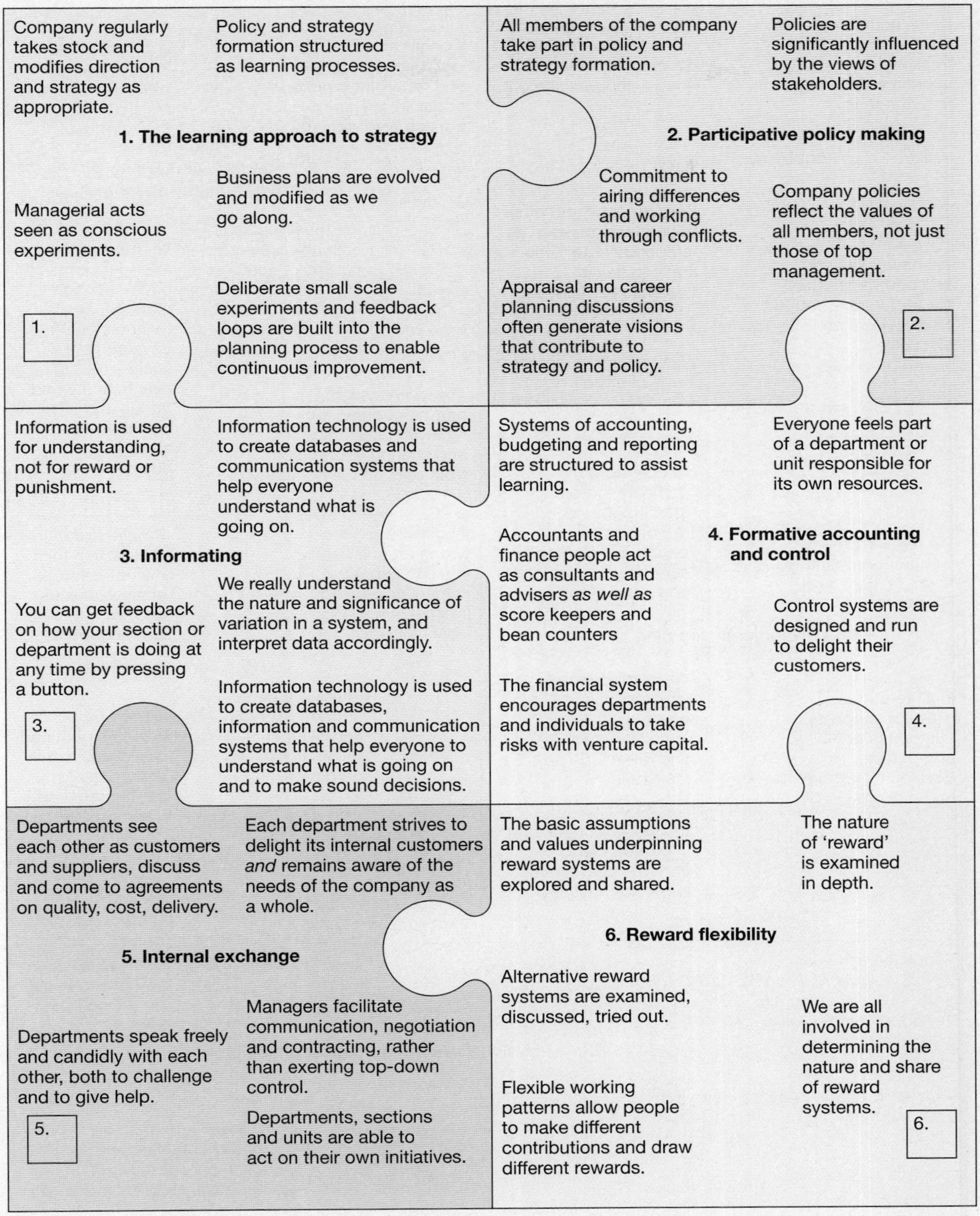
Company regularly takes stock and modifies direction and strategy as appropriate.
Policy and strategy formation structured as learning processes.
1. The learning approach to strategy
Managerial acts seen as conscious experiments.
Business plans are evolved and modified as we go along.
Deliberate small scale experiments and feedback loops are built into the planning process to enable continuous improvement.
1.
All members of the company take part in policy and strategy formation.
Policies are significantly influenced by the views of stakeholders.
2. Participative policy making
Commitment to airing differences and working through conflicts.
Company policies reflect the values of all members, not just those of top management.
Appraisal and career planning discussions often generate visions that contribute to strategy and policy.
2.
Information is used for understanding, not for reward or punishment.
Information technology is used to create databases and communication systems that help everyone understand what is going on.
3. Informating
You can get feedback on how your section or department is doing at any time by pressing a button.
We really understand the nature and significance of variation in a system, and interpret data accordingly.
Information technology is used to create databases, information and communication systems that help everyone to understand what is going on and to make sound decisions.
3.
Systems of accounting, budgeting and reporting are structured to assist learning.
Everyone feels part of a department or unit responsible for its own resources.
Accountants and finance people act as consultants and advisers as well as score keepers and bean counters
4. Formative accounting and control
Control systems are designed and run to delight their customers.
The financial system encourages departments and individuals to take risks with venture capital.
4.
Departments see each other as customers and suppliers, discuss and come to agreements on quality, cost, delivery.
Each department strives to delight its internal customers and remains aware of the needs of the company as a whole.
5. Internal exchange
Departments speak freely and candidly with each other, both to challenge and to give help.
Managers facilitate communication, negotiation and contracting, rather than exerting top-down control.
Departments, sections and units are able to act on their own initiatives.
5.
The basic assumptions and values underpinning reward systems are explored and shared.
The nature of 'reward' is examined in depth.
6. Reward flexibility
Alternative reward systems are examined, discussed, tried out.
We are all involved in determining the nature and share of reward systems.
Flexible working patterns allow people to make different contributions and draw different rewards.
6.

Source: from *The Learning Company*, McGraw-Hill (Pedlar, M., Burgoyne, J. and Boydell, T. 1991) pp. 26–7 © 1991, reproduced with the kind permission of The McGraw-Hill Companies. All rights reserved.

Figure 8.7b The learning company profile

7. Enabling structures

Roles and careers are flexibly structured to allow for experimentation, growth and adaptation.

Appraisals are geared more to learning and development than to reward and punishment.

We have rules and procedures but they are frequently changed after review and discussion.

Departmental and other boundaries are seen as temporary structures that can flex in response to changes.

We experiment with new forms of structures.

7.

8. Boundary workers as environmental scanners

It is part of the work of all staff to collect, bring back, and report information about what's going on outside the company.

All meetings in the company regularly include a review of what's going on in our business environment.

We meet regularly with representative groups of customers, suppliers, community members and so on to find out what's important to them.

We receive regular intelligence reports on the economy, markets, technological developments, socio-political events and world trends and examine how these may affect our business.

There are systems and procedures for receiving, collating and sharing information from outside the company.

8.

9. Inter-company learning

We regularly meet with our competitors to share ideas and information.

People from the company go on attachments to our business partners, including suppliers, customers and competitors.

We engage in joint ventures with our suppliers, customers and competitors, to develop new products and markets.

We participate in joint learning events with our suppliers, customers and other stakeholders.

We use benchmarking in order to learn from the best practice in other industries.

3.

10. Learning climate

If something goes wrong around here you can expect help, support, and interest in learning lessons from it.

People make time to question their own practice, to analyse, discuss and learn from what happens.

There is a general attitude of continuous improvement – always trying to learn and do better.

When you don't know something, it's normal to ask around until you get the required help or information.

Differences of all sorts, between young and old, women and men, black and white, etc. are recognized and positively valued as essential to learning and creativity.

10.

11. Self-development opportunities for all

People here have their own self-development budgets – they decide what training and development they want, and what to pay for it.

There are lots of opportunities, materials and resources available for learning on an 'open access' basis around the company.

With appropriate guidance people are encouraged to take responsibility.

Self-development resources are available to external stakeholders.

The exploration of an individual's learning needs is the central focus of appraisal and career planning.

11.

Source: from *The Learning Company*, McGraw-Hill (Pedlar, M., Burgoyne, J. and Boydell, T. 1991) pp. 26–7 © 1991, reproduced with the kind permission of The McGraw-Hill Companies. All rights reserved.

STOP and think

Pedlar et al. (1991, 1997) explain that the diagnostic jigsaw ought to be used by organisations to test how they measure up against the concept of the learning organisation. Apply the jigsaw to your organisation.

Questions

1 *To what extent is my company like this?*

2 *If this is how my company is at the moment, how would I like it to be in the future?*

There are, however, criticisms of the concept. Its popularity peaked in the early 1990s, and since 2002 there has been considerably less discussion of the impact of the idea than in previous years. Even strong supporters point to the fact that it has not lived up to 'all our aspirations . . . or delivered its full potential' (Burgoyne, 1999). Garvin (1993: 78) identifies that important writers' work, Senge and Nonaka particularly, is 'utopian . . . filled with near mystical terminology'.

Garvin (1993: 50) also highlights the aspirational nature of the ideas:

. . . idyllic? Absolutely. Desirable? Without question. But does it provide a framework for action? Hardly. These recommendations are far too abstract, too many questions remain unanswered. How, for example, will managers know when their companies have become learning organisations? What concrete changes in behaviour are required? What policies and programmes must be in place? How do you get from here to there?

Sloman (1999: 31) agrees – 'the concept of the learning organisation should be redefined or declared redundant'. In its current manifestations, 'The idea of learning organisations cannot be said to be capable of operationalisation in any meaningful sense' (Stewart and Sambrook, 2002: 183).

Overall, the models lack a convincing link between theory and practice (Lahteenmaki *et al.*, 1999), practice and outcomes. However, it must be noted that the original authors did not promise the learning organisation as a quick fix or simple solution (Pedlar *et al.*, 1991) and that organisations face challenges of culture, time, ownership and commitment (Chase, 1997) is hardly surprising given the nature and size of the task.

However, the debate is still live on how to promote individual learning for organisational advantage. Organisations still place 'enormous importance' on the creation of cultures that support learning and development for individuals, and for business benefit (CIPD, 2004c: 14), but the discussion has moved on, in part at least to the development of a coaching culture.

Making evaluation work: closing the loop

The initial diagrams for planning learning and development represented the process as a loop, where evaluation ultimately fed into the development of future plans.

Easterby-Smith and Mackness (1992) state that 'Training evaluation is commonly seen as a feedback loop, starting with course objectives and ending by collecting end-of-course reactions which are then generally filed away and not acted on' and the same likely applies to other learning and human resource development activities.

Closing the loop gives purpose to the evaluation activities, and without that there is little point in engaging in what is potentially difficult, complex and judgemental.

STOP and think

How can HRD evaluation make a contribution to the development of future plans and approaches?

HRD and national frameworks for vocational education and training

Against this backdrop, the dramatic fall in the financial fortunes of the UK since the start of 2008, the growth in unemployment and issues in the UK banking system, have made an emphasis on developing skills now seem more critical to the success of the UK. Thus, National Vocational Education and Training (NVET or VET) comes into focus as a key way of increasing national productivity and competitiveness. NVET is about country-wide perspectives on HRD, focusing on developing the skills needs of different sectors across a country. Considering the broader national and international context of skills development has clear relevance for organisational HRD strategies often, the approaches spoken about here are how new recruits have acquired and continue to acquire knowledge and skills relevant to work. Making the right choices about NVET is central to a country's national competitiveness (Finegold and Soskice, 1999, Van den Berg *et al.*, 2006) and reflecting on long-term policies for skills development helps develop our understanding of why there are skills gaps, shortages and gluts. Furthermore, analysing NVET systems allows consideration of how weaknesses in the national approach to skills development translate into skills deficiencies and shortages in organisations and correspondingly how strengths translate into innovation and organisational strength and helps to underline the increasing importance of workplace learning as a source of competitiveness and supports similar arguments in previous sections.

Evidence suggests that organisational differences in human resource (HR) practices, including training and development, are related to variations in national legislation and cultural frameworks of a country and the national context is a primary factor which must not be ignored in the examination of determinants of training and development activity (Tregaskis and Dany, 1996). Learning and development are not solely the concern of individuals and their employers. To ensure that a country achieves the level of skills it needs to compete internationally, they ought also to be the concern of governments and European bodies (Leitch, 2006). Trends in technology, the decline in the need for traditional skills, the aging of the population and changes in career and life spans are international issues and comparison works to aid comprehension of the issues and the position of vocational education in the UK as it appears to its competitors.

Box 8.6 Global warming, terrorism, avian flu and skills shortages

In a thought-provoking article in 2007, Kingston argued that companies are disproportionately concerned with emerging, headline-grabbing issues such as avian flu, global warming or terrorim. In 2009/10, we can see a similar pattern in the obsession of employers with contingency planning for so-called swine flu. Such issues are played up in the media as harbingers of disaster and national decline and as something that ought to be a preoccupation for employers and employees alike.

However, even in the face of a significant shift in the financial fortunes of most developed economies, almost no attention is given in the press to the developing skills shortage, particularly in the UK. The economic risk posed by a lack of emphasis on training and skills is significant in terms of the capability of the country's businesses to compete in a challenging marketplace. The lack of credible news articles about the impact of poorly-trained workers on the economy is tangible. Moreover, inadequate management rarely captures attention. Yet, both combined are indicative of national skills shortage of catastrophic levels.

Source: Kingston (2007: 28).

Since 1996, the UK government has published National Employers Skill Surveys (**www.lsc.gov.uk**) bi-annually which identify, among other things, the skills gaps and shortages experienced by the UK. Academics have for many years drawn attention to the link between skills development and national productivity (e.g. Keep and Mayhew, 1996b; Steedman and Wagner, 1987; Finegold and Soskice, 1988; Finegold and Levine, 1997). Most attention has been focused on discovering the elements of education and training that can create successful companies, which then contribute to the economic strength of the nation. Wilson and Briscoe (2004) attribute a 1–3 per cent increase in GDP per capita growth to a 1 per cent increase in school enrolment rates and it is asserted that since 'some education makes some of us rich, more would make more of us richer' (Wolf, 2002: 28). However, the relationship is complicated and controversial as the emphasis on academic participation in the UK has not resulted in sound economic growth: 'The explosion in graduate output over the last 15 years has not been accompanied by any concomitant uplift in productivity growth' (Keep and Mayhew, 2004: 299).

Finegold and Soskice (1988) discussed the two-way relationship between education and training and international competitiveness. They characterised Britain as trapped in a low skills equilibrium, which means 'a self-reinforcing network of societal and state institutions which interact to stifle the demand for improvements in skill levels' (1988: 22). The notion of and trend in developing a low-skills equilibrium meant that many UK organisations persisted in producing low added-value products and services that demanded low skills, so that UK employers had little incentive to invest in skills development (Hendry, 1994: 102). Hall and Soskice (2001) provide another international perspective and a different dimension by placing the UK in a broader economic landscape. They examine critically the link between national level institutional structures and organisation level skills strategies. Using international data and drawing international comparisons, they identify two types of economy, namely *coordinated* market economies, and *liberal* market economies. The strength of the relationship between the national structures and organisational strategies determines the skills levels of the employees, and thus the competitiveness of the national economy.

Coordinated market economies, typified by Scandinavian countries such as Denmark, Sweden and the Netherlands, as well as Germany, are underpinned by strong inter-organisational relationships between investors and organisations, product differentiation strategies and cooperative networks between organisations. They rely on the development of high-value skills and task or sector specific skills development. *Liberal* market economies (e.g. the UK, Australia and the US) by contrast have less well-structured relationships between national structures and organisational strategies, employment security and protection is weaker, and as such economies rely on the development of portable and generic skills, fundamental shifts in products and services are more likely to be supported. (For a more detailed discussion of cross-national variety in employment policy and practice, see the section in Chapter 15 entitled 'National employment systems' page 573.)

However, researching the link between education and training and economic growth is limited by the poor quality of data, particularly in intercountry comparisons, and by the fact that human capital is mostly measured by *formal* education, training and qualifications (Descy and Tessaring, 2005: 16). Moreover, rapidly changing economic conditions makes learning and replication difficult if not impossible. Furthermore, the research underemphasises macro-social outcomes (crime, social cohesion, citizenship, civic and political participation) and individual benefits of education and training beyond the impact on company performance (Green *et al.*, 2004). Drawing conclusions about the link between education and macro-social outcomes is difficult as these 'effects are mostly indirect and conditional on other – often more powerful – contextual determinants' (Descy and Tessaring, 2005: 37). Furthermore, for the individual, there are likely to be substantial personal benefits – including better health, parenting, crime reduction and social inclusion (Descy and Tessaring, 2005: 39).

Education and training are complex systems that do not exist in isolation but have social and economic roles. Reforming them is a process that requires debate and compromise on what is to be changed and for what reasons, not only between those in the systems but also other stakeholders, especially social partners. It is essential to envisage and to evaluate the internal consistency of a new policy with other elements of the system . . . but reforms also have to take into account the needs – and be coherent with the modes of functioning – of the productions system and of society more generally (external consistency). Traditional evaluations of policies or programmes focus strictly on policy as a separate entity, treating it as if it were self-contained and independent from the historical, structural and institutional context. This reinforces the tendency to design policies that are limited in scope and do not take into account the existing institutions and interventions as well as the modes of functioning of economic and social systems. (CEDEFOP/Descy and Tessaring, 2005: 21).

At the level of the business, there is strong evidence that investment in training and development generate substantial gains for firms (Descy and Tessaring, 2005: 38; Ballot, 2003; CIPD, 2005d; Bassi *et al.*, 2001). The consideration of NVET systems is therefore complex and context bound, however, it is essential to ensure an understanding of the extent to which, on an increasingly competitive international stage, individual countries can meaningfully compete.

The European dimension – VET in Europe

National vocational education and training systems (NVETs), providing training beyond compulsory school age and exist internationally, but with differences in key features, aims and objectives and underlying principles. Particularly within Europe, the difficulty with this area is not that there is a dearth of information available, but that there is so much, in so many places. The European Commission (EC), the Organization for Economic Co-operation and Development (OECD), the European Centre for the Development of Vocational Training (CEDEFOP) and the Chartered Institute of Personnel and Development (CIPD) all provide information across a range of national systems of vocational education and training. However, because of the variety of information available, realistic comparison is *not* easy given different political, social, economic, technological and legal development paths as well as different styles of management and cultural understanding.

This section of the chapter will consider comparative aspects of selected national systems of VET across Europe. There are a number of uniting themes in this context which allow side-by-side consideration of national VET systems, policies and procedures, not least because the European context is one which faces particular labour market challenges and changes (Descy and Tessaring, 2005: 21):

- Higher skills levels are needed, especially in modern, knowledge intensive, global economies.
- At the same time labour markets are becoming more polarised, with more precarious and repetitive jobs for the less educated.
- The population of the EU is ageing, and this trend will be accelerated by the accession of new countries.
- The initial education level of the EU population is improving, but a substantial proportion is still typified by a low level of formal education.
- Unemployment is a concern, particularly after enlargement of the EU.
- Skill renewal through lifelong learning is becoming increasingly desirable in EU countries.

However, Europe is united by common goals in this area. The Lisbon European Council in 2001 set a strategic goal to make the EU, by 2010 'the most competitive and dynamic knowledge-based economy in the world, capable of sustainable economic growth with more and better jobs and greater social cohesion'. Subsequently, the Barcelona European Council in 2002 set the goal of making 'Europe's education and training systems a world quality reference by 2010'. These goals were to be achieved through comprehensive systems of lifelong learning, from nursery school to retirement.

Common objectives for education and training were established to measure five reference levels of European average performance in education and training. These educational benchmarks (the 'Lisbon Goals') are intended to provide all citizens with the basic education they need in a knowledge-based society (EC, 2002).

By 2010:

- at least 85 per cent of 22-year olds should have completed upper secondary education;
- no more than 10 per cent of those aged 18–24 should have left school before completing upper secondary education or vocational or other training;
- the total number of graduates in mathematics, science and technology should have increased by 15 per cent while the gender imbalance should decrease;
- the percentage of 15-year olds with low achievement in reading literacy should have decreased by at least 20 per cent compared to 2000 levels;
- the average level of participation in lifelong learning of those aged 25 to 64 should be at least 12.5 per cent.

However, as 2010 and the expiry of the Lisbon Goals approaches, a number of developments (e.g. the Copenhagen Declaration in 2002 and the Bordeaux Communique in 2008) have refocused this strategy in recognition of the challenging economic conditions and the likelihood that the original Lisbon goals will not be met (CEDEFOP, 2009) This has opened the door for a greater level of Europe-wide comparison and provided common targets for the EU.

Activity

On the web (1)

There is a range of websites from which you can begin to explore comparative aspects of VET. A list of useful websites is provided at the end of this chapter. For comparative aspects of VET in Europe particularly, visit the European Centre for the Development of Vocational Training (CEDEFOP) European Training Village at:

http://www.trainingvillage.gr/etv/Information_resources/Bookshop/list.asp

CEDEFOP has published reports on vocational education and training research since 1998, presenting a comprehensive review of current research, its results and the implications for policy, practice and future research. They also attend to the theoretical and methodological foundations with reference given to economic, sociological, pedagogical and other fields of research.

Questions

One of the themes of this section of the chapter is that the VET system is embedded in its national context. Consider the following questions:

1 What features of the German national context make its particular VET system so successful?

2 What aspects of the VET system in Germany could be transferable to the UK context?

3 What challenges could be faced in doing so?

4 What are the limitations of seeking to transfer ideas from other national contexts?

Within this context then, this section attempts to outline the main components of Germany and France, to allow comparison with the UK approach to NVET considered later in this section.

The German system of VET

Germany's 'dual system' has remained one of the most frequently copied training systems in the world (Deissinger, 2000: 605) and is often given as an example of best practice in vocational education. Germany, like France, takes a process-oriented approach to education; that is, education paths are largely anchored in institutional (vocational or academic) communities. This contrasts with the fundamentally outcomes-oriented approach taken by English-speaking countries that is an essential element of vocational education and training (Deissinger, 2000). Germany's vocational education system is based on learning on the job (Hippach-Schneider *et al.*, 2007). It is a centralised, highly structured system which relies on a dualism of learning venues, funding and legal responsibilities, placing responsibility for the funding and development of the programmes on a number of stakeholders (Dybowski, 2005). Training is workplace led and practical and skill requirements are defined around the workplace. Over the three years of the process, participants spend 30 per cent of their time in a vocational school (at least 12 hours a week), and 70 per cent in the workplace. The cost of the system is split between the employers and the state, in fact, employers have a legal responsibility to provide funding and resources for training. This 'dual system' is determined by the involvement of the federal and state administration, as well as employers' associations and trade unions, making occupational standards and conditions of apprenticeship legally enforceable.

Some 53 per cent of school leavers take part in one of the 370 training vocations across 23.3 per cent of all companies who provide training (Hippach-Schneider, Martina, & Woll, 2007). For the employers, the cost of recruitment is low and businesses have an influence on the content and organisation of training. The trainees have the opportunity to earn while they are learning and acquire labour market relevant training. The on- and off-the-job instruction is carefully coordinated, producing a vocational course that provides development of three areas of skills: occupational competence (of systems and equipment), methodological competence (in reasoning and problem solving) and personal and social competence (team working and creativity) (Dybowski, 2005: 16).

Underpinning this is a strong sense of cooperation between the state and private organisations which is envied by the UK. The LSC's second (2005) Statement of Priorities (LSC, November 2005: 1) argues:

> . . . we have to take a more collaborative, less transactional approach if we are to get the provision of learning right. That means building meaningful relationships with colleges, schools, providers and employers. Increasingly, our business will feature strategic discussions with local partners that recognise the need to channel resources to our priority areas for funding.

The German system is augmented by continuing vocational education and training either to allow advancement in a particular occupation (further training for advancement) or to extend or update vocational knowledge, for example in line with legislative changes (adaptive further training). The Federal Institute for Vocational Education has a key role in both initial and continuing vocational education (**www.bibb.de**).

Activity **On the web (2)**

The German Federal Institute of Vocational Education and Training has a multi-language website which provides a substantial amount of information and context on the German system of VET (**www.bibb.de**), including a short film which gives a thorough overview of the system (**http://www.bibb.de/en/wlk32526.htm**)

Explore this website for current issues and debates in the German system.

Over 100 years old, the system has only infrequently been reviewed or updated, the most recent being in 2005 when the Vocational Training Reform Act 2005 comprehensively amended the 1969 Vocational Education and Training Act to allow more flexibility and responsiveness in the rigid and legally framed system (**http://www.bmbf.de/en/**). In 2006, a VET Innovation Group, composed of senior representatives of companies, academia, employers associations, trade unions and local governments to ensure the continued development of the system in pace with challenges associated with changes in demographic (e.g. migration and ageing) and employment trends as well as the challenges of globalisation and international recession (Hippach-Schneider *et al.*, 2007) However, despite recent developments and while much envied and mimicked, the German system is not immune to the pressures being faced across Europe, and is challenged with resisting stagnation and decline (Moraal *et al.*, 2009).

Deissinger (2000: 605) argues that Germany's 'dual system' continues to exist because of a 'deeply rooted disinclination to reform' and because 'it has remained one of the most frequently copied training systems in the world'.

What are the disadvantages of the German system?

The French system of VET

The French system of vocational training is a complex and comprehensive one, with a long period of development, including substantial reforms between 2000 and 2009 (Bousquet, 2008), starting with the introduction of an Education Code to replace prior education Acts.

In short, the French Government's commitment to VET and lifelong learning (la formation professionnelle permanente) is embodied in three levels of provision:

1 The secondary education system:
   - Baccalauréat Professionelle: a four-year course which confers a qualification in a given occupation;
   - the Baccalauréat Technologique: which confers a qualification in a given technology.
2 Higher education: which offers job-related courses.
3 Formation Professionnelle Continué (CVT): continuing education post school.

Like other European countries, France has been hit by a slowdown in economic growth and substantial demographic change. To combat this, greater flexibility within the system has been sought, for example there is a growing emphasis in France on *alternance* training or apprenticeship which involves the employer in the provision of training, gives the participant the status of employee rather than student, and has the aim of bringing training closer to practice and ease the transition to working life. Furthermore, the introduction of the recognition of vocational experience through the *validation des acquis de l'experience (VAE)* system and the increased provision of professionalisation courses has built the provision of vocational training for people already established in work (Bousquet, 2008).

The French system of continuing vocational training relies on the principles of the training tax or levy introduced in 1971 and the need for the provision of training to be measurable and accountable has resulted in an emphasis on the use of formal courses at the expense of informal on-the-job learning (CIPD, 2001c). While this has been overhauled substantially, the system of entitlement and a statutory obligation to provide continuing training at work endures. Since 2004, compulsory training leave of at least 20 hours per year, mostly funded by employers, has been enforced. Each company and the self-employed, pay a percentage of their wage bill to fund employee training and leave, initial vocational training, and encourage the development of training plans.

The French system is, like others, under some considerable pressure. Rising, and dramatic, youth unemployment, with 20 per cent of 18- to 25-year-olds unemployed (more than twice the national average) is being tackled under the 'Battle for Jobs' (**www.premier-ministre.gouv.fr**, 16 March 2006). However, the French Prime Minister was forced to abandon a new first-job contract or CPE (contrat première embauche) on 10 April 2006, after prolonged and extensive public demonstrations and unrest. Furthermore, extensive legislation, introduced in 2007, intended to improve the labour market has had little success, and unemployment rose 19 per cent in the year to February 2009 (Reuters, 7 April 2009).

Greinert (2002) presents three paradigms which lend shape and form to the institutions in the countries they relate to. How far can you see Greinert's paradigms reflected in the NVET systems in France, Germany and the UK?

- *In Britain the production relationship is regarded as no more than a market process in which the market participants are members of society. The image of law is correspondingly negative.*

- *In France, the production relationship is seen as a political entity. Central control of working life is given to the state.*

In Germany the production relationship is regarded as a kind of community which has a tradition of reciprocal responsibility and consideration of the whole. It is based on active social partnership.

Implications of European comparisons for the UK

This section's introduction argued that the performance of the economy in the UK is dependent on the development of the skills required in the labour market. The internationalisation of markets means that this is done on a globally competitive stage, and the comparative state of the UK is one which sees a narrowing productivity gap between the UK and other nations, and lower unemployment, but still a lower output per hour than France, Germany and the USA (LSC, 2004).

Each country we have considered has a number of routes through education and training. While the sequential nature of the French system contrasts with the dual system of the German system, we will see from the next section that the UK's approach is the most diffuse, complex and lacking in clarity. Keep and Mayhew (2001) describe the UK approach as a 'blizzard of initiatives' with a system of qualifications that is a 'sprawling, complex mess, incomprehensible to employers and trainees alike' which involves 'near-ceaseless organisational change' that does not produce results, and fails to deliver lasting and significant change on a number of fronts. Arguably, the link between learning and work is less well cemented in the UK than in the other countries we have considered. Recent attempts at imposing order and reform (Leitch, 2006) have resulted in widespread rationalisation of the system, but some still challenge its impact or success (Kingston, 2007).

VET in the UK

Introduction

The history of workforce development pre-Leitch (Leitch, 2006) is well documented elsewhere (Cannell, 2004), and this section focuses on more contemporary aspects of government approaches and initiatives to developing an economically productive workforce.

This brief summary will help to outline the background to skills development and the nature of the changes in the last 35 years.

1973–1997: national survival

Until 1979 there was no clear vision for national education and training policy. Attempts to raise the national profile of the issues in 1973 were embodied in the Employment and Training Act which introduced the Manpower Services Commission (MSC) and a national Training Services Agency (TSA). This underlined the growing role of training in national competitiveness and indicated a stronger role for the government in regulating training. A major outcome of the MSC was the Youth Opportunities Programme (YOP) offering work experience and work preparation courses. This was a major part of the government's attempts to reduce unemployment as it grew dramatically in the late 1970s.

In 1979, the new Conservative government, led by Margaret Thatcher, heralded a less interventionist and market-led approach which continued the voluntaristic view of individual and employer responsibility for workplace training and development. However, the level of intervention grew as academic criticism of the UK's approach to training and skills development gathered pace. The 'cradle-to-grave' approach to skills development included the introduction of National Vocational Qualifications (NVQs) in 1986 and the Education Reform Act in 1988 which changed the system of GCSEs with the aim of enhancing educational standards and vocational choice and providing greater parity between vocational and academic qualifications. The notion of competence was central to these approaches and has remained at the heart of the UK's NVET since then.

Training Enterprise Councils (established in 1989 and replaced in 2001 by Learning Skills Councils) completed this tranche of changes and had as their aim to make training policy sensitive and responsive to local business needs, and to accelerate business growth.

The 1991 White Paper *Education and Training for the 21st Century*, although focused still on individual and employer responsibility, set out seven aims for national vocational education and training. Investors in People was launched in 1991 and provided national accreditation for workplaces who met a set of standards which valued learning and development. A piecemeal approach continued during the boom and bust entrepreneurial age of the late 1990s until the change of government in 1997.

1997–2006: national competitiveness and upskilling

The new Labour government in 1997 recognised that the approach taken by the previous government had had limited impact on the competitiveness of the nation, as, despite having the fourth largest economy in the world, the UK's productivity lagged, and lags, behind the most advanced countries. While the UK's productivity has improved significantly over the last 10 years compared with that in other countries, the level of productivity in the UK remains below that in other developed countries and on a Gross Domestic Product (GDP) per worker basis, is lower than that of France and the USA, similar to that of Germany, and above that of Japan (ONS, 2004, 2006). Economic growth rates in the UK are no higher now than at the end of the Second World War (Elliot, 2004). Combined with increased competition from the Far East and challenging demographic trends as the population ages, the UK faces new challenges in developing skills to match the global competitive environment (LSC, 2005: 6). That said, the UK labour market has been, since 1997, characterised by reducing unemployment, increased educational attainment and the increased participation of women in employment and in 2003/04, investment in education and training as a proportion of GDP rose from 4.7 per cent in 1996/7 to 5.3 per cent (Cuddy and Leney, 2005).

One of the first tasks of the Labour government which came to power in 1997 was to establish the National Skills Task Force (NSTF) which embraced the case, made for many years by academics and researchers, that developing the skills of the workforce was a way of improving the UK's productivity and competitiveness in the global marketplace. The problem has been a lasting one, as recent government documents highlight the issues still persists. *The National Employers Skills Survey* (LSC, 2004) reiterates the findings of previous years (LSC, 2001; LSC, 2003); one in five employers reported skills gaps in their workforce (representing 7 per cent of the total workforce in England), and, specifically, employers identify shortages among applicants for vacant posts in technical and practical skills, communication skills, customer handling, team-working and problem-solving skills. While overall, there has been little change in the proportions of vacancies attributed to shortages in these main skill areas, there has been 'a relatively large increase in the incidence of literacy and numeracy skill shortages being reported' (LSC, 2004: 8).

In order to combat the limitations of previous approaches, the focus in the last decade in the UK has been one of up-skilling the workforce and developing a focus on lifelong learning through a variety of initiatives which have had a major effect on HRD in the UK (Lee, 2004: 334). Some 94 per cent of employers agree that up-skilling their workforce is important to achieving their business strategy (CIPD, 2005a), so at both an organisational and national level, the development of workforce skills is vitally important. *Learning to Succeed 1999*, the government's White Paper on lifelong learning specifies local authorities, employers, the voluntary sector and trade unions as vital partners in up-skilling the workforce in the context of lifelong learning.

Since 1997, the Labour government has taken a proactive approach to developing the skills base of the UK's workforce. The new millennium has seen a proliferation of initiatives in order to raise the bar on workforce development. The Learning and Skills Act 2000, the February 2005 White Paper, *14–19 Education and Skills*, the *Skills Strategy White Papers* in 2003 and 2005, which followed the launch of *Skills for Life* in 2001, and the Strategy Units comprehensive action plan for skills development to 2010 (Strategy Unit, 2001, 2002) set out the government's agenda for the demand-led development of workforce skills at a national, organisational and individual level. The *Skills Strategy* is at the heart of the government's attempts to improve skills in the UK and runs alongside specific reforms aimed at 14–19-year-olds. It aims to 'ensure that employers have the right skills to support the success of their businesses and individuals have the skills they need to be both employable and personally fulfilled (Strategy Unit, 2003: 11).

The strategy, which is essentially demand- and market-led, and is still voluntary for the most part, is underpinned by a number of government initiatives and bodies which are outlined below. There is very little substantive legal regulation in this area and almost without exception the government's role is one of providing a policy context rather than a legal one. However, there is clear evidence of increasing involvement by the state (Cuddy and Leney, 2005).

Finally, the government commissioned the Leitch Review of Skills 'to identify the UK's optimal skills mix in 2020 to maximise economic growth, productivity and social justice, and to consider the policy implications of achieving the level of change required' (**www.hm-treasury.gov.uk**, 5 April 2006). It published its interim report 'Skills in the UK: The long-term challenge' on 5 December 2005, and was due to report to the government during 2006 on the gap between the likely skills profile in 2020 and the skills profile that ought to be aimed for, and the consequences of this.

However, despite this activity to raise levels of qualification in the population, to increase employability and improve competitiveness and productivity in the UK, major decisions about workplace training and HRD are still in the hands of employers and the VET system is still a voluntaristic one (Leney *et al.*, 2004).

2006–2010: Order from chaos to exceed the Lisbon goals?

In 2004, as discussed above, Lord Leitch was commissioned to identify the UK's optimal skills mix in 2020 and the policy implications of achieving the level of change required (repetition from previous page). Additionally he was asked to consider how to better integrate employment and skills at a local level. This task was undertaken against a background of comparatively poor economic and educational performance of the UK compared to other developed countries – for example at the time of writing the interim report, Leitch identified that 'More than one third of adults do not hold the equivalent of a basic school leaving certificate. Almost half of adults are not functionally numerate and one sixth are not functionally literate. This is worse than our principal comparator nations.' (2005: 1). Without addressing these issues we faced the prospect of a long-term fall in our ability to compete in global markets (CIPD, 2008b). On publication of the final report in 2006, and the government response in 2007 (DIUS, 2007a), a number of key recommendations were accepted which have led to policy and structural changes in the management and implementation of VET. These include:

- that the UK achieve world class skills by 2020 built on a partnership between government, employers and individuals;
- that all publicly funded, adult vocational skills in England are routed through Train to Gain (**www.traintogain.gov.uk**) reinforcing the demand led nature of the system;
- that the employers voice is strengthened through a Commissions for Employment and Skills (**www.ukces.org.uk**) and a clearer remit for Sector Skills Councils;
- that all employers are encouraged to make a skills pledge that all employees are enabled to gain and be qualified in basic skills and drive up the attainment of intermediate and higher skills;
- that a culture of learning is embedded across the country;
- that there is an integrated employment and skills service.

From these recommendations fell several key initiatives to be rolled out between 2007 and 2011 which demonstrated the government's commitment to building skills in the UK. These include an increased commitment to apprenticeships, the redevelopment of aspects of the school curriculum to include Diplomas to replace some A-level subjects and provide a more vocational education, Welfare to Work initiatives, Train to Gain, the UKCES and a redevelopment of standards in vocational education. Additionally, the policy structure was redrawn and backstage, a complicated set of arrangements divides policy responsibility between three government departments, namely:

- The Department for Children, Schools and Families (DCSF);
- The Department for Innovation, Universities and Skills, and (DIUS);
- The Department for Business, Enterprise and Regulatory Reform (BERR).

In developing the skills agenda in the UK the former two have an express mandate in pre- and post-19 learning respectively. This separation between vocational and academic learning has been criticised as being counter to the reality of people's lives where 'individual, societal and industrial challenges are interwoven' (Stevenson, 2003: 34).

The front stage view is, arguably clearer since the increased emphasis on Train to Gain (**www.traintogain.gov.uk**) which followed the Leitch Review, but there is still a plethora of initiatives and bodies which facilitate access to and provision of NVET in the UK. The UKCES continue to attempt to 'hide the wiring' (UKCES, 2008) to make the system clearer to employers and individuals.

Much of this new approach has been lauded as a sea-change in UK skills development, however, it has been criticised by organisations such as the CIPD (CIPD, 2008b) as being too focused on basic skills and missing a broader, and essential, level of skills development at professional and managerial levels. Moreover, the systems of access to the training initiatives have been branded 'the skills maze' (Phillips, 2009). Furthermore, unlike the systems in France and Germany, there is no legislative compulsion in the law that facilitates the system. While the government are committed to ensuring an entitlement to training, the details of this are sketchy. The next sections provide an overview of the key aspects of NVET in the UK as developed in the light of the Leitch Review.

UK Commission for Employment and Skills (UKCES)

As identified above, the UKCES was a key recommendation in the Leitch Review (2006) and has a mandate to benefit employers, individuals and government by advising how improved employment and skills can help the UK become a world-class leader in productivity, in employment and in having a fair and inclusive society. Opening in April 2008, the key element of the Commission's activities to assess progress towards goals in employment and skills by 2020 and the UKCES is a central part of the UK government's skills strategy. As an advisory body, it has influence, rather than authority across a range of policy and practice areas such as:

- *14–19 Development*: the development of diplomas which incorporate functional and employability skills has provided a structured vocational element to A-levels and GCSEs. Available initially in 5 subject areas from September 2008, a range of 17 will be available by 2013.
- *Apprenticeship (formerly known as Modern Apprenticeships)*: this framework offers 180 different types of apprenticeship over 80 different sectors leading to key skills and vocational, technical or other occupational qualifications alongside industry practice and experience.
- *National Occupational Standards (NOS)*: occupational standards describe the skills, knowledge and understanding needed to do a particular task or job at a national level of competence. They form the basis of National Vocational Qualifications (NVQ) and Vocationally Related Qualifications (VRQs).
- *Vocational Qualifications Reform Programme (UKVQRP)*.
- *Sector Skills Councils*: formed as an Alliance in January 2009, their existence previously had been piecemeal and slow to develop. Covering 25 sectors, their role is to represent industry employers to address sectoral issues in skills development.
- *Credit and Qualifications Frameworks*: Approved for implementation in January 2009, the new Qualifications and Credit Framework (QCF) aligned all skills and qualifications to make it easier to understand the level of qualification help, their content and comparison with other qualifications. While the framework includes all qualifications, it is central to understanding vocational qualifications (see below).

Train to gain

Another central plank of the Leitch Review, Train to Gain (**www.traintogain.gov.uk**) is intended to provide the gateway to VET in the UK by linking employers to appropriate training through Skills Brokers who give advice on appropriate responses to skills needs. Train to Gain can also provide advice on funding opportunities and other related services.

Vocational qualifications

While there is no required distinction between academic and vocational qualifications in the UK, there is a clear inequality between them. Vocational qualifications are viewed as second-class to the academic and disadvantaged groups are badly served, with staying-on rates poor, and drop-out rates high among low-income learners (DfES, 2005b: 21). In the UK, vocational education and training includes a wide range of qualifications, structures and awarding bodies. Broadly speaking, vocational qualifications offer an introduction to a career or industry sector, are practically focused and result in a recognisable qualification or award. The awards are based on the achievement of competencies.

> At the core of the term skill is the idea of competence or proficiency . . . skill is the ability to perform a task to a pre-defined standard of competence . . . but also connotes a dimension of increasing ability . . . skills therefore go hand in hand with knowledge. (NSTF, 2000: 6)

This competency-based approach is at the heart of vocational qualifications in the UK and across the world. While this approach is sometimes criticised (Armstrong, 1996; Kandola, 1996) there is no sign of it disappearing. Following the Leitch Review, a substantial review of the QCF was approved for implementation in January 2009 which began with the application of the framework to VQs (all general qualifications are intended to be included by 2013). This included developing the modular nature of VQs meaning that employees can take parts of qualifications with them when they move jobs, and allows employers the potential to have their in house training recognised under the new system. Vocational qualifications include:

- vocational subjects at GCSE level;
- Vocational Certificates of Education (VCE) which are groups of A-levels in a range of work-related subjects;
- National Vocational Qualifications (GNVQs and NVQs) which demonstrate the skills and knowledge required for particular occupations, covering the main aspects of an occupation, including current best practice, the ability to adapt to future requirements and the knowledge and understanding to enable an employee to perform well. At the heart of NVQs are National Occupational Standards which describe the work competencies required of an individual in a range of occupations;
- Higher National Certificates and Diplomas (HNCs and HNDs) which are vocational higher education qualifications. They are an alternative route for students who want to get a higher education without studying for a degree and normally last two years, as opposed to the three years normally required of an academic higher education qualification;
- Vocational Qualifications (VQs) offered by a number of other awarding bodies with the National Qualifications Framework (NQF) ensuring the consistency and reliability of all the qualifications. There are vocational qualifications covering almost every industry sector, and every level of the NQF (**www.directgov.co.uk**).

All qualifications are included in the 'National Qualifications Framework' introduced in 2000 and updated in 2006 to classify all qualifications from entry level to level 8. Entry level qualifications recognise basic knowledge and skills and the ability to apply learning in everyday situations under direct guidance or supervision. Learning at this level involves building basic knowledge and skills and is not geared towards specific occupations. Level 8 qualifications by contrast recognise leading experts or practitioners in a particular field. Learning at this level involves the development of new and creative approaches that extend or redefine existing knowledge or professional practice. This scale makes the qualifications transparent for users, learners and potential employers so that the former know what they have to learn and the latter know what they can expect.

Apprenticeships as part of the VET framework provide work-based training in a range of sectors and combine working with gaining recognised qualifications. They consist of three elements – an NVQ (an occupationally specific qualification assessed and delivered in the workplace), Key Skills at an appropriate level (including communication, ICT, application of number) and a technical certificate (underpinning knowledge of the technical or business terms, delivered in an FE college). They are not age limited. Funded and managed by the LSCs, they had as a central aim the reduction of the 'skills gap' in the UK and a target of getting 28 per cent of 16–21 year-olds entering apprenticeships by 2005 (**http://www.apprenticeships.org.uk**). There are over 60 apprenticeships and advanced apprenticeships available in over 80 different industries (Cuddy and Lenny, 2005). By 2010 all key VQs will be approved by Sector Skills Councils and available to learners in smaller, credit-based units of learning.

Academic qualifications

The government's growing reliance and emphasis on the importance of tertiary (university/higher) education in the UK is not without consequence. Keep and Mayhew (2004: 298) argue that underpinning the government's policy of expanding higher education are the beliefs that it is necessary to transform economic performance and that it can aid social justice by opening up higher-earning jobs to those from lower socio-economic backgrounds.

However, they go on to argue that the evidence for a positive economic impact is at best ambiguous (Keep and Mayhew, 1996b; Keep *et al.* 2002), and the rest of the vocational and educational system is likely to suffer as a result. This ambiguity is evidenced in the fact that, 'There will remain a substantial number of jobs with vocational requirements below degree level, not least in craft and technical operations. It is doubtful whether graduate courses (honours or foundation) are an effective or efficient means of meeting such demand' (Keep and Mayhew, 2004: 299; Mayhew, *et al.*, 2004).

Additionally, the emphasis on academic participation has not resulted in sound economic growth. 'The explosion in graduate output over the last 15 years has not been accompanied by any concomitant uplift in productivity growth (Keep and Mayhew, 2004: 299).

Foundation degrees, introduced in 2001, are an attempt at bridging the gap between the skills required by employers and the skills acquired during academic qualifications. They are degree-level qualifications designed in partnership with employers to create the knowledge and skills to improve business performance and profitability (**www.foundationdegree.org.uk**). They offer work placement opportunities within them, and are assessed on a blend of academic and vocational ability, through part-time distance learning, e-learning, workplace learning, modular provision and where students do need to attend college or university, local provision. There is some resemblance between these and the German 'dual system' considered earlier in the chapter.

Lifelong learning

In the UK, the decision on access to further education beyond statutory school age is left to the individual except in cases where a job requires certain entry qualifications (an individualistic approach). Although government places increasing importance on upskilling the workforce, training policies are left to employers (a voluntaristic approach). The UK performs comparatively well on short, workplace training courses, but overall levels of qualification compare unfavourably with several other EU countries (Cuddy and Leney, 2005: 36).

The notion of lifelong learning embodies the greater attention paid to vocational education by policy makers in the UK. In the most recent government White Paper on this area *Skills: Getting on in Business, Getting on at Work* (March 2005) the government outlines its plans to increase skills levels through lifelong learning initiatives. Lifelong learning is

---

Box 8.7   **Too much apple pie?**

Thompson (2001) argued that 'Lifelong learning is something of an "apple pie" concept. Hardly anyone is actively against the encouragement of perpetual access to education and training, but, beyond the warm rhetoric, lifelong learning proves to be a tricky term, full of tensions, contradictions and questions about what sort of learning is valued, who it's for and who ought to be funding it . . . Equally depressing is the suspicion, voiced recently by John Field, professor of lifelong learning at the University of Warwick, that the share of all learning taken by people aged over 25 may have fallen dramatically over the past five years, while the share among the 16–24 age group has risen. Indeed, government policies may be making little, if any, difference to opportunities for learning later in life . . . It is not unreasonable for a business to focus training and development on areas of immediate benefit and to concentrate learning opportunities among those who might be expected to deliver the greatest short-term returns on its investment. The problem is that, overall, this results in a volume and pattern of opportunity distribution that everyone agrees is insufficient, wasteful of human potential and not conducive to an inclusive business culture.'

understood to mean 'the provision of an interconnected, universal system of education and training that permits high quality learning from early years to retirement. It allows learners to earn recognised and clearly understood qualifications, and to build on them over their lives' (DfES, 2005b: 6).

The UK has a comparatively high level of participation in adult learning, with the largest percentage in the OECD of workers aged 30–39 who report having been enrolled in full- or part-time training (OECD, 2004).

Learning and Skills Council

The Learning and Skills Act (2000) overhauled the funding and planning of post-compulsory education and training in the UK by establishing the Learning and Skills Council (LSC) to be the primary funding body for all post-16 education (but not university education) and training in England. In the financial year 2006/07, the LSC received £10.4 billion to invest in learning and skills, £11.4 billion in 2007/08 rising to £12.6 billion in 2010 (LSC, 2005). This expenditure covers (LSC, 2005):

- school sixth forms;
- 16–19 further education;
- work-based learning;
- 19+ further education;
- National Employer Training Programmes (NETP);
- personal and community development learning;
- learners with learning disabilities and/or difficulties;
- learner support funds;
- University for Industry/learndirect;
- 14–19 years skills and quality reform.

A network of local LSCs serve counties across England and the priorities are delivered through an array of local and national bodies, both government and private bodies (LSC, 2005). Plans have been announced to dissolve the LSC in 2010, and replace it with a smaller Skills Funding Agency in recognition of the shift of responsibility of 16–19 education to local authorities and the substantial development of Train to Gain (**www.dius.gov.uk**).

Trade Union Learning Representatives

Trade unions play a growing role in the government's learning and skills agenda. Union Learning Representatives (ULRs) were established by legislation in 2002 to provide advice and guidance to union members on their training, education and development needs. Particularly, their role is to encourage members to think about the benefits of learning and training, understand the options available to them, encourage the low-skilled into education and training and to support those with higher level skills to engage in continuing professional development (Cuddy and Lenny, 2005). Their role is increasing in importance with the launch of Unionlearn (**www.unionlearn.org.uk**) in 2006 which has responsibility for the Union Learning Fund.

Sector Skills Councils

The Sector Skills Development Agency (SSDA), launched in September 2002, is a UK-wide non-departmental body network of 25 (and increasing) employer-led sector skills councils covering 85 per cent of the UK's workforce. They have undergone several revamps and overhauls and relaunched as the Alliance of Sector Skills Councils in 2009 under the watchful eye of the UKCES.

The aims of the agency are to reduce skills gaps and shortages; improve productivity, business and public service performance; increase opportunities to boost the skills and productivity of everyone in the sector's workforce and improve learning supply including apprenticeships, higher education and National Occupational Standards (NOS). SSC provide a forum for discussion and network building to ensure that skills and productivity needs of employers and employees are met by course providers.

Investors in People

The Investors in People (IiP) Standard was developed in 1990 and revised in 2004 (placing emphasis on employee involvement and on maximising their potential) and is a national quality standard setting a level of good practice for improving an organisation's performance and competitiveness through a planned approach to setting and communicating business objectives and developing people to meet these objectives.

The IiP Standard is based on three principles:

- *Strategy*: developing strategies to improve the performance of the organisation.
- *Action*: taking action to improve the performance of the organisation.
- *Evaluation*: evaluating the impact on the performance of the organisation.

There are ten indicators grouped under these key principles which form the basis of measurement against the standard. Organisations are assessed against the standard on the basis of evidence and self-assessment. Once the organisation has achieved the standard, and been recognised as such, this can be maintained through reassessment at no more than three-yearly intervals. The achievement of the standard requires investment and effort on the part of the business, but the processes followed to achieve this and the outcomes are likely to have considerable organisational benefits (Taylor and Thackwray, 1995; Bourne *et al.*, 2008). From Summer 2009, the IiP standard and its administration will fall under the remit of the UKCES

Despite the popularity of the Standard, particularly among larger employers, in 2001, IiP had reached only 1.5 per cent of all employers 11 years after its creation (CIPD, 2001c: 56). However, Spellman (2001) estimates that this represents a third of the working population, as most organisations that have achieved recognition are larger, prominent, high-profile businesses with high numbers of employees. In 2006, around a quarter of employees worked in organisations with IiP (IDS, 2006).

Scotland, Wales and Northern Ireland

Throughout this section, the predominant view has been that of the UK, but in many sections this applies only to England as the devolution of governance in the UK means that the government and institutional frameworks differ between England, Wales, Northern Ireland and Scotland. For example, in Scotland, the government has launched its own skills agenda coordinated by Skills Development Scotland (**www.skillsdevelopmentscotland.co.uk**).

Conclusions

It is easy to find criticisms of the UK's 'myriad of national, regional and local agencies' (Unwin, 2004: 147) which make up its approach to vocational education and training. Critics reflect on (Unwin, 2004):

- employer inertia;
- lack of investment and interest in training;
- policy makers' short-sightedness and ultimate failure;
- low quality training provision;

- lack of information for employees;
- the dual standards between academic and vocational learning and training.

The UK government is investing heavily in developing its skills strategy, yet the proliferation of initiatives underneath these bodies mean that employers are often confused by what is available (Phillips, 2009), or reluctant to invest where the outcomes are not clear. The continuity of the systems in France and German are examples of where consistency has meant strength and clarity.

What ought to be done to improve the UKs system of VET? What practical recommendations would you make to policy makers to clarify the system and the responsibilities of the key players within it?

What are the challenges ahead?

The UK now has the emergent institutional infrastructures to move from a low-skills/low-tech equilibrium to a high-skills/high-tech economy. Given the rapidity and strength of the competitive challenges globalisation is bringing, the case for this is unanswerable. However, much political and institutional will is required to ensure that the UK, along with the rest of the European Union, becomes a dynamic knowledge economy in the future . . . Despite the widespread perception that the UK's training system is largely dysfunctional, the cumulative impact of reforms undertaken since 1997 is beginning to be significant – if so far largely unremarked on. Action is being taken . . . and the UK can close our 'human capital gap'.

(Hutton and The Work Foundation, 2005)

Whether the UK can or cannot close the 'human capital gap' remains a pressing issue. The following issues are proposed as the main themes for debate on the future of HRD:

- *Skills and knowledge.* Britain can (probably) never compete with the 'large armies of inexpensive offshore workers' (Gentleman, 2005) offered by countries in the Far East and Africa and so it must find other ways of differentiating itself in the global market place to be competitive and successful as a nation. For some time now, the role of knowledge as a strategic resource has been recognised:

    Many writers argue that there has been a profound change in the nature of work so that there is a reliance on 'creativity . . . and intellective skills' (Frenkel *et al.*, 1995: 780). If this is the case then, the future of UK skill development is likely to be twofold: developing the 'intellective' skills of the workforce, and in capturing the knowledge on which they rely.

    The rise in interest in 'knowledge management' over the years is evidence of the growing importance of this area. (Issues relating to this are covered in the previous chapter.)

- *The link between workplace training and competitiveness.* This section identifies that the problematic relationship between workplace training and development and national competitiveness remains.

First, Crouch and Sako (2001) argue that improved skills levels do not necessarily solve unemployment, and improved levels of education and training may simply produce overqualified workers. Furthermore, if employers, as they do in the UK, provide skills training independent of government initiatives, then the government is left to sweep up the 'bottom third, the less able' (Unwin, 2004) who have been excluded from the investment of their employers in the past and may be unemployed in the present. The contribution that this level of development makes to national competitiveness is unclear. We have seen from the French VET system that high unemployment, especially among young people has proved problematic and can note the challenges that now face the German system as unemployment rises. Third, while most recognise the value and worth of training and development, few claim to be able to isolate the effects of it on economic growth. Attempts have been made with varied results.

> Knowledge and information are becoming the strategic resource and transforming agent of the post-industrial society . . . just as the combination of energy, resources and machine technology were the transformational agencies of industrial societies.
>
> (Bell, 1980: 531)

> The productivity of knowledge and knowledge workers will not be the only competitive factor in the world economy. It is however, likely to become the decisive factor, at least for most industries in the developed countries.
>
> (Druker, 1998: 17)

> Knowledge-based industries (e.g. financial services, information technologies etc.) . . . operate by . . . selectively appropriating information as a key resource to be exploited . . . [with] highly specialised knowledge as a key resource from which . . . significant returns on investments can be earned.
>
> (Cooke, 2002: 71)

It remains to be seen then, whether the continuing voluntarist approach of the Labour government can carry the country forward in an increasingly competitive global market.

Summary

- This chapter has considered the shifts in the HRD landscape, especially the change in rhetoric and reality from training to learning, and the contribution that learning can make to business performance.
- The discussion of practical issues of HRD in an organisational context provided a clear structure for the strategic assessment of the contribution of HRD to organisational performance: from establishing needs, through designing and delivering learning and training, to closing the loop through evaluating the value added by the interventions. There was also an outline of the central methods for the delivery of training and their relative effectiveness.
- Of particular contemporary interest were the issues which surround coaching and e-learning, and the enduring interest in 'learning organisations'.
- Then, the chapter set the scene for the discussion of NVET by considering the link between education and economic growth and then discussed the European context of vocational education and training (VET) and provided a comparative analysis of the approaches in Germany, France and the UK, drawing critical conclusions in assessing the value and effectiveness of the individual national approaches as they strive to achieve the Lisbon Goals.
- Finally, the chapter concluded with identifying the key challenges ahead if the UK is to be competitive in a global marketplace.

Questions

1 The learning cycle is aspirational and textbook and does not bear comparison with messy organisational reality. How far would you agree with this statement?

2 To what extent is the evaluation of HRD interventions truly possible? How can businesses demonstrate the contribution to the 'bottom line'?

3 To what extent is there a business benefit in developing a coaching culture? Is it just the latest management fad or are there demonstrable benefits for businesses?

4 What impact do government initiatives really have on business performance?

Exercises

1 The notion of the learning organisation – is it alive or dead? Is it something that is worth working towards? Working in two groups, prepare your case for each side of the argument and present it to the whole group.

2 What steps would you take if you were tasked with achieving Investors In People status for your organisation? What would be the benefits of achieving it? What would be the spin-off benefits of simply going through the process?

3 Compare the UK, French and German systems of VET. Read further in the CEDEFOP, CIPD and other information. What can the UK learn from the approaches of other nations? What does the UK do well, or less well than other countries?

Case study

Recruiting, training and developing referees at the Football Association

The Football Association (F.A.) is the governing body for the game of association football in England. As football is the most popular sporting activity in the country the F.A. has a very high public profile.

The laws of football are agreed internationally through the federal governing body, FIFA, which has 206 member associations. In March of each year, these member associations have an opportunity to agree amendments to their laws. However they have remained fairly static, with the last major change implemented in the 90s – this concerned 'denial of the obvious goal-scoring opportunity'.

Football must be conducted according to these laws in a huge number of games that occur every day. These range from school football and six-aside games in leisure centres through to amateur competitive leagues, the professional football and premiership leagues to the international and world cup compe-

titions. One of the essential, but less recognised roles of the F.A. is to ensure that sufficient referees are recruited, trained, retained and developed. In total in England, there are some 3,500 referees currently registered to operate at the most senior professional levels and another 28,000 who are registered to referee at the lower levels.

Ian Blanchard, Head of National Referee Development at the F.A., works with a team of seven regional staff to ensure that this refereeing facility is available and the required standards are maintained. According to Ian Blanchard, the qualities of a good referee are 'good communication, a strong personality and clear and confident decision-making, a great awareness of what is happening and empathy for the game'. Such interpersonal skills are, to an extent, innate (not everyone could make a good referee, however highly motivated) but can be identified, developed and

Case study continued

assessed through their application in practice. Two other obvious pre-requisites for a capable referee are knowledge of the laws of the game and physical and mental fitness.

Some 7,000 new referees undergo initial training through the F.A. each year and a similar number leave the system. Given the total figure of 28,000 operating below the most senior levels, this is a high rate of attrition. However, a significant number, over 60 per cent of those entering the system, are under 16 and many of these are acquiring a referees' license in support of a leadership qualification – for example, the Duke of Edinburgh's Award – and do not intend to referee any games. In addition significant numbers drop out after they have refereed their first few games. To ensure an adequate pipe-line of referees, there is a constant programme of recruitment with advertisements in local newspapers, at leisure centres and in libraries. University career fairs have produced a good source of recruitment as a higher percentage of the populations enter full-time education.

An internal project team, led by Ian Blanchard, has recently redesigned the subsequent training programme after recruitment. One of the challenges has been that referee training must be delivered at local levels, by County Associations and the system relies on the commitment of volunteers. Nevertheless, standards must be maintained if the game is to be supported and developed.

It should be added that the F.A. is considered a world leader in the training of referees and there are frequent requests to support emerging associations overseas – particularly from developing countries.

Perhaps the most striking feature of referee training is the complete dependence on volunteers to deliver the system. There is a need for a cohort of trainers and mentors (where these can be found) at Module 3, and of independent assessors to maintain standards at the higher levels. Referees are paid (£300 at professional level to £30 at the most junior), but it is the level of commitment to the game that produces this pipe-line of enthusiasts.

Enthusiasm however is not enough and standards must be maintained. Regular checks are made and continuing training and development opportunities are in place. The F.A operates an assessment scheme for all referees who are offered advice on their performance detailing strengths and development points. Also in place is an annual appraisal system designed to maintain standards as well as assist Instructors development. On occasions licenses are withdrawn because of poor practices.

Source: from CIPD, Recruiting, training and developing referees at the Football Association, http://www.cipd.co.uk/helpingpeoplelearn/_lrncltreftbss.htm, with the permission of the publisher, the Chartered Institute of Personnel and Development, London (www.cipd.co.uk).

Questions

1 How do you think this training programme contributed to improving the referees commitment to the job?
2 What are the issues involved in using volunteers to deliver the training?
3 How could the effectiveness of this training be evaluated?

Useful websites

URL	Organisation	Summary of contents
www.cipd.co.uk	Chartered Institute of Personnel and Development (CIPD)	Professional organisation for HR professionals
www.managers.org.uk	Chartered Management Institute	Professional organisation for managers
www.iipuk.co.uk	Investors in People	Validating body for the IIP standard
www.qca.org.uk	Qualifications and Curriculum Authority	Maintains and develops school curricula and associated assessments, as well as accrediting and monitoring qualifications in schools, colleges, and at work
www.ssda.org.uk	Sector Skills Councils	The Skills for Business network is made up of 25 Sector Skills Councils (SSCs). Each SSC is an employer-led, independent organisation that covers a specific sector across the UK

URL	Organisation	Summary of contents
www.learndirect.co.uk	University for Industry/Learn Direct	Government-driven, hundreds of online courses, 1,350 learndirect centres to help deliver learning to excluded sections of the population
www.qca.org.uk/nq/framework	National Qualifications Framework	Explains how the National Qualifications Framework (NQF) works
http://www.cedefop.eu.int	The European Centre for the Development of Vocational Training	Established in 1975, is a European agency that helps the European Union (EU). It is the EU's reference centre for vocational education and training
www.trainingvillage.gr	Training Village	Sponsored by CEDEFOP
www.oecd.org	Organisation for Economic Co-operation and Development (OECD)	An international organisation helping governments tackle the economic, social and governance challenges of a globalised economy

References and further reading

Alberga, T. (1997) 'Investors in People: Time for a check up', *People Management*, 30–32.

Anderson, V. (2007) *The Value of Learning.* London: CIPD.

Argyris, C. (1992) *On Organizational Learning.* Oxford: Blackwell Business.

Argyris, C. and Schön, D.A. (1978) *Organizational Learning: A Theory in Action Perspective.* Needham Heights, MA: Allyn & Bacon.

Armstrong, G. (1996) 'A qualifications cuckoo in the competency nest?', *People Management*, 23.

Ashworth, L. (2006) 'Training needs analysis is better carried out at an individual level than as a "sheep-dip"', *People Management*, 12, 6: 1.

Ballot, G. (2003) 'Firms investment in human capital: sponsoring and effect on performance', *European Conference on The Future of Work: Challenges for the European Employment Strategy.* Athens.

Barnes, M. and Asogbon, G. (2004) *International Comparisons of Productivity: Better Data Improve UK Productivity Position: Detailed Results for the February 2004 Release of International Comparisons of Productivity covering 1990 to 2002.* London: Office for National Statistics.

Barrington, H. and Reid, M.A. (1999) *Training Interventions: Promoting Learning Opportunities.* London: IPD.

Bartram, D., Foster, J., Lindley, P.A., Brown, A.J. and Nixon, S. (1993) *The Learning Climate Questionnaire.* London: Employment Service and Newland Park Associates Ltd.

Bassi, L.J. *et al.* (2001) *Human Capital Investments and Firm Performance.* Washington, DC: Human Capital Dynamics.

Becker, B.E. and Huselid, M.A. (1998) 'High performance work systems and firm performance: a synthesis of research and managerial implications' in G.R. Ferris (ed.) *Personnel and Human Resource Management.* Greenwich, CT: JAI Press. 16: 53–101.

Beer, M., Spector, B., Lawrence, P.R., Quinn Mills, D. and Walton, R.E. (1984) *Managing Human Assets.* New York: Free Press.

Bell, D. (1980) 'The social framework of the information society' in T. Forester (ed.) *The Microelectronics Revolution.* Oxford: Blackwell.

Blake, R.R. (1995) 'Memories of HRD', *Training and Development*, 49, 3: 7.

Blyth, A. (2003) 'A worthwhile investment?', *Personnel Today*, 21–22.

Bourne, M., Franco-Santos, M., Pavlov, A., Lucianetti, L., Martinez, V. and Mura, M. (2008) *The Impact of Investors in People on Management Practices and Firm Performance.* Milton Keynes: Cranfield University.

Bousquet, S. (2008) *Vocational Education and Training in France* Luxembourg: Office for Official Publications of the European Communities.

Brewster, C. and Hegewisch, A. (1993) 'A continent of diversity', *Personnel Management*, January: 36–40.

Brinkerhoff, R.O. (2005) 'The success case method: a strategic evaluation approach to increasing the value and effect of training', *Advances in Developing Human Resources*, 7, 1: 86–102.

Burgoyne, J. (1999) 'Design of the Times', *People Management*, 3 June.

Cannell, M. (1997) 'Practice Makes Perfect', *People Management*, 26–33.

Cannell, M. (2004) *Training – A Short History.* London: CIPD.

CEDEFOP (2000) *Vocational Education and Training in France.* Luxembourg: Office for Official Publications of the European Communities.

CEDEFOP (2002) *Towards a History of Vocational Education and Training in Europe in a Comparative Perspective: Proceedings of the First International Conference*: Vols 1 and 2. Florence/Luxembourg: Office for Official Publications of the European Communities, 2004.

CEDEFOP (2009) *Continuity, Consolidation and Change: Towards a European Era of Vocational Education and Training.* Luxembourg: Office for Official Publications of the European Communities.

Chase, R. (1997) 'The knowledge based organisation: an international study', *Journal of Knowledge Management*, 1, 1: 38–49.

CIPD (2001a) *The Learning and Development Generalist Standard: CIPD Practitioner-Level Professional Standards*. London: CIPD.

CIPD (2001b) *The Future of Learning for Work: Executive Briefing*. London: CIPD.

CIPD (2001c) *Workplace Learning in Europe*. London: CIPD.

CIPD (2002) *Who Learns At Work? Survey Report*. February. London: CIPD.

CIPD (2004a) *E-learning Survey Results Report*. London: CIPD.

CIPD (2004b) *Quarterly Trends and Indicators: Survey Report Autumn 2004*. London: CIPD.

CIPD (2004c) *Reflections: New Trends in Training and Development: Experts' Views on the 2004 Training and Development Survey Findings*. London: CIPD.

CIPD (2004d) *Trade Union Learning Representatives: the Change Agenda*. London: CIPD.

CIPD (2004e) *Why Accessible e-learning Makes Business Sense: Inclusive Learning for All*. London: CIPD.

CIPD (2005a) *A Barometer of HR Trends and Prospects 2005: Overview of CIPD Surveys*. London: CIPD.

CIPD (2005b) *Basic Skills in the Workplace: Opening Doors to Learning*. London: CIPD.

CIPD (2005c) 'An informal approach gets better results', *People Management*, 11, 13: 14.

CIPD (2005d) *Latest Trends in Learning, Training and Development: Reflections on the 2005 Training and Development Survey*. London: CIPD.

CIPD (2005e) *Quarterly HR Trends and Indicators: Survey Report 2004/5*. London: CIPD.

CIPD (2005f) *Training and Development: Annual Survey Report 2005*. London: CIPD.

CIPD (2005g) *Professional Standards*, London: CIPD.

CIPD (2005h) *Training and Development: Annual Survey Report 2005*, London: CIPD.

CIPD (2006) *Learning and Development: Annual Survey Report 2006*. London: CIPD.

CIPD (2007) *Learning and Development: Annual Survey Report 2006*, London: CIPD.

CIPD (2008a) *Learning and Development: Annual Survey Report 2008*, London: CIPD.

CIPD (2008b) *The Skills Agenda in the UK*, London: CIPD.

CIPD (2009) *Learning and Development: Annual Survey Report 2009*, London: CIPD.

Clutterbuck, D. and Megginson M.D. (2005) *Making Coaching Work: Developing a Coaching Culture*. London: CIPD.

Cooke, P. (2002) *Knowledge Economies*. London: Routledge.

Crouch, C.F.D. and Sako, M. (2001) *Are Skills the Answer? The Political Economy of Skill Creation in Advanced Industrial Nations*. Oxford: Oxford University Press.

Cuddy, N. and Leney, T. (2005) *Vocational Education and training in the United Kingdom*. Luxembourg: Office for Official Publications of the European Communities.

Dee, K. and Hatton, A. (2006) 'How to face training evaluation head-on', *People Management*, 12, 6: 40–41.

Deissinger, T. (2000) 'The German "Philosophy" of linking academic and work-based learning in Higher Education: the case of vocational academies', *Journal of Vocational Education and Training*, 52, 4: 605–26.

Deming, W.E. (1986) *Out of Crisis*. Cambridge: Cambridge University Press.

Department for Education and Skills (2002) *Delivering Skills for Business*. London: Department for Education and Skills, Skills Sector Development Agency: 8.

Department for Education and Skills (2004) *The Story So Far*. London: Sector Skills Development Agency.

Department for Education and Skills (2005a) *Skills Sector Agreements*. London: Skills Sector Development Agency.

Department for Education and Skills (2005b) *White Paper – Skills: Getting On in Business, Getting On at Work*. London: Department for Education and Skills.

Department for Education and Skills (2005c) *Department for Education and Skills: Departmental Report 2005*. London: Department for Education and Skills.

Descy, P. and Tessaring, M. (2005) *The Value of Learning: Evaluation and Impact of Education and Training. Third Report on Vocational Training Research in Europe*. Luxembourg: Office for Official Publications of the European Communities.

DIUS (2007a) *World Class Skills: Implementing the Leitch Review of Skills in England*, Norwich: The Stationery Office.

DIUS (2007b) *World class skills: implementing the Leitch review of skills in England: Government Response to Leitch, Cm7181*, Norwich: The Stationery Office.

Downey, M. (2003) *Effective Coaching*. New York: Thompson Texere.

Druker, P. (1998) 'The future has already happened', *The Futurist*, 32, 8: 16–18.

Dybowski, D.G. (2005) *The Dual Vocational Education and Training System in Germany*. Keynote speech on Dual Vocational Training International Conference, Taiwan.

Easterby-Smith, M. and Mackness, J. (1992) 'Completing the cycle of evaluation', *Personnel Management*, June: 50–55.

Edwards, C. (2005) 'An informal approach gets better results', *People Management*, 11, 13: 14.

E-Learning Strategy Unit (8 July 2003) *Towards a Unified e-learning Strategy*. London: Department for Education and Skills.

Elliot, L. (2004) 'Why we shouldn't just be topping up the number of graduates', *The Guardian*, 12 January, p. 23.

Ellis, J. and Williams, D. (1995) *International Business Strategy*. London: Pitman.

Ernst & Young (1997) *Measures that Matter*. London: Ernst & Young.

European Commission (2002) *Communication from the Commission – European Benchmarks in Education and Training: Follow-up to the Lisbon European Council*. Luxembourg: EUR–OP.

Finegold, D. and Levine, D.I. (1997) 'Institutional incentives for employer training', *Journal of Education and Work*, 10, 2: 109–27.

Finegold, D. and Soskice, D. (1988) 'The failure of training in Britain: analysis and prescription', *Oxford Review of Economic Policy*, 4, 3: 21–53.

Finegold, D. and Soskice, D. (1999) 'Creating self-sustaining high-skill ecosystems', *Oxford Review of Economic Policy*, 15, 1: 60–79.

Ford, D. J. (1993) *Benchmarking HRD*. London: ASTO.

Frenkel, S., Korczynski, M., Donoghue, L. and Shire, K. (1995) 'Re-constituting work: trends towards knowledge work and info–normative control', *Work, Employment and Society*, 9, 4: 773–96.

Gallwey, T. (1986) *The Inner Game of Golf*. London: Pan.

Garavan, T.N. (1991) 'Strategic human resource development', *Journal of European Industrial Training*, 15, 1: 17–30.

Garavan, T.N. (2007) 'A Strategic perspective on human resource development', *Advances in Developing Human Resources*, 9, 11: 11–30.

Garavan, T.N., Costine, P. and Heraty, N. (1995) 'The emergence of strategic human resource development', *Journal of European Industrial Training*, 19, 10: 4–10.

Garavan, T.N., Heraty, N. and Morley, M. (1998) 'Actors in the HRD process', *International Studies of Management and Organization*, 28, 1: 114–35.

Garvin, D. (1993) 'Building a Learning Organisation' in P. Druker and D. Garvin (eds) *The Harvard Business Review on Knowledge Management*. Boston, MA: Harvard Business School Press, pp. 47–80.

Gentleman, A. (2005) 'Painful truth of the call centre cyber coolies', *The Observer*, 30 October. Available online at **http://www.guardian.co.uk/business/2005/oct/30/india.internationalnews**

Gibb, S. and Megginson, D. (2001) 'Employee development' in, T. Redman and A. Wilkinson (eds) *Contemporary Human Resource Management*. London: FT/Prentice Hall, pp. 128–67.

Gilley, J.W. and Eggland, S.A. (1989) *Principles of Human Resource Development*. Wokingham: Addison-Wesley.

Green, A., Preston, J. and Malmberg, L.-E (2004) 'Non-material benefits of education, training and skills at the macro level' in P. Descy and M. Tessering (eds) *Impact of Education and Training*. Luxembourg: Office for Official Publications of the European Communities (CEDEFOP Reference Series 54), pp. 119–77.

Green, F., Felstead A. and Gallie, D. (2002) *Works Skills in Britain 1986–2001*. Nottingham: DfES Publications.

Green, K. (1999) 'Offensive thinking', *People Management*, 5, 8: 27.

Greinert, W.-D. (2002) 'European vocational training systems: the theoretical context of historical development' in CEDEFOP, *Towards a History of Vocational Education and Training in Europe in a Comparative Perspective: Proceedings of the First International Conference*, Vol. 1. Luxembourg: Office for Official Publications of the European Communities, pp. 23–33.

Grieves, J. (2003) *Strategic Human Resource Development*. London: Sage.

Guest, D. (1987) 'Human resource management and industrial relations', *Journal of Management Studies*, 24, 5: 503–21.

Hall, D.T. (1984) 'Human resource development and organisational effectiveness' in C. Fobrum, N. Tichy and M. Devanna (eds) *Strategic Human Resource Management*. New York: John Wiley.

Hall, L. (2005) 'Coach class', *People Management*, 1 September: 46.

Hall, P.A. and Soskice, D. (2001) *Varieties of Capitalism: The Institutional Foundations of Comparative Advantage*. Oxford: Oxford University Press.

Hamblin, A.C. (1974) *Evaluation and Control of Training*. Maidenhead: McGraw-Hill.

Harrison, R. (2005) *Learning and Development*. London: CIPD.

Harrison, R. (2009) *Learning and Development*, 5th edn. London: CIPD.

Harrison, R. and Kessells, J. (2004) *Human Resource Development in a Knowledge Economy: An Organisational View*. Basingstoke: Palgrave Macmillan.

Hendry, C. (1994) 'The Single European Market and The HRM Response' in P.A. Kirkbride (ed.) *Human Resource Management in Europe: Perspectives for the 1990s*. London: Routledge, pp. 93–113.

Hippach-Schneider, U., Martina, K., and Woll, C. (2007). *Vocational Education and Training in Germany*. Luxembourg: Office for Official Publications of the European Communities.

Hirsch, W. and Reilly, P. (1998) 'Cycling proficiency: how do large organisations identify their future skill needs among their thousands of employees?', *People Management*, 9 July: 36–41.

Holden, L. and Liviad, Y. (1993) 'Does strategic training policy exist? Evidence from ten European countries', in A. Hegewisch and C. Brewester (eds) *European Development in HRM: The Cranfield Management Research Series*. Aldershot: Kogan Page.

Holton, E.R., III. (1996) 'The flawed four-level evaluation model', *Human Resource Development Quarterly*, 7: 5–21.

Honey, P. (1999) 'A declaration on learning', *Human Resource Development International*, 2, 1: 9–17.

Honey, P. and Mumford, A. (1989) *Manual of Learning Opportunities*. Maidenhead: Peter Honey.

Huselid, M.A. (1995) 'The impact of human resource management on turnover, productivity and corporate financial performance', *Academy of Management Journal*, 38: 635–72.

Hutton, W. and The Work Foundation (2005) *Where are the Gaps? An analysis of UK Skills and Education Strategy in the Light of the Kok Group and European Commission Midterm Review of the Lisbon Goals*. Department for Education and Skills.

IDS (2004) 'TNT UK recognised as an IiP champion', *IDS HR Studies Update*, 782: 19–23.

IDS (2006) 'Investors in People'. *IDS HR Studies 816*, February 2006.

Investors in People, UK (2001) *A Decade of Success: 10 Years of Making a Difference to Working Life in the UK*. London: IIP UK.

Jarvis, J. and Hooley, A. (2004) 'Access all areas', *People Management*, 9 December: 40.

Kandola, B. (1996) 'Are competences too much of a good thing?', *People Management*, 2 May: 21.

Kanter, R.M. (1989) *When Giants Learn to Dance*. New York: Simon & Schuster.

Kearns, P. (2005) 'From return on investment to added value evaluation: the foundation for organizational learning', *Advances in Developing Human Resources*, 7, 1: 135–46.

Keep, E. and Mayhew, K. (1996a) 'Economic demand for Higher Education: a sound foundation for further expansion?', *Higher Education Quarterly*, 50, 2: 89–190.

Keep, E. and Mayhew, K. (1996b) 'Evaluating assumptions that underlie training policy' in A. Booth and D.J. Snower (eds) *Acquiring Skills*. Cambridge: Cambridge University Press, pp. 305–34.

Keep, E. and Mayhew, K. (2001) *The Skills System in 2015. The Future of Learning for Work*. Executive Briefing. London: CIPD.

Keep, E. and Mayhew, K. (2004) 'The economic and distributional implications of current policies on higher education', *Oxford Review of Economic Policy* 20, 2: 298–314.

Keep, E., Mayhew, K. and Corney, M. (2002) *Review of the Evidence on the Rate of Return to Employers of Investment in Training and Employer Training Measures*. SKOPE Research Paper. Coventry: University of Warwick.

Kenney, J. *et al.* (1979) *Manpower Training and Development*. London: Institute of Personnel Management.

Kessels, J. and Harrison, R. (1998) 'External consistency: the key to management development', *Management Learning*, 29, 1: 39–68.

Kingston, P. (2007) 'Short changed', *People Management*, 13, 16: 28–31.

Kirkpatrick, J. (1960) 'Techniques for evaluating training programmes', *Journal of American Society for Training and Development*, 14, 13–18: 25–32.

Knights, A. and Poppleton, A. (2008) *Developing Coaching Capability in Organisations: Research into Practice*. London: CIPD.

Kolb, D. (1984) *Experiential Learning: Experience as the Source of Learning and Development*. Englewood Cliffs, NJ: Prentice-Hall.

Lahteenmaki, S., Holden, L. and Roberts, I. (eds) (1999) *HRM and the Learning Organisation*. Turku, Finland: Turku School of Economics and Business Administration.

Learning and Skills Council (2001) *National Employers Skills Survey: Key Findings*. London: Department for Education and Skills.

Learning and Skills Council (2003) *National Employers Skills Survey: Key Findings*. London: Department for Education and Skills.

Learning and Skills Council (2004) *National Employers Skills Survey: Key Findings*. London: Department for Education and Skills.

Learning and Skills Council (2005) *Transforming Learning and Skills: Our Annual Statement of Priorities*. London: Department for Education and Skills.

Learning and Skills Council (2008) *National Employers' Skills Survey 2007* (published 8 May 2008). London: Learning and Skills Council.

Lee, M. (2004) 'National human resource development in the United Kingdom', *Advances in Developing Human Resources*, 6, 3: 334–45.

Leitch, S. (2005) *Skills in the UK: The Long-term Challenge*. London: HM Treasury.

Leitch, S. (2006) *Prosperity for all in the Global Economy: World Class Skills: Final Report* (**www.dcsf.gov.uk/furthereducation**) Norwich: Stationery Office.

Leney, T., Cuddy, N., May, T. and Hall, J. (2004) *Thematic Overview of VET in England and the Devolved Administrations of the UK*. CEDEFOP.

Luoma, M. (2000) 'Investigating the link between strategy and HRD', *Personnel Review*, 29(6): 769–90.

Mankin, D. (2009) *Human Resource Development*. London: Oxford University Press.

Marchington, M. and Wilkinson, A. (2005) *Human Resource Management at Work*. London: CIPD.

Matthews, J.-J., Megginson, D. and Surtees, M. (2004) *Human Resource Development*. London: Kogan Page.

Mayhew, K., Deer, C. and Dua, M. (2004) 'The move to mass higher education in the UK: many questions and some answers', *Oxford Review of Education*, 30, 1: 65–82.

Mayo, A. (2000) *Building a Training and Development Strategy*. **www.cipd.co.uk/subjects/training/trnstrgy/buildtdstr.htm**

McCracken, M. and Wallace, M. (2000) 'Towards a redefinition of strategic HRD', *Journal of European Industrial Training*, 24, 5: 281–90.

McGoldrick, J., Stewart, J. and Watson, S. (2002) *Understanding Human Resource Development: A Research Based Approach*. London: Routledge.

Miller, R. and Stewart, J. (1999) 'Opened University', *People Management*, 17 June: 42–44.

Millward, N., Bryson, A. and Forth, J. (2000) *All Change at Work: British Employee Relations 1980–1998*. London: Routledge.

Moraal, D., Lorig, B., Schreiber, D. and Azeez, U. (2009) *BiBB Report: A look behind the scenes of continuing vocational training in Germany*. BIBB (Federal Institute for Vocational Education and Training)

Nadler, L. (1984) *The Handbook of Human Resource Development*. New York: John Wiley.

NAO (2005) *Employer Perspectives on Improving Skills for Employment*. London: National Audit Office.

National Skills Task Force (2000) *Skills for All: Proposals for a National Skills Agenda*. London: Department for Education and Employment.

Noon, M. and Blyton, P. (2002) *The Realities of Work*. Basingstoke: Palgrave.

OECD (2004) *Education at a Glance*. Paris: OECD.

OECD (2005) *The Role of Qualifications Systems in Promoting Life-long Learning*. Paris: OECD.

Office for National Statistics (2004) *Economic Trends*, December 2004, available from **www.statistics.gov.uk**.

Office for National Statistics (2006) *Economic Trends*, March 2006, available from **www.statistics.gov.uk**.

Overton, L. (2004) 'Fighting fit', *E-Learning Age*. December 2003–January 2004, **www.elearningage.co.uk**.

Parsloe, E. and Wray, M. (2000) *Coaching and Mentoring: Practical Methods to Improve Learning*. London: Kogan Page.

Payne, J. (2003) *Vocational Pathways at Age 16–19*. DfES Research Report. Nottingham: DfES.

Pearn, M., Roderick, C. and Mulrooney, C. (1995) *Learning Organisations in Practice*. Maidenhead: McGraw-Hill.

Pedlar, M., Burgoyne, J. and Boydell, T. (1991) *The Learning Company*. Maidenhead: McGraw-Hill.

Pedlar, M., Burgoyne, J. and Boydell, T. (1997) *The Learning Company*, 2nd edn, Maidenhead: McGraw-Hill.

Peters, T.J. and Waterman, R.H. (1982) *In Search of Excellence: Lessons from America's Best Run Companies*. New York: Harper & Row.

Pettigrew, A. and Whipp, R. (1991) *Managing Change for Competitive Success (ESRC Competitiveness Surveys)*. Oxford: Blackwell.

Pfeffer, J. (1994) *Competitive Advantage Through People: Understanding the Power of the Workforce*. Boston, MA: Houghton Mifflin.

Pfeffer, J. (1998) *The Human Equation: Building Profits by Putting People First*. Cambridge, MA: Harvard Business School Press.

Pfeffer, J. (2003) *Understanding the People and Performance Link: Unlocking the Black Box*. London: CIPD.

Phillips, J. (2002) *How to Measure Training Success: A Practical Guide to Evaluating Training*. New York: McGraw-Hill.

Phillips, J. (2005) 'Measuring up', *People Management*, 7 April: 42–43.

Phillips, L. (2008) 'Council rolls out diversity e-learning course', *People Management*, 27 February. **http://www.peoplemanagement.co.uk/pm/articles/2008/02/councilrollsoutdiversityelearningcourse.htm**.

Phillips, L. (2009) 'The skills maze', *People Management*, 7 May: 20.

Pullinger, D. (2004) 'Capture learning to capitalise value', *People Management* (Study notes, 27 October): 69–70.

Purcell, J. (2003) *Understanding the People and Performance Link: Unlocking the Black Box*. London: CIPD.

Rae, L. (2002) *Assessing the Value of Your Training: The Evaluation Process from Training Needs to the Report to the Board*. London: Gower.

Reid, M. A., Barrington, H. and Brown, M. (2004) *Human Resource Development: Beyond Training Interventions.* London: CIPD.

Reuters 7 April 2009, **http://www.france24.com/en/20090420-french-unemployment-deficit-ofce-government-recession-economy-shrink-financial-crisis**.

Revans, R. (1982) *The Enterprise as a Learning System. Action Learning in Practice.* Aldershot: Gower.

Revans, R. (1983) *The ABC of Action Learning.* Bromley: Chartwell Bratt.

Reynolds, J., Caley, L. and Mason. R. (2002) *How do People Learn?* London: CIPD.

Reynolds, J. (2004) *Helping People Learn: Strategies for Moving from Training to Learning. Research Report.* London: CIPD.

Rothwell, W.J. and Kanazas, H.C. (1989) *Strategic Human Resource Development.* Englewood Cliffs, NJ: Prentice-Hall.

Saggers, R. (1994) 'Training climbs the corporate agenda', *People Management*, July: 55–57.

Schön, D. (1983) *The Reflective Practitioner: How Professionals Think in Action.* New York: Basic Books.

Scott, A. (2008) 'Seven-way collaboration produces modular, customised package', *People Management*, 20 June **http://www.peoplemangement.co.uk/pm/articles/2008/ob/nhs-trust-launch-e-learning-course-for-mental-healthcare-professionals.htm**.

Seibert, K. (1999) 'Reflection in action: tools for cultivating on the job learning conditions', *Organizational Dynamics*, 27, 3: 54–66.

Senge, P. (1990) *The Fifth Discipline.* London: Random House Business Books.

Shury, J., Davies, B., Riley, T. and Stanfield, C. (2008) *Skills for the Workplace: Employer Perspectives.* London: UKCES.

Sloman, M. (1999) 'Learning centre: seize the day', *People Management*, 20 May: 31.

Sloman, M. (2002) 'Don't believe the hype', *People Management*, 21 March: 41.

Sloman, M. (2005) *Change Agenda: Training to Learning. Research Report.* London: CIPD.

Sloman, M. and Rolph, J. (2003) *E-learning: The Learning Curve. Change Agendas.* London: CIPD.

Smethurst, S. (2006) 'Course of treatment', *People Management*, 12, 5: 34–36.

Soskice, D.W. (1993) 'Social skills from mass Higher Education: rethinking the company based initial training paradigm', *Oxford Review of Economic Policy*, 9, 3: 101–13.

Spellman, R. (2001) 'Training for success: the case for IiP.' *Training Journal*, 14–16.

Steedman, H. and Wagner, K. (1987) 'A second look at productivity, machinery and skills in Britain and Germany', *National Institute Ecomonic Review*, November.

Stevenson, J. (2003) *Developing Vocational Expertise.* London: Crows Nest, Allen & Unwin.

Stewart, J. (1999) *Employee Development Practice.* London: FT/Pitman Publishing.

Stewart, J. and McGoldrick, J. (1996) *Human Resource Development: Perspectives, Strategies and Practice.* London: Pitman.

Stewart, J. and Sambrook, S. (2002) 'Reflections and discussion' in J. Stewart, S. Tjepkema, S. Sambrook, M. Mulder, H. Horst and J. Schreerens (eds) *HRD and Learning Organisations in Europe.* London: Routledge, pp. 178–87.

Storey, J. (ed.) (1989) *New Perspectives on Human Resource Management.* London: Routledge.

Storey, J. (1992) *Developments in the Management of Human Resources: an Analytical Review.* Oxford: Blackwell.

Storey, J. (1995) *Human Resource Management: A Critical Text.* London: Routledge.

Strategy Unit (2001) *In Demand: Adult Skills in the 21st Century.* London: Strategy Unit.

Strategy Unit (2002) *In Demand: Adult Skills in the 21st Century – Part 2.* London: Strategy Unit.

Strategy Unit (2003) *Skills Strategy White Paper.* London: Department for Education and Skills.

Sung, J. and Ashton, D. (2004) *Achieving Best Practice in Your Business: High Performance Work Practices: Linking Strategy and Skills to Performance Outcomes.* London: DTI.

Swanson, R.A. (2001) *Assessing the Financial Benefits of Human Resource Development.* Cambridge, MA: Perseus.

Swanson, R.A. and Holton, E.F. (2001) *Foundations of Human Resource Development.* San Francisco, CA: Berrett-Koehler.

Symon, G. (2002) 'The "reality" of rhetoric and the learning organization in the UK', *Human Resource Development International*, 5, 2: 155–74.

Taylor, J. (2008) *Identifying Learning and Training Needs.* London: CIPD.

Taylor, P. and Thackwray, B. (1995) *Investors in People Explained.* London: Kogan Page.

Thompson, A. (2001) 'Too much apple pie?', *People Management*, 3 May. **http://www.peoplemanagement.co.uk/pm/articles/2001/05/932.htm**.

Thompson, I. (2005) *Training Evaluation: Making it Happen.* **http://www.cipd.co.uk/subjects/training/trneval/treva.htm**.

Tracey, W.R. (1968) *Evaluating Training and Development Systems.* New York: American Management Association.

Tregaskis, O. and Dany, F. (1996) 'A comparison of HRD in France and the UK', *Journal of European Industrial Training*, 20, 1: 20–30.

UKCES (2008) *Simplification of Skills in England: Expert Advice to Government on Simplification of the Post-compulsory Skills System for Employers.* Norwich: The Stationery Office.

Ulrich, J.G., Flemming, S., Granath, R.O. and Krekel, E.M. (2006) 'Number of newly concluded training contracts drops to lowest level since German reunification', **www.bibb.de**, 16 March.

Unwin, L. (2004) 'Growing beans with Thoreau: rescuing skills and vocational education from the UK's deficit approach', *Oxford Review of Education*, 30, 1: 147–60.

Van den Berg, N., Meijers, F. and Sprengers, M. (2006) 'More vocational education and supplementary training through equalisation of costs?', *Human Resource Development International*, 9, 1: 5–24.

Walton, J. (1999) *Strategic Human Resource Development.* Harlow: Pearson Education.

Wang, G.G. and Spitzer, D.R. (2005) 'Human resource development measurement and evaluation: looking back and moving forward', *Advances in Developing Human Resources*, 7, 1: 5–16.

Warr, P., Bird, M.W. and Rackham, N. (1970) *Evaluation of Management Training.* Aldershot: Gower.

Warren, C. (2006) 'Curtain Call', *People Management*, 23 March. **http://www.peoplemanagement.co.uk/pm/articles/2006/03/curtaincall.htm**.

Westwood, A. (2001) 'Drawing a line – who is going to train our workforce?' in D. Wilson, E. Lank, A. Westwood, E. Keep, C. Leadbetter and M. Sloman (eds) *The Future of Learning for Work: Executive Briefing.* London: CIPD, pp. 17–22.

Whitmore, J. (2002) *Coaching for Performance*. London: Nicholas Brearley.

Whittington, R. (1993) *What is Strategy and Why Does it Matter?* London: Routledge.

Wilson, J. (ed.) (1999) *Human Resource Development*. London: Kogan Page.

Wilson, R.A. and Briscoe, G. (2004) 'The impact of human capital on economic growth: a review' in *Impact of Education and Training: Third Report of Vocational Training Research in Europe: Background Report*. Luxembourg: Office for Official Publications of the European Communities, pp. 13–65.

Wolf, A. (2002) *Does Education Matter: Myths About Education and Economic Growth*. London: Penguin.

Wolf, A. (2004) 'Education and economic performance: simplistic theories and their policy consequences', *Oxford Review of Economic Policy*, 20, 2: 315.

Woodall, J. and Winstanley, D. (eds) (2004) 'New frontiers in HRD', *Routledge Studies in Human Resource Development*. Abingdon: Routledge.

Yeung, A. and Berman, B. (1997) 'Adding value through human resources: reorienting human resource management to drive through business performance', *Human Resource Management*, 36, 3: 321–35.

Young, M.F.D. (2003) 'National qualifications frameworks as a global phenomenon: a comparative perspective', *Journal of Education and Work*, 16, 3: 223–37.

For multiple-choice questions, exercises and annotated weblinks related to this topic, visit **www.pearsoned.co.uk/mymanagementlab**.

Chapter 9

Management and leadership development

Mairi Watson

Objectives

- To explain the meanings and nature of management and leadership development in organisations.
- To acknowledge the significance of management and leadership development to organisational success.
- To contrast key conceptual approaches to management and leadership development.
- To examine the methods, techniques and processes used to develop managers and leaders.
- To draw attention to the way management and leadership development can be varied to meet different needs and in different contexts.
- To speculate about the future direction of management and leadership development in the UK and beyond.

Introduction

> The development of management and leadership skills is seen as most the important priority in meeting business objectives in the next two years.
>
> (CIPD 2009: 2)

While there has been significant interest in the field of management and leadership development (MLD) in recent years, there are still many questions unanswered, and areas unexplored. This chapter will assist you in developing your understanding of MLD within increasingly complex and diverse organisational contexts and challenging economic circumstances. To this end, the chapter identifies issues that must be explored in order to develop a critical analysis of MLD and concludes with questions, exercises and a case study. These will help you to review and consolidate what you have learned.

Defining management and leadership development (MLD)

The changing nature of management and leadership

Practically, managers and leaders have to deal with the ambiguities and complexities that arise from tensions in their position in the organisation. They have to deal with the different aims, expectations and interests of those they manage and those who set their goals. Furthermore, conceptions of 'management' or 'leadership' have changed significantly. Recent work has suggested that the required competences of managers and leaders are converging (Salaman, 2004) and neat distinctions between the roles of managers and leaders are not possible. In the 1990s it was common to see typologies which dichotomised the nature of management and leadership roles, emphasising the visionary and inspirational nature of leadership functions against the practical and controlling nature of management. While appealing, this type of work caricatures rather than describes the roles and functions of managers and leaders. Furthermore, this leadership and management split is based on dubious assumptions about the structure of organisations as long hierarchical chains (Mabey & Finch-Lees, 2008). Arguably the dominance of a Western view of leadership that reinforces the split between leadership and management does so without considering the potential range of leadership behaviours that can be observed across the globe (House *et al.*, 2002; Mabey and Finch-Lees, 2008). Increasingly, the blurring of management and leadership roles has led to a redefinition of the roles and competences of those who organise, control and inspire across organisations (Salaman, 2004). For example, Boddy (2005: 13) identifies several different positions in a hierarchy for managers in organisations with the amount of management, leadership and non-management work varying within these positions:

● *Performing direct operations*: this is likely to contain some element of managerial work but in lower level jobs this will be limited. Managerial work may be greater where this applies to professions such as lawyers, accountants or to small business owners who may perform significant levels of direct operations alongside managerial work.

● *Managing staff on direct operations*: this includes supervisors or first line managers who have responsibility for staff performing the daily operations of the business.

● *Managing managers*: usually this means 'middle managers' who are expected to ensure supervisors achieve organisational goals through monitoring and supporting. They also provide a link to the board/those who manage the business and ensure information flows up and down appropriately

● *Managing the business*: this is the work of a small group of people at the top of the organisation who are most responsible for the overall performance and direction of the organisation.

If, as Boddy argues, leadership is the activity of generating effort and commitment towards meeting organisational objectives, at which level does leadership start and management end?

While it is difficult to draw a clear line between management and leadership, using Boddy's typology you can see that there are leadership *and* management responsibilities at all levels of the organisation. Thus leadership is no longer the preserve of senior figures in the organisation. Leadership acts can be observed at all levels, and leadership is dispersed rather than concentrated in the hands of managers. Current thinking, therefore, favours a line of argument that sees 'leadership is a necessary quality of managers at all levels' (Salaman, 2004: 77; Lee, 2003). MLD therefore has to address the complexities of varied managerial and leadership roles and the diverse needs of the individuals who occupy them (Hales, 1993). In other words, any investment in development has to be congruent with the 'reality' of what managers do, and not (however well intentioned) be rooted in abstract or increasingly redundant models of what others might think they should do or used to do (Salaman, 1995). In short, MLD has to 'measure up' (Tyler, 2004: 152).

In addressing issues in *management and leadership development* (MLD) this chapter therefore conflates the titles of management and leadership on purpose. This signifies that the roles, responsibilities and development of managers and leaders are best considered as one single topic, which may, over history have been popular as one (management development 1985–1990s) and then another (leadership development 1990s–2000s), but now there is a clear recognition in the literature of the overlapping and intertwining nature of the roles which makes distinguishing between the two less important. This is appropriate since management and the work of managers and leaders is not a simple process but a complex matter which is individual and organisation specific (Mumford and Gold, 2004).

What is management and leadership development?

There are many definitions of MLD but most contemporary definitions share the characteristics contained in the view of development suggested by Thomson *et al.* (2001: 10):

> We have used the term in a comprehensive sense to encompass the different ways in which managers improve their capabilities. It includes management education, which is often taken to refer to formal, structured learning in an institutional context, and management training which is often used to mean acquiring knowledge and skills related to work requirements, also by formal means. But our use of the term 'development' goes beyond the sum of these to mean a wider process than the formal learning of knowledge and skills, which includes informal and experiential modes of human capital formation. Management development is thus a multi-faceted process in which some aspects are easier to identify and measure than others.

This definition emphasises the multifaceted nature of MLD as something that involves not just formal training but also broader, informal processes of learning, including learning from experience. We shall discuss these in more detail later in the chapter.

Moreover, MLD has a diverse range of purposes (Burgoyne and Jackson, 1997; Hill and Stewart, 2007). As well as organisations ensuring that development is linked to their philosophies and strategic objectives, decision makers must also take account of individual needs, expectations and aspirations. This can often be a difficult balance to achieve and frequently becomes a source of tension (Sturges, 2004; Currie, 1999; Woodall and Winstanley, 1998). Narrowly defined, its central purpose is to provide the structures and systems necessary for individual development. From this individual perspective, engaging in MLD is linked to personal career, self-esteem, prestige and job security. From an organisational perspective, MLD serves a much broader agenda. For example, it is viewed as a 'tool' or device for attaining competitive advantage by enhancing knowledge and skills which in turn lead to improvements in efficiency, productivity and innovation. It can also be used as a device to 'engineer' organisational change, especially culture change. However, reconciling and managing the contradictions and incongruities that sometimes emerge when organisations seek to balance organisational goals and personal aspirations is a major challenge. For instance, senior managers who are seeking a quick-fix solution to a deep-rooted managerial or organisational problem will often consult with development 'experts', who are only too pleased to solve the problem by introducing them to the latest development fad. When the 'quick-fix' solution fails to produce the anticipated results or (worse) exacerbates an existing problem, MLD is at risk of being undermined and discredited (Roberts and McDonald, 1995; Currie, 1999). It is therefore vital that organisations view MLD as a long-term investment and select an approach that is suited to their specific needs and requirements.

The strategic significance of MLD

> Competition and the pace of change in business require continuous improvement – and that means continuous learning . . . Today learning and development opportunities rank high among the concerns of talented employees. Support for management development in whatever form is perhaps the strongest weapon that a business can use in its struggle to retain the best employees. (Stern, 2002: 2)

While the rhetoric of the strategic significance of MLD is appealing, unravelling this in practice is challenging. There are two issues that emerge in the discussion of the extent to which MLD can support the achievement of business goals and intentions:

- Can MLD contribute to business goals?
- To what extent do organisations invest in MLD?

These are related and significant issues in establishing the business contribution of MLD and each will now be considered in turn.

Can MLD contribute to the achievement of business goals?

There are those who argue strongly in favour of MLD's contribution to the achievement of strategic goals. There is evidence to suggest that some employers identify strategically driven MLD, implemented over time, as making a significant difference to business performance (CIPD, 2004). MLD is usually credited with a role in organisational success and strategic achievement as it can develop successful business leaders. On the other hand, many organisations do not understand the relationship between management capability and business performance (CIPD, 2002: 5) nor the value of the processes of MLD (Clarke *et al.*, 2004). Thus, while crediting MLD with positive business effects is appealing, it is by no means settled (Tyler, 2004) and a belief in its effectiveness is not always supported by evidence of tangible successes (Clarke *et al.*, 2004). Thus, while investment in MLD in some larger organisations (see Unilever example below) often amounts to a sizeable proportion of the HR budget, it can be argued that companies continue to support such training and development largely as an as an act of faith (Tamkin and Hillage, 1999). To be fair, in part this reliance of faith can be explained by the challenges in evaluating MLD (Barker, 1997), which while important, is not always fatal to the argument that MLD makes a difference:

> Despite all these difficulties, it can be predicted with some confidence that if an organization carefully cultivates the development of its managerial cadre, this will, in time, lead to improvements in morale, motivation and corporate capability, which will in turn, and other things being equal, lead to a more productive organization. (Mabey and Ramirez, 2005: 1068)

Furthermore, a number of research studies have identified characteristics of organisations that report a link between MLD and business performance. While this does not prove the link between MLD and performance, it develops our understanding of the powerful rhetoric that surrounds MLD and its strategic halo (Mabey & Finch-Lees, 2008).

- A careful alignment between MLD and a longer-term strategic focus (Clarke *et al.*, 2004; Brown, 2005; Mabey, 2005; Mabey and Ramirez, 2005), rather than with the shorter-term learning needs of individuals (Tate, 2004).
- A sustained, proactive investment in MLD as an organisational priority with board level support (Mabey, 2005).
- Learning linked to identified behavioural competences which support business purposes (Salaman, 2004).

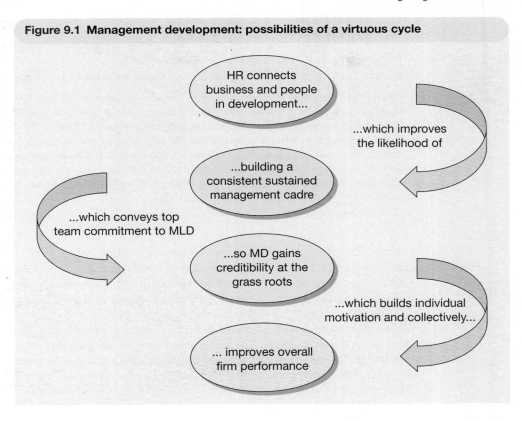

Figure 9.1 Management development: possibilities of a virtuous cycle

- An emphasis on learning tied to the workplace, or particular context, or the managers and leader being developed (Antonacopoulou and Bento, 2004; Mole, 2004; Brown, 2007).
- An understanding and appreciation of the multiple stakeholders and their multiple interests in HRD (Burgoyne and Jackson, 1997; Stansfield and Stewart, 2007).

These four aspects strengthen the 'virtuous cycle' sometimes argued for MLD (Figure 9.1) to support the link between investment in MLD and organisational performance.

To what extent do organisations invest in MLD?

Some organisations, as suggested in the previous section, invest heavily in MLD. An illustration of how MLD is being integrated with and used to support business strategy can be found in the major international company Unilever (see Box 9.1).

Box 9.1   A management development strategy for Unilever

Unilever is a huge international organisation with 1000 brands, employing some 255,000 people in 300 operating units across 88 countries. In recent years the business strategy has been refocused to achieve significant economies of scale, reduce the number of products offered and increase penetration in successful product markets.

This refocusing has had a major impact on HR strategies and policies. One area that the company has identified as a priority has been the development of its managers as 'global players' with the ability to implement the new business plan.

Success in developing managers is based on the following principles:

- Management development is a business responsibility.
- Responsibility for development is shared between Unilever and the manager.

Box 9.1 continued

- Individuals drive their own learning and development.
- Explicit responsibilities are placed on line and senior managers for developing their managers.

Unilever aims to create a 'seamless' system of management development – delivered in one language worldwide in a way that facilitates the transfer of people across different operating units. A framework of worldwide competences and skills is available on the Internet for managers to plan their personal development. An emphasis is placed on managers developing both professional and generalist skills that are transferable to different global contexts. Development activity is closely linked to performance management and measurable outcomes. Managers are required to produce an improvement development plan and advancement is tightly linked to meeting performance targets.

Source: Adapted from Reitsma (2001).

Unilever is representative of one type of approach to MLD evident in the UK context. However, Mumford and Gold (2004) and Burgoyne (1988) paint a picture that is representative of a broader spectrum of organisational behaviours in UK MLD, which argues that while some organisations invest heavily, a more piecemeal, unstructured approach is more common.

Mumford and Gold (2004) describe three different types or 'levels' of approach (see Box 9.2) which emphasise a generic approach to MLD allowing portability of skills between management jobs (Ramirez, 2004). The increasing emphasis on planning as the levels progress supports the development of a strategic approach outlined above. In a similar manner, Burgoyne's (1988) early work argued that MLD may be considered as progressing through different levels of maturity (see Table 9.1). At Level 1 there is no systematic approach to MLD, and at Level 6 MLD not only shapes and informs corporate strategy, it actually enhances the process of strategy formation. Both argue that in practice, MLD approaches for most organisations rarely extend beyond informal levels of development. Those who reach Levels 5 and 6 in Burgoyne's model find it is 'often precariously achieved and lost' (1988: 44). Burgoyne argues that to progress through the levels of maturity to the point where MLD is making the fullest contribution to organisation development demands a much more holistic approach. In this approach, both 'hard' (roles, duties, technical competence, etc.) and 'soft' (career, quality of life, ethos, values, etc.) managerial issues are considered when framing approaches to development.

Activity

Study Mumford and Burgoyne's models. Identify where you believe your organisation is positioned in relation to the different 'types' and 'levels of maturity'.

- What action would they have to take to develop a strategic approach to MLD?

Box 9.2

Type 1: 'Informal managerial' – incidental and accidental processes
Characteristics:
- occurs within manager's activities
- explicit intention is task performance
- no clear development objectives
- unstructured in development terms
- not planned in advance
- owned by managers.

Development consequences:
- learning real, direct, unconscious, insufficient.

> **Box 9.2 continued**
>
> **Type 2: 'Integrated managerial' – opportunistic processes**
> *Characteristics:*
> - occurs within managerial activities
> - explicit intention is both task performance and development
> - clear development objectives
> - structured for development by manager and direct report
> - planned beforehand or reviewed subsequently as learning experiences
> - owned by managers.
>
> *Development consequences:*
> - learning is real, direct, conscious, more substantial.
>
> **Type 3: 'Formalised management development' – planned processes**
> *Characteristics:*
> - often away from normal managerial activities
> - explicit intention is development
> - clear development objectives
> - structured for development by developers
> - planned beforehand or reviewed subsequently as learning experiences
> - owned more by developers than managers.
>
> *Development consequences:*
> - learning may be real (through a job) or detached (through a course)
> - is more likely to be conscious, relatively infrequent.
>
> *Source*: Mumford and Gold (2004).

Sadly, fragmented approaches to MLD are all too common (Mole, 2000; Clarke *et al.*, 2004). Such approaches contribute to the failure of MLD to fulfil personal and organisational expectations (Temporal, 1990; Mumford, 1997; Mole, 2000). Not only do they waste investment, time and effort, there is also a risk of damage to existing levels of morale and commitment among managers as efforts to develop them founder on organisational barriers to change (Doyle, 1995, 2000a). As Molander and Winterton (1994: 89) contend:

> Where such conditions exist, what is required is an organisation-wide assessment of the elements in the culture which require changing, followed by an effective change programme. Focusing attention on individual managers . . . will not bring about required change. In this case the organisation itself should be the focus of change.

The need for a broader and more contextualised perspective of MLD is central to a strategic approach (Hill and Stewart, 2007). Many approaches to development have characteristics similar to Mumford's Type 1 and Type 3 development and Burgoyne's Levels 1 and 2 and accordingly may be labelled as *piecemeal*. Implementing piecemeal approaches will almost certainly lead to inefficient and ineffective development.

Piecemeal approaches to development are characterised by the following:

- There is no MLD infrastructure. Development is not linked to business strategy. Activities are unrelated, and lack overall direction or philosophy. They fail to reinforce each other, and reduce the potential for organisational effectiveness.

Table 9.1 Levels of maturity or organisational management development

1 No systematic management development	2 Isolated management development	3 Integrated and coordinated structural and development tactics	4 A management development strategy to implement corporate policy	5 Management development strategy input to corporate policy formation	6 Strategic development of the management of corporate policy
No systematic or deliberate management development in a structural or developmental sense; total reliance on , *laissez-faire* uncontrived processes of management development	There are isolated and ad hoc tactical management development activities, of either structural or developmental kinds, or both, in response to local problems, crises, or sporadically identified general problems	The specific management development tactics that impinge directly on the individual manager, of career structure management, and of assisting learning, are integrated and coordinated	A management strategy plays its part in implementing corporate policies through managerial human resource planning, and providing a development strategic framework and direction for the tactics of career structure management and of learning, education and training	Management development processes feed information into corporate policy decision-making processes on the organisation's managerial assets, strengths, weaknesses and potential, and contribute to the forecasting and analysis of the manageability of proposed projects, ventures, changes	Management development processes enhance the nature and quality of corporate policy-forming processes, which they also inform and help implement

Source: from Management development for the individual and the organisation, *Personnel Management*, June, pp. 40–44 (Burgoyne, J, 1988), with permission from Dr J. G. Burgoyne.

- Development often focuses on the needs of the organisation, and fails to meet the learning needs and aspirations of individuals and groups.
- Development is largely defined in terms of a range of universal, off-the-shelf internal or external courses.
- There is tacit support for management education and training because it is seen as a 'good thing to be doing' irrespective of organisational needs.
- There is a lack of common vision among those responsible for MLD. For instance, some managers see development as a central part of their job, others see it as peripheral and a nuisance.
- MLD effort can be wasted because it is used as a solution to the wrong problem. Rather than developing managers, the correct solution may be to change aspects of organisation structure or systems.
- It is difficult to evaluate the effectiveness of a piecemeal approach that lacks clear direction and established objectives.

Designing MLD

MLD policies

> Management development will fail if there is no clear policy.   (Margerison, 1991: 3)

We saw in the previous section the importance of organisational commitment to MLD. Policy statements are useful because they express an organisation's commitment to development, and set out clearly a framework within which it can take place (Mabey, 2002). They make explicit who is responsible for development, the support that is available, methods used etc. Research has also suggested that those organisations having a formal policy for developing their managers undertook significantly more management training than did companies without (Thomson *et al.*, 2001).

An MLD policy will normally include the following (Mumford and Gold, 2004; Clarke *et al.*, 2004):

- *A statement of purpose for MLD.* Why are we undertaking MLD? How does it link to our strategic intentions? What is the framework that supports our MLD?
- *Definition of those to be identified as managers/leaders.* Who will be targeted? Will our provision be tailored or standardised?
- *A list of the processes to be used in MLD.* What will be done? When will it be done? Who will be responsible and accountable?

Each of these issues will be considered as this chapter progresses.

However, what is sometimes less clear is the extent to which organisations are committed to and prepared to implement their policies. Policies may be viewed with some scepticism – especially during times of radical downsizing involving the loss of managerial jobs (Thomson *et al.*, 2001). Moreover, organisations face challenges in aligning their needs with individual career requirements as careers become more individualised (Sturges, 2004). There are also difficulties in evaluating the effectiveness of policies in achieving desired outcomes (Tyler, 2004; Hamblin, 2007). The difficulties associated with evaluating MLD outcomes will be explored later in the chapter.

Does your organisation have an MLD policy? If so, locate it and identify the extent to which these three aspects are present? If it does not have a policy, what has been the impact on MLD outcomes?

Stakeholders in MLD

Having determined its policy guidelines, the next step for the organisation is to consider how it should *approach* the development of its managers. If a development programme is to be successfully planned and implemented, there has to be clear and unambiguous allocation of responsibility and a willingness to accept that responsibility by the parties involved. Traditionally, responsibility for development has rested with the HR function, with some input from the manager's boss through the performance management system (Duerden, 2006) (see below and Chapter 13). The individual manager was often passive in the process: they were only required to 'turn up and be developed'.

However, to be effective, development demands the involvement of a range of stakeholders, or 'helpers', each of whom will have an impact on the development process and its outcomes (Mabey and Salaman, 1995; Mumford, 1997; Burgoyne and Jackson, 1997). Figure 9.2 identifies a number of key stakeholders who each share a measure of responsibility. Clarifying these at the outset is central to ensuring continued support for the process and for minimising resistance.

An active process of discussion and negotiation should ensure that each set of stakeholders accepts and owns a share of the responsibility for supporting the process, for example through supporting the manager, setting development objectives, planning and implementing the process. However, as Mabey and Salaman (1995: 176) point out, the

Figure 9.2 Stakeholders in MLD

Reasons for supporting	Stakeholder	Reasons for resisting
Personal development, status/prestige, improved career, break from the norm	**Manager/leader**	Waste of time, unwillingness to accept new responsibilities
Improved management and direction, expresses commitment to development	**Team**	Resistance to changes, absence of manager when training, waste of time
Solves performance problems, commitment to development, reward/incentive	**Line managers**	Creates line problems (manager's absence)
Strengthens skills, opportunity to demonstrate professional knowledge, improves political ties in organisation	**HR Professionals**	Might be able to see better alternative
Demonstrates action to other stakeholders, improves financial performance	**Senior managers**	Might not be sufficiently tied to the bottom line
Concrete message about commitment to employees, improved financial performance	**Boards**	May be disruptive, cause divisions
Financial opportunity	**External**	Limited involvement in design
Demonstrates commitment to improving national skills	**Funding agencies**	Doesn't generate sufficient new knowledge or skills, not tied to national standards

Source: Adapted from Burgoyne and Jackson (1997: 63).

linkages between each stakeholder are complex and each will 'help shape the ethos and practice of training and development within organizations'.

Activity

Prepare a list of those who are responsible for your development.

● How clearly are their roles delineated and communicated?

● How effective is the support you receive?

● Does it need to be improved in any way?

Supportive frameworks for MLD

In those organisations that take a structured approach to MLD, there are a number of frameworks that can be used to support MLD policies and their implementation. Three will be considered here: competency frameworks, career development and appraisals.

Competency frameworks in MLD

Competency-based development (CBD) in MLD provides a formalised and structured method for informing the development of managers and leaders. Competency frameworks describe the knowledge, skills and behaviours that are required for an individual to perform their role effectively (Woodruffe, 1992). Their strengths lie in accepting the argument that while it may not be possible to teach leadership, it is possible to develop the skills and competencies of leadership (Mole, 2004) This approach to development was introduced with the aim of improving the overall effectiveness of UK managers following severe criticism of their performance and its impact on the national economy in the late 1980s. National standards for management competency (competency here is defined as an ability to apply knowledge and skills to a required standard of performance) were originally devised in the early 1990s by the then lead body for management standards – the Management Charter Initiative (MCI). These national standards have undergone several periods of redevelopment and renegotiation and now, as standards for Management and Leadership, are part of the National Occupational Standards Framework (**www.ukstandards.org**) and form the basis for NVQs, SVQs and VRQs. There has been considerable effort in the development of the standards to introduce some contextualisation – for example, the Management and Leadership Standards for 2008 are divided into nine further categories to take account of different trade, sector and professional specialisms in management.

Locate the National Occupational Standards for Management and Leadership at **www.ukstandards.org**.

Which category is most relevant for your occupational specialism? Could you find one that fits?

Since their inception, competence-based national standards have attracted considerable criticism. Some have questioned how far competences can be generalised beyond a particular organisational context (Woodall and Winstanley, 1998; Mole, 2004). As Kilcourse (1994: 14) remarks: 'competencies thought to have general application will fit where they touch when it comes to specific organisations'. Thus CBD can generate frustration and resentment when the competence-based approach is seen not to be appropriate or relevant to the needs of managers in their organisational situation (Stewart and Hamlin, 1992a; Currie and Darby, 1995; Antonacopoulou and Fitzgerald, 1996; Loan-Clarke, 1996). or where managers who may be viewed as competent in one contextual setting are deemed 'incompetent' when reviewed in another context.

Others have also argued that there has been too much emphasis on assessment and not enough on learning (Antonacopoulou and Bento, 2004) or have expressed concerns about the way competence-based approaches are seen to operate (cost, time, bureaucracy, inflexibility etc.). Further, the view that competences are either scientifically neutral or objectively measurable has been challenged (Mabey and Finch-Lees, 2008) especially where they reinforce gender stereotypes of management behaviour (Rees and Garnsey, 2003).

Despite the criticisms, the notion of competence-based development has now been established within the framework of UK MLD (Thomson *et al.*, 2001). Recent evidence suggests that there are moves away from the generic model originally developed by MCI to a more flexible and contextually based approach such as that defined in the latest standards. However, alongside the national standards, many organisations prefer to 'do their own thing'. Rather than engage with a somewhat costly, bureaucratic, prescriptive and rigid framework of national standards, some organisations have developed competence frameworks for managers that are more fragmented and differentiated as they seek to adapt to changing individual circumstances, (Sparrow and Bognanno, 1994; Roberts, 1995).

If one considers organisational competency frameworks as simply 'high-level job analysis' (Mole, 2004), competencies can be used as predictors of successful management and leadership behaviour and form the basis for formal learning interventions, particularly if they are not considered to be 'a panacea for all management development ills but . . . one approach which may be taken with others' (Currie and Darby, 1995: 17). Thus competency based development can provide a framework for decision making about the most appropriate ways to develop managers and leaders and inform policy making and implementation.

Activity	List what you see as the pros and cons of Competency Based Development (CBD).

- To what extent would CBD make a difference to the way managers in your organisation are currently being developed?

- If your organisation already operates CBD, how effective has it been?

Career development and MLD

MLD policies can only be effective if careful consideration is given to career paths and opportunities for promotion and progression (Mumford, 1997; Margerison, 1994a). In the past, career development very much reflected more traditional organisational structures and cultures. Hierarchical progression was seen to be upwards through clearly defined junior, middle and senior management roles based on tenure and the possession of specialist skills and the display of patterns of expected behaviours. However, in the face of radical organisational change such pathways are now giving way to a more uncertain and less clearly defined progression where 'automatic' promotion is no longer available to many. Citing research by Benbow, Thomson *et al.*, (2001: 181) capture the mood amongst UK and US managers about their future career development:

> A high proportion of respondents do not feel in control of their future career development. The pace of change over the last decade has shattered career and financial expectations, generating a need for individuals to re-examine many of the inherited wisdoms of the past. The demise of the job for life and the trend towards a wholly flexible employment market are clear examples of the extent to which new agendas are being set.

Such concerns reflect in part the emphasis now being placed on managers to ensure their employability and marketability. This in turn reflects a redefinition of the psychological contract that exists between managers and their employing organisation (Herriot and Pemberton, 1995). In terms of career progression, the emphasis is shifting towards individuals who display greater flexibility, adaptability and personal characteristics such as emotional resilience (Watson, 2002). Some will find themselves facing a 'boundaryless' career in which there will be less job security and career progression opportunities will be limited. Instead, career progression is likely to involve a greater emphasis on horizontal or diagonal rather than vertical movement, e.g. projects, overseas secondments and postings, departmental and job shifts, internal consultancy roles, acting as mentors and coaches etc. (Arnold, 1997; Thomson *et al.*, 2001). The career, in short, is now an individual rather than a corporate experience (Sturges, 2004).

Performance management and MLD

The principles and structures of performance management are covered in detail in Chapter 13 but performance management systems can also provide the basis of MLD and allow a more individualised approach. They have the potential to motivate and reward managers who contribute to strategic goals and objectives and, by implication, to exert sanctions on or 'punish' those who fail to deliver anticipated performance levels. This is leading a number of organisations to link their systems of reward more closely to the attainment of higher levels of competence, which is one way of overcoming 'the subjectivity and arbitrariness of assessment' (Hendry, 1995: 309). The achievement of objectives is closely linked to management training and education, which act to provide the skills and knowledge required to meet objectives. Performance appraisal provides the forum for identifying development needs. It also serves as the mechanism for feeding back information to managers about their current levels of performance, enabling them to identify and negotiate adjustments or further development needs. However, as Thomson *et al.* (2001) point out, issues such as lack of line manager support and weaknesses in the appraisal process mean that 'individuals rarely walk away from such discussions with clear plans for personal development' (p. 126).

Activity	Have you got a personal development plan? If you haven't, make a mental note to discuss this with your boss at your next appraisal interview. If you have got a plan, when was it last reviewed? Is it still valid and up to date?

In addition to performance appraisal, another method of establishing a personal development plan is through a development centre (DC). DCs are used to determine career development needs and talent potential (Harrison, 2009). These 'centres' are 'workshops which measure the abilities of participants against the agreed success criteria for a job or role' (Lee and Beard, 1994) and diagnose individual training needs (Munchus and McArthur, 1991). They are quite distinct from assessment centres, which are used to inform decisions about selection or promotion. The main aim of a development centre is to 'obtain the best possible indication of people's actual or potential competence to perform at the target job or job level' (Woodruffe, 1993: 2). In that sense they are useful both to the organisation and the individual in clarifying values, motivation and potential. The result is the crafting of a development plan.

Most development centres operate in the following way:

- There is careful selection of job-related criteria. These may be in the form of competences, dimensions, attributes, critical success factors, etc.
- A group of managers is identified and brought together in the form of a workshop normally lasting one or two days. In the workshops a series of diagnostic instruments and/or multiple assessment techniques are administered that aim to measure an individual's ability to perform against the job-related criteria. These can take the form of psychometric tests, planning exercises, in-tray exercises, interviews, games, or simulations.
- A team of trained assessors observe and measure performance, evaluate and provide structured feedback and guidance to individuals.
- After the workshop, line managers and/or trainers utilise the feedback to help the individual construct a personal development plan.

Although the use of development centres is growing, there have been a number of criticisms which tend to revolve around: assessment techniques that do not relate to the task or job, poor organisation, poorly trained assessors, ineffective feedback and the lack of follow-up action (Dulewicz, 1991; Whiddett and Branch, 1993).

Choosing who to develop

A growing interest in 'talent management' (Tansey *et al.*, 2007; CIPD, 2009; see also Chapter 5) has fostered an exclusive/targeted approach in many organisations where high potential individuals are the focus of considerable development investment (Clarke *et al.*, 2004). As businesses

Figure 9.3 MLD strategy framework

		Who?	
		Targeted	*Inclusive*
What?	*Individualised content*	**High potential tailored:** structured, targeted, individual, tailored activities to aid succession planning	**Self-motivated:** no prescribed methods or content, development open to all, individual motivation central
	Corporate consistency	**High potential programme:** planned and consistent activities driven by business needs and corporate message	**Generic programmes:** develops organisational capabilities, available to all

Source: Adapted from Clarke *et al.* (2004: 287).

become contextually more complex, those with talent and leadership potential are more difficult to find (Strack and Krinks, 2008) and so identifying and developing internal staff with high potential becomes vital to business success. Clarke *et al.*, (2004) argue that there are alternative ways in which to development high potential managers, and that these ought to run alongside more inclusive approaches to develop a balanced approach to MLD. They identify four separate approaches (Figure 9.3) that support strategic objectives in businesses. These approaches are not mutually exclusive, rather they identify that each are appropriate for different purposes and different levels of managers and leaders.

However, many organisations are not sufficiently focused when identifying their target population for MLD (Mabey, 2002; Clarke *et al.*, 2004). Given the sensitivity that surrounds role identification and the prestige that is often attached to inclusion in MLD programmes (Mabey and Finch-Lees, 2008), issues of power and identity influence decision makers. However, having devised and communicated a clear policy for MLD, those responsible for implementing development need to think through and be able to justify why they are developing an individual manager (or a group of managers).

One way to assess the extent of MLD needs is suggested by Odiorne (1984), who advocates a *portfolio* approach to development to improve the overall efficiency of the process and ensure the optimal allocation of resources (see Box 9.3). This requires organisations to make a range of decisions and develop a 'mix' of contingent objectives and techniques arranged to match the profile of the management team in the organisation.

Box 9.3	A portfolio approach to development

'Stars': high-performing, high-potential managers

Aim:
- create challenge
- provide incentives and reward
- allocate adequate resources and effort.

'Workhorses': high-performing, limited-potential managers

Aim:
- emphasise value and worth of experience
- motivate and reassure
- utilise experience on assignments, projects, coaching.

'Problem employees': high-potential, underperforming managers

Aim:
- identify weaknesses
- channel resources to address weaknesses
- regular performance monitoring and feedback.

'Deadwood': low-performing, low-potential managers

Aim:
- identify weaknesses, resolvable?
- if not, consider release, early retirement, demotion.

Source: Adapted from Odiorne (1984).

Choosing what to do

Once the target population has been identified, a number of questions can be asked so as to tailor provision for the groups or individuals (Odiorne, 1984).

What is being developed?

- Does the programme seek to develop new attitudes and values, for example after a takeover or merger?
- Does the programme aim to develop technical, financial, business or interpersonal skills? What are the priorities?
- Does the programme seek to change existing managerial behaviours and styles to reflect an internal organisational restructuring, such as the introduction of new technology?

Where will the development take place?

- Should development be on-the-job in the office, factory or sales territory, or off-the-job in a residential hall, academic institution or individual's home, or a combination of all of these?

What are the most appropriate techniques to achieve the best fit between individual and organisational requirements?

- What are the most cost-effective/appropriate techniques available?
- How much scope is there to accommodate individual learning needs and preferences?

- How much choice is delegated to the individual over the choice of development techniques?
- How is conflict resolved between individual and organisational needs?

Answering these questions will help the business decide the most appropriate range of activities to undertake, for when people refer to MLD, they usually refer to the activities that are planned and deliberate (Mumford and Gold, 2004). However, there is more to MLD than that. MLD methods are often divided into formal and informal (Woodall and Winstanley, 1998), in house or external (Storey, 2004), or taught and experiential (Antonacopoulou and Bento, 2004) and MLD delivery can be as individual as the organisation in which it is based. However, MLD usually includes (Mabey and Thompson, 2000; Mabey, 2004; CIPD, 2008b):

- *Formal learning and education*: specific interactions designed to address and achieve specific competences e.g. internal skills programmes, external courses, seminars or conferences, e-learning, formal qualifications(from NVQs to MBAs).
- *Informal learning*: work-based methods designed to structure the informal learning that takes place in the workplace e.g. mentoring or coaching, in company job rotation, external assignments, placements or secondments.

Most of the interventions that are available, be they formal or informal, contain one or more of the following aspects (Storey, 2004): first, learning about leadership theory and its application, second, self and/or team analysis through questionnaires and instruments, and third, experiential learning and simulation through team based activities (often outdoor). The transitional process from learning through analysis to application forms the core of best practice MLD. It is widely recognised that central to the success of MLD is contextualisation to the role and organisation of the individual (Duerden, 2006).

Formal methods of delivering MLD

Formal methods of MLD rely heavily on input from trainers, teachers and other 'experts' and the MLD industry is big business (Mole, 2004). MLD is often seen as synonymous with formal education. The emphasis on formal education makes it easier to demonstrate MLD's link to the strategic intentions of the organisation as participation can be clearly identified and tracked through performance management systems. Such formal MLD can take place 'on-the-job' – within the workplace environment, for instance at a training centre, or it can take place 'off-the-job' – away from the workplace in a college, university or conference/seminar (Woodall, 2000; Mumford and Gold, 2004). The previous chapter explained the differences in on and off the job approaches to learning generally, but here we consider MLD specifically.

However, there is considerable debate about whether 'teaching' leadership is an effective way of developing managers (Antonacopoulou and Bento, 2004). Programmes or courses may be the least appropriate way to develop individuals or groups of managers and may even generate resistance and frustration (Roberts and McDonald, 1995; Mole, 1996, 2000; Currie, 1999). Furthermore, it is debatable whether leadership can be taught, or must be developed experientially (Burgoyne and Reynolds, 1997; Antonacopoulou and Bento, 2004). While formal programmes may be effective in giving knowledge about leadership, they are less effective at developing leadership skills *per se* (Doyle and Smith, 1999). Typically, formalised methods are less contextualised or applied, yet the most effective are those that take account of both the specific organisational contexts in which the managers and leaders operate, and the outcomes for which those leaders and managers are responsible (Mole, 2004). One way in which to build this comprehensive picture to effectively inform MLD is through competency frameworks, described and discussed in the previous section.

Research by Burgoyne and Stuart (1991) reveals that the following methods are likely to be used in more formalised and structured approaches (in order of predominance of use):

- lectures;
- games and simulations;
- projects;
- case studies;
- experiential (analysis of experience);
- guided reading;
- role playing;
- seminars;
- programmed instruction (computerised/packaged).

Although these methods are widely used in education and training, they can often appear to be abstract, detached and somewhat artificial in nature (Burgoyne and Stuart, 1991). Criticisms have been levelled at the relevance of much of the taught material and the problems of transferring knowledge and skills into the reality of the workplace (Roberts and McDonald, 1995; Mumford, 1997).

Corporate universities

Corporate universities (CUs) have, for some larger organisations, been the vehicle for delivering in-house formal MLD (Paton *et al.*, 2004). CUs vary in structure and arrangements, but have as their purpose the meeting of corporate learning requirements through a highly structured and visible in-house provision, usually based in corporate headquarters. They often rely on competency frameworks to structure the delivery of MLD and in that sense there is a clear link between the activity of the CU and organisational performance (Paton *et al.*, 2004). In the UK where there are now an estimated 200 organisations professing to have established a corporate university. Organisations include: Anglian Water, Unipart, Lloyds TSB and British Aerospace.

There are a number of factors that have led to this expansion:

- Dissatisfaction with the generic nature of academic programmes which do not always address localised and unique management problems and issues.
- Technological development facilitating new approaches to learning and networking that can be delivered with ease and cost-effectively.
- As organisations grow increasingly more complex and ambiguous, the establishment of a corporate university becomes an important symbol and mechanism for knowledge management.
- It raises the status and prestige of the HRD department.
- It delivers HR benefits, e.g. access to a high standard of development facilities, aiding recruitment by demonstrating commitment to develop.

We can see that corporate universities represent a coherent attempt by organisations to plan and organise the whole panoply of training and MLD in such a way that it meets the needs of the organisation and the individuals within their workplace reality. In other words, it becomes a way of directly addressing the issue of strategic fit and overcoming the problem of how to meet the needs of contextual diversity and complexity by customising and shaping HRD to suit contingent circumstances. Their aim is 'to align training and development with business strategy while also sending out a clear message to employees that the organisation is prepared to invest in them' (Arkin, 2000: 42). However, there are a number of issues to address. First, there is a risk that some so-called corporate universities may be nothing more than re-badged training departments where the motive is more political or PR than learning or development (Prince and Beaver 2001). Second, at forecasted rates of growth, there is a fear that corporate universities will overtake and become a challenge to traditional universities (Vine, 1999). However, organisations refute this. Rather, what they say they are seeking is a collaboration with Higher Education institutions, e.g. to validate their degree offerings. But there are fears that the values that underpin university education (independence of thought and critical analysis and debate) may not be welcome in certain types of organisational culture. Third, there are practical concerns too. What happens if students are part-way through their studies and the company decides to close its corporate university as a cost-cutting exercise? Universities too may be chary of linking themselves too closely to a single partner when there is a risk of commercial failure (Arkin, 2000). It remains to be seen how far this ideal will evolve in the years to come.

Informal methods for developing managers

There is a growing interest in informal, but planned methods for developing managers and a parallel interest in capturing unplanned learning (Marsick and Watkins, 1997; Moon, 2004). Such methods are proving increasingly effective as their key strength lies in contextualising the learning to the managers' particular situations (Thomson *et al.*, 2001; Duerden, 2006). As we saw earlier, this may in part reflect a general dissatisfaction with generic, formal off-the-shelf courses or education programmes when they do not meet unique organisational, contextual or individual needs (Thomson *et al.*, 2001; Mole, 2004). It may also reflect the desire by individuals and organisations to take advantage of more flexible and cost-effective methods, often using innovative technologies (Scott, 2004) that fit with changing lifestyles and rapidly changing organisational situations. A range of informal, planned methods will be considered here alongside methods for capturing unplanned learning. These are:

- coaching and mentoring;
- action learning;
- reflective practice;
- projects and secondments;
- outdoor MLD;
- self-development.

Coaching and mentoring

Coaching and mentoring are described in detail in the previous chapter, where the dual concerns of raising awareness and developing responsibility (Whitmore, 2002) were identified and explained. As an MLD tool it has received significant attention (Lee, 2003) for its role in raising self-awareness and focus on achieving specific outcomes. Furthermore, significant value rests on the process of capturing learning from the day-to-day activities of managers. There has been considerable investment by some organisations in providing external, or developing internal, coaches to support managers and leaders at all levels and it is part of management development activities in 55 per cent of organisations (CIPD, 2009). For managers and leaders the provision of coaching can signify the organisation's commitment to their development (see also Chapter 8).

Action learning

Action learning, attributed to Reg Revans, is based on learning by doing, reflecting on personal actions and experience to improve performance. Action learning is common in leadership development models. Revans' key principles of action learning are that:

1 Management development must be based on real work projects.

2 Those projects must be owned and defined by senior managers as having a significant impact on the future success of the enterprise.

3 Managers must aim to make a real return on the cost of the investment.

4 Managers must work together and learn from each other.

5 Managers must achieve real action and change.

6 Managers must study the content and process of change.

7 Managers must publicly commit themselves to action.   (Margerison, 1991: 38)

Revans saw learning (L) as a combination of what he terms 'programmed knowledge' (P) and 'questioning insight' (Q): thus $L = P + Q$. When facing unprecedented changes, managers cannot know what programmed knowledge they will need. Instead, they need to 'understand the subjective aspects of searching the unfamiliar, or learning to pose useful and discriminating questions'. Therefore action learning becomes a 'simple device of setting them to tackle real problems that have so far defied solution' (Revans, 1983: 11).

Revans argues that managerial learning has to embrace both 'know-how' and 'know-that', and be rooted in real problem solving, where 'lasting behavioural change is more likely to follow the reinterpretation of past experiences than the acquisition of fresh knowledge' (p. 14). Managers will be more able to make their interpretations, which are 'necessarily subjective, complex and ill-structured' (p. 14), and reorder their perceptions by working with colleagues who are engaged in the same process, rather than with non-managers such as management teachers who are 'not exposed to real risk in responsible action'. In other words, managers form 'learning sets' (groups of four to six people) who with the aid of a facilitator, work together and learn to give and accept criticism, advice and support. Margerison (1994b), citing Revans, likens this approach to 'comrades in adversity'. Managers will only 'learn effectively when they are confronted with difficulties and have the opportunity to share constructively their concerns and experiences with others' (p. 109).

Margerison (1991), drawing on case studies and personal experience of supervising action learning programmes, points out that managers learn a considerable amount:

- about themselves;
- about their job;
- about team members; and most of all
- about how to improve things and make changes.

However, there are some doubts about the efficacy of action learning. For example, in the extent to which managers will truly engage in action learning if this challenges current management cultures and political structures with concomitant risks for the individual (Pedler, 1997). That said, interest is still alive in the benefits of action learning to the manager's experience (Kesby, 2008).

Reflective practice

Introduced by The Reflective Practitioner (Schön, 1984) and closely associated with action learning, the ideas associated with reflective practice have gained ground in the last 25 years. Schön's work argued that the gap between theory and practice was widening and in order to address that, managers ought to be encouraged to be reflective practitioners. In Chapter 8, the significance of experiential learning processes to the development of managers was identified. Much of the theory relating to experiential learning is drawn from the theoretical work of Kolb (1984) and Honey and Mumford (1986), who introduced the concept of a learning cycle in which managers learn through a process of:

- implementation;
- reflection;

- making changes;
- initiating further action.

Burgoyne and Stuart (1991) point out that a greater focus on experiential learning in the workplace, coupled to a reaction against the 'remoteness', complication and institutionalisation of MLD, has encouraged organisations to adopt new methods of learning, which include reflective practice. While the process is not without its critics (well articulated by Hunt, 2005), the value of reflecting on practice is well established in many professions (e.g. HRM, nursing, teaching) and underlines the notion of the manager as practitioner, rather than scientist (Gold *et al.*, 2007; Moon, 2004).

Projects and secondments

Project management is increasing in prominence as the role and function of a manager changes within an increasingly turbulent, uncertain and often ambiguous world (Watson and Harris, 1999). Managers are developing new skills and having to take on board new values (Rosenfeld and Wilson, 1999). Buchanan and Boddy (1992) highlight the need to develop the notion of the 'flexible manager' who has the ability to:

- understand and relate to the wider environment;
- manage in that environment;
- manage complex, changing structures;
- innovate and initiate change;
- manage and utilise sophisticated information systems;
- manage people with different values and expectations.

One way to develop these attitudes and competences is to delegate responsibility for managing a cross-functional team of people, tasked with achieving a specific organisational goal within a fixed time-scale and to a set budget. This cross-functional project management role not only improves core management skills such as communication and motivation but also helps develop 'higher order' diagnostic, judgemental, evaluative and political skills (Buchanan and Boddy, 1992).

Secondments are being used increasingly for manager development. Multinational companies have highly sophisticated management exchange programmes that are used not only to develop important language and cultural skills in managers, but also to reinforce the organisation's central belief and value systems (see the example of Unilever earlier in this chapter and the later section that explores international MLD). Exchange programmes also exist between public and private sector organisations to transfer knowledge and broaden understanding. Some larger organisations are seconding their managers to various initiatives designed to assist small business ventures and community programmes.

Activity
Projects and secondments offer many developmental benefits. Identify a possible project or secondment opportunity that you could take advantage of in your organisation.

Outdoor MLD

OMD can be used to describe anything from an afternoon of activities on a hotel lawn to a month of outdoor adventure training in the Scottish Wilderness. (Jones and Oswick, 2007: 327)

During the 1980s and 1990s increasing attention was focused on the benefits of outdoor management development (OMD) as a development tool. OMD has its roots in the Outward Bound movement founded by Kurt Hahn (Burnett and James, 1994). The aim is to provide opportunities for personal growth and for managers to realise the potential of their 'inner resources' (Irvine and Wilson, 1994). In OMD, managers are exposed to emotional, physical and mental risks and challenges in which skills such as leadership and teamwork become *real* to the individuals and groups concerned (Burnett and James, 1994) and where 'the penalties for wrong decisions are painful; the consequence of bad judgements can be as real as being lost in a cold rainstorm at the edge of a dark forest' (Banks, 1994: 11).

While the consequences may be real during the experience of OMD, it is not always clear what the longer term benefits are or how likely learning is to be transferred to the workplace:

> Depending on your bent or glee at seeing a difficult colleague disappear down a river without a paddle, the experience [of OMD] invariably delivered 'war stories' of hilarity and terror with widely questioned benefits to the team at the real coalface back at the office.
>
> (Tarrant, 2005: 25)

With this issue in mind, Jones and Oswick (2007) identify that the most effective OMD aims to improve participants management of themselves and others, is embedded in a broader process of MLD, addresses the *specific* learning needs of the individuals and teams involved and requires both individual discretion and cooperative effort. Furthermore, tasks have to increase in difficulty as the OMD progresses and review and feedback is regular and focused on process, rather than technical, issues.

While physical challenges are still popular, there has been a noticeable shift to more sophisticated forms of OMD that focus on problem solving, innovation and changing behaviour in the classroom and beyond. For example, Arkin (2003) describes how Sony (Europe) took its senior managers on a 'leadership journey' across Europe linked to team and individual exercises designed for them to experience the anxiety and uncertainty their employees felt during radical change. Allen also describes how managers are engaging with community-based projects linked to corporate social responsibility, arguing that OMD is moving towards 'experiences that are carefully designed to provide a true metaphor for the workplace' (Allen, 2003: 36).

Self-development

Organisations that invest in effective MLD programmes are encouraging their managers to take more responsibility for and control of their own development. As Boydell and Pedler (1981: 3) remark:

> Any effective system for management development must increase the manager's capacity and willingness to take control over and responsibility for events, and participating for themselves in their own learning.

If managers take responsibility for their own development they are likely to:

- improve career prospects;
- improve performance;
- develop certain skills;
- achieve full potential/self-actualisation.

STOP and think

What arrangements have you made for your self-development?

A range of techniques exists for managers to undertake self-development. Some involve managers helping each other by sharing experiences in self-managed learning groups (see the previous section on action learning). Other approaches are more personally focused, using techniques such as distance learning materials, computer-based training and interactive videos. (For a fuller discussion of the methods used for self-development, see Pedler *et al.*, 1990.)

In summary, this section has outlined some of the formal and informal methods that are currently being used to develop managers. However, it must be borne in mind that a great deal of development takes place in ways that are not only less formal, they are incidental and opportunistic (Mumford, 1997). There may be times when the individual manager is unaware that development has even taken place, e.g. trial and error, learning from mistakes, playing political games etc. This suggests that development may have as much to do with the provision of organisational support and facilitation for the creation of a learning culture (Woodall, 2000) and managing the influence of organisational context (social, political, cultural) in which managers operate (Doyle, 2000a) as it does with the selection and implementation of specific development methods.

Evaluating MLD

Measuring MLD is vital to demonstrate the value of the programme in terms of monetary value or achievement of organisational goals (Mabey and Finch-Lees, 2008). Organisations undertake MLD with the assumption that there will be some beneficial outputs (Tyler, 2004). With increased pressure on resources, being able to demonstrate the contribution is vital. Aside from financial measures, other success criteria are possible and identifying these in advance is vital if there is to be effective evaluation (Tate, 2004; Hamblin, 2007). If MLD is to be effective in meeting individual needs and delivering organisation goals, the whole process must be effectively evaluated to make judgements about its cost-effectiveness and aid ongoing organisational learning and improvement (Easterby-Smith, 1994). Traditionally, the literature on evaluation has focused heavily on the training and education 'components' of development (Warr *et al.*, 1970; Rae, 1986). Evaluation of HRD generally is covered in detail in Chapter 8 and should be referred to to help answer the next Activity.

Activity

Identify a recent MLD initiative that you were involved in.

- What were the desired outcomes of this initiative?
- How could these be measured?

In attempting to evaluate MLD, a number of issues emerge. Most evaluation is short-term in outlook – captured in the ubiquitous 'happy sheet' questionnaire where questions focus on the immediacy of development activity rather than its longer-term outcomes (Kirkpatrick, 1960). To be effective, development must permit managers (a) the opportunity to transfer and apply new knowledge and skills and (b) a period of learning and adjustment in respect of newly acquired attitudes and behaviours. This implies that any evaluation of development outcomes has to have a longer-term orientation.

In addition to assessing changes in the performance and behaviour of individual managers, evaluation must include some assessment of the impact of the organisational context in which managers are seeking to apply their new knowledge, e.g. the cultural and political environment that may promote or inhibit development. As Smith (1993: 23) observes, 'management development programmes are not context free but dependent on the cultural baggage of the participants and the organisation'. Therefore any judgement about the outcomes of MLD programmes must be viewed in the context in which they are embedded (Tyler, 2004). This raises further issues about the way MLD outcomes themselves are interpreted and justified. For example, any claims about the efficacy of MLD investment may fall prey to political games. As Fox (1989: 192) explains, 'because a pseudo-scientific approach [to evaluation] does not deal with human issues and value judgements, it is not surprising that they fall into disuse or are simply done by token [then] politics takes over'. Both Fox (1989) and Currie (1994), who have examined the evaluation of MLD programmes in the NHS, conclude that political and cultural factors were heavily influential in shaping the evaluation process.

Another issue relates to the way development outcomes are measured. It is common to encounter evaluation methodologies that are striving to display some form of pseudo-scientific objectivity to win or protect investment in development activity. For example, those responsible for development might be tempted to make unsubstantiated causal links between an investment in development and some aspect of organisational performance, e.g. annual sales. Another problem is that the environment in which evaluation is taking place is often highly complex and subjective and evaluation methodologies may be judged simplistic and inadequate (Smith, 1993; Mole, 1996, Mole, 2000). For example, some of the criticisms levelled at competency-based development discussed earlier revolve around the doubts and reservations over supposedly objective and structured internal and external verification procedures as a means of determining the level of an individual's competency (Loan-Clarke, 1996). In other words, 'the complexity of management training and development demonstrates the point that measuring its effectiveness cannot be adequately accomplished by using a single, generic formula' (Endres and Kleiner, 1990: 4).

Concerns surround the need to ensure that emotional, attitudinal and behavioural outcomes are measured and have an equal validity alongside harder aspects such as financial performance and technical competence. This necessitates the use of carefully constructed and focused methodologies incorporating ethnographic, interpretative techniques (Fox, 1989; Currie, 1994). However, this presupposes that those tasked with evaluation have the time, commitment and skills to conduct research in these areas.

Looking at all these issues, it seems inevitable that the evaluation of MLD will always be a somewhat difficult, complex and at times contentious process. One way to improve evaluation is for organisations to adopt a more systemic, holistic perspective of evaluation. This can be done by:

- Examining the extent to which development activity fits with individual needs and organisational context.

- Assessing how far new behaviours can be transferred and applied in the workplace, whether or not new behaviour corresponds with espoused organisational culture and values.

- Adopting methodologies that can measure both hard and soft aspects of performance (Easterby-Smith, 1994; Mole, 1996).

- From a more practical perspective, rather than focus on the benefits of development, consider the ramifications of not doing development.

- Rather than looking forward to eventual outcomes, it might be more prudent to look back at, for example, past mistakes, which can often be quantified. Improvements can be measured from that point, i.e. how mistakes and associated cost have been eliminated through development activity.

But are we asking too much? Is evaluation a chimera? As Easterby-Smith (1994: 143) states:

Thus attempts to evaluate development methods may fail to satisfy the purist, and much of this stems from the diffuseness of the target that is being examined and the difficulty of isolating procedures from the real constraints and politics of the organisations in which they are taking place.

MLD systems in Europe

It is difficult to separate development approaches from the cultural, social and economic context in which they are located (Geppert *et al.*, 2002). Furthermore, the impact of industrial relations, social protection (Estevez-Abe *et al.*, 2001), professional associations and legislation or regulation will play a part in determining MLD practices at a national level (Mabey and Finch-Lees, 2008). In short, the national context will frame the choices that businesses make about investments in MLD (Thompson *et al.*, 2001). In order to explore this further a short review of practices across Europe is presented. As with the previous chapter, a close focus is given to the UK, Germany and France in comparison (Table 9.2). In Table 9.2, MLD is across five categories. Column 1 identifies the skills type predominantly developed, and column 2 explains how this links to career progression. Column 3 identifies who resources the MLD with column 4 outlining those who drive the process. Finally, column 5 describes the characteristics that distinguish managers in a particular national context. For a fuller review, see Ramirez (2004), who broadens the discussion to include Spain, Norway and Denmark.

UK

MLD in the UK is often viewed as a separate, discrete and heavily individualised activity, aimed at correcting identified 'weaknesses' in skills and knowledge or 'deviances' in individual attitudes and behaviour (Mumford, 1997; Ramirez, 2004). In essence, development approaches are dominated by a powerful rational-functional philosophy, which views the main justification for any development programme as being its direct contribution to business strategy and organisational performance. In other words, the view is that MLD must add value to the business and maintain competitiveness in the face of environmental threats (Woodall and Winstanley, 1998; Thomson *et al.*, 2001; Mabey and Finch-Lees, 2008).

Increasingly, the aim is to develop generalist managerial, rather than narrow, specialist skills to improve mobility and the ability to take on new assignments and challenges – especially in a global environment (Heisler and Benham, 1992) – and maintain their skills when moving jobs (Ramirez, 2004). Development has often been synonymous with management education and/or short, intensive training courses. For example, both countries now focus attention on competence-based approaches. In the UK such approaches are institutionalised and championed through competency based development (see above for the earlier discussion on competency-based development). However, as we have seen in this chapter, there is now a growing emphasis on more holistic, contextual, work-based forms of development that are experientially based, e.g. action learning projects, coaching and mentoring (Vicere, 1998). Additionally, there is an increasing emphasis on individual funding and express links to professional bodies for recognition or accreditation (Ramirez, 2004).

Germany

In contrast to the Anglo-Saxon model described above, many continental European approaches have in the past been less concerned with MLD as a discrete activity. In Germany, the approach to development is much more functional, with specialist expertise, especially in engineering and science, being closely linked to the vocational system of education built around the concept of 'Technik' and the production of 'Technikers' – technical experts who dominate in management (Randlesome, 2000). Within this highly structured system, there is little organisational mobility and a strong emphasis on career progression within one or a few organisations (Ramirez, 2004).

In terms of the content of MLD activity, there is less perceived need for generalist skills development and generalist business education such as that represented by the MBA, which in the past has been 'regarded with great suspicion' (Randlesome, 2000). Discrete MLD activity is

Table 9.2 European management development systems

	Skills type	Career paths	Who pays for training?	Agents driving training and status of training Institutions	Distinguishing national characteristics of managers
UK	Managers can maintain skills when moving jobs.	Less emphasis on firm-level career development (Bournois *et al.*, 1994). Managers exposed to losing jobs in hostile takeovers.	Growing general business educations financed by employee (Barnett, 1997).	High status of chartered instutions. Low status of vocational training (Tregaskis, 1997).	High premium on the 'gifted amateur' (Bennett, 1997). Managers are 'specialist coordinators' (Lam, 1994).
Germany	VET for managers and employees' technical/scientific skills prior to becoming managers (Streeck, 1993). Formal management education emphasizes scientific, theoretical principles.	Strong emphasis on succession planning (Bournois *et al.*, 1994). Low mobility between firms (Lane, 1989).	Hands on managerial training funded by firms (Lane, 1989).	High status of VET for managers (Streeck, 1993). Formal management training routes lie in the *Diploma Kaufman* and *BWL* in the university system (Shenton, 1996). High-level CEOs would have PhDs.	Managers are subject to intense monitoring. Managers are 'players' (Lam, 1994). High concensus between managers and workers.
France	*Grandes Ecoles* vocational origins and proximity to business world (Shenton, 1996).	More likely to lose skill status when moving jobs (Eyraud *et al.*, (1990)). Job hierarchies and seniority. Internal labour markets (Maurice *et al.*, 1986). Promotion into *cadre* status is rare (Tregaskis, 1997).	Law requires firms to spend at least 1.5 per cent of wage bill on training.	*Grandes Ecoles* technocratic elite (Shenton, 1996). 75 per cent of senior executives in large firms have *Grandes Ecoles* qualification (Bennett, 1997)	Managers are 'coordinators' (Lam, 1994). Comparitively weak retention and short-term training plans.

Source: Adapted from Ramirez (2004: 438–40).

seen as less salient, and does not flourish to the same extent (Lawrence, 1992). Where MLD is carried out it is mainly in-house (Thomson *et al.*, 2001). For instance, German managers tend to favour 'structured learning situations with precise objectives, detailed assignments and strict timetables' (Hill, 1994).

France

In France, the development of managers is linked more closely to its social and historical context. Rather than management being something that can be explicitly developed in individuals, it is perceived as 'more a state of being' (Lawrence, 1992). Those who become managers form part of a social elite (*cadre*), and much of their development begins within the higher education institutions (*grandes écoles*), where the study of natural sciences and mathematics predominates. However, concerns are now being expressed about the ethnocentrism and insularity that is permeating French business schools (*grandes écoles de commerce*), creating structural and cultural barriers to a wider system of management education that is adapted to global market situations (Kumar and Usunier, 2001). However, this elitism permeates the whole system of MLD in France and despite recent emphases on linking MLD to strategic outcomes, evidence of a shift is meagre (Le Deist *et al.*, 2007).

As in Germany, the concept of management is not considered as something to be seen as separate, but more as part of the overall functional system within the organisation. Managers have less mobility than in the UK, tending to stay in their functional role much longer.

Despite their relatively weak tradition and the problem of 'cultural insularity' in terms of MLD, France, Germany and other European countries are beginning to establish institutions specifically aimed at developing managers. For example, despite past reservations, there has been a growth of MBA activity in both Germany and France (Easterby-Smith, 1992; Randlesome, 2000). In major German companies such as Siemens and BMW there is a greater awareness of the importance of managerial competencies (Randlesome, 2000) and in France there is a belated emergence of US-style business schools (Hill, 1994; Kumar and Usunier, 2001).

MLD for different needs and contexts

This section will explore a variety of different contexts in which development takes place and looks at the needs of different managers.

Senior manager development

The separate treatment of the most senior managers in an organisation is a well-established approach (Trehan and Shelton, 2007). Arguably, their position high in the organisational hierarchy, their strategic responsibilities and special benefits linked to their status means that they require special consideration (CIPD, 2008a). However, many of those involved in planning, organising and facilitating MLD in organisations encounter a paradox when they seek to address senior MLD. On the one hand, senior managers are viewed as a valuable and critical resource to the survival and success of the organisation (Woodall and Winstanley, 1998; Syrett and Lammiman, 1999). Logic therefore dictates that during periods of radical change their knowledge and skills must be maintained at levels consistent with meeting the challenges of change. On the other hand, their development often appears to be inadequate or neglected. For instance, a survey of 295 HR specialists in the 1990s revealed that 50 per cent of organisations surveyed did not have a strategy for developing their senior managers (Industrial Society, 1997). That they are likely to be far fewer in number will mean that their development will need to be more tailored and specific, requiring additional planning and investment (CIPD, 2008a). Explanations for the poor provision of senior manager development range from the pressure of work and a lack of time to deeper emotional and political attitudes about their perceived need for development (Syrett and Lammiman, 1999). Their isolation – often without a peer group on whom to draw for learning and support – makes their role even more difficult to develop (CIPD, 2008a) and solutions harder to identify. There may, however, be a deeper reason inhibiting some senior managers from participating in development activity. Simply put, they do not believe they need it, or argue that if they were to admit they needed their credibility would be negatively affected.

Individually, the role of a senior manager demands a considerable emphasis on strategic leadership coupled to legal and regulatory duties that are not found in other management roles. Collectively, senior managers have to be developed to work as an effective team while at the same time maintaining a required independence of thought and behaviour (Mumford, 1988).

Woodall and Winstanley (1998) identify four stages in the process of developing senior managers:

- *Grooming*: managers are prepared for the transition to the boardroom by giving them wider responsibilities and exposure to a range of managerial experiences.

- *Induction*: having entered the boardroom, senior managers are familarised with the cultures, processes and practices that prevail there – both formal and informal.

- *Competencies within the role*: an assessment of the individual's current level of skills and ability benchmarked against what is required to develop senior manager competence. Individual development plans are prepared through joint discussion and negotiation.

- *Team effectiveness*: the collective development needs of the senior manager team are assessed in areas such as group interaction, team roles etc. and a development plan for the top team is implemented.

In many ways, development for senior managers mirrors the approaches that are used at lower levels. For senior managers, a careful analysis of needs is of primary importance and in particular 360-degree feedback, psychometric tests, development reviews, coaching, action learning, shadowing and external input may form the basis for effective intervention (CIPD, 2008b). However, it is important to note that the content and emphasis given to aspects such as political, leadership and change skills are likely to differ markedly to reflect strategic, legal, regulatory and fiduciary roles as well as the added emotional and psychological burden that is inherent in such roles (Syrett and Lammiman, 2003).

Developing professionals as managers

Woodall and Winstanley (1998) identify professionals as having the following characteristics:

- expertise based on a distinct body of knowledge;
- altruistic service orientation to work;
- autonomy and independence;
- restrictive entry;
- collective peer group collegiate relations;
- code of professional ethics;
- power through expertise;
- professional goals above the organisation.

Arguably, these special characteristics means a tailored approach to MLD. A number of research projects have examined leadership training in, for example, education (Glatter, 2004), the National Health Service (NHS) (Bristow, 2007), and the HR profession and have considered the specific challenges exist in the MLD of professionals.

Activity

- Think about the way that professionals are being developed in your organisation (this may include you).

- List what you see as the challenges facing developers in your organisation.

Bittel (1998) argues that the main challenge for developers stems from the highly individualistic approach that professionals have towards their work. They view professional work as rewarding and intellectually challenging and are generally loyal to their profession and its values. However, when faced with the challenge of moving into management, they may display a number of what Bittel deems are 'counterproductive characteristics'. They:

- over-apply their analytical skills and can become paralysed by analysis;
- are insensitive to others and feel they are above organisational politics;
- expect their technical expertise to solve organisational problems;
- respect logic and intuition over emotion;
- lack feeling and empathy;
- lack awareness of common-sense solutions to problems.

There is, of course, a danger of generalising too far here and becoming a prey to stereotyping. Undoubtedly, some professionals make very good managers and are particularly good with people (Woodall and Winstanley, 1998). Yet others face conflict between their role as professional and their role as manager. For example, research in secondary education amongst heads of department and deputy heads highlights the clash between the professional role as teacher and the role of middle manager (Adey, 2000). In the NHS, similar clashes were identified. Some doctors who found themselves moving into management by default became more concerned with protecting their corner and loyalty to their professional colleagues. However, other doctors welcomed their move into management, were loyal and committed to the organisation and viewed themselves as a member of the management team (Woodall and Winstanley, 1998).

As we have seen, one area that demands close attention is the conflict between professional and managerial value systems. Clearly, approaches to development that challenge these values are likely to be resented and resisted. For example, in the NHS, competence-based approaches that were seen to be generic, highly prescriptive and structured did not go down well with professional groups (Currie and Darby, 1995). As Currie (1999: 58) remarks:

> Whilst recognising that every organisation is unique, the history and professional elaboration of groups in the public sector make a hospital particularly unique. The weakness of the competence approach and insensitivity of delivery to context reinforce the ideological gap between managerial and professional values.

Other research highlights the potential dangers of using what are perceived to be generic, simplistic, off-the-shelf training courses for developing professionals as managers. For example, in education, the government has made the MLD of head teachers a key priority. But amongst some head teachers management theory is seen as 'applied social science' offering simplistic recipes to complex problems. Research suggests that overall, professionals in education may prefer a more contingent, personalised approach to their development and the issues it raises (Bolam, 1997) and in particular, action learning in the development of leaders in the NHS has been well received (Bristow, 2007). The 'environmental complexity' inherent in many professional environments makes tailored provision particularly important (Glatter, 2004: 208).

The spirit of this personalised approach is captured in the notion of continuous professional development (CPD).

> The essential principles of CPD are that development should be continuous; it should be owned and managed by the learner; learning objectives should be clear and wherever possible, serve both organisational needs as well as individual goals. And regular investment of an individual's time in learning should be seen as an essential part of professional life.
>
> (Little, 1997: 28)

What arrangement have you made/are you making for your professional development to include management knowledge and skills?

In summary, it would seem that in terms of developing professionals as managers, the issue is not so much one of access and the availability of MLD but recognising that professionals have special needs and prefer to plan and organise their own MLD to meet them. For developers the message is clear: resist the temptation to direct professionals into structured, mechanistic and simplistic approaches. Instead, offer advice and support within the framework and spirit of CPD where reflective and experiential on-the-job approaches such as multidiscipline projects and individual assignments linked to coaching and mentoring seem to work best in developing their managerial skills.

Graduate MLD

Research has revealed that 67 per cent of organisations surveyed viewed graduate recruitment and development as a key feature of their business strategy (CIPD, 2009). Graduates are recruited – usually directly from university or shortly after they graduate – for broadly two purposes. First, they provide essential specialist knowledge and skills, e.g. scientific, engineering, computing etc. Second, they 'create a pool of intelligent people with high potential as a means of providing for management of the future' (Mumford, 1997: 222). What they lack are organisation specific skills (Boyatzis *et al.*, 2002), which poses particular issues for MLD.

Following a rigorous selection process – usually involving an assessment centre – successful graduates will work with their organisation to prepare a personal development plan. The plan will normally focus on the development of both hard and soft managerial skills – building on the information obtained at the assessment centre and other identified needs, and often supported by a mentor or supervisor. In respect of the way in which graduates are developed as managers, Mumford (1997: 223) argues:

> There is no mystery about what to do with graduates. There needs to be a formal development programme for them which will include appropriate courses; they need to have assignments in particular units or departments long enough to establish that they have done a definable piece of work.

Many large organisations (see Box 9.4) will have graduate MLD schemes designed to take graduates with potential to senior management roles quickly and successfully.

Box 9.4

The National Offender Management Service (NOMS) Graduate Programme

This probably isn't the first graduate scheme you've looked into and, more than likely, it won't be the last. However, what will make our programme stand out from the rest is the truly exceptional careers we can offer.

To see if the Prison Service is right for you, ask yourself the following questions.

- Do I want my work to make a real difference to people's lives?
- Do I want to work with people from all walks of life?
- Do I want a career where no two days are the same?
- Do I want a career with real responsibility early on?
- Do I want to progress as high as I can, as fast as I can?

If the answer to one, or more, of these questions is 'yes' – we strongly recommend you read on.

What is it like working in the Prison Service?
People are often shocked by how 'normal' life is on the inside. But with around 80,000 prisoners in our care at any one time – 99.9% of whom will return to society – maintaining routine and 'normality' is vital.

Box 9.4 continued

Like most other organisations, we realise that our staff are our biggest asset. That's why we guarantee to recognise talent at all levels, tailor career development opportunities to meet individual needs and provide effective support and training wherever, and whenever, it's needed.

What does the NOMS Graduate Programme involve?
Firstly you'll complete full training to become a Prison Officer, followed by up to 12 months in an establishment as a Prison Officer.

Then you will progress to Senior Officer with responsibility for a group of staff. Your next move will then be to an Operational Manager (a middle management governor position). Your speed of progression will be determined by your own ability, but we are looking for people with the potential to progress to senior management positions within a very short time frame.

Within 2½–3 years of joining the scheme you could be head of a busy unit, or function, within a prison. Beyond that, progression will only be limited by your potential.

Source: www.hmprisonservice.gov.uk (accessed 24 May 2009).

MLD in the small firm

Small and medium-sized enterprises account for 99 per cent of firms in the UK (Hall, 2004) and thus the economic role of such firms in creating wealth and employment is widely acknowledged in the UK and beyond. Given the wide range of firms that fall under this umbrella, knowledge is limited and generalisations difficult (Mayson and Barrett, 2005).

However, despite the relatively upbeat account of SMEs from some quarters, with managers being judged as good or very good and high levels of trust and participation (Forth *et al.*, 2006; Stone *et al.*, 2006), in the UK 65–75 per cent collapse or are sold during first-generation ownership tenure (Williams and Cowling, 2008). While there are many factors that may contribute to this high failure rate, the lack of management knowledge and expertise is viewed as a major factor (Saee and Mouzytchenko, 1999; Fuller-Love, 2006) and many small businesses fail to reach their potential because of the way their people are managed (Leach and Kenny, 2000).

There appears to be sound evidence to suggest that few managers in small firms receive formal management training (Thomson *et al.*, 2001) and while there have been improvements in the development of managers in small firms in recent years, one in five managers receive no training at all (Fuller-Love, 2006).

STOP and think

To what extent are the problems facing the development of managers in small firms similar or different to those in larger firms?

Research has identified a number of reasons why small firms rarely invest in MLD. The main barriers are:

- lack of time;
- lack of resources to fund formal training;
- lack of previous formal education;
- concerns about realising returns on investment in management training;
- not knowing where or how to get advice and assistance;
- complicated procedures and bureaucracy when applying for assistance.

(Saee and Mouzytchenko, 1999; Kerr and McDougall, 1999; Thomson *et al.*, 2001; Fuller-Love, 2006).

Another significant barrier arises from the peculiarities, idiosyncrasies and diversity of the small firm sector. This often makes the transfer and take-up of mainstream, large-organisation-focused methods problematical (Mayson and Barrett, 2005). Problems also emerge when MLD is reduced to the provision of 'enterprise training', focusing on basic skills in operations, HRM marketing, finance etc.

> This view however, springs from an economic model of small businesses as large firms scaled down, a model which many consider to be deeply flawed . . . Management development is seen as a subordinate priority to the need to improve the institutional and structural framework within which small firms operate.
> (Thomson *et al.*, 2001: 205)

Other barriers may arise from the attitudes and values that are to be found in small firms. Kerr and McDougall (1999), researching 130 small firms in Scotland, found that a short-term outlook, pragmatism, a desire for informality and the need to survive were considerations that often took precedence over training or business planning. In another study of small firms in the hotel and leisure industry, Beaver and Lashley (1998: 234) found that 'managers running small firms have a wider variety of roles and different priorities than those running larger enterprises'; for instance, the assumption that all owner/managers are motivated solely by commercial objectives 'is naïve'. Many in fact attach more significance to personal lifestyle considerations. In the same vein, Tolentino (1998) makes the point that small firm managers have a different outlook to managers in larger firms in areas such as entrepreneurship, risk-taking, personal achievement and control. They have a much closer identification with the business and the family/community in which it is located.

Considerations for a strategy for developing managers in the small firm would include the following:

- identifying the knowledge and skills required by small firm owner/managers;
- delivering development in a way that acknowledges the sector's diversity and uniqueness;
- finding ways to overcome the bureaucracy and provide accessible and affordable approaches to development.

In terms of the knowledge and skills required, these are seemingly well understood and documented. Thomson *et al.* (2001) cite Bolton's list of skills as typical of those that are felt to be required:

- raising and using finance;
- costing and control information;
- organising and delegating;
- marketing;
- using information;
- personnel management;
- dealing with technological change;
- production scheduling and purchase control.

Other studies showed that while these areas were important, they were ones in which many small firm managers lacked the required level of knowledge and skills. For example, one survey found that small firm managers were particularly lacking in the ability to appraise performance, strategic planning, teamworking and communication (IRS Employment Review, 1997).

In terms of support to facilitate development of managers, the role of the CEO/owner is seen as a crucial factor, as is the support given by experienced external consultants/advisers

(Wong *et al.*, 1997; Kerr and McDougall, 1999). Other studies highlight the role of various government agencies, tax incentives and loans, and the impact of the Investors in People initiative in promoting and supporting MLD in small firms (Beaver and Lashley, 1998).

In summary, it is clear that the needs of the small firm manager have similarities to those of managers in larger organisations but they also differ sharply in a number of important respects. Success in developing these managers has to begin with a careful and considered examination of the context in which they are managing, allied to an understanding of their individual and collective motives and needs; and ensuring that whatever methods or approaches that are adopted are relevant and affordable.

Management development in the public sector

Management in the UK public sector has often been the butt of criticism from politicians, journalists and other commentators about its seemingly bureaucratic, inefficient and unfocused approach to organisation and management. Cooper (2002: 17) captures the mood in identifying that:

> many senior public sector managers thought that 'management' was about changing organisational systems, committee structures, and hierarchy charts rather than developing and investing in their vision/long-term objectives and the people who achieve them. For them management meant bureaucratic action, fiddling with committees, setting up control systems and dealing with detail.

This reflects a tradition that has underplayed management skills so that a focus on targets and strategy is comparatively new but is 'staggeringly complex' (Alimo-Metcalfe and Alban-Metcalfe, 2004: 178). Developing leadership skills has therefore been a key plank of the Government's Modernisation Agenda (PIU, 2001) in, for example, the NHS, Education, Policing and the Civil Service.

Within the public sector, there is a huge range of contexts and work environments within which leaders face many challenges (Flynn, 2007). These can include:

- the management of limited resources that accompany the provision of a 'free' service;
- maintaining a public service ethos in a commercial society;
- managing complex environments with multiple goals and functions and different types of staff (e.g. professional and managerial);
- working within the constraints of unionised environments;
- managing professionals working in environments that may be substandard to that available in the private sector;
- performance standards and goals 'imposed' externally which cover issues not always within the control of the service.

These challenges and contradictions make for an interesting environment in which to develop the manager, often where there are limited funds available. That said there are noteable examples where considerable investment has been made in developing public sector managers, for example:

- the NHS Leadership Qualities Framework – **www.nhsleadershipqualities.nhs.uk**;
- the National College for School Leadership (**www.ncsl.org.uk**);
- the National Police Leadership Faculty at Bramshill.

International MLD

Information and communication technologies have made working with suppliers, customers and connections across the globe part of everyday life for most managers (Melkman and Trotman, 2005). Moreover, for some multinational organisations such as Unilever, the ability to manage across boundaries is a core competence and MLD has focused on the creation of elite cadres of international managers tasked with building efficient networks of organisations operating across national boundaries (McCall and Hollenbeck, 2002). We saw earlier in this chapter that Unilever's aim is to develop a common philosophy and system of MLD that is 'seamless' and permits managers to move easily between different countries (Reitsma, 2001). The main challenges that international managers face are cultural, whereby different cultural groups typify different 'orientations to the world' (Kluckhohn and Strodtbeck, 1961; Adler, 1997), giving rise to differences in expectation and behaviour regarding:

- the nature of individuals and their relationship to society;
- people's relationship to the world;
- the importance of religion and custom;
- social protocols;
- orientation to activity;
- language and non-verbal communication.

Western managers are often accused of 'cultural blindness' which seemingly limits their ability to work in multicultural environments (Miroshnik, 2002). It is clear that an inability to address cultural diversity has the potential to undermine MLD strategies in an international context (Liu and Vince, 1999). Therefore the primary focus for international MLD must be to ensure that 'working effectively in multiple cross-cultural contexts is . . . a vital competence' (Harris and Kumra, 2000: 604). As Miroshnik (2002: 524) points out, 'Different cultural environments require different managerial behaviours . . . managing relations between multicultural organisations and cultural environments is thus a matter of accurate perception, diagnosis and appropriate adaptation.' It is clear that to be effective, this process of cultural awareness must begin well before the manager arrives at their international destination (Harris and Kumra, 2000).

Phillips (1992) summarises the views of most commentators and practitioners in the following list:

- *technical skills and experience* often beyond those normally required at home, for example the engineer who needs sound financial management skills;
- *people skills* – cultural empathy, team-building and interpersonal skills;
- *intellectual skills* – seeing the big picture, and thinking in a macro not micro way;
- *emotional maturity* – being adaptable, independent, sensitive, self-aware;
- *motivation* – drive, enthusiasm, stamina, resilience and persistence.

Despite the recognition of the importance of softer skills, there is a risk that technical expertise may come to dominate and dictate the development agenda at the expense of softer skills. Other risks include:

- the reliance on selection processes that rest heavily on personal recommendations;
- a successful track record in a national rather than an international context;
- selection criteria based on Western competences and personality traits which may have to be for an overseas appointment.

If such risks are not addressed, organisations may be in danger of setting their international managers up to fail, with serious consequences for the organisation and the individual.

Methods to develop international skills are eclectic and will vary according to the organisation, the type of international assignment that is planned, the nature of the host country etc. They will include formal programmes of management education to develop language skills and cultural awareness. They will also include on-the-job activities such as international exchanges, projects and action learning programmes to develop technical expertise, communication and interpersonal skills (Melkman and Trotman, 2005).

MLD and diversity issues

In the past, substantial attention has been paid to the differential treatment of women managers and their progression through organisations (Vinnicombe and Colwill, 1995). Much less has been said about the position of the other diverse groups in society, and in microcosm in management. Much MLD is 'diversity-neutral' (Mabey and Finch-Lees, 2008) and fails to recognise how current approaches reinforce current prejudices and limitations. MLD is after all, about conformity – building managers who reinforce corporate messages and approaches (Clarke *et al.*, 2004) and difference is viewed as 'a liability' (Mabey and Finch-Lees, 2008). Taking a balanced view to MLD and recognising diversity requires asking hard questions. Diversity issues are covered in detail in Chapter 7 and ought to be explored before embarking on designing MLD.

The future for MLD: the need for new thinking and new practices?

Activity

- Before you read this section of the chapter, list what you believe to be the way in which MLD might evolve over the next 10–15 years. Add a short sentence against each point to explain your reasoning.

- If time and/or circumstances permit, discuss your ideas with a colleague(s). How do your ideas compare with theirs?

In concluding this chapter, we speculate on the future direction of MLD. Perhaps the first thing to note is that the development of managers – like so many aspects of organisational life – is in a state of considerable flux and transformation. This is giving rise to a number of issues and tensions that are continuing to influence the way MLD is interpreted, planned, organised and implemented across a wide range of contexts.

Is MLD worth the money?

As the economy contracts at record rate and a new financial order is emerging, any investment in employee development has to be worth the money invested in it. One of the challenges identified in this chapter was in evaluating MLD. If a clear case cannot be made for the link between MLD and organisational performance, and if this cannot be demonstrated within each organisation, then it will not be a priority in cash-strapped businesses. MLD will only be worth the money if clear links can be made with the business and its purposes (Tate, 2004). As such, MLD poses a 'strategic challenge':

- *Strategy must be put ahead of training*: business leaders must take an informed view about what aspects of MLD support the business directly and jettison those that do not.

- *Development has to look outwards*: at customers, markets, brands, products and competition, and inwards – at organisation, culture, structure, systems, relationships and rules.

- *MLD has to be targeted carefully*: not all managers need the same level or quantity of development over the same time scales. Identifying specific behaviours that have to change in which individuals will allow a much more tailored offering.

- *Assumptions have to be challenged*: however 'self-evident' the value of MLD may be, it should not escape serious challenge.

- *The focus should be on leadership as it is practiced, rather than as its learned*: and solutions tailored to make this its business purpose.

In those ways, MLD can become a resource for the organisation, rather than a drain on its resources. This challenges the notion that MLD should meet individual as well as organisational needs and will be discussed shortly.

Can MLD be truly strategic?

A clear case has been made in this chapter that MLD to be effective, must be linked to strategic goals and intentions. Chapter 2 introduced some of the realities of strategic flux and change in organisations – where intended strategies were not always realised and emerging strategies replaced those intended as the strategic environment changed over the process of planning cycles. If we are to achieve and maintain the required level of strategic fit, MLD has to be managed in a way that accepts and accommodates contextual diversity and organisational complexities. 'Managing' development therefore has to be seen as being just as important as 'doing' development.

So to what extent is MLD fulfilling its strategic role in this contextual and contingent manner? The answer has to be a qualified one. There is evidence of success (Clarke *et al.*, 2004; Mabey and Ramirez, 2005; Brown, 2007) but there is also evidence that in some situations MLD might be considered to be 'failing' in the sense that it is not fully delivering anticipated organisational and individual outcomes (Meldrum and Atkinson, 1998; Currie, 1999; Doyle, 1995, 2000a).

To what extent do you feel that MLD is 'failing' to deliver anticipated outcomes in your organisation?

While investment and commitment may have increased, there are still reservations and doubts about the overall *efficacy* of MLD and its ability to deliver increased performance and organisational success during times of radical and far-reaching change (Doyle, 1995, 2000a; Tate, 2004). Any shift towards a more systemic perspective on MLD may require a significant reorientation in thinking and practice amongst the professionals involved. For instance, one such reorientation emphasises the greater use of work-based approaches to development (Woodall, 2000).

In order to meet the challenge to be strategic, organisations have to address several challenges Clarke *et al.*, 2004):

- they must be clear about the nature of leadership and the qualities they value in the leaders in their business;

- they need clear evaluation strategies that demonstrate the multiple values of MLD;

- they must engage high quality professionals to support MLD internally and to build networks externally;

- they must be 'in it for the long term' rather than following financial trends which drive piecemeal and partial investment.

Can MLD be individualised while still meeting organisational needs?

As careers become more individualised, the challenges in balancing individual and organisational needs become more acute (Sturges, 2004). For example, the key way to increase the effectiveness of MLD is to place an emphasis on developing *managers within the context in which they manage* rather than just in the classroom, the training suite or the hotel conference room. However, this is likely to make managers' skills less portable if their organisation is no longer able to employ them. While the UK system has traditionally relied on developing generic, rather than specific, management skills (Ramirez, 2004) this may suit individuals' career plans, but not do so much for organisations. However, this emphasis on mobility and portable skills has been strengthened further by the emergence of 'the new career'; and the associated 'new psychological contract'.

The emergence of the new career is characterised by three points of difference from the 'traditional' career (Sturges, 2004):

● an increase on individual (rather than organisational) management, making self-development more important in MLD;

● an emphasis on career mobility where security with one employer is no longer guaranteed, meaning an increased desire for the individual to develop generic, portable skills;

● an increasing recognition that work is just one part of life, meaning individuals are not prepared to devote long periods away from work to development and training that could take place in work time.

Thus, as the challenges have changed the landscape for individuals, so has it changed for organisations: as management structures have delayered, so opportunities for progression have reduced and organisations no longer treat individuals as indispensible or irreplaceable, nor are inclined to invest highly in their development.

Summary

● The terms 'management' and 'leader' have different meanings within different contexts. The role and 'reality' of managing in organisations is often more complex, confusing and chaotic than many management texts would suggest.

● Management and Leadership Development is more than just management education and training. It involves the holistic development of the manager, taking account of such factors as: the needs, goals and expectations of both the organisation and the individual; the political, cultural and economic context; structures, and systems for selection, reward and monitoring performance.

● As part of an overall human resource strategy, MLD is now identified by many organisations as a source of competitive advantage and one of the key ingredients for success. However, if MLD is to be effective it must link to, and support, the organisation's business strategy. This enables those responsible for development to respond to the question, 'Why are you developing this manager?'

● Development is more effective when a stakeholder partnership exists between the individual, their boss and others in the organisation. A wide range of development techniques exists. The selection of the most appropriate techniques will depend upon the learning preferences and needs of managers. To be effective, development must reflect organisational context and the 'reality' of managerial work. An increasing reliance is being placed on the use of experiential techniques.

- A greater emphasis is now required on MLD attending to contextual complexity and diversity and meeting the needs of diverse groups of individuals, e.g. public sector, international managers and professionals.
- Like many aspects of organisational life, MLD cannot be isolated from controversy and debate. New challenges, conflicts, tensions and ambiguities continue to emerge.

Questions

1 What do you understand by the term 'Management and Leadership Development'?

2 To what extent can MLD support the business strategy?

3 Who are the stakeholders in MLD? Where can they support or block the process?

4 What are the important issues to consider in developing an MLD policy?

5 What are the challenges and issues that face MLD in the coming years?

Exercises

1 List the different methods and techniques used to develop managers and leaders. How would you judge and evaluate their effectiveness?

2 Organisations are increasingly turning to self-development as a management technique. Imagine you are the manager responsible for a group of young graduates about to embark upon your organisation's graduate development programme. Working in groups, develop an action plan for achieving a self-learning culture.

Case study 1

Ebay bids for a makeover

Meg Whitman, chief executive of Ebay, does not mince her words about the extent of the repair work needed at the company she has led for a decade.

'We have retooled Ebay a number of times over the years – this may be the biggest retooling we have to do,' she said earlier this week, after announcing that she would step down at the end of March.

Her comments indicate the scale of the task ahead for her chosen replacement: John Donahoe, 47, a former Bain management consultant who Ms Whitman brought in to run Ebay's main e-commerce businesses three years ago.

While insisting that 'it was definitely me that called the time' of the departure, Ms Whitman, speaking in an interview, was characteristically candid about why Ebay needs a change at the top. After 10 years, she said, it was hard for any chief executive to stay 'fresh' – and that was particularly true in an industry that moved as fast as the internet. She denied that the timing of her retirement, at 51, was directly linked to Ebay's circumstances, but left no doubt that it could use some new blood after falling behind.

'The web has evolved dramatically,' she said. 'The competitive position has changed, the technology has really changed. The industry keeps moving, you've got to pick up the pace.'

Some of Ms Whitman's own recent attempts to pick up the pace have fizzled. Her controversial acquisition of Skype, intended to lubricate Ebay's markets by making it easier for buyers and sellers to communicate, has failed to have an impact. A foray into China flopped, and Ebay later handed over control of its operations there to a local partner.

Most significant of all, though, has been Ms Whitman's fruitless struggle to rekindle the growth rate of her company's core auction and fixed-price

Case study continued

e-commerce businesses. In spite of attempts to lure more buyers by clamping down on fraudsters and making its sites easier to use, and to attract sellers by tinkering with its fees, Ebay has seen a steady decline in growth.

The company's latest quarterly figures this week pointed to the extent of the problem. While revenues and earnings were a little better than expected, the barometer of Ebay's underlying health swung in an ominous direction. In the US, transaction fees grew by 11 per cent, half the level of recent quarters, and the value of goods traded on the site – known as gross merchandise value – increased by only 5 per cent.

Mr Donahoe believes he now has a prescription for this. Over the next few weeks, he said, Ebay would announce a series of changes to its fee structure and to the way its search engine sifts through its millions of listings and chooses which to present most prominently. He warns that this is likely to attract bad publicity in the short term, as some sellers who lose out complain and competitors try to sow confusion. It will also dent the company's earnings this year, with growth falling to about 12 per cent as the company changes its

pricing formulae. Yet it was the only way, he added, to promote the site's best sellers and lure more buyers.

So far, Ebay's attempt to bill this management succession as a new page has been only partially successful. Mr Donahoe has already been in charge of the marketplace division for three years, and in that time 'we have not yet seen an improvement in the platform', said Youssef Squali, an analyst at Jefferies. If Mr Donahoe is to emulate Ms Whitman's decade at the top, his first job will be to prove to Wall Street he can start running faster.

Source: from Ebay bids for a makeover, *Financial Times*, 25 January 2008 (Waters, R.).

Questions

1 What challenges do organisations face in developing senior managers?

2 To what extent do senior managers present a special case in MLD?

3 As most organisations now prefer to develop internal managers through management succession, than to recruit from outside, how can Ebay effectively develop Donahoe's successor?

Case study 2

Alignment and trust in the learning function at Tesco.com: the role of metrics and measures

Tesco plc is one of the world's leading international retailers. Since its formation in 1919 the group has developed and expanded into a range of markets and has utilised different ways to deliver its retail services to customers. Tesco.com was formed in 1999 to drive forward its on-line retail processes in UK. Tesco.com operates as a 'business within a business' employing around 1,500 people. It is the most successful on–line grocery shopping service in the world. Sales growth (currently almost £1 billion) has been at about 30 per cent year on year since its inception whilst profits have also increased year on year to over £55 million in 2006.

Tesco's core purpose is 'to create value for customers' and so learning, like all other business processes is judged by its ability to contribute to this purpose. In the context of the rapid expansion and the imperative of growing profit margins, learning makes a strategic contribution at Tesco.com in three ways.

First, learning contributes to the development of a leadership framework that can manage a 30 percent year-on-year growth. Laura Wade-Gery, Chief Executive of Tesco.com highlights the importance of managers having the skills and abilities to 'do the right thing for customers, take people with you and live our values'.

Second, learning contributes to wider issues of talent management and development within the organisation. As Therese Procter, the Personnel Director puts it: 'talent planning, talent spotting, bringing the right people through, and moving people on is key for us'.

A further value contribution that learning makes is to the development of an appropriate culture for the Tesco.com business itself to reflect the specific fast-paced environment of dot.com businesses; technologically and competitively. Recruitment, employee

Case study continued

engagement and retention of IT, marketing and electronic commerce specialists are key issues for this part of the Tesco business.

This close alignment of learning to business priorities has enabled senior decision makers to have more trust in the ability of the learning function to add value. Laura Wade-Gery explained that 'What I've got is, I suppose, a belief that by producing managers/leaders who are that much more capable of doing things through others, we end up standing a better chance of getting what we need done.' This belief, however, is only sustained as a result of visible links between learning and business results. A significant investment in management and leadership development was sought, for example, that included the opportunity for managers at all levels to spend time in stores, with customers and staff 'to understand exactly what is going on' and then to convert their learning into action leading to tangible operational savings or product or service improvements. Given the close alignment of the proposed programme with business priorities, this investment in learning was supported by the Board without a full 'up-front' return on investment (ROI) business case.

In a business like Tesco.com the need for metrics and targets as a feature of management decision-making is taken for granted. A Tesco 'steering wheel' as a form of balanced scorecard forms the basis for measurement and performance improvement. The steering wheel includes five segments which indicate a balanced range of perspectives through which organisational performance can be measured:

'customers'; 'finance'; 'operations', 'community'; and 'people'. Within the 'people' segments regular measurement takes place and targets for continuous improvement are also established.

The focus of learning measures is firmly on outcomes rather than inputs. Therese Procter has targets for talent development and retention, therefore, as well as targets relevant to other features of the people segment of the steering wheel. Assessing the value of learning at Tesco.com, therefore, involves using business-relevant and aggregate measures including regular data from an annual staff survey ('Viewpoints') as well as from a quarterly 'Pulse' survey and measures of absence and staff turn-over. The effective use of a range of types of information that is relevant to the priorities of senior decision makers is, therefore, key to ensuring ongoing alignment and to developing and sustaining trust in the ability of learning function to add value.

Source: from Alignment and trust in the learning function at Tesco.com: the role of metrics and measures, http://www.cipd.co.uk/helpingpeoplelearn/_vlvtsc.htm, with the permission of the publisher, the Chartered Institute of Personnel and Development, London (www.cipd.co.uk).

Questions

1 What methods of evaluation are Tesco using to demonstrate the value of the MLD programme?

2 What assumptions are they making about its value?

3 How could their approach be improved?

References and further reading

Those texts marked with an asterisk are recommended for further reading.

Adey, K. (2000) 'Professional development priorities: the views of middle managers in secondary schools', *Educational Management and Administration*, 28, 4: 419–31.

Adler, N. (1997) *Organizational Behaviour*. Cincinnati, OH: South-Western College Publishing.

Alimo-Metcalfe, B. and Alban-Metcalfe, J. (2004) ' Leadership in public sector organisations' in J. Storey (ed.), *Leadership in Organizations: Current Issues and Key Trends*. London: Routledge, pp. 173–202.

Allen, A. (2003) 'Out of the ordinary', *People Management*, 9, 24: 36–38.

Antonacopoulou, E. and Bento, R. (2004) 'Methods of learning leadership: taught and experiential', in J. Storey (ed.), *Leadership in Organizations: Current Issues and Key Trends*. London: Routledge, pp. 81–102.

Antonacopoulou, E. and Fitzgerald, L. (1996) 'Reframing competency in management development', *Human Resource Management Journal*, 6, 1: 27–48.

Arkin, A. (2000) 'Combined honours', *People Management*, October, 6, 20: 42–46.

Arkin, A. (2003) 'Shaken and stirred', *People Management*, 9, 24: 32–34.

Arnold, J. (1997) *Managing Careers into the 21st Century*. London: Paul Chapman.

Baddeley, S. and James, K. (1990) 'Political management: developing the management portfolio', *Journal of Management Development*, 9, 3: 42–59.

Banks, J. (1994) *Outdoor Development for Managers*, 2nd edn. Aldershot: Gower.

Barker, R. (1997) 'How can we train leaders if we do not know what leadership is?' *Human Relations*, 50, 4: 343–62.

Beaver, G. and Lashley, C. (1998) 'Barriers to development in small hospitality firms', *Strategic Change*, June, 7, 4: 223–35.

Bicker, L. and Cameron, A. (1997) 'From manager to leader: facing up to the challenge of change', *EFMD Forum*, 1: 30–32.

Bittel, L. (1998) 'Management development for scientific and engineering personnel', in J. Prokopenko (ed.) *Management Development: A Guide for the Profession*. Geneva: International Labour Office, pp. 426–45.

Boddy, D. (2005) *Management: An Introduction*. London: FT/Prentice Hall.

Bolam, R. (1997) 'Management development for head teachers: retrospect and prospect', *Educational Management and Administration*, 25, 3: 265–83.

Boyatzis, R., Stubbs, E., and Taylor, S. (2002) 'Learning cognitive and emotional intelligence competencies through graduate management education', *Academy of Management Learning and Education*, 1, 2: 150–62.

Boydell, T. and Pedler, M. (1981) *Management Self-Development*. Westmead: Gower.

Bristow, N. (2007) 'Clinical leadership in the NHS: evaluating change through action learning' in R. Hill and J. Stewart (eds), *Management Development: Perspectives from Research and Practice*. Abingdon: Routledge, pp. 302–16.

Brown, P. (2005) 'The evolving role of strategic management development', *Journal of Management Development*, 24, 3: 209–22.

Brown, P. (2007) 'Strategic management development' in R. Hill and J, Stewart (eds) *Management Development: Perspectives from Research and Practice*. London: Routledge, pp. 40–59.

Bu, N. and Mitchell, V. (1992) 'Developing the PRC's managers: how can Western Europe become more helpful?', *Journal of Management Development*, 11, 2: 42–53.

*Buchanan, D. and Badham, R. (1999) *Power Politics and Organisational Change: Winning the Turf Game*. London: Sage.

*Buchanan, D. and Boddy, D. (1992) *The Expertise of the Change Agent*. Hemel Hempstead: Prentice Hall.

Buchanan, D., Claydon, T. and Doyle, M. (1999) 'Organisation development and change: the legacy of the nineties', *Human Resource Management Journal*, 9, 2: 20–37.

Burgoyne, J. (1988) 'Management development for the individual and the organisation', *Personnel Management*, June: 40–44.

Burgoyne, J., and Jackson, B. (1997) 'The arena thesis: management development as a pluralistic meeting point' in J. Burgoyne and J. Reynolds (eds) *Management Learning: Integrating Perspectives in Theory and Practice*. London: Sage.

Burgoyne, J., and Reynolds, J. (1997) *Management Learning: Integrating Perspectives in Theory and Practice*. Sage: London.

Burgoyne, J. and Stuart, R. (1991) 'Teaching and learning methods in management development', *Personnel Review*, 20, 3: 27–33.

Burnett, D. and James, K. (1994) 'Using the outdoors to facilitate personal change in managers', *Journal of Management Development*, 13, 9: 14–24.

Caligiuri, P. and Cascio, W. (1998) 'Can we send her there: maximising the success of Western women on global assignments', *Journal of World Business*, Winter, 33, 4: 394–416.

Chak-Ming Wo and Pounder, J. (2000) 'Post-experience management education and training in China', *Journal of General Management*, 26, 2: 52–70.

Chapman, J.A. (2001) 'The work of managers in new organisational contexts', *Journal of Management Development*, 20, 1: 55–68.

Chong, J., Kassener, M.W. and Ta-Lang Shih (1993) 'Management development of Hong Kong managers for 1997', *Journal of Management Development*, 12, 8: 18–26.

CIPD (2002) *Developing Managers for Business Performance*. London: CIPD.

CIPD (2004) *Learning and Development Survey*. London: CIPD.

CIPD (2008a) *Developing Senior Managers: Factsheet*. London: CIPD.

CIPD (2008b) *Management Development: Factsheet*. London: CIPD.

CIPD (2009) *Learning and Development: Annual Survey Report 2009*. London: CIPD.

Clarke, M., Butcher, D. and Bailey, C. (2004) 'Strategically aligned leadership development', in J. Storey (ed.), *Leadership in Organizations: Current Issues and Key Trends*. London: Routledge, pp. 271–92.

Constable, J. and McCormick, R. (1987) *The Making of British Managers*. London: BIM/CBI.

Cooper, C. (2002) 'Wanted: leaders to transform public services', *Sunday Times*, 13 January, p. 17.

Cumber, M., Donohoe, P. and Ho Sai Pak (1994) *Making Asian Managers*. Hong Kong: The Management Development Centre of Hong Kong.

Currie, G. (1994) 'Evaluation of management development: a case study', *Journal of Management Development*, 13, 3: 22–26.

*Currie, G. (1999) 'Resistance around a management development programme: negotiated order in an NHS Trust', *Management Learning*, 30, 1: 43–61.

Currie, G. and Darby, R. (1995) 'Competence-based management development: rhetoric and reality', *Journal of European Industrial Training*, 19, 5: 11–18.

Davidson, M. (1991) 'Women managers in Britain: issues for the 1990s', *Women in Management Review*, 6, 1: 5–10.

Davidson, M. and Burke, R. (eds) (1994) *Women in Management: Current Research Issues*. London: Paul Chapman.

Davidson, M. and Cooper, C. (1992) *Shattering the Glass Ceiling: The Woman Manager*. London: Paul Chapman.

Davis, T. (1990) 'Whose job is management development: comparing the choices', *Journal of Management Development*, 9, 1: 58–70.

Dearlove, D. (2002) 'Why workers distrust bosses', *The Times*, 31 October, p. 11.

Doyle, M. (1995) 'Organisational transformation and renewal: a case for reframing management development?', *Personnel Review*, 24, 6: 6–18.

*Doyle, M. (2000a) 'Management development in an era of radical change: evolving a relational perspective', *Journal of Management Development*, 19, 7: 579–601.

Doyle, M. (2000b) 'Managing careers in organisations', in A. Collin and R. Young (eds) *The Future of Career*. Cambridge: Cambridge University Press, pp. 228–42.

Doyle, M. (2002) 'From change novice to change expert', *Personnel Review*, 31, 2: 465–81.

Doyle, M., Claydon, T. and Buchanan, D. (2000) 'Mixed results, lousy process: contrasts and contradictions in the management experience of change', *British Journal of Management*, 11, special issue: 59–80.

Doyle, M., and Smith, M. (1999) *Born and Bred? Leadership, Heart and Informal Education*. London: YMCA George Williams College/Rank Foundation.

Duerden, D. (2006) *Management Development Activities*. London: CIPD.

Dulewicz, V. (1991) 'Improving assessment centres', *Personnel Management*, June: 50–55.

Easterby-Smith, M. (1992) 'European management education: the prospects for unification', *Human Resource Management Journal*, 3, 1: 23–36.

*Easterby-Smith, M. (1994) *Evaluation of Management Education, Training and Development*. Aldershot: Gower.

Endres, G. and Kleiner, B. (1990) 'How to measure management training and effectiveness', *Journal of European Industrial Training*, 14, 9: 3–7.

Estevez-Abe, M., Iversen, T., and Soskice, D. (2001) 'Social protection and the formation of skills: a reinterpretation of the welfare state' in P. Hall and D. Soskice (eds), *Varieties of Capitalism: The Institutional Foundation of Comparative Advantage*. Oxford: Oxford University Press, pp. 145–83.

Ferner, A. (1994) 'Multi-national comparisons and HRM: an overview of research issues', *Human Resource Management Journal*, 4, 3: 79–102.

Fischer, M. and Gleijm, H. (1992) 'The gender gap in management', *Industrial and Commercial Training*, 24, 4: 5–11.

Flynn, N. (2007) *Public Sector Management*. London: Sage.

Forth, J., Bewley, H. and Bryson, A. (2006) *Small and Medium Sized Enterprises: Findings from the 2004 Workplace Employment Relations Survey:* **www.niesr.ac.uk**.

Fox, S. (1989) 'The politics of evaluating management development', *Management Education and Development*, 20, 3: 191–207.

Fuller-Love, N. (2006) 'Management Development in small firms', *International Journal of Management Reviews*, 8, 3: 175–90.

Geppert, M., Matten, D. and Williams, K. (2002) *Challenges for European Management in a Global Context: Experiences from Britain and Germany*. Basingstoke: Palgrave Macmillan.

Glatter, R. (2004) 'Leadership in education' in J. Storey (ed.), *Leadership in Organizations: Current Issues and Key Trends*. London: Routledge, pp. 203–22.

Gobell, D., Przybylowski, K. and Rudelius, W. (1998) 'Customising management training in Central and Eastern Europe', *Business Horizons*, May/June, 41, 3: 61–72.

Gold, J., Thorpe, R. and Holt, R. (2007) 'Writing, reading and reason: the three Rs of manager learning' in R. Hill and J. Stewart (eds.), *Management Development: Perspectives from Research and Practice*. Abingdon: Routledge, pp. 271–84.

Greco, J. (1997) 'Corporate home schooling', *Journal of Business Strategy*, May/June, 18, 3: 48–52.

Hales, C. (1993) *Managing Through Organisation*. London: Routledge.

Hall, G. (2004) 'Work in Progress', *People Management*, 10, 19: 25.

Hamblin, B. (ed.) (2007) *Towards Evidence-based Management Development*. London: Routledge.

Hammond, V. (1998) 'Training and developing women for managerial jobs' in J. Prokopenko (ed.) *Management Development: A Guide for the Profession*. Geneva: International Labour Office, pp. 446–62.

Handy, C. (1987) *The Making of Managers*. London: MSC/ NEDO/BIM.

Hansen, C.D. and Brooks, A.K. (1994) 'A review of cross cultural research on human resource development', *Human Resource Development Quarterly*, 5, 1: 55–74.

Harris, H. and Kumra, S. (2000) 'International manager development: cross-cultural training in highly diverse environments', *Journal of Management Development*, 19, 7: 602–14.

Harrison, R. (1997) *Employee Development*, 2nd edn. London: IPM.

Harrison, R. (2009) *Learning and Development*, 5th edn. London: CIPD.

*Harzing, A.-M. and Van Ruysseveldt, J. (1995) *International Human Resource Management*. London: Sage.

Heisler, W.J. and Benham, P. (1992) 'The challenge of management development in North America in the 1990s', *Journal of Management Development*, 11, 2: 16–31.

Hendry, C. (1995) *Human Resource Management: A Strategic Approach to Employment*. Oxford: Butterworth-Heinemann.

Herriot, P. and Pemberton, C. (1995) *New Deals: The Revolution in Managerial Careers*. Chichester: John Wiley.

Hilb, P. (1992) 'The challenge of management development in Western Europe in the 1990s', *International Journal of Human Resource Management*, 3, 3: 575–84.

Hill, R. (1994) *Euro-Managers and Martians*. Brussels: Euro Publications.

Hill, R., and Stewart, J. (eds). (2007) *Management Development: Perspectives from Research and Practice*. London: Routledge.

Hollingshead, G. and Michailova, S. (2001) 'Blockbusters or bridge builders? The role of Western trainers in developing new entrepreneurialism in Eastern Europe', *Management Learning*, 32, 4: 419–36.

Honey, P. and Mumford, A. (1986) *Manual of Learning Styles*, 2nd edn. Maidenhead: Peter Honey.

Hopfl, H. and Dawes, F. (1995) 'A whole can of worms! The contested frontiers of management development and learning', *Personnel Review*, 24, 6: 19–28.

House, R., Javidan, M., Hanges, P. and Dorman, P. (2002) 'Understanding cultures and implicit leadership theories across the globe: an introduction to Project Globe', *Journal of World Business*, special issue, 37, 1: 3–10.

Hunt, C. (2005) 'Reflective practice' in J. Wilson (ed.), *Human Resource Development*. London: Kogan Page, pp. 234–51.

Hyland, T. (1994) *Competences, Education and NVQs: Dissenting Perspectives*. London: Cassell Education.

Industrial Society (1997) 'Senior management development', *Managing Best Practice*, 80, London.

Industrial Society (1998) 'Graduate recruitment and development', *Managing Best Practice*, 53, London.

International Labour Organization (1997) *Breaking Through the Glass Ceiling: Women in Management*. Geneva: ILO Publications.

IRS Employment Review (1997) 'Developing managers in small firms', April, 630: 15–16.

Irvine, D. and Wilson, J.P. (1994) 'Outdoor management development: reality or illusion?', *Journal of Management Development*, 13, 5: 25–37.

Jones, P. and Oswick, C. (1993) 'Outcomes of outdoor management development: articles of faith?', *Journal of European Industrial Training*, 17, 3: 10–18.

Jones, P. and Oswick, C. (2007) 'Inputs and outcomes of outdoor management development: of design, dogma and dissonance', *British Journal of Management*, 18, 4: 327–41.

Kakabadse, A. and Myers, A. (1995) 'Qualities of top management: comparisons of European manufacturers', *Journal of Management Development*, 14, 1: 5–15.

Kast, F.S. and Rosenzweig, J.E. (1985) *Organisation and Management: A Systems Approach*, 4th edn. New York: McGraw-Hill.

Kerr, A. and McDougall, M. (1999) 'The small business of developing people', *International Small Business Journal*, January/March, 17, 66: 65–74.

Kesby, D. (2008) 'Exploring the power of action learning', *Knowledge Management Review*, 11, 5: 26–29.

Kilcourse, T. (1994) 'Developing competent managers', *Journal of European Industrial Training*, 18, 2: 12–16.

Kirkbride, P. and Tang, S. (1992) 'Management development in the Nanyang Chinese societies of S.E. Asia', *Journal of Management Development*, 11, 2: 54–66.

Kirkpatrick, J. (1960) 'Techniques for evaluating training programmes', *Journal of American Society for Training and Development*, 14, 13–18: 25–32.

Kluckhohn, F. and Strodtbeck, F. (1961) *Variations in Value Orientations*. New York: Peterson.

Kolb, D. (1984) *Experiential Learning*. New York: Prentice-Hall.

Kumar, R. and Usunier, J.C. (2001) 'Management education in a globalising world', *Management Learning*, 32, 3: 363–91.

Kwiatkowski, S. and Kozminski, A. (1992) 'Paradoxical country: management education in Poland', *Journal of Management Development*, 11, 5: 28–33.

Larwood, L. and Wood, M. (1995) 'Training women for changing priorities', *Journal of Management Development*, 14, 2: 54–64.

Lawrence, P. (1992) 'Management development in Europe: a study in cultural contrast', *Human Resource Management Journal*, 3, 1: 11–23.

Leach, T., and Kenny, B. (2000) 'The role of professional development in stimulating changes in small growing businesses', *Continuing Professional Development Journal*, 3: 7–22.

Le Diest, F., Dutech, A., Klarsfeld, A. and Winterton, J. (2007) 'Management training and development in France: will elitism give way to strategic development?' in R. Hill and J. Stewart (eds) *Management development: Perspectives from Research and Practice*. Abingdon: Routledge, pp. 79–94.

Lee, G. (2003) *Leadership Coaching*. London: CIPD.

Lee, G. and Beard, D. (1994) *Development Centres: Realising the Potential of Your Employees through Assessment and Development*. Maidenhead: McGraw-Hill.

Lee, M. (1995) 'Working with choice in Central Europe', *Management Learning*, 26, 2: 215–30.

Lewis, A. and Fagenson, E. (1995) 'Strategies for developing women managers: how well do they fulfil their objectives?', *Journal of Management Development*, 14, 2: 39–53.

Linehan, M. and Walsh, J. (2000) 'Work–family conflict and the senior female international managers', *British Journal of Management*, 11, special issue: S49–58.

Little, B. (1997) 'I have a plan', *Management Skills and Development*, September: 26–30.

Liu, S. and Vince, R. (1999) 'The cultural context of learning in international joint ventures', *Journal of Management Development*, 18, 8: 666–75.

*Loan-Clarke, J. (1996) 'The Management Charter initiative: critique of management standards/NVQs', *Journal of Management Development*, 15, 6: 4–17.

Mabey, C. (2002) 'Mapping management development practice', *Journal of Management Studies*, 39, 8: 1139–56.

Mabey, C. (2004) 'Developing managers in Europe: policies, practices and impact', *Advances in Developing Human Resources*, 6, 4: 404–27.

Mabey, C. (2005) 'Management development works: the evidence', *Achieving Management Excellence Research Series 1996–2005*. London: Chartered Management Institute, pp. 1067–82.

Mabey, C., and Finch-Lees, T. (2008) *Management and Leadership Development*. London: Sage.

Mabey, C., and Ramirez, M. (2005) 'Does management development improve organizational productivity? A six-country analysis of European firms', *International Journal of Human Resource Management* 16, 7: 1067–82.

Mabey, C. and Salaman, G. (1995) *Strategic Human Resource Management*. Oxford: Blackwell.

Mabey, C., and Thompson, A. (2000), 'Management development in the UK: a provider and participant perspective', *International Journal of Training and Development*, 4, 4: 272–86.

Margerison, C. (1991) *Making Management Development Work*. Maidenhead: McGraw-Hill.

Margerison, C. (1994a) 'Managing career choices' in A. Mumford (ed.) *Gower Handbook of Management Development*, 4th edn. Aldershot: Gower, pp. 65–78.

Margerison, C. (1994b) 'Action learning and excellence in management development' in C. Mabey and P. Iles (eds) *Managing Learning*. London: Routledge, pp. 109–17.

Marsick, V. and Watkins, K. (1997) 'Lessons from informal and accidental learning' in J. Burgoyne and J. Reynolds (eds), *Management Learning: Integrating Perspectives in Theory and Practice*. London: Sage, pp. 295–311.

Mattis, M. (2001) 'Advancing women in business organisations: key leadership roles and behaviours of senior leaders and middle managers', *Journal of Management Development*, 20, 4: 371–88.

Mavin, S. and Bryans, P. (2000) 'Management development in the public sector: what role can universities play?', *International Journal of Public Sector Management*, 13, 2: 142–52.

Mayson, S. and Barrett, R. (2005) 'The science and practice of HRM in small firms', *Human Resource Management Review*, 16, 4: 447–55.

McCall, M.W. and Hollenbeck, G.P. (2002) *Developing Global Executives: The lessons of International Experience*. Boston, MA: Harvard Business School Press.

McFarlin, D., Coster, E. and Mogale, P. (1999) 'South African management development in the twenty-first century: moving towards a more Africanised model', *Journal of Management Development*, 18, 1: 63–78.

*Meldrum, M. and Atkinson, S. (1998) 'Is management development fulfilling its organisational role?', *Management Decision*, 36, 8: 528–32.

Melkman, A. and Trotman, K. (2005) *Training International Managers: Designing, Deploying and Delivering Effective training for Multi-cultural Groups*. Aldershot: Gower.

Miroshnik, V. (2002) 'Culture and international management: a review', *Journal of Management Development*, 21, 7: 521–44.

Mitiku, A. and Wallace, J. (1999) 'Preparing East African managers for the twenty-first century', *Journal of Management Development*, 18, 1: 46–62.

Molander, C. and Winterton, J. (1994) *Managing Human Resources*. London: Routledge.

Mole, G. (1996) 'The management training industry in the UK: an HRD director's critique', *Human Resource Management Journal*, 6, 1: 19–26.

*Mole, G. (2000) *Managing Management Development*. Buckingham: Open University Press.

Mole, G. (2004) 'Can leadership be taught?' In J. Storey (ed.), *Leadership in Organizations: Current Issues and Key Trends*. London: Routledge, pp. 125–37.

Moon, J. (2004) *A Handbook of Reflective and Experiential Learning*. London: Routledge.

*Morgan, G. (1997) *Images of Organisation*, 2nd edn. Beverley Hills, CA: Sage.

Mumford, A. (1988) *Developing Top Managers*. Aldershot: Gower.

*Mumford, A. (1997) *Management Development: Strategies for Action*, 3rd edn. London: IPD.

Mumford, A. and Gold, J. (2004) *Management Development: Strategies for Action*. London: CIPD.

Munchus, G. and McArthur, B. (1991) 'Revisiting the historical use of assessment centres in management selection and development', *Journal of Management Development*, 10, 1: 5–13.

Neelankavil, J. (1992) 'Management development and training programmes in Japanese firms', *Journal of Management Development*, 11, 3: 12–17.

Odiorne, G.S. (1984) *Strategic Management of Human Resources: A Portfolio Approach*. San Francisco, CA: Jossey-Bass.

Ohlott, P., Ruderman, M. and McCauley, C. (1994) 'Gender differences in managers' developmental job experiences', *Academy of Management Journal*, 37, 1: 46–67.

Owen, C. and Scherer, R. (2002) 'Doing business in Latin America: managing cultural differences in perceptions of female expatriates', *SAM Advanced Management Journal*, Spring, 67, 2: 37–41, 47.

Paauwe, J. and Williams, R. (2001) 'Seven key issues for management development', *Journal of Management Development*, 20, 2: 90–105.

Paton, R., Taylor, S. and Storey, J. (2004) 'Corporate univerisities and leadership development' in J. Storey (ed.), *Leadership in Organizations: Current Issues and Key Trends*. London: Routledge, pp. 103–24.

Pedler, M. (1997) 'Interpreting action learning' in J. Burgoyne and M. Reynolds (eds) *Management Learning: Integrating Perspectives in Theory and Practice*. London: Sage, pp. 248–64.

Pedler, M., Burgoyne, J., Boydell, T. and Welshman, G. (1990) *Self-Development in Organisations*. Maidenhead: McGraw-Hill.

Phillips, N. (1992) *Managing International Teams*. London: Pitman.

PIU (2001) *Strengthening Leadership in the Public Sector*. London: Cabinet Office Performance and Innovation Unit.

Prince, C. and Beaver, G. (2001) 'Facilitating organisational change: the role of the corporate university', *Strategic Change*, June/July, 10, 4: 189–99.

*Prokopenko, J. (1998) *Management Development: A Guide for the Profession*. Geneva: International Labour Office.

Puffer, S. (1993) 'The booming business of management education in Russia', *Journal of Management Development*, 12, 5: 46–59.

Rae, L. (1986) *How to Measure Training Effectiveness*. Aldershot: Gower.

Ramirez, M. (2004) 'Comparing European approaches to management education', *Advances in Developing Human Resources*, 6, 4: 428–50.

Randlesome, C. (2000) 'Changes in management culture and competences: the German experience', *Journal of Management Development*, 19, 7: 629–42.

*Ready, D., Vicere, A. and White, A. (1994) 'Towards a systems approach to executive development', *Journal of Management Development*, 13, 5: 3–11.

Rees, B. and Garnsey, E. (2003) 'Analysing competence: gender and identity at work', *Gender, Work and Organization*, 10, 5: 551–78.

Redman, T., Keithley, D. and Szalkowski, A. (1995) 'Management development under adversity: case studies from Poland', *Journal of Management Development*, 14, 10: 4–13.

Reitsma, S.G. (2001) 'Management development in Unilever', *Journal of Management Development*, 20, 2: 131–44.

*Revans, R. (1983) *ABC of Action Learning*. Bromley: Chartwell-Bratt.

*Roberts, C. and McDonald, G. (1995) 'Training to fail', *Journal of Management Development*, 14, 4: 1–16.

Roberts, G. (1995) 'Competency management systems: the need for a practical framework', *Competency*, 3, 2: 27–30.

Rosenfeld, R. and Wilson, D. (1999) *Managing Organisations: Texts, Readings and Cases*, 2nd edn. London: McGraw-Hill.

Saee, J. and Mouzytchenko, O. (1999) 'The role of multinational entrepreneurs within the Australian economy: strategic entrepreneurs management training and institutional responses and solutions', *Journal of European Business Education*, December, 9, 1: 62–79.

*Salaman, G. (1995) *Managing*. Buckingham: Open University Press.

Salaman, G. (2004) 'Competences of managers, competences of leaders' in J. Storey (ed.) *Leadership in Organizations: Current Issues and Key Trends*. London: Routledge, pp. 58–78.

Schon, D. (1984) *The Reflective Practitioner: How Professionals Think in Action*. Massachusetts: Basic Books.

Scott, P. (2004) 'Innovative technologies and leadership development' in J. Storey (ed.) *Leadership in Organizations: Current Issues and Key Trends*. London: Routledge, pp. 138–51.

Simpson, P. and Lyddon, T. (1995) 'Different roles, different views: exploring the range of stakeholder perceptions on an in-company management development programme', *Industrial and Commercial Training*, 27, 4: 26–32.

Smith, A. (1993) 'Management development evaluation and effectiveness', *Journal of Management Development*, 12, 1: 20–32.

Smith, A. and Porter, J. (1990) 'The tailor-made training maze: a practitioner's guide to evaluation', *Journal of European Industrial Training*, 14, 8: complete issue.

*Snyder, R. (1993) 'The glass ceiling for women: things that don't cause it and things that won't break it', *Human Resource Development Quarterly*, 4, 1: 97–106.

Sparrow, P. and Bognanno, M. (1994) 'Competency forecasting: issues for international selection and assessment' in C. Mabey and P. Iles (eds) *Managing Learning*. London: Routledge, pp. 57–69.

Stansfield, L. and Stewart, J. (2007) 'A stakeholder approach to the study of management development' in R. Hill and J. Stewart (eds), *Management Development: Perspectives from Research and Practice*. London: Routledge.

Stern, S. (2002) 'Enhancing your talent', *Management Today*, October: 2–3.

*Stewart, J. and Hamlin, B. (1992a) 'Competence-based qualifications: the case against change', *Journal of European Industrial Training*, 16, 7: 21–32.

*Stewart, J. and Hamlin, B. (1992b) 'Competence-based qualifications: a case for established methodologies', *Journal of European Industrial Training*, 16, 9: 9–16.

Stone, I., Braidford, P. and Houston, M. (2006) *Insights from Studying the 2004 Sunday Times 50 Best SMEs to Work for*, **www.berr.gov.uk**.

Storey, J. (1992) 'Making European managers: an overview', *Human Resource Management Journal*, 3, 1: 1–10.

Storey, J. (2004) 'Changing theories of leadership and leadership development' in J. Storey (ed.) *Leadership in Organisations: Current Issues and Key Trends*. London: Routledge, pp. 11–38.

*Storey, J., Mabey, C. and Thomson, A. (1997) 'What a difference a decade makes', *People Management*, June: 28–30.

Storey, J., Okazaki-Ward, L., Gow, I., Edwards, P.K. and Sisson, K. (1991) 'Managerial careers and management development: a comparative analysis of Britain and Japan', *Human Resource Management Journal*, 1, 3, Spring: 33–57.

Strack, R., and Krinks, P. (2008) 'The talent crunch', *People Management*, 14, 13: 30–31.

Sturges, J. (2004) 'The individualisation of the career and its implications for leadership and management development' in J. Storey (ed.) *Leadership in Organisations: Current Issues and Key Trends*. London: Routledge, pp. 249–68.

Syrett, M. and Lammiman, J. (1999) *Management Development: Making the Investment Count*. London: Profile Books.

Syrett, M. and Lammiman, J. (2003) *Boardroom Education*. Oxford: Capstone.

Tamkin, P. and Hillage, J. (1999) *Employability and Employers: The Missing Piece of the Jigsaw*. Brighton: Institute for Employment Studies.

Tansey, C., Turner, P., Foster, C., Harris, L., Sempik, A., Stewart, J. and Williams, H. (2007) *Talent: Strategy, Management and Measurement – Research into Practice*. London: CIPD.

Tarrant, D. (2005) 'Building a better team', *Management Today Australia*, May 14: 25–27.

Tate, W. (2004) 'Linking development with business' in J. Storey (ed.) *Leadership in Organisations: Current Issues and Key Trends*. London: Routledge, pp. 293–318.

Templer, A., Beatty, D. and Hofmeyer, K. (1992) 'The challenge of management development in South Africa: so little time, so much to do', *Journal of Management Development*, 11, 2: 32–41.

Temporal, P. (1990) 'Linking management development to the corporate future: the role of the professional', *Journal of Management Development*, 9, 5: 7–15.

*Thomson, A., Mabey, C., Storey, J., Gray, C. and Iles, P. (2001) *Changing Patterns of Management Development*. Oxford: Blackwell Business.

Thornhill, A. (1993) 'Management training across cultures: the challenge for trainers', *Journal of European Industrial Training*, 17, 10: 43–51.

Thurley, K. and Wirdenhuis, H. (1991) 'Will management become European? Strategic choice for organisations', *European Management Journal*, 9, 2: 127–35.

Tijmstra, S. and Casler, K. (1992) 'Management learning for Europe', *European Management Journal*, 10, 1: 30–38.

Tolentino, A. (1998) 'Training and development of entrepreneur–managers of small enterprises' in J. Prokopenko (ed.) *Management Development: A Guide for the Profession*, Geneva: International Labour Office, pp. 471–92.

Torrington, D., Weightman, J. and Johns, K. (1994) *Effective Management: People and Organisations*, 2nd edn. Hemel Hempstead: Prentice Hall.

Trehan, K. and Shelton, R. (2007) 'Leadership development: a critical evaluation' in R. Hill, and J. Stewart (eds.) *Management Development: Perspectives from Research and Practice*. London: Routledge, pp. 285–301.

Tyler, S. (2004) 'Making leadership and management development measure up' in J. Storey (ed.), *Leadership in Organizations: Current Issues and Key Trends*. London: Routledge, pp. 152–70.

Varma, A., Stroh, L. and Schmitt, L. (2001) 'Women and international assignments: the impact of supervisor–subordinate relationships', *Journal of World Business*, 36, 4: 380–88.

Veale, C. and Gold, J. (1998) 'Smashing into the glass ceiling for women managers', *Journal of Management Development*, 17, 1: 17–26.

Vecsenyi, J. (1992) 'Management education for the Hungarian transition', *Journal of Management Development*, 11, 3: 39–47.

Vicere, A. (1998) 'Changes in practice, changes in perspectives: the 1997 international study of executive development trends', *Journal of Management Development*, 17, 7: 526–43.

Vine, P. (1999) 'Back to school', *British Journal of Administrative Management*, March/April: 18–21.

Vineall, T. (1994) 'Planning management development' in A. Mumford (ed.) *Gower Handbook of Management Development*, 4th edn. Aldershot: Gower, pp. 23–32.

Vinnicombe, S. and Colwill, N. (1995) *The Essence of Women in Management*. Hemel Hempstead: Prentice Hall.

Wah, L. (1998) 'Surfing the rough seas', *American Management Association*, September: 25–29.

Warr, P., Bird, M. and Rackham, N. (1970) *Evaluation of Management Training*. London: Gower.

*Watson, T. (1994) *In Search of Management*. London: Routledge.

*Watson, T. (2002) *Organising and Managing Work*. Harlow: Financial Times/Prentice Hall.

*Watson, T. and Harris, P. (1999) *The Emergent Manager*. London: Sage.

Whiddett, S. and Branch, J. (1993) 'Development centres in Volvo', *Training and Development UK*, 11, 11: 16–18.

Whitaker, V. and Megginson, D. (1992) 'Women and men working together effectively', *Industrial and Commercial Training*, 24, 4: 16–19.

Whitmore, J. (2002) *Coaching for Performance*. Nicholas Brearley.

Williams, M. and Cowling, M. (2008) *Annual Small Business Survey 2007/8*. Institute for Employment Studies: **www.berr.gov.uk**.

Wong, C., Marshall, N., Alderman, N. and Thwaites, A. (1997) 'Management training in small and medium-sized enterprises: methodological and conceptual issues', *International Journal of Human Resource Management*, 8, 1: 44–65.

Woodall, J. (2000) 'Corporate support for work-based management development', *Human Resource Management Journal*, 10, 1: 18–32.

*Woodall, J. and Winstanley, D. (1998) *Management Development: Strategy and Practice*. Oxford: Blackwell.

Woodruffe, C. (ed.) (1992) *What is Meant by Competency?* Maidenhead: McGraw-Hill.

Woodruffe, C. (1993) *Assessment Centres: Identifying and Developing Competence*. London: IPM.

Zaleznik, A. (1992) 'Managers and leaders: are they different?' *Harvard Business Review*, March–April: 126–35.

For multiple-choice questions, exercises and annotated weblinks related to this topic, visit **www.pearsoned.co.uk/mymanagementlab**.

Transforming Anglian Water

The history

Anglian Water is geographically the largest of the ten regional water companies in the UK, delivering clean drinking water and removing sewage and waste-water from the homes and premises of some 5 million customers. Throughout the 1980s there were growing concerns over the standards and level of service delivery afforded by public sector organisations, and in line with the then government ideology and policy Anglian Water was privatised in 1989. Following privatisation, the company introduced a major reorganisation of its business, involving a rationalisation of existing structures and a diversification into new markets – many of them overseas operations. Between 1993 and 1995 the company reduced management layers from eleven to five, and 33 per cent of white-collar jobs were eliminated, bringing a saving of £40 million. However, senior management were conscious that if the organisation was to transform itself into a successful, high-performing international company, a fundamental realignment of its existing culture was required.

Prior to privatisation, the company's culture could be described as 'militaristic' – and with some justification. The risks were high. Any mistake in delivering water to customers could prove disastrous, and the company abided by the principle that 'contaminated water cannot be recalled'. The management solution was to introduce strict rules and procedures that were to be followed to the letter and obeyed without question. Any diversion from routine procedures was alien to an organisation where small risks or mistakes could rapidly and seriously jeopardise health and safety. The result was a culture in which playing by the rules, obeying orders, the acceptance and non-questioning of procedures was (and in the eyes of many had to be) the norm.

Forging a learning organisation

Senior management were under no illusions: the company's future success and survival in an increasingly competitive and aggressive marketplace depended on replacing the company's command-and-control culture with a more outward-looking, entrepreneurial, customer-focused, innovative approach to doing business. But how could this be achieved?

Philosophically, the company's approach was rooted in the need to reorient and prepare its employees for continuing and radical change, and to do this meant creating a more flexible, empowering, learning culture. The need to move in this direction was highlighted by a series of employee attitude surveys carried out after the restructuring of the early 1990s. Among other things, the surveys highlighted a discontent with the existing management style and communication policies. This led the senior management of Anglian Water into a considered debate about the future cultural direction of the business and the decision to create what they termed a *learning organisation.*

As a learning organisation the company would move away from the old public sector, keep your head down, jobs for life, follow the procedure mentality towards an environment in which employee creativity, innovation and challenge would be encouraged and valued. Employees would be empowered to take the lead in change. Individually and in cross-functional teams they would involve themselves in continuous improvement, not only in the area of technological development but – more significantly for a highly rational, technical organisation – in the area of customer service to meet changing needs and demands.

Steps along the way

There were two central, interlocking components designed to transform Anglian Water into a learning organisation. The first was the Transformation Journey. The concept of the Journey evolved from a development programme for attitudinal and behavioural change among senior managers. Following its success, a decision was taken to roll it out to all employees. The Journey was not a training programme. Instead it was a holistic strategy designed to prepare and equip employees for the technical and emotional challenges of operating in a turbulent and uncertain environment. The Journey was aimed at changing mindsets and creating self-awareness. It sought to promote teamworking and cooperation, and ultimately to have a direct bearing on operational effectiveness and business performance.

Any employee could 'sign up' for the Journey, and participation was entirely voluntary. However, clear signals were sent to the workforce that individuals were expected to participate, and enrolment on the Journey was regarded as an indication of their commitment to the company and its future.

Employees formed themselves into teams. Sometimes these were work related, but on other occasions individuals from disparate backgrounds came together. The only proviso was that any activity they engaged in was to benefit themselves, their group, and Anglian Water. There were four guiding principles for 'Travellers':

- a willingness to get to know myself;
- a desire to develop myself;
- a desire to realise my full potential with and through others;
- an ability to link my personal development to the development of Anglian Water.

A typical Journey lasted two years and was an essentially self-managed exercise. Each group was expected to acquire its own funding and sponsorship and to arrange its own support and skills development. Regular reviews along the way ensured that there was a basis for learning and reflection.

Journeys included groups who went outside Anglian Water, for example to build a toilet block on top of England's highest mountain, to refurbish a children's hospice, or to dig a well in Africa. Other groups focused on internal projects to improve overall business functioning and 'make things happen'. They involved themselves in more cross-functional teamworking, sought to improve their business knowledge and commercial awareness, became more creative and lateral in their thinking, conducted detailed research into business problems, and explored different options for change.

Between 1995 and 1997, 3000 employees had enrolled on the Journey, with some 300 groups being formed. In a 1996 survey, 88 per cent of respondents felt the Journey had benefited Anglian Water, and 99 per cent said that participation in a Journey had been a 'good learning experience'. Coincident with this survey, it was reported that customer satisfaction ratings had risen from 70 per cent in March 1995 to 90 per cent in March 1996.

The second component in Anglian's strategy to transform itself into a learning organisation was the establishment of the *University of Water* (colloquially known as Aqua Universitas). Knowledge creation and sharing were seen as vital in promoting best-practice networks and better customer service, and in enhancing commercial success. The University was aimed at acknowledging, integrating, supporting and accrediting all forms of learning taking place in the company. Its role was to define and develop the skills and competences – especially management skills – that were required to move Anglian into the twenty-first century and ensure its future as a global player. To this end, considerable resources were made available – for example, a dedicated 'campus' on the shores of Rutland Water and the installation of an intranet to promote information exchange and communication.

Around these two central components throughout the 1990s the company introduced a raft of supporting initiatives, including total quality management, leadership coaching, mass communication strategy development, change agent networks, new HR performance management policies, and vision and values statements designed to inculcate new attitudes and behaviours.

So have efforts to transform Anglian Water into a learning organisation culture been a success? Certainly there are considerable references to the 'old Anglian Water' and the 'new Anglian Water', reflecting a perception of behaviour and attitudinal change. And according to Clive Morton, ex-HR Director of Anglian, there is no doubt that a change in culture has occurred:

> The combination of the Journey and the University of Water with its universal access has created the conditions for a learning business, helping to assure the future for Anglian Water and its stakeholders.
>
> (Morton, 1998: 98)

The future

In 1998 Ofwat (the government's regulatory body for the water industry) recommended a price reduction of at least 17.5 per cent (about £45 on the average bill) in 2000. This one-off cut in charges represented about £130 million loss of revenue, and compares with 1998 profits of £268 million on turnover of £850 million. 'Costs must come down', the company warned. During 1999 the company initiated a major cost-reduction strategy, and this has translated into 400 job losses (10 per cent of the workforce).

Reference

Morton, C. (1998) *Beyond World Class*. Basingstoke: Macmillan Business Press.

Source: Extracts from *Anglian Water News*.

Questions

You are an external consultant(s) advising a company facing similar challenges to those experienced by Anglian Water. It has read an account similar to the one described above, and is interested in exploring the whole concept of the learning organisation as a way of helping it to transform and succeed in the face of radical change. However, the board is cautious, and slightly sceptical of the cultural transformation process that Anglian has undergone. It has asked you to make an assessment. Specifically, they want you to report:

1 on the extent to which Anglian Water's claim to be a learning organisation can be justified. On what grounds should any claims or justifications be made?

2 against the backdrop of recent major job losses, whether or not Anglian can/should sustain the ideals and practices of a learning organisation. Are there any factors that might eventually undermine the concept and call into question the massive investment Anglian has made?

You are to prepare a report for the board of between 1000 and 1500 words, and follow this up with a short presentation (ten minutes).

Part 4

THE EMPLOYMENT RELATIONSHIP

Introduction to Part 4

The employment relationship is key to understanding how employment is managed. It brings together the sources of power and legitimacy and rights and obligations that management and employees seek for themselves and apply to others. This part of the book is concerned with explaining the employment relationship and examining how it works out through a variety of applications such as the law, collective bargaining, performance and reward, and employee involvement.

Chapter 10 deals with the role and influence of the law in determining the nature of contract. The contract of employment is not simply a document that is presented to employees on appointment, but is a complex set of formal and informal rules which govern the whole basis of the employment relationship. Thus, the way employees and managers conform with, or break, those rules determines how that relationship works out in practice. Moreover, the nature of contract can have an important bearing on whether such newer concepts as human resource management can fundamentally change a relationship that is so dependent upon the interaction of formal and informal legal regulation.

Chapter 11 examines the changing pattern of employment regulation in the UK. It starts by examining changes in collective bargaining in the context of its overall decline, looking at how pressures for management decentralisation, labour flexibility and public sector modernisation have influenced the extent nature and effectiveness of collective bargaining. This is followed by a critical discussion of how since 1997 Labour governments have extended the regulation of employment in order to promote its agenda of 'partnership' and 'fairness at work'. The key issue here is how successfully the New Labour administration has balanced this agenda with its concern to promote labour market flexibility as the basis for international competitiveness. Finally, the chapter examines the various ways in which terms and conditions of employment are established in the non-union firms that are now predominant in the private sector, looking at both large and small organisations and exploring distinctive patterns of employment regulation in small non-union firms.

Chapter 12 reviews approaches to performance measurement, in particular appraisal, and distinguishes between performance management and the broader concept of performance management. It goes on to consider the extent to which there has been a significant shift away from equating performance measurement with 'individual employee' effort and achievement to seeing it as something that encompasses and involves the 'whole organisation'.

Chapter 13 examines developments in employee reward and the practical ways in which reward management can be used in conjunction with other HRM practices to promote employee engagement and drive individual and organisational performance. After tracing the historical development of reward systems the chapter moves on to explore the contemporary meaning of reward, focusing on its role as a potential strategic lever to orient individuals and teams in the direction of business goals and values. The chapter also considers the economic and legal environment for reward and the challenges associated with designing a reward strategy that is affordable, equitable and relevant, paying particular attention to pragmatic reward choices and dilemmas experienced by today's organisations. These include decisions about the relative importance of internal equity and external pay comparability, the role of job evaluation, the factors which tend to be influential in shaping the reward 'mix', where to pitch pay and how to design pay structures and manage pay progression.

Chapter 14 is concerned with the development of employee involvement. This is a topic that has seen great interest recently, but there are contradictory elements within it which this chapter explores, among them whether involvement can genuinely bring employee and managerial interests together and whether involvement is a vehicle for 'empowerment' or simply a further way in which the managerial prerogative is asserted in the employment relationship.

Chapter 10

The employment relationship and employee rights at work

Ian Clark and Alan J. Ryan

Objectives

- To introduce readers from a variety of backgrounds to the central significance of contract in the employment relationship.
- To examine the contractual and statutory regulation of employment contracts in a manner that is reader friendly, taking as its central focus the manner in which employment rights need to be regulated and proceduralised in the workplace.
- To provide the HR practitioner or other interested reader with the necessary basic information to enable them to make fair and reasonable decisions within the employment relationship.
- To add critical observations on the limitations of employee rights in the UK.

Introduction

This chapter examines the employment relationship and its contractual regulation. In particular, it outlines the central significance of contractual regulation in the employment relationship, and how this legitimises the managerial prerogative. The employment relationship should be seen as a process of socio-economic exchange. By this we mean that, unlike other contractual relationships such as the purchase of a railway ticket, the act of hiring an employee does not complete the exchange; instead it simply initiates it as both parties intend the contract to continue until one of them decides to end it. As a socio-economic exchange the employment relationship not only contains an economic component – the exchange of work for payment – but also includes a sociological dimension centred on power and authority. The economic and sociological components of the employment relationship are structured by the contract of employment. In addition, the employment relationship is subject to a range of other processes, for example management competence and efficiency, work group control, management and worker motivation and the potential for workplace conflict and disagreement. These factors make the apparently rational process of economic exchange much more complicated and to some extent indeterminate – that is, a relationship in which the specific details are subject to ongoing negotiation and change.

All employees are protected by a series of basic contractual and statutory employment rights which employers must respect. In order to provide readers with the necessary basic information on these matters the chapter is divided into seven sections:

- Distinguishing contractual and statutory employment rights;
- The contract of employment;
- Discrimination in employment;
- The regulation of working time;
- Termination of the employment contract;
- Enforcement of contractual and statutory employment rights;
- Current issues.

Throughout the chapter there is a series of Activity boxes and Stop and Think boxes that aim to assist the reader apply and digest particular points. Readers should work through these individually, in conversation with their peers or in discussion with their teachers. The material in each part of the chapter, although necessarily legal in nature, is explained as far as possible in terms that are general and straightforward to assist the reader in their application. Some points are repeated as they affect areas of employment regulation detailed in successive parts of the chapter. Because the aim is to present the material in a 'reader friendly' manner there are few direct references to legal texts or statutes; however, at the end of the chapter a list of law texts is provided for further reading. The reader should view this chapter as a general introduction to the contract of employment and its regulation and readers should be aware that more specialist information may be required in applying the general principles to specific situations.

Distinguishing contractual and statutory employment rights

In a chapter such as this, it is not possible to provide a complete and comprehensive analysis of the employment relationship and its legal regulation – employment contracts and employment statutes are subject to change as practices that were previously 'outwith the law' become subject to legal regulation, for example the recent emergence of paid paternity leave for fathers and more recently still, protection against discrimination in employment due to age. Hence the law may be further updated after this edition is published. Equally, many areas of contractual and statutory regulation are extremely complicated and disputes between an employer and an employee may require specialist analysis by employment lawyers. Examples of these areas include discrimination claims with respect to pension rights for part-time women employees, disability discrimination claims that relate to the status of an employee as HIV positive and the interpretation of working time regulations for a particular group of employees. Thus, bearing in mind that contractual and statutory regulation of the employment relationship is a 'moving target', our examination of regulation within the employment relationship divides between a discussion of contractual and statutory employment rights.

Contractual rights

All employees have a contract of employment that governs the relationship between the employer and an individual employee. A key element in relation to these rights is the definition of the difference between an employee and a worker found in the Employment Rights Act 1996 (ERtsA) s. 230. As we discuss below, an employment contract has two types of terms and conditions within it – express terms that are usually written down and which govern the specific details of the employee's contract of employment and implied terms, which fall into two groups and are unlikely to be written down but which nevertheless are considered to be part of an employee's contract of employment. For example, terms implied by statutory provision include the requirement that an employer is under a legally enforce-able duty to provide a healthy and safe workplace. Further terms are implied under what is commonly referred to as the 'business efficacy' rule – in simple terms they are implied as a matter of fact and are needed in order for the contract to work. These are often derived from custom and practice arrangements in the workplace even though many of them may be unwritten. The core principle, in relation to 'business efficacy' is therefore the extent to which the parties would have agreed to the term had the issue involved been put to them at the outset of the contract (Holland and Burnett, 2009). In summary, contractual rights flow from the express and implied terms and conditions that create an individual contract of employment. It is important to point out that while employees receive protection via ele-ments of these terms and conditions they are also subject to regulation by them; hence the contract of employment is made up of a balance of rights and obligations between the employer and the employee.

Statutory rights

Statutory employment rights have been enacted in an attempt to provide a basic floor of rights for all workers – so the distinction between 'employees' and 'workers' becomes irrele-vant. Statutory employment rights are created by legislation in the form of Acts of Parliament, statutory instruments, and increasingly, European Union directives that must be incorporated into UK law. An example of the latter is the emergence in the UK of the statu-tory regulation of working time.

In the drafting process, government and European Union civil servants seek to ensure that the legislation covers most eventualities. However, because legislation is necessarily general in its coverage of a particular issue an employer, trade unions and the judiciary must interpret legislation. Interpretation of legislation is a complicated and controversial matter and often turns on the issue of what is 'reasonable'. For an employer's interpretation of a statute to be rea-sonable the employer must be able to demonstrate to an employee, trade union or, in a matter of dispute, an employment tribunal that another employer faced with the same or a similar situation would have acted in the same way. In a matter of dispute an employee or a trade union must be able to demonstrate that another employer would not have acted in a particular manner. For example, it was common practice for many employers to exclude their part-time workforce from occupational pension schemes on the basis that the salary or wage level of part-timers was too low to generate a sufficient pension fund, particularly as this would reduce the take-home pay of such workers because of the necessary deduction of an employee's contri-bution to the pension scheme. After a long legal campaign several trade unions, supported by the then Equal Opportunities Commission, established that this practice was unreasonable because many part-time workers were women and their exclusion from company pension schemes amounted to indirect sex discrimination. This was the case because, although the exclusion of part-time workers from pension schemes appears to be sex neutral in its effects, such exclusion has a disproportionate effect on women, so the practice is discriminatory. (See *R v Secretary for Employment ex parte Seymour-Smith* [1999] IRLR 253). Common law precedent, that is, judicial decisions of interpretation, guide decisions in disputes where there is no rele-vant Act of Parliament and thus has the status of an Act of Parliament.

Summary

A central principle of the English legal system operative in contract law, the common law and statute law is that of *reasonableness*. In employment contracts, the common law terms and conditions and statutory interventions both have to be reasonable in their effects on the employer and employee. Thus in many cases judgments in disputes between employer and employee often turn on the question of reasonableness. The notions of reasonable and unreasonable behaviour or instructions are questions of interpretation in the circumstances of particular cases. As explained above, an express, or implied term in a contract of employment is reasonable if, in a matter of dispute, it is held that a similar employer would have done the same thing, for example discipline or dismiss an employee, in similar circumstances. The discussion of this point is important for the following reasons. As statutory rights are subject to interpretation, challenge and eventual updating either in the form of statutory amendment or a binding precedent created by a court or employment tribunal, personnel practitioners must keep abreast of developments in employment law to ensure that the procedures set in place by their employer reflect the spirit and the letter of the law.

Try to think of five contractual rights and five statutory rights that you have or that your parents or partner have in employment.

The importance of the contract of employment

As indicated throughout this chapter the regulation of the employment relation is fundamentally a matter of legal interpretation. It matters not whether we are focusing on wage, performance, or termination; a key element on which the answer will turn is the status of the individual concerned. In simple terms we are asking whether the individual concerned is a 'worker' or an 'employee' because the law attaches different levels of protection to each. As Freedland (2003) argues, the common law principles which establish a valid contract (see below) have both a different format and an alternative function in the framework relating to personal employment contracts. The existence of a contract of employment, and hence the classification of an individual as an employee, determine the availability of employment rights. As indicated in Figure 10.1 below, the legal categorisation of an individual as an 'employee' opens access to all employment rights, while other groups have restricted rights.

As can be seen, the division of rights between three different arrangements for offering and obtaining labour gives organisations options – some of which reduce the extent of their obligations to those undertaking the labour. Throughout the rest of this chapter this division of rights will be highlighted where appropriate in order to draw out the importance of the contract of employment, and the extent to which there has been progression in the development of a more 'fluid relationships between organisations and those who carry out work for them' (von Prondzynski, 2000: 103). These more fluid relationships, such as those involving self-employed workers and sub-contract workers, are not well suited to regulation through the employment contract in its current form (Collins *et al.*, 2000; Blanpain and Weiss, 2003; Conaghan and Rittich, 2005; Davidov and Langille, 2006; Njoya, 2007; Freedland and Kountouris, 2008; Bercusson and Estlund, 2008). Thus while this traditional – contractual – approach to the employment relation may have provided a useful explanation of the relationship in the past we can argue (see below on current debates) that a new approach is needed for the twenty-first century. This new approach has been variously portrayed as the law relating to 'subordinate labour' (Davidov, 2005a; Hyde, 2006), the law of 'the personal employment contract' (Freedland, 2003) or the 'private/property law model' (Collins, 2000; Njoya, 2007). These various models are included in the following analysis at appropriate points.

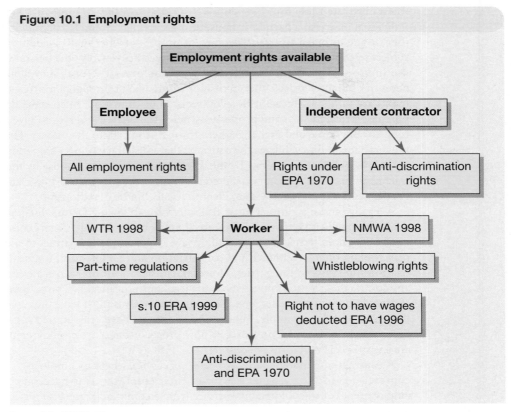

Figure 10.1 Employment rights

Source: Cabrelli (2008: 11).

The contract of employment

This part of the chapter primarily adopts the traditional analysis of the employment relation and therefore divides into six subsections. The first distinguishes employment contracts from commercial contracts; this is followed by a brief discussion of contract theory. The third subsection examines the effects of the common law on employment contracts; this is followed by a discussion of different types of employment contracts. The fifth subsection discusses terms and conditions of employment contracts, and finally statutory rights that relate to employment contracts are examined in some detail.

Distinguishing commercial contracts and employment contracts

In order to explain the concept of contract, it is useful to distinguish between commercial contracts and employment contracts, our particular area of focus. Commercial contracts, for example something as simple as buying a bus ticket or something as complex as a house purchase, contain four elements:

- offer;
- acceptance;
- consideration; and
- an intention to create legal relations.

To illustrate these four elements we can draw on the example of a house purchase. An individual may visit a particular house and decide they would like to buy it. As a result of this they decide to make an *offer*. The current property owner may decide to accept this offer – subject to contract. 'Subject to contract' will necessarily involve the person who wishes to buy the house – the offeror – receiving a satisfactory structural survey and acquiring the necessary purchase price either in cash or (more likely) through a mortgage. If these requirements are fulfilled satisfactorily, a contract can be drawn up. In consideration for the agreed purchase price, the existing property owner – the offeree – agrees to give up their property rights in the house and exchange them through contract to the offeror. Thus *consideration* is the mechanism that validates the contract: that is, each party gives something to the contract, in this case a house for money by the offeror and money for a house by the offeree. If a contract contains offer, acceptance and consideration, the presence of these factors indicates that the parties to the contract wish to create a legally binding relationship.

A legally binding contract must also satisfy the following factors. First, the contents of the contract, to which the parties have agreed, must be reasonable. Second, the contract in itself must be legal, in terms of the prevailing law. For example, a contract to assassinate a person may contain offer, acceptance and consideration and an intention to create a legally binding relationship between the parties. However, conspiracy to murder is a criminal offence, thus any contractual relationship is void – the legal term for invalid. Third, there must be genuine consent between the parties, and the parties themselves must have the capacity to consent to the agreement. For example, minors and bankrupts have only limited capacities in contract. From this brief introduction we can now proceed to look at employment contracts, which are a very specialised form of contract.

A contract of employment is a *contract of service*, where an employee – the subject of the contract – is in the personal service of their employer. It is necessary to distinguish an employment contract of personal service from a commercial *contract for services*. As Wedderburn (1986: 106) makes clear, the law marks off the employee under a contract of service from independent contractors – self-employed workers – who may provide services to an organisation under a commercial contract. For example, a commercial contract whereby catering or cleaning services are provided to one firm by a second firm is a contract for services, not an employment contract, even though the work is performed by labour. Catering staff may be employees in the offeror firm, but the offeree firm has bought their services under a commercial contract for catering services.

A contract of employment differs from a commercial contract for services in the sense that an employment contract of personal service to an employer is intended to be an open-ended relationship. It is a relationship that continues until either party decides to end it through due notice, whereas a commercial contract is more likely to be a precise exchange of services over a clearly defined period of time. Some employment contracts today are of a temporary or fixed-term nature, but nonetheless an employment relationship is created, whereas in commercial contracts of a long-term duration, for example computer or photo-copier servicing, an employment relationship is not created. Equally, such commercial contracts are likely to contain clear and precise contractual duties for each party. Thus commercial contracts are a purely contractual relationship and, unlike employment contracts, are not subject to the *common law duties* of an employer and employee which operate as implied terms and conditions within the contract of employment. The common law refers to areas of law that are not covered by parliamentary or European Union legislation. The common law has been developed by the judiciary: that is, the common law is *judge-made law*. Now that we have defined contract and distinguished between commercial and employment contracts, it is possible to proceed with a discussion of the underlying assumptions behind contract theory.

Activity List the differences between commercial and employment contracts. Explain how commercial contracts might create employment. Compare and contrast your views with those of a colleague or the teacher.

Equality and freedom of entry: market individualism

The philosophical basis of contract is derived from the principle of market individualism (see Atiyah, 1979; Deakin and Wilkinson, 2005). Market individualism suggests that the individual is the best judge of his or her own interests. From this suggestion the notion of *freedom of contract* is introduced, which assumes that individuals are self-determining agents who are primarily self-interested and are best able to fulfil their interests if they are free to enter into contracts with other parties in a free market.

Freedom of contract suggests that individuals act as free agents when they enter into contracts as both parties to a contract have equal status before the law and they jointly determine the terms and conditions of the contract. It follows from this assumption that the component elements of a contract – offer, acceptance and the consideration between the parties – are arrived at through a process of negotiation and then agreement to create legal relations. This may be the situation in the case of a house purchase, but in relation to employment the situation is somewhat different. As Fox (1985: 6) points out, contract theory alone, with all that it entails in terms of equality and references to adjudication by an outside body, cannot be an effective method of regulating terms and conditions of employment if the parties to the contract are in dispute. In the UK this is because the employment relationship remains one in which the status of the parties to the contract is unequal. The notion of status derives from paternalism in the master and servant relationship inherent in 'employment' prior to the rise of industrial economies. Examples of paternal employment include domestic service and tied cottages for estate farmers and general agricultural labourers. In the nineteenth century, domestic servants and agricultural labourers were not employees in the modern sense of the word; rather they were subject to a crude form of commercial contract whereby they provided their labour services to a master in return for board and lodgings. However, once employment became contractually determined in a formal legal sense it did not constitute a clean break with the past. Consequently the contractual process incorporates characteristics from pre-industrial 'paternal' employment: for example, the status bias of the master and servant relationship.

Fox (1985: 3–5) identifies paternalism as the basis of status within employment. Paternalism refers to a situation of subordination to legitimate authority. Prior to the development of the contract of employment, the process of subordination to legitimate authority was entirely within the master–servant relationship. Within contractually determined employment, the employee subordinates him or herself to the greater legal authority of the employer, the superiority of which is derived from the status-based relationship of master and servant. So, although employment contracts provide employees with a degree of independence from their employer – for example, employees can terminate their employment through due notice – employees remain subordinate parties to the employment contract. They are subject to the reasonable and legitimate authority of their employer, to whom they provide personal service.

From the above discussion it is clear that equality before the law in employment contracts is a fiction because employers' authority is derived from their paternal status which underpins the employment relationship. This is often referred to as the *managerial prerogative*. In most contracts the agreeing parties are assumed to be the best judges of their own interests. However, in employment the status bias of the employer gives them the privilege of determining their self-interest *and* having a partial say in the determination of employee interests. This privilege derives from the concept of *subordination*, which implies that the junior partner to the employment contract cannot perceive all their real interests. Kahn-Freund (1984:

15) described the individually based contract of employment as an act of submission on the part of the employee:

> In its operation it is a condition of subordination, however much the submission and the subordination may be concealed by that indispensable figment of the legal mind known as the contract of employment.

An employer may determine the organisation of work, levels of payment and duration of working time. The employee is bound by such impositions if they are reasonable. Thus the notion of free employment contracts bears little resemblance to the real world (Hyman, 1975: 23). Relatedly, although all employees have an individual contract of employment, the terms and conditions of an individual's contract of employment are likely to be determined and regulated by means of a collective agreement, the details of which are normally incorporated in an individual's contract of employment. These agreements are often negotiated by a trade union through the process of collective bargaining. In the absence of a trade union and collective bargaining 'collective agreements' are unilaterally determined by management on behalf of the employer; they are not the subject of negotiation. This point again illustrates that the notions of individual negotiation and freedom of contract exist at only a superficial level of relations between employer and employee.

Activity

- Summarise what you understand by the terms 'managerial prerogative' and 'subordination' in the employment relationship. Provide two examples of the managerial prerogative and subordination in your employment.

- Explain how the notion of 'equality before the law' is not necessarily the same as equality in law within the employment relationship.

Common law regulation of employment contracts

There are two features of the English legal system that highlight the contexts within which all aspects of the law operate. First, the English legal system, unlike most other legal systems (for example, those of other European Union states), does not operate in conjunction with a written constitution or a Bill of Rights. In the specific area of employment the absence of a written constitution or a Bill of Rights means that British subjects do not possess any specific inalienable rights as employees: for example, the right to strike. Second, and relatedly, the system is very conservative – some would say obsessed with the past. This conservatism explains why 'precedent' has so prominent a role in the common law. Precedent operates on the basis of decisions previously arrived at in a higher court. It is judge-made law that creates a rule for lower courts and subsequent future cases of a similar nature. Thus a precedent creates an example for subsequent cases or acts as a justification for subsequent decisions.

Advocates of Britain's unwritten constitution argue that its major benefit is adaptability over time, which contrasts with the rigid mechanism of a written constitution around which new developments have to be moulded. In matters of employment many of the rights held by British subjects result from case law and precedent and from trade union activity in collective bargaining. Equally, trade unions have a consultative role in the formulation of statutory protections and provisions such as the national minimum wage or the statutory procedure for trade union recognition under the Employment Relations Act 1999.

Common law duties of employer and employee

Earlier in this part of the chapter, the concept of 'freedom of contract' was introduced. This concept assumes that individuals are self-determining agents who are primarily self-interested. It follows from this that individuals both freely enter into contractual arrangements and jointly determine the terms and conditions of an employment contract. In the case of employment, the notion of freedom of contract operates in conjunction with the common law duties of employer and employee. That is, although contracts of employment may be entered into freely, the contract of employment itself incorporates the common law duties of employee and employer.

Common law duties of the employer

These are to:

- Take reasonable care to ensure that all employees are safe at the workplace, and indemnify any employee for injury sustained during employment. Employers have both a common law duty and a statutory duty to provide a safe working environment for their employees. Aspects of this liability are codified in statute under the Health and Safety at Work Act 1974.

- Treat all employees in a manner which is in line with the duty of mutual trust and confidence – arguably therefore in a courteous and polite manner. That is, employers should not 'bully' or abuse their employees, or subject them to racist or sexist remarks. Aspects of this liability are codified in the Sex Discrimination Act 1975 (as amended) and the Race Relations Act 1976 (as amended). The common law duties of the employer contrast with those of an employee.

- Provide a reasonable opportunity for the employee to work and pay the agreed wages as consideration for work performed. It is a matter of some debate as to whether the employer has a common law duty to actually provide work; the issue appears to turn on two distinct arguments. First, the notion of reasonableness, which will depend on the details of any particular case, and second, the operation of common law principles. The courts have held, for example, that the duty to provide work is a matter of fact rather than a matter of law. Thus in specific factual circumstances related to the nature of the work such a duty may be implied into the contract of employment. The courts have indicated that where an employee needs to

> - maintain or develop key skill levels;
> - keep up to date with developments in the industry, sector or trade within which they work; or
> - there was an understanding between the parties that the employee would be given a reasonable amount of work in order that they could enjoy a specific level of earnings; or
> - the failure to provide work may lead to a loss of reputation or publicity on the part of the employee.
>
> (Adapted from Cabrelli, 2008)

they are willing to find the existence of an implied duty to provide work (for examples see *Breach* [1976] IRLR 180, and *William Hill* [1998] IRLR 313).

Activity Taking the four points listed above make a list of jobs which may fall into any of these categories and therefore be covered by such an implied duty.

Common law duties of the employee

These are to:

- be ready and willing to work for their employer;
- offer personal service to the employer – that is not to send a substitute without agreement;

- offer exclusive service to their employer – that is not hold a second job without agreement;
- take reasonable care in the conduct and performance of their personal service;
- work in the employer's time;
- carry out all reasonable instructions during that time, except that the employee is not required to carry out instructions which are outwith his/her contract (for a discussion see *O'Brien* v *Associated Fire Alarms Ltd* [1969] 1 All ER 93);
- undertake not to disrupt the employer's business on purpose;
- not disclose any trade secret to a third party. (for a discussion see *Faccenda Chicken Ltd* v *Fowler* [1986] IRLR 69).

The common law duties of the employee and employer are not always detailed in the written particulars of a contract of employment, indeed they are more often terms implied in the contract which are derived from custom and practice or statutes.

In market economies, the law assumes that the contract of employment is entered into freely; however, the terms and conditions, whether they are express or implied, are not jointly determined, and in terms of employee and employer obligations they are not equal in terms of their scope and coverage. In most cases the employer is in the dominant bargaining position because they are offering employment. Hence the employer is able unilaterally to determine how the common law duties of the employee are to be fulfilled. The common law duties of the employee, as listed above, are clear and precise but open to considerable interpretation. In contrast to this, the common law obligations of the employer are imbued with the tenet of limited reasonableness: that is, the obligations imposed on the employer should not be unreasonable. Thus the general concept of reasonableness can only be tested in individual cases. As Hyman (1975: 24) argues, the status equality implied by the concept of self-determining individuals freely entering into contracts of employment is really status *inequality* because of the way the principles of equality before the law and freedom of entry operate in practice. Clearly, equality before the law belies the market power held by an employer. Individual equality before the law places firms that have access to necessarily expensive legal advice on the formulation of employment contracts and individuals bereft of such a capability on the same plane. As we pointed out earlier, within the contract of employment freedom and equality are fused with the traditional status bias of employment, with the result that the reality of the employment relationship is that, rather than being one of exchange between equals, it is one of subordination of one party – the employee – to another – the employer.

Types of employment contract

Every employee has a contract of employment. However, as indicated above, not all *workers* have a contract of employment. Where an employer provides regular work, defines working hours, the place of work, determines holiday and sick pay arrangements, requires personal service, and deducts income tax and National Insurance through the PAYE system, the courts are predisposed to a finding that a contract of employment – an hence an employment relationship – exists and anyone engaged on these terms is likely to be an employee. In contrast, a worker who is not an employee will often pay their own income tax and National Insurance contributions, decide when, where and how they work, be allowed to arrange for a substitute to undertake their work, and make their own holiday and sick pay arrangements. However, in addition to self-employed contractors and freelance IT specialists, journalists, consultants etc., some agency workers, casual workers and 'home workers' may be classified as having worker status rather than employee status (see 'Current issues' below). A contract of employment is not always written down in one document, and sometimes the contract may not be written down at all.

There are several types of employment contract, as detailed below.

Permanent, ongoing or open-ended contracts

This type of employment contract is assumed to continue until either side gives notice of an intention to terminate the contract.

Temporary contract

This type of contract has no specified duration; therefore it does not contain any restrictive fixed term, or limiting event. It often does not contain waivers, for example, the requirement that the employee waive their right to statutory protection in relation to redundancy. A temporary contract may be made permanent and the time served under the temporary contract will constitute continuity of service. Hence in the case of employment rights that are based on an employee's length of service – for example, unfair dismissal, which is currently set at one year's length of service – it is unnecessary for the employee to serve another full year to acquire this protection. However, although the general principle is clear, it is a complex area of law subject to the particular circumstances of individual cases. This complexity, in many cases, is the result of the triangular nature of such temporary contracts which involve the use of employment agencies (see 'Current issues' below).

Fixed-term or limiting event contract

This type of contract has a specified duration: that is, a clear start date and a clear and unequivocal termination date or event which occasions termination. Examples of this might include situations where employment is subject to 'funding arrangements' that are not renewable, a specific one-off project or matters such as maternity and paternity leave. Both parties to such contracts should be aware that the contract is not renewable once the event or date occurs. More significant than this, many employees who are subject to such contracts are required to waive their statutory protections against unfair dismissal and redundancy. The Employment Relations Act 1999 (ERA) now prohibits employers from using waiver clauses against unfair dismissal; however, redundancy waivers continue. Since November 2001, employees under such contracts have equal rights to those of permanent employees in terms of pay rates and pension provision. Further the *Fixed-Term Employees (Prevention of Less Favourable Treatment) Regulations 2002* now provide that an individual who has worked on two or more such contracts over a period of four years has a right to a permanent contract (for further discussion see 'Current issues' below).

'Casual', 'spot' or zero hours contracts

Under this type of contract the employee must be available for work, but the employer does not have to guarantee work: for example, a retired teacher may be on call to cover for sick colleagues. Equally, banks use on-call staff to cover busy periods such as lunchtime, whereas the Post Office employs many casual workers at Christmas. In most situations this type of contract is mutually beneficial and not open to abuse; however, if a worker is required to be at work but clock off during slack periods – a practice once common in many fast-food outlets – zero hours contracts are open to abuse. For example, such a worker could remain at the workplace for long periods yet have a very low rate of hourly pay owing to continual clocking off. In an effort to overcome some of the abuses of zero hours contracts a person employed on such a contract is now entitled to the national minimum wage, whereas the Working Time Directive entitles the person to a paid holiday provided they worked during the preceding 13 weeks. The vast majority of individuals who are engaged under a zero hours contract will be classified as an employee; however, some employers have attempted to argue that engagement under a zero hours contract is compatible with worker status. The basis of this argument centres on the 'mutuality of obligation' between the employer and the worker or employee. If someone engaged under a zero hours contract does not have regular hours of work and is able to decline offers of work and/or work elsewhere, there is unlikely to be a mutuality of obligation between the two parties. It is the presence of mutual obligation that creates the employment relationship establishing the employer and employee. This is a controversial area and the distinction between worker status and employee status is persistently criticised by the TUC and other employee groups. It has been the subject of much judicial comment and continues to cause concern amongst a wide range of organisations (see 'Current issues' below). Up to 9 million workers in the UK may have worker status, many of whom are arguably *de facto* employees, for example, long-term agency workers or temps engaged in one organisation. The TUC is campaigning for all workers to have the status of an employee and therefore receive the basic contractual and statutory protections outlined earlier in the chapter. On the specific issue of agency and temporary workers, the UK's forthcoming adoption of European Union directives may provide the basis of some improvement in employment protection.

STOP and think

What types of employment might be offered on the basis of a casual, spot or zero hours contract of employment?

What reasons might an employer have to engage an employee on a fixed-term contract of employment?

We have established that in the vast majority of cases the employer is the dominant party in the employment relationship. This dominance enables the employer to determine many terms and conditions contained within the employment contract.

Terms and conditions within employment contracts

There are two types of terms and conditions within a contract of employment.

Express terms and conditions

These form an explicit part of an individual contract of employment. They are often referred to as the *written* terms and conditions of the contract that are included in the written *statement of the contract*. Any employee, irrespective of the number of hours they work, must be given a statement of the written terms and conditions of their contract within two months – eight weeks – of starting work (s.1(2) ERtsA 1996). The statement must include the following items:

- Name and address of employer.
- Name of the employee
- Date employment began.
- Place or places of work.
- Rate of pay or salary point: for lower-paid employees the rate must adhere to the statutory national minimum wage, from 1 October 2008, £5.73 per hour for workers aged 22 or over, £4.77 per hour for those aged 18–21 and £3.53 for 16- and 17-year-olds. This rate is adjusted annually by amounts which are determined in consultation with the Low Pay Commission.
- Hours of work: as a result of the Human Rights Act, 1998 it may be necessary for employers to specify the reasons for, frequency of and need to telephone employees at home. This legislation establishes that an employer does not have an automatic right to demand an employee's home phone number unless the express terms of an employment contract state that an employee has a duty to be available outside normal working hours.
- Holiday entitlements: as a result of the working time regulations all full-time employees are now entitled to 28 days paid holiday, part-time workers on a pro-rata basis. The situation with respect to temporary or agency workers is more complicated. All employees are entitled to a minimum of 28 days paid holiday but to qualify for this an employee must work for an employer for 13 weeks. Temps employed by an agency are entitled to paid holidays if they work for 13 weeks. This is the case even if they move between differ-

ent workplaces as long as the employment is continuous. The introduction of this right to paid holidays presented problems in relation to casual and part-time workers. One way employers – in some cases in agreement with recognised trade unions – sought to deal with this issue was the use of a system known as 'rolled-up holiday pay'. In simple terms this was a system whereby the hourly rate was supplemented by an agreed amount which was to represent holiday pay. In relation to casual – short-term assignments the worker is then deemed to take holiday at the end of the assignment, having already been paid for the time. The courts and the EAT in Scotland held such arrangements to be void as a form of contracting out of the legal requirements, In *Robinson-Steele* v *R D Retail Services* [2006] IRLR 14 the English court finally referred the matter to the European Court of Justice (ECJ) having previously held such arrangements to comply with the WTR's. The difference in approach was a result of the Scottish courts arguing that the principle in 'rolled-up' schemes of 'receive as you earn' acted as a disincentive to take leave, whilst the English Tribunals argued that if the amount was genuine, sufficient, and transparent the WTR permitted such arrangements. The ECJ reasoned that as the purpose was to put the worker in the same position as regards payment, that the Directive prohibited the replacement of the period of leave by payment alone, and the 'rolled-up' scheme may lead to the replacement of leave with payment in lieu, such arrangements were excluded by the Directive. The ECJ went on to hold that the Directive does not outlaw "the use of 'rolled-up' pay from being set off against any liability to pay in respect of any specific leave taken by the worker" (LexisNexis, 2009: A [922]). This in part offers legitimacy to the practice at least in situations where the scheme currently exists, in relation to its continued used of Reg. 35 of the Directive – which makes void any provision excluding rights provided by the Directive – seals the demise of rolled-up holiday pay.

- Sick pay arrangements.
- Notice entitlements.
- Pension rights.
- Details of the grievance procedure – including the identity of the person to whom the employee can apply for the purpose of seeking redress.
- Details of the discipline procedure.
- Job title.
- Period of employment if job not permanent.
- Details of any collective agreements which directly affect the terms and conditions.

Implied terms and conditions

These are terms and conditions that are not explicitly stated in an individual contract of employment but which are assumed to be included in the contract: for example, workplace custom and practice arrangements and the common law duties of the employer and employee.

Terms implied by Statutory Provision

These are terms and conditions that are incorporated into individual contracts of employment as either express or implied terms. Incorporated terms and conditions of employment include the statutory protections passed by the UK Parliament or the European Union. In English law, collective agreements negotiated between employers and trade unions through the process of collective bargaining are not legally binding. However, elements within collective agreements are legally binding if they are incorporated into individual contracts of employment: for example, working hours and pay rates.

Changing terms and conditions of employment

Employers are able to change terms and conditions of employment; however, employees have some rights if an employer seeks to change terms and conditions without consultation and agreement. A unilateral change in pay rates represents a serious breach of contract, as does the unilateral removal of a company car, reductions in holiday entitlements and suspension of an employer's pension contribution. Employees can accept unilateral changes and work normally under protest, i.e object to the changes and seek to minimise the effects of the unilateral change. However, a recent case *Robinson* v *Tescom* Corporation [2008] IRLR 408 made it clear that such objection, even if in writing and following the wording suggested by ACAS, is still acceptance of the change. Therefore, objecting to the new terms and conditions in writing and refusing to work to them when they are introduced later, still amounts to gross disobedience which may lead to summary dismissal. Such a dismissal could well be judged to be reasonable and fair under the 'some other substantial reason' provision (see discussion on dismissal below). This has the effect of allowing employees who object to the variation only one option; leave and claim 'constructive dismissal'.

STOP and think

Ensure that you are clear on the differences between express, common law implied and statutory implied terms and conditions of employment. Check your understanding with a class colleague and the teacher.

Activity

Examine the points above on express and implied terms and conditions of employment against your own job and see if you can state what your express terms are or where details of them can be found.

Statutory rights relating to employment contracts

All employees have a contract of employment; equally, all employees receive some level of statutory protection against arbitrary and unreasonable treatment by an employer. Statutory protection can be framed in individual terms, for example protection against sexual and racial discrimination in the workplace; alternatively, rights may be collective, for example the statutory procedure for trade union recognition introduced by the Employment Relations Act 1999.

Since 1995 all workers, either full-time or part-time, have been subject to the same *day one statutory rights* irrespective of how many hours they work. Statutory day one rights provide a minimum level of protection to all workers. Some workers may have additional contractual rights negotiated by their employer and a recognised trade union. In addition to day one rights, other rights depend on an employee's length of service.

Day one employment rights

Equal pay/equal value

Section 1(1) of the Equal Pay Act 1970 (EqPA) inserts an *equality clause* into contracts of employment that can be enforced by an employment tribunal. Under the EqPA terms within contracts of employment must be equal between the sexes. The equality clause enforces equal terms and conditions in the contracts of men and women in the same employment. The clause covers pay and all other contractual terms of employment. The EqPA is applicable in three situations:

● *Like work*. Where men and women are employed to perform like work, that is, the same work or work that is broadly similar, men and women must receive the same rate of pay or be paid on the same salary scale. This is the case even if part-time men and women work fewer hours than full-time men and women, that is, a part-time worker may compare themselves to a full-time employee.

- *Work rated as equivalent under an analytical job evaluation scheme.* Job evaluation describes a set of methods that compare jobs with the view to assessing their relative and comparative worth (see Chapter 13). The process of job evaluation ranks jobs based on rational and objective assessment of key factors – such as skill, effort and decision-making – from a representative sample of jobs in a particular organisation. The purpose of job evaluation is to produce a reasonable and defensible ranking of jobs. By formalising and making explicit the basis of payment systems and associated differences in pay levels, employers can expose discriminatory practices and remove them; for more detail on job evaluation see Chapter 13 pp. 512–3.

- Where work is of *equal value*, even though it is not like work or work covered by a non-discriminatory job evaluation scheme in the same employment. Equal value is measured in terms of the demands upon the worker in terms of skill levels, effort and decision-making. If different work is held to be of equal value under these criteria then the two groups of workers must have the same pay levels. Pay is constituted in its widest sense and includes salary scales or pay rates, access to occupational pension schemes, redundancy protection, sick pay, travel concessions and other perks. In the 1980s, USDAW (the shop workers' trade union) and the Equal Opportunities Commission successfully fought equal value cases on behalf of supermarket checkout workers, who are predominantly women, against delivery dock and warehouse workers who were predominantly men. An employer may defend an equal value case on the grounds that differences in pay between men and women are justified on the grounds of a genuine material factor that is both relevant and significant in the particular case. The fact that a particular group of workers who are predominantly women includes a male worker does not constitute a genuine material factor: that is, men who receive lower pay than other men employed in the same organisation are able to claim that their work is of equal value. For example, the presence of a 'token' male checkout worker or school lunch assistant appears insufficient to defeat a claim for equal value. In summary, a claim to equal pay for work of equal value normally involves women in comparison to men; however, the presence of lower-paid men cannot undermine a claim because men are also protected in respect of equal pay for work of equal value.

Sex discrimination/harassment

It is unlawful to discriminate against an employee, that is offer them less favourable treatment on grounds of their sex or marital status, or because of maternity or pregnancy. Employment protection legislation covers discrimination in respect of pay, whereas the Sex Discrimination Act 1975 as amended (SDA) in s. 6 covers discrimination in respect of selection, training, promotion, termination (e.g. selection for redundancy) or any other detriment in employment. The SDA applies equally to men and women except with respect to pregnancy provisions, and defines discrimination in four ways:

- *Direct discrimination* (SDA s.1(1)(a)). For example, denying a woman a job or promotion on the grounds that she is a woman, a married woman, a single woman, is pregnant and/or has children. Such discrimination is often said to be covered by the 'but for' description. That is the treatment would not have been received 'but for' the fact of gender.

- *Indirect discrimination* (SDA s.1(1)(b) and (2)). This category refers to apparently sex-neutral job requirements, provisions, criterion, or practices that have a disproportional effect on men or women, for example height requirements, dress codes or age and length of service requirements for promotion that may preclude married women with children from having sufficient length of service to apply by an upper age limit. Some cases of indirect discrimination appear to be intentional, whereas other cases result from a failure to update Human Resource Management procedures in accordance with the law: for example, dress codes that prevent women from wearing trousers (see *Schmidt* v *Austicks Bookshops Ltd* [1977] IRLR 360). An employer may choose to defend a charge of indirect discrimination on the grounds that the apparently discriminatory provision is a necessary requirement of the job or there is what can be classed as objective justification for the provision, criterion or practice. For example, in selection exercises for the fire service candidates must be able to expand their lung capacity by a certain measurement. Many women applicants are unable to meet this requirement: hence it appears to have a disproportionate effect on women. However, many men are unable to meet the requirement. Lung expansion is a requirement of a firefighter's job because it plays a part in assessing whether or not a candidate would be able to escape from a variety of smoke-filled situations. Claims of direct and indirect sex discrimination are in the majority of cases launched by women; however, the law is equally applicable to men and women, an equality that was recently demonstrated in the decision of an employment tribunal. In this case a male worker in a Stockport job centre won a claim for sexual discrimination because he refused to wear a tie at work. The basis of this claim was that he was told what to wear whereas female colleagues were not and that female colleagues were allowed to wear tee-shirts as opposed to more formal blouses. The Department of Work and Pensions appealed this decision to the EAT at which time it was overturned. The EAT held that requiring members of one sex to wear clothing of a particular kind, when members of the other sex are not does not necessarily mean the former are treated less favourably than the latter (see *The Department for Work and Pensions* v *Thompson* [2004] IRLR 348), as a result of the case a settlement was reached on a voluntary basis that involved re-working the dress codes for both male and female employees. As Tolleys (2009: B2001) notes "[a]s years go by, attitudes to acceptable dress and appearance alter and the courts have shown a willingness to take into consideration modern views and aspirations".

Activity

Make a list of the HR policies and procedures adopted by an organisation with which you are familiar. How many could be said to be 'out of date' and how would you modernise them?

Talk to your peers and develop a wider list.

- *Victimisation.* (SDA s. 4). In terms of legal definitions this is a situation where a person discriminates against another because that other has brought proceedings, given evidence, or indicated an intention to bring proceedings against the former under the various statutory provisions (i.e. Equal Pay, SDA and Pensions Act). The offence is committed by treating the individual less favourably than one treats other people on the broad range of issues covered with section 6 of the Act. (See *St Helen's Borough Council* v *Derbyshire* [2007] IRLR 540)

- *Harassment* (SDA s. 4A). This category covers verbal abuse, suggestive behaviour, or conduct that has either the purpose or effects mention and is founded on the grounds of sex. Harassment and bullying occur when a person engages in such unwanted conduct which has the purpose or effect of violating another's dignity, creating an intimidating, hostile, degrading, humiliating or offensive environment for that individual. As an example an employer who tolerates sexist jokes and or pornography images around the work place might be said to have created an offensive environment, even if the employee is not able to claim the remark or image was aimed specifically at them. A key factor in determining whether such behaviour does have the effects indicated is the perception of the victim and reasonableness. This does not however, give free rein to the oversensitive individual. In *Driskel* v *Peninsula Business Services Ltd* [2000] IRLR 151 the EAT held that those who "take offence at a perfectly innocent comment will probably not be considered as having been harassed" thus the legal concept of 'reasonable' plays an important role in the determination of both the purpose and the effect of a particular incident or pattern of behaviour.

It should be noted that certain types of employment are exempt from the provisions of the SDA: for example, employment that is mainly or wholly outside the UK, photographic modelling, and some areas of social work such as child protection from abuse and rape counselling.

Racial discrimination and harassment

The Race Relations Act 1976 (as amended) (RRA) follows the model set by the SDA and defines racial discrimination under the same headings and with the same definitions. Cases of direct racial discrimination in employment on the grounds that a person is black, Asian or Afro-Caribbean are less in evidence than during the 1960s. However, examples of indirect racial discrimination in employment turn on the relevance of apparently race-neutral job requirements that have a disproportionate effect on ethnic minorities: for example, requirements that preclude candidates on the basis that their grandparents were not British, or English language requirements. If these requirements are unrelated to the job they may well be indirectly discriminatory. Racial harassment in employment covers matters such as racial abuse, suggestive behaviour or the effects of tokenism. Certain types of employment are exempt from the provisions of the RRA: for example, staff in specialised restaurants and community social workers who are required to speak particular ethnic languages.

Activity

Think of two examples of employer or organisational behaviour that might constitute direct discrimination, indirect discrimination and harassment in employment in terms of racial and sexual discrimination. Compare your list with one of your class colleagues.

Maternity, adoption, and paternity rights

The rules and regulations in respect of maternity rights are very complicated. It is important that both the employer and the employee follow them carefully. Some employees have better maternity arrangements than the statutory arrangements; this is usually the result of collective bargaining arrangements in the workplace.

All women are entitled to maternity leave, which under the provisions of the ERA was set at 26 weeks and was further extended by the maternity and paternity leave regulations to 52 weeks, of which up to 39 weeks are paid maternity leave. In April 2007 paid maternity leave was extended to nine months and the government has made a further commitment to increase paid leave to one year by the end of this Parliament (at the latest 2010). In addition to this the government is also examining a new right for mothers to transfer up to three months of their paid maternity leave entitlement to fathers. The entitlement to paid maternity leave is unrelated to the number of hours worked or length of service. A pregnant employee must conform to the following requirements:

- provide written notice of pregnancy and due date;
- provide a medical certificate if requested;
- indicate the date the employee intends to begin leave – this cannot be before the 11th week;
- return to work within 39 weeks which is the maternity pay period or 52 weeks if the employee is taking a further 13 weeks unpaid maternity leave.

Maternity leave may be extended if the employee is sick or has an illness related to confinement. The day one employment rights listed above and below establish that employees who are either pregnant or on maternity leave cannot be dismissed or made redundant because of pregnancy or a pregnancy-related illness contracted or diagnosed as commencing before or after the birth of the child.

An employee who fulfils the following criteria is entitled to *statutory maternity pay* when:

- their average weekly earnings are at least equal to the lower earnings limit;
- the employee provides the employer with a maternity certificate giving the due date;
- they were employed up to and including the 15th week before the baby was due;
- they have stopped working;
- they have given the employer 28 days' notice of their intention to stop working;
- at the end of the 15th week of confinement before the baby was due, the employee had worked for this employer for 26 weeks.

Statutory maternity pay is calculated on the basis of 6 weeks at 90 per cent of average earnings plus 33 weeks at 90 per cent of average earnings or the basic rate – currently £123.06 per week – whichever is the lower. Employees who do not qualify for maternity pay may receive maternity allowance from the Department of Social Security. Awards for maternity allowance depend on an employee's National Insurance contribution. Finally, an employer can compel a new mother to take maternity leave. There is a two-week period of compulsory maternity leave (four weeks for employees who work in a factory) following the birth of a child. It is unlawful for an employer to allow or compel a new mother to work during this period. After a period of maternity leave an employee is entitled to return to the same job they held before going on leave. In the case of extended maternity leave for employees working in a firm employing fewer than five workers, an employer may be able to demonstrate that keeping a job open is unreasonable and offer the returning employee a similar job. In April 2007 provisions were introduced that allow employers to 'keep in touch' and for employees to undertake a limited number of work days in order to keep up to date. In relation to the former it is now considered good practice for the employer to inform the employee of any vacancies that arise during the maternity leave period. Indeed in *Visa International Service Association* v *Paul [2004]* IRLR 42 an employee who was not told about a vacancy won her claim for discrimination and constructive dismissal despite a finding by the tribunal that she would not have stood any chance of success in obtaining the position. HR managers ought therefore to make it part of the maternity procedure to ensure they keep individuals on maternity leave informed. The same amendments to the regulations allow for a period of 10 working days during the maternity pay period when individuals could 'return to work' without losing the right to maternity pay.

After a great deal of pressure from family groups, the EOC, trades unions and adoption agencies, the government enacted the Paternity and Adoption Leave Regulations (2002). These regulations provided, for the first time, rights to adoptive parents on the same footing as birth parents. Adoptive parents can now claim 39 weeks paid adoption leave and are entitled to extend that to 52 weeks adoption leave. The rules about returning to work are identical to those for maternity leave as are all the contractual protections. Provisions for contact and 'return to work' days mimic the maternity provisions allowing employees to keep their skills current.

The same legislation introduced a period of two week paternity leave which must be taken within 56 days of the date of birth. The leave can be taken either as two one week blocks or a single two week block. It is intended – under provisions in the Work and Families Act 2006 – to make arrangements for parents to choose additional paternity leave of up to 26 weeks – in simple terms sharing the 52 weeks family leave.

Disability discrimination

There are approximately 9 million disabled working age people in the UK but only one third of that figure are actually in employment, while many more would like to work but are unemployed or in receipt of incapacity benefit. The Disability Discrimination Act 1995 (as amended) (DDA) makes it unlawful for an employer to discriminate against applicants for employment and employees who have a disability in relation to job applications, promotion, training and contractual terms and benefits. The UK legislation has been influenced by both the Americans with Disabilities Act and, more recently, the European Framework Equal Treatment Directive (FETD) 2000/78/EC (see 'Current issues' below for further discussion of the effects of the FETD).

There are two primary theories of disability, the most dominant of which has been the 'medical model'. Under this model an individual is disabled as a direct consequence of a physical or mental impairment. The alternative model (the 'social model') has a fundamentally different concept of disability. In contrast to the medical model it views disability as the result of a complex interrelationship between "individual biomedical impairment, individual reactions to that impairment and the associated functional limitations, and a social environment which is not responsive to the needs of that person" (Hosking, 2007: 229). The UK legislation is firmly rooted in the medical model and we are presented with a number of legal and HR policy options – basically aimed at improving individual circumstances and caring for those unable to adapt to their social environment by facilitating changes to that environment. In *Mangold* v *Helm* (Case C-144/04, [2005] ECR) the ECJ advocated a broader approach to disability more in line with the social model and argued that the FETD advocated this wider understanding. The adoption of this definition opens the coverage of anti-disability discrimination legislation to a far wider group of individuals than a traditional medical model. In so doing it places responsibilities on employers to eliminate structural barriers to participation, develop programmes of integration and create working conditions of individual empowerment. This moves beyond the current requirements of the DDA to make 'reasonable adjustments', covers a wider group to include the 'long-term sick' and hence adds to the operating costs imposed on organisations. The UK government has currently made no announcement of changes to the law and appears to be relying on a more recent ECJ decision (in *Chacon Navas* v *Eurest Colectividades SA* [2007] ICR 1) in which the ECJ regarded an individual as 'sick' rather than as having a 'temporary disability' – as though by labelling her long-term sick it excluded her from being labelled disabled. Thus the adoption of the medical model restricted the development of broader employer responsibilities. In the discussion that follows we adopt the medical model as currently used within UK legislation but note the existence of an increasingly successful campaign by the disability rights movement to promote the social model.

The provisions of the UK statute cover all employees from permanent to casual. In addition, subcontract workers are also covered. The DDA is now universal in application, since October 2004 employers with fewer than 15 workers are now covered by its provisions. The 2005 Disability Discrimination Act further extends the coverage of disability in the workplace, for example, the framework of protection now covers employees with 'asymptomatic' conditions such as MS, HIV, ADDHS and some forms of cancer from the time they are diagnosed by a doctor. This provision detailed in the 2005 legislation is intended to cover so-called 'hidden disabilities'. In some respects this is a response to the developing pressure to apply the social model, despite a continued use of the medical definition.

The DDA (s.1(1)) defines *disability* as mental or physical impairment that has a long-term and substantial adverse effect on the ability of an individual to perform normal daily activities. The legislation goes on in Schedule 1 to amplify this definition under several headings. First, the nature of impairment is broadly interpreted in terms of its daily impact on an employee rather than being confined to those that are recognised medical conditions, for example, HIV-positive status, schizophrenia, ADDHS and other forms of mental illness. Second, the requirement for a substantial effect rules out minor complaints such as hay fever or colour-blindness. Third, and related, a condition of impairment must last at least a year or the rest of a person's life to qualify as a long-term effect. This requirement rules out impairments such as whiplash resulting from minor motor accidents and other temporary debilitating illnesses. Last, the ability to undertake normal daily activity covers issues such as the ability to hear and learn, comprehend the perception and risk of physical danger, continence, eyesight, hearing, manual dexterity, memory, speech and physical coordination.

The DDA (ss.3A – 4A) outlines the tests for disability discrimination:

- *Less favourable treatment.* As with other anti-discrimination legislation the law provides for a range of prohibited acts – in relation to employment these are found in s. 4. Contravention of this regulation results in an individual being considered to have received less favourable treatment. This situation arises when a disabled employee is able to demonstrate less favourable treatment – in comparison with an able-bodied person – that is related to their disability that cannot be objectively justified by the employer. An employer can defend a claim for disability discrimination on the grounds of less favourable treatment if they can demonstrate a relevant or substantial justification for the treatment.

- *A duty to make reasonable adjustments.* This duty comes into play when the employer could be reasonably judged to know that an individual with a disability would be placed at a substantial disadvantage by their work arrangements or premises. In such a situation a failure to make reasonable adjustments in the workplace may result in disability discrimination. It is likely to be unlawful and unreasonable where a disabled employee is substantially disadvantaged by work arrangements or the layout of the workplace when compared with an able-bodied employee. In this situation the employer is under a legal duty to make reasonable adjustments: for example, the installation of wheelchair ramps and the provision of ground floor office space for wheelchair users. An employer cannot justify the discrimination on the grounds that they were unaware that a job applicant or employee was disabled (see *HJ Heinz & Co Ltd* v *Kenrick* [2000] IRLR 144), this means that employers should consistently consider whether there may be a reason for the employees' behaviour (absence, low performance etc.) that relates to a disability of which the employer is not yet aware. In addition to this, an employer can no longer justify disability discrimination with a substantial reason; they must rather demonstrate objective justification for their action or lack of action. Lastly, from December 2006 public sector employers were charged with a duty to promote disability equality as best practice.

- *Harassment.* It is unlawful under the DDA to harass a person for a reason that relates to the persons' disability. The definition of harassment in s.3B mirrors the definition discussed above in relation to gender harassment in terms of having the purpose or effects listed in that legislation.

- *Victimisation.* As with harassment the provisions relating to victimisation mirror the provisions in the other anti-discrimination legislation in that they protect individuals who have asserted a statutory right or instigated proceedings under the legislation.

Under the provisions of the EU Framework Employment Directive (FED) the UK extended the coverage of anti-discrimination legislation to include groups previously excluded or poorly covered. A good example of this relates to the Lesbian, Gay, Bi-sexual and Transgender (LGBT) community. Despite the existence of the SDA it was still possible to discriminate on the basis of sexual orientation and/or gender re-assignment – indeed what case law existed in this area was generally an attempt to stretch the SDA to cover orientation and/or re-assignment. In order to honour our obligations under the FED the government enacted a series of Statutory Instruments to address the specific issues of sexual orientation, religion and belief (2003) and age (2006).

Sexual orientation

The Employment Equality (Sexual Orientation) Regulations (2003) put in place provisions which attempt to prohibit discrimination on the basis of sexual orientation. The forms of discrimination echo the older provisions by including direct, indirect, harassment and victimisation. The regulations define sexual orientation as an attraction to a person of the same sex, the opposite sex or both, as such covering the whole of the LGBT community. Unlike the SDA, which refers to less favourable treatment 'on the ground of her sex', this regulation defines discrimination merely 'on grounds of'. In principle this means that all forms of discrimination can be based on the discriminator's perception, even where that perception is not accurate, or the perpetrators know the individual is not lesbian, gay, bi-sexual or transgender (see *English* v *Thomas Sanderson Ltd* [2008] EWCA 1421). Further, individuals can be deemed to have discriminated against others where the action relates to someone with whom the victim of discrimination associates. Whilst direct discrimination can never be justified, the regulations provide for objective justification of indirect discrimination in much the same way as the previous legislation. Similarly, harassment and victimisation are covered by wording that reflects the standard approach. Amendments were enacted to the regulations in 2005 in order to take into account the Civil Partnership Act 2004 by making it unlawful to treat an individual less favourably because they were a 'civil partner' rather than a married person.

Religion and belief

The Employment Equality (Religion and Belief) Regulations (2003) employ much the same approach to the prohibition of discriminator behaviour on the grounds of religion or belief. The FED does not contain any definition of 'religion or belief' and the UK government adopted a wide ranging definition in Article 2 of the regulations. By adopting a deliberately wide terminology ('any religion' and 'any religious or philosophical belief') the regulations use a concept in line with Article 9 of the European Convention on Human Rights (Rubenstein, 2004). The effect of avoiding discrimination because of an individuals' religion or belief should not be discrimination against the non-believer – thus it is unlawful for a Christian employer to refuse to employ an individual of no belief simply on that basis. The regulations do provide for an objective justification defence where belief is central part of the role under the same interpretation as is found in relation to indirect discrimination under the SDA. Recent case law has highlighted that these regulations are designed to cover identifiable groups (see *Ewieda* v *British Airways plc* [2009] IRLR 78) and that belief is separate from actions (see *Chondol* v *Liverpool CC* [2009] EAT1298/08 and *Islington LBC* v *Ladele* [2008] EAT1453/08).

Age discrimination

Until October 2006 age discrimination was regulated by a voluntary code of practice but is now regulated due to the implementation of the Employment Equality (Age) Regulations (2006). The age discrimination regulations contain the following provisions. They make it unlawful for employers to specify age when recruiting staff, promoting staff or training staff. Similarly terms such as 'youngish', 'recently qualified' 'under forty' become unlawful unless an employer is able to provide a clear business-related reason for the specification of the requirement. In addition to these provisions the regulations suggest that advertisements which seek 'experienced' workers will require careful wording and person specifications to ensure that it is clear that recruitment decisions are not made on the basis of age and experience. Centrally, in relation to HR policies and employer behaviours the regulations introduce procedures in relation to retirement. While the statutory age limit of 65 in relation to unfair dismissal and redundancy payments no longer applies, it is still possible to enforce retirement at 65 providing the procedural requirements are satisfied. The regulations require employers who intend to retire staff at 65 or a lower age if that is the normal retirement age (below 65 may be unlawful unless such an age can be justified) to write to the employee no more than 12 months and no less than 6 months prior to the intended retirement date. They must indicate to the individual that they have the right to seek to work beyond the retirement age and such a request must be made at least three months before the date of retirement. The request must state whether the employee desires to continue:

- indefinitely;
- for a stated period; or
- until a stated event or date.

The employer is required to consider the request and respond before the retirement date. Such a response may be to agree, or to request a meeting at which an alternative may be discussed or a reason given for a refusal.

Activity

In relation to all the above anti-discrimination legislation organisations should adopt policies/procedures in order to ensure they follow the legislative requirements. Looking at your own organisation identify the extent to which such policies/procedures have been adopted and identify any gaps.

Try writing a policy which would meet the needs of:

- the Employment Equality (Sexual Orientation) Regulations;
- the Employment Equality (Religion and Belief) Regulations;
- the Employment Equality (Age) Regulations.

Miscellaneous day one rights

In addition to the above day one rights, all employees have the following day one rights where relevant:

- time off for trade union duties;
- protection against victimisation due to involvement in trade union duties – for example, unfair selection for redundancy;
- protection against victimisation due to involvement in health and safety activity;
- the right to itemised payslips;
- protection against unlawful deductions from wages and or claims that relate to entitlements under the provision of the national minimum wage or the provisions of the working time directive, for example, entitlements to paid holidays;
- written reasons for dismissal during pregnancy or maternity leave;
- time off for antenatal visits;
- Sunday working rights, where relevant;
- protection against victimisation for enforcing a day one or length of service statutory right;
- disclosure of wrong-doing under the provisions of the Public Interest Disclosure Act (1998) that is 'whistle-blowing'.

Ensure that you are clear on the day one rights, and the terms that statutory provision requires to be given to all employees within eight weeks. Check your understanding with a class colleague and the teacher.

Rights that depend on length of service

Access to the following statutory rights is dependent upon an employee's length of service, but is unrelated to how many hours they work.

- *Written statement of main terms and conditions of employment.*
- *Written reasons for dismissal:* 1 year.
- *Protection against unfair dismissal:* 1 year.
- *Protection against unfair dismissal due to 'whistle-blowing', i.e. public interest disclosure:* 1 year. Such cases can be expensive for an employer because the public interest disclosure legislation does not impose a cap on tribunal awards. Connex, the train operating company, was ordered to pay £55,000 to a train driver who successfully demonstrated his victimisation after he published concerns over safety risks. £18,000 of the award was for aggravated damages and injury to feelings. Connex declined to appeal the tribunal decision.
- *Dismissal due to job redundancy:* 2 years.
- *Guaranteed lay-off pay:* 1 month.
- *Medical suspension pay:* Absence or suspension from work on medical grounds – 1 month.

Employers are required to provide employees with the periods of paid notice listed in Table 10.1. Employers must give employees full pay for the notice period even if the worker is off sick or on maternity leave.

Activity

On the basis of the material on day one and length of service rights, discuss with your class colleagues any situation in your employment where such rights may have been infringed. The discussion should test your argument against the law. In areas of disagreement between you and your class colleagues, confer with the teacher.

Table 10.1 Minimum notice periods

Length of service	Notice	Length of service	Notice
4 weeks–2 years	1 week	7–8 years	7 weeks
2–3 years	2 weeks	8–9 years	8 weeks
3–4 years	3 weeks	9–10 years	9 weeks
4–5 years	4 weeks	10–11 years	10 weeks
5–6 years	5 weeks	11–12 years	11 weeks
6–7 years	6 weeks	Over 12 years	12 weeks

Discrimination in employment

As the second part of this chapter has shown, employees have statutory protection against discrimination on grounds of sex, race, disability and unequal treatment in terms of pay. However, the presence of discrimination in employment is still evident (see Dickens, 2005 for general discussion of the problem and Chapter 4 of this textbook for details of the relative positions of women and members of ethnic minorities in the labour market). There are three possible explanations for the continued presence of discrimination in employment.

First, much discrimination goes unreported and is tolerated by employees, who feel that they have no voice mechanism to complain about such treatment; this is particularly the case in small firms and some non-union employers. That is, some employers know they are breaking the law but hope to get away with ignoring it. However, it is necessary to point out that even in workplaces that have collective bargaining and otherwise well-ordered human resource management policies, discrimination may still occur.

A second explanation for the continued presence of discrimination relates to the rather limited nature of employment protection legislation during the 1980s. For much of its period of office the Conservative government operated differential employment protection legislation for full-time and part-time workers. The results of much of this legislation, for example the lawful exclusion of part-time workers from occupational pension schemes, are now unlawful as the result of new legislation since 1997. However, many claims against this type of discrimination, unequal pay and indirect sex discrimination, lodged on the basis that more part-time workers were women than men, remain in the process of redress and resolution.

In an effort to reduce discrimination between full-time and part-time employees, the Part-time Workers' (Prevention of Less Favourable Treatment) Regulations came into force in July 2000. These regulations state that part-time workers should receive the same pay rates as full-time colleagues and receive the same hourly overtime rate once they exceed normal working hours. In addition to these equal rights, part-time workers must receive the same holiday, maternity and paternity leave entitlements as full-time colleagues on a pro-rata basis. Finally, part-time workers must be included in the provision of workplace training; that is, there must be a single framework for training in the workplace and not separate sets of arrangements for full-time and part-time workers. The regulations, although a marked improvement on the previous situation – which forced female part-timers who alleged discrimination to seek redress through the indirect route of the Sex Discrimination Act – remain limited. For example, while the regulations call for comparability of pay between full-time and part-time workers, they contain no mechanism to measure or quantify such comparison. Currently a 'comparable worker' – a comparator that a part-time employee uses for comparison – is defined as 'a full-time worker with the same type of employment contract doing the same or similar work'.

A third explanation for the emergence of newly defined forms of discrimination in employment is the UK's further integration within the EU and the adoption by the incoming Labour government of the EU's Social Charter of employment and social rights in 1997. This accession further exposed the limited protection provided for many British employees; for example, prior to November 2001 individuals employed on fixed-term contracts did not have the same rights as full- and part-time employees in terms of pay, pension entitlement and paid holidays. Some of these omissions were remedied by the adoption of the Fixed-term Employees (Prevention of Less Favourable Treatment) Regulations in 2002. The regulations also encourage the use of more permanent arrangements by requiring that individuals who have worked on two or more such fixed-term contracts over a continuous period of four years (the 2 + 4 rule) become permanent employees.

The issue of workplace bullying further demonstrates the limited nature of the UK's discrimination and employment protection laws. It has been reported that every year 18.9 million working days are lost as a direct result of workplace bullying, costing the UK economy some 6 billion pounds (see **www.bullyingatwork.com**). A 2002 survey of 3500 employees found that 20 per cent of the sample had experienced workplace bullying in the past year, with 8 per cent of the sample claiming to have experienced bullying on a regular basis. Bullying is not confined to employees further down the organisational hierarchy; 24 per cent of middle managers and 17 per cent of senior managers reported that they had been bullied at least once over the past year (Mercer Human Resource Consulting, 2002). A more recent survey of 10,000 employees, by the Andrea Adams Trust (2008) found that the situation had worsened, with 92 per cent reporting that they had been bullied at work. Equally disturbingly, they report that 47 per cent of organisations either do not have in place a policy on bullying or do not follow any policy when it is reported and 60 per cent stated they did not believe reporting it would lead to a solution. The sample used consisted of predominantly female (71 per cent), white (90 per cent), full-time workers (85 per cent), who were longer-term employees (45 per cent having been in place over five years). There was a significant number reporting verbal abuse on a weekly basis (32 per cent) and occasional physical abuse (88 per cent). The figures also indicate the rise in workloads, with over 45 per cent reporting managers setting unrealistic targets on a regular basis and imposing unreasonable levels of monitoring. The respondents placed the blame on poor management skills (50 per cent) and in particular they blamed line managers (56 per cent). Not surprisingly a significant percentage (65 per cent) thought bullying at their workplace was a serious problem (see **andreaadamstrust.org.uk**). Despite this feeling of an increase in bullying at work, it is still not specifically categorised in employment legislation, and while the practice may constitute discrimination or indirect discrimination, in other cases employees may have to resign (47 per cent of those reporting bullying in the survey reacted by leaving their job) and possibly lodge a claim for constructive dismissal.

It is important for the Human Resource Management practitioner to note that an employer is liable to defend an allegation of discrimination in the workplace and act upon it even if the employer is not directly responsible for it but where another employee is responsible for the discriminatory behaviour. As some cases in City of London financial institutions demonstrate, it is not sufficient for an employer to argue that racist and sexist behaviour constitutes workplace 'banter' or that they were unaware that such behaviour occurred or that it is not discriminatory because all employees are subject to it. Further, other recent cases in financial institutions demonstrate the continued presence of indirect sex discrimination due to unequal pay, such as in the calculation of bonus payments. For example, a female analyst employed by Schroder Securities won £1.4 million damages in a sex discrimination case where she successfully argued at employment tribunal that her results were similar to those of male colleagues but her bonus payments (£25,000) were significantly lower than those of her colleagues who received 'six-figure' bonuses, and that she had been underpaid because she was a woman (see *Bower* v *Schroders Securities* [2002] IRLR 235). The employer, while denying the claim, accepted the tribunal decision and withdrew its application to the

Employment Appeal Tribunal. Since April 2003, employees have had the right to require employers to complete equal pay questionnaires on co-workers. The evidence suggests that employers who conduct regular pay reviews and those who are committed to pay transparency are far less likely to have pay systems that discriminate against women workers.

The main themes that emerge from this part of the chapter centre around three issues, each of which is pertinent to the Human Resource Management practitioner. First, statutory protection is updated at Parliamentary or EU level and it is essential that human resource managers audit and monitor workplace practices and procedures that are likely to be affected by new legislation. Second, workplaces that have proceduralised systems for human resource management must be vigilant and act quickly to prevent apparently one-off incidents developing into persistent behaviour consistent with emergent bullying or harassment. Finally, much remains to be done in order to remove discriminatory practices in the workplace and it is clear that the discrimination agenda gets not only longer but wider as new areas of activity have been drawn into the scope of existing measures; for example, the extension of equal pay legislation to cover pension entitlements and before that, in the 1980s, the introduction of the equal value amendments for different work of equal value to an employer in terms of skill, effort and decision making.

STOP and think

Is it fair and reasonable to argue in the twenty-first century that lawful discrimination actually exists?

The regulation of working time

As Chapter 11 demonstrates, historically the UK's industrial relations system exhibits only a few areas of specific regulation. The voluntary nature of the British system witnessed a reliance on the negotiation of voluntary agreements over pay and conditions of employment and working time arrangements in particular (see Clark, 2000 and Edwards, 2003 for a general discussion of voluntarism). The 1998 Working Time Regulations (WTR) provide one of the first serious attempts to provide for the regulation of hours at work. However, the voluntary and unregulated nature of the British industrial relations system remains significant. Currently, the UK's application of the EU working time directive illustrates the pervasive nature of voluntarism via the inclusion of opt-outs that allow employers – sometimes unilaterally, sometimes in negotiation with trade unions – to regulate working hours as they see fit.

The UK's working time regulations provide the following working time rights for all employees. These include a maximum of 48 hours for each seven days averaged over a 17-week period. By article 2 of the regulations 'working time in relation to a worker, means any period during which he is working, at his employer's disposal and carrying out his activities or duties' (Working Time Regulations, 1998). This therefore includes overtime, workplace training provided by the employer, work time travelling to meet clients or business partners when this is a regular part of a job and hospitality arrangements such as attendance at receptions and working lunches.

One aim of the working time regulations that remains unfulfilled is a reduction in the effects on employees, of all grades, of the burden of the UK's previously poorly regulated work culture. In 2004 the Workplace Employment Relations Survey (WERS) found that 11 per cent of employees continued to work more than 48 hours, down from 13 per cent in 1998, and that men were still more likely to work longer hours than women. British working hours continue to be the longest in Europe and even in face of the provisions contained in the Working Time Directive (see European Commission, 2003). The long-hours work culture prevalent in the UK has resulted in the emergence of workplace stress as a major issue for

British employers, with work overload often cited as the main cause of stress. The Labour Force Survey (2007/08) indicates that some 13.5 million working days were lost to self-reported stress and some 237,000 people reported suffering depression and/or anxiety due to work-related stress, an incidence rate of 780 cases per 100,000 workers. The extent of the long-hours culture and workplace stress can be seen amongst all workers, with nurses, teachers and professional groups reporting a higher prevalence (13.6 per cent) than other areas. In part this is because whilst the length of the average full-time working week has been falling, the overall development of a long hours work culture remains in evidence (see Burke and Cooper, 2008). Just under a quarter of the employed population (6.3 million people) worked more than 45 hours per week in 2005 with British workers on average also having fewer paid holidays than employees in other EU states, 20 compared to 25–30 in most EU nations, see (CIPD, 2009a).

The limit of opt-out arrangements

An employer cannot require employees to opt-out of the provisions listed below:

- 28 days paid holiday;
- a single work time break where the working day exceeds 6 hours – this does not increase where the working day exceeds 12 hours. (see *Corps of Commissionaires Management Ltd* v *Hughes* [2008] UKEAT|196|08);
- a rest period of 11 consecutive hours in every 24 hours;
- a rest period of 24 continuous hours once every 7 days;
- a maximum of an average of 8 hours' night work in every 24 hours and free health assessments for night workers.

Unlike other EU nations, the British government provides a number of exceptions which restrict the application of specific provisions within identified groups of workers. The WTR also allows employers to seek voluntary modifications in relation to the detailed application of some elements of the protection provided, although not the other provisions within the working time directive. Specific categories for which exceptions are available include:

- domestic employees who work in private households, e.g. cleaners, domestic staff and servants;
- workers where the employer's activities involve the need for continuity of service or production;
- members of the police and the armed forces;
- junior doctors;
- employees who have 'unmeasured or undetermined' working time.

The last category represents a catch-all mechanism that covers many white-collar workers who have some measure of autonomy over how and when they perform their work. Junior doctors have voiced strong opposition to their exclusion from the regulations, the British Medical Association has negotiated reductions in the length of their working week and have been successful in removing their exclusion from the 48-hour rule; a situation which under EU law must be remedied by 1 August 2012 at the latest.

The regulation of working time in the UK demonstrated the partial nature of an apparently inalienable right – the provision of opt-outs creates voluntary exclusion and illustrates the persistence of aspects of Britain's voluntary industrial relations system. In contrast to this, the exclusion via exemptions of many groups of autonomous workers renders working time unregulated in several sectors of employment. Further, low-paid workers who earn only the basic national minimum wage per hour are in effect forced to sign opt-outs to earn a living wage. Lastly, young workers over 15 but younger than 18 are beyond the regulations and covered by the Young Workers' Working Time Directive, which is similar to the regulations for older workers but provides for better rest breaks during working time.

Activity

In what ways are the exceptions (WTR 18–27A) from some of provisions within the WTR reasonable? Is your job included in these exceptions?

If your job is included in these exceptions or you are subject to an opt-out clause in your contract of employment, consider the implications for your employer if, in the future, your job were to be included in the regulations. If your work is 'unmeasured' would a maximum 48hour week affect you or your employer?

Termination of the employment contract

Employment contracts can terminate in a variety of ways, for example job redundancy, voluntary resignation, death in service, non-renewal of a fixed-term contract and summary termination due to conduct – 'the sack'. This part of the chapter examines the issue of termination due to dismissal under the headings of fair dismissal, unfair dismissal, wrongful dismissal and constructive dismissal.

Fair dismissal

The days of 'at-will' contracts of employment, when employers could sack people for any or no reason arguably came to an end with the introduction of the concept of 'unfair dismissal' in the Industrial Relations Act 1971 (IRA). Since then employers can be required to demonstrate that the termination was for one of the reasons listed in s.98(1) of the ERtsA 1996. In general it is correct to say that to be fair a dismissal must be contractually lawful, that is not in breach of any contractual provision and must also be lawful according to statute. In most situations when an employee is dismissed, the reasons for the dismissal are likely to be fair. An employer can fairly dismiss an employee on several grounds; dismissal is likely to be fair if it relates to the categories shown in Figure 10.2.

- *Employee conduct* (s.98(2)(b)). Theft or fraud in the workplace, gross insubordination, fighting etc.

Figure 10.2 Potentially fair reasons for dismissal

- *Redundancy* (s.98(2)(c)). Where a job is classed as redundant under s. 139 meaning that the employee is dismissed due to job redundancy through no fault of their own and has been correctly consulted about the situation and fairly selected for redundancy via an agreed process of selection. If an employee has two years of continuous service with the employer, they must be compensated for the redundancy.

- *Capability and qualifications* (s.98(2)(a)). An employer can fairly dismiss an employee on these grounds but must demonstrate that dismissal relates to job capability, not the employee. For example, to obtain dismissal due to capability on the grounds of illness or disability an employer must demonstrate that they have already made changes to the work situation of an employee and cannot make further changes. Without this evidence the employee may have a claim under the Disability Discrimination Act. If an employee has falsified their qualifications or if they lose a practitioner qualification, for example, by being struck off the medical register if they are a doctor, dismissal is likely to be fair. If an employee is deemed to be incompetent it will be necessary to demonstrate this, for example, that they have been through an internal disciplinary procedure and been given a reasonable opportunity to improve their performance but failed to do so.

- *Contravention of a duty or restriction imposed under or by an enactment* (s.98(2)(d)). For example, if an employee is a driver or needs to be able to drive to perform their job, the loss of a driving licence is likely to be a fair reason for dismissal. Similarly, if there is another legal requirement that the employee can no longer meet, dismissal is likely to be fair; for example, for deep sea divers there are strict age and hours limits due to health and safety considerations. Equally, lorry drivers may have to pass eyesight checks and pilots meet strict health requirements. While dismissals may be fair in some situations, an employer may be expected to offer the employee another job. This is more likely if the firm has a collective bargaining agreement with a trade union.

- *Some other substantial reason* (s.98(1)(b)). Here an employer must demonstrate, in a case where a dismissal is disputed, that the dismissal, while it does not relate to the categories listed above, is nonetheless substantive, fair and reasonable. Often this will be connected to re-organisation, and/or variation of contractual terms (for an example see *Robinson* v *Tescom Corporation* [2008] IRLR 408).

- *Retirement* (s.98(2)(ba)). As indicated above since the introduction of the Employment Equality (Age) Regulations in 2006 the enforced retirement of an employee is considered a dismissal. Where the employer follows the set procedures it is probable this will be a fair dismissal.

Unfair dismissal

As distinct from 'wrongful dismissal', see below, unfair dismissal is a statutory creation based originally in the IRA 1971, and now found within ss 94–132 of the ERtsA 1996. Where an employee believes that they have been dismissed unfairly they have the right to lodge a claim at an employment tribunal (s. 111) and seek compensation, re-engagement or re-instatement. In order for us to understand the process of presenting a claim it is possible to break it down into a number of issues and indicate on whom the burden to prove these issues falls:

Issue	Burden of proof
1 Qualification (an employee with 12 months service)	Employee
2 Dismissal (under ERtsA s. 95)	Employee
3 Reason (under ERtsA s. 98)	Employer
4 Reasonableness (under ERtsA s. 98(4))	Neutral

(Adapted from Jefferson 1997)

By ss 94 and 108 all employees with 12 months service are given the right not to be unfairly dismissed. Whilst these points are not often difficult to prove, the development of 'flexible' working arrangements, including the extension of the use of casual, part-time, and/or fixed-term contracts has led to the development of extensive case law on the issue of status (see discussion below on 'Current issues').

Having demonstrated that the individual is qualified to make a claim, the next issue is whether or not there was actually a dismissal. Section 95(1) lists three situations in which a dismissal will be deemed to have occurred:

- the contract under which he is employed is terminated by the employer (whether with or without notice);
- he is employed under a limited-term contract and that contract terminates by virtue of the limiting event without being renewed under the same contract; or
- the employee terminates the contract under which he is employed (with or without notice) in circumstances in which he is entitled to terminate it without notice by reason of the employer's conduct.

(Section 95(1) ERtsA 1996)

Where the employer has followed a dismissal procedure, a redundancy procedure, or formally written to the employee stating the contract is terminated, proof that the situation meets the requirements of sub-section (1)(a) is not difficult. In many cases the same can be said of sub-section (1)(b). The final definition relates to what is commonly referred to as 'constructive dismissal' and poses many more difficulties. In these situations the employee has to show that the employers' behaviour was such as to amount to a 'repudiation' of the contract – put simply that the employer no longer intends to be bound by the terms of the contract. There is extensive case law on this issue which is founded on the decision in *Western Excavating (ECC) Ltd* v *Sharp* [1978] IRLR 27. In order for an employee to be able to mount a successful claim for constructive dismissal, four circumstances must be proved:

- There must be a breach of contract by the employer.
- That breach must be sufficiently important to justify the employee resigning, or else it must be the last in a series of incidents which justify his leaving.
- The employee must leave in response to the breach and not for some other, unconnected reason.
- The employee must not delay too long in terminating the contract in response to the employer's breach, otherwise he may be deemed to have waived the breach.

(Adapted from *Harvey on Industrial Relations and the Law* Vol. 1 section D1 @ [403])

It is clear therefore that it is insufficient for the employee to terminate the contract because the employer has acted unreasonably, the conduct needs to be a breach of a fundamental term of the contract of employment.

Attention then turns to the stated reason for the dismissal which, in order to be potentially fair, has to be one of the six reasons detailed above. In many cases this is not at issue as the employer will have stated in the letter of termination what the reason was, or the employee will have indicated the reason for his resignation on the claim form. The tribunal must then decide whether the employer acted reasonably or not in treating the reason as a sufficient cause for dismissal. However, as pointed out earlier in the chapter, many aspects of employment law turn on questions of interpretation and the reasonableness of a particular interpretation. So while an employer may deem a dismissal fair, an employee may disagree.

For example, they may claim that they were unfairly selected for redundancy, or that they have been victimised for whistle-blowing or that their dismissal on any of the grounds listed above was motivated by discrimination such as disability, race, sex, marital status, pregnancy etc. In these situations an employment tribunal applies a 'several tests' rule on the fairness of a dismissal. A tribunal will examine the dismissal against the facts of a particular case to test whether the dismissal was *fair in the particular circumstances of the case*. If the details of a particular case do not meet the criteria for a potentially fair dismissal then the dismissal is unfair. In some circumstances a reason for dismissal may be fair yet the dismissal may have been conducted in an unfair manner, that is, a dismissal may be *procedurally unfair*. Hence, if there are internal procedures that should be followed that relate to grievance and discipline in the workplace it is vital that an employer follows these procedures and is further able to demonstrate to the employee, their representatives and a tribunal that they have done so.

Unfair dismissals that relate to discriminatory behaviour, including those for unequal pay and those that relate to pregnancy, are automatically unfair and remedies are available to employees as day one rights. For example, a group of part-time women workers employed on a particular pay grade made redundant after six months' service may be able to demonstrate unfair selection for redundancy if no male employees were made redundant and they can establish that they were made redundant because they were the cheapest employees to terminate. Other situations where no length of service is necessary to claim unfair dismissal include those that relate to trade union membership, participation in lawful industrial action that lasted less than eight weeks, participation as an employee representative for purposes of consultation (where there is no trade union presence), refusal to work on grounds of health and safety or where an employee seeks to assert a statutory right.

Wrongful dismissal

A wrongful dismissal is a dismissal that is in breach of contract, for example dismissal without notice or a failure to pay all due wages and remuneration during the notice period. It is settled law that the damages awarded for wrongful dismissal are the amount equivalent to that which would have been due in wages, together with the value of any fringe benefits, during the period between actual termination and when the contract could have been lawfully terminated (see *Silvey* v *Pendragon plc* [2001] IRLR 685). Many wrongful dismissal cases relate to highly paid business executives who are dismissed but denied some aspect of their remuneration package. Other cases may relate to employees in government service who are dismissed by ministers. In the early 1990s, Michael Howard, the Conservative government Home Secretary, dismissed Derek Lewis, head of the prison service, without notice in a dispute about who held overall operational responsibility for prisons. Mr Lewis sued for wrongful dismissal and the Home Office later met his claim.

Constructive dismissal

As indicated above, claims for constructive dismissal are risky because an employee has to satisfy a tribunal that they had no alternative but to leave and in the majority of cases it is unlikely that the employee will get their job back.

Redundancy rights

Under current legislation – ss 105 and 162–170 ERtsA – employees require two years of continuous service in a particular employment to qualify for a lump sum compensation award. Such compensatory awards are detailed within the statutory provision in relation to age and years of service on the effective date of termination (EDT). For each complete year of service under the age of 22 they will receive half a week's pay. This increases to one week's pay for each completed year of service during which the employee was aged between 22 and 40 and rises to one and a half week's pay for each completed year of service during which the employee was over the age of 41. Redundancy payments and unfair dismissal compensation are unaffected by the number of hours an employee works but the statutory limit for one week's pay is £350 and redundancy payments up to the value of £30,000 are tax free. An employer must make the payment as soon as the employee is dismissed.

Employers are required to consult the workforce about redundancy and, where collective bargaining is present, a trade union must be consulted in specific circumstances. In non-union workplaces employers must establish a representative body of the workforce to consult over redundancy, for example multinational corporations may use existing European Works Councils for this purpose. The employer must consult with the consultative body or the trade union, giving information as to the reasons for redundancy, the numbers involved, mechanisms to minimise the numbers affected, the grades of job affected, the method of determining which jobs are redundant and how any payments that supplement the statutory requirements are to be worked out. If an employer has collective bargaining it is likely that there will be an established redundancy procedure negotiated with the trade union. Whilst there is a statutory period for consultation that relates to the number of jobs being made redundant, the timing of these consultations is often a matter of dispute – see 'Current Issues' below. The statute (Trade Union and Labour Relations (Consolidation) Act 1992 ss 188–196 – TULR(C)A) provides that if over 100 jobs are made redundant the employer must consult over a 90-day period, but only 30 days of consultation are necessary where the number of job redundancies is fewer than 100. Throughout the consultation period an employer must seek alternatives to job redundancy and act in good faith. Both these issues are controversial. Many trade unions argue that it is easier to dismiss British employees than employees in other EU nations because consultation occurs once the decision to make jobs redundant is taken rather than before the decision is made, as is required by law in most other EU nations. In extreme cases, some employees, for example those employed at Vauxhall's Luton plant, have first heard of their impending redundancy through the local and national media.

The first section of this chapter, 'The contract of employment' detailed the contractual and statutory rights of employees; the following section 'Discrimination in employment' examined the continued presence of discrimination, whilst the third section 'The regulation of working time' demonstrated the difficulty of establishing employee rights that relate to working time. This part of the chapter has illustrated how employers can fairly dismiss employees and how employees can respond by making a claim to an employment tribunal. The next section examines the issues that relate to the enforcement of employee rights in the employment relationship.

Activity

Provide two potential examples of unfair, wrongful and constructive dismissal. In each case suggest how an employer might avoid the situation.

Enforcement of contractual and statutory employment rights

For the vast majority of employees, enforcement of employment rights is not an issue. Good employers, large and small, ensure that employment contracts reflect existing and new employment rights. In general, larger employers are likely to have a dedicated human resource management function to do this and in some cases they are likely to recognise trade unions for the purposes of individual and collective representation. This union presence is likely to ensure that terms and conditions of employment and internal procedures reflect employee rights, be they contractual or statutory. In general, it is not in employers' interests to 'short change' their employees, particularly when staff recruitment and retention are recognised human resource management problems. Equally, if, as many employers claim, employees are the most valued assets within a firm, demonstrating this through good employment practice is one way to be recognised as an employer of choice. However, some employers do seek to short-change employees by withholding certain rights, such as the minimum wage, or subjecting employees to arbitrary and unreasonable treatment.

If employees feel that a contractual or statutory employment right is absent, incorrectly proceduralised, or not enforced, they have three main options. Discussion of the situation with a supervisor, line manager or the Human Resource Management Advisor may result in corrective action. Alternatively, an employee can raise their grievance through their trade union representative or other employee representative. Lastly, and more often in cases of alleged unfair dismissal, an employee can instigate proceedings against their employer or former employer by making an application to an employment tribunal. In many cases such an application may be sufficient to persuade the employer that they need to take corrective action. However, some cases will go to tribunal either because the dispute cannot be settled in any other way due to employer intransigence or because an employer feels the case must be defended because of its future implications for themselves and other similar employers.

Employment tribunals are now long established and operate as specialist employment 'courts'. Tribunals have a legally qualified employment judge and two lay members acting as employee and employer nominees. Tribunals are meant to be less formal than other courts but over the years they have become increasingly legalistic and much more time-consuming, particularly in situations where a test case is being heard. Virtually all claims in relation to the employment relationship are heard in tribunals; however some, notably claims for wrongful, constructive, and unfair dismissals that involve a breach of contract, may be heard in civil courts.

To begin an application to a tribunal an employee or former employee must complete an application form ET1 within the time limit specified for the particular jurisdiction covering the event they intend to complain about (see Bowers *et al.*, 2009 for a detailed list of time limits). The ET1 will contain details of the employee's claim and the remedy they are seeking – reinstatement, re-engagement or compensation. The tribunal service will send the ET1 and an ET2 to the employer or former employer; the ET2 summonses the employer to appear before the tribunal. The employer must also complete an ET3, stating their side of the case and return it to the tribunal service within 28 days of the date it was sent to them. Failure to return it within this time may result in either a default judgment against the employer or the employer being barred from participating in the proceedings.

In 2008 there was a rise of approximately 45 per cent in applications to the tribunal service – 189,303, up from 132,577 in 2007, and 115,039 in 2006 (Employment Tribunal Service Annual Report 2009). Whilst this increase was spread across a number of jurisdictional areas, notable increases were seen in the areas of Working Time (where 10,000 claims from airline employees were resubmitted on a number of occasions), Age Discrimination (up by 2,000) and Equal Pay (up by nearly 20,000). This constant rise seems difficult to stop because as employers and government address one area (unfair dismissal claims reduced by 4,000) other areas increase. Employers continually claim that many of these applications are frivolous or vexatious. Even so, the introduction in July 2001 of a fine of up to £10,000 for making such applications has apparently had little long term effect, despite being increased in line with awards; the median amount awarded as costs in 2008 was £1,000 with the highest being £17,775.

The statutory award for unfair dismissal is made up of two components. First, the basic award of up £350 for each year of completed employment (making the maximum 30 × 350 = 10,500) and second the compensatory award of up to a maximum of £66,200 (making the maximum combined award £76,700). However, in cases that relate to discrimination there is no upper limit on tribunal awards. For example the average and highest awards in 2007/08 were:

Jurisdiction	Maximum	Average
Race discrimination	£68,991	£14,566
Sex discrimination	£131,466	£11,263
Disability discrimination	£227,208	£19,523
Religious dicrimination	£5,750	£3,203
Sexual orientation	£22,850	£7,579
Age discrimination	£12,124	£3,334
Unfair dismissal	£76,536	£8,058

(*Source*: ETS Annual Report 2007/08)

While the maximum compensation awards may seem large, the table shows that the average award is much lower in the majority of cases. In 2007/08 only 60 unfair dismissal cases saw awards above £50,000 while 148 saw awards below £500 and over 1,500 were awarded less than £4,000. Equally, in most cases former employees do not get their job back; for example, in 2007/08 in a total of 8 (or less than 1 per cent) of unfair dismissal cases was the applicant re-employed. The figures show that some 80 per cent of unfair dismissal claims never reach the tribunal – being either conciliated or withdrawn prior to the hearing, and of those that get to the tribunal only 10 per cent are successful. In those cases compensation, as opposed to re-employment or re-engagement, is the preferred remedy of most tribunals. Tribunals are not, it would appear, the easy 'lottery win' for those who make a claim.

There is, in addition to these arguments, evidence that employers, and small employers in particular, lack confidence on the issue of employee rights. Edwards *et al.* (2003) in a survey of SMEs found that despite the growth of legislation, the impact on this sector appears relatively small. They wonder whether this is a result of lack of awareness rather than lack of impact. Their findings reflect those of Blackburn and Hart (2002) in which they noted only 20 per cent of small employers have confidence in their knowledge of employment legislation, with only 50 per cent aware of the employee right to paid paternity leave.

In the Employment Act 2002 the government sought to take some steps to regulate the exercise of employment rights more effectively by introducing a statutory Dismissal and Disciplinary procedure and by compelling employees to follow the minimum statutory grievance procedure within the organisation before taking a case to tribunal. These measures, while at the time appearing to be a sensible and reasonable approach, rested on the premise that all employers would put these procedures in place. In reality, far fewer employers implemented these procedures than expected. This uneven implementation of the statutory procedures, created additional legal arguments and appeared to increase ET claims rather than reduce them as planned. The statutory procedures were repealed by the Employment Act 2008 (see 'Current issues' below).

The evidence suggests that employers' claims of 'excessive red tape' and the burden of defending unnecessary tribunal applications are not proven. Many employees are denied the opportunity to go through internal grievance procedures, either through fear of reprisals or the non-existence of clear procedures. Equally, the growth in employment rights caught some employers – good and bad – off guard, particularly in the area of unfair dismissal. Employer claims of red tape and the cost of defending at a tribunal must be measured against better regulation of the employment relationship and the need for improved best practice. While the majority of applications to tribunals to enforce employee rights are settled on a voluntary basis and withdrawn, the growth in the number of applications demonstrates the absence of best practice in many areas of employment. Lastly, claims that a 'compensation culture' is emerging which is likely to damage the competitiveness of British industry is a very doubtful argument, because if employees win a case at tribunal it demonstrates that their rights were in some way infringed. Alternatively, if an employer settles a claim or takes corrective action in the workplace, this demonstrates that not all procedures were adequate. High-profile compensation awards involving large sums, such as those associated with the 'sexism in the City' cases, are rare, despite being of great interest to the media, but they do demonstrate that poor employment practice occurs in all types of employment and that enforcement can be expensive for employers. Furthermore, the actions of some employers in recent cases undermine claims of bureaucracy, red tape and time wasted in having to defend applications to employment tribunals. Applications to tribunals that are withdrawn or settled voluntarily may have been settled 'out of court' by employers. For example, Nomura International reached an out of court settlement with an employee made redundant while on maternity leave, who prior to that had been asked to wear short skirts at work and give a male colleague a massage. The former employee dropped her discrimination claim but reached a £70,000 out-of-court settlement with Nomura, who maintained that the claim was unfounded. In a similar City case, Cru Publishing settled a case of constructive dismissal out of court even though an employment tribunal found that the employee was 75 per cent to blame for her dismissal.

While the growth of out-of-court settlements does undermine employers' claims of red tape and excessive costs in employment regulation, there are three specific problems with them in respect to the enforcement of employment rights. First, out-of-court settlements often prevent full disclosure of the facts and while a former employee may be generously compensated, the provisions of a settlement usually remain confidential. Second, withdrawing a claim and settling out of court often enables employers to deny the charges made against them and, more importantly, prevents the creation of what might be a reference point – a precedent for future cases. Third, an employer that settles a case out of court but denies the basis of the claim may fail to improve human resource management procedures – a measure often enforced by tribunals or the Equalities and Human Rights Commission.

In summary, a well-resourced human resource management function staffed by CIPD-qualified practitioners is one route to employer best practice in the area of employment rights; trade union recognition is another, and the latter is likely to lead to negotiation and partnership in the management of employee rights. Both routes are likely to become more fruitful for employers, bearing in mind the likelihood of further growth in employee rights and the medium- to longer-term impact of the membership of the EU.

Current issues

This final part of the chapter examines the expansion of legal rights alongside the drive for higher performance and the continued development of human resource management techniques. In straightforward terms HRM practices arguably increase management control over labour while at the same time using the language of partnership, empowerment, and performance management. This section considers the manner in which the courts have addressed some of the key themes and practices within HRM. Whatever description of HRM is used, there are some recurrent themes and practices. Ryan and Pointon (2007: 510) referred to it as a mantra, which included ideas such as 'productivity through our people, strong(er) leadership, cohesive cultures, flatter structures, and customer focus'. Gilmore (2009) suggests HRM is best understood as the development of the six themes of strategy, performance, commitment, flexibility, culture, and power. Having laid out the basic legal rights and protections for employees, we now look at some of the problems this move to extend managerial control currently presents in the case reports and how the decisions arrived at by the courts might affect the development of HRM practices.

The flexicurity debate

The flexicurity debate can be summed up as follows: on the one hand, encouraged by policy makers, employers want to make more flexible use of labour to increase productivity and competitiveness but the opposite side of this coin is the worker's desire for job security and stability. As Philips and Eamets (2007) noted '[e]mployers are demanding wider deregulation in order to cope with global competition . . . [w]orkers are searching for better job security during a time of rapid structural change and job reallocation' (2007: 5). These two forces pull in opposite directions as employers seek loyalty and commitment from a flexible workforce and employees strive for stability of employment. In contemporary organisations this conflict is manifest in debates over the status of workers raised by the increased use of agency staff and other 'flexible' forms of labour deployment.

As we noted above, the existence of a contract of employment is critical in deciding what legal protection is afforded to individuals. From a legal perspective this debate concerns the labelling of the relationships for the provision of labour. Freedland (2003) argues that we need to remove the classifications of 'employee and worker' and adopt a broader definition of 'dependent labour' thus extending the range of protective legislation. Njoya (2007) suggests a legal solution based in the concept of property rights developed from the decision of Hawkins J in *Allen* v *Flood* [1898], which postulates a regime of protection based on 'the full benefit of the valuable interest they (workers) have in a probable expectation of continuing employment' ([1898] at 16).

The courts have adopted, at various times, both a wide and a narrow interpretation of the concept of status. It was possibly seen at the broadest in *Dacas* v *Brook Street Bureau* [2004] in which the Court of Appeal established that a temporary/agency worker could become an employee of the client company, despite a clause in the agreement to the contrary. These relationships can be visualised as 'triangular relationships'.

Whilst these arrangements provide numerical, functional and financial flexibility for the Client Company (CC) they provide no security for the worker (W). In this model, while there are plenty of contracts floating around, the worker is not regarded as an employee of either of the other parties because none of these contracts is a contract of employment. These 'temp' workers began to receive some form of protection in the late 1990s as the Courts sought to identify an 'umbrella' contract of employment. Using this idea in *McMeechan* v *Secretary of State for Employment* [1997] ICR 549 the Court of Appeal determined that, in specific circumstances, there could be two contracts between the worker and the employment business: (a) an 'umbrella contract', referred to as 'being on the books' and (b) separate contracts for each assignment. They felt the latter was more likely, but that if sufficient assignments were undertaken over a long enough period of time the 'umbrella contract' would make the worker an employee of the employment business (see also the decision in *Consistent Group Ltd* v *Kalwak* [2008] IRLR 505). In *Dacas*, on similar facts, they

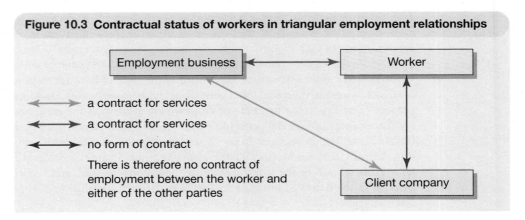

Figure 10.3 Contractual status of workers in triangular employment relationships

Employment business ← → Worker

→ a contract for services

← → a contract for services

← → no form of contract

There is therefore no contract of employment between the worker and either of the other parties

Client company

reached the conclusion that the 'umbrella contract' would be with the client company, a decision that presents more acute problems for HR managers in terms of workforce planning and flexibility. The key issue, in both circumstances, appeared to be the length of time the worker had been engaged either as 'on the books' or within a specific client company. This length of service it was held, creates obligations – notably based around issues of control and payment – for one or other of the organisations in relation to specific workers. The Courts have now decided that such an 'umbrella contract' can only be implied where it is *necessary* to give the arrangement business sense (see *James* v *London Borough of Greenwich* [2008] IRLR 302). HR managers can at present, therefore develop flexibility plans which make extensive use of 'temps' without fear that these people will gain employment protection rights in relation to their organisation; that is pending the next twist in this complex debate. This twist may come in relation to the development of the discussions about 'vulnerable workers' currently in progress and focusing on changes made by the Employment Act 2008 in relation to Employment Businesses and Employment Agencies. BERR (2008) noted that there are some 16,000 agencies making use of between 1.1 and 1.5 million temporary workers, that a larger proportion of the UK workforce (some 5 per cent) engages in temporary employment than in our major EU competitors (an average of 2.25 per cent), that some 225,000 of these workers are regularly on assignments of less than one week, while 55 per cent of engagements are less than 12 weeks. The report suggests that while a cornerstone of the recent achievements in the UK economy have been secured through the application of flexible workers, the vulnerable agency workforce is significantly slanted towards members of the minority ethnic groups. The results of this wide-ranging discussion can be seen in sections 8–18 of the Employment Act 2008 which address issues of minimum wages, enforcement of existing protections, and information sharing between agencies. Despite these changes, the approach can still be described as 'light-touch' in terms of regulation of this sector which reflects a policy towards vulnerable workers that conflicts with any move to provide substantive rights for agency workers or a change in the Governments' extended opposition to the implementation of the EU Temporary Agency Worker Directive (Wynn, 2009).

A similar story can be told in relation to homeworkers. While the current case law tends to involve textile workers (see *Nethermere of St Neots* v *Gardiner* [1984] ICR 612) or assembly workers (see *Airfix Footwear Ltd* v *Cope* [1978] ICR 1210), the arguments can be extended to cover casual workers (see *O'Kelly* v *Trust House Forte* [1983] ICR 728). Indeed, it is possible to note that the two most litigated issues in the last decade, especially in relation to status, concern 'temps' and 'casual/homeworkers'. For twenty-first century HR managers these issues are likely to be more related to individuals using information technology at home as a means of managing work–life balance issues. Removing the work (and hence the worker) away from the normal place of work allows the individual to gain more self-control over pace, timing and organisation of work and increases the likelihood that the courts will view the relationship as a contract of services rather than of service. The issue of status therefore continues to turn on the implied obligation of mutual trust and confidence (Brodie, 2008). Whether the HR manager is dealing with a casual worker, a homeworker or a temporary worker provided by an employment business it is arguable that the application of this obligation is consistent with the protection of people's 'dignity, autonomy, respect, status or security' (Oliver, 1999: 86); values upon which the modern (ethical) HR manager would place importance and significance.

Job security in these terms can be defined as the right to have access to remedies for unfair dismissal, wrongful dismissal, discrimination, and harassment, As Deakin and Morris (2005) suggest '[t]he key to the meaning of employment security is the existence of some form of regulatory intervention designed to protect workers against arbitrary managerial decisions' (2005: 338). Despite pressure from various interest groups and trades unions, such protection within UK law is hard to identify, leaving much of the responsibility for ensuring this vulnerable section of the workforce enjoy the dignity, respect, and security afforded other workers in the hands of business leaders; a particular challenge for CIPD qualified, ethical HR managers.

Grievance, discipline and dismissal

It is arguable that no better example of 'arbitrary managerial decisions' (Deakin and Morris, 2005) can be found than in the areas of grievance, discipline and dismissal. Despite extensive case law, this area remains one of the largest single areas of dispute and tribunal workload. In order to reduce the extent to which individuals resorted to tribunal applications following unsuccessful internal grievance procedures and/or disciplinary procedures, the government put in place statutory procedures in 2004. The Dispute Resolution Regulation (2004) required both parties to follow specific procedures before they could lodge a tribunal claim. For example, after lodging a grievance employees had to allow employers 28 days to it before they could raise a tribunal complaint in relation to constructive dismissal. These requirements were meant to encourage resolution of disputes in the workplace and were part of a broader policy of enterprise confinement in relation to employment relations which New Labour continued from the previous Conservative administration. By placing more emphasis on internal resolution, the procedures enhanced the role of HR managers in dispute resolution and, initially at least, reduced the number of tribunal applications. However, as had happened before with tribunals more generally, solicitors became more involved and tribunal workload was swelled by technical arguments relating to the interpretation of specific provisions within the regulations. The number of tribunal applications became so large that in 2006 the government set up a review under the leadership of Michael Gibbons. The Gibbons report was published in 2007 and reported that the statutory procedures were widely condemned because they were seen to exacerbate disputes, create expectations of failure to secure a resolution, and to be impractical. The report therefore recommended the repeal of the procedures and their replacement with clear, simple, non-prescriptive guidelines developed within the stewardship of the Advisory, Conciliation and Arbitration Service (ACAS). A key message from the report was that:

> [i]nflexible, prescriptive regulation has been unsuccessful in this context and it follows that the measures used in the future should be much simpler and more flexible – and therefore will offer rather less certainty and predictability in their operation   (Gibbons 2007: 6)

It is unsurprising therefore, that the Employment Act 2008, which implements many of the reports recommendations, should include provisions to allow 'monetary disputes' (mainly under the NMWA and provisions covering Unlawful Deductions) to be settled without a hearing by an employment judge alone. The Act also provides for more 'free' dispute resolution services to be provided by ACAS along with an enhanced helpline that will advise on the pitfalls of following the tribunal route, and an extension of the time allowed for ACAS involvement before the hearing.

The new scheme was introduced from April 2009, although many commentators class it as being a case of 'Back to the future'. For HR managers the system should be simpler, if less transparent, as the statutory procedures have been removed without replacement. The new system relies heavily on the new ACAS code issued in November 2008 as a standard against which tribunals should gauge the behaviour of both employers and employees. The shortened Code of Practice maintains the basic structure of 'letter, meeting, appeal' found in the statutory procedure, but does not require either party to follow this Code or the associated and extensive guidance because the Act re-introduces the rule in *Polkey* v *AE Dayton Services* [1988] AC 344 or 'no-difference' concept. Put simply, an employer who fails to follow the procedure set out in the Code of Practice may now argue that it would have made 'no-difference' to the outcome and avoid a finding of unfair dismissal. As Sanders (2009: 42) notes, 'This is a significant decline indeed when employees' protection against dismissal is nearly exclusively procedural, given tribunals' reluctance to examine the substantive fairness of dismissals'. The manner in which tribunals will handle the change in terms of increasing the award (now 25 per cent) will also affect the willingness of employers to abide by the Code of Practice. The statutory procedures were introduced in part because of a realisation that up to 40 per cent of employers had no procedure for handling discipline and even fewer had procedures for handling grievances. This was especially true outside the public sector and larger private sector companies. The danger is that replacing statutory procedures with a Code of Practice may return us to this situation – meaning a diminution of protection for employees in SMEs. As Blackburn and Hart (2002) noted, the situation before the introduction of the statutory procedures was that SMEs found themselves defending tribunal claims on a far more regular basis than other sectors of the economy. In part this was seen to be because of the lack of awareness amongst this group of the basic legislative provisions.

In relation to grievances, the removal of the statutory procedure also removes the need for employees seeking to claim 'constructive dismissal' or any other detriment to write to the employer at least 28 days before lodging a tribunal claim, hence returning us to a situation where the first an employer knows of a grievance may be when the ET1 arrives in the post. While the guidance associated with the Code of Practice suggests an internal procedure which necessitates the use of various mechanisms – including the use of informal procedures for trivial matters – failure to follow them does not prevent an employee making a claim to a tribunal.

The introduction of an extended period for ACAS conciliation before the tribunal date is designed to encourage the use of third-party mediation. This is surprising bearing in mind the failure of the existing ACAS scheme, which was used a mere 44 times during 2001–2004. Whether and to what extent the introduction of such a scheme, supported by the improved service on the ACAS helpline and the development of training programmes for internal mediators, will reduce tribunal claims – which appears to be the policy goal – is open to question. It is true that in recent times a dispute resolution structure which is significantly different from the one we understand has arisen in non-union firms, the major difference being that it has not evolved from negotiation between parties of comparatively equal terms, but has been unilaterally imposed by employers. It is also accurate to argue that the new scheme appears to support the development of managerially determined disputes procedures within larger firms, but this does nothing to address two key problems; first, the lack of procedures within SMEs, identified by all parties, and second, the number of so-called 'vexatious litigants'. What is missing is a realisation that discipline and grievance may represent a form of reactive conflict which stems primarily from the deteriorated state of the relationship between the parties (Lewin, 1999) and that workplace conflict resolution mechanisms need to address the imbalance of power within organisations. What appears to have been created by these regulations is a 'new era in unfair dismissal law in which "economy prosperity" dominates "social justice" to a degree not seen before' (Sanders, 2009: 32). For the CIPD-qualified, ethical HR manager, the challenge will be to implement and apply internal mechanisms that meet the organisations' needs whilst retaining the dignity, respect and security required by employees.

Framework equal treatment directive

The introduction of the Framework Equal Treatment Directive (FETD) in 2002 has led to a number of significant changes in UK legislation. These have included the enactment of regulations relating to discrimination on the grounds of Religion and Belief (2003), Sexual Orientation (2003) and Age (2006). It is also possible to suggest that the FETD was part of the driving force behind the introduction, in April 2009, of the Equality Bill. The Bill aims to simplify the existing range of anti-discrimination legislation by consolidating it within one Act. This could mean the introduction of a more clearly defined category of indirect discrimination within the area of disability (Keen, 2008). The Bill further proposes a duty, at least on public bodies, to disclose internal pay audits in full (including all pay levels) for the purpose of equality assessment – there are indications that this would be extended to all organisations with over 250 staff, using a voluntary measure until 2013. Interestingly, the Bill proposes a duty on public bodies not to discriminate on the basis of 'class' in the provision of opportunities. This requires them to have procedures that allow access for all groups. While initially this appears limited to the provision of services to service users, the use of the word 'opportunity' suggests a possible expansion to include employment opportunities.

STOP and think

Imagine a restaurant owner prevents a blind person from bringing his dog into his restaurant, merely because he wishes not to have a dog in his restaurant. If this is the reason for prohibiting entry would it be related to the customer's disability?

What about dismissing a one legged postman for slowness?

*If you are sure of the answers (or unsure) look at the judgements of Bingham LJ and Scott LJ in **London Borough of Lewisham** v **Malcolm** [2008] HL 43.*

Other developments in brief

Other recent changes have included the provision of Statutory Sick Pay for agency workers with assignments lasting three months or more and the removal of 'tips' from calculations of the NMW. A further requirement will be that all employers cooperate with school leavers under the age of 18 if they are desirous of participating in education or training. While at the other end of the working life from 2012 workers will either automatically qualify and be included in the organisations pension scheme or the employer will need to arrange for deductions of the same amount to be paid into the Personal Account Scheme on their behalf. The position of Agency Workers is further enhanced with the publication of the Temporary Agency Workers Directive (2008/104/EC), which will need to be implemented in the UK by 2011 and provides additional protections for such workers. These rights include that they will have equal rights to comparable permanent workers after 12 weeks. There have also been changes to the right to request flexible working arrangements, which now covers parents of children up to the age of 16, although full implementation is yet to be detailed.

Conclusion

While many see the employment relationship as a private exchange between an employer and an employee, they are actually subject to significant contractual and statutory regulation. All employees have a contract of employment and some measure of statutory protection against unfair and unreasonable treatment by an employer. However, since 1997 the contractual and statutory regulation of the employment relationship has tightened. As a result of this, employees have greater protection than previously; this creates the need for improved vigilance from employers and reinforces the need in all areas of employment for an effective human resource management function. In large and small employers, a human resource management function staffed by CIPD-qualified, ethical professionals is likely to increase employer confidence in the regulation of employment and may help avoid the infringement of employee rights. Equally, trade unions have a role to play in the enforcement of employee rights at work through collective bargaining. This is the case because, although there has been a significant growth in statutory protection for individual employees since 1997, a question remains about its effectiveness. The growth in the number of applications to employment tribunals illustrates that the application of best practice principles in the regulation of the employment relationship is far from universal. Similarly, the continued search for labour market flexibility, as demonstrated by the UK's idiosyncratic application of the Working Time Directive and the weakness in the framework for applications for flexible working, may infringe the employment rights of some workers but go unnoticed. Therefore, there is an issue of how to enforce recent additions to individual employment rights. Notwithstanding the drive for flexibility, the dignity and respect rightly desired by workers, alongside the need for employment security, means that legislation must seek to establish enforceable rights and safeguards for workers. This is especially true in light of the relative weakness of trade unions across the employed labour force.

If, as many employers assert, employees are the most valued assets within an organisation, fair and reasonable treatment consistent with contractual and statutory rights regulated on an individual basis is one measure of good employment practice. Moreover, the voluntary enforcement of employee rights by employers demonstrates the 'good employer' ethos – best practice in the regulation of the employment relationship. Employees who receive fair and reasonable treatment in the employment relationship are more likely to be retained by an employer, better motivated, more committed and deliver higher productivity than those employees who are not. As this chapter demonstrates, employee rights are extensive but not prohibitive in terms of coverage or the 'red tape' they create. Reasonable treatment requires regulation and enforcement. The evidence suggests that what some employers term 'red tape' actually results from problems created when unreasonable treatment occurs; that is, when employers deviate from the good employer ethos and fail to follow best practice procedures.

Summary

This chapter examined the employment relationship and its regulation through the contract of employment under six different headings.

Distinguishing contractual and statutory employment rights

- All employees have a contract of employment.
- All employees are protected by some statutory rights – these include day one rights and other rights that require some qualifying length of service.

The contract of employment

- Employment contracts are contracts of personal service between an employer and an employee.
- Employment contracts are based on the theory of market individualism, where individuals are seen as rational and self-interested.
- Employment contracts are subject to the common law.
- There are different types of employment contract.
- Employment contracts contain express, implied and statutory incorporated terms and conditions.

Discrimination in employment

- Discrimination remains a persistent feature of the employment relationship.
- Some types of 'discrimination' remain lawful.

The regulation of working time

- Traditionally, working time has been unregulated in the UK.
- The Working Time Directive regulates hours of work but contains many exceptions and allows employees to opt out from the provision.

- The Working Time Directive has failed to counter the UK's 'long-hours' culture.
- The UK's application of the directive may soon be challenged.

Termination of the employment contract

- Employees can be fairly, unfairly, wrongfully or constructively dismissed.
- Dismissals may be fair and potentially fair, otherwise they are unfair.

Enforcement of contractual and statutory employment rights

- Most employees are treated fairly.
- If employees are treated unreasonably or unfairly they can complain to an employment tribunal.
- Tribunals, Human Resource Management departments, Commission for Equality and Human Rights (established by the Equality Act 2006 and combining the Equal Opportunities Commission, the Commission for Racial Equality and the Disability Rights Commission), trade unions play a role in enforcing employment rights.

Current issues

- The development of a flexible workforce generated a long-standing debate between the rights of employers and the security of employment desired by employees. We are left to consider just who's rights hold the trump card?
- The changes in the legislation relating to grievance, discipline and dismissal mark a return to a less regulated regime.
- The development of the new ACAS Code of Practice and the associated guidance offer new challenges for the CIPD-qualified, ethical HR manger.
- Further employment rights are constantly in the process of development and introduction, meaning that an understanding of the basic provisions becomes more important for a CIPD qualified, ethical HR manager.

Questions

1 How is a contract formed in the following situations?
  (a) Buying a magazine in a newsagent's.
  (b) An offer of full-time permanent employment.
  (c) The hiring of a subcontractor to perform maintenance work on a firm's computers.

2 How does employment protection legislation actually protect full-time and part-time employees?

3 Do you think that the employment protection legislation provides for effective and reasonable protection of employees?

Case study

The pitfalls that follow a failure of best practice

In June 1996 Jane Smith was engaged by the department of media studies at Cromwell University as a part-time administrative assistant. For non-academic staff and casual employees decisions over recruitment, selection, remuneration and terms and conditions of employment are decentralised to departmental managers who should follow procedures laid down in best-practice manuals supplied by the Human Resource Management function. At the time, Jane was given a 'casual contract' that excluded her from the terms and conditions of employment applied to permanent staff and academic staff employed by the university. Jane was not given a copy of the contract even though she regularly asked for a copy. Two years later, Jane was given a copy of the casual contract. On examining the contract Jane noticed that, although the contract specified that a termination date must be included, no termination date was included. In addition to this omission, Jane's hours of work were not specified. Jane queried both these omissions but was told by her line manager, Professor Clarke, not to worry about them. On average Jane worked 15 hours per week and was paid at an hourly rate of £10. By June 1999 the hourly rate had risen to £11. In order to receive her pay Jane merely had to include a code on her wage claims and get the signature of Professor Clarke. The code related to funds held and controlled by the department of media studies and as long as this was included on wages claims the wages and salaries section would not query any claims.

In June 1999 Jane became pregnant, and she informed her line manager Professor Clarke, indicating that she would soon seek maternity leave, and asked him what procedures she needed to follow in order to do this. Professor Clarke replied that he didn't know but would find out for her. Since her engagement Jane had worked continuously at the university and had been allowed to take holidays by arrangement with her line manager even though at the time of her engagement this was clearly prohibited within the terms of her casual contract.

Eventually, Jane approached the wages and salaries section of the Human Resource Management function to inquire about maternity leave and maternity pay. She was told that as a casual employee she was not entitled to these benefits because she was engaged by the university on a term-by-term basis. Jane countered this argument by stating that she had worked at the university for the past three years, had a staff pigeon-hole and an entry in the university telephone directory. The staff in the wages and salary section, although nominally part of the Human Resource Management function, are actually controlled by the university treasury function and are not qualified Human Resource Management practitioners. They refused to process her inquiry because as she had no employee reference number she must be an hourly paid casual worker. An argument ensued and Jane was told to stop wasting their time and go away.

Jane went directly to see the head of Human Resource Management but found that he was away on holiday; perplexed, Jane sought legal and trade union assistance. Her representatives contacted the pro vice chancellor responsible for staff relations and demanded a meeting. At the meeting, all the above information was presented to the pro vice chancellor, who was unable to deal with it effectively because the head of Human Resource Management was on holiday. However, he promised to get this matter sorted out by the middle of the following week and arranged a meeting for the Wednesday.

Activity

Assume you are the Human Resource Management manager and a summary of the above lands on your desk when you return from holiday on the Monday morning together with a note from the pro vice chancellor asking you to sort all this out by Wednesday. How would you sort the situation out? And how would you diagnose the situation? The following pointers may help guide you in this task:

- Does the university have to provide Jane with maternity leave and maternity pay? If so, why?

- Is Jane an employee? Does it matter that she is a casual employee?

- Does Jane have continuous service with the university?

- Does Jane's situation suggest that there might be a wider problem in the university? For example, would the apparently less than satisfactory situation concerning Jane's employment go unnoticed if she had not become pregnant or if Jane was a male employee?

- How will you rectify Jane's situation?

Useful websites

www.cbi.org.uk   Confederation of British Industry
www.equalityhumanrights.cm   Equality and Human Rights Commission
www.cipd.org.uk   Chartered Institute of Personnel and Development
tuc.org.uk   Trade Union Congress
andreaadamstrust.org   Andrea Adams Trust

References and further reading

ACAS (2004) *Employment Relations Matters*, 1. London: ACAS, p. 6.

Anderman, S. (2000) *Labour Law, Management Decisions and Worker Rights*. London: Butterworths.

Armstrong, P. and Baron, A. (1995) *The Job Evaluation Handbook*. London: CIPD.

Atiyah, P.S. (1979) *The Rise and Fall of Freedom of Contract*. Oxford: Oxford University Press.

Barnet, D. and Scrope, H. (2002) *European Employment Law*. London: Butterworths.

Barmes, L. (2007) 'Common law implied terms and behavioural standards at work', *Industrial Law Journal*, 36, 1: 35–47.

Barmes, L., Collins, H. and Kilpatrick, C. (2007) 'Reconstructing employment contracts', *Industrial Law Journal*, 36, 1: 1–12.

Benson, E. (2009) *Jordans Employment Law Precedents*. Bristol: Jordan Publishing.

Bercusson, B. and Estlund, C. (2008) *Regulating Labour in the Wake of Globalisation: New Challenges, New Institutions*. Oxford: Hart Publishing.

BERR (2008) *Agency Working in the UK: A Review of the Evidence*. BERR October 2008.

Blackburn, R. and Hart, M. (2002) *Small Firms' Awareness and Knowledge of Individual Employment Rights*. DTI Employment Relations Research Series No. 14.

Blanpain, R. and Weiss, M. (eds) (2003) *Changing Industrial Relations and Modernisation of Labour Law: Liber Amicorum in Honour of Professor Marco Biagi*. The Hague: Kluwer Law International.

Bowers, J., Brown, D., Korn, A., Mansfield, G., Palca, J. and Taylor, C. (2009) *Blackstone's Employment Law Practice 2009*. Oxford: Oxford University press.

Brodie, D. (2008) 'Mutual trust and confidence: catalysts, constraints and commonality', *Industrial Law Journal*, 37, 4: 329–75.

Brown, E. (2008) 'Protecting agency workers: implied contract or legislation?', *Industrial Law Journal*, 37, 2: 178–96.

Bryden, C. and Salter, M. (2009) 'Overstepping the Mark' *New Law Journal*, 159: 491.

Burke, R. and Cooper, C. (eds) (2008) *The Long Work Hours Culture*. Bingley: Emerald.

Cabrelli, D. (2008) *Law Express: Employment Law*. London: Pearson Longman.

Casebourne, J., Regan, J., Neathey, F. and Tuohy, S. (2006) *Employment Rights at Work – Survey of Employees 2005*. DTI Employment Relations Research Series No. 51.

CIPD (2009a) *Reward Management: A CIPD Survey*. London: CIPD.

CIPD (2009b) *Pay and Reward: An overview*. CIPD Factsheet. London: CIPD.

Clark, I. (1996) 'The state and new industrial relations', in I. Beardwell (ed.) *Contemporary Industrial Relations: A Critical Analysis*. Oxford: Oxford University Press, pp. 37–64.

Clark, I. (2000) *The State, Regulation and Industrial Relations*. London: Routledge.

Collins, H. (2000) 'Justifications and techniques of legal regulation of the employment relation' in H. Collins, P. Davies and R. Rideout (eds) *Legal Regulation of the Employment Relation*. London: Kluwer Law International, pp. 2–30.

Collins, H., Davies, P. and Rideout, R. (eds) (2000) *Legal Regulation of the Employment Relation*. London: Kluwer Law International.

Conaghan, J. and Rittich, K. (2005) *Labour Law, Work and Family*. Oxford: Oxford University Press.

Craig, J. and Lynk, M. (2006) *Globalization and the Future of Labour Law*. Cambridge: Cambridge University Press.

Daniels, G. and McIlroy, J. (eds) (2009) *Trade Unions in a Neoliberal World: British Trade Unions Under New Labour*. London: Routledge.

Davidov, G. (2005a) 'Who is a worker', *Industrial Law Journal*, 34: 57–72.

Davidov, G. (2005b) 'Joint employer status in triangular employment relationships', *British Journal of Industrial Relations*, 42: 727–50.

Davidov, G. and Langille, B. (2006) *Boundaries and Frontiers of Labour Law*. Oxford: Hart Publishing.

Davies, A. (2007) 'The contract for intermittent employment', *Industrial Law Journal*, 36, 1: 102–20.

Davis, P. and Freedland, M. (2007) *Towards a Flexible Labour Market: Labour Legislation and Regulation since the 1990s*. Oxford: Oxford University Press.

Deakin, S. (2007) 'Does the 'Personal Employment Contract' provide a basis for the reunification of employment law?', *Industrial Law Journal*, 36, 1: 68–90.

Deakin, S. (2008) 'Timing is everything: industrialization, legal origin and the evolution of the contract of employment in Britain and Continental Europe' in B. Bercusson and C. Estlund. *Regulating Labour in the Wake of Globalisation: New Challenges, New Institutions*. Oxford: Hart Publishing, pp. 86–115.

Deakin, S. and Morris, G. (2005) *Labour Law*, 4th edn. Oxford: Hart Publishing.

Deakin, S. and Wilkinson, F. (2005) *The Law of the Labour Market: Industrialization, Employment and Legal Evolution*. Oxford: Oxford University Press.

Dickens, L. (2005) 'Walking the talk? Equality and diversity in employment' in S. Bach (ed.) *The Management of Human Resources: Personnel Management in Britain*. Oxford: Blackwell, pp. 178–209.

Discrimination Law Review (2007) *A Framework for Fairness.* Department of Communities and Local Government.

Eaton, A. and Keefe, J. (eds) (1999) *Employment Dispute Resolution and Workers' Rights in the Changing Workplace.* Illinois: IRRA.

Edwards, P. (ed.) (2003) *Industrial Relations: Theory and Practice.* Oxford: Blackwell.

Edwards, P., Black, J. and Ram, M. (2003) *The Impact of Employment Legislation on Small Firms: A Case Study analysis.* DTI Employment Relations Research Series No. 20.

Employment Tribunals Service (2009) *Employment Tribunal and EAT Statistics (GB) 1 April 2007 to 31 March 2008* available at **www.ets.gov.uk**.

Equal Opportunities Commission (2002) – evidence submitted to the Hicks' Inquiry into Non-Executive Directors' Pay. Manchester: EOC.

ETS Annual Report (2007/08) available at **www.employmenttribunalservice.gov**.

Fox, A. (1985) *History and Heritage.* London: Allen & Unwin.

Fredman, S. (2004) 'Women at work: the broken promise of flexicurity', *Industrial Law Journal*, 33: 299–310.

Freedland, M. (2003) *The Personal Employment Contract.* Oxford: Oxford University Press.

Freedland, M. and Kountouris, N. (2008) 'Towards a comparative theory of the contractual construction of personal work relations in Europe', *Industrial Law Journal*, 37: 49–60.

Gibbons, M. (2007) *Better Dispute Resolution: A Review of Employment Dispute Resolution in Great Britain.* London: Department of Trade and Industry.

Gilmore, S. (2009) 'Introducing Human Resource Management' in S. Gilmore and S. Williams *Human Resource Managment.* Oxford: Oxford University Press.

Gilmore, S. and Williams, S. (2009) *Human Resource Management.* Oxford: Oxford University Press.

HMSO (2008) *Framework for a Fairer Future – The Equality Bill* (Cm 7431) 27 June 2008.

Holland, J. and Burnett, S. (2009) *Employment Law: Legal Practice Course Guides.* Oxford: Oxford University Press.

Horton, R. (2008) 'The end of disability-related discrimination in employment?', *Industrial Law Journal*, 37, 4: 376–400.

Hosking, D. (2007) 'A high bar for EU disability rights' *36 Industrial Law Journal: 228–50.*

Hyde, A. (2006) 'What is labour law?' in G. Davidov and B. Langille. *Boundaries and Frontiers of Labour Law.* Oxford: Hart Publishing, pp. 37–62.

Hyman, R. (1975) *Industrial Relations: A Marxist Introduction.* London: Macmillan.

Jefferson, M. (1997) *Principles of Employment Law*, 3rd edn. London: Cavendish Publishing.

Kahn-Freund, O. (1984) *Labour and the Law*, 2nd edn. London: Stevens.

Keen, S. (2008) 'Discrimination: blame it on the dog', *New Law Journal*, 158, September: 1216.

Kersley, B., Carmen, A., Forth, J., Bryson, A., Bewley, H., Dix, S. and Oxenbridge, S. (2004) *Inside the Workplace – First Findings from the 2004 Workplace Employment Relations Survey.* London: DTI, ESRC, ACAS, PSI and Routledge.

Kidner, R. (2008) *Blackstone's Statutes on Employment Law 2008–2009.* Oxford: Oxford University Press.

Koukiadaki, A. (2009) 'Case law developments in the area of fixed-term work', *Industrial Law Journal*, 159, January: 89–103.

Lawson, A. and Gooding, C. (eds) (2005) *Disability Rights in Europe: From Theory to Practice.* Oxford: Hart Publishing.

Lewin, D. (1999) 'Theoretical and empirical research on the grievance procedure and arbitration: a critical review' in A. Eaton and J. Keefe (eds) *Employment Dispute Resolution and Workers' Rights in the Changing Workplace.* Illinois: IRRA, pp. 137–86.

LexisNexis (2009) *Harvey on Industrial Relations and Employment Law* (5 vols) London: LexisNexis.

Ley, C. (2009) 'Back to the future', *New Law Journal*, 159, April: 537.

Luhmann, N. (2004) *Law as a Social System.* Oxford: Oxford University Press.

McCann, D. (2008) *Regulating Flexible Work.* Oxford: Oxford University Press.

McKay, S. (2008) 'Employer motivations for using agency labour' *37 Industrial Law Journal 296.*

Mercer Human Resource Consulting (2002) *The Prevalence of Bullying in the Workplace.* London: MHRC. Mercer. Pressoffice@mercer.com.

Metcalf, H. and Rolfe, H. (2009) *Employment and Earnings in the Finance Sector: A Gender Analysis.* London: Equality and Human Rights Commission.

Monaghan, K. (2007) *Equality Law.* Oxford: Oxford University Press.

National Association of Citizens Advice Bureau (2002) *Report on Equal Opportunities OECD Economic Outlook.* Paris: OECD.

Njoya, W. (2007) *Property in Work: The Employment Relationship in the Anglo-American Firm.* Aldershot: Ashgate.

O'Leary, S. (2002) *Employment Law at the European Court of Justice: Judicial Structures, Policies and Processes.* Oxford: Hart Publishing.

O'Dempsey, D., Jolly, S. and Harrop, A. (2006) *Age Discrimination Handbook.* London: Legal Action Group.

Oliver, D. (1999) *Common Values and the Public Private Divide.* London: Butterworths.

Oliver, M. and Barnes, C. (eds) (1998) *Disabled People and Social Policy: From Exclusion to Inclusion.* London: Longman.

Palmer, C., Wade, J., Wood, K. and Heron, A. (2006) *Maternity and Parental Rights: A Guide to Parents' Legal Rights at Work*, 3rd edn. London: Legal Action Group.

Peninsula (2003) *Survey on Flexible Hours.* London: Peninsula.

Philips, K. and Eamets, R. (2007) *Approaches to Flexicurity: EU Models.* Dublin: European Foundation for the Improvement of Living and Working Conditions.

Pigott, C. (2009) 'Justifying unequal pay', *New Law Journal*, 159, July: 55.

Public Affairs (2001) *A Women's Place.* **public.affairs@imgt.org.uk**.

Reich, C. (1964) 'The new property', *Yale Law Journal*, 73, 5: 733–87.

Reynold, QC. F. and Palmer, A. (2007) 'What place for hindsight in deciding whether a claimant was disabled?', *Industrial Law Journal*, 36, 4: 486–99.

Rubenstein, M. (2004) *Discrimination: The New Law: Harvey Special Report Series.* London: LexisNexis.

Ryan, A.J. and Pointon, J. (2007) 'Reward and performance management' in J. Beardwell and T. Claydon (eds) *Human Resource Management: A Contemporary Approach*, 5th edn. Harlow FT/Prentice Hall, pp. 487–524.

Sanders A. (2009) 'Part One of the Employment Act 2008: "better" dispute resolution?', *Industrial Law Journal*, 159, January: 30–42.

Schiek, D. (2006) 'The ECJ Decision in Mangold: a further twist on effects of directives and constitutional relevance of community equality legislation', *Industrial Law Journal*, 35: 333–50.

Simler, I. (ed.) (2009) *Jordans Employment Law*. Bristol: Jordan Publishing.

Smith, I. (2009a) 'Hitting the buffers', *New Law Journal*, 159, February: 215.

Smith, I. (2009b) 'Presidential protection', *New Law Journal*, 159, March: 369.

Tolley (2009) *Tolley's Employment and Personnel Procedures*. London: Reed Elsevier.

TUC (2000) *Trade Union Recognition*. London: TUC.

TUC (2002) *Focus on Recognition*. London: TUC.

TUC (2005) 'Government Should Investigate Cause of Tribunals Drop', press release, 12 July.

TUC (2008) *Hard Work, Hidden Lives, the Full Report of the TUC Commission on Vulnerable Employment*. London: TUC.

Upex, R., Benny, R. and Hardy, S. (2009) *Employment Law; Core Text Series*. Oxford: Oxford University Press.

Various (2008) *New Developments in Employment Discrimination Law*. Tokyo: The Japan Institute for Labour Policy and Training.

Von Prondynski, F. (2000) 'Labour law as business facilitator' in H. Collins, P. Davies and R. Rideout (eds) *Legal Regulation of the Employment Relation*. London: Kluwer Law International, pp. 3–145.

Von Wachter, V. (2009) 'Rearing its ugly head', *New Law Journal*, 159, February: 296.

Waddington, L. (2005) 'Implementing the disability provision of the framework employment directive' in A. Lawson and C. Gooding (eds) *Disability Rights in Europe: From Theory to Practice*. Oxford: Hart Publishing, pp. 67–105.

Wedderburn, W. (1986) *The Worker and the Law*. London: Penguin.

White, R. (2008) 'Notes: working under protest and variation of employment terms', *Industrial Law Journal*, 37: 365–80.

Willey, B. (2009) *Employment Law in Context*, 2nd edn. Harlow: Prentice Hall.

Work Stress Management (2002) *Survey on Workplace Stress*. **www.workstressmanagement.com**.

Wynn, M. (2009) 'Regulating rouges? Employment agency enforcement and sections 15–18 of the Employment Act 2008', *Industrial Law Journal*, 38, 2: 64–72.

Wynn-Evans, C. (2009) 'Age Discrimination and Redundancy', *Industrial Law Journal*, 38, 1: 113–26.

For multiple-choice questions, exercises and annotated weblinks related to this topic, visit **www.pearsoned.co.uk/mymanagementlab**.

Chapter 11

Establishing the terms and conditions of employment: changing forms of voice and influence

Susan Marlow, Bob Carter and Trevor Colling

Objectives

- To describe, evaluate and critically analyse the manner in which the terms and conditions of employment are imposed, negotiated and agreed within the private and public sectors of the UK economy.
- To explore differing avenues for employee voice and influence within this process.
- To critically evaluate the impact of contemporary state regulation upon agreeing the terms and conditions of employment.
- To explore how terms and conditions are agreed and implemented within the small firm sector.

Introduction

Establishing the terms and conditions of employment is a fundamental component of the employment relationship. What an employee is expected to do, when and how tasks are undertaken and critically, the rewards commanded are central. Some years ago, analyses of such aspects within the modern era would have focused overwhelmingly upon the theory and practice of collective bargaining (Brown and Nash, 2008). However, since the early 1980s, the influence of trade unions and their associated collective bargaining activities have diminished markedly (Kersley *et al.*, 2006; Blanchflower *et al.*, 2007; Guest *et al.*, 2008). It is notable that no clear mode of effective employee representation or partnership relationship has yet emerged as a dominant model to replace that of collective bargaining (Tailby *et al.*, 2007, Brown and Nash, 2008). Accordingly, agreeing the terms and conditions of employment is now a far more fractured and diverse process influenced by firm context, state regulation, managerial prerogative and still, in over 30 per cent of workplaces, collective bargaining (Charlwood and Terry, 2007; Kersley *et al.*, 2006). In exploring how the terms and conditions of employment are agreed within the workplace, this chapter reflects the changes which have occurred within this process over time and then, explores contemporary approaches.

We begin with an overview of collective bargaining. As noted above, although this is no longer the dominant model regarding terms and conditions, it remains influential and its heritage certainly deserves consideration. To explore the growing diversity of working conditions within the contemporary economy, we follow our analysis of collective bargaining with a brief overview of recent Labour government employment regulation. Such regulation has offered some opportunities to trade unions to regain legitimacy and a bargaining presence while also strengthening alternative avenues for non-union representation and managerial prerogative (Smith and Morton, 2006). It is notable that collective bargaining has retained a strong presence within the public sector, where the government is the employer; consequently, we explore terms and conditions in this sector in some detail. In contrast to this, we then consider how employee voice is articulated in non-union firms and discuss ensuing implications for the terms and conditions of employment. Finally, acknowledging the influence of context and the considerable attention now afforded to the contribution of the small firm sector to the economy, we conclude with an exploration of employment conditions within such firms.

Collective bargaining – a short overview

As the capitalist system of production evolved, the foundations of a wage economy were established. This process was not without contention; given the openly exploitative nature of early capitalist production there was much debate, discussion and indeed, violence between labour, employers and the state in determining how the rights of workers should be represented (Coates and Topham, 1986). Eventually, by the late nineteenth century, trade unions had emerged as legitimate collective organisations which aimed to protect the employment conditions of skilled labour; by the early part of the twentieth century, unions had expanded their influence to cover many semi- and unskilled workers (Hyman, 2003). Consequently, the concept of negotiating the terms and conditions of employment emerged into modern society such that in the post-1945 period, until the mid 1980s, collective bargaining was taken as the basis of institutional industrial relations (Coates and Topham, 1986).

Collective bargaining is a process of voluntary negotiation undertaken between employers' federations and/or managerial representatives and elected trade union representatives to agree the terms and conditions of employment. Each 'side' within this bargaining relationship acts as an agent to represent the collective interests of their stakeholders. Essentially, collective bargaining, through the auspices of trade union representation, offers employees a voice within the employment relationship which, in itself, is inequitable as the owners and representatives of capital (employers and managers) have more power than that of the individual employee (Hyman, 2003). By acting collectively through a trade union, employees can also exercise limited sanctions in the form of industrial action, to support their claims. Hence, collective bargaining is a mechanism which, to some extent, redistributes power within the employment relationship, offering employees a legitimate voice to influence their own terms and conditions of employment. As such, it is argued that collective bargaining promotes greater fairness and equity without unduly compromising efficiency (Freeman, 2005).

The term 'collective bargaining' was first utilised by Sidney and Beatrice Webb (Webb and Webb, 1902) who believed that this activity was the collective equivalent to individual bargaining, the prime aim being to achieve economic advantage. So, bargaining had an *economic* function and was undertaken between trade unions and employers or employers' organisations. This classical definition of collective bargaining has been subject to a number of critical analyses. In the late 1960s, Flanders (1968) argued that this view was erroneous; rather, collective bargaining should be understood as a *rule-making process* which established the rules under which the economic purchase of labour could initially take place. Flanders also argued that collective bargaining entails a power relationship; the imbalance of economic power, status and security between the single employee and that of the management can, to some degree, be addressed by collective pressure such that agreements are compromise settlements of power conflicts. Fox (1975) disputed Flanders' argument that an individual bargain is an economic exchange which always concludes with an agreement, whereas collective bargaining is essentially a process to establish rules for exchange. In fact, Fox argued that there is no assurance that either process will achieve agreement on terms acceptable to the parties involved in negotiation. Drawing from these arguments, it is useful to recognise that Flanders moves the discussion forward with the emphasis on regulation, but the contrast between collective regulation, and individual bargaining is debateable.

Rather than isolating one major function of collective bargaining, Chamberlain and Kuhn (1965) offer an analysis which outlines three distinct activities which interact to form the bargaining process:

● *Market or economic function*: this determines the price of labour to the employer, thus the collective agreement forms the 'contract' for the terms under which employees will work, i.e. the *substantive terms* of employment.

● *Decision-making function*: in this role, collective bargaining offers employees the opportunity, if they wish, to 'participate in the determination of the policies which guide and rule their working lives' (Chamberlain and Kuhn, 1965: 130).

● *Governmental function*: collective bargaining establishes rules by which the employment relationship is governed. Thus, bargaining is a political process as it establishes a 'constitution' (Rose, 2004).

From the above points it is clear that collective bargaining is concerned with the establishment of:

● *Substantive rules*: these regulate all aspects of pay agreements and hours of work.

● *Procedural rules*: these establish the rules under which negotiation over the terms and conditions of employment can take place and establish grievance and dispute procedures.

Bargaining principles

The aim of collective bargaining is to reach negotiated agreements; accordingly there is some potential for conflict as essentially, the distribution and division of scarce resources are under negotiation (for example, division of profit as dividends or wage increase). Others agreements however, will have mutual benefits (for example, introduction of health and safety procedures). These differences were noted by Walton and McKersie (1965) who outlined two approaches to collective bargaining:

● *Distributive bargaining*: one party will seek to achieve gains at the expense of the other; the aim is the division of a limited resource between groups both of whom wish to maximise their share. Pay bargaining is distributive bargaining as one party's gain is the others loss.

● *Integrative bargaining*: this approach seeks mutual gains in areas of common interest with a problem-solving approach from the parties involved. Successful integrative bargaining depends upon a relatively high level of trust between parties and a willingness to share information.

What do you think are the advantages to employees and managers or engaging with collective bargaining to establish the terms and conditions of employment?

Summary

Historically, collective bargaining was considered to embody notions of fairness and equity in determining how employment conditions were to be agreed. As such, the process offers employees, through trade union representation, some collective leverage to challenge the basic power imbalance with capitalism. The rationale behind collective bargaining has been subject to some debate; whether it has operated as primarily an economic process to ensure fairer distribution of profits to employees as wages or, whether as a governmental and regulatory process. In essence, it encompasses all three. However, the importance of collective bargaining in offering employees a voice within the employment relationship should not be underestimated. There has been considerable debate regarding the fundamental nature and purpose of the bargaining process, but any definition of collective bargaining must take account of historical and contemporary influences which impinge upon those involved in bargaining practices.

The collective agreement

At the end of the negotiating and bargaining process, collective agreements are reached. Traditionally, British collective bargaining has been notable for the informality of such agreements but from the early 1970s, there has been a growing trend to establish formal written contracts to avoid any potential problems given the possibility of differing interpretations of negotiation outcomes. Written agreements also contribute to the rationalisation and codification of employment relations procedures but the existence of such agreements will not prevent informal bargaining at local level (Rollinson and Dundon, 2007). Indeed, there are a number of levels, outlined below, at which collective agreements can be reached.

Multi-employer agreements

Such agreements cover specific groups of employees (described within the contract) from a particular industry and are negotiated by employers' associations or federations and full-time national trade union officials. Multi-employer agreements also form guidelines for employers who are not members of the industry association, and for firms who do not recognise unions.

Single-employer bargaining (organisational bargaining)

Organisational bargaining may occur at a number of levels for example:

- *Corporate*: all those employed by the organisation are covered by agreements bargained by the company and relevant trade union officials.
- *Plant*: the collective agreement is negotiated for a specific site or plant within the corporate structure affecting only the employees of that location. These agreements may be totally independent of national terms or constructed upon an industry agreement.

Determinants of bargaining level within organisations

Company-level bargaining is associated with large organisations and the presence of professional HR specialists in corporate-level management. Site bargaining is associated with firms where labour costs are a high percentage of total costs and there are substantial numbers of workers on each site. At present, the choice of bargaining level falls within managerial prerogative influenced by a number of variables; for example, corporate-level bargaining may be favoured as one channel to neutralise potentially powerful plant-based union pressure and avoid inter-plant comparisons (Rose, 2004).

A brief historical analysis of collective bargaining in Britain 1945–1980

During the immediate postwar period, the influence of corporatism, where joint negotiations between employers and trade unions were encouraged by the state, ensured that industry-level collective bargaining became firmly established. The nationalisation programme and the advent of the welfare system ensured that the state became a major employer; the post-war Labour government enacted legislation which obliged management in the newly nationalised industries to establish negotiating procedures for all employees. It is incorrect however, to assume that local bargaining ceased to be of relevance because of the formal establishment of national bargaining machinery for the majority of employees. In fact, by the 1960s, the conditions of full employment, coupled with high demand for goods, offered considerable leverage for local bargaining by shop stewards in the less bureaucratic, private manufacturing sector. The toleration of local bargaining eventually led to 'wages drift' which occurred when national agreements were utilised as a bargaining floor upon top of which local agreements were added, leading to inflationary pressures (Edwards, 2003). This latter point generated concern from the Labour government of the time, given the problems of introducing and operating incomes policies in the face of informal, unregulated local bargaining and growing inflation. The growth and economic effect of domestic bargaining was deemed an 'industrial relations problem' (Rose, 2004).

Domestic bargaining was a problem for employers who, facing increasing international competition, found wage costs difficult to control. It was also a threat to government economic policy given the impact on inflation and a Royal Commission was established to examine industrial relations practices and procedures in both the public and private sector. The Donovan Commission reported in 1968, arguing that Britain had two systems of industrial relations, the formal and informal (Donovan Commission, 1968: 12). In private-sector manufacturing, the formal system was based upon national bargaining between employers' organisations and full-time trade union officials. The informal system was based upon local bargaining between management and shop stewards under the influence of full employment and buoyant demand for goods. Overall, the Donovan Commission argued that workplace bargaining had become of greater importance than national bargaining. This local level of bargaining was described as 'largely informal, largely fragmented, and largely autonomous' (Flanders, 1970: 169) as it was based upon verbal agreements between shop stewards and line managers backed by custom and practice. The Commission argued that multi-employer bargaining on a national industry level could no longer effectively accommodate differentiated working practices throughout the private sector. The responsibility for introducing reform lay with management however, local informal agreements were not dismissed rather, they were afforded a level of formality such that they could no longer ignore and undermine national agreements. What was required was a rationalisation of the existing system which would effectively combine the two systems of industrial relations into one coherent, ordered process which did not then undermine the formal rules in multi-employer agreements.

The reform of local-level bargaining

Consequently, most organisations, encouraged by the Conservative government (1970–74) and the Labour government (1974–79) undertook voluntary reform of collective bargaining procedures. This involved the formalisation of domestic bargaining through the recognition of shop stewards, supporting union organisation through closed shop agreements and check-off procedures (whereby union subscriptions are deducted by the company from wages and then paid to the trade union account). The reform of collective bargaining during the 1970s offered clear benefits to trade unions with increased formal recognition and better facilities (for a critique of the incorporation of shop stewards into formal management/trade union bargaining hierarchy – 'the bureaucratisation thesis' – see Hyman, 1977). Despite such changes, rising inflation, growing international competition and greater foreign ownership, combined with state intervention in industrial relations issues, prompted management to press for further reforms. So, for example, there emerged a trend towards decentralisation of bargaining and a growth in formal recognition of domestic bargainers, but there remained considerable variation in collective bargaining processes within British industry during the 1970s.

STOP and think

When the Donovan Committee (1968) reported that the UK had two approaches to bargaining, informal and formal, what do you think this meant?

Summary

In the post-war period there was a rapid expansion in domestic bargaining at local level in private sector manufacturing industry despite the existence of national agreements negotiated by multi-employer organisations and full-time trade union officials. The Labour government of 1964–70 was concerned that local bargaining was adding to inflationary pressure and adversely affecting Britain's competitive performance. The Donovan Commission was charged with investigating contemporary industrial relations and concluded that Britain had two systems of industrial relations, informal and formal. The solution was to incorporate the two, establishing formal bargaining processes and procedures at the domestic level with an emphasis upon productivity bargaining.

Changes in collective bargaining since the 1980s

From the late 1970s to the mid 1990s the British economy suffered cyclical economic recession and volatile levels of unemployment (Rollinson and Dundon, 2007). Such structural changes, combined with the influence of successive Conservative governments (1979–97) hostile to the ethos of collective trade union representation, prompted substantial changes in the nature of collective bargaining in both the public and private sector. It is important to note that such changes arose from joint pressures from industry, the policies of successive Conservative governments and a failure by unions to develop strategies to protect their presence in the workplace. It was a combination of such factors which prompted substantial changes within the scope and influence of the collective bargaining process (Brown and Nash, 2008). Contemporary workplace studies (Blanchflower *et al.*, 2007; Kersley *et al.*, 2006; Charlwood and Terry, 2007) have found that, while the nature, scope and processes of collective bargaining have changed, it remains an important vehicle for fixing pay and conditions in the public sector, and for a growing minority of private sector employees.

Decentralisation of bargaining

There has been a growing trend towards the decentralisation of collective bargaining away from multi-employer/industry-level, to organisation or plant-level. From the corporate stance, decentralised bargaining offers the opportunity to link pay and productivity together at local level where regional variations and conditions can be accounted for accurately by local management and trade union officials. The weakened state of contemporary trade unions ensures they are less able to resist managerial strategies to utilise local bargaining to review labour costs and reform working practices, for example, the introduction of new technology, flexible working practices, etc. (Rose, 2004). In their assessment of shifts within contemporary collective bargaining, Brown and Nash (2008: 96) argue that, 'employers have been permitted to feel freer to match pay to the contours of local labour markets and to develop performance related pay'. Kersley *et al.* (2006: 191) note that the incidence of performance related pay rose from 20 per cent in 1998 to 32 per cent in 2004.

Flexibility issues

The introduction of flexible working has been made possible by the deregulation of the labour market, the weakness of trade unions and the growth of managerial prerogative, market pressure to cut costs and the desire to embed 'family friendly' policies (see Chapter 4 for further discussion). Where changes aimed at promoting flexibility within the labour process have been introduced, the following points have emerged:

- If a company introduces flexible working, not subject to statutory regulation, such changes usually form an overlapping agreement to become part of a complete package which constitutes a flexibility agreement. The terms and conditions of contemporary flexibility agreements will depend on such factors as the state of union–management relations, the bargaining environment and the nature of technology employed.

The implications for collective bargaining of flexibility agreements are as follows:

- Trade unions are no longer bargaining terms and conditions for a specific craft or activity. Flexibility between tasks blurs lines of demarcation such that the possession of a specific skill or talent is no longer exclusive as tasks are spread throughout the workforce. Thus, bargaining leverage is reduced.
- As employees undertake a wider range of tasks throughout the labour process, fewer 'core' workers are required with an increasing dependence upon numerically flexible labour, thus leading to redundancies and a consequent fall in trade union membership.
- Growth in atypical labour (employees not working under a standard employment contract) has implications for union membership given the difficulties of attracting and retaining such employees as union members.
- The growing links between flexibility bargaining and pay increases means that there is a growing trend to bargain around issues of exchange, for example, for wage increases in exchange for changes in work organisation, manning levels and redundancies.
- Regarding family-friendly policies, there may be some scope for increased union influence when supporting employees to access such rights.

In return for accepting flexibility agreements, some employees have been offered a range of benefits including pay increases, enhanced status and greater job security (Rose, 2004). Trade unions have been forced to bargain for better conditions on the basis of making concessions allowing significant changes in the labour process (Legge, 2005). Indeed, a reflection of this stance can clearly be seen in the Labour government's attitude toward the 2002–03 fire fighters' dispute, where agreement to changed working practices was demanded in order for meaningful negotiations to ensue. More recently, the market downturn particularly among car manufacturers, has seen unions actively working with employers to agree a reduced working week and extended layoffs in order to preserve jobs (BBC Radio 4: World at One: 31 March, 2009).

Successive Labour administrations from 1997 have offered continued support for flexible working while recognising the need to ameliorate the most exploitative effects of such initiatives (Dickens, 2004). It was intended that the statutory protection offered in the Minimum Wage Act (1998), the Employment Relations Act (ERA) (1999), the Employment Acts (2002, 2004 and 2008) plus the recognition and adoption of relevant EU directives would go some way towards offering vulnerable labour greater protection. Moreover, there has been a clear focus upon the development of family friendly policies which aim to allow parents (primarily mothers) to accommodate both work and family commitments (Davies and Freedland, 2007). It is recognised that statutory provision for individual employment rights might challenge the need for collective bargaining (if not for collective representation to ensure rights are observed: see below). This stance is indicative that contemporary Labour governments have focused mainly upon regulation and individualisation with considerable sensitivity towards business needs rather than supporting free collective bargaining and any ensuing collaboration with trade unions (Legge, 2005; Dickens *et al.*, 2005; Smith and Morton, 2006). However, such agreements may be used as a floor of rights in some organisations while scope exists for unions to police the provisions and ensure they are properly represented within the collective bargaining agenda or act to support individual employees should they decide to pursue their new rights.

Recent bargaining initiatives

Since the reform of collective bargaining in the 1980s, a number of discrete initiatives have emerged which have, on the whole, enabled management to reform the bargaining process quite considerably. A number of these are briefly considered.

- Single-union deals are largely associated with Japanese management strategies given their initiation within Japanese subsidiaries locating on greenfield sites in the UK (Rollinson and Dundon, 2007). The single-union agreement occurs where management grants recognition to only one trade union to represent employees in the bargaining process. Quite clearly, limiting union presence reduces effective representation for differing groups of employees whilst such agreements are clearly linked to no-strike deals and pendulum arbitration (Rose, 2004).

- A no-strike clause, once accepted by a trade union on behalf of the membership, effectively deprives union negotiators of the threat of strike action should bargaining break down and, moreover, denies employees the option of withdrawing their labour unilaterally.

- Pendulum arbitration facilities, where a third party will arbitrate on behalf of the two principals should they fail to reach agreement, stands instead of industrial action. (Singh, 1986; Milner, 1993). The limited use of this practice in Britain makes it difficult to assess the impact upon the bargaining process.

- Single table bargaining offers employers similar benefits to single-union deals whilst maintaining a multi-union site. Bargaining takes place between unions to establish a negotiation proposal, which is then articulated by one bargaining unit which negotiates on behalf of all employees (Rollinson and Dundon, 2007).

- Narrowed bargaining agendas have emerged since the 1980s; managers have exerted their prerogative to narrow the scope of collective bargaining (Brown and Nash, 2008). The Workplace Employment Relations Survey (WERs) 2004 data indicate that issues included within collective bargaining agendas have fallen considerably reflecting a growth in managerial prerogative to replace negotiation with consultation or indeed, unilateral implementation.

- Shifting time frames are more evident within contemporary agreements. Whereas the *annual* pay negotiation was a feature of the British system of industrial relations of the past, within the contemporary economy, employers favour longer-term agreements linked to inflation and changed working practices. These do not always work to employer advantage however. Three-yearly agreements linked to inflation forecasts made with the University and College Union prior to the rapid fall in inflation in 2008, have resulted in advantageous pay increases for university lecturers, much to the consternation of the employers (Newman, 2009).

HRM and collective bargaining

The early conceptual notion of HRM embedded within the notion of the unitary firm has not emerged in practice within the modern British economy. In contemporary usage, HRM is employed as a set of policies and practices focused upon the efficient management of labour (Marlow, 2006). Depending upon strategic orientation, HRM may be effectively utilised to improve competitiveness (see Chapter 2 for further discussion) or be seen as synonymous with general personnel management. However, there is some agreement that HRM initiatives are aimed at encouraging individual commitment and raising productivity. So, introducing and managing HRM practices in a collective bargaining environment was considered contentious within the 1990s (Storey, 1995). It is now evident that HRM and collective bargaining are not mutually exclusive. Given that the majority of organisations describe their labour management practices through the lens of HRM, it is no longer feasible to suggest that such policies are incompatible with collective representation. Even analyses of sophisticated and strategic HR approaches, which may go beyond the normative model of employee management, found that 'high commitment management practices going hand in hand with a union presence' (Cully *et al.*, 1999: 294). Consequently, it is simplistic to suggest that where employees are managed through policy and practices labelled as 'HRM' that collective bargaining will be removed from the agenda. Considering the issue of HRM and collective bargaining processes specifically, it appears that the former can coexist with the latter and indeed, HRM initiatives may be introduced through bargaining channels. In established plants, while HRM initiatives are evident, they have not seriously challenged the main focus of collective bargaining upon pay issues, but the scope of bargaining has been narrowed, with consultation being employed as a preferred channel of communication (Kersley *et al.*, 2006).

Summary

A number of bargaining initiatives have emerged during the 1980s and 1990s which have changed the level and structure of the collective bargaining process. These initiatives have facilitated the exercise of managerial prerogative in the bargaining relationship and further narrowed the scope of bargaining channels. Overall, where it persists, the collective bargaining function remained intact but constrained in scope.

STOP and think

How has the shifting social, political and economic environment affected the reach and scope of collective bargaining from the 1980s–1997?

'New Labour' and the regulatory agenda: implications for the terms and conditions of employment

With the election of 'New Labour' in 1997 there has emerged a rather contradictory programme of change and continuity in employment relations. A modernising agenda has been adopted which moves away from the traditional Labour philosophy of state-sponsored wealth redistribution through social ownership to support for private capital, private enterprise, individualism and a continuation of Conservative expenditure limits (Edwards, 2003; Smith and Morton, 2006). The new administration made it quite clear that the majority of the reforming regulation enacted by the previous Conservative administration would remain in place. Hence, the anti-union legislation enacted in the last 20 years remains largely untouched so that Britain still has the most restrictive regime of any Western developed nation towards collective representation at work (Howell, 2004; Smith and Morton, 2001). There has been no noticeable resurgence of the special relationship between Labour and unions evident in previous administrations, while the government has retained an enthusiasm for a de-regulated labour market with flexibility as a key factor (Legge, 2005). However, while retaining some of the frameworks which shaped employment relations over the previous 20 years, successive Labour governments have introduced policies which necessitate the state to develop a model of 'good' employment relations. The key focal points of the administration to date have been the notions of fairness at work for the individual, social partnerships and the constrained recognition of European employment regulation (Smith and Morton, 2006).

Successive Labour governments have brought a considerable body of employment regulation to the statute book which affects terms and conditions. Thus, the Minimum Wage Act (1998), Employment Relations Act (1999), the Employment Act (2002) and Employment Relations Act (2004), Transfer of Undertakings Act (2006) constitute major pieces of legislation and these have been accompanied by around 50 statutory instruments (see Chapter 10 for further detail). As a political administration however, Labour have not demonstrated any great enthusiasm for enhancing the rights of trade unions and expanding the coverage of collective bargaining (Charlwood, 2004). The main focus of employment regulation has been on the individual employee in the workplace, with the ambition to create 'fairness at work', generate greater labour market efficiency and promote minimum standards (HM Treasury, 2002). A cornerstone of the effort to support greater fairness was through the national minimum wage (NMW). However, some critics argued that it was set at such a low level to appease the small firm lobby and it did little to address poverty while excluding unions from setting and policing the NMW, once again undermining their traditional role as wage negotiators (Rollinson and Dundon, 2007). As Gennard (2002: 590) notes, through their approach, 'the government has annoyed everyone and protected only the few'.

As a whole, this body of regulation represents, 'a major reordering of employment law' (Smith and Morton, 2006: 401). Its constitution however, affords considerable legitimacy to the interests of employers, aiming, 'not [to] impose labour market rigidities or disproportionate costs on the employers' (ibid: 404). Within this modernising regime, trade unions are not completely excluded – hence there is weak support to pursue statutory recognition in the ERA (1999) – but union rights are afforded no special privilege or place (DTI, 2003; Charlwood and Terry, 2007). The reluctance to restore trade union influence combined with a notable sympathy towards employer prerogative has prompted Hall (2003: 19/22) to describe this approach as, 'a hybrid regime' and a 'social democratic variant of neo-liberalism'. Difficult choices have faced the trade union movement in reaching a compromise with this new Labour administration, reluctant to abandon the Thatcherite foundation of the contemporary employment relationship (McIlroy, 1998; Buckler and Dolowitz, 2000). This has led to fractious relationships between the government and the trade union movement with critical debate and in some cases, a substantial reduction in financial contributions to Labour Party funds (EIRO: 2009).

Although the Labour government has recognised the European social agenda by signing up to the provisions of the Maastricht Treaty, the introduction of subsequent EU employment regulation into law has been tardy, with diluted provisions in order to placate employers (Smith and Morton, 2001; Ford and Slater, 2005). Examples of 'foot dragging' and intent to only partially implement provisions can be seen in the initial outlines of the Part-Time Workers Directive, the Agency Workers Directive and the Information and Consultation for Employees Directive. This diluted commitment to EU regulation is, according to the government, necessary to ensure economic competitiveness yet, for Smith and Morton (2006) it is indicative of a reluctance to challenge or alienate employer interests. Rollinson and Dundon (2007: 139) support this argument, 'Labour's claim to fairness at work is questionable . . . the government has had a consistent record of opposing some of the major employment law interventions at a European level'.

There are different perspectives on the Labour government's record on employment relations. Smith and Morton (2001; 2006) are scathing in their critique of the actions of successive Labour government in terms of their approach to employment regulation, particularly their failure to support the role and legitimacy of trade unions within the work place. Brown and Nash (2008) however, describe the Labour government as, 'cautiously supportive' of trade unions and collective bargaining given the enactment of the ERA (1999) which offered a route for statutory recognition. Upon closer examination of the contemporary influence of trade unions and collective bargaining upon the terms and conditions of employment, it is evident that, despite the weak support offered by the Labour government, there has been some expansion in reach and impact (Blanden *et al.*, 2006; Charlwood and Terry, 2007). Drawing upon survey data from over 650 private sector firms, Blanden *et al.* (2006: 183) concluded that 'the post-1997 period has been characterised by a sharp increase in the number of new recognition agreements'. Much of this activity occurred in the period surrounding the enactment of the ERA (1999), which brought statutory union recognition into law (for a critical analysis of the restrictions of this Act, see Chapter 10). While this may be encouraging for trade union activists it appears that new recognition agreements are concentrated in sectors where unions already have a presence. Consequently, the data set developed by Blanden *et al.* suggests that unions have gained ground where they already had a presence so, new recognition agreements will not necessarily lead to a notable expansion of membership. As Gall (2004: 267) argues, 'the concentration of recognition campaigns in areas of traditional strength and the continued growth of union-union sectors may suggest that unions in Britain are running very fast to stand still'.

Blanchflower *et al.* (2007) agree with this analysis; drawing from the larger 2004 WERS data set, they found that unions are failing to access new and small work places. Accordingly, collective bargaining coverage remains firmly sited in traditional areas of union strength; within the economy as a whole, around 35 per cent of employees are subject to collective bargaining to negotiate the terms and conditions of employment (Kersley *et al.*, 2006: 186). While the rate of decline in collective bargaining has steadied, there are notable differences between the public sector and the private manufacturing and service sector. There has been some expansion of coverage in the first two but collective bargaining is largely absent within services. In terms of the scope of the bargaining agenda, Brown and Nash (2008) suggest this has not narrowed substantially since 1998 but it is notable that both union representatives and managers agree that *consultation and information* exchanges define bargaining practices to a greater extent than traditional *negotiation*. The emergence of social partnerships has also affected the practice of collective bargaining (Collins, 2003) by encouraging more consultative and less adversarial approaches to agreeing terms and conditions.

The Labour government has actively promoted the notion of social partnership (Tailby *et al.*, 2007), in which employers and employees have a mutual responsibility to engage in dialogue to introduce change, improve productivity and resolve disputes. Partnership agreements may be formed between management and established trade unions and/or Non-Union Employee Representatives (NURs). Exploring the management/union model first, there was enthusiasm for social partnership during the 1990s (Collins, 2003; Guest *et al.*, 2008) as it appeared to be a channel through which unions could revive their influence and voice. Moreover, the mutual gains emphasis within social partnership was presented as a useful management tool to motivate employees and increase performance (DTI, 2002). Some degree of impetus has also been added to the partnership model through the enactment of the Information and Consultation of Employees regulations (ICE) (2005). However, there is evidence that the union movement has grown disillusioned with the notion of partnership under the auspices of the Labour government. Based on their disappointment with the nature of proposed changes in the public sector, in July 2001 the TUC openly expressed doubts about the government's ability to generate meaningful partnerships. If the union movement feels those who are supposed to be most supportive of the notion of partnerships are not committed to them, this must surely raise questions regarding the whole ethos. Union disillusionment with this process has become more evident in the 2000s with contemporary union leaders losing enthusiasm (Guest *et al.*, 2008). Drawing upon evidence from the 2004 WERS survey, Guest *et al.* (2008) found that the partnership related practices remain undeveloped despite the impetus of the ICE legislation. It is also interesting to note that Guest *et al.* found that work place partnerships, even when formally established, do not automatically generate mutuality and trust to inform productive relationships between management and employees

A more radical critique of social partnerships questions the whole feasibility of such relationships in the first instance; Kelly (1996) for example, argues that it is difficult to form meaningful relationships within the inequitable power relations which define capitalism. As such, the likelihood of a real partnership is impossible unless far reaching coercive measures can be applied to employers to share information and consult meaningfully. Briefly, Kelly believes that given the current state of management strength and the ambivalence towards unions from the current government, that there is little rationale for employers to enter into true partnerships with unions when they can achieve their goals through flexing their prerogative. This argument is supported by contemporary evidence when Guest *et al.* (2008: 150) state that, 'although enthusiasm for partnership flickered briefly, capturing the spirit of the early days of New Labour, as with many of the other ideas of the time, this initially appealing idea was snuffed out by the cold wind of reality'.

STOP
and
think

To what extent has the new regulatory framework enacted by successive Labour governments (1997+) offered 'fairness not favours' to both employees and employers regarding the agreement of the terms and conditions of employment?

Summary

When the Labour government was elected to power in 1997, it was anticipated that there would be some revival of trade union influence over policy and economic development. However, successive Labour administrations have not demonstrated any enthusiasm to develop a close relationship with the trade union movement. Rather, they have enacted legislation which has strengthened union rights but the overall focus has been upon the individual at work and incorporating weak versions of European regulation rather than supporting collective labour rights. The outcome of this distancing stance has been a growing disillusionment by the union movement with successive Labour governments. There can be little doubt that the ERA (1999) did strengthen unions' ability to influence terms and conditions of employment. However, this fell short of what the trade union movement expected of the Labour government and it appears unlikely that any further government support will be forthcoming. Another outcome of the emphasis upon individuality has been a notable expansion in cases brought to the Employment Tribunal as traditional collective solutions to disputes have declined, 'the collapse in union membership and collective bargaining coverage of the past two decades have forced the tribunal system to undertake work previously handled by voluntary collective procedures' (Howell, 2004: 11). It should be noted that the government has taken action through recent Employment Acts (2002/2004/2009) as a response to the increase in tribunal cases. The aim being to compel greater formality around the grievance and discipline process, encourage other routes to avoid tribunals through the auspices of ACAS for example and offer greater leeway to employers to resist tribunal applications. Although it is evident that collective bargaining has declined in scope, importance and popularity within the UK economy, it still remains of considerable importance within the public sector which we explore within the next section.

Activity

Stanier Enterprises has grown rapidly over the last 10 years; it now employs 350 people and is set to grow further. The family owners have recently employed a professional HR team to manage policy and practice; traditionally they have depended upon managerial prerogative to establish terms and conditions of employment and used rather informal methods of communication – the grape vine – as a mode of consultation. This has caused some disquiet amongst employees about 30 per cent of whom have recently joined a trade union. As the newly appointed HR director, outline the presentation you would make to the family owners on the following issues:

(a) the rationale for having a formal process to review and amend the terms and conditions of employment;

(b) the advantages and disadvantages of recognising a trade union for bargaining purposes;

(c) the statutory obligations surrounding trade union recognition according to the ERA (1999);

(d) the nature of an effective social partnership.

Establishing the terms and conditions of employment in the public sector

For much of the period following the Second World War, public sector employment relationships were distinctive. Unlike in the private sector, managers were held accountable through political and administrative mechanisms, rather than through the market, and links between management practice and public policy were viewed as obvious and entirely legitimate. Public organisations were required to exemplify 'model employer' practice. Employment procedures were prescribed explicitly, sometimes by statute, and were subject to informal ministerial influence. Collective bargaining and consultation with trade unions were well established with national bargaining forums sitting atop complex local and regional structures setting uniform national pay rates and conditions of service.

Since 1979, there has been considerable reform of these processes. Successive Conservative governments were intent on privatisation, cost cutting and the introduction of market forces into service provision; successive Labour governments have broadly supported many of the Conservative ideas and reforms but within a new framework of a modernising agenda that recognises the need for increasing investment if service provision is to be improved and recruitment and retention problems addressed. Whilst demonstrating more sympathy towards the notion of public sector provision, subsequent Labour governments have been determined to continue to foster increasing cooperation with the private sector through the private finance initiative (PFI) and public private partnerships (PPP) (Bach, 2002) whilst also demanding changes to working practices. To explore these issues in more detail, this section will outline the 'golden era' of public sector development, consider how this has changed in recent years and discuss current government initiatives regarding pay and conditions for public sector employees.

The 'golden era': Morrisonian organisations and model employment

That which until recently was recognised as the public sector developed in the immediate postwar period (Winchester, 1983). Between 1945 and 1950, the Labour government took into public ownership a number of basic industries including coal, steel and the railways. Together these accounted for approximately 10 per cent of the country's total productive capacity (Dearlove and Saunders, 1984: 268). Services that were to constitute the welfare state, including health and social security, were established under public administration and expanded rapidly. By 1959, almost a quarter (23.9 per cent) of the labour force worked in the public sector (Fairbrother, 1982: 3). Over the next 30 years this diverse range of enterprises, utility industries and services was gradually restructured more or less according to the principles of public corporations established by the Labour politician, Herbert Morrison. During this 'golden era', there was little doubt that employment practice in the public sector was different from that prevailing elsewhere in the economy (Winchester, 1983).

Morrisonian principles were informed by two policy objectives: first, to ensure that the priorities pursued by key industries and services were consistent with macroeconomic, industrial and social policy; and second, to provide within this framework some autonomy for professional managers. These large, integrated organisations were managed therefore, through independent industry boards that had responsibility for day-to-day operational matters. But these boards were accountable directly to the relevant ministers, who were also empowered to give 'general direction' (Pendleton and Winterton, 1993). In the interests of equality of treatment, uniform standards of product or service were a priority, and departments would be deployed to ensure consistency across the organisation. Guaranteeing probity in the public interest required complex internal control systems and hierarchies of management and committee structures (Pratchett and Wingfield, 1995).

The public sector as a whole was also assigned a particular industrial relations mission: to be a 'model employer' and implement 'a range of practices which today constitute good management' (Priestly Commission, 1955, cited in Farnham and Horton, 1995: 8). The state sector's role in macroeconomic policy was important in this regard. Though the depth of the postwar consensus can be exaggerated, commitments to full employment and the welfare state structured the programmes of both of the key political parties for as long as they could be combined with economic growth (Hills, 1990). The public sector was assigned a key role in job creation, 'mopping up' underemployment created by restructuring in the broader economy.

'Model employer' practices also implied a range of procedures, which included promoting collective employment relations, intended to set an example to organisations across the economy. Union growth was consequently stimulated directly (through the promotion of trade union membership) and indirectly (through the involvement of unions with collective bargaining). This growth continued in the 1970s as union membership expanded alongside the growth in public sector employment. Given the strategic importance of public industries in particular, great emphasis was also attached to the collective involvement of employees as a means of identifying and resolving grievances, and thereby avoiding potentially costly disruption. The requirement on public enterprises 'to consult with organisations which appear to them to be representative' was legally specified in their respective nationalisation acts (Pendleton and Winterton, 1993: 3). Elaborate, formal and bureaucratic systems for negotiation and consultation, often referred to as Whitleyism, also developed across the public services. Created with the brief to establish viable industrial relations systems following the end of the First World War, the Whitley Committee advocated centralised bargaining through joint industrial councils with a view to securing 'cooperation in the centre between national organisations' (Clegg, 1979: 31).

Consequently, industrial relations were marked by a significant degree of centralisation but there were important variations in this general picture (Fogarty and Brooks, 1986). For example, traditions of local bargaining in some of the nationalised industries (such as coal, docks and steel) remained entrenched long into the golden era, and local government employers came to full national bargaining relatively late in the day (Kessler, 1991: 7). Such centralisation was also evident in influencing the determination and negotiation of terms and conditions and cost constraints, and their ramifications for the management of the public sector, were more prominent features of the 'golden era' than is often acknowledged. Ministerial responsibilities for containing public expenditure generated a compelling interest in the outcome of collective bargaining. So, 'model employer' principles developed during this period resulted in relatively coherent frameworks for bargaining and consultation and a prominent role for trade unions in the management of change. It is important to maintain an appropriately nuanced perspective however, and exhortations to 'good management' were laced intermittently with cost pressures backed by ministerial pressure. Whilst public employment was secure, low pay and discriminatory employment procedures remained characteristic of large parts of the public sector (Thornley, 1994).

The Conservative era and market reform

From 1979 to 1997 international pressures on the economy led to a major reversal of government policies and the undermining of the tenets of the post-Second World War settlement that had underpinned the growth and stability of the public sector. Public enterprises such as the utilities, telecommunications and transport were transferred to the private sector. Where institutions remained within the public sector, the focus shifted from what Ackroyd *et al.* (1989) described as custodial management to market-based approaches, with expansion first halted by public expenditure constraints and then reversed, as 'rolling back the frontiers of the state' became a priority (Hutton, 1996). The unified Civil Service was broken into a large number of discrete 'agencies' (Fairbrother, 1994), thus facilitating the variation of terms and conditions through market mechanisms and competitive pressures, features that were generalised throughout public services. Organisations were fragmented into business units as distinct roles were created for service purchasers and providers (Bach and Winchester, 2003). Conservative ministers from 1979, and the New Right thinkers who influenced them, were inclined to view trade unions as an impediment to the effective operation of markets (Rose, 2004). At a more pragmatic level, they also recognised that public sector unions had become a potent source of opposition to government policy, and had contributed in no small measure to the downfall of both the early 1970s Conservative government of Edward Heath and the 1974–79 Labour government.

Promoting national collective bargaining and trade union organisation became less of a priority. More important perhaps, the very notion of a single set of employment principles was not attractive to policy makers, who regarded the ability to tailor terms and conditions of employment to specific trading contexts as the hallmark of effective management. During the period of market-based reform, the emphasis shifted from promoting 'model employment' to providing the space in which managers could assume the *right* to manage (Bach and Winchester, 2003). The extent to which this philosophy was reflected in governments' changed management practice is open to debate. Colling (1997) argues that government's interest in employment levels and pay remained undiminished and constrained the extent to which decision-making could be left entirely to local actors. Paradoxically, promoting market pressures in these and other areas often required government to intervene more determinedly rather than stand back. Alongside measures promising greater discretion therefore, such as local management of schools, initiatives were developed to test performance and to set targets for change and improvement. These contrary trends are best understood as part of what has been widely described as New Public Management (NPM) in which policy determination is centralised and enforced through the setting of targets but managers are allowed some discretion over how to achieve them and are held accountable for their performance. Bureaucratic and administrative relations within workforces are thus transformed into much more managerially driven ones (Carter and Fairbrother, 1999).

Reform of the centralised bargaining and consultation structures, characteristic of the Morrison era, has been one of the most tangible indicators of changing employment practice. After 1979, market orientations fostered an approach to pay determination founded on aligning pay with local labour markets and affordability considerations at the level of service providers. Decentralisation was thus the primary motif of Conservative governments throughout the 1980s and 1990s. It was pursued pragmatically (rather than strategically), however, and was held in tension by a contending desire to maintain central control of the overall pay bill (Bach and Winchester, 2003).

The growth of indexation and independent pay review mechanisms played a significant role in reducing the scope of collective bargaining (Bach, 2002). Where they have been introduced, pay issues are decided through either predetermined formulae, in the case of indexation, or the deliberations of a panel following the submission of evidence from managers, unions and government. While some argue that the latter amounts to 'quasi-bargaining forums' (Winchester, 1996: 10), the removal of formal collective bargaining, and notionally thereby, the threat of strike action, was a common element. Although it was reserved initially for judges, doctors and the armed forces, other significant occupational groupings were incorporated gradually. The fire and police services were surprisingly late additions at the end of the 1970s, and schoolteachers, nurses and midwives were added subsequently. One third of public sector employees were no longer affected by collective pay bargaining by the end of the period of market-based reform (Bailey, 1996: 136).

Throughout the 1980s, centralised bargaining structures came under informal pressure through changes to public sector financial procedures. The switch to cash, rather than volume planning, required employers to balance increases in pay against levels of service. From the late 1980s, managers in the NHS used the discretion available to them to vary starting salaries and job descriptions for ancillary and administrative staff (Grimshaw, 1999). The creation of market relationships, such as those stemming from competitive tendering, provided additional impetus. Decisions about the allocations of service contracts were based primarily on price, of which labour costs are usually a substantial element. Quests for savings prompted service managers locally to redesign work organisation and terms and conditions of employment (Colling, 1993). Ad hoc adjustments to employment packages became common, irrespective of whether or not the work was retained by public sector employers. In local government, for example, reform of bonus payments and working hours disorientated pay and grading structures and increased pay inequalities (Escott and Whitfield, 1995).

From the early 1990s, attempts were made to extend decentralised bargaining and upgrade structures to include professional and technical staff whose pay and conditions remained subject to national negotiations. This required a more direct approach to reform. The 1992 White Paper *People, Jobs and Opportunity* promised to:

> encourage employers to move away from traditional, centralised collective bargaining towards methods of pay determination which reward individual skills and performance; respond to the wish of individual employees to negotiate their own terms and conditions, and take full account of business circumstances. (Cited in White, 1994: 7)

The government's determination to decentralise is further illustrated by the escalation of pressure on NHS trust managers. Local managers, aware of the considerable opposition of the unions and professional associations, sought initially to innovate through job redesign and to maximise the grading flexibility offered by existing national agreements rather than negotiate locally for professional groups (Bach and Winchester, 1994). Following the 1992 election, however, burgeoning entrepreneurial spirit was galvanised by increasingly explicit exhortations from ministers and the NHS Executive and, after a protracted stand-off with the unions, the 1995 pay settlement eventually permitted some element of local bargaining for health service staff with the exception of doctors (Grimshaw, 1999).

Activity   Make a note of the key elements which differentiate the 'golden era' of public sector development from the market reform era of successive Conservative governments 1979–97.

Decentralisation and market-based reform contributed significantly to changing expectations surrounding public sector pay. Comparability gave way to affordability, and earnings growth considerably fell behind that of the private sector (Elliot and Duffus, 1996; Winchester, 1996). Such changes also generated difficulties of their own; the inequalities that emerged subsequently (Escott and Whitfield, 1995) did little for morale and provided the basis for substantial legal challenges. The Acquired Rights Directive and its UK variant, the Transfer of Undertakings (Protection of Employment) Directive (TUPE), provide rights to consultation and prohibit changes to pay and conditions when staff are transferred from one employer to another (e.g. from the public sector to a private contractor). Equal pay legislation makes it illegal to pay different rates to women and men when they carry out similar work, work rated as equivalent by a job evaluation scheme, or work that is of equal value in terms of effort or skill (see Chapter 7). Though the extent and security of such protections have been far from total (Napier, 1993; Dickens, 2000), unions became adept at selecting test cases to inhibit or reverse market-driven reform of pay systems, and won some notable victories in both domestic and European courts (Colling, 2000). The threat of further proceedings underpinned subsequent bargaining strategies, particularly in health and local government, where potential equal value cases became intertwined with union demands for coordinated reviews of pay and grading.

'New Labour' and the modernising agenda

According to Howell (2004) New Labour's modernisation agenda reveals a 'third way' approach to managing the public sector based on a combination of planning and market-driven strategies. It is certainly true that the open mantra of 'public sector bad, private sector good' so evident under the Conservatives (Carter, 1997) has ceased, although the government's frustration with the public sector is still frequently and strongly voiced. Just days before leaving office, for instance, the former Prime Minister Tony Blair called for a 'permanent revolution' in public service reform to meet the public's 'high expectations'. He went on to reinforce the government's frequent characterisation of public sector unions as conservative forces: 'The danger sometimes is that public service unions and associations get into a competition over who can flag up the most resistance to change' (Blair, 2007). It may be hard to establish a qualitatively different 'third way' therefore. What is being witnessed might be better conceived as continuity with Conservative market strategies together with increased financing and performance demands on those services that remain in the public sector.

The pressure for public sector modernisation stems from its perceived role in promoting national competitiveness in a globalised world. This perception is utilised to demand fundamental reforms in its structure and functioning. There have been increases in central government funding, particularly in health and education, but in return New Labour has demanded reforms of working practices and terms and conditions of work, and these demands, together with other developments, have caused growing tensions with the still entrenched public sector unions. The continued push for privatisation of funding for capital projects and service delivery, via the Private Financial Initiative (PFI), has resulted in projected government revenue payments to PFI contractors by 2028 of more than £110 billion, a colossal sum equivalent to about a tenth of then current GDP (Meacher, 2004; for an account of its affect on hospitals see Pollock, 2004). In addition, wage restraint and restructuring have further resulted in a strong perception of continuity of government policies with the previous Conservative administrations. The sharp economic recession that began in 2008 is, at the time of writing, still developing but is unlikely to change direction. Indeed, the (delayed) need for lowering public sector borrowing might reinforce present tendencies.

Modernisation and the continuation of New Public Management

Much of the policy towards the public sector that has flowed from New Labour has come from under the rubric of modernisation. This is a deliberately disarming concept, suggesting technicality and value-neutrality (Fairclough, 2000). Faced with a welter of ideological resources, it is difficult for groups on the receiving end of policy change to deny the need for 'modernisation': who could appear to argue for stasis or going back in the face of obvious service deficiencies? The concept therefore, needs some unpacking and this is best done through a general examination of the continuity of 'new public management' and the way this has evolved in parts of the public sector. NPM is variously defined and much has been made of the importation of private sector business methods such as individual performance related pay, benchmarking and outsourcing. Others have been relatively supportive of the direction of change seeing it as bringing about the transformation of the public sector into being efficient, responsive and consumer orientated (Ranson and Stewart, 1994). More critical evaluations have been common, with Pollitt (1993: 26) claiming that NPM amounts to the 'injection of an ideological "foreign body" into a sector previously characterised by quite different traditions of thought'. Pollitt defines the new emphasis on 'managerialism' as an ideology which believes that increasing the powers of professional managers leads to productivity increases and social progress.

New Labour's development of such policies is best examined in particular services, such as the NHS, one of the two main beneficiaries of increased government spending on public services. Increased finance has been advanced together with demands and targets, with profound affects on the service. According to Harrison's (2002: 466) account, one result has been 'the development of a medical labour process which embodies many of the specific characteristics of Fordism and . . . scientific-bureaucratic medicine'. Although the Conservatives had promoted central regulation, Harrison (2002: 472) maintains that the real innovation was to create a mechanism for the implementation of the model: 'specifically "clinical governance" a mechanism for controlling the health professions, most obviously Doctors'. New legislation has placed a statutory duty on hospitals for the quality of care, effectively making Chief Executives responsible for the clinical, as well as the financial performance. Outside hospitals, the National Institute for Clinical Excellence (NICE), the Department of Health and the Commission for Health Improvement (CHI) play key roles. The former appraises treatments not only for clinical effectiveness, but also for *cost*-effectiveness, while the latter has begun to conduct rolling programmes of reviews, visiting every hospital trust over a period of about three to four years, in much the same way that Ofsted inspects schools. The parallels with education go further:

> CHI will also become responsible for publishing comparative performance information about NHS organisations, on the basis of which the latter are publicly awarded performance 'stars' . . . Persistent poor performance will lead to sanctions, including possible mergers or replacement of the managerial and clinical leadership (Secretary of State 2000: 62–7).
>
> (Harrison 2002: 473)

It would be wrong, however, to view changes as introducing rigidities through central control of doctors. Changes in control of the workforce, especially beneath the level of senior doctors have largely reflected a flexibility offensive designed to get more for less. Nursing has a central place in hospital care and according to Cooke (2006: 224) 'this flexibility offensive has been accompanied by a narrative that has emphasised the empowering nature of these changes'. The introduction of the Health Care Assistant grade had led to greater division of labour and inequality (Grimshaw, 1999). The consequence for nurses was that they were put under pressure to take on more routine managerial and medical work:

> Ward sisters have been widely re-titled 'ward managers' taking on a wide range of management functions, formerly performed by middle managers. As well as undertaking more routine administration and paperwork during office hours, ward nurses now provide most onsite and out of hours management cover. (Cooke 2006: 226)

Cooke's study showed that role extension, presented as a positive opportunity for nurses, signalled in practice growing workloads and intensification of labour. Nor is it just hospitals that have been subject to changing skill mixes. Jabareen (2009) has shown how changes in general practice service delivery have led to shifts in routine care from doctors to nurses. As new roles for practice nurses have evolved, GPs have been able to focus on treating more complex problems that need medical diagnosis and intervention. Targets and incentives of the new contract have made chronic disease management a predominant activity for practice nurses.

The second beneficiary of New Labour's increased spending was education and here again large sections of its workforce have been ambivalent about the results. Again earlier Conservative reforms that increased centralisation have been strengthened. The introduction of the national curriculum, for instance, has been reinforced by the addition of the literacy and numeracy hours. Teachers are now not only told what to teach but, especially in the case of literacy, how to teach it. Similarly, the opt-out of schools from already weakened, local authority control has been encouraged via the growth of Academy and Trust schools, and schools' infrastructures have been improved by a massive Private Finance Initiative rebuilding and refurbishment programme (*Building Schools for the Future*). What is distinctive about New Labour's policy is again workforce reform. From 2001, when faced with both recruitment and retention crises and the prospect of teacher industrial action over workload, New Labour turned to the idea of workforce remodeling, believing that standards could be improved and workload reduced by stripping teachers of non-core work and assigning it to teaching assistants and other support workers. In 2003, the government, employers and all but one of the teacher unions signed a national agreement, *Raising Standards, Tackling Workloads*, that had the following provisions:

- A requirement that a range of administrative tasks (the so-called '25 tasks') were to be performed by support staff and were not to be carried out by teachers. These included, amongst other things, bulk photocopying, data entry, collecting money from students and mounting displays.

- The provision of a guaranteed 10 per cent of a teachers' normal timetabled teaching time for planning, preparation and assessment (PPA).

- A ceiling of 38 hours per year that a teacher could be required to cover for absent colleagues, with an expectation that over time there would be 'a downward pressure on the burden of cover' (DfES, 2003: 7).

The National Union of Teachers (NUT), the largest classroom teachers' union in England and Wales, refused to sign because of opposition to the use of teaching assistants (TAs) to take whole classes – a development that undermined the union's desire for teaching to be an all-graduate profession – and because of reservations about the agreement being the centre piece of a long-term Social Partnership with the government.

The 'partnership' unions contrast their years of marginalisation with current access to and influence with ministers. There are, however, dangers in the new relationships for all parties. The unions have subscribed to the principle of integrative, 'win–win' bargaining and agreement based on consensus rather than votes (Walton and McKersie, 1965). The corollary of this approach is an abandonment of interest bargaining and an identifiable trade union position. When decisions are reached all parties adhere to confidentiality about positions and compromises and are bound by the agreement to promote and promulgate the decisions. The consequence is that unions can appear to be the executive arm of the government's strategy, or as McIlroy (2000: 16) characterised unions' positions in partnership agreements, 'junior partners in change management'. This can lead to a democratic deficit within unions, with tensions generated with their members who are not mobilised over issues and who cannot see their interests being represented in a transparent manner.

The dangers posed to unions are not just in the processes of employment relations but also the outcomes. Not only have the hours of work of teachers not significantly reduced (STRB, 2008), but it appears that the very restructuring of their jobs has given routine work to poorly paid TAs and other support staff, only to load teachers with additional expectations. The inspection regime, the tests and the league tables have increased the pressure on teachers to perform, and these pressures have been made more effective by the extension of management posts (Carter *et al.*, 2009). As a result of the confluence of these pressures, teacher union conferences in 2009 reflected growing anger and threats of action.

STOP and think

To what extent have public sector unions established effective partnerships with government to establish a dialogue regarding changes to terms and conditions?

Developments within the NHS and schools are not universal, but there are parallels elsewhere in the public sector. The continued privatisation of prisons, the expansion of community support officers performing routine police work, and other developments such as the expansion of call centres in civil service sectors and the introduction of 'lean production' in processing in Revenue and Customs' work highlight the issues of workforce restructuring. Targets are commonly imposed and are subject to a number of criticisms including the narrowing of service provision and the distortion of public sector values. One commentator summed up the issues thus:

> The Health Commission's finding last week that pursuing targets to the detriment of patient care may have caused the deaths of 400 people at Stafford between 2005 and 2008 simply confirms what we already know. Put abstractly, targets distort judgment, disenfranchise professionals and wreck morale. Put concretely, in services where lives are at stake – as in the NHS or child protection – targets kill. (Caulkin, 2009: 6)

There are also other generic issues that continue to impact on employment relations. The government is setting pay targets and increasingly influencing the recommendations of pay review boards. Equal pay continues to be a problem for employers and unions. In local government in particular, single status and the harmonisation of the conditions of 1.5 million white collar and manual employees, and its promise of equal pay for work of equal value, welcomed by unions when it was proposed and agreed in 1997, has become a contentious issue. Agreed without any additional funding, local authorities were slow to implement it and many missed a subsequently imposed deadline of 2007. Where implementation has taken place it has often been in the face of fierce local union opposition, reflecting the fact that budgets can only be maintained by lowering some higher salaries, including female administrators, by as much as £12,000 to the level of lower ones in order to equalise pay. In Birmingham, for instance, 4500 appeals have been lodged against the outcomes, and the figure will be higher because some are group actions by people carrying out the same job. The council is also defending 2400 employment tribunal unfair dismissal claims resulting from the pay and grading review.

Summary

The scope and depth of public sector activity grew dramatically during the 'golden era' from the 1940s to the late 1970s. Principles established by Herbert Morrison underpinned management structures and behaviour. A key feature was the need to ensure some degree of congruence between the goals of particular public organisations and espoused public policy. Organisations were highly integrated, characterised by bureaucratic procedures, and managed by professional specialists subject to general direction by the relevant government ministers with a clear emphasis on centralised bargaining and collective industrial relations.

The election of successive Conservative governments during the 1980s and 1990s saw the introduction of far-reaching reform into the public sector. There was a marked shift from the centralised, 'model employer' policy to that which focused upon market forces and cost constraints. This stance, combined with the government's evident hostility toward organised labour, substantially reduced the influence of trade unions upon employment issues. The uneven implementation of Conservative policies, however, led to a degree of confusion and problems in achieving desired outcomes regarding cost savings, productivity and performance.

Public anger at the previously feted role of the City and private sector bankers has given the public sector a new status and importance but one that is already under attack. Public sector borrowing has risen steeply with long term fears that taxes will have to be increased and public services cut; voices are already being raised against the sector for having greater security of employment, higher wage settlements and better pension provisions (for an attack and a defence, see Tebbit, 2009 and Toynbee, 2009, respectively). It is therefore, likely that the government will persist with its version of new public management with its emphasis on 'performativity' (Bach, 2002) and equally likely that public sector unions will resist what they consider to be further detrimental reforms. Having explored historical shifts within the public sector where trade unions retain some influence, we now turn to consider how terms and conditions are implemented in non-union organisations.

STOP and think

Compare and contrast the approach of successive Conservative governments (1979–97) and successive Labour governments (1997+) to managing terms and conditions in the public sector.

Establishing the terms and conditions of employment in non-union organisations

It is important to remember that even when collective bargaining coverage was at its peak in the 1970s, at least a third of the labour force was excluded from such agreements. In reality, the figure was probably greater given the tendency to ignore the small firm sector and exclude it from employment surveys prior to the late 1990s. However, it is evident that the non-union sector has grown over the last 25 years given the decline of trade unions and political encouragement for greater managerial prerogative. Yet while non-union organisations may share a non-recognition status, the way this is articulated depends on managerial style, size, sector, markets, location etc. To facilitate an overview of the non-union sector, the useful distinction based upon the notion of substitutionists and suppressionists, outlined by Flood and Toner (1997), will be adopted as a descriptive tool. The particular characteristics of smaller firms will be considered separately. It is acknowledged that a crude categorisation of firms will be a blunt tool at best; as Dundon and Rollinson (2004: 152) argue, this leads to a tendency to 'obscure the dynamic processed within these relationships'. Therefore these categories are better seen as forming ends of a continuum with differing degrees of coercion and consent evident throughout.

Substitutionist strategies involve developing sophisticated policy and practice to ensure that employees will not want to seek union recognition because a collectively bargained agreement will be unlikely to improve terms and conditions. Such an approach must ensure that, for the majority of employees, terms and conditions are at the least as good as, if not better than, those in comparable firms that recognise trade unions for bargaining purposes (Kim and Kim, 2004). Clearly, the aim is to ensure that employees will not find a union presence or collective bargaining beneficial. Such firms might be described as having a 'soft' HRM style with a focus upon employee involvement, consultation and participation to ensure high performance and individual commitment to the firm. To maintain this situation, the organisation must be able to provide what are perceived as a floor of excellent terms and conditions of employment and promote an environment which rewards individuality while offering effective channels for employee involvement (Dundon and Rollinson, 2004).

This stance has been described as a somewhat 'pyrrhic' victory by Flood and Toner (1997) who argue that if one of the aims of non-unionism is cost containment through the avoidance of collective bargaining and collective leverage, this is unlikely to be achieved through such costly substitution policies. Given the investment required in terms of finance and management time for high reward, consultation, communication etc., the rewards do seem uncertain. However, in many cases the key strategic focus will be on retaining managerial prerogative with respect to decision making, change management and flexibility, and the avoidance of disruptive collective resistance. Moreover, in the absence of unions there is scope for a blurring of the divisions between management and employees, promoting the unitarist ethos of shared focus and ambition. It might be expected that if there has been a growth of non-union firms developing this type of substitutionist strategy to avoid recognition, there should be some evidence for the spread of 'soft' HRM practices and policies in the UK. However, drawing on the WERS data, the presence of high commitment practices remain relatively rare and indeed, are most frequently found in unionised firms (Kersley *et al.*, 2006). Thus it seems that this type of 'soft' HRM, non-union organisation remains rare in the UK and most non-union firms are not pursuing these strategies.

Organisations which have neither derecognised unions nor employed substitutionist strategies are most likely to be found in sectors where unions have been traditionally weak, such as private services (Blanchflower *et al.*, 2007). These firms are unlikely to have considered union recognition or have been able to ignore any approaches from a relatively weak union movement. They either avoid employing or else intimidate those who might pursue recognition. As such, these firms *suppress* moves to achieve union recognition. Within such organisations, managerial prerogative, with limited avenues for consultation and commitment is likely to dominate (Dundon and Rollinson, 2004). The recently enacted ICE legislation appears to have had limited impact upon this tendency although the full implications of the regulation upon smaller organisations has yet to be assessed (Tailby *et al.*, 2007).

STOP
and
think

Contrast and compare suppressionist and substitutionist approaches to preventing a trade union presence in the workplace

Within the non-union sector, the opportunity for employee voice to influence their terms and conditions of employment is contingent upon a number of issues. These include the organisation's preferred management style regarding the employment relationship and the manner in which management prerogative is exercised, issues which are themselves contingent upon the firm's market position, sector, product and the perceived value of their employees. However, as Dundon and Rollinson observe, even where employees enjoy relatively extensive provisions for involvement in decisions over their terms of employment, 'these schemes were all designed and controlled by management and where employees could contribute, it is important to recognise that these contributions were on matters deemed appropriate by management' (2004: 157). In other words, management set the agenda and the boundaries for employee voice which in itself, remains very limited. Recent WERS data reveal that only 5 per cent of workplaces have independent, elected non-union representatives (Kersley *et al.*, 2006: 125).

It is important to note, however, that in recent years management prerogative has been somewhat constrained by employment regulation introduced by successive Labour governments and also by their recognition and implementation of European regulation. For example, the Employment Relations Act (1999) legislated for statutory recognition of trade unions where the necessary degree of support could be demonstrated and the Works Council Directive requires representation and consultation in multinational enterprises. While there was some argument that works councils, reflecting an established European model, might prove more effective than weakened trade unions in giving workers voice this has not proved to be the case (Gollan, 2002). There is little evidence that this European model has emerged in the British economy, so works councils remain constrained in reach and influence (Tailby *et al.*, 2007).

Of some interest for this discussion is the impact of ICE (2005). After some delay, this was transposed into legislation in April 2005 for undertakings with at least 150 people eventually covering all undertakings with more than 50 employees by 2008, with employment calculated upon an annual average. The aim of the European Directive (2002/14/EC) was to 'establish a general framework for informing and consulting employees' and to strengthen opportunities for dialogue between management and employees. Storey (2005: 7) summarises these aspects into three categories:

1 Information on the recent and probable development of the undertakings . . . activities and economic situation.

2 Information and consultation on the situation and probable development of employment – in particular, if there is a threat to employment.

3 Information and consultation on decisions likely to lead to substantial changes in work organisation or in contractual relations.

In terms of the relevance of ICE for the non-union organisation, it should be noted that unless at least 10 per cent of employees (or a minimum of 15 and maximum of 2500) request an agreement – described as 'pulling the trigger', employers are not obliged to introduce new arrangements or amend those in existence. Tailby *et al.* (2007) describe this as a challenging 'trigger' for employees, particularly without the support of union coordination. Where a pre-existing agreement exists, a ballot is required to endorse that agreement, which has to be a formal, written agreement extending to all employees. If a new agreement is concluded, it must meet the minimum standards laid down in ICE in order to comply with the legislation, which again requires a written agreement covering all employees. It must also provide for the election or appointment of employee representatives or establish how direct information and consultation is to be provided (ACAS, 2004). While ICE does offer employees the right to be informed and consulted regarding their employment conditions and makes provision for the election of employee representatives, as Storey (2005: 11) argues there is, 'considerable scope for interpretation of the meaning and implications of much of this new legislation. These spaces for ambiguity are likely to be exploited'. There is, of course, the 'trigger' issue in that unless employees request a change to existing provision, no actions will be taken.

Smith and Morton (2006: 409) are again highly critical of the provisions of ICE; even if the 'trigger' hurdle is overcome, they argue that there is only a 'narrow right of employees [itself a restrictive criterion] to received information, subject to commercial confidentiality'. Once again, the decision rests with employers regarding what information might be shared and discussed, 'the employer is the judge of employees' interests: a unitary perspective with a vengeance!' (*ibid*: 410). In suppressionist organisations it is difficult to envisage a full and open spirit of cooperation with elected representatives consulting freely with management. Finally, the use of the notion 'undertaking' – a public or private venture undertaking an economic activity – leaves some uncertainty regarding the level at which engagement will take place given the complexity of the contemporary organisation. Consequently, it is likely that, although ICE will have some impact upon the opportunities for employee voice, as Storey (2005: 5) suggests, the 'outcome in the medium term . . . is that organisations will introduce a series of adjustments to current arrangements, but these will in all probability be of a "bolt-on" nature'.

Activity   Prepare a brief presentation outlining the aims of ICE and the conditions necessary to 'trigger' its implementation.

There has been relatively little research exploring and comparing the effectiveness of union and non-union representatives in the workplace. However, a study by Tailby *et al.* (2007) explores partnership practices in financial organisations which recognised unions and others that had a 'partners' council in place. Drawing from their findings, they found that in both types of organisation employees felt informed rather than involved. However, union representatives felt they had more power on the basis of collective voice in comparison to non-union council members – in effect, they were not so easy to ignore. This did not mean that they were notably more effective; regarding proposed reforms to terms and conditions, management proved adept at using superior communication networks to bypass union representatives. Yet it was noted that during a period of redundancies at the partnership organisation, representatives become more militant as they were clearly being ignored. However, as Hall and Terry (2004) note, it is difficult to establish the impact of any such militancy as non-union representatives cannot make any credible threats to impose sanctions; they can protest but not act.

The idea of 'partnership' approaches to employment regulation has become increasingly influential and we reviewed the debate concerning union/management social partnerships earlier in this chapter. In non-union organisations, what actually constitutes a 'partnership' in non-union firms is very difficult to define but Guest *et al.* (2008) argue that it must revolve around mutuality and trust. Moreover, there must be acknowledgement of a partnership arrangement and this in turn must be linked to specific action – putting a policy in place that is translated into practice. Finding such partnerships is rather challenging; studies by Gollan (2002) and Dundon and Rollinson (2004) suggest that most partnership agreements are often restricted and shallow; much rests upon managerial willingness to engage with non-union representatives. Rather paradoxically therefore, partnerships appear only to be feasible if managerial prerogative permits – there are of course, some very successful examples such as the John Lewis Partnership – but these would appear to be exceptions to the norm.

STOP and think — *Under what conditions can non-union representatives offer effective voice to employees?*

Summary

Since the 1980s, the political environment in the UK has supported the growth of the non-union sector. The manner in which non-unionism has emerged in larger enterprises has taken a number of forms; for some firms, there has been the adoption of clear substitution policies to avoid union recognition in the first instance. For others, active forms of suppression have been adopted; such strategies are slightly more tenuous given the provision of the ERA (1999) for statutory recognition. However, it appears that such provisions have enabled unions to expand their influence where they are already in place rather than make inroads into established non-union sectors such as the private service sector. Given the level of political encouragement and union weakness, a relatively small number have pursued (either strategically or in an ad hoc fashion) derecognition policies with only limited resistance from unions and their members. There has been some speculation that the ICE (2005) regulations may have increased the scope for non-union voice regarding terms and conditions. However, given the trigger mechanisms, managerial resistance and general employee ignorance of the provisions, the impact has been limited (Smith and Morton, 2006). Overall, it would appear that what Towers (1997) described as the 'representation gap' arising from the demise of union voice and a lack of any effective mechanism to take its place, persists.

Activity — Make a list of advantages and disadvantages of working in a non-union firm from the perspective of the HR manager and from that of a production worker.

Establishing the terms of employment in small firms

There are several different definitions of a 'small' firm. In 1971, the Bolton committee report referred to criteria of independence and a small market share, the Companies Act of 1985 combined turnover and employment criteria, while the EU uses the most comprehensive criteria of turnover, employees and independence. In the UK, governments rely on the somewhat simplistic measure of the number of employees within the enterprise such that:

- small firm = 0–49 employees
- medium firm = 50–249 employees
- large firm = over 250 employees (DTI, 2004).

Given the heterogeneity of small and medium-sized firms (SME) sector, it is difficult to find a definition which adequately encompasses all relevant firms. Regardless of how the sector is defined, it is appropriate to consider small firms as a separate entity within the economy. For some time they have been recognised as being essentially different from their larger counterparts in their approach to management, markets and business outlook; it is no longer presumed that such firms are enterprises which have merely failed to grow to corporate dimensions (Carter and Jones-Evans, 2007). As Cully et al. (1999: 251) remark, 'small businesses occupy a distinct part of the lexicon in academic and policy debates'. They also have their own associations and government representative at ministerial level. This is not to suggest that small firms can be easily studied as a single entity. A significant challenge in analysing small firm behaviour is identifying common themes and trends in a sector noted for its heterogeneity. So, any conclusions drawn and observations made must always be qualified with the same caution applied to large firms, that there will always be a substantial number of enterprises which do not conform to wider trends.

The number of small businesses in the UK economy has grown since the early 1980s, levelling out in the early 1990s (Stanworth and Purdy, 2003). As the DTI (2004) notes, SMEs account for 99.8 per cent of all private sector businesses, 58 per cent of employment and 52 per cent of turnover, although it should be noted that the majority of these are sole traders. It is apparent that small firms are important employers in the modern economy and so insight into how labour is managed in such firms is critical. It is generally accepted that within small firms, informality is more likely to be the managerial norm as the organisation is usually overseen by the owner or one general manager, often working without formal professional understanding and few formalised systems (Harney and Dundon, 2006). In place of formal policies and procedures, idiosyncrasy and managerial prerogative dominate and standard models of best practice are not followed. Marchington et al. (2003) however, suggest that informality should not be dismissed as ineffective in that it can be an appropriate response to organisational context. Others argue that social and spatial proximity can be drawn upon to engender employee commitment, enable swift decision making, facilitate mutual problem solving and so add to competitive advantage (Edwards et al., 2006).

Smaller firms are particularly vulnerable to market pressures, so their approach to managing labour is shaped by external influences to a greater extent than in large firms (Harney and Dundon, 2006). Rainnie (1989) argued that labour management in small firms was largely determined by the market, as managers were constrained by the competitive environment in which they are marginal price takers. Rainnie argued that the market vulnerability and pressure to minimise costs that affect small firms meant that autocratic management was the rule. However, Rainnie's argument has been repeatedly challenged by findings and analysis that suggest there is an uncertain interaction between market forces and the internal social relations of production, leading to a more negotiated employment relationship (Moule, 1998; Ram et al., 2001; Ram and Edwards, 2003; Edwards and Ram, 2006). Gilman et al. (2002: 54) summarise this succinctly: 'the whip of the market is likely to be mediated by employee skill, scarcity value and the extent to which there are fraternal or familial relationships within a firm'.

STOP and think

Outline some of the characteristics of small firms: how will these affect the employment relationship?

As firms grow and become more organisationally complex, formality emerges and terms and conditions of employment are inscribed within written policies and articulated through a more professionalised form of management. In such contexts, as Marlow (2002: 27) notes, 'both labour and management have recourse to a set of rules, should they feel it appropriate to use them'. Care must be taken however, not to construct a simplistic dichotomy between informality/formality and small/large firms respectively (Marlow *et al.*, 2005). As Ram *et al.* (2001: 846) argue, informality and formality are dynamic constructs which co-exist in differentiated forms in time and space such that 'informality in small firms is a matter of degree and not kind'. The distinction compared with larger, more formalised organisations lies in the manner in which formal policy and procedure surrounds and orders the employment relationship.

Dating back at least to the Hawthorne studies (Roethlisberger and Dickson, 1939), we know that employment relations in the largest organisations operate through both formalised policies and informal interactions or negotiation (Brown, 1973; Edwards, 1986). Managers must navigate a path between rationality and intuition, formality and informality, professional norms and personal preference or idiosyncrasy. The toleration of informality and custom and practice that persists in the context of a contested labour process (Burawoy, 1979) contributes to the structured antagonism that shapes the employment relationship. Within smaller firms, the absence of professional HR managers and a context of social and spatial proximity creates a fertile environment for the persistence and dominance of informality when shaping and agreeing the terms and conditions of employment.

Survey evidence such as that drawn from WERS (Forth *et al.*, 2006) finds that many of those who work in smaller firms have poorer terms and conditions than their counterparts in larger organisations. Paradoxically however, small firm employees report higher levels of job satisfaction (Tsai *et al.*, 2007). There has been some speculation that this may arise from informality and a lack of regulation which encourages direct personal negotiation between employers and employees (Saridakis *et al.*, 2008). The likelihood is however, that the social and physical proximity between owners and employees enables clearer insight into the reality of what can and cannot be afforded so fuels a stronger sense of organisational justice despite limited formal voice and poorer employment prospects (Edwards *et al.*, 2009; Cox, 2005).

Within all firms there are varying degrees of emphasis on informal and formal labour management approaches which suggests that it is too simplistic to develop an uncritical correlation between firm size and these concepts. Whilst recognising this, Marlow *et al.* (2009) draw attention to the fact that in larger firms, the dynamic of control and consent is bounded by formality in that if, and when, line managers have to overtly assert authority, they have the channels by which to do so or indeed, where necessary or preferred, they can even delegate this task to the professional HR function. Equally, recourse to formal policy and practice is available to employees or their trade union representatives should they wish to individually, or collectively, assert their rights within the employment relationship.

Empirical evidence relating to the manner in which regulatory compliance is managed by smaller firms is a good illustration of the impact of external change upon the articulation and accommodation of informality (Marlow, 2002). Overall, the introduction of an increasing tranche of employment regulation has been seen as particularly problematic for smaller firms (Federation of Small Business (FSB), 2006). If, as the evidence would indicate, many such firms rely on differing degrees of informal, flexible, even idiosyncratic labour management, adopting a regulatory approach will be challenging as it is axiomatic that compliance is demonstrated by inclusion within existing, established policy (Marlow *et al.*, 2009). There has been considerable resistance to the regulation agenda by pressure groups representing small businesses in particular (FSB, 2006) with dire predictions made regarding the impact of increasing regulation upon the performance of the small firm sector (Oldfield, 1999). However, the empirical evidence on this issue so far suggests that the impact of compliance has been considerably less disastrous than predicted (Blackburn and Hart, 2001: 264).

This brief overview of some of the critical developments in the literature pertaining to employment relations in small firms serves to demonstrate the growing sophistication of analysis in this area. As evidence has accumulated on the nature of employment relations in small firms, knowledge has become more detailed and far more sensitive to issues of heterogeneity within the sector as well as to the dynamic between these enterprises and their larger counterparts. What has emerged is an argument which suggests that the effort wage bargain is an outcome of the interaction between the external market positioning of the firm and the internal dynamics of the enterprise.

STOP and think

How does a firm's size impact upon its propensity to recognise a trade union for bargaining purposes?

To summarise, although there will always be exceptions, it is apparent that establishing terms and conditions of employment in small firms is more likely to be conducted on an informal basis, focused on the individual in a framework unilaterally devised by the firm owner. For some employees, there will still be room to construct their own social relations of production and engage in mutual adjustment strategies but for many there will be little opportunity to exercise any discretion over the manner in which they work and are rewarded. To some extent, increasing employment regulation should address these issues but this does depend upon employer awareness and observation of the legislation. As Blackburn and Hart (2001) found, increasing regulation and legislation is not a problem for many small owners because they simply do not know about it. In terms of the ICE (2005) regulations which now apply to firms with more than 50 employees, the necessity of the 'trigger' mechanism is likely to prove an impediment to adoption in firms where the proximity between employers and employees dominates the social relations of production. Given the number of employees within the small firm sector, there is some cause for concern regarding the level of informality and ignorance that persists surrounding the management of labour. However, this overview must again be qualified with the recognition of heterogeneity amongst small firms such that exceptions to these generalisations will be evident throughout the sector.

Summary

- Collective bargaining has customarily been defined in Britain as the process of joint regulation of job control, undertaken by management and trade unions which negotiate to establish the terms and conditions which govern the employment relationship. Human resource management might be viewed as posing a threat to this joint process by its emphasis on the managerial dominance of the relationship which requires that employees accept a managerially derived employment agenda.

- Contemporary developments in collective bargaining in the private sector have seen a narrowing of its coverage as a result of the decline in unionisation and managerial pressure to limit its scope amongst employees. In the public sector, there have been considerable changes regarding the 'model employer' perception during the post war period. The 'golden era' associated with centralisation, trade union influence and collectivity was replaced in the 1980s with a market approach which focused far more on cost constraints in a context of privatisation and decentralisation. Since 1997, a modernising agenda has been developed to bring greater coherence between cost issues, performance elements and service provision with implications for pay-setting where emphasis is upon 'performativity' with some evident resistance from public sector employees.

- The current Labour government promoted 'social partnerships' based on fairness, equity, information sharing, employee representation and consultation and a consensual approach to problem solving. Some trade unions and employers embraced the ethos of partnership but recently, the failure of these to deliver in regard to improved conditions of employment and clear avenues of information sharing has led to some discontent and indeed, disaffection from the notion by the trade union movement. In becoming a full signatory to the Maastricht agreement, the Labour government has committed the UK to the implementation of European Directives on employment but as Smith and Morton (2006) have observed, a dilute, weakened form of adoption would seem to be preferred by the present government adding to cynicism regarding the desire to establish a new, strong framework of employee rights.

- There has been a significant increase in the number of organisations in the UK where there is no form of union representation or voice for employees. Within this non-union sector, whilst there is evidence for a range of strategies and initiatives employed to establish the terms and conditions of employment, the overwhelmingly preference is for the exercise of managerial prerogative. Larger non-union firms have, to some degree, had the overt exercise of prerogative bounded by employment regulation in recent years. This would not appear to be the case in small firms.

- Within small firms, managerial prerogative also dominated but the defining feature within the sector is informality. The social and physical proximity between owners and employers supports this informal approach whilst the absence of professional HR managers and ignorance of regulation ensures its continuance. Given the embedded social relations of production supported by proximity, despite poorer conditions of employment in general, small firm employees report a higher degree of job satisfaction than their counterparts in larger firms.

Questions

1 What has fuelled the changes to British collective bargaining since 1979?

2 To what extent is collective bargaining the only effective form of employee voice in shaping the terms and conditions of employment?

3 Smith and Morton (2006) suggest that the manner in which contemporary employment regulation has been enacted in the UK serves to preserve managerial prerogative at the expense of employee voice. Evaluate this claim.

4 Outline and discuss the challenges non union representatives have in establishing effective partnerships with management.

5 Compare and contrast the approach of successive Conservative governments (1979–97) and sucessive Labour governments (1997+) to the management of terms and conditions of employment in the public sector?

6 Critically evaluate why those in small firms might express higher levels of job satisfaction despite having poorer terms and conditions of employment.

Exercises

1 Debate the proposition that 'collective bargaining is the most appropriate channel to redress the power imbalance within the employment relationship'.

2 You are the HR director of a private firm wishing to bid for a public sector project as part of the private finance initiative. If the bid were successful, what new challenges would arise in the management of the employment relationship under such circumstances?

3 You have just been employed by a small firm as their first HR professional; your priority task is to make a presentation which convinces the small management team of the need to elect formal employee representatives for information and consultation purposes. Outline this presentation.

4 Prepare a workshop presentation which outlines the provisions of the Information and Consultation for Employees (2005) legislation.

Case study

'Betrayed teachers demand 10 per cent pay rise. We were underpaid during the boom years.' says NUT

The National Union of Teachers demanded a 10 per cent pay rise yesterday, saying that it refused to take 'lessons in morality' on money from the Government. Its annual conference in Cardiff voted to press for a rise of £3,000 or 10 per cent, whichever is the greater, because teachers had been underpaid during the country's boom years. Other unions have accepted pay rises of 2.3 per cent this year and next year. One delegate at the NUT conference Ian Murch, made a thinly veiled gibe against Jacqui Smith, the Home Secretary. 'Teachers have not forgotten that between 2004 and 2008, while the sun was shining on the Fred Goodwins of this world and while real pay was rising in most of the economy, we experienced a cut in the real value of our pay of more than 6 percent' he said.

'The last time I went on a deputation to see a government minister about pay, she gave us a brief lecture about how well off we were, told us that performance-related pay was the way forward and showed us the door. She now has a more high-profile job. 'We take no lessons in morality from government ministers who fit out their homes with stone sinks from Habitat on their expenses and who pay their husbands more than a teacher earns to be their personal assistants and who don't appear to engage in even a hint of performance management of what they get up to.' Dave Clinch, who proposed the motion, said that young teachers were having to leave the profession because they could not afford to live. 'Teachers are being forced to grovel for money that's rightfully

theirs.' He said that teachers had been betrayed by the School Teachers' Review Body, which negotiated the 2.3 per cent deal. He added that public sector workers should not be made to feel guilty for the financial crisis by the 'fat cats of global capitalism'.

Joe Flynn, from Croydon, who seconded the resolution, suggested that the 2.3 per cent pay deal had been accepted when people were in shock but said that there was now 'real anger'. Anyone who thought 10 per cent was too much should look at the rail workers' union that recently won 29 per cent for threatening to go on strike, he said.

One teacher opposed the motion because so many other people were being made redundant or not receiving any pay rise. Michael Rought-Brooks, from North Yorkshire, said 'Are we going to tell them we want 10 per cent while they claim £90 a week in benefits? If we take more than we need then we're stealing from some-one'. Another, Becky Williams, said that she had resigned and was going to work at a British school in Kenya because it was better paid. In response, Sarah McCarthy-Fry the Schools Minister, said 'The average teacher is on nearly £33,000. We have cut teachers' working hours, dramatically reduced the amount of administrative tasks they are expected to do, doubled the number of support staff and given them time outside the classroom to plan or prepare lessons.'

Source: from Teachers demand 10 per cent pay rise, *The Times*, 14 April 2009 (Woolcock, N.), © The Times 14 April 2009.

References and further reading

Those texts marked with an asterisk are particularly recommended for further reading.

ACAS (2004) 'Information and consultation', **www.acas.org/ infoconsut/consultation.html**.

Ackroyd, S., Hughes, J. and Soothill, K. (1989) 'Public sector services and their management', *Journal of Management Studies*, 6, 4: 603–19.

Audit Commission (2003) 'Early PFI schools not significantly better, says Audit Commission', **www.audit-commission. gov.uk/** reports, 30 January 2003.

Bach, S. (2002) 'Public sector employment relations reforms under Labour: muddling through on modernization?' *British Journal of Industrial Relations*, 40, 2: 319–41.

Bach, S. and Winchester, D. (1994) 'Opting out of pay devolution? Prospects for local pay bargaining in the UK public services', *British Journal of Industrial Relations*, 32, 2: 82–96.

Bach, S. and Winchester, D. (2003) 'Industrial relations in the public sector' in P. Edwards (ed.) *Industrial Relations: Theory and Practice*. Oxford: Blackwell.

Bailey, R. (1996) 'Public sector industrial relations' in I.J. Beardwell (ed.) *Contemporary Industrial Relations: A Critical Analysis*. Oxford: Oxford University Press, pp. 121–51.

Bates Report (1997) 'Review of the Private Finance Initiative', 30 October, London: HMSO.

BBC Radio 4, 'Honda lays off workforce', World at One, 31 March: 2009.

Beaumont, P.B. (1995) *The Future of Employment Relations*. London: Sage.

Blackburn, R. and Hart, M. (2001) 'Ignorance is bliss, knowledge is blight? Employment rights and small firms', Proceeds of the 24th ISBA National Small Firms Conference, Leicester: November, pp. 261–80.

Blair, T. (2007) in 'Blair sets out EU treaty demands' BBC News 24. Retrieved 12 January 2007 from **http://news.bbc. co.uk/go/pr/fr/-/1/hi/uk_politics/6763121.stm**.

Blanchflower, D., Bryson, A. and Forth, J. (2007) 'Workplace industrial relations in Britain, 1980–2004', *Industrial Relations Journal*, 38, 4: 285–302.

Blanden, J, Machin, S. and Van Reenen, J. (2006), 'Have unions turned the corner? New evidence on recent trends', *British Journal of Industrial Relations*, 44, 2: 169–90.

Bolton, J.E. (1971) *Report of the Command of Inquiry on Small Firms*, Cmnd. 0811. London: HMSO.

Brown, W. (1973) *Piecework Bargaining*. London: Heinemann.

Brown, W. (1993) 'The contraction of collective bargaining in Britain', *British Journal of Industrial Relations*, 31, 2: 145–62.

*Brown, W. and Nash, D. (2008) 'What has been happening to collective bargaining under New Labour? Interpreting WERS 2004', *Industrial Relations Journal*, 39, 2: 91–103.

Buckler, S. and Dolowitz, D.P. (2000) 'New Labour's ideology: a reply to Michael Freedon', *Political Quarterly*, 70, 2: 102–109.

Burawoy, R. (1979) *Manufacturing Consent: Changes in the Labour Process under Monopoly Capitalism*. Chicago, IL: University of Chicago Press.

Carter, b. (1997) 'Restructuring state employment: Labour and Non Labour in the Capitalist State', *Capital & Class*, 63: 1: 65–84.

Carter, B. and Fairbrother, P. (1999) 'The transformation of British public sector industrial relations: from 'model employer' to marketized relations and the impact on trade unionism', *Historical Studies in Industrial Relations*, 7, 1: 119–46.

Carter, B., Stevenson, H. and Passy, R. (2009) *Industrial Relations in Education: Transforming the School Workforce*, London: Routledge.

Carter, S. and Jones-Evans, D. (2007) (eds) *Enterprise and the Small Business: Principles, Policy and Practice*, London: Prentice Hall.

Caulkin, S. (2009) 'This isn't an abstract problem. Targets can kill', *The Observer*, Sunday 22 March.

Chamberlain, N.W. and Kuhn, J.W. (1965) *Collective Bargaining*. New York: McGraw-Hill.

Charlwood, A. (2004) 'The new generation of trade union leaders and prospects for union revitalisation', *British Journal of Industrial Relations*, 42, 3: 379–97.

Charlwood, A. and Terry, M. (2007) '21st-century models of employee representation: structures, processes and outcomes', *Industrial Relations Journal*, 38, 4: 320–37.

Clegg, H. (1979) *The Changing Systems of Industrial Relations in Great Britain*. Oxford: Blackwell.

Coates, K. and Topham, T. (1986) *Trade Unions and Politics*. Blackwell: Oxford.

Colling, T. (1993) 'Contracting public services: the management of CCT in two county councils', *Human Resource Management Journal*, 3, 4: 1–15.

Colling, T. (1997) 'Managing human resources in the public sector' in I. Beardwell and L. Holden (eds) *Human Resource Management: A Contemporary Perspective*. London: Pitman, pp. 654–79.

Colling, T. (2000) 'Personnel management in the extended organisation' in S. Bach and K. Sisson (eds) *Personnel Management: A Comprehensive Guide to Theory and Practice*. Oxford: Blackwell, pp. 70–91.

Collins, H. (2003), *Employment Law*. Oxford: Oxford University Press.

Cooke, H. (2006) 'Seagull management and the control of nursing work', *Work, Employment and Society*, 20, 2: 223–43

Cox, A. (2005) 'Managing variable pay systems in smaller workplaces: the significance of employee perceptions of organisational justice' in S. Marlow, D. Patton and M. Ram (eds) *Managing Labour in Small Firms*. London: Routledge, pp. 124–45.

Cully, M., Woodland, S., O'Reilly, A. and Dix, G. (1999) *Britain at Work: As Depicted by the 1998 Workplace Employee Relations Survey*. London: Routledge.

Davies, P. and Freedland, M. (2007) *Towards a Flexible Labour Market: Labour Legislation and Regulation since the 1990s*. Oxford: Oxford University Press.

Dearlove, J. and Saunders, P. (1984) *Introduction to British Politics*, Cambridge: Polity Press.

Department of Trade and Industry (2002) *High Performance Workplaces: The Role of Employee Involvement in a Modern Economy*. London: HMSO.

Department of Trade and Industry (2003) *Review of the Employment Relations Act, 1999*. London: HMSO.

Department of Trade and Industry (2004) *Small and Medium Enterprise, SME – Definitions*. London: HMSO.

Department of Trade and Industry: Small Business Service (2004) 'SME statistics for the UK, 2003', **www.sbs.gov.uk/ content/statistics/stats2001.xls**.

DfES (2003) 'Raising standards and tackling workload: a national agreement', **http://www.tda.gov.uk/upload/resources/na_standards_workload.pdf**, accessed 2 September 2009.

Dickens, L. (2000) 'Doing more with less: individual conciliation' in W. Brown and B. Towers (eds) *Employment Relations in Britain: Twenty-five Years of the Advisory, Conciliation and Arbitration Service*, Oxford: Blackwell.

Dickens, L. (2004) 'Problems of fit: changing employment and labour regulation', *British Journal of Industrial Relations*, 42, 4: 595–616.

*Dickens, L., Hall, M. and Wood, S. (2005) 'The impact of employment legislation: reviewing the research', *DTI Employment Relations Series*, 45, URN 05/1257, London.

Donovan Commission (1968) *Report of the Royal Commission on Trade Unions and Employers' Associations, 1965–68*, Cmnd. 3623. London: HMSO.

Dundon, T. and Rollinson, D. (2004) *Employment Relations in Non-union Firms*. London: Routledge.

Edwards, P., Sengupta, S. and Tsai, C. (2009) 'Managing low skill workers: a study of small UK food manufacturing firms', *Human Resource Management Journal*, 19, 1: 40–58.

Edwards, P. (1986) *Conflict at Work*. Oxford: Blackwell.

Edwards, P. (2003) *Industrial Relations Theory and Practice in Britain*. Oxford: Blackwell.

Edwards, P. and Ram, M. (2006) 'Surviving on the margins of the economy', *Journal of Management Studies*, 43, 4: 895–916.

Edwards, P., Ram, M., Sengupta, S. and Tsai, C.J. (2006) 'The structuring of working rlationships in small firms: towards a formal framework', *Organization*, 13, 5: 701–24.

EIRO (2009) 'Unions review financial contribution to Labour', European Industrial Relations Observatory, **http://www.eurofound.europa.eu/eiro/site_map.htm**; accessed April, 2009.

Elliott, R. and Duffus, K. (1996) 'What has been happening to pay in the public services sector of the economy? Developments over the period 1970–1992', *British Journal of Industrial Relations*. 34, 1: 51–85.

Escott, K. and Whitfield, D. (1995) *The Gender Impact of Compulsory Competitive Tendering in Local Government*. Manchester: Equal Opportunities Commission.

Fairbrother, P. (1994) *Politics and the State as Employer*. London: Mansell.

Fairbrother, P. (1982) *Working for the State*, Studies for Trade Unionists, 8.29. London: Workers Educational Association.

Fairclough, N. (2000) *New Labour, New Language?* London: Routledge.

Farnham, D. and Horton, S. (1995) 'The new people management in the UK's public services: a silent revolution?'. Paper presented to the International Colloquium on Contemporary Development in HRM, École Supérieure de Commerce, Montpellier, France, October.

Federation of Small Business (2006) 'FSB delivers damning "red tape" dossier to government', 23 May, **www.fsb.org**.

Flanders, A. (1968) 'Collective bargaining: a theoretical analysis', *British Journal of Industrial Relations*, 6, 1: 1–26.

Flanders, A. (1970) 'Collective bargaining: prescription for change', *Management and Unions: The Theory and Reform of Industrial Relations*. London: Faber.

*Flood, P. and Toner, B. (1997) 'Large non-union companies: how do they avoid a Catch 22', *British Journal of Industrial Relations*, 35, 3: 257–77.

Fogarty, M. and Brooks, D. (1986) *Trade Unions and British Industrial Development*, London: Policy Studies Institute.

Ford, C. and Slater, G. (2005) 'Agency working in Britain: character, consequences and regulation', *British Journal of Industrial Relations*, 39, 2: 207–36.

*Forth, J., Bewley, H. and Bryson, A. (2006) *Small and Medium-sized Enterprises: Findings from the 2004 Workplace Employment Relations Survey*. London, Routledge.

Fox, A. (1975) 'Collective bargaining, Flanders and the Webbs', *British Journal of Industrial Relations*, 13, 2: 151–74.

Freeman, R. (2005) 'What do unions do? The 2004 M-Brane Stringtwister Edition', *Journal of Labor Research*, 24, 4: 641–68.

Gall, G. (2004), 'Trade union recognition in Britain 1995–2002: turning a corner?', *Industrial Relations Journal*, 35, 3: 249–70.

Gennard, J. (2002) 'Employee relations and public policy developments 1997–2001: A break with the past?' *Employee Relations*, 24, 6: 581–94.

Gilman, M. Edwards, P., Ram, M. and Arrowsmith, J. (2002), 'Pay determination in small firms in the UK: the case of the response to the National Minimum Wage', *Industrial Relations Journal*, 33, 1: 52–68.

Gollan, P. (2002), 'So, what's the news? Management strategy towards non-union representation at News International', *Industrial Relations Journal*, 33, 4: 316–31.

Grimshaw, D. (1999) 'Changes in skills-mix and pay determination among the nursing workforce in the UK', *Work, Employment and Society*, 13, 2: 295–328.

Guest, D., Brown, W., Peccei, R. and Huxley, K. (2008) 'Does partnership at work increase trust?', *Industrial Relations Journal*, 39, 2: 124–52.

Hall, M. and Terry, M. (2004) 'The emerging system of statutory worker representation' in G. Healy, E. Heery, R. Taylor, and W. Brown (eds) *The Future of Worker Representation*. Basingstoke Palgrave, pp. 207–28.

Hall, S. (2003) 'New Labour's double shuffle', *Soundings*, 24, 1: 10–24.

Harney, B. and Dundon, T. (2006) 'An emergent theory of HRM: a theoretical and empirical exploration of determinants of HRM among Irish SMEs', *Advances in Industrial and Labor Relations*, 15, 1: 109–59.

Harrison, S. (2002) 'New Labour, modernisation and the medical labour process', *Journal of Social Policy*, 31, 3: 465–85.

Hills, J. (1990) *The State of Welfare: The Welfare State in Britain since 1974*. Oxford: Oxford University Press.

HM Treasury (2002) *Full and Fulfilling Employment: Creating the Labour Market for the Future*. London, HMSO: The Treasury Office.

Hood, C. (1991) 'A public management for all seasons', *Public Administration*, 69, 1: 3–19.

Howell, C. (2004) 'Is there a third way for Industrial Relations?', *British Journal of Industrial Relations*, 42, 1: 1–22.

Hutton, W. (1996) *The State We're In*. London: Vintage.

Hyman, R. (1977) *A Marxist Introduction to Industrial Relations*. London: Macmillan.

Hyman, R. (2003) 'The historical evolution of British Industrial Relations' in P. Edwards (ed.) *Industrial Relations: Theory and Practice*. Oxford: Blackwell, pp. 37–57.

Jabareen, M. (2009) 'Skill mix development in general practice: a mixed method study of practice nurses and general practitioners'. Unpublished PhD thesis, University of Glasgow.

Kelly, J. (1996) 'Union militancy and social partnership', in J. Kelly (1996) (ed.) *Rethinking Industrial Relations*. London: Routledge, pp. 26–39.

*Kersley, B. Alpin, C., Forth, J., Bryson, A. Bewley, H., Dix, G. and Oxenbridge, S. (2006) *Inside the Workplace: Findings from the 2004 Workplace Employment Relations Survey*. London: Routledge.

Kessler, I. (1991) 'Workplace industrial relations in local government', *Employee Relations*, special issue, 13, 2: complete issue.

Kim, D.O. and Kim, H. (2004) 'A comparison of the effectiveness of union and non-union works councils in Korea', *International Human Resource Management Journal*, 15, 6: 1069–93.

Legge, K. (2005) *HRM: Rhetoric and Realities,* 2nd edn. London: Routledge.

Marchington, M., Carrol, M. and Boxall, P. (2003). 'Labour scarcity and the survival of small firms', *Human Resource Management Journal*, 13, 1: 5–22.

Marlow, S. (2002) 'Managing labour in smaller firms', *Human Resource Management Journal*, 12, 3: 26–47.

Marlow, S. (2006) 'HRM in smaller firms, fact or fiction?' *Human Resource Management Review* 16, 4: 467–77.

Marlow, S. (2007) 'People in the small firm' in S. Carter and D. Jones-Evans (eds) *Enterprise and Small Business: Principles, Policy and Practice*. London: Prentice Hall, pp. 385–405.

Marlow, S. and Patton, D. (2002) 'Minding the gap: managing the employment relationship in smaller firms'. *Employee Relations*, 24, 5: 345–60.

*Marlow, S., Patton, D. and Ram, M. (2005) (eds) *Managing Labour in Small Firms*. London: Routledge.

Marlow, S., Taylor, S. and Thompson, A. (2009) 'Informality and formality in medium-sized companies: contestation and synchronization', *British Journal of Management*, 20, 4: 313–26.

*McIlroy, J. (1998) 'The enduring alliance: trade unions and the making of New Labour, 1994–1997', *British Journal of Industrial Relations*, 36, 4: 537–64.

McIlroy, J. (2000) 'New Labour, New Unions, New Left', *Capital & Class*, 71, 1: 11–45.

McKay, S. (2001) 'Between flexibility and regulation: rights, protection and equality at work', *British Journal of Industrial Relations*, 39, 3: 285–303.

McLoughlin, I. and Gourlay, S. (1994) *Enterprise Without Unions: Industrial Relations in the Non-Union Firm*. Buckingham: Open University Press.

Meacher, M. (2004) 'Picking up the tabs for the PFI', *The Times*, 14 December.

Milner, S. (1993) 'Dispute deterrence: evidence on final offer arbitration', in D. Metcalf and S. Milner (1993) *New Perspectives on Industrial Disputes*. London: Routledge, pp. 143–56.

Moule, M. (1998) 'Regulation of work in small firms: a view from the inside', *Work, Employment and Society*, 12, 4: 635–53.

Napier, B. (1993) *CCT, Market Testing and Employment Rights: The Effects of TUPE and the Acquired Rights Directive*. London: Institute of Employment Rights.

Newman, M. (2009) 'Alarm grown as jobs go', *Times Higher Education*, 1, 889: p. 10.

Oldfield, C. (1999) 'Red tape is strangling enterprise', *Sunday Times*, 31 October, p. 7.

Pendleton, A. and Winterton, J. (1993) 'Public enterprise industrial relations in context', in A. Pendleton and J. Winterton (eds) *Public Enterprise in Transition*. London: Routledge, pp. 3–17.

Pollitt, C. (1993) *Managerialism and the Public Services: The Anglo-American Experience*. Oxford: Blackwell

Pollock, A. (2004) *NHS plc*, London: Verso.

Pratchett, L. and Wingfield, M. (1995) *Reforming the Public Service Ethos in Local Government: A New Institutional Perspective*, Leicester Business School Occasional Paper 27. Leicester: De Montfort University.

Rainnie, A. (1989) *Industrial Relations in Small Firms*. London: Routledge.

Ram, M. (1999) 'Managing autonomy: employment relations in small professional service firms', *International Small Business Journal*, 17, 2: 26–37.

Ram, M. and Edwards, P. (2003) 'Praising Caesar not burying him: what we know about employment relations in small firms', *Work, Employment and Society*, 17: 719–30.

Ram, M., Edwards, P., Gilman, M. and Arrowsmith, J. (2001) 'The dynamics of informality, employment regulations in small firms and the effects of regulatory change', *Work, Employment and Society*, 15, 5: 845–61.

Ranson, S. and Stewart, J. (1994) *Management for the Public Domain*. London: Macmillan.

Roethlisberger, F and Dickson, W. (1939) *Management sector and the Worker*. Cambridge, MA: Harvard University Press.

Rollinson, D. and Dundon, T. (2007) *Understanding Employment Relations*, London: McGraw-Hill.

Rose, E. (2004) *Employment Relations*. London: Prentice Hall.

Saridakis, G., Sen-Gupta, S. Edwards, P. and Storey, D. (2008) 'The impact of enterprise size on Employment Tribunal incidence and outcomes', *British Journal of Industrial Relations*, 46, 3: 469–99.

Singh, R. (1986) 'Final offer: arbitration in theory and practice', *Industrial Relations Journal*, Winter: 329–30.

*Smith, P. and Morton, G. (2001), 'New Labour's reform of British Employment Law: the devil is not only in the detail but in the values and policy too', *British Journal of Industrial Relations*, 39, 1: 119–38.

*Smith, P. and Morton, G. (2006) 'Nine years of New Labour: neoliberalism and workers rights', *British Journal of Industrial Relations*, 44, 4: 401–20.

Stanworth, J. and Purdy, D. (2003) *SME Facts and Figures, Report to the All-Party Parliamentary Small Business Group*, Westminster.

Storey, D.J. (1994) *Understanding the Small Business Sector*. London: Routledge.

Storey, J. (ed.) (1995) *HRM A Critical Text*. London: Routledge.

Storey, J. (ed.) (2005) *Adding Value Through Information and Consultation*. London: Palgrave.

STRB (2008) *Teachers' Workloads Diary Survey*. London: BMRB Research.

Tailby, S., Richardson, M., Upchurch, M, Danforth, A. and Stewart, P. (2007) 'Partnership with and without trade unions in the UK financial services', *Industrial Relations Journal*, 38, 3: 210–28.

Tebbit, N. (2009) 'A nation of haves and have-nots', *Daily Mail*, 1 April. **http://www.dailymail.co.uk/debate/article-1166252/LORD-TEBBIT-A-nation-haves-nots.html**, accessed 2 September 2009.

Thornley, C. (1994) 'Nursing pay policy: chaos in context'. Paper presented to Employment Research Unit Annual Conference, Cardiff Business School, September.

Timmins, N. (2000) 'PRP: team bonuses for civil servants'. *Financial Times*, 12 February, p. 11.

Towers, B. (1997) *The Representation Gap: Change and Reform in the British and American Workplace*. Oxford: Oxford University Press.

Toynbee, P. (2009) 'The clamour to cut public sector pay is based on myth', *The Guardian*, 3 March **http://www.guardian.co.uk/commentisfree/2009/jul/06/public-sector-private-pay**, accessed 2 September 2009.

Tsai, C-J., Sengupta, S. and Edwards, P. (2007) 'When and why is small beautiful? The experience of work in the small firm', *Human Relations*, 60, 1779–808.

Walton, R. and McKersie, R. (1965). *A Behavioural Theory of Labor Negotiations: An Analysis of a Social Interaction System.* New York: McGraw-Hill.

Webb, S. and Webb, B. (1902) *Industrial Democracy.* London: Longman.

White, G. (1994) 'Public sector pay: decentralisation versus control'. Paper presented to Employment Research Unit Annual Conference, *The Contract State: The Future of Public Management*, September.

Winchester, D. (1983) 'The public sector' in G.S. Bain (ed.) *Industrial Relations in Britain.* Oxford: Blackwell, pp. 155–79.

Winchester, D. (1996) 'The regulation of public services pay in the United Kingdom'. Paper presented to the Industrial Relations in the European Community (IREC) Network Annual Conference, *Industrial Relations in Europe: Convergence or Diversification?* University of Copenhagen: FAOS.

For multiple-choice questions, exercises and annotated weblinks related to this topic, visit **www.pearsoned.co.uk/mymanagementlab**.

Chapter 12

Performance management

Julia Pointon

Objectives

- To explain the distinction between performance measurement and performance management.
- To present an overview of performance appraisal including reference to some of the limitations of appraisal.
- To review the links between performance management and human resource management.
- To consider how organisations manage performance in relation to collaborative working, a diverse workforce, an ageing workforce and a volunteer workforce.

Introduction

It is fair to say that in the past there has been a tendency for the term performance measurement, and specifically the term performance appraisal, to become synonymous with, and sometimes used interchangeably with, the term performance management, but that is slightly misleading and obscures the subtle but important differences between the two concepts. In this chapter we review approaches to performance measurement, in particular appraisal, and make a clear distinction between it and the broader concept of performance management. We consider the extent to which there has been a significant shift away from equating performance measurement with 'individual employee' effort and achievement towards a conceptualisation of performance management that encompasses and involves, the 'whole organisation'.

This shift in focus has been stimulated by changes in the marketplace. As business has become more global and aggressive, organisations have sought to survive by achieving and sustaining a distinct competitive advantage. They are increasingly aware of value for money along with the need to make cost reductions and efficiency savings. They are experiencing increasing demands from customers and external stakeholders for a more rapid service of ever higher quality with increasingly competitive pricing. As a consequence, organisations are demanding even higher levels of performance from their employees. In short, employer's expectations about employee competence, organisational commitment and performance contribution are escalating.

This reconfiguration of the competition and performance agenda has extended what was once a relatively straightforward process of assessing an individual's performance against predefined criteria, into a more integrated, holistic and developmental exercise spanning the entire organisation. In so doing, attention has been placed on the contribution human resource management (HRM) makes to the management of performance.

This chapter starts by providing an overview of the more traditional approaches to measuring performance, in particular performance appraisal and the growth of 360-degree feedback. We consider what performance appraisal is and how it is used in organisations. We will also reflect on some of the associated limitations of appraisal, in particular from a Foucoudian perspective. We then extend the focus to consider the wider and more sophisticated application of performance management. In this context, we review the association between HRM and performance management and again consider some of the associated limitations. Finally, the chapter reviews some of the specifics of managing performance in different organisational contexts, for example in collaborating organisations and in relation to specific groups of employees, for example a diverse workforce, an ageing work force and volunteer workers.

The history of performance measurement?

Many of the roots of performance measurement can be traced back to Taylor's 'time and motion' studies. More recently, measurement has been influenced by the development of other business systems, for example, programming and budgeting, zero-based budgeting (ZBB) and in the UK in particular, 'management by objectives' (MBO). This approach, advocated by Drucker (1999), gained much popularity because it encouraged management to set individual objectives for employees at the commencement of the defined time period and to review progress at the end of the period. It provided a relatively easy and clear indication of the extent to which the employee had performed and achieved their predefined targets. In the late 1990s and early 2000 performance measurement became more extensive and, arguably, more intensive, to the point where some authors (see Adair *et al.* 2003, Harris *et al.*, 2007; Hyde *et al.*, 2006 and Bourgon, 2008) considered that performance measurement became one of the most striking features of the business agenda and, in particular, a central feature of the public sector reform agenda.

Workplace Employment Relations Survey (WERS) data for 2004 suggest that appraisals constitute one of the main tools used in measuring performance. The use of performance appraisals has increased since 1998. In 2004, 78 per cent of managers in workplaces reported that performance appraisals were undertaken compared with 73 per cent in 1998. However,

---

Box 12.1 | **Defining performance measurement**

In the context of performance measurement, performance appraisal represents just one tool in the toolkit. It is a way of eliciting information about the performance of one or more employees against certain predefined criteria or dimensions.

DeNisi (2000: 121) defines performance appraisal as 'the system whereby an organization assigns some "score" to indicate the level of performance of a target person or group'.

Fletcher (2001: 473) defines performance appraisal more broadly as 'activities through which organisations seek to assess employees and develop their competence, enhance performance and distribute rewards'. The focus was on performance ratings and other such limited and measurement-focused issues, but more recently has broadened and currently addresses social and motivational aspects of appraisal. Fletcher's definition reflects this shift in focus.

Mondy *et al.* (2002: 58) define performance appraisal as a system of review and evaluation of an individual's (or team's) performance and the process of appraising performance (who appraises and how is it done) within organisations. The emphasis on the organisations signals a further evolution in the nature of performance appraisal.

Table 12.1 Performance appraisal in UK workplaces

Private 1998	Public 1998	All 1998	Private 2004	Public 2004	All 2004
72	79	73	75	91	78

Base: All workplaces with 10 or more employees.

Figures are weighted and based on responses from 2191 managers in 1998 and 2024 managers in 2004.

Source: WERS 2004 (Kersley *et al.*, 2006).

performance appraisals were not always conducted on a regular basis or used for all employees. Two-thirds (65 per cent) of all workplaces conducted regular appraisals for most (60 per cent or more) non-managerial employees. This represented an increase since 1998, when the equivalent figure was 48 per cent.

The growth in the use of performance appraisal has been linked to a raise in performance-related pay schemes (PRP), but as Bach (2005) comments, this is not really the full picture as there is in fact, 'little evidence to suggest that performance appraisal was introduced to support individual performance pay' (2005: 297). Rather, Bach (2005) suggests, the increased use is more closely associated with the commitment of successive Conservative and, more recently, Labour governments to introduce private sector 'best practice' into the public sector in response to the need to increase efficiency and enhance managerial authority noted above. A further stimulus to organisations to review the performance of their employees came in the mid to late 1990s with the expansion of interest in gaining externally accredited recognition awards, for example Investors in People (IiP) and BSO 5750, ISO 9000. The need to evidence that training and development needs were regularly reviewed against organisational aims and objectives was a central feature of IiP and could be demonstrated through the use of a formal appraisal scheme.

This however, is only one purpose for appraisals, in 2003a, the Industrial Relations Services (IRS) found that approximately 15 per cent of respondents considered one of the main purposes for introducing appraisals was to help identify and deal with poor or underperformance.

Other reported purposes of performance appraisal were:

- promotion, separation and transfer decisions;
- feedback to the employee regarding how the organisation viewed the employee's performance;
- evaluations of relative contributions made by individuals and entire departments in achieving higher level organisation goals;
- criteria for evaluating the effectiveness of selection and placement decisions, including the relevance of the information used in the decisions within the organisation;
- reward decisions, including merit increases, promotions and other rewards
- ascertaining and diagnosing training and development decisions;
- criteria for evaluating the success of training and development decisions;
- information upon which work scheduling plans, budgeting and human resources planning can be used.

In many instances the actual appraisal is undertaken via a face-to-face discussion, but it is important to note that this may be changing as the use of information technology and software packages such as 'Performance Pro' means that appraisals can easily be undertaken on line (see Case study).

The case of TRW

TRW Inc., is a global automotive, aeronautics, electronics and information-systems company with 100,000 employees, based in 36 countries on five continents and with four core businesses. It was originally called 'Thompson Ramo Wooldridge Inc.', but was shortened to TRW Inc. in 1965.

In 2001, the company had a heavy debt load following a large acquisition in the automotive sector and in the face of current adverse market conditions, TRW was challenged to become more competitive and performance-driven and to provide greater value to shareholders. To reach those goals, the senior management committee instituted dramatic change throughout the company. Business units were empowered to operate more autonomously than they had in the past, and the corporate headquarters itself was renamed the 'Business Support Centre.'

To guide the creation of a new and energised work culture, a new set of company-wide TRW 'Behaviours' was developed and communicated throughout the company. The aim was to organise and operate a performance-appraisal, professional-development and succession-management system that not only attempted to create a more performance-driven, customer-oriented organisation, but also command respect and workers acceptence. The solution was to select a team of IT experts and key HR people from each of the businesses. Each member was faced with the task of allowing their own particular business's way of doing things (some were used to working with two-page appraisal forms, others had ten) to be incorporated into a single system. The employee performance and development process they came up with, although common to the entire organisation, was allowed to flow within particular units as was felt best, both standardisation and flexibility being recognised as essentials.

To position TRW competitively for the twenty-first century, the company stands committed to excellence and quality, exploring new markets, and satisfying its customers, shareholders and employees. To meet those commitments, TRW has created a set of six behaviours that distinguishes it in the marketplace through performance and technology.

The six behaviours that guide performance management are:

1 **Create trust**:
   - create an open and constructive environment;
   - deal with reality;
   - communicate with candour and honesty;
   - honour commitments;
   - take personal accountability for results.

2 **Energise people**　　:
   - rigorously select, empower and grow people who demand the best of themselves and others;
   - reward performance and initiative.

3 **Performance driven**
   - deliver profitable growth;
   - develop and achieve demanding goals . . . short and long term;
   - continuously improve productivity and quality;
   - execute with facts, urgency and decisiveness;
   - create energy that doesn't tolerate bureaucracy.

4 **Embrace change**
   - passion for innovation;
   - a thirst for new ideas;

- be adaptable and flexible;
- know your markets . . . lead your competitors.

5 Customer-oriented

- understand our customers;
- relentlessly focus on their needs;
- develop lasting relationships.

6 Build teamwork

- share information and best practices;
- speak up;
- encourage diverse views;
- get the facts . . . make decisions;
- ACT!
- support it.

Note: The TRW behaviours were instituted in 2001 to guide the culture of the company (Neary, 2002).

Approaches to performance appraisal

The scope and method for reviewing performance varies between organisations, but in general, appraisal takes a 'free text' form, in which the appraiser and the appraisee review performance in general, although the problem with such qualitative forms of appraisal is that they have the potential to ignore important areas that would benefit from being appraised, thereby making them highly selective and highly subjective.

An alternative is to undertake a straight ranking of performance against predefined criteria or traits. On the basis of an assessment against the dimensions, employees are given the final rankings. Any approach using predetermined criteria has limitations, especially if the same criteria are employed across a wide range of job roles, as not each criterion may be relevant. Traits such as resourcefulness, loyalty or enthusiasm may be open to different interpretations by different appraisers and the appraisee, leaving them open to bias and prejudice. Finally, the criteria may become obsolete, for example in the banking sector the use of creativity, innovation and imagination may not be as desirable in the first half of the twenty-first century as it was in the latter half of the twentieth century.

A critical incident method is one in which the appraiser rates the employee on the basis of critical events and how the employee behaved during those incidents. It includes both negative and positive points. The drawback of this method is that the appraiser has to note down the critical incidents and the employee behaviour as and when they occur.

A checklist approach is one in which the appraiser is given a list of statements or descriptions of the desired knowledge, skills competences and behaviours of the employees. The list may be drawn from key aspects of the role or directly from the job description. Often the appraisee and appraiser indicate which description most closely reflects the job performance of the employee. This is often undertaken independently of each other at the start of the process, but later, during a formal discussion, the appraiser and appraisee seek to reach agreement as to which description is most appropriate. This approach is referred to as 'Behaviourally anchored rating scales (BARS)' or 'behaviourally observed rating scales (BOS)', and is a reasonably equitable method, as the possibility of personal bias is reduced, especially if there is a requirement to reach a consensus decision.

Another approach, and one that seeks to make the process even more equitable, establishes job objectives or goals, and each year reviews the extent to which they have been met to a satisfactory level. In this style of appraisal, the CIPD suggest the following points should be considered:

● What they have achieved during the review period, with examples and evidence.

● Any examples of objectives not achieved with explanations.

● What they most enjoy about the job and how they might want to develop the role.

● Any aspect of the work in which improvement is required and how this might be achieved.

● Employee learning and development needs with arguments to support their case for specific training.

● What level of support and guidance employees require from their manager.

● Employees aspirations for the future, both in the current role and in possible future roles.

● Objectives for the next review period (CIPD, 2009a).

Have you ever been appraised? How did you find the experience? How could the experience have been improved?

The extent to which the appraisee is involved in establishing performance goals varies between organisations, but motivational theory suggests goals are most effective in terms of motivating performance when the employee has been directly involved in setting them (see Box 12.2). A variation on this theme is to use a competency based framework as the basis against which performance is appraised. Many schemes use a combination of competency assessment, objectives and role accountabilities.

Performance may also be measured by gathering raw data (see Box 12.3). It is frequently used, for example to monitor activity rates of computer operators, call handling speed and ability of operators in call or throughput rates for staff in fast food restaurants. Performance measurement or employee monitoring can also be conducted in other ways that were not possible until very recently. For example, some cellular telephones have built-in global positioning systems that enable employers to track the physical location of employees at all times. Employers can then track every physical and electronic move an employee makes. Furthermore, employers can now

Box 12.2   Goal setting theory and performance management

Goal setting theory was established by Latham and Locke in 1984 in which he argued that goals pursued by employees can play an important part in motivating improved performance. In striving to achieve the goals employees reflect upon their behaviour and performance, and if they surmise that their goals may not be realised they will modify their behaviour. Heslin *et al.* (2009) suggest a prime axiom of goal setting theory is that specific, difficult goals lead to higher performance than when people strive to simply 'do their best' (Locke, 1966; Locke and Latham, 1990). The performance benefits of challenging, specific goals have been demonstrated in laboratory and field studies (Locke and Latham, 1990, 2002). Specific challenging goals do not, however, necessarily lead to such desirable personal and organisational outcomes. Rather, contribution goal setting can make to effective performance management depend on issues pertaining to goal commitment, task complexity, goal framing, team goals and feedback. For goals to be motivating they need to:

● be specific rather than vague;

● be demanding but attainable and realistic;

● generate feedback that is timely and meaningful;

● be accepted by the employees as desirable.

Box 12.3

Wireless real-time production and employee performance measurement

The system is referred to as 20/20 Data Collection/Monitoring & Management System and is used in any production or manufacturing context, from assembling computers, to answering telephone calls in a call centre, to packing chocolate biscuits. It is a wireless real-time shop floor data collection and management system that is designed to enhance the production management to a higher level thereby allowing productivity gains. It works by constantly monitoring the work rate of the operators to show if specific operators or assembly stations are constraining overall production throughput. Performance and line balancing reports rank the bottleneck operators and stations according to their constraint on system output. With real-time data access, managers are able to make well-informed decisions, such as reprioritising a job or reallocating staffing. Productivity analysis allows managers to measure individual employee performance and analyse labour costs by employee, department or work assembly station. In terms of performance management real time measurement data enables managers to:

- improve productivity by leveraging production monitoring and motivating the workers to meet the standards;
- access detailed analysis allowing managers to monitor performance and labour costs in terms of each employee;
- indicate and monitor individual operator efficiency and output;
- use the reported information to determine the precise cause of any defect and the action necessary to resolve the issue;
- identify poor operator performance before it causes a problem;
- use the data as part of a continuous total quality improvement programme.

conduct their own private investigations into employment applicants, partly because of the reluctance of former employers to give references. So, instead, employers may collect information about prospective employees from driving records, vehicle registration records, bankruptcy proceedings. Social Security records, property ownership records, military records, sex offender lists, incarceration records, drug testing records, professional licensing records, workers' compensation records and credit reports. In performance measurement, electronic monitoring and surveillance of employees has grown, especially the monitoring of email and web browsing (Sipor and Ward, 1995; Stanton, 2000). The ethical implications of such an approach will be discussed later when we consider some of the limitations of performance appraisal.

What, if any, are the ethical implications of wireless real-time production and employee performance measurement?

The CIPD suggest there are five key elements of the performance appraisal:

- *Measurement*: assessing performance against agreed targets and objectives.
- *Feedback*: providing information to the individual on their performance and progress.
- *Positive reinforcement*: emphasising what has been done well and making only constructive criticism about what might be improved.
- *Exchange of views*: a frank exchange of views about what has happened, how appraisees can improve their performance, the support they need from their managers to achieve this and their aspirations for their future career.
- *Agreement*: jointly coming to an understanding by all parties about what needs to be done to improve performance generally and overcome any issues raised in the course of the discussion (CIPD, 2009a).

Box 12.4 | **Performance appraisal at Tata Sons**

Mr Satish Pradhan, Executive Vice President – HR at Tata Sons, based in Mumbai, and with over 20 years of international and national experience in human resource management, explained how performance appraisal at Tata Sons was built on two principles:

● no surprises;
● reward for performance.

Mr Pradhan took time to explain that effective performance appraisal was all about trust and development. He stated: 'If our employees trust that we have their best interests at heart and that we genuinely want them to succeed in their careers at Tata Sons, then their commitment to us and performance for us; will excel.' He said that at no stage in the performance appraisal process should an employee be told anything they were not already aware of or had not had sufficient time to reflect upon. He was also keen to demonstrate that while financial incentives were part of the reward for performance, money was not the whole story. For Tata Sons, non-financial rewards, for example being chosen to represent the company on the platform of an international convention, are held in as much, if not more esteem among the employees, than a salary increase.

How far do you agree with Mr Satish Pradhan, Executive Vice President – HR at Tata Sons, that there should be 'no surprises' in a performance appraisal?

Why do you think he is so keen to emphasise that non-financial rewards are also part of the system of performance recognition?

Limitations of performance measurement

Over recent years, there has been a growing discomfort with measuring performance through the use of appraisal indicators and targets. Callahan (2007) provides a clear steer to all managers involved in measuring performance through such traditional indices, to start to think outside the performance box. He suggests that performance measurement is inadequate because it fails to recognise the key concepts of accountability and citizen participation and fails to emphasise the critical importance of their relationship. In other words, performance appraisals are compromised because they are used for a range of often conflicting purposes. In addition, they are undertaken by stakeholders who themselves have a range of roles and responsibilities – which, again, may be conflicting (Wilson, 2002). To illustrate, the appraiser can be placed in the position, described by McGregor (1957) as being required to 'play God'. Appraisers invariably judge and rate the performance of their staff member. This role sits at odds with their responsibility to motivate and develop the same staff member, and may sit in opposition to their role as employee counsellor. Newton and Findlay (1996) make the point that employees are less likely to confide their limitations, development needs or anxieties about job competence to their appraiser because it could adversely affect their rating at the next performance review and may affect reward levels if performance is linked to remuneration.

Appraisers may equally be reluctant to give their staff a poor review because it might prove demotivating, could create conflict and might suggest they lacked the necessary management skills to elicit high performance. Additional limitations relate to what is known as the 'halo effect', which, as the name implies, causes managers to see only an 'angel' in an employee and blinds them into ignoring smaller problem areas that require growth and development. The 'comparing employees effect', in which a manager evaluates one employee against another without considering the different tasks they are required to perform, and the 'recency effect', when managers rate employees on the basis of their most recent encounter with them or on their most recent knowledge of their performance, and the 'central tendency' effect, when managers are reluctant to be overly lenient or harsh – so they opt for the safe midway or central point, may all reduce the effectiveness of appraisal. Research undertaken by Geddes and Konrad (2003) and Thornton and Rupp (2007) indicate that appraisal ratings are also influenced by gender, ethnic origins and physical attractiveness.

According to Bach (2005: 304), one of the most common responses to rater bias is to 'redouble training efforts to ensure managers are trained in conducting appraisals, and be aware of some of the potential limitations'. Another response has been to seek multiple sources of data from multiple stakeholders. One such example is the use of the 'balanced scorecard' (Kaplan and Norton, 1992, 1996). The balanced scorecard is a performance management approach to monitor progress toward an organisation's strategic goals. Each major unit throughout the organisation is tasked with establishing its own scorecard which, in turn, is integrated with the scorecards of other units to achieve the scorecard of the overall organisation. It focuses on various overall performance indicators, often including:

● financial perspective;

● customer perspective;

● internal process perspective; and

● innovation and learning perspective.

360-degree appraisal

A second approach to performance appraisal is the use of 360-degree feedback, or 'multi-rater feedback'. This approach was first developed and used by General Electric in the USA in 1992, and despite Newbold's (2008) suggestion that it went out of fashion for a while, it is now back in vogue with many organisations using it. Aswathappa (2005: 234) lists GE (India) Reliance Industries, Godrej soaps, Wipro, Infosys, Thermex and Thomas Cook as examples of organisations currently using the 360-degree system of performance appraisal. It is an approach in which performance data is sought from peers, subordinates, superiors and nominated significant others who may be internal or external to the organisation.

Self-assessment is an indispensable part of 360-degree appraisals; they therefore have high employee involvement and also have the strongest impact on behaviour and performance. As it provides a '360-degree review' of the employees' performance, it is often considered to be one of the most credible performance appraisal methods. The 360-degree appraisal is also a powerful developmental tool because, when conducted at regular intervals, it helps monitor changes in the perceptions of others' about particular employee's performance, and so hold greater surface validity.

STOP and think

What might be the advantages and limitations of 360-degree appraisal?

The points noted above relate to limitations in the design and operational implementation of performance appraisal. Another level of critical commentary has emerged which draws attention to the ethical and philosophical limitations of performance appraisal and the fact that appraisal can be seen as a means of manufacturing consent among employees. These accounts reject the unitary assumptions and managerialist prerogatives that underpin traditional approaches to performance appraisal and replace them with a radical ideology that questions managerial objectives, their power to control, manipulate and direct employee behaviour and the extent to which they have a right to engage in the covert surveillance of employees. Bach (2005) provides an excellent summary of this proposition, in which he suggests that those influenced by the work of French philosopher Michel Foucault view trends in appraisal as part of a more sinister management regime to control all aspects of employee behaviour and eliminate any scope for employee resistance or misbehaviour.

Understanding Foucault

Foucault's work involves reference to Bentham's panopticon. Bentham was a utilitarian theorist, believing human beings are intrinsically bound to seek pleasure and avoid pain, wherever possible, and that 'good' and 'bad' are defined by what is pleasurable and painful. The object of legislation therefore, according to Bentham, should be to secure the greatest happiness for the greatest number of people; consequently, the pain of punishment should be proportional to the happiness that it secured. As a part of his vision of rational social control, Bentham devised an architectural device he called the 'Panopticon', which is Greek for 'all seeing'. The panopticon was based on the design for a Russian factory that minimised the number of supervisors required, it was proposed by Bentham for the design of prisons, workhouses, mental asylums and schools. The supervisors were able to view and monitor the inmates, but the inmates could not see the supervisors. The underlying principle is that the total and constant surveillance of inmates or workers would encourage them to conform to all the desired behaviours and beliefs and eventually each individual would themselves become an overseer of others. The strong illusion of a powerful, controlling and all-seeing eye would become an inner reality of self-policing. Bentham believed this approach could be successfully adopted in any environment, including work organisations, which involved any level of supervision – i.e. of employees. (**http://www.mdx.ac.uk/www/study/ybenfou.htm**).

The same principles about power, control and observation were enshrined in much of Foucault's (1977) thinking about the role of managers controlling the behaviour and thoughts of their employees. In the example we saw earlier of the 20/20 data collection used as a wireless real-time production and employee performance measurement system, it is easy to appreciate how this distant but all embracing surveillance of the action, speed of work quality and production can be regarded as an example of why Foucault exhibited concern over the extent to which employees were being manipulated, controlled and monitored by others and saw appraisal as epitomising a desire for observation in order to make every employee a knowable, calculable and administrative object (Miller and Rose, 1990: 5). Foucault, like Townley (1993b) and Grey (1994) in their work on appraisals and career management, questioned the ethics of such close and consistent intrusion into an employees working life and saw such involvement as a negative feature of performance appraisal. However, to leave the story at that junction would be to tell only half of it as others, in particular Findlay and Newton (1998), use their discussion of performance appraisal to highlight Foucault's apparent neglect of human agency (Newton, 1994) and to suggest that to see all aspects of intervention as a negative use of power is to ignore the mutuality of interests that characterise many aspects of the modern labour process.

To what extent do you share the view of Townley (1993a, 1993b, 1994, 1997) and Grey (1994) about the 'negative' aspects of performance appraisal?

Performance management

As the limitations of performance measurement and some aspects of appraisal became more apparent, and as the role of HRM became more accepted and respected, the agenda shifted to embrace a more strategic, systematic, integrated and organisationally focused approach to the management (rather than measurement) of performance. As an area of academic study and research, performance management dates back to the late 1980s with commentators such as Johnson and Kaplan, 1987; Lynch and Cross, 1991; Eccles, 1991; Kaplan and Norton, 1992; and Thorpe, 2004, setting the scene. Den-Hartog *et al.* (2004: 556) describe performance management as being concerned with the:

> challenges organizations face in defining, measuring, and stimulating employee performance with the ultimate goal of improving overall organisational performance. Performance management involves multiple levels of analysis and is clearly linked to the topics studied in strategic human resource management (HRM).

Armstrong and Baron (2005: 15) define performance management as a process rather than an event, and so it operates in a continuous cycle. It 'contributes to the effective management of individuals and teams in order to achieve high levels of organizational performance'. They go on to stress that it is 'a strategy which relates to every activity of the organization set in the context of its human resource policies, culture, style and communications systems. The nature of the strategy depends on the organizational context and can vary from organization to organization' (Armstrong and Baron, 2005: 16). Armstrong and Baron argue the principle value of performance management is to:

- communicate a shared vision of the purpose of the organisation;
- define expectations of what must be delivered and how;
- ensure employees are aware of what high performance means and how they can achieve it; and
- to enhance levels of motivation and enable employees to monitor their own performance and understand what needs to be done to improve their overall level of performance.

To quote from the CIPD *Fact Sheet on Performance Management* (2009b), it should be:

> - *strategic*: it is about broader issues and longer-term goals;
> - *integrated*: it should link various aspects of the business, people management and individuals and teams.
>
> And incorporate:
>
> - *performance improvement*: throughout the organization, for individual, team and organizational effectiveness;
> - *development*: unless there is continuous development of individuals and teams, performance will not improve;
> - *managing behaviour*: ensuring that individuals are encouraged to behave in a way that allows and fosters better working relationships.

Armstrong and Baron (2004) stress that, at its best, performance management is a tool to ensure that managers manage effectively; that they ensure the people or teams they manage:

- know and understand what is expected of them;
- have the skills and ability to deliver on these expectations;
- are supported by the organisation to develop the capacity to meet these expectations are given feedback on their performance; and
- have the opportunity to discuss and contribute to individual and team aims and objectives.

Human resource management and performance management

Human resource management, and in particular strategic HRM (SHRM), has developed since the early 1980s and provides us with a framework to understand the contribution HR practices can make – directly or indirectly – to individual and organisational performance. We have already read about the different approaches to HRM, but to recap there are essentially three major perspectives that emerge from the existing literature:

1 Universalistic
2 Contingency
3 Configuration.

The universalistic or 'best practice' perspective posits there are certain policies and procedures which, if followed, will always result in higher performance. The aim of HR practitioners is to identify precisely what these are. Although there is no undisputed list of high involvement/performance/commitment HRM practices, it has been claimed that rigorous recruitment and selection processes, performance-contingent compensation systems, extensive development and training activities and commitment to employee involvement are generally considered key to 'best practice'

The contingency, or 'external fit', perspective suggests that different HR policies and practices are required to ensure high performance depending on the type and nature of the organisation in which they are being operated. In other words, perspective emphasises the 'fit' between business strategy and HRM practices, implying that business strategies are followed by HRM practices in determining business performance.

The configurational perspective posits a simultaneous internal and external fit between a firm's external environment, business strategy and HRM strategy, implying that business strategies and HRM practices interact according to organisational context in determining business performance.

At its most basic, HRM is about aligning the management of people with the needs of the business. This, according to Roberts (2001), involves the organisation being clear about its mission, its values, its strategic direction and its goals. It involves establishing and articulating specific organisational, departmental, team and individual objectives designed to meet the stated goals and translating those into a meaningful set of targets for every individual involved. This can involve a panoply of specific actions and processes: performance appraisal, strategic approaches to reward, training and development, sophisticated communication and feedback mechanisms, coaching and individual career planning, mechanisms for monitoring the effectiveness of performance management systems and interventions, and even cultural management techniques.

So far our discussion has focused on the performance of the individual; we now move on to consider the links between individual performance and that of the organisation as a whole. The relationship between performance management and human resource management practices is longstanding, if not always evidence-based or consistent. In fact, since the concept of HRM first emerged in the early 1980s, two basic paths of research have developed. The first approach assumes there is a 'direct' relationship between individual HRM practices and organisational performance (see Schuler and Jackson, 1987, 1999). The second is based on the assumption that there is no quantifiable direct link, but there is an 'indirect' relationship between individual HRM practices and organisational performance (see Ferris *et al.*, 1998; Edwards and Wright, 2001).

To illustrate this difference in opinion, international authors such as Boselie *et al.* (2001) from the Netherlands, argue there is an obvious and direct link between HRM and performance management, in particular in relation to employee involvement and internal regulation. Seeking to confirm or refute the link, Boselie *et al.* (2005) analysed 104 referred journal articles between 1994 and 2005. They concluded that there were a number of hidden assumptions in most of the conceptual models developed in the research; and that in most of the studies there was empirical evidence to confirm that human resource management does affect organisational performance. However, they also pointed out that the variety of methods used in the research made it impossible to compare results and concluded overall that there is no consistent picture of what human resource management is or what it does. Björkman and Budhwar (2007) were similarly interested in exploring whether the proposed effects of HRM were universalistic or contingent on the national context of the organisation. Based on an analysis of companies in India, they concluded the key message for practitioners is that HRM systems do improve organisational performance in the Indian subsidiaries of foreign firms, but that an emphasis on the localisation of HRM practices can further contribute in this regard. In a further research study undertaken in India, Chand and Katou (2007) sought to demonstrate the operational link between HRM and performance and concluded that the financial and commercial success of hotels in India is positively related to their HRM systems of recruitment, selection, HR planning, job design, training and development, quality circles and pay systems. Other commentators, notably Legge (1995) and more recently Hall (2004) from the UK, are less convinced. While we are, therefore, advised to treat clear proclamations of cause and effect with a degree of caution, the general consensus developed among researchers is that HRM practices and/or HRM systems do not influence business performance directly (Budhwar *et al.*, 2006; Katou and Budhwar, 2007). Rather, they influence firm resources, such as human capital, or employee behaviours, and it is these resources and behaviours that ultimately lead to performance. This implicit model assumes that there are variables that mediate a link between HRM practices and business performance, although only a few researchers (Huselid, 1995; MacDuffie, 1995) have measured these mediators and addresses their importance.

Critique of links between HRM and performance

Links between HRM and performance management have a natural logic about them: good HRM practices can improve employee commitment; higher levels of commitment can positively affect employee performance, which in turn impacts on the organisation's financial performance and ultimately competitive advantage and success. The central concerns are ability, motivation and opportunity to participate and practice or AMO for short (see Chapters 1 and 2 in this volume and Boxall and Purcell, 2008). The successful organisation not only has to have better than average human capital, through recruitment (where organisational reputation is important), selection and development and then appropriate job design, motivation, communication and involvement systems, but also better processes or capabilities. These combine human and non-human resources together in ways highly appropriate for end-users and markets and in ways which other firms find hard to copy. In terms of managing performance Purcell, in a paper from Bath University refers to ability, motivation and opportunity as the prime building blocks of HR architecture if employees, individually and collectively are to engage in the sort of discretionary behaviour that is beneficial to the organisation. Purcell states that effective performance management must recognise and make provision for three conditions of AMO:

- There must be enough employees with the necessary ability (skills, experience, knowledge) to do current, and perhaps future, jobs.

- There must be adequate motivation for them to apply their abilities. These motivation factors may be financial but will almost certainly include social rewards (and sanctions) and recognition of contribution as applied by co-workers and immediate bosses.

- There must be an opportunity to engage in discretionary behaviour (thus the importance of job cycle time). Opportunity is the invitation to participate and take part, or get involved. This occurs both within the job itself in terms of how the job can best be done (known as 'online participation') and outside the job as a member of a team or work area, and a 'citizen' of the organisation (offline participation). This is where opportunities may exist, and certainly can be created, which provide space for wider participation and involvement, so employees contribute knowledge and ideas on how things should be done and how to respond to the change. AMO is therefore considered to be at the heart of effective performance management and strategic human resource management.

This intricate relationship between the individual and the organisation epitomises that espoused by Guest (2000) and embodies the essential elements in his earlier, more detailed model developed in 1997. It too has an innate appeal.

However, authors Richardson and Thompson (1999) and, in particular Hall (2004) identify a number of problems with research which claims to demonstrate a significant relationship between 'progressive' HR practices and internal and external performance outcomes. First, Hall notes that the way HR practices are assessed lacks reliability, consistency, depth and breadth; in particular, the line manager's and the employee's perspectives are excluded and the samples inadequate. The assessment of performance outcomes are also criticised in terms of relevance, unhelpfully narrow limits, short-termism and manipulability. She also suggest that while some significant relationships have been found between HR practices and performance outcomes, these are variable and suggests the relationships should be treated with caution. Hall (2004) also advises caution is needed as the statistics do not provide any evidence of a causal relationship. This leads her to conclude that progressive HR practices may lead to higher performance outcomes or higher performance outcomes may lead to investment in more progressive HR practices, or these factors may both be influenced by something else which has yet to be identified and measured.

The set of assumptions underpinning the body of research also warrants caution. Studies are carried out with an implicit or explicit assumption that 'best practice' can be revealed and then used to guide other companies in their choices; such an unquestioned universalist perspective is contested (see Legge, 1995) as is the unitarist assumption – and as employee views were not sought in the majority of the research examples, this raises questions about their validity. Looking at the internal measure of employee performance from a completely different perspective, Patterson *et al.* (1997) found that the greatest influence on employee performance was not HR practices per se, but rather the culture of the organisation – a factor not reported on in some studies, although it was discussed by Guest (1997). Patterson *et al.* (1997) also found that welfare provision of all HR policies had the greatest influence on employee performance.

Finally, Hall (2004) identifies a further difficulty in making a definitive and direct link between the impact of HR practices and performance, namely that the majority of research was collected without the use of a theoretical framework, and in particular with no regard to the intervening mechanism which mediates HR practices and performance outcomes. This, she concludes, leaves the existing research with no explanatory power.

Collaborative performance management

So far in this chapter we have focused on the measurement and management of performance within an organisation. We have noted that in order for organisations to make the most effective use of performance measurement outcomes they must be able to make the transition from simply *measuring* performance to actually *managing* performance and be able to anticipate needed changes in the strategic direction of the organisation and have a methodology in place for effecting strategic change. To put it another way, effective performance management provides organisations with the opportunity to refine and improve their development activities. In this next section we consider some of what Waggoner *et al.* (1999: 52) call the 'various forces that shape organisational performance management systems'. In particular, we will consider the challenges of managing performance in a diverse workforce, an ageing workforce and whether managing the performance of a volunteer is in any respect different from managing the performance of salaried employees.

The fact that today's marketplace is more fiercely competitive than ever before is indeed widely acknowledged (Fawcett and Magnan 2002; Patterson *et al.* 2003). Globalisation, technological change and demanding customers constantly push the performance bar upward. In response to this new global economic order Bititci *et al.* (2004) suggest that over the past decade or so, businesses have been forced to become more responsive and adapt to a continuously changing business environment, to be more agile and persistently restructure themselves and find new ways of continuously improving processes, systems and performance. Longnecker and Fink (2001) and Longnecker *et al.* (1999) suggest that in response to both recognising the potential limitations of performance measurement and responding to the demands inherent in a new global business world, organisational processes and delivery systems are being re-engineered and streamlined so that cycle-times are reduced and efficiencies are improved. Relationships with both customers and suppliers are being redefined so that 'strategic partnerships' may be forged and leveraged. Workforce effectiveness and productivity initiatives are being developed to improve employee performance. Total quality and customer service are no longer viewed as individual programmes but rather are being integrated into organisational cultures and operating practices as 'simply a way of life'. In addition, technology is 'exploding' in most industries and must be properly integrated and implemented if it is to be leveraged to provide competitive advantage. Enlightened approaches to human resource management are also being used as a vehicle to leverage human capital in the emerging global workplace.

Burgess *et al.* (1997) cited in Busi and Bititci (2006: 10) summarised the impact of this new territory by suggesting that in order 'to cope with today's increasing competitive marketplace, companies have, and should, become more collaborative' and to form a network that boasts as a whole all those resources and competencies needed to satisfy the end-customer. In short, to survive and meet new demands, organisations will struggle to go it alone; collaboration and networking have been earmarked as key themes of success. The collaborative model is based on breaking down traditional physical boundaries and getting the partners to behave as a single unit. Integrating different organisations implies forming teams of different people with different cultures, policies and routines (Holmberg, 2000). Managing multidisciplinary teams poses a number of challenges related to communication, the psychological contract, trust and behaviour.

Amaratunga and Baldry (2002) argue that in order for organisations to achieve the level of collaboration and competitive advantage they seek, they will need to move away from an approach to performance management that seeks to optimise internal activities and applied within the tight organisational boundaries of a specific firm, towards an approach that recognises their relationship with other stakeholders and their respective performance. As Busi and Bititci (2006) suggest, the move toward more collaborative types of networks calls for new processes, new strategy, new measures and new way of managing performance. In the collaborative enterprise, companies will be closer than ever and, unlike in the past, the performance of an enterprise will depend as much on the performance of its partners in the value chain as on its own performance. Collaborative performance measurement and management means that customers and suppliers get access to performance information beyond their own firm and give access to performance information to the other partners in the network. By sharing performance data with partners, firms can identify bottlenecks and 'weak links' (2006: 11).

In other words, collaborative organisations will need to move away from an isolated, internally focused 'performance measurement' to 'performance management'. Armstrong and Baron (1998) see performance management as a continuous process involving performance reviews focusing on the future rather than the past. They emphasise the strategic and integrated nature of performance management, which in their view focuses on: 'increasing the effectiveness of organisations by improving the performance of the people who work in them and by developing the capabilities of teams and individual contributors' (1998: 38–39). The definition offered by Busi and Bititci (2006) retains a strong sense of measurement, while nonetheless acknowledging the strategic goal-orientation of the process:

the use of performance measurement information to effect positive change in organizational culture, systems and processes, by helping to set agreed-upon performance goals, allocating and prioritising resources, informing managers to either confirm or change current policy or programme directions to meet those goals, and sharing results of performance in pursuing those goals.   (Busi and Bititci, 2006: 11)

In determining the manner in which a collaborative/networked organisation should approach performance management Longnecker and Fink (2001) suggest HR practitioners should ask the following critical questions, the answers to which will greatly influence the quality of performance management:

- Do all of our managers have a clear and unambiguous understanding of their role in our changing organisation?
- Do we provide all of our managers with ongoing and balanced performance feedback?
- Do we have a systematic approach to helping our managers 'learn by doing'?
- Is management development truly a management priority at our organisation?
- Do we take active steps to ensure that our management development efforts are designed to meet the actual needs of our managers?

Busi and Bititci (2006) build on this foundation and characterise a network-wide collaborative approach to performance management as focusing on:

- managing extended processes within and beyond the single company's boundaries;
- managing the collaborative enterprise performance, rather than only measuring it;
- creating and managing cross-organisational multidisciplinary teams;
- deploying integrated ICT across organisations;
- creating and sharing knowledge.

As Busi and Bititci (2006) summarise, the supporting collaborative performance management system would include the following key elements:

- a structured methodology to design the performance measurement system;
- a structured management process for using performance measurement information to help make decisions, set performance goals, allocate resources, inform management, and report success (see also Amaratunga and Baldry, 2002);
- a set of requirements specifications of the necessary electronic tools for data gathering, processing and analysis (see also Waggoner *et al.* 1999);

Box 12.5   The aims of collaborative performance management

- Translate organisational vision into clear measurable outcomes that define success, and which are shared throughout the organisation and with customers and stakeholders.
- Provide a tool for assessing, managing and improving the overall health and success of performance management systems.
- Continue to shift from prescriptive, audit and compliance-based oversight to an ongoing, forward-looking strategic partnership.
- Include measures of quality, cost, speed, customer service and employee alignment, motivation and skills to provide an in-depth, predictive performance management system.
- Replace existing assessment models with a consistent approach to performance management.

Source: Adapted from Procurement Executives' Association (1999).

- theoretical guidelines on how to manage through measures. (As Adair *et al.*, 2003) point out, performance management systems are used to apply the information and knowledge arising from performance measurement systems);
- a review process to ensure that measures are constantly updated to reflect changes in strategy and/or market conditions (see also Waggoner *et al.*, 1999).

As we have seen, the traditional focus of performance measurement has been on process operations within the organisational boundaries of one particular firm. With changes in the structure and economy of the global business world, collaboration became a necessary business development, capable of rendering single-business and internally focused performance measurement systems inappropriate. However, the difficulty of developing a collaborative culture and the difficulty of developing appropriate cross-cultural and translational performance indices have been identified as major barriers to the successful implementation of collaborative performance management systems.

Busi and Bititci (2006) advise that various studies that analyse the issue of local versus overall performance measures conclude that collaborative performance measurement systems should evaluate both local measures and business network-wide measures in order to maintain relevance and effectiveness in the collaborative enterprise business model. As the collaborative enterprise business model is based on breaking down traditional physical boundaries and getting the partners to behave as a single unit, integrating different organisations implies forming teams of different people with different cultures, policies and routines. Managing such multidisciplinary teams poses a number of ongoing challenges, indicating that future research should continue to investigate collaboration performance management in more detail.

Managing performance in a diverse workforce

As the composition of the workforce continues to become more inclusive and diverse, understanding how this dimension affects performance has become an increasingly significant issue for HRM, and a number of organisations across different sectors have begun efforts to understand workforce diversity in relation to performance. Both scholars and practitioners have begun to explore the consequences of increased diversity on work-related outcomes. Indeed, emphasis on diversity and its management has become a primary theme in the public management research literature, with inquiry devoted to diversity management programmes (Kellough and Naff, 2004; Naff and Kellough, 2003), the impact of diversity on performance outcomes (Pitts and Wise, 2004; Pitts, 2005; Wise and Tschirhart, 2000), the status of minority groups in public employment (Lewis and Smithey, 1998), and the role of diversity in public administration education (Pitts and Wise, 2004; Tschirhart and Wise, 2002).

In the USA, for example, Pitts (2009) suggested that almost 90 per cent of federal agencies reported they were actively managing diversity but, despite this high level of interest, there remained little empirical research to test the relationships between diversity management, job satisfaction and work group performance. To address this deficit Pitts (2009) conducted a study among 140,000 federal government employees. His findings indicated that diversity management was positively and significantly related to job satisfaction. The most satisfied employees worked in units where they reported diversity management was strong. His work provides evidence for the argument that it is poor diversity management that is leading some segments of the workforce to be less satisfied with their jobs, rather than the jobs themselves.

The practical implications of his study are clear and direct: diversity management matters. At the organisational level, it means that resources should be devoted to diversity management programmes and training opportunities. Diversity should be viewed as a core competency for all employees, particularly managers. At the suborganisational level, it means that managers who are concerned with the effective management of performance should put time and energy into understanding the different perspectives of employee groups. The man-

479

agers who are likely to be most successful are those who effectively acknowledge and manage the diversity present in their groups. As a field, this means that HR practitioners must view diversity management as a core tool in the toolkit of performance management and should strive to include diversity-related competencies and raise levels of understanding and awareness across the entire organisation.

What features distinguish a diverse workforce and how, if at all, might they affect an organisations approach to managing performance?

Managing performance in an ageing workforce

As we have seen above, effective performance management demands that organisations confront many of the demographic changes occurring in the workforce, such as increasing racial and ethnic diversity, along with greater numbers of women workers. Calo (2008) identifies a further aspect of performance management in the context of diversity, which involves recognising that in many developed economies, the workforce is steadily ageing, a reflection of declining birth rates and the greying of the baby boom generation. Most HR practitioners are vaguely aware that a major demographic shift is about to transform their societies and their companies. The statistics are compelling. For example, in the US the percentage of the workforce between the ages of 55 and 64 is growing faster than any other age group. The situation is described by Strack *et al.* (2008), as being particularly acute in certain industries. In the US energy sector, more than a third of the workforce is already over 50 years old, and that age group is expected to grow by more than 25 per cent by 2020. In Japan, the number of workers over the age of 50 in the financial services sector is projected to rise by 61 per cent between now and then. Indeed, even in an emerging economy like China's, the number of manufacturing workers aged 50 or older will more than double by 2025.

An ageing workforce can also create a mismatch between labour supply and demand, for example, Germany currently faces an immediate shortage of qualified engineering graduates. Experienced engineers are retiring and because engineering ceased to be an attractive career option in the late 1980s, there is a massive shortage of new recruits. In 2006 the country had a deficit of approximately 48,000 engineers and that figure is expected to grow significantly in coming years. At the same time, the country has too many unskilled workers: the unemployment rate of unskilled labour is more than six times higher than that of university graduates and many industrialised countries face similar situations.

In terms of performance management, an ageing workforce has two important HR implications, namely: organisations must ensure the transfer of the valuable knowledge that older workers possess before they retire; and second, organisations must address the issue of how to maintain efficient levels of performance among the older workers while they remain in the organisation.

As the workforce driving the knowledge economy ages, new challenges arise, particularly the risk of a significant loss of valuable knowledge as older workers retire from the workforce. Researchers and practitioners have discussed the importance of knowledge transfer to an organisation's success, and knowledge has become recognised as the most strategically significant resource of organisations. When Drucker (1993) originally alerted organisational leaders to the rise of the knowledge society, he described the radical change in the meaning of knowledge and how knowledge had assumed even greater importance than either capital or labour for nations. O'Dell and Grayson (1998: 6) referred to knowledge management as a broad concept, defining it as 'a conscious strategy of getting the right knowledge to the right people at the right time' and as a way of putting knowledge into action to improve organisational performance. How to transfer knowledge from one person to others or to the broader organisational knowledge base is a challenging aspect of the performance management process because knowledge transfer does not occur spontaneously or naturally. While it is difficult to calculate accurately the financial consequences of losing critical knowledge, the risks certainly include lost productivity, increased errors, and diminished creativity. The essential point, argues Calo (2008), is that organisational leaders need to recognise that once knowledge and expertise have left their organisation, they are difficult to recover, so difficult as to make their recovery unlikely. Knowledgeable older workers will be leaving organisations in record numbers over the coming decade, so before they leave it is imperative that organisations take steps to retain their knowledge. Calo (2008) suggests that conducting a knowledge risk assessment is one such strategy. It would involve all managers within the organisation being tasked with the responsibility of first identifying the at-risk positions, and then of developing a plan to identify a successor, of having an accelerated learning plan for the identified successor, and of facilitating the transfer of knowledge from the incumbent workers to successors. This approach would serve to emphasise the overall institutional commitment to a knowledge transfer process.

As noted above, Calo (2008) has drawn our attention to many of the concerns that have been expressed regarding the risk of the ageing workforce involved in the loss of knowledge from the retirement of the baby boomers and the potential shortage of workers to fill the gaps left by exits from the workforce. A distinct, but related, concern is highlighted here and must be addressed: how to make the best use of older workers who remain in the workforce. Today, the workforce of most organisations has a higher overall age than at any time in history. While many older workers are members of the first wave of baby boomers, the 50–54 age group is the fastest growing segment of the population, and the 45–49 age group is the second fastest growing. The concerns, then, should not be only about the imminent retirement of the first wave of the baby boomers, but that organisations will need to confront many new performance issues as a result of having a larger number of older workers on their payrolls. As Cappelli (2008) advised, managing an ageing workforce is going to be an ongoing and integral component part of an organisation's approach to performance management.

Strack *et al.* (2008) suggest that initiatives that focus on performance management of older workers can help address the implications an ageing workforce has for productivity. They advise that conducting a systematic review of current HR policies and processes could alert the organisation to possible adjustments in a variety of areas to turn age-related challenges into competitive opportunities. The most obvious involves training programmes that help older workers update their skills and leverage their performance. However, in training older workers it is important to remember that one-age-fits-all courses are not necessarily geared to the particular needs, knowledge and strengths of older workers. For example, older manufacturing employees' lack of familiarity with the internet may make typical web-based or blended training programmes unappealing to them.

Another obvious area for performance enhancement is healthcare management. On average, older employees don't become ill more often than younger employees, they just are ill for longer periods. Proactive measures, designed to prevent sickness and injury, can reduce the problem significantly. Such measures should be targeted at employees with a high risk of health problems and tailored to the jobs they do. Strack *et al.* (2008) reviewed RWE's strategy for managing older workers. RWE Power is a German electric power and natural gas public utility based in Essen and is the second largest electricity producer in Germany. Strack *et al.* report that in 2006, RWE Power found that an older workforce reduced performance in production-related job families. To counter this trend it is managing the performance of older workers through personalised work schedules in which shift lengths are tailored to employees' abilities. It is also exploring the possibility of 'lifetime working programmes,' in which employees accumulate credit for overtime hours that can be used to reduce work hours when they are older.

The performance of older workers can also be enhanced through the development of creative performance incentives. For example, Strack *et al.* (2008) suggest older workers might serve as mentors to new workers, which can increase motivation and performance.

Employees with critical knowledge might be offered the chance to return to the company and work on special projects on a freelance basis after they have retired. This latter approach has demonstrated multiple benefits: reducing capacity shortfalls in a crucial job category and keeping valuable knowledge in the company, as well as motivating employees near retirement to perform well so that they will be considered for this post-retirement opportunity.

In summary, performance management of a diverse and ageing workforce is not a passing fad. It is a pressing and competitive priority for all organisations in this era of rapid demographic and social change.

What features distinguish an ageing workforce and how, if at all, might these affect an organisation's approach to managing performance?

Managing performance in a volunteer workforce

Volunteers are the lifeblood of many non-profit organisations. Non-profit organisations have traditionally relied on volunteers to perform crucial agency functions. As staffing costs continue to rise, and as job seekers continue to look for valuable experience, non-profits will continue to rely more heavily on volunteers and other unpaid staff than do their for-profit counterparts. To put this into context, Cilenti *et al.* (2007) estimate that in the United States in 2000, adult volunteers devoted 15.5 billion hours of time to non-profit organisations throughout the nation, representing a total dollar value of $239 billion in volunteer time. Between September 2004 and September 2005, more than 65 million people did some kind of volunteer work, up from 59.8 million people in 2002.

The author of this article contends that well-managed non-profits have become expert at several crucial components of running a successful organisation, and can serve as examples to the for-profit sector. In short, non-profits often have well-defined, unwavering missions; they make wise use of their board of directors as a resource; and they seem to know a lot about managing paid employees and volunteers. Geber (1991) suggests that because volunteers often come from the ranks of the employees it is vital to give them meaningful work that suits their level of expertise. This involves matching the volunteer's skills to an available position, preparing detailed job or project descriptions to facilitate a fast, thorough orientation, giving them high-quality but streamlined on-the-job training, and providing formal performance appraisals, while also offering less formal forms of feedback and recognition. Although these approaches may not sound much different from those that should be used with any paid employee, the importance of keeping volunteers satisfied and fulfilled with their assigned work, the necessity of expediency in their orientation and training, and the significance of giving recognition to their contribution accentuate the importance of these elements.

Performance Managing Volunteers at the CIPD

The Chartered Institute of Personnel and Development (CIPD), the professional lead body for all HRM practitioners, relies extensively on the use of volunteers to maintain the branch network and to operate as directors on the National Executive Board. In June 2008, under the Executive Leadership of Robin Jordan, the CIPD developed a series of competencies required at board level for all directors. In line with best performance management practice the competencies are regularly reviewed and currently comprise:

- *Strategic direction*: the ability to contribute to setting the vision, values and purpose for CIPD, and ensure CIPD has the resources – people and financial – to achieve its goals. A person with the ability to think and plan ahead strategically.

- *Business judgement*: the ability to weigh evidence and analyse ideas before reaching an independent and objective conclusion, including an understanding of financial information at a complex business level; also the ability to assimilate information quickly and effectively.

- *Governance*: the ability to ensure that the CIPD is managed with integrity and probity, and bring those qualities and independence of mind to the role.

- *Relationships*: the ability to work supportively and build team cohesiveness with fellow board members and executive management colleagues, while at the same time, constructively probing, challenging and adding value to the strategic direction, decision making and performance of CIPD.

The unique aspect of how the CIPD manage their volunteers at director level is that each volunteer board director has a 'conversation with purpose'. This is essentially a structured performance appraisal with the Chair. Whilst acknowledging the voluntary nature of Board appointments, the principles associated with good governance suggest that this 'conversation with a purpose' involves:

- The opportunity for at least an annual meeting between the Chair and each director. (Opting out of the annual meeting is possible, except where the director indicates an intention to seek re-election.)

- The meeting is a two-way conversation, with opportunity to discuss the contribution of the director and the Chair.

- Three areas should be covered: constructive feedback; aspirations for other roles or re-election; development needs:

  (i) *Constructive feedback*
  - consider examples to illustrate contributions made and behaviours apparent;
  - demonstrates appropriate preparation, attendance and commitment;
  - provides valuable input to board meetings;
  - asks demanding questions of the executive team;
  - challenges others constructively within the board;
  - contributes to strategy and policy discussion;
  - involved in promoting the work of the CIPD outside board meetings;
  - additional inputs in relation to feedback to the Chair may include management of board agendas;
  - encouragement and participation of board members.

  (ii) *Aspirations for other roles*
  - What aspirations or potential have you considered for another role on the board or its subcommittees?
  - Are you considering a second term (if applicable)? If so how do you meet the current requirements for non-executive directors?

  (iii) *Development needs*
  - What personal development would be appropriate and how might it be achieved?
  - How might the board's development be addressed?

- A record of the meeting is held by both the director and the Chair, to be used in subsequent discussions and within the context of succession and development planning.

The 'conversations with a purpose' have aided effective performance management by clearly establishing the requirements of the role the volunteer is committing to. The conversations have the benefit of providing a formal opportunity for the volunteer board director to discuss with the Chair their performance and contribution, needs and aspirations and development plans. This serves to ensure the volunteer is aware of their role and is able to fulfil the requirements satisfactorily. In this respect Robin Jordan, the retiring Chair suggested managing volunteers is no different from managing salaried staff, there is a role to be performed and there is an expectation about the way in which it will be undertaken. He said: 'There are roles and responsibilities and volunteers have a duty to undertake the performance of their work as effectively as possible.' In the approach to managing the performance of volunteers adopted by the CIPD, the level of support available from the host organisation is the same for volunteers and their needs and career aspiration are taken just as seriously as those of paid staff.

Managing the performance of volunteers is a vital part of managing organisational performance. The innovative, creative and responsive approach adopted by the CIPD is a role model for many organisations who will increasingly rely on the contributions and effort of non-paid associates.

In summary, the following points are advised when managing volunteers:

- Understand individuals' motivations;
- Find the right fit;
- Manage the relationship with full-time staff;
- Match roles to talents;
- Implement best practices;
- Keep volunteers in the loop.

 STOP and think

To what extent do you agree with Robin Jordan, the retiring Chair of the National Executive of the CIPD, that managing volunteers is the same as managing paid staff?

Conclusion

This chapter has focused on performance management. It has demonstrated how our understanding and appreciation of the difference between performance measurement and performance management has evolved over the years. It has demonstrated that despite a growing understanding of the limitations of performance appraisal, it remains one of the most widely employed approaches in the contemporary management of employees. The critique related to operational limitations – referring to manifestations such as rater bias, the recency effect and the tendency for raters to award grades in the middle of the scale to avoid overt conflict with the appraisee or to mitigate potential accusations concerning their own poor management techniques – a poor employee indicates a poor manager. The critiques also reflected the multiple and often conflicting applications to which appraisals are applied – and highlighted the inherent tensions of using essentially the same process to achieve different outcomes, for example, some are related to pay and development while others are related just to development. However, the growing awareness of possible limitations has hastened the search for alternatives, and the advent of 360-degree appraisal is possibly one such solution.

The application of technology is likely to hasten the evolution still further. The ability of organisations to undertake covert surveillance of workers by monitoring how long they take to process a particular piece of work or complete a call in a call centre leaves a hollow and cautious 'Big Brother' feel to some of the approaches to measurement techniques currently being developed. Concerns over the ethical probity of monitoring the work of employees so closely and of managers being in a position of such authenticated power left some commentators feeling rather nervous and just a little sceptical about the motivations behind performance appraisal to control human behaviour, thoughts and actions. While such fears may have some justification, there is a danger of underestimating employees' ability to influence the appraisal process and casting the manager as despot and villain – almost without trial.

Caution is needed here, because if we truly subscribe to the idea that effective HRM can lead to a genuine level of employee engagement and commitment, the desires, aims and objectives of the managers and the workers and their employment relationship ceases to be one characterised by antagonistic objectives, underpinned by adversarial and conflicting tensions and becomes one in which mutuality, trust and respect prevail. In such circumstances, any power held by the manager would be used to further consolidate the effectiveness of the working relationship – rather than jeopardise it by trying to subvert the worker or manipulate them through covert surveillance techniques. Performance appraisal does have the potential to be misused, but it also has the potential to help the development and career opportunities of many employees. In many respects it appears that the jury is still out, with the culture of the organisation perhaps being the single biggest factor to influence the direction of the path followed.

The chapter observed a trend in the extension of performance management from that concerned solely with individual employees to an approach that embraced the whole organisation. In this context, attention was drawn to the way in which organisational structures and operating boundaries are shifting, and bring new demands and a need for new ways of approaching performance management. Working across cultures and between collaborating organisations requires the effective management of knowledge and the ability to translate organisational visions into clear measurable outcomes that define success, and are shared throughout the organisation with customers and stakeholders. This emerging perspective on performance management continues the shift from prescriptive, audit- and compliance-based oversight to an ongoing, forward-looking strategic partnership. Managing the performance of older workers and the performance of volunteers were reviewed in the chapter and served to demonstrate the extent to which the management of performance will increasingly become an organisation focused rather than an individual-focused activity. For further evidence of this trend one only needs to review the press and observe the extent to which organisations are increasingly concerned with the effective management of their performance within society and within the community. The ability to demonstrate an active engagement with the corporate social responsibility agenda is growing rapidly. Perhaps therefore, in the future, performance management will be less about quantifying the output of individual employees and more about the effective performance of the organisation in society.

Summary

- There are differences between performance measurement and performance appraisal.
- Approaches to performance measurement are typically represented in a performance appraisal process.
- Performance appraisal has limitations which result in part resulting from the many competing aims it seeks to achieve.
- The ethics of probity of performance appraisal has been questioned and represented as a management tool which enables managers to monitor and engage in constant surveillance of their employees.
- Information and communication technology will change the nature and scope of performance management.

- Effective performance management will need to address changes in organisational structure and composition, in particular in relation to an increasingly global and competitive market, a diverse and ageing workforce and to manage a rising number of volunteer workers.

- In the future, performance management will be less about individual performance and more about the performance of the organisation as a world player and social partner with a conscience.

Questions

1 What are the organisational advantages and limitations of performance measurement?

2 For what reason has performance appraisal has been so severely critiqued?

3 What role do you envisage for ICT in the management of performance, are there any associated risks?

4 What are the theoretical links between HRM and performance appraisal?

5 What new challenges will organisations face in managing performance in the years to come?

6 What factors would you take into account if you were designing an approach to performance management?

Case study

Performance-based reward at DIY Stores

DIY Stores (DIYS) is a chain of large warehouse-style stores selling DIY equipment, self assembly furniture, plumbing appliances and garden tools. It is a wholly-owned subsidiary of a larger retail group and is ranked in the top five in terms of its UK market share. Its annual turnover exceeds £50 million and its annual profits are around £1million. DIYS currently runs 250 stores across the country, serves over a million customers a week and employs 12,000 people.

In response to a slight fall in market share over the past year, the board of directors has recently produced a new company mission statement. High on the list of core aims for the coming two years is the desire to substantially improve efficiency and performance levels. Ambitious targets have been set, and statements issued about the need to create a more dynamic, performance-focused corporate culture. Reform of the existing approach to performance management in DIYS is now very much on the agenda.

The present approach is well established and clearly understood by all DIYS employees. It is distinguished by the emphasis it places on the role of the store manager (i.e. the general managers responsible for running each of the 250 stores). Store managers are rewarded with a standard package of terms and conditions which is noticeably more generous than that offered to other managers and staff. In addition to the basic salary they enjoy a range of benefits (including private health care and additional holiday), the right to purchase share options and substantial discounts on products sold by DIYS and its parent company. In addition, they each receive an annual, individual, performance-related pay (PRP) award dependent on the extent to which their stores meet pre-agreed targets.

Performance objectives are all specific and measurable, being made up of targets in five categories:

- target increase in total store takings (e.g. 5% over the year)
- target reduction in stock loss (e.g. 7% over the year)
- target increase in average spend per customer (e.g. £3.00)
- target improvement in product availability (e.g. to 97%)
- target increase in customer care (e.g. by 10%).

This last measure is determined by the scores awarded to each store by 'mystery shoppers' employed by the company to visit stores incognito.

Other members of staff, including managers below store manager level, receive a considerably less generous reward package and no performance-based reward. Managers are expected to raise performance levels and achieve their targets through effective supervision, 'pats on the back' and, where necessary, the application of disciplinary measures. For senior staff, the expectation of promotion into a store manager role has for long been used as the main method of motivation.

A number of criticisms have been made of existing performance management arrangements. The most important are:

1 Managers working below store manager level can improve their financial position only through promotion. Those who are performing very effectively in their present roles and have no interest in promotion are not properly rewarded for their efforts. This leads to dissatisfaction and avoidable staff turnover. There is also a failure to maximise performance among this group.

2 Store managers are limited in the range of performance-management techniques available to them to apply within their stores. No financial incentives can be given, beyond a few pounds in the form of 'employee of the month' prizes and small gifts at Christmas. This means that managers have to rely on close supervision and the use of disciplinary approaches in order to achieve their targets. The result is de-motivated staff, high employee turnover and a low-trust employee relations culture.

3 Store managers themselves, because of the way the PRP system works, are encouraged to focus wholly on the performance of their own stores. Overall corporate performance is of less interest to them, as is the performance of their regional divisions. Indeed, there is huge competition between store managers in each locality, leading to situations in which they fail to co-operate with one another. Ideas are rarely shared and there is resistance to transferring staff from one store to another to cover sickness and holidays. More damaging is the tendency to hold on to stock, even when other stores have run short due to unexpected high demand.

Source: from CIPD case study site, with the permission of the publisher, the Chartered Institute of Personnel and Development, London (www.cipd.co.uk).

Your task

What changes would you suggest should be made to the established performance management and reward procedures? How would you justify the changes you have recommended if asked to do so at a presentation to the board of directors?

References and further reading

Adair, C., Simpson, L., Birdsell, J., Omelchuk, K., Casebeer, A., Gardiner, H., Newman, S., Beckjie, A. and Clelland, S. (2003) *Performance Measurement Systems in Health Care Services: Models, Practices and Effectiveness*. Alberta: The Alberta Heritage Foundation for Medical Research.

Amaratunga, D. and Baldry, D. (2002) 'Moving from performance measurement to performance management', *Facilities*, 20: 217–23.

Armstrong, M. and Baron, A. (1998) *Performance Management: The New Realistic*. London: IPD.

Armstrong, M. and Baron, A. (2004) *Managing Performance: Performance Management in Action*. London: CIPD.

Armstrong, M. and Baron, A. (2005) *Managing Performance: Performance Management in Action* London: CIPD.

Aswathappa, K. (2005) *Human Resource and Personal Management: Text and Cases*, 4th edn. Delhi: Tata McGraw-Hill.

Bach, S. (2005) *Managing Human Resources: Personnel Management in Transition*, 4th edn. Oxford: Blackwell.

Bentham, J. (1995) *The Panopticon Writings*, (ed. M Bozovic). London: Verso.

Bititci, U., Martinez, V., Albores, P. and Parung, J. (2004) 'Creating and maintaining value in collaborative networks', *International Journal of Physical Distribution and Logistics Management*, 34: 251–68.

Björkman, I. and Budhwar, P. (2007) 'When in Rome …?', *Employee Relations*, 29: 595–610.

Boselie, P., Dietz, G. and Boon, C. (2005) 'Commonalities and contradictions in HRM and performance research', *Human Resource Management Journal*, 15: 67–94.

Boselie, P., Paauwe, J. and Jansen, P. (2001) 'Human resource management and performance: lessons from the Netherlands', *International Journal of Human Resource Management*, 12: 1107–25.

Boxall, P. and Purcell, J. (2008) *Strategy and Human Resource Management*. Basingstoke: Palgrave Macmillan.

Bourgon, J. (2008) 'Performance management: it's the results that count', *Asian Pacific Journal of Public Administration*, 30, 1: 41–58.

Budhwar, P., Varma, A., Singh, V. and Dhar, R. (2006) 'HRM systems of Indian call centers in India: an exploratory study', *International Journal of Human Resource Management*, 17, 5: 881–97.

Burgess, T., Gules, H. and Tekin, M. (1997) 'Supply chain collaboration and success in technology implementation', *Integrated Manufacturing Systems*, 8: 323–32.

Busi, M. and Bititci, U. (2006) 'Collaborative performance management: present gaps and future research', *International Journal of Productivity and Performance Management*, 55: 7–25.

Callahan, K. (2007) *Elements of Effective Governance: Measurement, Accountability and Participation* New York: CRC Press: Taylor Francis.

Calo, T. (2008). 'Talent management in the era of the aging workforce: the critical role of knowledge transfer', *Public Personnel Management*, 37, 4: 403–41.

Cappelli, R. (2008) 'Talent management for the twenty-first century', *Harvard Business Review*, 86: 74–81

Chand, M. and Katou, A. (2007) 'Human resource management: organisational performance; Hotel and Catering Industry, India', *Employee Relations*, 29: 576–94.

Cilenti, M., Guggenheimer, E. and Kramnick, R. (2007) *The Volunteer Workforce: Legal Issues and Best Practices for Non-profits*. New York: Lawyers Alliance for New York.

CIPD (2009a) *Fact Sheet on Performance Appraisal*. Wimbledon: CIPD.

CIPD (2009b) *Fact Sheet on Performance Management*. Wimbledon: CIPD.

Den-Hartog, D., Boselie, P. and Paauwe, J. (2004) 'Performance management: a model and research agenda', *Applied Psychology: An International Review*, 53: 556–69.

DeNisi, A. (ed.) (2000) *Performance Appraisal and Performance Management: A Multilevel Analysis*. San Francisco, CA: Jossey-Bass.

Drucker, P. (1999) *The Practice of Management*, Oxford: Butterworth-Heinemann.

Drucker, R. (1993) 'The rise of the knowledge society', *Wilson Quarterly*, 17: 52–69.

Eccles, R. (1991) 'The performance measurement manifesto', *Harvard Business Review*, 69, 1: 131–37.

Edwards, P. and Wright, M. (2001) 'High-involvement work systems and performance outcomes: the strength of variable, contingent and context-bound relationships', *International Journal of Human Resource Management*, 12, 4: 568–85

Fawcett, S. and Magnan, G. (2002) 'The rhetoric and reality of supply chain integration', *International Journal of Physical Distribution and Logistics Management*, 32: 339–61.

Ferris, G., Arthur, M., Berkson, H., Kaplan, D., Harell-Cook, G. and Frink, D. (1998) 'Toward a social context theory of the human resource management–organization effectiveness relationship', *Human Resource Management Review*, 8: 235–64.

Findlay, P. and Newton, T. (1998) 'Re-framing Foucault: the case of performance appraisal', in P. Findlay and T. Newton (eds) *Foucault, Management and Organization Theory*. London: Sage.

Fletcher, C, (2001) 'Performance appraisal and management: the developing research agenda', *Journal of Occupational and Organisational Psychology*, 74: 473–88.

Foucault, M. (1977) *Discipline & Punish: The Birth of the Prison*. London: Penguin Books.

Geber, B. (1991) 'Managing Volunteers', *Training*, 28: 21–26.

Geddes, D. and Konrad, A. (2003) 'Demographic differences and reactions to performance feedback', *Human Relations*, 56: 1485– 514.

Grey, C. (1994) 'Career as a project of the self and labour process discipline', *Sociology*, 28: 479–97.

Guest, D. (1997) 'Human resource management and performance: a review and research agenda', *Journal of Human Resource Management*, 8: 263–76.

Guest, D. (2000) 'Human resource management, employee well-being and organizational performance', in D. Guest (ed.) *CIPD Professional Standards Conference 11th July*. Keele: Keele University.

Hall, L. (2004) 'HRM practices and employee and organizational performance: a critique of the research and guest's model', Department of Business and Management discussion paper No. 5. Manchester: Manchester Metropolitan University.

Harris, C. Cortvriend, P. and Hyde, P. (2007) 'Human resource management and performance in healthcare organizations', *Journal of Health and Organization Management*, 21: 448–59.

Heslin, P. Carson, J. and VandeWalle, D. (2009) 'Practical applications of goal setting theory to performance management', in J.W. Smither *Performance Management: Putting Research into Practice*. San Francisco, CA: Jossey Bass, pp. 89–114.

Holmberg, S. (2000) 'A system perspective on supply chain management', *International Journal of Physical Distribution and Logistics Management*, 30: 847–68.

Huselid, M. (1995) 'The impact of human resource management practices on turnover, productivity and corporate financial performance. *Academy of Management Journal*, 38: 635–70.

Hyde, P., Boaden, R. Cortvriend, P. Harris, C., Marchington, M., Sparrow, P. and Sibbald, B. (2006) *Improving Health Through Human Resource Management*. London: CIPD.

Industrial RS (2003a) 'Time to talk – how and why employers conduct appraisals', *Employment Trends*, 769: 8–14.

Johnson, H. and Kaplan, R. (1987) *Relevance Lost: The Rise and Fall of Management Accounting*. Boston, MA: Harvard Business School Press.

Kaplan, R. and Norton, D. (1992) 'The balanced scorecard – measures that drive performance', *Harvard Business Review*, 70, 1: 79–80.

Kaplan, R. and Norton, D. (1996) 'Using the balanced scorecard as a strategic management system', *Harvard Business Review*, January/February: 75–85.

Katou, A. and Budhwar, P. (2006) 'Human resource management systems and organisational performance: a test of a mediating model in the Greek manufacturing context', *The International Journal of Human Resource Management*, 17: 1223–53.

Katou, A. and Budhwar, P. (2007) 'The effect of human resource management policies on organizational performance in Greek manufacturing firms', *Thunderbird International Business Review*, 49: 1–35.

Kellough, J. and Naff, K. (2004) 'Responding to a wake-up call: an examination of Federal Agency diversity management programs', *Administration & Society*, 36: 62–90.

Kersley, B., Alpin, C., Bewley, H., Dix, G. and Oxenbridge, S. (2006) *Inside the Workplace: Findings from the 2004 Workplace Employment Relations Survey*. London: Routledge.

Latham, G. and Locke, E. (1984) *Goal Setting: A Motivational Technique that Works*. Englewood Cliffs, NJ: Prentice-Hall.

Legge, K. (1995) *Human Resource Management Rhetorics and Realities*. Basingstoke Macmillan.

Lewis, G. Smithey, P. (1998) 'Gender, race, and training in the Federal Civil Service', *Public Administration Quarterly*, 22: 204–08.

Locke, E. (1966) 'The relationship of intentions to level of performance' *Journal of Applied Psychology*, 50: 60–88.

Locke, E. and Latham, G. (1990) 'Work motivation and satisfaction: light at the end of the tunnel', *Psychological Science*, 1: 240–6.

Locke, E. and Latham, G. (2002) 'Building a practically useful theory of goal setting and task motivation: a 35-year odyssey', *American Psychologist*, 57: 705–17.

Longenecker, C. and Fink, L. (1997) 'Keys to designing and running an effective performance appraisal system: lessons learned', *Journal of Compensation and Benefits*, 13: 28–35.

Longnecker, C. and Fink, L. (2001) 'Improving management performance in rapidly changing organisations', *Journal of Management Development*, 20, 1: 7–18.

Longnecker, C. Simonetti, J. and Sharkey, T. (1999) 'Why organizations fail: the view from the front line', *Management Decision*, 15: 503–13.

Lynch, R. and Cross, K. (1991) *Measure Up! Yardstick for Continuous Improvement*. Cambridge, MA: Blackwell Business.

MacDuffie, J. (1995) 'Human resource bundles and manufacturing performance: flexible production systems in the world auto industry', *Industrial Relations and Labour Review*, 48: 197–221.

McGregor, D. (1957) 'An uneasy look at performance appraisals', *Harvard Business Review*, 5: 89–95.

Miller, P. and Rose, N. (1990) 'Governing economic life', *Economy and Society*, 19: 1–31.

Mondy, R., Noe, R. and Premeaux, S. (2002) *Human Resource Management*, 8th edn. Upper Saddle River, NJ: Prentice-Hall.

Naff, K. and Kellough, E. (2003) 'Ensuring employment equity: are federal programs making a difference?', *International Journal of Public Administration*, 26: 1307–36.

Neary, D.B. (2002) 'Creating a company-wide, on-line, performance management system', *Human Resource Management*, 41: 491–98.

Newbold, C. (2008) '360-degree appraisals are now a classic', *Human Resource Management International Digest*, 16: 38–40.

Newton, T. and Findley, P. (1996) 'Playing God: the performance of appraisal', *Human Resource Management Journal*, 6: 42–58.

Newton, T. (1994) 'Discourse and agency: the example of personnel psychology and assessment centers', *Organization Studies*, 15: 879–902.

O'Dell, C. and Grayson, C. (1998) *If Only We Knew What We Know*. New York: Free Press.

Patterson, K., Grimm, C. and Thomas, M. (2003) 'Adopting new technologies for supply chain management', *Transportation Research Part E*, 39: 95–121.

Patterson, M., West, M., Lawthom, R. and Nickell, S. (1997) *The Impact of People Management on Business Performance*. London: IPD.

Pitts, D. (2005) 'Diversity, representation, and performance: evidence about race and ethnicity in public organizations', *Journal of Public Administration Research and Theory*, 15: 615–31.

Pitts, D. (2009) 'Diversity management, job satisfaction, and performance: evidence from U.S. federal agencies', *Public Administration Review*, 69: 328–39.

Pitts, D. and Wise, L. (2004) 'Diversity in professional schools: a case study of public affairs and law', *Journal of Public Affairs Education*, 10: 142–60.

Procurement Executives Association (1999) *Guide to a Balanced Scorecard Performance Management Methodology*. Procurement Executives' Association. Available at **http://management.energy.gov/documents/BalancedScorecardsPerfAndMeth.pdf**.

Purcell, J. 'Sustaining the HR and performance link in difficult times', University of Bath. **http://www.bath.ac.uk/werc/pdf/toughCIPD_8_02.pdf**, accessed 3 June 2009.

Richardson, R. and Thompson, M. (1999) 'The impact of people management practices on business performance: a literature review', in CIPD *Issues in People Management*. London: CIPD.

Roberts, I. (2001) 'Reward and performance management', in I. Beardwell and L. Holden (eds) *Human Resource Management: A Contemporary Approach*, Harlow: FT/Prentice-Hall, pp 506–58.

Schuler, R. and Jackson, S. (1987) 'Linking competitive strategies with human resource management practices', *Academy of Management Executive*, 1: 207–19.

Schuler, R. and Jackson, S. (1999) *Strategic Human Resource Management: A Reader*. London: Blackwell.

Sipor, J. and Ward, B. (1995) 'The ethical and legal quandary of email privacy', *Communications of the Association for Computing Machinery*, 38: 8–54.

Stanton, J. (2000) 'Reactions to employee performance monitoring: framework, review and research directions', *Human Performance*, 13, 1: 85–113.

Strack, R., Baier, J. and Fahlander, A. (2008) 'Managing demographic risk', *Harvard Business Review*, 86: 119–28.

Taylor, F. (1911) *The Principles of Scientific Management*. New York, NY: W.W. Norton. Published in Norton Library 1967 by arrangement with Harper & Row, Publishers, Inc.

Thornton III G. and Rupp, D. (2007) *Assessment Centers in Human Resource Management: Strategies for Prediction, Diagnosis and Development*. London: Taylor & Francis.

Thorpe, R. (2004) 'The characteristics of performance management research, implication and challenges', *International Journal of Productivity and Performance Management*, 53: 334–44.

Townley, B. (1993a) 'Foucault, power/knowledge and its relevance for HRM', *Academy of Management Review*, 18: 518–45.

Townley, B. (1993b) 'Performance appraisal and the emergence of management', *Journal of Management Studies*, 36: 287–306.

Townley, B. (1994) *Reframing Human Resources Management: Power, Ethics and the Subject at Work*. London: Sage.

Townley, B. (1997) 'The institutional logic of performance appraisal', *Organization Studies* 18: 261–85.

Tschirhart, M. and Wise, L. (2002) 'Responding to a diverse class: insights from seeing a course as an organization', *Journal of Public Affairs Education*, 8: 165–77.

Waggoner, D., Neely, A. and Kennerley, M. (1999) 'The forces that shape organizational performance measurement systems: an interdisciplinary review', *International Journal of Production Economics*, 60: 53–60.

Wilson, F. (2002) 'Dilemmas of appraisal', *European Management Journal*, 20: 620–29.

Wise, L. and Tschirhart, M. (2000) 'Examining empirical evidence on diversity effects: how useful is diversity research for public sector managers?', *Public Administration Review*, 60: 286–395.

For multiple-choice questions, exercises and annotated weblinks related to this topic, visit **www.pearsoned.co.uk/mymanagementlab**.

Chapter 13

Employee reward

Amanda Thompson and Alan J. Ryan

Objectives

- To present the historical and theoretical foundations underpinning contemporary employee reward practice.
- To define employee reward and identify the key components of reward.
- To explore the concept of reward management and the benefits and difficulties associated with introducing a strategic approach to reward.
- To consider key employee reward choices facing organisations.
- To explore the economic and legal context for reward and the implications for employee reward practice.
- To identify the internal/organisational factors affecting organisational approaches to reward and the influence of sector.
- To consider key choices and emergent trends in terms of establishing pay levels, designing pay structures and determining criteria for pay progression.

Introduction

This chapter identifies and discusses developments in employee reward and considers the practical ways in which reward management can be used, as part of a suite of human resource practices, to elicit employee engagement and drive individual and organisational performance. The chapter traces the historical path of reward, focusing initially on the nature of the wage–effort bargain and previous, somewhat limited approaches to reward, revolving principally around the key construct of pay. The chapter then moves to identify and explore the meaning of reward in the contemporary setting, focusing upon reward as a potential strategic lever which can be used by organisations to orient individuals and teams in the direction of business goals and values. The overarching themes of the remainder of the chapter concern the economic and legal environment for reward and the challenges associated with designing a reward strategy that is affordable, equitable and relevant. Embedded within these themes, emphasis is placed on pragmatic reward choices and dilemmas experienced by organisations in the twenty-first century, including decisions about the relative importance of internal equity and external pay comparability, the role of job evaluation, the factors which tend to be influential in shaping the reward 'mix', where to pitch pay and how to design pay structures and manage pay progression.

The historical and theoretical foundations of employee reward

We now outline and examine the extent to which human resource management (HRM) has developed current practical and theoretical issues surrounding the management of reward systems within modern organisations. A critical element of these discussions is the management of structures and strategies. This chapter introduces the notion of reward(s) as a central function in the development of a strategic role for HR functionaries and offers some explanation of the objectives of current reward management structures, strategies and systems.

'There's only one reason we come here – the money' has not been an unusual comment heard from employees in all organisations since the period of industrialisation. Such comments echo the nature of the employment relationship as a reward/effort bargain (Chapter 11). Whether openly, covertly, personally or collectively, we all become involved in the resolution of this bargain at some time during our working life. This chapter discusses how management have resolved and continue to resolve their problem of converting the labour potential, obtained by their transactions in the labour market, into the labour performance they desire; simply securing the required effort levels without rewarding at levels detrimental to the generation of sufficient profit. In this sense we view reward as a core function for HR managers and rewards as composed of more than the mere 'notes' in the pay packet. Terms such as 'pay', 'compensation' and 'remuneration' are all recognisable expressions, but as we argue below 'reward' is something qualitatively different in that the issues covered encompass both financial and non-financial benefits.

The development of reward systems

As a distinctive concern for managerial functionaries, the topic of reward is a recent addition, indeed it is fair to say that reward management has often been viewed as the 'poor relation'. Within the early labour management literature, it was discussed in terms of the management of figures and procedures (Urwick, 1958; Yates, 1937). Such discussions clearly view 'reward' as solely a matter of financial benefits (wage/effort) rather than including consideration of the non-financial benefits. We can argue from this initial analysis that during the development of a 'factory-based' system, in the late nineteenth/early twentieth centuries, it appears wage, rather than effort, was the central concern. Further that this period was accompanied by a system within which owners frequently found difficulty in securing consistent levels of control of the effort side of the bargain (Hinton, 1986; Lovell, 1977; Zeitlin, 1983). Employees, who were until that time self-controlled and in many respects driven by subsistence needs, had worked in small 'cottage' industries within which the product of labour was owned by the producers (workers themselves; notably in regard to the skilled artisans) and they worked only as hard as necessary in order to meet their subsistence needs. As Anthony suggests, 'A great deal of the ideology of work is directed at getting men [sic] to take work seriously when they know that it is a joke' (1977: 5).

Owners found that getting workers to keep regular hours and to commit the effort owners considered to constitute 'a fair day's work' was problematic. In response to this dilemma they employed the 'butty' system of wage management. Under this system, owners committed a specific level of investment to a selected group of workers (normally skilled artisans) who then hired labour on 'spot contracts' by the day. The major problem for the owners with this system was that these 'subcontractors' had control over the effort/reward bargain and were able to enrich themselves at the expense of the owners. The owners enjoyed little or no control over the process of production so the system was economically inefficient and failed to deliver the returns (rents/profits) required or more importantly the returns that were possible from the process of industrialisation.

From this group of 'favoured' workers, along with the introduction of some university grad-uates there grew a new management cadre. This was a slow process, Gospel notes that generally, in UK industry, this group (management, technical and clerical) amounted to only 8.6 per cent of the workforce in most manufacturing organisations by the start of the First World War (1992: 17). It can be further argued that even within these organisations the development of a dedicated, specialised managerial function was uneven and patchy. These changes did little to address the problems associated with the wage/effort bargain, meaning productivity was below optimum levels. A key component in these problems was that they were underpinned by the actuality that 'the managers' brain was still under the workers' cap', or more precisely that these new managers rarely possessed the skills or knowledge of the production process held by the workers. This led to lower than optimum levels of production and reduced profits, a system F.W. Taylor described as 'systematic soldiering'. This activity was engaged in by workers, accord-ing to Taylor, 'with the deliberate object of keeping their employers ignorant of how fast work can be done' (Taylor, 1964: 74). From his observations Taylor took the view that workers acting in this manner were merely behaving as 'economically rational actors' desiring their own best interests. It was clear therefore that management needed to take the reins of the production process and reclaim their right to determine the outcome of the wage/effort bargain.

Taylor, as the so-called 'father of scientific management', developed a system of measuring work, which assisted the process of reclaiming managerial rights. Jobs were broken down into specific elements which could then be timed and rated, whilst in the process, returning the determination of the speed of work to management and allowing for the development of pay systems which reflected, however crudely, performance. This scientific system devised by Taylor became the basis of countless pay systems operating effectively alongside the routinisation and deskilling of work which is often associated with scientific management within the literature (see, for example, Braverman, 1974; Burawoy, 1985; Hill, 1981; Littler, 1982, 1985; Thompson, 1983; Wood, 1982). Whilst this allowed management to reassert their control over the level of outputs, to relocate the managers' brain under their own hats and hence the determination of the wage/effort bargain, it did generate problems in relation to managerial attempts to convince workers to take work seriously. In straightforward terms we can suggest that the 'measured-work' techniques advocated by adherents of Taylorism further separated conception from execution and led to feelings of alienation. Alienation can be defined as 'various social or psychological evils which are characterized by a harmful separ-ation, disruption or fragmentation which sunders things that properly belong together' (Wood, 2000: 24); in our terms that means the separation of workers from that which they produce. Blauner (1964) argued that such an objective state is created as an offshoot of the subjective feelings of separation which workers experience under modern production sys-tems. These feelings and their outcomes can be briefly outlined in the following manner:

- *Powerlessness*: the inability to exert control over work processes.
- *Meaninglessness*: the lack of a sense of purpose as employees only concentrated on a nar-rowly defined and repetitive task and therefore could not relate their role to the overall production process and end product.
- '*Self-estrangement*': the failure to become involved in work as a mode of self-expression.
- *Isolation*: the lack of sense of belonging (adapted from Blauner, 1964).

Although scientific management originated at the beginning of the twentieth century, its legacy has lived on in many areas. Similar experiences have been reported in the design of work in service industries and call centres (Ritzer, 1997, 2000; Taylor and Bain, 1999; Taylor and Bain, 2001; Callaghan and Thompson, 2001). The solution to this problem has been sought, following Taylor's notion of man as an economic actor, by the introduction of vari-ous reward systems and mechanisms, the core objectives of which were originally to operationalise effective control over the wage/effort bargain and later with current systems to alleviate the feelings of alienation and generate commitment to organisational goals.

In this regard it is possible to argue that such reward systems are not designed in the 'perfect world' that some commentators have imagined. Rather they are controlled by various external and internal stimuli and operate within a complex landscape. These incentives or pressures can be broken down and identified in simple terms which highlight some of the more complex debates we address within this chapter. In no particular order, we can see that they include the ability of the organisation to pay, which in the current times of financial restraint and turbulence is greatly reduced. To this we can add the bargaining strength – both internally and more widely – of trades unions. Whilst the decline in trade union membership alongside the rise in non-union forms of representation (Dundon and Rollinson, 2004; Gollan 2007), and the increased importance of small firms (Marlow *et al.*, 2005) especially within the private sector, may have weakened such power there are still sectors within the economy where organisations have to make a judgement about the residual power available to trade unions. Such residual power is also a dynamic force behind moves to maintain differentials in line with existing custom and practice. A further element in this consideration is the wider increase in the 'cost of living' which places strains on both the employer and the employees. This is not ameliorated by the recent period of rapid technological change which has influenced labour markets and available skills patterns. Whilst organisational and technological change may have increased productivity, and hence arguably created increased profits, employers must decide what percentage of such increases can be used to develop wage systems which reflect current effort (see the discussion below on new pay). These pressures have been crystallised into three main features which affect the quantity given:

- labour market pressures – supply and demand;
- product markets – competition and demand;
- organisational factors – sector, technology and size (Milkovitch and Newman, 1996).

These consideration lead to a discussion of the extent to which employers can develop, design, and control reward systems in an ever-changing (some would say globalised) economy.

Design and debates

Whilst this chapter often discusses reward systems in a manner which appears to offer a chronological explanation, we would note that the development of a 'new' system does not indicate the total removal of other older mechanisms. Evidence suggests that in many modern organisations we continue to find both 'old' and 'new' pay systems operating in tandem, delivering control on different levels for various groups of workers (Armstrong and Brown, 2006; Armstrong and Stephens, 2005).

In terms of the types of reward mechanism applied, we can note the application of a number of different mechanisms based on 'time worked'. Time rates are mechanisms whereby reward is related to the number of hours worked and are often applied to manual workers in the form of hourly rates and non-manual workers by the application of monthly or annual salaries. In the past, these rates were set in a number of ways which relied on the power of employers to unilaterally lay down the appropriate amount, by statutory enactment, or by collective bargaining. Employer discretion has been limited in a number of ways by the introduction of statutory rules and regulations ranging from the Truck Acts, enacted in the mid nineteenth century which required payment in cash – an attempt to prevent the misuse by employers of 'factory shop vouchers' – to the 1891 Fair Wages Resolution which obliged employers on local or national government projects to pay the standard/recognised rate for a job. Both of these measures, along with the Wage Councils, which were first established in 1909, were modified or repealed in the 1980s – with the Agricultural Wages Board, due in part to employer support, being the only survivor. More recently the government has put in place the National Minimum Wage Act (1999) which sets hourly rates across the whole economy for various groups of workers – primarily manual workers. These rates were set following meetings of the Low Pay Commission and graduated according to the age of the worker concerned.

A criticism of time-based mechanisms is that they are often related to historic rather than current value, and can result in discrimination, demarcation disputes and a sense of injustice. Such time-related mechanisms are often based on the notion of a pay hierarchy in which groups of jobs/skills are banded. Although widely applied basic versions of these instruments are poor in terms of relating wage to current effort; often rewarding effort which has been applied externally (gaining a recognised skill) and is inappropriate to current tasks. The advantages of these systems are that management can control wage costs by

(a) limiting the access to various grades in the hierarchy;

(b) by limiting the range of the grade (say 4 per cent top to bottom); and

(c) demonstrating they are fair in relation to agreed procedures.

The problems created are not necessarily with the pay hierarchy system per se but with the manner in which skills relating to specific grades are defined; solutions must then address the structure, strategy and rationale of the reward system rather than the application of such mechanisms.

Bowey and Lupton (1973) developed a scheme for highlighting the manner in which such hierarchies are built and sustained. They argued that five factors are in play when selecting, deciding the location of each job within the hierarchy. These were:

- skill;
- responsibility;
- mental effort;
- physical effort; and
- working conditions (Bowey and Lupton 1973).

Using these factors it is possible to identify similarities between jobs rather, than is the case with standard job evaluation schemes, differences. Following the identification of these similarities it is possible to locate various jobs within the pay hierarchy. What is more difficult is to translate this identification into a pay structure due to the various allocation or availability of the elements which make up an individual pay packet. Most conspicuous are the differences in the elements which are included in the individual pay packet at each level. So, for example, elements such as overtime, shift premium, individual bonus payments and other special allowances, lead to increased earnings for some groups but not others. It is possible, in part, to explain the gender differences in earnings by reference to these elements. Hellerstein and Newmark (2006) argue that the difference in directly observable reward maybe be founded on either productivity differences or pure (taste-based) discrimination. In adopting this residual wage approach to wage discrimination they suggest it is possible to estimate the true level of taste-based wage difference – whether looking at ethnicity, gender, age, disability or other forms of discrimination. (See discussion on equal pay below.)

Conboy (1976) noted that the key advantage of these time-based instruments is that both parties have a clear idea of the 'wage' element of the bargain. For management the problem is that these mechanisms do not give any clear indication of the 'effort' element of the bargain. This has led to time rate instruments being complicated by the addition of 'performance' elements, often in the form of 'piece-rates' or other complex 'bonus' calculations in an attempt to determine acceptable effort levels (e.g. predetermined motion time systems and measured-day-work). The traditional form of such schemes can be demonstrated using the diagram shown in Figure 13.1.

Figure 13.1 The traditional form of time rate instruments

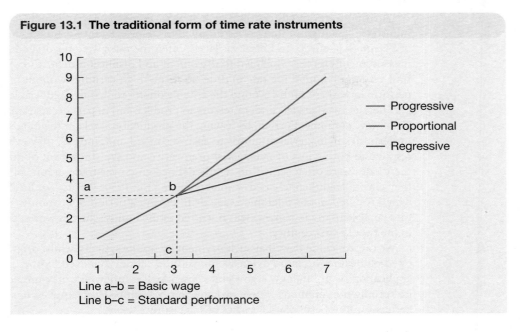

Line a–b = Basic wage
Line b–c = Standard performance

Many schemes give guaranteed basic earnings which are then supplemented in ways which we can class as proportional (wages increase in direct relationship to output), progressive (wages increase more than output) or regressive (wages increase at a slower rate than output).

An important element in this discussion regards the manner in which the 'base' element is decided. We have become familiar with the notion of a National Minimum Wage, which sets the minimum rate for specified groups; outwith this scheme, organisations need some mechanisms by which to assign values to various roles within the organisation. Traditional mechanisms (and in a slightly modified manner 'new pay' systems) have related to hierarchy calculations or simplistic forms of job evaluation scheme. A job evaluation scheme operates by allocating values to each of a series of elements (e.g. skill or responsibility) and then measuring each 'job' in order to arrive at an agreed 'score'. The scores are then placed on the pay spine in relation to accepted criteria. These criteria will be formed by the interaction of two sets of relativities. Scores will need to reflect 'external relativities', by which we mean the situation that appears to hold in relation to external markets and environmental conditions, and 'internal relativities', meaning an appearance of fairness in relation to other jobs/roles within the organisation. In the basic form, these schemes introduce us to the notion of reward packages under which different elements can be rewarded in various ways. However, these schemes fell out of favour in some respects because they are seen to 'pay-the-job' rather than 'pay-the-worker', and as such were difficult to relate to individual performance (see the discussion below).

Time-based pay is clearly the simplest form of wage payment system, easily understood by both parties; it allows the development of 'overtime' payments for work completed in addition to the contracted hours in any given period and formed the basis of the creation of systems classed as payment by results (PBR). Early PBR schemes were time based in that they used the time accumulated by the pace of work as a percentage of the time allowed to form a foundation for the calculation of performance payments. So, in a simple form, if a task is timed to take 8 minutes but is completed in 6 then there is a saving of 25 per cent, but the increase in performance is 33⅓ per cent in that if the job is completed in 6 minutes then the 2 minutes left is equal to a third of the new job time. From the employers point of view therefore paying a 25 per cent bonus leaves a surplus per piece of 8⅓ per cent. This adds to the perceived advantages of this style of PBR linked to hierarchical reward systems by providing increased worker effort because they see the resultant higher pay within weeks and higher output.

During the twentieth century such structures/systems were widely used within British industry in an attempt to increase productivity. However, they are associated with a number of detrimental effects and disadvantages. Often the rates were negotiated following a work-measurement exercise which led to discontent and disillusionment. Too often operators can find easy ways around the rate in order to secure high earnings without the expected higher performance; these routes around the scheme often resulted in a reduced level of quality – in part because workers felt under pressure to produce and in part because quality and speed do not always combine. Further, by leaving the production levels in the hands of the workers it undermines managerial attempts to secure control and, indeed, may even be said to have resulted in both a loss of managerial prerogative and the abrogation of managerial roles. As these rates were often set within tightly defined employer/trade union collective agreements they encouraged the increased – notably during the 1950s–1970s – of local shop agreements which resulted in considerable 'wage drift' during a period of economic restraint. Many of these problems are to some extent mirrored in the bonus schemes within the financial sector in the twenty-first century.

We can conclude then that such payment by results systems, whilst originally crude, developed alongside the more extensive division of labour achieved by the increasing use and application of technology, ergonomics (pseudo-scientific work measurement) and mechanical production methods. These early techniques can be easily applied to such divided work because of four basic characteristics of such work:

- short job cycles;
- high manual content (which, using sophisticated ergonomic processes, can be measured);
- batch production (with repeated orders/processes);
- no marked fluctuations in required outputs (adapted from Conboy, 1976).

The simplistic assumptions underlying these and other PBR systems are twofold. First, workers are motivated to increase performance (work harder) by money, and second, any increases in output will result in equivalent increases in wages. The schemes are intended to be self-financing and designed to reduce 'wasteful activity' in that they can be used to redesign the labour process. Whilst such schemes now enjoy less popularity than they have in previous decades, there is still evidence that they are used in relation to specific groups of workers.

Hierarchy schemes in general continue to find favour especially amongst salaried staff. A key element of such schemes is the practice of incremental progression. Such schemes operate on the simple premise that advancing years of service result in additional reward because of loyalty or greater experience. Whilst they have recently been challenged – on the basis that they discriminate on the grounds of age – they continue to form a foundation for the solution of the labour problem for many organisations.

STOP and think

To what extent do you think the solutions to the labour problem suggested so far reflect management's inability to clearly determine the 'effort' side of the bargain?

Having set out the basic framework within which the wage/effort bargain can be viewed, we now move on to consider developments that are more recent. In the discussion that follows we move from an analysis of solutions to the labour problem founded on the cash nexus to a series of arguments which indicate more complex and considered solutions.

Employee reward

The subject of reward is vast and continually evolving, in short it has been described as a 'bundle of returns offered in exchange for a cluster of employee contributions' (Bloom and Milkovich, 1996: 25). This is a rather loose definition and sheds little light on what form 'returns' might take or what contribution employees might make to reap such returns. Usefully, the definition does, however, capture the multiplicity of returns and possible employee contributions, suggesting that reward comprises a blend of offerings and that employees' contributions can be numerous and eclectic.

The notion of a *range* of different forms of return in exchange for employee contributions of various types signals a departure from a narrow focus upon wages and effort. Wages or monetary return for the effort expended by employees, as charted in the opening part of this chapter, remain central to the employment relationship; however, the advent of the concept of reward, and more pointedly reward management, prompts organisations to consider the differing ways in which employees positively impact the organisation via a range of contributions (not restricted to effort) and how best to signify organisational appreciation. The practice of reward veers away from a single dimensional focus on wages and instead encompasses a plethora of financial and non-financial returns employees might potentially receive in exchange for favourable contributions to the organisation. In terms of employee contributions to the organisation, effort becomes but one input amongst many potential offerings, indeed its value to the organisation may well be considered less important and less attractive than other employee behaviours, for example, measureable *outcome-related* contributions. It is clear thus that reward is a more inclusive term than wages or payment and that it is used to denote a diverse range of devices at the organisation's disposal to recognise the role individuals and teams play in the operation of, and ultimate success of the business. Reward steps beyond the perimeters of compensation, remuneration and benefits terminology where emphasis is placed on pay and other settlements which carry a monetary value to a new plane in which almost anything could be construed as a return to employees for exhibiting desirable behaviour, from a cash bonus or health care benefit to employee involvement in decision making, increased role responsibility, autonomy, access to more interesting work and other factors relating to the nature of the work itself and the environment in which it is carried out.

Components of reward

As indicated above, reward comprises several elements, extending beyond base pay thus presenting employers with a number of complex decisions. The first of these is which components to include in the reward package and the associated rationale for inclusion or rejection. Further decisions entail whether to permit employees a degree of choice in the reward 'mix' so that they can, for example, sacrifice salary in exchange for benefits or indeed choose from a menu of benefits to a defined value or cash limit. In addition, employers have fundamental decisions to make concerning whether the reward offering will be standardised and universal (applied to all employees) or tailored and status/seniority related (Marchington and Wilkinson, 2008). Such decisions will be influenced by the nature of the external operating environment, the behaviour of competitors and a range of internal organisational factors; these key determinants of the features of organisational reward systems will be explored later within the chapter.

For all workers, base pay forms the starting point in the reward package. The term is used to denote the hourly rate, wage or annual salary employees are paid for the work they do based either upon some measure of job size or some aspect of the person, for example, qualifications, skill set or demonstrable competencies. Base pay is a critical component as it is used as the anchor rate for calculating redundancy payment entitlement, sick pay, pension level in a final salary scheme, overtime rates, as applicable, and other such employee rights. Base pay might be set deliberately low if, for example, commissions can be earned in excess and the organisation is keen to incentivise sales activity, base pay might also be suppressed where benefits are generous and so the overall worth of the reward bundle is considered to be commensurate with market rates. As is detailed later, however, the introduction of the National Minimum Wage (NMW) in April 1999 imposed minimum limits on base pay in an attempt to curb the problem of low pay in the economy, as a result employers are now obliged to adhere to minimum rates and review pay in accordance with changes in the NMW rates. The level of base pay awarded to employees and movement in base pay can be individually negotiated between managers and employees, unilaterally determined by owners/management, the subject of collective bargaining with relevant trades unions recognised within the industry and /or organisation or as occurs in some cases, set by National Pay Review Bodies.

Over and above base pay, further decisions may be made concerning supplementary payments attributable to skill or performance, for example, and other additions such as overtime, danger or dirt money, shift premium, bonuses or commissions. Dominant reward terminology refers to supplementary payments which are consolidated into base pay as forms of contingent pay and those that are non-consolidated as elements of variable pay (Armstrong, 2002). In practice, both forms of pay described are event- and/or behaviour-dependent and therefore not an assured, regular form of payment. Variable pay in particular is sometimes described as 'at risk' pay by being non-consolidated employees are compelled to repeat activities and behaviours to trigger variable pay in each subsequent business period and so secure a consistent level of reward. In addition, employees are disadvantaged in the sense that base pay, the driver of other entitlements, remains unaffected by variable pay, regardless of how frequently variable pay is awarded or what portion of total salary variable pay comprises. The combination of base pay plus variable pay and/or contingent pay represents total earnings and is reflected in the employee pay advice slip, yet entitlement to employee benefits enables the employee to accumulate additional remuneration. Employee benefits, sometimes called 'perks' (perquisites) or fringe benefits carry a financial value or afford the recipient tax advantages which result in a net financial gain, however in contrast to earnings, benefits are often presented in non-cash form. Where benefits are particularly generous and constitute a substantial component of the reward package they tend to be identified in job advertisements to indicate the total financial value of the role to potential applicants (see Box 13.1).

Benefits can be classified as *immediate, deferred or contingent*. Employees derive value from immediate benefits instantaneously, such benefits might include the provision of a company car, a laptop computer, discounts, expensed mobile phone or subsidised meals. Where benefits are deferred their value accrues and has a future rather than present value to the employee, a clear example of such a benefit is a pension plan or share scheme. Contingent benefits are

Box 13.1

West Midlands Fire Service

HR Officer (Employee Relations)

Salary: £25,146–£26,706 per annum + relocation + benefits

Royal Mail

HR Business Partners

South East/South West and Home Counties
Salary up to £60,000 per annum + benefits to include car allowance and bonus

Trafford College

Director of Human Resources

£54k plus contributory pension scheme

Source: People Management, 15, 2, January 2009.

those that are triggered in certain circumstances, for example sick pay schemes, paternity and maternity pay and leave arrangements. Rather than deferring to the aforementioned classification, Wright (2004: 182) prefers to consider benefits in four distinct groupings:

- *Personal, security and health benefits*: for example, pension, company sick pay scheme, life cover, medical insurance, loans.

- *Job-, status- or seniority-related benefits*: for example, company car, holiday leave beyond statutory minimum, sabbaticals.

- *Family friendly benefits*: for example, childcare or eldercare facilities, nursery vouchers, enhanced maternity/paternity/parental leave arrangements.

- *Social or 'goodwill' or lifestyle benefits*: for example, subsidised canteen, gym/sports facilities, discounts, ironing collection/dry cleaning.

Benefits can be voluntary, affording employees the choice whether to 'opt in' and use them according to their personal needs and financial position. Should employees elect to purchase benefits such as childcare vouchers, cycle-to-work scheme loan, life cover or pension contributions, arrangements tend to be set up for deductions to occur at source, this can attract tax advantages for the employee, for example, where childcare assistance is purchased. The 'Advantages' benefits package operated by DHL Logistics is typical of voluntary benefit schemes. It incorporates the company's Voyager pension scheme, childcare savings via the 'Care-4' scheme, Denplan dental care, AXA PPP healthcare and a range of leisure, health, motoring and financial discounts and offers. Details of the scheme are presented in a booklet distributed to all employees and staff take up is encouraged. To promote the scheme, further value illustrations are available to demonstrate to individual employees the total worth of the benefits should they choose to make use of 'Advantages'. A recent CIPD survey reports that voluntary benefit schemes are in use in 27 per cent of organisations (CIPD, 2008a). In other organisations benefits are universal, in other words provided to all and regarded as 'perks' of the job. This is in direct contrast to status or seniority-related benefits, which employees only qualify for if they have accrued the requisite number of year's service or are employed at or beyond a prescribed grade or level. Flexible benefit schemes or 'cafeteria benefits', so named because of the choices presented to employees, have been around for a number of years in some organisations, however, data depicting the prevalence of such schemes would suggest a degree of employer reticence. Of all the organisations surveyed by the CIPD (2008a) just 13 per cent operated flexible benefits and a further 12 per cent indicated plans to introduce such a scheme. Flexible schemes were present in 22 per cent of organisations with over 5000 staff, possibly indicating that larger workplaces are more likely to be able to resource a system of flexible benefits, both financially and logistically. Earlier data (Employee Benefits, 2003) estimated adoption of flexible benefits in around 8 per cent of organisations, again suggesting that this mode of providing employee benefits enjoys relatively narrow appeal. The basic premise of a flexible or cafeteria benefits scheme is that employees can spend up to a points limit or cash total, purchasing benefits from a defined menu. Cafeteria schemes may comprise fixed (inflexible, core) benefits and flexible ones (a so-called 'core plus' scheme) or offer complete freedom of choice to the maximum cash value/points value. In other schemes pre-packaged sets of benefits may be on offer to employees; these schemes are referred to as modularised benefits (Wright, 2004: 207).

It is difficult to generalise the provision of benefits as part of the overall reward package and predict the types of benefits any one organisation will deem appropriate to adopt. The impetus for providing benefits can be viewed from a number of perspectives:

- Do organisations see benefits as a way of compensating for lower pay or do higher pay and generous benefits tend to co-exist as part of a deliberate strategy aimed at attracting and retaining staff?

- Do employers select benefits in the belief that they will motivate employees and instil a greater sense of loyalty and commitment?

● Is benefit provision enhanced by employers where trade unions lobby successfully to expand the reward package on behalf of their members?

● Are benefits a mechanism for employer branding, the costs of which some organisations are prepared to bear? (Wright, 2009.)

The answers to these questions are intricate and beyond the scope of this chapter. We do know, however, that whilst employee benefits in themselves are a fairly steadfast feature of reward in the UK, recent years have witnessed some shifts in the types of benefits more commonly provided by employers. Wright (2009: 175) detects 'cutbacks in the most costly benefits and at the same time a growth in low-cost lifestyle and voluntary benefits'. She attributes such trends to the dual influences of the changing composition of the labour force (particularly the influx of mothers) and the need for employers to be economically prudent and focus on value for money as competition intensifies. These trends would seem to be reflected to some extent in the benefits top-ten (see Table 13.1), particularly in the list of benefits most commonly provided to all employees.

Non-financial reward

Whilst the components of reward identified and discussed so far have a financial basis, reward can also be non-financial, or relational (Brown and Armstrong, 1999), for example praise, thanks, opportunities to develop skills and recognition awards such as 'employee of

Table 13.1 Top ten employer-provided benefits by provision

Provided to all employees	Provision dependent on grade/seniority	Part of a flexible benefit scheme only
Training and career development (71%)	Mobile phone (business use) (58%)	Dental insurance (9%)
25 days' or more paid leave (67%)*	Car allowance (50%)	Childcare vouchers (6%)
Tea/coffee/cold drinks (free) (62%)	Company car (49%)	Critical illness insurance (5%)
Christmas party/lunch (free) (62%)	Private medical insurance (32%)	Cycle-to-work scheme loan (5%)
On-site car parking (60%)	Relocation assistance (25%)	Health screening (5%)
Childcare vouchers (56%)	Fuel allowance (21%)	Private medical insurance (5%)
Life assurance (51%)	25 days' or more paid leave (20%)*	Healthcare cash plans (4%)
Eyecare vouchers (46%)	On-site car parking (14%)	Permanent health insurance (3%)
Enhanced maternity/paternity leave (43%)	Permanent health insurance (13%)	Life assurance (3%)
Employee assistance programmes (42%)	Health screening (12%)	Gym (on-site or membership) (2%)

Percentage of respondents in brackets.
*Excludes statutory leave.

Source: from *Reward Management: A CIPD Survey*, CIPD (2009) p. 13, with the permission of the publisher, the Chartered Institute of Personnel and Development, London (www.cipd.co.uk).

the month', 'going the extra mile' and service awards. Awards are often publicly acknowledged in ceremonies and/or in company newsletters and notice boards thus communicating to the wider workforce the employee behaviours the organisation values and is prepared to reward. Non-financial rewards also include the general quality of working life (QWL), for example the work environment, flexibility, work-life balance, managerial style/attitude, job-role autonomy and responsibility plus opportunities for employee involvement and employee voice; collectively these factors might be termed the work 'experience'. Definitions of non-financial rewards are bound up with the concept of total reward described below, emphasising the potential benefits to be derived from considering reward in the broadest of senses. As Perkins and White conclude (2008: 315),

> definitions of non-financial reward are multi-faceted and often complex, requiring dissection of the elements to facilitate detailed cost–benefit analysis while simultaneously seeking to promote 'holistic employment experience' value greater than the sum of the parts.

Total reward

In recent years there has been interest in the notion of managing rewards such that the various components are carefully crafted together to support one another and so maximise the satisfaction employees experience in the course of, and as a result of their employment. This approach is the essence of a total rewards process (Armstrong and Murlis, 1998). Worldat-Work (2000) loosely describe total rewards as all of the employer's available tools that may be used to attract, retain, motivate and satisfy employees, encompassing every single investment that an organisation makes in its people, and everything employees value in the employment relationship. The components of total rewards are succinctly presented in the model shown in Figure 13.2.

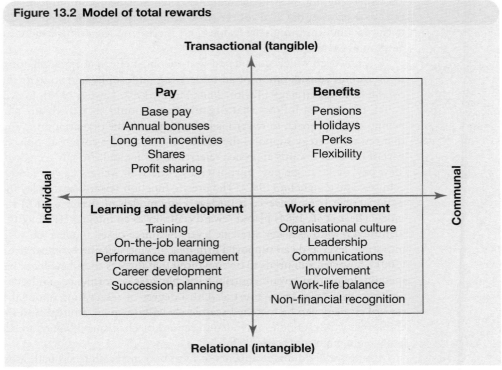

Figure 13.2 Model of total rewards

Transactional (tangible)

Pay	Benefits
Base pay	Pensions
Annual bonuses	Holidays
Long term incentives	Perks
Shares	Flexibility
Profit sharing	

Learning and development	Work environment
Training	Organisational culture
On-the-job learning	Leadership
Performance management	Communications
Career development	Involvement
Succession planning	Work-life balance
	Non-financial recognition

Individual ← → Communal

Relational (intangible)

Source: Brown and Armstrong (1999: 81).

Thompson and Milsome (2001) insist that the concept of total rewards is necessarily holistic and integrative, it should also provide an approach to reward in the organisation which augurs well with the business objectives and desired organisational culture and as such is conflated with strategic approaches to reward. In addition, it is people centred, customised, distinctive (offering support to a unique employer brand) and it is evolutionary, in the sense that it is developed incrementally as opposed to the product of drastic, sudden change. A total rewards approach is reputed to offer potential for organisations striving to reduce costs, heighten visibility in a tight labour market, recruit and retain successfully, increase flexibility and improve productivity (Armstrong, 2002: 10) and so would certainly seem to 'tick the boxes' for contemporary organisations. In practice however, the latest CIPD Reward Survey (CIPD, 2009a) reports that only one fifth of organisations claim to have implemented total rewards while a further 22 per cent plan to introduce it during 2009. It could perhaps be deduced from these findings that a total rewards approach is somewhat elusive and difficult for employers to establish.

Reward management and the emergence of strategic approaches to reward

The term 'reward management' was first used in 1988 by Armstrong and Murlis to denote the development of a new field or collective set of activities to emerge within the arena of HRM. The new term recognised that static techniques, principally concerned with salary administration, were fast giving way to a more dynamic approach emphasising the use of pay (and other rewards) in a flexible and innovative way with the aim of improving individual, team and organisational performance. The activity 'reward management', has been described as encompassing not only the development, maintenance, communication, and evaluation of reward processes, but also concerned with the development of appropriate organisational cultures, underpinning core values and increasing the commitment and motivation of employees (Armstrong and Murlis, 1998).

It is, however, widely considered that the most effective approaches to reward are based upon careful consideration of an underlying philosophy and strategy that corresponds to overall business strategy (Taylor, 2008; Storey, 1992; Lawler, 1990). In accordance with this belief, the mantra follows that organisations should seek to ensure that the philosophy behind their approach to reward is in keeping with the organisation's values and beliefs and that reward strategy supports the achievement of wider corporate objectives; indeed this is part of the total rewards approach referred to earlier and strongly conveyed in the rhetoric of 'new pay' or 'strategic pay' purported by American writers Lawler (1990, 1995, 2000) and Schuster and Zingheim (1992). The precise function reward has to play in advancing organisational objectives, however, is unclear. Early models of strategic HRM such as the Harvard model (Beer *et al.*, 1984) placed reward centrally as an integral HR activity and Storey (1992) identified reward as a 'key strategic lever'. Resource-based models too suggest pay acts as an important lever and can support a firm in achieving sustained competitive advantage. Kessler (2001), however, still needs to be convinced that there is sound evidence based upon credible methodologies that reward contributes to business performance and leads to sustained competitive advantage. There must also be a degree of reservation about the ease with which reward strategy can be matched seamlessly with business strategy and the extent to which employees will respond as intended to reward mechanisms designed to elicit certain desired behavioural patterns (Lewis, 2006).

Despite these doubts it appears to have become established orthodoxy that a strategic approach to reward can be used to leverage the kinds of employee behaviours that contribute to business goals (Marchington and Wilkinson, 2008). Proponents of strategic reward suggest it is possible for reward strategies, intentionally or otherwise, to signal what the organisation considers important and what it clearly does not value. For example, reward strategies that rest on service-related salary increments are likely to convey messages that the organisation values loyalty and long tenure above all else whereas the use of competence-related pay would suggest a need for employees to develop and demonstrate core competences and job-specific competences. Table 13.2 seeks to demonstrate a number of aligned relationships between the key thrust of business strategy and the direction of reward strategy.

Table 13.2 Examples of alignment: reward strategy and business strategy

Business strategy	Reward strategy
Achieve value added by improving employee motivation and commitment	Introduce or improve performance pay plans – individual, team, gain sharing
Achieve added value by improving performance/productivity	Introduce or improve performance pay plans and performance management processes
Achieve competitive advantage by developing and making best use of distinctive core competencies	Introduce competence-related pay
Achieve competitive advantage by technological development	Introduce competence-related or skills-based pay
Achieve competitive advantage by delivering better value and quality to customers	Recognise and reward individuals and teams for meeting/exceeding customer service and quality standards/targets
Achieve competitive advantage by developing the capacity of the business to respond quickly and flexibly to new opportunities	Provide rewards for multi-skilling and job flexibility. Develop more flexible pay structures (eg. broad-banding)
Achieve competitive advantage by attracting, developing and retaining high-quality employees	Ensure rates of pay are competitive. Reward people for developing their competencies and careers (for example, using the scope made possible in a broad-banded grading structure)

Source: from *Reward srategy: How to develop a reward strategy. A CIPD Practical Tool*, CIPD (CIPD 2005) http://www.cipd.co.uk/subjects/pay/general/tools.htm?IsSrchRes=1, with the permission of the publisher, the Chartered Institute of Personnel and Development, London (www.cipd.co.uk).

*What messages does the reward strategy in your own organisation convey? Are these the messages that the organisation **intends** to convey?*

Reward strategy in practice

Latest CIPD survey information (CIPD, 2009a) illustrates that 26 per cent of the sample acknowledges the existence of a reward strategy within their organisations while a further 24 per cent plan to adopt one in 2009. These figures seem to show a retraction when compared with the same survey a year and indeed two years earlier (CIPD, 2007, 2008a). In 2008, 33 per cent of respondents claimed to have a reward strategy, in 2007 the corresponding figure was 35 per cent with a further 40 per cent of respondents planning to introduce one in the course of 2007, the 2008 findings would suggest that this was not something they did in fact manage to do! The 2009 survey ponders whether the falling portion of respondents claiming to have a reward strategy could be attributed to some organisations perhaps questioning whether they had a reward strategy in the first place, a kind of crisis of confidence, or whether some employers did have a strategy but have recently had to relinquish it due to the fragility of the economic climate (CIPD, 2009a: 6). Of those organisations claiming to have a reward strategy, 85 per cent maintain that implementing their reward strategy has been difficult at times. The survey shows that overall the main inhibitors to the effective operation of the reward strategy are budgetary constraints/pressures, line managers' skills and abilities, line management attitudes and staff attitudes, although respondents from different sectors report notably different barriers to success.

Concerns over the ability of organisations to mount strategic approaches to reward are not new. In research conducted by the Institute for Employment Studies, Bevan (2000: 2) commented that having a reward strategy sounded like a 'tall order'. To be successful, he argues, reward strategy is supposed to be downstream from business strategy and reinforce business goals, drive performance improvements within the business, deliver cultural and behavioural change, integrate horizontally with other HR practices and keep pay budgets under control, so 'little wonder that so many employers under-perform in the design and delivery of a truly strategic approach to reward – if such a thing exists' (2000: 2). The same IES research (Bevan, 2000) detected ten common mistakes responsible for contributing to the under achievement of many reward strategies. The errors revolve around design or delivery and are summarised in Table 13.3.

Table 13.3 Reward strategy: ten common mistakes (Bevan, 2000)

1 Starting at the end	Trying to emulate the reward system used by competitors without recognising unique organisational drivers and what the business strategy requires
2 Having no success criteria	Failing to think through the underpinning reward philosophy and objectives and what success might look like so little idea whether the reward strategy is performing
3 Trusting the business strategy	Problems with the business strategy, for example failure to articulate it clearly and the chance that business strategy changes faster than reward is able to follow
4 Equating complexity with flexibility	Trying to build over-elaborate reward systems in an attempt to appeal to a diverse workforce, this can have the effect of confusing employees such that they fail to see a clear line of sight between performance and reward
5 Confusing speed with haste	Trying to rush in new reward systems, potentially damaging employee relations and harming the culture of the organisation
6 Focus on excellence	Focusing reward on excellence in the minority as opposed to encouraging performance improvements among the majority
7 Ignoring pay architecture	Getting weighed down in detail, for example wrangles over performance markings, rather than paying proper attention to pay structures and frameworks used to facilitate reward decisions
8 Failing to get real 'buy-in'	Failing to get full commitment from senior managers and line managers
9 Having too much faith in line managers	Relying on the skills and abilities of line managers to make difficult reward decisions without the necessary training and support
10 Failing to integrate reward with other strands of HR	Lack of logic between reward processes and systems and other HR practices, this can be due to a variety of reasons including conflicting process goals, process ownership issues and timing

Source: Bevan (2000: 3)

STOP and think

Do you recognise any of the above mistakes in your own organisation's efforts to design and implement a reward strategy capable of supporting and reinforcing strategic business objectives?

Which mistakes have occurred and how might they be rectified?

Key reward choices

Whilst accepting the notion of aligning reward to business strategy to optimise the utility of reward mechanisms a number of key, value-laden choices must be made in the process. Marchington and Wilkinson (2008: 464) suggest that there are five essential reward decisions an organisation needs to draw consensus on:

- what to pay for, job size, time, performance, skills/qualifications or some other person-centred attribute or behaviour;
- whether to place primary focus on internal equity when determining pay or be more concerned with external benchmarks;
- whether to operate a centralised or decentralised approach to reward or a hybrid with some central control and a degree of localised latitude;
- whether to build hierarchy into the reward system such that there are seniority or status related rewards or to devise a harmonised, single-status approach;
- the precise nature of the reward 'mix'.

Getting these decisions right is critical if reward is to reinforce the strategic direction of the organisation. Similarly, the decisions made need to be ones most likely to motivate individuals to orient their actions and behaviours towards business goals. This is demanding for any organisation given that motivation is individualised and complex. Thought needs to be invested in considering the extent to which different rewards are capable of motivating employees, the value of intrinsic and extrinsic motivation to employees, the role of pay in motivating people and the importance of equity in reward systems and reward management practices.

Motivation theory offers useful insight and can help guide the design and management of reward processes. Notably amongst the many theories of motivation, Herzberg's 'Two-Factor Theory' (Herzberg, 1966) suggests that pay is a *hygiene* factor rather than a motivator and so in itself it is unlikely to motivate. Herzberg contends that pay needs to be adequate to prevent dissatisfaction but other factors induce a motivational state such as responsibility and autonomy. This is, indeed, a salutary message particularly to those organisations that attempt to use pay or the prospect of financial rewards as an incentive for greater output, better quality or other outcomes they determine to be desirable.

Process theories of motivation such as 'Expectancy Theory' (Vroom, 1982) attempt to explain the internal thought processes that instil a motivational state. Expectancy theory offers us the insight that employee motivation is the result of a complex set of decisions and assumptions made by the individual. For an employee to be motivated and therefore to expend effort, the rewards on offer have to be something that the individual values (hold 'valence'), hence the importance of the reward 'mix. In addition, the individual must have belief that the rewards are achievable. An appreciation of expectancy theory encourages organisations to construct a clear 'line of sight' so that employees are in no doubt what it is they need to do in order to gain the rewards offered. If there is ambiguity or partiality disturbing the line of sight individuals are likely to be de-motivated, even if the potential rewards hold personal valence.

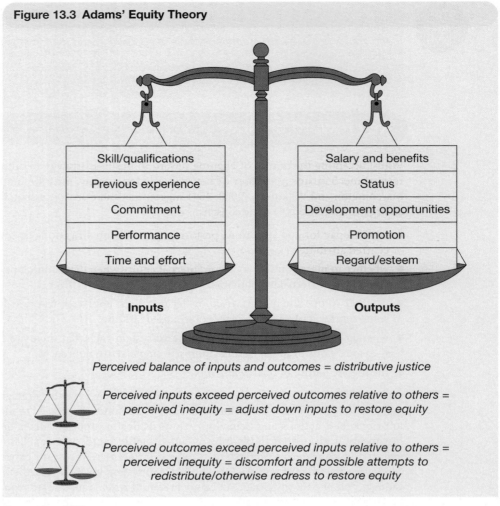

Figure 13.3 Adams' Equity Theory

Inputs	Outputs
Skill/qualifications	Salary and benefits
Previous experience	Status
Commitment	Development opportunities
Performance	Promotion
Time and effort	Regard/esteem

Perceived balance of inputs and outcomes = distributive justice

Perceived inputs exceed perceived outcomes relative to others = perceived inequity = adjust down inputs to restore equity

Perceived outcomes exceed perceived inputs relative to others = perceived inequity = discomfort and possible attempts to redistribute/otherwise redress to restore equity

Source: Adams (1965)

Finally, Adams' 'Equity Theory' (Adams, 1965) prompts organisations to consider the perceived fairness of rewards and their application. Adams suggests that employees will compare the rewards they receive (outputs) in return for their effort, skill, qualifications, time and other contributions (inputs). Employees will be motivated where they perceive 'distributive justice' and de-motivated where they perceive inequity. Employees may seek to adjust their inputs when they perceive inequity. Using the subliminal messages inherent in Adams' theory, organisations would be advised to take steps to ensure that their reward systems are fair, consistently applied and sufficiently transparent so that employees can see for themselves how reward decisions are determined (see Figure 13.3).

Factors influencing organisational approaches to reward practice and pay determination

An organisation's approach to reward generally, and to pay determination, will be shaped both by factors in the external environment within which it operates and an array of internal firm-specific characteristics, namely the nature of the business, the size of operation, organisational structure and culture, types of employees, jobs and technology, management and ownership and so forth. Each of the reward choices Marchington and Wilkinson (2008) posit in the segment above cascade a range of further ancillary choices thus creating the potential for multiple models of reward practice. Because of this it is difficult to generalise about approaches to reward and impossible to be prescriptive. More safely, an organisation's approach to developing a reward strategy ought to start from the standpoint 'what makes sense for this organisation?' (Wright, 2004: 8) whilst subsuming relevant knowledge relating to the internal and external factors influencing choice. In this segment of the chapter we briefly discuss the key factors in the external and internal environment that shape and influence organisational approaches to reward.

The economic climate

This chapter has already alluded to some of the ways in which the economic environment might influence reward, notably the way in which employers are likely to switch to less costly benefits in tougher economic conditions, and the way in which employers can reduce risk and financial burden by making more extensive use of variable pay. The economic context is an important determinant of pay levels and a barometer for future trends. In setting pay levels, employers cannot help but be influenced by the market rates for jobs. As Kessler (2007: 167) remarks 'organisations cannot survive if they fail to pay competitive labour market rates to attract employees with the skills needed to provide a service or manufacture a product'. Of course, there is no such thing as a single market rate for a job, rather several rates or a zone of discretion, the spread of which is influenced by the supply of and demand of labour, geographical factors and the actions of employers competing for labour. In tight labour markets, where competition for resources is intensive and supply is low, market rates are driven higher, affecting the price employers have to pay to attract adequate resources. Economic activity rates and unemployment indicators are thus key factors influencing pay levels. In addition, for most organisations the rate of growth in the economy is a critical benchmark for the salary review process and impacts upon organisations' ability to pay. According to the IRS (2008) employers use various measures of inflation to guide pay increases, of these the Retail Prices Index (RPI) is the most popular measure with more than eight in ten employers (81.7 per cent) saying they would refer to this measure during forthcoming pay reviews. In an economic downturn there is evidence to suggest that employers tighten their belts where pay is concerned and look to minimise or avoid pay increases. Cotton (2009) suggests that in the current climate of an economy in recession and mounting insolvencies, workers are not optimistic that they will receive a pay rise during 2009.

The legal context for reward

Since the rise of industrialisation there have been numerous legal interventions into the realm of reward management. These have ranged from the Truck Acts of the nineteenth century, which were designed to ensure skilled workers were paid in cash, through to more recent interventions in terms of minimum wage regulation. These demonstrate the ways in which legal regulation can be seen to shape reward practices. Statutory regulation has been in place in the United Kingdom for some 30 years which was intended to ensure pay equity in gender terms. More recently, legislation has been implemented to regulate pay at the lower extreme of the labour market, to impose minimum holiday entitlement and a restraint on working hours. Here we briefly discuss in turn the ways in which the Equal Pay Act 1970, The National Minimum Wage Regulations 1999 and the Working Time Directive 1998 constrain and influence employee reward practices.

The Equal Pay Act 1970 (EqPA)

> Labor market discrimination occurs when groups of workers with equal average productivity are paid different average wages.
>
> (Baldwin and Johnson 2006: 122)

Equal Pay regulations have a history founded in the Convention on Equal Pay approved by the International Labour Organisation in 1950–51, a regulation that had antecedents within the Treaty of Versailles in 1919, if not before (Jamieson, 1999). In the UK the EqPA was enacted as part of the move towards membership of the European Economic Community (now the EU) in the early 1970s. Employers were allowed five years' 'grace' to voluntarily adjust and to permit them to get their reward structures in order before the legislation came into force in 1975. Broadly, the legislation is designed to grant everyone the right to equal terms and conditions of employment in situations where they do the same work as a colleague of the opposite sex. Over the ensuing period this has been widened by the application of European Law to the extent that the UK has modified its laws (see the Employment Act 2002 s 42 for example) to include in this group colleagues of the opposite sex who do work that has been rated as equivalent under a job evaluation scheme or where it can be proved by other mechanisms that the work is of equal value. The manner in which this is achieved is to imply into all contracts of employment an 'equality clause', which has the consequence of requiring the employer not to treat persons of different genders less favourably simply on the basis of gender. In spite of this legislation, there still exist very significant inconsistencies between men's and women's pay. It does not matter whether wages are measured hourly or weekly, women currently receive approximately 83 per cent of the full-time male average, whilst in part-time work 'almost 50 per cent of women who work part-time earn nearer 60 per cent' of their average for their male counterparts (McColgan, 2008: 401). As McColgan (2008) notes, bringing equal pay claims is a sluggish, unwieldy and costly process, especially as the government refuses to go along with the development of class actions and shows even less willingness to implement legislation which places a positive obligation on employers to eliminate pay discrimination.

In spite of this lack of legislative backing to pursue equal pay, some employers seek to address such inequality within their reward structures. This can be achieved by the introduction of a number of reward polices and practices such as:

- ensuring employees reach the top of a given scale within a reasonable timescale;
- setting targets for all staff to reach pay points within a specific timescale;
- setting competency *and* experience criteria for each pay point;
- shortening the scales;
- reducing the number and range of performance measures (Equality and Human Rights Commission, 2009).

As Fredman (2008) suggests, the fact that the current difference in gender-related pay is down to 12.6 per cent when measured using the median figure (rather than the usual mean which rates it at 17.2 per cent) following 34 years of equal pay legislation gives no reason for satisfaction. Indeed, the change in the mechanisms for calculation merely masks the continuing inability of some groups to secure equality of treatment especially where 'the median part-time gender pay gap was a scandalous 39.1% in 2007' (Fredman 2008: 193). The continuing gap indicates the need for a more complex response which addresses both government and employer unwillingness and the narrow coverage of the current legislation.

STOP and think

Whilst some inroads have been made, to what extent do you think the continued reliance upon the three requirements for equal pay claims (same or equivalent establishment, same employer and equal work) continue to limit the progress towards equal pay?

Consider an organisation of which you are aware and indicate mechanisms they could institute in order to address inequalities in terms and conditions.

National Minimum Wage Regulations 1999

The regulation of wages is a central debate within the realm of 'worker protection, globalization, development and poverty reduction' (Evain, 2008: 20). These were put in place in order to develop the dual goals of fairness and efficiency. As the report of the Low Pay Commission suggested it can be argued that low wages lead to a malevolent cluster which comprises low morale, low performance and low productivity. The introduction of a national minimum wage is said to have benefited some 1.3 million workers (Low Pay Commission, 2001). Many of those affected worked in organisations where pay setting was inexact and did not recognise the need for formal systems, further the new wage levels benefited women more than men due to inequality and the extent of part-time work amongst women. The UK currently has three rates covering those over compulsory school age but under 18, those aged between 18 and 21 and those aged 22 and above. The rates are changed in October each year and from 2008 they were £3.53, £4.77 and £5.73 respectively. As with the Wage Council rates before them these rates are poorly policed and many small employers, especially those in the service sector, avoid enforcement (Arrowsmith and Gilman, 2005). Arrowsmith and Gilman argue that in such small firms 'Pay levels reflect not only economic, product and labour market factors but also the informality of internal pay structures' (2005: 169). As we note below, such indeterminacy and informality support existing pay bias, as it is often based on pre-determined skill patterns, time worked and length of service.

The level within the UK is set at above the equivalent of US$1,000 per month (in the period 2006–07) which locates the UK within the top 18 per cent of countries where such a minimum is set (Evain, 2008) and within a group of industrialised countries where the rate is set other than by government alone. Evain (2008) notes more than 100 countries in membership of the International Labour Organisation (ILO), which have ratified the Minimum Wage Fixing Convention 1970 (No 131), either enact minimum wage legislation, set such rates following the recommendation of a specialised body, or through collective bargaining. World-wide, the average range of minimum rates vary from US$30 in Africa, US$75 in many Asian countries, US$480 in Eastern Europe and Latin America to the US$1,000 or above in the majority of industrialised countries. These rates reflect national, regional, sectored and/or global imperatives and satisfy many competitive pressures. By removing wage calculation out of competition organisations can, in domestic and global settings, strive for alternative means of differentiation in terms of product or service. The issue then becomes the enforcement mechanism, Eyraud and Saget (2005) suggest that these regulations are often poorly enforced leading to a continued decline in working conditions across the globe. The extent to which the legislation in the UK is enforced, and the individualised mechanisms for enforcement, tend to support the view that whilst the existence of such regulation is designed to ensure a high level of protection, the continued avoidance of such rules as indicated by Arrowsmith and Gilman (2005) is wide spread.

STOP and think

Minimum wage legislation is said to advance a wide range of policy goals.

What do you think such goals might be and how effectively does the current UK regulation achieve these goals?

Working Time Regulations 1998

Placing limits on working hours is an essential activity in the quest for worker protection and ensuring the health and safety of those at work. In the current climate it has also become a touchstone of the movement towards securing a sustainable work-life balance. In terms of the latter, there are two discourses which each have a separate focus. These uses of the concept cover the *personal control of time* on the one hand and the notion of *workplace flexibility* on the other (see Humbert and Lewis, 2008). In terms of the reward agenda, we concentrate primarily on the latter in that we are seeking solutions to the question of providing options for people with a work place focus who also enjoy non-work (chiefly family) commitments. In that respect the Working Time Regulations (1998) [WTR] offer some attempt to balance the demands of the employer with the needs of family life by placing limits on a range of working time issues. At a glance the key provisions are:

- maximum 48-hour working week for many groups;
- An average eight-hour shift in each 24-hour period for night workers;
- A rest break after six consecutive hours' work;
- Rest periods of 11 continuous hours daily and 35 continuous hours weekly; and
- A minimum of 5.6 weeks' leave per annum.

The UK regulations have their basis in the EU Directive (93/104/EC), which is said to have introduced the new principle of 'humanisation' into EU social regulations, under which employers should be required to take into account the general principle of adapting work and wage in order to alleviate monotonous work and work at a pre-determined rate. The fact that the UK has implemented the directive subject to a number of derogations does not alter the fact that reward managers need to consider the effects of the regulations. That the Employment Appeals Tribunal (EAT) could in a recent case (*Corps of Commissionaires Management Ltd* v *Hughes* [2008] EAT|196|08) hold that the rest break is only triggered after six hours and not multiples thereof, is a simple indication of the minimalist approach of the UK government and the reluctance of management to extend the protection within the UK. During 2009 elements of the EU Directive relating to the definition of 'working time' – notably in relation to 'on-call' time and junior doctors – will come into force and change the options for UK reward managers. The development of 24/7 production and 'rolling shifts' has not been unduly limited by the daily or weekly rest periods due to the availability of opt-outs, however, as these opt-outs are withdrawn it will present fresh challenges for reward managers in the UK.

World-wide most members of the ILO have some form of regulation on working time. In a recent survey (Evain, 2008), attention is drawn to the fact that working time regulation was the subject of the very first ILO convention (Convention 1: 1919) and that the topic has been a major regulatory concern since that date. The general rule, where a normal hourly figure is placed on the working week, is that the figure of 40 or less is applied. In the UK we have no universal normal working limit because the WTR exclude 'professional workers' and/or workers who are not paid in relation to time. The latter group includes many clerical workers, most managers and almost all professional workers. This limitation is not unique to the UK as it can be found in some 24 per cent of industrialised countries. A key result of such exceptions has been the development of 'extreme work' hours most of which are unpaid. It is reported that managers in the UK work the longest hours in Europe, with 42 per cent working in excess of 60 hours a week; this phenomenon runs alongside evidence that work has also intensified (Burke and Cooper, 2008). Hewlett and Luce (2006) describe the amalgamation of these two factors, in the work of 'high earners', as the basis for the creation of 'extreme work'. Such work is portrayed as combining elements such as:

- unpredictable workflow;
- fast pace under tight deadlines;
- scope of responsibility that amounts to more than one job;

- work-related events outside regular working hours;
- availability to clients and/or more senior managers 24/7;
- large amounts of travel;
- large (and increasing) number of direct reports;
- physical presence at the workplace on average at least 10 hours a day (adapted from Hewlett and Luce, 2006).

For reward managers, these elements present few problems because they tend to either describe the role chosen and adopted by the individual or take place within the terms of the existing contract of employment. As such, they are rewarded by existing reward structures including PBR or other personalised reward agreements. In their survey of US business managers and professionals, Hewlett and Luce found that 91 per cent cited unpredictability as a key pressure point whilst 86 per cent also included increased pace within tight deadlines, 66% included work-related events outside normal hours and 61 per cent 24/7 client demands (2006: 54). Perhaps the words of the eighteenth-century washer-woman Mary Collier better fit modern managers and professionals both male and female;

> Our toil and labour daily so extreme,
> that we have hardly ever the time to dream.
>
> (Quoted in Thompson 1991: 81)

From this discussion we can begin to see that legislative activity, whilst a key source for elements which influence reward structures, are not the only, nor perhaps the most important, influences.

Internal/organisational factors and the influence of sector

In addition to reflecting factors in the external environment, organisations' chosen approach to reward will be shaped by the idiosyncratic nature of the firm and sector-specific factors. There are no hard and fast rules, so the full plethora of reward choices is theoretically at the disposal of the organisation. As far as its capabilities stretch, the organisation must develop an approach to reward that is compliant, cost-effective and capable of attracting, retaining and motivating employees commensurate with the needs of the business. It is beyond the boundaries of this chapter to discuss in detail the complex configurations of reward and corresponding internal drivers that are likely to be significant in each case. Instead, a more general stance is adopted, which notes some of the discernable differences between reward practices according to workplace characteristics such as ownership/sector, unionisation and workplace size. We return to these themes in the final part of the chapter, where contemporary trends in pay and reward practices are discussed against rhetoric of heightened strategic use of reward.

Large-scale surveys such as the Workplace Employment Relations Survey (WERS) (Kersley et al., 2006) and the CIPD Annual Reward Survey allow changes and trends in employee reward practice to be tracked over time; they also provide a snapshot of employee reward practices at the time of the survey. CIPD research provides analysis by firm size (number of employees), firm sector (manufacturing and production, private sector services, voluntary sector and public services) and by occupation (senior management, middle/first-line management, technical/professional and clerical/manual), whilst WERS provides further industry breakdown and in addition, considers the variance between reward practices in unionised and non-unionised workplaces and foreign-owned and UK-owned workplaces. A sample of observations is drawn from WERS 2004 (Kersley et al., 2006) and the latest CIPD survey (2009a) and shown in Table 13.4.

Table 13.4 Trends in reward practice

Reward strategy	• The incidence of reward strategy shows little variance by sector but does appear to be more closely correlated to workplace size – 48 per cent of respondents in workplaces of 5000+ employees reported the existence of reward strategy compared with 20 per cent of repondents where there were between 50 and 249 employees
Pay structures	• In the public sector and to a lesser extent in the voluntary sector, employers are far more likely to us pay spines • The most common approach to pay structures taking all sectors into account is the use of individual pay rates/ranges and spot salaries although there are variations by sector and by occupation • Broad-banding is most prevalent in manufacturing and production • Most senior managers are paid according to individual pay rates/ranges/spot salaries as are most clerical and manual workers
Pay progression	• The CIPD report that the most common approach to pay progression is to use a combination of factors (combined approach) in contrast to a single factor such as length of service, skills or individual performance • Combination approaches are more common in manufacturing and production and private sector services than they are in the voluntary sector and public services • Where combination approaches are used, the most common combination in the public sector is individual performance and length of service, individual performance is the most popular factor across all sectors, market rates feature strongly in the private sector and competency is more typical in the voluntary sector
Pay/salary determination	• Market rates are shown to be more important in determining salaries in private sector firms • In the public sector collective bargaining was the dominant form of pay setting • In the private sector, the percentage of employees with pay set through collective bargaining was much higher in foreign-owned workplaces than in UK-owned workplaces • Clerical and manual staff are more likely to be covered by collective bargaining arrangements than managerial staff • The views of the owner/managing director are more likely to be a factor in setting salary levels in small firms than in large organisations (CIPD, 2009a) • Pay set by management where this is the sole method of pay determination is a growing phenomenon in private sector workplaces (43 per cent of private sector workplaces in 2004 compared with 32 per cent in 1998) (Kersley *et al.*, 2006) • Job evaluation processes are more likely to underscore salary determination in the public sector and voluntary sectors than in the private sector • Job evaluation is more likely to be used by large employers than small employers • Public sector organisations are far more likely to have conducted an equal pay reviews (EPR) to audit internal pay equity than private sector employers

Pay determination – internal or external focus?

As the final segment of Table 13.4 demonstrates, a key decision when setting levels of pay is whether to place emphasis on comparability with the external market or internal equity. The lure of the external market would appear to be more compelling for private sector organisations, whereas the greater use of tools such as job evaluation and the Equal Pay Review process in the public sector suggests internal equity is more paramount here. Ultimately, however, any approach must try and reconcile the need to keep pace with external market rates with due concern for internal equity.

Job evaluation has come in for criticism in recent years for being excessively paperwork-driven and costly and too rigid to be of value to organisations trying to be adaptable and flexible in the face of intensive competitive pressures. The notion of conceiving tightly defined job descriptions, of the kind needed for traditional job evaluation schemes is also heralded in some quarters as incompatible with flatter organisational structures and associated desire to create flexible ways of rewarding employees. Job evaluation consequently is supposed to have withered away, at least from mainstream use. On the contrary, IDS (2000) suggest that much of the criticism directed at job evaluation is unsupported by hard empirical evidence and that in practice organisations are showing signs of using it to complement broad-banding and in conjunction with role profiling and competencies. Brown and Dive (2009: 29) would appear to agree,

> By evolving to meet the needs of organisations for more fluid structures, more market- and person-driven pay and more talented leaders – as well as performing its traditional function as a foundation for fair pay management – job evaluation seems to be securing its place in the HR professional's toolkit for the foreseeable future.

Typically, job evaluation schemes attempt to fairly address issues of internal comparability in terms of pay. Job evaluation is defined as 'the process of assessing the relative size of jobs within an organisation' (Armstrong and Murlis, 1998: 81). The term 'size' in this context means the value of the job to the organisation.

Armstrong and Murlis identify the defining characteristics of job evaluation (JE) as:

- *A judgemental process*: always (to some extent) reliant on the exercise of judgement in interpreting facts and situations and applying these to decisions about the relative 'size' of jobs.

- *An analytical process*: it is about making informed judgements based upon an analytical process of gathering facts about jobs (based on job analysis techniques).

- *A structured process*: a framework is provided to help evaluators make consistent and rational decisions.

- *A job-centred process*: JE focuses on jobs, not on the people doing them and/or how well they do them. This aspect has clearly raised questions about the value of JE to organisations that adopt a person-based approach as opposed to job-based approach to reward.

Job evaluation is therefore, not a 'perfect' determinant of job relativities. As we can see, it relies to some extent on subjective judgements and it may present some challenges in contemporary workplaces where there is likely to be greater fluidity in job roles.

Devising pay structures

Whether or not organisations engage systematically with the process of job evaluation or take a stronger lead from benchmarking salaries in the external market without recourse to job evaluation techniques, most would agree with Armstrong (2002: 204), that 'pay structures are needed to provide a logically-designed framework within which equitable, fair and consistent reward policies can be implemented'. Perkins and White (2008: 98) argue that grading structures are 'the core building blocks of any organisation's human resource management system, not just for pay but often for conditions of service and career development as well'. The degree of sophistication characterising the design of pay structures in organisations can vary considerably according to firm size, sector and occupational group. For example, smaller firms are generally less likely to operate formal pay structures especially during the formative stages of the business, relying perhaps instead on management discretion to set individual rates of pay for employees (Perkins and White, 2008). However, research in small and medium-sized organisations (SMEs) would indicate that as small firms grow, an informal approach to HRM becomes less tenable (Barrett and Mayson, 2007; Barrett *et al.*, 2008; Mazzarol, 2003); it is at this point that SMEs are likely to begin to inject greater levels of formalisation across a range of human resource practices, including reward. Further, the 2009 CIPD Reward Survey points to sectoral differences and occupational differences.

Responses indicate that pay spines with fixed incremental points are common at all levels in the public sector, while individual pay rates or ranges, which allow for greater flexibility, are more prevalent in the private sector. By occupation, senior managers are most likely to be subject to individual pay rates or ranges.

According to Armstrong (2002: 203) a pay structure:

- defines the different levels of pay for jobs or groups of jobs by reference to their relative internal value as established by job evaluation, to external relativities as established by market rate surveys and, where appropriate, to negotiated rates for the job;
- except in the case of 'spot rates', provides scope for pay progression in accordance with performance, skill, contribution or service;
- contains an organisation's pay ranges for jobs grouped into grades, individual jobs or job families; or pay scales for jobs slotted into a pay spine; or the spot rates for individual jobs where there is no scope for progression.

In essence, a pay structure defines the rate, or range of the payment rate, for jobs within the organisational structure. Whilst this might sound a relatively simple task, there are a number of design choices to be made:

- Should the organisation establish spot rates for individual jobs or devise a more complex structure or series of pay structures?
- How many pay structures are necessary?
- What types of pay structures are suitable?
- If a grading structure is deemed appropriate, how many grades should there be; how wide should each grade or band be; and how close should grade differentials be?

Further decisions must subsequently be made about 'whether, or on what basis, employees will progress through the pay structure' (Perkins and White, 2008: 152).

General design features

As a rule, pay structures need to be flexible enough to accommodate change in the organisation or in the external market and sufficiently clear for individuals to understand where in the structure they are placed and how pay progression is achieved. Spot rates, as referred to in Armstrong's definition above, are set rates of base pay for individual jobs, independent to one another and not tied to a scale or range. Where there is a spot rate for a job, all employees incumbent in the role are paid the same base rate for the job; this may be supplemented by forms of variable pay such as overtime and shift premium or attendance bonus. Spot rates tend to preside in manufacturing and warehouse/distribution centres and in other forms of manual work (Armstrong, 2002). It is difficult to regard a series of spot rates as a pay structure per se, however, spot rates can be customised to personify typical features of a pay structure, for example a mini-series of spot rates (generally referred to as an individual pay range) could be assigned to a role such that there is scope to pay a lesser training or learning rate to individuals new to the role, a target spot rate for a fully competent employee and a further (higher) rate to recognise superior skill, experience or performance. In other circumstances, organisations may elect to manage spot rates in such a way as to incentivise consistently high levels of output, this might be attempted in a somewhat punitive fashion, by dropping lower performing employees to a less favourable spot rate until such a time as higher productivity is resumed.

Whilst, as illustrated, a degree of tailoring is possible, spot rates do not readily offer scope for pay progression; rather they supply a series of detached job rates. Such an approach may be eminently suitable where jobs are fairly static in nature and career development opportunities and expectations are limited. In contrast grading, pay spines and job families, more aptly fit the description of a framework for the enactment of pay policy, in addition, they offer options for pay progression, through the spine, grade or family of jobs based upon length of service or other criterion best suited to the organisation's strategic business objectives.

A single structure or several structures?

An organisation may be able to design and implement a single pay structure to incorporate the entire range of jobs (or the vast majority of jobs) across the organisation, alternatively two or more structures may be in place to assimilate different groups of roles represented within the organisation (for example, a manual pay scale and an office and managerial salary structure). In recent years, both the National Health Service (NHS) and the Higher Education (HE) sector have untaken extensive pay reform, underpinned by job evaluation to develop single pay structures. The NHS scheme, 'Agenda for Change', succeeded in introducing a single national pay scale for NHS hospital employees (with the exception of doctors and consultants), similarly the National Framework Agreement in Higher Education has created a single pay spine for support staff and academic staff in HE institutions.

What benefits do you think hospitals and universities are likely to derive from the formulation of single pay structures in their respective organisations?

Pay spines

A pay spine is a series of fixed incremental salary points reflecting all jobs from the highest paid through to the lowest paid incorporated in the structure. Incremental points may increase at an evenly distributed rate throughout the spine, for example each increment might be set 2.5 per cent above the next from the bottom to the top of the structure. Alternatively, increments might be wider at higher levels in the organisation (Armstrong, 2002). Pay spines are common in the public services sector including education, health, local government and the police service (Perkins and White, 2008). In these work environments, pay grades are superimposed upon the pay spine to form a structure in which a series of increments apply within each grade. Employees' annual salaries are typically automatically raised to the next incremental point on the basis of length of service, this either occurs on an individual basis, triggered by the anniversary of the employee joining the organisation or collectively at a fixed date in the calendar. Except in extreme cases of poor performance, where an increment might be withheld or where progression 'gateways' have to be crossed, employees continue to receive automatic annual increments (and possibly accelerated increments awarded according to performance criteria) until such a time as they reach the top point in the grade. Pay progression thereafter, in the form of increments, is contingent on the employee gaining promotion to a higher grade. In some organisations further additional discretionary points may be available beyond the upper limit of the grade boundary, reserved for those employees who have performed exceptionally throughout the year or those who have made a special contribution. In public services, where pay spines are prevalent, uplift to the pay spine is the subject of national pay bargaining between trade unions and employers; where a cost of living percentage increase in pay is agreed the incremental scale is adjusted upwards accordingly. Pay spines offer employees a degree of pay progression certainty and give employers certainty in terms of total salary expenditure, but may be perceived as bureaucratic and excessively rigid.

Try to think of other potential benefits and disadvantages associated with pay spines.

Graded pay structures

Aside from the use of a central pay spine, organisations opting for a formal pay structure are likely to use some form of grading. The general principles of a pay-grading structure are that jobs are grouped together into grades or bands, often according to some measure of job size. Graded structures require firms to determine how many grades or bands to build into the structure, the width of each grade ('bandwidth'), the degree of overlap to configure between grades and the size of grade differentials to apply throughout the structure. Jobs should be grouped together such that a distinction can be made between the characteristics of the jobs in different grades and the grade hierarchy should broadly take account of the organisational hierarchy. Additionally, there should be a significant step in demands on job holders in the next highest grade such that salary differentials can be suitably justified (www.e-reward.co.uk, January 2007).

Narrow-graded pay structures

Narrow-graded pay structures, or 'traditional' graded structures as they are sometimes referred to, comprise a large number of grades, typically ten or more with jobs of broadly equivalent worth slotted into each of the grades (Armstrong, 2002). As the name would suggest, the width of each grade within the structure ('bandwidth') is narrow, perhaps amounting to a range where the upper salary limit of the grade is anywhere between 20 per cent and 50 per cent higher than the lower salary limit (www.e-reward.co.uk, January 2007). Salary differentials between pay ranges are invariably around 20 per cent (Armstrong, 2002), calculated with reference to the grade mid-point. There is usually an overlap between ranges, which can be as high as 50 per cent (www.e-reward.co.uk, January 2007). The purpose of an overlap is to provide the employer with the scope to recognise and reward a highly experienced and/or qualified employee at the top of a grade more generously than someone who is still in the learning curve zone of the next higher grade (see Figure 13.4). Ultimately, however, the individual placed in the higher grade has greater scope for salary progression. He/she will be able to move closer towards, and eventually, beyond the target rate for a fully competent employee within the grade, contingent upon on satisfying the criteria for pay progression used by the organisation.

For illustrative purposes Figure 13.5 shows a single narrow grade with a bandwidth of 40 per cent, while Figure 13.6 shows an extract of a narrow graded pay structure where the bandwidth is 40 per cent throughout the structure, a grade overlap of 20 per cent is applied and the differential between grades is set at 20 per cent.

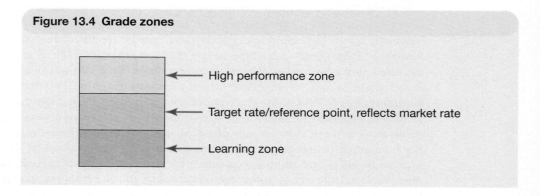

Figure 13.4 Grade zones

High performance zone

Target rate/reference point, reflects market rate

Learning zone

Figure 13.5 Narrow salary grade (40 per cent bandwidth)

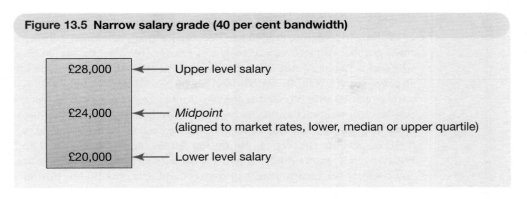

£28,000 ← Upper level salary

£24,000 ← *Midpoint*
(aligned to market rates, lower, median or upper quartile)

£20,000 ← Lower level salary

Figure 13.6 Extract of narrow-graded pay structure

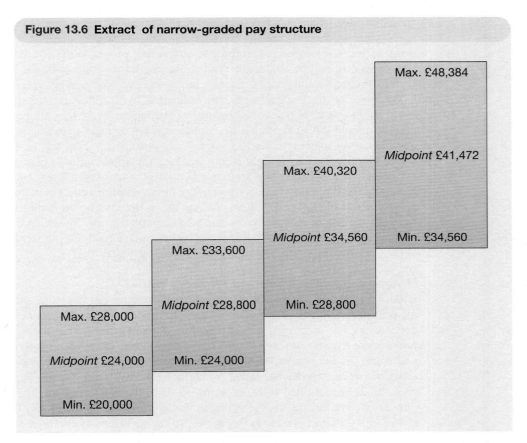

Max. £28,000

Midpoint £24,000   Min. £24,000

Min. £20,000

Max. £33,600

Midpoint £28,800   Min. £28,800

Max. £40,320

Midpoint £34,560   Min. £34,560

Max. £48,384

Midpoint £41,472

Min. £34,560

It is practice to identify a reference point or target rate in each grade which is the rate for a fully competent individual who is completely qualified and experienced to execute the job to the required standard. This target rate is frequently, but not always, the *midpoint* in the range, aligned to market rates for similar jobs and set in accordance with the organisation's pay stance (upper, median or lower quartile), (www.e-reward.co.uk, January 2007). Analysis seems to show that among private sector service employers, the target rate does tend to be the mid-point in the range, whereas in the public sector the target rate is close to the top of the range. In the manufacturing and production sectors and across the voluntary sector employers are broadly divided as to whether the target salary is at the mid-point or towards the top end of the pay band (CIPD, 2009b).

517

Broad-banded pay structures

In contrast to a narrow-graded pay structure, a broad-banded structure involves the use of a small number of pay bands, usually just four or five (Armstrong, 2002), each with a band-width of between 70 and 100 per cent (Perkins and White, 2008). The broader salary range attached to bands in the structure gives employers greater flexibility than is possible in a narrow-graded structure and is arguably more suitable for use in flatter organisations where employee development and career progression is not inextricably linked to vertical movement through the hierarchy. Flatter organisations tend to develop a more flexible outlook as far as careers are concerned, promoting lateral career development and 'zig-zag' careers. Whilst narrow grades might inhibit such moves, broad bands allow employers to recognise and reward non-vertical career movement and role growth. For this reason broad-banded pay structures are sometimes labelled career-based structures (CIPD, 2000). The CIPD (2000) is keen to point out, however, that some organisations claiming to have made the transition to a broad-banded structure have simply collapsed several narrow grades into fewer wider grades and crucially failed to re-position their own and their workforce's percep-tions in terms of career development and salary progression. The CIPD suggests pay structures of this type ought to be called broad-*graded* because of their attachment to the vertical progression mentality more closely associated with narrow-grading structures, the CIPD also offers the less flattering term 'fat-graded' to describe such structures.

A further feature of true broad-banded pay structures is that they afford employers greater latitude in establishing starting salaries and so the opportunity to pay more to attract suitably qualified and experienced staff to 'hard to fill' positions. Whilst this facility might be per-ceived useful, especially in tight labour markets, the opportunity to place an employee on a salary anywhere within the wide range between the band minimum and maximum gives managers the discretion to apply individual differentiation and therein license to cloud any notion of transparency (IDS, 2006). Where this is the case, broad-banding would appear to heighten the risk of an equal pay claim whilst simultaneously loosening the employer's rein on the pay budget, potentially leading to higher reward costs. So can pay levels be managed fairly and cost-consciously within a broad-banded pay structure?

Managing pay within a broad-banded pay structure

Perkins and White (2008) suggest employers have indeed been anxious about the potential for untrammelled pay progression as a result of wide pay bands. In an effort to curb costs and manage pay more systematically within a broad-banded structure, some organisations have sought to mark out zones within bands to indicate the expected salary range for partic-ular roles. The salary level reflected in the zone is likely be arrived at by benchmarking with comparators in the external market. Similarly, a series of target rates for particular jobs in the band could be identified and superimposed upon the band to denote the market rate for a fully competent individual performing in the job. Further, a series of bars or gateways can be etched into the band to serve as thresholds. To cross a threshold and thereby access the higher salary zone beyond the bar, job holders might be required to demonstrate defined compe-tency levels or reach particular standards of performance. These methods of managing pay within a broad-banded pay structure would appear to improve transparency and provide a surer basis for ensuring equal pay for work of equal value. The role for job evaluation in establishing a hierarchy of jobs within a broad-banded structure is also more apparent where zones or target rates for roles are incorporated.

- *Is there a grading structure within your organisation?*
- *How many grades/bands exist within your own organisation?*

Number of bands	Senior executives	Managerial/professional	Staff /manual
3 or less	☐	☐	☐
4–5	☐	☐	☐
6–9	☐	☐	☐
10+	☐	☐	☐

- *Would you classify your own organisation's pay structure as* **broad-graded, broad-banded** *or* **traditional (narrow-graded)***?*
- *What advantages and disadvantages are associated with the pay structure in place within your own organisation?*

Job families

Finally, pay structures can be characterised wholly or partially by the use of job family structures, or labour market structures as they are sometimes called. Armstrong (2002: 206) maintains that

> a job family structure consists of separate grade or pay structures for jobs which are related through the activities carried out and the basic skills used, but are differentiated by the level of responsibility, skill or competence required.

There may be six to eight levels within each job family, representing the range of jobs in the family from lower ranking jobs through to higher ranking posts (CIPD, 2008b). In essence, this approach to devising pay structures treats different occupations or functions separately and results in a series of pay ladders for different sets of jobs. Alternatively, a single job family structure could co-exist with a main stream pay structure in an organisation where the family of jobs concerned cannot easily be assimilated in the mainstream structure without giving rise to anomalies. In practice, job family pay structures are beneficial where an organisation needs to recruit to job roles within a particular occupational group and there is fierce competition in the labour market forcing the price of wages up. A job family pay structure allows the organisation to align to the external market more closely and so improve its chances of attracting and retaining adequate resources (CIPD, 2008b).

Pay progression

As Wright (2004: 78) argues 'there is little point in organisations having elaborate pay structures unless they are offering employees some progression opportunities for their pay *within* the pay structure' (original emphasis). A number of means are at the organisation's disposal to manage employees' movement within the salary structure, indeed, the way in which this is done in different types of organisations tends to vary far more than actual levels of wages and salaries (Perkins and White, 2008). *How* organisations pay portrays their stance on reward and is in many ways a more strategic decision than *how much* to pay. Where a strategic approach to reward is manifest, methods of pay progression will be informed by a clear notion of the organisation's values and strategic imperatives such that the 'right' individuals are recognised and rewarded for the 'right' behaviours. As was suggested earlier in this chapter, strategic approaches to reward are not universally applied, and even where they are, weaknesses and difficulties often mire best efforts. Where pay progression is concerned sometimes pragmatic decisions, underscored by the lack of resources and expertise to design and manage more elaborate pay progression mechanisms, drive organisations to apply blanket solutions such as automatic annual increments linked to employee service and across-the-board percentage pay increases. Indeed, for some organisations, and the stakeholders involved in the particular employment relationship, annual service-related increments and unified pay awards may signify equity, parity and transparency and therefore be viewed more positively than other means of salary progression.

However, whilst service-related pay progression rewards the build-up of expertise in the job and may help employers with retention, it risks signalling to employees that longevity of service is more important than the quality and/or quality of the work undertaken and the manner in which work is conducted. Similarly, universal pay increases, resulting in the same pay award to everyone regardless of their contribution, fail to take into account other factors that might justifiably be used to determine the speed and scale of individual salary progression. Service-related increments are a traditional method of pay progression in the public sector, but they are less frequently used by private sector employers who tend to prefer mechanisms that reward other factors such as performance, competence and skill (CIPD, 2008c). Similarly the 2009 CIPD Reward Survey shows that the use of collective bargaining, resulting in the same percentage pay increase for represented groups of employees, is far more prevalent in the public sector than it is in private sector and voluntary sector organisations.

In contrast, a number of alternative means of managing salary progression are available including:

Individual performance-related pay (PRP)

PRP links individual pay progression with employee performance. The basic notion of individual PRP is that the promise of rewards contingent on performance will incentivise employees to perform optimally thus raising individual performance and leading to improved levels of organisational performance. Within a PRP scheme, employee performance is typically assessed against pre-set targets or pre-agreed objectives often at appraisal time, although a separate pay review meeting could be used to determine a PRP increase. PRP payments may be consolidated into base pay or paid as a bonus (variable pay). PRP schemes ebb and flow in popularity and have been the subject of much controversial debate in the reward literature. In particular the supposed causal link between PRP and performance or productivity has been heavily questioned (Thompson, 1992; Marsden and Richardson, 1994; Kessler and Purcell, 1992). Indeed, rather than glowing accolades heralding the benefits of PRP, much attention has been drawn to the potential negative ramifications associated with using it. Reservations tend to revolve around the following issues:

- PRP schemes operate on the basis that employees will be motivated by money whereas motivational theories suggest money is not the only motivator, or even necessarily an effective motivator.
- The size of the 'pay pot' and how to divide this appropriately commensurate with individual performance achievements.
- Problems associated with measuring performance in a fair and objective manner.
- The ability of managers to manage the award of PRP; to make, communicate and justify difficult and potentially divisive reward decisions.
- Potential for pay discrimination/bias.
- Potential harm to efforts to engender team-work as individual PRP encourages employees to focus on their own performance targets or objectives without concern for the greater good of the team, department or wider organisation.
- Focus on output/outcomes, but not the means used to accomplish performance outcomes.

Further, Kessler and Purcell (1992) argue that linking assessments of performance to pay can induce tunnel vision whereby employees concentrate on those aspects of their job that trigger pay increases and ignore other parts of their job role. They also suggest that the limitations of the pay pot may mean that even employees with positive appraisal ratings only receive relatively small pay-outs that fail to measure up to the 'felt-fair' principle. In view of the criticisms individual PRP has attracted, the CIPD (2008c) indicates that some employers are moving towards a broader concept of contribution-related pay which not only measures outcomes but takes into account how employees achieved the performance outcome. Pay schemes related to contribution propose a more holistic view of individual performance taking into account processes and behaviour.

Contribution-related pay

As indicated above, interest in contribution-related pay is partly prompted by concern that individual performance-related pay takes too narrow an interpretation of performance by focusing upon outcomes in isolation. Organisations expressing a preference for contribution-related pay signal an interest in how the results are achieved as well as the results themselves. Indeed, the way in which employees conduct their work and the attitudes and behaviours they display may have been identified by such organisations as a critical factor in securing competitive advantage, so to try to match pay to softer measures of behaviours as well as harder results data would seem to indicate an attempt to design a pay progression mechanism that places due emphasis on strategic fit. Armstrong (2002: 309) defines contribution-related pay as 'a process for making pay decisions which are based on assessments of both the outcomes of the work carried out by individuals and the level of skill and competence which have influenced these outcomes'. It is thus an attempt at a mixed, blended or hybrid method incorporating the ethos of performance-related pay and competence based pay. It means paying for results (outcomes) and competence, for past performance and potential for future success (see Figure 13.7).

The mechanisms used to pay for contribution can vary considerably. Recognising that contribution-related pay incorporates multi-dimensional measures, some organisations reward the acquisition and display of required competencies in base pay, and reward results achieved with an unconsolidated bonus (variable pay) whilst others arrive at a composite increase in base pay taking into account both competence and results pay-outs (Brown and Armstrong, 1999).

Competence-related pay

Competence-related pay, used alone as means of pay progression, adopts a relatively narrow focus akin to the use of individual performance-related pay, however, emphasis is placed on employees' input to the job, rather than performance or output. The aim of competence-related pay is to encourage and reward the development of particular competencies desired by the organisation; it amounts to a method of paying employees for *the ability to* perform as opposed to paying *for* performance (Armstrong, 2002). Perkins and White (2008: 176) comment that 'whereas individual performance related pay can appear to be simply a punitive system to

Figure 13.7 Contribution-related pay

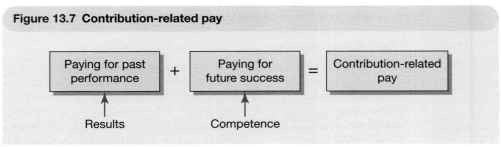

Source: Adapted from Brown and Armstrong (1999: 137).

Table 13.5 The advantages and disadvantages of competence-related pay

Advantages	Disadvantages
• Encourages competence development	• Relies on appropriate, relevant and agreed competence profiles
• Fits de-layered organisations by facilitating lateral career moves	• Assessment of competence levels may be difficult
• Helps to integrate role and organisational core competencies	• Might pay for irrelevant competencies
• Forms part of an integrated, competence-based approach to people management	• Links to pay may be arbitrary
• Delivers message that competence is important	• Costs may escalate if inappropriate or unused competencies are rewarded

Source: from *Employee Reward*, 3rd ed., CIPD (Armstrong, M. 2002) p. 306, with the permission of the publisher, the Chartered Institute of Personnel and Development, London (www.cipd.co.uk).

penalise workers, competency-based systems can in contrast appear positive for employees' own career development'. The introduction of competence-based pay requires a competency framework to be in place and means for measuring individual competence levels to be agreed and understood by managers and employees alike. Table 13.5 summarises the advantages and disadvantages of competence-related pay.

> Skills based pay provides employees with a direct link between their pay progression and the skills they have required and can use effectively.   (Armstrong, 2002: 314)

Skills-based pay

Skills-based pay is sometimes referred to as 'pay for knowledge' or 'knowledge-based pay' (Perkins and White, 2008: 181). The aim of skills-based pay is to encourage employees to acquire additional skills, units of skill or specific qualifications that are deemed important to meet business needs. Skills-based pay might be closely tied to NVQs (National Vocational Qualifications) and the units and levels of qualifications set out in modular qualification frameworks of this type, alternatively the organisation may identify discernable skills or blocks of skills and arrange these in a hierarchy to indicate progressive skill levels. Marchington and Wilkinson (2008) identify both constraints and benefits in the use of skills-based pay. They argue that in order for skills-based pay to aid the efficiency and effectiveness of the organisation, thorough skills-needs analysis needs to be conducted to ensure only those skills critical to business success are encouraged and rewarded. Further, the organisation must pledge a clear commitment to training to underpin the scheme. Finally, whilst skills-based pay is likely to encourage a desire for upward mobility and thirst for skills acquisition amongst workers, care must be taken to ensure that only skills used are paid for, otherwise costs will escalate and the organisation will fail to profit. In addition to costs concerns, Armstrong (2002) suggests employees may become frustrated and de-motivated once they exhaust the skills hierarchy and pay progression grinds to a halt.

Team-based pay

Team rewards involve linking pay increases or a portion of individuals' pay increase to an assessment of performance at team rather than at an individual level. Team-based pay is essentially a variant of individual performance-related pay, designed to reinforce collaborative working and team results. Pay for the achievement of team objectives or targets can be distributed as a fixed sum to all team members or can be calculated as a percentage of base salary (Armstrong, 2002). Armstrong and Murlis (1998: 395) contest that 'the case for team pay looks good in theory but there are some formidable disadvantages':

- its effectiveness relies on the existence of well-defined and mature teams;
- distinguishing individual team members' contributions to the team could be problematic;
- it can be difficult to develop fair and objective methods for measuring team outcomes;
- team rivalry may develop;
- organisational flexibility may be hampered in the sense that employees in high-performing, well-rewarded teams might be unwilling to change roles;
- high performers in low-achieving teams may feel unduly penalised and dissatisfied.

Pay progression based on measures of organisational performance

Finally, there are a three main ways in which individuals' pay can be linked to organisational performance, namely gain-sharing, profit-related pay and share-ownership schemes. The general premise of all three schemes is that by linking pay to organisational performance, employees will be encouraged to focus on value-added activities and will identify more closely with the goals of the organisation. Where the organisation is successful as a result of employees' efforts and contributions, due rewards are passed to employees either in the form of a consolidated payment, a cash one-off payment (unconsolidated, variable pay) or the issue of company shares, and hence a financial stake in the organisation, where the preferred method of linking pay to organisational performance is a share-ownership scheme. Briefly, gain-sharing schemes apply a formula to award individuals a share of the financial gains made by the organisation as a result of improvements in quality, productivity enhancements or cost reduction strategies assisted by employees. Profit-related pay or profit-sharing, on the other hand, typically rewards employees with a slice of the company profits generated over and above a pre-specified profit target or level. The level of payouts varies between 2 and 3 per cent of salary and 10 per cent and more (Armstrong 2002: 356). CIPD data (2009a) would suggest that pay progression based on organisational performance is used as part of the pay progression criterion in around a half of all private sector organisations but that its use in the voluntary sector and in the public sector is limited.

Trends in reward practice – towards a strategic approach or more traditionalism?

Since the early 1990s 'new pay' enthusiasts (Lawler, 1990, 1995, 2000; Schuster and Zingheim, 1992) have consistently promoted the efficacy of transforming pay and reward such that it serves as a more effective driver of organisational performance. In essence, 'new pay' or 'dynamic pay' (Flannery *et al.*, 1996) advocate a far more managerialist view of the design and application of reward tools, resonating with the acclaimed superiority of strategic approaches to reward and the notion of 'total rewards'. Its key ingredients include a greater helping of variable pay, a move away from rigid payment structures to fluid and flexible ones, pay centred on the person not on the job, pay progression dependent on performance, competence, skills, contribution or some other form of contingent pay and a shift away from collectivism to individualism in reward. Such practices are considered to offer the organisation greater agility to reward individual employees commensurate with the impact they make upon critical business objectives and greater control over the pay budget. In this final part of the chapter, we discuss the extent to which organisations in the UK appear to echo the new pay rhetoric by marking out the support of business goals as the supreme priority governing reward objectives and throwing out traditional pay practices in favour of the new.

As we have learned throughout this chapter, there are a multitude of ways to do reward. At the same time, there is a strong tide running through business text books, the HR practitioner press and the professional body, persuading organisations that the right way to do reward is to align it with business strategy. Much of the evidence would suggest that despite the pressure to make the link to business strategy few have grasped the nettle firmly. Indeed, the 2009 CIPD Reward Survey indicates a smaller proportion of respondents with a reward strategy in place than the year before and no more enthusiasm to devise one in the year ahead. The CIPD attributes the drop to the current economic turmoil but their reward adviser, Charles Cotton, considers this foolhardy, 'I believe that during these difficult times it becomes even more important for practitioners to determine whether their reward practices support the objectives of the business' (2009a: 35).

Whilst there might be loose attachment to fully fledged reward strategy, there is evidence that elements of 'new pay' are permeating reward practices, particularly in the private sector. Here we see greater use of broad-banded pay structures, greater reference to market rates when determining salary levels and a higher propensity to use more varied and individualised methods of pay progression, 'Only in the public sector and the not for profit sector is seniority-based pay still the most common form of progression' (Perkins and White, 2008: 193). The decline of collective bargaining in the private sector and the rise in performance-related pay would also seem to indicate that a managerial agenda of individualism and greater use of contingent pay in place of uniform rates for jobs is winning through (Kersley *et al.*, 2006). In contrast, much of the public sector, at least in non-managerial roles, remains riddled with traditionalism.

Summary

This chapter began by outlining seven key objectives and these are revisited here.

- Historically, the area of HRM that we now recognise and understand as employee reward, majorly concerned wages and payment systems and the ways in which these could be used to exert control over both sides of the wage/effort bargain, enlarge the area of managerial control and so maximise organisational profitability.

- Contemporaneously, employee reward is defined more broadly to include base pay, variable pay, benefits and non-financial rewards.

- Reward is now recognised by many employers as a key strategic lever which can be used to mould and direct employee behaviour such that it supports and reinforces business goals. Strategic approaches to reward emphasise the importance of matching reward systems and practices to corporate strategy and integrating reward such that it complements other HR policies and practices. Debates persist, however, as to the precise contribution reward can make to business performance and doubts are cast on the ability of employers to design and implement reward strategy effectively.

- There are no right and wrong approaches to employee reward, rather, a myriad of choices are available to organisations. Key choices entail whether to pay for the person or pay for the job, whether to centralise or decentralise reward decision making, whether to place primary focus on internal equity when determining pay or be more concerned with external benchmarks, whether to build hierarchy into the reward system such that there are seniority or status related rewards or to devise a harmonised, single-status approach and how to determine the precise nature of the reward 'mix'.

- Reward decisions are influenced by a range of factors in the external operating environment. In particular, the economic climate affects employers' ability to pay and it guides organisations in determining salary levels/size of the pay review. The legal framework surrounding reward is designed to protect the low paid, set standards for hours of work and holiday entitlement and to ensure equal pay for work of equal value.

- In practice, approaches to reward are influenced by the size and nature of the organisation, the presence of trade unions, ownership/sector and types of workers employed

- Notable differences emerge between the public sector and private sector in terms of favoured methods for establishing pay levels, the design of pay structures and the criteria for pay progression.

- Despite the rhetoric of 'new pay' and the resounding case for strategic approaches to reward, traditionalism remains pervasive alongside experimentation with the new.

Case study

Changes to reward and recognition at KCLSU

King's College London Students' Union (KCLSU) is an independent, voluntary-sector organisation, affiliated to the National Union of Students (NUS). It enjoys a close relationship with King's College London (KCL), the organisation's current regulator and principal source of funding. KCLSU's purpose is to represent the voice of students at KCL and provide services and facilities to both support and enrich students' lives. KCLSU employs a number of permanent staff in a range of managerial and support roles, in addition, four students are elected annually by the student body to serve a sabbatical year as officers of the union. Elected officers join the payroll of KCLSU during their period of office. This case study captures the process of reviewing reward at KCLSU and poses two alternatives for the future direction of reward strategy within the organisation.

Background

Pay structures and reward strategy at KCLSU need to be reviewed for three main reasons:

- KCLSU currently uses the pay structure in place at King's College London (KCL), an arrangement that has persisted for many years. Along with much of the higher education sector, KCL is currently undergoing a process of modernisation within its pay structures and the current structure is in the process of being phased out. KCLSU is unsure whether the new KCL pay framework will be appropriate for adoption in the students' union. Also, a reconsideration of the logic of KCLSU sharing the KCL pay structure is timely as the organisation is on the brink of becoming regulated by the Charity Commission, rather than the college, and subject to more diversified funding.

- The recognition that there is a need for a modern pay structure to reflect the values of KCLSU, such as contribution and development, and the fact that KCLSU is a modern, forward thinking organisation

- KCLSU needs to be a competitive employer within the voluntary sector, this is essential for staff recruitment and retention purposes

Current system

As indicated above, KCLSU currently utilises the pay scales and process in operation at KCL. The current pay structure is based on the following criteria:

- Several pay spines exist for different grades of staff within the college. KCLSU currently uses two of the existing KCL pay spines: 'Academic and related', which is used primarily for the senior management team and 'Clerical and related' for all other staff.

- The pay spines are divided into overlapping grades; each grade has up to nine increments including discretionary increments at the top of each of grade.

- Individual salary progression is via automatic annual increment to the top of a grade.

- A cost of living increase is awarded annually in August (usually in the region of 3 per cent).

- Discretionary increments are subject to authorisation by a staff member's line manager, historically these have been awarded without question and there is an expectation in place that they will be granted.

- Once a staff member has reached the top of their grade, a proposal for progression to the next grade can be submitted to the HR Committee, who will make a decision as to whether progression will be authorised or not. Currently, the President, Chief Executive and Human Resources Manager sit on the HR Committee.

- If progression to the next grade is not authorised, the staff member will stay at the top of their current grade. The HR Committee will automatically review their salary annually.

- Salaries for new staff members are determined through comparison with existing roles.

This system has a number of inherent problems.

Case study continued

Issues with the current system

There are a number of significant issues with the current pay structure:

- *Progression*: currently, progression through the grades and the award of annual increments is primarily automatic and based on length of service rather than individual contribution. Several staff members will reach the upper limit of their current grade or scale within the next 12–18 months.
- *CEO remuneration*: the KCL pay scales have historically proved unsuitable for the remuneration of the KCLSU Chief Executive due to their upper limits. Therefore KCLSU has developed its own scale for this post and advises the KCL payroll for pay-processing purposes.
- *Benchmarking*: historically benchmarking has only taken place within the students' union sector and not against charity, not-for-profit or public sector equivalents. Increasingly, staff are being attracted to public sector/charity roles as opposed to staying with the students' union world. A recent salary benchmarking exercise drawing information from *Charity Rewards 2005/2006: A Comprehensive National Survey of Pay and Benefits in the Voluntary Sector*[1] has highlighted that current KCLSU salaries may be uncompetitive within the voluntary sector, especially at junior and middle management level i.e. 42 per cent of staff. In fact, the current upper limits of the salary ranges for KCLSU middle and junior managers are below the lower quartile for the charity sector. Taking a wider view, all the upper limits of the current salary ranges are below the median for the charity sector with the exception of the Skilled Manual and Specialist Clerical roles, where the upper limit of the salary range sits £617 above the median. All the lower limits of the current salary ranges are below the lower quartile for the sector, except that for Skilled Manual and Specialist Clerical roles. Elected officer remuneration is typically below that of graduate entrants.
- *Pay and performance*: the KCL pay scales have no latitude for relating pay to performance; there is no reward for good performance other than discretionary rises; there is no organisational imperative added to personal performance. The pay structure has no 'bonus' mechanism.

Observations and developments

KCL pay and modernisation programme

The pay and modernisation programme is KCL's response to the National Framework Agreement

(NFA), which focuses on modernising pay within the Higher Education sector. The guiding principles of the programme are those of equal pay for work of equal value and consistency of grading.

- The programme also aims to harmonise terms and conditions of employment for all job roles within the college.
- The new pay structure will focus on rewarding individual contribution; progression will be linked to satisfactory performance and tied into a new appraisal scheme.
- Individual contribution will be measured by both performance (outputs) and competence (inputs).
- The new pay structure will provide the ability to make annual additional payments for rewarding outstanding individual performance.
- The new pay structure will use a single set of pay grades for all staff. Position of a role on the pay spine is to be determined by a single job evaluation scheme. The scheme in use is HERA (Higher Education Role Analysis).
- There are five job families of associated job roles, which are designed to aid job evaluation and underpin career paths.

Considerations – stay with KCL or 'go it alone'?

KCL has indicated that KCLSU is welcome to assimilate to the new KCL pay structure and continue to use college payroll services, however, KCLSU is unsure whether continuing to mirror KCL's pay structures and philosophy will adequately reflect and support the competencies and values KCLSU is striving to embed. KCLSU is also concerned that the issues it currently experiences as a result of adopting KCL's reward framework will prevail with the new, modernised version.

KCLSU want to adopt a reward strategy capable of harnessing the skills and enthusiasm of KCLSU staff to provide a fantastic service to students at KCL, through a clear and sustainable link between reward and achievement. In particular they are keen to ensure that the new approach will:

- provide the flexibility to respond to different demands in a way that is simple, clear and free from bureaucracy, recognising that different parts of the business have different needs;
- provide predictable or guaranteed earnings that give financial certainty, but with the opportunity to reflect upon business success, and reward people for the passion or creativity that contributes to that success;

Case study continued

- value people for what they do and how they do it, so that KCLSU delivers on its promises and makes a difference to the quality of student life at KCL;
- act as an effective magnet to attract good people, recognising the need for a steady influx of fresh thinking and new approaches, alongside the development of existing talent;
- support KCLSU values and reward employees for living KCLSU values (see Table).

KCLSU values

Value	Examples of how this might be demonstrated
Making sure every person in the organisation matters	• Communicates openly and honestly, always giving consideration to the views and feelings of others • Listens to others, questions when unclear to ensure mutual understanding and allows for discussion • Gives and receive feedback sensitively creating an environment where issues can be discussed constructively • Acts as a team player, actively supports team and organisation objectives • Demonstrates cross-organisational understanding • Shows respect and consideration for the needs of others, and the context within which they work • Demonstrates an understanding of the value of diversity, and the strengths and skills of others
Focusing on our students	• Has a clear understanding of role, and how it relates to the team's and KCLSU's objectives • Demonstrates dedication and enthusiasm towards students • Represents KCLSU positively to students • Seeks and acts upon feedback from both students and internal/external sources.
Continually striving to improve	• Is focused on meeting and exceeding objectives • Is prepared to ask for support from colleagues/line manager when required, to help meet objectives • Sets challenging targets that encourage personal development • Committed to innovation, developing new ideas and solutions • Demonstrates adaptability, flexibility, and a willingness to experiment • When required is entrepreneurial and willing to take appropriate risks
Not being complacent, overcoming unnecessary bureaucracy	• Actively seeks and shares information for the benefit of themselves, team and KCLSU • Seeks to develop effective and efficient ways of working at individual, team and organisational level • Sees mistakes as an opportunity to learn and encourages others to think in the same way
Being confident of our role	• Promotes positive understanding of the aims of KCLSU • Acts as a role model inspiring, supporting, motivating and encouraging others • Raises awareness and understanding of issues affecting students • Values the contribution of others, and recognises and celebrates others' achievements
Managing people well	• Articulates a clear vision for staff; establishes clear aims and objectives for individuals and teams • Ensures that every team member has a clear understanding of their role and how it relates to KCLSU's objectives • Manages individuals and teams consistently, objectively and fairly • Carries out constructive performance reviews with team members • Encourages colleagues to continue their professional development • Listens to feedback and forms recommendations to improve service, develop ideas and deal with issues • Helps develop a culture in which people are valued and able to reach their full potential

1. Croner Reward 2005.

Source: KCLSU

Case study continued

Questions

1 Critically assess the degree to which KCL's pay and modernisation programme is likely to address the issues and concerns KCLSU currently experiences as a result of using the KCL pay framework

2 Consider the benefits and risks associated with KCLSU 'going it alone'.

3 Identify the immediate and on-going/longer-term resource implications for KCLSU if the organisation decides to break away from the KCL pay framework and supporting infrastructure.

4 Using your knowledge and understanding of reward options identify and justify a set of preliminary proposals for a KCLSU 'tailor-made' reward strategy.

References and further reading

Adams, J. (1965) 'Inequity and social exchange' in L. Berkowitz (ed.) *Advances in Experimental Social Psychology 2*, New York: Academic Press, pp. 267–96.

Anthony, P.D. (1977) *The Ideology of Work*. London: Tavistock Publications.

Armstrong, M. (2002) *Employee Reward*, 3rd edn. London: CIPD.

Armstrong, M. and Brown, D. (2006) *Strategic Reward*. London: Kogan Page.

Armstrong, M. and Murlis, H. (1998) *Reward Management; A Handbook of Remuneration Strategy and Practice*. London: Kogan Page.

Armstrong, M. and Stephens, T. (2005) *A Handbook of Employee Reward Management and Practice*. London: Kogan Page.

Armstrong, M., Cummins, A., Hastings, S. and Wood, W. (2003) *Job Evaluation: A Guide to Achieving Equal Pay*. London: Kogan Page.

Arrowsmith, J. and Gilman, M. (2005) 'Small firms and the national minimum wage' in S. Marlow, D. Patton and M. Ram (eds) *Managing Labour in Small Firms*. London: Routledge, pp. 159–77.

Baldwin, M. and Johnson, W. (2006) 'A critical review of studies of discrimination against workers with disabilities' in W. Rodgers III (ed.) *Handbook on the Economics of Discrimination*. Gloucester: Edward Elgar, pp. 119–60.

Barrett, R. and Mayson, S. (2007) 'Human resource management in growing small firms', *Journal of Small Business and Enterprise Development*, 14, 2, 307–20.

Barrett, R., Mayson, S. and Warriner, M. (2008) 'The relationship between small firm growth and HRM practices' in R. Barrett and S. Mayson (eds) *International Handbook of Entrepreneurship and HRM*. Cheltenham: Edward Elgar, pp. 186–204.

Beer, M. (1984) *Managing Human Assets*. New York: Free Press.

Beer, M., Spector, B., Lawrence, P., Mills, D. and Walton, R. (1984) *Human Resource Management; A General Manager's Perspective*. New York: Free Press.

Bevan, S. (2000) *Reward Strategy: 10 Common Mistakes*. London: Institute for Employment Studies.

Blauner, R. (1964) *Alienation and Freedom: The Factory Worker and his Industry*. Chicago, IL: University of Chicago Press.

Bloom, M.C. and Milkovich, G. (1996) 'Issues in managerial compensation research' in C.L. Cooper and D.M. Rousseau (eds) *Trends in Organizational Behavior*, Vol. 3. Chichester: John Wiley, pp. 23–47.

Bowey, A. and Lupton, T. (1973) *Job and Pay Comparisons*. Aldershot: Gower.

Braverman, H. (1974) *Labour and Monopoly Capital: The Degradation of Work in the Twentieth Century*. London: Monthly Review Press.

Brown, D. and Armstrong, M. (1999) *Paying for Contribution; Real Performance-Related Pay Strategies*. London: Kogan Page.

Brown, D. and Dive, B. (2009) 'Level-pegging'. *People Management*, 15 January: 26–29.

Burawoy, M. (1985) *The Politics of Production*. London: Verso.

Burke, R. and Cooper, C. (2008) *The Long Work Hours Culture: Causes, Consequences and Choices*. Bingley: Emerald.

Callaghan, G. and Thompson, P. (2001) 'Edwards revisited; technical control and call centres' *22 Economic and Industrial Democracy*, 22: 13–40.

CIPD (2000) *A Study of Broad-banded and Job Family Pay Structures*. CIPD Report. London: CIPD.

CIPD (2003) *Total Reward*. Research Summary. London: CIPD.

CIPD (2005) *Reward Strategy: How to Develop a Reward Strategy. A CIPD Practical Tool*. London: CIPD.

CIPD (2007) *Reward Management*. A CIPD Survey. London: CIPD.

CIPD (2008a) *Reward Management*. A CIPD Survey. London: CIPD.

CIPD (2008b) *Market Pricing; Approaches and Considerations*. CIPD Factsheet. London: CIPD.

CIPD (2008c) *Pay Progression*. CIPD Factsheet. London: CIPD.

CIPD (2009a) *Reward Management*. CIPD Survey. London: CIPD.

CIPD (2009b) *Pay and Reward: An Overview*. CIPD Factsheet. London: CIPD.

Conboy, B. (1976) *Pay at Work*. London: Arrow Books.

Cotton, C. (2009) 'Workers gloomy about their pay prospects', *Impact: Quarterly update on CIPD Policy and Research*, 26: 18–19.

Druker, J. and White, G. (2009) 'Introduction' in G. White and J. Druker (eds) *Reward Management: A Critical Text*. Abingdon: Routledge, pp. 1–22.

Dundon T. and Rollinson, D. (2004) *Employment Relations in Small Firms*. London: Routledge.

Employee Benefits/MX Financial Solutions (2003) 'Flexible Benefits Research 2003', *Employee Benefits*, April: 4–9.

Equality and Human Rights Commission (2009) **www.equalityandhumanrights.org**.

e-Reward (2007) *Graded Pay Structures*, factsheet. **www.e-reward.co.uk**.

Evain, E. (2008) *Working Conditions Laws 2006–2007*. Geneva: ILO.

Eyraud, F. and Saget, C. (2005) *The Fundamentals of Minimum Wage Fixing*. Geneva: ILO.

Flannery, T.P., Hafrichter, D.A. and Platten, P.E. (1996) *People, Performance and Pay*. New York: The Free Press.

Fredman, S. (2008) 'Reforming equal pay laws', 37 *Industrial Law Journal 193*.

Fudge, J. and Owens, R. (2006) *Precarious Work, Women and the New Economy*. Oxford: Hart Publishing.

Gollan, P. (2007) *Employee Representation in Non-Union Firms*. London: Sage.

Gospel, H. (1992) *Markets, Firms and the Management of Labour in Modern Britain*. Cambridge: Cambride University Press.

Heery, E. (2000) 'The new pay: risk and representation at work' in D. Winstanley and J. Woodall (eds) *Ethical Issues in Contemporary Human Resource Management*. Basingstoke: Palgrave, pp. 172–88.

Hellerstein, J. and Newmark, D. (2006) 'Using matched employer-employee data to study labor market discrimination' in W. Rodgers III (ed.) *Handbook on the Economics of Discrimination*. Gloucester: Edward Elgar, pp. 29–60.

Herzberg, F. (1966) *Work and the Nature of Man*. Cleveland, OH: World Publishing.

Hewlett, S. and Luce, C. (2006) 'Extreme jobs: the dangerous allure of the 70-hour work week', *Harvard Business Review*, (December): 49.

Hill, S. (1981) *Competition and Control at Work*. London: Heinemann.

Hinton, J. (1986) *Labour and Socialism*. London: Wheatsheaf Books.

Humbert A.L. and Lewis, S. (2008) 'I have no life other than work – long working hours, blurred boundaries and family life' in R. Burke and C. Cooper *The Long Work Hours Culture: Causes, Consequences and Choices*. Bingley: Emerald, pp. 159–82.

IDS (2000) 'Job evaluation', *Incomes Data Services StudyPlus*; Autumn.

IDS (2002) 'Kingsmill recommends a package of measures to address the gender pay gap', *Incomes Data Services Report 848*, January: 4–5.

IDS (2006) *Developments in Occupational Pay Differentiation. A Research Report of the Office for Manpower Economics*, October 2006. London: Incomes Data Services.

IRS (2003) 'Employers value job evaluation', *IRS Employment Review 790 /Employment Trends*, 19 December: 9–16.

IRS (2008) 'Survey of pay prospects'.

Jamieson, S. (1999) 'Equal Pay' in A. Morris and T. O'Donnell (eds) *Feminist Perspectives on Employment Law*. London: Cavendish, pp. 223–40.

Kersley, B., Alpin, C., Forth, J., Bryson, A., Bewley, H., Dix, G. and Oxenbridge, S. (2006) *Inside the Workplace: Findings from the 2004 Workplace Employment Relations Survey*. Abingdon: Routledge.

Kessler, I. (2001) 'Reward system choices' in J. Storey (ed.) *Human Resource Management: A Critical Text*, 2nd edn. London: Thomson Learning, pp. 206–31.

Kessler, I. (2007) 'Reward choices: strategy and equity' in J. Storey, (ed.) *Human Resource Management: A Critical Text*, 3rd edn. London: Thomson Learning, pp. 159–76.

Kessler, I. and Purcell, J. (1992) 'Performance related pay; objectives and application'. *Human Resource Management Journal*, 2, 3, Spring: 16–33.

Kohn, A. (1993) 'Why incentive plans cannot work', *Harvard Business Review*, September–October: 54–62.

Lawler, E. (1990) *Strategic Pay*. San Francisco, CA: Jossey-Bass.

Lawler, E. (1995). 'The new pay; a strategic approach', *Compensation and Benefits Review*, July/August: 46–54.

Lawler, E. (2000) 'Pay and strategy; new thinking for the new millennium', *Compensation and Benefits Review*, January/February: 7–12.

Lewis, P. (2006) 'Reward management' in T. Redman and A. Wilkinson (eds) *Contemporary Human Resource Management*, 2nd edn. London: FT/Pearson, pp. 126–52.

Littler, C. (1982) *The Development of the Labour Process in Capitalist Societies*. London: Heinemann.

Littler, C. (ed.) (1985) *The Experience of Work*. Aldershot: Gower.

Lovell, J. (1977) *British Trade Unions 1875–1933*. London: MacMillan.

Low Pay Commision (2001) *1st Report of the Low Pay Commission*. London: HMSO.

Marchington, M. and Wilkinson, A. (2008) *HRM at Work; People Management and Development*, 4th edn. London: CIPD.

Marlow, S., Patton, D. and Ram, M. (2005) *Managing Labour in Small Firms*. London: Routledge.

Marsden, D. and Richardson, R. (1994) 'Performing for pay? The effects of "merit pay" in a public service', *British Journal of Industrial Relations*, June: 243–61.

Mazzarol, T. (2003) 'A model of small business HR growth management', *International Journal of Entrepreneurial Behaviour and Research*, 9: 27–49.

McCann, D. (2005) *Working Time Laws: A Global Perspective*. Geneva: ILO.

McColgan, A. (2008) 'Equal pay' in P. Cane and J. Conaghan, *The New Oxford Companion to Law*. Oxford: Oxford University Press, pp. 401–02.

Milkovitch, G. and Newman, J. (1996) *Compensation*, 5th edn. Burr Ridge: Irwin.

Murlis, H. (2004) 'Managing rewards' in D. Rees and G. McBain (eds) *People Management: Challenges and Opportunities*. Basingstoke: Palgrave, pp. 152–70.

Perkins, S.J. and White, G. (2008) *Employee Reward: Alternatives, Consequences and Contexts*. London: CIPD.

Pfeffer, J. (1998) 'Six dangerous myths about pay', *Harvard Business Review*, May–June: 108–21.

Ritzer, G. (1997) *The McDonaldization Theory*. London: Sage.

Ritzer, G. (2000) *The McDonaldization of Society*. London: Sage.

Schuster, J. and Zingheim, P. (1992) *The New Pay: Linking Employee and Organisational Performance*. New York: Lexington Books.

Storey, J. (1992) *Developments in the Management of Human Resources*. Oxford: Blackwell.

Taylor, F.W. (1964) *Scientific Management*. New York: Harper & Row.

Taylor, P. and Bain, P. (1999) 'An assembly line in the head' *Industrial Relations Journal*, 30: 101–17.

Taylor, P. and Bain, P. (2001) 'Trade unions, workers rights and the frontier of control in UK call centres', *Economic and Industrial Democracy*, 22: 29–41.

Taylor, S (2008) *People Resourcing*, 4th edn. London: CIPD.

Thompson E.P. (1991) 'Time, work-discipline and Industrial Capitalism' in E.P. Thompson *Customs in Common*. Harmondsworth: Penguin, pp. 68–92.

Thompson, M. (1992) 'Pay and performance; the employer experience', *Institute of Manpower Studies*. Report No. 218, London.

Thompson, M. (2009) 'Salary progression systems' in G. White and J. Druker (eds) *Reward Management; A Critical Text*. Abingdon: Routledge, pp. 120–47.

Thompson, P. (1983) *The Nature of Work*. London: Macmillian.

Thompson, P. and Milsome. S. (2001) *Reward Determination in the UK*. Research Report, London: CIPD.

Urwick, L. (1958) *Personnel Management in Perspective*. Oxford: Oxford University Press.

Vroom, V. (1982) *Work and Motivation*. New York: John Wiley.

White, G. (2009) 'Determining pay' in G. White and J. Druker (eds) *Reward Management: A Critical Text*. Abingdon: Routledge, pp. 23–48.

Wood, A.W. (2000) 'Alienation' in *Concise Routledge Encyclopedia of Philosophy*. London: Routledge, p. 24.

Wood, S. (ed.) (1982) *The Degradation of Work?* London: Hutchinson.

WorldatWork (2000) *Total Rewards: From Strategy To Implementations*. Scottsdale, AZ: WorldatWork.

Wright, A. (2004) *Employee Reward in Context*. London: CIPD.

Wright, A. (2009) 'Benefits' in G. White and J. Druker (eds) *Reward Management: A Critical Text*. Abingdon: Routledge, pp. 174–91.

Yates, M.L. (1937) *Wages and Labour Conditions in British Engineering*. Cambridge.

Zeitlin, J. (1983) 'The labour strategies of British engineering employers 1890–1922' in H. Gospel and C. Littler, *Managerial Strategies & Industrial Relations*. Aldershot: Gower, pp. 25–54.

For multiple-choice questions, exercises and annotated weblinks related to this topic, visit **www.pearsoned.co.uk/mymanagementlab**.

Chapter 14

Employee participation and involvement

Peter Butler and Linda Glover

Objectives

- To provide definitions of employee involvement, participation and industrial democracy.
- To examine why the concept of employee involvement is closely allied to 'soft' HRM.
- To clarify the difference between 'cycles' and 'waves' of participation.
- To review evidence in respect of downwards communication, upwards problem solving, financial participation and representative participation.
- To examine recent developments in workplace consultation emanating from the EU.
- To critically evaluate the implications of selected new management initiatives for organisations and employees.

Introduction

This chapter focuses upon employee participation and involvement (EPI). Employee involvement is central to mainstream models of HRM and, as such, is an extremely important component of the contemporary study of HRM. However, as we shall see, EPI initiatives are characterised by ambiguity – both in terms of academic terminology, their application in the field and in terms of the outcomes for organisations and employees. Given the potential for confusion, this chapter will begin by unpacking the EPI construct. As will become clear, the subject matter is broad and actually covers three distinct but related fields of study: employee involvement, employee participation and industrial democracy. Our first section focuses upon definitions of each of these terms. Armed with some conceptual clarity the second section moves on to discuss the history of EPI. It will become evident that while managerially inspired employee involvement is currently ascendant, this is a relatively recent development – over the years the other components have occupied far more column inches in the annals devoted to the topic. The third section focuses upon the managerial motives for EPI and shows that interpretations of managerial purpose range from those that view EPI interventions as positive for managers and employees (i.e. unitarist), to those who view managerial intent with suspicion and regard motives as primarily exploitative. There are also those who believe that managerial goals are not so clear-cut and fall somewhere between these two extremes. The fourth section explores the precise nature of EPI practices in more depth and reviews some of the evidence relating to trends for the various mechanisms. The fifth section reviews contemporary developments at EU level. It will be argued that some of these are significant in heralding a potential renaissance for collective systems of employee participation.

The chapter closes with a discussion of the highly topical area of the implications for organisations and employees of new management initiatives. Here we focus on the move from quality circles to quality management to high performance management.

Definitions

The topic of employee participation and involvement (EPI) has been a perennial feature of writing on the management of human resources. The resilience of EPI and its capacity for reinvention over the last 100 years or so has been one of the more enduring features of studies of the employment relationship. Richardson (2003: 374) likens EPI to Cinderella in its ability to attract and enthral new audiences from one year to the next; a fixation that shows little sign of waning. A key problem facing students of EPI, however, is ambiguity in terminology; indeed Marchington and Wilkinson (2005: 392) comment that 'employee participation and involvement are somewhat elastic terms and are amenable to a range of definitions'. EPI is often treated as a loosely specified concept within which a myriad of managerial interventions are collapsed.

Involvement and participation, while closely related, are conceptually and philosophically distinct and have similarly achieved prominence during differing historical periods. While writers in this field have long lamented the absence of universally accepted definitions (see Hespe and Little, 1971; Pateman, 1970) we are today fortunate in that the terrain of EPI is far less theoretically impoverished than it was a generation or so ago. Indeed, following the emergence of the topic as discrete field of study it is possible to construct a reasonably precise set of concepts, bringing some much needed order to the subject matter. Lewis *et al.* (2003: 248) have argued that 'important differences . . . exist between the concepts in relation to the exercise of power, the locus of control, the nature of employee influence, and the driving force behind each approach in practice'. More empirically, Marchington *et al.* (1992: 7–8) suggest that it is possible to draw distinctions in terms of the degree of employee involvement; the form which the involvement takes; the level in the organisational hierarchy at which individuals are involved; and the range of subject matter dealt with. In the final analysis these models suggest that the essence of any distinction centres on issues of power and influence.

Employee involvement

Employee involvement (EI) is central to most models of HRM. For example, employee involvement is seen as a central tenet of 'soft' HRM, where the focus is upon capturing the ideas of employees and securing their commitment. Storey (1992: 46) suggests that 'soft' HRM 'connotes a style of approach whose touchstones are the careful nurturing of, and investment in, the human stock'. Legge (2005: 105–06) comments that the soft 'developmental humanism' model involves 'treating employees as valued assets, a source of competitive advantage through their commitment, adaptability and high-quality (of skills, performance and so on) . . . the stress is therefore on generating commitment via "communication, motivation and leadership"'. As with HRM, the concept of employee involvement is strongly grounded in unitary theory – put simply it is assumed that managers and employees will 'march to the same tune'. Characteristically, employee involvement initiatives are promoted by management with a view to mobilising the support and tacit knowledge of employees towards corporate goals. Marchington and Wilkinson (2005: 390) observe that employee involvement has 'focused on direct participation of small groups and individuals, it is concerned with information sharing at work-group level, and it has excluded the opportunity for workers to have any inputs into high-level decision-making'.

Box 14.1   Employee involvement

Practices and policies which emanate from management and sympathisers of free market commercial activity and which purport to provide employees with the opportunity to influence and where appropriate take part in the decision making on matters which affect them.

Source: Hyman and Mason (1995: 21).

Critics have argued that employee involvement has management firmly in the driving seat and very limited real influence is relinquished or ceded to non-managerial actors. That is, employee involvement schemes 'extend little or no input into corporate or higher level decision making' and generally do not entail any significant sharing of power and authority (Hyman and Mason, 1995: 22). Simply put, employee involvement is 'soft on power' (Blyton and Turnbull, 2004: 272) the hallmark being that the 'range' (Marchington *et al.*, 1992: 8) of subject matter dealt with is non-strategic in nature and of only localised operational importance. To the extent that there is any granting of influence to employees, the locus is restricted to task or work-group level (Lewis *et al.*, 2003: 259). Any employee 'involvement' in higher order decisions is restricted to top-down information provision.

Participation

Employee participation, as distinct to employee involvement, is grounded in pluralist thinking – a perspective that acknowledges the presence of divergent interests between different organisational stakeholders. Henceforth, when using the term 'participation', we refer to *indirect* forms such as consultative committees. Operationally speaking participation may be contrasted with employee involvement in that it derives invariably from employees, or their organisations (i.e. trade unions), as opposed to being employer led (Harley *et al.*, 2005: 13). As Hyman and Mason (1995: 29) acknowledge, employee participation 'emerges from a collective employee interest to optimize the physical security and aspirational conditions under which employees are contracted to serve'. The motivation for participation therefore differs fundamentally from employee involvement in that it is borne of a desire to increase the influence of employees *vis-à-vis* the employer rather than being concerned with technical issues of corporate efficiency (see Box 14.2). Two outcomes follow. First, in contrast to the task-centred menu of practices that normally surround employee involvement, participation is more fundamentally power-orientated – it is typically about joint decision making or co-determination (Blyton and Turnbull, 2004: 59). While mechanisms of participation are concerned with the 'institutionalisation of conflict', industrial action may occur in the absence of agreement. This could take the form of strikes, stoppages, working-to-rule or an employer lock-out. Recent examples of industrial discord include the Royal Mail dispute of 2009, which began over disagreements about pay, pensions and flexible working. Second, participation is likely to give employees (usually via the agency of their representatives) access to a relatively higher order 'range' of decisions (e.g. wage rates, introduction of new technology and training etc.) than that provided by the machinery of employee involvement. In Abrahamsson's (1977: 189) terminology, participation can be viewed as a political process contributing to high level decision making as opposed to the 'socio-technical nature' of employee involvement which restricts tangible employee influence to narrow production issues.

Because participatory schemes generally involve some dilution of managerial influence there is a long history of employers seeking to resist their encroachment. Consequently, the more enduring examples, such as the works council format found in many European countries, tend to have a strong statutory underpinning and have often been initiated by social democratic governments sensitive to the needs of labour (Payne and Keep, 2005).

Box 14.2   Workers' participation

Workers' participation is about the distribution and exercise of power, in all its manifestations, between the owners and managers of organisations and those employed by them. It refers to the direct involvement of individuals in decisions relating to their immediate work organisation and to indirect involvement in decision making, through representatives, in the wider socio-technical and political structures of the firm.

Source: Brannen (1983: 16).

Within the UK, participation has traditionally found expression through the medium of collective bargaining, rather than via mandated works councils. Collective bargaining is the mechanism through which trade unions and employers jointly regulate certain aspects of the employment relationship (for example, negotiating over pay and conditions such as leave entitlements, pensions and working hours). In terms of the level of influence exerted via this process, the traditional trade union preoccupation with wage issues or 'economism' (Hyman, 1989: 45) has ensured that strategic matters, for example, decisions pertaining to capital investment, have rarely figured as substantive items on the bargaining agenda. Table 14.1 summarises some of the key differences between employee involvement and employee participation.

Industrial democracy

Industrial democracy is distinct from participation in that the goal is a more radical sharing of power within the employment relationship. Throughout the course of capitalist history various radical movements (e.g. the guild socialists, see below) have sought to greatly extend employee influence via calls for industrial democracy. The goal here is to effect a wholesale reshaping of power within the employment relationship. Drawing on Marxian principles, fundamentalist adherents to this approach argue that nothing less than the transfer of ownership and the means of production to workers is consistent with true workplace democracy (see Hyman and Mason, 1995: 9–12). The Israeli kibbutz, experiments in self-management in the former Yugoslavia and the Mondragón corporation in the Basque region of Spain (see Cheney, 1999) have, at various times, been lauded as exemplars of this approach.

With one or two exceptions, e.g. the John Lewis Partnership (Flanders, 1968), British experiments in industrial democracy have tended to be relatively modest affairs, for example, the appointment of worker directors in some public sector enterprises in the 1960s and 1970s (see below). The goal has been to give employees some strategic influence via boardroom representation, not overturn the structure of corporate governance, i.e. working for

Table 14.1 Employee involvement and participation compared

Employee involvement	Employee participation
Management inspired and controlled	Government or workforce inspired; some control delegated to workforce
Geared to stimulating individual employee contributions	Aims to harness collective employee input through market regulation
Employees often passive recipients	Employee representatives actively involved
Tends to be task based	Decision making at higher organisational levels
Assumes common interests between employer and employees	Plurality of interests recognised and machinery for their resolution provided

Source: Adapted from Hyman and Mason (1995: 25).

Box 14.3 Industrial democracy

Adherents to this approach would argue that democratic procedures need to be 'injected at the highest organisational levels in order to restructure authority relations within industry and thereby make all aspects of industrial decision making available and accountable to the majority of the participants who are disenfranchised from existing structures'.

Source: Hyman and Mason, (1995: 18).

rather than owning the company. In view of the traditional antipathy of employers towards any serious extension of employee influence, the state or super state (in the form of the EU) has typically been the driver behind any change to the status quo.

The 'escalator of participation' (see Figure 14.1), as originally devised by Marchington *et al.* (1992), allows us to clarify visually the terrain of both participation and industrial democracy. The latter concept occupies the top step on the escalator. Participation conversely resides on the second step, possibly spreading onto the third depending on the precise nature of consultation. Consultation is itself a term that raises immense definitional problems; in part this is avoided by presenting the term as a continuum. Following Shuchman (cited in Poole, 1978: 26–27) and Bernstein (1976) the consultation 'step' contains three levels of consultation. Of these genuine participation only occupies the green shaded region. Following Pateman (1970) the other forms of consultation are best viewed as 'pseudo participation', i.e. it is only in high-level consultation that management take workers' views seriously and are likely to modify plans accordingly.

STOP and think

- *Why is employee involvement described as 'unitarist'?*
- *Why is employee involvement central to HRM?*
- *What are the differences between direct participation via employee involvement and indirect participation?*
- *Why might management resist moves towards greater industrial democracy?*

Figure 14.1 The escalator of participation

INFORMATION	COMMUNICATION	CONSULTATION	CO-DETERMINATION	CONTROL
		High-level consultation: workers initiate criticism and suggestions. Management still has sole power to decide, but usually adopt worker proposals		
		Mid-level consultation: same as below, but the outcome may stimulate managerial reconsideration		
		Low-level consultation: managers give prior notice of certain changes, representatives have chance to voice their views		

Source: Adapted from Marchington *et al.* (1992: 7).

History of EPI

The following sections trace the history of EPI from the early capitalist period to contemporary times. The purpose is to give an overview of key developments and to show that EPI has a long history.

The early capitalist period

As Brannen (1983: 33) notes, issues of EPI have been 'articulated, fought over, conceded and rejected since the earliest years of industrial society'. This is inevitably so given the initially precarious position of collective labour relative to capital. Workers 'combining' to further their interests were potentially subject to criminal prosecution until the repeal of the Combinations Acts in the nineteenth century. Exhortations by enlightened thinkers such as John Stuart Mill that the provision of industrial democracy would provide the working classes with a stake in the capitalist system and so mediate any tendency to engage in revolt against it (Richardson, 2003: 376) went mostly unheeded. Accordingly, while most recent initiatives in the field of EPI have been brokered by management, early developments were very much worker driven. Aside from one or two radical experiments in cooperative production, initiated by utopian socialists such as Robert Owen (Richardson, 2003: 376), labour was at the vanguard of the emergence of – or at least calls for – EPI.

During the nineteenth century the disenfranchisement of the working classes from all matters relating to workplace regulation gave rise to a radicalisation of employee demands in the form of syndicalism, i.e. demands for the means of production to be placed under worker control and later, guild socialism, i.e. a desire for the state ownership of industry. While philosophically distinct, there was common ground in that both denied the legitimacy of the principles of ownership and control embodied within capitalism (Brannen, 1983: 46) and emphasised the necessity for workers' self-government of industry (Brannen, 1983: 39) – that is a pure form of industrial democracy. Influenced by the Bolshevik revolution in Russia, this period witnessed a considerable growth in left-wing ideology (Holden, 2001: 565). However, tangible employee influence only emerged through the growth of the pluralist practice of collective bargaining (i.e. indirect participation) – an institution that seeks *accommodation* with capital – not its overthrow. Interestingly, the growth in coverage of collective bargaining and the increased institutional strength of trade unions ushered in the first 'cycle' (Ramsay, 1977) of employee involvement. As far back as the 1860s, firms were pioneering profit-share schemes as a means of 'detaching workers from their unions' (Ramsay, 1977: 483). Such practices, however, were not to gain widespread currency for a century or more.

The inter-war period: Whitleyism and joint consultation

The emergence of industrial syndicalism, while short lived, was not without legacy and it was a factor motivating both politicians and employers to give more thought to issues pertaining to EPI (Ramsay, 1977: 486). Set against a backdrop of widespread industrial conflict in the immediate aftermath of the First World War, a government subcommittee of enquiry under J.H. Whitley made up of employer and trade union representatives was established to consider how to achieve a permanent improvement in relations between employers and workers (Marchington *et al.*, 1992: 5). The key policy outcome was the suggestion that workers should be able to participate more fully in the regulation of employment conditions of most concern to them (Marchington *et al.*, 1992). The upshot was the creation of 73 joint industrial councils with over 1000 local committees, the aim being to discuss not only wages and conditions but also problems of industrial efficiency and management. Opinion regarding whether Whitleyism was ever intended to impinge significantly upon managerial prerogative has been a source of some controversy. Brannen (1983: 41) has argued that 'Whitleyism was the officially sponsored *compromise* with demands for worker control' (emphasis added) while for Ramsay the machinery was more about illusory worker control and union incorporation (see Ramsay, 1977: 487–88). Whatever the potential rationale, the initiative was short lived and by 1925 much of the Whitley infrastructure had fallen into disuse.

During the Second World War, EPI again witnessed something of a renaissance. Given the demands placed upon a vastly depleted labour force, the government encouraged the creation of workplace Joint Production Committees (JPCs), both as a means of increasing production and efficiency and according to Ramsay (1977: 490), neutralising militants. By 1943 there were over 4000 JPCs operating in private firms in engineering and related industries covering around 2.5 m workers (Brannen, 1983: 44). It has been estimated that around half of the committees succeeded in relation to their terms of reference (Ramsay, 1977: 490). Nevertheless, as with Whitleyism, enthusiasm for consultation proved ephemeral. Brannen (1983: 44) notes that by 1948 there were only 550 councils in existence. The reason for the brief longevity of such a major, and at times successful, EPI initiative has attracted significant academic comment. Ramsay (1977: 490) gives precedence to worker disillusionment with the way in which the JPCs were used to bolster management power as disciplinary bodies and the like. That is, the original pluralist intent was subverted for an essentially unitary *raison d'être*, i.e. management trying to reorientate control. Brannen (1983: 44–45) argues, however, that such an interpretation sits uneasily with TUC exhortations made via its General Council in 1944 that consultation should be kept as a *permanent* feature of industrial organisations (Brannen, 1983). In any event, as with Whitleyism, widespread interest in EPI was again to move into another lengthy period of torpor as the consultation machinery was wound down.

- Why was the Whitley committee convened?
- What was its main contribution?
- Why were JPCs discredited in the eyes of workers?

The 1970s 'High Noon' of industrial democracy

Much has been written about the 1970s revival of interest in industrial democracy. It warrants highlighting at the outset, however, that this version bore little resemblance to the syndicalism that enjoyed a brief but ultimately unfruitful vogue a century before. Where the syndicalism of the nineteenth century denied the legitimacy of capitalist ownership, the premise that management should wield ultimate authority was never seriously challenged in the 1970s.

Renewed interest in issues of workplace democracy arose because of a triple configuration of events. First, the early 1970s marked Britain's accession to the then Common Market where there were already plans afoot for a 'Fifth Directive' on company law. Under these proposals companies with over 500 employees were to have supervisory boards, with one third of their members representing employees (Clegg, 1979: 438). Powers were to be far reaching with a second-tier management board required to ask the approval of the supervisory board on major decisions such as closure and reorganisation (Brannen, 1983: 59).The British government circles felt that a considered response was needed if Britain was not to be 'swamped by alien policies' (Elliot, cited in Brannen, 1983: 59). A second impetus was provided by the election of a Labour government in 1974. Six years earlier a Labour working party report, *Industrial Democracy*, had been adopted by the 1968 Party Conference (Ramsay, 1977: 494). In its election manifesto Labour pledged itself to implementing many of the report's recommendations via a specific industrial democracy Act (Brannen, 1983: 59). Third, as Clegg (1979: 438) has noted, this period witnessed a 'remarkable reversal' in the attitude of the TUC. Previously the unions had never supported TU representation on company boards, the guiding philosophy being famously captured in Clegg's (1951: 22) dictum that 'trade unions are an opposition which can never become a government'. As Lewis *et al.* (2003: 25) note, under this view, participation in decision making would have compromised the essentially oppositional role that unions had traditionally played. However, sensing a sea-change, TUC policy shifted to one of support for worker directors with prominent unionists, such as Jack Jones, calling for a real transfer of power and responsibility to workers (Ramsay, 1977: 494). This change of heart was significantly driven by the growing complexity of the financial structure of organisations – the emergence of multinational enterprise was making it difficult for unions to bargain knowledgeably. As Crouch (1979: 109) noted at the time, union officials were increasingly coming to believe that they would need to gain more of an 'insiders' view to pursue matters satisfactorily.

These factors led to the setting up of the Bullock Committee of Inquiry charged with looking at ways of *achieving* boardroom participation (Brannen, 1983: 60). The terms of reference were an immediate source of controversy amongst the committee members comprising trade unionists, academics and employers. The latter argued that they had been forced to consider not *whether* but *how* employee directors should be appointed (Hyman and Mason, 1995: 143, emphasis in original). Reflecting this split, the output was actually two reports. The majority report (representing the views of the chairperson and the trade unions and academic committee members) supported the creation of so called 'unitary boards' in private sector organisation. The formula $2x + y$ was devised, meaning parity representation of worker directors ($2x$) plus one or more neutral board member recommended by bodies such as ACAS (Hyman and Mason, 1995: 140). The minority report argued that any system should be based on a two-tier model as in Europe, with employee representatives sitting on a supervisory, i.e. policy, board (Hyman and Mason, 1995: 143).

Unsurprisingly, British private sector management was 'vehemently opposed' (Brannen, 1983: 60) to the proposals. Indeed, Cressey (cited in Lewis *et al.*, 2003: 251) has argued that the minority report was itself a 'pale reflection' of the rancour felt by British employers. Several ministers, including the Secretary for Trade, Edmund Dell, shared the employers' views and pressed the government for the dilution of any legislation (Crouch, 1979: 111). The resultant White Paper in 1978 largely affirmed the minority position, proposing the establishment of two-tier boards with employees being given a statutory right, if they wished, of representation on a supervisory board (Crouch, 1979: 60). Ultimately, however, some brief public sector experimentation with employee boardroom representation was the only tangible legacy of the Inquiry. Attempts were made to introduce worker director schemes into both British Steel and the Post Office (see Batstone *et al.*, 1983 and Brannen *et al.*, 1976). Even here, however, any involvement was mostly restricted to industrial relations issues and the schemes did little to extend the 'range' of employee influence. Failure to make progress meant that Britain remained one of the few western European countries without a statutory framework for consultation or participation (Lewis *et al.*, 2003: 251). Political events ensured that any such change remained a generation away.

- *What factors sparked the renewed interest in workplace democracy?*
- *Why do you think private sector managers were 'vehemently opposed' to the proposals of the Bullock report?*

Thatcherism and beyond

The 1980s represented a distinct watershed for EPI. The coming of Thatcherism and economic structural change provided a fertile climate for managerial experimentation with practices of employee involvement. The Conservatives were committed to the principles of voluntarism. That is, the premise that management should be allowed to introduce forms of involvement that they saw fit rather than having an external source imposed (Lewis *et al.*, 2003: 258). Thus, from the outset the incoming administration was opposed to the Bullock recommendations. The Conservatives *were*, however, committed by their manifesto to encourage employee involvement through consultation, communication and financial involvement (Brannen, 1983: 60). The upshot was a legislative programme that *inter alia* sought to significantly diminish *collective* trade union power *and* encourage *individual* involvement, e.g. by granting tax relief for approved corporate employee share-ownership and profit-related pay schemes. As Blyton and Turnbull (2004: 263) acknowledge, 'in this the Conservative government sought to promote material rather than participative–democratic forms of employee involvement'.

That this period of Conservative rule saw levels of the trade union membership plunge to a post-war low needs no rehearsing. A variety of factors including the weakening of the manufacturing base and the rise of the service sector (much of which being historically non-union) contributed to the decline. Hyman and Mason (1995: 53) have argued that union weakness at political, industrial and organisational level provides employees with opportunities to contemplate alternative arrangements for employee relations. Perhaps unsurprisingly, therefore, the use of employee involvement increased substantially between 1984 and 1990. The overall form that employee involvement took was greater willingness to communicate directly with employees and an enhanced recognition of the potential contribution that employees could make to organisational performance (Marchington, *et al.*, 1992: 6). Employee involvement initiatives such as team briefings, quality circles, suggestion schemes, profit share and share ownership all grew after the late 1970s (Marchington *et al.*, 1992). The growth of employee involvement coincided with the rise of 'HRM' as a distinct approach to management.

While the Thatcherite era represented a permissive climate, the requirement for employee involvement was ultimately conditional on the move to a distinctive human resource management approach. Blyton and Turnbull (2004: 258) make the point well:

> For managers, support for 'involvement' stems largely from the principles of human relations management, which draws attention to the importance of the social aspects of organisation in general, and the connection between, on the one hand, communication and consultation between management and workforce, and on the other, increased worker commitment, higher job satisfaction and motivation, and reduced resistance to change.

As Holden (2001: 561) notes, under various influential HRM models, such as that proposed by the Harvard Business School, employee involvement was expounded as a key component of HRM strategies. In addition, the management gurus Tom Peters and Robert Waterman published their influential book, *In Search of Excellence*, in 1982, which very much expounded the managerial and organisational benefits of promoting employee involvement (and were openly dismissive of trade unions). Their books emphasised the value of employee involvement and echoed neo-human relations strictures in respect of their theories about motivation (i.e. make people feel valued and respected by management by walking around and encouraging bottom-up problem solving groups) – and higher commitment and motivation will necessarily follow because people feel valued and respected etc. In essence, HRM provided the philosophical compass for alterations to people management with employee involvement cast as a core component of the hardware and HRM's ascent was assisted by changes in the political and business environment and the influence of management gurus.

Surveying the scene in the late 1990s students of this field might have been forgiven for engaging in Fukuyamaesque 'end of history' pronouncements. The prospects for the rejuvenation of 'power centred participation' appeared bleak within the context of 'ascendant management, and individualistic and competitive values' (Harley *et al.*, 2005) wholly supportive of employee involvement. Indeed, as recently as 2000 Millward *et al.* (2000: 124) were able to confidently state: 'there has been a major shift from collective, representative, indirect and union based voice, to direct, non-union channels'. Broadly put, a shift from employee participation to employee involvement. However, the new millennium ushered in a renewal of interest in employee participation. Following the signing up of the New Labour government to the Social Chapter in 1999 the UK became increasingly touched by the EU's social agenda. More particularly, the consultation and participatory rights of British employees have been enhanced by the European Works Council and Information and Consultation Directives. The workings of these institutions will be afforded critical coverage later in the chapter.

STOP and think

- *Why did the Thatcher government try to encourage employee share ownership via tax incentives?*
- *Why did trade union numbers fall in the Thatcher period?*
- *Why is employee involvement central to HRM?*

EPI: managerial motives

EPI and managerial motive

The subject of managerial motive has long been a source of controversy in the field of EPI. Reviewing the literature, we can identify a range of theoretical orientations that may explain managerial interest in the 'social technology' (Scholl, cited in Dachler and Wilpert, 1978: 2) that EPI represents. These theories, or 'vocabularies of participation' (Brannen *et al.*, 1976: 29), are derived from distinctly different value systems and may be bracketed under three headings: (i) a unitary approach which, following Delmotte (cited in Bolle De Bal, 1992: 614), may be termed *idyllic participation*, (ii) a *conflictual* model, and (iii) a *contingency* approach.

Idyllic participation

This essentially unitarist perspective is so-called because it treats EPI as wholly benign and unproblematic from both a managerial and workforce standpoint. It is both a technique and an overarching managerial philosophy; positive-sum outcomes are envisaged as areas of common interest between employers and employee are highlighted. This position, to which many paragraphs have been devoted in both the academic and the more prescriptive management journals, draws its inspiration from the human relations school; the central postulate is that *both* management and worker interests are served through EPI. As Dachler and Wilpert (1978: 8) observe, 'increases in innovative behaviour and economic efficiency and productivity are seen as a correlate of individual and group development'. In a similar vein, Argyris (1964) has argued that EPI leads to greater self-actualisation and higher levels of performance and hence the *integration* of individual and organisational needs. This intellectual tradition has spawned a mighty prescriptive literature, e.g., *The Human Side of Enterprise* (McGregor, 1960); *New Patterns of Management* (Likert, 1961); *Integrating the Individual and Organization* (Argyris, 1964) in which EPI is eulogised as a panacea capable of correcting a variety of corporate dilemmas and difficulties that arise from the 'debilitating effects of traditionally designed organisations' (Dachler and Wilpert, 1978: 7). Latterly, of course, these broad ideas have been given further impetus from the contemporary interest in HRM, and phrases such as 'job enrichment' and 'good communications' have become *de rigueur* amongst 'forward-looking' organisations.

In sum, all these subtle variations on a theme incorporate the common notion that the apparatus of EPI, in its broadest sense including job enrichment, participative styles of management, work group re-organisation and improved communications, has the potential to deliver a range of both individual *and* organisational benefits.

Notwithstanding the vast body of work derived from this paradigm, it has crucial theoretical shortcomings. A fundamental problem lies in the uncritical acceptance of unitary theoretical presuppositions that underpin the idyllic orthodoxy – a position that seems 'out of sync' with much of the empirical evidence. In recent years, management has been the primary actor behind such initiatives. Within the idyllic rubric EPI practices are treated implicitly as neutral interventions, participation being depicted as mutually advantageous with attendant benefits accruing to both capital and labour. It is necessary merely to recognise that the employment relationship is at least partly distributive to expose the problems with such a position. By ignoring the potential for conflict within labour management relations, the idyllic position obscures the significant implications that participation schemes may have, not simply for efficiency and productivity *per se*, but for the pattern of intra-organisational social relations. This stance thus conceals the incorporative and manipulative functions that EPI may potentially serve when imposed as a managerial tool. Grenier and Hogler (1991: 314) make the point well:

> The structure and power underlying participative processes is complex, ambiguous, and manipulable and far from bestowing meaningful authority on workers, such techniques may enable managers to maintain a relationship of dominance and control (emphasis added).

This is not to suggest that EPI cannot give rise to attendant benefits to both capital and labour in certain settings, but rather that positive employee outcomes do not *automatically* flow from the very act of employee participation or involvement.

What are the key assumptions underpinning the idyllic view of EPI? What are the limitations of this approach?

The conflictual model

Over the last 25 years or so a body of more critical work emanating from an industrial sociology perspective has emerged to question the underlying unitary and positive sum assumptions of the idyllic position. Central to this was Harvie Ramsay's seminal work. His 'cycles' thesis (Ramsay, 1977) was founded on Marxist analysis of production relations in capitalist societies. Contrary to the unitary assumptions underpinning 'idyllic' EPI, Ramsay takes as his point of departure the centrality of conflict and antagonism within the employment relationship.

Central to Ramsay's writings was the notion that management was most pre-disposed towards EPI when its authority was under threat from below – the aim being 'to nullify pressures to change the status quo' (Ramsay, 1977: 496). Managerial interest in EPI was seen to be a function of historical conjunctures in the ongoing conflict between capital and labour that gave rise to 'clear waves or cycles of interest' (Ramsay, 1980: 50) in response to working class resistance; 'interest' was seen to ebb once the managerial crisis had passed. For example, a discrete wave or cycle identified by Ramsay in his original 1977 paper was the industrial democracy movement of that period (see earlier discussion). This and other initiatives of this era were dismissed by Ramsay as an incorporative means of countering the growth in shopfloor power. The thrust of Ramsay's critique was that systems of EPI were somewhat underhand creations, 'presented as concessions by superordinates . . . of some real degree of influence over decisions to those classed as subordinates' (Ramsay, 1980: 46), the ultimate purpose being to incorporate the workforce through a system of 'phantom participation', i.e.

'a skilful con-trick' (Ramsay, 1980: 49) – or more poetically – 'honeyed flypaper dangled out to capture the unwitting worker' (Ramsay, 1993: 79).

While highly influential, the cycles thesis is open to criticism. The tone of the original paper is of data being used to illustrate theory rather than test propositions. Ultimately managerial motivation cannot be assumed or rejected on philosophical grounds, but must be subjected to a rigorous analysis on a case-by-case basis. Ramsay's empirical reliance upon time series data to track the apparent 'cycles', and secondary qualitative accounts, of varying rigour and merit, to impute a causal relationship is strongly suggestive of the illustrative approach, undermining the validity of the conclusions reached.

The most significant critique of Ramsay's work has come from members of the UMIST industrial relations team (Ackers *et al.*, 1992). Fundamentally Ramsay's focus on issues of workplace control is seen to be undermined by the renaissance of participation from the 1980s onwards, a period in which any 'threat from below' is broadly viewed as having dissipated. The 'cycles' thesis is seen to oversimplify the employment relationship, reducing it to one of an overriding desire by management to control workers more effectively when increasingly management want employee commitment and motivation. This said, it would be wrong to suggest that the essence of the cycles thesis is flawed in *all* cases. Indeed, there is much evidence that the introduction of EPI, or subsequent re-invigoration of EPI structures, may be stimulated by a perceived threat to managerial prerogatives (Marchington *et al.*, 1993). As Ackers *et al.* (1992: 274) argue, ultimately Ramsay's account is simply 'too narrow and partisan to serve as a useful *general* test for participation' (emphasis added).

STOP
and
think

What were the key elements of Ramsays 'cycles of control' thesis? How does this differ from the idyllic view? What were the criticisms of the 'cycles' thesis?

Contingency approach

The above literatures represent competing viewpoints on EPI. They are based upon highly partisan frames of reference invoking the notion that managerial intent is founded upon either progressive or reactive and defensive goals. A more subtle formulation has been afforded by the UMIST team, elements of which have been alluded to above (cf. Ackers *et al.*, 1992; Marchington *et al.*, 1992). Using an in-depth study of 25 separate organisations they stress the indeterminate nature of the functionality of EPI. From within their resultant 'explanatory matrix' (Ackers *et al.*, 1992: 268), it is possible to derive two dominant drivers of EPI. The first encapsulates elements of Ramsay's position, fulfilling his zero-sum expectations; participation is 'industrial relations' centred (Ackers *et al.*, 1992: 277), aimed at incorporating or bypassing unions, the underlying rationale being concerned with control issues. Alternatively, the importance of 'market participation' is stressed where 'economic pressures other than labour control and union avoidance considerations motivate participation' (Ackers *et al.*, 1992: 278). In these settings, influences such as the need for customer care in the service sector or labour market problems (e.g. recruitment and retention) are viewed as pre-eminent. Here labour and product market pressures 'impact upon the human resource problem without having to pass through the distorting lens of industrial relations problems' (Ackers *et al.*, 1992: 278).

The UMIST team goes on to describe specific scenarios in which management assumes that participation will yield tangible benefits, shedding light on the logic of the latter approach. Mostly, they are scenarios where the quality and efficiency of production is heavily dependent on the constructive initiative, commitment and support of employees. This is captured, for example, in the above references to 'customer care' within the service sector. Ackers *et al.* (1992) likewise provide the example of the invocation of a quality culture within a broader TQM manufacturing environment. Participation is also viewed in these settings as an adjunct to loyalty and hence employee retention, contributing further to effective production or service delivery.

The above position, implicitly drawing its analytical inspiration from contingency theory, represents a useful counter to the 'grand theory' catalogued earlier. It complements a growing body of literature suggesting that management is a strategic actor synchronising HR policies to wider business goals, although the extent to which such adjustments are genuinely strategic rather than tactical remains controversial.

As distinct from Ramsay's 'cycles' metaphor, the UMIST team moved on to develop the notion of 'waves' (Marchington *et al.*, 1993). This marked a further important theoretical contribution because it allowed the ebb and flow of organisational EPI initiatives to be related not necessarily to corporate goals, but managers' own career objectives. As Marchington (2005: 31–32) recollects, 'by treating each technique individually, it became possible to chart the dynamics of [employee] participation [and involvement] over time in relation to the growth and decline of different schemes rather than as a whole'. Via this route it was often possible to apportion specific techniques to internal 'champions' (Marchington *et al.*, 1993: 565) of EPI. That is, the waves were driven by a myriad of factors. Sometimes these related to business contingencies but in other instances the driver was naked careerism or 'impression management' (Marchington *et al.*, 1993: 570). Hence, ultimately managerial intent in EPI is likely to be driven by a complex array of factors and recent research by Butler (2009) underlines the need to build micro-, macro- and indeed, sector-level analyses into explanatory models of EPI.

STOP and think

- *What are the key elements associated with the contingency approach?*
- *What is meant by 'waves of participation'?*
- *Why is the notion of 'waves of participation' useful in terms of explaining the ebb and flow of EPI initiatives?*

EPI practices in the workplace

We will now examine a range of EPI practices used in contemporary organisations. Marchington *et al.* (1992) identify four categories of EPI initiatives:

- *Downward communications.* This refers to top–down communication from management to employees. Typical practices include company newspapers, team briefing, communication meetings, video briefing, employee reports and the use of the intranet.

- *Upward problem solving forms and teamworking.* Upward problem solving refers to bottom-up communication and involvement structures that are generally designed with the aim of capturing ideas and solving production/service problems (either individually or in small groups). Typical mechanisms include suggestion schemes, and quality circles/problem solving groups. This category could also include attitude surveys which management may implement (or commission) to try to understand more about the general climate within the company and as a mechanism to allow employees to raise concerns and/or ideas for future changes that they would like to see. In addition to the typical forms of upwards problem solving already cited, Marchington and Wilkinson (2005) also identify the following forms, task-based participation and teamworking and self-management.

- *Financial participation.* This refers to schemes that allow employees a financial stake in the company. Typical mechanisms include employee share ownership schemes and profit related pay.

● *Representative participation*. This refers to mechanisms for indirect participation, for example, through trade unions, works councils and consultative committees. It means that employees are represented by elected representatives that have been drawn from their number.

Before we move on to discuss each of these categories in more detail, it is important to highlight once more points raised by Marchington *et al.* (1992) in respect of mechanisms for EPI. They argue that the mechanisms for EPI must be considered in respect of four dimensions:

1 The *degree* of involvement (the extent to which employees influence the final decision).

2 The *level* of involvement (whether at job, departmental or organisational level).

3 The *forms* of involvement (direct participation, indirect participation and financial).

4 The *range* of the subject matter being considered in the involvement scheme.

By considering each of these four dimensions, one can appreciate the relative levels of power and influence that the respective mechanisms allow. As we have already highlighted, a criticism of employee involvement initiatives (that are central to HRM) is that they afford very limited power and influence to employees. This is primarily because such mechanisms are essentially controlled by management, who has the final say as to what they will or will not accept. For example, in terms of *degree*, employees may have little influence over a final decision. In terms of *level* of involvement, employee involvement initiatives may essentially be dealing with locally based production issues (for example, problem solving activities). The *form* that employee involvement practices take will essentially be determined by management and the *range* of subject matter may, for example, revolve around work-based production problems rather than tackling higher-level issues of pay, conditions, redundancies etc.

In contrast, representative participation (here we refer especially to trade unions activities) are not primarily controlled by management and in the case of trade unions, their organisation and structure are not circumscribed by management. We can contrast employee involvement to representative participation by considering once more the four levels identified by Marchington *et al.* (1992). Taking trade unions as the example – trade unions are more likely to wield power and influence. They tend to have a higher *degree* of influence (if negotiations get tough, trade unions may coordinate industrial action), they may be negotiating at company or sector level (i.e. a high *level* of involvement), their *form* is not dictated by management, participation is indirect and they are likely to be involved in and negotiating on a wide *range* of subjects. Once the four dimensions are taken into account, one can understand why critics have argued that the employee involvement initiatives associated with HRM represent 'pseudo-participation'.

We will now discuss each of the four categories in more detail. As already highlighted, the terminology in this area is somewhat elastic (Marchington and Wilkinson, 2005) and the same issue applies to some of the practices, for example, the exact form and use of problem solving groups could vary both within and between organisations. However, the Workplace Employment Relations Surveys (WERS) give an indication of the general trends for each of the categories. The WERS surveys are particularly useful in that they are large scale. The initial survey was conducted in 1980 (when it was called the Workplace Industrial Relations Survey) and it was repeated in 1984, 1990, 1998 and again in 2004. This means that one can identify trends over a period of years. We will now discuss each of the categories in more detail.

Why do critics argue that employee involvement as part of a wider HRM approach represents 'pseudo-participation'?

Downward communication

Downward communication means top–down communication from management to employees. As indicated, this includes company newspapers, communication meetings, team briefings and the use of the intranet. Table 14.2 is taken from the first findings of the 2004 WERS.

A noteworthy result from the survey is the popularity of meetings with the entire workforce or team briefings. The instance of these rose in both the private and the public sector. Holden (2004) explains that team briefing systems are normally used to cascade managerial messages down the organisation. Although team-briefing arrangements may vary, they are normally given to relatively small groups and (in terms of content) often focus on issues affecting production or service, targets etc. Team briefings are essentially a top–down form of communication, but there is often some opportunity for employees to ask questions or perhaps even to lodge comments, queries or concerns. Evidence tends to show that team-briefing systems work better when the briefers are properly trained. Whilst evidence indicates that team-briefing sessions are generally welcomed, problems can also emerge. For example, some studies have shown a tendency for team briefing sessions to be cancelled when production pressures are high (Glover, 2001). Also, critics have noted that team-briefing sessions can be used to brief against existing trade unions or to try to dissuade employees from seeking union recognition in non-union firms.

Table 14.2 also shows that newsletters remain fairly widespread, especially in the public sector. Holden (2004) notes that newsletters can often be welcomed, but a potential limitation is that management retain editorial control – as such it is less likely that newsletters would be used as a forum to air employee grievances. The latest WERS also included questions about the use of noticeboards, e-mail and intranet. Use of the e-mail and intranet was reported by more than 30 per cent of organisations. It is likely that the instances of usage of e-mail and intranet will increase in years to come as more companies make use of these facilities. The use of employee surveys was captured by WERS 2004, and these were particularly popular in the public sector.

The rhetoric of HRM is that companies will focus on maintaining effective communication. Table 14.2 shows that many companies have the infrastructure in place for various forms of downward communication; however, whether employees view these mechanisms as effective is a different question (Glover, 2001).

Table 14.2 Direct communication by sector of ownership

Direct communication	Percentage of workplaces					
	1998			2004		
	Private sector	Public sector	All	Private sector	Public sector	All
Meeting with entire workforce or team briefing	82	96	85	90	97	91
Systematic use of management chain	46	75	52	60	81	64
Regular newsletters	35	59	40	41	63	45
Noticeboards	–	–	–	72	86	74
E-mail	–	–	–	36	48	38
Intranet	–	–	–	31	48	34
Employee surveys	–	–	–	37	66	42

Source: Adapted from Kersley *et al.* (2005: 18).

Upward problem solving and teamworking

Upward problem solving mechanisms (such as suggestion schemes and problem solving groups) are generally designed for the purpose of capturing ideas and solving production and service problems. Task-based participation, teamworking and self-management can also be considered here. They are more substantive in nature as they are 'integral to the job and part of everyday working life' (Marchington and Wilkinson, 2005: 388).

Suggestion schemes work on the principle that employees submit suggestions (for example, into a suggestion box), the suggestion is then reviewed by managers, a decision will be made as to whether to accept the suggestion or reject it. If the suggestion is accepted the employee will generally receive a direct financial reward. Such rewards may equate to a percentage of the overall saving that the suggestion will bring. Some companies may put a cap on the amount of cash that can be rewarded, but may 'top-up' with other products or services (for example, Ford had a suggestion scheme which had a cap on the amount of cash that would be awarded, but if the suggestion was particularly good and the value of the savings was particularly high, the 'top-up' could be a car). The WERS of 1998 and 2004 indicated that around 30 per cent of organisations reported the use of suggestion schemes.

Upward problem solving also includes problem solving groups (often referred to as quality circles in the 1990s). Problem solving groups (PSGs) are generally small in nature (for example, 6–8 people) and normally meet on a voluntary basis. The purpose of such groups is to identify quality or work-related problems and to produce a solution to the problem. Some organisations will offer problem solving groups administrative support, training and trained facilitators. Also, most groups will meet in work time. However, in contrast to suggestion schemes, there is not normally a direct financial reward for the solutions and ideas generated by such groups. Again, evidence shows that these initiatives can be welcomed, but problems can emerge if groups feel that their ideas are not listened to, or fail to be actioned. In terms of coverage, WERS 2004 indicated that 21 per cent of organisations had problem-solving groups that comprised of non-managerial employees. It also found that PSGs were more common (44 per cent) in organisations where the core group of employees were in professional occupations. Interestingly, WERS 2004 found that training in problem solving was more common than the existence of formal groups – and concluded that while many workplaces may encourage problem-solving, they may not necessarily set up formal groups dedicated to problem-solving activities (Kersley *et al.*, 2006). Overall, they found that 45 per cent of workplaces either had PSGs, and/or had trained employees in problem solving.

In addition to these more traditional forms of upwards problem solving, Marchington and Wilkinson (2005) identify task-based participation and teamworking and self-management, which, they argue, are integrated into normal working life rather than being 'bolt-on' initiatives. They explain that task-based participation can occur 'both horizontally and vertically' (2005: 390). The former means that employees engage in a wider variety of tasks, but these are at a similar skill level. Vertical participation means that employees, 'may be trained to undertake tasks at a higher skill level or they may be given some managerial and supervisory responsibilities' (2005: 392).

The concept of teamworking is closely linked to task-based participation and is now seen as a central feature of HRM (Mueller and Proctor, 2000). For example, the term 'multi-skilling' is similar to horizontal task-based participation, essentially meaning that employees will move around tasks and will not be bound by strict job demarcation. Again, 'teamworking' can mean different things in different organisations. WERS 1998 and 2004 give an insight into what companies are reporting in terms of teamworking practices. Table 14.3 provides a summary of some of the findings.

Table 14.3 shows that over 70 per cent of organisations in 1998 and 2004 reported teamworking structures for core employees. The surveys also indicated that functional flexibility (multiskilling) was evident and that core employees had received some training for these activities. The 2004 survey showed that only 21 per cent of organisations reported having

Table 14.3 Work organisation by sector of ownership

| | Percentage of workplaces | | | | | |
| | 1998 | | | 2004 | | |
	Private sector	Public sector	All	Private sector	Public sector	All
Some core employees in formally designated teams	72	85	74	68	88	72
Some core employees trained to be functionally flexible	69	67	69	67	64	66
Problem solving groups involving non-managerial employees	–	–	16	19	33	21
Some core employees trained in teamworking, communication or problem solving	35	65	41	45	65	48

Source: Adapted from Kersley *et al.* (2005: 11).

problem solving groups that involved non-managerial employees – but that instances were higher in the public sector. Finally, 48 per cent of organisations reported organising training courses for general teamworking activities but again, instances were higher in the public sector.

The 1998 survey revealed an interesting finding in respect of teamworking. Again, while it found a large percentage of organisations reporting the use of teamworking, only 3 per cent seem to be allowing teams real autonomy – meaning that team members had responsibility for a specific product, had autonomy in terms of deciding how the job was done and had some authority to appoint their own team leaders. Therefore, while teamworking is widely reported in Britain, evidence still suggests that much of this is fairly low-level (for example, team members working together) and that instances of semi-autonomous teams and self-managing teams are less common (Geary, 2003). Some would argue that self-managing teams are the ultimate in direct participation (and as such there is quite some way to go in the UK). Others however, would argue that self-managing teams represent the ultimate form of management control in that they work on the basis of peer pressure and surveillance and are not genuinely liberating because they are always under the control of management (Garrahan and Stewart, 1992; Sewell and Wilkinson, 1992a; Taylor *et al.*, 2002). Yet others have argued that teamworking tends to offer mixed consequences – and it is too stark to argue that the outcomes of it are either 'all good' or 'all bad'.

Financial participation

The third category is financial participation. This means that employees have a financial stake in the company. Given the constraints of space, we will now provide a brief review of mechanisms for financial participation.

Holden (2004: 554) explains that 'the general aim of financial participation schemes is to enhance employee commitment to the organisation by linking the performance of the organisation to that of the employee'. He goes on to explain that various governments over the years have tried to encourage the growth of financial involvement schemes. For example, the Conservative government of 1979–97 introduced a range of tax incentives for schemes including profit-related pay and employee share option schemes. The current Labour government has also introduced various schemes to try to stimulate financial involvement (Holden, 2004). One presumption is that if employees have a financial stake in the company, they are more likely to be committed to the success of the company and (perhaps) will be less likely to engage in forms of industrial action. Some would regard financial involvement as a 'win-win' scenario, i.e. that employees share some of the financial gains from success and that the employer will have a hard-working workforce that is interested in the overall perform-ance of the company.

The three main forms of financial participation are profit-sharing, profit-related pay and employee share ownership schemes. Deferred profit-sharing schemes work on the basis that 'profits are put in a trust fund to acquire shares in the company for employees' (Gennard and Judge, 2005). The overall aim of such a scheme is to increase motivation and commitment, but Gennard and Judge (2005: 195) observe that one of the problems can be creating a clear, identifiable link between effort and reward. For example, problems may emerge if individuals feel that they have worked hard, but that this effort is not adequately reflected in the profits that they share. Also, there will be an inevitable delay between the day-to-day behaviours of employees and the final calculation of profit and the rewards that flow back as a conse-quence. Again, this may mean that employees find it difficult to relate effort and reward.

Profit-related pay works on the basis that a proportion of an employee's pay is linked to the overall profits of the company. Again, the goal is to increase commitment and motivation and various governments have introduced tax breaks to try to encourage this type of scheme. In practice, profit-related pay can be difficult to calculate and some companies found that government tax-break schemes were not easy to administer.

The final form of financial participation is share ownership. This means that employees own shares in the company. Again, various governments have introduced incentives for share ownership schemes and these have sometimes been difficult to administer. For example, employee share ownership plans (ESOPs) were devised as a way of dealing with tax liability from share ownership schemes (Gennard and Judge, 2005).

Again, the WERS are useful in that they give some indication into the relative spread of these schemes. There was a rise in profit sharing schemes from 19 per cent in 1984 to 46 per cent in 1998 (Millward *et al.*, 2000: 214) and the WERS 2004 revealed little change (Kersley *et al.*, 2006). Millward *et al.* (2000) go on to suggest that this rise from 1984–98 could probably be attributed to government intervention (certainly in the 1980s). They also observed that the UK multinationals were more likely to have a profit-related pay scheme, but the most influential factor appeared the size of the enterprise to which the workplaces belonged, and that profit-related pay was much more likely in enterprises that had 1000 or more employees. The survey also asked about why profit-related schemes had either been introduced or with-drawn and several reasons were noted:

- If a scheme had been withdrawn, the most common reason was a change of ownership.
- The second most common reason for withdrawal was that the scheme was too expensive to run (the costs of administration being a cited factor).
- The most common reason for the introduction of a profit-related pay scheme was that the workplace had undergone a change of ownership.
- The reason for implementing schemes varied. Some reported that a scheme had been implemented for tax relief reasons. Others reported that profit sharing was part of wider organisational changes where companies have been attempting to develop more sophisti-cated reward systems (Millward *et al.*, 2000).

The surveys have also given an insight into the spread of share ownership schemes. They show, for example, that 13 per cent of workplaces had share ownership schemes in 1980, 22 per cent in 1984, 30 per cent in 1990 a slight drop to 24 per cent in 1998 (Millward *et al.*, 2000: 216) and little change by 2004 (Kersley *et al.*, 2006). However, they found that the exis-tence of employee share ownership schemes were related to size and were more likely in the financial services sector (where four out of five companies had employee share option schemes). The general conclusion was that increases in profit sharing and employee share ownership schemes were seen in the 1980s then tailed off for a period, but coverage has remained relatively unchanged between 1998 and 2004 (Kersley *et al.*, 2006).

Representative participation

The final category is representative participation and this refers to mechanisms for indirect participation. Such mechanisms include works councils and trade unions. We discuss works councils in more detail elsewhere in this chapter, so will restrict ourselves to a brief review here. The main difference between representative participation and the other categories that we have discussed is that these structures are firmly based on the principles of pluralism. Early HRM models tended to be unitarist in nature and there was an assumption that unions and HRM 'don't mix'. However, recent evidence questions the early assumptions (Cully *et al.*, 1999; Glover, 2000) and trends towards partnership signal changing times (Guest and Peccei; 2001, Martinez Lucio and Stuart, 2002; Tailby *et al.*, 2004). Trade unions are clearly an important mechanism for representative participation and the field of industrial relations has historically been devoted to their study. In this section, we will reflect upon some general issues around the theme of trade unions and will introduce the concept of 'social partnership' that is becoming part of the mainstream debate (Bacon, 2006; Martinez Lucio and Stuart, 2002; Tailby and Winchester, 2005). Again, the WERS are very useful in terms of identifying general trends over a number of years and we will review some of the evidence.

One of the issues that we will raise here is the relative decline of forms of representative participation. In some ways, the climate for representative participation is more conducive when compared to the recent past. New Labour's early legislative programme (1997–99) included a statutory route for union recognition, an extension of rights for individual employees, a national minimum wage and closer engagement with the social policies of the European Union. These policy initiatives represent an effort 'to replace the notion of conflict between employers and employees with the long term promotion of partnership (DTI, 1998)' (Bacon, 2006: 195). In addition, legislation has come into force in respect of works councils (see below). However, although these developments appear to be more positive for trade unions, evidence continues to chart a decline in membership (see Kersley *et al.*, 2006: 109) and the growth of a 'representation gap' (Towers, 1997). We will return to this theme as the section unfolds.

Employee consultation has a long history, first coming to prominence as 'joint consultative committee' (JCC) during the Second World War. There was a decline during the 1950s and 1960s followed by an increase in the 1970s. WERS has been able to capture trends in terms of the coverage of consultative committees since 1980. The changes from 1980–98 are summarised in Table 14.4. We can see that the coverage of functioning consultative committees fell over the period from 1980–98. Twenty-five per cent of workplaces did not have a workplace-level committee but had 'a consultative forum that operated at a higher level in the organisation' (Kersley *et al.*, 2005: 14) and that JCCs were much more common in larger workplaces. The survey also gives insights into the operation of these committees. For example, 96 per cent had met at least twice in the previous year and 75 per cent had met at least four times. Topics discussed by such committees included: future plans (81 per cent), work organisation (81 per cent), employment issues (78 per cent), production issues (71 per cent) and financial issues (65 per cent) (Kersely *et al.*, 2005: 14). Interestingly, the survey found that financial issues and employment issues were more likely to be discussed if the

Table 14.4 Percentage coverage of functioning consultative committees as shown by WIRS/WERS surveys

Survey date	All establishments (%)			
	1980	1984	1990	1998
Functioning Consultative Committee	30	31	26	23

Source: Adapted from Millward *et al.* (2000: 109).

committee contained trade union representatives. WERS 2004 indicated that there had been a decline in the incidence of JCCs since 1998 to just 14 per cent of workplaces (Kersley *et al.*, 2006). The decline was most marked in workplaces with under 100 employees. Thus the long-term downward trend of JCCs has continued.

The next form of representative participation that we will discuss is trade unions. As indicated, the field of industrial relations was traditionally devoted to the study of trade unions and we will necessarily have to restrict ourselves to discussing certain themes and will refer once more to WERS in order to give an indication of some of the trends in respect of trade union coverage.

In the early 1980s, 'HRM' tended to be viewed as unitarist. Indeed, one of the distinctions that Storey (1992) drew in his 'ideal types' continuum between personnel management/ industrial relations (PM/IR) on the one hand and HRM on the other was that the nature of relations in PM/IR was characterised as pluralist and HRM as unitarist. At the time there was much debate about the role of trade unions under HRM and Guest commented that 'the rising interest in HRM throughout the 1980s coincided with a steady decline in the significance of industrial relations as a central feature of economic performance and policy' (Guest in Storey, 1995: 110). During this period there was a wave of union derecognition by companies (Claydon, 1996). The climate of the 1980s was harsh for unions. In addition to the rise of anti-union legislation by the Thatcher government (for example, legislation covering balloting arrangements and secondary action – contravention of which could mean the courts could impose the sequestration of union assets), the same period saw the decline of manufacturing and the increase in the service sector. The manufacturing sector was a traditional stronghold for trade unions, while the service sector was viewed as more difficult to organise (given the fact that it often included small businesses, part-time (women) workers etc.). At the same time as structural, economic and political changes were taking place, HRM came into ascendancy. Some of its key tenets were direct participation, unitarism, the importance of customer orientation etc. and some felt that trade unions struggled to adjust to the changing context.

There have been some interesting changes more recently in terms of the relationship between trade unions and HRM. Traditionally, the relationship between trade unions and employers was often typified as 'them and us'. We can contrast this to some of the findings of WERS 1998 where Cully *et al.* (1999: 111) note that 'an active and strong trade union presence is compatible with the broad suite of high commitment management practices', i.e. the opposite that one would expect under previous stereotypes of 'them and us'. Indeed, WERS 1998 indicated positive links between high performance practices and trade union representation. There have been changes in the discourse about management and trade union relationships in recent years and now terms such as 'social partnership' and 'partnership' are widely referred to (Ackers and Payne, 1998; Guest and Peccei, 2001; Martinez Lucio and Stuart, 2002; Tailby *et al.*, 2004). As the term implies, the overall meaning is that management and trade unions (or employee representatives) or management and employees will (try to) work cooperatively. However, 'partnership' is an ambiguous term and tends to be used differently by different stakeholder groups. For example, the CBI, TUC and IOD all interpret the term in different ways (Undy, 1999). Bacon (2006) observes that the CIPD adopted a rather unitarist perspective in 1997, emphasising partnership between employers and employees rather than advocating the role of trade unions, whilst the TUC emphasises the importance of trade union involvement in partnership arrangements.

Despite the ambiguity, the partnership debate does seem to signal that the unions have at least begun to (try to) reclaim the agenda, after the 'wilderness years' when numbers were declining and they were unsure of how to respond to HRM (Storey, 1995). The notion of partnership has offered some potential for unions to re-legitimise their role, not least because it is often linked to notions of increasing competitiveness. However, Bacon (2006) notes that the number of signed partnership agreements remains relatively low and that such agreements are only likely to be successful if managers are willing to work closely with the unions on a long-term basis and that managers refrain from making attacks on trade unions. He goes on to observe that it remains unclear as to whether such agreements deliver returns to managers and unions. For example, Guest and Peccei (2001) found that management enjoyed the main benefits from partnership, Martinez Lucio and Stuart (2002) found that concerns over employment security and the quality of working life remained problematic and that there was often a gap between the rhetoric of partnership and experiences of trade unionists on the ground. Suff and Williams (2004: 33) concluded that 'the reality of market relations and the balance of power in the employment relationship imply that genuine mutuality is likely to be unobtainable in practice'. However, overall the partnership debate represents a shift in emphasis and the outcomes of such agreements for employers and employees will remain a key area of research.

We turn now to the empirical evidence on trade union coverage. Once again, WERS are especially useful because they offer insights into historical trends relating to trade union recognition. Table 14.5 summarises developments from 1980 to 1998 and shows quite clearly the extent of the decline in coverage of union recognition from 1980 to 1998. WERS 2004 indicates that recognition had fallen to 27 per cent for all workplaces and to 15 per cent in the private sector, and 82 per cent in the public sector (Kersley *et al.*, 2006)). One can see that while recognition remains high in the public sector there were huge drops in recognition in the private sector, which was down to 15 per cent of private service companies by 2004. This trend is particularly significant given the overall increase in service sector employment in the UK. Indeed, union density fell from 39 per cent of employees in 1990 to 37 per cent in 1998 and 34 per cent in 2004 (Cully *et al.*, 1999: Kersley *et al.*, 2006).

Reflecting on the first findings of WERS 2004, Kersley *et al.*, (2005: 35–36) observe that

> most striking of all, perhaps, was the continued decline of collective labour organisation. Employees were less likely to be union members than they were in 1998; workplaces were less likely to recognise unions for bargaining over pay and conditions; and collective bargaining was less prevalent.

The overall rate of decline seems to have slowed and 50 per cent of employees were employed in workplaces with a recognised trade union, approximately 33 per cent were union members and approximately 40 per cent had pay set via collective bargaining (Kersley *et al.*, 2005). However, there remain large sections of the British workforce that are not covered by trade union representation. Significantly, private services remain low in terms of unionisation, but tend to employ many women often on relatively low rates of pay – but such employees do not enjoy the backing of trade unions. Millward *et al.*, (2000: 236) reflect upon some of these themes and conclude that in future, the British economy is likely to generate more workplaces where, 'the nature of employment relationships is almost exclusively a matter for managerial choice'. Managerial choice could include approaches on a continuum from enlightened HRM to authoritarian regimes with few opportunities for the employee voice. The conclusion they draw is that

> should the current reforms also prove insufficient, we see a yet more extensive floor of employee rights, rigorously enforced by state agencies, as the most feasible method of preventing the more extreme forms of exploitation that an unregulated labour market can produce in the increasingly competitive world in which Britain operates.
>
> (Millward *et al.*, 2000: 236)

Table 14.5 Trade union recognition by broad sector, 1980–1998

	Percentage			
Year of survey	1980	1984	1990	1998
All establishments	64	66	53	42
Public sector	94	99	87	87
Private sector	50	48	38	25
Private services	41	44	36	23

Source: Adapted from Millward *et al.* (2000: 96).

- *What are the main trends in representative participation since 1980?*
- *What are the implications of these trends for organisations, managers and employees?*
- *Why do Millward et al. (2000) argue that a more extensive floor of employment rights may be needed to protect British employees?*

Works councils and consultation in the European Union

At this point we will pause to consider some of the more recent developments in respect of employee consultation. A recurrent theme within this chapter has been the ascendance of managerially inspired employee involvement. By and large, systems of indirect *participation*, that is mechanisms that seek to involve employees more fundamentally in the 'political structures of the firm' (Brannen, 1983: 16) fared less well throughout the 17-year period of Conservative government from 1979 to 1997. However, the decision of the incoming Labour government to sign up to the European Agreement on Social Policy (the Social Chapter) put employee participation firmly back on the agenda.

There is a long history of a European level of interest in employee participation. As discussed, plans for a 'fifth directive' that sought to provide workers with boardroom representation were suspended inconclusively in 1982. A new framework for a European Company Statute was again launched in 1989 (Hyman and Mason, 1995: 33). This also called for workers to have board-level input. However, pressure from employers and the British Conservative government ensured that the draft directive was never ratified (Hyman and Mason, 1995). As Leat (2003: 245) notes, ultimately such initiatives ran counter to the UK's voluntarist tradition and even more so to the *neo-laissez faire* approach adopted by British governments after 1979. Consequently, the decision of the Blair government to bind Britain to the European Social Policy Protocol under the Treaty of Amsterdam (1999) marked a fundamental change in policy. Following this move, the directives agreed between 1994 and 1998 and all subsequent legislation under the social chapter became applicable to British companies. In terms of EPI, the most far-reaching of these measures have been the directives on European Works Councils (1994) and Information and Consultation (2002).

The European Works Council directive

Background

The EWC directive, transposed into UK law in 1999, requires a EWC to be established in companies with at least 1000 employees within the EU and at least 150 employees in each of at least two member states. It is thus explicitly aimed at multinational enterprises (MNCs). It has been estimated that the directive covers around 1850 MNCs (Kerckhofs, 2002). By 2003,

639 MNCs had negotiated agreements (Waddington and Kerckhofs, cited in Hall and Marginson, 2005: 208). The directive is a response to the concerns of the European Commission regarding the power of MNCs to take decisions in one member state that affect employees in others without their being involved in the decision-making process (Leat, 2003: 250). The legislation is thus intended to bridge the 'representation gap' between the growth of transnational decision making and employees' hitherto strictly nationally defined information and consultation rights (Hall and Marginson, 2005). The EWC directive is significant in that the requirement for mandated consultation (see Box 14.4) suggests some potential for the extension of employee influence.

Impact of the directive

Over a decade after the directive's inception a reasonable amount of research has been conducted exploring the workings of these institutions. Reviewing the data, Blyton and Turnbull (2004: 373–74) argue that EWCs overwhelmingly tend to be management-led with restrictions placed on the consultation procedure. These findings chime with Hall and Marginson's overview of the terrain, where they conclude that very few agreements depart from the formalised definition of consultation as set out in the directive, viz. 'the exchange of views and establishment of dialogue' between employee representatives and management (Hall and Marginson, 2005: 207). Only sporadically are firmer consultation rights provided such as the right of employee representatives to be allowed to respond formally to managerial proposals and receive a considered response *before* management acts (Hall and Marginson, 2005). The balance of evidence is that limited headway has been made by EWCs in extending employee influence over strategic issues, with any impact restricted to the *implementation* of decisions rather than their actual substance (see, in particular, Stirling and Fitzgerald, 2000).

A plausible interpretation of the current situation is that companies operating EWCs have aligned them with their own organisational requirements rather than those of their employees. Hall and Marginson (2005) cite a study by Wills in which British managers generally had a positive view about the contribution of EWCs, seeing them as a way of reinforcing corporate communications and downplaying their consultative and representative role. Similarly, in Nakano's study of 14 Japanese MNCs (again cited in Hall and Marginson, 2005) managers perceived EWCs as providing benefits in terms of information provision, the fostering of cooperation between management and employee representatives and the development of a wider corporate identity among employee representatives (see also Timming, 2007 for a useful overview of the literature). Taken together, these studies suggest that the EWC machinery is prone to be hijacked by management, who then reconstruct these ostensibly pluralist structures along unitary lines to form part of the employee involvement apparatus. Arguably this stems from the original legislation that gave organisations considerable latitude in how to implement the directive. More alarmingly, Timming (2007: 251) points to the 'dark side' of the operation of EWCs, suggesting management may use divide

---

Box 14.4 **The competence of EWCs**

EWCs have the right to meet with central management once a year. There must be information or consultation on:

- the structure, economic and financial situation of the business;
- developments in production and sales;
- the employment situation;
- investment trends; and
- substantial changes concerning the introduction of new working methods or production processes, transfers of production, mergers, cutbacks or closures of undertakings.

and rule tactics to 'encourage competition between geographically dispersed workforces'. Under such a scenario managers are able to 'convert an ostensibly labour-friendly institution into a business friendly managerial tool'. So far the creation of EWCs appears to have done little to significantly improve the participation rights of British workers. Indeed, it is conceivable that, albeit unintentionally, mandated employee participation has significantly buttressed the employee involvement arrangements.

- *When did the EWC directive transpose into law and what were the main implications of this directive?*
- *Does the evidence suggest that the directive has significantly increased the degree of employee influence? If not, why not?*

The Information and Consultation directive

Background

These new regulations make provision for employees to be consulted and given information on major developments in their organisation. They differ from the EWC directive, as here coverage extends to *all* companies in the EU with over 50 employees – not just MNCs. Within the British context the directive has been portrayed as a useful corrective to the failure of voluntarism (Sisson, 2002: 2) and the consequent 'representation gap' (Towers, 1997). The key significance of the legislation is that it is a vehicle for the extension of participation for employees without trade union representation. As such it has the potential 'to transform the UK industrial relations environment' (see Gollan and Wilkinson, 2007: 1145).

The original proposals were strongly backed by the French amid objections from Germany, Ireland, Denmark and the UK. Although the directive was initiated under the social chapter, and hence subject to qualified majority voting, these four dissenters comprised a sufficient blocking minority to initially keep the proposals off the statute book. The UK's objection was based on the notion of 'subsidiarity', the doctrine that the EU should only legislate where the objectives cannot be reached by legislation at national level (**www. eurofound.eu**). The proposals were, however, accepted by the European Parliament in February 2002. Under a compromise position the UK (along with Ireland) had dispensation to phase in the legislation over a four-year period. Initially, only companies with 150 employees were covered.

Organisations with existing information and consultation arrangements that have the support of employees can continue operating them. In other circumstances employees must 'trigger' negotiations with their employer to agree new information arrangements. If the negotiations do not produce an agreement, statutory information and consultation arrangements become applicable (see Box 14.5).

Box 14.5 The right to information and consultation covers

- Information on the recent and probable development of the organisation's activities and economic situation;
- Information and consultation on the situation, structure and probable development of employment within the organisation;
- Information and consultation on decisions likely to lead to substantial changes in work organisation.

Source: **www.eurofound.eu**.

Impact of the directive

To date there has been limited research exploring the effectiveness of the directive. What evidence there is, however, mirrors much of the EWCs output. Thus, Hall *et al.*'s (2007) 'provisional' study of Information and Consultation (I&C) arrangements in 13 case study organisations highlights how the fora 'were dominated by information provision by management' (p. 75). Developing this theme it is noted that 'evidence of consultation as discussion *before* a decision and the even tougher criterion of influencing management plans were fairly sparse' (p. 75, emphasis added). While induction training was provided in most instances, there was only 'limited evidence of subsequent training' (p. 72) and little indication that management went out of their way to build up representative effectiveness (p. 73). Alarmingly, a significant proportion of workers across the study organisations were actually ignorant of the presence of the representative bodies.

Gollan and Wilkinson (2007: 1152) caution that there is a danger of viewing the legislation as a 'single shock to the system that will have a once and for all effect'. The argument here is that learning on all sides may develop the participation process. Consequently, 'managers may become more comfortable and employees more confident, changing an ineffectual consultation process into something with real meaning' (*ibid.*). Hall *et al.*'s later (2008) 'interim' findings lend guarded support to this line of argument. In the emerging evidence, four of the ICE bodies under review had actually declined in effectiveness. Evidence of weakness and marginality was seen *inter alia* in a lack of weighty agenda issues, lack of consultation on major organisational change and a lack of training for new members. None the less, in five cases there were signs of growing effectiveness being invoked through 'experiential learning' (*ibid.* 7). Taken as a whole – and in line with the emphasis on legislatively prompted voluntarism (Hall, 2005) – the emergent evidence suggests a variegated and complex set of outcomes rather than any sort of wholesale transformation to structures of participation and systems of corporate governance.

STOP and think

- *What are the key differences between the EWC directive and the Information and Consultation directive?*
- *Given the history of EPI initiatives reviewed in this chapter, what impact do you think the Information and Consultation directive will have on levels of employee influence?*

New management initiatives: from quality circles, to quality management, to 'high performance management'?

We now bring this chapter to a close by reflecting upon a range of new management initiatives that have employee involvement as a central feature, i.e. our focus turns primarily to direct participation. By reference to WERS, we have laid out some of the contemporary trends in employee involvement (for example, in respect of downwards communication and upwards problem solving) and have catalogued a variety of employee involvement techniques routinely utilised by management. Over the last two decades, there has been a range of managerial initiatives that have incorporated employee involvement, primarily as a way of increasing organisational effectiveness by capturing ideas, eliciting commitment etc. Indeed Collins (2000) provides an extremely useful overview of a range of management 'fads and fashions', including TQM, Business Process Re-engineering and the Excellence phenomenon. He reflects upon the discourse associated with each of the chosen initiatives and upon empirical evidence (in particular, highlighting the gaps between the rhetoric of such initiatives and workplace 'reality'). Due to the confines of space, we focus on quality circles, quality management and one of the latest trends, high performance management (HPM). The reason for this choice is that one can see linkages between each of these developments. More importantly, quality management and high performance management are generally regarded as holistic interventions, rather than 'bolt on' practices.

Quality circles to quality management

We have already noted that quality circles (QC) are a form of upward problem solving. Quality circles have a long history in the UK and Holden (2004) notes that they can be traced back to the period after the Second World War. The concept was originally developed in the USA, but popularised by the Japanese. QCs became very popular in the 1980s, but activity declined towards the end of that decade. Some of the reasons for the decline included a lack of training, management failing to action ideas and (as a result) employees regarding them as a 'waste of time' (Heller *et al.*, 1998; Holden, 2004). One of the main limitations of the QC movement was that QCs tended to be a 'bolt-on' management initiative, rather than part of a wider management approach (Hill, 1995).

The significance of QM was that it was conceptualised as an organisation-wide approach, i.e. a way of doing business rather than a particular set of techniques or practices (Hill, 1995). In common with HPM, the terminology is fluid and open to interpretation (Dawson, 1998) and the terms 'world-class manufacturing', 'lean production', 'just-in-time' are often subsumed under the QM banner, but in practice the outcomes of each (certainly for employees) could be quite different. In essence, Wilkinson *et al.*, (1998) suggest that QM tends to be characterised by three common principles: a customer orientation, a process orientation and an emphasis on continuous improvement. There are clear implications for HRM in that QM requires that employees actively engage in activities such as problem solving and that they orientate their behaviours and actions towards satisfying the customer (Alvesson and Willmott, 2002). As a result, employee involvement initiatives are generally regarded as central to QM, for example, continuous improvement can be facilitated by the activities of problem solving groups via upward problem solving. Another outcome of QM was that it spurred the move towards teamworking structures that have become so popular of late (Kersley *et al.*, 2005) and are now seen as part of a HPM approach.

The outcomes of QM for organisations and employees have been a matter of much debate (we will return to the latter in due course). In respect of the former, Jong and Wilkinson (1999) draw attention to the fact that while companies tended to report the use of QM, evidence shows that many adopted a 'pick and mix' approach and as a result may not have enjoyed the full business benefits of QM. Studies suggest that whilst (T)QM became very fashionable in the late 1980s to mid-1990s, levels of 'successful' take-up and sustainability were quite low. However, there is some evidence that organisational benefits did accrue when companies were able to implement and sustain QM (Wilkinson *et al.*, 1998). Typical barriers to sustaining QM included; a lack of support and commitment from senior and middle management, business short termism, a lack of integration between QM and HR practices and a lack of contextual application (Redman and Grieves, 1998; Bradley and Hill, 1987; Dale and Cooper, 1994; Wilkinson *et al.*, 1997). Pertinent observations are that QM tended to have a particular blind-spot in terms of industrial relations (Wilkinson *et al.*, 1998) and that it failed to 'model the political realities of organisation' (Collins, 2000: 212).

Despite the fact that the term 'QM' has fallen from fashion, Wilkinson *et al.* (1998: 188) observe that many of the practices associated with QM such as teamworking, employee involvement, and continuous improvement have become embedded within the normal functioning of organisations. Dawson (1998: 8) goes on to observe that 'institutional (for example, the European Foundation for Quality Management) and business market requirements' have created a climate within which QM will continue to exist. Essentially, the term 'QM' may have fallen from its height of popular usage, but has left the legacy of practices that continue to merit further study. Indeed, there is a relationship between QM thinking and HPM, to which we turn now.

High performance management

Despite HPM achieving increasing prominence over the last few years, there is still confusion as to its precise nature. As Lloyd and Payne (2004: 13) observe, 'not only is there no clear definition of the model, but there is also a fundamental lack of agreement about the specific practices it should and should not incorporate, as well as the meanings that are ascribed to those practices'. Developing this theme Butler *et al.* (2004) argue that academic accounts of the phenomenon use a wide range of terms, thereby heightening the uncertainty surrounding its underlying tenets. Thus, in addition to HPM there is also reference to high performance work systems (Danford *et al.*, 2004), high involvement work systems (Harmon *et al.*, 2003), high commitment management (Baird, 2002) and similar formulations (see Table 14.6). Butler *et al.* (2004) suggest that the significance of this is more than just semantic (see also Boxall and Macky, 2009). For example, a focus on high performance work systems suggests a mechanistic route to sales and revenue growth through quality management techniques such as statistical process control and conformity evaluation. This is the agenda popularised by quality gurus including Crosby, Deming, Feigenbaum, and Duran. Early models of QM often emphasised the important role of senior managers and quality professionals. Conversely, high commitment management, given formal expression via the concept of (soft) HRM, emphasises the importance of *all* organisational players (in rhetoric at least). From the perspective of resource-based HRM, competitive advantage is derived not from the formal organisation and shaping of work *per se*, but the constituent workforce (see Chapter 2 in this volume).

Table 14.6 The lexicon of high performance management

Terminology	Studies	Dominant emphasis
High-performance work systems	Appelbaum *et al.* (2000) Danford *et al.* (2004) Farias *et al.* (1998) Harley (2002) Ramsay *et al.* (2000) Thompson (2003)	Production management
High-performance work practices	Handel and Gittelman (2004)	
High-performance work organisation	Ashton and Sung (2002) Lloyd and Payne (2004)	
High-involvement work systems	Edwards and Wright (2001) Felstead and Gallie (2002) Harmon *et al.* (2003)	Work organisation
High-involvement work practices	Fuertes and Sanchez (2004)	
High-performance practices	Goddard (2004)	
High-involvement management	Forth and Millward (2004)	
High-performance employment systems	Brown and Reich (1997)	
High-commitment management	Baird (2002) Whitfield and Poole (1997)	Employee relations

Source: Butler *et al.* (2004: 4).

Notwithstanding this apparent confusion, following the work of Bélanger *et al.* (2002) HPM may be viewed as combination of three elements. The first dimension, production management, is concerned with aspects of productive flexibility and process standardisation. A key facet here is *hard* quality management which characteristically involves the use of statistical tools to analyse variance from tolerance margins at each stage of the production process (Wilkinson *et al.*, 1998), which is subsumed within a wider TQM format. A quite distinct second dimension relates to work organisation. Here there has been a trend towards production activities based on knowledge, cognition and abstract labour. The centrepiece of the new approach is teamworking and again one can see the linkages between HPM and earlier models of QM. The practice of sharing skills across traditional demarcations 'is thus a fundamental feature of the emergent model' (Bélanger *et al.*, 2002: 39). The third sphere, 'employment relations', very much underpins the coherence of the former two components given the requirement for a committed, rather than merely compliant workforce (Bélanger *et al.*, 2002: 42–48). Two significant features emerge. First, Bélanger *et al.* (2002) state there is a desire to align and support task flexibility via terms and conditions of employment. This is typically sought by making pay contingent on group performance (Appelbaum, 2002: 124). Second, HRM professionals are charged with the pursuit of social adhesion and commitment to the new production format and wider organisational goals. This involves 'efforts to fashion employment conditions and the modes of regulation of those conditions in such a way as to elicit the tacit skills of the workers and tie them more closely to the goals of the firm' (Bélanger *et al.*, 2002: 44). In other words, the central task becomes the inculcation of a unitary organisational culture, or in Guest's (2002: 338) terms, the creation of a social system in support of the technical system.

Controversy: the impact of HPM on organisational performance

The driving force behind the introduction of HPM is to enhance organisational performance. In recent years the underlying assumption that HPM necessarily gives rise to positive improvements in performance has been subject to detailed investigation. That HPM has the *potential* to enhance organisational performance appears to be well settled. Thus, Whitfield and Poole (1997: 755) have concluded that extant research is 'strongly supportive of the notion that firms adopting the high performance approach have better outcomes than those which do not'. These conclusions do, however, come with reservations. First, these scholars argue that the perennial issue of causality needs to be considered (Truss, 2001). It is possible that the findings reflect that more successful firms use their competitive success as a basis to build more innovative practices.

A more significant second charge made by Whitfield and Poole (1997) concerns the narrow base on which the existing research has been undertaken. This is dominated by manufacturing, typically organisations competing on the basis of product quality and differentiation, as well as price. Building upon this theme, Ashton and Sung (2002: 165) have argued 'we still do not know the extent to which HPWP (high performance work practices) are only appropriate for certain types of industry or product market strategy'. In Wood's (1999: 368) terms, the debate is whether high-performance systems will *universally* outperform all other systems or whether the optimal system depends on the circumstances of the firm. Pursuing this theme, Wood (1999) draws upon Porter's conceptual distinction between two generic approaches, cost minimisation and innovative/quality strategies, as a basis on which to differentiate contexts. Schuler and Jackson (cited in Wood, 1999) have highlighted the need to link a Taylorist control approach with cost minimisation, and HPM to a quality-oriented strategy. In other words, HPM is only seen to be a suitable solution in certain circumstances; in others it may be economically rationale to combine low involvement with low employee skill and commitment (see Boxall and Macky, 2009: 11).

Controversy: the impact of new managerial practices on employees

In contrast to the increasing research on organisational outcomes there is far less systematic data on employee experiences of new management initiatives (especially drawn from qualitative data). However, there have been attempts in recent years to 're-focus attention on the worker' Guest (2002: 335).

As explained, the direct intellectual antecedent of HPM was QM. Much of the sociological literature dealing with employee experiences of this production format can be allotted to one of four broad streams: optimistic perspectives (e.g. Piore and Sabel, 1984) exploitation perspectives (e.g. Sewell and Wilkinson, 1992b), contingency perspectives (Hill, 1991) and the re-organisation of control (Rees, 1998). The optimistic perspective is that QM tends to be regarded as a 'win–win', i.e. employees and employers both benefit so employee experiences are likely to be positive. For example, Peccei and Rosenthal (2001) identified positive outcomes flowing from a service excellence initiative and found that employees broadly welcomed the initiative. The exploitation perspective argues that QM is essentially typified by peer pressure, increased surveillance and management by stress. For example, in a classic article, Sewell and Wilkinson (1992b) use the metaphor of a panopticon to drive home the theme that QM increases surveillance in organisations. Wilkinson *et al.* (1997) argue that the early debate tended to cluster around the polar extremes of 'bouquets or brickbats' as summarised in Table 14.7.

One can see the clear contrast between these two perspectives. More recently 'middle-ground' perspectives have emerged that tend to argue that QM is neither 'all good' nor 'all bad' and is likely to bring mixed consequences for employees. The contingency perspective focuses mainly on the way that contextual factors (for example, management intransigence, lack of training etc.) affect QM and a central theme tends to be that QM often fails to live up to expectations. The re-organisation of control approach has links with a labour process perspective in that

> the nature of production and the organisation of work tasks are considered to be the crucial factors in determining the boundaries of employee autonomy and discretion. However, it stops short of concluding that the implications of QM for employees tend invariably to be negative. Rather, QM is here seen as one among the series of changes, which also embrace new technology and new payment systems, which re-organise the shop floor so that in some respects commitment is enhanced while in others control is also tightened. (Rees, 1998: 38)

Table 14.7 Employee involvement and TQM: contrasting perspectives

Bouquets	Brickbats
Education	Indoctrination
Empowerment	Emasculation
Liberating	Controlling
Delayering	Intensification
Peer group pressure	Surveillance
Responsibility	Surveillance
Post-Fordism	Neo-Fordism
Blame-free culture	Identification of errors
Commitment	Compliance

Source: Wilkinson *et al.* (1997).

Evidence from studies from the contingency and re-organisation of control perspectives show that while aspects of QM are often welcomed, there is often a gap between rhetoric and the day-to-day reality in the workplace and the outcomes for employees are often ambiguous (Bacon and Blyton, 2000; Edwards *et al.*, 1998; Glover and Noon, 2005; Storey and Harrison, 1999). Overall, we can see that there is a diversity of perspectives on how QM affects employees, ranging from the optimistic to exploitation at the extremes and a middle-ground that emphasises mixed consequences. In many ways the debate about the impact of HPM on employees is following similar lines and it is to this that we now turn.

As explained, HPM has become increasingly popular, both as managerial rhetoric and a focus for academic research and one angle has been to investigate the implications of HPM for employees. Butler *et al.* (2004) observe that elements of the 'bouquets or brickbats' tradition are present in the HPM debate (Wilkinson *et al.*, 1997). For example, proponents of HPM use the rhetoric of empowerment and increased intrinsic rewards to claim that it benefits employees. Much, but not all, of this literature is contained within prescriptive accounts (see, for example, CIPD, 2004). We also find an exploitation perspective that centres upon the work intensification thesis and views HPM simply as a managerial ruse intended to extract greater effort from employees. Interestingly, there is common ground between these competing claims. This is that techniques of HPM, mediated by worker outcomes, are likely to contribute to enhanced organisational performance. What *is* disputed, however, is how this is generated.

As with QM, the optimistic perspective argues that the impact of HPM is mostly positive (for example, CIPD, 2004). Employees' experiences of work are enhanced and the outcomes are thus beneficial to both capital and labour. Increased task discretion and autonomy engender commitment, which, in turn, feeds into performance gains. The exploitation perspective also assumes a positive association between HPM and performance gains. However, the distinction is that any benefits take the form of minor gains in discretion, granted as a means of securing compliance with managerial aims. Such advances are far outweighed by work intensification, insecurity and stress (see Ramsay *et al.*, 2000: 505). Stress arises because of the added responsibility associated with the new production mode allied to increased pressure within the working environment due to the absence of buffers within lean production formats.

Unfortunately, there are only a handful of studies that have collected systematic data informing this debate. One of the most cited accounts in support of the optimistic thesis is provided by Appelbaum *et al.* (2000). This study investigated the effects of HPM in three manufacturing sectors: steel, clothing and medical products, with data collated from around 4000 workers. HPM was associated with positive performance gains and evidence was found linking various HPM practices to job satisfaction. This study provides support for David Guest's (2002: 354) assertion that 'there is consistent evidence that workers respond positively to practices associated with what is described as a high performance work system'. This said, there is an emergent body of contrary case study evidence that points towards heightened employee stress (see, for example, Danford *et al.* 2004; McKinlay and Taylor, 1996; Brown, 1999).

As with the debate about the effect of QM for employees, some have adopted a more middle-ground position. Edwards and Wright (2000: 570) have argued that, 'polarizing the issue between critics and supporters is not helpful'. Such exhortation chimes with an increasing body of literature indicating that HPM is likely to give rise to more complex outcomes for employees than those suggested above. Utilising the 1998 Workplace Employee Relations Survey (WERS98), Ramsay *et al.* (2000) found that, on the one hand, the data pointed to some association between HPM and higher job discretion and commitment. However, on the other, job strain was also reported. This confirms Edwards and Wright's (2000: 569) assertion that the links between HPM and employee outcomes represent a 'shifting and variable complex whole', which cannot be reduced to employee enhancing or damaging effects. For Edwards (2001: 3) one key to explanation lies in understanding the balance between the need for creativity and control within the contemporary workplace under the new production system. Thus, 'the fundamental tension is between work design which provides responsibility and autonomy and that which calls for predictable work outcomes based on defined tasks and monitoring (Edwards, 2001: 3).

One managerial solution to the above dilemma has been a shift away from command-and-control towards more indirect methods of tracking employee performance; that is, 'a change in the means of control' (Edwards, 2001: 16) not a move away from all forms of control. Under new forms of work organisation the control system is based upon outcomes, not specific instructions to detail. Via the techniques of human resource management, risks and responsibilities are internalised in the sense that employees are held responsible for their own actions (Edwards, 2001: 23). Thus, task discretion does not mean the lifting of organisational controls, rather the widespread use of HRM as opposed to more direct methods of control (i.e. the reorganisation of control). This is one means of reconciling the 'puzzle'. The contradictions are tapping into different aspects of a given worker's experiences arising from the multi-dimensional nature of HPM as identified by Bélanger and his colleagues. That is, increased responsibility (autonomy) arises from changes in work organisation, but so also does greater stress as risks are internalised via performance management and techniques of HRM. Mirroring the debate about the implications of QM for employees, evidence remains contrasting. As Boxall and Macky (2009: 17) caution, 'the current state of knowledge ... implies there are *possibilities* for win–win ourtcomes in *certain* contexts but not without careful managment of inherent tensions for both parties' (emphasis added).

Summary

- The terrain of EPI is broad and actually comprises three distinct but related concepts: employee involvement, employee participation and industrial democracy. The difference between these constructs is best understood in terms of variations in employee power and influence. Broadly speaking, there is a continuum ranging from narrow task-based employee input (employee involvement (EI)) through to elements of co-determination or joint decision making (participation) extending to full-blown employee ownership (industrial democracy).

- The topic of EPI has a long history. Interestingly while employee involvement (EI) is nowadays ascendant this is a relatively recent phenomenon. In the past the field has been dominated by the themes of participation and industrial democracy. The current hegemony of employee involvement can be tracked to the 1980s and the emergence of neo-liberalism and various influential HRM models. While employee involvement is currently riding high, developments at EU level have served to bolster the flagging fortunes of employee participation. The European Works Council and Information and Consultation directives provide employees with statutory rights to consultation hitherto denied to British workers. Academic commentators, however, have expressed reservations as to whether the legislation has the potential to seriously challenge managerial prerogative.

- Direct participation is generally geared towards capturing the creativity of employees so that organisational performance improves.

- WERS shows a trend towards an increase in direct forms of participation and a decline in representative participation. An outcome of this trend is that large swathes of the British workforce are not covered by trade union representation. Often these workers are based in service sector organisations that offer minimal pay and conditions. There is a concern that their plight is largely determined by managerial choice and approaches can range from enlightened HRM to authoritarian management.

- In the field of EPI the topic of managerial motive has been a longstanding area of controversy. Ramsay's (1977) 'cycles of control' thesis is regarded as seminal. According to

Ramsay, management was only interested in employee involvement when there were threats to managerial power. This stance has now been discredited. It is now widely acknowledged (e.g. Ackers *et al.*, 1992) that managerial goals are much more complex and cannot be reduced to issues of crude labour control. More creative goals that may be followed include the enhancement of customer care, employee recruitment and retention, and the invocation of a quality culture.

● The impact of a range of new management initiatives upon organisations and employees were reviewed. Evidence remains inconclusive as to the direct organisational benefits of the selected schemes. Evidence is also split as to the outcomes of these initiatives for employees.

Case study

Advanced Components

Advanced Components (AC) are a subsidiary of a large Anglo/French MNC called CarCo. AC produce specialist components for the car industry. AC are based in the north of England. CarCo went through a massive programme of rationalisation in the late 1970s, the mid-1980s and more recently in the late 1990s. They are beginning to explore opportunities for future growth and are in early talks about a potential joint venture in China. If this went ahead, the future of AC would be uncertain and the unions suspect that CarCo could close AC and relocate production in China.

The AC subsidiary has been on the same site since the industrial revolution, albeit under different names and different ownerships. AC employs 800 employees on a single site. The site employed 8000 in 1970. Over the years it has reduced its headcount, via early retirement, voluntary redundancies and compulsory redundancies. The workforce are mainly male, the average age is 48 and the average length-of-service is 15 years. AC produces specialist products and the workforce comprises a mix of production and craft workers (such as electricians). Average pay is £28,000 and comprises a mix of basic salary, overtime and bonuses.

Advanced Components is strongly unionised and had a reputation for being one of CarCo's industrial relations blackspots of the 1960s and 1970s. During this period, relationships between management and unions were conflictual. However, trade union activity has been less militant in recent years. Indeed, many feel that AC adopted a 'bullying' and autocratic form of management in the 1980s when much of the downsizing took place. However, management now seem keen to promote more cooperative relationships for the future. Shop stewards realise that the long-term future is made more precarious by CarCo's

negotiations within China. The trade unions have begun to express an interest in exploring the possibilities for a 'social partnership' agreement.

AC changed the name of their personnel department to the human resource department in 1995. The emphasis of the old personnel department had been very much upon industrial relations, health and safety and record keeping. There has been no system of appraisal or systematic training for the shopfloor or administrative staff. The apprenticeship system was the traditional training vehicle for shopfloor workers, but AC have not taken any new apprentices for 12 years. Any training that occurs tends to be on-the-job 'sitting with Nellie' but this approach is not formally managed. There is a corporate level, fasttrack management development scheme for identified high fliers, who are normally graduates. The high fliers are entered onto an MBA programme that is run by one of the UK's top business schools. The scheme has been very successful in terms of developing these individuals and tends to lead to accelerated careers for the individuals concerned and is still used today. There was no such formalised scheme for other white collar/managerial employees.

The change of label from the 'personnel department' to the 'human resources department' coincided with the implementation of quality management. The espoused strategy was QM would be supported by 'soft' HRM (including an emphasis on training and involvement). This signalled a change in management style (in rhetoric at least) and a more participative style was promised. However, many employees feel that this tends to be rather patchy and some managers maintain an autocratic style. The company have been trying to improve direct participation for over a decade. They have a company newsletter, a suggestion scheme, a team briefing system and have tried to encourage problem-solving groups. However, the success of these has been mixed. The newsletter is read by about 30 per cent of employees. The suggestion scheme generated a lot of interest initially and one large award of £5000 was made. However, the number of suggestions has fallen and there is a perception that it is extremely difficult to win awards and that management are slow to process the paperwork and feedback on proposals. The team briefing system is mainly welcomed, but the satisfaction levels are very much affected by the quality of the team briefers. Some are naturally good, but others struggle and there is no training for team briefers. AC do have problem-solving groups, but in reality only a handful are active and productive. Levels of problem-solving group activity tends to ebb and flow according to how much encouragement individual managers offer.

AC now wish to implement a programme of changes to take them forward. They are calling the programme 'Towards 2010'. AC have analysed their current position and have identified key issues:

- Car components is an increasingly competitive market sector with threats from the Asia.
- AC must continue to decrease costs whilst increasing quality.
- AC believe that there is significantly more potential within their employee ranks than is currently being utilised.
- AC believe that they need to increase flexibility, particularly on the shopfloor.
- They will be investing in improved IT to improve the site operations. An IT system will be linked to the production lines and will track all aspects of the progress of raw stock to the point at which it leaves the site. The system will give all departments (e.g. sales, marketing, finance) access to information regarding the status of customer orders, stock levels etc. The implementation of the system will lead to a consequent reduction in white collar administrative staff. The system will be launched in January 2007.

AC wish to achieve the following in relation to its human resources:

- increase productivity;
- improve the customer focus;
- increase quality;
- reduce labour costs;
- create a training and development strategy that covers all employees;
- increase and broaden all employee skills at all levels;
- encourage employee involvement.

The task

1 Advanced Components have asked you to summarise the EPI implications of 'Towards 2010'.

2 They have asked you to devise the following:

(a) An EPI *strategy* that will guide all activities. You are required to write a briefing paper that will be distributed to all managers that summarises the key content of this strategy.

(b) Outline the *operational objectives* that describe what EPI practices should be implemented (or sustained) within the organisation by the year 2010.

3 You must explain the rationale for your strategy, indicating why it would be appropriate for implementation at AC.

4 AC recognise trade unions. What approach should AC take in respect of the unions?

5 What do you perceive to be the main barriers in terms of taking the EPI strategy forwards and how would you suggest that AC deal with these?

References and further reading

Abrahamsson, B. (1977) *Bureaucracy or Participation*, London: Sage.

Ackers, P., Marchington, M., Wilkinson, A. and Goodman, J. (1992) 'The use of cycles: explaining employee involvement in the 1990s', *Industrial Relations Journal*, 23, 4: 268–83.

Ackers, P. and Payne, J. (1998) 'British trade unions and social partnership: Rhetoric, reality and strategy', *International Journal of Human Resource Management*, 9, 1: 529–50.

Alvesson, M. and Willmott, H. (2002) 'Identity regulation as organizational control: producing the appropriate individual', *Journal of Management Studies*, 39, 5: 619–44.

Appelbaum, E. (2002) 'The impact of new forms of work organisations on workers', in G. Murray, J. Bélanger, G. Giles and P. Lapointe. *Work and Employment Relations in the High Performance Workplace*. London: Continuum, pp. 120–49.

Appelbaum, E., Bailey, T., Berg, G. and Kelberg, G. (2000) *Manufacturing Advantage*. Ithaca, NY: Cornell University Press.

Argyris, C. (1964) *Integrating the Individual and Organization*. New York: Wiley.

Ashton, D. and Sung, J. (2002) *Supporting Workplace Learning for High Performance Working*. Geneva: International Labour Office.

Bacon, N. (2006) 'Industrial relations' in T. Redman and A. Wilkinson (eds) *Contemporary Human Resource Management*. Harlow: FT/Prentice Hall, pp. 188–208.

Bacon, N. and Blyton, P. (2000) 'Worker responses to workplace restructuring'. Paper presented at the BUIRA study group: What about the workers? Employee perspectives on HRM, King's College, London.

Baird, M. (2002) 'Changes, dangers, choice and voice: understanding what high commitment management means for employees and unions', *Journal of Industrial Relations*, 44, 3: 359–75.

Batstone, E.. Ferner, A. and Terry, M. (1983) *Unions on the Board: An Experiment in Industrial Democracy*. Oxford: Blackwell.

Bélanger, P., Giles, A. and Murray, G. (2002) 'Workplace innovation and the role of institutions', in G. Murray, J. Bélanger, A. Giles, and P. Lapointe. *Work and Employment in the High Performance Workplace*. London: Continuum, pp. 150–80.

Bernstein, P. (1976) *Workplace Democratization*. New Jersey: Transaction Books.

Blyton, P. and Turnbull, P. (2004) *The Dynamics of Employee Relations*, 3rd edn. Basingstoke: Palgrave.

Bolle De Bal, M. (1992) 'Participative management' in G. Szell (ed.) *Concise Encyclopedia of Participation*. Berlin: Walter de Gruyter, pp. 603–10.

Boxall, P. and Macky, K. (2009) 'Research and theory on high performance work systems: progressing the high involvement stream', *Human Resource Management Journal*, 19, 1: 3–23

Bradley, K. and Hill, S. (1987) 'Quality circles and managerial interests', *Industrial Relations*, 26, 1: 66–82.

Brannen, P. (1983) *Authority and Participation in Industry*. London: Batsford.

Brannen, P., Batstone, E., Fatchett, D. and White, P. (1976) *The Worker Directors: A Sociology of Participation*. London: Hutchinson.

Brown, C. and Reich, M. (1997) 'Micro-macro linkages in high performance employment systems', *Organizational Studies*, 18, 5: 765–81.

Brown, T. (1999) 'Restructuring teams and learning: the case of a clothing company', *Studies in Continuing Education*, 21, 2: 239–57.

Burchill, F. (1997) *Labour Relations*. Basingstoke: Macmillan.

Butler, P. (2004) 'Employee representation in non-unions firms: a critical evaluation of managerial motive and the efficacy of the voice process'. Unpublished PhD Thesis, University of Warwick.

Butler, P. (2009) 'Riding along on the crest of a wave: tracking the shifting rationale for non-union consultation at FinanceCo', *Human Resource Management Journal*, 19, 2: 176–93.

Butler, P., Felstead, A., Ashton, D., Fuller, A., Lee, T., Unwin, L. and Walters, S. (2004) 'High performance management: a literature review', *Learning as Work Research Paper No. 1*, Centre for Labour Market Studies, University of Leicester.

Cheney, G. (1999) *Values at Work: Employee Participation Meets Market Pressure at Modragon*. Ithaca, NY: ILR Press.

CIPD (2004) *Maximising Employee Potential and Business Performance*. London: CIPD.

Claydon, T. (1996) 'Union decognition: a re-examination' in I. Beardwell (ed.) *Contemporary Industrial Relations: A Critical Analysis*. Oxford: Oxford University Press, pp. 151–74.

Clegg, H.A. (1951) *Industrial Democracy and Nationalization: A Study Prepared for the Fabian Society*. Oxford: Blackwell.

Clegg, H. (1979) *The Changing System of Industrial Relations in Britain*. Oxford: Blackwell.

Collins, D. (2000) *Management Fads and Buzzwords: Critical Practical Perspectives*. London: Routledge.

Crouch, C. (1979) *The Political Economy of Industrial Relations*. Glasgow: Fontana.

Cully, M., Woodland, S., O'Reilly, A. and Dix, G. (1999) *Britain at Work: As Depicted by the 1998 Workplace Employee Relations Survey*. London: Routledge.

Dachler, P. and Wilpert, B. (1978) 'Conceptual dimensions and boundaries in organizations', *Administrative Science Quarterly*, 23: 1–39.

Dale, B.G. and Cooper, C. (1994) 'Total quality management: Some common mistakes made by senior management', *Quality World Technical Supplement*, March: 4–11.

Danford, A., Richardson, M., Stewart, P, Tailby, S., Upchurch, M. (2004) 'High performance work systems and workplace partnership: a case study of aerospace workers', *New Technology, Work and Employment*, 19, 1: 14–29.

Dawson, P. (1998) 'The rhetoric and bureaucracy of quality management: A totally questionable method', *Personnel Review*, 27, 1: 5–14.

Edwards, P. (2001) 'The puzzle of work: autonomy and commitment plus discipline and insecurity', *SKOPE Research Paper No. 16*, University of Warwick.

Edwards, P. and Wright, M. (2000) 'High involvement work systems and performance outcomes', *International Journal of Human Resource Management*, 24, 4: 568–85.

Edwards, P., Collinson, M. and Rees, C. (1998) 'The determinants of employee responses to total quality management: six case studies', *Organization Studies*, 19, 3: 449–75.

Farias, G.F. and Varma, A. (1998) 'High performance work systems: what we know and what we need to know', *Human Resource Planning*, 21, 2: 50–55.

Felstead, A. and Gallie, D. (2002) 'For better or worse? Non standard jobs and high involvement work systems', *SKOPE Research Paper No. 28*, University of Warwick.

Flanders, A. (1968) *Experiment in Industrial Democracy: A Study of the John Lewis Partnership*. London: Faber.

Forth, J. and Millward, N. (2004) 'High involvement management and pay in Britain', *Industrial Relations*, 43, 1: 98–119.

Fuertes, M. and Sanchez, F. (2003) 'High involvement practices in human resource management: concepts and factors that motivate their adoption', *International Journal of Human Resource Management*, 14, 4: 511–29.

Garrahan, P. and Stewart, P. (1992) *The Nissan Enigma: Flexibility at Work in a Local Economy*. London: Mansell Publishing.

Geary, J.F. (2003) 'New forms of work organisation: still limited, still controlled, but still welcome?' in P.K. Edwards (ed.) *Industrial Relations: Theory and practice in Britain*. Oxford: Blackwell, pp. 338–67.

Gennard, J. and Judge, G. (2005) *Employee Relations*, 4th edn. London: CIPD.

Glover, L. (2000) 'Neither poison nor panacea: shop floor responses to TQM', *Employee Relations*, 22, 2: 121–41.

Glover, L. (2001) 'Communication and consultation in a green field site company', *Personnel Review*, 30, 3: 297–316.

Glover, L. and Noon, M. (2005) 'Shop-floor workers' responses to quality management initiatives: broadening the disciplined worker thesis', *Work, Employment and Society*, 19, 4: 727–45.

Goddard, J. (2004) 'A critical assessment of the high performance paradigm', *British Journal of Industrial Relations*, 42, 2: 349–78.

Gollan, P. and Wilkinson, A. (2007) 'Implications of the EU Information and Consultation Directive and the Regulations in the UK – prospects for the future of employee representation. *International Journal of Human Resource Management*, 18, 7: 1145–58.

Grenier, D. and Hogler, R. (1991) 'Labour law and managerial ideology: employee participation as a control system', *Work and Occupations*, 16, 3: 313–33.

Guest, D. (2002) 'Human resource management, corporate performance and employee well-being: building the worker into HRM', *Journal of Industrial Relations*, 44, 4: 335–58.

Guest, D. and Peccei, R. (2001) 'Partnership at work: mutuality and the balance of advantage', *British Journal of Industrial Relations*, 39, 2: 207–63.

Hall, M. (2005) 'How are employers and unions responding to the information and consultation of employee regulations', *Warwick Papers in Industrial Relations*, No. 77.

Hall, M. and Marginson, P. (2005) 'Trojan horse or paper tiger? Assessing the significance of European Works Councils' in J. Hyman and P. Thompson (eds) *Participation at Work: Essays in Honour of Harvie Ramsay*. Basingstoke: Palgrave Macmillan, pp. 204–21.

Hall, M., Hutchinson, S., Parker, J., Purcell, J. and Terry, M. (2007) 'Implementing information and consultation: early experience under the ICE Regulations', *Employment Relations Research Series*, No. 88, London: Department for Business Enterprise and Regulatory Reform.

Hall, M., Hutchinson, S., Parker, J., Purcell J. and Terry, M. (2008) 'Implementing information and consultation in medium-sized organizations', *Employment Relations Research Series*, No. 97, London: Department for Business Enterprise and Regulatory Reform.

Handel, J. and Gittleman, M. (2004) 'Is there a wage payoff to innovative work practices?', *Industrial Relations*, 43, 1: 67–97.

Harley, B. (2002) 'Employee responses to high performance work system practices: An analysis of the AWIRS95 data', *Journal of Industrial Relations*, 44, 3: 418–34.

Harley, B., Hyman, J. and Thompson, P. (2005) 'The paradoxes of participation' in B. Harley, J. Hyman and P. Thompson (eds) *Participation and Democracy at Work: Essays in Honour of Harvie Ramsay*. Basingstoke: Palgrave Macmillan, pp. 1–19.

Harmon, J., Scotti, D. and Behson, S. (2003) 'Effects of high performance work systems practices: an analysis of the WIRS95 data', *Journal of Industrial Relations*, 44, 3: 418–34.

Heller, F. (1992) 'Competence' in G. Szell (ed.) *Concise Encyclopedia of Participation*. Berlin: Walter De Gruyter.

Heller, F., Pusic, E., Strauss, G. and Wilpert, B. (1998) *Organisational Participation: Myth and reality*. Oxford: Oxford University Press.

Hespe, G. and Little, S. (1971) 'Some aspects of employee participation' in P. Warre (ed.) *Psychology at Work*. Harmondsworth: Penguin, pp. 325–47.

Hill, S. (1991) 'Why quality circles failed but total quality might succeed', *British Journal of Industrial Relations*, 29, 4: 541–68.

Hill, S. (1995) 'From quality circles to total quality management' in A. Wilkinson and H. Willmott (eds) *Making Quality Critical: New Perspectives on Organisational Change*. London: Routledge, pp. 33–53.

Holden, L. (2001) 'Employee involvement and empowerment' in I. Beardwell, L. Holden and T. Claydon (eds) *Human Resource Management: A Contemporary Approach*, 3rd edn. Harlow: Prentice Hall, pp. 559–82.

Holden, L. (2004) 'Employee involvement and empowerment' in I. Beardwell and L. Holden (eds) *Human Resource Management: A Contemporary Approach*, 4th edn. Harlow: Prentice Hall, pp. 539–78.

Hyman, R. (1989) *The Political Economy of Industrial Relations: Theory and Practice in a Cold Climate*. Basingstoke: Macmillan.

Hyman, J. and Mason, B. (1995) *Managing Employee Involvement and Participation*. London: Sage.

Jong, J. and Wilkinson, A. (1999) 'The state of total quality management: A review', *International Journal of Human Resource Management*, 10, 1: 137–50.

Kerckhofs, P. (2002) *European Works Councils; Facts and Figures*. Brussels: European Trade Union Institute.

Kersley, B., Alpin, C., Forth, J., Bryson, A., Bewley, H., Dix, G. and Oxenbridge, S. (2005) *Inside the workplace: First findings from the 2004 Workplace Employment Relations Survey*. ESRC, ACAS, PSI, DTI. Abingdon: Routledge.

Kersley, B., Alpin, C., Forth, J., Bryson, A., Bewley, H., Dix, G. and Oxenbridge, S. (2006) *Inside the Workplace: Findings from the 2004 Workplace Employment Relations Survey*. Abingdon: Routledge.

Leat, M. (2003) 'The European Union' in G., Hollinshead, P. Nicholls and S. Tailby (eds) *Employee Relations*. Harlow: Prentice Hall, pp. 202–61.

Legge, K. (2005) *Human Resource Management: Rhetorics and Realities* (Anniversary ed.). Basingstoke: Palgrave Macmillan.

Lewis, P., Thornhill, A. and Saunders, M. (2003) *Employee Relations: Understanding the Employment Relationship*. Harlow: Prentice Hall.

Likert, R. (1961) *New Patterns of Management*. New York: McGraw-Hill.

Lloyd, C. and Payne, J. (2004) 'The only show in town (if a pretty pathetic one at that) . . . Re-evaluating the high performance workplace as a vehicle for the UK High Skills Project', Paper presented to the International Labour Process Conference, Amsterdam.

Marchington, M. (2005) 'Employee involvement: patterns and explanations' in B. Harley, J. Hyman and P. Thompson (eds) *Participation and Democracy at Work: Essays in Honour of Harvie Ramsay*. Basingstoke: Palgrave Macmillan, pp. 20–37.

Marchington, M. and Wilkinson, A. (2005) 'Direct participation' in S. Bach (ed.) *Personnel Management: A Comprehensive Guide to Theory and Practice*. Oxford: Blackwell, pp. 382–404.

Marchington, M., Goodman, J., Wilkinson, A. and Ackers, P. (1992) *New Developments in Employee Involvement*. Department of Employment Research Series No. 2. London: HMSO.

Marchington, M., Wilkinson, A., Ackers, P. and Goodman, J. (1993) 'The influence of managerial relations on waves of employee involvement', *British Journal of Industrial Relations*, 31, 4: 553–76.

Martinez Lucio, M. and Stuart, M. (2002) 'Assessing the principles of partnership: Workplace trade unions representatives' attitudes and experiences', *Employee Relations*, 24, 3: 305–20.

McGregor, D. (1960) *The Human Side of Enterprise*. New York: McGraw-Hill.

McKinlay, A. and Taylor, P. (1996) 'Power surveillance and resistance: inside the factory of the future' in P. Ackers, C. Smith and P. Smith (eds) *The New Workplace and Trade Unionism*. London: Routledge, pp. 279–300.

Millward, N., Bryson, A. and Forth, J. (2000) *All Change at Work? British Employment Relations 1980–1998, as Portrayed by the Workplace Industrial Relations Survey Series*. London: Routledge.

Mueller, F. and Proctor, S. (2000) *Teamworking*. Basingstoke: Macmillan.

Pateman, C. (1970) *Participation and Democratic Theory*. Cambridge: Cambridge University Press.

Payne, J. and Keep, E. (2005) 'Promoting workplace development: Lessons for UK policy from Nordic approaches to job redesign and the quality of working life' in B. Harley, J. Hyman and P. Thompson (eds) *Participation and Democracy at Work: Essays in Honour of Harvie Ramsay*. Basingstoke: Palgrave Macmillan, pp. 145–65.

Peccei, R. and Rosenthal, P. (2001) 'Delivering customer-orientated behaviour through empowerment: An empirical test of HRM', *Journal of Management Studies*, 38, 6: 831–57.

Piore, M. and Sabel, C. (1984) *The Second Industrial Divide: Possibilities to Prosperity*. New York: Basic Books.

Poole, M. (1978) *Workers' Participation in Industry*. London: Routledge.

Ramsay, H. (1977) 'Cycles of control', *Sociology*, 11, 3: 481–506.

Ramsay, H. (1980) 'Phantom participation: patterns of power and conflict', *Industrial Relations Journal*, 11, 3: 46–59.

Ramsay, H. (1993) 'Recycled waste? Debating the analysis of worker participation: a response to Ackers *et al.*', *Industrial Relations Journal*, 24, 1: 76–80.

Ramsay, H., Scholarios, D. and Harley, B. (2000) 'Employees and high performance work systems: testing inside the black box', *British Journal of Industrial Relations*, 38, 4: 501–31.

Redman, T. and Grieves, J. (1998) 'Managing strategic change through TQM: Learning from failure', *New Technology, Work and Employment*, 14, 1: 64–80.

Rees, C. (1998) 'Empowerment through quality management: employee accounts from inside a bank, a hotel and two factories' in C. Mabey, D. Skinner and T. Clark (eds) *Experiencing Human Resource Management*. London: Sage, pp. 33–53.

Richardson, M. (2003) 'Employee involvement and participation' in G. Hollinshead, P. Nicholls and S. Tailby (eds) *Employee Relations*. Harlow: Prentice Hall.

Sewell, G. and Wilkinson, B. (1992a) 'Empowerment or emasculation? Shopfloor surveillance in a total quality organisation' in P. Blyton and P. Turnbull (eds) *Reassessing Human Resource Management*. London: Sage, pp. 271–90.

Sewell, G. and Wilkinson, B. (1992b) 'Someone to watch over me: surveillance, discipline and the just-in-time labour process', *Sociology*, 26, 2: 271–90.

Sisson, K. (2002) 'The Information and Consultation Directive: unnecessary regulation or an opportunity to promote partnership', *Warwick Papers in Industrial Relations*, No. 67.

Stirling, J. and Fitzgerald, I. (2000) 'European works councils: representing workers on the periphery', *Employee Relations*, 23, 1: 13–25.

Storey, J. (1992) *Developments in the Management of Human Resources: An Analytical Review*. London: Blackwell.

Storey, J. (1995) *Human Resource Management: A Critical Text*. London: Routledge.

Storey, J. and Harrison, A. (1999) 'Coping with world-class manufacturing', *Work, Employment and Society*, 13, 4: 643–64.

Suff, R. and Williams, S. (2004) 'The myth of mutuality? Employee perceptions of partnership at Borg Warner', *Employee Relations*, 26, 1, 30–43.

Tailby, S. and Winchester, D. (2005) 'Management and trade unions: towards social partnership?' in S. Bach (ed.) *Human Resource Management: Personnel Management in Transition*. Oxford: Blackwell, pp. 365–88.

Tailby, S., Richardson, M., Danford, A. and Upchurch, M. (2004) 'Partnership at work and worker participation: an NHS case study', *Industrial Relations Journal*, 35, 5: 403–18.

Taylor, P., Mulvey, G., Hyman, J. and Bain, P. (2002) 'Work organization, control and the experience of work in call centres', *Work, Employment and Society*, 16, 1: 133–50.

Thompson, P. (2003) 'Disconnected capitalism: or why employers can't keep their side of the bargain', *Work Employment and Society*, 17, 2: 359–78.

Timming, A. (2007) 'European Works Councils and the dark side of managing worker voice', *Human Resource Management Journal*, 17, 3: 248–64.

Towers, B. (1997) *The Representation Gap: Change and Reform in the British and American Workplace*. Oxford: Oxford University Press.

Truss, C. (2001) 'Complexities and controversies in linking HRM with organizational outcomes', *Journal of Management Studies*, 38, 8: 1121–49.

Undy, R. (1999) 'Annual review article: New Labour's 'Industrial Relations Settlement': the Third Way?', *British Journal of Industrial Relations*, 37, 2: 315–36.

Whitfield, K. and Poole, M. (1997) 'Organizing employment for high performance theories, evidence and policy', *Organisational Studies*, 18, 5: 745–64.

Wilkinson, A., Godfrey, G. and Marchington, M. (1997) 'Bouquets, brickbats and blinkers: TQM and employee involvement in practice', *Organisation Studies*, 18, 5: 799–819.

Wilkinson, A., Redman, T., Snape, E. and Marchington, M. (1998) *Managing with Total Quality Management: Theory and Practice*. London: Macmillan.

Wood, S. (1999) 'Human Resource management and Performance', *International Journal of Management Review*, 1, 4: 367–413.

 For multiple-choice questions, exercises and annotated weblinks related to this topic, visit **www.pearsoned.co.uk/mymanagementlab**.

Malone Superbuy Ltd

Malone Superbuy is a large food retail company that has been established since the beginning of the twentieth century. Over the last 100 years the organisation has built a reputation for quality foods, and so depends on relatively discerning shoppers for its market; most of its outlets are in the South-West and South-East of Britain. The organisation is a large employer (more than 4000 employees); it is highly dependent upon part-time, female labour and casual student workers for shopfloor employees, with full-time management staff consigned to given stores. The firm does experience costly medium-to-high labour turnover, largely because of the unsocial hours to which all employees are rostered, and the transient nature of student labour. Wage rates are average for the sector, and were unaffected by the Minimum Wage Regulation. The organisation has never recognised trade unions, but has had a fairly informal system of local employee representation committees, many of which have fallen into disuse in recent years.

The food retail sector has recently experienced growing competition between the market leaders as attention has been drawn to the differentials between the price of food in the UK and in other European countries. British farmers have also been active in publicly denouncing the profiteering that has been evident in the retail food sector. Consequently, the big firms are engaged in 'price wars' and are actively increasing the quality and variety of goods on offer while also focusing on the level of service offered within their stores. Malone Superbuy is not in the top league, but nevertheless has been affected by increasing competition in the sector. To add to its troubles, the TGWU is actively recruiting employees, and it looks as if Malone's will be presented with a recognition claim for bargaining rights in the near future. To remain competitive in the market the firm must:

- improve the quality of service offered to customers throughout the organisation;
- find ways of cutting labour costs.

Further to developing a strategy for change to deal with market pressures, the firm must also decide whether it intends to:

- accept a trade union presence and attempt to build a partnership agreement;
- adopt a substitution or suppressionist approach to union recognition.

Activity

You are a member of an external team of HR consultants employed by the company to outline a strategy which will achieve employee support for increased competitiveness in an environment of change. The Managing Director has already decided that he wants a comprehensive report to indicate how the firm will move forward and this will be presented under the title, 'Superbuy shapes up for the future!'. As a team your remit is to construct that report and your particular responsibility is to write the following sections:

1 Outline and discuss an appropriate HR Strategy (see also Chapter 2) for this organisation which will facilitate the coherent development of the firm within its particular context.

2 Suggest policy initiatives to address the labour turnover problems currently affecting the firm.

3 Develop a training programme which will enhance customer service skills amongst shopfloor staff.

4 Address the issue of employee representation with a reasoned consideration of whether to adopt substitution/exclusion approaches or to negotiate a recognition agreement with trade unions.

5 Consider how employee reward policies might be re-evaluated to encourage greater employee motivation and loyalty (without substantially affecting the wages bill!).

Part 5

INTERNATIONAL HUMAN RESOURCE MANAGEMENT

Introduction to Part 5

The considerable growth of interest in international human resource management stems from the rise of globalisation over the past half century, a phenomenon that has accelerated considerably over the last decade. This term describes the proliferation of international trading links, foreign direct investment, worldwide mergers and acquisitions and a burgeoning of telecommunications, faster and cheaper transport and rapid technological change. Globalisation has involved the integration of markets world-wide and on a regional level and is being stimulated further by the rise of new and potentially powerful markets in China, India and Eastern and Central Europe.

The rise of the multinational company (MNC) has been one of the most visible manifestations of globalisation. As companies and organisations expand their cross-border activities there has been a concomitant increase in business activity together with an increase in cross-border integration of their production processes. This in turn has created growing interest in the ways in which they achieve international management coordination and control and what effect such coordination has on HRM in the countries in which their operations are based.

The possible role of MNCs as forces for change in national HRM systems is just one element in a wider debate that is developing concerning the effects of globalisation on national economic and business systems. Are there varieties of capitalism that are each efficient in their own national contexts, or is globalisation creating new conditions in which some of those varieties cease to be sustainable, causing convergence towards a dominant global model?

The chapters that comprise this part cannot do justice to the complexity and scale of these issues. They merely serve to give you a flavour of some of the developments in the field and some of the debates that are now emerging. The section begins with a system-level comparative perspective on HRM that takes up the question of international convergence by looking at pressures for change in Germany, Japan and the USA to see how far the highly institutionalised German and Japanese business and employment systems are being forced to move towards the more loosely regulated and managerially dominated US system.

The following chapter extends the comparative theme and the discussion of possible global convergence by examining the way HRM is developing in China and India. It uses cultural and institutional perspectives to explore how historically rooted national characteristics interact with international, globalising influences to shape HRM in these potentially huge global players.

The final chapter combines a range of firm level perspectives to examine how human resources are managed in MNCs. It starts by showing how international operations offer firms advantages in terms of gaining access to human resources and knowledge. It then explores the different ways in which MNCs might choose to structure the international HR function and discusses how HR networks and expatriate managers are used to generate and transfer HR knowledge internally. Finally, it explores how their HRM practices are influenced by characteristics of their country of origin and of the countries in which they operate.

Chapter 15

Trends and prospects in HRM systems: a comparative perspective

Ian Clark and Tim Claydon

Objectives

- To demonstrate the nationally distinctive character of employment systems with reference to Germany, Japan and the United States.

- To show how patterns of employment regulation are embedded within wider features of societies, specifically their business systems.

- To examine the nature and extent of change occurring in the German, Japanese and American employment systems.

- To identify and explain recent pressures for change in employment systems, for example the adoption and diffusion of new business models.

- To examine the debate concerning whether change in national employment systems is leading to convergence towards the American model.

Introduction: divergence, change and convergence in employment systems

Variations between national employment systems reflect wider differences in national culture and institutions. They are the outcome of nationally distinctive histories of how national identity and statehood were forged, how industrialisation developed, and how the nature and outcomes of class conflicts shaped political institutions and relations between capital, labour and the state. For many analysts, who we might summarise as the 'divergence school', this means that national systems of employment regulation will always differ from each other in important respects, as will the employment relations practices of firms in different countries, since they embody nationally specific historical developments (Hall and Soskice, 2001; Maurice *et al.*, 1986; Whitley, 2000). Others, however, who we can summarise as the 'convergence school' have argued that powerful socio-economic forces such as technological change, industrial development and more recently, the global diffusion of new business models focused on shareholder and investor interests, force nation states along convergent paths. Because of this, national differences in respect of economic and social organisation, including employment regulation, become less and less significant (Kerr *et al.*, 1960; Streeck, 1997). However, if this is the case, what are national systems converging towards?

In this chapter we look at three nationally based systems of employment regulation, those of Germany, Japan and the USA. There are two main reasons for focusing on the employment systems of these particular countries. First, at different points in recent history each has been seen as an example of excellence and a model to be emulated. Second, each of these models currently embodies a different paradigm of employment relations and HRM. The USA represents the liberal market model, Germany represents a model of social partnership and Japan is a model of enterprise-based partnership.

In Germany, constitutional law has provided workers with rights to collective representation and participation in decision making as well as individual rights. Trade unions wield significant albeit declining influence and workers' representatives have a legal right to negotiate or to be consulted on a wide range of issues including pay, hours, training, new investment and technology, work organisation and workforce adjustments. This emphasis on joint regulation of the employment relationship has provided the basis for a high degree of worker–management cooperation in the workplace and has underpinned a production system based on high productivity and high quality output.

In Japan, management and unions have developed a cooperative relationship that is based on mutual commitment to the enterprise. Historically, leading Japanese employers have provided workers with wide-ranging welfare benefits, long-term employment security and internal training, and promotion prospects and salaries that reflect length of service as well as ability. The dependence of Japanese workers on their employers for so many aspects of their welfare has encouraged a high degree of cooperation with management. This in turn has supported a system of production that relies on workers supplying high levels of effort, taking responsibility for monitoring quality, solving production problems and identifying ways of improving the efficiency of the production process and the quality of the product.

In the USA, trade unions are weak, state intervention in employment matters is limited and management has a lot of freedom to determine most elements of the employment relationship; hiring and firing procedures, hours of work, wages and salaries, pay systems, work organization and training. This has given rise to varied approaches to regulating the employment relationship.

Since the 1970s the US employment system has developed in ways that embody a business model which promotes an outsider-shareholder-focused approach to capitalism; in contrast to this, the German and Japanese employment systems reflect, albeit in different ways, an insider-stakeholder business model of capitalism (Dore, 2000). However, the German and Japanese systems have come under increasing economic and financial strain during the last 25 years and there is debate about the sustainability of nationally distinctive stakeholder approaches to capitalism in a globalised world economy currently dominated by the USA (Dore *et al.*, 1999). This raises a fundamental question about the future viability of stakeholder forms of capitalism and the employment systems that have been associated with them. This has been reflected in the recent worldwide 'credit crunch' and national responses to it. The loss of international liquidity and dramatic reductions in bank lending associated with the credit crunch demonstrated how American business models, particularly those in the financial sector which were so closely attuned to the cheap credit conditions of the global economy, were increasingly emulated in the UK (Northern Rock), Germany (Hypobank), France (Société Générale), Japan and in the rapidly developing economies in Asia, notably China and India. However, responses to the crisis have demonstrated national differences; the UK and the USA have been more willing to increase government budget deficits in order to stimulate the economy than has Germany or France, where there is a stronger emphasis on the need for stricter regulation of financial institutions.

In the next sections of the chapter we shall:

- Describe the hitherto distinctive and divergent national characteristics of the German, Japanese and US employment systems.

- Explain how these nationally distinctive employment systems are connected to other social institutions as part of wider national business systems.

- Discuss the nature and significance of the main currents of change in the German, Japanese and US employment systems.

- Review the debate over whether the changes that are taking place in national employment systems are leading to convergence towards a particular model.

National employment systems

In this section of the chapter we describe what are seen as the key features of the German, Japanese and American systems of employment relations. Before we do so however, we need to issue a health warning. Any attempt to generalise about a country involves a degree of simplification. In reality, there are considerable variations in the way work and employment are organised and managed within individual countries. Descriptions of the American, German and Japanese employment systems usually focus on formal institutions of employment regulation and on the employment practices that characterise the leading sectors of the economy. This does not give a complete picture of employment practice since the extent to which different types of organisation are subject to formal regulation differs and practices that are typical of leading sectors may be much less so of others in the same country. However, it does mean that we can identify the key features of national employment systems and compare them.

Germany: the social partnership model

In 1993 the German car manufacturer Volkswagen faced a crisis brought about by a sharp drop in sales.* The decline meant that 30,000 of the company's German workforce of just over 102,000 had become surplus to requirements. It was clear to VW management that they had to reduce labour costs but how could this be done in a way that was acceptable to employees? Traditional options of early retirement, voluntary redundancy and temporary reductions in working hours were unworkable because of the scale and immediacy of the problem. At the same time, the dismissal of 30,000 workers was unacceptable, particularly given that unemployment in the Lower Saxony region, where VW was located, was already running at 15 per cent. VW management therefore asked itself, how could VW reduce employment costs and improve productivity, competitiveness and financial performance while protecting jobs and conditions of employment?

Its response was to try to get employees and their representatives to agree to a new employment model for VW that involved a considerable element of shared sacrifice by workers in order to preserve jobs. Employees were asked to accept a move to a four-day week with matching reductions in annual pay. They were asked to accept retraining and redeployment to different job grades where necessary. They were also asked to accept relocation to other VW factories in the region if required. The broad outline of the scheme was negotiated between VW senior management and the main trade union, IG-Metall. The details of the plan and how it would be implemented in VW's six German factories were decided in specially established negotiating committees and in discussions between management and works councils at company and factory level. The negotiation process was initially difficult as the unions and most employees were resistant to reductions in hours if they meant lower earnings. Therefore, management put a lot of effort into meetings and seminars with employees to convince them of the necessity for this. Works council representatives also met with employees to get their views and suggestions to form the basis of a negotiating agenda that they took to management.

The new employment model that was finally agreed involved the reduction from a five- to a four-day week with a proportionate reduction in annual pay. To ease the impact of this on employees' monthly income, bonuses that had previously been paid once a year, such as holiday pay, annual and Christmas bonuses were incorporated into monthly pay. A second feature of the model was a block release system whereby employees could interrupt their employment to continue their education and training for a period of three to six months, although they would not be paid during that time. Finally, the model included a scheme

---

* This description of events at Volkswagen draws heavily on Kothen et al. (1999).

where newly trained workers would work for just 20 hours a week during their first year, thereafter increasing to 28.8 hours (the four-day week) over the next three and a half years. Older workers nearing retirement age would decrease their weekly hours in the same way.

As well as making changes to its employment pattern, VW management also introduced measures to increase productivity through a just-in-time production system that was linked to flexible hours working. This meant that employees could be required to work more than 28.8 hours in any one week. The extra hours worked would be counted as overtime hours that could be taken as time off at a later date. Employees were also organised into continuous improvement teams to find ways of improving productivity and efficiency.

Gaining acceptance of the plan and agreeing the details of its implementation were not easy. Nevertheless, VW was able to maintain employment of over 100,000 workers and by 1996, 49 per cent of the workforce stated that they were satisfied with the new scheme while just 16 per cent said that they were dissatisfied, the remaining 35 per cent being neutral (Kothen *et al.*, 1999). Thus, while the workforce in general was far from being in love with the new regime, there was a high level of acceptance based on the recognition that it was a jointly negotiated change that had protected employment.

In 1993, VW was not typical of German companies. For one thing, it was part publicly owned. The state of Lower Saxony was a major shareholder and the governor of the region was a member of VW's Supervisory Management Board. VW is also unusual, although increasingly less so, in that it negotiates with unions at company level. Usually companies negotiate indirectly with the unions through their employers' associations at regional industry level to establish industry level collective agreements. Nevertheless, this story about VW illustrates the key features of the German employment system and the German model of capitalism very well because it raises the questions of why VW management were so reluctant to implement mass sackings and how they were able to construct, through negotiation and consultation, a broad consensus in support of radical change. As we shall see, these issues can only be explained by looking at wider features of the German employment system and how it reflects broader features of the German model of capitalism. As we shall also see later on in the chapter, VW has recently undergone a significant transformation in ownership and this change, whilst taking place at firm level, may reflect the nature and extent of pressures on the German business and employment systems more generally.

The German employment system

Germany's system of employment relations was established in the aftermath of the Second World War but some of its features can be traced back to the Bismarck era of the late nineteenth century. The basic principle of the German system is one of collective self-regulation by employer and employee organisations within a framework of law. The German system has five key characteristics (Jacobi *et al.*, 1998). These are:

- *A framework of law* that supports and regulates interest representation in employment relations. German employment relations law has established basic principles and institutional arrangements that allow employers and workers to regulate their own affairs with little direct interference from the state. Thus the 1949 Collective Agreement Act established collective bargaining rights for workers. The Works Constitution Act of 1952 and the Code-termination Acts of 1951 and 1976 give workers the right to elect Works Councils in workplaces employing five or more workers. They also provide for workers to be represented on the Supervisory Boards (see Glossary) of companies having more than 500 employees. In providing workers with legal rights to collective representation, the law made an important distinction between collective bargaining and co-determination, effectively creating the second key feature of the system, a dual structure of interest representation.

- *A dual structure of interest representation.* German employment relations law makes important distinctions between collective bargaining and co-determination in terms of their functions, institutions and the levels at which they operate.

Collective bargaining establishes basic terms of employment such as wages and hours, what the Germans have called *issues of interest*. Co-determination deals with issues that arise from the application of industry-wide collective agreements to individual enterprises. These issues are known as *issues of rights*. Collective bargaining takes place at industry/regional level between trade unions and employers' associations. Co-determination is conducted between works councils and management at enterprise/workplace level. Trade unions and works councils are therefore separate legal entities, with distinct functions and separate arenas of action. In practice however, there has always been some overlap between the two. The majority of works councillors are trade union members and works councils have for a long time engaged in informal workplace bargaining with management over pay (Jacobi *et al.*, 1998). Since the 1980s the role of works councils in negotiating terms and conditions of employment has increased owing to decentralising tendencies in German industrial relations (see below, pp. 594–5).

The dual system of interest representation is reflected in the law on industrial action in Germany. Trade unions may call strikes in the event of disputes arising from a failure of collective bargaining negotiations to reach agreement on terms and conditions of employment (*disputes over issues of interest*). Works councils, on the other hand, have a legal obligation to work cooperatively with management for the good of the employees and the enterprise. Once a collective bargaining agreement has been concluded there is a peace obligation on both sides for as long as the agreement lasts and strikes during the currency of a collective agreement are unlawful. Disputes that may arise over the interpretation or application of the agreement (*disputes over issues of rights*) must be dealt with through co-determination procedure or by arbitration in the Labour Courts.

- *Centralisation and co-ordination of collective bargaining at sectoral level* has been a third key feature of the German model. In the private sector collective bargaining has generally taken place in each region (*Lande*) between the trade union and the regional employers' association for the industry/sector concerned. In the public sector, collective bargaining is conducted at national level. The centralisation of collective bargaining is a crucial aspect of the dual system of representation since it means that collective bargaining operates at industry/sector level while co-determination operates at enterprise or workplace level. If collective bargaining took place at company or workplace level, as is the case in the USA or the UK, it would be much more difficult to differentiate between trade union activities and works committee activities. However, in recent years there has been a move towards decentralisation of bargaining in much of German industry (see below, p. 594).

- *Encompassing organisations of workers and employers.* Unions are legally required to represent all workers, not just their own members. Works councils represent all workers in a workplace. Also, although not legally required to do so, employers' associations have historically represented all employers in their industries. Collective agreements have therefore tended to cover all workers in each sector. This is recognised in law, so that workers effectively have a right to collective representation on basic terms and conditions of employment. Consequently, while the proportion of workers who are union members has always been relatively modest at around 35–37 per cent, 90 per cent have been covered by collective agreements (Jacobi *et al.*, 1998).

- *Social partnership.* While the German system recognises that there are legitimate differences of interest between capital and labour, there is also a strong emphasis on labour–management cooperation supported by the state. At the level of the economy the social partners, i.e. peak confederations of employers' associations and trade unions, participate in a three-way 'political exchange' with government on issues of national economic and social policy. At the sectoral level trade unions have developed a role as mediators between employer and employee interests rather than simply pursuing adversarial strategies against employers through collective bargaining (Jacobi *et al.*, 1998). At enterprise level, while works committees can constrain management actions on issues such as payments systems, work schedules, recruitment, transfer and dismissal, they are legally obliged to consider company aims and interests and not simply pursue immediate employee interests. This has supported the concept of the *professional enterprise community* (Lane, 1989). This term expresses a sense in which managers, employees and their representatives see themselves as the key stakeholders in the enterprise, acting as a coalition to guide its future.

These features of the German system of employment relations mean that employment issues are subject to a high degree of *institutional regulation*. In other words, the ability of management to exercise unilateral control over terms and conditions of employment is constrained by individual employment rights provided by state legislation and employees' rights to collective representation in decision-making through collective bargaining and co-determination.

The employment system and 'Deutschland AG': the wider German business system

The German approach to employment regulation is an integral part of its broader approach to organising and regulating economic activity, i.e. its wider business system. This is often referred to as Deutschland AG, which describes a intricate web of cross-shareholdings between banks, founding families, insurance companies and leading industrial firms which as in the VW case is designed to protect many of Germany's leading firms from overseas corporate predators. In addition to the employment relations system, key elements of the wider business system in Germany are:

● *The nature of state regulation.* Since the 1960s *bargained corporatism* (Strinati, 1982) has been a guiding principle for state action in Germany. Compared with the United States, where market individualism exerts a powerful influence on government policies for the labour market, there is much greater direct state intervention to regulate aspects of employment. Germany's employment protection laws are noticeably stricter in the way they constrain employers' freedom to dismiss workers than those of the USA or the UK, although not as strict as those in Italy, Spain or France. The second crucial element of bargained corporatism in Germany is active state support for the collective organisation and representation of workers and employers. This support takes the form of statutory rights to collective organisation, collective bargaining and other forms of collective worker participation in decision making. Finally, as noted above, collective organisations of workers and employers have a role in negotiating with government over aspects of labour market regulation and wider issues of economic and social policy. Taken together, these three elements support a dense framework of institutional regulation of employment and in this way bargained corporatism supports and is in many ways synonymous with the concept of social partnership in Germany.

● *Corporate governance and finance.* German firms operate a 'stakeholder' model of governance in which management's obligation is not only or even primarily to shareholders but to the various needs of a range of stakeholders in the company, including employees. The stakeholder principle is supported by the German system of company finance. German companies obtain finance through long-term bank loans and cross-investments by other companies rather than share flotations. This pattern of company finance has meant that enterprises have not been subject to strong pressure to maximise short-term profits. As long-term creditors, banks have focused more on long-term growth and performance than on immediate profits. This in turn has meant that firms have been able to make significant long-term investments in research and development and employee training, leading to high productivity, which supports high wages and good working conditions. It has also meant that German employers have been willing to 'balance the pursuit of profit by a consideration of social justice' (Lane, 2000: 211). This has been manifested in co-determination rights, employee involvement in decision-making on the shop floor, commitment to long-term employment security, and generous welfare benefits financed through company payroll taxes. This particular version of the stakeholder model has been termed 'insider capitalism', reflecting the priority given to the interests of those working inside the firm, both management and employees, in good working conditions, long-term security and career prospects, relative to those of 'outside' interests such as the owners of the company. In this way the system of corporate governance underpins the ideologies of the professional workplace community and social partnership at enterprise level.

● *The vocational education and training system (VET).* Most school leavers who do not go on to higher education spend three years as apprentices in the vocational education system. The system combines classroom-based training in vocational schools with practical training in companies. This provides apprentices with broadly based training for a defined occupation, e.g. engineer, baker. The costs of training are shared between employers, who are legally obliged to provide funding and resources for training, government and apprentices themselves. Firms finance the provision of practical, on-the-job training in the workplace, the state funds the vocational schools, and trainees accept relatively low wages. Trainees have to meet standards that are laid down by employers' organisations and trade unions and receive certificated qualifications that are universally recognised by employers.

The broad-based occupational nature of vocational training in Germany means that jobs are designed to match the range of occupational skills acquired by workers through formal training. Compared to the system of work organisation in the USA, where workers are fitted to jobs, under the German system jobs are designed to fit workers (Marsden, 1999). It also means that German workers are competent over a relatively wide range of tasks, some of which may include planning and coordination of production. The system also means that German workers are not tied to a single firm, as their skills are transferable across firms.

Germany's system of VET has not only resulted in a large supply of highly skilled workers. It has also helped to generate the high levels of worker–management cooperation that are characteristic of German industry. The apprenticeship system has historically enjoyed high regard in Germany and many German managers have been through apprenticeships, often in addition to taking higher education qualifications. Foremen, supervisors and many middle managers will have completed apprenticeships before obtaining further qualifications as a condition for promotion. This common grounding in technical education leads to workers, supervisors and managers sharing a common understanding of production issues and a common technical language. This in turn lays a basis for cooperation in the workplace that is founded on respect for superiors' technical expertise. In doing so, it contributes to the concept of the professional enterprise community, which is part of the ideological basis for the high level of worker–management cooperation at workplace level (Lane, 1989).

Activity Review the VW case at the start of the chapter and then make a list of the features of the German employment system and wider business system that help to explain why VW dealt with its crisis in the way that it did.

The German employment system and national competitiveness

The features of the German employment system and the wider business system described above have underpinned a distinctive strategy for competing in international markets.

● The high level of institutional regulation in Germany has made it difficult for employers to treat labour simply as a disposable commodity. Collective bargaining, co-determination and state legislation have resulted in high wages and restrictions on employers' freedom to dismiss workers. This means that employers have had to achieve competitiveness by ensuring that high wages are matched by high productivity and by competing on the basis of product quality rather than price. This has meant placing a relatively high emphasis on skill in the workforce and the production process.

- The consequences of the German system of VET are that German workers' broad skills mean that they are able to adapt to new technologies relatively easily and acquire additional skills within their occupational fields. They are also able to undertake aspects of production planning and problem solving to a higher degree than in many other countries. This, together with the high level of cooperation that is partly due to the training system, means that workers need relatively little supervision. Therefore, firms employ fewer staff not directly engaged in production, which contributes to high productivity levels.

- The centralisation of collective bargaining and its formal separation from co-determination, together with the influence of social partnership ideology, have resulted in low levels of industrial conflict and have also kept inflationary wage pressures low. In this way, the industrial relations system has contributed to quality of output in terms of reliability of supply and also to the control of wage costs.

The results have been high labour productivity and a competitive advantage in markets for sophisticated, innovative, high-value products based on high levels of research and development expenditure and sophisticated production techniques. This has allowed German firms to pay high wages without becoming uncompetitive and also to fund, through taxation, a comprehensive and generous welfare state.

Japan: the enterprise-based model

The following extract is taken from an article printed in *The Economist* in December, 1995.

The Japanese employment system has been described as *welfare corporatism* or *corporate paternalism*. One way in which this has been expressed is in the diffuse nature of the relationship between the large Japanese company and its employees. As Box 15.1 shows, it is not just about paying workers for their effort; it also includes company responsibility for key areas of the employees' welfare. Moreover, this responsibility extends beyond the employee himself to

---

Box 15.1 **Mitsubishi's company man**

You could hardly find a better example of 'company man', that besuited creature who trades stolid loyalty for lifetime security, than Minoru Makihara, the president of Japan's Mitsubishi Corporation. Mr Makihara is a company man both by birth and marriage: his father spent his life with Mitsubishi; his wife is the great-grand-daughter of the firm's founder. He even grew up in the corporation's giant villa on what was then the outskirts of Tokyo, moving there after his father's death in 1942. He joined the company in 1956, aged 26, and happily admits that, for him, working in a large firm 'amounts to living life to the full'.

Never mind that company man may be on the way to extinction in Western firms, as they try to reinvent themselves as nimble, focused entrepreneurs. And never mind that even in Japan, after years of recession, lifetime employment is under unprecedented threat. At Mitsubishi Corporation, a huge, diversified trading house, company man still flourishes contentedly. The corporation gets the pick of Japan's best graduates. It offers them dormitories when they are young and single and social clubs throughout their lives; it even tries, informally, to find them a wife from within the corporate family.

Mitsubishi man has every reason to believe that, in his company at least, jobs for life will survive. After all, Mitsubishi is the world's biggest company, measured by sales ... it is also the leading spirit in a *keiretsu* industrial group containing 29 companies (including Mitsubishi Bank and Mitsubishi Heavy Industries) which help each other to avert disaster. And, as a quintessential company man, Mr Makhara is an unqualified supporter of lifetime employment.

Source: from Mitsubishi's company man, *The Economist*, © The Economist Newspaper Limited, London (9 December 1995).

include his family members. Thus Dore (1973) reported that at the Hitachi company during the 1950s and 1960s, all permanent employees were eligible for retirement bonuses, company pensions, social clubs and activities for retired workers, rented accommodation provided by the company, savings and loan schemes to aid house purchase, transport subsidies, sickness pay, educational loans for employees' children, gift payments made for weddings, births, marriages of children, and condolence gifts on an employees' death or the death of a family member.

The strength of welfare corporatism is largely due to the relative absence of a welfare state in post-Second World War Japan. In these circumstances, the provision of extensive welfare benefits by large Japanese companies was a way of attracting the best employees at a time of labour shortage. The range and level of welfare benefits also rapidly became an important issue for trade unions in negotiations with employers as it did in the United States, where state welfare provision is also minimal.

Welfare corporatism has helped to foster what Sako (1997) described as *community consciousness* among Japanese workers and managers. This is expressed in high levels of employee commitment and cooperation with management and low levels of industrial conflict. It has been said that Japanese workers see their relationship with their company as a 'partnership of fate' that involves a strong element of personal loyalty to the company and feelings of responsibility to colleagues and superiors in return for long-term material security provided by the firm (Matanle, 2003).

Three key structural features of the employment system, often referred to as its 'three pillars', have underpinned welfare corporatism in Japan:

- lifetime employment.
- seniority-based pay and promotion.
- enterprise unionism.

Lifetime employment

Large Japanese corporations have filled the vast majority of their permanent vacancies by recruiting school-leavers and university graduates as trainees. Once hired, these workers have usually remained with the company until retirement. Essentially they have entered an internal labour market (see Chapter 4) that provides long-term employment security and fills vacancies by internal promotion rather than external recruitment. Historically, Japanese employers have gone to great lengths to avoid dismissing workers during slack production periods. Depending on how long the slack period lasts, employers have used the time to provide workers with additional training or they have transferred workers internally or to other companies either temporarily or permanently rather than simply dismiss them. Some firms have even set up new subsidiary companies to absorb redundant employees. This reluctance among large firms to dismiss workers on grounds of redundancy has been attributed to three factors:

- fear that dismissals would damage their reputation and make it harder for them to recruit high quality university graduates in the future;
- legal restrictions that make dismissals difficult to defend in the Courts;
- desire to avoid conflict with the union, which could lead to immediate disruption of production and weaken the basis for long-term cooperation (Rubery and Grimshaw, 2003).

STOP
and
think

Go back to the description of Mitsubishi at the beginning of this section of the chapter. How do you think Mitsubishi's keiretsu group helps it to avoid dismissing workers?

Seniority-based pay and promotion

Historically, the distinctive feature of the Japanese approach to pay has been that instead of pay being job-related, i.e. determined by the nature of the job being performed, it is person-related. A key person-related criterion for determining pay is *seniority* measured by age and length of service. Basic salaries are agreed for employees in different age bands, and annual salary increases are also related to seniority, with longer-serving workers receiving larger increases. In addition to basic salary, workers receive merit bonuses based on evaluation by their superiors. However, while merit bonuses mean that workers with the same length of service are paid different amounts, merit payments still incorporate a seniority element. This is because of agreements between employers and unions that specify that workers with longer service receive higher average merit ratings. Seniority-based promotion from one grade to another does not mean that the workers' function changes, it just means 'more status and a higher level of annual salary increases' (Dore, 1973: p. 99). In recent years, employers have increased the weight attached to ability as opposed to age when determining pay, but how ability is determined is often vague (Matanle, 2003).

Enterprise unionism

While American trade unions are organised on an occupational or industrial basis and German trade unions on an industrial or sectoral basis, Japanese union organisation is based around individual enterprises. Thus corporations such as Nissan or Toyota have their own enterprise unions and enterprise union federations. Unions do coordinate their wage bargaining activity on a sectoral and national basis through the annual pay bargaining round – the 'spring wage offensive' (*shunto*). However, collective bargaining is essentially conducted at enterprise level. There is debate over the effectiveness of enterprise unions as representatives of employees' interests. Critics have argued that enterprise unionism means that trade union power is fragmented and thus weakened. They have also argued that enterprise-based unions identify too closely with the employing organisation and are too susceptible to interference from employers (Shirai, 1983). Supporters argue that enterprise-based unions make it easier for management and union to work together to resolve problems. They also argue that Japanese enterprise unions exert considerable influence on management decision making, to the benefit of workers (Nakamura, 1997).

Dualism in Japan's employment system

The features discussed above have not applied equally to all enterprises and all workers in Japan. They are found in the large-firm corporate sector to a far greater extent than among small and medium-sized firms. Moreover, even within the corporate sector, not all employees enjoy lifetime employment and seniority-based pay and promotion. These conditions only apply to 'standard' employees, i.e. permanent, 'core' workers. A significant proportion of workers employed by large corporations in Japan are non-standard workers, i.e. seasonal, temporary and part-time workers. The exact proportion of Japanese workers who enjoy lifetime employment status has been a matter of debate. A common estimate during the 1980s was 35 per cent, but some estimates were as low as 10 per cent (Oliver and Wilkinson, 1992). Inagami (1988) however, reported that long-term, if not lifetime employment was becoming increasingly common among smaller firms as well as large ones. This was the result of the development of close, long-term relationships between large corporations and their smaller suppliers, which gave the latter long-term commercial security and supported long-term employment contracts.

Why are lifetime employment and seniority wages less common in small firms than in the large corporations?

The employment system and the wider Japanese business system

As in Germany, Japan's employment system is embedded in a wider framework of institutionalised relationships, the most important of which are the role of the state, the principles of corporate governance and the system of vocational education and training.

State regulation

Japanese employment relations have sometimes been described as micro-corporatist. This refers to the close links between unions and management and the degree of union involvement in business decision making at enterprise level. There are also close links between employers and government and Japanese employers see their responsibilities as being not just to their shareholders but also to their employees and the nation as a whole. However, the absence of an authoritative central trade union confederation and the decentralised nature of collective bargaining have prevented Japanese trade unions from engaging in political exchange with employers and the government, so bargained corporatism has not developed in Japan. The absence of trade unions from policy making has led to Japan being described as having 'corporatism without labour' (Shinoda, 1997). However, from the late 1980s some observers argued that this situation was beginning to change and that Japanese trade unions were developing a more coherent political voice at national level following the formation of a unified peak organisation, Rengo (Shinoda, 1997).

In Japan, as in Germany, government legislation supports workers' right to organise and act collectively although, unlike Germany, it has not laid out formal procedures for co-determination. Legislation also regulates labour market activity in Japan by establishing minimum standards with regard to wages, working time, dismissal and health and safety, although the operation of the law is nationally distinctive. For example, there is no statute that obliges employers to give valid reasons for dismissing workers. Nevertheless, despite the absence of a specific statute, the courts have developed strict standards governing employers' conduct regarding dismissals on the basis of case law, so the law has developed so as to reinforce the practice of lifetime employment (Sugeno and Suwa, 1997).

Corporate governance and finance

Japanese firms, like their German counterparts, operate on the stakeholder principle of governance. It can be argued that Japanese corporations operate a stronger version of the insider variant of this model than German firms, given their formal commitment to lifetime employment and to providing for the social welfare of their employees. This is supported by the system of corporate finance. As in Germany, Japanese corporations obtain most of their finance through bank loans and cross-investments (Oliver and Wilkinson, 1992). This reduces the pressure on Japanese managers to maximise short-run profits and encourages them to take a long-term view of company performance and underpins Japanese employers' commitment to providing long-term employment security, training and career development for workers. Moreover, as shown in Box 15.1, the tendency to prioritise insider interests is reinforced by the fact that senior managers have themselves been part of the lifetime employment system, promoted from more junior positions within the company (Matanle, 2003).

The vocational education and training system

In contrast to German practice, new recruits are not selected on the basis of the occupational skills they possess but their ability to conform to company values, work cooperatively with others and benefit from training in company-specific skills. The Japanese training system and the system of lifetime employment are closely interlinked. Unlike Germany, Japan does not have a well-developed national system of vocational training. Instead, training is enterprise-based. Employers take school leavers and college graduates and provide them with initial and continuing vocational training in sets of skills that are specific to the firm. Workers are trained using a mixture of formal training off the job and informal on the job training. A distinguishing feature of the enterprise-based system is its emphasis on continuing training over the employee's career in the firm. Permanent workers' careers typically involve gaining training and experience in a range of jobs within the company, updating and broadening their skills over time. Tasks are allocated on the basis of how workers are ranked in terms of their firm-specific skills and experience rather than their formal occupational qualifications (Marsden, 1999). Workers who are more highly ranked by their supervisors in terms of length of service and ability are allocated the more demanding tasks, which may include the design and control of production processes and the management of quality (Lincoln and Kalleberg, 1992; Nakamura, 1997). The Japanese approach to training supports the seniority-based pay and promotion system as longer-serving workers are competent across a wider, more demanding range of tasks and therefore warrant higher pay.

The Japanese employment system and national competitiveness

The key features of the Japanese employment system are widely seen as underpinning Japan's success in manufacturing, in particular the *lean production* system. Lean production is a method of mass production that achieves competitiveness by combining high quality with low costs of production. High quality is achieved through close attention to product and process design and continuous improvement of both the product and the production process (*kaizen*). This involves teams of production workers taking responsibility for product quality, problem solving and making suggestions for quality improvements through quality circles and suggestion schemes. Low cost is achieved by making full use of equipment, minimising the amount of capital tied up in stocks of materials, parts, and finished products, and by intensive working. However, the use of low wage subcontractors from the non-corporate sector as suppliers is also an important source of cost competitiveness for Japanese corporations (Rubery and Grimshaw, 2003).

Lean production has been described as a 'fragile' system of production (Rubery and Grimshaw, 2003). This is because the minimisation of stocks requires so-called 'just-in-time' production, where raw materials, parts and components arrive as they are needed. Buffer stocks, which guard against interruptions to supply, are minimal. Therefore disruption at a supplier or at any stage in the actual production process has an almost immediate effect on production and output. Lean production is also fragile in the sense that it operates with minimum staffing levels. This makes attendance at work an important issue and requires workers to cover for absent colleagues when necessary, something that contributes to the high levels of work intensity associated with lean production. It also relies on workers sharing their detailed job knowledge with management in order to achieve continuous quality improvement.

Because of all this the Japanese production system requires a highly disciplined and cooperative workforce that is functionally flexible and willing to accept considerable work intensification. The employment system enables these requirements to be met in the following ways.

- The lifetime employment system encourages workers to share their knowledge with management in the interests of continuous improvement. This is because long-term employment security means that workers are not afraid that sharing their detailed knowledge of production with management to improve efficiency will lead to job losses.

- More broadly, the lifetime employment system reinforces the workers' sense of being in a 'partnership of fate' (see above, pp. 578–9) in which their personal interests are inextricably intertwined with those of their company. This high level of personal identification with the firm means that workers have been willing to accept strict discipline and high work intensity, demonstrating what observers have called high commitment despite having limited autonomy and low job satisfaction (Lincoln and Kalleberg, 1992).

- The enterprise-based union structure also contributes to worker–management cooperation. Inevitably unions identify closely with their companies because the union's organisation is limited to the company and dependent on it in the long run. More positively, the involvement of enterprise unions in management decision making helps to create a climate of mutual trust that underpins union and worker cooperation with management (Nakamura, 1997). Fujimura (1997) also claims that the presence of a single union within the enterprise avoids demarcation disputes and makes it easier to deploy and redeploy labour so as to achieve functional flexibility of labour.

- Continuing training and job rotation mean that Japanese workers are functionally flexible, i.e. they can perform a range of tasks and thus cover for absent colleagues.

Activity

Germany and Japan are both noted for high levels of cooperation on the shop floor between workers and management, but this cooperation is achieved in different ways. Review the previous sections and try to identify the differences in the nature of workplace cooperation in Germany and Japan.

The American employment system: a managerial model

The American employment system differs fundamentally from the German and Japanese systems, reflecting the particular nature of American capitalism with its strong emphasis on individualism, private property rights and free market competition (Chandler, 1977, 1990; Lazonick, 1991). Business associations that play a significant role in regulating markets and relations among firms in other national systems are less prominent in the USA and firms prefer to 'go it alone'. This is because American business never had to define itself collectively in opposition to aristocratic or feudal interests (other than the conflict over slavery) in the way European capitalists did. Consequently, the American business system is characterised by a relative absence of collective organisation among American businesses and therefore weak 'collective governance' in the private sector (Hollingsworth, 1997).

The ideology of egalitarian individualism is diffused throughout American society. Individual property rights are seen to be the foundation of democracy, creating a strong presumption against state regulation. In the field of employment relations this has translated into a strong bias against external interference with the rights of management whether by the state or trade unions. Therefore, compared with their counterparts in Germany and Japan, American managers are less constrained by legislation and social norms that restrict the employer's freedom to hire and fire and provide workers with rights to collective representation and participation in decision making.

This relative freedom resulted in a comparatively poorly developed labour movement in the USA and allowed American employers to adopt a variety of managerially led approaches to workplace HRM and industrial relations. These included relatively sophisticated unitarist and pluralist approaches to employment regulation as well as traditional approaches based on 'hire and fire'. The remainder of this section summarises the three main approaches to HRM and industrial relations in the American business system.

Pluralism: the New Deal System

The late 1920s through to the early 1930s were a period of sustained economic collapse in the United States; often referred to as the 'Great Depression', this period witnessed the collapse of agriculture in the mid-west and California and the collapse of employment in many elements of manufacturing industry. Despite heavy unemployment and weak trade unions however, there were pockets of sustained resistance to some of the worst excesses of management control and de-skilling within the American model of management. The perceived paralysis of Republican President Herbert Hoover in the face of the slump led to the Democrat Franklin D. Roosevelt being elected as President in 1933 on the basis of his promise of a 'New Deal' for America. Recognising the threat of a total collapse of American capitalism, Roosevelt promised a series of government interventions to create jobs, provide a measure of social security and address the historic imbalance of power in the employment relationship.

New Deal legislation in the form of Section 7a of the 1933 National Industrial Recovery Act and the 1935 National Labor Relations Act gave employees the legal right to organize and bargain collectively through representatives of their own choosing, free from employer coercion and interference (practices that were common during the 1920s). The New Deal approach to workplace trade unionism and collective bargaining introduced truly independent trade unions into American workplaces for the first time, but provided no authoritative enforcement procedures. The effect of this was both to stiffen employer resistance to collective bargaining and stimulate militant worker resistance to management control. This led to a low trust, adversarial system of industrial relations characterised by highly codified industrial relations practices such as:

- written contracts;
- detailed job descriptions;
- formalised grievance and disciplinary procedures;
- seniority rules to determine lay-offs and promotion between grades;
- provision for disputes arbitration and in some cases no-strike clauses (see Clark and Almond, 2006; Towers, 1997; Rupert, 1995).

In many respects the New Deal system created a constitutional framework for workplace industrial relations, yet employer resistance to the system saw the development of employer-led, managerially controlled alternatives. A good number of large corporations had never accepted New Deal collective bargaining and kept unions out of their plants through a combination of paternalism and authoritarianism that came to be known as *welfare capitalism* (see below). Moreover, from the 1970s the New Deal system came under increasing strain due to increased international competition, the declining significance of domestic mass production and pressure for more flexible deployment of labour across work tasks as a way of improving competitiveness. In some cases, for example at General Motors and Delta Airlines, this led management and unions to seek a more cooperative relationship in which unions accepted new, more flexible working patterns and pay restraint in return for improved employment security, employee involvement and union participation in decision making. More commonly however, competitive pressures encouraged employers to turn towards non-union strategies that involved relocating operations away from the traditional industrial regions of the North-East to greenfield sites in tax- and employer-friendly states in the South where New Deal industrial relations were much less entrenched. At the same time, a shift in the labour force away from blue-collar towards white-collar and professional occupations encouraged employers to develop more individually focused human resource management policies, reinforcing the non-union trend (Kochan *et al.*, 1993).

Sophisticated unitarism: welfare capitalism

Welfare capitalism is a management approach to labour relations based on non-unionism and strong mutual commitment between employer and employees. It is characterised by an ideological opposition to trade unions and collective bargaining in the workplace. Developed and extended during the 1920s and 1930s, welfare capitalism co-existed with the New Deal model of labour relations. In many respects, welfare capitalist employers, in adopting sophisticated non-unionism, laid the origins for what is now termed HRM, developing an authoritarian yet paternalist approach to labour relations where the firm, rather than the state, trade unions or other third parties such as the Courts or arbitration panels, should provide for the security and welfare of employees.

Welfare capitalist employers devised strong corporate cultures and branding techniques. Examples of welfare capitalist employers that you might be familiar with include Kodak, Procter & Gamble, Standard Oil, Heinz and IBM. To keep trade unions and collective bargaining out of their workplaces, welfare capitalist employers developed sophisticated union substitution strategies, including personnel management innovations such as provisions for employment security, severance pay, unemployment insurance, pensions and health care insurance (Foulkes, 1980). These strategies were supported by profits generated in strong, stable markets and often by being the dominant employer in a 'company town', which was an additional source of employee loyalty. More recently, welfare capitalist firms have been associated with the deployment of team working, profit sharing and share ownership, workplace appraisals and employee rankings and performance-related pay schemes for both teams and individuals, in other words with the techniques associated with HRM (Jacoby, 1997). However, welfare capitalist firms have not relied exclusively on sophisticated union substitution strategies; they have not hesitated to use more authoritarian methods to suppress attempts at unionisation when these have occurred. There is a thriving union avoidance industry made up of specialist consultants and law firms that advise companies on how to resist union recruitment drives and suppress union activity, and 'strike management' firms that provide workplace security in situations where an employer has replaced economic strikers. For more detail on union avoidance see Logan (2006).

Traditional unitarism: 'lower road approaches'

American management has been influenced by the highly competitive nature of product markets and the attendant pressures for cost and price reduction. This, together with a scarcity of skilled labour, has encouraged the development of systems of management control over work organisation and product assembly that intensify and de-skill labour. In some sectors of employment, such as fast-food, apparel and food retailing, meat-packing, laundry services and delivery, cut-throat cost and price-based competition has encouraged employers to minimise labour costs by taking 'low road' non-union approaches to HRM and industrial relations, (Katz and Darbishire, 2000). Here management focuses on standardisation, strict job controls and de-skilling, provides low wages and limited fringe benefits and only limited access to employee development and training. Initially lower road approaches, sometimes summarised as 'hire and fire', predominated in areas of employment not covered by New Deal and welfare capitalist employers. The retail giant Wal-Mart has often been portrayed as an example of this approach.

In what ways might de-skilling and management control systems manifest themselves? For example, what role might information and communication technologies have in aiding management control and employee surveillance in lower road approaches to HR?

Varieties of employment regulation – and a dominant model

We have seen that the USA is characterised by a variety of systems of employment regulation. However, by the 1970s the typical large American corporation, whether unionised or not, had developed an employment system that featured the elements of an internal labour market. These were:

- tightly specified job descriptions and working methods;
- job security provisions;
- internal training and promotion for core workers;
- seniority rules to govern lay-offs and promotions;
- Pay linked to the job rather than individual or company performance
- Company-financed pensions and health insurance.

Internalised systems developed partly in response to trade union pressure to provide secure jobs with predictable earnings, opportunities to increase earnings over the time spent in the company's employment, and social benefits in the absence of a developed welfare state. Some firms responded through New Deal collective bargaining. Others responded by developing internalised systems in the form of Welfare Capitalism as a substitute for unionisation (Cappelli *et al.*, 1997). However, internalised systems also grew for reasons of managerial efficiency, i.e. they reduced supervision and turnover costs in ways that reflected wider features of the American business system that are outlined in the next section.

The internalised employment systems developed by large US companies differ in important respects from those in Germany and Japan. First, the commitment to providing long-term employment security is less strong than in Japan. Second, managed employees in American companies have far less influence over management decisions, even those affecting their own employment, than their counterparts in German and Japanese firms. Both of these differences reflect the relatively low level of institutionalised regulation of employment in the USA.

The employment system and wider aspects of the American business system

The nature of state regulation

American individualism is reflected in political commitment to the principles of the *liberal market economy*, i.e. free competition and as little state regulation of business as possible. Thus government has undertaken minimal regulation of the labour market. It has supported the 'hire at will' doctrine, which means that workers have few statutory protections against dismissal other than on grounds of unfair discrimination. Also, while the National Labor Relations Act provides workers with a legal right to vote for union representation, it leaves many avenues open to employers who wish to resist unionisation so the law is of limited effectiveness (Kochan, *et al.*, 1993). Weak statutory regulation of employment and weak statutory support for collective bargaining results in a very flexible labour market that enables employers to make swift adjustments to the size of their labour force and also makes it easy for them to adopt 'low road' employment strategies. However, at the time of writing, an Employee Free Choice Bill is being considered by the US legislature. If the Bill survives stiff opposition from the Republicans in the US Congress and is passed, it will make it easier for employees to build union organisation and demand legal recognition from employers.

The financial system and corporate governance

Although some long-term inter-firm collaboration typical of more coordinated market economies is to be found in certain sectors such as defence, health care and electronics (Hollingsworth, 1997; Locke, 1996), for the most part relations between firms are arm's-length and contractual rather than long-term and relational (Chandler, 1977, 1990; Lazonick, 1991; Hall and Soskice, 2001). The arm's-length character of relations between firms in competitive demand-driven markets applies to the financial system too. In contrast to the close, long-term links between banks and firms typical of the post-war German and Japanese business systems there is a much greater development of equity markets in the USA. Historically, share ownership has been much wider in the United States than elsewhere and as enterprises grew in size and complexity, professional managers replaced owner–managers.

This separation of ownership from control led to sophisticated hierarchies of professional managers exercising considerable discretion in defining and achieving the goals of the firm and causing economists to develop new 'managerial theories' of the firm (Baumol, 1959; Williamson, 1964). These theories developed what O'Sullivan (2000) later termed the 'retain and reinvest' pattern of corporate governance in the American business system. Although heavily focused on short-term results, managers nevertheless balanced the claims of shareholders against the need to retain profits to invest in product innovation. Professional managers also secured close control over labour through systematic mechanisation, labour de-skilling and bureaucratic forms of control (Braverman, 1974; Edwards, 1979; Littler, 1982).

Consider your workplace – is it an American-owned firm? If it is, you should be able to identify examples of direct, technical and bureaucratic control systems.

Even if your workplace is not American-owned it is likely to have direct, technical and bureaucratic control systems.

In addition, it could be the case that the presence of these types of controls in non-American firms demonstrates the wider impact of American management techniques.

The system of vocational education and training

The United States does not have a strongly developed system of vocational education and training. In particular, there is little organised training provision for high school leavers, who have to pick up skills through a mixture of informal and formal training once they enter employment (Cappelli *et al.*, 1997). In the absence of a training system that produces workers with formal occupational qualifications, employers design jobs to their own specifications and then fit the workers to the jobs (Marsden, 1999). Company-provided training has therefore aimed at providing workers with narrow skills related to their particular job rather than the broad occupational skills produced by German apprenticeships or the combinations of firm-specific skills generated by in-company training in Japan. This is in line with the tendency to substitute capital equipment for skilled labour and rely on systematic technical and bureaucratic control over workers rather than providing for their involvement in decision making on the shop floor. This in turn has reinforced the 'arm's-length' relationship between management and labour.

The American employment system and national competitiveness

The wider impact of individualism on the American state, its financial institutions and patterns of industrial relations demonstrate that the central drivers of the American business system make it very dynamic. The institutional constraints on management are much weaker than in the German or Japanese business systems, so different models of company organisation, patterns of finance and employment relations can emerge alongside one another. The managerially led institutional features of the American employment system described above have underpinned a distinctive strategy for domestic and international competition.

● The low level of institutional regulation in the American employment system enables employers to treat labour as a disposable commodity and adjust wages and headcount in response to changes in labour and product market conditions. Also, workers work longer hours and have shorter holidays than in the UK and EU (although not Japan), which contributes to high labour productivity in the USA.

● The development of superior management capabilities, including systems for the management of people, meant that American firms developed a more systematic approach to work organisation and the control of labour than those in other countries in the twentieth century. More significantly still, superior management capability, in terms of business and HR strategies, results from the early adoption business models, focused on shareholder and investor value associated with 'leveraged' buy-outs supported by private equity investors. Within these approaches a central focus of business and HR strategies is short-term performance management.

● An emphasis on investment in technological innovation. The competitive nature of domestic product markets in the USA forces management to introduce the latest technology as quickly as possible (McGuckin and van Ark, 2005). American management has also been more aggressive and quicker to deploy new technologies to control and monitor workers than management in other countries (ESRC, 2004; CIPD, 2006). This has been a further factor in the USA's productivity lead over other countries.

- Higher levels of capital per worker in the USA that underpin high productivity levels (ESRC, 2004).

The visible hand of management has moulded a business system and employment system where management control and coordination of work organisation has combined with substitution of capital for labour to create sustained international competitive advantage in terms of productivity and unit labour costs.

How does the ability to treat labour as a disposable commodity shape US companies' competitive strategies?

In the light of this why might some US companies decide to treat labour as a valued resource instead?

Three national systems: a summary

Our examination of American, German and Japanese employment systems has shown that while each is distinctive, the German and Japanese systems have more in common with each other than they do with the American system. In both Germany and Japan, albeit in different ways, there is a stronger emphasis on institutionalised regulation of the employment relationship as a basis for generating worker–management cooperation than there is in the USA, where the emphasis is much more on using the managerial prerogative to gain workers' compliance. This is explained by the more active role the state plays in Germany and Japan compared with the USA, particularly the stronger political and legislative support for employment protection and collective worker representation. Consequently, to a much greater extent than in USA, workers are recognised as stakeholders whose interests have to be recognised alongside those of managers and owners. Analysts have argued that each of these systems has been successful in enabling the countries concerned to establish patterns of competitive advantage that have been the basis for their long-run economic growth and prosperity (Whitley, 2000; Hall and Soskice, 2001). Recently however, each system has come under strain and this has created pressures for change.

Patterns of change in national systems: the emergence of a neo-liberal business model?

Since the 1970s national business systems and in turn national employment systems have experienced sustained pressures for change in the direction of a more contractual and free market approach to the regulation of business and HR:

- the oil shocks and slowing down of economic growth in the 1970s;
- the return of mass unemployment in the 1980s and 1990s;
- the effects of radical technological change, in particular digital and micro-chip technologies;
- financial deregulation in the 1980s, which led to the global dominance of the free market ideology and ideological challenges to established national business systems;
- by the 1990s financial deregulation had stimulated the internationalisation of capital markets and multinational and transnational patterns of investment, leading to:
- the prominence of multinational companies and competition between and within them. This prominence and competition saw:

- the emergence and diffusion of new organisational paradigms in multinational firms, e.g. lean production, HRM and performance management;
- by the first years of the twenty-first century the spread of industrialisation and the emergence of new competitor nations led to firms in Brazil, China and India challenging the dominance of Western multinationals;
- following from this, the recent past has witnessed an intensification of international competition in markets for goods and, increasingly, services.

These forces have created pressures for change at the level of individual firms and at the level of national employment systems, focusing on:

- *flexibility* – in labour use strategies;
- *decentralisation* – of established patterns of job regulation, in particular collective ones;
- *deregulation* – of established patterns in employment protection and collective governance.

At firm level, management has sought functional, numerical and financial flexibility of labour. This has led to increased emphasis on training, skills development and team working (functional flexibility), greater use of non-standard employment contracts and out-sourcing (numerical) and increased use of contingent pay (financial).

Employers' search for labour flexibility has also been linked to government policies for the labour market. In order to encourage employers to create more new jobs and reduce unemployment, governments have, to varying degrees legislated to:

- make it easier for employers to make use of non-standard employment contracts;
- make it easier for employers to dismiss workers for reasons of redundancy;
- increase incentives to work and put more pressure on the unemployed to take work on offer or to retrain.

Changes at firm level and labour market level mean that changes are occurring in national employment systems.

Change in the USA: taking the low road?

We saw earlier that, despite the diverse approaches to employment regulation in the USA, internalised employment systems became characteristic of the typical large US corporation by the 1970s. Since the 1980s however, internalised employment systems have been eroded as many welfare capitalist and New Deal employers have implemented cost reduction strategies such as downsizing and concentration on core competencies. This restructuring has reduced the size of core work groups, weakened internal labour markets and exposed more workers to lower road approaches to HRM. This is reflected in:

- withdrawal of commitments to job security;
- cut-backs in pension benefits;
- the increased use of *contingent labour* – part-time, fixed term contract and temporary agency workers.

This has polarised experience of the employment relationship. A growing number of workers, particularly low-skilled workers, are subjected to lower road, commodity labour approaches to HRM. Meanwhile, higher road, resourced-based approaches to HRM, currently labelled high performance work systems (see Chapter 2), have also become more widespread. However, while these resource-based HRM systems provide employees with more rewarding work they also offer less security than the New Deal or Welfare Capitalist systems that they have replaced. To a great extent the commitment to providing long-term employment security has been replaced by provisions aimed at helping employees maintain their employability through training. One recent study noted that

> HRM firms have been distinguished from other non-union employers in the late 1980s and 1990s not by their employment security but rather by the extent to which they subsidise their employees' investments in skill development or job transfers.   (Katz and Darbishire, 2000: 23)

What this tells us is that even among those employers that value their employees more highly, an erosion of commitment to internalised employment systems has taken place and there is a greater readiness to hire and fire as corporate circumstances change. Employers are requiring employees to bear more of the risks of employment. This has also been reflected in the spread of payment systems that link pay to company profits and in widespread cutbacks in company-financed pension schemes (Cappelli *et al.*, 1997).

Reasons for shifts in the US employment system

The decline of internalised employment systems in the USA reflects the collapse of the conditions that supported them up to the 1970s, i.e. stable, steadily expanding mass markets that were relatively protected from overseas competition and the way in which American capitalists responded to it.

Economic crisis

The American economy experienced a crisis in the 1970s and early 1980s. Economic growth slowed down, profits fell and inflation accelerated. At the same time foreign competition was intensifying. The Japanese in particular, secured a technological and productivity lead over the USA in the consumer electronics and automobile industries and began to penetrate deeply into the US market. This put pressure on US firms to cut costs, improve quality and become more responsive to changes in market demand. This meant that more and more managers came to believe that the benefits obtained from internal labour markets, i.e. stability and ease of management control, were outweighed by the costs, i.e. rigid job classifications that prevented the introduction of more efficient, productivity enhancing forms of work organisation, rigid wage structures that made it difficult to reward high performance, costly commitments to long-term employment and, in unionised companies, the length of time required to negotiate change (Kochan *et al.*, 1993; Cappelli *et al.*, 1997). The lack of political and legislative support for trade unions and collective bargaining meant that employers were able to take advantage of the recession and the threat of job losses arising from foreign competition to demand concessions from trade unions and increasingly, to move from unionised to non-unionised employment relations.

Shareholder and investor value and changes in corporate governance

During the late 1990s new pressures were exerted on American managers by US financial and stock markets, often in the form of hostile takeovers by what were previously termed 'leveraged buy-out firms' but which are now more commonly termed private equity firms. Private equity is a pool of money that is raised on private rather than public markets and managed for the specific purpose of investing directly in private companies. A private equity fund is a fund management company either in the form of a limited partnership or a plc business that actively manages the pool of money. In addition to venture capital and mid-market private equity funds, larger, multinational private equity funds acquire listed firms or divisions of listed firms by buying all the shares or a controlling percentage of the shares which are listed on a public stock market such as the New York Stock Exchange. The purchase of a controlling percentage of the available shares is often the first move to complete control and once a fund has control of all the shares in a portfolio company then it becomes the single shareholder and the firm is no longer a publicly tradable listed company, this is what is referred to as the take private, private equity business model (see Clark, 2007).

Once in control of a previously listed firm, private equity owners give management teams financial incentives in the form of 'sweet equity' (free future shares) or share options, which enable them to buy shares at a later date at the issue price. This will be extremely lucrative if the financial performance of the firm is successful and reflected in a highly valued share price. Together, these factors, combined with the low transaction costs of the highly efficient US stock market, encourage rapid trading and since the 1980s have generated a sometimes aggressive 'hostile' market for takeovers or mergers and acquisitions. Expressed as the principle of 'shareholder value', these developments, rhetorically at least, aim to ensure that management works in the interests of the owners (investors in and shareholders) of the company (O'Sullivan, 2000).

Consequently, senior managers in the USA have become increasingly preoccupied with maximising the short-term financial performance of their companies (Boyer, 2005; Jensen and Murphy, 1990). This represents a shift from the 'retain and invest' pattern of governance to what has been called the 'down-size and distribute' pattern, in which the workforce is cut back and work is intensified for those remaining in order to cut costs and boost profits, which are then distributed to shareholders in the form of higher dividends or capital gains realised as a result of an increase in the share price. The announcement of job cuts, which used to be seen as a sign of a company in trouble, is now more often taken as evidence of action to improve profitability through cost reduction and more effective work organisation. This has contributed to the extension of 'lower road' approaches to employment relations in firms that were once associated with New Deal or welfare capitalist approaches.

Forced by competition towards the US model? Where the USA leads does the rest of the world follow?

The changes that have taken place in the USA are of particular significance since many analysts have argued that the USA is setting the pattern for the new century; this may remain the case even allowing for the recent 'credit crunch'. Analysts suggest that the changes that took place in the USA during the 1980s led to the resurgence of the US economy and its political domination of the processes of political and economic globalisation, for example in the World Trade Organization where the United States pushed for and secured a global commitment (for membership of the WTO) to international trade on the basis of free and open multilateral market principles for businesses and labour. Meanwhile, the more institutionally regulated economies of Germany and Japan experienced low economic growth and historically high levels of unemployment throughout the 1990s. Their productivity also declined relative to the USA and they are said to lag behind the USA in the development of new technologies and the adoption of new business models. This has led many to argue that the problems of Germany and Japan are due to patterns of regulation that put too many constraints on business, raise the cost of employment, slow down decision making and deter new investment. This has made them less competitive in globalised markets, where they face competition from high quality, lower cost competitors. The recommended solution is to reform social welfare systems and labour market institutions so as to reduce employment costs, allow for greater wage flexibility and more flexible utilisation of labour and allow managers to initiate and implement change more quickly in response to market threats and opportunities.

Second, it has been argued that the emergence of global financial markets and the sustained growth of foreign direct investment by US-owned multinational companies are causing the shareholder value concept to take hold in countries such as Germany and Japan, which have hitherto operated a stakeholder form of corporate governance. Given the incompatibility of these two approaches and that key features of Germany and Japan's employment systems are embedded in the stakeholder model, the development of shareholder value pressures would undermine their existing patterns of institutional regulation and force them along the path of market liberalism. Recently, the OECD has advocated the primacy of shareholder interests, demonstrating the widening influence of the shareholder value principle (OECD, 2004) and in the American and British business systems debates over corporate governance now appear resolved in favour of investor and shareholder value approaches (see Dore, 2000; Hansmann and Kraakman, 2001; FSA, 2006). The policy reaction of the American and British governments to the recent credit crunch in letting only one financial institution collapse – Lehman Brothers – has only confirmed this resolution. A key question is how far this Anglo-American transition to shareholder capitalism will be diffused to stakeholder systems such as those in Germany and Japan. Gulger *et al.*, (2004) argue that 'American' measures of efficiency and competitiveness on the shareholder model are emerging as a growth regime for all western business systems and multinational companies irrespective of country of origin. Similarly, Carr (2005) argues that to compete globally German firms must develop 'professional management' on the Anglo-American business school model. Carr concludes that as German and Japanese firms globalise they become more similar in operations and strategies to British or American multinational firms.

Change in Germany: the erosion of social partnership?

Since the 1980s there has been growing criticism of key features of the German employment system. Once seen as underpinning German economic success, it has come to be viewed by many economic policy advisers and financial and business interests as a hindrance to renewed economic growth, competitiveness and job creation. There are several reasons for this disenchantment with the German model.

Economic stagnation and unemployment

Over the last 25 years Germany has experienced slow economic growth and high, persistent unemployment. Unemployment in West Germany rose from 2.6 per cent in 1980 to 7.2 per cent in 1985 and did not drop below 5 per cent until the early 1990s, when there was a short economic boom following German reunification in 1990 (OECD, 2006). Since 1995, the unemployment rate in Germany as a whole has not fallen below 7 per cent and during 2005 it stood at 11.5 per cent before falling back to 7.4 per cent in 2008. However, the effects of the world economic crisis meant that it climbed rapidly to 8.6 per cent by March 2009 (Federal Statistical Office Germany, 2006, 2008; OECD, 2008; DW.World, 2009).

The underlying reasons for Germany's unemployment problem are much debated. There is a strong case for arguing that it stems from the problems of economic adjustment in the old East Germany, where unemployment reached an official level of 18 per cent in 1999, with observers suggesting that the true level was nearer 25 per cent (Tuselman and Heise, 2000), and a monetary policy that has depressed levels of demand rather than being caused by features of the labour market (Teague and Grahl, 2004). However, economic advisers and financial and business interests became increasingly critical of aspects of the employment system in general, particularly the level of employment protection and social welfare benefits for workers and the centralised system of collective bargaining, and demanded reforms to increase labour market flexibility.

The case against strong employment rights and social protection is that they raise the costs of employing labour and therefore discourage firms from creating more jobs. For example, because workers' strong employment rights make workforce reductions difficult and costly, employers prefer to achieve increases in output by raising the output of their existing workforce rather than hiring additional workers. Generous social welfare benefits are financed largely out of payroll taxes levied on employers. This means that non-wage costs of hiring workers are high as well as wage costs. This reinforces employers' reluctance to add to the size of their workforces and also deters new business start-ups. They also contribute to high unemployment among low-skilled workers by setting a 'floor' to wages that prevents them from falling to a level that would lead to more unskilled jobs being offered.

The criticism of centralised collective bargaining is that it sets too high a minimum wage, which together with the social welfare system prevents wages for unskilled workers adjusting to a level that would lead to more jobs being created. It is also argued that it prevents enterprises from addressing the need to develop more flexible ways of using labour in order to raise productivity and reduce costs. The reforms that have been demanded are that restrictions on the use of flexible forms of employment such as temporary and fixed term employment should be eased, the level of social benefits should be cut back to ease the tax burden on employers and enable wages to be more flexible at the lower end of the market and that collective bargaining should be decentralised to allow for greater wage flexibility and permit negotiations on company-specific issues.

From stakeholder to shareholder principles?

Pressures for labour market reforms along American lines have been reinforced by the diffusion of the concept of shareholder value into the German business system. A number of developments have led some analysts to argue that strong pressures are developing to force Germany to converge towards the Anglo-American model of corporate governance based on shareholder value. Given the incompatibility of shareholder value with the existing stakeholder principle, its diffusion among German companies could lead to the eventual abandonment of the German employment system and convergence towards the liberal market model. Whether such a convergence is happening is under debate. A recent review of the literature by Edwards, (2004) has identified three positions. The first argues that shareholder value principles are taking hold in Germany as foreign ownership of German share capital increases, the proportion of firms' value added distributed to shareholders rises and more senior managers are rewarded with stock options and profit-related bonuses. This is said to be undermining key institutions such as codetermination, with works councils becoming 'empty shells'. The second position stresses the limited extent of change in German corporate finance, with ownership still being highly concentrated, and the continued strength of codetermination as a 'central pillar' of corporate governance. The third view is that significant changes are occurring but there has been no transformation of the German system. Edwards' own case study of Volkswagen tends to support the argument for continuity. While VW has paid more attention to the interests of shareholders since the early 1990s and set higher target rates of return on capital, this did not lead to US-style down-sizing or to attempts to weaken codetermination (Edwards, 2004). However, the VW story has recently taken a further twist: VW is now mainly owned by Porsche, which has sought to reform VW's organisational structure and extend managers' freedom of action on Anglo-American lines, something that poses a considerable threat to established forms of co-determination at VW. You can find out more about the background to this change and its implications in the end of chapter case study.

After reading the material on the American business system and the German business system are you able to suggest why the German business system might be able to develop a more enlightened approach to shareholder value than that found in the UK or the USA?

What role might the German employment relations model have in hindering or encouraging this development?

The main currents of change in German employment relations are discussed overleaf.

Changes to employment law aimed at increasing labour market flexibility

As we noted above, the ongoing failure to create jobs and reduce unemployment has led to growing demands within Germany for measures to increase labour market flexibility to encourage job creation, attract foreign investment and stimulate economic growth (Teague and Grahl, 2004). The result has been a gradual and limited relaxation of restrictions on contingent forms of employment such as fixed term contracts and the use of temporary agency workers. The 1985 Employment Promotion Act and subsequent amendments have made it easier for employers to hire workers on fixed term contracts. The maximum length of time that an employer can keep a worker on a temporary agency contract has also been gradually extended from 3 months in 1972 to 6 months in 1985, 9 months in 1993 and 12 months in 1997. However, German employers have not rushed to hire contingent workers as a result. Fixed term contract workers and agency temps together accounted for 7.8 per cent of employment in 1998 compared with 7.1 per cent in 1991. Moreover permanent workers continue to enjoy strong employment protection rights, with dismissal still regarded as a last resort and employers are expected to explore all possible alternatives, including redeployment (Peuntner, 2003).

Weakening support for collective bargaining and co-determination

The proportion of workers who are trade union members has fallen in Germany. At the same time, a growing number of small and medium-size businesses do not have works councils, so that at the end of the 1990s an estimated 60 per cent of German workers were outside co-determination (Teague and Grahl, 2004). Among employers, the coverage of employers' associations is declining. Many companies in the East either did not join or else withdrew from employers' associations after unification in order to avoid centralised wage bargaining. In the West a number of small and medium-sized enterprises have quit employers' associations in order to negotiate their own individual agreements with the trade unions and many new companies are not joining employers' associations. Nevertheless, trade unions retain considerable influence and the percentage of workers covered by collective agreements in the West is still very high – around 90 per cent – although substantially lower in the East (Tuselman and Heise, 2000).

Decentralisation of collective bargaining

More significant than any overall decline in collective bargaining coverage has been the trend towards decentralisation of collective bargaining. This has reflected the growing relative importance of 'qualitative issues' concerning changes in working practices, new technology and flexibility, which are specific to companies or workplaces, compared with wage bargaining. At the same time however, there have been examples of 'disorganised decentralisation' arising out of 'wildcat cooperation' between works councils and company management whereby they (illegally) agree to undercut or ignore the terms of collective agreements, usually on the grounds of preserving jobs. In an effort to eliminate wildcat cooperation and achieve a more coordinated and controlled decentralisation of bargaining, formal 'opening clauses' are being inserted into industry level agreements that allow enterprise managements and works committees to negotiate over more flexible working time arrangements or to undercut sectoral agreements on pay for limited time periods and in defined circumstances (Tuselman and Heise, 2000). This controlled decentralisation not only reflects the interests of the unions in maintaining an over-arching structure of centralised bargaining. It also owes much to the fact that employers continue to value the way that centralised bargaining moderates wage pressure and acts as a force for stability in industrial relations.

Changes in co-determination

The role of co-determination has been strengthened by legislation that has provided stronger support for works council organisation and extended the influence of works councils over training and employment protection matters. Furthermore, decentralisation of collective bargaining has increased the role of works councils in establishing terms and conditions of employment. In particular, they became closely involved in company modernisation programmes during the 1980s that focused on the introduction of new technologies, more flexible forms of working and new forms of employee involvement, such as quality circles and team working. While this evolution of the role of works councils can be seen as an extension of the social partnership model in the workplace, it has been viewed by some as threatening to undermine their role as defenders of workers' employment rights. High unemployment and increasingly intense competition mean that works councils are under pressure to cooperate with management in 'building up an organisational consensus around corporate plans to succeed in global markets' that serves the interests of management, shareholders and the elite 'core' group of employees but exposes other workers to increasing insecurity (Teague and Grahl, 2004: 566).

Germany's economic difficulties have strengthened the critics and weakened the defenders of its employment system, most notably the German trade unions. As some of the material in this chapter has sought to demonstrate, the high wages, comparatively low inequality in and between capital and labour, and high living standards that were once seen as strengths of 'Deutschland AG' are increasingly being represented as the source of persistent unemployment and comparatively weak growth. High unemployment has created fear of job loss and, as in the VW case, created a climate in which unions and works councils are on the defensive. At the same time, German firms are becoming more open to the disciplines of the stock market and influenced by the principle of shareholder value. However, while significant changes have taken place, reform of the German system has so far been gradual, hesitant and, at times, strongly resisted, particularly in the area of welfare reform, where there is strong continuing public support for Germany's excellent welfare state provision. Even so, pressure on the German system has been intensified recently by the effects of the credit crunch and world recession. Before the credit crunch and associated world recession Germany's trade surplus sustained resistance to full-blown domestic reforms in business and employment regulation to meet the demands of globalisation, which were considered by many Germans to mean greater economic insecurity and stagnating wages. However, the recession has damaged Germany's export trade, weakening the trade balance. This has rendered Germany's combination of export-led manufacturing strategy and internationalisation of German capital less effective, at least in the short term and may force further, more radical reform.

STOP and think

Why might German employers be wary of abandoning the German model of employment relations?

Change in Japan: the crumbling of the 'three pillars'?

Japan experienced an even more marked slowing down in economic growth after 1990 than Germany, with an annual average growth rate of GDP of 1.6 per cent during 1991–98. Unemployment in Japan also hit record levels of around 5 per cent, peaking at 5.3 per cent in 2003. It fell back to 3.9 per cent in 2007 but then rose again to 4.4 per cent in February 2009 (Inoue, 1999; OECD, 2008; *Wall Street Journal,* 2009). While this appears low by European standards it has to be viewed in the context of the Japanese employment system and the extreme reluctance to dismiss workers. The unemployment figures mask a higher level of hidden unemployment and under-employment. The stagnation of Japan's economy, coupled with demographic and social changes, put considerable strain on the employment system. As in Germany, this led a growing number of observers, inside and outside of Japan, to argue that while the employment system may have underpinned Japan's economic success during the 1970s and 1980s it was an obstacle to recovery in an increasingly globalised world economy. Thus in 1998 the Japanese Congress on Economic Strategy, an advisory body to the government, argued that the Japanese system attached too much importance to equality and fairness and that Japan needed to restructure itself as a 'more competitive' society' (Inoue, 1999). Critics also argued that the lifetime employment system had become socially and economically divisive. While older workers continued to enjoy the benefits of lifetime employment, such opportunities for young workers had become increasingly limited. The lifetime employment system was also criticised for being based on an outdated male model of employment that was increasingly at odds with Japanese women's changing aspirations (Schoppa, 2006).

The economy began to recover from 2002–03, with improved growth of GDP and the unemployment rate fell to 3.8 per cent in 2007 (OECD, 2007). However, Japan has been hard hit by the global economic crisis caused by the 'credit crunch'. The value of exports fell by 49 per cent in the first quarter of 2009 and unemployment climbed again, hitting 4.4 per cent in February 2009. After the 'lost decade' of the 1990s observers commented on how the economic crisis had initiated or accelerated currents of change in Japan's employment system and questioned its long-term viability (Hattori and Maeda, 2000; Hanami, 2004). The impact of the 'credit crunch' is almost certain to produce further challenges to the Japanese version of stakeholder capitalism and its associated employment system.

From stakeholder to shareholder capitalism?

As we have seen, the Japanese employment system is underpinned by a 'stakeholder capitalism' approach that is reflected in a system of corporate finance and governance that encourages a long-term management orientation and gives a relatively low priority to 'outsider', i.e. shareholder interests compared with those of 'insiders', i.e. managers and managed employees. However, over the last 20 years changes in patterns of ownership and changes in corporation law have raised the possibility that the stakeholder model is being eroded by growing shareholder influence.

The most important developments, described by Araki (2005) are:

- a decline in long-term and cross-shareholding in Japan, which, if it spreads, will destabilise the long-term relations between and within companies that have supported the Japanese employment system;
- a rising proportion of equity owned by foreign shareholders;
- legal reforms that have strengthened the power of shareholders over managers and made it possible for corporations to adopt new governance structures that include external, non-executive directors on boards of directors to represent shareholder interests.

On the other hand Araki (2005) concludes that these changes 'can best be viewed as the realignment of the priorities of different stakeholders within the framework of the stakeholder model' (p. 281) rather than indicating the collapse of the stakeholder approach. This is because 80 per cent of companies maintain cross-shareholding and remain committed to long-term, cooperative relations with other companies and the share of equity owned by foreign shareholders fell slightly during 2000–02. Also, while some leading corporations such as Sony, Toshiba and Mitsubishi have adopted the new model of corporate governance, most firms continue to operate the traditional model in which boards of directors are dominated by people promoted from inside the firm.

The decline of enterprise unionism

The proportion of Japanese workers who are union members fell from 34.7 per cent in 1975 to 20.7 per cent in 2001. In addition, enterprise unions and their confederations have been subject to a growing criticism that they serve only the interests of the elite group of workers in the leading corporations (Hanami, 2004). In the past, enterprise unions have played an important role as a channel for employee voice in Japanese companies and as such have helped to create the basis for the high levels of worker-management cooperation that has been a characteristic of Japanese employment relations for most of the post-war period. Therefore, the decline of enterprise unionism could threaten to weaken the system as a whole.

The decline of seniority-based pay and promotion

An ageing workforce and slow economic growth since 1990 have undermined the seniority pay system. This is because seniority-based pay depends on the balance in the workforce between younger, junior employees and older, more senior employees. Younger workers are paid less than is warranted by their productivity, while older workers are paid more. As long as the proportions of younger and older workers are balanced, the overall wage bill is in line with the productivity of the workforce. However it means that more young workers have to be hired each year to offset the effects of seniority-based wage increases for existing workers. But to be able to do this the company has to keep expanding to create new vacancies at entry level. The economic stagnation of the Japanese economy has meant that corporations have cut back on their recruitment of young workers. Therefore the overall age profile of the workforce has increased, causing company wage bills increasingly to be out of line with workers' productivity, thus increasing production costs and reducing profitability and competitiveness (Hattori and Maeda, 2000).

Reform of the wage and promotion system has also been encouraged by the increased pace of change in organisations. This means that skills and knowledge gained through seniority are at less of a premium. Therefore promotion is being linked more to individual performance. Finally, it is claimed that moves to base pay on individual performance are in tune with changing social attitudes as younger generations of workers have developed more individualised sets of values and are less collectively oriented (Kusuda, 2000).

The outcome is that most Japanese corporations claim to be reducing the extent to which pay is determined by seniority and increasing the weight given to performance. A survey of large firms carried out by the Japan Productivity Centre for Socio-Economic Development in 1998 found that 76 per cent of respondents planned either to do away completely with seniority based pay or move to predominantly performance-based pay systems for their managerial employees (Hattori and Maeda, 2000). Regarding promotions, a survey carried out in 1999 for the Ministry of Labour found that over 80 per cent of companies said that they used ability and performance as criteria for promotions to managerial grades while 48 per cent used seniority. Also, more companies claim to have introduced 'fast track' promotion routes and are promoting people at a younger age (Matanle, 2003; Conrad and Heindorf 2006). At the same time however, the extent of team-working makes individual performance hard to measure, so some companies focus on team rather than individual performance. Also, skills and qualifications have become more rather than less important in determining basic pay. As employees need to have spent specified periods of time acquiring prescribed skills and abilities in order to gain promotion to the next grade, this blurs the distinction between seniority and ability/performance and managers may continue to use age as a convenient proxy for performance. Moreover the shift from seniority to performance-based pay has been concentrated on managerial staff (Inoue, 1999; Matanle, 2003; Conrad and Heindorf 2006).

A retreat from lifetime employment?

The long period of economic stagnation throughout the 1990s has led companies to increase their use of fixed term contracts and temporary agency workers. Between 1990 and 2002 the proportion of 'atypical' workers, i.e. those on part-time and fixed-term contracts rose from 20.2 per cent in 1990 to 29.8 per cent (Araki, 2005). This included a three-fold increase in the number of registered temporary agency workers from 0.5 million in 1992 to 1.7 million in

2002 (Hanami, 2004; Macnaughtan, 2006). This has been encouraged by legislation that has relaxed restrictions on the use of fixed term contracts and made it easier to set up and run temporary employment agencies. At the same time however, an amendment to the Labour Standards Law in 2003 tightened the restrictions on employers' right to dismiss workers (Hanami, 2004).

The late 1990s also saw household name companies being forced to make major cuts in their workforces. In 1999 Nissan Motor Corporation, which had just been taken over by Renault, announced the closure of five sites in Japan with the loss of over 10,000 jobs. This, together with other job cuts in Japanese corporations, was widely interpreted as signalling the end of the lifetime employment system in Japan. However, what was not so widely reported was that Nissan promised to achieve the reductions through natural wastage, early retirement, increasing part-time employment and selling non-core subsidiaries (Symonds, 1999). More generally, research has found that large Japanese companies remain reluctant to lay off workers, even when there is a need to cut jobs. As at Nissan, natural wastage, early retirement and temporary or permanent transfer of workers to subsidiaries are still the preferred methods of reducing headcount (Watanabe, 2000; Kato, 2001; Matanle, 2003). A Ministry of Labour survey of large firms in 1999 found that roughly a third of respondents planned to maintain their existing lifetime employment systems while a little under half said that they planned to make partial revisions to their lifetime employment systems. Less than a fifth planned to make major changes (Hattori and Maeda, 2000; Matanle 2006). Signs of a revival of the Japanese economy during 2003–07 gave a further boost to confidence in the virtues of long-term employment (see Box 15.2).

We can see that some of the key principles that defined the Japanese employment system are being eroded. The principle of seniority in determining pay and promotion is being downgraded and companies have cut jobs and made more use of non-standard workers, i.e. temporary, fixed-term and part-time, when hiring. It may well be that these changes are having long-term effects on levels of trust and employee commitment, weakening the established basis for management–worker cooperation that has existed in Japan (Kwon, 2004). However, we can also see evidence of continuing commitment to the principle of long-term if not lifetime employment and we have noted the limits to the shift from seniority to performance in determining pay and promotion. Even where changes are being made, they continue to be constrained by features of the existing system.

Box 15.2 'Keidenran's Okuda lauds Japanese management for revival'

'Japan was able to overcome the protracted recession because companies focused on long-term growth and did their best to avoid massive lay-offs even while grappling with the need to restructure', Japan Business Federation Chairman Hiroshi Okuda said . . .

'Japanese society has finally survived the long-standing economic slump because we, private firms, have stuck to the two bases of Japanese management: respect for people and long-term perspective.'

But Okuda's lecture was not an endorsement of the traditional management style. The corporate sector 'has been making necessary adjustments to accommodate the globalisation of the economy while giving consideration to job security', he said. Companies have 'tackled various reforms, for example, reviewing their seniority systems and introducing merit-based compensation'.

Source: *The Nikkei Weekly*, 16 January 2006 (*note*: the rest of the article is omitted)

Activity

Discuss why Japanese employers have been readier to reform the seniority wage system than retreat from lifetime employment.

Conclusion: divergence, change and convergence in employment systems?

The employment systems of the USA, Germany and Japan have each undergone change in response to economic crises during the late twentieth century. In each case, internalised employment systems have come under strain as a result of pressures to increase flexibility and reduce costs. America was the first country to adjust, prompted by deterioration in economic performance in the face of German and Japanese competition. The relative weakness of institutionalised regulation of the US business and employment system meant that the shift away from the bureaucratised internal labour market, which had in any case been gathering pace during the 1970s, was relatively rapid and complete. The story in Germany and Japan has been different, owing to the deeply embedded nature of institutionalised regulation of the employment relationship in those countries. In both cases change has been hesitant and uneven, with employers reluctant to abandon completely the systems that have yielded significant benefits in the past. As the extract in Box 15.2 shows, in Japan's case economic revival has led to the reaffirmation of a reformed lifetime employment model. Yet debate about the future direction of employment systems and, more fundamentally, the future direction of capitalist development continues. The debate is framed round the question of whether, in an increasingly globalising world economy, diverse forms of capitalism that support nationally distinctive employment systems will continue to survive.

The debate concerning whether countries' business and employment relations systems are converging or not is not a new one. It has its origins in the 'industrialisation debate' of the 1960s. The convergence argument was advanced first by Clark Kerr and his colleagues (Kerr *et al.*, 1960). They argued that as countries became more industrially developed, their industrial relations systems would mature also. Specifically, they argued that industrial relations would become increasingly subject to institutional regulation through collective bargaining. Industrial conflict would wither away to be replaced by social consensus. Implicitly Kerr *et al.*, assumed that nations would converge towards America's 'New Deal' industrial relations system.

Kerr's thesis came increasingly to be rejected during the 1970s as it was apparent that industrial relations systems remained widely diverse. The dominant view was that there were persistent national differences in:

- the strength and pattern of organisation among workers and employers;
- the level at which collective bargaining was conducted;
- the role of law in industrial relations;
- ideological features of industrial relations.

These differences would remain because they were embedded in wider societal institutions so that change would follow nationally distinctive paths (Maurice *et al.*, 1986).

Since the 1980s however, the debate over whether national employment and business systems are converging has been renewed in the light of a trend change towards globalisation of the world economy. The argument is that first, increased international competition in markets for goods and services and also for capital investment is forcing firms to adopt the most efficient production methods in their sectors, e.g. lean production. This means that firms will increasingly tend to adopt, on the basis of efficient markets, similar approaches to work organisation, training, pay, employee involvement, etc. Where existing features of national systems of employment regulation are seen to prevent or hinder firms from adopting new techniques, they will come under growing pressure for reform, what might be termed managed change or defensive modification. This tendency will be reinforced by the growing importance of multinational companies as they transfer practices developed in foreign subsidiaries back to their home country (see Chapter 17).

Second, international mergers and takeovers mean that companies are becoming increasingly international in their ownership, leading to the spread of arm's-length relations between owners and managers and the consequent spread of investor and shareholder value principles of governance. As we have seen, these principles are at odds with the stakeholder approach that has underpinned social partnership and welfare corporatist systems of employment regulation.

Third, the internationalisation of investment has meant that countries are in competition to attract and retain foreign direct investment. This means that there is pressure on governments to ensure that fiscal and monetary policies, industrial and labour market policies are 'business-friendly'. In particular, it is argued that countries with high levels of regulation such as Germany and Japan are being forced to move towards the more lightly regulated liberal market model of the USA (Streeck, 1997).

Against this line of argument are those who argue that, despite the fact that national employment systems are subject to the same pressures arising from globalisation, their responses will be shaped by their historically developed patterns of institutional regulation. Smith and Meiksins (1995) identified three aspects of change that influence the possible extent of convergence:

- *System imperatives*: changes in the conditions of capitalist competition;
- *Societal effects*: how national institutional frameworks mediate system imperatives;
- *Dominance effects*: the influence of particular paradigms or countries in shaping production and employment systems.

System imperatives force change but change does not necessarily mean convergence. Societal effects imply divergence; dominance effects imply convergence. The question is whether societal effects outweigh or moderate dominance effects. If it is the case that the system imperative favours a particular type of employment system, this creates a strong dominance effect. Other systems become less competitive and under increasing pressure to move closer to the favoured model. Convergence advocates argue that today's system imperatives seem to favour the type of employment system associated with liberal market economies, creating a dominance effect that is putting pressure on other systems to converge on the US model.

What are the main dominance effects operating on the German and Japanese employment systems? What societal effects might limit the Americanisation of the German and Japanese employment systems?

Work by American scholars Katz and Darbishire (2000) suggests that it might be misleading to think in simple terms of convergence versus divergence. They found that in all of the countries they looked at – USA, UK, Australia, Italy, Japan and Sweden – employment systems were becoming more diverse. In each country four patterns of employment were spreading – a low wage pattern, i.e. the 'lower road' approach, a high performance-based HRM model, the Japanese lean production model, and a joint team-based model. As a result, they claimed there was evidence of convergence, but in the sense that employment systems in all countries were becoming more internally diverse. This may suggest that the frameworks of institutionalised regulation are weakening in countries where they have been strong, i.e. in Sweden, Italy, Japan and Germany, allowing managers more freedom to innovate as has been the case in the USA. However, the relative balance between each of the four patterns varied across countries and was influenced by national institutions, providing evidence of continued divergence.

This picture of 'converging divergences' (Katz and Darbishire, 2000) suggests that simple notions of convergence or divergence are inadequate to describe contemporary patterns of change across countries. A more useful concept might be *hybridisation* (Kwon, 2004). In terms of Smith and Meiskins' framework, hybridisation can be seen as the interplay of dominance effects and societal effects. Dominance effects mean that national employment systems come to share more common influences such as lean production, shareholder value and labour flexibility but societal effects mean that the way governments, employers and other actors use these influences to achieve change continues to reflect features of the existing system.

In looking at recent patterns of change in Germany and Japan, we have seen that there is some evidence that dominance effects are at work in the diffusion of shareholder value ideas and pressures to increase labour flexibility. However, we have also noted the limited and partial nature of the changes that have taken place. Societal effects mean that there is still support for the social partnership principle in Germany and for welfare corporatism in Japan. While we cannot rule out the possibility that Germany and Japan will move closer to the American model in the future, the fact that employment systems are deeply embedded in wider societal institutions suggests that while the German and Japanese systems are likely to evolve in response to new global pressures, this is not to say that they will come to replicate the US model. Indeed, the difficulty of predicting the future shape of employment systems is compounded when we consider the possible effects of the emergence of China and India as leading players in the new global economy and the unfolding effects of the recent credit crunch and national and global responses to it.

Summary

- There are noticeable differences in the way the employment relationship is regulated in different countries such that we can identify different national employment systems.

- National employment systems can be compared on the basis of similarities and differences in the extent and patterns of institutionalised regulation of the employment relationship.

- Different countries' employment systems are embedded in and shaped by their wider business systems.

- Historically, Germany, Japan and the USA have adopted different employment paradigms based on respectively social partnership, welfare corporatism and a managerially led model.

- Each of the three paradigms has been embedded in distinctive business systems that have in turn produced and supported distinctive strategies for achieving competitiveness in domestic and international markets.

- Since the 1980s, each system has come under intense pressure to change in response to forces that many observers believe are encouraging the convergence of all employment systems towards the current US model.

- Globalisation if it means anything means that international competitive pressures and reactions to them override the priorities of national business and employment systems leading to the further marketisation of corporate governance and employment relations.

- In a global context financial performance becomes much more important than previously, particularly as the stock market and the market for corporate control increasingly discipline management to ensure managerial efficiency on the basis that investors and shareholders are the dominant stakeholders.

- The diffusion of investor and shareholder approaches to corporate performance, combined with external shocks such as the recession caused by the credit crunch, encourage employers to see labour as a cost rather than a productive resource, leading to changes in HRM. At the same time however, national systems of institutional regulation moderate this pressure.

Questions

1 Explain the terms 'social partnership', 'welfare corporatism' and 'managerial capitalism'. What is their significance for the regulation of the employment relationship?

2 How have the German, Japanese and American employment systems shaped the ways in which these countries compete in international markets?

3 Compare any two of the three systems discussed in this chapter to discuss how national differences in employment systems reflect wider institutional differences.

4 What have been the main pressures for change in the American, German and Japanese employment systems?

5 In what ways and how fundamentally are the German and Japanese systems changing?

6 In the light of the country studies in this chapter, consider the arguments for and against the likely convergence of national employment systems.

Case study

The VW scandal, Porsche and the VW law

Throughout 2006 and 2007 VW was embroiled in a scandal and subsequent legal case that threatened to derail the authority of Germany's co-determination laws. VW's head of Human Resources was found guilty of bribing the head of VW's works council to cooperate with the introduction of the four-day working week and a new production system. As well as shocking the German business community and the public in general, the scandal exposed the degree to which co-determination at VW sustained massive inefficiencies compared with other automobile manufacturers in Germany. Worse still for VW, it led to the removal of the 'VW law'. This law had not only limited individual shareholder voting rights to a value set at 20 per cent of share capital irrespective of actual shareholding but also guaranteed the State of Lower Saxony (where 76,000 of VW's 98,000 employees live) two seats on the Supervisory Board irrespective of the overall value of its shareholding. The European Commission outlawed this arrangement on the basis that it prevented the free movement of capital.

The fallout from the bribery case and the end of the VW law saw a power struggle within the firm resulting in Ferdinand Peich becoming VW chairman. Peich is a member of the Porsche family who controlled over 30 per cent of VW shares in early 2008. Since becoming VW chairman Peich has seen off an attempt by the German government to re-

formulate the VW law, gained control of a third seat on the VW supervisory board and in October 2008 ensured that 74 per cent of VW shares are now directly or indirectly controlled by the Porsche family.

Porsche have made it clear that they want to modernise the VW organisational structure to give management a freer hand along Anglo-American lines and improve the technical sophistication of the VW brand by putting all its luxury marques (Audi, Bentley, Bugatti, Lamborghini) in one division and its mass market badges (VW, Seat, Skoda) in a second division. The IG Metall union stated that the change in the VW law clearly favoured shareholders over workers. Peich has succeeded in retaining VW as a German firm – something that was clearly under threat by the end of the VW law, but has transformed VW from a state controlled (blocking minority) company back to a founding family business.

Questions

1 In what ways does this case illustrate the pressures for change in the German employment system being generated by globalisation?

2 What kind of changes do you think Porsche have been looking to make to give management 'a freer hand'? What is the significance of continued German ownership of VW in this context?

Activity

Using documentary and internet sources, do some research to find out more about the changes being introduced at VW in the wake of the Porsche takeover and their implications for the management of people in the firm. A good source is the European Industrial Relations Observatory On-line, which can be found at **www.eiro.eurofound.ie** Go to 'browse by country' and click on Germany. The *European Industrial Relations Review* is another useful source.

References and further reading

Araki, T. (2005) 'Corporate governance, labour and employment relations in Japan: the future of the shareholder model?' in H. Gospel and A. Pendleton (eds) *Corporate Governance and Labour Management: An International Comparison.* Oxford: Oxford University Press, pp. 254–83.

Baumol, W.J. (1959) *Business Behaviour, Value and Growth.* New York: Macmillan.

Boyer, R. (2000) 'Is a finance-led growth regime a viable alternative to Fordism? A preliminary analysis', *Economy and Society,* 29, 1: 114–45.

Boyer, R. (2005) 'From shareholder value to CEO power: the paradox of the 1990s', *Competition and Change,* 9, 1: 7–47.

Braverman, H. (1974) *Labour and Monopoly Capital.* New York: Monthly Review Press.

Cappelli, P. Bassie, L., Katz, H. Knoke, D., Osterman, P. and Unseem, M. (1997) *Change at Work: How American Industry and Workers Are Coping with Corporate Restructuring and What Workers Must Do to Take Charge of Their Own Careers.* Oxford: Oxford University Press.

Carr, C. (2005) 'Are German, Japanese and Anglo-Saxon strategic decision styles still divergent in the context of globalization?', *Journal of Management Studies,* 42, 6: 1155–88.

Chandler, A. (1977) *The Visible Hand: The Managerial Revolution in American Business.* Cambridge: Cambridge University Press.

Chandler, A. (1990) *Scale and Scope: The Dynamics of Industrial Capitalism.* Cambridge: Cambridge University Press.

CIPD (2006) *People, Productivity and Performance – Smart Work.* London: CIPD.

Clark, I. (2007) 'Private equity and HRM in the British business system', *Human Resource Management Journal,* 17, 3: 218–26.

Clark, I. and Almond, P. (2006) 'An introduction to the American business system' in P. Almond and A. Ferner (eds) *American Multinationals in Europe: Human Resource Policies and Practices.* Oxford: Oxford University Press, pp. 37–56.

Conrad, H. and Heindorf, V. (2006) 'Recent changes in compensation practices in large Japanese companies: wages, bonuses and corporate pensions' in P. Matanle and W. Lunsing (eds) *Perspectives on Work, Employment and Society in Japan.* Basingstoke: Palgrave, pp. 79–97.

Dore, R. (1973) *British Factory – Japanese Fcatory: The Origins of National Diversity in Industrial Relations.* London: Allen & Unwin.

Dore, R. (2000) *Stock Market Capitalism: Welfare Capitalism. Japan and Germany Versus the Anglo-Saxons.* Oxford: Oxford University Press.

Dore, R., Lazonick, W. and O'Sullivan M., (1999) 'Varieties of capitalism in the twentieth century', *Oxford Review of Economic Policy,* 15, 4: 102–20.

DW.World (2009) *DW.World.DE* 31 March **http://www.dw-world.de/dw/article/0,,4143056,00.html**.

Edwards, R. (1979) *Contested Terrain.* New York: Basic Books.

Edwards, T. (2004) 'Corporate governance, industrial relations and trends in company-level restructuring in Europe: convergence towards the Anglo-American model?' *Industrial Relations Journal,* 35, 6: 518–35.

ESRC (2004) *The UK's Productivity Gap – What Research Tells Us and What We Need To Know.* Swindon: ESRC.

Federal Statistical Office Germany (2006) **www.destatis.de**.

Federal Statistical Office Germany (2008) Press release 136/1 April 2008, 'Upward trend on labour market undiminished'.

Financial Services Authority (2006) 'Private equity: a discussion of risk and regulatory engagement', *Discussion Paper,* 06/6, November, London: FSA.

Foulkes, F. (1980) *Personnel Management in Large Non-Union Companies.* Englewood Cliffs, NJ: Prentice Hall.

Fujimura, H. (1997) 'New unionism: beyond enterprise unionism?' in M. Sako and H. Sato (eds) *Japanese Labour and Management in Transition: Diversity, Flexibility and Participation.* London: Routledge, pp. 296–314.

Grahl, J. and Teague, P. (2000) 'The regulation school, the employment relation and financialisation', *Economy and Society,* 29, 1: 160–78.

Grahl, J. and Teague, P. (2004) 'The German model in danger', *Industrial Relations Journal,* 35, 6: 557–74.

Gulger, K., Mueller, D. and Yurtoglu, B. (2004) 'Corporate governance and globalization', *Oxford Review of Economic Policy,* 20, 1: 129–56.

Hall, P. and Soskice, D. (2001) 'An introduction to varieities of capitalism' in P. Hall and D. Soskice (eds) *Varieties of Capitalism: The Institutional Foundations of Comparative Advantage.* Oxford: Oxford University Press.

Hanami, T. (2004) 'The changing labour market, industrial relations and labour policy' *Japan Labor Review,* 1, 1: 4–16.

Hansmann, H. and Kraakman, R. (2001) 'The end of history for corporate law', *Georgetown Law Review,* 43: 439–41.

Harris, H. (1982) *The Right to Manage.* Madison, WI: University of Wisconsin Press.

Hattori, R. and Maeda, E. (2000) 'The Japanese employment system (summary)' *Bank of Japan Monthly Bulletin* (January), **www.boj.or.jp/en/type/ronbun/ron/research/data/ron0001a.pdf**.

Hollingsworth, J.R. (1997) 'The institutional embeddedness of American capitalism' in C. Crouch and W. Streeck (eds) *The Political Economy of Modern Capitalism.* London: Sage.

Inagami, T. (1988) *Japanese Workplace Industrial Relations,* Japanese Industrial Relations Series 14. Tokyo: Japanese Institute of Labour.

Inoue, S. (1999) 'Japanese trade unions and their future: opportunities and challenges in an era of globalisation', *International Institute for Labor Studies Discussion Paper* No. 106. Geneva: ILO.

Jacobi, O., Keller, B. and Muller-Jentsch, W. (1998) 'Germany: facing new challenges', in A. Ferner and R. Hyman (eds) *Changing Industrial Relations in Europe*. Oxford: Blackwell, pp. 190–238.

Jacoby, S. (1997) *Modern Manors: Welfare Capitalism since the New Deal*. New York: Princeton University Press.

Jensen, M. and Murphy, K. (1990) 'Performance pay and top-management incentives', *Journal of Political Economy*, 98, 2: 225–64.

Kato, T. (2001) 'The end of lifetime employment in Japan? Evidence from national surveys and research', *Journal of the Japanese and International Economies*, 15: 489–514.

Katz, H. and Darbishire, O. (2000) *Converging Divergences: World Wide Changes in Employment Systems*. New York: Cornell University Press.

Kerr, C., Dunlop, J., Harbison, E. and Myers, C. (1960) *Industrialism and Industrial Man*. Cambridge, MA: Harvard University Press.

Kochan, T., Katz, H. and McKersie, R. (1993) *The Transformation of American Industrial Relations,* 2nd edn. New York: Cornell University Press.

Kothen, G., McKinley, W. and Scherer, G. (1999) 'Alternatives to organisational downsizing: a German case study' *M@n@gement* 2, 3 (special issue): 263–86.

Kusuda, K. (2000) 'Trends in wage systems in Japan', *Japanese Institute of Labor Bulletin*, April.

Kwon, Hyeong-ki (2004) 'Japanese employment relations in transition' *Economic and Industrial Democracy*, 25, 3: 325–45.

Lane, C. (1989) *Management and Labour in Europe*. Aldershot: Edward Elgar.

Lane, C. (2000) 'Globalization and the German model of capitalism: erosion or survival?', *British Journal of Sociology*, 51, 2: 207–34.

Lazonick, W. (1991) *Business Organization and the Myth of the Market Economy*. Cambridge: Cambridge University Press.

Littler, C. (1982) *The Development of the Labour Process in Capitalist Economies*. London: Heinemann.

Locke, D. (1996) *The Collapse of American Management Mystique*. Oxford: Oxford University Press.

Logan, J. (2006) 'The union avoidance industry in the United States', *British Journal of Industrial Relations*, 44, 4: 651–75.

Lincoln, J. R. and Kalleberg, A.L. (1992) *Culture, Control and Commitment: A Study of Work Organization and Attitudes in the United States and Japan*. Cambridge: Cambridge University Press.

Macnaughtan, H. (2006) 'From "post-war" to "post-bubble": contemporary issues for Japanese working women', in P. Matanle and W. Lunsing (eds) *Perspectives on Work, Employment and Society in Japan*. Basingstoke: Palgrave, pp. 31–57.

Marsden, D. (1999) *A Theory of Employment Systems*. Oxford: Oxford University Press.

Matanle, P. (2003) *Japanese Capitalism and Modernity in a Global Era: Refabricating Lifetime Employment Relations*. London: Routledge Curzon.

Matanle, P. (2006) 'Beyond lifetime employment? Re-fabricating Japan's employment culture', in P. Matanle and W. Lunsing (eds) *Perspectives on Work, Employment and Society in Japan*. Basingstoke: Palgrave, pp. 58–78.

Maurice, M., Sellier, F. and Silvestre, J.J. (1986) *The Social Foundations of Industrial Power*. Cambridge, MA: MIT Press.

McGuckin, R. and van Ark, B. (2005) *Performance 2005: Productivity, Employment and Income in the World's Economies*. New York: Conference Board.

Nakamura, K. (1997) 'Worker participation: collective bargaining and joint consultation', in M. Sako and H. Sato (eds) *Japanese Labour and Management in Transition: Diversity, Flexibility and Participation*. London: Routledge, pp. 280–95.

OECD (2004) *Principles of Corporate Governance*. Paris: OECD.

OECD (2006) *OECD Factbook*. **www.sourceoecd.org**.

OECD (2007) *OECD Economic Outlook 82*. Paris: OECD Publishing.

OECD (2008) *OECD. Statextracts*. **http://stats.oecd.org. WBOS/Index.aspx?DatasetCode=ALFS_SUMTAB**.

Oliver, N. and Wilkinson, B. (1992) *The Japanization of British Industry: New Developments in the 1990s*, 2nd edn. Oxford: Blackwell.

O'Sullivan, M. (2000) Contests *for Corporate Control and Economic Performance in the United States and Germany*, Oxford: Oxford University Press.

Peuntner, T. (2003) 'Contingent employment in Germany' in O. Bergstrom and D. Storrie (eds) *Contingent Employment in Europe and the United States*. Cheltenham: Edward Elgar, pp. 136–62.

Rubery, J. and Grimshaw, D. (2003) *The Organization of Employment: An International Perspective*. Basingstoke: Palgrave.

Rupert, M. (1995) Producing Hegemony: The Politics of Mass Production and American Global Power. Cambridge: Cambridge University Press.

Sako, M. (1997) 'Introduction: forces for homogeneity and diversity in the Japanese industrial relations system', in M. Sako and H. Sato (eds) *Japanese Labour and Management in Transition: Diversity, Flexibility and Participation*. London: Routledge, pp. 1–26.

Schoppa, L. (2006) 'Race to the bottom? Japanese multinational firms and the future of the lifetime employment system' *Japan Focus*, February, **www.japanfocus.org**.

Shinoda, T. (1997) 'Rengo and policy participation: Japanese-style neocorporatism?' in M. Sako and H. Sato (eds) *Japanese Labour and Management in Transition: Diversity, Flexibility and Participation*. London: Routledge, pp. 187–24.

Shirai, T. (1983) *Contemporary Industrial Relations in Japan*. Madison, WI: Wisconsin University Press.

Smith, C. and Meiksins, P. (1995) 'System, societal and dominance effects in cross-national organisational analysis', *Work, Employment and Society*, 9, 2: 241–67.

Streeck, W. (1997) 'German capitalism: does it exist? Can it survive?' in C. Crouch and W. Streeck (eds) *Political Economy of Modern Capitalism*. London: Sage, pp. 33–54.

Strinati, D. (1982) *Capitalism, the State and Industrial Relations*. London: Croom Helm.

Sugeno, K. and Suwa, Y. (1997) 'Labour law issues in a changing labour market: in search of a new support system' in M. Sako, and H. Sato (eds) *Japanese Labour and Management in Transition: Diversity, Flexibility and Participation*. London: Routledge, pp. 53–78.

Symonds, P. (1999) 'Nissan announces 21,000 jobs to go in Japan's first major downsizing' World Socialist Website, October, **www.wsws.org**.

Towers, B. (1997) *The Representation Gap*. Oxford: Oxford University Press.

Teague, P. and Grahl, J. (2004) 'The German model in danger', *Industrial Relations Journal*, 35, 6: 557–73.

Tuselman, H. and Heise, A. (2000) 'The German model at the crossroads: past, present and future', *Industrial Relations Journal*, 31, 3: 162–77.

Wall Street Journal, 31 March 2009, 'OECD expects Japan 2009, GDP at −6.6% Vs −0.1% November forecast' **http://wsj.com/article/BT-CO-200090331-70342.html**.

Watanabe, S. (2000) 'The Japan model and the future of employment and wage systems', *International Labour Review*, 139, 3: 307–34.

Whitley, R. (2000) *Divergent Capitalisms: The Social Structuring and Change of Business Systems*. Oxford: Oxford University Press.

Williamson, O. (1964) *The Economics of Discretionary Behaviour: Managerial Objectives in a Theory of the Firm*. Englewood Cliffs, NJ: Prentice Hall.

For multiple-choice questions, exercises and annotated weblinks related to this topic, visit **www.pearsoned.co.uk/mymanagementlab**.

Chapter 16

Human resource management in China and India

Linda Glover and Anita Hammer

Objectives

- To examine the convergence–divergence debate with respect to HRM in Asia.
- To apply cultural and institutional perspectives to understand HRM in China and India.
- To explore the developments in human resource management in the People's Republic of China.
- To explore the nature and development of human resource management in India.

Introduction

This chapter focuses upon China and India. It explores the general business context of each of these countries and reflects upon some of the human resource issues that are relevant to each. The chapter is designed to give readers an overview of the key issues for each country. Further reading is recommended if a detailed understanding of either/both countries is required and the reference list is offered as a useful starting point.

China and India are in the process of rapid development and together hold two fifths of the world's population. They are becoming increasingly important in economic terms. As well as receiving inward foreign investment, developing countries are becoming important sources of foreign direct investment (World Investment Report, 2005). China has been called the 'factory of the world' as manufacturers increasingly locate operations there. India has become a popular base for IT-enabled services, such as call centre operations for the HSBC bank, Microsoft, British Telecom and British Gas. Chinese and Indian firms are becoming more established and some are buying well-known brands or forming strategic alliances in order to become global players. Examples include Lenovo's acquisition of IBM's PC division, Nanjing Automotive's acquisition of part of the Rover group and the Tata group's acquisition of Tetley tea, Jaguar and Land Rover, and Corus Steel.

Some have argued that India and China face similar challenges in dealing with unemployment, regional disparities and the 'enduring poverty of farmers' (*The Economist*, 2005). China is often portrayed as more advanced in terms of economic development and India as 'big, lumbering and slow off the mark'. However, others have argued that India is emerging as a new 'Asian Tiger' (*The Economist*, 2005) and that while India could learn lessons from China in terms of economic growth, the Chinese model has been one of political authoritarianism and India's tradition of democracy has much to commend it (*The Economist*, 2005). Until quite recently, China and India were considered to be relatively immune to the world economic crisis. Some hoped that these huge emerging markets might provide the engines that could pull the world out of recession. Others however, fear the reverse: that the global downturn is going to drag China and India down with it, bringing massive unemployment. While China is the bigger economy, some have argued that India has an advantage over China in terms of coping with the economic slowdown. India has a democratic state embedded enough to cope with disgruntlement without its foundations being challenged. Though India pays an economic price for its democracy (and as in China, unrest and insurgency are widespread), its political system has resilience and flexibility that China's own leaders, it seems, believe they lack (*The Economist*, 2008).

The structure of the chapter is as follows. The first section considers the evidence for convergence or divergence among economies in Asia. The second section moves on to discuss China and includes an overview of the country, its economic growth and a brief history of the 'iron rice bowl' to 'socialism with Chinese characteristics'. The discussion then moves on to discuss HRM issues including: employment contracts, labour market concerns, recruitment selection and training, reward systems and employee relations, some cultural issues and problems around management skills, labour discipline and motivation. This is followed by a brief overview of Hong Kong, as it has a different history from mainland China.

The next major section focuses on India and includes an overview of the country and its economic development, and issues related to the national business system and the Indian business environment, in particular the rise of Indian multinational firms. It then moves on to consider HRM in India including legal provisions, industrial relations, recruitment, reward and wages, training and skill development and finally the challenges, advantages and prospects for the future.

Convergence or divergence in Asia?

The assumption in the past was that management and employee relation practices could be transposed to any international context with requisite training and the implementation of proper systems of management, usually American. Another assumption by many Westerners was that Asian cultural influences on management could largely be ignored. This was a perspective strongly informed by imperialist attitudes that assumed that what was good for Western economies could automatically be transplanted into any socio-cultural context. As has already been noted in Chapter 15 on international HRM, these convergence assumptions have been rigorously challenged by divergence theorists from a cultural and institutional perspective, as well as by Whitley (1992) and his followers, who believe that each national context throws up its own unique business system. However, more recently there has been a return to the convergence view, much influenced by the phenomenon of 'globalisation' (a concept still largely ill-defined and subject to much misunderstanding) and the relative decline of Japan in relation to the United States in the latter part of the 1990s.

Others have gone beyond the simplistic suppositions of convergence and divergence to capture the complexities that underpin HRM in a national context as it interacts with global processes and practices. They have come to the general conclusion that divergence of HRM practices remains predominant. This is due to socio-cultural differences, varied investment patterns and financial institutional practices, and political and historical factors that have led to different stages of economic development (Warner, 1993; Easterby-Smith *et al.*, 1995; Leggett and Bamber, 1996; Paik *et al.*, 1996; Rowley, 1997; Sparrow and Wu, 1999; Warner, 2000).

Leggett and Bamber (1996) claim that despite enormous growth, high investment from foreign companies and closer cooperation through the Association of South East Asian Nations (ASEAN) and the Asia-Pacific Economic Cooperation (APEC) forum, Asia Pacific economies diverge into three tiers or levels of development.

- *The top tier*: led predominantly by Japan, also includes Australia, Hong Kong, New Zealand, Singapore, Taiwan and South Korea. The non-Anglo-Saxon countries are generally known as the *Asian tigers*, and are made up of so-called *newly industrialised economies* (NIEs). These have witnessed impressive growth rates over the past 20 years, and are moving into a second phase of development where the reliance on cheap labour is being superseded by investment in high technology and service industries.

- *The second tier*: a second generation of tigers, comprising Malaysia, the Peoples Republic of China (PRC) and Thailand. They reflect the earlier experience of the older tigers, and are at present at the stage of being 'caught in a "sandwich trap" of cheap labour competition from below and exclusion from higher value-added markets from above' (Deyo, 1995: 23).

- *The third tier*: made up of Burma, India, Indonesia, the Philippines and Vietnam, comprises a diverse range of economies that have not reached the overall developmental stages of the first two tiers. What characterises this tier is the availability and abundance of cheap and unskilled labour.

However, as the case of India shows, the tier model does not accommodate variations in levels, rates and nature of growth. Sections of the Indian economy have experienced enormous growth in the past ten years. Some sectors like information technology, software, computing and the services sector are highly developed. Today, it is the fastest growing economy along with China and aiming to capitalise on its competitive advantage of a relatively young, English-speaking, skilled workforce to move up the value chain.

In sum, to put these economies into one all-embracing category does not do justice to the diversity of their cultures, nor the political and social structures that create their unique business systems. As Warner (2000: 177) states: 'There is hardly any evidence to support the classic convergence hypothesis . . . it is hard to argue that Asian HRM is fast converging to a common model.' In separating forms of convergence into 'hard' and 'soft' ('hard' being labour market and economic influences exemplified by deregulation and privatisation and institutional structures, and 'soft' being more concerned with sociocultural variables) Warner (2000: 181) concludes that:

> the Asia-Pacific model is far from homogeneous [and that there is] a vast range of geographical and demographic variation. The economic systems range from emerging from a communist planned economy to fully fledged liberalised market-based ones. The political systems also differ greatly, as do the social arrangements. There is probably less cultural variation but more variety than acknowledged by many writers in the field. There is in this sense a fair degree of residual cultural diversity in the Asia-Pacific region that is likely to continue into the new millennium. On the other hand, if there is a common direction in which the HR systems are moving, it is most likely to be towards business restructuring, deregulation and liberalisation vis-à-vis the challenges of globalisation.

STOP and think

What factors would prevent a true convergence of HRM practices in the Asia Pacific region?

China: economic growth and HRM

Introduction

The People's Republic of China (PRC) has an area of 9,561,000 square kilometres, and had an estimated population of 1.3 billion people in 2004. China contains 22 provinces, 5 autonomous regions and 4 municipalities. Its capital is Beijing, which has a population of 7,610,000 (*Financial Times*, 2005). It has borders with countries including India, Burma and Russia. China has one-party rule by the Chinese Communist Party (CCP). The National Peoples Congress (NPC) is the organ of supreme power and contains 2989 delegates selected by provinces, municipalities, autonomous regions and the armed forces. The main functions of the NPC include formulating and revising the constitution, approving members of the Standing Committee of the NPC, approving the president and the vice president and examining and approving plans for economic and social development. The Politburo of the CCP sets policy and controls administrative, legal and executive appointments. The nine-man standing committee of the Politburo is the focus of power (*Financial Times*, 2005).

China has experienced rapid economic, political and social development over more than two decades. The death of Mao Zedong in 1976 heralded the beginning of a period of economic reform led by Deng Xiaoping. During this period China adopted an 'open door' policy for encouraging trade and technology transfer. The management of the economy moved from a centrally planned *command economy* to a *socialist market economy* (CCCC, 1993). Annual economic growth has averaged 9 per cent since 1978. Domestic spending rose by five times in the 1990s. GDP growth remained impressive until the world economy went into recession in 2008, indeed real GDP growth was running at 10.4 per cent in 2005, 11.6 per cent in 2006, and 11.9 per cent in 2007 (World Bank, March 2009). Despite the economic downturn the World Bank reported real GDP growth of 9 per cent in 2008 and predicted growth of 6.5 per cent for 2009 (World Bank, March 2009). While this seems relatively low for China, the predictions remain impressive compared with many leading economies.

There has been a rapid increase in the number of foreign-invested enterprises in China (Ding and Warner, 1999). Foreign investment in early 1996 was US$7.74 billion. This had risen to US$46.8 billion by 2001 and to US$55 billion in 2004 (Thornhill, 2002a; OECD, 2005). China was the largest recipient of foreign investment after the United States and received US$60 billion in FDI in 2004 (*The Economist*, 2005). However, the World Bank warned that the economic recession meant that foreign firms were reducing their investment plans, and noted that FDI had fallen by 26 per cent in the first two months of 2009 (World Bank, March 2009).

China has often been called 'the factory of the world'. In 2001, China's main trading partners were the United States, Japan and the EU, to which it exported goods totalling 20.4, 16.9 and 15.4 per cent of its output respectively in 2001 (Thornhill, 2002a). Merchandise exports were US$593.4 billion in 2004 and were expected to rise from US$761.3 billion to US$889.6 billion in 2005 and 2006 respectively. Merchandise imports were $534.4 billion in 2004 (*Financial Times*, 2005). However, the economic crisis began to bite in Autumn 2008 and trade volumes declined sharply. For example, exports were down by 21 per cent in the first two months of 2009 and imports also fell (World Bank, March 2009). The slowdown in China was identified as one of the key reasons for the sharp falls in global commodity prices from October 2008 onwards. One of the outcomes of the reduced economic activity was a rise in domestic unemployment, which was predicted to run around 9 per cent in 2008–9 (*Financial Times*, 24 November 2008).

Despite the extent and depth of the economic crisis of late 2008, most commentators agree that China has been relatively less affected (compared to many other economies) largely because it does not rely heavily on external financing. However, a key challenge has been the decline of Chinese exports (and related unemployment, particularly in the manufacturing sector). After the Asian economic crisis of the late 1990s, the World Bank high-lighted three main problems (World Bank 1999). These were:

- weaknesses in corporate governance, and a poor definition of ownership and accountability;
- government interference in investment decisions;
- slow progress in setting up satisfactory mechanisms by which to regulate the financial sector.

Concerns remain around each of these perceived problems, including the need for satisfactory mechanisms by which to regulate the financial sector. However, this observation looks rather rich given the parlous state of the financial sector in the UK and beyond – around which a debate about increased regulation rages!

In conjunction with the institutional weaknesses highlighted above, there remain associated problems of corruption within the system. It was estimated that one fifth (Rmb 117 bn) of central government revenues had been misused in the first eight months of 1999 (Kynge, 1999). The lack of legal regulation meant that foreign businesses often experienced problems when setting up businesses within China (Murray, 1994; Peng, 1994). These included dealing with broken contracts, incurring bad debts, and completing property developments. However, there is evidence that government is beginning to make progress with such issues, spurred by the need to implement rules and regulations in order to comply with its membership of the World Trade Organization (WTO). For example, Cody (2006) reports that the CCP disciplined more than 115,000 members for corruption and related violations in 2005 and that more than 15,000 were sent to court for prosecution. For example, a series of accidents in coal mines killed almost 6000 workers in 2005. Investigators found that local officials were not enforcing health and safety regulations due to the fact that they were either part-owners of the mines or were 'paid to look the other way' (Cody, 2006). Similarly, there was the well-publicised baby milk scandal in 2008 where tainted milk made more than 6000 infants sick and resulted in four deaths (*The Economist*, 18 September 2008). Therefore, corruption remains a problem in China.

Accession to the WTO (in December 2001) has increased the pressure to deal with issues such as labour rights, trade union rights, employment conditions and human rights more generally. Zhu and Warner (2005) observe that China has received both praise and criticism from interest groups both within and outside of China. In respect of the latter, they observe that one of the critical areas of debate has centred upon employment relations. They argue that criticism has centred on issues such as,

> the implementation of international labour standards, the role of trade unions, working conditions, wage-price factors in relation to the cost of production and export competition in global market, social protection and social inequality, 'efficiency' vs 'fairness and justice' . . . 'industrial democracy' vs 'power, control and corruption'
>
> (Zhu and Warner, 2005)

China is a developing economy and labour is one of its key resources. Zhu and Warner (2005: 355) explain that critics regard globalisation as part of a 'zero-sum game' that leads to an uneven distribution of benefits, where many employees work in poor conditions and exist on poverty wages. However, they also observe that accession to the WTO will bring increasing pressure from international governing bodies such as the ILO and organisations such as the International Confederation of Free Trade Unions (ICFTU) to improve employment rights and conditions (and the broader context of human rights).

China is now facing a more challenging climate in which export opportunities and foreign investment have declined and unemployment is emerging as a key concern – especially given the lack of an adequate social security net at present (Mok *et al.*, 2002).

The 'iron rice-bowl' to 'socialism with Chinese characteristics'

An historical overview serves to provide a framework for understanding some of the contemporary human resource issues that are impacting upon China. The historical review begins by focusing upon the period during which Mao Zedong was in power. Child (1994: 36–38) suggests that one can identify four main phases of industrial governance during this period. These are summarised below.

Phase 1: Central planning, 1953–56

Mao Zedong came to power in 1949. He advocated that China should move to an economy based upon socialist ownership. The Five Year Plan was launched in 1953. This included moves towards centralised planning and control from the state. Trade unions did exist, but their role was confined to dealing with welfare issues. Complicated piece-rate systems were used to reward many workers.

Phase 2: Decentralisation and the Great Leap Forward, 1957–61

The system of industrial governance that developed as part of the five-year plan was influenced by the Soviet system. Child argues that this tended to be very hierarchical, and as such was not in sympathy with a Chinese culture in which collectivism was a central feature. The Great Leap Forward was a period when many of these collectivist values came to the fore. During 1957–61, control of much of industry passed from central to provincial government. However, great emphasis was placed upon allegiance to the Communist Party, and factory directors had to report to Party committees. The system of bonus payments was reduced.

Phase 3: The period of readjustment, 1962–65

1959–61 saw a drop in agricultural output, followed by a famine. This was partly caused by an over-emphasis on expanding the manufacturing sector during the Great Leap Forward. The period of readjustment saw moves back towards more centralised planning; however, factory directors were given more control over day-to-day production issues.

Phase 4: The Cultural Revolution, 1966–76

The Cultural Revolution was a distinctive period, during which politics and ideology were the predominant concerns. There was a great emphasis upon allegiance to the Party. Factories moved away from hierarchical control towards using factory revolutionary committees as the management mechanism. In terms of rewards, 'competitive, individual and material incentive was rejected in favour of cooperative, collective and moral incentive' (Child, 1994: 37). Therefore, a context of collectivism and control developed. Child (1994: 39) comments that

> The Cultural Revolution was seen to have dissipated incentive and responsibility for economic performance through egalitarianism, the weakening of management, the general devaluation of expertise and the claim that ideological fervour and inspired leadership could substitute for technical knowledge . . . The xenophobia of the period had denied the country opportunities for inward investment and technology transfer.

Child's summary of the four phases of industrial governance gives an insight into the context that developed during the rule of Mao Zedong. The role of the state was central throughout. The state managed the economy, and increasingly enforced its ideology upon the citizens. China was relatively undisturbed by foreign influence during this period. Child notes that social and political discipline was used as an effective force for controlling the Chinese people.

One of the legacies of Mao's rule was the system that became known as the 'iron rice-bowl'. This related to the provision of lifetime employment and cradle-to-grave welfare structures (Ding *et al.*, 2000). The enterprise played both an economic and a social role, and provided its employees with housing, medical support and education. Central to the enterprise were work units (*danwei*). The *danweis* formed the core of the community. Ding *et al.* (2000: 218) comment that a number of writers have suggested that the iron rice-bowl encouraged a high degree of 'organisational dependency'. They argue that organisational dependency is a deep-seated feature of the Chinese system, and that it has encouraged attitudes and behaviours that are difficult to change. The implications of organisational dependency interlinked with many of the HR issues that are discussed below.

China's industrial production was dominated by state-owned enterprises. These accounted for 80 per cent of industrial production in 1978 (Warner, 1997). Under the full employment system that emerged, the dismissal of workers was allowed only if a worker had committed 'gross negligence', but this term was open to interpretation, and the sanction was rarely used even if the individuals concerned were undisciplined. In order to avoid the problems that are associated with unemployment, a system of 'featherbedding' was used, which resulted in enterprises that were overstaffed, with low levels of productivity (Child, 1994). Wages were based on seniority, and there was no real incentive for employees to strive for promotion. There was no concept of a labour market, and individuals were not allowed to move within China to 'follow work'. Trade unions existed, but had a different role from their Western counterparts:

> The All China Federation of Trade Unions (ACFTU) were assigned two functions: by top-down transmission, mobilisation of workers for labour production on behalf of the State, and by bottom-up transmission, protection of workers' rights and interests.
>
> (Chan, quoted in Warner, 1997: 37)

Therefore, the union role centred on production and welfare issues. They would not be involved in negotiations on pay and conditions, as would be the norm in Western countries.

What are the key characteristics associated with the 'iron rice-bowl'? What behaviours did it encourage? Identify some of the key HR issues related to this period.

Post-1976: 'Socialism with Chinese characteristics'

After the death of Mao Zedong in 1976, Deng Xiaoping assumed power in China. Under his leadership China embarked on an economic reform programme. This included the commencement of an 'open door' policy in which international trade and the influx of foreign technology were encouraged. From the early 1980s onwards China allowed joint ventures to operate and from this point, foreign invested enterprises (FIEs) became widespread. Foreign companies provided technology and managerial knowledge (Ding *et al.*, 2000). In 1982 Deng Xiaoping coined the phrase 'socialism with Chinese characteristics' to describe this approach to economic reform.

In 1999 the government amended the constitution to formally recognise the concept of private ownership. Employment in the private sector rose from 150,000 to 32.3 million in the period from 1980 to 1999 (Montagnon, 1999a). FIEs were important in terms of providing employment, technology and modern management techniques.

The process of modernisation has not been painless. One of the key problems was that the state-owned enterprises (SOEs) were overmanned and underinvested. Reports suggest that the number of bankruptcies in the PRC rose from 98 in 1989 to 8939 in 2001 and approximately 60 per cent of these were in SOEs (Thornhill, 2002a). In the period between 1998 and 2001, 25 million employees lost their jobs in SOEs. In 2002, 150,000 SOEs remained, employing 50 million workers and these numbers had fallen to 36 million by 2005. Workers in the SOEs had been socialised into the iron rice-bowl mentality, in which they expected that the organisation would provide cradle-to-grave employment and welfare. One of the aims of the modernisation programme was to move away from this. In 1992 personnel legislation was introduced that became known as the *three systems reforms*. The three key areas were: the introduction of labour contracts, performance-related rewards, and social insurance reforms. Warner (1996) provides a useful summary of the key differences between the traditional system and the emerging system of labour reforms within China (see Table 16.1).

The 1994 Labour Law provided a further spur to the modernisation. It aimed to provide regulation for 'a labour system compatible with a social market economy' (Warner, 1997: 33). The law covered a variety of issues, including the right for workers to choose jobs, equal opportunities, minimum wage levels, directives on working hours, and provisions for dispute handling and resolution. Warner comments that one of the implications of the 1994 Labour Law was that the distribution of power would be readjusted so that the trade unions could have more autonomy from the state.

The process of modernisation has meant that there is no longer a 'job for life'. Other aspects of the iron rice-bowl are also beginning to wane. From 1998 the *danweis* were no longer allowed to allocate subsidised housing, and allowances for education and medical support were slowly being reduced (Kynge, 1999). The modernisation programme led to SOEs being restructured and downsized. It was estimated that SOEs had 20 million employees excess to requirements in 1999 (Montagnon, 1999a) and Ministry of Labour and Social Security figures indicate that 21 million SOE workers were laid off between 1994 and 2005 (Anon. 2007). Mok *et al.* (2002: 411) found that a 'strong sense of destitution and betrayal [was] experienced by most state workers who used to be the "labour aristocracy" in China'. They go on to note that the sense of inequity has been fanned by the media attention that has focused upon successful millionaires. There is a concern that unemployed workers from the SOEs may not pass easily into the labour market – and while the state and local governments have created various mechanisms to try to encourage re-employment (for example, re-employment centres and redeployment contracts when SOEs were sold) estimates indicate that only around 30 per cent of SOE workers were redeployed via official channels (Anon., 2007). Evidence of worker unrest is emerging; for example, 216,750 strikes and demonstrations involving 3.5 million workers were recorded in 1998. Within this number, there were some instances of violence and 78 deaths occurred (Mok *et al.*, 2002).

The government has set up a system of social security. The cost of the social security bill rose by 23 per cent in 1998, and unemployment rose from 3.1 per cent in 1998 to 5.5 per cent

Table 16.1 Summary of the differences in characteristics of the labour-management reforms

System characteristic	Status quo	Experimental
1 Strategy	Hard-line	Reformist
2 Employment	Iron rice-bowl	Labour market
3 Conditions	Job security	Labour contracts
4 Mobility	Job assignment	Job choice
5 Rewards	Egalitarian	Meritocratic
6 Wage system	Grade based	Performance based
7 Promotion	Seniority	Skill-related
8 Union role	Consultative	Coordinative
9 Management	Economic cadres	Professional managers
10 Factory party-role	Central	Ancillary
11 Work organisation	Taylorist	Flexible
12 Efficiency	Technical	Allocative

Source: Warner (1996: 33).

in 1999 (Montagnon, 1999a). More recently, unemployment figures have risen sharply as a result of the global economic crisis and were expected to run at 9 per cent by 2009 (*Financial Times*, 28 November 2008)). Clearly, unemployment will remain as a key concern for some time to come, partly due to levels of surplus labour within the SOEs, but also because of the general economic downturn. Indeed, one of the features of China's economic boom was the movement of migrant workers from rural areas to the cities (Glover and Siu, 2000). Some have noted the potential for further unrest in the cities as migrant workers become laid off – particularly if such workers are unable to return home (for example, if they have leased their land etc). Some have predicted that there will be 'a spike in localised riots resulting in the mobilisation of armed police all over the country' (Branigan, 2009). A process of modernisation is taking place, but the size and historical development of China mean that this is a slow process. We will return to some of these issues as the chapter progresses. Overall, the legacy of the iron rice-bowl is still apparent, and complete reform is still a long way off.

STOP and think

Identify key strengths and weaknesses in the Chinese economy. What human resource issues emerge from this context?

HRM with 'Chinese characteristics'?

Economic reforms in China have allowed the influx of foreign interests and have set a new context in which both indigenous Chinese and foreign invested companies manage the employment relationship. There is a debate as to whether employment systems in the Asian bloc are converging towards common approaches to HRM or, alternatively, whether they are becoming more divergent as time goes by. Some have argued that an Asian model of HRM exists. The Asian model has been characterised by: non-adversarial relationships; low union density, or unions (as in China) that are closely controlled by the state; and low instances of overt industrial conflict. However, as we have already noted, academics are now beginning to appreciate that the Asian bloc is far from homogeneous, and differences in IR/HRM systems reflect different national histories and cultures (Leggett and Bamber, 1996; Rowley, 1997; Warner, 2000). Part of the remit of this section is to explore the extent to which employment systems in China are becoming more 'Westernised'. This seems possible for two main reasons: first, the high levels of foreign investment in the country, and second, the fact that the modernisation programme has increasingly subjected the SOEs in particular to the logic of the market.

The debate regarding the extent to which Chinese enterprises are adopting HRM is a problematic one. Academic perspectives on this issue relate back to the wider debate about the nature of HRM itself. Child (1994: 157) questions the extent to which one can utilise the term 'HRM' as a descriptor for the management of personnel in Chinese enterprises:

> Although definitions of personnel management and human resource management vary considerably, modern Western thinking tends to be predicated upon assumptions such as the primary contribution of competent and motivated people to a firm's success, the compatibility of individual and corporate interests, the importance of developing a corporate culture which is in tune with top management's strategy for the firm, and the responsibility of senior management rather than employees' own representative bodies for determining personnel practices. It attaches importance to systematic recruitment and selection, training and development (including socialisation into corporate culture), close attention to motivation through personal involvement and participation in work and its organisation, appraisal and progression procedures and incentive schemes . . . This concept of human resource management is not found in Chinese enterprises.

Therefore, authors such as Child believe that the term 'HRM' is unsuitable as an analytical model for use in the Chinese context. Others, however, are explicitly using mainstream HRM models in order to analyse human resource issues within China (Ahlstrom *et al.*, 2005; Zhu and Warner, 2004). For example, Benson and Zhu (1999) use Storey's model of HRM, which identifies four key elements of HRM (beliefs and assumptions, strategic aspects, management role and key levers), in order to evaluate the extent to which six SOEs were adopting HRM practices. They refute Child's assertion that the concept of HRM is not found within Chinese enterprises. By reference to the Storey model, they conclude that there were three models of HRM within their sample. The first model was a minimalist approach, in which two of the SOEs had made few attempts to adopt an HRM approach. The second model was one in which two companies had attempted to adopt an HRM paradigm. Part of this was related to the fact that both of these companies were relatively small, and had strong connections with foreign companies via joint ventures or contracting arrangements. The third model represented a transitional stage between the old and the new. Benson and Zhu argue that there is evidence that some enterprises had developed the concept of and practices associated with HRM, and the extent to which this had happened depended upon factors such as market forces and changes in legislation. Their evidence does not, however, suggest that HRM is the dominant paradigm, and they acknowledge that factors such as China's historical development and cultural traditions can act as a barrier to the development of a Western model of HRM.

Clearly, the extent to which China is adopting an 'HRM' approach is a matter of some debate. The evidence suggests that some enterprises may be adopting some of the practices that are associated with Western models of HRM, but full-blown models are not widespread. Some authors have focused upon the linkages between HRM and organisational performance within the Chinese context. Bjorkman and Xiucheng (2002), for example, found some support for the notion that organisational performance appeared to be positively influenced where companies had a strong integration between HRM and strategy. They also suggested positive relationships between performance-based rewards, individual performance appraisal and organisational performance. They do, however, acknowledge the relatively small size of their sample and the relative lack of understanding at present about the intervening variables that 'knit together' HRM and organisational performance. The following sections will review some of the evidence regarding different aspects of contemporary HR/personnel practice within China.

Employment contracts, surplus labour, social insurance and labour market concerns

Part of the modernisation process has included the shift to a more decentralised and flexible labour market. Indeed Zhu and Warner (2005: 360) comment that the Chinese labour market is still in a 'nascent' state. The employment contract system was formally implemented in 1986 and it gave employers the ability to hire employees on contracts that specified the terms of employment. Under this system, enterprises were able to downsize and remove problematic employees (Ding and Warner, 1999). The drive to modernise the labour market was further progressed by the provision of subsequent legislation such as the personnel legislation of 1992 and the 1994 Labour Law. This meant that both individual and collective labour contracts could be set up. The collective contracts would cover employees belonging to an enterprise, and would be arranged via the trade union. Collective contracts would cover areas such as pay and conditions, working hours, holidays and welfare (Ding and Warner, 1999: 249).

New labour legislation entitled *The Labor Contract Law of the Peoples Republic of China* came into effect in January 2008. One of the key points is that the legislation emphasises the protection of employees' interests. For example, it requires employers to produce a written contract of employment, puts more constraints upon labour contract termination by employers, includes provisions for severance pay if a labour contract is terminated early, and specifies rules for collective bargaining and dealing with part-time employees (Anon., 2008b)

Social insurance is emerging as a critical issue in China. As highlighted, one outcome of the reform programme has been that a substantial number of redundancies have been made and 21 million SOE workers were laid off between 1994 and 2005 (Anon., 2007). Prior to the economic reforms, the enterprise took responsibility for welfare issues such as pensions and medical cover. Since the reforms, the government has had to set up a system of social insurance. The funds for social insurance are contributed to by the state, the enterprise and individual employees (Ding and Warner, 1999). Social insurance is designed to act as a safety net, particularly for employees who are made redundant. One of the issues that China will have to deal with is the rising cost of social insurance (Montagnon, 1999a) and there is some concern that the social security fund will not be strong enough to support claims from it. The reasons for this include that: the system is fairly new and as a result, a mass of contributions has not built up; many retirees did not make contributions into the scheme, but are now drawing from it; SOEs that have closed no longer make contributions for their employees and the government did not make enough compensation for employees who were employed during the centrally planned period (Zhu and Warner, 2005: 363). It has been estimated that the cost of moving towards a fully funded pension system by 2030 could reach Rmb 3000 billion (Thornhill, 2002a). Zhu and Warner (2005) comment that the problem is likely to be exacerbated in the future (by the ageing population) and that the government will have to consider injecting more money into the social security fund. However, the government is actively considering this issue and it is anticipated that it will pass a new Social Security Law in 2009. As well as concerns about the levels of social security cover, there is a fear of further social unrest resulting from mass redundancies (Mok *et al.*, 2002; Branigan, 2009).

In addition to concerns about social security, there are tensions in respect of general labour market issues. Generally, there is a shortage of skilled labour and an oversupply of unskilled labour in China – the latter has been exacerbated by the global economic downturn (with particular concerns already noted about migrant labour). Zhu and Warner (2005) identify a number of key labour market concerns. First, the imbalance in the labour market is likely to lead to increased competition for qualified workers between domestic private enterprises (DPEs), SOEs and foreign-owned enterprises. Second, FDI has tended to flow into the coastal regions and large cities (and that this has been accelerated by WTO accession). This has led to regional disparities in terms of 'employment opportunity, income and engagements with a global economy' (2005: 360). They comment that while the government has a policy to develop the western regions, so far there has been limited foreign investment in these areas and that this is likely to lead to more domestic political tensions. Third, there is a growing income gap between the top 20 per cent and bottom 20 per cent of the population. Fourth, a large unregulated labour market of internal migrant workers exists and this 'floating population' generally does not have proper registration or work permits and in this way has less protection against poor working conditions and exploitation. For example, it was estimated that there were 42 million migrant workers in Guangdong – larger than the population of Poland (Harney, 2005). Fifth, the move from workers being regarded (in state rhetoric) as 'masters' of SOEs to 'employer and manager' relationships will require adjustment and 'competition and insecurity among employees have become even more serious since China's WTO accession' (Zhu and Warner, 2005: 361). Overall, the economic downturn has exacerbated underlying labour market problems – with particular concerns around migrant labour and recent graduates (who are not well covered by the unemployment benefits programme (World Bank, March 2009).

Recruitment, selection and training

One of the impacts of the reforms has been that there is now greater mobility within the labour market. Prior to the reforms, workers were assigned to firms from labour bureaus.

This often meant that workers were assigned even when they did not hold the requisite skill and knowledge for the job. There is greater labour mobility now, but some studies indicate that mobility remains low for shopfloor workers (Tsang, 1994; Ding and Warner, 1999; Benson *et al.*, 2000) and as noted, a recent phenomenon has been the surge in numbers of unregistered migrant workers. Table 16.2 demonstrates the continuing role of external agencies in the recruitment process.

There is contrasting evidence in respect of recruitment and selection practices in China. For example, Zhu and Dowling (2002) found that recruitment and selection were becoming less influenced by political bureaucracy and more by economic and market concerns. For example, there was more emphasis on personal competency as a criterion, rather than an individual's political background. This trend was more evident within foreign invested enterprises. In contrast, Ahlstrom *et al.* (2005) revealed fascinating insights into how personal networks and connections affected recruitment and selection practices in 16 foreign firms in China. They found, for example, that managers perceived potential benefits in strategic 'overstaffing'. The reason for this was to curry favour with local government officials by taking on workers from SOEs that were downsizing. In effect, if companies took on additional staff they could expect to 'negotiate some reciprocal benefits from the local government' (2005: 272), for example, a more helpful approach in respect of property deals. Managers also reported that recruiting members from retrenching SOEs could also bring useful industry contacts, for example, an SOE could be a customer of the foreign firm and deals could be lubricated by networks of personal contacts. This was particularly the case in respect of senior positions. The selection of well-connected individuals to management teams and boards of directors was seen as a paramount issue by some firms (not only to lubricate deals but also to impart knowledge about local rules and regulations so that the company could understand which rules had to be complied with). Finally, the study found that it was not unusual for companies to ask prospective employees for their list of connections with key officials and that, 'by hiring such connected individuals, firms ensure that they have a voice as officials at various levels and in different regions help to overcome difficulties' (2005: 277). This shows that *guanxi* (a concept relating to relationships outside a person's immediate family (Child, 1994: 30)) continues to affect the processes such as recruitment and selection and it is a subject that we return to below.

One of the HR problems confronting China is the huge scale of training and development that is needed to ensure that industry and commerce can continue to develop. China has a

Table 16.2 Multiple recruitment methods in state-owned enterprises (SOEs) and joint ventures (JVs)

	SOEs N = 12	JVs N = 11
Sources for recruiting workers		
Secondary/technical school	11 (92%)	7 (64%)
Allocated by labour bureau	9 (75%)	2 (18%)
Labour market	7 (58%)	9 (82%)
Transferred from Chinese partner firm	NA	3 (27%)
Internal recruitment	2 (17%)	NA
Sources for recruiting managers		
Promoted from within the firm	12 (100%)	11 (100%)
Appointment by superior government body	7 (58%)	11 (100%)
Open recruitment	4 (33%)	7 (64%)
Appointed by parent firm	0	3 (27%)
University graduates	0	1 (9%)

Source: Ding and Warner (1999: 247).

large pool of unskilled and semi-skilled labour from which to draw, but there is a dearth of managerial employees and engineers with the skills and knowledge that modern industry and commerce require (Ding and Warner, 1999). Warner (1992) suggests that this stems from two key factors. First, education and development were severely disrupted during the Cultural Revolution; for example, management development and training were banned during this period. The lack of effective training and development meant that there was a lack of educated managers and engineers, and the legacy of this still remains today. Second, the speed of economic development in China (incredibly rapid until Autumn 2008) meant that there has been a great demand for educated, skilled staff. The state has responded by encouraging the development of an infrastructure for management development and training (Child, 1994). However, Gronewald (2008) observes that of the 1.5 to 2 million university graduates, only a small percentage have qualifications in business related subjects and McKinsey have estimated that only 10 per cent of graduates could be immediately deployed to international businesses (Groenewald, 2008: 132). In addition, evidence suggests that there remains a lack of systematic training within companies. Foreign investors in joint ventures (JVs) can find that Chinese partners often request an enormous amount of overseas training for indigenous employees. Training and development issues are likely to remain as continuing concerns for the future within China (Glover and Siu, 2000).

Reward systems and employee relations

The review above has highlighted some of the changes in relation to reward systems. The seniority-based flat rate system is now being replaced by systems that often have some link to performance. Wages were determined by legislation and regional agencies until the mid-1980s, and seniority was the most important factor in terms of employee earnings, but other aspects were entering the equation by the mid 1990s. Factors such as responsibility and qualifications have started to be taken into account (Benson *et al.*, 2000). However, the evidence remains that SOEs are often unwilling to increase wage differentials. State enterprises have tended to pay equal bonuses to all employees regardless of the performance of individual employees. They have also retained a great degree of harmonisation of work conditions (Benson *et al.*, 2000). This appears to be an example of the way in which the principle of equality has endured post-Mao.

From around 2004 until mid 2008 reports indicated that the labour market was extremely tight and companies experienced labour shortages. As a result, salary and wage levels surged (but started from a very low base for some!), indeed there were some reports of 40 per cent increases in salaries during 2005 (Roberts, 2006). Many companies experienced high labour turnover – for example, turnover in multinationals averaged 14 per cent in 2005. One of the outcomes of the situation was that companies were not only boosting wages but were also having to improve living conditions for workers and Roberts (2006) reported that it was no longer sufficient to expect workers to work 12 hour days, 7 days a week and to be accommodated in 8 to a room dormitories. The onset of the economic crisis will doubtless feed in and it is likely that the level of pay increases will abate (at least until the economic crisis begins to ease).

In summary, whilst there have been overall moves to increase flexibility within reward systems and linkages between pay and performance, some aspects of the old system endure, including the reluctance of SOEs to penalise poor performers (Benson *et al.*, 2000).

The discussion will now turn to employee relations. Trade unions have historically tended to play a different role within Chinese enterprises (compared with Western counterparts) and have tended to concentrate on welfare issues and assisting in production issues. Benson *et al.* (2000) comment that trade unions were traditionally 'relegated' to the role of 'watchdog' over issues such as health and safety and workers' rights. In addition, unions have historically been more 'pro-management' than 'pro-labour' in the private sector, partly due to management involvement in the leadership selection processes. However, there are some signs that changes are beginning to happen. Zhu and Warner (2005) observe that the role of trade unions seems to have been strengthened in some ways since the accession to the WTO. For example, the All China Federation of Trade Unions (ACFTU) has been involved in establishing a 'tripartite negotiation system' at national level, as such legitimising the role of trade unions in protecting the economic interests of employees and representing them at state level. The first National Tripartite Committee was held in 2001 and contained representatives from the Ministry of Labour and Social Security, the China Enterprises Association and the ACFTU.

Zhu and Warner (2005) also observe that union activities are changing at enterprise level and in addition to their traditional welfare role trade unions are becoming involved in issues around lay-offs, re-employment and dispute settlement. However, downsizing in the SOEs has also affected union numbers and FOEs as DPEs tend to be less unionised. Indeed, Zhu and Warner observe that management in the private sector enjoy 'extraordinary powers' over employment relations issues 'without being greatly concerned about workers' rights in those non-union enterprises' (2005: 361). However, the 'Labour Contract Law of the Peoples Republic of China' which came into effect in 2008, now offers more protection (given that one of its aims is to protect employees' interests) – indeed, it has been called 'the biggest change in Chinese labour law in the reform period' (Anon., 2008b).

Despite the fact that the state remains a powerful hegemonic force, Zhu and Warner (2004: 314) comment that

> . . . there are indications that the party/state also makes compromises from time to time in order to gain support from the masses, in particular through institutions such as ACFTU. The revision of trade union law in 2001, promoting tripartite negotiation system by recognising the legitimate role of the ACFTU, developing a national social security network (which has faced huge difficulties), and encouraging new investment and the creation of employment opportunities are some of the state initiatives.

The New Labour Contract Law could be added to the list. Lee Cooke (2002: 22) observes that China is 'plagued by large-scale unemployment, low skills, low investment, management prerogatives and ineffective institutional intervention' and that the repercussions for workers are severe. Developments in respect of a tripartite system of control should help institutionalise industrial relations and legitimise the participation of groups such as trade unions – but overall it is likely that the state will seek to retain a high degree of control for the foreseeable future.

The preceding review has given an overview of the current situation in key areas such as employee resourcing, development and relations. It seems that China is beginning to use techniques that are derived from Western and Japanese practices. However, the full-scale adoption of Western-style techniques is unlikely, at least in the short term, as these would be incongruent with Chinese culture and the historical development of their business traditions. The following section will highlight some of the issues that impact upon the management of people in China.

STOP and think

- *Why has the number of redundancies increased in China in recent years?*
- *Why is training and development likely to be a key issue in years to come?*
- *What are some of the key trends in terms of rewarding employees in China?*

Some issues influencing HRM in China

Culture

This section will provide an overview of some of the issues that influence the management of people in China. These include the impact of culture, the lack of managerial skills, problems of labour discipline, and dealing with low motivation. Warner (2000) has noted that a great deal of divergence remains within the Asian bloc, and that one of the explanatory variables for this is the impact of national cultures upon human resource systems. Culture is a notoriously difficult concept to define, and it is hard to make broad generalisations that would fit all individuals and groups within a particular country. China, for example, comprises a huge land mass, and many argue that one can find differences in culture between people from the north compared with those of the south. For example, northern Chinese tend to speak Mandarin, while many southerners speak Cantonese. However, it is useful to outline some of the features that are associated with Chinese culture, in order to understand some of the HR issues that are affecting both SOEs and FIEs.

Child (1994: 28–32) provides an overview of some of the key aspects of Chinese culture. He points out that there is a degree of agreement that Confucianism is the basis for many Chinese traditions. An understanding of Confucianism does help one to understand certain values, attitudes and behaviours within the Chinese context. Fan (1995) suggests that Confucian ideologies are relevant to contemporary studies for four main reasons:

- Confucian ideology has become firmly rooted as an 'undeniable' system that governs many aspects of Chinese lives;
- thousands of years of a feudalistic system have dominated the Chinese view of themselves and the world;
- to gain acceptance in China, new ideas have to be proved to be compatible with classics and tradition;
- the current economic reforms are not necessarily changing Chinese people's fundamental mentality or behaviour.

Kong Fu Ze (551–479 BC) was called Confucius by Jesuit missionaries. His philosophy on life became popular some 300 years later. The fifth Han Emperor, Wu, found that Confucian ideologies fitted well with the need to create a strong, centralised monarchy. Confucianism emphasised a respect for elders and the family, order, hierarchy, and a sense of duty. Confucius believed that individuals had a fixed position in society, and that social harmony could be achieved when individuals behaved according to rank (Jacobs *et al.*, 1995). There was an emphasis upon the 'correct and well-mannered conduct of one's duties, based upon a sound respect for the social conventions of a patrimonial society' (Child, 1994: 29). Age was respected, particularly in the case of male elders.

Child quotes Lockett (1988), who identified four values that are central to Chinese culture, and which are based upon Confucian ideologies:

- respect for age and hierarchy;
- orientation towards groups;
- the preservation of 'face';
- the importance of relationships.

'Face' is an important concept, and it relates to a person's social standing, position and moral character. Child (1994: 30) comments that the Chinese attach great importance to how they are viewed by others. 'Face' means that conflicts within a group would be kept private, as the group would be demeaned in the eyes of the wider community if conflict were overt. The importance of relationships is captured in the concept known as *guanxi*. Luo and Chen (1997: 1) note that '*guanxi* refers to the concept of drawing on connections or networks to secure favours in personal or business relations'. The concepts of *guanxi* and 'face' are intertwined, and some have argued that they can act as inhibitors to the modernisation programme (Chen, 1995).

The preceding paragraphs have given a short overview of a complex subject. There is much evidence that FIEs often find it difficult to operate within China, and that some of the problems are caused by a lack of appreciation of Chinese culture (Chow, 2004). The examples quoted have highlighted some of the underlying tensions that have developed between foreign and Chinese partners. Peng (1994) has commented that foreign investors have complained that Chinese managers lack initiative, are unwilling to delegate, and are perceived to be unsystematic. Lockett (1988) argues that such behaviours reflect aspects of Chinese culture: for example, he reminds us that during the Cultural Revolution managers were promoted according to Party allegiance rather than on the basis of merit. He argues that this legacy has hampered the level of management skill in China. The tendency towards collective rather than individual orientation often leads to behaviours that clash with the behaviours expected by foreign counterparts. Chinese managers will often avoid taking individual responsibility, and Child (1994) argues that this is due to a combination of Chinese traditions and the Cultural Revolution. On the other hand, Jacobs *et al.* (1995) argue that there is too much emphasis upon the negative implications of Chinese culture and that Confucian-based philosophies can lead to positive outcomes in the workplac, because of the emphasis upon 'diligence, responsibility, thrift, promptness, cooperation and learning' (p. 33). More research is needed in order to evaluate the impact of Chinese culture upon business performance.

Management skills, labour discipline and motivation

As highlighted, one of the issues affecting China today is a dearth of appropriate management skills. Tsang (1994) argues that the lack of skills relates to four main factors. First, the Cultural Revolution severely disrupted education, training and development. Second, central planning meant that managers had little autonomy. For example, all products were sold to the state at a predetermined price. Therefore managers did not have the scope to develop entrepreneurial skills. Third, mistakes were severely penalised, but achievements were not rewarded. Fourth, important decisions were made by collective consensus, managers saw themselves as an information conduits' and individuals were unwilling to take risky decisions (relating back to the danger of losing face). Again, these behaviours relate back to a combination of Confucian ideology and the legacy of the Cultural Revolution. The development of adequate levels of managerial skill is likely to remain as a key issue for the future.

Two linked issues are the problems of labour discipline and low motivation. Evidence suggests that Chinese managers are often unwilling to discipline staff, as they prefer to avoid overt conflict and maintain harmony (Tsang, 1994). While Chinese culture emphasises the importance of hard work and diligence, the system of featherbedding in SOEs meant that the enterprises were overstaffed and productivity was low. Tsang quotes from the *China Daily*:

> Labour discipline in our enterprises is very lax. Some workers don't work eight hours a day, a few are absent for a long time to engage in speculation and profiteering. Others even turn to street brawling and stealing of state property. There are also technically incompetent people who do not seek improvement, but just drift along, wasting their own and other people's time.
>
> (Tsang, 1994: 5)

This comment reflects the fact that China is going through the equivalent of an industrial revolution, in that many workers are being drawn from agricultural work to factory work. The problems highlighted above are reminiscent of those that faced nations such as the USA, Japan and the United Kingdom as they went through their own industrial revolutions and sought to find ways in which to control and motivate agricultural/migrant workers (Zuboff, 1988; Buchanan and Huczynski, 1997).

Glover and Siu (2000) have pointed out that foreign invested enterprises (FIEs) based in southern China often employ migrant workers from the north, whose numbers have grown dramatically (Harney, 2005). Their case study evidence suggested that the main aim of the migrant workers was to accumulate money and return home as quickly as possible. For this reason, they were not motivated by the prospect of career development, had a purely instrumental attachment to the company, and no real stake in the long-term prosperity of the firm. It is also important to point out that part of the attraction of the joint venture was that the company could take advantage of the low pay levels in China. In other words, the company was also operating in an instrumental way in respect of its use of manual labour in China. Glover and Siu identify a range of problems that were being encountered by the company, many of which were related to human resources issues. Burrell (1997) argues that although many of the world's workers are, in fact, peasants, traditional organisational theory has ignored this, leading to a lack of knowledge and understanding about the motivations and aspirations of a numerically significant group of workers.

How might an understanding of Chinese culture and traditions help FIEs when setting up new businesses in China?

Hong Kong: economic growth and HRM

It is relevant to refer to Hong Kong separately here, as it has a different history from that of mainland China. Hong Kong has a relatively small land mass of 1095 square kilometres. It has an estimated population of 6,687,200. It enjoyed rapid economic growth until the Asian crisis of 1997–98 when the economy dipped and unemployment rose. This was followed by an upturn during 2003–07 and although the economy has been affected by the current world recession, projected growth of GNP for 2008–09 was still strong by the standards of Western economies (see below, p. 623). This section will give a short review of Hong Kong's historical development, and will highlight some of the issues that face the territory after its reunification with China.

Hong Kong became a British colony in 1843. The British wanted to secure a base from which to trade. Initially, one of the key exports to China was opium, which proved to be a lucrative business for the British. Drug taking was illegal, but there was a high demand for opium within China in the mid- to late 1800s. The Japanese invaded China and subsequently Hong Kong in the Second World War, and occupied Hong Kong between 1941 and 1945. They surrendered in 1945. The Communist Party came to power in China in 1949, and this provoked a wave of migration from China to Hong Kong. Many of the immigrants were traders and businessmen. Many had fought against the Communists during the civil wars in China, and tensions remained between the two factions. Hong Kong became wealthy in the period after the Second World War. Central to its success were the Asian 'tycoons', many of whom were immigrants who had left mainland China in 1949–50. The tycoons preferred to work with family members or close contacts, relating back to the Chinese concept of *guanxi*. However, there is an argument that Hong Kong will slowly move away from its patriarchal culture. Four main reasons have been highlighted. First, the first generation of Chinese businessmen are preparing to hand over to their children, many of whom have been educated in the West. Second, the financial crisis of 1997–98 made the businesses more reliant on Western capital. Third, the internet may pose a threat to more traditional ways of doing business in Hong Kong. Finally, Asia's maturing legal and financial framework may undermine the influence of Chinese networks overseas (Anon., 2000a).

Hong Kong was under British sovereignty until 1997. As a result, it developed a capitalist business system that was influenced by Chinese culture and traditions. Sovereignty was handed back to mainland China in 1997 and China adopted a 'one country, two systems' approach in terms of Hong Kong, which became a Special Administrative Region (SAR) with agreement that it would maintain its legal system and capitalist approach for at least 50 years. There were many concerns that the agreement would not protect the democratic rights of the people of Hong Kong, or that reunification would affect the economic progress of Hong Kong. In the event, the handover appeared to run smoothly. Hong Kong now has an executive-led, non-elected government and a legislative council (elected by universal suffrage). The system has not been without its problems, and Hong Kong must decide in 2008 whether or not it wishes to move to a fully elected government (*Financial Times*, 1999).

Hong Kong's economy was badly hit by the Asian economic crisis. GDP growth fell by 5.1 per cent in 1998 and by 1.5 per cent in 1999. Unemployment levels rose from 4.7 per cent in 1998 to 7 per cent in 1999 (*Financial Times*, 1999). Indeed, when South Korea, Singapore and the Philippines began to emerge from the Asian crisis, Hong Kong's GDP continued to fall. After 1997, Hong Kong began to be regarded as having an uncompetitive cost base (for reasons including high property values, high property rental prices, high service charges at ports and airports and spiralling wage levels within the territory without concomitant increases in productivity (Lucas, 1999a). Hong Kong's economy experienced two economic slowdowns in the five-year period from 1997/8 to 2002 (Leahy, 2002). During this period, property prices fell by 65 per cent and this contributed to a four-year period of deflation. In addition, unemployment rose and hit 7.8 per cent in 2002 (Leahy, 2002). Large companies, including Motorola, the Bank of Asia and Swire Pacific, continued to shed staff (Grammaticas, 2002). Hong Kong's ports continued to lose market share to mainland China by 2002, but air cargo exports rose and tourist arrivals increased in 2002.

Hong Kong's economy did rebound and GDP rose by 8.6 per cent in 2004, 7.3 per cent in 2005 and 6.4 per cent in 2007 (Anon., 2008a). Unemployment hit a peak of almost 9 per cent in 2003, but fell back to 5.6 per cent in 2005. Exports grew by 11.4 per cent in 2005 and the major export markets were the Chinese mainland (45 per cent), the US (16 per cent), the EU (15 per cent) and Japan (5 per cent) (Hong Kong Trade Development Council, 2006). The UNCTAD World Investment Report indicated that Hong Kong was the second largest recipient of inward foreign direct investment (FDI) in Asia and the seventh in the world in 2004. However, Hong Kong has also been hit by the global economic downturn and exports fell to their lowest level since 2002 in October 2008 (Anon., 2008a). The government reduced their growth forecasts for 2008 from 4–5 per cent to 3–3.5 per cent and unemployment was expected to run at around 4.6 per cent in January 2009 (Anon., 2008a; Chan, 2008).

Hong Kong has acted in recent years as 'a 'half-way' house between a modern Western business society and the mainland China context' (Selmer *et al.*, 2000: 237). However, this role may diminish as the process of modernisation and openness in China continues to develop. Some of the specific HR issues include the fact that historically, Hong Kong had strictly limited the importation of labour. Businesses were allowed to import construction workers and domestic help, but it was difficult to import potential managers (Fields *et al.*, 2000). However, this was recognised as a problem and as a result the government relaxed the rules making it easier for foreigners to work in Hong Kong from 2006. Some studies have suggested that labour turnover among educated workers and managers tends to be high and can pose a problem for Hong Kong businesses. Some companies are placing more emphasis upon internal development and promotion to try to alleviate this problem. Fields *et al.* (2000) found that retention rates were higher in these cases. However, an adequate supply of skilled managers will be critical for Hong Kong's future, especially in the information technology sector.

Improving human capital remains a key issue for Hong Kong (Chan, 2008). Fields *et al.* (2000) found, for example, that some companies were reluctant to invest in training, and this was possibly linked to the problem of 'job-hopping' in Hong Kong. In addition, evidence suggests that training budgets tend to be cut in periods of economic slowdown (Chu and Siu, 2001) so there is further potential for investment in training to fall as a result of the economic slowdown.

This short review has highlighted some of the key differences in the historical and economic context of Hong Kong. It is clear that differences remain between the system in Hong Kong and that of its mainland counterpart. It is also clear that Hong Kong's role of 'middle-man' between the West and the East may be further compromised as China continues to modernise.

STOP and think

What are the current challenges for Hong Kong's economy?

India

Introduction

India is one of the largest democracies in the world with a strategic location in South Asia. Spread over 3.3 million square kilometers with a population of over a billion, it shares international borders with eight countries. India is a secular, sovereign, socialist, democratic republic with a parliamentary form of government. Comprising twenty-five states and seven Union territories, it is home to all main religions of the world and has sixteen officially recognised languages, over 150 other languages and more than 500 dialects. Hindi and English are the two official languages. The multi-ethnic, multi-lingual and multi-religious nature of the Indian society is both its asset and its challenge.

Today, India is the second fastest growing economy in the world with an average annual growth rate of 8.8 per cent (see Figure 16.1). Services, which contribute more than half of GDP, have grown fastest, especially computer-services firms such as Infosys, TCS and Wipro. Indian manufacturing has also done well as is evident in the pharmaceutical sector and in the launch by Tata Motors of an ultra-cheap family car, the Nano.

After undertaking economic reforms in the 1990s, India has increasingly moved towards external trade liberalisation and efforts to attract foreign direct investment, marketing itself as a large market with a vast labour force. Its major trading partners are China, USA, UAE, UK, Japan and the European Union. That India has one of the largest English-speaking populations in the Asia-Pacific region with a high level of skill in engineering, computing and software is a significant reason for its attraction to investors. It is also one of the largest exporters of skilled migrants in areas of software engineering and financial services. At the other end of the spectrum, it offers a massive pool of readily available cheap labour.

As the second-most favoured destination for foreign direct investment (FDI) in the world after China, the US, South Korea, Japan and the EU are major investors in the country, with sectors such as automobiles, telecommunications and software attracting most FDI. Despite

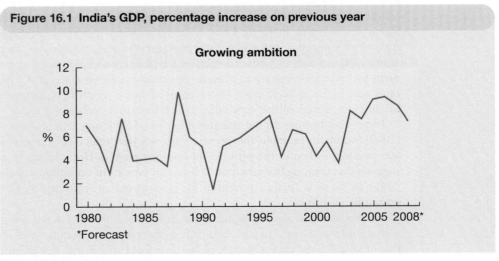

Figure 16.1 India's GDP, percentage increase on previous year

Source: CEIC data.

624

far-reaching changes to attract foreign investment, inward FDI flows, though consistently increasing, are still modest compared to China (World Investment Report, 2005). The industrial and the services sector have registered growth of around 8 per cent and an overall growth of about 7 per cent, which is good but below its potential. This is because of a number of challenges that India faces:

- the need for a more developed infrastructure;
- increasing corruption in government and politics;
- lack of adequate intellectual property protection;
- unemployment, poverty and increasing inequality;
- instability of output in agriculture and related areas;
- a low literacy rate; 57 per cent but unevenly distributed;
- lack of national consensus on the extent, nature and role of FDI in the economy.

Yet, in the current global crisis, although India is likely to face harder times, a recession should hurt it less than other emerging markets. Compared with its neighbours in Asia, it relies little on exports, which are only about 22 per cent of India's GDP, against 37 per cent of China's. Also, it relies less on foreign capital than the overstretched economies of Eastern Europe; its gross saving rate reached 37.7 per cent of GDP in the past fiscal year (*The Economist*, 2008). Moreover, Indian MNCs in information technology, pharmaceuticals and manufacturing, continue to grow and show resilience in the economic downturn. The next section outlines the economic and political trajectory of India post independence (in 1947), the ongoing transformations since the 1980s and 1990s, and India's role in the global economy with an aim to understand the nature of its business system and practices.

Approach: culture, institutions and varieties of capitalism

The debate in the business literature has been whether business systems and practices are progressively converging or national differences remain. It has been given added impetus by the developments associated with 'globalisation'. On one hand, trends towards liberalisation, deregulation and privatisation and the growth of multinational firms are ostensibly integrating and standardising work and work practices worldwide. On the other, those that question convergence argue that history, polity and culture of a country influence the route that it takes to industrialisation and the evolution of its business institutions, which remain distinctive despite global pressures towards convergence (Whitley, 1999; Hall and Soskice, 2001).

A number of studies have examined the influence of 'cultural assumptions' that shape employer–employee relations, organisational culture and managers' actions in India. Hofstede (1991) found a high power distance society marked by low to moderate uncertainty avoidance, low individualism and a low masculinity culture. This is attributed to India being a tradition-bound society that values ties of family and extended family, interpersonal relations, age, seniority and status. It is a hierarchical society segmented by caste, religion and other group affiliations and a desire for proximity to sources of power. For business, this translates into a paternalist management style in largely family owned businesses and a preference for personalised relationships rather than a performance orientation. Individuals display fear of power, obedience to superiors, tenacity, resilience, indiscipline, and a submissive, modest, unreserved and collectivist orientation. There is an unwillingness to accept organisational change, a reluctance to take risks, lack of initiative in problem solving and disinclination to accept responsibility. A 'soft work culture' and a 'nurturant–task–leadership' style employ familial, cultural and moral means at the workplace. Recruitment, rewards and career progression are through family and social networks and based on loyalty, status and political connections for both the employer and the employee (Sharma, 1984; Singh, 1990; Sinha and Sinha, 1990; Tayeb, 1988; Budhwar and Debrah, 2001; Budhwar and Khatri, 2001).

Though culture helps to explain the variation in the business environment and management practices between countries, it is difficult to measure and varies within a country and over time. Moreover, a cultural approach does not accommodate change and tends towards stereotypes (Rubery and Grimshaw, 2003; McSweeney, 2002). 'Institutions' on the other hand, are tangible and easier to study and accommodate the cultural as well as the politico-economic evolution of the country. Thus, each country has its own basis of 'competitive advantage' in its politico-economic system, legal provisions, industrial relations, training and other provisions for firms and workers in their relation with the state and society. The resultant 'varieties of capitalism' in different countries mediate the influences of global economy and multinational practices in specific ways (Lane, 1995; Whitley, 1999; Hall and Soskice, 2001). A more sophisticated approach accommodates the influences of the global economy with continued significance of societal influences and national institutions (Smith and Meiksins 1995; Rubery and Grimshaw 2003). This approach is adopted here to understand the Indian business system and human resource practices. However, it is important to remember that as a large and diverse country with a federal structure, India has sub-national variations of culture and institutions within its national context that pose a challenge to understanding the resultant sub-national variations in its human resource practices.

Activity

The preceding sections have provided an overview of India. Take a moment to think over the size and the nature of the Indian state and economy.

Questions

1 What does it tell us about its role and position in the global economy?

2 What role do culture and institutions play in understanding the Indian business system?

Route to industrialisation: from a 'mixed' to an 'open' economy

India adopted the model of a planned and mixed economy after independence in 1947 that emphasised both public and private sector. Economic planning is carried out through five-year national plans. This section outlines the evolution of Indian economic policy in a historical perspective and its influence on the business environment.

Post-colonial India inherited gross inequality and imbalances in regional development. While encouraging private initiative, government used the public sector to develop, generate employment and provide access to basic facilities in the hitherto underdeveloped areas that might not be attractive to private investment. While it aimed at a faster rate of growth the emphasis was on regulation to protect domestic industry from foreign competition and to promote self-reliance through a policy of import substitution. This was evident in the first two five-year plans:

- *First plan (1951–56).* This plan focused on agriculture to ensure self-sufficiency in food grains and to address poverty since a majority of population relied on agriculture for subsistence.

- *Second plan (1956–61).* Also known as the 'Mahalanobis' plan, the plan focused on industry and industrialisation. The main thrust of the plan was to install capacity in heavy industry. Initially successful in creating capacity and a move from a predominantly agrarian economy to one that produces a wide variety of consumer and industrial goods, reliance on regulatory mechanisms ultimately led to under-utilisation of capacities and the emergence of a licence-quota regime based on political patronage.

- *In a number of successive plans from 1961–91*, the performance progressively declined due to inflation, poverty and unemployment though there were some achievements in defence and agriculture (for details on five-year plans see Datt and Sundharam, 1999). According to Dreze and Sen (1995):

Indian economic planning offered a good illustration of horrendous over activity in controlling industries, restraining gains from trade, and blighting competitiveness; and, soporific under activity in expanding school education, public health care, social security, gender equity and land reform.

For the Indian economy the economic crisis of the 1980s meant a decline in industrial production, high rate of inflation, fiscal indiscipline and a very low level of foreign exchange reserves by 1991. A turnaround in the Indian economy came with the economic reforms of 1991. These were engendered by a globalising world economy with trends towards liberalisation and privatisation that accompanied structural adjustment programmes proposed by the World Bank and the International Monetary Fund (for an assessment of industrial development post reform see Kaplinsky, 1997).

- *Eighth plan (1992–97); Ninth plan (1997–2002).* The outcomes were deregulation and introduction of a series of economic reforms that have carried on in successive plans. The currency was devalued and new industrial, fiscal and trade policies formulated. Reforms were undertaken in the public and the banking sectors. Foreign investment was liberalised (for details on reforms see the special issue of *Columbia Journal of World Business*, 1994).

  Aware of India's comparative advantage in information and communication technology and its export potential, barriers to the entry of foreign firms and technology transfer were removed, and finance for software development through equity and venture capital was provided along with institutional interventions. A number of software technology parks and training institutes have been set up to provide infrastructural and manpower support to the industry.

- *Tenth plan (2002–07).* The tenth plan carried on the spirit of reforms of the 1990s. The Indian economy was not adversely affected by the Asian crisis of 1997–98 because of control on capital flows, on disinvestments and on full convertibility as well as continued foreign exchange remittances by migrant workers. The government has undertaken further reduction in state control and in addressing fiscal imbalance. The economy is being made more open to foreign direct investment in key sectors. Substantial reforms have been made in the financial, telecommunications and the shipping sector with increasing focus on energy infrastructure and supply. Some 51 per cent FDI is now allowed in single brand products in the retail sector and 100 per cent allowed in a number of new sectors (**www.ibef.org**).

To sum up, the historical experience of colonialism, the vision of constitution makers, and the influence of global economic changes, especially since the 1980s, all contribute to the way the Indian business system continues to evolve. The next section focuses on the nature of the Indian production and business environment.

Indian production and business environment

In the light of an uneven and unequal development, it is not surprising that the public sector dominated the Indian business environment until quite recently. It continues to be significant as the largest employer of organised labour in India and in its envisaged role as harbinger of social and economic change. It is state controlled, offers lifetime employment, places emphasis on training and seniority and displays relatively standardised and sophisticated HRD, for example in Defence and Steel. At the same time, it is also marked by excessive bureaucracy, under-utilised capacity, surplus labour, inefficient technology often associated with reduced productivity, quality and high costs – all leading to uncompetitive organisations. These factors influence recent efforts at downsizing and disinvestments in the sector.

Conversely, the private sector suffered. Though receiving some state support, excessive regulation and the licence-quota regime resulted in benefiting a few at the cost of stifling most private initiative. 'Protection' meant firms did not have the initiative to upgrade technology and training, mobilise resources or improve productivity and quality. Further, a policy of import substitution provided a captive market and removed the threat of competition for indigenous firms. Despite this, there is a strong industrial base in some areas. The management style is paternalist, with suspicious firms that rely on family, caste and community for recruitment and management. Increasingly however, there is a discernable move towards performance and merit in the management of private sector firms.

Liberalisation of policies has meant increased competition for both public and private firms from foreign ones. Privatisation has permitted entry of the private sector in areas that were hitherto reserved for the public sector, e.g. transport, telecom, banking, electricity among others. This requires them to change the infrastructure, technology, production methods and work organisation to increase productivity, improve quality and reduce costs. For corporate management, it implies a shift from protective regulation to market-driven competition that has created opportunities for resource mobilisation from new sources, expansion, diversification and internationalisation (Venkata Ratnam, 1995; Krishna and Monappa, 1994; Rao *et al.*, 1994). This is particularly evident in the large Indian conglomerates like Tatas, Reliance, Ranbaxy and the new computer firms like Infosys, Wipro and Satyam. At the same time, labour law is being liberalised and the power of trade unions is declining.

Today, the services sector is the fastest growing, with a growth rate of 7.5 per cent per annum over 1991–2000, and it provides employment to 23 per cent of the workforce. A significant development has been the growth of information communication technology, financial services, community services and software exports. Software exports have grown by over 45 per cent during the decade 1989–2000, substantially higher than the global software industry. Indian software firms include TCS, Infosys, Wipro and Silicon Automation. Business Process Outsourcing from developed economies has also seen the rise of call centres. Microsoft, Dell, Ford, GE, Oracle, Compaq, Lucent and Nortel are scaling up their operations and American Express, IBM and foreign airlines like British Airways are offshoring their services to India. Some European and US firms are considering outsourcing their human resource and accounting departments to India as well (Bagchi, 1999; Joseph, 2001).

Accompanying the above developments, the period (1980s–90s) has seen the influence of Japanese and US styles of management on the Indian business environment via the adoption of practices/terminologies of 'lean production', 'just-in-time', 'teamwork', 'total quality management' and 'performance-based pay' among others. This stems in part from the training of many Indian managers abroad and adoption of Western management systems of teaching by institutes of management learning in India, and in part from the influx of MNCs into India (for an overview of government policy, structure and issues pertaining to MNCs see Venkata Ratnam, 1998; for the impact of reforms on different groups of companies see Vachani, 1997).

Before moving on to examine the regional disparities in industrial development and management styles and their implications for human resource policies and practices in India, it is important to consider the relatively recent rise of Indian MNCs on the global scene and implications of such developments on human resources in India as well as in an international context.

Indian multinationals: evolution and implications

Recent decades have seen MNCs from India expanding their operations around the world. They include information technology and computer firms such as Infosys, Wipro, Satyam and TCS as well as manufacturing firms such as Tata, Reliance and Asian Paints, among others. This development has both theoretical and practical implications. Literature on multinational firms and FDI outlines five stages of investment development paths (Dunning, 1993; Dunning and Lundan, 2005). According to this, composition of FDI changes from low technology and resource based investment to high technology and efficiency seeking. It progresses from:

- very little FDI;
- inward FDI increases, outward FDI low;
- inward FDI declines, outward FDI faster;
- outward FDI more than inward FDI;
- inward FDI = outward FDI.

However, many newly emerging economies, such as China, India and Brazil, have begun to internationalise at an early stage in their overall economic development, moving rapidly to a pattern of outward FDI that is high-tech and efficiency seeking. This is in contradiction to Dunning's stages and raises the possibility that new economies are not just sources of cheap labour and that MNCs from new economies have their own advantages and motives for internationalisation (Lecraw, 1977). In terms of sources of advantage, Indian MNCs have production process capabilities in low-cost, high-quality production as well as in distribution and delivery in electronics, automobile components, textiles and footwear industries; for example, Bharat Forge is the second largest producer of forgings in the world. Advantages also derive from expertise and technology-based specialisation. They often enjoy 'late-comer' advantage, for example in IT, heavy industries (Reliance) and transportation equipment (Tatas). In addition, they rely on home country resources, such as clusters of knowledge/resources: IT hubs in Bangalore or Hyderabad; early adoption of new technology (telecommunications); access to funds from state owned banks, and high personal savings/funds from family ownership. Networks of family, diaspora and cultural and institutional affinity play a role as well, for example Indian MNCs invest in Malaysia and South Africa, countries with which India has had a historical link. There is wide range of motives for Indian firms to internationalise – from resource seeking (such as Oil and Natural Gas Company expanding into Africa and Latin America), to market seeking as in the case of IT firms. Firms in electronics and automobile sector often expand for efficiency seeking purposes, while pharmaceutical firms like Dr Reddy's and Ranbaxy internationalised for created-efficiency seeking (World Investment Report, UNCTAD, 2005, 2006).

The evolution of Indian MNCs is likely to have implications for human resources both in India as well as the countries into which they expand. The Tata group is an example. It is a significant player in the Indian economy as one of the largest business group as well as being at the forefront of the internationalisation by Indian firms. Almost 150 years old, the Tata group consists of 96 companies in seven major business lines: information system and communications, engineering, materials, services, energy, consumer products and chemicals. It has operations in 54 countries and its companies export products and services to 120 countries. The main drivers of its internationalisation include market access for exports, sourcing of raw materials and horizontal and vertical integration. Apart from being one of the earliest firms to adopt a corporate structure and management style, Tatas also have rich experience of managing highly politicised industrial relations in the Indian context (Tata Steel at Jamshedpur) and place a strong emphasis on corporate social responsibility. These two factors may influence its HR policy and practices in Corus in the UK (for details see Goldstein, 2008).

Activity

Take a moment to reflect on the nature of the Indian economic policy and business environment.

Questions

1 In what ways have the historical evolution of the Indian economy and globalisation influenced its business environment?

2 Do Indian MNCs enjoy some advantages arising from their context? What implications does it have for human resources?

Human resource management in India

Human resource management in India incorporates both indigenous firms (public and private) as well as MNCs (foreign and Indian). Most HRM literature on India emphasises the need for indigenous organisations to modernise, mechanise, introduce new technology and cope with workforce reduction, retention, skills and career development issues to become competitive. Such developments are visible in all sectors of economy, in particular traditional sectors like steel, pharmaceuticals and public sector organisations. Enhanced human resource planning, along with customer satisfaction, ranks high among the priorities of Indian managers (Venkata Ratnam, 1995; Sparrow and Budhwar, 1997; Budhwar and Sparrow, 1997).

MNCs, for their part, transfer and standardise management practices but also often modify and alter their policies and practices in response to the context (Amba-Rao *et al.*, 2000 and Trivedi, 2006; for a comparative analysis of HRM practices in Indian public and private sector organisations see Budhwar and Boyne, 2004; between India and Britain see Budhwar and Khatri, 2001; between India and Thailand see Lawler *et al.*, 1995; within MNCs in India see Trivedi, 2006). This is discussed in detail in subsequent sections.

Firms in the high-technology sector such as software, information technology and Business Process Outsourcing (BPO) have their own specific patterns of human resource practices that are significantly different from other sectors. In view of the higher level of academic and other requirements specific to this sector, especially software, the tight labour market and rapid growth, salary and benefits are very high. Yet, so is the attrition rate. The software industry suffers 20–30 per cent attrition every year. The rapid growth of the industry also demands more skilled manpower that would help brand India as a quality destination rather than a low-cost one, enabling it to counter threats of other cost effective destinations like China, Philippines and South Africa as well as a slowdown of demand.

Though convergence is observable in the trends towards liberalisation, changing business environment and the influx of MNCs and their management practices, such developments are varied in their implementation and outcome and contested and negotiated by different actors. Thus there are also visible limits to convergence. Organisations face the challenge of managing differences of region, religion, caste, language, age, gender, skills, nationality, sector and types of plants. Union influence remains strong. That 'labour' is a 'concurrent' subject, i.e. both central and provincial governments can legislate on it, is a significant reason for the observable heterogeneity. These aspects are explored below with respect to the labour market, legal provisions, industrial relations and specific practices of recruitment, rewards, training and skill development that exist in both indigenous and multinational firms.

Labour market

There is a vast labour force in India, with the number of people of working age growing rapidly. Roughly 14 million Indians are now being added to the labour market each year, and that number is rising. Half of India's people are under 25 and 40 per cent under 18 (see Figure 16.2). Skill levels vary considerably. On one hand, with underinvestment in education in the country, many are not obviously skilled at anything. Approximately only 20 per cent of job seekers have had any sort of vocational training (*The Economist*, 2008). On the other, there is a growing number of educated and skilled personnel. India produces 2.5 million new university-level graduates per year, 10 per cent of whom are in engineering (World Development Indicators, 2005).

Of the total workforce, only 7–8 per cent are organised i.e. have formal employment and are covered by legislative and social security provisions. The majority (more than 90 per cent) are in unorganised informal employment, with no labour or social protection. Women are predominantly in unorganised employment. Child labour, though illegal, prevails in some sectors. This results in inequality at work and social discrimination (Breman, 1996; Harriss-White, 2003).

The challenge for India is to create employment. In recent years it has been creating more jobs. Between 2000 and 2005 its rate of employment growth doubled, to 2.6 per cent a year.

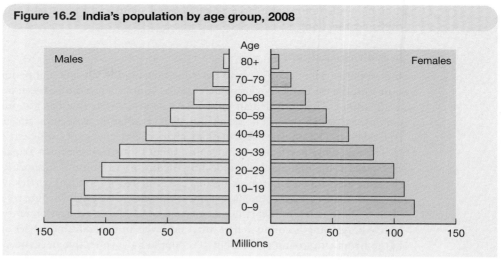

Figure 16.2 India's population by age group, 2008

Source: US Census Bureau.

But that is still insufficient and invokes fears of instability arising from growing inequalities, and there are also fears about the quality of jobs being created. The latter has become prominent through anti-globalisation movements, trade union agitations and anti-SEZ (Special Economic Zone) struggles.

Legal provisions

Labour being a concurrent subject, a plethora of laws on work and employment exist but are weak on implementation (Harriss-White and Gooptu, 2001). From the 1920s to the 1940s a number of legal provisions for workers and trade unions were instituted. Some of the prominent ones included the Trade Union Act 1926, Factories Act 1948, Industrial Disputes Act 1948, Minimum Wages Act 1948. Others followed like Apprenticeship Act 1961, Maternity Benefit Act 1961, Payment of Bonus Act 1965 and the appointment of First National Commission on Labour 1969. It is considered that the pro-labour laws favour the workers and trade unions in India (Venkata Ratnam, 1995; Sparrow and Budhwar, 1997; Sengupta and Sett, 2000).

The situation has begun to change post economic reforms, with increasing withdrawal of the state from the employment arena. There are pressures to reform labour laws to ensure flexibility and remove restrictions on firms' freedom to close sites and withdraw investment. The second National Commission on Labour (2002) was instituted to recommend comprehensive reforms in labour laws and provisions for labour in line with the requirements of economic liberalisation. Managerial rights are becoming more dominant in collective bargaining relationships and the power of unions is declining. These developments have accorded greater flexibility to the managers in their human resource policies with respect to adjustments of wages and benefits, suspension of trade union rights, and provided more freedom to modernise and increase productivity.

Increased flexibility and greater control over labour and trade unions are marketed as major attractions to foreign investors, especially in Special Economic Zones (SEZ) but they can also be used by firms to practice indiscriminate hiring and firing of employees, avoid payment of minimum wages and other benefits, and create an environment of fear by penalising any attempts at collective organisation by workers (Trivedi, 2006; Hammer, 2010). On a positive note, however, globalisation of the economy has also put increasing pressure on firms to conform to international labour standards, occupational and health safety, and address child labour and human rights issues, environmental concerns, working conditions and social security mechanisms. This pressure has been exerted through international and national trade unions to a large extent. Trade Unions and Industrial Relations are the focus of the next section.

Industrial relations

Indian industrial relations system developed during the late colonial period and in conjunction with the freedom struggle, which created common ground between political leaders and trade unions. This accorded an influential role to the state that has not only been the largest employer through the public sector but also a regulator, prosecutor and mediator in industrial relations (Ramaswamy, 1984; Bhattacharjee, 2001; Sengupta and Sett, 2000).

The following key features underpin Indian industrial relations. Tripartite consultations take place at the national level, reflecting the history of political support for trade unions by the state and the fact that most unions are affiliated to political parties. Works committees and joint management councils operate at the enterprise level. Dispute resolution machinery operates at four levels: bipartite negotiation, conciliation, arbitration and adjudication. Collective bargaining is conducted at different levels in different industries and is size specific. Large firms employing more than 300 people have collective bargaining, including most MNCs, with the exception of those in electronics and a few in banking. At the managerial level, individual bargaining is more prevalent (Bhattacharjee, 2001; Kuruvilla and Erickson, 2002; Kuruvilla *et al.*, 2002; Frenkel and Kuruvilla, 2002).

The extent and role of unions in India varies according to geography, sector and industry. While the state of West Bengal has a dominance of politically affiliated left-leaning trade unions, in Maharashtra enterprise-level unions, independent and unaffiliated, have a major presence. Gujarat has seen the rise of 'footpath unionism' and social-movement unions of unorganised workers, e.g. SEWA (Self-Employed Women's Association), whereas industrially and socially backward states of Andhra Pradesh and Bihar have radical and militant trade unions. Unionism is stronger in manufacturing units and in the chemical, pharmaceutical and automobile industries than in electronics units. Both public and private sector banks have entrenched unions but not foreign banks.

The great influence exercised by trade unions over the human resource policies of firms has begun to weaken with increasing withdrawal of state support and labour law reforms. Many unions are becoming more cooperative and less militant (Venkata Ratnam, 1995, 2001). There is a marked trend towards enterprise-based unions in response to the inability of central trade union organisations to address workers' everyday concerns (Ramaswamy, 1994; Hammer 2010). Different motives also underpin the unions' varied responses to the introduction of schemes of employee empowerment in Indian enterprises (Ramaswamy and Schiphorst, 2000).

Venkata Ratnam (2001) has identified multiple trends in industrial relations outcomes based on employer and trade union responses that are contextually dependent:

● conflictual industrial relations arising from limited resources, increasing costs and decreasing output;
● an increase in managerial control over vulnerable trade unions;
● worker cooperatives taking over and managing bankrupt companies;
● cooperative unions making concessions in bankrupt firms;
● takeover of plants by workers;
● non-union workforce in new industries and new workplaces.

Another significant reason for the growing weakness of unions is the creation and development of new industrial areas – Export Promotion Zones and Special Economic Zones specifically to attract FDI – free of union influence. It is common practice in such new industrial areas to circumvent the labour laws through the use of executive regulations. This limits unionisation in the firms located within them. Some firms allow enterprise-based unions but resist and restrict cross-industry or wider political alliances, i.e. in Japanese MNCs. In some cases, firms follow a vehement 'non-union' policy, i.e. in Korean MNCs (Trivedi, 2006; Hammer, 2010). Hindustan Lever and Philips have been hostile to any attempts to form federations of their company's unions (Venkata Ratnam, 1998).

In the climate of ongoing economic reforms, business interests are demanding major structural changes such as reduction in the political influence of unions and inter-union rivalry, stopping multiple subscription of union membership and amendment of pro-labour laws such as the Trade Union Act 1926 (for details about the debate on reforms in industrial relations laws see Sengupta and Sett, 2000). This is to allow managers greater power and flexibility to determine their human resource policies and practices and these are discussed below.

Activity   Take a moment to review the legal and industrial relations system in India.

Questions

1 Are they similar across the country or show differences?
2 Is the inflow of FDI and MNCs influencing labour laws and trade unions?

Recruitment

The vast labour force in India and the varied nature of the skills available allows firms flexibility in their recruitment patterns. Variations in recruitment policies of firms are also observable based on ownership, sector, industry, geographical location and skills.

The public sector has always had a formalised personnel system that uses standardised formal examinations and interviews to recruit its employees. The aim was to create a Weberian impersonal bureaucracy free of prejudice and discrimination based on a technical/rationalist approach. There are special provisions of quotas to recruit disadvantaged groups and communities and a specified percentage of local to broader population in recruitment. The personnel function has evolved from welfare and industrial relations to human resource development during the 1980s.

In indigenous private firms, forms of recruitment vary though social networks have been predominant. In largely family-owned firms like the Birlas and the Singhanias, community and family networks played a major role in recruitment. Predominantly from the traditional trading *Marwari* community, such firms were concentrated in particular industries like textile and cement, and in particular regions like Kanpur and Nagpur. At the same time, there were others like the Tatas, another family-based firm, which was among the earliest to adopt a more corporate style of management with diversification in the nature of its workforce and recruitment policies. At the managerial level, there is a move towards merit-based recruitment, particularly of junior managers, among private firms.

Greater variation in recruitment policies and practices is observable in the MNCs operating in India. It stems from a combination of economic-strategic approach of the firms towards cost-minimisation; institutional influences; societal expectations; the role of social networks and power within the organisation and its wider operating context. Areas developed to attract FDI have a concentration of workers, especially migrants, and are free from union influence. MNC policies vary from a simultaneous use of internal and external labour market for recruitment to reliance largely on external ones. Many segment the workforce by region (local/migrant), skill, age and gender. The segmentation often sees human resource managers travelling to recruit skilled workers from other regions of the country. For example, an Indian MNC recruits its permanent workers from other regions of India and temporary workers locally (Trivedi, 2006). On the other hand, recruitment of unskilled workers largely from local external labour market relies on the *strength of weak ties* (Granovetter, 1994) of region, community, friends and acquaintances among workers. Permanent workers are normally older than the young temporary workers. While production firms employ a predominantly male workforce, export units employ mainly women.

Similar variation is observable at the management level in MNCs. Some MNCs, e.g. Korean firms, rely more on expatriates as senior managers with Indians in middle management, but the overwhelming majority employ and train Indian managers as senior executives (Trivedi, 2006). In high-tech industries like software and telecommunications, India has a comparative advantage in having highly skilled manpower and on-campus recruitment is the norm.

In the services sector, especially business process outsourcing (BPO), the high rate of attrition of around 40 per cent poses a challenge for human resource management. Some of the reasons are the age profile, expectations of employees and the working conditions at the workplace (for call centres, see Taylor and Bain, 2005). The industry has concentrated on recruiting from the younger age group who join to make 'quick money' and leave for a better working environment and career development options than those provided in these 'internet sweatshops' that 'overlook talent'. To address these issues, BPO firms have begun to recruit mature talent, i.e. people over 35 years of age. Often these are outstation candidates (from small towns) and they are provided with shared accommodation. This also translates into changes in compensation and training policies to retain employees discussed in the following sections.

Rewards and wages

The theme of variation observed in industrial relations and recruitment practices above continues in remuneration and reward practices. It varies by the nationality of firms (indigenous/MNC), sector (public/private), industry (new/old; high-tech/low-tech) and skill and nature of employment contract of employees.

There is no uniform wage policy for all sectors of the economy. Although the Minimum Wages Act 1948 is a centrally legislated act, minimum wages vary widely across states. The public sector is still largely characterised by standardised wages with other social benefits and security of employment. Increasingly, there is a move towards performance-related pay and promotion in private firms (Bordia and Blau, 1998). While public sector workers are much better off than private sector workers, the reverse is true in the case of senior managers (Venkata Ratnam, 2001). Some private firms also use labour laws to shift to temporary and contractual labour and often avoid payment of minimum wages or any other statutory benefits (Trivedi, 2006).

Variations in wages and benefits exist between and within a firm. Ownership of the firm often determines its remuneration policy. MNCs pay higher wages than local firms and the working conditions are usually better in MNCs. This is true for employees at both ends of spectrum: cheap labour for cost-minimisation in manufacturing and call centres as well as the highly skilled workforce in computing and software. Korean firms are usually the highest paymasters followed by Japanese and then indigenous firms. Segmentation of the workforce into permanent, company casual, trainee and contract workers spells different packages for each group, thus reinforcing segmentation. Social security measures mandated by law, e.g. gratuity and provident fund are provided to all workers, but pension funds are instituted only for senior executives. This is evident both in manufacturing and the services sector. Higher wages serve the twin purpose of employing better skilled personnel and at times as a means to curtail trade union developments. Young graduates are willing to work in the call centres for their comparatively higher remuneration packages. Workers are willing to work for higher wages and benefits even in the face of what they call an 'environment of fear and control' especially in manufacturing units while others prefer 'to earn less but be freer at the workplace'. The differences in remuneration and rewards that exist between workers and managers can be a major source of dissatisfaction also (Venkata Ratnam, 2001; Trivedi, 2006).

In rapidly growing new industries such as information and communication technology where the supply of technical skill is constrained and employee mobility very high, salary and benefits are very high. There is a growing realisation that higher pay cannot be enough to retain employees and schemes such as profit sharing, share option and other perks as well as a secure career and better communication are often offered to retain employees in such sectors.

Training and skill development

The nature of the training infrastructure and skill level varies considerably in India. Training infrastructure is more extensive in the public sector but the quality is steadily declining. At the same time, the emphasis on training is increasing in private firms. This is because high quality skills exist in the software industry and in business management but not in others.

In keeping with a welfare state and the social role of public sector, the state in India provided the training infrastructure, i.e. Industrial Training Institutes form the basis of organised industrial training in India. Apprenticeship systems are instituted in all public sector firms. For management, there has been a move from personnel administration to human resource development in the last decade. This is evident in provisions for systematic training schedules, identification of core competencies and multi-skilling in public sector firms.

Along with engineering and medical skills, recent decades have witnessed an increase in business and management institutes and courses in India, as well as students obtaining business degrees from other countries like the US, UK, France and the Philippines. More organisations for providing technical skills required by the software and communications industry have been opened. More than 100,000 engineering graduates and 70,000 software professionals join the industry, both indigenous private and multinational firms, every year. According to Microsoft, India ranks second world-wide in the number of Microsoft Certified Engineers produced. These graduates represent the comparative advantage that India enjoys in terms of skilled professionals over other countries like China (Bagchi, 1999).

At the same time, low literacy, inadequate provision for health and education, a bias against vocational skills and an occupational preference for non-production jobs has created an uneven skill base. While the quality of skilled labour is good, it remains scarce in relation to the working population as a whole. Even in the information and communication technology industry where the highly skilled manpower is available, middle and lower level skilled personnel are in short supply. The training infrastructure is ageing and the technology obsolete. The emphasis on general education and insufficient interaction with industry has exacerbated these trends. More education of higher quality is provided to a few rather than a sound one for all. This leads to even greater inequality (Venkata Ratnam, 2001).

The literature on learning and development argues that for developing countries like India, learning requires borrowing from industrially advanced countries with consequences for the distribution of skills. Following economic reforms and liberalisation of economy, it is envisaged that the role played hitherto by the public sector in employment creation and training will be supplemented and/or replaced by MNCs. It is assumed that skills upgrading will occur in response to the requirements of new, technologically sophisticated industries. Individual workplace-based learning will, over time, enhance the social stock of knowledge and skills, thereby promoting growth (Okada, 2004).

While this may be true at managerial level where Indian managers in MNCs are sent to the company's parent country for training, such as in Japanese MNCs or in the software industry, at junior management and worker level it is more doubtful, especially in manufacturing MNCs. Elger and Smith (1998) found that work processes in international firms are being simplified to minimise training requirements and facilitate the substitutability of labour. This reduces the dependence on experienced workers. Rationalisation and deskilling of jobs enhance the inter-changeability of workers, who do not need specific skills. Deskilling and multi-tasking rather than multi-skilling and use of trainees for job completion rather than actual training, appear more the norm in most MNCs (Trivedi, 2006).

Even in new industries, like software and information technology, the comparative advantage has been based on labour cost advantage rather than innovation and quality. The focus has been mostly at the lowest end of the value chain, i.e. low-level design, on-site export of services and associated customised software development. There has been an increase in sales, exports and the number of firms but a decline in research and development intensity. Thus a move up the value chain through enhanced skills is necessary to retain comparative advantage. Wipro, India's second largest software services exporter, now recruits maths and science graduates and trains them for three years through on-the-job and classroom training at its Wipro Academy of Software Education. In the BPO firms, there is increasing focus on talent recognition and prospects for career development through offers of places on MBA courses and management diplomas (Bagchi, 1999; Joseph, 2001).

Activity

Foregoing sections have highlighted the variations in the recruitment, reward and training practices in Indian as well as multinational firms. Try to identify some of the factors responsible for such variations.

Questions

1 Does the relative power of employees, based on their skill level, have any implication on their rewards and remuneration?

2 Why does India need to upgrade its skill level?

Challenges

The major challenges identified at the beginning of this section can be attributed to the imposition of reform policies without recognising the diversity of the country circumstances, as well as the inability to address the social costs of reforms that have become more acute. The one size fits all approach and the consequent lack of national consensus on reforms exacerbates these shortcomings.

Infrastructure

A combination of weak regulatory mechanisms and nature of FDI flow that is largely in non-core sectors has restricted the flow of investment in core sectors like infrastructure and energy. The government has demarcated additional investment of almost US$200 billion for energy infrastructure development and set up an Investment Commission. It has prioritised power generation and distribution, telecommunications, national highway and ports development, rural electrification and higher education, as well as setting up a $5 billion infrastructure development fund. Wider skills upgrading is an imperative if India is to take advantage of the contemporary economic climate, e.g. in the information and communication technology industry, an area of comparative advantage.

Corruption

One of the reasons for greater flow of FDI to China has been the lower prevalence of corruption in its polity and executive compared with India. A study by Transparency International (2005) places India at the lower end of the table in terms of the ease of doing business and the average time taken to secure clearance for a start-up or to invoke bankruptcy. Corrupt practices are inherited from the licence-quota regime of earlier economic phases and there is a perception that reforms have been and continue to be introduced in India via covert means. The Rights to Information Act (2005) and setting up of vigilance commissions are attempts to address this through greater accountability and transparency.

Growth with equity

While jobs have been created, most of the new jobs are in the unorganised sector with low wages, poor working conditions, low job security and increased risk of safety and occupational health. Absence of adequate social security mechanisms have further increased and polarised inequalities. Some 65 per cent of Indians live on agriculture, which accounts for less than 18 per cent of GDP. Assuring more productive livelihoods for them – and so reducing poverty – requires attention. The government has instituted special programmes and fund allocation for addressing poverty, child development, mass education for the poor, the disadvantaged and women. However, more effort is required to increase employment opportunities, augment skill development, ensure rights of workers and trade unions, provision of education and health for all and the need for wider social dialogue among all.

Advantages

Despite the above-mentioned challenges, India enjoys certain advantages that, if built upon, would equip it to manage and benefit from the ongoing economic changes.

Language

Advantages arising from knowledge of the English language, increasingly a lingua franca of globalisation, are evident in more than a million graduates that Indian universities produce regularly. Many of them work in the mushrooming call centres that have resulted from outsourcing of services to India. There is also an ever-increasing percentage of senior executives from India in multinational firms and international organisations.

Skills

Higher-end spectrum training and skills, especially computing, software, heavy engineering and information technology is India's other comparative advantage. India, though a source of unskilled cheap labour, nevertheless produces a large number of graduates in mathematics and science as well as engineers and doctors from its vast network of engineering and medical colleges. Recent decades have seen a formidable rise in the number of graduates from management and business institutes and middle-level professionals for the software and communications industry. These form the Indian diasporas to the developed economies, e.g. software engineers in Silicon Valley; doctors in the UK; business managers; and researchers in universities. Nevertheless, further upgrading of skills and wider vocational training base is crucial for the country to remain competitive and to weather the economic crisis.

Democracy

The democratic character of the Indian state provides a sustainable framework to manage diversity with an equitable distribution of resources and opportunities. Empowerment of the weak and the disadvantaged that a democratic process engenders, however slowly, would redress the imbalances created by a differentiated globalisation. The power of the electoral ballot restrains the excesses of global capitalism by exercising control over a national system that may favour it indiscriminately. This may help India address the challenges of poverty and inequality and strive towards a fairer society. It may also counter the corruption that is seeping into governance and polity.

Diversity

Diversity is the key to understanding the Indian context. It is diverse in its social makeup as well as the nature of its workforce, business practices, industrial relations and skill levels. This diversity, if harnessed properly, can yield good returns in the long run in terms of good business practices and a workforce with varied skills. Managers with an experience of diversity are often better equipped to adjust as well as respond to the increasingly diverse international workplace and to global competition.

Prospects

The ongoing transformations are overshadowing and often replacing the post-colonial identity of India, indeed of the developing world, though what the alternative may be remains uncertain. It could be that India on account of its comparative advantage continues to gain employment within the global division of labour between MNCs, nevertheless also growing its own MNCs and brands that will in turn seek global reach, like Mittal Steels, Tatas, Reliance and Infosys. From this a new set of business practices and human resource policies may emerge. The probability of this happening is high, with a projected growth of 9–10 per cent predicted by the World Bank. On the other hand, it might be that movement up the value chain is limited and India remains in a subordinate interdependent position within global capitalism. Continued analysis of the material issues and social struggles associated with global capitalism as it interacts with the Indian business system, keeping in mind that social processes are iterative and that the global economy continuously changing, would yield a clearer picture of the nature of human resource practices in firms in India.

Activity

Identify the major challenges and advantages facing the Indian business environment and practices in the globalising world economy.

Questions

1 What do you think are the future prospects for India?

2 Reflecting on the whole section, what advantages does India have in weathering the economic crisis?

Summary

- The section on the People's Republic of China discussed key issues relating to human resource management, and outlined some of the key points in China's historical development under Mao. It illustrated the way the system known as the 'iron rice-bowl' continued to exert some degree of influence over contemporary practices. While China has enjoyed rapid economic growth, it is now confronting a number of problems, including restructuring, downsizing and unemployment. In response to this, it is having to develop a system of social insurance. There is a debate as to the extent to which HR practices within China are converging with Western approaches. This section concluded that while there is some degree of similarity, full-blown Westernised models of HRM are unlikely to take hold because of cultural and institutional differences. There are a number of issues that are impacting upon people management in China, including skills gaps, problems of labour discipline, and low motivation.

- The short review of Hong Kong highlighted the clear differences from the PRC, its mainland counterpart. It is also clear that Hong Kong's role of 'middleman' between the West and the East may be further compromised as the PRC continues to modernise.

- The section on India presented an overview of human resource management as it has evolved in the recent past, with special emphasis on the nature of changes in the Indian business environment and practices on account of current transformations in the global economy. Both cultural and institutional perspectives were employed to understand the similarities with standard global HR practices and the differences that persist. The overarching theme was of variations in HR practices based on region, sector, industry, ownership and skill. Challenges and advantages were identified with some possible implications for India's role in the global economy. Based on this some speculations are made on the prospects for India in weathering the economic downturn in particular.

China

As a member of the human resource development department of a large multinational corporation you have been given responsibility to devise a programme to prepare managers and other parent company employees who will be working in China.

Prepare a presentation that you might give to these employees, including general information on the country, history, culture, language and customs and work-related attitudes. Use anecdotes and solid examples to illustrate your presentation.

Questions

1 To what extent would you agree with the contention that existing models of HRM fail to recognise cultural differences, and that this is a weakness given the rapid rate of globalisation?

2 Outline the similarities and differences in terms of the approaches to the management of people in India and China.

3 To what extent would you agree with the view that there is an 'Asian model of HRM'?

Case study

Yummee Biscuits: Part 1

Yummee Biscuits is a large UK-based snack manufacturer that was set up in the nineteenth century. It is now one of the largest snack manufacturers in the UK. Over the past two decades it has been internationalising its operations, and has acquired companies in the USA and Australia. In 1995 it became involved in a joint venture in the south of the People's Republic of China (PRC). The Chinese partners were local businessmen who had no prior experience in biscuit-making. Yummee pumped in money and resources, and the Chinese partners set up the land deal. The biscuit factory was built on a greenfield site, and was equipped with state-of-the-art machinery. Work was organised on scientific management (Taylorist) lines, with strictly demarcated jobs and close supervision. Yummee took the view initially that it would be best to employ local Chinese managers to run the factory. However, in the following two years numerous problems occurred within the factory. These included problems of quality control, stock control, and failing to deliver orders to customers on time.

Yummee sent out a delegation of senior managers to investigate the problem. They found that many of the problems were related to a lack of managerial skill and poor coordination between different departments. They realised that it had been a mistake to assume that the indigenous Chinese managers could

run the factory to British standards with little support or training. Yummee put all managers through management development training. This included topics such as leadership skills, communication skills, time management skills and dealing with conflict. The training programmes were adapted from programmes that were delivered in the UK. Individual training needs were not assessed. The managers said that they had enjoyed the training, but the trainer felt that there could be an element of politeness involved. There was little improvement in the performance of the subsidiary one year later.

A senior executive from Yummee travelled to the subsidiary to inspect the plant. He sent a report outlining the key problems in the factory. These were the main points of his report.

Shopfloor problems

- There were low levels of motivation within the shopfloor ranks. Most of the shopfloor workers were from the north of China.
- Shopfloor workers seemed unwilling or unable to take on any level of responsibility.
- There seemed to be little interest in promotion or development opportunities.
- There was no appreciation of hygiene rules and regulations.

Case study continued

Management problems

- Many managers seemed unwilling to take responsibility.
- Managers would often prefer to hire members of their family rather than the best person for the job.
- Managers were often unwilling to discipline subordinates.
- Interdepartmental communication was poor.
- Managers seemed to spend a lot of time dealing with the personal problems of subordinates.

Questions

1 Does a knowledge of the historical and cultural development of China help you to understand the problems experienced in the PRC subsidiary? Give examples.

2 You have been asked to take over the running of the PRC subsidiary. What managerial initiatives would you implement to help resolve the above problems? What barriers would you face and how would you deal with them?

3 To what extent could a Western model of HRM be applied to the context of this factory? If not, why not? Give specific examples.

Yummee Biscuits: Part 2

Yummee Biscuits is now interested in opening a new biscuit factory in Shanghai. It is predicted that the factory will require 800 employees at all levels from senior management to shopfloor workers. The new factory will contain the following departments: human resource management, finance, sales and marketing, food production and distribution and quality control. Yummee will install new German biscuit-making machines, as it feels that these are the best on the market at the moment. The machines will be shipped in from Germany. The factory will produce a range of savoury and sweet biscuits.

Yummee has already purchased a site and expects the building to be complete by December 2007. It would like to put in place a skeleton staff in November and have full staffing in place by the end of December. It is especially keen to ensure that the factory produces quality products from the beginning and that production is brought online as smoothly as possible. The new factory will include a fully equipped training centre and the company will supply a learning resource centre as part of this development. It believes that training is crucial to the success of the venture. It is also keen to attract high-calibre staff, particularly at management levels. It expects to utilise some expatriate staff, but is keen to employ a high percentage of indigenous Chinese staff. It is also keen to avoid the problems that it experienced in its factory in the South of China.

Questions

Yummee has asked for guidance on the following issues:

1 How should it go about recruiting workers for the new factory? What recruitment channels would you recommend and why?

2 How would it organise the selection process for managers and shopfloor workers?

3 Provide guidance that focuses upon how it would develop a reward system for managers and shopfloor workers.

4 Produce a plan that focuses on meeting training and development needs. This should include the following details: timescale, resourcing requirements and staffing needs.

5 Are there any training programmes that would be compulsory for all?

6 What systems should be put in place to ensure that individual training needs are met?

7 Identify the critical success factors and barriers that would be related to each of these activities.

References and further reading

Those texts marked with an asterisk are particularly recommended for further reading. The issues covered in this chapter are also addressed in Chapters 8, 13 and 15.

There are also regular articles on Asian countries in the *International Journal of Human Resource Management* and the *Asia Pacific Business Review*. These two journals and the *Human Resource Management Journal* have had special editions on HRM in the Asian region in recent years. There are also occasional articles on Asian HRM in the many other journals that cover HRM subjects.

*Ahlstrom, D., Foley, S., Young, M.N. and Chan, E. (2005) 'Human resource strategies in post-WTO China', *Thunderbird International Business Review*, 47, 3: 263–385.

Amba-Rao, S.C., Petrick, J.A., Gupta, J.N.D. and Von der Embse, T.J. (2000) 'Comparative performance appraisal practices and management values among foreign and domestic firms in India', *International Journal of Human Resource Management*, 11, 1: 60–89.

Anon. (2000a) 'The end of tycoons', *The Economist*, 29 April.

Anon. (2000b) 'Let the good times roll', *The Economist*, 18 April.

Anon. (2007) 'Reform of state-owned enterprises', *China Labour Bulletin*, 19 December.

Anon. (2008a) 'Hong Kong slides into recession', *BBC News*: 14 November: London. Available at **http://news.bbc.co.uk/1/hi/business/7729652.stm**.

Anon. (2008b) *An Overview of PRC's New Labour Contract Law*. Beijing: BMU Consulting.

Ashton, D. and Sung, J. (1994) *The State Economic Development and Skill Formation: A New Asian Model?* Working Paper 3. Leicester: Centre for Labour Market Studies, Leicester University.

Bagchi, S. (1999) 'India's software industry: the people dimension', *IEEE Software Magazine*, May/June.

Benson, J. (1996) 'Management strategy and labour flexibility in Japanese manufacturing enterprises', *Human Resource Management Journal*, 6, 2: 44–57.

Benson, J. and Zhu, Y. (1999) 'Markets, firms and workers in Chinese state-owned enterprises', *Human Resource Management Journal*, 9, 4: 58–74.

Benson, J., Debroux, P., Yuasa, M. and Zhu, Y. (2000) 'Flexibility and labour management: Chinese manufacturing enterprises in the 1990s', *International Journal of Human Resource Management*, 11, 2: 183–96.

Bhattacharjee (2001) 'The evolution of Indian industrial relations: a comparative perspective', *Industrial Relations Journal*, 32, 3: 244–63.

Björkman, I. and Xiucheng, F. (2002) 'Human resource management and the performance of Western firms in China', *International Journal of Human Resource Management*, 13, 6: 853–64.

Bordia, P. and Blau, G. (1998) 'Pay referent comparison and pay level satisfaction in private versus public sector organisations in India', *International Journal of Human Resource Management*, 9, 1: 155–67.

Branigan T. (2009) 'China fears riots will spread as boom goes sour', *The Observer*, 25 January London. Available at **http://www.guardian.co.uk/world/2009/jan/25/china-globaleconomy**.

Breman, J. (1996) *Footloose Labour: Working in India's Informal Economy*. Cambridge: Cambridge University Press.

Buchanan, D. and Huczynski, A. (1997) *Organisational Behaviour: An Introductory Text*. Hemel Hempstead: Prentice Hall.

Budhwar, P.S. and Boyne, G. (2004) 'Human resource management in the Indian public and private sector: an empirical comparison', *International Journal of Human Resource Management*, 15, 2: 346–70.

Budhwar, P.S. and Debrah Y.A. (eds) (2001) *Human Resource Management in Developing Countries*. London: Routledge.

Budhwar, P.S. and Khatri, N. (2001) 'A comparative study of HR practices in Britain and India', *International Journal of Human Resource management*, 12, 5: 800–26.

Budhwar, P.S. and Sparrow, P.R. (1997) 'Evaluating levels of strategic integration and development of human resource management in India', *International Journal of Human Resource Management*, 8, 4: 476–94.

Burrell, G. (1997) *Pandemonium: Towards a Retro-Organisation Theory*. London: Sage.

Burton, J. (1999a) 'Economic squeeze calls for change', *Financial Times*, 20 October.

Burton, J. (1999b) 'The chaebol: the empire strikes back', *Financial Times*, 20 October.

Burton, J. (1999c) 'Banking: still reluctant to change', *Financial Times*, 20 October.

Burton, J., Jonquieres, G., Kazmin, A. and Mandel-Campbell, A. (2001) 'Enter the dragon: economic uncertainties raised by China's accession to the WTO are likely to put pressure on international trade relations for years to come', *Financial Times*, 10 December.

CCCC (1993) *The Work Report of the 14th Conference of the Central Communist Party*. Peoples Republic of China.

Chan, H. (2008) *2008 Economic Background and 2009 Prospects*. Hong Kong Special Administrative Region Government. **http://ww.hkeconomy.gov.hk/en/home/**.

Chen, M. (1995) *Asian Management Systems: Chinese, Japanese and Korean Styles of Business*. London: Thunderbird/Routledge Series in International Management.

Child, J. (1994) *Management in China in the Age of Reform*. Cambridge: Cambridge University Press.

Chow, I. Hau-Siu (2004) 'The impact of institutional context on human resource management in three Chinese societies', *Employee Relations*, 26, 6: 626–42.

Chu, P. and Siu, W. (2001) 'Coping with the Asian economic crisis: the rightsizing of small and medium sized enterprises', *International Journal of Human Resource Management*, 12, 5: 845–58.

Cody, E. (2006) 'China cracks down on corruption', *Washington Post Foreign Service*, 15 February.

Datt, R. and Sundharam, K.P.H. (1999) *Indian Economy*. New Delhi: S. Chand & Co.

Deyo, F. (1995) 'Human resource strategies in Thailand' in S. Frenkel and J. Harrold (eds) *Industrialization and Labor Relations: Contemporary Research in Seven Countries*. Ithaca, NY: ILR Press, pp. 23–36.

Ding, D.Z., Ge, G.L. and Warner, M. (2004) 'HRM in China after the Asian financial crisis', *International Studies of Management and Organisation*, 34, 1: 10–31.

Ding, Z. and Warner, M. (1999) 'Re-inventing China's industrial relations at enterprise level: an empirical field study in four major cities', *Industrial Relations Journal*, 30, 3: 243–60.

*Ding, Z., Goodall, K. and Warner, M. (2000) 'The end of the "iron rice-bowl": whither Chinese human resource management?', *International Journal of Human Resource Management*, 11, 2: 217–36.

Dreze, J. and Sen, A. (1995) *India – Economic Development and Social Opportunity*. Delhi: Oxford University Press.

Dunning, J. (1993) *Multinational Enterprises and the Global Economy*. Aldershot: Edward Elgar.

Dunning, J. and Lundan, S. (2005) *Multinational Enterprises and the Global Economy*. Aldershot: 2nd edn. Aldershot: Edward Elgar.

Easterby-Smith, M., Malina, D. and Yuan, L. (1995) 'How culture sensitive is HRM? A comparative analysis of practice in Chinese and UK companies', *International Journal of Human Resource Management*, 6, 1: 31–59.

Elger, T. and Smith, C. (1998) 'New town, new capital, new workplace? The employment relations of Japanese inward investors in West Midlands New Town', *Economy and Society*, 27: 578–600.

Fan, X. (1995) 'The Chinese cultural system: implications for cross-cultural management', *SAM Advanced Management Journal*, 60, 1: 14–20.

Fields, D., Chan, A. and Akhtar, S. (2000) 'Organisational context and human resource management strategy: a structural equation analysis of Hong Kong firms', *International Journal of Human Resource Management*, 11, 2: 264–77.

Financial Times (1999) 'Country survey of Hong Kong', 30 June.

Financial Times (2005) 'World report: China', 7 November.

Financial Times (2008) 'China: special report', 24 November, p. 1.

Frenkel, S. (1993) *Organized Labour in the Asia-Pacific Region: A Comparative Study of Trade Unions in Nine Countries*. Ithaca, NY: ILR Press.

Frenkel, S. and Harrod, J.A. (1995) *Industrialization and Labor Relations: Contemporary Research in Seven Countries*. Ithaca, NY: ILR Press.

Frenkel, S. and Kuruvilla, S. (2002) 'Logics of action, globalisation and changing employment relations in China, India, Malaysia and the Philippines', *Industrial and Labor Relations Review*, 55, 3: 387–412.

Glover, L. and Siu, N. (2000) 'The human resource barriers to the management of quality in China', *International Journal of Human Resource Management*, 11, 4: 867–82.

Goldstein, A. (2008) 'Emerging economies' transnational corporations: the case of Tata', *Transnational Corporations*, 17, 3: 85–108, UNCTAD.

Government HKSAR. (2008) *2008 Economic Background and 2009 Prospects*. http://www.hkeconomy.gov.hk/en/home/

Government of India data from **www.ibef.or**; **www.mea.nic.in** and **www.commerce.nic.in**.

Grammaticus, D. (2002) 'Hong Kong unemployment surges', BBC News, 17 January.

Granovetter, M. (1994) *Getting a Job: A Study of Contacts and Careers*. Chicago, IL: Chicago University Press.

Groenewald, H. (2008) 'Maintaining Chinese management talent in Western subsidiaries', *Journal of Current Chinese Affairs*, 4: 131–46.

Hall, P.A. and Soskice, D. (eds) (2001) *Varieties of Capitalism: The Institutional Foundations of Comparative Advantage*. Oxford: Oxford University Press.

Hammer, A. (2010, forthcoming) 'Trade unions in a constrained environment: workers' voices from a special economic zone in India', *Industrial Relations Journal*, 41, 3.

Harney, A. (2005) 'Guangdong: paying the price of rapid development', *Financial Times*, 7 November.

Harriss-White, B. (2003) 'Inequality at work in the informal economy: key issues and illustrations, *International Labour Review*, 142, 4: 459–69.

Harriss-White, B. and Gooptu, N. (2001) 'Mapping India's world of unorganised labour' in L. Panitch and C. Leys (eds) *Socialist Register 2001: Working Classes. Global Realities*, Canada: Merlin.

Heller, P. (1999) *The Labor of Development: Workers and the Transformation of Capitalism in Kerala, India*. Ithaca, NY: Cornell University Press.

Hofstede, G. (1991) *Cultures and Organisations: Software of the Mind*. London: McGraw-Hill.

Hong Kong Trade Development Council (2006) 'Economic and trade information on Hong Kong', 22 February. Available at **http://www.hktdc.com/info/vp/a/hke/en/1/4/1/1x000KNP/Economic-Trade-Information-On-Hong-Kong.htm**.

Jacob, R. (2002) 'From lavish parties to pessimism: businessmen say they feel "awful" but believe their prospects are good', *Financial Times*, 1 July.

Jacobs, L., Gao, G. and Herbig, P. (1995) 'Confucian roots in China: a force for today's business', *Management Decision*, 33, 9: 29–35.

Joseph, K.J. (2001) 'ICT, economy and labour', *Labour and Development*, 7, 2: 1–36.

Kaplinsky, R. (1997) 'India's industrial development: an interpretive survey', *World Development*, 25, 5: 681–94.

Krishna, A. and Monappa, A. (1994) 'Economic restructuring and human resource management', *Indian Journal of Industrial Relations*, 29, 4: 490–501.

Kuruvilla, S. (1996) 'Linkages between industrialisation strategies and industrial relations/Human Resource Policies: Singapore, Malaysia, The Philippines and India', *Industrial and Labor Relations Review*, 49, 4: 635–57.

Kuruvilla, S. and Erickson, C.L. (2002) 'Change and transformation in Asian industrial relations', *Industrial Relations*, 41, 2: 171–227.

Kynge, J. (1999) 'Reflections on half a century', *Financial Times*, 1 October.

Lane, C. (1995) *Industry and Society in Europe*. Aldershot: Edward Elgar.

Lardy, N. (2002) 'Problems on the road to liberalisation: China has joined the WTO on stricter terms than fellow members. If it is to succeed in opening its markets, the world should resist using protectionist provisions', *Financial Times*, 15 March.

Lawler, J.J., Jain, H.C., Venkataratnam, C.S. and Atmiyanandana, V. (1995) 'Human resource management in developing economies: a comparison of India and Thailand', *International Journal of Human Resource Management*, 6, 2: 319–46.

Leahy, J. (2002) 'Still waiting for the correction: Hong Kong property prices have fallen 65 per cent in the bubble years, but they remain expensive and could slide further', *Financial Times*, 30 November.

Lecraw, D. (1977) 'Direct investment by firms from less developed countries', *Oxford Economic Papers*, 29, 3: 442–57.

Lee Cooke, F. (2002) 'Ownership change and reshaping of employment relations in China: a study of two manufacturing companies', *Journal of Industrial Relations*, 44, 1: 19–39.

Leggett, C. and Bamber, G. (1996) 'Asia Pacific tiers of change', *Human Resource Management Journal*, special issue: *HRM in the Asia Pacific Region*, 6, 2: 7–19.

Li, L. (2006) 'Labor contract law likely to pass this year', China Update, *Squire Sanders and Dempsey L.L.P.*, February 2006.

Lockett, M. (1988) 'Culture and the problems of Chinese management', *Organisation Studies*, 9, 4: 475–96.

Low, L. (1993) 'From entrepôt to a newly industrialising economy', in L. Low, T.M.H. Heng, T.W. Wong, T.K. Yam and H. Hughes (eds) *Challenge and Response: Thirty Years of the Economic Development Board.* Singapore: Times Academic Press.

Low, L., Toh, M.H. and Soon, T.W. (1991) *Economics of Education and Manpower Development: Issues and Policies in Singapore.* Singapore: McGraw-Hill.

Lucas, L. (1999a) 'Still lingering in negative territory', *Financial Times*, 30 June.

Lucas, L. (1999b) 'Tiger rivalry: jury still out on best methods', *Financial Times*, 15 September.

Luo, Y. and Chen, M. (1997) 'Does *guanxi* affect company performance?', *Asia Pacific Journal of Management*, 14, 1: 1–16.

Mamkoottam, K. (1982) *Trade Unionism: Myth and Reality: Unionism in the Tata Iron and Steel Company.* Delhi, Oxford: Oxford University Press.

McSweeney, B. (2002) 'Hofstede's model of national cultural differences and their consequences: A triumph of faith – a failure of analysis', *Human Relations*, 55, 1: 89–118.

Mok, K., Wong, L. and Lee, G. (2002) 'The challenges of global capitalism: unemployment and state workers reactions and responses in post-reform China', *International Journal of Human Resource Management*, 13, 3: 399–415.

Montagnon, P. (1999a) 'Agonising choices accompany change', *Financial Times*, 1 October.

Montagnon, P. (1999b) 'Banking: still reluctant to change', *Financial Times*, 20 October.

Morden, T. and Bowles, D. (1998) 'Management in South Korea: a review', *Management Decision*, 36, 5: 316–30.

Murray, G. (1994) *Doing Business in China.* Kent: China Library.

Okada, A. (2004) 'Skills development and interfirm learning linkages under globalisation: lessons from the Indian automobile industry', *World Development*, 32, 7: 1265–88.

Ouchi, W. (1981) *Theory Z.* New York: Avon.

Paik, Y., Vance, C. and Stage, D. (1996) 'The extent of divergence in human resource practice across three Chinese national cultures: Hong Kong, Taiwan and Singapore', *Human Resource Management Journal*, 6, 2: 7–19.

Park, W. and Yu, G. (2000) 'Transformation and new patterns of HRM in Korea', Conference paper at the International Conference on Transforming Korean Business and Management Culture, Michigan State University, 19–20 September.

Parry, J.P., Breman, J. and Kapadia, K. (eds) (1999) *The Worlds of Indian Industrial Labour.* New Delhi: Sage.

Peng, F.C. (1994) 'China: managers can learn from the methods of venture partners', *South China Morning Post*, April, 13, 15.

Ramaswamy, E.A. (1984) *Power and Justice: The State in Industrial Relations.* Delhi: Oxford University Press.

Ramaswamy, E.A. (1994) *The Rayon Spinners: The Strategic Management of Industrial Relations.* Delhi: Oxford University Press.

Ramaswamy, E.A. (1997) *A Question of Balance: Labour, Management and Society.* Delhi, New York: Oxford University Press.

Ramaswamy, E.A. and Schiphorst, F.B. (2000) 'Human resource management, trade unions and empowerment: two cases from India', *International Journal of Human Resource Management*, 11, 4: 664–80.

Rao, T.V., Silvera, D.M., Shrivastava, C.M. and Vidyasagar, R. (eds) (1994) *HRD in the New Economic Environment.* New Delhi: Tata McGraw-Hill.

Report of the First National Commission on Labour (1969), Ministry of Labour, Government of India, Delhi.

Report of the Second National Commission on Labour (2002), Ministry of Labour, Government of India, Delhi.

Roberts, D. (2006) 'How raising wages are changing the game in China', *Business Week*, 27 March.

Rowley, C. (1997) 'Conclusion: reassessing HRM's convergence', *Asia Pacific Business Review*, special issue: *Human Resource Management in the Asia Pacific Region: Convergence Questioned*, 3, 4: 197–210.

Rowley, C. and Bae, J. (2002) 'Globalisation and transformation of human resource management in South Korea', *International Journal of Human Resource Management*, 13, 3: 522–49.

Rubery, J. and Grimshaw, D. (2003) *The Organization of Employment: An International Perspective*, Basingstoke: Palgrave Macmillan.

Selmer, J., Ebrahimi, P. and Mingtao, L. (2000) 'Personal characteristics and adjustment of Chinese mainland business expatriates in Hong Kong', *International Journal of Human Resource Management*, 11, 2: 237–50.

Sengupta, A.K. and Sett, P.K. (2000) 'Industrial relations law, employment security and collective bargaining in India: myths, realities and hopes', *Industrial Relations Journal*, 31, 2: 144–53.

Sharma, I.J. (1984) 'The culture context of Indian managers', *Management of Labour Studies*, 9, 2: 72–80.

Singh, J.P. (1990) 'Managerial culture and work-related values in India', *Organisation Studies*, 11, 1: 75–101.

Sinha, J.B.P. and Sinha, D. (1990) 'Role of social values in Indian organisations', *International Journal of Psychology*, 25: 705–14.

Smith, C. and Meiksins, P. (1995) 'System, societal and dominance effects in cross-national organisational analysis', *Work, Employment and Society*, 9, 2: 241–68

Sparrow, P.R. and Budhwar, P.S. (1997) 'Competition and change: mapping the Indian HRM recipe against worldwide patterns', *Journal of World Business*, 32: 224–42.

Sparrow, P. and Wu, P-C. (1999) 'How much do national value orientations really matter? Predicting HRM preferences of Taiwanese employees' in S. Lahteenmaki, L. Holden and I. Roberts (eds) *HRM and the Learning Organisation.* Turku, Finland: Turku School of Economics, pp. 239–84.

Tayeb, M. (1988) *Organisations and National Culture*, London: Sage.

Taylor, P. and Bain, P. (2005) 'India calling to the far away towns' the call centre labour process and globalisation', *Work, Employment and Society*, 19, 2: 261–82.

The Economist (2005) 'The insidious charms of foreign investment, the tiger in front: A Survey of India and China', 5–11 March, p. 7.

The Economist (2008) **http://www.economist.com/opinion/displaystory.cfm?story_id=12749375**.

The Economist (2008) Special edition on China and India: Asia's wounded giants, 11 December.

Thornhill, J. (2002a) 'Private enterprise seen as way forward', *Financial Times*, 12 December.

643

Thornhill, J. (2002b) 'Companies rush in with the cash', *Financial Times*, 12 December.

Thornhill, J. (2002c) 'Asia's recovery "exposed to oil price volatility"', *Financial Times*, 10 April.

Thornhill, J. (2002d) 'Rebuilding the tiger: five years after East Asia suffered a devastating financial crisis, John Thornhill finds that the region has gone a long way towards improving corporate governance', *Financial Times*, 5 June.

Transparency International (2005) See Global Corruption Barometer: Corruption Perceptions Index; and Regional and national surveys and indices on **www.transparency.org**.

Trivedi, A. (2006) 'Global factory, Indian worker', unpublished PhD thesis, University of London.

Tsang, E.W.K. (1994) 'Human resource management problems in Sino-foreign joint ventures', *Employee Relations*, 15, 9: 1–14.

Vachani, S. (1997) 'Economic liberalisation's effect on sources of competitive advantage of different groups of companies: the case of India', *International Business Review*, 6, 2: 165–84.

Venkata Ratnam, C.S. (1995) 'Economic liberalisation and the transformation of industrial relations policies in India' in A. Verma, T.A. Kochan and R. Lansbury (eds) *Employment relations in the growing Asian economies*. London, New York: Routledge.

Venkata Ratnam, C.S. (1998) 'Multinational companies in India', *International Journal of Human Resource Management*, 9, 4: 567–89.

Venkata Ratnam, C.S. (1999) 'The case of India' in ILO (1999/3) *Trade Unions in the Informal Sector: Finding their Bearings: Nine Country Papers*. Geneva: ILO Bureau for Workers Activities.

Venkata Ratnam, C.S. (2001) *Globalisation and Labour-management Relations: Dynamics of Change*. New Delhi: Response Books.

Ward, A. (2002a) 'Hailed as an example to other Asian countries: economic transformation by Andrew Ward: But despite dramatic progress, economic weaknesses remain', *Financial Times*, 29 October.

Ward, A. (2002b) 'Country's largest company shifts upmarket and wins accolade: Samsung Electronics', *Financial Times*, 29 October.

Ward, A. (2002c) 'Benefits of restructuring are starting to filter through', *Financial Times*, 29 October.

Ward, A. (2002d) 'Strike hits Korean car makers', *Financial Times*, 6 November.

Ward, A. (2002e) 'South Korean unions set for privatisation protest', *Financial Times*, 25 February.

Warner, M. (1992) *How Chinese Managers Learn: Management and Industrial Training in China*. London: Macmillan.

Warner, M. (1993) 'Human resource management with Chinese characteristics', *International Journal of Human Resource Management*, 4, 1: 45–65.

Warner, M. (1996) 'Human resources in the People's Republic of China: the "three systems reforms"', *Human Resource Management Journal*, 6, 2: 32–43.

Warner, M. (1997) 'Management–labour relations in the new Chinese economy', *Human Resource Management Journal*, 7, 4: 30–43.

Warner, M. (2000) 'Introduction: the Asia-Pacific HRM model revisited', *International Journal of Human Resource Management*, 11, 2: 171–82.

Whitley, R. (1992) *Business Systems in East Asia*. London: Sage.

Whitley, R. (1999) *Divergent Capitalisms: The Social Structuring and Change of Business Systems*. Oxford: Oxford University Press.

World Bank (1999) 'China: weathering the storm and learning the lessons', *Country Studies*, 8 January: 114.

World Bank (2009) China Quarterly Update, March 2009, **www.worldbank.org/china**.

World Development Indicators (2005) **http://devdata.worldbank.org/wdi2005/cover.htm**.

World Investment Report (2005) UNCTAD; **www.unctad.org/wir**.

World Investment Report (2006) UNCTAD; **www.unctad.org/wir**.

Zhu, C. and Dowling, P.J. (2002) 'Staffing practices in translation: some empirical evidence from China', *International Journal of Human Resource Management*, 13, 4: 569–97.

Zhu, Y. and Warner, M. (2004) 'Changing Chinese patterns of human resource management in contemporary China: WTO accession and enterprise responses', *Industrial Relations Journal*, 35, 4: 311–28.

Zhu, Y. and Warner, M. (2005) 'Changing Chinese employment relations since WTO accession', *Personnel Review*, 34, 3: 354–69.

Zuboff, S. (1988) *In the Age of the Smart Machine: The Future of Work and Power*. Oxford: Heinemann.

 For multiple-choice questions, exercises and annotated weblinks related to this topic, visit **www.pearsoned.co.uk/mymanagementlab**.

Chapter 17

International HRM

Phil Almond and Olga Tregaskis

Objectives

- To examine factors that help explain the strategy and structure of MNCs.
- To examine the structure, role and activities of international HRM functions in MNCs and the factors influencing these configurations.
- To consider the role of international HR networks and expatriates in generating and transferring HR knowledge in MNCs.
- To examine the influence of MNC country of origin and country of operation on HRM practice.

Introduction

This chapter deals with issues relating to the management of human resources within multinational corporations (MNCs), that is, firms that directly employ people in at least two countries. Such firms represent a substantial proportion of employment. In the UK, more than 25 per cent of manufacturing employment is in the subsidiaries of foreign multinationals, as well as 11.6 per cent of total employment in services (OECD, 2006). In addition, of course, many UK-owned firms also have international operations, and therefore have to engage in international human resource management, even if, as we will see, the issues faced by UK managers will be to some extent different in British-owned to foreign-owned MNCs. Finally, it is often argued that the management practices of foreign MNCs have a wider influence on HRM in domestic firms (cf. Dunning, 1958; Oliver and Wilkinson, 1992). This is particularly the case when firms are part of the supply chain to foreign MNCs. Overall, then, a large proportion of UK managers and workers are, directly or indirectly, affected by the human resource decisions of MNCs.

Of course, from an HR perspective, this only matters if the human resource issues facing managers in MNCs are somehow different to those in purely domestic firms. In other words, does the diverse group of firms that are MNCs have something in common, that is distinctive from other firms, which means we should analyse them together? This chapter will argue that MNCs should be considered as a distinct group of organisations, in a way that has some parallels with the way in which employment relations academics have long recognised that we need to treat, say, public sector organisations as a distinct group of employers.

The chapter will therefore explain what makes the process of human resource management distinctive in an MNC. It will, for instance, reflect the fact that managing the human resources of a firm becomes more complex when those human resources work in different national societies, for reasons which can be related back to the cross-national differences in employment relations systems introduced in the previous chapter. Differences in employment law and industrial relations systems between countries mean that some HR policies and practices may be legally and socially acceptable in a firm's operations in one country, but not in another. Equally, differences in national training and education systems are likely to mean that the skill and competence profile of the workers available on the labour market will differ from one country to another. Finally, differences in national management cultures may mean that some management styles are more appropriate in some national settings than others.

These national differences, though, are not just a 'problem' for the managers of MNCs to deal with; they can also be exploited to the advantage of the firm. Indeed, much of the literature on international HRM is dominated by a concern to identify and understand how MNCs manage their geographically dispersed workforces for both local and global competitive advantage. Questions typically asked in this literature concern the circumstances in which MNCs broadly attempt to pursue uniformity of HR policies across their international operations, and those in which there are advantages to having different policies in different countries. Such differentiation may in some cases be useful in order to meet the demands of local product markets, where national differences in customer demands mean that firms have to adapt their management of labour. In other cases, differentiation may take place in order to exploit most efficiently the local labour market; MNCs which originate in high-cost, highly regulated economies may well choose not to transfer important elements of their HR systems to lower wage, lightly regulated economies, for example.

Despite the demands for and benefits that MNCs can accrue from differentiation there are strong competitive reasons for these organisations to want to coordinate and integrate their activities across geographical boundaries. To maximise economies of scale MNCs attempt to coordinate activities involving scarce and/or costly resources. Equally, it is argued that the more management processes and activities can be integrated across geographical boundaries the easier it is to share resources and knowledge. The HRM function in MNCs play a critical role in developing systems and process that promote internal consistency in how employees are treated. They also need to consider how they can identify and best use the skill and management talent that exists across the distributed MNC network. At the same time the desire for standardisation and integration in HRM needs to take account of the country differences that give rise to different employee expectations, perceptions and skills levels. This raises questions about how the international HR function can organise itself to address both the demands for integration and localisation. Which HRM activities should be coordinated or controlled by the corporate HR function and which activities should be localised? How can the HR function structure itself to best address these competing demands for integration and localisation? And more recently the literature in the field has been concerned with how HR knowledge can be transferred across the MNC and whether global HR practices can be created from knowledge drawn from the subsidiaries as much as from that generated by the centre or corporate HR function.

These varying literatures and debates are considered in this chapter. We begin with the organisational-focused literature by introducing the international strategic context MNCs operate within which then leads into the alternative models that have been proposed to explain how the international HR function is organised and its role. We then consider how HR knowledge is transferred, focusing specifically on the role of international HR networks and expatriates. The chapter then shifts its focus to the national context literature and moves on to analyse the extent to which international HRM is affected by the national ownership of firms, and by the countries in which they operate. The role of managers in dealing with different national systems of employment relations (see Chapter 15) is highlighted here.

The international strategic context

The introduction to this chapter indicated that additional insights are necessary in order to understand HR management in MNCs, for the simple reason that one thing that all MNCs share is the challenge of coordinating managers and workers in more than one country. At the most basic level, this creates dilemmas for managers about the extent to which the firm should pursue consistent HR policies across its different national operations, or allow foreign subsidiaries to pursue the policies which are seen as appropriate for the specific national employment systems involved.

Clearly, however, all MNCs are not the same; they vary enormously along dimensions such as size, the number of foreign countries in which they have workforces, and in their degree of internationalisation (that is, the proportion of the firm's workforce, and of its sales, which are outside the original home country) and these differences impact greatly on the nature of management within such firms.

Differences in MNC structure

It is sometimes argued that some of the differences between international firms mean that, when discussing international management, we should distinguish between MNCs with different structural forms, and discuss the nature of management processes within each, rather than simply referring to 'multinational corporations' as if this group of firms were homogenous.

International business strategists have attempted to generate theory that makes it easier to interpret the complex world of international business. One of the best known is Prahalad and Doz's (1987) Integration–Responsiveness (IR) Grid. They argue that MNCs are faced with pressures to integrate and coordinate their activities on the one hand and on the other to respond to local (national) variations. The pressures driving integration and responsiveness faced by MNCs are summarised in Table 17.1.

These two pressures, namely integration and responsiveness, form the Integration–Responsiveness grid and MNCs adopt different strategies and structures depending on where they sit within this grid (see Harzing, 1999 for an in-depth review). So for example in a multi-domestic industry, such as utilities (e.g. water services) consumer demands and service provision are highly context specific. Thus, the competitive strategy of a multinational's French subsidiary, for example, is in this case largely independent of that of its UK counterpart. This is necessary because regulatory requirements, customer norms or government policy require a strategy that is responsive to local conditions. As such these subsidiaries compete in domestic markets and frequently with domestic companies. Equally, a decentralised organisational structure where subsidiaries are given a high degree of strategic and operational autonomy from its parent is the most efficient. However, often the parent retains some degree of control through setting performance targets. This type of organisation would be located in the bottom right-hand side of the grid (Figure 17.1). By contrast, in a global industry, such as consumer electronics, standardised product/service demands by customers and economies of scale dominate. The organisation's strategy prioritises efficiencies by producing standardised products, locating in the most cost effective economies and coordinating expensive resources such as equipment, or R&D. These organisations tend to centralise resources and responsibilities to the parent company, while the role of the subsidiaries tends to be sales and services. The strategic responsibility and operational freedom of subsidiaries is usually fairly tightly controlled by the parent. This type of organisation would be located in the top left-hand side of the grid.

There is a considerable degree of empirical evidence supporting the existence of multi-domestic and global organisational forms (Bartlett and Ghoshal, 1989; Harzing, 2000; Leong and Tan, 1993; Moenaert *et al.*, 1994; Roth and Morrison, 1990). And the I–R grid is a simple and effective tool for explaining the key priorities shaping these organisations' strategies and structures. However, it is less effective at capturing the significance of the transfer of learning and innovation, which is an important strategic priority for the third type of international organisation, namely the transnational.

Table 17.1 Summary of the pressures making up the I–R grid

I–R grid	Pressures
Strategic coordination need is high where:	• Multinational customers are a large proportion of the customer base. For example, it is important to coordinate pricing, service and product support worldwide as the multinational customer has the ability to compare prices on this basis • Global competition is likely. If companies operate in multiple markets global competition is highly likely. As such it is important to monitor and collect information on competitors' activities in the different countries in readiness for an appropriate and timely strategic response • Investment in one or more parts of the business is high. For example, high-tech manufacturing or R&D are common high fixed costs. To maximise the benefits and yield the best return on capital investments global coordination is necessary
Operational integration need is high where:	• Technological intensity is high. Technology intensive businesses often require a small number of manufacturing sites that enable quality and costs to be centrally controlled while • serving wide geographically dispersed markets. • Cost reduction is a priority. This can be achieved through locating in low cost economies or building plants designed to maximise economies of scale. • The product is universal and requires minimal adaptation to local markets. This is typical in consumer electronics. • Manufacturing needs to be located close to essential raw materials or energy such as in the petrochemicals business.
Local responsiveness is high where:	• Customer demands vary across nations or regions. • Distribution channels need to be tailored to the characteristics of the country or region. For example, marketing of products may need to be nationally specific. • There are other similar products or where the product needs to be adapted to local needs. • Local competitors rather than multinational competitors define the market competition. • The host country places restrictions on the operating subsidiary.

● *What is the business case for global integration by a multinational? Explain.*

● *What consequences does the pursuit of economic efficiencies have on local economies?*

● *What issues does global integration by multinationals raise in terms of the wider environment and social consequences for local economies?*

Suggested reading: Ghoshal and Bartlett (1998).

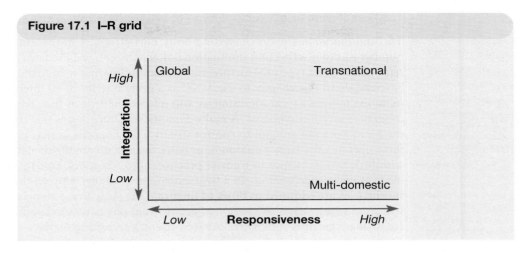

Figure 17.1 I–R grid

Another prominent model in the international management literature is that developed by Bartlett and Ghoshal (1989). Their work elaborates on issues around innovation and knowledge transfer in MNCs. Like Prahalad and Doz (1987) they identify the different pressures facing firms, which push them towards different structural forms. Two of the pressures they identify share much in common with Prahalad and Doz's concepts of integration and responsiveness. However, they also identify a third pressure, namely, worldwide innovation. Each of these are discussed in more detail below.

- *Local differentiation.* This refers to pressures emanating from 'local' (which usually in this context means national) markets to offer distinctive products, or to offer services in a distinctive way. This can be caused by consumer tastes; for example, a supermarket chain seeking to operate in both the UK and Spain would have to take account of the fact that there is a much higher demand for fresh produce, and regional products, in Spain, and a higher demand for packaged meals in the UK. This might affect the necessary skills profile of the workforce in the two countries, and also would be likely to affect the way in which the national operations think about distribution and marketing. In other cases, pressures for local differentiation are brought about by national regulations; this is often the case in the utilities sector, for example.

- *Global integration.* Bartlett and Ghoshal argue that the technological developments of the last half-century mean that economies of scale became increasingly crucial to competitive success. In order to achieve the scale necessary to gain competitive advantage, firms may seek to create integrated production processes in different parts of the world. For example, in automobile production it is common for different parts of vehicles to be manufactured in different national subsidiaries of the major companies.

- *Worldwide innovation.* Here, the argument is that firms have come under increasing pressure to increase the pace of innovation, as markets and technologies evolve rapidly. In this context, Bartlett and Ghoshal argue that a logical response for many international firms is to encourage and support innovation in a coordinated way across their different inter-national operations, rather than simply to rely on the innovative capacities of the original home country operations of the firm.

Bartlett and Ghoshal further argue that these different pressures exist to differing extents. This will partly depend on which sector(s) the MNC is operating in; national differences in markets, for example, may be important in food retail, but far less so (if at all) in the market for computer chips, while economies of scale and the extent of radical innovation will also be greater in some sectors than others. They also argue that the nature, and extent, of these pressures has altered over time, with greater pressures for global integration and particularly for worldwide innovation, meaning that the predominant structural forms of MNCs should change to fit these.

They identify four main structural forms of international firms. These are:

- *The multinational ('multi-domestic') form.* Bartlett and Ghoshal, in common with a number of other writers on international management, use the term 'multinational' to refer to a specific type of structure, rather than to international firms in general. As we have chosen in this chapter to use MNC as a generic term for all international firms, to minimise terminological confusion we will refer to the type of firm Bartlett and Ghoshal mean here as 'multi-domestic'. A multi-domestic structure means that the headquarters of the MNC does not attempt to control strictly what happens in overseas subsidiaries, so these operate on a largely autonomous basis. Such firms are highly decentralised in HR, with little or no attempt to transfer practices across borders. Equally, few attempts are made at knowledge transfer. To a large extent, the relations between the HQ and foreign subsidiaries are confined to flows of finance. This structure is associated with circumstances in which customer tastes vary greatly from one nation to another, or where there are strong regulatory differences between countries, creating markets which are strongly national in nature. Bartlett and Ghoshal associate this form with the first half of the twentieth century, but it should be noted that the multi-domestic form of MNCs continues to exist in markets such as utility sectors, where national regulation makes extensive attempts at international coordination by HQ largely counterproductive.

- *The global form.* This is essentially a model in which HQ management takes home country management approaches, and tries to replicate them abroad in order to achieve economies of scale. In this model, there is a clear hierarchy, with HQ instructing foreign managers how to manage their operations, or using a high number of expatriate managers for the same reason. Strategic decisions will exclusively be taken at HQ level, with research and development also concentrated in the home country. This model of international management is most likely in markets where economies of scale are critical to competitive advantage. Bartlett and Ghoshal associate this model with the period between 1950 and 1980, although cases where HQ strongly directs policy abroad, and concentrates knowledge in the home base, continue to exist.

- *The international form.* In the global form, MNCs replicate a production technology worldwide, in order to produce an identical product in different national operations. The international firm goes one step beyond this, in that HQs become increasingly cognisant of cross-national differences in consumer demands. They export knowledge and expertise to foreign subsidiaries, but allow local management the ability to alter the nature of products and services to suit the nature of the local market. In these firms, control is somewhat less tight than in global firms, but the general tone of policy is still likely to flow from the HQ to subsidiaries.

- *The transnational firm.* In this final type of MNC, the firm moves away from being a hierarchy, with the HQ at the top and the various national subsidiaries below, and towards what is sometimes referred to as a 'heterarchy' (Nohria and Ghoshal, 1997), or network form of organisation. In such 'transnational' firms, then, management control is dispersed across the corporation, rather than being concentrated at HQ. Unlike in the previous three forms of international organisation, the various international units of the enterprise are highly interdependent. Because of this, there are extensive flows of people, knowledge and resources not just from HQ to foreign subsidiaries (as is frequent in the global and international forms), but also from foreign subsidiaries to HQ, and between different foreign subsidiaries. Such firms achieve coordination through shared decision making, aided by attempts to create a common managerial culture across the firm (sometimes referred to as 'normative integration', see Birkinshaw and Morrison, 1995: 737), rather than through rule-making from HQ. According to Bartlett and Ghoshal (1989), this network form of organisation allows international firms systematically to transfer learning and knowledge across their various international operations, while offering a more flexible, responsive form of coordination than the three previous models of organisation.

- *How do heterarchic structures differ to hierarchical-based structures?*

- *How might an HR manager support learning and knowledge flows in heterarchial structures?*

As we mentioned above, Bartlett and Ghoshal argue that the most appropriate structure for MNCs has altered over time, with a broad movement from the multi-domestic through to the transnational form. In the current context of internationalised markets, rapid transformations in production technology and product markets, and the need to combine global economies of scale with local or regional adaptability, they clearly argue that large MNCs, at least, should follow the transnational model.

In reality, though, many of even the larger MNCs do not follow the transnational model. There are several reasons for this. First, as Bartlett and Ghoshal would acknowledge, there remain product markets which are so nationally specific as to make the transnational structure an inappropriate organisational structure. Second, their models downplay the importance of organisational politics (Edwards and Rees, 2006: 77–81); the transnational structure is difficult to coordinate as, in reality, managers in different countries are liable to pursue their own objectives, with the result that the strategy of an international organisation which is not strongly hierarchical is more likely to be the result of continual negotiation rather than of rational planning. In other words, it is difficult for the senior executives of an organisation to create a rational network structure; how the network operates in reality will be affected by the range of managerial actors within the international organisation. Finally, Bartlett and Ghoshal largely ignore the extent to which MNC structures and strategies are affected both by the countries they originate from, and the countries they operate in. Such effects will be examined in a later section of this chapter.

Section summary

In summary, Prahalad and Doz provided an effective and simple model for appreciating the two competing pressures, integration and responsiveness, and their impact on MNC structures. However, their work underemphasised the importance of global innovation and knowledge transfer. This is addressed to a greater extent by Bartlett and Ghoshal who offer a fourfold typology of MNC structures; some of the effects of positioning along these dimensions on HRM and the international transfer of knowledge and learning will be explored below. They argue that pressures on such organisations to combine local differentiation, global integration and worldwide innovation mean that the transnational model is increasingly the most appropriate model to follow. However, it is increasingly argued (Ferner, 1997; Edwards and Rees, 2006) that Bartlett and Ghoshal's typology underestimates the roles of organisational politics and of national setting in determining how MNCs really operate. For this reason, many MNCs, even if they are seeking to achieve local differentiation, global integration and worldwide innovation, may not in reality operate according to the transnational model.

Configuration of the international HRM function

International HRM is defined as:

> The set of distinct activities, functions and processes that are directed at attracting, developing and maintaining an MNC's human resources. It is thus the aggregate of the various HRM systems used to manage people in the MNC, both at home and overseas.
>
> (Taylor, *et al.*, 1996: 960)

Here we consider the models of international HRM that have been put forward to explain how the HR function is configured, the activities and roles undertaken and the factors affecting these. It is interesting to consider how external and institutional factors are treated within these models, an issue that will be explored in more detail in the latter part of this chapter. Since the early 1990s the international HRM literature has been dominated by models and typologies aimed at identifying the role and structure of international HRM functions aligned with organisational strategy. As a result of the attempt to 'explicitly link IHRM with the strategy of the MNC' (Taylor *et al.*, 1996: 960), this body of work is tightly tied to developments in multinational strategy-structure and is 'built on antecedents that are decades old' (p. 961). The human resource management systems at the international and national levels are seen as the mechanisms through which competitive demands are potentially realised. The key theoretical work in the field of international HRM thus draws heavily on the strategy-structure work of the international management researchers, most notably Bartlett and Ghoshal (1989), Hedlund (1986) and Prahalad and Doz (1987). The questions that dominate this field include: how can such organisations most efficiently structure their geographically dispersed operations to meet both global and local competitive demands? What is the nature of the control relationship between the parent and its subsidiaries? These questions in turn raise issues for international HRM in terms of what types of human resource management activity should be centralised to maximise integration and meet globalisation strategic imperatives, and what should be decentralised to allow localisation of policy and practice and to maximise local competitive advantage.

The five approaches reviewed here have each had a profound effect on the debates and theoretical development in this field. However, they each differ in the nature of the contribution they make. First, we will consider the Schuler *et al.* model which was developed as an analytical framework pulling together various conceptual and empirical work in the field providing researchers with a potential roadmap of the internal and external organisational factors influencing the issues, function, practices and impacts of international HRM. The importance of national context is recognised but not specified. Second, Taylor and colleagues (1996) focused on the conditions under which the parent was more likely to exercise control over its subsidiaries' activities. In particular the model emphasised the resource dependencies that existed between the parent and its subsidiaries. This says little about national contextual issues, but is important as, unlike much previous writing in the field, it recognises that subsidiaries of multinationals have considerable ability to control their own action and influence the degree of parent control over them by using resources that the parent needs as a means of trading or negotiating. The third model shifts its focus from the international HR function to the influence of management perceptions on multinational strategy. Perlmutter identifies variation in the mindsets or ways of thinking about the international environment, which he argues can affect the international nature of the organisation's management processes. This model has had a profound effect on international HRM debates for it underpins much of the theorising on the role of corporate HR functions in multinationals (e.g. Schuler, Dowling and De Cieri, 1993). The fourth and fifth models, by Adler and Ghadar (1990) and Milliman and Von Glinow (1990) respectively, are models of organisational change. They focus more on the relative influence of host and home country factors in shaping the role of the international HR function and in particular the role of expatriate managers in enabling international strategy. Both models adopt a similar perspective in terms of seeing the multinational progress through various stages of internationalisation, with each stage bringing into focus the importance of home and host country priorities. Here we see the potential for overlap between much of the comparative work and international HR theory, however as will be illustrated the discussion of home and host contextual issues is scant.

Schuler, Dowling and De Cieri (1993): integrative framework of international HRM

The Schuler *et al.* (1993) integrative framework of international HRM was, in essence, a conceptual framework that attempted to map HRM activity to the varying strategic requirements for integration and local responsiveness which define MNC strategy (Figure 17.2). Because of this it is extremely comprehensive in terms of the breadth of issues addressed, although this is at the expense of depth in the explanation of these issues. This framework built upon the work of strategic HRM theorists researching HRM in domestic companies (Boam and Sparrow, 1992; Schuler, 1992; Lengnick-Hall and Lengnick-Hall, 1988; Wright and McMahan, 1992). As such, Schuler *et al.* (1993: 422) define strategic international HRM as:

> Human resource management issues, functions, policies and practices that result from the strategic activities of multinational enterprises and that impact the international concerns and goals of those enterprises.

Figure 17.2 Integrative framework of strategic international HRM in MNEs

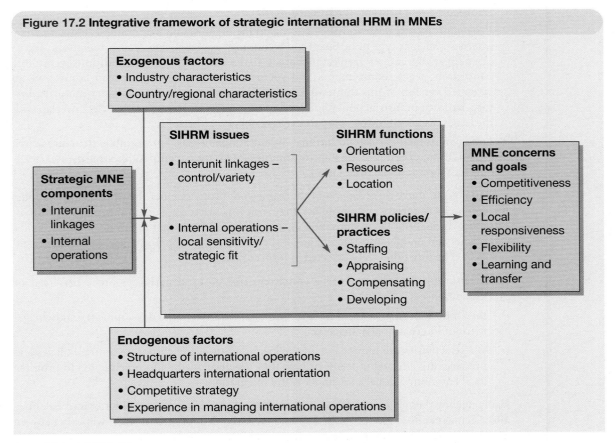

Source: Schuler *et al.* (1993: 423).

The overlap between the study of domestic and international HRM is discussed explicitly by Taylor *et al.* (1996: 960):

> Strategic Human Resource Management (SHRM) . . . is used to explicitly link with the strategic management processes of the organisation and to emphasise coordination or congruence among various human resource management practices. Thus, SIHRM is used to explicitly link IHRM with the strategy of the MNC.

This integrative framework of SIHRM identifies a series of strategic MNE (multinational enterprise) components, endogenous factors and exogenous factors that shape the issues, policy, practices and functions of HRM in international organisations. These determinants are explained, briefly:

1 Strategic MNE components include interunit linkages and internal operations. Inter-unit linkage is concerned with the need to differentiate or integrate several operations which are geographically dispersed (Ghoshal and Bartlett, 1998; Prahalad and Doz, 1987). Internal operations refer to how each unit operates within its local environment. The restrictions of national institutional or legislative frameworks are recognised along with the cultural diversity in attitudes towards work, management, authority and so forth (Hofstede, 1980; Laurent, 1983; Schein, 1984).

2 Exogenous factors relate to issues external to the organisation. For example, industry characteristics such as type of business and technology available, nature of competitors, degree of change; and country/regional characteristics such as political conditions, economic conditions, legal requirements and socio-cultural context. They also argue that an extended version of this framework would include issues such as industry maturity, history, national industrial policy and level of unionisation. Here there is a clear overlap with the issues discussed by the comparative researchers.

3 Endogenous factors relate to internal organisational issues. For example, structure of the organisation, experience, or stage of internationalisation, competitive strategy and headquarter's international orientation.

Essentially, the above three aspects of the framework bring together the work of international management theorists and argue for their impingement on the management of human resources throughout the organisation. Specifically, they argue that the strategic components, exogenous and endogenous factors affect the SIHRM function and associated policies and practices. The function can be affected in terms of its:

(a) orientation, i.e. the extent to which control of local activities are centralised or decentralised;

(b) the amount of financial and time resources committed to the development and management of international managers;

(c) where activities are located, i.e. in the local unit or at the corporate centre. Policies and practices are affected in terms of how they are developed and implemented to promote local autonomy, global coordination and integration.

Using agency theory (Jones, 1984) and resource dependency theory (Pfeffer and Salancik, 1978) Schuler *et al.* (1993) propose that an organisation's approach to HRM will vary between using a high level of parent country nationals and normative control measures to direct local behaviour versus high levels of local or third-country nationals and normative control measures to enable the centre to guide policies while still allowing for local adaptation. HR philosophy will play a key role in providing local sites with general statements to guide their practices so they are in tune with the corporate approach but locally sensitive. There is also a need for local HR policy to fit with corporate policy if personnel are to be able to be selected, transferred and developed as an organisational resource as opposed to a subsidiary resource. As such they argue that in order for multinational companies to be flexible and adaptable to local circumstance, transfer learning and to retain strategic integration HR practices need to match strategic and cultural demands at the local level. A *modus operandi* needs to be developed to enable HR practices to fit changing circumstances. While global HR policies need to be developed to be flexible enough to be applied to local HR practice. This perspective therefore not only focuses on HR policies and practices for the management of international managers but HR policies and practices for the management of local employees.

As indicated earlier, the role of national institutional factors is incorporated within the framework. Specifically, they argue uncertain political environments and high economic risk demand greater monitoring and control from the parent. While, high levels of heterogeneity, and complexity in legislative conditions affecting labour relations are likely to lead to the greater utilisation of local employees, rather than expatriates, in senior management positions at the subsidiary level. They also recognise that cultural diversity will demand greater attention by HR professionals in contexts where there is a business demand for integration and coordination. Thus the effects of the national institutional context are recognised in terms of the degree of control or autonomy given to the subsidiary by the parent and in terms of the centrality of expatriates.

The relationship between organisational structures and strategic international HRM policy and practice is discussed in relation to four organisational strategy-structure configurations, namely, the international divisional structure, the multinational structure, the global and the transnational. They state:

> Different structures of international operations create different requirements for autonomy, localisation and co-ordination, thus affecting the nature of and extent of SIHRM policies and practices; and the structures of the international operations of the MNE will impact the need for the units to develop mechanisms to respond to local conditions and to develop a flexible capability.
> (Schuler *et al.* 1993: 446)

Given this, Schuler and colleagues propose that international divisional structures result in a strategic international HRM orientation that focuses on a single issue, namely the selection of senior managers to head up local operations. The multinational structure focuses on selecting managers from anywhere in the company that can run local operations autonomously and with sensitivity to local conditions. The global structure requires a strategic international HRM orientation that selects managers who can operate under centralised control conditions. The transnational structure requires selecting and developing managers that can balance both local and global perspectives. Here again we see that the focus of the model is on explaining and matching the internal HR resources, via recruitment, selection or development, to meet the strategic needs of the organisations.

Schuler *et al.* (1993: 451) conclude that strategic international HRM is concerned with:

> Developing a fit between exogenous and endogenous factors and balancing the competing demands of global versus local requirements as well as the needs of coordination, control and autonomy.

Whilst the model is comprehensive it has been criticised for failing to explain the micropolitical processes that underpin parent–subsidiary relations (Quintanilla, 1999) and for being overly descriptive (Holden, 2001). In addition, whilst the model alludes to the impact of international HRM on both the international and local workforces, in reality the discussion tends to focus on management employees only (Ferner, 1994).

Using Schuler et al*.'s framework of SIHRM:*

(a) *In what ways does the HRM function at the headquarters level and the subsidiary level differ in their priorities and roles?*

(b) *How might these differences impact on the competencies of HR professionals in the different functions, if at all?*

(c) *What is the role of the HR philosophy in MNCs?*

(d) *Why might it be important to understand the mirco-policitical processes underpinning parent-subsidiary relations. Justify?*

Suggested reading: Schuler et al*. (1993).*

Taylor, Beechler and Napier (1996): exportive, integrative and adaptive model

Taylor *et al.* (1996) apply the resource-based theory of the firm to explain and predict why international organisations adopt different forms of strategic international HRM. Resource-based theory of the firm (Barney, 1991) applied to HR issues (Lado and Wilson, 1994) argues that HR can facilitate strategic goals by developing competencies within the organisation that are valuable, rare, hard to imitate and non-substitutable. Competencies are:

- *valuable* if they are differentiated and provide the company with something that they lack;
- *rare* if they are scarce or in short supply;
- *hard to imitate* where, for example, they are embedded within the firm's culture or history and thus based on collective values;
- *non-substitutable* where they cannot easily be replaced through recruitment, for example, in the case of tacit knowledge.

Applying this perspective, Taylor *et al.* suggested that the multinational could leverage resources at the national, firm and subsidiary level that could contribute to competitive advantage. Some of these resources would be context specific while others were context gener-alisable. This is illustrated by the exportative, integrative and adoptive strategic international HRM orientations towards corporate, subsidiary and employee group level HR issues, policies and practices. The concepts of these three SIHRM forms are based on previous work in international management and SIHRM (Hedlund, 1986; Perlmutter, 1969; Rosenzweig and Nohria, 1994; Rosenzweig and Singh, 1991). Each of these three orientations are explained below:

- *Adaptive.* HRM reflects subsidiary HRM systems designed to match the local environment. Differentiation is emphasised and HRM is concerned with the appointment of local senior managers but with little transfer of HRM philosophies, policies, or practices from the parent to subsidiary or between subsidiaries. This approach focuses on attending to local differentiation needs and is polycentric in nature.
- *Exportive.* HRM focuses on replication of parent HR systems in subsidiaries. Integration is a key priority and all HRM functions are affected not just the international 'cadre' (managers). This approach focuses on maximising global integration and is ethnocentric in nature.
- *Integrative.* HRM is based on the notion of taking the best HRM systems from anywhere in the company and allowing for both global integration and local differentiation and is geocentric in nature.

At the level of the subsidiary the strategic international HRM orientation determines the level of transfer of parent HRM systems, which is based on the resource-dependency relationship between the parent and subsidiary. For example, exportive HRM leads to high control by the parent which promotes a high level of transfer of its HRM systems to achieve global integration. Under these conditions the subsidiary is highly dependent on the parent for HR systems and processes to enable integration. In contrast, the adaptive HRM orientation demands little control and transfer of practices by the parent as differentiation is the priority. Under these conditions resource-dependency by both the parent and subsidiary is low. In the middle we have the integrative orientation which demands a balance between the transfer of some systems while maintaining the flexibility in the system to allow the subsidiary to adapt to the local context. Under these conditions, there is a parent–subsidiary interdependency. Finally, from the resource-dependence perspective they argue that parent control and standardisation of parent and subsidiary practice will be greater in those areas affecting employees 'most critical to the MNC's performance' (Taylor *et al.*, 1996: 978).

Taylor *et al.* also recognise that there are a number of factors that are likely to constrain the degree of parent control over subsidiary behaviour, namely method of subsidiary establishment, cultural and legal distance of host country from the parent or home country of the multinational. With respect to the first of these points the evidence suggests that subsidiaries that have been acquired have less in common with their parent HR systems than those that are greenfield sites, although this pattern may change over time. Equally, the greater the dissimilarity between the parent company's national culture and legal context, the less commonality between the parent and subsidiary's HR systems. This would follow from many of the institutional arguments outlined in Chapter 15.

Their work raises a number of implications. First, unlike much of the previous work Taylor *et al.* (1996) are more explicit about the impact of SIHRM on different occupational groups. They recognise that not all employees provide the same level of value to the company or provide the same level of critical resources. Traditionally, broad distinctions have been made between white-collar and blue-collar workers. However, there is a need to refine this further by looking at other occupational groups that may be critical to competitive advantage, such as research staff or product designers. Second, their work raises a key question about the generalisability of HR practice beyond the context in which it was developed. What aspects of HRM practice are generalisable? Why? Third, and finally, their model lacks specificity with regard to what is transferred and how.

Activity

Read the section below on Perlmutter's mindsets and consider the following question. Taylor *et al*. (1996) argued that the exportive, adaptive and integrative SIHRM orientations are linked to Perlmutter's ethnocentric, polycentric and geocentric mindsets respectively. Explain why and what this means for HRM practice in the case of each of the three orientations.

Suggested reading: Taylor *et al*. (1996).

Perlmutter (1969): mindsets

Perlmutter (1969) is widely recognised as one of the first theorists to propose a network-based model of how international companies organise globally. Perlmutter's classification has been applied primarily in the international human resource management literature rather than the international business field, from where it originated. Kobrin (1994) explains that Perlmutter's adoption by the international HRM theorists is largely because the classification is defined in terms of human resource management issues (e.g. training, recruiting, selecting people and resources). Perlmutter initially defined three organisational types based on senior management's cognitions or mindsets: the ethnocentric, polycentric and geocentric organisation. Later he defined a fourth mindset namely, the regiocentric. He argues that senior management mindsets reflect the extent to which home, host, global or regional values are perceived as important and in turn influence the international nature of management processes used in the company. These mindsets have been adopted by many in the international HRM field as a way of classifying different HRM approaches, for example:

- *The ethnocentric mindset* reflects a focus on home country values and ways of operating. As a consequence key positions in subsidiaries are filled by parent country nationals (i.e. expatriates). This gives the parent a high degree of direct control over the subsidiaries' operations.

- *The polycentric mindset* focuses on host country values and ways of operating. As a result key positions in the subsidiary are more likely to be filled by local employees and the parent company is less interested in controlling and homogenising the organisational culture.

- *The geocentric mindset* focuses on global values and ways of operating. These global values are not nationally specific but instead transcend national boundaries and become almost acultural. This approach looks to use the best people for the job selecting from all over the global organisation.

- *The regiocentric mindset* focuses on regional values and ways of operating. As a result the organisation is usually structured along regional geographical lines (e.g. Europe, America, and the Asia/Pacific Rim) and employees move around within these regions. This approach allows some degree of integration, but recognises regional diversity.

Schuler *et al.* incorporate Perlmutter's ideas into their framework arguing that these attitudes underpin a multinational's strategic international HRM orientation in terms of autonomy and standardisation of local HR practice (e.g. staffing, appraisal, compensation and training). The ethnocentric mindset promotes control and centralisation of HR activity, the polycentric mindset is aligned with local decentralisation, the geocentric mindset does not develop HR activity on the basis of nationality. We also saw how these mindsets were associated with Taylor *et al.*'s integrative, adaptive and exportive orientations. While these relationships are somewhat scant in their detail they allude to the widening scope of the role of a corporate strategic international HRM function as organisational structures become more complex and network-like rather than hierarchical in nature. One of the primary problems with Perlmutter's approach is that it provides little explanation of how or why the organisation may move from one type of mindset orientation to another.

Adler and Ghadar (1990) and Milliman and Von Glinow (1990): organisational change models

Two models have been put forward that are based on organisational change models namely the product lifecycle model of Adler and Ghadar (1990) and the organisational lifecycle model of Milliman and Von Glinow (1990). These models have been designed to explain how and why the international HRM orientation of a multinational change over time in line with changes in its corporate strategy. Both approaches also recognise the variable importance of the parent or home country context and the host country context throughout each stage. In doing so they take a largely cultural approach.

The Adler and Ghadar (1990) model is based on the product lifecycle (PLC) during internationalisation, first observed and described by Vernon (1966), and is a stage model of organisational change. In Adler and Ghadar's model they describe how the role of culture changes in salience and how HRM activities are modified at each stage in response to product strategic requirements and cultural requirements. These phases are described briefly in Table 17.2.

- *Phase I: Domestic.* Here the focus is on the home market. The products/services are unique, they have not been available before, therefore the price is high relative to cost and competition is minimal. As the products are unique there is no need for cultural sensitivity and if they are exported they are in a significantly strong position not to need adaptation. Indeed exportation of the product/service is based on the premise that 'foreigners' want the product/service unadapted. The HR needs are therefore not that demanding in international terms, i.e. expatriate assignments, internal business trips, cross-cultural training are not warranted for the export market. The international work is

Table 17.2 Globalisation and human resource management

	Phase I Domestic	Phase II International	Phase III Multinational	Phase IV Global
Primary orientation	Product or service	Market	Price	Strategy
Strategy	Domestic	Multi-domestic	Multinational	Global
Worldwide strategy	Allow foreign clients to buy product/ service	Increase market internationally, transfer technology abroad	Source, produce and market internationally	Gain global strategic competitive advantage
Staffing expatriates	None (few)	Many	Some	Many
Why sent	Junket	To sell control or transfer technology	Control	Coordination and integration
Whom sent		'OK' performers, salespeople	Very good performers	High-potential managers and top executives
Purpose	Reward	Project 'To get job done'	Project and career development	Career and organisational development
Career impact	Negative	Bad for domestic career	Important for global career	Essential for executive suite
Professional re-entry	Somewhat difficult	Extremely difficult	Less difficult	Professionally easy
Training and development	None	Limited	Longer	Continuous throughout career
For whom	No one	Expatriates	Expatriates	Managers
Performance appraisal	Corporate bottom line	Subsidiary bottom line	Corporate bottom line	Strategic positioning
Motivation assumption	Money motivates	Money and adventure	Challenge and opportunity	Challenge, opportunity, advancement
Rewarding	Extra money to compensate for foreign hardship		Less generous, global packages	
Career 'fast track'	Domestic	Domestic	Token international	Global
Executive passport	Home country	Home country	Home country, token foreigners	Multinational
Necessary skills	Technical and managerial	Plus cultural adaption	Plus recognising cultural differences	Plus cross-cultural interaction, influence and synergy

Source: Adler and Ghadar, 1990.

restricted to product or project specific technical competence (Mendenhall *et al.*, 1989). As domestic sales tend to dominate profits international aspects of management are not given to the best people nor seen as a valuable career move. International organisational development is not seen as relevant.

- *Phase II: International.* Here competition increases and international markets become more important for profit. There is a shift in focus from product development (R&D) to manufacturing and plants are set up locally and divisional structures emerge. Cultural sensitivity becomes critical to effective corporate strategies. However, decision making and control tend to remain with the parent. HR performs a vital role in attaining control of local operations. Home country personnel are used to transfer technology and management systems overseas where replication, rather than innovation, is the prime objective. Training in cultural sensitivity and adaptability is key at this stage.

- *Phase III: Multinational.* Here the product/service reaches maturity, competition is intense and the price has fallen. Coordination of resources becomes a vital tool in the reduction of costs. The role of culture becomes less important as the issue of reducing costs takes central position. As such the best people are usually chosen for international posts to increase profits and control costs. The management assumption at this phase is that organisational culture is more important than national culture therefore sensitivity to local cultures is seen to be less important and recruitment of international managers tends to be from those familiar with the parent culture.

- *Phase IV: Global.* The three prior phases were based on hierarchical structures. This phase is based on the assumption that the organisation will need to operate in all three phases simultaneously and therefore build 'complex networks of joint ventures, wholly owned subsidiaries and organisational and project defined alliances' (Adler and Ghadar, 1990: 240). Under such conditions the role of culture comes again to the fore. These organisations operate at a strategic level to combine responsive design and delivery quickly and cheaply. This negates the development of global R&D, production and marketing and therefore requires the management of culture and relationships external to the organisation. Success is based on international managers being able to communicate effectively in a culturally diverse environment. The delineation between expatriate and local managers disappears and the organisation needs to manage the dual demands of integration and local responsiveness (Doz and Prahalad, 1986).

Activity

Drawing on your understanding of the PLC model consider the role of expatriates, local employees, host national culture and organisational training during each phase.

	Phase I	Phase II	Phase III	Phase IV
Expatriates	• Expatriates are from the parent company • Focus on the transfer of technical competence to overseas operations; otherwise input is limited			
Local employees				
Host national culture				
Organisational training				

Suggested reading: Adler, N. and Ghadar, F. (1990).

However, the Adler and Ghadar (1990) model is criticised for its emphasis on the role of the expatriate manager and management expertise, with little reference to other employee groups. Milliman and Von Glinow (1990) also argue that as it focuses on a product lifecycle it is too narrow. International organisations often have multiple products and the stage of the cycle may vary across the strategic business units (SBU) changing the parent–SBU relationship. Therefore in response Milliman and Von Glinow (1990) apply the organisational lifecycle (OLC) approach to provide a more general framework to understanding SIHRM at the parent and subsidiary level. This model was further refined in the paper by Milliman, *et al.* (1991). The OCC approach is based on the premise that HRM responses will predictably vary in line with stages of organisational development. Milliman and Von Glinow's work highlights the importance of recognising the inter-relationships between the parent and subsidiary level in defining the nature of international HRM. They note that:

> The degree to which the corporate business and human resource strategies affect the SBU's strategic choices and practices depends on a number of fundamental characteristics of the MNC, such as its organisational culture, management style, and control systems.
>
> (Milliman and Von Glinow, 1990: 28)

The Milliman and Von Glinow (1990) model identifies four international HRM objectives, namely, timing, cost versus development, integration and differentiation:

- *Timing* refers to whether the organisation takes a short-term or long-term perspective in its business and international HRM strategy. The former requires quick responses the latter allows a longer period for implementation, which can mean longer international assignments and commitment to overseas operations.

- *Cost* refers to whether the organisation needs to focus on lowering costs or can focus on longer-term development issues in its overseas operations and the career paths of its expatriate managers.

- *Integration* relates to the use of expatriate managers in implementing informal control systems.

- *Differentiation* refers to the development of a network of home and host country managers to facilitate communication and control between the parent and subsidiary.

These four objectives change over four OLC stages leading to a different pattern of international HRM. These stages are now explained in brief:

- *Stage 1.* As the firm starts out most of the international HRM is conducted on an ad hoc basis and international assignments focus on technical work skills with little emphasis on cultural training. The need for integration or differentiation is minimal.

- *Stage 2.* The number and extent of commitment in overseas operation increases. Short-term savings remain a priority and the need of integration is minimal. However, for successive growth of the overseas markets greater knowledge of the local environment is needed. Thus expatriate training in cultural sensitivity and languages becomes more important.

- *Stage 3.* As the business becomes well established, the organisation can take a longer-term perspective and integration becomes key, particularly for controlling costs. Home country expatriates provide control along with the transfer of home HRM systems and organisational culture. But as cultural sensitivity is less important training in this area for expatriates diminishes and career development for this group is not so long term. Sophisticated control systems such as socialisation, mentoring and succession planning are vital for promoting a unified organisational culture and integration.

- *Stage 4.* The demands for both integration and differentiation are evident. In response organisations need to invest in training and development to enhance the flexibility of the organisation to meet these demands. They also need to evolve a 'multicentric cultural perspective' (Milliman and Von Glinow, 1990: 32) which ensures awareness of the national cultures and subcultures at the subsidiary level.

The Milliman and Von Glinow (1990) model parallels closely the stages models proposed by Adler and Ghadar (1990). Both models provide prescriptions of international HRM types. While Stages 1 to 3 are themselves supported by empirical work the associated international HRM forms are theoretically extrapolated. Stage 4, like the work of the international management theorists is largely a theoretical concept. Mayrhofer and Brewster (1996) argue that in practice MNCs, irrespective of their need for integration or diversity, adopt an ethnocentric approach to IHRM with many relying heavily on the use of expatriate managers to control overseas operations. Another problem with the stages model is that it has become less relevant as MNCs adopt both domestic and international markets simultaneously (Taylor and Beechler, 1993) and with acquisitions, mergers and de-mergers there is less evidence that multinationals have to pass through each of these phases in order to internationalise.

Section summary

In this part we have looked at the organisational processes, policies and practices adopted by MNCs to address their international strategic goals. This has considered the question of the role of the international HR function, how it is organised and the activities undertaken. Furthermore complex relationships between the internal configuration of organisational strategies and structures have been considered in terms of how these meet variable external influences. The resource-dependent nature of parent–subsidiary relations as a mechanism of influence highlighted the multiple levels at which international HRM operate, and its differential impact on home and host country employees.

Knowledge and the transfer of HR policy and practice in international organisations

The models outlined in the section above emphasise the importance of integrating HRM and creating global HRM practices that transcend national boundaries. This presupposes that HR knowledge can be easily packaged and transferred across multinational units and across national borders. A recent survey conducted by Brewster, Harris and Sparrow (2002) for the CIPD found that 45 per cent of organisations in their study identified knowledge management as a central plank of their international HRM strategy. In this section we consider some of the difficulties associated with knowledge transfer and the role of international HR networks and expatriates in facilitating the transfer of HR policy and practice.

The nature of knowledge

Knowledge is most frequently defined in terms of its explicit and tacit qualities (Nonaka and Takeuchi, 1995). This classification is based on Polanyi's (1962) expression of knowledge as having two complementary elements: the tacit which cannot be articulated and the explicit which can be articulated. Most of our knowledge is tacit in nature, particularly when we think of operational skills or know-how (Lam, 2000). This point is illustrated by Athanssiou and Nigh (2000: 474) when they suggest that while an individual may know how to ride a bike, they may not be able to explain how this is possible in relation to the laws of physics, thus, often, 'one knows more than one can tell'. In contrast, explicit knowledge, because it can be articulated, can be codified which makes it easier to transfer (Lam, 2000).

In terms of the transfer of knowledge it is argued that the transfer of tacit and explicit knowledge require different mechanisms. While the latter can be accumulated or stored at a central location or 'repositories' (Argote and Ingram, 2000), the former is dependent on close interaction. Tacit knowledge is personal and not subject independent. As such, it is scattered throughout an organisation. Its transfer is highly dependent on the transferor's 'deeper aware- ness of the communicable details' (Athanassiou and Nigh, 2000: 474) and the transferee's ability to understand what is being communicated. Developing a shared understanding, or what Polanyi (1966: 61) refers as the 'same kind of indwelling', is fundamental to the effective transfer of tacit knowledge. Such shared understandings can best be generated through close interaction. There is a significant body of evidence that suggests developing a common under- standing of the tacit dimension of knowledge is best achieved via face-to-face personal communications or strong social interaction (Nohria and Eccles, 1992).

Both modes of knowledge also demand differing methods for acquisition and accumu- lation purposes (Lam, 2000). It is argued that explicit knowledge can be generated through reasoning and deduction, and can be acquired from formal learning mechanisms such as reading, training, educational programmes. In contrast, tacit knowledge is dependent on practical context-specific experience. Thus in organisations tacit knowledge is acquired through personal experiences of different environments and face-to-face communications, and close interactions are critical for the diffusion of this knowledge.

In sum, the tacit or explicit nature of knowledge requires alternative mechanisms for its effective transfer, accumulation and generation. Because explicit knowledge can be codified it becomes a public as opposed to an individual or private possession. In so doing this makes it easier to copy or replicate. As a result organisations are particularly interested in harnessing tacit knowledge for competitive purposes, which is by its nature much more difficult for competitors to replicate. However, the context-specific nature of tacit knowledge and its non- articulation places emphasis on personal interaction as a means of transferring and generating tacit knowledge. It is argued that the HR function is a source of a considerable degree of tacit HR knowledge (Lado and Wilson, 1994; Huselid, 1995).

The role of the social context in generating and transferring HR knowledge

Many of the models of international HRM discussed previously imply that explicit HR knowledge is contained within the policies and practices of the company, but clearly over- look *how* this knowledge is transferred. Building on the earlier debates this section considers the importance of the social context for the generation and transfer of HR knowledge.

Taylor (2006) argues that HR functions play an important role in building social capital as a means of developing and transferring HR policies to achieve strategic integration. Social capital is defined as 'an asset embedded in relationships, communities, networks or societies' (Leana and van Buren, 1999: 539). It potentially provides a means through which tacit knowledge can be transferred because it creates a conducive social or relational context (Tre- gaskis, *et al.* 2005). Nahapiet and Ghoshal (1998) identified three dimensions of social capital underpinning knowledge creation and diffusion in organisations: structural, cognitive and social dimensions (Box 17.1). This work emphasises the importance of personal interaction in networks for harnessing tacit knowledge.

Implications for the generation and transfer of HR knowledge

The knowledge and social capital literature suggests that the generation and transfer of knowledge is socially embedded. As such one of the key mechanisms for the generation and diffusion of HR knowledge is the network. There has been an increasing body of work exam- ining the role of transnational teams or networks in multinationals in knowledge creation and diffusion (Athanassiou and Nigh, 2000). However, less work has looked at networks involved in developing HR-related knowledge in international organisations. One of few studies to explore this issue in detail was conducted by Tregaskis *et al.* (2005) who examine

Box 17.1

Dimensions of social capital

Structural dimension of social capital

This refers to the structure of the network, the nature of the ties in terms of being weak or strong, how they are combined to transfer knowledge and to combine knowledge. Evidence suggests that weak ties facilitate the search for information; however, they can hinder the transfer of knowledge particularly tacit knowledge. When the network is dealing with tacit knowledge strong ties have been found to be more effective (Hansen, 1999). The intensity of ties, their density, connectivity and hierarchy all influence the level of contact among network members and the ease with which information can be exchanged. The structural elements are also important in terms of the opportunity they offer to exchange knowledge more quickly than would be the case in the absence of such a network, and in facilitating flows of knowledge providing network members with opportunities to combine and exchange knowledge that would not arise if the network did not exist.

Cognitive dimension of social capital

This refers to the resources that foster the shared meanings and understanding among network members, such as common codes and language or shared narratives that represent the way things are done. This cognitive dimension provides a shared context between group members that facilitates more effectively and efficiently the sharing of tacit knowledge and the potential to combine this knowledge in new and novel ways (Gulati *et al.*, 2000).

A number of studies have found that network members that have worked together longer tend to work better together because they have developed shared routines and understandings that enable them to leverage the distinctiveness of group members for organisational purposes (Bantel and Jackson, 1989; Fisher and Pollock, 2004).

Relational dimension of social capital

This refers to the nature of the personal relationships that exist between network members in terms of, for example, the degree of trust, identification with others, a sense of obligation to others and the norms or expectations within the group regarding cooperation. These elements can affect access to knowledge, and the motivation to engage in knowledge exchange and combination activities.

Source: Tregaskis *et al.* (2005: 10).

the role of international HR networks in 13 multinational organisations. This research identified companies that had explicitly adopted formal international HR networks comprising headquarter-level (e.g. parent or regional) HR directors and senior-subsidiary-level HR managers. The case study evidence revealed that these forums had seven primary functions:

- global policy development;
- global HR policy implementation;
- best practice creation and sharing;
- exploitation of the distributed HR expertise;
- creating buy-in to policy initiatives;
- information exchange;
- socialisation of the HR community.

These functions reflected the organisation's desire to achieve integration in certain areas of HR activity, such as performance management, succession planning, talent spotting, expatriate careers. They also reflected the ambition by some of the companies to generate new global HR knowledge by drawing together expertise and tacit knowledge of how HR issues operated in divergent national contexts. There was also evidence of two alternative decision making processes (i.e. top–down *vs* collaborative) at play in the performance of these functions. The collaborative decision-making process embraced national variation as part of the process toward integration. In contrast, the top–down decision-making process tended to ignore or sideline national variation. The implication for the generation of new HR knowledge was stark. In the collaborative networks there was more opportunity for tacit knowledge to be exchanged among network members that had spent considerable time building the structural, relational and cognitive dimensions of the network. This tacit knowledge was used to create new global policies based, to a greater extent, on the joint experiences of the network members. The top-down model relied more heavily on HR knowledge that was generated at the centre, then codified and transferred through extensive implementation measures.

The value of networks for the rapid transfer of knowledge has also been explored by Brown and Duguid (1991) through what they refer to as 'communities of practice' (COP). Unlike the formal networks examined in the research by Tregaskis *et al.*, a COP may be informal in nature. Desouza (2003: 29) defines a COP as 'a group of people who have common tasks, interact and share knowledge with each other, either formally or informally'. These communities have a tacit and shared understanding of the group's identify and generate knowledge that is unique because the membership and the tacit knowledge of its membership is unique. Sparrow, Brewster and Harris (2004: 97) argue that the types of structures needed to support such communities include 'team processes for learning, reflection and appreciative enquiry, and co-enquiry, as opposed to simple expert–student relationships (headquarter-country operation)'. This suggests the generation of global HR practices within international HR communities of practice would require collaborative relations across subsidiary HR functions and between headquarters and subsidiary-level HR functions. It also challenges the nature of the parent–subsidiary control relationship that underpins many of the models explaining the configuration of the international HRM function.

Activity

You work in the UK HR function of a French owned chemical MNC. The headquarters HR function in France is keen for its subsidiary-level HR functions to exchange best practice ideas. However, you have found communication with HR functions in other countries very difficult. These difficulties are not due to language, instead there seems to be a reluctance on the part of your counterparts in the other countries to talk to each other and exchange ideas.

Questions

1 How might the company move toward more network-based relations across the international HR community?

2 How might the relational context of these networks be advanced?

3 What are the costs associated with building social capital in firms?

Another significant mechanism for the generation and transfer of international HR knowledge is the expatriate manager. The role of the expatriate manager in knowledge diffusion in transnational organisations was recognised by Bartlett and Ghoshal (1995). However, work in this area is generally limited (but see Bonache and Brewster, 2001; Cerdin, 2003). Kostova and Roth (2003) suggest social capital is accumulated by international managers because of their boundary-spanning roles. Boundary-spanning roles refer to management roles that cross networks, functional or geographical boundaries. These individuals often act as the lynchpin between horizontal or vertical structures within the multinational network. As such international managers can act to help diffuse HR practices across these boundaries. But equally, there is a need for the HR function to consider utilising international HR professionals in boundary-spanning roles to facilitate the diffusion and generation of tacit HR knowledge (Tregaskis *et al.*, 2005).

Section summary

This section has considered how HR knowledge is generated and transferred across the international organisation. It is suggested that the tacit nature of knowledge and its context-specificity, demands organisational structures and processes that enable a social context for the generation and transfer of knowledge. In terms of the international HR function this raises possibilities for the role of formal networks, communities of practice and boundary spanning international HR roles. These are all issues relevant to the future direction of international HR research.

Country effects

This section considers influences on the international human resource management policies and practices of MNCs that are related to the country from which they originate, and the foreign countries in which they operate. As we will see, there is evidence that countries of ownership, and of subsidiary operation, have effects both on processes of international learning within MNCs, and on specific HRM practices such as the management of pay or collective industrial relations.

It should be noted that some writers on international management downplay the importance of such influences, or even, in some cases, virtually deny their existence. Particularly, some writers on globalisation often make the claim that globalising trends in the world economy militate against cross-national differences in management in general, driving a convergence of capitalisms generally towards a single model, heavily influenced by the American model. At the extreme, the work of authors such as Kenneth Ohmae (1991) suggests a 'borderless world', or 'interlinked economy' in which the globalisation of production chains, product markets, corporate structures and financial flows makes national boundaries and the nation-state largely irrelevant. Following a similar logic, Reich (1991: 3) speculates about a future with 'no national products or technologies, no national corporations, no national industries'.

Against this, however, arguments are frequently made that the vast majority of MNCs retain a national identity. For example, the capital on which MNCs depend for investment remains predominantly based in the country of origin (Doremus *et al.*, 1998). Equally, in general, managerial control tends to be exerted by nationals of the original home country; for example, Ruigrok and van Tulder (1995) found that 25 of the 30 largest American-owned MNCs had no foreign nationals on their boards of directors. Additionally, it has often been argued that MNCs are often less 'transnational' than they may appear to be at first glance. Frequently, operations, particularly strategic functions such as research and development centres, remain disproportionately concentrated in the country of origin (Pauly and Reich, 1997; Hirst and Thompson, 1999).

Additionally, there are both economic and sociological reasons to expect that MNCs with their origins in different national systems of business and employment may operate in somewhat distinctive ways, with effects on the nature of HR policies in their subsidiary operations across the world. From an economic perspective, it is commonly argued that the ways in which firms choose to internationalise, as well as their use of specific management practices, is a result of their embeddedness in specifically national institutional contexts which coincide with the firms' country of origin (c.f. Porter, 1990; Morgan, 2001; Whitley, 1999; Lane, 2001; Kristensen and Morgan 2007). The basic argument here is that firms' competitive advantage is rooted in their home country business systems, and that they will seek to replicate such advantages abroad. A good example of this can be found in the early development of the automobile industry. Faced with a lack of craft workers, but a plentiful supply of semi-skilled workers, and a large domestic market with relatively homogenous tastes due to (at the time) relatively small class distinctions compared with European countries, American firms such as

Ford developed a mass production system which they later sought to internationalise. More recently, Japanese firms developed a competitive advantage in some areas of manufacturing, which can be related to elements of the Japanese business and employment systems such as the close links between companies within supply chains, enterprise unionism and employment security for core workers in large firms. This permitted the development of the employee involvement and quality management programmes necessary to achieve more flexible forms of mass production (see Chapter 15). Again, in many cases, Japanese companies abroad have sought to replicate (or provide equivalents for) some of these policies.

In the international HRM literature, then, the term 'country of origin effects' (Ferner, 1997), sometimes referred to as 'home country effects', means those elements of the behaviour of MNCs which can be traced back to the characteristics of the national business system from which the MNC originates. Country of origin business systems can influence HRM in many areas. For example, the preferred nature of industrial relations management may well be affected by senior executives' domestic experiences, affecting both how MNCs deal with trade unions in foreign subsidiaries, and policies in areas such as employee involvement and participation. Equally, the nature of training and education in the home country may affect managers' understandings of the appropriate competencies of workers and managers, and of work organisation. Employment-related policy may also be affected by business system effects outside the direct area of employment. For example, the nature of corporate finance in the country of origin may affect the extent to which senior executives adopt a short-termist 'shareholder value' mentality, which in turn may affect the extent to which they adopt a short-term or long-term approach to employment issues, with American or British firms perhaps, all other things being equal, being less willing to offer secure employment in subsidiaries than their Japanese counterparts, as managers in the latter group of firms have generally had less need to worry about short-term fluctuations in profitability (Whitley, 1999; Hall and Soskice, 2001).

Evidence on country of origin effects

Research into the HR and industrial relations practices and policies of foreign firms in the UK has revealed a number of ways in which subsidiary policy is often influenced by firms' embeddedness in their country of origin business system. Here, we review evidence on the influence of such 'country of origin effects' in foreign-owned firms in the UK. We particularly use evidence from a recent research project (Almond and Ferner, 2006), which examined employment relations and human resource management in the European subsidiaries of US MNCs. This identified that the 'Americanness' of US MNCs affected the nature of their management of human resources in a number of ways.

First, the management of the majority of the US MNCs is quite highly centralised (Ferner, Gunnigle, Wachter and Edwards, 2006). In contradiction to predictions that MNCs are evolving into devolved networks (cf. Nohria and Ghoshal, 1997), centralised rule-setting from the US headquarters of firms remained commonplace. Most of the firms involved in the research pursued uniformity of HR policies across countries, and subsidiary managers had to give strong arguments to global HQ when they wished to deviate from 'global' policy, which, as we argue below, was often fairly 'American' in nature. Control was achieved by measuring outcomes (such as the achievement of diversity targets, number of employees in each grade, etc.) at the HQ, rather than by high numbers of expatriate managers. This pattern of centralisation across international operations is an extension of the way American firms developed formalised, bureaucratic control systems in order to coordinate their varied activities across the USA, as analysed by Chandler (1976). Recently, the increased need for business units within US MNCs to be financially accountable in the short term, due to pressures for 'shareholder value' (O'Sullivan, 2000), has probably led to a tightening of central control in some US MNCs.

Given this pattern of centralisation, it is perhaps unsurprising that, for nearly all of the organisations studied, there was a considerable amount of 'forward' policy transfer of HR

667

policy (that is, transfer of US policy to foreign subsidiary operations), but relatively little evidence of 'reverse' transfer from subsidiaries to the USA (Edwards *et al.*, 2006). In this respect, most of the firms resembled Bartlett and Ghoshal's (1989) global, or international forms, more than the transnational form. Edwards and his co-authors argue that this pattern of organisational learning in the area of HR is influenced by the fact that US management theories and policies emanate from a liberal business and employment system, where there are relatively few 'constraints' on management decision making in the area of HR. This means that US managerial techniques are seen as relatively independent of the context in which they operate, when compared to HR policies developed in societies which are more actively regulated. For example, many German firms, and German subsidiaries of foreign MNCs, develop policies which allow them to develop high levels of functional flexibility, in response to their relative lack of freedom to compete on labour cost due to the nature of German collective bargaining, the need to consult with their workers through codetermination institutions, and the skills available to firms because of the nature of the co-determination system. However, such policies are difficult to export to countries such as the USA and UK which do not share these institutions, as the appropriate skills might not be so readily available, and the forms of cooperation between local workers and managers which are said to characterise large German firms might not be replicable in countries with substantially different industrial relations systems. Evidence from German MNCs suggests, for example, they make relatively little attempt to 'export' elements of the German system of employment to their UK operations (Ferner and Varul, 2000).

With regard to specific HR practices, the first area of policy on which US MNCs often exhibit country of origin effects is that of collective industrial relations. It is well known that employers in the USA are, on average, more resistant to trade union organisation than their counterparts in other developed industrial democracies (Colling *et al.* 2006) and that the legal supports for trade union organisation and collective bargaining in the USA are weak in comparison to those in other countries. Both these facts reflect a variety of historical factors in the pattern of industrialisation in the United States (for more details, see Colling, 2000) which are distinct to those in Europe.

There have long been large subsidiaries of US MNCs in the UK which have operated non-union, human relations style policies (what would now be termed 'soft HRM'), even before the 1980s, when changes to the UK industrial relations climate made large non-union workplaces somewhat less unusual. The prototypical example here would be a firm such as IBM, which would historically offer relatively high pay and employment security to its workers, but would strongly resist efforts at trade union organisation. These firms generally were monopolistic firms in which the founding family retained substantial influence, under an ideology, often known as 'welfare capitalism' (Jacoby, 1997), that the firm, rather than trade unions or the state, should be responsible for the welfare of workers. Although changes to the American business system, and increased global competition, meant that firms from this group no longer offered 'jobs for life' well before the current economic crisis, there continue to be a substantial number of US MNCs that make the avoidance of trade unions abroad a central part of their HR strategy (see Colling *et al.*, 2006; Ferner *et al.*, 2005). In some cases, the American HQ of such firms makes explicit written guidelines, sometimes even published on corporate websites, that subsidiary managers should discourage trade union organisation. Additionally, as the above authors reflect, a number of firms which have not been able to avoid unionisation in the USA are anxious to do so abroad, perhaps due to their experience of highly conflictual industrial relations in their home country. Finally, of course, there are a number of 'low road' MNCs such as McDonald's which are strongly anti-union (cf. Royle, 2000). This is not to say, however, that all foreign subsidiaries of US firms operate non-union or anti-union policies. Some US MNCs, although seeking to avoid trade unions in the USA, make little effort to intervene in foreign industrial relations systems, providing that such systems do not impinge too heavily on their ability to pursue their desired HR policies (Ferner *et al.*, 2005).

Further effects can be seen in the management of pay and performance (Almond, Muller-Camen, Collings and Quintanilla, 2006). In particular, US MNCs were innovators in the area of formalised systems of performance-related pay in Europe (Muller, 1998), which can be seen as a reflection of the particularly market-oriented American employment system. This practice is now also diffused widely among large non-American firms (Faulkner *et al.*, 2004). It can still be argued, however, that the form the practice often takes in US MNCs, with forced distributions pushing given percentages of employees into high and low performing categories, and in some cases the threat of dismissal or reduced job security for lower performing groups, reflects specifically American managerial beliefs about employment. In particular, this type of practice can be related to the American notion of 'employment at will' meaning there is, for most US employees, little protection from unfair dismissal (cf. Almond *et al.*, 2006). Systems of performance management tend to be tightly controlled by US HQ, with relatively little freedom for national subsidiaries to adopt distinctive policies.

STOP and think

What are the advantages and disadvantages to a firm in attempting to pursue a uniform system of performance management across its international operations?

A number of US MNCs also export workforce 'diversity' policies from the USA. These are clearly linked to the social and legislative context of equal opportunity law, and to US firms' attempts to interpret equal opportunity law to their own advantage (Ferner *et al.*, 2006). In many cases, US firms, having devised diversity policies for the USA, chose to export these abroad, thus imposing targets for the proportion of women, and sometimes other disadvantaged labour market groups, in management positions. This reflects how the nature of country of origin effects can change over time, as the home country institutional context changes. Political sensitivities to equality issues in the USA, prompted by the civil rights movement and reactions to it, have led to the development of a range of diversity policies, which have in many cases been internationalised through the formal management systems of US firms.

It has also frequently been argued that Japanese MNCs betray specifically 'Japanese' characteristics when operating abroad. Japanese economic success in the 1970s and 1980s sparked considerable academic interest in Japanese management methods, with a wave of interest both in the HR policies of Japanese subsidiaries themselves (cf., for example, Kenney and Florida (1993) and Milkman (1991) for US subsidiaries of Japanese MNCs; Morris, Wilkinson and Munday (2000) and Elger and Smith (1994) for their UK subsidiaries), and, in Britain, in 'Japanese' practices which were being imitated by UK firms (cf., for example, Oliver and Wilkinson, 1992).

It is difficult to compare the HR policies of the UK subsidiaries of Japanese MNCs directly with those of US MNCs. The main reason for this is that the overwhelming majority of Japanese Foreign Direct Investment in the UK has taken place in the last 25 years, into a UK industrial relations environment which had already been affected by Thatcherism and the economic crisis of the late 1970s/early 1980s. Much US investment is much older, going back in some cases to the Victorian era, meaning that many UK subsidiaries of US MNCs such as, say, Ford or General Motors, have a much more substantial 'British' heritage than Toyota or Nissan. Equally, much Japanese investment has involved so-called 'greenfield' sites, meaning that the Japanese MNCs involved had the opportunity to 'start from scratch' in terms of their management systems, and to recruit and select an entire, new workforce.

Indeed, one of the notable features of many Japanese subsidiaries investigated in this period was their very selective recruitment procedures, in many cases focusing on the recruitment of a young workforce with the ability to learn, rather than looking for experienced workers with substantial experience of other UK firms (Oliver and Wilkinson, 1992). This reflects practice among core workers in the largest Japanese firms, where workers are selected directly from school or university and expected to remain with the same employer for the majority of their career.

At least some of the larger Japanese inward investors also sought to replicate Japanese-type structures in their industrial relations policies. Rather than taking advantage of the 1980s industrial relations climate by seeking to exclude trade unions, some Japanese MNCs sought to reach single union agreements, whereby one trade union, usually the very moderate AEEU, represented all the different workforce groups within the firm. This differs from the more typical UK pattern in manufacturing, in which different occupational groups are represented by different trade unions, and replicates, to the extent that this is possible in a UK context, the company unionism present in the core Japanese firms at home. One 1990s survey of Japanese subsidiaries in South Wales found that 75 per cent had a single union deal (Innes and Morris, 1995). The Japanese firms in the same survey tended to have fewer job grades, reflecting a lesser degree of job demarcation than in US firms, and were less likely to have performance-related pay (see above), but slightly more likely to have elements of single-status practices such as equal holiday leave, and the wearing of company uniforms by all employees. Perhaps surprisingly, however, in view of the 'Japanisation' literature, flexible work organisation arrangements such as teamworking were only slightly more prevalent, and employee involvement systems such as quality circles no more prevalent, than in US-owned firms. This is in spite of the fact that considerable case study evidence from the larger Japanese subsidiaries in the UK does suggest that these policies are used.

Part of the explanation for this could lie with the extent to which Japanese practices, then seen as a model to be emulated (Womack *et al.*, 1990), were being copied by rival firms. If this is the case, it remains possible that the nature of policies such as teamworking is qualitatively different in Japanese-owned and American-owned firms. At least equally importantly, however, as an important recent book, based on a long-term study of Japanese firms in Telford, argues (Elger and Smith, 2006), the portrait of Japanese management generally found in the English-language management literature is somewhat stereotypical. Specifically, the commonly understood Japanese HRM model only really applies to core workers in a small number of well-known firms. Elements of the model such as employment security and internal career structures do not extend to peripheral firms in supply chains, or to peripheral groups of the workforce, and very often Japanese MNCs used foreign workforces as part of this periphery. The picture Elger and Smith present of Japanese management in Telford, of union avoidance and intensified assembly line work and modest wages, is much more reminiscent of the less glorified peripheral work systems of Japan, than of the more paternalist HRM policies experienced by the core workers of core firms.

Finally, country of origin effects are likely to be stronger where the home country retains a substantial proportion of the MNC's operations. This is usually the case with US and Japanese firms, but, for obvious reasons, is less common with large MNCs based in smaller countries. In these cases, internationalisation of the firm may mean a much greater degree of internationalisation of its management cadre, and often of its capital base (i.e. the larger continental European MNCs will tend to raise, finance from the US stock market as well as from domestic sources), meaning that country of origin effects may tend, over time, to diminish. The work of Hayden and Edwards (2001) examines this process in the Swedish case.

Overall, one can say that the various effects of firms and their managers originating from one particularly national business system may lead them to be more likely to choose some policies than others. This is not an automatic process, however. One cannot simply say that firms will adopt a certain style of HRM just because they are from a given country, but they may predispose managers to certain choices over others in given contexts. A major survey of HR practices shows the extent of some of these tendencies (Edwards *et al.*, 2007).

Host country effects

'Host country effects' is the term used to describe elements of MNC HR policy which are shaped by the context of the foreign countries that subsidiaries are located in. In other words, this concerns the way in which subsidiary HR policies and practices are shaped by a foreign

MNC's interaction with employees, and host-country managers, working under different national rules and different national cultural and social systems. These rules and systems, along with levels of economic development and ease of access to markets, also provide countries with different competitive advantages. MNCs may sometimes choose to (or need to) deviate from their original, home country, policies, in order to exploit these advantages fully, while dealing with societal and cultural differences.

The broad term of 'host country effects' can perhaps be usefully split into a number of groups. First, there are effects which are imposed on the foreign MNC by host country constraints. These may arise directly from labour market regulation; as the previous chapter illustrates, host countries, even within European Union countries, still differ considerably in their regulation of core elements of the employment relationship such as wage protection, working time, employment security, worker participation and the trade union and collective bargaining rights of employees. In most European countries, for example, MNCs cannot simply choose to refuse to offer union recognition to employees. Equally, it is much harder, and more expensive, to dismiss permanent employees in some countries than in others. In other words, certain policies are either obligatory or prohibited in some societies, which has the effect of reducing the (legitimate) scope for strategic choice for foreign MNCs.

To this group of effects, one can also add elements of national cultural/societal understandings of the employment relationship which may not be written down in law, but which will affect the ways in which given HR practices will be interpreted by workers. For example, due to the nature of gender relations in Britain (see Chapter 4), employers in the UK, including foreign MNCs, benefit from a large workforce that is eager to take part-time employment with flexible working hours (i.e. working-class women, and, increasingly, students) (Almond and Rubery, 2000). In France, while it is possible to recruit flexible part-timers due to the current high levels of unemployment in that country, most women in employment have historically tended to work full-time hours, meaning that part-time workers may be less content with their situation. While this does not, of course, stop a foreign MNC from employing a part-time workforce in France, managers should not be surprised if, as a result, their French employees display less 'commitment' than their British counterparts.

Second, host country effects are not only constraints on foreign MNCs. Indeed, if they were, there would be much less foreign direct investment. In fact, MNCs are constantly taking advantage of differences between different host countries (and other potential host countries) (Kristensen and Morgan, 2007). Much production, and, indeed, increasing proportions of service provision, takes place in global supply chains which seek to exploit national socio-economic differences. If the employment system of one country offers expensive, but skilled workers, with a high capacity for learning, while that of another offers largely untrained, but cheap labour, then MNCs may locate the higher skilled work in the first, and the less skilled in the second. Similarly, the policies required to be seen as a 'good' or 'fair' employer in contemporary China, say, are clearly not as high as those in Germany, meaning that many firms will not choose to employ the same types of HR policies in these two very different environments. It should also be noted that MNCs' coordination of work extends beyond workplaces they directly own, through various forms of contractual and alliance relationships in global value chains (Coe et al., 2008; Herrigel and Zeitlin, forthcoming). While issues concerning subcontracted work are not generally well integrated within the international HRM literature, it is necessary to recognise their importance in a fuller analysis of how MNCs manage human resources.

Finally, where an MNC locates a subsidiary in a country partly or mainly in order to exploit the national or regional product market, differences in consumer demand between nations may necessitate different ways of managing human resources. This was discussed briefly above in relation to the 'multi-domestic' form of MNC organisation, but will also apply to many firms which do not share that type of structure. While market differences may equally well be present in manufacturing as in the service sector, they are perhaps more likely to impact on HRM where there is direct contact between the employee and the customer.

The extent to which host country effects will cause differentiation in HR policies obviously depends on the nature of host country patterns of employment relations, and how different these are from those in the country of origin. This is sometimes referred to as 'institutional distance' (Kostova, 1999). For example, a US firm attempting to export a non-union system of HRM with a high performance-related element to pay would probably face far more difficulties in Germany than it would in the UK (for an example, see Almond *et al.*, 2005). By the same token, if the training system of one host country supplies the firm with a plentiful quantity of workers who have an otherwise scarce skill, it might well not choose to export all the elements of its corporate training programme to that country.

However, it should be noted that the strength of host country effects cannot simply be read off from a broad understanding of the nature of its institutions. In particular, the degree to which national economies depend on foreign MNCs for their success varies quite considerably from country to country. In countries such as Hungary or Ireland, where nearly half the manufacturing workforce works directly for foreign MNCs, one would expect this group of firms to have considerable lobbying power, and thus potentially a substantial collective impact on the nature of the overall business and employment systems (cf. Gunnigle *et al.* 2003 for the Irish case).

At a more micro-level, the impact of 'constraining' host country effects may in practice be reduced if the MNC has a substantial choice about which countries it is located in. If the firm can produce credible threats that it may move part or all of its operations to more lightly regulated and/or lower cost countries, it is possible that some host country constraints can be 'negotiated' (particularly with local unions and local/regional governments), lessening their real impact. Less dramatically, the practice of 'coercive comparisons' (Marginson and Sisson, 2002), by which MNCs threaten (explicitly or implicitly) to withdraw investment in one subsidiary unless it matches the performance of another, is commonplace.

Another way of dealing with undesirable host country regulations, of course, is simply to disobey them. This is commonplace in the multinational fast food industry (Royle, 2000), but also happens in firms which do not follow 'hard', cost minimisation strategies quite so obviously (cf. Almond *et al.*, 2005; Colling *et al.*, 2006). The subsidiaries of MNCs, whose home country practices may challenge the assumptions behind host country employment relations systems, will frequently attempt to find ways of exploiting the 'malleability' of those systems (Muller-Camen *et al.*, 2001). When foreign MNCs succeed in avoiding the constraints of host country systems, they may begin to alter the nature of those systems, in that their practices may well be imitated by domestic firms. For instance, while some medium-large British non-union firms did exist in the post-war era, one might argue that US MNCs became a template for later attempts to create non-union 'soft HRM' workplaces in the UK. More recently, German employers have followed closely the attempts of German subsidiaries of US multinationals to create more flexible pay structures.

The negotiation of home and host country effects

Neither home or host country effects are automatic in their operation. It is important to take into account the fact that different organisational members, such as national and local managers, down to groups of shopfloor employees, have interests and goals of their own, which cannot simply be reduced to those of the 'Corporation'. In particular, it is important to take account of the ways in which host country socialisation affects the rationality of host country managers (Broad, 1994). In other words, host country managers may, because of their own 'embeddedness' in their own society, have different ideas about what is 'good management', and what is 'fair' and 'just', than their foreign superiors. For example, in the recent study of US MNCs in Europe discussed above, German and British subsidiary managers, both coming from countries with much more pluralist industrial relations traditions than their American counterparts, often applied HQ industrial relations policy in a fairly pragmatic and accommodating way, allowing more role for collective labour than a strict reading of corporate policy might suggest (Colling *et al.*, 2006). Similar processes can be seen to operate in the UK subsidiaries of Japanese firms (Elger and Smith, 2006)

In other words, HR outcomes at subsidiary level result from different actors, at different levels of the organisation, with different power resources negotiating on the extent to which it is desirable to follow a 'global' policy, or to make allowances for local contingencies. In particular, local managers should have specific knowledge about the local situation and will have their own interpretations of the realities of what is likely to work in the local context. It may be difficult for an HQ manager to tell exactly how a foreign subsidiary workforce is likely to respond to a given HR initiative, or how strictly an element of employment law is enforced. Local managers therefore have a role in interpreting and negotiating precisely what the nature of 'host country effects' are in a given context. In other words, any analysis of policy transfer within MNCs needs to take account of organisational politics and the power resources of various actors (Edwards, 2004).

Summary

- This chapter has analysed international HRM by combining a range of academic perspectives in the area, from strategic approaches, to those focusing more on MNCs relations with their institutional environment. It highlights the fact that internationalised operations offer firms advantages in terms of access to human resources and to knowledge, while also dealing with the increasingly complicated nature of HRM when firms internationalise.

- The chapter highlights how HRM decisions in MNCs may be related to business strategy and structure, but with the added complication that global as well as national strategic factors would need to be taken into account by senior managers. It then examines the ways in which MNCs might choose to structure their international HR function in order to cope with the complexities of international management and the role of networks and expatriates in the generation and transfer of HR knowledge. The final section examines the potential effects on HRM strategies and structures of the country of ownership of MNCs, as well as of the countries in which they operate.

- As the chapter reflects, the coordination of human resources in MNCs is a socially complex affair. It should be emphasised that none of the models, or explanations, presented above to explain MNCs behaviour in HRM fully succeeds in unwrapping this complexity. In examining the process of human resource management in the international firm, it is necessary to take account of strategies, internal structures and institutions together.

Questions

1 Explain what is meant by the terms integration and responsiveness in the context of MNCs. What effect can these have on how the MNC is structured, the nature of the parent–subsidiary control relationship and the flow of knowledge across the MNC?

2 Outline and explain, the key internal and external organisational factors that influence an MNC's approach to international strategic human resource management.

3 Explain why HR knowledge is difficult to transfer across an MNC.

4 How and why are the extent and direction of HR policy transfer likely to differ between multi-domestic, international, global and transnational companies?

5 Examine the nature of HR policies in the UK subsidiaries of US and/or Japanese MNCs. What evidence is there of a 'country of origin' effect?

6 To what extent, and how, do you believe that British patterns of HRM have been affected by reports of the activities of foreign-owned MNCs in the UK?

Case study

All change at Linkz

Linkz is a German-owned transnational telecommunications company. It was established in 1935 as a domestic company. Since then the company has expanded internationally. It now operates in 140 countries, employs 104,000 people worldwide, including 22,000 in design centres spread across 25 countries. Approximately 40 per cent of the staff are employed within Germany, but expansion in employee numbers over the past 10 years has been greater outside of Germany.

Linkz began as a wireline telecomunications network supplier. In recent years it moved into wireless software design and it is in this, the area of mobile phones and networks that the business has expanded rapidly in the last 15 years. Linkz has 30 per cent of the global market share in mobile systems making it one of the leading mobile communications suppliers worldwide. Sales figures are largest for the Europe, Middle East, Africa region, followed by the Asia Pacific region, Latin America region and finally the North America region. Sales figures increased in 2007 by 10 per cent on the previous year. Japan is the company's largest market for third generation mobile phones. However, the European markets have shown some increase during 2006–07. In 2005 Linkz invested 20 per cent of its sales revenue in technical development.

The telecommunications industry has changed significantly in recent years. In the past Linkz sold telecommunications equipment to large monopolistic operators. Datacom and computer companies are venturing into traditional areas of the telecommunications market, as these voice and data industries converge a single multimedia industry is emerging. In addition, wireline and wireless phone technology has moved toward increasingly advanced digital technology and internet technology giving rise to 'third generation' technology and products, e.g. mobile phones with video and internet services. Worldwide deregulation has enabled the merging of wireline and wireless operators with global capabilities. As a result the market is becoming more transnational in nature. The number of global operators is shrinking, while at the regional or local level the number of operators is expanding. This means there is greater pressure for global standards across the industry that enables compatibility between datacom and telecom systems. While at the local level the advances in technology have led to fierce competition between companies to deliver the latest innovations in products and services

to customers. All this leaves Linkz with the demand for increased global efficiency and learning transfer to maximise on its investment in design capability. And the need to be highly sensitive to the demands of local customers given the nature of the competition.

Faced with these many pressures Linkz restructured in a bid to move away from strong parent hierarchical control over its subsidiary operations, whilst still building on its global strengths and capability. It established four additional corporate headquarter offices, one for each of its regions (Europe, Middle East and Africa with a corporate office in London; North America with a corporate office in Texas; Asia Pacific with a corporate office in Hong Kong; Latin America with a corporate office in Miami) in addition to the home headquarters in Hamburg. The majority of the senior managers in these offices are German. The corporate offices hold responsibilities for finance, technology, supply and information technology, human resource management (HRM), marketing and strategic business development, corporate communications, and legal affairs.

The restructuring had notable implications for the design and HRM functions. In terms of design a corporate function was created with responsibility for coordinating R&D across the multinational network, particularly in relation to standardisation, patents, and strategic partnerships. In addition, a research centre was established in Hamburg responsible for advanced early 'blue sky' research. The role of design in the subsidiaries was reduced and shifted toward the development of highly specialised products for local customer markets.

The corporate HRM function had the responsibility of creating a global philosophy that enabled best practice and policy from across the network to define the organisational culture. Diversity was seen as a feature of the organisation to be built upon rather than smoothed over. To facilitate this philosophy annual audits were carried out whereby HR teams from the regional corporate offices would visit subsidiaries to gain evidence of local best practice that they deemed useful for global dissemination. In addition, HR professionals across the network would attend an annual internal HR conference where issues and experiences faced by the HR teams were discussed. The HR intranet bulletin board and chat room provided additional mechanisms for the spread of innovation and networking among the internal HR community.

The Linkz Management Academy (LMC) was established in Hamburg mandated to develop the managerial capability of its worldwide workforce. The LMC designed management development programmes for graduates and junior managers through to its senior managers. These involved academic and practitioner guest speakers from all over the world and usually combined off-site development with on-the-job learning, international transfers or secondments.

This restructuring created many challenges for how the corporate HR functions would achieve their mandate, and the competency requirements of these HR professionals to deliver in this changed context. The changes also created a trade-off between greater autonomy for the subsidiary in some areas versus the loss of control in others. For example, the subsidiary design functions now had almost total control over their activities relating to product design for local customers. However, they were no longer permitted to engage in long-term strategic R&D as this responsibility now lay with corporate R&D. For the design function the reorganisation also brought new challenges for local managers with regard to how to motivate and develop the necessary technical capability to cope with the changes in the industry and the organisation. While it also changed the career landscape for local senior managers in terms of their opportunity for local and international career advancement.

Given the reorganisation and changes in the market context faced by Linkz, consider the following:

1 What types of competencies do you feel the HR professionals in the corporate and regional headquarter offices would need to demonstrate to deliver against the international strategic demands of the organisation?

2 If you were tasked with designing a Linkz management development programme for middle managers what types of issues would it address and how would it be delivered?

3 Assess the nature of the motivational problems the design function's managers are likely to face, given the organisational changes and changes in the external context. As an HR manager working in partnership with design what solutions would you suggest?

4 What opportunities and threats might an international career structure bring to local managers?

References and further reading

Adler, N. and Ghadar, F. (1990) 'Strategic human resource management: a global perspective' in R. Pieper, *Human Resource Management: An International Comparison*. Berlin: Walter de Gruyter, pp. 235–60.

Almond, P., Edwards, T., Colling, T., Ferner, A., Gunnigle, P., Muller-Camen, M., Quintanilla, J. and Wachter, H. (2005) 'Unraveling home and host country effects: an investigation of the HR policies of an American multinational in four european countries', *Industrial Relations (Berkeley)*, 44, 2: 276–306.

Almond, P. and Ferner, A. (eds) (2006) *American Multinationals in Europe: Managing Employment Relations Across Borders*. Oxford: Oxford University Press.

Almond, P. and Rubery, J. (2000) 'Deregulation and societal systems' in M. Maurice and A. Sorge (eds) *Embedding Organisations*. Amsterdam: John Benjamin, pp. 277–94.

Almond, P., Muller-Camen, M., Collings, T. and Quintanilla, J. (2006) 'Pay and performance' in P. Almond and A. Ferner (eds) *American Multinationals in Europe: Managing Employment Relations Across Borders*. Oxford: Oxford University Press, pp. 119–45.

Argote, L. and Ingram, P. (2000) 'Knowledge transfer: a basis for competitive advantage in firms', *Organisational Behaviour and Human Decision Processes*, 82: 152–69.

Athanassiou, N. and Nigh, D. (2000) 'Internationalization, tacit knowledge and the top management teams of MNCs', *Journal of International Business Studies*, 31, 3: 471–88.

Bantel, K.A. and Jackson, S.E. (1989) 'Top management and innovations in banking: does the composition of the top team make a difference?', *Strategic Management Journal*, 13: 338–55.

Barney, J. (1991) 'Firm resources and sustained competitive advantage', *Journal of Management*, 17: 99–120.

Bartlett, C.A. and Ghoshal, S. (1989) *Managing Across Borders: The Transnational Solution*. Boston. MA: Harvard Business School Press.

Bartlett, C.A. and Ghoshal, S. (1990) 'The multinational corporation as an interorganisational network', *Academy of Management Review*, 15, 4: 603–25.

Bartlett, C.A. and Ghoshal, S. (1995) *Transnational Management*, 2nd edn. Boston, MA: Irwin.

Birkinshaw, J. and Morrison, A. (1995) 'Configurations of strategy and structure in subsidiaries of multinational companies', *Journal of International Business Studies*, 26, 4: 729–54.

Boam, R. and Sparrow, P. (1992) *Designing and Achieving Competency*. London: McGraw-Hill.

Bonache, J. and Brewster, C. (2001) 'Knowledge transfer and the management of expatriation', *Thunderbird International Business Review*, 43, 1: 145–68.

Brewster, C., Harris, H. and Sparrow, P.R. (2002) *Globalizing HR: Executive Brief*. London: CIPD.

Broad, G. (1994) 'The managerial limits to Japanisation: a manufacturing case study', *Human Resource Management Journal*, 4, 3: 52–69.

Brown, J.S. and Duguid, P. (1991) 'Organisational learning and communities-of-practice: towards a unified view of working, learning and innovation', *Organisation Science*, 2, 1: 40–57.

Cerdin, J-L. (2003) 'International diffusion of HRM practices: the role of expatriates', *Beta: Scandinavian Journal or Business Research*, 17, 1: 48–58.

Chandler, A. (1976) *The Visible Hand: The Managerial Revolution in America*. Cambridge, MA: Belknap.

Coe, N. M., Dicken, P. and Hess, M. (2008) 'Global production networks: realizing the potential', *Journal of Economic Geography*, 8 (3): 271–95.

Colling. T. (2000) 'In a state of bliss there is no need for a ministry of bliss. Power, consent and the limits of innovation in American non-union companies'. Occasional paper, Leicester Business School, De Montfort University.

Colling, T. (2001) 'In a State of bliss, there is no need for a Ministry of Bliss: Some further thoughts on welfare capitalism', Occasional Paper, Leicester Business School, De Montfort University.

Colling, T., Gunnigle, P., Quintanilla, J. and Tempel, A. (2006) 'Collective representation and participation', in P. Almond and A. Ferner (eds) *American Multinationals in Europe: Managing Employment Relations Across Borders*. Oxford: Oxford University Press, p. 95–118.

Desouza, K.C. (2003) 'Knowledge management barriers: why the technology imperative seldom works', *Business Horizons*, January–February: 25–29.

Doremus, P., Keller, W., Pauly, L. and Reich, S. (1998) *The Myth of the Global Corporation*. Princeton, NJ.: Princeton University Press.

Doz, Y.L. and Prahalad, C.K. (1986) 'Controlled variety: a challenge for human resource management in the MNC', *Human Resource Management*, 25, 1: 55–72.

Dunning, J. (1958) *American Investment in British Manufacturing*. London: Allen & Unwin.

Dunning, E. (1998) *American Investment in British Manufacturing Industry*. London: Routledge.

Edwards, P., Edwards, T., Ferner, A, Marginson, P. and Tregaskis, O. (2007) 'Employment practices of MNCs in organisational context: a large-scale survey. Report of Main Survey'. **http://www2.warwick.ac.uk/fac/soc/wbs/projects/mncemployment/conference_papers/full_report_july.pdf**.

Edwards, T. (2004) 'The transfer of employment practices across borders in multinational companies', in A.-W. Harzing and J. van Ruysseveldt (eds) *International Human Resource Management*, 2nd edn. London: Sage pp. 389–410.

Edwards, T., Collings, D., Quintanilla, J. and Tempel, A. (2006) 'Innovation and the transfer of organisational learning', in P. Almond and A. Ferner (eds) *American Multinationals in Europe: Managing Employment Relations Across Borders*. Oxford: Oxford University Press, pp. 223–47.

Edwards, T. and Rees, C. (eds) (2006) *International Human Resource Management: Globalization, National Systems and Multinational Companies*. London: FT/Prentice Hall.

Elger, T. and Smith, C. (eds) (1994) *Global Japanization? The transnational transformation of the labour process*. Oxford: Oxford University Press.

Elger, T. and Smith, C. (2006) *Assembling Work. Remaking Factory Regimes in Japanese Multinationals in Britain*. Oxford: Oxford University Press.

Faulkner, D., PitKethley, R. and Child, J. (2004) 'International mergers and acquisitions in the UK 1985–1994: A comparison of national HRM practices', *International Journal of Human Resource Management*, 13, 1: 94–111.

Ferner, A. (1994) 'Multinational companies and human resource management: an overview of research issues', *Human Resource Management Journal*, 4, 2: 79–102.

Ferner, A. (1997) 'Country of origin effects and HRM in multinational enterprises', *Human Resource Management Journal*, 7, 1: 19–37.

Ferner, A., Almond, P., Colling, T. and Edwards, T. (2005) 'Policies on Union Representation in US Multinationals in the UK: Between micro-politics and macro-institutions', *British Journal of Industrial Relations*, 43, 4: 703–28.

Ferner, A., Gunnigle, P., Wachter, H. and Edwards, T. (2006) 'Centralization' in P. Almond and A. Ferner (eds) *American Multinationals in Europe: Managing Employment Relations Across Borders*. Oxford: Oxford University Press, pp. 197–222.

Ferner, A., Muller-Camen, M., Morley, M. and Susaeta, L. (2006) 'Workforce diversity policies', in P. Almond and A. Ferner (eds) *American Multinationals in Europe: Managing Employment Relations Across Borders*. Oxford: Oxford University Press, pp. 146–71.

Ferner, A. and Varul, M. (2000) 'Vanguard' subsidiaries and the diffusion of new practices: a case study of German multinationals', *British Journal of Industrial Relations*, 38, 1: 115–40.

Fisher, H.M. and Pollock, T.G. (2004) 'Effects of social capital and power on surviving transformational change: the case of initial public offerings', *Academy of Management Journal*, 47, 4: 463–82.

Ghoshal, S. and Bartlett, C.A. (1998) *Managing Across Borders*. London: Random House, Part 1, pp. 1–81.

Ghoshal, S. and Westney, D.E. (1993) 'Introduction and overview', in S. Ghoshal and D.E. Westney (eds) *Organisation Theory and the Multinational Corporation*. New York: St Martin's Press, pp. 1–23.

Gulati, T., Nohria, N. and Zaheer, A. (2000) 'Strategic networks', *Strategic Management Journal*, 21: 203–15.

Gunnigle, P., Collings, D., Morley, M. and McAvinue, A.O. (2003) 'US multinationals and human resource management in Ireland: towards a qualitative research agenda', *Irish Journal of Management*, January: 7–25.

Hall, P. and Soskice D. (2001) *Varieties of Capitalism: The Institutional Foundations of Comparative Advantage*. Oxford: Oxford University Press.

Hansen, M.T. (1999) 'The search-transfer problem: the role of weak ties in sharing knowledge across organisation subunits'. *Administrative Science Quarterly*, 44, 1: 82–111.

Harzing, A.-W. (1999) *Managing the Multinationals: an International Study of Control Mechanisms*. Cheltenham: Edward Elgar.

Harzing, A.-W. (2000) 'An empirical analysis and extension of the Bartlett and Ghoshal Typology of Multinational Companies', *Journal of International Business Studies*, 31, 1: 101–19.

Hayden, A. and Edwards, T. (2001) 'The erosion of the country of origin effect: a case study of a Swedish multinational company', *Relations Industrielles*, 56, 1: 116–40.

Hedlund, G. (1986) 'The hypermodern MNC – a heterarchy?' *Human Resource Management*, 25, 1: 9–35.

Herrigel, G. and Zeitlin, J. (forthcoming) 'Inter-firm relations in global manufacturing: disintegrated production and its globalization' in G. Morgan, J. Campbell, C. Crouch, P.H. Kristensen, O. Pedersen and R. Whitley (eds) *The Oxford Handbook of Comparative Institutional Analysis*, Oxford: Oxford University Press.

Hirst, P. and Thompson, G. (1999) *Globalization in Question*, 2nd edn. Cambridge: Polity Press.

Hofstede, G. (1980) *Culture's Consequences: International Differences in Work-Related Values*. Beverly Hills, CA: Sage.

Holden L. (2001) 'International human resource management', in I. Beardwell and L. Holden, *Human Resource Management*. London: Prentice Hall, pp. 633–76.

Huselid, M. (1995) 'The impact of human resource management practices on turnover, productivity and corporate financial performance', *Academy of Management Journal*, 38, 3: 635–72.

Innes, E. and Morris, J. (1995) 'Multinational corporations and employee relations: continuity and change in a mature industrial region', *Employee Relations*, 17, 6: 25–42.

Jacoby, S. (1997) *Modern Manors: Welfare Capitalism since the New Deal*. Princeton, NJ: Princeton University Press.

Jones, G. (1984) 'Task visibility, free riding, and shirking: explaining the effect of structure and technology on employee behaviour', *Journal of Financial Economics*, 3: 305–60.

Kenney, M. and Florida, R. (1993) *Beyond Mass Production*. New York: Oxford University Press.

Klein, N. (2000) *No Logo*. London: Harper Collins.

Kobrin, S.J. (1994) 'Is there a relationship between a geocentric mind-set and multinational strategy?' *Journal of International Business Studies*, third quarter: 493–511.

Kostova, T. (1999) 'Transnational Transfer of Strategic Organisational Practices: A Contextual Perspective', *Academy of Management Review*, 24, 2: 308–24.

Kostova, T. and Roth, K. (2003) 'Social capital in multinational corporations and a micro-macro model of its formation', *Academy of Management Review*, 28, 2: 297–317.

Kristensen, P. and Morgan, G. (2007) 'Multinationals and institutional competitiveness', *Regulation and Governance*, 1: 197–212.

Lado, A. and Wilson, M. (1994) 'Human resource systems and sustained competitive advantage: a competency based perspective', *Academy of Management Review*, 19: 699–727.

Lam, A. (2000) 'Tacit knowledge, organizational learning and societal institutions: an integrated framework'. *Organization Studies*, 21, 3: 487–513.

Lane, C. (2001) 'Understanding the globalization strategies of German and British multinational companies: is a "societal effects" approach still useful' in M. Maurice and A. Sorge (eds), *Embedding Organisations*. Amsterdam: John Benjamins, pp. 189–208.

Laurent, A. (1983) 'The cultural diversity of Western conceptions of management', *International Studies of Management and Organization*, 13, 1–2: 75–96.

Leana, C. and van Buren, H. (1999) 'Organizational social capital and employment practices', *Academy of Management Review*, 24, 3: 538–55.

Lengnick-Hall, C. and Lengnick-Hall, M. (1988) 'Strategic human resource management: A review of the literature and proposed typology', *Academy of Management Review*, 13: 454–70.

Leong, S.M. and Tan, C.T. (1993) 'Managing across borders: an empirical test of the Bartlett and Ghoshal [1989] organizational typology', *Journal of International Business Studies*, 24, 3: 449–64.

Marginson, P. and Sisson, K. (2002) 'Coordinated bargaining – a process for our times?', *British Journal of Industrial Relations*, 40, 2: 197–220.

Mayrhofer, W. and Brewster, C. (1996) 'In praise of ethnocentricity: expatriate policies in European multinationals', *International Executive*, 36, 6: 749–78.

Mendenhall, M., Dunbar, E. and Oddou, G. (1989) 'Expatriate selection, training and career pathing: a review and critique', *Human Resource Management*, 26: 331–45.

Milkman. R. (1991) *Japan's California factories: Labor relations and economic globalization*. Berkeley, CA.: Institute Industrial Relations, UCLA.

Milliman, J.F. and Von Glinow, M.A. (1990). 'A life cycle approach to strategic international human resource management in MNCs', *Research in Personnel and Human Resources Management*, Supp. 2: 21–35.

Milliman, J.M., Von Glinow, A. and Nathan, M. (1991) 'Organizational life cycles and strategic international human resource management in multinational companies: Implications for congruence theory', *Academy of Management Review*, 16, 2: 318–39.

Mintzberg, H. and Waters, J.A. (1989) 'Of strategies, deliberate and emergent' in D. Asch and C. Bowman, *Readings in Strategic Management*. Milton Keynes: Open University and Macmillan, pp. 4–19.

Moenaert, R.K., Souder, W.E., De Meyer, A. and Deschoolmeester, D. (1994) 'R&D-marketing, integration mechanisms, communication flows and innovation success', *Journal of Product Innovation Management*, 11, 1: 31–45.

Morgan, G. (2001) *The Multinational Firm*. Oxford: Oxford University Press.

Morris, J., Wilkinson, B. and Munday, M. (2000) 'Farewell to HRM? Personnel practices in Japanese manufacturing plants in the UK', *International Journal of Human Resource Management*, 11, 6: 1047–60.

Muller, M. (1998) 'Human resource and industrial relations practices of UK and US multinationals in Germany', *International Journal of Human Resource Management*, 9, 4: 732–49.

Muller-Camen, M., Almons, P., Gunnigle, P., Quintanilla, J. and Tempel, A. (2001) 'Between home and host country: multinationals and employment relations in Europe', *Industrial Relations Journal*, 32, 5: 435–48.

Nahapiet, J. and Ghoshal, S. (1998) 'Social capital, intellectual capital, and the organization advantage', *Academy of Management Review*, 23: 243–66.

Nohria, N. and Eccles, R.G. (1992) 'Face-to-face: making network organisations work' in N. Nohria and R.G. Eccles (eds) *Networks and Organizations: Structure, Form and Action*. Boston, MA: Harvard Business School Press, pp. 288–323.

Nohria, N. and Ghoshal, S. (1997) *The Differentiated Network: Organizing Multinational Companies For Value Creation*. London: Routledge.

Nonaka, I. and Takeuchi, H. (1995) *The Knowledge Creating Company*. New York: Oxford University Press.

OECD (2006) OECD *Factbook 2006: Economic, Environmental and Social Statistics*. Paris: OECD.

Ohmae, K. (1991) *The Borderless World*. London: Macmillan.

Oliver, N. and Wilkinson, B. (1992) *The Japanization of British Industry*. Oxford: Blackwell.

O'Sullivan, M. (2000) *Contests for Corporate Control: Corporate Governance and Economic Performance in the United States and Germany*. Oxford: Oxford University Press.

Pauly, L. and Reich, S. (1997) 'National structures and multinational corporate behaviour: enduring differences in the age of globalization', *International Organization*, 51, 1: 1–30.

Perlmutter, H.V. (1969) 'The tortuous evolution of the multinational corporation', *Columbia Journal of World Business*, 8–18.

Pfeffer, J. and Salancik, G.R. (1978) *The External Control of Organizations*. New York: Harper and Row.

677

Polanyi, M. (1962) *Personal Knowledge.* Chicago, IL: University of Chicago Press.

Polanyi, M. (1966) *The Tacit Dimension.* Garden City, NY: Doubleday.

Porter, M. (1990) *The Competitive Advantage of Nations* (with a new introduction). Basingstoke: Macmillan.

Prahalad, C.K. and Doz, Y. (1987) *The Multinational Mission: Balancing Local Demands and Global Vision.* New York: The Free Press.

Quintanilla, J. (1999) 'The configuration of human resource management policies and practices in multinational subsidiaries: the case of European retail banks in Spain'. Unpublished PhD Thesis, University of Warwick.

Reich, R. (1991) *The Work of Nations: Preparing Ourselves for 21st Century Capitalism.* New York: Alfred A. Knopf.

Rosenzweig, P.M. and Nohria, N. (1994) 'Influences on human resource management practices in multinational corporations', *Journal of International Business Studies,* second quarter: 229–51.

Rosenzweig, P.M. and Singh, J.V. (1991) 'Organizational environments and the multinational enterprise', *Academy of Management Review,* 16, 2: 304–16.

Roth, K. and Morrison, A.J. (1990) 'An empirical analysis of the integration-responsiveness framework in global industries', *Journal of International Business Studies,* 22, 4: 541–61.

Royle, T. (2000) *Working for McDonald's in Europe.* London: Routledge.

Ruigrok, W. and van Tulder, R. (1995) *The Logic of International Restructuring.* London: Routledge.

Schein, E. (1984) 'The role of the founder in creating organizational culture', *Organizational Dynamics,* Summer: 13–28.

Schuler, R. (1992) 'Strategic human resources management: linking the people with the strategic needs of the business', *Organizational Dynamics,* Summer: 18–32.

Schuler, R., Dowling P. and De Cieri, H. (1993) 'An integrative framework of strategic international human resource management', *Journal of Management,* 19, 2: 419–59.

Sparrow, P., Brewster, C. and Harris, H. (2004) *Globalising Human Resource Management.* London: Routledge.

Taylor, S. (2006) 'Emerging motivations for global HRM integration' in A. Ferner, J. Quintanilla and C. Sanchez-Runde (eds) *Multinational, Institutions and the Construction of Transnational Practices.* London: Palgrave, pp. 109–30.

Taylor, S. and Beechler, S. (1993) 'Human resource management integration and adaption in multinational firms' in S. Prasad and R. Peterson (eds) *Advances in International Comparative Management,* 8. Greenwich, CT: JAI Press, pp. 155–74.

Taylor, S., Beechler, S. and Napier, N. (1996) 'Toward an integrative model of strategic international human resource management', *Academy of Management Review,* 21, 4: 959–85.

Tregaskis, O., Glover, L. and Ferner, A. (2005) *International HR Networks.* London: CIPD.

Vernon, R. (1966) 'International investment and international trade in the product cycle', *Quarterly Journal of Economics,* May: 190–207.

Whitley, R. (1999) *Divergent Capitalisms.* Oxford: Oxford University Press.

Womack, J., Jones, D. and Roos, G. (1990) *The Machine that Changed the World.* New York: Rawson.

Wright, P. and McMahan G. (1992) 'Theoretical perspectives for strategic human resource management', *Journal of Management,* 18, 3: 295–320.

For multiple-choice questions, exercises and annotated weblinks related to this topic, visit **www.pearsoned.co.uk/mymanagementlab**.

Global and local: the case of the inoperable HRM strategy

Medical Precision Systems (MPS) is a US-owned company based on the outskirts of Birmingham, Alabama, USA. It has been producing medical precision tools used in surgery since 1972, and has built up a well-respected business in the USA with a turnover of $150 million annually. Its Birmingham plant employs 2000 staff made up of skilled and semi-skilled workers. Most staff are employed in production process work, but a significant number work in research and development and other highly skilled and knowledge-based areas.

There are no unions and the Human Resources Department has consciously followed a policy of best-practice HRM to keep out union influence. There is a an excellent pensions scheme, a successful profit-sharing scheme, and a share options scheme whereby employees can choose to have bonuses in the form of company shares if they have worked at MPS for more than two years. Laying employees off is avoided as much as possible during slack periods in order to retain staff loyalty.

However, a performance management culture is strong at MPS, and there is an astringent appraisal system linked to remuneration and promotion. Target setting for groups and individuals has been strongly implemented for the past 20 years and refined over that time. A total quality management (TQM) programme has been in operation for the past 15 years, and work areas or cells are operated by teams. Under the TQM system groups of ten workers are allowed to elect a leader, who organises feedback sessions and reports to senior production managers. Annual staff opinion surveys are conducted on a range of employment and production issues. Training is taken seriously, and all employees attend sessions to train in teamworking and people skills, as well as sessions and courses of a more technical nature. MPS prides itself on its strong culture, and likes to communicate its values and vision clearly and frequently to the workforce. The mission statement 'MPS – working for the health of America' is printed on all pay packets and slips, and most communication bulletins.

There are excellent canteen and recreational facilities, the employees have a number of sports teams, and social events take place regularly.

Expanding overseas

Since the early 1990s, MPS has decided to set up plants overseas, but in doing so is conscious that it needs a fairly educated workforce that can cope with the highly technical nature of the work. In addition, it has recognised that its major markets are in Europe, where it has been exporting since the early 1980s. The MPS board thus decided to open subsidiaries in the UK initially, followed by Sweden and later France.

The UK operation was acquired by taking over a medical engineering company in 1991 near Bath and initially employed 150 people rising to 350 by the end of the decade. The Swedish subsidiary was set up on a greenfield site in a business park on the outskirts of the university city of Uppsala in 1994, employing 50 and then 250 staff by the end of the decade. A new plant was set up in Lyon, France, in 1997 that employs fewer than 200 staff.

In 2001, the MPS HQ in Alabama was revamping its strategy in line with its global developments and commitments. The production and marketing side of the business were doing well, and there had been steady growth in the UK subsidiary in Bath and the Swedish subsidiary at Uppsala. Preliminary reports also indicated that the French subsidiary had enormous potential. However, the Director of Human Resources, Jim Grant, commissioned a full report on the overseas HRM operations as there had been difficulties experienced in HRM. Jim wanted to create an HRM strategy that would complement the new business strategy and at the same time solve the problems in the overseas subsidiaries.

The existing international HRM strategy

Using Perlmutter's typology, MPS international HRM strategy can only be described as ethnocentric (see Chapter 17). It attempts to exert strong controls over its subsidiaries through the extensive use of expatriate managers in both technical and managerial areas of the business. Its goals in financial and production terms have been set by the parent company, and the local subsidiaries have little say. The feedback mechanisms have been implemented from the USA, backed with training programmes for all employees.

Expatriate managers have been told either to keep the unions out or to ensure that their influence is as minimal as possible. Loyalty schemes such as profit sharing have been introduced, and it is planned that the company share scheme will be introduced in 2002 across all subsidiaries. Annual staff opinion surveys have been implemented, and communication is emphasised as being fluid and as frequent as possible between expatriate managers, host country managers and employees.

TQM programmes have also been introduced, and are run with the teamworking systems and workplace feedback and improvement mechanisms. The strong MPS culture has been effectively reinforced through regular staff bulletins, and local company magazines in the language of the subsidiary company country. The mission statement is widely displayed, and a strong public relations image also supports the company culture.

While many of these initiatives have had success, there has been some reluctance and even opposition to others in the three European subsidiaries. In 2001, Jim Grant carried out a full review, and was able to make the following points in a report to the US HQ board.

HRM overseas in MPS: report by Jim Grant

One of the problems we have faced is the diversity of conditions in the subsidiaries, and the practices we follow in the USA do not always translate well in the local context. These problems concern expatriate managers, industrial relations, management style and the degree of control that subsidiaries believe is being exerted over them. Expatriate managers faced a considerable degree of difficulty when given assignments, particularly in the European subsidiaries. While all the senior managers in France and Sweden spoke excellent English, there were considerable communication barriers between the American expatriates and their subsidiary workforces. Common problems were incomprehension of each other's culture and working practices.

Expatriate manager feedback, Bath, UK

Joe Mendes, who runs the English operation, also commented that, despite the common language, he didn't always understand the British mentality. There was considerable resentment when it was suggested that weekend working be brought in to fulfil some emergency orders.

He also said the plant we inherited was highly unionised, with several technical and other unions operating. When he suggested having one union for negotiating purposes there was nearly a mass walk-out, and union officials became very obstructive. Another problem was the performance management system, which met with considerable initial difficulties in being set up. The unions and many employees felt the targets were too harsh and divisive, and they also felt that they had little control over them.

Expatriate manager feedback, Lyons, France

Andy Smith, who runs the French operation, had no problems in regard to the unions, as it was a greenfield site and it was relatively easy to exclude unions by recruiting new staff, although some of the technical staff had union membership. The major problem concerned management style. While there were some initial difficulties in setting up the performance management system, the main problem was with the feedback mechanisms. The French workforce could not see the point of the cellular feedback mechanisms, and preferred to have a line manager with an authoritative air, technically proficient and capable of directing the workforce towards work tasks.

Andy also had problems in getting the workforce to work extra hours, and he felt there were excessive holidays in France. 'Every time production seemed to be up running perfectly, another saint's day holiday would put out our schedule,' he said.

A works council was set up in accordance with French law, but in the eyes of most of the French workforce did not operate very effectively.

Expatriate manager feedback, Uppsala, Sweden

Gary Alder, head of the Swedish operation, reported that despite the subsidiary being a greenfield site start-up operation the workforce very soon joined unions, and by the end of the first year over 65 per cent of employees were union members. As in France and the UK, the Swedish workforce baulked at the targets set under the performance management scheme. However, there was considerable enthusiasm for the feedback mechanisms in the cellular manufacturing processes, and many interesting ideas and innovations emerged as a result of this.

The Swedes, like the French and the British, were not impressed by the attempts by American management to engender a 'gung ho' culture through culture training and attitudinal orientation sessions. Most employees in all three countries paid lip service to these sessions.

Under Swedish and EU law a works council had to be set up for management and employees, but the Americans, although having to conform to European and national laws, resented these meetings and tended to treat them with less than enthusiasm. They appeared in the eyes of one Swedish union organiser at times to be almost non-cooperative.

The general conclusion that Jim drew was that some HRM policies had been more successful than others.

Questions

1 Given the report, what would you advise Jim to recommend to the board in drawing up a new international HRM strategy?

2 How could this strategy be locally responsive and yet global in its scope?

Academy Schools State-maintained independent schools set up with the help of external sponsors – usually business, religious or voluntary organizations.

Advisory, Conciliation and Arbitration Service (ACAS) Founded in 1975, aims to improve employment relations. It provides information, advice and training and will work with employers and employees to solve problems.

ACFTU The All China Federation of Trade Unions.

Added value Technically the difference between the value of a firm's inputs and its outputs; the additional value is added through the deployment and efforts of the firm's resources. Can be defined as FVA (financial value added), CVA (customer value added) and PVA (people value added).

AEL Accreditation of Experiential Learning.

Alienation Marx suggests it is a condition in which a worker loses power to control the performance, processes and product of his/her labour. Thus the very worker becomes a thing rather than a human being, in which state they experience powerlessness, meaninglessness, isolation and self-estrangement.

Androgogy 'The art and science of helping adults learn' (Knowles *et al.*, 1984: 60).

Annualised hours contract Relatively novel form of employment contract that offers management, and sometimes workers, a considerable degree of flexibility. The hours that an employee works can be altered within a very short time frame within a day, a week, or even a month. So long as the total hours worked do not exceed the contractually fixed annual amount an employee can be asked and expected to work from 0 up to anything in excess of 80 hours in any one week.

APL Accreditation of Prior Learning.

Appraisal The process through which an assessment is made of an employee by another person using quantitative and/or qualitative assessments.

Appraisal (360 degree) A system of appraisal which seeks feedback from 'all directions' – superiors, subordinates, peers and customers.

Attitude survey Survey, usually conducted by questionnaire, to elicit employees' opinions about issues to do with their work and the organisation.

Balanced scorecard An integrated framework for balancing shareholder and strategic goals, and extending these balanced performance measures down the organisation.

BERR Department for Business, Enterprise and Regulatory Reform, now part of the Department for Business, Innovation and Skills.

Best fit Models of HRM that focus on alignment between HRM and business strategy and the external context of the firm. Tend to link or 'fit' generic type business strategies to generic HRM strategies.

Best practice A 'set' or number of human resource practices that have the potential to enhance organisational performance when implemented. Usually categorised as 'high commitment', 'high involvement' or 'high performance'.

BIS Department for Business, Innovation and Skills.

Broadbanding Pay systems which have a wide range of possible pay levels within them. Unlike traditional narrow systems, there is normally a high degree of overlap across the grades.

BS 5750 British standard of quality, originally applied to the manufacture of products but now also being used to 'measure' quality of service. Often used in employee involvement (EI) as a way of getting employees to self-check their quality of work against a standardised norm.

Bundles A coherent combination of human resource practices that are horizontally integrated.

Business process re-engineering (BPR) System that aims to improve performance by redesigning the processes through which an organisation operates, maximising their value-added content and minimising everything else (Peppard and Rowland, 1995: 20).

Cabinet Office A senior government department alongside the Treasury, the Cabinet Office supports the Prime Minister, the Cabinet and the Civil Service in managing government policy.

Career 'The evolving sequence of a person's work experiences over time' (Arthur *et al.*, 1989: 8); 'the individual's development in learning and work throughout life' (Collin and Watts, 1996: 393).

Causal ambiguity The cause or source of an organisation's competitive advantage is ambiguous or unclear, particularly to the organisation's competitors.

CBI Confederation of British Industry. Powerful institution set up in 1965 to promote and represent the interests of British industry. Financed by subscription and made up of employers' associations, national business associations and over 10,000 affiliated companies. Works to advise and negotiate with the government and the Trades Union Congress.

CCT Compulsory competitive tendering.

Chaos and complexity theories In contrast to traditional science, these more recent theories draw attention to the uncertainty, non-linearity and unpredictability that result from the interrelatedness and interdependence of the elements of the universe.

CIPD Chartered Institute of Personnel and Development – the professional organisation for human resource and personnel managers and those in related fields such as training and development. Website: **www.cipd.org.uk**.

Closed system System that does not interact with other subsystems or its environment.

Collective bargaining Process utilised by trade unions, as the representatives of employees, and management, as the representatives of employers, to establish the terms and conditions under which labour will be employed.

Competence 'The ability to perform the activities within an occupational area to the levels of performance expected in employment' (Training Commission, 1988).

Competences Behavioural repertoires that people input to a job, role or organisation context, and which employees need to bring to a role to perform to the required level (see also **Core competences**).

Competency-based pay An approach to reward based on the attainment of skills or talents by individuals in relation to a specific task at a certain standard.

Competitive advantage The ability of an organisation to add more value for its customers than its rivals, and therefore gain a position of advantage in the marketplace.

Configurational approach An approach that identified the benefits of identifying a set of horizontally integrated HR practices that were aligned to the business strategy, thus fitting the internal and external context of the business.

Constructivism Concerned with individual experience and emphasises the individual's cognitive processes.

Contingent pay Elements of the reward package which are contingent on other events (performance, merit, attendance) and are awarded at the discretion of the management.

Cooperatives Organisations and companies that are collectively owned either by their customers or by their employees.

Core competences Distinctive skills and knowledge, related to product, service or technology, that can be used to gain competitive advantage.

Cost minimisation This refers to a managerial approach that perceives human resources as costs to be controlled as tightly as possible. HR practices are likely to include low wages, minimal training, close supervision and no employee voice mechanisms.

CPSA Civil and Public Servants Association.

Culture The prevailing pattern of values, attitudes, beliefs, assumptions, norms and sentiments.

Danwei Central to the state-owned enterprises in China were work units or *danweis*.

DCSF Department for Children, Schools and Families.

DfES Department for Education and Skills now subsumed into the Department for Business, Innovation and Skills – see **BIS**.

Deskilling The attempt by management to appropriate and monopolise workers' knowledge of production in an effort to control the labour process. To classify, tabulate and reduce this knowledge to rules, laws and formulae, which are then allocated to workers on a daily basis.

DETR Department of the Environment, Transport and the Regions.

Development The process of becoming increasingly complex, more elaborate and differentiated, by virtue of learning and maturation, resulting in new ways of acting and responding to the environment.

Development centres Normally used for the selection of managers. They utilise a range of intensive psychological tests and simulations to assess management potential.

Discourse The shared language, metaphors, stories that give members of a group their particular way of interpreting reality.

DIUS Department for Innovation, Universities and Skills. Now part of the Department for Business, Innovation and Skills.

Downsizing Possibly the simplest explanation is given by Heery and Noon (2001: 90) as 'getting rid of employees'. A modern 'buzzword' used to indicate the reduction of employment within organisations.

Double-loop learning *See* **Single-loop learning**.

DTI Department for Trade and Industry, now subsumed into the Department for Business, Innovation and Skills.

Dual system German system of vocational training for apprentices, which combines off-the-job training at vocational colleges with on-the-job training under the tutelage of *meister* (skilled craft) workers.

Efficiency The sound management of resources within a business in order to *maximise* the return on investment.

Efficiency wages Wages paid above the market rate to attract better workers, induce more effort and reduce turnover and training costs.

Effectiveness The ability of an organisation to meet the demands and expectations of its various stakeholders, albeit some more than others.

EI Employee involvement; a term to describe the wide variety of schemes in which employees can be involved in their work situation.

EIRO European Industrial Relations Observatory – produces regular reports on employment relations in EU Member States.

e-Learning Use of new technology such as e-mail, the internet, intranets and computer software packages to facilitate learning for employees.

Emergent Strategies which emerge over time, sometimes with an element of trial and error. Some emergent strategies are incremental changes with embedded learning, others may be adaptive in response to external environmental changes.

Employability The acquisition and updating of skills, experience, reputation – the investment in human capital – to ensure that the individual remains employable, and not dependent upon a particular organisation.

Empowerment Recent term that encompasses EI (employee involvement) initiatives to encourage the workforce to have direct individual and collective control over their work processes, taking responsibility for improved customer service to both internal and external customers. Generally confined to workplace-level issues and concerns.

Enterprise unions Japanese concept of employee unions associated with only one enterprise and the only one recognised by the company. One of the 'three pillars' of the Japanese employment system.

Epistemology The assumptions made about the world which form the basis for knowledge.

ESOPS Employee share option scheme, whereby employees are allowed to purchase company shares or are given them as part of a bonus.

ET Employment Training.

EU European Union, so named in 1992 (formerly EC).

Exit policy Policy/procedures that facilitate prompt and orderly recovery or removal of failing institutions through timely and corrective action. There were restrictions placed on closure and retrenchment in view of the social costs and their political ramifications that are now being eased.

Factor of production An input into the production process. Factors of production were traditionally classified as *land* (raw materials), *capital* (buildings, equipment, machinery) and *labour*. Labour is usually seen as a variable factor of production because labour inputs can be varied quite easily at short notice, unlike capital, the amount of which cannot be varied easily in the short run. Internalising the employment relationship transforms labour into a *quasi-fixed factor of production* because it restricts the employer's freedom to cut jobs at short notice.

FIEs Foreign invested enterprises.

Firm-specific skills Skills that can be used in only one or a few particular organisations.

Fit The level of integration between an organisation's business strategy and its human resource policies and practices. 'Fit' tends to imply a top–down relationship between the strategy makers and the strategy implementers.

Forked lightning, the Mae West Language and concepts used by city financiers working on the international currency and commodity markets. Used to describe the patterns formed by fluctuating price movements as they get represented on dealers' screens.

Foundation schools State-financed schools that own school land and other physical assets of the school, are the employers of school staff and which have authority over admissions.

FSB Federation of Small Businesses.

FTSE The FTSE Group provides a series of indices (measures) relating to share prices and other aspects of economic activity. The **FTSE100 index** is an index of the share prices of the top 100 firms by share value.

Functional flexibility The ability of management to redeploy workers across tasks. Functional flexibility can be horizontal – redeployment across tasks at the same level of skill, and/or vertical – the ability to perform tasks at different (higher) levels of skill.

GDP Gross domestic product – a measure of the total value of goods and services produced within a country, excluding income from investments abroad.

Globalisation A controversial term that has generated considerable debate as to its meaning. Generally seen to involve increased internationalisation of investment and production, the growing importance of multinational companies and the emergence of transnational regulation of economic activity.

GNVQs General National Vocational Qualifications.

Guanxi Chinese term that refers to the concept of drawing on connections or networks to secure favours in personal or business relations.

Hard HRM A view of HRM that identifies employees as a cost to be minimised, and tends to focus on 'flexibility techniques' and limited investment in learning and development (see also **Soft HRM**).

Hegemony The imposition upon others of a powerful group's interpretation of reality.

High-commitment management Used to describe a set of HR practices aimed at enhancing the commitment, quality and flexibility of employees.

High-performance work practices A term that gained currency in the 1990s that sought to link bundles of HR practices with outcomes in terms of increased employee commitment and performance which in turn enhances the firm's sustained competitive advantage, efficiency and profitability.

HMSO Her Majesty's Stationery Office. Publishers of parliamentary proceedings, official government documents and reports. Privatised in 1996 and now known as The Stationery Office (TSO).

Holistic Treatment of organisations, situations, problems as totalities or wholes as opposed to a specific, reductionist approach.

Horizontal integration Level of alignment across and within functions, such that all functional policies and practices are integrated and congruent with one another.

HRD Human resource development.

Human capital The knowledge, skill and attitudes, the intangible contributions to high performance, that make employees assets to the organisation.

Human relations Associated with the pioneering work of Roethlisberger and Dickson, Elton Mayo and others, who studied the importance of community and collective values in work organisations. These studies first identified that management needed to attend to the 'social needs' of employees.

Ideology The set of ideas and beliefs that underpins interpretations of reality.

IIP Investors in People.

ILO International Labour Organization. International body set up in 1919 to promote employment rights and decent employment standards. Now an agency of the United Nations.

IMS The Institute of Manpower Studies. Located at the University of Sussex.

Independent Pay Review Bodies are in place to offer expert advice to the government on the pay of certain groups of public sector employees: armed forces, doctors and dentists, school teachers, certain groups of NHS nursing and healthcare staff, police officers and highly paid public officials such as judges and senior civil servants.

Indexation procedure linking pay, pensions or other financial benefits to changes in the retail price index to protect against inflation or in some cases to the growth of average earnings to protect the relative as well as the absolute value of pay etc.

Institutional vacuum/representation gap Situation in which collective bargaining is no longer the dominant form of establishing terms and conditions of employment, but no recognisable or regulated channel of employee representation or employee voice has emerged to replace it.

Intellectual capital The hidden value, and capital, tied up in an organisation's people (knowledge, skills and competencies), which can be a key source of competitive advantage and differentiate it from its competitors.

IPD Institute of Personnel and Development; see also **CIPD**.

IRDAC Industrial Research and Development Advisory Committee of the Commission of the European Communities.

IRS Industrial Relations Services. A data gathering and publications bureau that collects and analyses movement in key variables of importance to the study and practice of industrial relations.

ITBs Industrial Training Boards. Set up in 1964 to monitor training in various sectors of the economy. Most were abolished in 1981, but a few still survive.

JCC Joint consultative committee; body made up of employee representatives and management, which meets regularly to discuss issues of common interest.

Job enlargement Related to job rotation, whereby a job is made bigger by the introduction of new tasks. This gives greater variety in job content and thereby helps to relieve monotony in repetitive jobs such as assembly line working.

Job enrichment Adds to a cycle of work not only a variety of tasks but increased responsibility to workers. Most associated with autonomous work groups introduced into Volvo's Kalmar plant in Sweden in the 1970s.

Job rotation Originally introduced in the 1970s for members of a team to exchange jobs to enliven work interest, but also used recently to promote wider skills experience and flexibility among employees.

JV Joint venture.

Keiretsu A form of inter-company organisation in Japan that consists of a set of companies that hold shares in each other and have shared business relationships.

Knowledge-based age Reflects the move to a global environment, where tacit and explicit knowledge becomes a key source of competitive advantage for organisations.

Knowledge-based organisation One that manages the generation of new knowledge through learning, capturing knowledge and experience, sharing, collaborating and communicating, organising information and using and building on what is known.

Labour process The application of human labour to raw materials in the production of goods and services that are later sold on the free market. Labour is paid a wage for its contribution, but capital must ensure that it secures value added over and above what it is paying for. Some call this efficiency. Others prefer the term 'exploitation'.

Learning Complex cognitive, physical and affective process that results in the capacity for changed performance.

Learning cycle Learning seen as a process having different identifiable phases. Effective learning may be facilitated if methods appropriate to the various phases are used.

Learning style Individuals differ in their approaches to learning, and prefer one mode of learning, or phase of the learning cycle, to others.

Learning organisation (LO) 'A Learning Company is an organisation that facilitates the learning of all its members and consciously transforms itself and its context' (Pedler *et al.*, 1997: 3).

LECs Local Enterprise Companies. Locally based agencies in Scotland whose function is to promote training and business and wider economic development. There are 22 in existence. For the UK see **LSC**.

Leverage The exploitation by an organisation of its resources to their full extent. Often linked to the notion of stretching resources.

Licence-quota regime The practice in a state-regulated economy where a business has to obtain permission to manufacture (licence) as well as the quantity to produce (quota) from the licensing authority (state) before commencing production.

Lifetime employment Japanese concept whereby in large corporations employees are guaranteed a job for life in exchange for loyalty to the organisation. One of the 'three pillars' of the Japanese employment system.

LMS Local management of schools.

LSC Learning and Skills Council. Set up in 2001 to replace the Training and Enterprise Council the LSC is responsible for funding and planning post-16 education and training in England. The equivalent body in Wales is Education and Learning Wales (ELWa). The LSC has 47 local offices known as Local Learning and Skills Councils (LLSCs) and ELWa has 4 regional offices.

Maastricht Protocol Part of the Maastricht Treaty dealing with the Social Chapter (Social Charter), allowing Britain to sign the treaty without signing the Maastricht Protocol or Social Chapter.

Maastricht Treaty The content was agreed at a meeting at Maastricht in the Netherlands and signed in a watered-down form in Edinburgh in 1992. It was rejected and then accepted by the voters of Denmark in two referendums. It concerns extending aspects of European political union (EPU) and European and Monetary Union (EMU).

Management gurus Phenomenon of the 1980s, when academics, consultants and business practitioners began to enjoy celebrity status as specialists on the diagnosis of management problems and the development of 'business solutions'. Includes people such as Tom Peters, Rosabeth Moss Kanter, John Harvey Jones and M.C. Robert Beeston.

McDonaldisation The reduction of organisation to simple, repetitive, and predictable work processes that make the labour process more amenable to standardised calculation and control.

MCI (Management Charter Initiative) Employer-led initiative with the aim of developing recognised standards in management practice.

Measured day work MDW is a system within which pay is fixed against specific levels of performance during the 'day' rather than by the hourly performance or piece-rates.

Mentor More experienced person who guides, encourages and supports a younger or less experienced person.

MSC Manpower Services Commission. Previously had responsibility for training but was abolished in 1988.

Mission statement A statement setting out the main purpose of the business.

NACETT National Advisory Council for Education and Training Targets now incorporated into the Learning and Skills Councils.

NALGO National and Local Government Officers Association. *See* Unison.

NASUWT National Association of School Masters/ Union of Women Teachers.

National curriculum Obligatory subjects of the UK school system, introduced via the Education Reform Act 1989.

National minimum wage Introduced by the National Minimum Wage Act 1998, this sets the minimum rate of reward any worker can receive on an hourly basis. The scale is age-related and linked to inflation through an annual upgrade.

NATO North Atlantic Treaty Organization. Western defensive alliance set up originally in 1949 to promote economic and military cooperation among its members. The original members were Belgium, Britain, Canada, France, Italy, Norway, Portugal and the Netherlands. Greece and Turkey joined in 1952, and the former West Germany in 1955.

NCU National Communications Union.

NCVQ (National Council for Vocational Qualifications) Government-backed initiative to establish a national system for the recognition of vocational qualifications.

Nenko Japanese term meaning seniority and ability. One of the 'three pillars' of the Japanese employment system.

Networking Interacting for mutual benefit, usually on an informal basis, with individuals and groups internal and external to the organisation.

New Deal Government initiative that provides training for 18–24-year-olds who have been out of work for more than six months, and 25-year-olds and over who have been unemployed for longer than two years.

New Deal in America Programme of economic and social reconstruction initiated by President F.D. Roosevelt in 1933 that aimed to lift the USA out of the Great Depression that hit the country in 1929.

NHS National Health Service.

NHS Trusts Local NHS organisations responsible for distributing NHS funds and managing services. Primary Care Trusts (PCTs) are responsible for managing 80 per cent of NHS funds and they cover GP services, dentists, opticians and pharmacists. Other trusts are ambulance trusts, hospital trusts and mental health and social care trusts.

Non-union firms Organisations which do not recognise trade unions for collective bargaining purposes; this may be throughout the organisation or at plant or business unit level. So, for example, IBM, frequently quoted as an example of a soft-HRM non-union firm, does, in fact, recognise unions in Germany, as does McDonald's, another organisation strongly associated with an anti-union stance.

NSTF National Skills Task Force.

Numerical flexibility The ability of management to vary headcount in response to changes in demand.

NVQs National Vocational Qualifications. An attempt to harmonise all VET qualifications within the UK by attributing five levels to all qualifications, from level 1, the lowest, to level 5, the highest.

ONS Office of National Statistics.

Open system System that is connected to and interacts with other subsystems and its environment.

OSC Occupational Standards Council.

Paired comparisons A system of appraisal that seeks to assess the performance of pairs of individuals, until each employee has been judged in relation to each other.

Paradigm A well-developed, and often widely held, set of associated assumptions that frames the interpretation of reality. When these assumptions are undermined by new knowledge or events, a 'paradigm shift' occurs as the old gives way (often gradually and painfully) to a new paradigm.

Payment by results Reward systems under which worker output or performance determines elements of the package.

PCT Primary Care Trust – see **NHS Trusts**.

Performance-related pay Payment systems which in some way relate reward to either organisational or individual performance. Often used as a way to motivate white-collar workers, usually based on a developed appraisal system.

PFI Private Finance Initiative.

Phenomenology Concerned with understanding the individual's conscious experience. It takes a holistic approach and acknowledges the significance of subjectivity.

Pluralism Theoretical analysis of the employment relationship that recognises inequality between capital and labour where each of the interest groups has some conflicting and some common aims. To address these issues, pluralists argue that employees should be facilitated to act collectively, usually as a trade union, to redress such imbalances. Management, as the representatives of employers, should engage in collective bargaining with trade unions to establish consensual agreements on issues of conflict and commonality.

Positivism The orthodox approach to the understanding of reality, and the basis for scientific method.

Post-Fordism A claimed epochal shift in manufacturing that sees a move away from mass production assembly lines and the development of flexible systems that empower and reskill line workers. Associated with the move towards niche products and volatile consumer demand.

Postmodernism A term used (often loosely) to denote various disjunctions from, fragmentations in, or challenges to previously common understandings of knowledge and social life.

PRB Pay review body.

Predetermined motion time systems A member of the time-rate pay systems family under which rewards are calculated based on time and piece. As a standard form of incentive bonus scheme, PDMT schemes rewards are set using the pseudo-scientific measurement of activity.

Profit sharing Scheme whereby employees are given a bonus or payment based on a company's profits.

Private Finance Initiative Where the government contracts out projects such as prison management, hospital building, road construction etc. to the private sector, then leases back the service over an extended period of time.

Privatisation The transfer of productive activities from public to private ownership and control. Privatisation was a key element of economic policy under the Conservative governments of the 1980s and 1990s when the coal and steel industries, the telephone service, water, gas and electricity supply and railways among others were transferred from public to private ownership.

Psychological contract The notion that an individual has a range of expectations about their employing organisation and the organisation has expectations of them.

Psychological (psychometric) testing Specialised tests used for selection or assessing potential. Usually in the form of questionnaires. They construct a personality profile of the candidate.

Public–Private Partnerships (PPP) Collaboration between public bodies, e.g. government or local authorities and private businesses to provide goods and services. See Private Finance Initiative.

Quality circle (QC) Group made up of 6–10 employees, with regular meetings held weekly or fortnightly during working time. The principal aim is to identify problems from their own area.

Ranking A method of assessing and ordering individual performance using a predetermined scale.

Rating A determined measure or scale against which an individual's performance is measured.

Reification The conceptualisation and treatment of a person or abstraction as though they were things.

Resource-based view Strategy creation built around the further exploitation of core competencies and strategic capabilities.

RCN Royal College of Nursing.

Rhetoric The often subtle and unacknowledged use of language to 'persuade, influence or manipulate'.

Rightsizing – see **Downsizing**.

Scientific management – see **Taylorism**.

Single-loop learning Detection and correction of deviances in performance from established (organisational or other) norms. Double-loop learning is the questioning of those very norms that define effective performance. (Compare efficiency and effectiveness.)

Single-table bargaining Arrangement under which unions on a multi-union site develop a mutually agreed bargaining agenda, which is then negotiated jointly with management.

Single-union deal Arrangement under which one trade union operates to represent all employees within an organisation; this is usually a preferred union sponsored by management.

Social Chapter Another name for the Social Charter, which emerged from the Maastricht meeting in 1989.

Social Charter A programme to implement the 'social dimension' of the single market, affording rights and protection to employees.

Social complexity The complex interpersonal relationships that exist within organisations, within and between teams and individuals.

Social constructionism Holds that an objective reality is not directly knowable. The reality we do know is socially constructed through language, discourse and social interaction.

Social partnership Process whereby employers and employees establish a framework of rights based upon minimum standards in employment, flexibility, security, information sharing and cooperation between management and employees' representatives.

Social relations of production The patterns and dynamics produced and reproduced in action by individuals and collectives employed in the labour process.

Sociotechnical The structuring or integration of human activities and subsystems with technological subsystems.

SOE State-owned enterprise.

Soft HRM A view of HRM that recognises employees as a resource worth investing in, and tends to focus on high-commitment/high-involvement human resource practices; see also **Hard HRM**.

Stakeholders Any individual or group capable of affecting or being affected by the performance and actions of the organisation.

Stakeholder society One in which individuals recognise that only by making a positive contribution to contemporary society can they expect a positive outcome from society.

Stakeholders in social partnership Those groups with an interest in promoting strong social partnerships at work, i.e. the state, employers and their organisations, employees and their organisations.

Strategic management The process by which an organisation establishes its objectives, formulates strategies to meet these objectives, implements actions and measures and monitors performance.

STRB School Teachers review Body – the pay review body for teachers in schools; see also **Independent Pay Review Bodies**.

Suggestion scheme (box) Arrangement whereby employees are encouraged to put forward their ideas for improving efficiency, safety or working conditions. Payment or reward is often given related to the value of the suggestion.

Supervisory boards Part of the dual management board structure required by law in all German enterprises listed on the German stock exchange. Day-to-day management is the responsibility of the management board, which is accountable to the supervisory board. The supervisory board appoints, oversees and advises the management board. It also participates directly in key strategic decisions. Supervisory boards are elected by shareholders and where firms employ more than 500 employees in Germany, membership of the board must also include employee representatives. Employee representatives make up one-third of the supervisory board membership in companies having 500–2000 employees and half of the membership in companies having over 2000 employees.

Sustainable competitive advantage The ability of an organisation to add more value than its rivals in order to gain advantage and maintain that advantage over time.

SVQs Scottish Vocational Qualifications.

Synergy Added value or additional benefit that accrues from cooperation between team members, or departments, such that the results are greater than the sum of all the individual parts.

System Assembly of parts, objects or attributes interrelating and interacting in an organised way.

Systemic Thinking about and perceiving situations, problems and difficulties as systems.

Tacit knowledge Knowledge that is never explicitly taught, often not verbalised, but is acquired through doing and expressed in know-how.

Taylorism, Taylorist a systematic approach to work organisation named after Frederick Winslow Taylor. Involves time and motion study, specialised subdivision of labour and close management control. Also referred to as 'scientific management'.

Team briefing Regular meeting of groups of between 4 and 15 people based round a common production or service area. Meetings are usually led by a manager or supervisor and last for no more than 30 minutes, during which information is imparted, often with time left for questions from employees.

TECs Training and Enterprise Councils. These operated in England and Wales and were made up of local employers and elected local people, to create local training initiatives in response to local skill needs. Their function was taken over in 2002 by Learning and Skills Councils.

Theory 'X' & 'Y' Based on McGregor's thesis on managerial change. Two contrasting views of people and work. Theory X sees people as inherently lazy, unambitious and avoiding of responsibility. Theory Y sees work as natural as rest or play and being capable of providing self-fulfilment and a sense of achievement for those involved.

Thinking performer A set of competencies that should guide CIPD members (Chartered Institute of Personnel and Development) through their careers.

TQM Total quality management, an all-pervasive system of management-controlled EI based on the concept of quality throughout the organisation in terms of product and service, whereby groups of workers are each encouraged to perceive each other (and other departments) as internal customers. This ensures the provision of quality products and services to external customers.

Transferable skills Skills that can be used anywhere in the economy.

Tripartism Systems of industrial relations whereby the state, employers associations and trade unions oversee and govern labour market initiatives and related policies, e.g. wage levels and increases.

Trust Schools State-funded schools supported by a charitable trust that has enhanced freedom to manage its own operations; see also **Foundation schools**.

TUC Trades Union Congress.

TUPE Transfer of Undertakings (Protection of Employment) Regulations.

UNICE Union of Industrial and Employers Confederations of Europe.

Unison Public service union formed following merger of COHSE, NALGO and NUPE.

Unitarism Theoretical analysis of the employment relationship based on managerial prerogative, valuing labour individually according to market assessments, and which views organised resistance to management authority as pathological.

Value chain A framework, for identifying where value is added and where costs are incurred.

VDU Visual display unit – a computer screen, for example. That component of a computer that transmits often dangerous levels of radiation.

VET Vocational education and training.

Vertical Integration In terms of SHRM, the level of alignment between an organisation's business strategy and its HR strategy, policies and practices.

Vision (statement) A desired future state, or an attempt by an organisation to articulate that desired future state.

VQs Vocational qualifications.

Wa Japanese term for harmony.

Wage drift A gradual and uneven increase in wages in certain sectors of the economy resulting from variable, informal bargaining activities reflecting areas of localised union strength. Such increases are supplementary to any formally agreed wages formula. If allowed to grow unchecked, this practice can lead to inflationary measures.

Weberian bureaucracy Associated with the research and writing of the sociologist Max Weber (1864–1920), who observed and studied the growth of vast organisational bureaucracies. Notable for the extreme degree of functional specialisation, formal rules and procedures, and long lines of command and authority. Staffed by professional, full-time, salaried employees who do not own the resources and facilities with which they work.

Works councils Committees made up either solely of workers or of joint representatives of workers, management and shareholders, which meet, usually at company level, to discuss a variety of issues relating to workforce matters and sometimes general, wider-ranging organisational issues. Usually supported by legislation, which compels organisations to set them up.

YOP Youth Opportunities Programme. A programme initially set up in 1978 and revived in 1983 to help unemployed youth to gain employment skills.

YT Youth Training (formerly Youth Training Service, YTS).

Zaibatsu Large, diversified Japanese business groups, which rose to prominence in the early twentieth century, such as Mitsubishi, Mitsui and Sumitomo.

References

Arthur, M.B., Hall, D.T. and Lawrence, B.S. (eds) (1989) *Handbook of Career Theory.* Cambridge: Cambridge University Press.

Collin, A. and Watts, A.G. (1996) 'The death and transfiguration of career: and of career guidance?', *British Journal of Guidance and Counselling*, 24, 3: 385–98.

Heery, A. and Noon, M. (2001) *Dictionary of Human Resource Management.* Oxford: Oxford University Press.

Knowles, M.S. and Associates (1984) *Androgogy in Action.* San Francisco, CA: Jossey-Bass.

Pedler, M., Burgoyne, J. and Boydell, T. (1997) *The Learning Company: A Strategy for Sustainable Development.* London: McGraw-Hill.

Peppard, J. and Rowland, P. (1995) *The Essence of Business Process Re-engineering.* Hemel Hempstead: Prentice Hall.

Training Commission (1988) *Classifying the Components of Managing Competencies.* Sheffield: Training Commission.

Index

GET THE INSIDE TRACK TO ACADEMIC SUCCESS

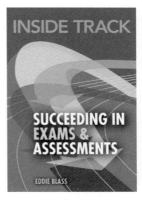

Written by a team of highly experienced authors, this series equips students with effective and practical ways to improve their academic skills across all subject areas.